Columbia Pictures Horror,
Science Fiction and Fantasy
Films, 1928–1982

ALSO BY MICHAEL R. PITTS
AND FROM MCFARLAND

Western Film Series of the Sound Era (2009)

Poverty Row Studios, 1929–1940: An Illustrated History of 55 Independent Film Companies, with a Filmography for Each (1997; paperback 2005)

Charles Bronson: The 95 Films and the 156 Television Appearances (1999; paperback 2003)

Horror Film Stars, 3d ed. (2002)

Western Movies: A TV and Video Guide to 4200 Genre Films (1986; paperback 1997)

Hollywood and American History: A Filmography of Over 250 Motion Pictures Depicting U.S. History (1984)

Columbia Pictures Horror, Science Fiction and Fantasy Films, 1928–1982

Michael R. Pitts

McFarland & Company, Inc., Publishers
Jefferson, North Carolina, and London

LIBRARY OF CONGRESS CATALOGUING-IN-PUBLICATION DATA

Pitts, Michael R.
Columbia Pictures horror, science fiction and
fantasy films, 1928–1982 / Michael R. Pitts.
p.   cm.
Includes bibliographical references and index.

ISBN 978-0-7864-4447-2
softcover : 50# alkaline paper ∞

1. Columbia Pictures Corporation — Catalogs.
2. Motion pictures — United States — Catalogs.   I. Title.
PN1999.C57P58   2010   016.79143'75 — dc22   2010031648

British Library cataloguing data are available

© 2010 Michael R. Pitts. All rights reserved

*No part of this book may be reproduced or transmitted in any form
or by any means, electronic or mechanical, including photocopying
or recording, or by any information storage and retrieval system,
without permission in writing from the publisher.*

On the cover: Cary Guffey as Barry Guiler in a scene from the 1977
film *Close Encounters of the Third Kind* (Columbia Pictures/Photofest)

Manufactured in the United States of America

*McFarland & Company, Inc., Publishers
Box 611, Jefferson, North Carolina 28640
www.mcfarlandpub.com*

To the Memories of
Richard Bojarski
(1935–2009)
and
Dr. Karlen Mooradian
(1935–1990).
And for Jasmine, a book of her own.

TABLE OF CONTENTS

Preface 1

Feature Films 3
Serials 288
Short Subjects 328
Telefeatures 352

Chronology 359
Bibliography 363
Index 367

Preface

Columbia Pictures Corporation has been one of the most long-lasting of Hollywood film studios, having been incorporated in 1924. Originally it was C.B.C. Pictures and was founded in 1920 by brothers Harry and Jack Cohn and Joe Brandt. Harry Cohn became the president of Columbia in 1932 and until his death in 1958 he ruled the company with an iron fist, bringing it up from a Poverty Row studio to one of filmdom's major players. Cohn considered Columbia to be a factory that made motion pictures and as a result it had a diverse product: feature films, short subjects, serials and cartoons. The studio survived Cohn's passing and continued to be a viable competitor in the film market. Unlike some of its contemporaries from the golden age of Hollywood, Columbia Pictures still exists, although under other ownership.

Columbia was never a major competitor with Universal in the horror film field. But, aware there was money to be made from horror, science fiction and fantasy movies, the studio turned out more than 200 features, nearly three dozen serials, 70 short subjects and a dozen made-for-television films from 1924 to 1982 (the years when it was a publicly traded company) that were in these genres.

This volume covers those movies released between 1928, the year Columbia issued its first genre film, *Ransom*, until it ceased to exist as a public company in 1982. Feature films, serials, short subjects and telefeatures are discussed in separate sections in alphabetical order with cast, credits, plot synopsis and critical analysis. The films are in black and white unless noted. A Chronology lists the titles in order of their release.

All the films included in the text were produced or distributed in the United States by Columbia Pictures Corporation. Not included are films made at its studios in England and never released in the United States like *The Feathered Serpent* (1934), *Dracula A.D. 1972* (1972), etc. Two 1959 films co-produced with England's Hammer Films, the feature *The Ugly Ducking* and the short subject *Operation Universe*, probably never got U.S. release but are included. On the other hand, another Hammer co-production, *Two Faces of Dr. Jekyll* (1961), is not in the text although Columbia did release it in its homeland. The film, however, was issued in the U.S. by American International Pictures.

As noted, Columbia released more than 200 genre-related feature films in the United States from 1928 to 1982. Most of these were also produced by the company but after World War II the studio began importing features from Italy and in the late 1950s from Mexico. It also signed a deal with Hammer Films, co-producing and releasing some of that outfit's genre product from the late 1950s into the early 1970s. With so many films involved, the quality naturally varied greatly, running the gamut from top-notch outings to bottom-of-the-barrel. The analysis of these films is simply the author's opinions.

What may be enjoyment to one person can be boredom to another, and vice versa. Films were, and are, made for entertainment and profit, with the emphasis on the latter for their makers.

Columbia did not get into the serial field until 1937, after the genre had dried up in the independent market. The studio rivaled Universal and Republic in turning out cliffhangers and, in fact, survived them by making its last chapterplay in 1956, after the other two had ceased serial production. Columbia's initial serials were produced by Jack Fier; he was followed by Larry Darmour and Rudolph C. Flothow. These maintained good production values. When Sam Katzman took over the unit in 1945, the budgets took a hit from which they never recovered. Still, Katzman was able to make 32 cliffhangers, including reportedly the biggest money-making serial of all time, *Superman* (1948).

The studio's short subject department was run by Jules White from 1934 to 1958 and it churned out scores of popular theatrical fillers, some 70 of which had horror, sci-fi or fantasy elements. Nearly all of these were "scare comedies" produced as part of series starring various comics. By far the most popular and prolific of these comedians were the Three Stooges, a team that turned out nearly 50 genre-related two-reelers between 1938 and 1958. In the early 1950s, when White was able to oust another producer, Hugh McCollum, the short subject department took to cannibalizing its own product, issuing "new" films that were mainly made up of old footage. By incorporating scenes from past shorts with smaller budgets, the new shorts became cheap-looking.

Columbia was one of the first major studios to enter the new field of making feature films for television with *Shadow on the Land* (1968). While it kept up a steady pace of producing telefeatures, most of them were not genre-related.

Columbia Pictures made some wonderful horror, science fiction and fantasy films such as *Curse of the Demon, Earth vs. the Flying Saucers, Homicidal,* the first *Lost Horizon, The Return of the Vampire, The 7th Voyage of Sinbad, Strait-Jacket, A Thousand and One Nights* and *The Werewolf,* just to name a few. Add to these its exciting serials and delightful scare comedies, and the result is a body of films that continue to delight. While Columbia may not have had Universal's reputation in the horror, sci-fi and fantasy film fields, it more than held its own when it came to making entertaining genre productions.

FEATURE FILMS

Africa Speaks

1930; 75 minutes. PRODUCERS: Walter Futter and Paul L. Hoeffer. DIRECTOR-SCREENPLAY-EDITOR: Walter Futter. PHOTOGRAPHY: Paul L. Hoeffer. CREW MEMBER: Harold Austin. CAST: Paul L. Hoeffer, Harold Austin (Themselves), Lowell Thomas (Narrator).

Documentaries had been constant film fare since the beginning of the cinema, and the coming of sound did not to undermine their popularity. While true to life, these armchair adventures sometimes contained more horror than anything Hollywood could concoct. *Africa Speaks*, issued by Columbia in the summer of 1930, was no exception. In its tale of an expedition into Equatorial Africa, it presents strange customs and rituals, orgiastic dances, religious rites to pagan gods, duck-billed Ugangi women who disfigure themselves to avoid Arab slavers, and lions killing and devouring a native guide. Made by Walter Futter Productions and the Colorado African Expedition, the documentary billed itself onscreen as "The Strangest Adventure Ever Filmed."

The feature follows the exploits of Colorado explorer Paul L. Hoeffer, who took 14 months to journey 14,000 miles across Central Africa, beginning at the Niger River with a steam wheeler and a foot safari of over 200 natives. After going through the fever country of Lakoja, Hoeffer photographed elephants and pygmies, whom he bribed with salt. Welcomed by the Iti tribe, he found they were made up of various clans ruled by a king. After a stay with the tribe, photographing their customs and use of poisoned arrows to kill elephants and other prey, the expedition heads to the Uganda plains (to photograph wildlife) and then to Lake Albert (to see millions of flamingos). At Rigon Fall near Lake Victoria, Hoeffer and his crew photographed White Rhino and survived an attack by millions of locust which decimated the area. They next visited the cattle-herding tribe of the Masai and then retraced their steps back north to see the duck-billed Ugangis. They returned to Masai country and photographed lions but were attacked by the beasts; one of their guides was killed and eaten by the big cats. After the Masai lion hunters ventured forth for revenge, surrounding and killing two lions, Hoefler and his crew reached the Indian Ocean.

Photoplay dubbed the film an "[i]nteresting travelogue with animal thrills, considerably dramatized. But it has a kick." Mordaunt Hall in the *New York Times* noted, "The explorer [Hoefler] shows that he has a keen eye for photographic effects as well as dramatic clashes with wild animals.... This *Africa Speaks* is the most thrilling of travel pictures that have come to the screen."

The year after the film was released, Paul L. Hoefler published a book called *Africa Speaks*, dealing with the safari and hunting expedition he filmed in the Serengeti in 1928 that made up most of the footage of the film.

Air Hawks

1935; 68 minutes. DIRECTOR: Albert S. Rogell. SCREENPLAY: Griffith Jay and Grace Neville. STORY: Ben Pivar. PHOTOGRAPHY: Henry Freulich. EDITOR: Richard Cahoon. MUSIC DIRECTOR: Louis Silvers. CAST: Ralph Bellamy (Barry Eldon), Tala Birell (Rene Dupont), Wiley Post (Himself), Douglass Dumbrille (Victor Arnold), Robert Allen (Bill Lewis), Billie Seward (Mona Greenwood), Victor Kilian (Tiny Davis), Robert Middlemass (Martin Drewen), Geneva Mitchell (Gertie Dunlap), Wyrley Birch (Holden), Edward Van Sloan (Professor Schulter), Egon Brecher (Leon), Bill [William] Irving (Jerry), Harry Strang (Taxi Driver), Peggy Terry (Blondie), Al Hill (Pete), C. Franklyn Parker (Ed Burbank), George Offerman, Jr. (Office Boy), Charles C. Wilson (Newspaper Editor), Guy Usher (Detective Shelton), Arthur Rankin (Pilot), Inez Courtney, Elise Cavanna (Nurses), James Farley (Harrington), Marianne Edwards (Dorothy Dunlap), Charles King (Ambulance Driver), Pat Flaherty (Frank Dunlap), Bob Stanley (Friend), John Irwin, Charles Marsh, James A. Guifoyle, Earle Bunn (Mechanics), Billy West, Steve Clark, Parker McConnell, Don Roberts, Sam Finn (Newsmen), Frank O'Connor (Ambulance Bystander), Yvonne Bertrand, Jeanne Lawrence, Ethel Bryant (Girls in Night Club), Roscoe Turner (Aviator), Niles Welch (Dispatcher McCoy), William Lally (Waiter), Frank Fanning (Detective), Gino Corrado (Headwaiter), Eddie Foster (Dancer), Joseph Sawyer, Ed Hart (Men), Elaine Walters (Woman).

Ben Pivar, who later produced several 1940s horror pictures for Universal, wrote "Air Fury," the story that served as the basis for this aviation thriller which contained a science fiction subplot. With advertising proclaiming "Super-Flyer of the Stratosphere," *Air Hawks* provided aerial thrills mixed with a love story and espionage. Noted pilots Wiley Post and Roscoe Turner performed the film's flying stunts and appeared in the feature (third-billed Post came in only briefly at the finale). About three months after the film's spring 1935 release, Post was killed in the air crash near Point Barrow, Alaska, which also took the life of Will Rogers.

Consolidated Airlines owner Martin Drewen (Robert Middlemass) wants to buy out rival Barry Eldon's (Ralph Bellamy) Independent Transcontinental Lines but Eldon intends to prove his belief that mail can be profitably carried by airplanes. Eldon meets beautiful Renee Dupont (Tala Birell) in a taxi and later sees her again at a casino run by Victor Arnold (Douglass Dumbrille), where she dances. Arnold makes a deal with Consolidated to use a ray gun invented by Professor Schulter (Edward Van Sloan) to take down rival planes and control the airways. During an experimental flight with the ray gun, Shulter destroys one of Eldon's planes. The air patrol urges Eldon to ground his craft.

As Eldon decides to back a new plane designed to break the transcontinental flight record, his friend, news hawk Tiny Davis (Victor Kilian), locates the professor's laboratory. A phone number found there leads Eldon and Tiny to Arnold's casino where they find a map of Independent's air routes and components for the ray gun. Arnold and Drewen plan to eliminate Eldon, but Renee warns him and then leaves with her boss on a plane piloted by Eldon. He reveals himself after they are in the air and makes Arnold identify the truck that Schulter uses to carry the ray gun; he then bombs the vehicle. Tiny and aviator Wiley Post (himself) fly Eldon's plane and break the flight record. Martin Drewen is apprehended, and Eldon and Renee fly to Washington, D.C., to sign the first aviation mail contract.

A fast-paced and entertaining effort, with fine performances, *Air Hawks* was a good dual biller which acquitted itself well in the popular field of aviation movies. Still, Andre Sennwald of the *New York Times* thought it a "headstrong tale" that "spends most of its time on the minor side of film entertainment." A highlight of the feature was the work of Edward Van Sloan as the European (the plot hints at both German and Russian) scientist who gleefully aids the greedy Arnold and Drewen, using his ray gun to destroy American aircraft with electricity. This marked his second mad scientist role at Columbia, having earlier portrayed the madman in 1932's *Behind the Mask* (q.v.). Prior to the release of *Air Hawks*, Ralph Bellamy starred in Columbia's *Below the Sea* (1933) and *Before Midnight* (1933) (qq.v.), and he would go on to headline *The Man Who Lived Twice* (1936) (q.v.).

The Ambushers

1968; 102 minutes; Color. PRODUCER: Irving Allen. ASSOCIATE PRODUCER: Douglas Netter. DIRECTOR: Henry Levin. SCREENPLAY: Herbert Baker, from the novel by Donald Hamilton. PHOTOGRAPHY: Edward Colman and Burnett Guffey. EDITOR: Harold F. Kress. MUSIC: Hugo Montenegro. SONG: Hugo Montenegro and Herbert Baka. ART DIRECTOR: Joe Wright. SOUND: James Flaster and Jack Haynes. SETS: Richard Spero. COSTUME DESIGN: Oleg Cassini. MAKEUP: Ben Lane. UNIT PRODUCTION MANAGER: Howard Pine. SPECIAL EFFECTS: Danny Lee. CHOREOGRAPHY: Mary Jane Mangler. SECOND UNIT DIRECTOR: James Havens. ASSISTANT DIRECTOR: Jerome M. Siegel. CAST: Dean Martin (Matt Helm), Senta Berger (Francesca Madeiros), Janice Rule (Sheila Sommers), James Gregory (MacDonald), Albert Salmi (Jose Ortega/Leopold Caselius), Kurt Kasznar (Quintana/Chidrick), Beverly Adams (Lovey Kravezit), David Mauro (Nassim), Roy Jenson (Karl), John Brascia (Rocco), Linda Foster (Linda), Annabella, Kyra Bester, Penny Brahms, Lena Cederham, Dee Duffy, Karin Fedderson, Terry Hughes, Yumiko Ishizuka, Alena Johnston, Ulla Lindstrom, Susannah Moore, Marilyn Tindall, Jann Watson (Slaygirls), Mauritz Hugo (Foreign Agent). Alexandra Hay (Quintana's Secretary), John Indrisano (Assassin Rapist), Edit Angold (Old Woman), Nick Dimitri (Parking Lot Thug).

The Ambushers, the third of four Matt Helm spy spoofs starring Dean Martin, was based on Donald Hamilton's 1963 novel and was filmed in Mexico. Grossing nearly $5 million, the production received a critical lambasting but was popular with theatergoers who enjoyed Martin's boozy, light-hearted antics and its bevy of beautiful young women. *Variety* complained about the feature's "tedious plot resolution right out of old serials.... Acting, writing and direction are pedestrian." Howard Thompson in the *New York Times* called it "[s]easonal junk" and complained about "its air of tired stupidity and professional staleness." In *The Espionage Filmography* (2001), Paul Mavis adjudged, "Columbia's answer to the Bond craze, the Helm films have shoddy production values, a heavy reliance on clichéd sex jokes, a constant parade of anonymous beauties, and tired old Dino, who looks as if he's disgusted with us for watching this drivel. Some of the last scenes in Mexico do have a certain comic-book look, utterly spoiled by the abysmal process shots." Containing the usual array of Martin wisecracks, the feature failed to let its star croon (outside of a bit of "Everybody Loves Somebody Sometime," his theme song). The feature title tune was sung by Tommy Boyce and Bobby Hart, who recorded it for AandM Records. This time the outing showcased futuristic weaponry like a retractable gun, a metal destroyer, camera pistol, heat camera and a handheld object control weapon.

When Intelligence Counter-Espionage (ICE) conducts a test flight of a new flying disc piloted by Sheila Sommers (Janice Rule), the craft is brought down by a mysterious ray and disappears along with its pilot. Six months later, at a field training school, agent Matt Helm (Martin) sees Sheila, who is in deep shock. Helm's beautiful secretary Lovey Kravezit (Beverly Adams) arrives with a message from his boss, MacDonald (James Gregory), with orders to get close to Sheila, who once pretended to be his (Helm's) wife on a mission, and find out what she can remember. When a male nurse tries to inject Sheila, she is saved by Helm and MacDonald and she regains her memory—but thinks she is married to Helm. In the guise of a photographer, Helm goes to Acapulco with Sheila in order to infiltrate the brewery of Montezuma Beer manufacturer Quintana (Kurt Kasznar), whose real name is Chidnick, a suspect in the theft. They are given a tour of the business by Quintana and at a party they meet swinger Francesca Madeiros (Senta Berger). Quintana informs cohort Jose Ortega (Albert Salmi) that Helm's wife is really Sheila.

Helm gets word from MacDonald that Ortega is actually international criminal Leopold Caselius. Sheila shoots Ortega, whom she recognizes as the man who tortured her after he sabotaged ICE's space mission and stole the flying saucer. She is unaware that the gun she used contains blanks. An attempt is made to kill her and Helm but it is thwarted by Francesca. Helm visits Francesca who wants to find Caselius, not knowing he is Ortega, because she wants to kill him for causing trouble in her country. When Helm refuses to tell her his whereabouts, she drugs him by kissing him with tainted lipstick. Sheila arrives and at gunpoint forces Francesca to give Helm an antidote. The trio agree to work together to bring in Ortega. Later, Sheila informs Helm that she has totally regained her memory and she too wants to kill Ortega for what he did to her. That night the two agents sleep together in a tent on the beach and the next day they masquerade as Mexicans and try to spy on Ortega. Helm follows him into the brewery but falls into a beer vat where he finds a drowning Quintana. Helm saves Quintana after he reveals where Ortega is headquartered. Helm and Sheila then drive inland and along the way they pick up Francesca, who is also heading to Ortega's fortress retreat. Nearing the location, Helm and Sheila proceed on foot and send Francesca alone since Ortega is unaware she wants to kill him. Using an infrared camera, Helm locates the flying disc hidden near the compound but at the fortress he is captured and taken to Ortega, as is Sheila. Foreign agent Hassim (David Mauro) wants to buy the craft for his country. After informing Francesca and Hassim that he has sold the saucer to an Oriental for $100 million, Ortega orders Helm shot by a firing squad. Helm uses mind-altering smoke from a cigarette to stop Quintana and his guards from shooting him and makes a getaway. Francesca finds the craft, but before she can board it she is strangled by Hassim. When he tries to fly the disc, he is fried by its electro-magnetic force to which only women are immune. When Ortega questions Sheila about ICE, she uses the lipstick drug to put him out of commission. As she heads for the saucer, he takes the antidote and orders Quintana to lock the ship's control device. Ortega follows Sheila to the saucer but is killed by its magnetic force. Quintana pulls a switch sending the craft, which is mounted on a railroad car flatbed, careening over tracks that lead to a cliff above the ocean. Helm follows the disc on a motorcycle, and when Sheila tries to use the car's brake to halt it, he lifts her off the flatbed with a ray gun and brings her to safety with him as the saucer crashes over the cliff.

Preceded by the Matt Helm flicks *The Silencers* and *Murderer's Row* (both 1966) [qq.v.], *The Ambushers* was followed by *The Wrecking Crew* (1969) [q.v.].

Arañas Infernales (Hellish Spiders)

1968; 85 minutes. PRODUCER-SCREENPLAY: Luis Enrique Vergara. DIRECTOR: Federico Curiel. PHOTOGRAPHY: Eduardo Valdez. EDITOR: Jose Juan Mungula. MUSIC: Jorge Perez Herrera. SONGS: Alvaro Carrillo, Federico Curiel and Amando Manzaneo. PRODUCTION DESIGN: Artis Gener. SOUND: Jesus Sanchez. PRODUCTION MANAGER: Raul Manjarrez. UNIT PRODUCTION MANAGER: Jose Rodriguez Rivera. MAKEUP: Amando Islas. SPECIAL EFFECTS: Ricardo Sainz. ASSISTANT DIRECTOR: Angel Rodriguez. CAST: Blue Demon (Himself), Blanca Sanchez (Hilda), Martha Elena Cervantes (Arianec), Ramon Bugarini (Police Lt. Robles), Sergio Virel (Jose), Jessica Mungula (Victim), Fernando Oses (Prince Ocram), Frankenstein [Nathanael Leon] (Moloc), Rene Barrera, Enrique Ramirez, Vincent Lara "Cacama," Juan Garza, Marco Antonio Arzate, Jose Luis Fernandez, Octavio Munoz, Jose E. Vergara.

Between 1966 and 1969, Columbia Pictures released several genre films made in Mexico by producer Luis Enrique Vergara for Spanish-language theaters on the U.S. side of the U.S.-Mexico border. In addition, Columbia also distributed the Filmica Vergara productions in Mexico and other locales. *Arañas Infernales* headlined masked professional wrestler Blue Demon, as did *La Sombra del Murciélago* (The Shadow of the Bat) [q.v.], issued the same year. Vergara, who often came up with the ideas for his features, wrote the screenplay.

The feature proved to be one of his tackier productions with the alien spiders of the title being little more than black blobs with oversized eyes and legs. The feature had long, drawn-out sequences and was padded with wrestling footage, and the scenes aboard the alien spaceship are dark and murky. The humans who are hypnotized into aiding the alien arachnids sometimes wear black capes with spider insignias on the back. The feature included brief shots from *Plan 9 from Outer Space* (1958) and *Teenagers from Outer Space* (1959), and footage from it cropped up in the compilation *It Came from Hollywood* (1982).

As flying saucers invade the country, Blue Demon (himself) wins a wrestling match. Later, as he and his friend Jose (Sergio Virel) are driving, they are attacked by a saucer and find a skeleton inside a car, the driver having been a victim of a ray from the object.

The aliens are spiders from the galaxy Aracnea who feed on human brains. A spider in human form, Arianec (Martha Elena Cervantes), leads the invasion while getting orders from her superiors on their home planet. After Blue Demon enters and helps win a tag team match, alien-controlled humans kidnap a woman (Jessica Mungula) who is sacrificed to a giant spider. Blue Demon and Jose are questioned by Police Lt. Robles (Ramon Bugarini) about their seeing the saucers. Along with Jose's girlfriend Hilda (Blanca Sanchez), the men search the area for a saucer and are observed by Arianec and her minions. She uses a ray to paralyze the quartet but Blue Demon revives and defeats the zombies who attack him. The aliens send Prince Ocram (Fernando Oses) to the area where he easily defeats a trio of grapplers. Hilda trails him to castle catacombs where she is caught in a giant spider web but manages to escape. She later tells Blue Demon and Jose what happened. When Blue Demon meets Ocram in the ring, he finds him nearly invincible. After Ocram is knocked out of the ring during the match, his right hand turns into a huge spider. He tries to kill Blue Demon with its venom but the masked man forces him to run from the arena as the crowd stampedes. Jose and Hilda are kidnapped by the zombies. Robles attempts to stop Ocram but dies from the spider's venom. The abducted couple are taken to the castle where Ocram meets with his leader. Hilda is caught in the giant spider web as Blue Demon revives and rescues Jose. As Blue Demon battles with Ocram, Jose frees Hilda. The masked man destroys the ship's control panel, causing it to take off and explode. Blue Demon, Jose and Hilda leave the castle knowing the alien invasion has failed.

While not as popular as his arch-rival, sometimes cinema monster fighter Santo, Blue Demon (Calejandro Munoz Moreno; 1922-2000) was one of Mexico's great wrestling heroes. He appeared in some two dozen horror movies including *Blue Demon Contra el Poder Satánico* (Blue Demon vs. the Satanic Power) (1966), *Santo Contra Blue Demon en la Atlantida* (Santo vs. Blue Demon in Atlantis) (1969), *El Mundo de los Muertos* (The Land of the Dead) (1970), *Las Momias de Guanajuato* (The Mummies of Guanajuato) (1972), *Santo y Blue Demon Contra Dracula y el Hombre Lobo* (Santo and Blue Demon vs. Dracula and the Wolfman) (1973), *Santo y Blue Demon Contra el*

Doctor Frankenstein (Santo and the Blue Demon vs. Dr. Frankenstein) (1974), *La Mansión de las 7 Momias* (The Mansion of the 7 Mummies) (1977) and *Misterio en las Bermudas* (Mystery in the Bermudas) (1979).

Bait

1954; 79 minutes. PRODUCER-DIRECTOR: Hugo Haas. ASSOCIATE PRODUCER: Robert Erlik. SCREENPLAY: Samuel W. Taylor. ADDITIONAL DIALOGUE: Hugo Haas. PHOTOGRAPHY: Eddie Fitzgerald. EDITOR: Robert S. Eisen. MUSIC: Vaclav Divina. ART DIRECTOR: William Glasgow. SPECIAL EFFECTS: Jack Rabin and Lee Zavitz. CAST: Cleo Moore (Peggy), John Agar (Ray Brighton), Hugo Haas (Marko), Emmett Lynn (Foley), Bruno VeSota (Webb), Jan Englund (Annie), George Keymas (Chuck), Sir Cedric Hardwicke (Satan/Narrator).

Working title: *Fever*.

Hugo Haas (1901–1968) was a Czech stage and film actor who directed five features in Hungary in 1937–38 before coming to the United States, eventually going to Hollywood in the mid–1940s as a character actor. In the early 1950s he produced, directed and starred in a quartet of features for Columbia, three of which he scripted. *Bait*, the final one, is introduced and narrated by Sir Cedric Hardwicke as Satan. It also starred Haas' busty, blonde protégé Cleo Moore, who headlined his earlier studio efforts *Strange Fascination* (1952) and *One Girl's Confession* (1953) and would again work with him in *Hold Back Tomorrow* (1955), which reunited them with *Bait* co-star John Agar, and *Hit and Run* (1957).

Down-on-his-luck laborer Ray Brighton (John Agar) agrees to help aging prospector Marko (Hugo Haas) locate a gold mine he discovered years before. (Marko and his partner found the mine but the other man died in a blizzard. Marko survived but cannot remember the mine's locale.) Despite the warnings of others, Ray and his dog Mike go into the mountains with Marko in search of the claim. At a remote store run by Foley (Emmett Lynn) they meet beautiful Peggy (Cleo Moore), a single mother whose son is in an orphanage. Shunned by society, the only work she can get is with Foley. Marko warns Ray to avoid her.

The two men set up camp in an old cabin and begin searching for the mine. After a few weeks Peggy comes to the cabin to restock their supplies. Ray asks her for a date which she refuses. Not long afterward, Ray finds the lost mine shaft and he and Marko being working it. As winter approaches, Marko schemes how to cheat Ray out of his share of the gold and settles on a plan that involves Peggy. Going to Foley's store, Marko stops the old man from forcing himself on the girl and then asks her to marry him. The two are wed and she returns to the cabin with Marko, who then plays a cat-and-mouse game as he accuses Ray of wanting his wife. While Peggy remains true to Marko, she admits to having feelings for Ray. Marko poisons Ray's dog when the canine spoils his plans to spy on his wife and partner. Marko pretends to head to the store, only to secretly stay and watch the two. Realizing that Marko is outside, Ray has Peggy turn out the light. When Marko breaks into the cabin, the two men fight. Peggy decides to leave with Ray, who splits the gold three ways. Marko tries to kill him and instead ends up with a broken leg. As Peggy and Ray make it to the highway, Marko goes out into the blizzard and perishes.

Hardwicke's brief but pleasing work as Satan puts *Bait* in the fantasy film category. Otherwise it is a cheaply made, mundane and rather boring little effort and hardly one of Haas' better cinema undertakings. Bosley Crowther in the *New York Times* called the story "a pitifully meager affair," the acting "leanly and laughingly done"; according to Crowther, the film's brevity was its "one shining virtue."

Battle in Outer Space

1960; 90 minutes; Color. PRODUCER: Tomoyuki Tanaka. DIRECTOR: Ishiro Honda. SCREENPLAY: Shinichi Sekizawa. STORY: Jojiro Okami. PHOTOGRAPHY: Hajime Koizumi. EDITOR: Kazuji Taira. MUSIC: Akira Ifukube. SOUND: Choschichiro Mikami. SPECIAL EFFECTS: Eiji Tsuburaya. PRODUCTION MANAGER: Yasuaki Sakamoto. PRODUCTION DESIGN: Teruski Abe. ASSISTANT DIRECTOR: Koji Kajita. CAST: Ryo Ikebe (Dr. Ichior Katsumiya), Kyoko Anzai (Etsuko Shiraishi), Yoshio Tsuchiya (Yuicki Iwamura), Hisaya Ito (Engineer Kogure), Koreya Senda (Professor Kenjiro Adachi), Leonard Stanford (Dr. Roger Richardson), Harold Conway (Dr. Immerman), George Wyman (Dr. Achmed), Elise Ritcher (Sylvia), Nadao Kirino (Okada), Kozo Nomura (Squadron Captain), Fuyuki Murakami (Inspector Ariake), Ikio Sawamura (Railroad Inspector), Jiro Kumagi (Lieutenant General), Katsumi Tezuka (Maritime Forces General), Miksuo Tsuda (Air Maritime Forces General), Tadashi Okabe (Adjutant), Rinsaku Ogata, Koichi Sato, Saburo Kadowaki (Astronomers), Osman Yusuf, Tatsuo Araki, Yoshiyuki Uemura (Crew Members), Heinz Bolmer (Advisor), Yutaka Oka (Scientist), Kisao Hatamochi (Communications Officer), Ed Keane (U.S. Army General), Yasuhisa Tsutsumi (Train Engineer), Shigeo Kato (Assistant Train Engineer), Minoru Takada (Commander), George Whitman (Roger), Roma Carlson (Roger's Wife), Yukihiko Gondo (Official), Shinjiru Hirota, Yokikose Kamimura, Jirya Kimagaya, Ketsumi Yamada (Aliens).

A semi-sequel to Toho Productions' *The Mysterians* (1957), *Battle in Outer Space* was a co-production of Columbia and Toho, filmed in Japan and issued there in 1959 as *Uchu Daisenso*. It was the first Japanese film offered stateside to list its native cast on posters and in other advertising material. It brought back the character of Professor Adachi from the first film; its heroine, Etsuko Shiraishi, was the sister of the heroine in *The Mysterians*. The two features had some of the same filmmakers, including producer Tomoyuki Tanaka, director Ishiro Honda (the helmsman of scores of Japanese science fiction outings), music composer Akira Ifukube and special effects artist Eiji Tsuburaya. The film's plot also brought back the Earth Defense Force from the original, with the nations of the world again uniting to fight off an alien invasion.

The story begins with flying saucers attacking a space station and then terrorizing various Earth cities. At the United Nations, Japan's Professor Adachi (Koreya Senda) leads a forum on the planet's defenses while Iranian representative Dr. Achmed (George Wyman) attempts to take a ray gun. When he fails, he runs outside and is disintegrated by a beam from a saucer. When an alien chip is found among the scientist's ashes, Adachi realizes that Achmed was under the control of the attackers.

A team of astronauts and scientists, including Adachi and Dr. Roger Richardson (Leonard Stanford), takes two rockets to the Moon. One of the crew members, Iwamura (Yoshio Tsuchiya), is under the control of the aliens. As the ships are being bombarded by a meteor shower, Iwamura unsuccessfully tries to destroy one of the spacecraft. On the lunar surface, the teams find a huge cave which houses the headquarters of the invaders, who are from the planet Natal. Using advanced laser guns, the Earthlings attack the base as Iwamura is ordered by the aliens to destroy the rocket ships. He blows up one of the vessels before the aliens lose control of his mind and he realizes the harm he has done. He now helps his allies return to the remaining ship, destroying three saucers before being killed. Back on Earth, defense forces unite to fight the aliens who attack and badly damage San Francisco, Gotham and Tokyo, the latter with an anti-gravity weapon. Using powerful laser cannons, the Earthlings destroy the invaders' main ship and the Natalians retreat.

The highlights of the

Poster for *Battle in Outer Space* (1960).

feature includes Honda's fast-paced direction, Tsuburaya's wonderful special effects and the Ifukube score, which was later reused in *Godzilla vs. Gigan* (1972). In 1963 a photo novel of the film called *Querra no Espaco* appeared as an edition of the Brazilian magazine *Cosmos Adventuras*. Interestingly, the aliens in the film, while they appear to be humanoid, are not seen outside their spacesuits.

When Columbia Pictures released *Battle in Outer Space* in the U.S. in the summer of 1960, it was usually screened as part of a double feature, often in tandem with *12 to the Moon*, *The Electronic Monster* (qq.v.) or MGM's *The Time Machine*. Although the public liked the space adventure, critics were mixed in their reactions. While *New York Times* critic Howard Thompson felt "the plot is absurd and is performed in dead earnest," he thought "some of the artwork is downright nifty.... [T]he lunar landscape is just as pretty as it can be." *Variety* called it a "rousing exploitation entry" while the *Monthly Film Bulletin* dubbed it an "[a]imless, witless war-of-the-worlds story."

In 1977 Toho produced *Wakusei Daiseno*, which Gold Key Entertainment issued to U.S. television as *Battle in Outer Space 2*.

Before I Hang

1940; 62 minutes. PRODUCER: Wallace MacDonald. DIRECTOR: Nick Grinde. SCREENPLAY: Karl Brown and Robert D. Andrews. PHOTOGRAPHY: Benjamin H. Kline. EDITOR: Charles Nelson. MUSIC: Morris Stoloff. ART DIRECTOR: Lionel Banks. SOUND: J.S. Westmoreland. ASSISTANT DIRECTOR: Milton Carter. CAST: Boris Karloff (Dr. John Garth), Evelyn Keyes (Martha Garth), Bruce Bennett (Dr. Paul Ames), Edward Van Sloan (Dr. Ralph Howard), Ben Taggart (Warden Thompson), Pedro de Cordoba (Victor Sondini), Wright Kramer (George Wharton), Bertram Marburgh (Stephen Barclay), Don Beddoe (Police Captain McGraw), Robert Fiske (District Attorney), Kenneth MacDonald (Anson), Frank Richards (Otto Kron), John Tyrrell (Sanders), Eddie Laughton (Guard), Stanley Brown (Gate Guard), Frederick Burton (Governor Prentiss), Ernie Adams (Sam), Richard Fiske (Mandish), Edward Earle (Dr. Nichols), James T. Mack (Butler), Charles Trowbridge (Judge Braden), Gohr Van Vieck (Dispatcher), George McKay (Officer Reardon), Jack Cheatham (Patrolman Olson), Bert Moorhouse (Defense Counsel), Edmund Mortimer, Sam Harris (Men in Courtroom).

Working title: *The Wizard of Death*.

Before I Hang was the third of five Columbia films that Boris Karloff starred in between 1939 and 1942. Like its predecessors *The Man They Could Not Hang* and *The Man with Nine Lives* (qqv.) it was directed by Nick Grinde and produced by Wallace MacDonald. Although it moved quickly and was well made, it was a dour affair with its main asset being the re-teaming of Karloff and Edward Van Sloan, who had previously worked together in *Frankenstein* (1931) and Columbia's *Behind the Mask* and *The Black Room* (qqv.).

The feature opens with elderly scientist Dr. John Garth (Karloff) on trial for the mercy killing of a senile patient. Despite his humanitarian explanation for the crime he is sentenced to hang, much to the sorrow of his daughter Martha (Evelyn Keyes) and her fiancé, Dr. Paul Ames (Bruce Bennett), Garth's assistant. Once Garth is incarcerated, the prison physician, Dr. Ralph Howard (Edward Van Sloan), convinces the warden (Ben Taggart) to let Garth continue his experiments in perfecting a serum which will indefinitely prolong life. Just before he is about to be executed, Garth has Howard inject him with the serum which contains the blood of a hanged killer. Garth collapses after the injection and awakens to find his sentence has been commuted to life in prison, thanks to the efforts of Martha and Paul, and that he now looks 20 years younger. Under the spell of the serum, however, Garth murders Howard and a prison trusty (Frank Richards); he is not later connected to the crimes and does not remember committing them. Soon Garth's sentence is commuted and he returns home to live with Martha, who notices a difference in his demeanor. Garth tries to convince three old friends, concert pianist Victor Sondini (Pedro de Cordoba), businessmen George Wharton (Wright Kramer) and Stephen Barclay (Bertram Marburgh), to let him inoculate them with the serum. When they refuse he kills them, one by one, but comes under the suspicion of Police Captain McGraw (Don Beddoe). After Barclay's killing, Martha confronts her father who almost attacks her but the girl faints and is saved by the arrival of Paul and McGraw and his men. Realizing the horror of nearly murdering his own child, Garth goes back to prison where he confronts the gate guard (Stanley Brown) and is shot and killed. Later Martha tells Paul that her father would have wanted him to continue his work.

Issued in the fall of 1940, *Before I Hang* appealed to its intended audience. *Variety* noted, "[It] is well geared to b.o. [box office] in the action districts, patronized by youngsters and elders who spend for this kind of thriller.... There's not much room for anyone save Karloff, who lumbers about amongst an array of bubbling gadgets, fiddles and hypodermics the first half, and then goes calling with murder his purpose during the second half." The *New York Post* opined, "The picture is fanciful pseudo-science which builds to an exciting murder orgy," while the British *Kinematograph Weekly* concurred, calling it a "Grand Guignol thriller with a pseudo-scientific background.... Boris Karloff takes himself seriously as Garth and his sincere acting helps to cloak much of the incredibility of the part."

Before Midnight

1933; 63 minutes. DIRECTOR: Lambert Hillyer. STORY-SCREENPLAY: Robert Quigley. PHOTOGRAPHY: John Stumar. EDITOR: Otto Meyer. SOUND: George Cooper. COSTUMES: Robert Kalloch. CAST: Ralph Bellamy (Inspector Trent), June Collyer (Janet Holt), Claude Gillingwater (John Fry/Edward Arnold), Bradley Page (Howard B. Smith), Betty Blythe (Mavis Fry), Arthur Pierson (Dr. Anthony R. Marsh), George Cooper (Officer Stubby), William Jeffrey (Edward Arnold/John Fry), Joseph Crehan (Captain Frank Flynn), Otto Yamaoka (Kono), Edward LeSaint (Harry Graham), Mary Foy (Housekeeper), Robert Kortman (Detective), Fred "Snowflake" Toones (Taxi Driver), Kit Guard (Taxi Driver Jack).

In 1933 Columbia initiated a series of detective programmers featuring the character of Trent, played by studio workhorse Ralph Bellamy. For the initial outing, *Before Midnight*, released in November, the studio chose a vehicle which starts off like a horror picture. It opens during a terrible thunderstorm and takes place in a creepy, gloomy mansion which houses a curse by which its owners are murdered after the appearance of a bloodstain and the stopping of a clock just before midnight. Following these events, however, the feature settles into a typical murder mystery, with the case being handled in a methodical manner by the rather surly, chain-smoking Trent. Mordaunt Hall in the *New York Times* claimed that it "is never exciting," adding, "It is just a puerile puzzle in which a zealous attempt is made to deceive the audience." On the other hand, the Jefferson City, Missouri, *Sunday News and Tribune* felt, "It is guaranteed to provide enough chills and thrills and gasps to satisfy the most jaded mystery fan.... Ralph Bellamy has a colorful role as the brilliant Trent."

During a violent storm, private detective Trent (Bellamy) arrives at the mansion of Edward Arnold (William Jeffrey), located near the town of Forest Lake, over 50 miles outside New York City. He is greeted by John Fry (Claude Gillingwater), Arnold's secretary, and he also meets Arnold's ward Janet Holt (June Collyer). Arnold tells Trent he is afraid of being murdered like his ancestors. Not long afterward he dies, with his physician, Dr. Anthony Marsh (Arthur Pierson), ruling the death a heart attack. Trent feels that Arnold was poisoned and orders an autopsy. It confirms his belief and he teams up with local police detective Stubby (George Cooper) to investigate the homicide.

Fry informs him that Arnold made a fortune in China and had only been home for a year. Janet tells Trent that she and Dr. Marsh are in love but that Arnold had forbidden them to wed. When Trent informs Janet that he suspects Marsh killed Arnold with a hypodermic injection, she tells him that Mavis Fry (Betty Blythe), John's wife, also knows how to use a syringe. Mavis denies killing Arnold but admits he gave her a check for $3,000 to leave after she told him she hated her husband. That night Arnold's lawyer, Howard Smith (Bradley Page), sneaks into Arnold's study and locates a diary but is stopped by Mavis, and struggle ensues. The events are overheard by houseman Kono (Otto Yamaoka). Mavis lets Smith escape and claims she does not know her assailant. Trent then arrests banker Harry Graham (Edward LeSaint) for the killing since he was seen in the Arnold house just before the man died (Arnold had threatened to withdraw a million dollars from Graham's troubled bank). After receiving a telegram from China, Trent confronts Fry, who admits he is really Arnold and that his best friend, Fry, had changed places with him in order to combat the family curse. Arnold, still pretending to be Fry, then informs Janet that she has inherited the Arnold estate. That night Trent enters Arnold's study and finds Kono, who is killed as he is about to reveal the murderer. After Trent tells the household about Kono's murder, Mavis goes to Smith's office and demands the diary at gunpoint. As she is leaving, she is abducted by a man (Robert Kortman) who is really a policeman. He takes the diary to Stubby who, in turn, gives it to Trent, who reads it and learns the motive for Fry's murder. Trent then figures out that the pen used by Fry to write Mavis' check housed a poisoned needle. He confronts Arnold, who admits to killing both Fry and Kono. Arnold also tells him he planned to murder Smith to stop him from blackmailing Janet, who is really his illegitimate daughter. In order to avoid a scandal, Arnold shoots himself.

Before Midnight opened and closed with a police captain (Joseph Crehan) talking about the case. The feature was followed by three others, all released in 1934 and co-starring Shirley Grey: *One Is Guilty*, *The Crime of Helen Stanley* and *Girl in Danger*.

Both *Before Midnight* and *One Is Guilty* were directed by Lambert Hillyer while the last two were helmed by D. Ross Lederman. Best known for making Westerns, Hillyer also directed two Universal horror features, *The Invisible Ray* and *Dracula's Daughter* (both 1936).

Harrison's Reports declared that *Before Midnight* was "fair to poor" in box office performance.

Behind the Mask

1932; 68 minutes. DIRECTOR: John Webb Dillon. SCREENPLAY: Jo Swerling, from his story "In the Secret Service." CONTINUITY: Dorothy Howell. PHOTOGRAPHY: Teddy [Ted] Tetzlaff. EDITOR: Otis Garrett. SOUND: Glenn Rominger. ASSISTANT DIRECTOR: Edward Sloman. CAST: Jack Holt (Jack Hart/Quinn), Constance Cummings (Julie Arnold), Boris Karloff (Jim Henderson), Claude King (Mr. Arnold), Edward Van Sloan (Dr. Munsell/Dr. August Steiner/Mr. X), Bertha Mann (Nurse Edwards), Willard Robertson (Captain E.J. Hawkes), Tommy [Thomas E.] Jackson (Burke), Harry Tenbrook (Gorman), Martha Mattox (Hotel Maid), Jessie Arnold (Nurse), Louis Natheaux (Office Assistant/Man in Cemetery), Rodney Hildebrand (Guard), Sherry Hall (Secretary).

Working titles: *The Man Who Dared* and *Secret Service*.

"Who Is the Murdering Monster?" and "A Slinking Fiend ... Skulking Terror ... Mad Murder!" were two of the taglines given *Behind the Mask*, which came to theaters late in February 1932. Issued just a couple of month's after Universal's blockbuster *Frankenstein* (1931), but made before it, this production featured two of the stars of that film, Boris Karloff and Edward Van Sloan. As a result, Columbia played up the horror angles of the plot which included a mad scientist, a cavernous old house during a terrible storm, electrical laboratory equipment, a spooky graveyard, the exhumation of a body, and threatened human vivisection. Through it all, though, the film was basically part of the solid series of action features that Jack Holt starred in for the studio during the 1930s. *Variety* noted, "Exploited as another horror picture, this doesn't horrify sufficiently to class with previous baby-scarers" but added it was a "not-so-bad Secret Service story."

Convict Quinn (Holt), who is really Secret Service agent Jack Hart, tells his cellmate Jim Henderson (Karloff) that he plans to make a prison break. After making his escape, he meets with another agent (Harry Tenbrook) who provides him with a flesh wound and directions to the estate of Arnold (Claude King), who is suspected of being part of a dope ring. There he meets Arnold's beautiful daughter Julie (Constance Cummings), who tends his wounds. Telling Arnold that he is an escaped convict sent by Henderson, he gets a job as his chauffeur. Captain Hawkes (Willard Robertson), the head of the Secret Service, instructs another agent, Burke (Thomas E. Jackson), to tail the recently released Henderson, who goes to see the bewhiskered Dr. August Steiner (Van Sloan). Steiner tells him to take over Arnold's job with the gang. Henderson spots his "tail" Burke and tells Steiner he is a SS man, and the doctor orders Burke killed.

Hawkes is presiding over a meeting of a citizen's council, headed by Dr. Munsell (Van Sloan), when he gets word of Burke's murder. After Jack takes Arnold to see Henderson, he gets orders from his former cellmate to fly a sea plane and get $10,000 for picking up a ship's cargo, which is really narcotics. Steiner spies Hart and tells Henderson he is a federal man, and Jim sets up a plot to kill Jack. Before going on his mission, Jack informs Julie about her father's activities. When Arnold tells her Jack has been set up by Henderson, she drives to stop him from making the flight but arrives too late. Hart carries out his orders and delivers the cargo to Henderson and his men aboard a boat; he is told to take off again and then parachute out of his plane, and they will pick him up. He fools them, however, by dropping a dummy in a parachute. When Julie goes to Hawkes to tell him what happened to Jack, she is relieved when he arrives and tells her and his boss about the intended double cross. Jack also informs Hawkes that he and Julie have fallen in love. Julie asks Hawkes and Jack to arrest her father for his own protection. When they go back to his mansion they find he has been taken to the Eastland Hospital where he dies following an emergency operation performed by Dr. Steiner, aided by Nurse Edwards (Bertha Mann). The nurse has been living in the Arnold home as a spy for Mr. X, the head of the dope ring.

Jack moves Julie to the Hotel Ansonia and after her father's funeral he goes to Steiner's office and locates a Dictaphone cylinder which implicates the doctor in the gang's operations. He has Arnold's body exhumed and taken to Dr. Munsell for an autopsy. When the coffin is opened it is found to contain narcotics. Returning to the hotel, he finds Julie has been removed to the hospital; when he goes to get her he is attacked by Steiner's men. The sadistic Steiner plans to eliminate Hart by performing a vivisection on him but Julie uses chloroform to subdue Nurse Edwards and arrives in time to save Jack by shooting Steiner. Hart unmasks him as both Dr. Munsell and Mr. X.

Van Sloan pretty much dominates *Behind the Mask* as the cold, calculating and sadistic villain who masquerades as three different people. Along with his roles as Van Helsing in *Dracula* and Professor Waldman in *Frankenstein* (both 1931), the film gave Van Sloan a chance to give one of his best portrayals in a horror part. While the first two were basically heroic ones, he was outstanding as the evil villain in this effort.

To further back the feature's reputation as a horror film, it was one of eleven Columbia releases included in the Screen Gems television package "Son of Shock," issued to TV stations in the late 1950s.

NOTE: An actor who fleetingly appears as a drug counter clerk bears a resemblance to John Wayne. Two months prior to the release of *Behind the Mask*, Wayne had an unbilled bit as a corpse in Columbia's *The Deceiver* (1931).

Bell Book and Candle

1959; 102 minutes; Color. PRODUCER: John Blaustein. DIRECTOR: Richard Quine. SCREENPLAY: Daniel Taradash, from the play by John Van Druten. PHOTOGRAPHY: James Wong Howe. EDITOR: Charles Nelson. MUSIC: George Duning. ART DIRECTOR: Cary Odell. SOUND: Franklin Hansen, Jr. SETS: Louis Diage. GOWNS: Jean Louis. MAKEUP: Ben Lane. ASSISTANT DIRECTOR: Irving Moore. CAST: James Stewart (Shepherd "Shep" Henderson), Kim Novak (Gillian "Gil" Holroyd), Jack Lemmon (Nicky Holroyd), Ernie Kovacs (Sidney Redlitch), Hermione Gingold (Mrs. Bianca de Passe), Elsa Lanchester (Aunt Queenie Holroyd), Janice Rule (Merle Kittridge), Philippe Clay (French Singer), Bek Nelson (Tina), Howard McNear (Andy White), The Brothers Candoli [Conte Candoli, Pete Candoli] (Musicians), Wolfe Barzell (Club Owner), James Lanphier (Waldo), Joe Barry (Exterminator), Gail Bonney

Poster for *Behind the Mask* (1932).

(Maid Betty), Monty Ash (Herb Store Owner), Don Brodie (Annoyed Cab Driver), John Traux (Cab Driver), Ollie O'Toole (Elevator Operator), Ted Mapes (Customer), Dick Crockett (Ad-Libber), Joe Palma, Maurice Marks, William Bloom (Men), Pyewacket the Cat (Himself).

John Van Druten's fantasy comedy *Bell Book and Candle* opened on Broadway in November 1950, starring Rex Harrison and Lilli Palmer, and ran 233 performances. The play proved popular enough to have two road companies, one in 1951-52 starring Rosalind Russell and Dennis Price and a second running for over a year in the 1952-53 theatrical season headlining Joan Bennett and Zachary Scott. Both road companies featured William Windom as Nicky Holroyd and Dorothy Sands as Aunt Queenie Holroyd. There was also a production staged in Vienna, Austria, in the fall of 1952. Rex Harrison and Lilli Palmer repeated their Broadway roles in the London version of the show which opened in October 1954 for 485 performances. Harrison and Palmer were married at the time but during the run they separated and Joan Greenwood took over the female lead. Following his divorce from Palmer in 1956, Harrison married Kay Kendall and they did a tour of the play in England.

Columbia released the film version, *Bell Book and Candle* early in 1959. This Phoenix Production was nominated for two Academy Awards: Best Art Direction-Set Decoration and Best Costume Design. In New York City on Christmas Eve, lonely primitive art store owner Gillian Holyrod (Kim Novak) finds herself attracted to book publisher Shepherd "Shep" Henderson (James Stewart), who lives in the apartment above hers. Returning home, Shep catches another neighbor, Queenie Holroyd (Elsa Lanchester), snooping in his apartment. Finding his telephone out of order he asks to use Gillian's, not knowing that Queenie is Gillian's aunt, and both are witches. While he is there, Queenie shows up and tells him she and her niece are planning to go to the Zodiac Club. After Shep leaves, Gillian makes her aunt promise to refrain from practicing witchcraft.

That evening, Shep and his fiancée Merle Kittridge (Janice Rule) go to the Zodiac Club, where Gillian's warlock brother Nicky (Jack Lemmon) plays bongos. Gillian recognizes Merle as a former rival from Wellesley College and uses her

Janice Rule and James Stewart in *Bell Book and Candle* (1958).

powers to make the music so loud, Merle and Shep are forced to leave the club. Later Gillian, Nicky and Aunt Queenie exchange Christmas gifts and Nicky gives his sister a love potion which causes flames to shoot up from a bowl. Arriving home, Shep sees the fire and rushes into Gillian's apartment. After Nicky and Queenie leave, Gillian puts him under her spell and he falls in love with the young woman. The next day he breaks off his marriage plans with Merle. At work, he finds author Sidney Redlitch (Ernie Kovacs) waiting to see him. When they first met, Shep expressed an interest to Gillian in publishing Redlitch's next book, since his current one on witchcraft in Mexico had become a best seller, and she invoked a spell bringing the author to New York. Redlitch, a neurotic drunk, proposes a book on witchcraft in Manhattan. He later talks with Shep, Gillian, Nicky and Aunt Queenie about the subject, telling them witches cannot blush, cry, drown or fall in love. He also says they hang out at the Zodiac Club. That evening, the always broke Nicky tells Sidney he is a warlock and offers to collaborate with him on the project.

Afraid she may lose Shep, Gillian asks Nicky to give up the book. When he refuses she puts a spell on it, causing Shep to reject the author's manuscript. Gillian then informs Shep that she is a witch and this is later confirmed by Aunt Queenie. Upset, Shep goes to the Zodiac Club where he meets Nicky and Sidney and they take him to Bianca De Pass (Hermoine Gingold), an established witch. Bianca brews a foul-tasting potion for Shep to drink and it removes Gillian's spell over him. He then confronts Gillian, who threatens to hex Merle. Shep goes to inform his ex-fiancée, who thinks he is insane. Gillian is unable to cast her spell because her cat Pyewacket, whom she uses to channel her powers, runs away. When it later appears at Shep's office, he takes it back to Gillian and finds out she has lost her powers by falling in love with him. As a result, the two are reunited, with Shep not knowing if his love for Gillian is magic or not.

Despite rather posh production values, *Bell Book and Candle* is an ordinary comedy fantasy which is not helped by Kim Novak's stoic performance. The rest of the cast is fine, especially Elsa Lanchester and Hermoine Gingold as eccentric witches. The feature does offer one rather amusing line: When Shep tells Merle that Gillian is a witch, she replies he is mistaken because he never learned to spell. Both *Photoplay* and the *New York Times* were taken with James Wong Howe's photography; the latter enthused, "The real magic is that color." *Variety* pinpointed the feature's main deficiency: "The hazard of the story is that there is really only one joke. This was sustained in the play by Van Druten's witting dialog. It is undercut in the picture by the fact that the backgrounds are too often as weird as the situations."

The feature does give a brief glimpse of noted jazz musicians Conte Candoli and his brother Pete. Its soundtrack was issued on Colpix Records (CP-502). In 1976 it was reissued on Citadel Records (CT-6006) and two years later resurfaced on the same label, as CT-7006.

In 1976 Columbia Pictures Television made the series pilot *Bell Book and Candle*, which was telecast September 8 of that year as an "NBC Comedy Special." Directed by Hy Averback, it featured Yvette Mimieux as Gillian, Michael Murphy as Alex Brandt, Doris Roberts as Aunt Enid and John Pleshette as Nicky. The tepid comedy failed to sell as a series.

Below the Sea

1933; 78 minutes. DIRECTOR: Albert S. Rogell. SCREENPLAY: Jo Swerling. PHOTOGRAPHY: Joseph Walker. EDITOR: Jack Dennis. SOUND: George Cooper. UNDERWATER TECHNICIAN: E. Roy Davidson. ASSISTANT DIRECTOR: Art Black. CAST: Ralph Bellamy (Steve McCreary), Fay Wray (Diana Templeton), Frederick Vogeding (Karl Schlemmer/Captain Von Boulton), Esther Howard (Lily), Paul Page (Bert Jackson), Trevor Bland (Horace Waldridge), William J. Kelly (Dr. Chapman), Richard Alexander, Kenneth MacDonald (Crew Members), Paul McVey (Party Guest).

Working title: *Beneath the Sea*.

During the early and mid–1930s, beautiful Fay Wray was menaced by a variety of screen monsters, most famously by *King Kong* (1933). She was also the object of intimidation by the evil *Doctor X* (1932), a human hunter in *The Most Dangerous Game* (1932), mad scientist Lionel Atwill in *The Vampire Bat* and *Mystery of the Wax Museum* (both 1933), and a voodoo curse in Columbia's *Black Moon* (1934) (q.v.). In *Below the Sea*, which was alternately released as *Hell's Cargo*, she is nearly done in by a giant octopus.

The feature, which Columbia issued in March 1933, begins in 1914 with German U-boat 170 carrying a cargo of gold bullion valued at three million dollars. When the commander, Von Boulton (Frederick Vogeding), orders an attack on a British clipper ship, both vessels are destroyed with Von Boulton and his first mate escaping. Having made a map of the location of the sunken U-boat, Von Boulton kills the other survivor before being rescued. Fourteen years later in San Francisco, the German now calls himself Karl Schlemmer and he teams with waterfront bar owner Lily (Esther Howard) in trying to find the treasure. They enlist the aid of loutish diver Steve McCreary (Ralph Bellamy), who demands an equal share of the gold. Deserting Lily, Schlemmer takes command of a ship which is sunk during a storm with the captain and McCreary escaping on a lifeboat. McCreary takes half the chart locating the treasure and three years later they go to work for the Chapman Expedition on the *S.S. Adventure*, a ship carrying out the underwater exploration being financed by socialite and oceanographer Diana Templeton (Wray). At first Steve and Diana do not get along but eventually they are attracted to each other as Schlemmer, the ship's captain, alerts McCreary to the fact that Lily is onboard as a stowaway.

Diana disobeys Steve's orders and goes underwater in his diving suit; she gets the bends and he rescues her. When Chapman (William J. Kelly) and fellow oceanographer Walbridge (Trevor Bland) try to get him fired, Diana comes to his rescue and the two fall in love. Schlemmer and McCreary locate the gold and chain the strongbox containing it to a buoy. The next day Schlemmer and Lily give Steve knockout drops and go for the treasure while Diana and photographer Bert Jackson (Paul Page) use a diving bell for underwater photography. Steve comes to and finds his partners gone just as a giant octopus wraps itself around the diving bell, cutting both its chain and air hose. Steve dons his diving suit and uses an underwater torch to attack the octopus, which nearly squeezes him to death before he finally kills it. He is able to re-attach the bell's chain and Diana and Bert are rescued. Through binoculars, Steve sees Schlemmer and Lily bring up the strongbox but it breaks and the gold bars drop to the bottom of the sea. The German, caught in a chain, falls overboard and drowns. Steve tells Diana she cost him a million dollars as they embrace.

The giant octopus takes *Below the Sea*, an otherwise average marine melodrama, in the realm

Lobby card for *Below the Sea* (1933) picturing Ralph Bellamy and Fay Wray.

of early cinema science fiction. The monster is a precursor of the giant squid in Columbia's *It Came from Beneath the Sea* (1955). While the creature is seen only briefly, the scenes in which McCreary battles the beast in order to keep Diana and Paul from suffocating are quite suspenseful. Also well staged is the battle scene between the German U-boat and the British ship and the storm sequence. Four minutes of the feature was filmed in two-color Technicolor but these underwater scenes are missing from the movie's television print.

Berserk

1968; 96 minutes; Color. PRODUCER: Herman Cohen. ASSOCIATE PRODUCER: Robert Sterne. DIRECTOR: Jim O'Connolly. SCREENPLAY: Aben Kandel and Herman Cohen. PHOTOGRAPHY: Desmond Dickinson. EDITOR: Raymond Poulton. MUSIC: Patrick John Scott. ART DIRECTOR: Maurice Pelling. SOUND: John Cox. Costumes: Jay Hutchinson Scott. WARDROBE: Joyce Stoneman. MAKEUP: George Partleton. PRODUCTION MANAGER: Laurie Greenwood. ASSISTANT DIRECTOR: Barry Langley. CAST: Joan Crawford (Monica Rivers), Ty Hardin (Frank Hawkins), Diana Dors (Matilda), Michael Gough (Albert Dorando), Judy Geeson (Angela Rivers), Robert Hardy (Detective Superintendent Brooks), Geoffrey Keen (Commissioner Dalby), Sydney Tafler (Harrison Liston), George Claydon (Bruno Fontana), Philip Madoc (Laszlo the Illusionist), Ambrosine Phillpotts (Miss Burrows), Thomas Cimarro (Gaspar the Great), Peter Burton (Gustavo), Golda Casimir (Bearded Lady), Ted Lune (Skeleton Man), Milton Reid (Strong Man), Marianne Stone (Wanda), Mike Iveria (Fortune Teller), Howard Goorney (Emil), Reginald Marsh (Sergeant Hutchins), Bryan Pringle (Constable Bradford), Billy Smart Circus Performers (Themselves).

Working titles: *Circus of Blood* and *Circus of Terror*.

Joan Crawford's 80th feature film, and her penultimate theatrical outing, was *Berserk*, which she made for her friend, producer Herman Cohen. Released early in 1968, it gave the veteran star the meaty role of the owner of a traveling circus plagued by a series of mysterious murders. Past 60, Crawford was still strikingly attractive; the part allows her to wear her accustomed chic wardrobe, and she also cuts quiet a figure in a top hat, red-spangled jacket and leotard as she introduced the circus acts. In the *New York Times*, Howard Thompson called her "certainly the shapeliest ringmaster ever to handle a ring microphone."

Monica Rivers (Crawford) has run the traveling Great Rivers Circus for the six years since her trapeze artist husband was killed. During a performance, high wire artist Gaspar the Great (Thomas Cimarro) dies when his rope splits, and Monica tells Albert Dorando (Michael Gough), her business partner, to make the most of the murder via publicity in order to shore up a bad financial season. Although Dorando objects, he does what he is told. He is unhappy when Monica hires newcomer Frank Hawkins (Ty Hardin) to replace Gaspar. Frank's act consists of working 60 feet above the ground, with steel bayonets below, doing "the walk of death" across a tightrope blindfolded. His act is a big success but Dorando becomes jealous because Frank has replaced him as Monica's lover. One night while stalking the newcomer, Dorando is killed when a spike is driven through his head. While the murder takes place, Monica steals her partnership agreement with Dorando and burns it. Illusionist Laszlo (Philip Madoc) calls a meeting of the circus performers and his partner and lover Matilda (Diana Dors)

Advertisement for *Berserk* (1968).

accuses Monica of the crimes. When midget Bruno (George Claydon) and the circus strong man (Milton Reid) stand up for their boss, the performers soon begin accusing each other of the crimes. Monica arrives and confronts Matilda, telling her to stop stirring up trouble.

Scotland Yard Commissioner Dalby (Geoffrey Keen) assigns Detective Superintendent Brooks (Robert Hardy) to investigate the murders. Brooks arrives at the circus and questions everyone, including Monica and Frank, who is demanding a portion of the enterprise. Monica's daughter Angela (Judy Geeson) shows up, having been expelled from private school, and Monica agrees to let her stay. Matilda is killed during a performance when the tool Laszlo uses to saw her in half malfunctions; Brooks finds out the apparatus was tampered with. Angela joins Gustavo (Peter Burton) in his knife-throwing act, but has an argument with her mother over Frank after the circus moves to London. On opening night there, Frank is stabbed in the back during his act. The killer is revealed and meets death by electrocution in the rain while being chased by Brooks.

Berserk proved to be an entertaining blend of drama, horror and circus acts with Crawford being ably supported, especially by Ty Hardin as her lover, Michael Gough as her ex-paramour, Judy Geeson as her daughter and Diana Dors as the bitchy, promiscuous Matilda. When Dorando accuses Monica of being "inhuman" when she wants to use Gaspar's death to drum up publicity, she asserts, "We're running a circus, not a charm school." Adding to the flavor of the film is the inclusion of several acts from the Billy Smart Circus, including trained elephants, horses and poodles, high wire and aerial feats, and Ingemar the Fearless and his lions. On the lighter side was the song "It Must Be Me," performed by the circus' skeleton man, bearded woman, midget and strong man.

Despite the entertaining plot with its hard-to-spot killer and the colorful circus acts, *Berserk* belonged to Crawford, as noted by Lawrence J. Quirk in *Hollywood Screen Parade* magazine: "Her figure is as trim as ever, her voice as warm and compelling, her legs rival Dietrich's, and her tigress' personality puts to shame most of the mewing kittens who call themselves 1968-style screen actresses. She is all over the picture, radiant, forceful, authoritative, a genuine movie star whose appeal never diminishes." Page Cook wrote in *Films in Review*, "Miss Crawford is still striking looking, and, by this time, can give a good performance in almost anything, even in such dreck as this." Two years after the film's release, Crawford did her last movie, *Trog*, her second horror feature for Herman Cohen. Her first genre outing came more than 40 years earlier when she was Lon Chaney's leading lady in *The Unknown* (1927).

Beware Spooks!

1939; 65 minutes. PRODUCER: Robert Sparks. DIRECTOR: Edward Sedgwick. SCREENPLAY: Richard Flournoy, Albert Duffy and Brian Marlow. STORY: Richard Flournoy. PHOTOGRAPHY: Allen G. Siegler. EDITOR: James Sweeney. MUSIC DIRECTOR: M.W. [Morris] Stoloff. ART DIRECTOR: Lionel Banks. SOUND: Edward Bernds. CAST: Joe E. Brown (Roy L. Gifford), Mary Carlisle (Betty Lou Winters Gifford), Clarence Kolb (Commissioner Lester Lewis), Marc Lawrence (Slick Eastman), Don Beddoe (Nick Bruno), George J. Lewis (Danny Emmett), Frank M. Thomas (Captain Wood), Iris Meredith (Babe), Stanley Brown (Johnny), Eddie Dunn (Police Sergeant), Walter Sande, Robert Williams, Chuck Hamilton, George Gould (Policemen), Eddie Laughton (Dr. Johnson), Robert Sterling (Bellboy), Howard C. Hickman (Judge Roth), Frank Dee (Politician), Edythe Elliott (Radio Announcer), George McKay (Cab Driver), Byron Foulger (Cashier), Joe Devlin, Joe Palma (Men at Shooting Gallery), Dickie Jones, Tommy Bupp (Boys), Charles Lane (Moore), James Blaine (Detective Adams), Ray Johnson (Popcorn Man), Claire Rochelle (Candy Girl), Ethelreda Leopold (Pretty Girl), Frank Moran, Pat McKee (Moving Men), Charles Regan, Al Rhein, Cy Schindell, Harry Bailey, Frank Bruno, Jack Egan, Stanley Mack, Harry Anderson, Anthony Merrill, Eddie Sturgis, Gene Stone, Johnnie Morris (Barkers).

Rubber-faced, big-mouthed comedian Joe E. Brown came to films in 1928 and during the years of the early talkies he developed quite a following. But by the time he starred for Columbia in *Beware Spooks!* his vogue was on the wane. Although his screen persona would have easily fit into horror and fantasy comedies, his only previous genre appearances were as Flute in Warner Bros'. *A Midsummer Night's Dream* (1935) and in *The Gladiator* (q.v.). *Beware Spooks!* did not bolster Brown's popularity and after the early 1940s his film appearances became sporadic.

Coming to theaters in the fall of 1939, it had bumbling police newcomer Roy L. Gifford (Joe E. Brown) planning a honeymoon trip to Bermuda with his new bride Betty Lou (Mary Carlisle). The newlyweds have to settle for Coney Island after Roy mistakenly helps crook Danny Emmett (George J. Lewis) pull off a bank heist.

When Roy then blunders and helps Slick Eastman (Marc Lawrence), a convicted murderer, get out of jail, he is fired by Police Commissioner Lewis (Clarence Kolb).

At their Coney Island hotel, Roy is knocked unconscious by a falling window shade. Betty Lou goes for help and returns with Danny, who helps him regain consciousness. Recognizing the thief, Roy summons the police, but upon their arrival he finds both his wife and Emmett gone and he is accused of lying. Leaving a trail of toffee, Betty Lou is tracing Danny to a spook house owned by crook Nick Bruno (Don Beddoe), and Roy soon follows her. When Roy finds Danny's corpse at the funhouse he decides to investigate. The body disappears and he accuses Nick of the killing. Sending Betty Lou to bring back help, Roy then finds Bruno has been bumped off and Slick gets the drop on him. Roy tries to escape from the killer and the two go on a wild chase through the various rigged spook house rooms before sliding down a chute and being met by Lewis and his men. Slick is arrested, Roy is reinstated into the police force and he a Betty Lou leave for their Bermuda honeymoon.

Variety termed the film a "formula comedy," adding, "Edward Sedgwick's direction keeps the comedy interest moving, despite some sagging spots in the first half. When the director gets Brown into the spook house, he utilizes every prop available to generate physical gags for laughs." *The New York Times* opined, "[F]or pure silliness, with practically no humorous justification, this flagrant misuse of the orally talented Joe E. Brown is, in its modest way, a new high in low comedy."

Birds Do It

1966; 88 minutes; Color. PRODUCERS: Ivan Tors and Stanley Colbert. EXECUTIVE PRODUCER: Ben Chapman. DIRECTOR: Andrew Marton. SCREENPLAY: Art Arthur and Arnie Logen. STORY: Leonard Kaufman. PHOTOGRAPHY: Howard Winner. EDITOR: Erwin Dumbrille. MUSIC: Stanley Matlovsky. SONG: Howard Greenfield and Jack Keller. ART DIRECTOR: Mel Bledsoe. SOUND: Howard Warren. PRODUCTION MANAGER: Edward Haldeman. SCRIPT SUPERVISOR: Joseph Gannon. MAKEUP: George Fiala. SETS: Don Ivey and Preston Roundtree. ASSISTANT DIRECTOR: James Gordon McLean. CAST: Soupy Sales (Melvin Byrd), Tab Hunter (Lieutenant Porter), Arthur O'Connell (Professor Wald), Edward Andrews (General Smithburn), Doris Dowling (Congresswoman Clanger), Beverly Adams (Claudine Wald), Louis Quinn (Sergeant Skam), Frank Nastasi (Cab Driver), Burt Taylor (Devlin), Courtney Brown (Arno), Russell Saunders (Clurg), Julian Voloshin (Professor Nep), Bob Bersell (Doorman), Warren Day (Curtis), Jay Laskay (Willie), Burt Leigh (Radar Operator), Natalie Moore (Redhead), Jack McDermott (Hired Killer).

Slapstick comedian Soupy Sales was a product of television, beginning in Detroit in 1953 and coming to ABC-TV to do a weekday series in the summer of 1955. His trademark was pie-throwing and various types of crude physical comedy along with a cast of puppets. He was back on ABC-TV from 1959 to 1961 in the Saturday series *Life with Soupy*; in the first four months of 1962 he had a weekly series on the network. Two years later he headlined a New York City TV program which was syndicated as *The Soupy Sales Show* and it generated his greatest popularity. As a result, Columbia signed him to star in *Birds Do It*, which came to theaters in the late summer of 1966. From 1968 to 1975 Sales was a regular on the syndicated version of *What's My Line?* and in the late 1970s he headlined another syndicated outing of *The Soupy Sales Show*.

Zany janitor Melvin Byrd (Sales) is employed at Cape Kennedy with self-propulsion cleaning tools after a rocket is contaminated by dust. Spies led by Lieutenant Porter (Tab Hunter) think he is crucial to the space program and try to kill him but he is saved by chimp Judi. By accident he is physically changed so that he can float and fly — and becomes a sex symbol. After being viewed flying over the space complex by various dignitaries, employees and foreign agents, he is chased by Claudine (Beverly Adams), the beautiful daughter of his boss, Professor Wald (Arthur O'Connell). Melvin has been in love with Claudine for some time but she hardly noticed him before his ionization. Flying over nearby waters he causes problems with airplanes and boats and the Coast Guard is called out to capture him. When the machine which causes his condition is turned off, he lands and is accosted by various people, including the spies. The Coast Guard arrests the spies, Melvin is declared a hero, and he and Claudine fall in love.

Writing in *The Columbia Story* (2001), Clive Hirschhorn said the script "wasn't exactly busting with ideas, though the film's big set-piece, which found Byrd 'negatively ionized' and flying his way around Florida, was moderately amusing." In *The Family Guide to Movies on Video* (1988), Henry Herx and Tony Zaza called it a "[h]armless comedy.... Innocuous story which young children may find amusing."

Ivan Tors Productions made *Birds Do It* and, like many of his films and TV shows, it involved an animal, in this case Judi the Chimp. Tors (1916–87) was a producer, director, writer and animal trainer who produced and wrote the stories for *The Magnetic Monster* (1953), *Riders to the Stars* and *Gog* (both 1954). He was best known for the various television programs he produced and sometimes scripted, including *Science Fiction Theatre*, *Sea Hunt*, *Men Into Space*, *Flipper*, *Gentle Ben* and *Daktari*.

Black Moon

1934; 68 minutes. PRODUCER: Harry Cohn. ASSOCIATE PRODUCER: Everett Riskin. DIRECTOR: Roy William Neill. SCREENPLAY: Wells Root, from the novel by Clements Riley. PHOTOGRAPHY: Joseph H. August. EDITOR: Richard Cahoon. SOUND: Edward Bernds. TECHNICAL ADVISOR: Don Taylor. DANCE DIRECTOR: Max Scheck. PROPERTY MASTER: Stanley Dunn. ASSISTANT DIRECTOR: Robert Margolis. CAST: Jack Holt (Stephen Lane), Fay Wray (Gail Hamilton), Dorothy Burgess (Juanita Lane), Cora Sue Collins (Nancy Lane), Arnold Korff (Dr. Raymond Perez), Clarence Muse (Lunch McClaren), Lumsden Hare (John Macklin), Henry Kolker (Psychiatrist), Madame Sul-Te-Wan (Ruva), Eleanor Wesselhoeft (Anna), Laurence Criner (High Priest Kala), Theresa Harris (Sacrificed Woman), Fred Walton (Butler), Edna Franklin (Sacrificed Girl's Mother), Lillian Smith (Nurse), Lillian West (Maid), Grace Chapman (Welfare Worker), William R. Dunn (Langa), Billy McClain, Charles R. Moore, Robert Frazier, Ada Penn, Anna Lee Johnson (Servants), Pierre Lufere (Killer).

Businessman Stephen Lane (Jack Holt), who is secretly loved by his secretary Gail Hamilton (Fay Wray), consults a psychiatrist (Henry Kolker) about his wife Juanita (Dorothy Burgess), who wants to return to her native home on the island of San Christopher near Haiti. Advised to let his wife work out her emotional problems, he allows her to return to the island with their daughter Nancy (Cora Sue Collins), in the company of the child's nurse Anna (Eleanor Wesselhoeft) and Gail. Before Juanita leaves, John Macklin (Lumsden Hare), the overseer of her family's plantation, arrives with a message from her uncle, Dr. Raymond Perez (Arnold Korff), who wants her to stay away due to recent voodoo sacrifices by the restless natives. When she refuses, Macklin goes to see Stephen but is murdered.

Returning to San Christopher, Juanita promises her uncle she will leave within three weeks but fails to do so and associates with her old nurse Ruva (Madame Sul-Te-Wan) and High Priest Kala (Laurence Criner), much to Perez's dismay. After Anna argues with Ruva over Nancy's care, Gail feels uneasy and sends for Stephen. He arrives on a schooner piloted by Lunch McClaren (Clarence Muse), whose girlfriend is an island native. After landing, Stephen and Gail find Anna murdered near a lava pit, and Juanita makes Ruva Nancy's nurse. Before Stephen can takes his family off the island, the schooner is stolen. When he tries to send for another boat, Kala destroys the wireless. Lunch tells Stephen he has learned that his girl (Theresa Harris) is going to become a voodoo sacrifice victim and the two go to the ceremony where he sees Juanita taking part in the proceedings. When Kala tries to kill the girl, Stephen shoots him and then sees Juanita commit the murder. Back at the plantation house, Perez tells Stephen that Juanita's parents were killed by the natives when she was two years old, and Ruva and Kala later initiated her into voodoo rituals and made her a high priestess. When he found out what was going on, Perez sent Juanita away to school, and she later met and married Stephen. That night Juanita says goodbye to Stephen and drugs his water pitcher. Nancy drinks the water instead and Perez gives her an antidote. With the priest only wounded, the natives plan to murder the whites but Lunch warns them and joins Stephen, Gail, Nancy and Perez in a fortified section of the house. When Juanita and the natives set a fire in the tunnel leading to the fortified area, the group tries to escape but Stephen and Gail are captured. Waiting to die, Gail tells Stephen she loves him. Perez sets them free and they escape to his yacht. Kala and Ruva force Juanita to give up Nancy for sacrifice, and when Stephen and Lunch go back to the island to rescue the little girl they find the house empty. They go to the voodoo ground and Stephen shoots Juanita as she is about to kill Nancy with a ceremonial sword. With their high priestess dead, the natives become peaceful, Perez buries his niece and Stephen, Gail, Nancy and Lunch leave the island.

Jack Holt was one of Columbia's most popular players and his action films did much to keep the studio financially afloat from the late 1920s to the mid–1930s. His relationship with studio boss Harry Cohn was adversarial, but Holt continued to headline programmers for Columbia until the early 1940s. Fay Wray had starred in RKO's *King Kong* the year prior to the release of *Black Moon*, and her addition to the cast did much to expand its box office pull. In 1933 she also was in Columbia's *Below the Sea* (q.v.). Director Roy William Neill had been directing films since 1916 and joined Columbia in 1930; he also helmed the studio's *The Menace* (1932), *The Ninth Guest* (1934) and *The Black Room* (1935) (qq.v) before going to England for the excellent *Dr. Syn* (1937), George Arliss' last feature. Neill is probably best known for directing the "Sherlock Holmes" series at Universal in the 1940s as well as that studio's *Frankenstein Meets the Wolf Man* (1943) and *Black Angel* (1946), his final feature.

The *New York Post* termed *Black Moon* "a humid melodrama" and *Variety* opined the "the direction in *Black Moon* is commendable and the acting is good, but the scenario possesses dubious elements." John T. Soister in *Up From the Vault: Rare Thrillers of the 1920s and 1930s* (2004) best summed up *Black Moon* when he called it "a competent thriller with inherent plot absurdities that are somewhat balanced by decent performances..."

The Black Room

1935; 70 minutes. PRODUCER: Robert North. DIRECTOR: R. [Roy] William Neill. SCREENPLAY: Arthur Strawn and Harry Myers. STORY: Arthur Strawn. PHOTOGRAPHY: Allen G. Siegler. EDITOR: Richard Cahoon. MUSIC DIRECTOR: Louis Silvers. ART DIRECTOR: Stephen Goosson. SOUND: Edward Bernds. COSTUMES: Murray Mayer. VISUAL EFFECTS: Jack Cosgrove. ASSISTANT DIRECTOR: C.C. Coleman. CAST: Boris Karloff (Gregor de Berghman/Anton de Berghman), Marian Marsh (Thea Hassel), Robert Allen (Lieutenant Albert Lussan), Thurston Hall (Colonel Paul Hassel), Katherine De Mille (Mashka), John Buckler (Beran), Henry Kolker (Baron Frederick de Berghman), Colin Tapley (Younger Lieutenant Paul Hassel), Torben Meyer (Peter), Egon Brecher (Karl), John Bleifer (Franz), Frederick Vogeding (Josef), Edward Van Sloan (Doctor), Phyllis Fraser, Lois Lindsay (Bridesmaids), George Burr Macannan (Majordomo), John Maurice Sullivan (Archbishop), Reginald Pasch (Tailor), Robert Middlemass (Prosecutor), Marion Lessing (Marie), George MacQuarrie (Chief Judge), Wilfred North, Count Rudolf von Steffenelli, Eric Mayne, Edward Davis, Edith Kingdon, Carrie Daumery (Court Members), Sidney Bracey (Hairdresser), Helena Grant (Anna), John Singer (Butler Raoul), Victor De Linsky (Footman Michael), Michael Park, Bert Sprotte, Paul Weigel (Peasants), Richard Lancaster, Bert Howard, James Gordon (Gentlemen), Hans von Morhart (Servant), Ivan Linow, Abe Dinovitch (Gatekeepers), Daniel Bleifer, Joseph Bleifer (Anton and Gregor as Boys), John Beck (Court Clerk), Enrique Acosta, Alex Melesh (Judges), John George (Waiter).

Poster for *Black Moon* (1934).

Working title: *The Black Room Mystery*.

Boris Karloff's first starring horror film for Columbia was *The Black Room*, which gave him dual roles, that of brothers under a family curse that says the younger will kill the older. Given rather lavish production values and sumptuous photography by Allen G. Siegler, the feature was one of the star's best non–Universal forays and proved to be a popular box office draw with the studio re-releasing it in 1955. It was ably directed by Roy William Neill, who had done the eerie *Black Moon* (q.v.) the year before, and it was greatly enhanced by the appearance of beautiful Marian Marsh, whose screen debut was as Trilby opposite John Barrymore in *Svengali* (1931). Robert Allen, as Marsh's love interest, had appeared in Columbia's *Air Hawks* (q.v.) a few months earlier. Veteran character actor Thurston Hall is quite good as an old family friend, as is Katherine De Mille in a brief role as a murdered mistress. Edward Van Sloan, who dominated Karloff's first studio genre effort, *Behind the Mask* (1932) [q.v.], only has a bit as the doctor who announces the birth of the twins.

Released in the summer of 1935, the feature began in late 19th century Hungary with the birth of two boys to Baron Frederick von Berghman (Henry Kolker), with the youngest of the infants having a paralyzed right arm. The baron has his friend, Lieutenant Paul Hassel (Colin Tapley), read a prophecy which says when twins are born to the von Berghmans, the younger will grow up to kill the older in the Black Room, a torture chamber in the family castle. The baron orders the entrance to the chamber sealed.

Forty years pass with the cruel older brother Gregor (Karloff) ruling the area with an iron hand and being hated by the peasants. Much to everyone's surprise he sends for his younger twin Anton (Karloff), who not only finds his sibling morose but also the target of assassinations because of the disappearances of young women in the area. Gregor wants to marry Thea (Marsh), the niece of the now aged Colonel Hassel (Hall), but she is in love with dashing Lieutenant Albert Lussan (Allen). Mashka (De Mille), Hassel's house servant, is secretly Gregor's mistress. When she realizes he wants Thea, she threatens to expose his crimes. He murders her and carries her body through a secret passage in a chimney to the Black Room where he dumps her body in a pit. Servant Peter (Torben Meyer) finds the girl's shawl and takes it to villager Karl (Egon Brecher) who leads the peasants in revolt against Gregor. To save his life, Gregor turns his title over to Anton and asks for time to settle his affairs before leaving the country.

Boris Karloff and Katherine De Mille in *The Black Room* (1935).

Later he takes Anton into the Black Room and pushes him into the pit, where he dies with the poignard that Gregor used to kill Mashka protruding from his paralyzed arm. Now only Anton's large loyal dog Thor knows that Gregor is not his master. Posing as Anton, Gregor sets out to romance Thea, which causes Lussan to become jealous. Lussan has words with Hassel over the girl. When the colonel spies Gregor using his supposed crippled right hand to sign papers making himself Thea's guardian, he confronts Gregor and is murdered. Lussan is blamed for the crime and is tried and sentenced to be shot. Thea agrees to marry the man she thinks is Anton, although she still loves Lussan. On their wedding day, Beran (John Buckler), a gypsy who loved Mashka, helps Lussan to escape jail. Thor chases Gregor to the church and attacks him during the ceremony. When those present see Gregor use his right arm, Lussan accuses him of murdering Hassel. Gregor escapes in a carriage and returns to the Black Room for sanctuary. Thor and the villagers follow him and, after the secret passage to the torture room is found, the mastiff attacks Gregor, pushing him into the pit where he falls on the dagger protruding from his brother. He dies with the family curse being fulfilled.

The Blonde Captive

1931; 76 minutes. DIRECTORS: Dr. Paul Withington, Clinton Childs, Ralph P. King and Linus J. Wilson. NARRATIVE-EDITOR: Lowell Thomas. PHOTOGRAPHY: George L. Crapp and Thornton P. Dewhurst. SOUND: Nathan C. Braunstein. CAST: Lowell Thomas, Dr. Paul Withington and Clinton Childs (Themselves).

It has just been issued on DVD. *The Blonde Captive* has a history more interesting than the documentary itself. Basically a travelogue, it does contain the subplot of searching for the remnants of the Neanderthal man and an Aborigines ghost legend. The feature was produced by the North Western Australian Expedition Syndicate under the auspices of the National Research Council of Australia and was first issued by William M. Pizor's Imperial Pictures in 1931 in a 59-minute version. *The Blonde Captive* was distributed by Columbia with an additional two reels of footage added following its New York City debut. Imperial reissued the feature in 1935 and Astor Pictures did the same in 1947. The main exploitation selling point was the inclusion of a subplot about a white woman shipwrecked in Australia's Arnhem Land and marrying one of the Aborigines.

Explorer-commentator Lowell Thomas, Dr. Paul Withington of Harvard University and archaeologist Clinton Childs lead an expedition to Australia in search of survivors from the age of the Neanderthal. Sailing from the West Coast, the trio makes stops in Hawaii, Bali, Pago Pago, Fiji and New Zealand. At each location the people and their customs are photographed and discussed. After landing in Sydney, Australia, the expedition travels to Ooldea where they find Australian Aborigines living in the desert, having been driven there by the encroaching settlement of their lands. Local wildlife like kangaroos and the duck-billed platypuses are filmed. Sailing the Timor Sea, they stop at an island with giant sea turtles and along the coast they stop at a native village, where they find a man who resembles a Neanderthal. There they also locate a white woman who has married a member of the tribe and given birth to a son, now 12 years old. (She was shipwrecked in the area where her sea captain husband's pearling ship capsized and she was the sole survivor.) The natives believe she is the pale ghost of their deceased wives. Although offered a way home, she prefers to stay with her native husband and son. With the coming of the monsoon season, the explorers decide to sail back to the United States.

Advertised as "An Absolutely Authentic Amazing Adventure," *The Blonde Captive*'s ads featured a scantily clad young woman. The film itself caused some controversy when various members of the scientific community denounced its final segments as fake; Dr. Withington issued a statement verifying the story of the shipwrecked white woman living with the natives. Lowell Thomas' participation in the feature added further credence since he had earlier narrated *Africa Speaks* (1930) (q.v.) and had won international fame for his interviews with Lawrence of Arabia. By the time the film was released, Thomas was broadcasting on NBC's Blue network and he would remain a radio staple until the mid–1970s.

The New York Daily News called the documentary "an unusually entertaining, educational and pictorial record," noting that it engendered an "enthusiastic public but critical reception." The Jefferson City, Missouri, *Daily Capitol News and Post-Tribune* announced, "Here is a picture that astounds you because it is real.... There is a variety of queer animals and the details of native customs are most intriguing.... [It] is excellent entertainment for jaded theatergoers — and those who are not jaded." *The Moberly (Missouri) Monitor-Index* said, "[T]he expedition meets all sorts of primitive people and animals. It will show you things you ever dreamed of before. The habits, customs and tribal rites they disclose will make you very happy you're civilized. But because there have been so many similar films released before this one, you may be a little disappointed."

Blondie Has Servant Trouble

1940; 70 minutes. PRODUCER: Robert Sparks. DIRECTOR: Frank L. Strayer. SCREENPLAY: Richard Flournoy. STORY: Albert Duffy. PHOTOGRAPHY: Henry Freulich. EDITOR: Gene Havlick. MUSIC: Leigh Harline. MUSIC DIRECTOR: M.W. [Morris] Stoloff. ART DIRECTOR: Lionel Banks. COSTUMES: Kalloch. ASSISTANT DIRECTOR: Abby Berlin. CAST: Penny Singleton (Blondie Bumstead), Arthur Lake (Dagwood Bumstead), Larry Simms (Baby Dumpling), Danny Mummert (Alvin Fuddle), Jonathan Hale (Mr. Dithers), Arthur Hohl (Eric Vaughn), Esther Dale (Anna Vaughn), Irving Bacon (Mr. Crumb), Ray Turner (Horatio Jones), Walter Soderling (Morgan), Fay Helm (Mrs. Fuddle), Eugene Anderson (Newsboy), David Newell (Nelson), Mary Jane Carey (Secretary Mary), Dick Durrell (Kirk), Tommy Dixon (Saunders), Frank Melton (Ollie), Murray Alper (Taxi Driver), Arthur Ritchie (Dr. Nolan), Ivan Miller (Police Commissioner), Eddie Laughton (Photographer), Daisy the Dog (Herself).

Working title: *Blondie Beware.*

Chic Young's popular comic strip "Blondie" served as the inspiration for 28 feature films made by Columbia between 1938 and 1950 with Penny Singleton as Blondie and Arthur Lake as her bumbling husband, Dagwood. *Blondie Has Servant Trouble*, also known as *Blondie Has Trouble*, was the sixth film in the series. It should have been called *Blondie Has Title Trouble* because its moniker kept hidden a delightful horror comedy. *Variety* noted that the film "is a good example of a title which keeps secrets, and a bad example of exploitation possibilities as viewed by the showman. Tag on this flicker is a considerable understatement, and only hints at the comedy contained in the piece."

Blondie (Singleton) wants to hire a maid and pesters her husband Dagwood (Lake) to get a ten dollar weekly raise so they can afford the luxury. Realty company owner Mr. Withers (Jonathan Hale), Dagwood's boss, nixes the request but instead offers to put the couple and their son Baby Dumpling (Larry Simms) in a large estate with servants for a two-week vacation. What he does not tell them is that the house was owned by the late magician Batterson and it is rumored to be haunted. He hopes by having the Bumsteads stay there, the rumors of ghosts will end and he will be able to unload the property. Arriving during a thunderstorm, Dagwood and Blondie become terrified when they see what appears to be a ghost, but it turns out to be teenager Horatio Jones (Ray Turner), who is staying overnight in the house as part of a lodge hazing. Then the house's ominous servants, Eric Vaughn (Arthur Hohl), who is really a crazy magician, and his wife Anna (Esther Dale), show up. Dagwood and Blondie find things like secret passages and sliding panels. Dagwood also finds an old newspaper with a story saying that Eric stabbed a lawyer, claiming he is the rightful owner of the estate since Batterson stole his illusions. No longer wanting a maid, Blondie decides to go home. Dagwood stops Eric from knifing her, he turns the madman over to the police and the newspapers dub him a hero, for which Dithers gives him a bigger salary.

The film's director, Frank L. Strayer, was no stranger to screen chillers, having previously done *Murder at Midnight* (1931), *The Monster Walks* and *Tangled Destinies* (both 1932), *The Vampire Bat* (1933), *The Ghost Walks* (1935) and *Murder at Glen Athol* (1936). *Variety* called *Blondie Has Servant Trouble* "the best of the series to date...More like this and the Blondies will be in the major leagues."

During the run of the film series, Arthur Lake also appeared as Dagwood on radio in "Blondie," which was broadcast from 1939 to 1950, with runs on the CBS, NBC Blue, NBC and ABC networks. Penny Singleton played the title role during the series' early years; the part was later played by Alice White, Patricia Van Cleve and Ann Rutherford. Hanley Stafford was Mr. Dithers. The series came to NBC-TV in 1954 for a year's run with Lake as Dagwood and Pamela Britton playing Blondie; it was revived for three months on the same network in 1958 with Lake and Singleton teaming again. A third TV *Blondie* series was telecast on CBS in 1968–69 with Patricia Harty in the title role with Will Hutchins as Dagwood.

The Boogie Man Will Get You

1942; 67 minutes. PRODUCER: Colbert Clark. DIRECTOR: Lew Landers. SCREENPLAY: Edwin Blum. ADAPTATION: Paul Gangelin. STORY: Hal Fimberg and Robert

B. Hunt. PHOTOGRAPHY: Henry Freulich. EDITOR: Richard Fantl. MUSIC: M.W. [Morris] Stoloff. ART DIRECTOR: Lionel Banks. SOUND: Charles Althouse and John Goodrich. SETS: George Montgomery. ASSISTANT DIRECTOR: Seymour Friedman. CAST: Boris Karloff (Professor Nathanial Billings), Peter Lorre (Dr. Arthur Lorentz), Maxie Rosenbloom (Maxie), Larry Parks (Bill Layden), Jeff Donnell (Winnie Slade Layden), Maude Eburne (Amelia Jones), Don Beddoe (J. Gilbert Brampton), George McKay (Ebenezer), Frank Puglia (Silvio "Jo-Jo" Bacigalupi), Eddie Laughton (Mr. Johnson), Frank Sully (Officer Joe Starrett), James C. Morton (Trooper Fred Quincy), Patrick McVey (Soldier), Frank Mitchell (Salesman Victim).

After having completed four of the five films he was to star in for Columbia Pictures, Boris Karloff headed to Broadway where he headlined *Arsenic and Old Lace*, which opened at the Fulton Theatre early in 1941. Karloff starred in the comedy-horror production for the next three years, taking time out only to film *The Boogie Man Will Get You*, which Columbia fashioned to take advantage of the star's Great White Way success. Colbert Clark took over as producer from Jack Fier on the film, which was issued theatrically in the fall of 1942. Karloff and Peter Lorre shared star billing; it was their second comedy-mystery after *You'll Find Out* (RKO, 1940). The movie also reunited Karloff with director Lew Landers, who as Louis Friedlander had helmed Universal's *The Raven* (1935).

The addled Professor Nathaniel Billings (Karloff) owns the debt-ridden Billings Tavern, an edifice built in 1764. The nearby town of Jenksville is run by Dr. Arthur Lorentz (Peter Lorre), who is the area's sheriff, coroner, banker, justice of the peace and insurance agent as well as the inventor of a hair restorer. Coming upon the quaint inn is Winnie Layden (Jeff Donnell), who decides to buy the place. Billings agrees on the condition that he be allowed to continue to work in his basement laboratory and that his housekeeper Amelia Jones (Maude Eburne) and farm hand Ebenezer (George McKay) be allowed to stay. Lorentz presides over the sale.

Billings tears up his mortgage and continues his experiments only to find out that Johnson (Eddie Laughton), a traveling salesman on which he has been experimenting in developing a superman, has expired. Winnie's estranged husband Bill (Larry Parks) tries to stop the sale but is too late but vows to stay on for ten days until he is drafted into the army. Choreographer J. Gilbert Brampton (Don Beddoe) arrives and signs in as a guest. At dinner that night the scream of Uncas, a ghost, is heard and Bill begins to think the locals are trying to scare Winnie away. He snoops in the lab and finds the body of Johnson. Bill and Winnie go to Lorentz who investigates and ends up joining Billings in his experiment. The doctor-lawman wants to use Bill as a specimen but is thwarted when Ebenezer accuses Brampton of trying to steal his pigs. A new potential subject arrives in the person of powder puff salesman Maxie (Maxie Rosenbloom) but he requires sedation before the experiment can be conducted and goes to Lorentz's home for medication. A new guest (Frank Mitchell) is murdered and the professor and Lorentz suspect Brampton. They call the police (Frank Sully, James C. Morton), but on their way to the tavern the lawmen are detained as spies by a soldier (Patrick McVey) as they speed by the local munitions plant. When Maxie returns with the sedative powder, it causes Billings and Lorentz to pass out. Maxie thinks he has killed them and goes for Winnie and Bill, who also faint after inhaling the powder. When the professor and Lorentz revive, they hide Bill and Winnie's bodies in a storage room, where Billings' other failures are housed. An intruder, enemy agent "Jo-Jo" (Frank Puglia), threatens to blow up the place but Maxie's return scares him into hiding. While the two doctors decide to turn Maxie into a superman to stop "Jo-Jo" from blowing up the munitions plant, Bill and Winnie come to and make their way upstairs where they find Brampton's body. He revives and tells them he is actually the curator of the Historical Society of America and offers Winnie $20,000 for the inn. The two police officers arrive and arrest Amelia (who tried to kill Brampton) and Ebenezer for the murders. "Jo-Jo" tries to set off his bomb but it is a dud and Maxie comes to as the supposedly dead victims return to life. Lorentz tells Billings he has discovered a suspended animation formula as the officers promise to commit everyone at the inn to the Idlewild Sanatorium — of which Lorentz is the director.

The Boogie Man Will Get You contains much hare-brained humor, such as Amelia sleepwalking and thinking she is a chicken and Lorentz constantly carrying a small kitten around in his pocket. Overall, though, the film fails to catch hold as a horror-comedy in the tradition of *Arsenic and Old Lace*. Kate Cameron noted in the *New York Daily News* that "frightening people in theatres takes more ingenuity and adroitness than the

Boris Karloff, Maxie Rosenbloom, Peter Lorre in *The Boogie Man Will Get You* (1942).

authors of this screenplay put into it." The British *Kinematograph Weekly* called the film a "[s]crewy comedy melodrama, a wild incursion into the macabre," adding, "Most of the characters are completely barmy, but somehow their insanity is a little too studio to promote spontaneous thrills or laughter." *Variety* said, "[T]his screwball comedy generates hearty laughs."

The cast of *The Boogie Man Will Get You* tries hard to sustain the comedy in the feature but in some cases, as with the young married couple portrayed by Jeff Donnell and Larry Parks, they sometimes try too hard. Former boxer Maxie Rosenbloom, billed here under his ring moniker "Slapsie" Maxie Rosenbloom, steals the show as the powder puff salesman with an inferiority complex. Rosenbloom (1903–76) was light heavyweight boxing champion of the world from 1930 to 1934 and his acting career of more than three decades included other genre efforts, *Harvard Here I Come* (1941) [q.v.], *Ghost Crazy* (1944) and *I Married a Monster from Outer Space* (1958) along with an hilarious performance in an episode of the mid–1960s CBS-TV series *The Munsters*.

Boston Blackie's Rendezvous

1945; 64 minutes. PRODUCER: Alexis Thurn-Taxis. EXECUTIVE PRODUCER: Irving Briskin. DIRECTOR: Arthur Dreifuss. SCREENPLAY: Edward Dein. STORY: Frederick Schiller. PHOTOGRAPHY: George B. Meehan. EDITOR: Aaron Stell. MUSIC DIRECTOR: Mischa Bakaleinikoff. ART DIRECTOR: Perry Smith. SOUND: Philip Faulkner. SETS: Fay Babcock. DIALOGUE DIRECTOR: Mel Ferrer. ASSISTANT DIRECTOR: Ivan Volkman. CAST: Chester Morris (Boston Blackie), Nina Foch (Sally Brown), Steve Cochran (Jimmy Cook), Richard Lane (Inspector Farraday), George E. Stone (Runt), Frank Sully (Sergeant Matthews), Iris Adrian (Martha), Harry Hayden (Arthur Manleder), Adele Roberts (Patricia Powers), Joe Devlin (Steve Caveroni), Dan Stowell (Desk Clerk), Philip Van Zandt (Dr. Volkman), Marilyn Johnson (Maid), John Tyrrell, Robert Williams, Joe Palma (Policemen), Clarence Muse (L.L. Cassington VIII), Frank Stephens, Perc Launders, Charles Jordan (Newsmen), Richard Alexander, Bing Conley, Charles Sullivan (Martha's Cousins), Tom Kennedy (Danceland Doorman), Bob Meredith, Eddie Hall (Ticket Buyers).

Working title: *Surprise in the Night*.

Within the confines of this glib, fast-paced, *noir*-style entry in Columbia's Boston Blackie detective series is a subplot about a psychotic killer, a precursor to the type of homicidal maniac who would populate horror films in later decades. In his fourth feature film, Steve Cochran gives a terrific performance as the madman, and studio contract player Nina Foch was never more fetching as his intended victim. The outing also featured the usual repartee between Blackie (Chester Morris) and his nemesis, Inspector Farraday (Richard Lane); the reformed safecracker performing a series of magic tricks to befuddle a shrink (Philip Van Zandt) trying to psychoanalyze him; and Blackie and his pal Runt (George E. Stone) masquerading as two black cleaning women in order to elude the law. Issued in the U.S. in the spring of 1945, the film was called *Blackie's Rendezvous* in England.

After a trip to Washington, D.C., Boston Blackie (Morris) returns to his rooms, which he shares with sidekick Runt (Stone), at the Park Madison Hotel only to be awakened by his friend Arthur Manleder (Harry Hayden) who asks his help in finding his nephew, Jimmy Cook (Cochran). Cook has escaped from a sanitarium after trying to kill a nurse; Manleder tells Blackie the young man is hopelessly homicidal as a result of an auto accident. Since Cook's brother is to be married in a week, Manleder wants to avoid a scandal. Blackie tells Runt to drive Manleder home and goes back to sleep, but is awakened by Cook, who has slipped into his room. Cook tells Blackie that he is not insane and that his family wants him committed so they can have the $230,000 he is about to inherit. Telling Cook he will help but advising him to return to the sanitarium, Blackie is choked by Cook, who then steals one of his suits and a hat, but drops a diary.

When Runt returns, he revives his pal. Blackie finds the diary which contains references to taxi dancer Sally Brown (Foch) with whom Cook has fallen in love. Cook goes to Danceland to meet Sally but her roommate, ticket taker Martha (Iris Adrian), tells him she has taken a few days off. He dances with pretty Patricia Powers (Adele Roberts), who leaves with him. When Blackie and Runt arrive at the club, Martha tells them Cook left with Patricia; the doorman (Tom Kennedy) says the two took a cab. They pay the same cabbie (Joe Devlin) to take them to the pair's destination, a deserted country lane, and there they find Inspector Farraday (Lane) and Sergeant Matthews (Frank Sully) investigating Patricia's murder. Cook goes back to Blackie's rooms and writes a letter — to Sally; when a maid (Marilyn Johnson) shows up, he murders her. Blackie pretends to be Sally's grandmother calling from out of state and gets her address from Martha. Just as Cook is about to knock on Sally's apartment door, Blackie shows up. Cook

Daybill for *Boston Blackie's Rendezvous* (1945).

hides while Sally, who has received the letter, mistakes Blackie for her admirer. When Farraday talks to Martha and finds out Runt was with her when she gave out Sally's address, he goes to their apartment as Martha calls her roommate and warns her about Cook. Thinking Blackie is Cook, Sally screams. As Farraday tries to get into the apartment, Blackie escapes through a window. After Farraday and his men leave, Cook shows up and tells Sally he is Boston Blackie, and she agrees to accompany him to his apartment. When Farraday returns, Martha tells him where the two have gone as Blackie and Runt go back to their rooms to pack in order to go into hiding. After the maid's body is found, they are arrested by Farraday for her murder. Blackie tells Farraday that Martha can identify him, not knowing she has gone to Brooklyn to visit her aunt. Escaping from the police chief, Blackie and Runt masquerade as black cleaning women and go through the hotel registration cards in order to match one of them with Cook's handwriting, since Blackie speculates he is also at the hotel. Finding the suite where he is staying, the two try to locate Cook and Sally. Cook calls the desk clerk (Dan Stowell) about an intruder and they go to Blackie's rooms. There Farraday again captures Blackie and Runt and makes them remove their makeup and costumes. Sally sees a picture of the real Boston Blackie and realizes Cook is an imposter. Matthews brings in Martha, who identifies Blackie. When Cook tries to kill Sally, she attempts to phone for help and the clerk alerts the law. Blackie and Farraday find Cook holding Sally at gunpoint but use the ruse of arguing to pull a rug and knock him off balance. Cook is handcuffed and Sally is saved.

The police psychiatrist who questions Blackie was given the name Volkman, the same surname as the film's assistant director, Ivan Volkman. Future star Mel Ferrer served as the movie's dialogue director. Boston Blackie confronted spiritualists in the ninth entry in the series, *The Phantom Thief* (q.v.), released the next year.

The Brotherhood of Satan

1971; 92 minutes; Color. PRODUCERS: L.Q. Jones and Alvy Moore. ASSOCIATE PRODUCER: Sheila Clague. DIRECTOR: Bernard McEveety. SCREENPLAY: William Welch, from the novel by L.Q. Jones. ORIGINAL STORY: Sean MacGregor. PHOTOGRAPHY: John Arthur Morrill. EDITOR: Marvin Walowitz. MUSIC AND SONGS: Jaime Mendoza-Nava. PRODUCTION DESIGN: Ray Boyle. PRODUCTION MANAGER: Bob Jones. SPECIAL EFFECTS: Steve Karkus. MAKEUP: Lou Lane. SCRIPT SUPERVISOR: Blair Brooke. CAST: Strother Martin (Doc Duncan), L.Q. Jones (Sheriff Pete), Charles Bateman (Ben Holden), Ahna Capri (Nicky), Charles Robinson (Father Jack), Alvy Moore (Deputy Sheriff Tobey), Helene Winston (Dame Alice), Joyce Easton (Mildred Meadows), Debi Storm (Billie Joe), Jeff Williams (Stuart), Judy McConnell (Phyllis), Robert Ward (Mike), Geri Reischi (K.T. Holden), Elsie Moore, Margaret Wheeler, Cicely Walper, Phillis Coghlan, Gertrude Garner, Ysabel MacCloskey, Lenore Shanewise (Witches), Anthony Jochim, John Barclay, Patrick Allen Burke, Donald Journeaux (Warlocks), Alyson Moore, Cindy Holden, Sheila McEveety, Scott Agular, Grant MacGregor, Jonathan Eisley, Brian McEveety, Robyn Grei, Linda Tiffany, Kevin McEveety, Debbie Judith (Children).

Working title: *Come In, Children.*

A car is run over by a tank but a young boy escapes and joins three other children. Traveling with his eight-year-old daughter K.T. (Geri Reischi) and girlfriend Nicky (Ahna Capri), Ben Holden (Charles Bateman) finds the wrecked car and goes to Hillsboro to report it to the sheriff, Pete (L.Q. Jones). After being forcefully questioned and released by the lawman, Ben witnesses Pete attacked by townsman Mike (Robert Ward) and drives away, but crashes his car into a pole trying to avoid hitting a little girl. After Ben and Nicky argue, they agree to return to Hillsboro with K.T. That night, the parents of the two Meadows children die suddenly and the siblings join three other children who take them to the deserted Barry home. Town physician Doc Duncan (Strother Martin), who pretends to be helping Sheriff Pete and Deputy Tobey (Alvy Moore) solve the crimes, conducts a black mass in the old house where children have been gathered along with several elderly witches. One of the witches, Dame Alice (Helene Winston), is denounced as an outcast by Doc and she is beaten to death by the other members of the coven. Finding the two dead bodies at the Meadows place, Ben, Nicky and K.T. spend the night with the sheriff as the local priest, Jack (Charles Robinson), warns them that witchcraft is being practiced in the area. The sheriff cannot understand why almost no one has been allowed in or out of town in the last three days in which six families have been attacked and their children have gone missing. After Nicky has a terrible dream, Ben decides to leave town. The sheriff loans him his car but along the road they have a flat tire and Ben and Nicky find that K.T. has disappeared. Reporting the event to the sheriff, Ben is told by the priest that witches have abducted the child. When the Mike follows his young son (Robert Ward) into a wooded area, he is decapitated by an armored horseman while Father Jack, who has seen the killing, loses his sanity. Having the needed number of children, Doc calls to the Devil to let the witches take over the youngsters' bodies so they can live for another lifetime serving evil. After coming across Mike's decapitated body, Ben, Nicky, the sheriff and his deputy find the crazed priest and go to the deserted house. When they break into the room where the sacrifices took place, they only find the now possessed children.

The Brotherhood of Satan was made by LQJAF (which stands for L.Q. Jones and Friends) Productions through Four Star–Excelsior Releasing Corporation and released theatrically by Columbia Pictures. It was the third feature produced by Jones and Alvy Moore, best known for playing the addled Hank Kimball on CBS-TV's *Green Acres* from 1965 to 1971. Their initial outing was 1964's *The Devil's Bedroom* and their next production, and first under the LQJAF banner, was *The Witchmaker* (1969). In 1975 they teamed again for the genre cult favorite *A Boy and His Dog*.

Jones told Justin Humphreys in *Psychotronic Video* #22 (1996) that *Brotherhood* was "one of those pictures that shows up on the ten best of the year. It is a very strange picture. If you look at it and realize what is happening. It's uneven. There's some good places in it and bad ones. But it really was a good attempt to work a story about witchcraft. It's stranger than first appears and it's one of the really enigmatic endings you will find in a motion picture." The film was based on Sean MacGregor's original story; in 1971 Jones turned into a novel called *The Brotherhood of Satan*, on which the film was based. The novel was published by Universal-Award; Ace Books issued it in paperback in 1980.

Poster for *The Brotherhood of Satan* (1971).

In *John Stanley's Creature Features Movie Guide Strikes Again* (1994), Stanley noted, "William Welch's script has many chilling moments as well as one eerie dream sequence." *The Phantom's Ultimate Video Guide* (1989) called it an "earnest, eerie, imaginative indie," while Mike Mayo in *Videohound's Horror Show* (1998) termed it "laborious.... The whole thing has an Ed Woodsian quality of enthusiastic incoherence that's irritating and endearing in about equal measures."

James O'Neill in *Terror on Tape* (1994) said it was "[o]ne of the better early '70s *Rosemary's Baby* spin-offs, with able acting from the great [Strother] Martin as the coven's leader and a creepily ambiguous ending." Henry Herx and Tony Zaza in *The Family Guide to Movies on Video* (1988) noted, "Director Bernard McEveety ladles out his witchcraft murders with remarkable ineptitude." The film does tend to drag with several long, drawn-out sequence that make little sense.

By Whose Hand?

1932; 65 minutes. DIRECTOR: Ben [Benjamin] Stoloff. SCREENPLAY: Harry Adler. PHOTOGRAPHY: Teddy [Ted] Tetzlaff. EDITOR: Maurice Wright. SOUND: Glenn Rominger. ASSISTANT DIRECTOR: Charles C. Coleman. CAST: Ben Lyon (Jimmy Hawley), Barbara Weeks (Alice Murray), Kenneth Thomson (Chambers), Ethel Kenyon (Maizie Wilson/Eileen Aylesworth), William V. Mong (J.W. Martin/Graham), Dolores Rey (Bride), Nat Pendleton (Killer Delmar), Tom Dugan (Drunk), Dwight Frye (Chick Lewis), William Halligan (Detective), Helene Millard (Mrs. Leonard/Mrs. Delmar), Lorin Raker (Bridegroom), Oscar Smith (Porter), Tom McGuire (Conductor), Eddie Kane (Accomplice), Martha Mattox (Spinster), DeWitt Jennings (City Editor), Kit Guard (Trainman), Buddy Roosevelt (Chauffeur Charles), Emma Tansey (Lewis' Mother), Florence Wix (Angry Woman), Lee Phelps (Ticket Agent), Polly Walters (Cigar Stand Attendant), Allen K. Wood, Matty Robert (Newsboys).

Working title: *Murder Express.*

Los Angeles newspaper man Jimmy Hawley (Ben Lyon) is assigned by his city editor (DeWitt Jennings) to try and find escaped hoodlum Killer Delmar (Nat Pendleton), who may leave the city aboard a train to San Francisco. At the station, Jimmy is kissed by pretty Alice Murray (Barbara Weeks), a member of a wedding party. Jimmy falls for the girl and follows her onto the train. The passengers include the newlyweds (Dolores Rey, Lorin Raker); rich double-crosser Chambers (Kenneth Thomson); Graham (William V. Mong), who served time for embezzlement based on Chambers' testimony; informer Chick Lewis (Dwight Frye), who sent Delmar to prison; an alcoholic pest (Tom Dugan); drug addict Mazie Wilson (Ethel Kenyon), using the name Eileen Aylesworth; and Killer's wife (Helene Millard), traveling incognito as widow Mrs. Leonard. Delmar is also aboard, hiding in a coffin.

After the train leaves, Chambers is found murdered and a diamond bracelet he was carrying is now missing. When the homicide is discovered, several of the passengers become suspects. The bracelet is found in Alice's purse; Maizie admits stealing it but denies killing Chambers. While the passengers are being questioned, Killer leaves the coffin and murders the train's engineer and fireman. When Chick realizes Delmar is on the loose, he tries to get away and is also knifed. Jimmy attempts to take control of the runaway train, Delmar tries to stop him, the newsman beats the hoodlum in a fight and makes him confess to Chick's murder. Delmar claims that Graham murdered Chambers for sending him to jail and then flees, but is captured by the other passengers. Bringing the train to a halt, Jimmy turns Delmar and Graham over to the law. Jimmy and Alice plan a trip to the altar.

Director Benjamin Stoloff went on to direct Columbia's *Night of Terror* (q.v.) with Bela Lugosi the year after making *By Whose Hand?* and in both films he infused a sense of mystery and terror in a claustrophobic setting, this time a moving train. The usual mysterious suspects, a killer hiding in a coffin and the presence of horror favorite Dwight Frye as a neurotic snitch add to the sinister atmosphere of the proceedings. The Jefferson City, Missouri, *Daily Capital News and Post Tribune* said, "It is difficult to conceive of more dramatic action than is paced into this unusual film.... The audience is kept on edge every minute as the logical but utterly baffling plot unfolds — and then gets a final thrill in the surprise ending."

Cannibal Attack

(1954; 69 minutes) PRODUCER: Sam Katzman. DIRECTOR: Lee Sholem. STORY-SCREENPLAY: Carroll Young. PHOTOGRAPHY: Henry Freulich. EDITOR: Edwin Bryant. MUSIC: Mischa Bakaleinikoff. ART DIRECTOR: Paul Palmentola. SOUND: John Livadary and Harry Mills. SETS: Sidney Clifford. UNIT MANAGER: Leon Chooluck. SPECIAL EFFECTS: Jack Erickson. ASSISTANT DIRECTOR: Abner [Abby] Singer. CAST: Johnny Weissmuller (Johnny), Judy Walsh (Luora), David Bruce (Arnold King), Bruce Cowling (Rovak), Charles Evans (Commissioner), Stevan [Steve] Darrell (John King), Joseph A. Allen, Jr. (Jason), Jack Perry (Henchman), Michael Granger (Narrator).

After making 13 features in its Jungle Jim series starring Johnny Weissmuller in the title role, Columbia dropped the character when the King Features comic strip on which it was based ceased publication. Producer Sam Katzman had a trio of series films yet to complete and for these the lead character became Johnny Weissmuller, although in *Cannibal Attack* he was simply referred to as Johnny. Originally released in sepia, the feature also marked the debut of Kimba, Johnny's pet chimp, who provides some amusing antics. It was basically a reworking of the earlier *Mark of the Gorilla* (q.v.) with crocodiles substituting for gorillas in the plot. Attractively filmed at Arcadia's Arboretum, the film incorporated a fight with a leopard from *Jungle Jim* (q.v.), the eagle attack from *Mark of the Gorilla* and a crocodile fray from *The Lost Tribe* (q.v.).

At a year-old settlement along Cannibal Valley's Magi River, mining operator John King (Stevan [Steve] Darrell) informs the local commissioner (Charles Evans) that the area's first cobalt shipment will be ready in about a week. At the same time, jungle denizen Johnny (Weissmuller) and his pet chimp Kimba find the body of David Renning but he is held at gunpoint by beautiful Luora (Judy Walsh). Johnny manages to get the weapon but the girl escapes by leaping into the nearby river. When he follows, Johnny is nearly run over by a boat manned by Rovak (Bruce Cowling), with Arnold King (David Bruce) helping him to escape. Going to the commissioner, Johnny finds out that the dead man worked for King, Luora's guardian, and that Rovak is also one of his employees. Looking into the theft of the cobalt shipment, Johnny is attacked by crocodile men — actually natives wearing croc skins. Luora tells Johnny that King and Arnold are brothers; John broke with his brother over the latter's drinking. Going to the mine, Johnny saves Arnold from being mauled by a leopard. Johnny tells him that he suspects that a former cannibal tribe, the Shenzis, may be responsible for the cobalt robbery since they are rumored to have power over crocodiles. At the mine, Arnold informs Johnny that he (Arnold) is in charge of the operation since he discovered the cobalt. Johnny is attacked by a native with a croc jaw club, the same type of weapon used to kill Renning. After seeing Rovak's henchmen (Joseph A. Allen, Jr., Jack Perry) with a Shenzi, Johnny tells the commissioner he thinks Rovak is involved in the theft. His theory is rejected; Luora states that Arnold is the hijacker. After suggesting that John King and the commissioner go with the next cobalt shipment, Johnny sees Rovak and his men steal the cobalt; before he can stop them he is attacked by a large eagle. Arnold meets up with his brother and the commissioner as the Shenzis provoke the crocodiles in attacking their boat. Several of the workers are killed as Arnold swims to freedom after killing a croc. When the commissioner announces that the Shenzis are responsible for the thefts, Johnny goes back into the jungle and is trailed separately by Arnold and Luora. After Johnny and Arnold find the supply cave where the stolen cobalt is being stored, Luora pretends she has been attacked by a crocodile man, whom Arnold kills. She then has Rovak and his men capture Johnny and Arnold and she tells them she is the half-caste princess of the Shenzi tribe. With Johnny and Arnold tied to stakes in the cave and tormented by the natives with a live croc, Luroa goes to her lover, John King, and tells him that the government Rovak represents will supply him with enough money from the cobalt to make them rulers of a jungle empire. When Rovak, his henchmen and the natives leave to transport the cobalt, Kimba rescues Johnny, who kills the crocodile. Johnny and Arnold locate the commissioner and King and inform them about Luora working with Rovak in stealing the cobalt. When the girl sees them, she fakes being killed in an elephant attack. She then goes to Rovak and joins him in the foray to steal a final cobalt shipment being led by King and the commissioner. They attack but are thwarted in a fight. When she sees John fighting against her, Luora throws a knife and kills him and is shot by the commissioner. Rovak attempts to escape in his boat but is overpowered by Johnny and drowns. The commissioner later congratulates Arnold on becoming the new chief of the mining operation.

Comely Judy Walsh was the highlight of *Cannibal Attack* with her ability to fill a sarong; her character was a half-caste princess of a onetime cannibal tribe of very light-skinned natives. The crocodile men were somewhat terrifying. *Variety* termed the feature "standard action-adventure material for juvenile audiences.... Weissmuller, although a little beefy, is still adept in the water." The *Motion Picture Herald* opined, "[T]he action tends to be repetitious and slow-moving."

Captive Girl

(1950; 73 minutes) PRODUCER: Sam Katzman. DIRECTOR: William Berke. SCREENPLAY: Carroll Young. PHOTOGRAPHY: Ira H. Morgan. EDITOR: Henry Batista. MUSIC: Mischa Bakaleinikoff. ART DIRECTOR: Paul Palmentola. SOUND: J.S. Westmoreland. PRODUCTION MANAGER: Herbert Leonard. SETS: James Crowe. ASSISTANT DIRECTOR: Paul Donnelly. CAST: Johnny Weissmuller (Jungle Jim), Buster Crabbe (Barton), Anita Lhoest (White Leopard Goddess/Joan Martindale), Rick Vallin (Chief Mahala), John Dehner (Hakim), Rusty Wescoatt (Silva), Frank Lackteen (Elder), Nelson Leigh (the Rev. E.R. Holcom), Stanley Price (Drummer).

Working titles: *Jungle Jim and the Captive Girl* and *Jungle Jim in Captive Girl*.

The fourth film in Columbia's Jungle Jim series, *Captive Girl* starred three swimming champions, Johnny Weissmuller, Buster Crabbe and

Anita Lhoest. Weissmuller and Crabbe were Olympic gold medalists and Lhoest won two national swimming championships in 1947. Other than the three lead players and the fact it was shot in sepia, the feature proved to be a barely standard jungle melodrama with horror overtones. *Variety* said it was "satisfactory" for juveniles, adding, "Producer Sam Katzman permits the footage to be prolonged far beyond its natural course by repetition and decisive scissoring is needed to trim 73 minutes down to requirements of secondary market." The *Motion Picture Herald* noted, "Except for some good animal shots, which have little to do with the development of the story, and some underwater photography, the picture emerges as a routine adventure film at best."

After studying abroad, tribal chief Mahala (Rick Vallin) returns to his jungle home with missionary Holcom (Nelson Leigh) and they encounter Jungle Jim (Weissmuller). They ask Jim to find the white leopard goddess (Lhoest) who has been attacking the tribe's witch doctor, Hakim (John Dehner). Holcomb believes the girl is the now grown daughter of archaeologists who were killed because they tried to find a sacrificial pool known as the Lagoon of the Dead. On the way to the native village, Jim and Mahala are nearly killed by a rock slide perpetrated by natives on Hakim's orders; Hakim wants to remain in control of the area and resents Mahala's return. In the village, Mahala is greeted fondly by the natives who tell him that Hakim has gone to kill the goddess. Jim sets out to locate the young woman and meets adventurer Barton (Crabbe), who believes there is fabulous treasure at the bottom of the sacrificial pool. Jim and Mahala find a cave concealed by a waterfall and there they locate photographs of the archaeologists, proving the girl is Joan Martindale, their daughter. They also find a letter which states that Hakim plans to sacrifice the couple at the Lagoon of the Dead. Barton joins Jim and Mahala in following a passage from the cave to the pool. As Barton and his party seek the treasure, Jim encounters the girl and saves her from quicksand. Barton convinces Hakim to murder Jim, Mahala and Joan; Jim falls from a cliff and is left for dead as Hakim takes Mahala and Joan to the pool for sacrifice. Regaining consciousness, Jim enlists the aid of group of monkeys and attacks Barton and Hakim, who are killed. Joan plans to return to civilization and Mahala takes the valuable lagoon relics back to his people.

The wild girl in the picture has a tiger for a pet although that large feline is not indigenous to Africa, the locale of the movie.

Casino Royale

(1967; 131 minutes; Color) PRODUCERS: Charles K. Feldman and Jerry Bresler. ASSOCIATE PRODUCER: John Dark. DIRECTORS: John Huston, Ken Hughes, Val Guest, Robert Parrish and Joe McGrath. SCREENPLAY: Wolf Mankowitz, John Law and Michael Sayers. ADDITIONAL DIALOGUE: Val Guest. PHOTOGRAPHY: Jack Hilyard. EDITOR: Bill Lenny. MUSIC: Burt Bacharach. SONG PERFORMERS: Herb Albert and the Tijuana Brass and Dusty Springfield. ART DIRECTORS: Lionel Couch, Ivor Beddoes and John Howell. COSTUME DESIGNER: Julie Harris. SOUND: Sash Fisher, Bob Jones, Dick Langford and John W. Mitchell. MAKEUP: Neville Smallwood. WARDROBE: Betty Adamson. TECHNICAL ADVISOR: David Berglas. CHOREOGRAPHER: Tutte Lemkow. SPECIAL EFFECTS: Cliff Richardson and Roy Whybrow. VISUAL EFFECTS: Les Bowie. Second Unit DIRECTORS: Richard Talmadge and Anthony Squire. ASSISTANT DIRECTORS: Roy Baird, John Stoneman and Carl Mannin. CAST: David Niven (Sir James Bond), Peter Sellers (Evelyn Tremble), Ursula Andress (Vesper Lynd), Orson Welles (Le Chiffre), Joanna Pettet (Mata Bond), Daliah Lavi (Detainer), Woody Allen (Dr. Noah/Jimmy Bond), Deborah Kerr (Agent Mimi/Lady Fiona McTarry), William Holden (Ransome), Charles Boyer (Le Grand), John Huston (McTarry/M), Kurt Kasznar (Smemov), George Raft (Himself), Jean-Paul Belmondo (French Legionnaire), Terence Cooper (Cooper), Barbara Bouchet (Miss Moneypenny), Peter O'Toole (Piper), Angela Scoular (Buttercup), Gabriella Licudi (Eliza), Tracey Crisp (Heather), Elaine Taylor (Peg), Jacky [Jacqueline] Bisset (Miss Goodthighs), Alexandra Bastedo (Meg), Anna Quayle (Frau Hoffner), Stirling Moss (Driver), Derek Nimmo (Hadley), Ronnie Corbett (Polo), Colin Gordon (Casino Director), Bernard Cribbins (Taxi Driver), Tracy Reed (Fang Leader), John Bluthal (Casino Doorman), Geoffrey Bayldon (Q), John Wells (Q's Assistant), Duncan Maccrae (Inspector Mathis), Graham Stark (Cashier), Chic Murray (Chic), Jonathan Routh (John), Richard Wattis (Army Officer), Vladek Sheybal, Jennifer Baker, Susan Baker (Le Chiffre's Assistants), Percy Herbert (First Piper), Penny Riley (Control Girl), Jeanne Roland (Guard Captain), Caroline Munro (Guard Girl), Dave Prowse (The Monster), Milton Reid (Temple Guard), Robert Rowland (M15 Agent), Valentine Dyall (Vesper Lynd's Assistant/Voice of Dr. Noah), Yvonne Marsh, Veronica Gardnier (Bond Girls), Bob Godfrey (Strongman), R.S.M. Brittain (Sergeant Major), Erik Chitty (Bond's Butler), Frances Cosslett (Michelle), John Hollis (Monk), Burt Kwouk (Chinese General), David Lodge, Alexander Dore, Arthur Mullard, Barrie Melrose (Men).

Following Sean Connery's huge success as Ian Fleming's super-agent James Bond in *Dr. No* (1962), *From Russia with Love* (1963), *Goldfinger* (1964), *Thunderball* (1966) and *You Only Live*

Twice (1967), Columbia released the spy spoof *Casino Royale*, based on Fleming's 1953 novel. That book had been adapted to television as an episode of *Climax*, telecast on CBS-TV on October 21, 1954, with Barry Nelson portraying Bond.

Famous Artists Productions made the $12 million big-screen feature which was lensed in England, France and Ireland. It had five credited directors, with the finale helmed by uncredited second unit director Richard Talmadge. Its script contained unacknowledged material by the film's stars Peter Sellers and Woody Allen along with Ben Hecht, Billy Wilder, Joseph Heller and Terry Southern. Despite a plethora of talent and a huge budget, the film proved to be a critical bust although it did well at the box office. Like the rest of the Bond series, it swerved into the area of sci-fi with its futuristic weapons and the usual sinister agents working for an outfit bent on world domination. For horror film fans there was the amusing scene near the finale when Bond asks the Frankenstein Monster (Dave Prowse) for directions out of SMERSH's underground complex. Prowse went on to play the creature in Hammer Films' *The Horror of Frankenstein* (1970) and *Frankenstein and the Monster from Hell* (1973) but gained his greatest fame as Darth Vader in the *Star Wars* features.

Long-retired agent James Bond (David Niven*) agrees to make a comeback to thwart the machinations of SMERSH, a murky crime gang out to control the planet. When his former boss, M (John Huston), is rubbed out, Bond attempts to console M's widow, Lady Fiona (Deborah Kerr), not realizing she works for SMERSH. When she tries to seduce James, he rejects her, causing the woman to give up spying and reside in a convent. Realizing the power of SMERSH, Bond decides to assign his name to several other agents, including wealthy vamp Vesper Lynd (Ursula Andress), gambling tycoon Evelyn Tremble (Peter Sellers), woman-resistant Cooper (Terence Cooper), the alluring Detainer (Daliah Lavi), and Mata Bond (Joanna Pettet), James' daughter from an affair with Mata Hari. Vesper and Evelyn try to thwart Le Chiffre (Orson Welles), a SMERSH agent out to win funds for the organization at the Casino Royale. Tremble beats Le Chiffre at gambling but is killed when he tries to stop Vesper from being kidnapped. In Berlin, Mata is taken by away by Dr. Noah (Woody Allen) in a flying saucer. Realizing that Casino Royale, run by his nephew Jimmy Bond (Woody Allen), aka Dr. Noah, is a front for SMERSH, James uses the Detainer to trick Jimmy into ingesting a delayed explosive. Calling into action American Indians, the French Foreign Legion, United Nations soldiers, the U.S. Cavalry and the Keystone Cops, Bond launches an invasion of the Casino Royale. During the fray, Jimmy's bomb goes off. James makes his escape before the casino is destroyed.

Karin J. Fowler in *David Niven: A Bio-Bibliography* (1995) wrote, "The film was a debacle. Much of the storyline made little sense and the editing made it seem disjointed. Audiences did not find the performances comedic or interesting. The best part of the film was its title song performed by trumpeter Herb Alpert." The *New York Times* noted, "This colorful grab-bag bulges with intrigue, many wise 'in' jokes, some genuine fun and at least 14 ranking stars." *Variety* called the film "a conglomeration of frenzied situations, gags and special effects, lacking discipline and cohesion. Some of the situations are very funny, but many are too strained." James Robert Parish and I opined in *The Great Spy Pictures* (1974), "The few virtues of this overlong, vulgar non-comedy were Burt Bacharach's score, a few of the elaborate sets used for idiotic sight gags, and the Berlin spy school sequence. James Bond purists and film-going realists who sat through *Casino Royale* sadly shook their heads and sighed over the good old days when a spy was a spy was a spy."

In 2006, *Casino Royale* was remade starring Daniel Craig as James Bond. Columbia co-produced with Metro-Goldwyn-Mayer and had the U.S. theatrical distribution rights.

El Castillo de los Monstruos (The Castle of the Monsters)

(1958; 89 minutes) PRODUCER: Jesus Sotomayor. Executive PRODUCER: A. Hernandez C. [Curiel]. ASSOCIATE PRODUCER: Heberto Davila G. [Guajardo]. DIRECTOR: Julian Soler [Jesus Sotomayor]. SCREENPLAY: Fernando Galiana, Carlos Oreland and Julian Soler. PHOTOGRAPHY: Victor Herrera. EDITORS: Sigfrido Garcia and Carlos Savage. MUSIC: Gustavo Cesar Carrion. ART DIRECTOR: Gunther Gherzo. SOUND: Luis Fernandez. SPECIAL EFFECTS: Juan Munoz Ravelo. MAKEUP: Rosa Guerrero. MONSTER MAKEUP: Antonio Neira. PRODUCTION MANAGER: Armando Espinoza.

---

*When Ian Fleming's "James Bond" books were acquired for films, he wanted his friend David Niven to portray Bond.

ASSISTANT DIRECTOR: Jaime L. Contreras. CAST: Antonio Espino Clavillazo (Clavillazo), Evangelina Elizondo (Beatriz), Carlos Orellana (The Lame One), German Robles (Vampire), Guillermo Orea (Dr. Sputnik/Mr. Melchor), Jose Munoz Wilhelmy, Jose Moreno Camacho (Clavillazo's Pals), Alejandro Reyna Garcia, Leopoldo Pineda Magana, Fernando Shewan, Cella Viveros, Arturo Cobo.

El Castillo de los Monstruos (The Castle of the Monsters) was one of several Mexican horror films that Columbia released in the United States from the late 1950s into the early 1970s. Some of the features, like this one, were not dubbed in English and released only to Spanish-language theaters, mostly in border states; others were dubbed for general distribution and a few were even co-produced by Columbia. Although the feature starred noted Mexican comedian Clavillazo, it is best known as German Robles' third outing as a vampire; he previously played bloodsuckers in *El Vampiro* (The Vampire) (1956) and *El Ataud del Vampiro* (The Vampire's Coffin) (1957). The film was released in Mexico in 1957 but was not shown stateside until the fall of 1958.

Made by Producciones Sotomayor at Mexico City's Churubusco–Azteca Studios, it opens with a wagon driven by the Lame One (Carlos Ortellana) bringing a coffin to a sinister castle and being admitted by a Frankenstein-like monster. In a nearby town, Clavillazo (Antonio Espino Clavillazo), who wears a baggy suit and a funny hat, works for a coffin business, the Lively Funeral Home. He meets lovely Beatriz (Evangelina Elizondo), whom he learns is homeless. She wants a coffin for her late aunt and Clavillazo lends her his small apartment. Beatriz helps the Lame One, who has fallen on the sidewalk.

Beatriz gets a job in a cleaning shop. Clavillazo proposes marriage and she accepts. That night she is abducted by Dr. Sputnik (Guillermo Orea) and the Lame One and is taken to the castle. Clavillazo finds Beatriz missing and goes to the police, but they arrest him. He is let go after his friends (Jose Munoz Wilhelmy, Jose Moreno Camacho) vouch for him. When the Lame One asks them about the girl, the trio decide to follow him as he goes to the castle, where they see a coffin being brought into the structure. The two friends smuggle Clavillazo into the castle in a coffin. The doctor plans to experiment on Beatriz and make her a superwoman by using telepathy. Searching the castle, Clavillazo is threatened by an ape man, a werewolf, a vampire (German Robles), a reptile man and a living mummy and nearly falls into an alligator pit. Finding Beatriz, Clavillazo brings her out of a stupor but her will is taken over again by the mad scientist, who turns out to be a supposed blind man, Mr. Melchor, who had earlier blessed their union. When Clavillazo objects to Sputnik's plans, the doctor summons his monsters and they tie up Clavillazo. When Lame One stops his master from harming Beatriz, the doctor strangles him. Beatriz releases her lover as the doctor calls in the reptile man; Clavillazo reduces him to a fish by throwing a powerful chemical on him. When the Frankenstein-like monster fights with Clavillazo he gets electrocuted, the mummy falls into the alligator pit and is devoured, and the ape man strangles the werewolf through its jail cell bars. The vampire nearly does in Clavillazo but dies with the coming of the dawn. Returning to confront the doctor, Clavillazo is imprisoned with Beatriz in a cell with closing walls, but the Lame One revives long enough to shoot the doctor. The lovers are nearly crushed before being saved by the arrival of Clavillazo's friends and the police.

With exception of German Robles as the vampire, the monsters in the feature are only fair imitations of the classic creatures. As Donald F. Glut noted in *The Frankenstein Legend* (1973): "Patterned after the Universal monster, Frentenstein had a stitched gash running horizontally across the high forehead and electrodes on the neck. But the white shirt and sport jacket were hardly the thing for a Frankenstein Monster, regardless of his name, to wear." The same author, in *Classic Movie Monsters* (1978), reported on the reptile man, "This Creature appeared more human than ever, as he was played by an actor in a shoddy Gill Man outfit resembling a pair of leathery pajamas. A mad doctor creates him from a tiny fish; the monster enjoys a brief career as the 'Creature from the Dry Lagoon' before returning to his original form."

Like most Mexican horror films of the 1950s and 1960s, *El Castillo de los Monstruos* was very atmospheric and creepy, but it does not pick up steam until its final quarter when Clavillazo battles the monsters in order to save his lady love. Prior to that, it is mostly a foolish romantic comedy which even includes a scene in which the star has a fight with a mentally disturbed young man. In one amusing sequence, Clavillazo serenades Beatriz via a recording only to have his friends switch songs, with the silly swain suddenly becoming a soprano.

Antonio "Clavillazo" Espino (1910–93) also headlined the Mexican horror-fantasy comedies *El Fantasma de la Casa Rojo* (The Phantom of the Red House) (1956), *Aladdin y la Lampara Maravillose* (Aladdin and the Marvelous Lamp) (1958), and *Conquistador de la Luna* (Conqueror of the Moon) (1960).

Chinatown Nights

(1938; 60 minutes) PRODUCER: Nell Emerald. DIRECTOR: Tony Frenguelli. SCREENPLAY: Nigel Byass and Frederick Reynolds. STORY: Kaye Mason. CAST: H. Agar Lyons (Dr. Sin Fang), Anne Grey (Sonia Graham), Robert Hobbs (Lieutenant John Byrne), Nell Emerald (Mrs. Higgins), Arty Ash (Professor Graham), George Mozart (Bill), Ernest Sefton, Louis Darnley (Henchmen).

Victory Film Productions made this British thriller, which was issued in its homeland by MGM as *Dr. Sin Fang* with Irish actor H. Agar Lyons in the title role. Lyons had already played the character of Sax Rohmer's Oriental master villain Dr. Fu Manchu in two English serials, *The Mystery of Dr. Fu Manchu* (1923) and *Further Mysteries of Dr. Fu Manchu* (1924). In 1928 he first portrayed the similar character of Dr. Sin Fang in the six-part series *Dr. Sin Fang Dramas*. Columbia distributed the feature in the U.S. in March 1938 as *Chinatown Nights*.

Chinese crime lord Dr. Sin Fang (Lyons) absconds from prison and kills the judge who sent him there. Returning to his secret headquarters in London's Chinatown, he tries to secure the formula for Professor Graham's (Arty Ash) "Silver Ray," a cancer cure. When he is unable to do so, he plans to blackmail Graham by kidnapping his sister Sonia (Anne Grey). The indomitable young woman joins forces with police detective Byrne (Robert Hobbs) and the two thwart the criminal's machinations, bring him to justice and save the world from Dr. Sin Fang's control.

Writing in *British Sound Films: The Studio Years 1928–1959*, David Quinlan called the feature "[i]ndescribably bad."

Chosen Survivors

(1974; 99 minutes; Color) PRODUCERS: Charles Fries and Leon Benson. DIRECTOR: Sutton Roley. SCREENPLAY: H.B. Cross and Joe Reb Moffy. PHOTOGRAPHY: Gabriel Torres. EDITOR: John F. Link II and Dennis Virkler. MUSIC: Fred Karlin. ART DIRECTOR: Jose Rodriguez Granada. SETS: Ernesto Carrasco. MAKEUP: Elda Loza. SOUND EFFECTS: Paul Laune. SPECIAL EFFECTS: Federico Farfan. PRODUCTION MANAGER: Joe Wonder. ASSISTANT DIRECTOR: Felipe Palomino. CAST: Jackie Cooper (Raymond Couzins), Alex Cord (Steven Mayes), Richard Jaeckel (Major Gordon Ellis), Bradford Dillman (Peter Macomber), Pedro Armendariz, Jr. (Luis Cabral), Diana Muldaur (Alana Fitzgerald), Lincoln Kilpatrick (Woody Russo), Gwenn Mitchell (Carrie Draper), Barbara Babcock (Dr. Lenore Chrisman), Christina Moreno (Kristin Lerner), Nancy Rodman (Claire Farraday), Kelly Lange (Mary Lou Borden).

Working title: *The Bat*.

Ten drugged people are taken by helicopter to a desert area and put on an elevator that takes them 1,700 feet into the Earth's surface where they are to be housed in a life-sustaining facility. They are shown a tape of a woman (Kelly Lange) who informs them that the world is being destroyed by a nuclear war and they have been chosen by computer to live in the facility for five years and then go back to the surface world to repopulate the planet. Major Ellis (Richard Jaeckel) is in charge of the facility and he is disliked by the other survivors, who include tycoon Raymond Couzins (Jackie Cooper), writer-artist Steven Mayes (Alex Cord), mysterious Peter Macomber (Bradford Dillman), Congresswoman Alana Fitzgerald (Diana Muldaur), Olympic gold medal winner Woody Russo (Lincoln Kilpatrick), and Dr. Lenore Chrisman (Barbara Babcock). The unit is hit with power failure and when the lights return the group finds several birds in a cage have been savagely killed. Later they find a bat, which is identified as a vampire bat, and kill it. One of the group, Kristin Lerner (Christina Moreno), goes into a state of shock over the attack while Couzins clashes with Macomber, whom he sees spying on the people in the unit. Getting drunk, Couzins damages the control room, causing another blackout which results in a swarm of vampire bats killing another survivor, Luis Cabral (Pedro Armendariz, Jr.).

Macomber tells the "chosen survivors" that they have been a part of a government experiment to test people on how they would react in case of a nuclear war. He declares that no such war took place and they will soon return to the surface. Thanks to Couzins' rampage, Macomber is unable to contact the military and the group will have to wait five days before being rescued. Kristin tries to kill herself with pills as Couzins offers Russo $100,000 to climb up the elevator shaft and manually bring it down. Macomber attempts to electrocute the bats but there are too many of them, and Kristin is killed by the invaders. Russo climbs the elevator shaft and manages to signal for help after being attacked by the bats and falling down the shaft. The vampire bats swarm into the facility and kill several of the people. Couzins, Mayes and Major Ellis manage to survive by finding shelter. A rescue party brings the survivors to the surface.

Produced by Metromedia at Mexico's Churubusco Studios and issued in late 1974, this is simply an overblown TV movie with the usual Hollywood Left stereotypes: a greedy, self-centered capitalist businessman, a good guy intellectual, a right-wing military man, a covert government agent, a proud black athlete and a highly competent female, in this case a doctor. Perhaps this is the reason why the *New York Times* dropped its usual vitriol regarding sci-fi films when A.H. Weiler wrote, "If the chills are intermittent, the combination of the voracious vampires and fumbling scientists as unwitting partners in disaster gives some novelty and a sardonic twist to this latest manufactured view of a possible doomsday.... [Director Sutton Roley] maintains a fair level of suspense gimmickry, technical effects and action sequences that accentuate the inmates' terror.... [The script has] some dialogue that realistically reflects on man's inhumanity to man."

The Circus Queen Murder

(1933; 65 minutes) DIRECTOR: Roy William Neill. SCREENPLAY: Jo Swerling, from the novel *About the Murder of the Circus Queen* by Anthony Abbot [Fulton Oursler]. PHOTOGRAPHY: Joseph August. EDITOR: Richard Cahoon. SOUND: Edward Bernds. CAST: Adolphe Menjou (Thatcher Colt), Greta Nissen (Josie La Tour), Ruthelma Stevens (Miss Kelly), Dwight Frye (The Great Flandrin), Donald Cook (Carlo "The Great" Sebastian), Harold [Harry] Holman (Jim Dugan), George Rosener (John T. Rainey), Adolph Milar (Krumptz), Clay Clement (Lubbell), Lee Phelps (Newman), Helene Chadwick (Crying Woman), Eddy Chandler, Kit Guard, Frank Mills (Roustabouts), Clarence Muse (Roustabout with Sledge Hammer), Esther Escalante (Aerial Performer).

New York City Police Commissioner Thatcher Colt (Adolphe Menjou) needs a vacation and decides to take two weeks off incognito. He throws a knife at a map of New York state and it lands on the small town of Gilead. He decides to go there and invites his secretary, Miss Kelly (Ruthelma Stevens), who is smitten with him, to go along. As they travel by train the two practice lip reading and along the way see the traveling Great John T. Rainey Show, which is also headed for Gilead. Rainey (George Rosener), who is partnered with Lubbell (Clay Clement) and star aerial attraction Josie La Tour (Greta Nissen), tells Josie they will close in Gilead unless he gets more financing from Lubbell and asks her to cozy up to the man. When she refuses he accuses her of having an affair with another aerial performer, The Great Sebastian (Donald Cook), even though she is married to her partner, Flandrin (Dwight Frye). She orders Rainey out of her wagon. But her husband confronts her about wanting a divorce and then he tells her he will not live without her. The next day in Gilead, Colt and Miss Kelly run into the circus' publicity man, Jim Dugan (Harry Holman), an old acquaintance of

Poster for *The Circus Queen Murder* (1933).

the commissioner. As they watch the circus performers parade through town, Flandrin uses his cigarette to pop a balloon, causing his wife's horse to run away, but she is saved by Sebastian. Dugan asks Colt to speak with Rainey about the show's troubles, one of which is the disappearance of a member of the cannibal act. Rainey tells Colt someone is trying to wreck the circus and all of the main performers have received threats and suspicion falls on Flandrin. Colt, Miss Kelly, Rainey and Dugan go to Flandrin's wagon where they find signs of a scuffle, a bullet hole in a window and blood, plus a warning note saying the aerialist will be the first to be eliminated. Colt then assures the circus performers they will have adequate police protection and the show will open as scheduled, on Friday the thirteenth. When Colt questions Josie, whose dog has been slain, she tells him her husband was mad. When Flandrin's clothes are found in animal trainer Krumpz's (Adolph Milar) wagon, Colt deduces the aerialist is still alive, that he killed the dog and is masquerading as one of the cannibals, since he counted fourteen of them sleeping in their tent when there should only have been thirteen. Fearing Flandrin, Lubbell runs away, and Colt wants to call off the show, but Josie says she does not fear her husband and is openly affectionate with Sebastian. During the performance Sebastian does his act but almost falls when one of the ropes breaks. He saves himself as Flandrin watches from the top of the tent. When Josie performs her trapeze act, Flandrin shoots her with a poison dart and she falls to her death. Miss Kelly sees a dark figure sliding down the outside of the circus tent and goes outside while Colt orders Josie to be taken to her tent. There he declares she was murdered by Flandrin but when he goes to look for Miss Kelly he finds she is the prisoner of the madman, who orders him at gunpoint to make sure Sebastian is in Josie's tent. Colt and Miss Kelly communicate by lip reading and Flandrin leads the young woman at gunpoint to the tent where he sees Sebastian holding Josie's body. Flandrin uses a blow pipe to kill Sebastian and then runs into the main arena where the circus is still being performed and climbs the high wire. Miss Kelly watches as Sebastian rises, but it is Colt dressed in the aerialist's costume and protected by a bulletproof jacket. The two go into the arena where Colt announces to the crowd that Flandrin will make his last public appearance before the aerialist shoots himself. Colt informs Miss Kelly he is going back to New York City for a vacation.

The *New York Times* termed *The Circus Queen Murder* "a competently managed mystery, a bit slow, but eventful." The *Hollywood Reporter* thought it "one of the best murder stories in many a moon." With its subplots of cannibalism, murder by poison darts, jealousy and madness, a voodoo doll, jungle drums and an eerie circus background, the film was a chiller with enough horror elements to satisfy genre fans. This feature gave sexy Ruthelma Stevens a lot of screen time as Thatcher Colt's loving secretary and she ends up stealing the show, making viewers wish Columbia had carried out its plans to make more Colt adventures, but this outing and the previous *The Night Club Lady* (q.v.) were the only two the studio produced. For horror buffs, the film's added attraction was Dwight Frye as the mad Flandrin, one of his best screen roles, and it allowed him to be disguised as a cannibal in addition to being the insane cuckold husband. The feature's circus footage was lifted from the studio's 1930 release *Rain or Shine*; *The Circus Queen Murder* was reissued in 1938.

Sidney Blackmer portrayed Thatcher Colt in the 1942 PRC release *The Panther's Claw* and the Colt character was also played by Hanley Stafford and Richard Gordon on the radio series "Thatcher Colt" (NBC, 1936–38).

City of Fear

(1959; 75 minutes) PRODUCER: Leon Chooluck. DIRECTOR: Irving Lerner. SCREENPLAY: Robert Dillon and Steven Ritch. PHOTOGRAPHY: Lucien Ballard. EDITOR: Robert Lawrence. MUSIC: Jerry Goldsmith. ART DIRECTOR: Jack Poplin. SOUND: Jack Solomon. SETS: Lyle B. Reifsnider. MAKEUP: Tom Cooley. COSTUMES: Norman Martien. ASSISTANT DIRECTOR: Louis Brandt. CAST: Vince Edwards (Vince Reicher/Vince Justin), Lyle Talbot (Chief Jensen), John Archer (Lieutenant Mark Richards), Steven Ritch (Dr. John Wallace), Patricia Blair (June Marlowe), Kelly Thorsden (Detective Sergeant Hank Johnson), Joseph Mell (Eddie Crown), Sherwood Price (Pete Hallon), Cathy Browne (Jeanne), Larry J. Blake (Police Sergeant), Jean G. Harvey (Landlady), Michael Mark (Restaurant Owner), Tony Lawrence (Sailor).

Two San Quentin inmates, Vince Reicher (Vince Edwards) and William Dapner, kill a doctor and two guards and make their escape in a prison ambulance. Reicher lifts a metal canister from the prison hospital thinking it contains heroin when in reality it is radioactive cobalt. Dapner suddenly dies and Vince switches cars, taking on the guise of salesman Vince Justin.

Driving to Los Angeles, Vince takes a room at a motor court while Police Chief Jensen (Lyle Talbot) and his associate Richards (John Archer) learn that Reicher probably has the deadly cobalt in his possession. Air Pollution Control official Dr. Wallace (Steven Ritch) informs the policemen that anyone getting close to the cobalt risks death.

Vince's girlfriend June Marlowe (Patricia Blair) visits him but he tells her to stay away because the police might be trailing her. As Geiger counters are used to locate the cobalt, the police question June but let her go. They also interrogate Vince's one-time employer, shoe store owner Eddie Crown (Joseph Mell), and a former associate, Pete Hallon (Sherwood Price). Crown later meets with Vince at the warehouse behind his store to discuss the sale of the heroin. Hallon interrupts them, and the next day his body is found by the police in a car which is radioactive. When Crown tries to convince the now-sick Vince to take the heroin to Miami, Reicher kills him. Richards interrogates June for the second time and, finding her suffering from radiation poisoning, gets her to tell him where Vince is hiding. The police go to the motor court. Hearing their sirens, Vince takes the canister to a café, which the law surrounds. Still holding on to what he thinks is heroin, Vince dies as he comes out of the eatery.

Although a well-made programmer, *City of Fear* is basically a reworking of Mickey Spillane's *Kiss Me Deadly* (1955) with heroin and radioactive cobalt in place of spies and atomic energy. In his pre–*Ben Casey* days, Vince Edwards is impressive as the cold-blooded killer Reicher, and veterans Lyle Talbot and John Archer match his work as lawmen. Co-scripter Steven Ritch, who played the Air Pollution consultant, had the title role in Columbia's *The Werewolf* (q.v.) three years earlier.

Close Encounters of the Third Kind

(1977; 135 minutes; Color) PRODUCERS: Michael Phillips and Julia Phillips. ASSOCIATE PRODUCER: Clark Paylow. DIRECTOR-SCREENPLAY: Steven Spielberg. PHOTOGRAPHY: Vilmos Zsigmond. EDITOR: Michael Kahn. MUSIC: John Williams. ART DIRECTOR: Dan Lomino. SETS: Phil Abramson. PRODUCTION DESIGN: Joe Alves. MAKEUP: Bob Westmoreland. SOUND EFFECTS EDITOR: Frank Warner. PROPERTY MASTER: Sam Gordon. ASSISTANT DIRECTORS: Chuck Myers and Jim Bloom. CAST: Richard Dreyfuss (Roy Neary), Teri Garr (Ronnie Neary), Francois Truffaut (Claude Lacombe), Melinda Dillon (Jillian Guiler), Bob Balaban (David Laughlin), J. Patrick McNamara (Project Leader), Warren Kemmerling (Major "Wild Bill" Walsh), Roberts Blossom (Farmer), Philip Dodds (Jean Claude), Carl Guffey (Barry Guiler), Shawn Bishop (Brad Neary), Adrienne Campbell (Sylvia Neary), Justin Dreyfuss (Toby Neary), Lance Henriksen (Robert), Merrill Connelly (Team Leader), George DiCenzo (Major Benchley), Howard K. Smith (Himself), Amy Douglass, Alexander Lockwood (Implantees), Gene Dynarski (Ike), Mary Gafrey (Mrs. Harris), Norman Barfold (Tollbooth Man), Josef Summer (Larry Butler), the Rev. Michael J. Dyer (Himself), Roger Ernest (Highway Patrolman), Carl Weathers (Military Patrolman), F.J. O'Neil (ARP Project Member), Phil Dodds (ARP Musician), Randy Hermann (Returnee Frank Taylor), Hal Barwood (Returnee Harry Walliclage), Matthew Robbins (Returnee Matthews McMichaels), David Anderson, Richard L. Hawkins, Craig Shreeve, Bill Thurman (Air Traffic Controllers), Roy E. Richards (Air East Pilot), Gene Rader (Hawker), Eumenio Blanco, Daniel Nunez, Chuy Franco, Luis Contreras (Federales), James Keane, Dennis McMullen, Cy Young, Tom Howard (Radio Telescope Team), Richard Stuart, Bob Westmoreland (Dispatchers), Matt Emery (Support Leader), Galen Thompson, John Dennis Johnson (Special Forces Troopers), John Ewing, Keith Atkinson, Robert Broyles, Kirk Raymond (Dirty Tricksters), Stephen Powers (United Nations Observer), Basil Hoffman (Longly), Monty Jordan (Helicopter Pilot), J. Allen Hynek (Pipe Smoker).

Muncie, Indiana, has been the site of a number of flying saucer sightings. Roy Neary (Richard Dreyfuss), a city electrical department employee, is sent to find and fix the source of a power blackout. After a saucer hovers over his stalled utility truck, he joins the state police in chasing it and other saucers along rural roads before the craft speeds away. Later at home, Roy tells his wife Ronnie (Teri Garr) what he saw but she does not believe him. He begins having visions of a large mountain.

A youngster, Barry Guiler (Cary Guffey), is abducted by aliens and his mother Jillian (Melinda Dillon) also starts seeing pictures of the mountain in her mind. Roy and Jillian meet, share their stories and travel west to Devil's Tower in Wyoming, the mountain in their visions. The military has surrounded the area, claiming a train wreck caused a chemical spill. The two try to climb the mountain and are taken by soldiers to a compound. There they meet Claude Lacombe (Francois Truffaut), the leader of an international top secret group looking into UFOs. Escaping, Roy and Jillian go back to Devil's Tower where they see a number of flying saucers and a gigantic leader craft. Alien beings emerge from the ship along with a number of human returnees, including Barry, who is reunited with his mother. When members of the investigative team are invited to board the spacecraft, Roy goes along. He is one of those chosen to leave with the aliens.

Made at a cost of $21 million (and eventually grossing well over four times that amount), *Close Encounters of the Third Kind* was a financial blockbuster which was nominated for nine Academy Awards. (It won two, for Vilmos Zsigmond's photography and Frank Warner's sound effects editing.) In *The Wordsworth Book of Movie Classics* (1996), Allan Hunter noted that director Steven Spielberg "used state-of-the art special effects (courtesy of Douglas Trumbull), colorful mixtures of blinding light and uplifting music to illustrate the quasi-religious simplicity of his childlike vision of loving extra-terrestrials who visit planet Earth. Unlike the classic science-fiction films of the 1950s that reflected the paranoia of the Cold War era in their depiction of bellicose aliens intent on destruction, Spielberg convincingly asserts that it is equally possible for their intentions to be peaceful and harmless, an assertion embellished in the subsequent *E.T.* (1982)." In *The Family Guide to Movies on Video* (1988), Henry Herx and Tony Zaza called it an "epic about UFOs and the humanistic, hopeful and, for some, religious theme of mankind's close encounter with an extragalactic life form. The scenes involving simple person-to-person relationships may be somewhat flat but the movie boasts some dazzling special effects and is tinged with a feeling of awe rare in science fiction works."

James Robert Parish and I wrote in *The Great Science Fiction Pictures II* (1990), "While the motion picture does sport magnificent special effects by Doug Trumbull, it is more often than not an overlong, confused, hard-to-follow psychological drama more remembered for specific scenes, than for the film as a whole.... The main drawback to *Close Encounters of the Third Kind* is that it tries to be too much: the ultimate sci-fi movie in a genre where each day finds new themes and effects to outshine past efforts. As a special effects diversion, the movie is highly satisfying! As a drama of human and alien interaction, it is a dud." It is difficult to call a film a classic when its hero cannot find his way around Muncie, Indiana, without a road map.

Close Encounters of the Third Kind "Special Edition" was released theatrically in 1980 with about two minutes of footage added to the finale showing the humans making contact in the foggy interior of the mother ship. It did nothing to enhance the feature's reputation.

The movie was the subject of two documentaries, both entitled "The Making of *Close Encounters of the Third Kind*." The first was done by Columbia in 1977; 30 years later it was issued on DVD by Sony Pictures Home Entertainment. Columbia Tri-Star Home Entertainment produced the second documentary for video release in 2001.

Clouds Over Europe

(1939; 79 minutes) PRODUCER: Irving Asher. EXECUTIVE PRODUCER: Alexander Korda. DIRECTORS: Tim Whelan and Arthur B. Woods. SCREENPLAY: Ian Dalrymple. STORY: Brock Williams, Jack Whittingham and Arthur Wimperis. PHOTOGRAPHY: Harry Stradling. EDITOR: Hugh Stewart. MUSIC DIRECTOR: Muir Mathison. ART DIRECTOR: Vincent Korda. SOUND: A.W. Watkins. ASSISTANT DIRECTOR: Jack Clayton. CAST: Laurence Olivier (Tony McVane), Ralph Richardson (Major Charles Hammond), Valerie Hobson (Kay Hammond), George Curzon (Jenkins), George Merritt (Mr. Barrett), Gus McNaughton (Blenkinsop), David Tree (MacKenzie), Sandra Storme (Daphne), Hay Petrie (Stage Door Man), Frank Fox (Karl), George Butler (Air Marshal Grant), Gordon McLeod (Baron), John Longden (John Peters), Reginald Purcell (Pilot), John Laurie (Editor), Pat Aherne (Officer), Ronald Adam (Aviation Engineer), Ian Fleming (Air Ministry Officer), Hal Walters (Driver), Mark Daly (John), David Farrar (Bosun), John Singer (Newsboy), John Vyvian (Police Sergeant), Roy Emerton (German Officer).

Several British war planes carrying top secret devices have vanished and Major Charles Hammond (Ralph Richardson) suspects sabotage. Aircraft manufacturer Barrett (George Merritt) scoffs at the warnings of test pilot Tony McVane (Laurence Olivier), who also thinks the company's craft are being attacked. When Barrett orders a test flight, the plane is shot down by a death ray from the *Viking*, a salvage boat. Germans on the ship search the downed vessel but fail to find the technical gear they are seeking (it was taken off the craft by Hammond before the test flight began). Tony blames his boss for the loss of the craft. Newspaper reporter Kay Hammond (Valerie Hobson), the major's sister, pursues the story by taking a job waiting tables at the Merritt plant. Merritt is unaware that his secretary, Jenkins (George Curzon), is in the pay of the saboteurs.

When the German spies fail to find what they want in the wreckage, the head of the gang, the Baron (Gordon McLeod), has Jenkins murdered. To make the crash look like an accident, the Baron lets the airplane wash ashore. Hammond and Tony, who are now working together, still believe it was sabotage. As a result, Hammond is taken off the case and Tony is ordered to pilot the next test flight. Hammond learns that all the planes were brought down near the salvage ship. McVane is shot down by the German radio beam and is taken prisoner, but he unites the other pilots who have survived and together they mutiny and fight to take over the *Viking*. Having commandeered a destroyer, Hammond rushes to join in the fight. The ship is taken and the Baron and his spies captured.

This Irving Asher production was made by Alexander Korda's London Films in England as *Q Planes*. When Columbia showed it in the U.S. as *Clouds Over Europe*, it was three minutes shy of its original running time. In 1947 it was reissued stateside by Film Classics. Its sci-fi angle is the radio beam death ray and the prediction that an all-too-soon future war would be partly fought in the air. In *Science Fiction* (1984), Phil Hardy called the film "routine hokum" but rated Ralph Richardson's performance "superb." David Quinlan in *British Sound Films: The Studio Years 1928–1959* (1984) termed it a "[s]py thriller with much good humor."

Corruption

(1968; 91 minutes; Color) PRODUCER-PHOTOGRAPHY: Peter Newbrook. DIRECTOR: Robert Hartford-Davies. SCREENPLAY: Derek Ford and Donald Ford. EDITOR: Don Deacon. MUSIC: Bill McGuiffie. PRODUCTION DESIGN: Bruce Grimes. COSTUMES: Hilary Pritchard. PRODUCTION SUPERVISOR: Robert Sterne. MAKEUP: John O'Gorman. SPECIAL EFFECTS: Michael Abrechtsen. ASSISTANT DIRECTOR: Ken Softley. CAST: Peter Cushing (Sir John Rowan), Sue Lloyd (Lynn Nolan), Noel Trevarthen (Dr. Stephen Harris), Kate O'Mara (Val Nolan), David Lodge (Groper), Anthony Booth (Mike Orme), Wendy Varnals (Terry), Billy Murray (Rik), Vanessa Howard (Kate), Jan Waters (Hooker), Philip Manikum (Georgie), Alexandra Dane (Sandy), Valerie Van Ost (Blonde on Train), Victor Baring (Mortuary Attendant Burt), Shirley Stelfox (Party Girl).

Columbia first distributed *Corruption* in the U.S. early in 1968. Not until the end of the year was it shown in Great Britain, where it was made by Oakshire Productions-Titan International. Its complete running time is 91 minutes; the feature has been shown at various lengths, mainly due to its inclusion of bloody surgeries, severed heads, sex and nudity. It also had some stateside release as *Carnage* and later was released on video in another version entitled *Laser Killer*. No matter its title or length, the feature mainly depended on the star power of Peter Cushing to carry it. It proved to be one of his lesser, but more graphic, outings. When released in England in December 1968, it was issued a Certificate X.

Sir John Rowan (Cushing), a noted surgeon, awakens from a nap in his London home and escorts his beautiful young fiancée Lynn Nolan (Sue Lloyd) to a party where they meet Mike Orme (Anthony Booth). A photographer, Orme wants fashion model Lynn to pose for him, making Rowan jealous. The two men fight and a floodlight falls on Lynn, burning her face. Rowan extracts pituitary fluid from a gland taken from a dead girl at a hospital, and with a laser beam manages to restore Lynn's beauty. They go on a vacation to celebrate, but the treatment goes into remission. Rowan kills a hooker (Jan Waters) and repeats the operation, again making Lynn beautiful. The effects are again temporary, but Rowan is urged by Lynn to keep on killing in order to find a permanent cure. Dr. Stephen Harris (Noel Trevarthen), Rowan's colleague, comes to realize what Rowan is doing and tells his fiancée, Lynn's sister Val (Kate O'Mara), and the two agree to inform Lynn. Rowan and Lynn go to his country house at Seaforth where they meet Terry (Wendy Varnals) on the beach. Since she has no family, Lynn wants Rowan to kill her so he can operate again but he refuses. Instead he murders a woman (Valerie Van Ost) on a train and takes her severed head back to the cottage. Terry returns and sees the head and runs to the beach, pursed by Rowan and Lynn. Eventually Rowan corners her and strangles the young woman.

When Rowan refuses to operate on Lynn again, she threatens to tell the police he is mad. They are interrupted by Terry's husband Rik (Billy Murray), who is with forceful Georgie (Philip Manikum), thuggish dimwit Groper (David Lodge) and blowzy Sandy (Alexandra Dane). They demand to know Terry's whereabouts and try to rob the place. Lynn offers Georgie money if she will force her husband to operate on her again. She tells him that Rowan murdered Terry. Next she takes Rik to the beach to see his wife's body and pushes him off a cliff. When she returns to the house, Georgie becomes suspicious and sends Groper and Sandy for the police. Rowan turns on the laser he uses to operate on Lynn. As Dr. Harris and Val arrive at the house, the beam goes out of

David Lodge, Peter Cushing and Billy Murray in *Corruption* (1968).

control and kills everyone, setting the place on fire. Rowan and Lynn then go to the party where she introduces him to Mike Orme.

The theme of a mad doctor restoring his lover's beauty by murdering comely young women for their body parts had been explored earlier in the European features *Les Yeux Sans Visage* (Eyes Without a Face) (1959) and Jess Franco's *Gritos en la Noche* (Cries in the Night) (1962), which was issued in the U.S. as *The Awful Dr. Orloff*. *Corruption*, however, was much sleazier than those two productions. Alan G. Frank stated in *Horror Movies* (1974), "With its gratuitous images of physical unpleasantness, such as a severed head in a polythene bag kept in a refrigerator next to the dairy products, the film was an unworthy vehicle for Cushing's talents." In *The Encyclopedia of Horror Movies* (1986), Phil Hardy noted, "This crude exploitative cocktail announces the gory potboilers which became so popular on video in the early eighties." On the other hand, in *John Stanley's Creature Features Movie Guide Strikes Again* (1994), the author felt *Corruption* was "[o]ne of Peter Cushing's best films and a treat with its gore murders."

Counterspy Meets Scotland Yard

(1950; 67 minutes) PRODUCER: Wallace MacDonald. DIRECTOR: Seymour Friedman. SCREENPLAY: Harold R. Greene, from the radio series "Counterspy" by Phillips H. Lord. PHOTOGRAPHY: Philip Tannura. EDITOR: Aaron Stell. MUSIC: Mischa Bakaleinikoff. ART DIRECTOR: Victor Greene. SETS: George Montgomery. SOUND: George Cooper. ASSISTANT DIRECTOR: Fred Briskin. CAST: Howard St. John (David Harding), Amanda Blake (Karen Michele), Ron Randell (Simon Langton/Mr. Wilbur), June Vincent (Barbara Taylor), Fred F. Sears (Agent Peters), John Dehner (Agent Bob Reynolds), Lewis Martin (Dr. Victor Gilbert/Hugo Borne), Rick Vallin (Agent "Mac" McCullough), Jimmy Lloyd (Agent Burton), Ted Jordan (Brown), Gregory Gay (Professor Schuman), Douglas Evans (Colonel Kilgore), Paul Marion (Paul Heisel), Don Brodie (Jimmy), Everett Glass (Dr. Ritter), Charles Meredith (Miller), Robert Bice (Agent Fields), John Doucette (Larry), Gloria Henry (Martha), Al Hill (Laundry Truck Driver), Taylor Reid (Agent Danning), Bill Hale (Agent), Harry Lauter (Agent Don Martin), Jack Rice (Power Company Man), Charles Williams (Taxi Driver), William Bailey, George Eldredge (Assistants), Kernan Cripps (Bancroft).

The radio drama "Counterspy," created by Phillips H. Lord, was broadcast from 1942 to 1957 with Don MacLaughlin as David Harding. It was

Advertisement for *Counterspy Meets Scotland Yard* (1950).

on ABC from 1942 to 1950, NBC from 1950 to 1953 and Mutual from 1953 to 1957. Columbia made the feature *David Harding, Counterspy* starring Howard St. John in the title role in 1950 and *Counterspy Meets Scotland Yard* was its follow-up. While the first feature was a drama detailing the Washington D.C.–based counter-espionage unit of the government thwarting spies at a defense plant, the sequel had some genre touches involving a somewhat futuristic atomic warhead carrying long-range missile and a graveyard sequence. St. John repeated the Harding role and Fred F. Sears, later director of the studio's sci-ef-forts *The Werewolf, Earth vs. the Flying Saucers* (both 1956) and *The Giant Claw* (1957) (qq.v.), and John Dehner, again appeared as his assistants.

This solid and well-acted programmer begins with the supposed suicide death of Counterspy agent Don Martin (Harry Lauter) who had been working undercover at a government missile production facility near the desert town of Cretona. He had phoned his boss in Washington D.C., David Harding (St. John), that he knew the identity of spies who had been relaying recent guided missile data out of the country. Harding moves his operation to Cretona and has agent Don Reynolds (John Dehner) attend Martin's funeral. He then has Reynolds go to the Thousand Oaks Cemetery at night to dig up Martin's body for an autopsy. At the cemetery, Reynolds fights with a man he finds opening the same grave. Reynolds and agents "Mac" McCullough (Rick Vallin) and Burton (Jimmy Lloyd) take the man to Harding, who greets him as his old friend, Scotland Yard operative Simon Langton (Ron Randell), there to deliver a new gyroscope type to Colonel Kilgore (Douglas Evans), the commander at the plant.

When the autopsy performed by Dr. Ritter (Everett Glass) shows that Martin was poisoned, Harding asks Simon to take over the dead man's job. At the office he meets Karen Michele (Amanda Blake), his chief assistant and Martin's girlfriend. Later Karen goes to the office of Dr. Victor Gilbert (Lewis Martin), who uses a truth serum to get her to provide missile test data under the guise of trying to help her overcome the horrors she faced while imprisoned in a European concentration camp. Aiding Gilbert is his nurse, Barbara Taylor (June Vincent), who claims to also be a war victim and Karen's best friend. The tape recording of Karen's information is hidden in the cork of a water bottle and taken to the head of the spy ring,

Miller (Charles Meredith), who operates a water company as a front. When Miller finds out that one of his men, Heisel (Paul Marion), attended Martin's funeral, he orders two thugs (Don Brodie, John Doucette) to kill him. Harding learns Gilbert is really an alien named Hugo Boren. On Harding's orders, Simon dates Karen and at her apartment he meets Barbara. On his way home, Miller's thugs try to run down Simon but McCullough comes to his rescue and kills one of the spies. Harding tells Langton to stay hidden as Kilgore informs Karen about the accident and asks her to sit in for Simon at the next day's missile test launch. Following the test, Karen goes to her weekly appointment with Gilbert, who drugs the young woman and gets the information about the test flight (which involved the firing of an atomic missile toward a target 1,500 miles away at a speed of 5,000 miles per hour). Harding and his men surround Gilbert's office and Simon takes on the guise of an old man seeking medical advice. Barbara recognizes Simon and warns Gilbert, who gives him a hypodermic injection. Langton uses spirits of ammonia to keep awake and signals the counterspies by throwing a chair out of a window. The spy operation is shut down with the arrest of Gilbert, Barbara and Miller and his men. With the case closed, Simon and Karen marry and plan to live in England.

Creature with the Atom Brain

(1955; 69 minutes) PRODUCER: Sam Katzman. DIRECTOR: Edward L. Cahn. STORY-SCREENPLAY: Curt Siodmak. PHOTOGRAPHY: Fred Jackman, Jr. EDITOR: Aaron Stell. MUSIC: Mischa Bakaleinikoff. ART DIRECTOR: Paul Palmentola. SOUND: J.S. Westmoreland. SETS: Sidney Clifford. SPECIAL EFFECTS: Jack Erickson. ASSISTANT DIRECTOR: Eddie Saeta. CAST: Richard Denning (Dr. Chet Walker), Angela Greene (Joyce Walker), S. John Launer (Captain Dave Harris), Michael Granger (Frank Buchanan), Gregory Gay (Dr. Wilhelm Steigg), Linda Bennett (Penny Walker), Tristram Coffin (District Attorney McGraw), Harry Lauter, Larry J. Blake (Reporters), Charles Evans (Police Chief Camden), Pierre Watkin (Mayor Bremer), Lane Chandler (General Saunders), Nelson Leigh (Dr. Kenneth C. Norton), Don C. Harvey (Lester Banning), Paul Hoffman (Tom Dunn), Edward Coch (Jason Franchot), Karl "Killer" Davis (Willard Pierce), Dick Cutting (Himself), Terry Frost (Officer Tom), Tyler McVey (Policeman), Michael Ross (Vernon Dunn), Eddie Foster (Bartender), Charles Horvath (Zombie), Dick Crockett (Caller).

Sam Katzman's Clover Productions made this slick, scary programmer that Columbia double-billed with the same producer's *It Came from Beneath the Sea* (q.v.) in the summer of 1955. Curt Siodmak's script combined a number of genre elements in its tale of zombies being powered by atomic energy. In this case, the scientist behind the experiments (Gregory Gay) is controlled by a vengeful gangster and the hero is a police doctor (Richard Denning) who quickly deduces what is behind a series of brutal murders but is unable to convince the press or his superiors. Director Edward L. Cahn nicely pilots the story, milking the horror of the scarred, indestructible creatures as they terrorize a city under the power of the mad gangster. Although economically budgeted, the feature shows no signs of cheapness.

When a gambling house operator is mysteriously murdered by having his spine snapped, Dr. Chet Walker (Denning), Police Captain Dave Harris (S. John Launer) and District Attorney McGraw (Tristram Coffin) are puzzled, especially when Chet discovers the footprints, fingerprints and blood of the killer are luminous. Unknown to them, the murderer (Karl "Killer" Davis) is really a dead body controlled by German scientist Dr. Steigg (Gregory Gay) and gangster Frank Buchanan (Michael Granger), the latter out to take revenge on the men who had him deported ten years before. Chet asks his wife Joyce (Angela Stevens) to keep the news of these events from their little daughter Penny (Linda Bennett), who is very partial to Dave. Next Buchanan orders one his zombies (Michael Ross) to kill McGraw, who successfully prosecuted him. After the D.A.'s murder is revealed, Chet finds out that several corpses have vanished from the city morgue. While the press scoffs at Chet's surmising that dead men are behind the killings, he and Dave meet with the mayor (Pierre Watkin), police chief (Charles Evans) and General Saunders (Lane Chandler), who agrees to use planes and trucks to track down the source of local radioactivity. Later Dave informs Chet that McGraw and the murdered gambler had worked together to deport Buchanan, a gangster kingpin, and that former assistant district attorney Lester Banning (Don C. Harvey), accountant Jason Franchot (Edward Coch) and hired gunman Tom Dunn (Paul Hoffman) had assisted the prosecution in the case. Dave provides the three men with police protection but Buchanan has one of the zombies dressed as a cop kill Franchot. Television newsman Dick Cutting (himself), who had formerly scoffed at Chet's theory, announces that the killings were perpetrated

Lobby card for *Creature with the Atom Brain* (1955), Don C. Harvey and S. John Launer.

by dead men. Leaving his laboratory to get medication for an injured hand, Steigg stops in a bar but departs when he spots military men taking radiation tests and leaves behind fingerprints which determine his identity. Buchanan telephones the mayor that he will destroy the city and then sends out a group of zombies who instigate mass destruction. The gangster wants Chet out of the way and sends Franchot after him, but instead the zombie brings back Dave, whom Steigg turns into one of the creatures. Buchanan sends Dave to Chet's house where he learns the whereabouts of Banning and Dunn, and also tears up Penny's doll. Banning and Dunn are in protective custody at the county jail, but Dave goes there and kills them. As Dave leaves the jail, Chet gets into the car with him but jumps out when a radio report announces the murders of Banning and Dunn. Dave wrecks the car and is taken to a hospital where x-rays reveal implanted electrodes in his brain. When Dave revives and drives to his power source at the laboratory, Chet, the police and the military follow him. With the lab surrounded, Steigg, who only wanted to use brain implants to help humanity, tries to destroy his work but Buchanan kills him. The gangster then sends out the zombies to destroy the police and soldiers. Dave breaks into the lab, followed by Chet, who is knocked out in a fight with Buchanan. Dave kills the gangster and then collapses as Chet awakens and destroys the laboratory, terminating the zombies. Later Chet gives Penny a new doll, telling her it is a gift from Uncle Dave.

Creatures the World Forgot

(1971; 92 minutes; Color) PRODUCER-SCREENPLAY: Michael Carreras. DIRECTOR: Don Chaffey. PHOTOGRAPHY: Vincent Cox. EDITOR: Chris Barnes. MUSIC: Mario Nascimbene. SOUND: John Streeter. SPECIAL EFFECTS: Syd Pearson. PRODUCTION DESIGN: John Stoll. COSTUMES: Rosemary Burrows. ANIMAL HANDLER: Uwe Schulz. ASSISTANT DIRECTOR: Ferdinand Fairfax. CAST: Julie Ege (Nala), Tony Bonner (Toomak), Robert John (Rool), Brian O'Shaughnessy (Mak), Sue Wilson (Noo), Rosalie Crutchley (Old Crone), Marcia Fox (Mute Girl), Gerard Bonthuys (Young Fair Boy), Hans Kiesouw (Young Dark Boy), Josje Kiesouw (Young Dumb Girl), Beverly Blake, Doon Baide (Young Lovers), Don Leonard (Old Leader), Frank Hayden (Killer Zen), Rosita Moulin (Dancer), Fred Swart (Marauder Chief), Ken Hare (Fair Tribe Leader), Derek Ward (Hunter), Christine Hudson, Tamsin Millard (Fighting Rock Women), Debbie Aubrey-Smith, Samantha Bates, Trudy Inns, Cheryl Stewardson, Heinke Thater (Rock Girls), Joan Boshier (Widow), Audrey Allen (Mother), Vera P. Crosdale, Mildred Johnston, Lilian M. Nowag (Old Women), Mike Dickman, Jose Manuel, Manuel Neto, Jose Rozendo, Mark Russell, Dick Swain, Alwyn Van Der Merwe (Rock Men).

A volcano destroys the village of the Stone Age Dark Tribe, and their leader (Don Leonard) is killed. Warriors Mak (Brian O'Shaugnessey) and Zen (Frank Hayden) do battle for the post with Zen being killed and beheaded. The tribe's witch, the Old Crone (Rosalie Crutchley), blesses Mak and he leads the survivors across the desert where they meet the Fair Tribe, with whom they dwell. The Fair Tribe's leader (Ken Hare) gives Noo (Sue Wilson) to Mak as a bride and she goes with him and his people to a green valley, where the tribe grows. Noo dies after giving birth to twins as the Old Crone takes a mute baby for her own.

The twins grow up to become sadistic Rool (Robert John) and intelligent Toomak (Tony Bonner) and the mute baby develops into the beautiful Mute Girl (Marcia Fox), whom Toomak likes. The Mute Girl gets away from Rool when he tries to rape her but she is captured by the Marauder Chief (Fred Swart) and his men. Rool kills the Marauder Chief whose daughter Nala (Julie Ege) attacks the Mute Girl; she is saved by Toomak. Rool wants Nala but Toomak takes her and Mak names him the tribe's new chief before dying from wounds suffered in the battle with the Marauder tribe. Rool then fights Toomak for the tribe's leadership but loses and suffers a leg injury. Fed up with the tribe's brutality, Toomak takes his people and Nala and leaves, with Rool and the remainder of the tribe planning to seek revenge. In a thick forest, Rool and his people are attacked by mud men but Toomak forces them to flee. Rool kidnaps Nala with the Mute Girl informing Toomak. The two brothers meet for a final battle on a mountaintop where Nala is nearly killed by a giant python. Toomak rescues her from the snake as the Mute Girl kills Rool. A spirit then beckons the trio into the future.

Released in the autumn of 1971, *Creatures the World Forgot* was Hammer Films' third prehistoric melodrama, preceded by *One Million Years B.C.* in 1966 and *When Dinosaurs Ruled the Earth* in 1970. Don Chaffey, who directed the 1966 release, returned to helm this outing which was filmed on location in the Namib Desert in Africa and contained no spoken dialogue, only grunts and gestures. It was produced and scripted by Michael Carreras, who also did the same chores on *One Million Years B.C.* In the *New York Times*, Howard Thompson opined, "The homestretch is quite lively, and the whole thing is considerably better than the Raquel Welch *One Million B.C.* [sic]. Make that less bad."

In *Little Shoppe of Horrors* (April 1978), Richard Klemensen commented, "Michael Carreras spent a year making this bomb?? What a waste of time for a basically talented filmmaker. Columbia must have wanted this film, but it is just another really dumb stone-age melodrama — without the special effects of a Ray Harryhausen or Jim Danforth to save it. All we have is the ever-popular Julie Ege who seems to strip at the drop of a hat.... A jerky film." James O'Neill, in *Terror on Tape* (1994), wrote, "Hammer's last prehistoric horror film has no dinosaurs and precious little excitement as well, instead concentrating on sex and sadism.... It's beautifully photographed but a real snooze." *Castle of Frankenstein* (October 1971) noted, "Hammer's playing the same tune too often these days, and *One Million Years B.C.* remakes' division, prehistoric kicks *et al.*, is running equally as dry as Hammer's Dracula, Frankenstein and Devil Cult factory. Ah, but for their zest for originality of former years."

The Creeping Flesh

(1973; 94 minutes; Color) PRODUCER: Michael Redbourn. EXECUTIVE PRODUCERS: Tony Tenser and Norman Priggen. DIRECTOR: Freddie Francis. SCREENPLAY: Peter Spenceley and Jonathan Rumbold. PHOTOGRAPHY: Norman Warwick. EDITOR: Oswald Hafenrichter. MUSIC: Paul Ferris. ART DIRECTOR: George Provis. MAKEUP: Roy Ashton. SETS: Peter James. COSTUME DESIGN: Anne Donne. WARDROBE: Bridget Sellers. CONTINUITY: Pamela Davies. CAST: Christopher Lee (James Hildern), Peter Cushing (Professor Emmanuel Hildern), Lorna Heilbron (Penelope Hildern), George Benson (Waterlow), Kenneth J. Warren (Charles Lenny), Duncan Lamont (Inspector), Harry Locke (Barman), Hedger Wallace (Dr. Perry), Michael Ripper (Carter), Catherine Finn (Emily), Robert Swann (Aristocrat), Maurice Bush (Kari), David Ballie (Doctor), Tony Wright (Sailor), Marianne Stone (Assistant), Alexandra Dane (Prostitute), Jenny Runacre (Marguerite Hildern), Larry Taylor, Martin Carroll (Warders), Dan Meaden (Lunatic), Sue Bond (Tavern Girl).

Victorian era archaeologist Professor Emmanuel Hildern (Peter Cushing) relates his discovery of a huge prehistoric subhuman skeleton in New Guinea and his returning with it to London. During his year's absence, his repressed daughter Penelope (Lorna Heilbron) has been in charge of his household. He has forbidden her to speak of her mother, who supposedly died two decades earlier, after turning to a life of debauchery. Unbeknownst to Penelope, her mother is still alive and a patient in Emmanuel's half-brother James Hildern's (Christopher Lee) asylum. There the cruel James conducts experiments on the inmates.

Emmanuel believes the skeleton represents ancient evil and by accident he finds out that water causes flesh to grow on it. Removing a finger from the skeleton, he re-grows it. To protect Penelope from going insane like her mother, he develops a mild serum from the finger and injects it into the girl. The injections causes Penelope to become sensuous. When she learns the truth about her mother by breaking into her sealed room, she puts on her mother's clothes, goes to a pub and, after several drinks, kills an attacker, Lenny (Kenneth J. Warren), who has escaped from her uncle's asylum. She too ends up in the asylum, where her uncle extracts blood and surmises the cause for the sudden change in her behavior. Wanting to experiment on the skeleton himself, James breaks into Emmanuel's laboratory and steals it during a storm. But the carriage carrying it overturns and the evil thing regains its flesh. The creature then seeks out Emmanuel, removes one of his fingers and departs. Emmanuel is then shown working in James' asylum where he is a patient.

The most haunting scene in *The Creeping Flesh* occurs at the finale with the giant prehistoric god briefly seen, clad in a hat and long coat, disappearing into the night. Otherwise the feature begins on a positive note but soon veers to the problems of Victorian sexual repression, with a dose of Nathaniel Hawthorne's "Rappaccini's Daughter." Surprisingly the film is lacking in both eroticism and violence, and the strong monstrous presence of the evil New Guinea god is mostly in the background. While it has some good moments, overall the feature is not particularly scary. It *is* quite visual, as noted by Phil Hardy in

Christopher Lee in *The Creeping Flesh* (1972).

The Encyclopedia of Horror Movies (1986): "Using a cool style, with many medium and long shots, [director Freddie] Francis gives the picture a sense of desolation and bleakness appropriate to the kind of 'decency' that must be accepted if the events recounted are to be viewed as disturbingly evil." *Castle of Frankenstein* (No. 21, 1974) said, "Effort to tell four different stories simultaneously gets a bit shaky, but the overall result is above average even if less than completely satisfying.... Properly moralistic and Victorian period piece features good production and some nice horror effects — though, as usual, they're on-screen too long for maximum effectiveness. The giant prehistoric skeleton is particularly swell." Henry Herx and Tony Zaza in *The Family Guide to Movies on Video* (1988) commented, "Horror buffs will find this adequate fair for a rainy afternoon." In *The Men Who Made the Monsters* (1996), Paul M. Jensen wrote, "The film's basic premise about the embodiment of evil has mythic power, but what holds the film together is Francis's clear, efficient storytelling, which conveys the complex plot... in little more than ninety minutes and does so without sacrificing mood or visual style.... *The Creeping Flesh* is far from a typical monster film, for its creature appears only at the end and is not a menace in and of itself. It is not the essence of evil, released to infect an innocent world. Rather, it embodies all the corruption that already pervades existence."

Made by Tigon Pictures and World Film Services, *The Creeping Flesh* was released internationally by Columbia. It was one of over 20 features in which Peter Cushing and Christopher Lee appeared together, most of them horror outings. Freddie Francis (1917–2007) replaced Don Sharp as the director; Francis had dual film careers as a cinematographer and director. In the later capacity he helmed nearly 30 horror features including *Torture Garden* (1968) (q.v.).

The Crime Doctor's Courage

(1945; 70 minutes) PRODUCER: Rudolph C. Flothow. DIRECTOR: George Sherman. SCREENPLAY: Eric Taylor. PHOTOGRAPHY: L.W. O'Connell. EDITOR: Dwight Caldwell. MUSIC: Mario Castelnuovo-Tedesco. ART DIRECTOR: John Datu. SOUND: Hugh McDowell, Jr. SETS: Sidney Clifford. CHOREOGRAPHY: Tito Valdez. ASSISTANT DIRECTOR: Leonard J. Shapiro. CAST: Warner Baxter (Dr. Robert Ordway), Hillary Brooke (Kathleen Massey Carson), Jerome Cowan (Jeffers "Jeff" Jerome), Robert Scott [Mark Roberts] (Bob Rencoret), Lloyd Corrigan (John Massey), Emory Parnell (Captain Birch), Stephen Crane (Gordon Carson), Charles Arnt (Butler), Anthony Caruso (Miguel Bragga), Lupita Tovar (Dolores Bragga), Dennis Moore (David Lee), Jack Carrington (Detective Fanning), King Kong [Abe Kashey] (Luga), Ken Carpenter (Master of Ceremonies), Edgar Dearing (Sheriff), William H. O'Brien (Caterer), John Maxwell (Headwaiter), Sam Harris (Club Patron).

While vacationing in Hollywood, psychiatrist Robert Ordway (Warner Baxter) is visited by Kathleen Carson (Hillary Brooke), a former acquaintance. She asks him to a dinner party in order that he may observe her new husband, Gordon Carson (Stephen Crane), who she fears may be insane because of the mysterious deaths of his two previous wives and twin suicide attempts. At the dinner that night the other guests include Kathleen's harness manufacturer father, John Massey (Lloyd Corrigan), Kathleen's confidant Bob Rencoret (Robert Scott), writer Jeffers "Jeff" Jerome (Jerome Cowan), and the brother-sister dance team of Miguel (Anthony Caruso) and Dolores Bragga (Lupita Tovar). One of the caterers turns out to be David Lee (Dennis Moore), the brother of Gordon's first wife; he accuses Carson of murdering his sister and also his second wife. The distraught Carson goes to his study; after a shot is heard, Ordway and Jeff break into the room and find Gordon dead. After observing the scene, Ordway calls the police and tells them that Carson has been murdered, despite the fact the room in which he was found has a locked door and barred windows. Kathleen leaves as Police Captain Birch (Emory Parnell) investigates the crime.

Later that evening, Jeff takes Ordway to a club, Ye Friar's Glen, to see the Braggas perform. During their dance Dolores vanishes and reappears again and the M.C. (Ken Carpenter) announces that the pair have the power of invisibility. Bob later informs Ordway that Kathleen is at the Braggas' house, and the doctor rides with the dancers to what turns out to be an old castle in the hills. Ordway sees a painting of Miguel and Dolores dated 1848 and Miguel tells him that his family in Spain practiced alchemy and learned the secret of eternal life. The doctor passes out from a spiked drink Miguel gave him, and the next day wakes up and explores their spooky mansion. He finds a note saying that Kathleen has returned to her father's home. Meeting Birch at Carson's house, Ordway learns that the dead man had left Kathleen his estate of over two million dollars as Bob visits the widow and asks her to marry him. She refuses, telling him she married Carson for his money and that she plans to wed Miguel. Bob then goes to Ordway and declares the Braggas are vampires, because they are never seen during the day and have the power of invisibility. Finding a trick lock under the window of the room where Carson was killed, Ordway tells Jeff how the murderer escaped. Back at the nightclub he sees the illusion the Braggas use to make Dolores disappear. Going to Jeff's bungalow, Ordway finds Kathleen there and he also sees the manuscript Jeffers is writing which states that Miguel and Dolores are vampires. The doctor calls Birch and tells him to meet him at the Braggas' mansion. He goes there with Kathleen and they find Jeff dying. They also see the drugged Braggas lying in coffins as someone tries to shoot the doctor. He gives chase and wounds the assailant, whom he turns over to Birch for killing Carson.

The Crime Doctor's Courage, released in February 1945, was the fourth of ten features starring Warner Baxter that Columbia made between 1943 and 1949, based on the popular radio series by Max Marcin. Like its predecessor, *Shadows in the Night* (q.v.), released the previous year, it had supernatural and horror overtones, with the possibility that a murder may have been committed by vampires. It was a well-paced and nicely acted mystery that included a non-too-likable heroine who married the victim for money, not love, and ends up with two million dollars. The *New York Times* called the melodrama "a woefully dull and uninspired conglomeration of whodunit clichés," claiming that the three leading players "are quite casual about the whole business."

Lupita Tovar, who portrayed one of the pseudo-vampires, had a turn as a bloodsucker's victim when she played the heroine in Universal's Spanish-language version of the 1931 *Dracula*. A year earlier she also had the lead in another Universal Spanish-language genre outing, *The Cat Creeps*. The part of the Braggas' assistant Luga was portrayed by an actor billed as King Kong. He was professional wrestler Abe Kashey, a native Californian of Syrian descent, who headlined grappling events from the early 1930s well into the 1950s.

Crime Doctor's Man Hunt

(1946; 61 minutes) PRODUCER: Rudolph C. Flothow. DIRECTOR: William Castle. SCREENPLAY: Leigh Brackett. STORY: Eric Taylor. PHOTOGRAPHY: Philip Tannura. EDITOR: Dwight Caldwell. MUSIC DIRECTOR: Mischa Bakaleinikoff. ART DIRECTOR: Hans Radon. SETS: George Montgomery. CAST: Warner Baxter (Dr. Robert Ordway), Ellen Drew (Irene Cotter/Jane Roberts), William Frawley (Inspector Harry B. Manning), Frank Sully (Bigger), Claire Carleton (Ruby Farrell), Bernard Nedell (Waldo), Jack Lee (Sergeant Bradley), Francis Pierlot (Gerald Cotter), Myron Healey (John Foster/Philip Armstrong), Olin Howland (Marcus Le Blane), Ivan Triesault (Alfred "Alfredi" Hempstead), Paul E. Burns (Gardner Tom), Mary Newton (Martha), Leon Lenoir (Herrara), Robert De Haven, Frank Cody (Sailors), Minerva Urecal (Disgruntled Landlady), Harry Hayes Morgan (Jervis), Cy Malis (Barker Joe), Wanda Perry (Miss White), Joe Palma (Policeman), Ralph Linn (Officer Reynolds), John Manning (Waiter), Ernest Hilliard (Head Waiter), Stella Le Saint (Woman).

Working title: *The Crime Doctor's Honor*.

The sixth entry in Columbia Pictures' popular "Crime Doctor" series, *Crime Doctor's Man Hunt* came to theaters in the fall of 1946. Like three of its predecessors, *Shadows in the Night* (1944), *The Crime Doctor's Courage* (1945) and *Just*

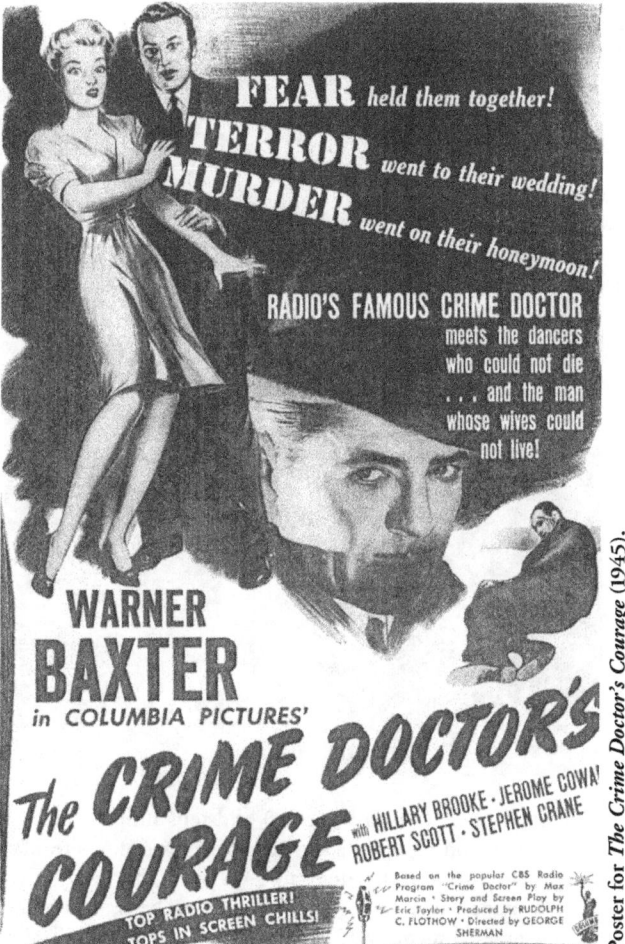

Poster for *The Crime Doctor's Courage* (1945).

Before Dawn (1946) [qq.v.], it possessed genre ingredients such as a spooky, deserted mansion and a homicidal woman with a split personality. In addition, the feature was done mostly in either indoor or night locales and was a compact, entertaining mystery deftly directed by William Castle, who gave it a number of *film noir* touches. Like the rest of the series outings, the production starred Warner Baxter as Dr. Robert Ordway, the character created by Max Marcin for the popular CBS radio series "The Crime Doctor" (1940–1947) starring Ray Collins in the title role. The script was written by mystery and science fiction author Leigh Brackett, whose screen work also included *The Vampire's Ghost* (1945) and *The Empire Strikes Back* (1980).

Wandering through a carnival, John Foster (Myron Healey) stops to talk with Ruby Farrell (Claire Carleton), who runs a shooting gallery that uses air guns. The man then goes to see psychia-

Warner Baxter, Ellen Drew, William Frawley in *The Crime Doctor's Man Hunt* (1946).

trist Dr. Robert Ordway (Baxter) and tells him about often ending up in a downtrodden part of town. He also says he does not his want his fiancée, Irene Cotter (Ellen Drew), to know he is having lapses of memory. Ordway suggests he may be suffering from bomb shock and battle fatigue and asks him to make another appointment. After Foster leaves, Irene, who has followed him to the doctor's office, consults with the psychiatrist, who tries to reassure her about Foster's condition. A week later, Ordway visits the carnival and on the way home walks through the tenement area Foster described. He sees his patient with a head wound being carried by two men, Bigger (Frank Sully) and Waldo (Bernard Nedell). When the duo spy the psychiatrist, he pretends to be drunk. They drive him to a rooming house where he claims to live and once there he telephones Police Inspector Manning (William Frawley). Meeting Manning and Sergeant Bradley (Jack Lee), Ordway leads them to another rooming house, the place he saw the two men emerge with Foster, whom he believes was murdered. They are admitted by the landlady (Minerva Urecal) and question several of the tenants, including phrenologist Le Blanc (Olin Howland) and Ruby. The police are not able to learn anything about Foster, and Manning thinks Ordway is mistaken about the homicide.

The psychiatrist recalls his patient speaking of going to a party where astrologer Alfredi (Ivan Triesault) predicted he would meet a violent end. Bigger and Waldo go to collect from a mysterious blonde woman with glasses who hired them to dispose of Foster's body but she puts off paying them. Ordway returns to the carnival where he talks with Ruby, who takes him to a deserted house across the street from her abode, saying she saw a light in the place the night of the murder. When the doctor goes inside to investigate, Ruby leaves. While looking through the house, Ordway is knocked out by Bigger who was hiding there with Waldo. Recovering, the psychiatrist goes to see Manning, who informs him that Foster has been found dead, that is real name was Philip Armstrong and he was killed by an air pistol. The two men go to see Gerald Cotter (Francis Pierlot), the owner of the abandoned house, whose daughter Irene was engaged to Armstrong. He is unable to help them. Irene becomes distraught when she finds out about Philip's killing. She tells the family housekeeper, Martha (Mary Newton), that her older sister Natalie had warned her not to marry

Advertisement for *The Crime Doctor's Man Hunt*.

Armstrong because he would only bring her sorrow. Upset that her father had sent her sister away three years before, Irene leaves the house and is told by the gardener (Paul E. Burns) that two men, Bigger and Waldo, had been asking about Natalie. Manning arrests Ruby for the murder since the victim was killed by an air gun but Ordway believes she is innocent. Bigger and Waldo again meet the blonde woman who promises to pay them.

Ordway has lunch with Irene and she tells him about her sister. As the doctor is informing the young woman there was no motive for her fiancée's killing, Manning calls him to say Bigger and Waldo are dead. Ordway goes to the hotel where the two men met the blonde woman, and determine that they died from asphyxiation. The apartment had been rented to a Jane Roberts. Finding a notebook with Alfredi's address in the apartment, Manning and Ordway question the astrologer at police headquarters but he denies any knowledge of the affair. Ordway again questions Ruby who says she remembers a blonde woman often coming to her shooting gallery; the doctor promises to get her out of jail. When Ordway and Manning query Alfredi a second time, he admits being hired by a blonde woman named Natalie to put a scare into Philip but he had nothing to do with his murder. Cotter informs Ordway and Manning that his older daughter Natalie controlled Irene since childhood and when the younger sister refused to break off her engagement with Armstrong, Natalie had angrily left town. An irate man, Herrera (Leon Lenoir), arrives at police headquarters and threatens to sue Manning since he gave out a newspaper story that Natalie, his late wife, was suspected of committing a murder. That night Ordway goes to the abandoned house where he meets Irene. Going inside, he pretends to find a clue and sends her to telephone Manning. The blonde woman shows up and attempts to kill the psychiatrist but is disarmed by Manning and Bradley. Ordway then removes the woman's glasses and blonde wig, revealing Irene, who he says assumed her sister's identity, resulting in a split personality. The young woman confesses to killing Philip because she was afraid he would discover her secret and that she also murdered Bigger and Waldo. As Bradley takes Irene into custody, Manning suggests Ordway talk with his wife, who he says has *no* personality.

Cry of the Werewolf

(1944; 63 minutes) PRODUCER: Wallace MacDonald. DIRECTOR: Henry Levin. SCREENPLAY: Griffin Jay and

Stephen Crane, Osa Massen and Nina Foch in *Cry of the Werewolf* (1944).

Charles O'Neal. STORY: Griffin Jay. PHOTOGRAPHY: L.W. O'Connell. EDITOR: Reg Browne. MUSIC: Mischa Bakaleinikoff. ART DIRECTORS: Lionel Banks and George Brooks. SOUND: Lambert Day. SETS: Robert Priestley. DIALOGUE DIRECTOR: Herman Rotsten. TECHNICAL ADVISOR: Dr. Fraime Sertoroclos. ASSISTANT DIRECTOR: Milton Feldman. CAST: Nina Foch (Celeste/Marie Latour), Stephen Crane (Bob Morris), Osa Massen (Elsa Chauvet), Blanche Yurka (Bianca), Barton MacLane (Lieutenant Barry Lane), Ivan Triesault (Yan Spavero), John Abbott (Peter Althius), Fred Graff (Pinkie), John Tyrrell (Mac), Robert Williams (Max), Fritz Leiber (Dr. Charles Morris), Milton Parsons (Adamson), George Eldredge (George Latour), Alan Bridge (Coroner), Ray Teal (Officer Ed), Frank O'Connor (Policeman), Al Thompson (Sheepman), George Magrill (Guard), Harry Semels, Hector Sarno, Tiny Jones (Gypsies).

Following the box office success of *The Return of the Vampire* (q.v.), Columbia put that film's co-star, Nina Foch, in *Cry of the Werewolf*. The feature was basically a reworking of Universal's blockbuster *The Wolf Man* (1941). Here there was a gender change, with the lycanthrope a female and the hero (Stephen Crane in his film debut) being the imperiled party. Blanche Yurka had the role of the older gypsy woman which Maria Ouspenskaya did in the Universal outing and Barton MacLane virtually repeated his role of a cop on the trail of the monster from Universal's *The Mummy's Ghost* (1944). For publicity value, Columbia claimed that Transylvanian psychiatrist Dr. Fraime Sertoroclos provided technical advice for the feature, which took the cheap way out and showed the heroine becoming a werewolf via shadows with an actual wolf substituting for the lycanthrope.

During a tour of the New Orleans Latour Museum, guide Peter Althius (John Abbott) tells the story of Marie Latour (Nina Foch), who murdered her husband (George Eldredge) when he found out she was a werewolf. Gypsy Celeste (Nina Foch), the daughter of the lycanthrope, is told by museum caretaker Yan Spavero (Ivan Triesault) that museum director Dr. Charles Morris (Fritz Leiber) plans to reveal the location of her mother's grave. Celeste then joins a tour of the museum but sneaks into a secret tunnel after leaving a devil doll on Morris' desk. The doll is found by the director's assistant, Elsa Chauvet (Osa Massen), a native of Transylvania. Morris tells Elsa to meet his son Bob (Stephen Crane) at the airport and drive him to the museum.

That night, Peter hears screams coming from

the secret passage. When Elsa and Bob arrive, they find Dr. Morris' manuscript has been burned and Peter in a trance. When the director is found murdered, Police Lt. Barry Lane (Barton MacLane) and his men arrive to investigate and first suspect Elsa but she is exonerated. After examining the remains of the manuscript, Elsa believes her boss was killed by a werewolf as Yan later destroys the work. The caretaker is then ordered killed by Celeste so as not to implicate her or her gypsy band. Later she is told to appear at his inquest. There Bob finds out that the gypsies return each year to bury their dead and he goes to see Adamson (Milton Parsons), the head of the funeral home where the bodies are stored before burial. When the undertaker refuses to help him, Bob sneaks into the cellar of the funeral parlor looking for the gypsies' records but finds himself stalked by a wolf-like presence and escapes by an elevator. He runs into Celeste at the Adamson establishment and they become friendly. She takes him back to her camp and tells him the history of her tribe. Bob comes under Celeste's spell and tells Elsa, now his fiancée, that she and the gypsies were not involved in his father's death. Suspicious, Elsa goes back to the museum and meets Celeste, who plans to make her a lycanthrope. Bob hears a noise emanating from the secret passage and finds a stunned Elsa, who claims she killed his father. Bob now feels Celeste is responsible for Elsa's behavior and tells Lane and his cohorts to investigate the secret passage leading to a basement, which houses Marie Latour's grave. While in the crypt, the cops fire at a fleeing wolf. The now wounded Celeste tries to get Elsa to murder Bob but he tells his fiancée to use her will to fight the demon. Although weak from loss of blood, Celeste transforms into a werewolf and attempts to eliminate Bob but is shot and killed by Lane. Elsa returns to normal and the police come to realize they have been hunting a werewolf.

Cry of the Werewolf was issued theatrically on a double bill with *The Soul of a Monster* (q.v.) and proved to be durable, continuing to be reissued into the early 1950s, often as a dual item for smaller theaters and drive-ins. The film got mixed reviews from critics. The *New York Times* scoffed at it ("[T]here is absolutely nothing original in this utterly suspenseless film") while the Zanesville, Ohio, *Sunday-Times Signal* claimed, "Horror fans are in for a thrill [with] the story of dread voodoo murders, horrifying tribal rites and a fantastic feast of death in which lovely and talented Nina Foch plays the woman werewolf whose mother terrorized millions and because of whose sins Nina can never marry."

Perhaps the best scene in the film is when Bob Morris sneaks into the catacombs of the funeral home and finds himself being stalked by a supernatural presence before finding escape via an elevator.

Curse of the Demon

(1958; 83 minutes) PRODUCER: Hal E. Chester. DIRECTOR: Jacques Tourneur. SCREENPLAY: Charles Bennett and Hal E. Chester, from the story "Casting the Runes" by Montague R. James. PHOTOGRAPHY: Ted Scaife. EDITOR: Michael Gordon. MUSIC: Clifton Parker. CONDUCTOR: Muir Mathison. PRODUCTION DESIGN: Ken Adam. SOUND: Arthur Bradburn. PRODUCTION MANAGER: R.L.M. Davidson. SPECIAL EFFECTS: George Blackwell and Wally Veevers. SPECIAL EFFECTS PHOTOGRAPHY: S.D. Onions. CONTINUITY: Pamela Gayler. ASSISTANT DIRECTOR: Basil Keys. CAST: Dana Andrews (Dr. John Holden), Peggy Cummins (Joanna Harrington), Niall MacGinnis (Julian Karswell), Maurice Denham (Professor Henry Harrington), Athene Seyler (Mrs. Karswell), Liam Redmond (Professor Mark O'Brien), Reginald Beckwith (Mr. Meek), Ewan Roberts (Lloyd Williamson), Peter Elliott (Dr. Kumar), Rosamund Greenwood (Mary Meek), Brian Wilde (Rand Hobart), Richard Leech (Inspector Mottram), Lloyd Lamble (Detective Simmons), Peter Hobbes (Police Superintendent), Charles Lloyd-Pack (Chemist), John Salew (Librarian), Janet Barrow (Mrs. Hobart), Percy Herbert, John Harvey (Hobart Brothers), Lynn Tracy (Stewardess), Ballard Berkeley, Michael Peake (Newsmen), Walter Horsbrugh (Butler Bates), Leonard Sharp (Ticket Man), Shay Gorman (Narrator).

Screenwriter Charles Bennett, who co-scripted Alfred Hitchcock's 1935 classic *The 39 Steps*, purchased the screen rights to Montague R. James' chilling short story "Casting the Runes" and worked with producer Hal E. Chester in bringing it to the screen. Made by Sabre Film Productions and Associated British Pictures Corporation, the feature was issued in its homeland in 1957 as *Night of the Demon* by Columbia. When the company released it stateside in July 1958 it was re-titled *Curse of the Demon* and was twelve minutes shy of its original 95-minute running time. Directed by Jacques Tourneur, who had helmed the Val Lewton classics *Cat People* (1942) and *I Walked with a Zombie* (1943) for RKO, the feature did not turn out the way Tourneur had intended. He and Bennett were especially unhappy with Chester for introducing the demonic creature very early in the proceedings; Tourneur claimed he did not film the sequence where the monster attacks Professor Harrington (Maurice Denham). The first appearance of the demon, however, is the only real drawback in what is otherwise an extremely well-made and frightening horror film.

Professor Henry Harrington (Denham) drives to the posh estate of Julian Karswell (Niall MacGinnis) with a promise to stop his investigation of Karswell's demonic cult in return for Karswell recanting a curse of death he put on Harrington. Karswell, when he finds out the parchment with runic symbols he gave the professor has since burned, agrees. As he arrives home, Harrington sees a huge flying fire demon and in his haste to escape in his car he backs into an electric pole; as he climbs from the car, the demon closes in.

On a plane from America, psychologist Dr. John Holden (Dana Andrews) meets a young woman whom he later learns is the professor's niece Joanna (Peggy Cummins). Holden is coming to England to speak at a conference on the paranormal and he is met at the airport by Harrington's assistant Lloyd Williams (Ewan Roberts), who tells him about Harrington's death. Holden also meets devil worship authority Professor Mark O'Brien (Liam Redmond) and Indian psychologist Dr. Kumar (Peter Elliott). O'Brien shows Holden some drawings of a demon made by Rand Hobart (Brian Wilde), an accused killer and a member of Karswell's sect who has been frightened into a catatonic state. Holden dismisses the professor's claims of devil worship but decides to look into the matter after receiving a telephone call from Karswell requesting he stop investigating his activities. He goes to the British Museum to look into Harrington's research and there meets Karswell, who gives him his card and invites him to his estate. At Harrington's funeral, Holden sees Joanna and that night she comes to his hotel and asks him not to delve into her uncle's research. When writing on the card Karswell gave him disappears without explanation, Holden asks Joanna to drive him to Julian's estate. When they arrive they find Karswell and his mother (Athene Seyler) hosting their annual Halloween party for local children. Karswell takes Holden for a walk around his estate and to show off his powers he conjures a thunderstorm and informs the American he will die in three days although he will stop the curse if the psychologist will give up his investigation.

That night John meets Joanna at her house for dinner and when he starts to show her some papers, a parchment with runic symbols flies out of his briefcase and gets caught in the fireplace grate. He keeps the paper and the next day goes into the country to get permission from Hobart's mother (Janet Barrow) to use hypnosis on her son to find out whey he committed murder. He obtains the needed consent, but when she and her family spy the runic parchment she tells him he has been "chosen." Holden travels to Stonehenge where he compares the runic symbols there with those on the parchment. That night Joanna, at the request of Mrs. Karswell, brings Holden to a séance conducted by a medium (Reginald Beckwith) and his wife (Rosamund Greenwood). In a trance, the medium speaks in Harrington's voice and tells Holden he must find the translation Karswell has done of the book on demons. John is skeptical but he lets Joanna drive him back to the estate where he breaks into the house and finds the book in the library. As he is about to examine it, a cat turns into a jaguar and attacks him. Karswell

The title monster in *Curse of the Demon* (1958).

shows up and the cat returns to normal. As Holden walks back to Joanna's car through the woods he sees a huge cloud materialize and then vanish. Holden and Joanna go to Scotland Yard and report the incidents to Inspector Mottram (Richard Leech) and Detective Simmons (Lloyd Lamble). The day Karswell predicted Holden will die, the psychologist conducts his lecture and then proceeds to hypnotize Hobart. When Holden shows Hobart the parchment, the formerly catatonic man says it must be returned to its giver or a demon will kill him. Going berserk, Hobart attacks Holden and his guards and then jumps from a window to his death below. Holden now realizes he must get the parchment back to Karswell or he too will die. Dr. Kumar tells him Mrs. Karswell informed him that her son was scheduled to leave for Southampton on a 9:45 train. Joanna gets a call from Mrs. Karswell saying Hobart knows the secret of the parchment and when she leaves to tell Holden, she is abducted. Holden races to the train and boards just as it leaves and he finds Joanna, under a spell, in Karswell's compartment. Julian releases Joanna from the trance and becomes nervous when he realizes that Holden is trying to slip him the parchment. As he tries to leave the compartment, Holden stops Karswell but Mottram and Simmons arrive and force Holden to let Karswell depart. As he does so, Holden puts the parchment into Karswell's overcoat. When Karswell realizes what happened, he searches the coat and the parchment escapes and glides out of the rail car. Outside, as Karswell is chasing it along the tracks, the fire demon materializes and mutilates him. The police conclude that Karswell was mangled by a passing train as Holden and Joanna depart.

In *The Encyclopedia of Horror Movies* (1986), Phil Hardy called *Curse of the Demon* "a brilliant adaptation" of the James story. He further expounded on director Tourneur's contribution to the movie:

> Here his extraordinary placing and handling of the camera imbue seemingly ordinary surroundings with a brooding sense of menace. The trees, objects or simply unlit areas darkly obtruding in the foreground suggest the presence of implacable forces waiting to pounce on vulnerable, isolated figures. Some of the suspense scenes, perfectly timed and staged, stand out as models of their kind.... The intensely rhythmic opening sequences, intended to set a tone impending doom, were ruined by the distributor's insistence on the need for early shock effects, but the rest of the movie is an object lesson in atmospheric horror."

David Quinlan, in *British Sound Films: The Studio Years 1928–1959* (1984), concurred by calling the feature a "[p]retty scary thriller; a pity they had to show the demon."

To be fair with both the producer and the distributor, the demon itself is indeed a frightening movie monster, and the finale when the huge thing picks up and shreds Karswell is terrifying. The shock of the scene is somewhat lessened by having seen the beast from Hell so early on in the film.

The Curse of the Mummy's Tomb

(1964; 78 minutes; Color) PRODUCER-DIRECTOR: Michael Carreras. ASSOCIATE PRODUCER: Bill Hill. SCREENPLAY: Henry Younger [Michael Carreras]. PHOTOGRAPHY: Otto Heller. EDITOR: Eric Boyd-Perkins. MUSIC: Carlo Martelli. SOUND: Claude Hitchcock. PRODUCTION DESIGN: Bernard Robinson. MAKEUP: Roy Ashton. WARDROBE: Betty Adamson and John Briggs. ASSISTANT DIRECTOR: Bert Batt. CAST: Terence Morgan (Adam Beauchamp/Pharaoh Re), Ronald Howard (John Bray), Fred Clark (Alexander King), Jeanne Roland (Annette Dubois), George Pastell (Hashmi Bey), Jack Gwillim (Sir Giles Dalrymple), John Paul (Inspector Mackenzie), Dickie Owen (Ra-Antef the Mummy), Michael McStay (Young Ra-Antef), Harold Goodwin (Fred), Michael Ripper (Achmed), Jill Mai Meredith (Jenny), Bernard Rebel (Professor Eugene Dubois), Vernon Smythe (Butler Jessop), Marianne Stone (Landlady), Jimmy Gardner (Cockney Workman), Olga Dickie (Housekeeper), Larry Taylor (Swordsman), Roy Stewart (Museum Bearer).

Between 1959 and 1971 Hammer Films made four Mummy movies: *The Mummy* (1959), *The Curse of the Mummy's Tomb* (1964), *The Mummy's Shroud* (1967) and *Blood from the Mummy's Tomb* (1971). *Blood from the Mummy's Tomb*, based on Bram Stoker's novel *Jewel of the Seven Stars*, was mostly helmed by Seth Holt although Michael Carreras took over for the final days of shooting after Holt's sudden death.

Filmed at Associated British Studios, *The Curse of the Mummy's Tomb* was a compact, fast-paced follow up to *The Mummy*. Of the quartet of Hammer Mummy movies, Columbia only released this one, on a double-bill with Hammer's *The Gorgon* (q.v.), in both the United States and Great Britain. Showings in its homeland began in the fall of 1964 with playdates in the U.S. beginning at the end of the year. In *The Curse of the Mummy's Tomb*, George Pastell (who was in the

1959 *The Mummy*) played Egyptian advisor Hashmi Bey.

Professor Dubois (Bernard Rebel) is murdered by native tribesmen in 1900 Egypt. Dubois, Sir Giles Dalrymple (Jack Gwillim) and John Bray (Ronald Howard) had excavated the long-lost tomb of Royal Prince Ra-Antef. Dubois' body is brought back to his daughter-assistant Annette (Jeanne Roland), who is loved by Bray. Bray accuses Egyptian advisor Hashmi Bey (Pastell) of trying to sabotage the expedition so his country can claim the wealth of treasure in the prince's tomb. The other member of the expedition and its financial backer, American showman Alexander King (Fred Clark), turns down Hashmi's offer of £70,000 from the Cairo Museum and plans to exhibit Ra-Antef's mummy and the treasure throughout the United States and Europe. As a result, Sir Giles resigns as leader of the expedition and assigns the task to Bray, who reluctantly agrees to go along with King's plans. That night the tomb's contents are ransacked and guard Achmed (Michael Ripper) is murdered. On the boat sailing for America, Annette tells Bray she has a bad feeling about the upcoming exhibition and later both Sir Giles and Bray are attacked by a stranger who tries to abduct Annette but is knocked overboard by another passenger, Adam Beauchamp (Terence Morgan). Adam, who is attracted to Annette, expresses an interest in Egyptian archaeology and she tells him the story of how 3,000 years ago Re, the younger son of Pharaoh Rameses VIII, ordered the murder of his brother Ra-Antef (Michael McStay) and she shows him a medallion from the tomb given to her by her father. That night she gives the medallion to Bray, who takes it to Sir Giles to be deciphered. Bray is knocked out by a stranger who steals the amulet.

The next day, King discusses the expedition and the finding of the mummy's tomb for the press and invited guests, but when he opens the sarcophagus the mummy is missing. Scotland Yard Inspector Mackenzie (John Paul) is called into the case, and Bray informs him and King that the stolen medallion was used to bring the mummy back to life to take revenge on all those who defiled its tomb. Both Mackenzie and King scoff at the assertion. That night the living mummy (Dickie Owen) kills King as Bray goes to Hashmi, whom he believes stole the amulet. The mummy murders Sir Giles. Adam informs Annette that he must leave the country and asks her to go with him, and she agrees. The mummy comes for Annette, knocks out Adam but leaves the house when Bray and Mackenzie arrive. When the mummy comes to kill Bray, it is caught in a net but escapes and crushes Hashmi, who asked for forgiveness for aiding infidels in opening its tomb. Adam shows Annette the Egyptian artifacts he has in his basement and then tells her he is really Re and that he was condemned to eternal life by his father for ordering the killing of his brother. He used the medallion to bring the mummy back to life, for it can kill him and then he and Annette can spend eternity together. He orders the mummy to kill the girl; when the mummy hesitates, Adam attempts to do so himself and the creature stops him. Bray and Mackenzie and his policemen arrive and Adam orders the mummy to carry Annette into the sewers but has his right hand severed when Mackenzie closes a heavy door on it. When Adam makes another attempt on Annette's life, the mummy kills him and then takes the medallion and walks away, pulling down the roof of the sewer on himself. The girl is rescued by Bray and Mackenzie.

The Devil Commands

(1941; 64 minutes) PRODUCER: Wallace MacDonald. DIRECTOR: Edward Dmytryk. SCREENPLAY: Robert D. Andrews and Milton Gunzburg, from the novel *The Edge of Running Water* by William Sloane. PHOTOGRAPHY: Allen G. Siegler. EDITOR: Al Clark. MUSIC DIRECTOR: M.W. [Morris] Stoloff. ART DIRECTOR: Lionel Banks. SOUND: Philip Faulkner, Jr. ASSISTANT DIRECTOR: George Rhein. CAST: Boris Karloff (Dr. Julian Blair), Richard Fiske (Dr. Richard Sayles), Amanda Duff (Anne Blair), Anne Revere (Mrs. Walters), Ralph Penney (Karl), Dorothy Adams (Mrs. Marcy), Walter Baldwin (Seth Marcy), Kenneth MacDonald (Sheriff Ed Willis), Shirley Warde (Helen Blair), Erwin Kaiser (Professor Kent), Lester Alden (Dr. Van Den), Jacques Vanaire (Dr. Hartley), Eddie Kane (Professor Walt), Wheaton Chambers (Dr. Sanders), Earl Crawford (Johnson), Ernie Adams (Elam), George McKay (Station Agent), John Tyrrell (Postmaster), Al Rhein (Truck Driver), Harrison Greene (Baker Booth).

Working titles: *The Devil Said No* and *When the Dead Commands*.

The Devil Commands, released early in 1941, was the fourth of five features Boris Karloff starred in for Columbia Pictures between 1939 and 1942. It was directed by Edward Dmytryk, who had previously done the borderline genre effort *Television Spy* (1939) for Paramount and would later helm Universal's *Captive Wild Woman* (1943). While the *New York Times* termed the thriller "a hodgepodge of scientific claptrap," the *Motion Picture Herald* called it "somewhat slow" but added, "[It] contains the necessary continuity to make it an interesting melodrama of horror and suspense." The British *Kinematograph Weekly* thought it a "[s]pectacular thriller," adding, "Whatever the mood, the film is good Karloff and that is good enough to promote excitement and win the approbation of the masses." It should be noted the feature was re-edited in several places by the British Censor to eliminate sequences it considered distasteful.

The film begins with the voice of Anne Blair (Amanda Duff) telling how her father, Dr. Julian Blair (Karloff), became the object of fear in the small town of Barsham Harbor. We flash back to two years earlier as Dr. Blair, chief of the science department at Midland University, shows four of his colleagues (Erwin Kaiser, Jacques Vanaire, Eddie Kane, Wheaton Chambers) his experiments in brain waves, with the help of his assistant, Dr. Richard Sayles (Richard Fiske). When Julian's wife Helen (Shirley Warde) arrives at his laboratory, Blair induces her to do a test that shows her brain waves on a screen. Following the test, Julian and Helen leave to pick up Anne, who has been out of town; on the way they stop at a bakery to get a cake for the girl's twentieth birthday. As Helen drives around the block in a rain storm, Julian gets the cake only to learn his wife has died after their car was hit by a truck. After his wife's funeral, Julian returns to his laboratory where he absentmindedly turns on some equipment and finds it is still transmitting Helen's brain waves. Believing he has found a means of communicating with the dead, he shares his findings with Anne, Richard and his colleagues and they all are skeptical. Julian's laboratory assistant Karl (Ralph Penney) induces the professor to attend a séance conducted by spirit medium Mrs. Walters (Anne Revere). While Julian proves the woman a fake, he also perceives that she houses high voltage electrical impulses and for pay she agrees to help him in his experiments. When the work goes awry, causing Karl brain damage, Julian resigns his university post, sends Anne away to New York City and he, Mrs. Walters and Karl move to the remote village of Barsham Harbor where he can continue his work in private.

Two years later, after five bodies have disappeared from the town cemetery, the disdain for the doctor in the village causes Sheriff Ed Willis (Kenneth MacDonald) to visit Blair's house. Both Julian and Mrs. Walters refuse him access to the laboratory but later he asks their housekeeper Mrs. Marcy (Dorothy Adams) to investigate. When the doctor forgets to lock the lab door, Mrs. Marcy enters and finds five cloaked bodies covered by metal suits. Karl locks the door from the outside, causing Mrs. Marcy to panic and accidentally set off the electrical equipment which brings the bodies to move, giving her heart failure. After her body is found, Mrs. Walters uses the dead woman's shoes to make false tracks that make it look as if she fell over a cliff while walking home. Not fooled, Mrs. Marcy's husband Seth (Walter Baldwin) accuses the doctor of murdering his wife.

The sheriff sends for Anne and she arrives with Richard. The three of them go to see Julian as Seth incites the villagers against Dr. Blair. During an experiment, Julian hears his wife's voice and increases the voltage to the point that it kills Mrs. Walters. When Anne arrives at the house with the sheriff and Richard, the doctor realizes that his daughter is the catalyst he needs to contact his dead wife. Richard tries to stop him but Karl knocks out the young man. Julian places his daughter in a metal suit and resumes his efforts in contacting Helen. Seth and the villagers, having overpowered the sheriff, break into the house and knock out Karl as Richard revives and tries to save Anne. This time Julian uses so much voltage that his machines blow up and destroy the house. Julian perishes but Richard is able to save Anne.

The Devil Commands was one of eleven Columbia films released to television in the late 1950s as part of Screen Gems' "Son of Shock!" package. Karloff's other four "Mad Doctor" features (*Before I Hang*, *The Boogie Man Will Get You*, *The Man They Could Not Hang*, *The Man with Nine Lives* [qq.v.]) were also included along with two of Karloff's earlier genre studio efforts, *Behind the Mask* and *The Black Room* (qq.v.).

Devil Goddess

(1955; 70 minutes) PRODUCER: Sam Katzman. DIRECTOR: Spencer G. Bennet. SCREENPLAY: George Plympton. STORY: Dwight Babcock. PHOTOGRAPHY: Ira Morgan. EDITOR: Aaron Stell. MUSIC DIRECTOR: Mischa Bakaleinikoff. ART DIRECTOR: Paul Palmentola. SOUND: Harry R. Smith. UNIT MANAGER: Leon Chooluck. SETS: Sidney Clifford. SPECIAL EFFECTS: Jack Erickson. ASSISTANT DIRECTOR: Leonard Katzman. CAST: Johnny Weissmuller (Johnny), Angela Stevens (Nora Blakely), Selmer Jackson (Professor Carl Blakely), William Tannen (Nels Comstock), Ed Hinton (Joseph Leopold), William M. Griffith (Professor Ralph Dixon),

Abel M. Fernandez (Teinusi), Frank Lackteen (Nkruma), Vera M. Francis [Viejah] (Sarab'na), Paul Marion (Matuas Chief Malu), John [Bob] Cason, Lynton Brent (Henchmen), George Berkeley (Bert), Max Reid (Kirundi Chief), Sue England (Girl), Kimba (Chimp).

The title *Devil Goddess* is a misnomer since the title character was a male; it should have been called *Devil God*. Such subtleties were lost on producer "Jungle Sam" Katzman, who used footage from seven previous Weissmuller-Columbia efforts to pad out the affair, along with grainy disaster scenes from other sources. A five-minute segment was lifted from *Savage Mutiny* (q.v.), which also co-starred Angela Stevens. The *Motion Picture Herald* dubbed the outing "a tongue-in-cheek adventure, in the best old-fashioned traditional classification" while *Variety* thought it was "a plodding, almost amateurish attempt at making a formula theme pay off." Overall, it was a hodgepodge of lots of trekking through the jungle, monkey antics and digging for treasure with borderline horror elements built around a demon of fire who was a volcano god in the Kirundi Valley.

Poster for *Devil Goddess* (1955).

After his pet chimp Kimba and two other simians get high after drinking from a bottle labeled "medicinal," Johnny Weissmuller (himself) meets pretty Nora Blakely (Angela Stevens), who has come to the jungle with her father, Professor Carl Blakely (Selmer Jackson), in search of Professor Ralph Dixon (William M. Griffith), an expert in the occult who disappeared four years before while on one of their expeditions. Since they feel he may have been lost while researching a tribe of fire worshippers near a volcano in the off-limits Kirundi Valley, Johnny agrees to lead them to the area. When the volcano erupts, the fire god, a manlike figure in a long robe with a white beard, makes an appearance, frightening the natives. One of the tribe, Nkruma (Frank Lackteen), finds a jewel-encrusted dagger which he sells to crook Nels Comstock (William Tannen) for tobacco. Comstock takes the artifact to Joseph Leopold (Ed Hinton), the manager of the Afro-European Metal Company, who decides to lead an expedition to the Kirundi Valley in search of more treasure. Upon their arrival in the forbidden land, the crooks make Nkruma and some of the other natives lead them to the place where the dagger was found and then put them to work excavating the area. Since a yearly human sacrifice is demanded by the fire god, native girl

Sarab'na (Vera M. Francis) is chosen; her lover Teinusi (Abel M. Fernandez) begs Johnny to save her. During the ceremony, the fire god appears but Johnny and Teinusi grab the girl and escape with her into the jungle. Sending the lovers for Nora and her father, Johnny goes to the volcano area where Leopold and his men have found a chest full of priceless relics. The natives attack them and Johnny is twice knocked out. The hunters are forced to take shelter in a cave. Nora and her father find Johnny and tell him they never saw Teinusi or Sarab'na. Kimba locates Teinusi, who has been injured. Nora stays to tend the native's wounds while Johnny and her father go to the mountain where Sarab'na is to be sacrificed to the fire god. They are too late, but go into a cave where they find Sarab'na, along with several other native girls, with an old man in a crude laboratory. The aged one thinks he is a god, but Blakely recognizes him as Professor Dixon, who believes the white men want to steal King Solomon's treasure. When Dixon tells Johnny and the professor that the volcano is about to erupt and destroy the native village, he is asked to scare the inhabitants into leaving the area. Exiting the cave, the group meets Leopold, Comstock and their men, but Dixon uses explosives to get away from them. The natives attack and kill Leopold and Comstock and capture the rest of their men. Nora and Teinusi are taken to their village for sacrifice. Dixon appears before the natives and tells them to depart while Johnny rescues Nora and Teinusi just as the volcano erupts, destroying the village. As a result, Dixon's memory returns and he agrees to go back with Nora, Professor Blakely and the treasure.

Devil Goddess proved to be the last of 16 features Johnny Weissmuller toplined for Sam Katzman, the first 13 being "Jungle Jim" outings. Following their demise, Weissmuller returned to the Alex Raymond–created character in the 1955–56 television season *Jungle Jim*.

The Devil's Mask

(1946; 65 minutes) PRODUCER: Wallace MacDonald. DIRECTOR: Henry Levin. SCREENPLAY: Charles O'Neal. ADDITIONAL DIALOGUE: Dwight Babcock. PHOTOGRAPHY: Henry Freulich. EDITOR: Jerome Thoms. MUSIC DIRECTOR: Mischa Bakaleinikoff. ART DIRECTOR: Robert Peterson. SOUND: George Cooper. SETS: George Montgomery. ASSISTANT DIRECTOR: Carl Hiecke. CAST: Anita Louise (Janet Mitchell), Jim Bannon (Jack Packard), Michael Duane (Rex Kennedy), Mona Barrie (Louise Mitchell), Barton Yarborough (Doc Long), Ludwig Donath (Dr. Karger), Paul E. Burns (Leon Hartman), Frank Wilcox (Professor Arthur Logan), Thomas E. Jackson (Captain Quinn), Richard Hale (Raymond Halliday), John Elliott (Butler John), Edward Earle (E.R. Willard), Frank Mayo (Quentin Mitchell), Coulter Irwin (Frank), Harry Strang (Brophy), Bud Averill (Museum Guard), Mary Newton (Nurse), Fred Godoy (Ybana), Frank Martin (Narrator).

Working title: *The Head.*

The third and final entry in Columbia's series based on the long-running radio program "I Love a Mystery," *The Devil's Mask* was preceded by *I Love a Mystery* (1945) and *The Unknown* (1946) (qq.v). With its spooky museum and taxidermist scenes, a stolen shrunken head, a mysterious murderer and an overall *film noir* atmosphere, *The Devil's Mask*

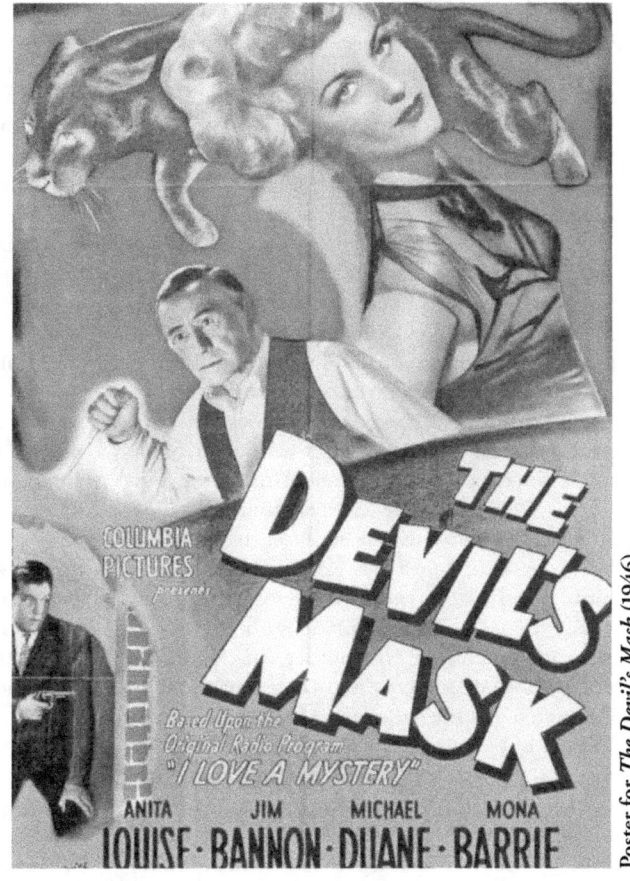

Poster for *The Devil's Mask* (1946).

proved to be a fairly satisfying and well-staged outing considering its limited budget. The film's main drawback is the casting of top-billed Anita Louise, who at 30 appears a bit long in the tooth to be portraying a 20-year-old with a father fixation.

Opening in a dark museum where a cloaked figure lurks, the picture details the crash of an airliner. The retrieved cargo is brought to the office of examiner E.R. Willard (Edward Earle) whose clerk (Coulter Irwin) opens a box and finds a shrunken head. San Francisco Police Captain Quinn (Thomas E. Jackson) decides to leave the head with Cordova Museum curator Raymond Halliday (Richard Hale), who plans to have it looked at by taxidermist Leon Hartman (Paul E. Burns), a close friend of missing museum director Quentin Mitchell (Frank Mayo). At the museum, Quinn meets detectives Jack Packard (Jim Bannon) and Doc Long (Barton Yarborough) who have come to meet a client, Louise Mitchell (Mona Barrie), the wife of the missing man. Arriving late, she tells them she is being followed by Rex Kennedy (Michael Duane), the boyfriend of her stepdaughter, Janet Mitchell (Anita Louise), and she is afraid the two are plotting to murder her. Janet and Rex go to see Hartman at his shop and she tells him she suspects her missing father was done in by her stepmother and her lover, Professor Arthur Logan (Frank Wilcox), during their recent expedition to the Jivaro headhunter country in South America. Rex tries unsuccessfully to get Jack and Doc to work with him on the case as the two detectives meet Louise at her house where she introduces them to Logan, who shows slides of the recent expedition. A mysterious figure fires a poison dart at the group and in escaping kills the butler (John Elliott), who recognized the assailant. Quinn suspects Kennedy and exposes him as a gambler, promoter and chiseler before Janet and holds him on a vagrancy charge. After getting out on bail, Rex goes to the Mitchell home and confronts Janet, who becomes so upset that he takes her to see neurologist Dr. Karger (Ludwig Donath), who places her under hypnosis during which she tells him she thinks her father is still alive and committed the murder. Jack and Doc tail Rex to Karger's office and Janet overhears the doctor tell Rex she has a father fixation. She tries to leave but is stopped by Rex. Janet asks the detectives to take her home. Jack discovers the doctor recorded his session with her and accuses him of being a blackmailer. Janet believes Rex is working with Karger and goes to Hartman, telling him she thinks her father is still alive and plans revenge on his wife and Logan. When a headless body is found in San Francisco Bay, the detectives asks Hartman if the shrunken head might be that of Quentin Mitchell but he dismisses the idea. Rex trails the gumshoes to the museum where the night watchman (Harry Strang) has been knocked out. Halliday arrives and they find that Mitchell's shrunken head is in a display case with other examples of the Jivaros' craft. Halliday also tells them that Quentin Mitchell had wanted him to recall Logan from the South American expedition. Jack finds words from the poem *The Rime of the Ancient Mariner* on beads sewn to Mitchell's shrunken head and he goes back to Hartman's shop as Rex tells the taxidermist he knows he murdered Janet's father. The girl arrives and thinks Rex is trying to blackmail Hartman. Rex tells her he saw Leon knock out the museum guard. Hartman informs Janet that he hated her father for killing animals and making him stuff them for the museum, and that he killed Quentin and shrunk his head. As Jack arrives at the shop, Hartman throws a knife into Rex's back and then knocks out the detective with a club. Hartman tells Janet he must eliminate Rex but Jack comes to as the taxidermist sets free his pet leopard Diablo. The beast stalks Jack but he runs into the shop and locks the door, leaving Hartman with the giant cat which attacks him. Jack shoots the animal, but not before it claws its owner to death. After explaining the case to Quinn, Jack and Doc go to the hospital to apologize to the recovering Rex, and they find him reunited with Janet who has made amends with Louise and Logan.

One of the highlights of the feature was its museum collection. Although the dinosaur replica was studio-built, the rest of the assemblage was authentic, including skeletons of an antelope, camel and chimpanzee, a taxidermy assortment of numerous South American jungle animals and Jivaro blow-guns and arrows. There were also funeral urns, several mummies, an Aztec sacrificial altar, and according to studio publicity, five real shrunken human heads. In addition, there was a display of South American Indian beads, bracelets and necklaces once owned by actor John Barrymore.

Die! Die! My Darling!

(1965; 96 minutes; Color) PRODUCER: Anthony Hinds. DIRECTOR: Silvio Narizzano. SCREENPLAY: Richard Matheson, from the novel *Nightmare* by Anne Blaisdell.

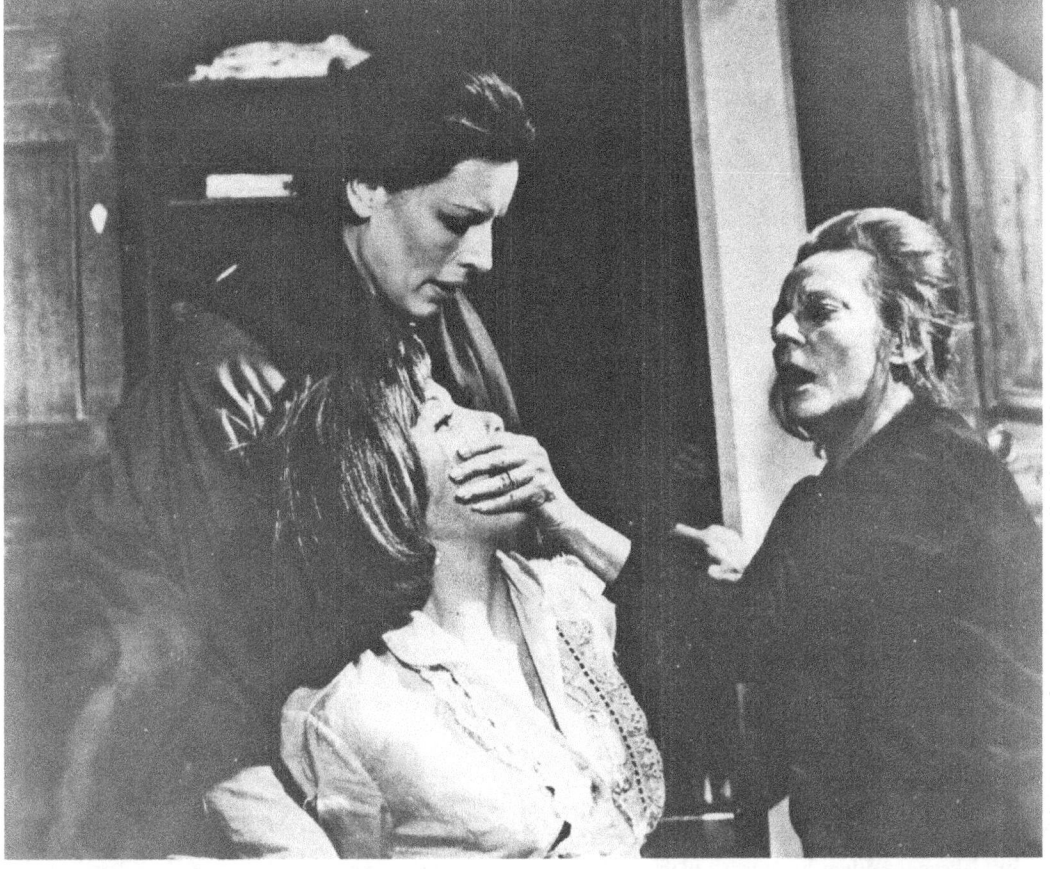

Yootha Joyce, Stefanie Powers and Tallulah Bankhead in *Die! Die! My Darling!* (1965).

PHOTOGRAPHY: Arthur Ibbetson. EDITOR: John Dunsford. MUSIC: Wilfred Josephs. SOUND: Ken Rawkins. MAKEUP: Roy Ashton and Richard Mills. PRODUCTION MANAGER: George Fowler. PRODUCTION DESIGN: Peter Proud. CONTINUITY: Renee Glynne. ASSISTANT DIRECTOR: Claude Watson. CAST: Tallulah Bankhead (Mrs. Trefoile), Stefanie Powers (Patricia "Pat" Carroll), Peter Vaughan (Harry), Maurice Kaufmann (Alan Glentower), Yootha Joyce (Anna), Donald Sutherland (Joseph), Gwendolyn Watts (Gloria), Robert Dorning (Ormsby), Philip Gilbert (Oscar), Winifred Dennis (Shopkeeper), Diana King (Shopper), Henry McGee (Rector).

Tallulah Bankhead's film career began in the silent days but, excepting a round of features in the early 1930s and her best-known cinema outing in Alfred Hitchcock's *Lifeboat* (1944), she is mainly remembered for her work on the London and American stages. Following the path of Joan Crawford, Bette Davis and Olivia de Havilland, she starred in this mid–1960s psychological horror effort made by Hammer Films at the Associated British Studios at Elstree. Based on Anne Blaisdell's 1961 novel *Nightmare*, it was shown in its homeland as *Fanatic* before reaching the U.S. in the spring of 1965.

Eschewing her usual off-center glamour, Bankhead played the character of Mrs. Trefoile as a plain, often well-meaning, but highly unbalanced religious fanatic. In *The New Biographical Dictionary of Film* (2002), David Thomson called her performance "a last gesture toward neglected extravagance." Although the feature had the makings of an entertaining thriller, it was too long and its emphasis on underplayed comedy offset the horror aspects of the plot. While Bankhead delivered a *tour de force* performance, the film itself, although pictorially satisfying, was like too many of her stage productions: It was piddling plot wise and unworthy of its star.

Arriving in London to be with her fiancé Alan Glentower (Maurice Kaufmann), American Pat Carroll (Stefanie Powers) tells him she plans to visit Mrs. Trefoile (Bankhead), the mother of her late boyfriend Stephen Trefoile. Pat drives to the small village where Mrs. Trefoile lives in a large but rundown house with her servants, groundsman Harry (Peter Vaughan), his housekeeper wife Anna (Yootha Joyce), and dimwitted gardener Joseph (Donald Sutherland). Mrs. Trefoile welcomes Pat, who soon learns the woman is a former actress who believes she lived a sinful past until she was saved by her late husband. She is also a religious fanatic who insists that Pat attend in-house religious services and dress in a reverential manner. Reluctantly Pat agrees to stay the night and the next day she accompanies Mrs. Trefoile to church so they can pray for Stephen's soul. There the woman informs Pat that she is Stephen's wife and must always remain a virgin and true to his memory. When Pat tells Mrs. Trefoile she never planned to marry her son, the woman locks her in her room and later at gunpoint she and Anna imprison Pat in the attic. Harry and Anna go along with the proceedings since he is a relative of Mrs. Trefoile's late husband and believes he will inherit the old woman's estate. During a scuffle with Anna, Pat is stabbed with a pair of scissors. To defy Mrs. Trefoile, the young woman tells her she is engaged to be married. Following a failed attempt to escape and after being brought back to the house by Harry, Pat is forced by the old woman to write Alan, saying she plans to stay in the country a while longer. Pat attempts another escape by trying to seduce Harry, but Mrs. Trefoile catches them and dismisses the groundskeeper. When he tries to blackmail her about Pat, she shoots him. Mrs. Trefoile informs Anna that her husband has gone to London for a few days in Pat's car. The defiant Pat tells the old lady that her son committed suicide because of her; Mrs. Trefoile goes berserk and locks her in the basement with Harry's corpse. Alan comes looking for Pat but Mrs. Trefoile tells him that Pat left the day before. At the local pub, Alan sees the barmaid (Gwendolyn Watts) wearing Pat's pin (given to her by Harry), so he returns to the house where he is attacked by Joseph. Finding Pat's car in the garage, Anna realizes that Harry has not gone to London and she revives Alan. He goes to the basement with her and Joseph and there they find Mrs. Trefoile planning to kill Pat in order to cleanse her soul. The old woman tries to shoot Alan but hits Joseph as Alan rescues Pat. Anna, who finds Harry's body, stabs Mrs. Trefoile, who dies before her son's portrait.

Sean Axmaker wrote in *The Scarecrow Movie Video Guide* (2004), "Bankhead pulls out all stops as the former stage actress twisted into fundamentalist severity by a terrible secret in her own dark past she dare not confront. It was her last screen appearance and she chews it up with the relish of an old scene stealer. Richard Matheson's screenplay ... owes inspiration to *Psycho* and *Baby Jane* but manages to stand on its own."

Doctor Faustus

(1968; 93 minutes; Color) PRODUCERS: Richard Burton and Richard McWhorter. DIRECTORS: Richard Burton and Nevill Coghill. SCREENPLAY: Nevill Coghill, from the play *The Tragical History of Doctor Faustus* by Christopher Marlowe. PHOTOGRAPHY: Gabor Pogany. EDITOR: John Shirley. MUSIC: Mario Nascimbene. ART DIRECTOR: Boris Jurage. SOUND: Aldo De Martini, John Aldred and David Hildyard. SETS: Dario Simoni. PRODUCTION DESIGN: John De Cuir. MAKEUP: Giannetto De Rossi, Frank La Rue and Ron Berkeley. COSTUME DESIGN: Peter Hall. PRODUCTION SUPERVISOR: Guy Luongo. UNIT MANAGER: Robert Cocco. CHOREOGRAPHER: Jacqueline Harvey. SPECIAL EFFECTS: Augie Lohman and Peter Harman. CONTINUITY: Elaine Schreyeck. TECHNICAL ASSISTANT: Nicholas Young. PRODUCTION ASSISTANT: Carlo Lastricati. ASSISTANT DIRECTOR: Gus Agosti. CAST: Richard Burton (Doctor John Faustus), Elizabeth Taylor (Helen of Troy), Andreas Teuber (Mephistopheles), Ian Marter (Emperor/Pride), Elizabeth O'Donovan (Empress), David McIntosh (Lucifer), Jeremy Eccles (Belzebub), Ram Chopra (Valdes), Richard Carwardine (Cornelius), Richard Heffer (First Disciple), Gwydion Thomas (Scholar/Lechery), Richard Durden-Smith (Knight/Evil Angel), Patrick Barwise (Wagner), Adrian Benjamin (Pope), Hugh Williams (Scholar), Jeremy Chandler (Emperor's Attendant), Angus McIntosh (Rector Magnificus), Ambrose Coghill (Professor/Avarice), Anthony Kaufman (Professor/Envy), Julian Wontner, Richard Harrison, Nevill Coghill (Professors), Michael Menaugh (Good Angel/Bishop), John Sandbach (Transformed Boy), Sebastian Walker (Idiot), Nicholas Loukes (Pride/Cardinal of Lorraine), Maria Aitken (Sloth), Valerie James (Idleness), Bridget Coghill, Petronella Pulsford, Susan Watson (Gluttony), Jacqueline Harvey, Sheila Dawson, Carolyn Bennett (Dancers), Jane Wilford (Court Lady/Nun), R. Peverello (Wrath).

Since 1897 there have been scores of films made about the Faust legend of a man selling his soul to the Devil in order to savor the pleasures and knowledge of the world. Columbia distributed this Nassau Films production, which its star Richard Burton also co-produced and co-directed. It was the seventh of 11 screen pairings of Burton with his then-wife Elizabeth Taylor; the rest of the cast was made up of members of the Oxford University Dramatic Society. Made in Rome, Italy, this fairly close adaptation of Christopher Marlowe's 1594 play "The Tragical History of Doctor Faustus" opened in the U.S. in

February 1968 and in London the following October. The feature is done entirely in darkened areas, not one scene showing the light of day. Taylor not only portrays Helen of Troy but also the incarnation of feminine beauty in several scenes.

In 16th-century Germany aged scholar Faustus (Burton) is given the University of Wittenberg's highest academic honors. Not satisfied with his life, he calls his friends Cornelius (Richard Carwardine) and Valdes (Ram Chopra) to aid him in carrying out magic. Later he conjures Mephistopheles (Andreas Teuber), a disciple of Lucifer (David McIntosh), but he is so ugly that the doctor commands him to return in the guise of a Franciscan friar. Faustus charges the spirit to attend to him while he lives and to follow all his commands. Mephistopheles tells Faustus to turn away from these wishes but the doctor orders the spirit to inform his master he wants 24 years to live the life he pleases with the spirit as his servant. Faustus battles within himself the concepts of good and evil but his overpowering desire for wealth changes the balance in favor of serving the Devil.

That night Mephistopheles returns with a promise from Lucifer that his wishes will be fulfilled but that he must promise to serve the evil one and give him his soul. Again overcome with second thoughts, Faustus finally signs the agreement with Lucifer in his own blood after being tempted by the sight of a naked woman. After signing, the now much younger Faustus questions Mephistopheles about Hell and then is given the prettiest maid in Germany but she turns ugly. His servant promises him an endless supply of concubines. When Faustus promises never to repent, Mephistopheles shows him the Seven Deadly Sins and with Pride (Nicholas Loukes) and his sons he joins in a battle between armies and ends up pierced by three swords. Before the emperor (Ian Marter) and empress (Elizabeth O'Donovan) the doctor conjures up the spirits of Alexander the Great and his paramour (Taylor), gives a doubting knight (Richard Durden-Smith) horns and then removes them, and is rewarded with gold. Faustus and his servant observe the Pope (Adrian Benjamin) and his cardinals on St. Peter's Holiday and have fun tormenting the holy men. A depressed Faustus gives his servant Wagner (Patrick Barwise) all his earthly goods. When three students (Richard Heffer, Hugh Williams, Gwydion Thomas) tell him they believe the most beautiful woman who ever lived was Helen of Troy (Taylor), he brings forth her image for them and falls in love with her. He begs Mephistopheles to make Helen his paramour and she is given to him. After the two decades have past, Faustus no longer casts a reflection in a mirror and he tells the student trio that he has lost Heaven and must remain in Hell forever and of his bargain with Lucifer. He also asks them to pray for him but not to try to rescue him from his fate. Faustus begs to Heaven to regain his soul but at midnight the gates of Hell open and a taunting Helen takes him downward.

Variety reported, "An oddity that may have some archive appeal, for at least it records a performance by Burton…that gives an insight into his prowess in classical roles. He is obviously captivated by Christopher Marlowe's 400-year-old verse, and speaks it with sonorous dignity and sense…One surprise is the general adequacy of the Oxford amateurs, with a good performance in any terms from Andreas Teuber as Mephistopheles." F. Maurice Speed in *Film Review* 1968–1969 (1968) called the production "[c]olorful, magical and with touches of sheer pantomime!," adding that Teuber was "brilliant as Mephistopheles." Speed also noted, "It was Burton himself, together with his wife Elizabeth Taylor, who made possible the screening of the Oxford University Dramatic Society's production of Christopher Marlowe's *Doctor Faustus*, for it was their company which put up the money to transfer it from stage success to screen. Burton directed himself to considerable effect…"

Dr. Strangelove, or: How I Learned to Stop Worrying and Love the Bomb

(1964; 93 minutes) PRODUCER-DIRECTOR: Stanley Kubrick. ASSOCIATE PRODUCER: Victor Lyndon. SCREENPLAY: Stanley Kubrick, Terry Southern and Peter George, from the novel *Red Alert* by Peter George. PHOTOGRAPHY: Gilbert Taylor. EDITOR: Anthony Harvey. MUSIC: Laurie Johnson. SONG: Ross Parker and Hughie Charles, sung by Vera Lynn. ART DIRECTOR: Peter Murton. PRODUCTION DESIGN: Ken Adam. PRODUCTION MANAGER: Clifton Brandon. MAKEUP: Stewart Freeborn. CONTINUITY: Pamela Carlton. TECHNICAL ADVISOR: Captain John Crewdson. ASSISTANT DIRECTOR: Eric Rattray. CAST: Peter Sellers (Group Captain Lionel Mandrake/President Merkin Muffley/Dr. Strangelove), George C. Scott (General Buck Turgidson), Sterling Hayden (Brigadier General Jack D. Ripper), Keenan Wynn (Colonel Bat Guano), Slim Pickens (Major T.J.

"King" Kong), Peter Bull (Alexi de Sadesky), James Earl Jones (Lieutenant Lothar Zogg), Tracy Reed (Miss Scott), Jack Creley (Mr. Staines), Frank Berry (Lieutenant H.R. Dietrich), Robert O'Neil (Ambassador Randolph), Glen Beck (Lieutenant W.D. Kivel), Roy Stephens (Frank), Shane Rimmer (Captain G.A. "Ace" Owens), Hal Galli, Laurence Herder, John McCarthy (Burpelson AFB Defense Team Members), Paul Tamarin (Lieutenant B. Goldberg), Gordon Tanner (General Faceman).

When *Dr. Strangelove* was released early in 1964, liberal film critics fell all over themselves with superlatives to describe this Stanley Kubrick–produced, –directed and –co-written production based on Peter George's 1958 novel *Red Alert*. The film's poking fun at the military, its use of cryptic and buffoonish character names and overall disdain for nuclear defense, placed it high on the year's list of film favorites for elitists and academics; it was nominated for an Oscar as Best Picture. The *New York Times* called it a "brilliantly-told sick joke...one of the cleverest and most incisive satiric thrusts into the awkwardness and folly of the military that has ever been screened."

Fearing that the Soviet Union plans to mentally demoralize and conquer the United States by putting fluoride in the nation's water supply, General Jack D. Ripper (Sterling Hayden) orders a nuclear attack on the Communist nation. Using a secret code, Ripper prevents his orders from being countermanded and he seals off his Burpelson Air Force base from the outside world. U.S. President Merkin Muffley (Peter Sellers) learns of the mission and convenes a meeting in the Pentagon's War Room, including Soviet Ambassador Alexi de Sadesky (Peter Bull). While General Buck Turgidson (George C. Scott) advises Muffley to conduct a limited nuclear war against the Russians, the president finally sends troops under the command of Colonel "Bat" Guano (Keenan Wynn) to arrest Ripper. In order to keep the mission alive, Ripper commits suicide but one of his group captains, R.A.F. Captain Lionel Mandrake (Sellers), deciphers the secret code and brings back the B-52s. The world appears to be saved from a nuclear holocaust until it is learned that a plane commanded by Major T.J. "King" Kong (Slim Pickens) did not get the order and is headed for Russia. Sadesky informs the president that his country has developed a Doomsday Device which will set off a global nuclear attack if an atomic bomb falls on the Soviet Union. The president then turns to his scientific advisor, former Nazi Dr. Strangelove (Sellers), a crippled scientist who calculates that the world will be inhabitable again in a century if the survivors live underground. As Kong's plane flies over Russia, he jumps on board the atom bomb and rides it, and when it explodes the Doomsday Devise is set off and the world is destroyed.

Sellers garnered critical acclaim for his work in *Dr. Strangelove*, as did George C. Scott, Sterling Hayden, Keenan Wynn and Slim Pickens as military men. The feature's most memorable scenes came at the end with Pickens' Major "King" Kong straddling the nuclear bomb as it heads toward Russia and the voice of Vera Lynn singing "We'll Meet Again" as the world dies in an atomic holocaust.

Writing in *Films in Review* (February 1964), Henry Hart stated, "The subtitle which Stanley Kubrick ... appends to *Dr. Strangelove* will warn off all who are aware of what the 'zeroes,' as non-'squares' can be fittingly called, are currently thinking. The subtitle: 'How I Learned to Stop Worrying and Love the Bomb.' Which is a twirpish twiddle, as is the film itself ... *Dr. Strangelove* is not really farce for farce's sake, but farce for the expression of the private world of Mr. Kubrick. And if you have been under any illusion about Kubrick's competence as a director, look at the absurd performance he allowed George C. Scott to give as a U.S. general, whose mind, what there is of it, is on his secretary-in-bed."

Dr. Strangelove, which poked fun at the military and nuclear defense, opened just little more than a year after the Cuban Missile Crisis had the world on the brink of an atomic war. In the third volume of his memoirs, *Khrushchev Remembers: The Glasnot Tapes* (1990), former Soviet leader Nikita Khrushchev recalled the event: "[Cuban President Fidel] Castro suggested that in order to prevent our nuclear missiles from being destroyed, we should launch a preemptive strike against the United States. He concluded that an attack was unavoidable and that this attack had to be preempted. In other words, we needed to immediately deliver a nuclear missile strike against the United States." Fortunately for the sake of the entire world, this real possibility, unlike the fantasy of *Dr. Strangelove*, never happened.

Down to Earth

(1947; 101 minutes; Color) PRODUCER: Don Hartman. DIRECTOR: Alexander Hall. SCREENPLAY: Edwin Blum and Don Hartman, from the play *Heaven Can Wait* by Harry Segall. PHOTOGRAPHY: Rudolph Maté. EDITOR: Viola Lawrence. MUSIC: George Duning and Heinz Roemheld. MUSIC DIRECTOR: Morris Stoloff. SONGS: Dorris Fisher and Allan Roberts. ART DIRECTORS: Stephen Goosson and Rudolph Sternad. SOUND: George Cooper. SETS: William Kiernan. COSTUMES: Jean Louis. MAKEUP: Clay Campbell. CHOREOGRAPHER: Jack Cole. ASSISTANT DIRECTOR: Wilbur McGaugh. CAST: Rita Hayworth (Terpsichore/Kitty Pendleton), Larry Parks (Danny Miller), Marc Platt (Eddie), Roland Culver (Mr. Jordan), James Gleason (Max Corkle), Edward Everett Horton (Messenger 7013), Adele Jergens (Georgia Evans), George Macready (Joe Mannion), William Frawley (Police Lieutenant), Jean [Willes] Donahue (Betty), Kathleen O'Malley (Dolly), William Haade (Spike), James Burke (Detective Kelly), Fred F. Sears (Orchestra Leader Bill), Dorothy [Hart] Brady (New Terpsichore), Lynn Merrick, Doris Houck, Shirley Molohon, Peggy Maley, Lucille Casey, Jo Rattigan, Virginia Hunter, Dusty Anderson (Muses), Cora Witherspoon (Woman on Street), Lucien Littlefield (Escort 3082), Myron Healey (Pilot Sloan), Harriette Ann Gray (Dancer), Rudy Cameron (Stage Manager), Arthur Blake (Nathaniel Somerset), Wilbur Mack (Messenger), Kay Vallon (Rosebud the Human Pretzel), Nicodemus [Nick] Stuart (Porter), Bob Ryan, Raoul Freeman (Policemen), Billy Bletcher (Conductor), Jean Del Val (Croupier), Frank Darien (Janitor), Matty Fain (Henchman), Jack Norton (Sleeper), Mary Forbes (Mrs. Fenimore Hume), Count Stefenelli (Frenchman), Eddie Acuff (Stage Hand), Alan Bridge (Police Sergeant), Tom Daly (Reporter), Francine Kennedy (Chorine), Mary Newton (Woman), Ottola Nesmith, Grace Hampton (Dowagers), Tom Hanlon (Radio Announcer), Sam Harris (Roulette Player), Dorothy Vernon (Wardrobe Mistress), Anita Ellis (Terpsichore's Singing Voice), Kay Starr (Georgia Evans' Singing Voice).

Rita Hayworth in *Down to Earth* (1947).

Rita Hayworth first got star billing in Columbia's *The Shadow* (q.v.) in 1937 and by the early 1940s she was one of the studio's top stars. Following her huge success in *Gilda* in 1946, she headlined *Down to Earth*, a musical follow-up to the acclaimed 1941 fantasy *Here Comes Mr. Jordan* (q.v.). Not only did Alexander Hall return to direct this semi-sequel but two of that film's players, James Gleason as Max Corkle and Edward Everett Horton as Messenger 7013, appear in *Down to Earth*. The feature also included the character of Mr. Jordan, played earlier by Claude Rains, and done here by a similar looking Roland Culver. Although containing mainly mediocre songs, the production offered Hayworth a fine role where she excelled as a dancer. Her singing was dubbed by Anita Ellis. Future best-selling recording artist Kay Starr dubbed co-star Adele Jergens' singing voice in the musical fantasy. Co-star Larry Parks, following his success in Columbia's *The Jolson Story* (1946), sang his own songs, after having been dubbed by Al Jolson in the latter's biopic.

Broadway agent-former boxing manager Max Corkle (James Gleason) is interrogated by the police regarding gambler Joe Mannion's (George Macready) killing. Telling the lawmen he is innocent, Corkle informs his questioner (William Frawley) about Danny Miller (Larry Parks), a one-time colleague of Mannion. Trying to go straight, Danny directs and plays one of the leads in a musical about nine Greek muses. On Mount Parnassus, an actual muse, Goddess of Dance Terpsichore (Hayworth), watches the rehearsals and becomes angered by the way she is shown to be vulgar by actress Georgia Evans (Adele Jergens). To get revenge, she plans to ruin Danny and his musical. Wanting to go to Earth to carry out her plans, the beautiful muse gets permission from heavenly travel czar Mr. Jordan (Culver) and he assigns Messenger 7013 (Horton) to accompany her. The two go to the theater where the play is being rehearsed, and Terpsichore interrupts by displaying her dancing and singing capabilities. Danny comes under the spell of the newcomer and, after Georgia becomes upset over the demonstration, he replaces her with Terpsichore, who uses the name Kitty Pendleton. The muse engages Corkle as her agent and begins work on the part, convincing Danny her role should be played as exalted rather than coarse. A Philadelphia tryout is not a success and Danny returns Kitty's part to that of a trollop. This infuriates Terpsichore and she demands that Mr. Jordan return her to Mount Parnassus. Instead he shows her how Danny lost a large sum of money to Mannion by gambling and was nearly bumped off by the gambler until he got the crook to invest in his show, giving him a suicide note as collateral. Terpsichore, to help Danny, agrees to resume her role in the musical. After the show is a big success on Broadway, Danny asks the muse to marry him. Although she loves Danny, Terpsichore realizes this cannot happen. When Corkle goes with the muse and the invisible Mr. Jordan for a ride around the city, the heavenly being envisions Mannion's shooting by rivals and has the goddess tell the agent to contact the police. Informing Terpsichore that she saved Danny from being killed, Mr. Jordan and the muse return home as Corkle is able to prove his innocence and gets a job representing Terpsichore's replacement (Dorothy [Hart] Brady). Looking into the future, Mr. Jordan shows Terpsichore that she and Danny will be together again.

Down to Earth met with both critical and audience success. Bosley Crowther in the *New York Times* called the musical "a good lot of song-and-dance shenanigans which have some rather striking screen vitality.... For color and music and movement — the coloring, incidentally, is superb — are combined here to stimulate the senses in a splashy, luxurious way." The *Motion Picture Herald* noted, "*Down to Earth* has all the indications of being one of the year's best musicals.... The film blends humor, drama, dance and music into a most enjoyable whole." *Newsweek* called it "entertaining fare.... [T]he music, dancing and sets are lively and imaginative." On the other hand, *Variety* termed it "a typical backstage story — and putting it in the *Jordan* setting is certainly the hard way of getting a twist on the old, standard musical." While the trade paper liked the stars, songs and dances, it claimed the plot "takes interminable time and constantly slows even the angels to a lazy walk. Making things worse is the fact that all the gags which should give the yarn a bit of pepper fall flat."

The musical was remade in 1980 by Universal as *Xanadu*, a colorful but flat production starring Olivia Newton-John, Michael Beck and Gene Kelly.

Earth vs. the Flying Saucers

(1956; 83 minutes) PRODUCER: Charles H. Schneer. EXECUTIVE PRODUCER: Sam Katzman. DIRECTOR: Fred F. Sears. SCREENPLAY: George Wortington Yates and Raymond T. Marcus [Bernard Gordon]. STORY: Curt Siodmak, from the novel *Flying Saucers from Outer Space* by Major Donald E. Keyhoe. PHOTOGRAPHY: Fred Jackman, Jr. EDITOR: Danny B. Landres. MUSIC: Mischa Bakaleinikoff. ART DIRECTOR: Paul Palmentola. SOUND: Josh Westmoreland. SETS: Sidney Clifford. SPECIAL EFFECTS: Russ Kelley. SPECIAL PHOTOGRAPHIC AND ANIMATION EFFECTS: Ray Harryhausen. UNIT MANAGER: Leon Chooluck. PRODUCTION COORDINATOR: Jack Erickson. ASSISTANT DIRECTOR: Gene Anderson, Jr. CAST: Hugh Marlowe (Dr. Russell A. Marvin), Joan Taylor (Carol Hanley Marvin), Donald Curtis (Major Huglin), Morris Ankrum (Brigadier General John Hanley), John Zaremba (Professor Kanter), Tom Browne Henry (Vice Admiral Enright), Grandon Rhodes (General Edmunds), Larry Blake (Motorcycle Policeman), Harry Lauter (Technician Cutting), Charles Evans (Dr. Alberts), Clark Howat (Sergeant Nash), Frank Wilcox (Mr. Cassidy), Alan Reynolds (Major Kimberly), Paul Frees (Narrator/Alien Voice), Forbes Murray, Nicky Blair (Officers at Rocket Firing), Holly Bane, Arthur Tovey, Bert Stevens, Fred Aldrich (Officers), Duke Green (Attendant), Don Marlowe (Running Man), Dale Van Sickel (Crushed Man), Beal Wong (Chinese Radio Listener).

Working titles: *Attack of the Flying Saucers*, *Flying Saucers from Outer Space* and *Invasion of the Flying Saucers*.

One of the great science fiction pictures of the 1950s was *Earth vs. the Flying Saucers*. Ray Harryhausen's special photographic and animated effects were stunning for their time and provided the basis for a visually exciting, highly entertaining and very scary feature film. Since UFOs were a major topic in the mid–1950s, the scenes of enemy aliens literally destroying the nation's capitol with death rays was an ironic twist to the possibility of a nuclear conflict as the Cold War was nearing its apex. Based on Major Donald E. Keyhoe's 1953 best seller *Flying Saucers from Outer Space*, the film's original story was written by Curt Siodmak, a noted science fiction writer-producer-director who is best known for penning Universal's classic horror thriller *The Wolf Man* (1941). Major

A saucer chases Joyce Taylor and Hugh Marlowe in *Earth vs. the Flying Saucers* (1956).

Keyhoe was one of the leading lights of an influential UFO organization, the National Investigation Committee on Aerial Phenomena (NICAP), whose members included broadcaster Frank Edwards, the first national network newsman to carry flying saucer sightings reports on radio. Edwards wrote the best-selling books *Flying Saucers—Serious Business* (1966) and *Flying Saucers—Here and Now* (1967).

Opening with a montage of UFO sightings around the world, the film shows Dr. Russell Marvin (Hugh Marlowe) and his new wife Carol (Joan Taylor) driving near a restricted military area when their car is buzzed by a flying saucer. Marvin works for the State Department's Project Skyhook rocket launch program and Carol is his secretary. At his laboratory at the Hemisphere Defense Command in Colorado, Marvin replays a tape he was making at the time of the incident and hears the sound of the saucer. That evening, over a cookout at their house, Russell and Carol tell her father, Brigadier General John Hanley (Morris Ankrum), about the sighting. The next day at the military base the general informs his son-in-law that all 11 rockets sent into space have disintegrated. When the twelfth rocket is about to be launched, Russell and Carol lock themselves in their underground laboratory and via television they see a flying saucer land and destroy the military base. Trapped in the lab, the two await rescue and while listening to the tape he made, the power slows down and he hears an alien voice telling him of the coming of the spaceship.

Upon their rescue, the couple are flown to the Pentagon where they tell General Edmunds (Grandon Rhodes), Vice Admiral Enright (Tom Browne Henry) and other officers about the aliens. Told to wait for government approval before he can contact the aliens, Dr. Marvin returns to his hotel room and uses a short wave radio to talk with the invaders. They tell him to meet them on a nearby beach and he leaves despite Carol's protests. She follows him with Major Huglin (Donald Curtis), who has been assigned to guard her husband. Along the way they are trailed by a motorcycle policeman (Larry Blake) and they all end up on the beach where a saucer lands. Boarding the craft, they are told by a voice (Paul Frees) that the aliens are the survivors of a disintegrating solar system and have come to Earth looking for a new home. Carol's father, who has been abducted by the spacemen, appears but his mind was destroyed when the aliens removed his memory and used it for their own knowledge. The cop tries to shoot at the voice control and the aliens read his brain and turn him into a zombie. The invaders want to meet with world leaders, and Russell is told he has 56 days to arrange it or an all-out invasion will take place. Russell, Joan and Huglin go to the Pentagon where it is determined that the invaders must be defeated. Dr. Marvin develops a weapon using sound to disrupt the magnetic field of the flying saucers and decides to get the plans to Washington, D.C. As the convoy with the weapon is leaving, a saucer appears and aliens disembark to search for the group. Marvin and technician Cutting (Harry Lauter) use the weapon to upset the craft's flight and the aliens escape but leave one of their own behind. The creature disintegrates Dr. Kanter (John Zaremba), who helped develop the weapon, but is shot and killed by Huglin. When Russell and the major remove the alien's space helmet, they find an almost mummified humanoid. The saucer returns, destroying the weapon and a fighter plane, setting a forest fire and dumping the bodies of General Hanley and the policeman.

Back at the Pentagon, Marvin and his associates are able to use the helmet to learn the aliens' plans but by now saucers are being seen all over the world. For 12 hours the alien voice warns that they will soon attack the Earth. Severe weather halts all transportation and communications but gives the army time to build weapons to combat the invaders. When the invasion comes, Marvin leads trucks carrying the weapons throughout Washington D.C. and a battle rages. The saucers destroy government buildings and monuments but the new weapons bring down many of the saucers. The last flying saucer is destroyed by Marvin and it falls into the Capitol building. With the invasion over, the president orders Project SkyHook reinstated with Dr. Marvin as its chief and he and Carol go to the beach for their belated honeymoon.

Ed Naha reported in *Horror from Screen to Scream* (1975), "Fascinating fluff with nonexistent plot but awesome special effect by Ray Harryhausen…. Great fun and released during a time when flying saucers were the *in* thing to worry about." Phil Hardy in *Science Fiction* (1984) was less complimentary: "Best remembered for Harryhausen's superior stop-motion special effects, that make the flying saucers look very convincing, and its fine title, this is an otherwise routine out from [director Fred F.] Sears, who was clearly more at home in the western. The script is closely influenced by [*The*] *War of the Worlds* (1953) but lacks the naïve grandeur of that film. In its place is an awkward plot that needed only the presence of Roy Barcroft for the film to be mistaken for *The Purple Monster Strikes* (1945)."

Director Sears also did *The Werewolf* (1956), *The Giant Claw* and *The Night the World Exploded* (both 1957) [qq.v.] but *Earth vs. the Flying Saucers* was his best genre outing. A very popular item with moviegoers, the feature found new life on television and later on tape and DVD. In 2008 Sony Pictures Home Entertainment issued *Earth vs. the Flying Saucers* in both its original and colorized versions.

The Electronic Monster

(1960; 72 minutes) PRODUCER: Alec C. Snowden. ASSOCIATE PRODUCER: Jim O'Connolly. DIRECTOR: Montgomery Tully. SCREENPLAY: Charles Eric Maine, from his novel *Escapement*. PHOTOGRAPHY: Bert Mason. EDITOR: Geoffrey Muller. MUSIC CONDUCTOR: Richard Taylor. PRODUCTION DESIGN: Wilfred Arnold. SOUND: Ronald Abbott and Keith Barber. PRODUCTION MANAGER: Bill Shore. MAKEUP: Jack Craig. WARDROBE: Eileen Welch. CONTINUITY: Marjorie Owens. DREAM SEQUENCE DIRECTOR: David Pallenghi. DREAM SEQUENCE PHOTOGRAPHY: Teddy Catford. ASSISTANT DIRECTOR: Peter Crowhurst. CAST: Rod Cameron (Jeff Keenan), Mary Murphy (Ruth Vance), Meredith Edwards (Dr. Phillip Maxwell), Peter Illing (Paul Zakon), Carl Jaffe (Dr. Hoff), Kay Callard (Laura Maxwell), Carl Duering (Blore), Roberta Huby (Verna Berteaux), Felix Felton (Police Commissaire), Larry Cross (Brad Somers), Carlo Borelli (Pietro Kalini), John McCarthy (Clark Denver), Jacques Cey (Police Doctor Pierre), Armande Guinle (Farmer), Malou Pantera (Clinic Receptionist), Pat Clavin (Studio Receptionist), Alan Gifford (Mr. Wayne).

Working titles: *The Dream Machine* and *Zex*.

A somewhat pedestrian and mercifully short British production, *The Electronic Monster* was issued in the U.S. by Columbia in the spring of 1960, double-billed with either *Battle in Outer Space* or *13 Ghosts* (qq.v.). Cut by eight minutes for its stateside release, the feature was originally shown in England as *Escapement*, the title of the 1956 novel which Charles Eric Maine adapted for the screen. An Anglo-Guild Production, it was filmed at Merton Park Studios in London in 1957. Its main draw was top-billed Rod Cameron, a stalwart action film hero who in the 1950s had

Advertisement for *The Electronic Monster* (1960).

great success starring in a trio of syndicated television programs, *City Detective*, *State Trooper* and *Coronado 9*. The film's associate producer, Jim O'Connolly, later directed Joan Crawford in another Columbia release, *Berserk* (q.v.). Basically a tired detective yarn entwined with a sci-fi subplot, *The Electronic Monster* had no monster other than a couple of obviously Teutonic villains experimenting with brain waves, some convoluted dream sequences and a boring electronic music track. *Variety* called it "strictly routine" and David Quinlan in *British Sound Films: The Studio Years, 1929–1959* (1984) said, "Main sufferers are the audience who have to sit through this unconvincing tosh."

Speeding along a road on the French Riviera, film star and expert racing driver Clark Denver (John McCarthy) has severe head pains and is killed when he loses control. Consolidated Assurance Company president Wayne (Alan Gifford) sends investigator Jeff Keenan (Rod Cameron) to look into the case since the film star was insured with their company for $250,000. Arriving at Hotel Memour, Jeff meets old friend Brad Somers (Larry Cross), the late star's publicity agent. He tells Jeff that two other men, along with Denver, also died after being patients at the d'American Clinic and that he should talk to actress Verna Bertreaux (Roberta Huby), who was involved with Denver. The woman denies any knowledge of the film star's death and Jeff is told by the police commissaire (Felix Felton) that Denver may have committed suicide because of an impending divorce. The police surgeon (Jacques Cey) informs him the actor died of cerebral thrombosis. Going to the clinic, the investigator runs into his former fiancée, actress Ruth Vance (Mary Murphy), who is engaged to film producer Paul Zakon (Peter Illing), the owner of the clinic. Dr. Phillip Maxwell (Meredith Edwards) explains to Jeff the clinic's therapy of using a metal electrode he has developed to clear patients' minds of worries and distractions. After Jeff departs, Dr. Maxwell uses the treatment on businessman Pietro Kallni (Carlo Borelli), a drug addict. With sequences filmed at Zakon's studio with a large picture of his face dominating the action, the dream machine is used by Maxwell to heal Kallni's mind. Unhappy with the results of the therapy on Kallni, Maxwell goes to Zakon, informing him that the psychotherapy may be dangerous and that he wants to close the clinic. Asking for proof, Zakon removes Maxwell as head of the project and makes him the assistant of Dr. Hoff (Carl Jaffe), since Zakon believes the dream machine will make him a fortune. Jeff finds that Somers has committed suicide and he visits Ruth telling her he thinks it was murder and that Verna is an agent working for her fiancé. Maxwell's wife and assistant, Laura (Kay Callard), finds evidence that all three of the clinic's dead patients were shown the same film as therapy and he decides to destroy the equipment but is stopped by Zakon who threatens to reveal that Maxwell has been practicing without a medical license. Zakon then subjects Kallni to another treatment and the high voltage kills him. When Maxwell fails to carry out his promise to Laura and destroy the dream machine, she goes to Zakon's studio. While going through his records she is captured by the producer and his thug, Blore (Carl Duering). A charm from her bracelet is left behind in Zakon's office. After being escorted out of the clinic by Zakon's security guards, Jeff goes to the film studio where he again meets Ruth. After they kiss, she tells him she still loves him. When Ruth returns Zakon's engagement ring, she finds Laura's charm on the floor. After she leaves, he orders Blore to abduct her. Jeff accuses Zakon of involvement in Denver's death and he is told to leave the studio. When he cannot locate Ruth, Jeff goes to the police but they will not help him until a hunter finds Laura's body and the coroner says she was strangled. He also admits that Clark Denver was killed as a result of an electric shock to the brain. That night, Jeff returns to the clinic and informs Maxwell about Denver's death and that his wife has been found murdered. When Ruth refuses to give up Jeff and return to Zakon, he has her prepared for a dream machine treatment by Dr. Hoff. Jeff and Maxwell stop the procedure and Keenan subdues Blore, who says Zakon ordered him to eliminate Mrs. Maxwell. Hoff tries to shoot Jeff but instead kills Blore as Keenan wrestles the gun away from the doctor. He forces Hoff to free Ruth as Maxwell takes revenge on Zakon, putting an electrode cap on his head and killing him with high voltage. Maxwell then destroys the dream machine, causing a fire which traps him in the conflagration. Jeff and Ruth escape and the police arrest Hoff.

Enigma de Muerte (*Secret of Death*)

(1969; 89 minutes; Color) PRODUCER: Luis Enrique Vergara. EXECUTIVE PRODUCER: Jorge Garcia Besne. DIRECTOR: Federico Curiel. SCREENPLAY: Ramon Obon, Jr. PHOTOGRAPHY: Alfredo Uribe. EDITOR: J. Juan Mungula. MUSIC: Gustavo Cesar Carreon. SOUND: Heinrich Henkel. PRODUCTION DESIGN: Jose Mendez and Octavio Ocampo. SETS: Raul Cardenas. MAKEUP: Eugenia Luna. SCRIPT SUPERVISOR: Jose Delfos. ASSISTANT DIRECTOR: Tito Novarro. CAST: John Carradine (El Payaso [The Clown]/Nazi General), Mil Mascaras (Himself), Maria Duval (Sandra), Isela Vega (Sara Carson), Eric del Castillo (Sandokan), David Silva (Police Inspector), Dagoberto Rodriguez (Carlos Martinez/Ringo), Patricia Ferrer (Marie), Santanon (Dwarf), Altia Mitchel (Mme. Marotte), Victor Junco (Master of Ceremonies), Frankestein [Nathanael Leon] (Weight Lifter), Juan Garza (Robles).

Producer Luis Enrique Vergara Cabrera began making films in Mexico in the early 1950s. After dropping his surname he specialized in horror thrillers, often featuring popular wrestlers like Santo and Blue Demon. Vergara is best known for producing Boris Karloff's final theatrical releases (*Fear Chamber, House of Evil, Incredible Invasion* and *The Snake People* [qq.v.]) in 1968 but one year earlier he made a quartet of movies with John Carradine, *Enigma de Muerte, Pacto Diabólico, Las Vampiras* and *La Señora Muerte* [qq.v.]. Columbia planned to release these movies in the United States with Carradine's name for box office draw but the best they did was play in Spanish-language theaters in border states with eventual release to the home video market.

Apparently *Enigma de Muerte* was made back to back with *Las Vampiras* since both movies co-star masked wrestler Mil Mascaras and Maria Duval and were directed by Federico Curiel. Mil Mascaras, which translates as One Thousand Masks, was born Aaron Rodriguez Arellano and made his wrestling debut in 1965. He held the World Wrestling Association heavyweight championship and also headlined such genre features

Lobby card for *Enigma de Muerte* (1969) with Mil Mascaras, Maria Duval, Victor Junco, Dagoberto Rodriguez, Isela Vega and Frankestein (Nathanael Leon).

as *Las Momias de Guanajuato* (The Mummies of Guanajuato) and *El Robo de las Momias de Guanajuato* (The Robbery of the Mummies of Guanajuato) (both 1972), *Las Bestias del Terror* (1973), co-starring Santo and Blue Demon; *Los Vampiros de Coyoacán* (The Vampires of Coyoacan) (1974), *Las Momias de San Angel* (The Mummies of San Angel) (1975), *Misterio en las Bermudas* (Mystery in the Bermudas) (1977), again with Santo and Blue Demon, and *Mil Mascaras contra la Momia Azteca* (Mil Mascaras vs. the Aztec Mummy) (2007).

More of an action crime thriller than a horror movie, *Enigma de Muerte* opens with Carradine sitting in front of a makeup mirror in a clown costume with white makeup on his chin and holding a lit cigarette. He proceeds to tell the audience that he made the film to support his acting troupe and delves slightly into the plot. Following the credits, black-and-white footage of aerial bombings is shown as two Nazis exchange rings and vow to continue the work of the Third Reich. Two decades later, Interpol investigates reports that Nazis are working in Mexico. Masked wrestler Mil Mascaras (Himself) is assigned to the case.

After winning a match in straight falls, the grappler flies his plane to the location of a carnival which he joins as a weight lifter. Among the performers are a tall, silly clown (Carradine) and his dwarf foil (Santanon), sharpshooter Ringo (Dagoberto Rodriguez), knife thrower Sandokan (Eric del Castillo) and his beautiful blonde assistant Sara (Isela Vega), and the master of ceremonies (Victor Junco). The local police inspector (David Silva) suspects that the performers are Nazis. When he is stabbed, Mil Mascaras chases the assailant. The two fight on a revolving Ferris wheel and the killer falls to his death.

In an underground bunker, the tall clown, who is really a Nazi general, preaches to his minions as some of the acts listen via short wave radios. When Sara defies the madman, he viciously whips her. Another member of the carnival, Sandra (Duval), tells Mil Mascaras that her father was murdered by the Nazis during the war. After Sara finds Nazi uniforms in a trunk in the carnival's prop room, an attempt is made on her life during her knife-throwing act. Mil Mascaras pursues the assailant but he escapes thanks to Sandokan's intervention. When the carnival's weight lifter (Frankestein) tries to strike the dwarf, Mil Mascaras stops him and the two men arm-wrestle with the masked grappler winning the contest. Later the jealous Sandokan finds Sara talking to Mil Mascaras and throws a knife at them. The two men fight and the wrestler subdues the knife thrower, who apologizes to Sara. During a western show, Sandokan is shot at by Ringo but he receives only a minor facial wound.

Because of his failure to kill the knife thrower, Ringo is taken to the bunker and incinerated by the Nazi leader with a death ray. Sandokan later overhears the general tells his officers of plans to take over the area. When they leave the bunker, a figure shoots at them from the Ferris wheel. The Nazis shoot the assailant and Mil Mascaras falls to the ground. When the dead man's mask is removed, he is revealed to be Sandokan. Mil Mascaras shows up, disperses the Nazis and follows their leader back to the bunker. There the madman tries to kill the wrestler with the death ray and an electric chair and then locks himself inside a glass chamber. Mil Mascaras accidentally turns on poison gas which fills the chamber and kills the Nazi.

Enigma de Muerte had hero Mil Mascaras wearing a different mask in each new scene and the film was enhanced by an elaborate carnival setting. It contained a lot of filler like a wrestling match, the various carnival acts and a western music show. The underground bunker was filled with Nazi regalia as well as futuristic machines and torture devices, including the death ray which turned Ringo into a skeleton.

The wrestling footage and the scenes with the masked grappler landing a twin engine airplane were lifted from *Los Canallas* (The Mobs) (1968) and *Mil Mascaras* (1969), the wrestler's first two films, both of which were produced by Filmica Vergara.

Escape in the Fog

(1945; 62 minutes) PRODUCER: Wallace MacDonald. DIRECTOR: Oscar [Budd] Boetticher, Jr. SCREENPLAY: Aubrey Wisberg. PHOTOGRAPHY: George Meehan. EDITOR: Jerome Thoms. ART DIRECTOR: Jerome Pycha, Jr. SOUND: Philip Faulkner. SETS: Joseph Kish. ASSISTANT DIRECTOR: Milton Feldman. CAST: Otto Kruger (Paul Devon), Nina Foch (Eilene Carr), William Wright (Barry Malcolm), Konstantin Shayne (Schiller), Ivan Triesault (Hausmer), Ernie Adams (George Smith), Mary Newton (Mrs. Devon), Ralph Dunn (Desk Sergeant), John Tyrrell (Detective Gil Brice), Charles Jordan (Detective Simmons), Noel Cravat (Kolb), John Elliott (Butler Thomas), Robert Williams (Bridge Policeman), Eddie Parker (Officer Sullivan), Wing Foo (Chang Yong), Leslie Denison (Hilary Gale), Elmo Lincoln, Dick Jensen, Joseph Palma (Policemen); William Yip, Jim Lim (Chinese); Leroy Taylor (Police Detective); Chuck Hamilton (Hotel Doorman); Emmett Vogan (Port Director); Edmund Cobb (Detective Jeff); Shelley Winters (Taxi Driver); Jessie Arnold (Screaming Woman at Accident); Victor Travers, Heinie Conklin (Accident Witnesses); Harrison Greene (Mr. Boggs); Tom Dillon (Lieutenant Commander); Chin Kuang Chow (Boy); Frank O'Connor (Harbor Patrol Officer); Frank Mayo (Bartender).

Working title: *Out of the Fog*.

On a foggy night, Eilene Carr (Nina Foch) is walking along San Francisco's Golden Gate Bridge when she sees a man threatened with a knife by a trio of men who pull up in a taxi cab. Screaming, she awakens at the Ye Rustic Dell Inn where she is a guest. Barry Malcolm (William Wright) and Mr. Boggs (Harrison Greene), who are also staying at the inn, hear her screams and she remembers Barry was the assaulted man in her dream. The next day while they dine, Eilene informs Barry she has been suffering from shock after the hospital boat on which she was serving as a nurse was torpedoed. He tells her he is involved in psychological warfare and had just worked with the freedom underground in Japanese-held territory. When Barry gets a call to come to San Francisco, he asks Eilene to go with him, with her staying with his aunt. His plans are overheard by another boarder, George Smith (Ernie Adams), who informs Chinatown watch repair shop owner Schiller (Konstantin Shayne). In San Francisco, Barry sees government agent Paul Devon (Otto Kruger), along with allies Hilary Gale (Leslie Denison) and Chang Yong (Wing Foo), who plan to send him to Hong Kong with a list of double agents working in Japan. Schiller shows up at Devon's house and informs the butler (John Elliott) that he has come to fix a grandfather clock. Behind the clock he finds a recording device and takes its cylinder. He and fellow Nazis Hausmer (Ivan Triesault) and Kolb (Noel Cravat) listen to it and find out about Barry's assignment. Barry tells Eilene he has leave but asks her to wait for him in the lobby of the Cumberland Hotel. Hausmer and Kolb use a ruse to abduct the agent when he gets into a taxi driven by one of their men. After Barry departs, Eilene goes for a walk and is hit by a car, the incident making her recall the dream, and she goes to see Devon. She meets the agent and his wife (Mary Newton) but he refuses

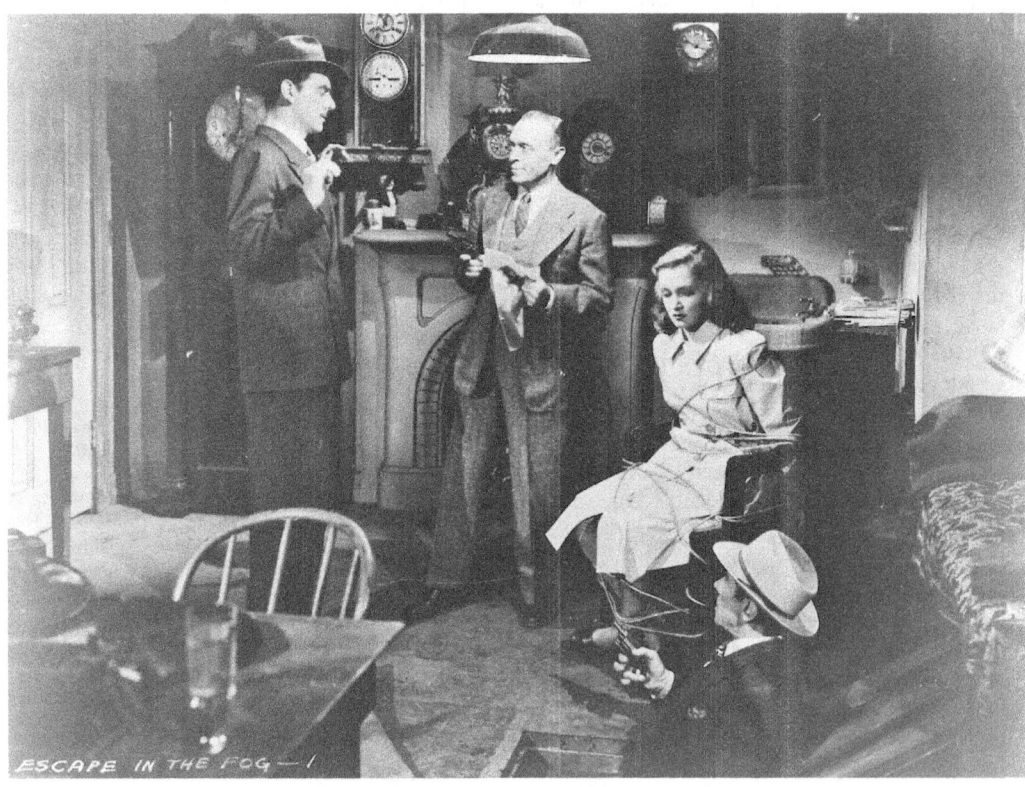

William Wright, Konstantin Shayne, Nina Foch, Ernie Adams in *Escape...* (1945).

to believe the young woman until he is informed that Barry has disappeared. At the Golden Gate Bridge, Eilene sees three men get out of a taxi and her screams bring a guard (Robert Williams). As Hausmer and Kolb escape in the vehicle, they find Barry, who has thrown the bag containing the agent list off the bridge. When the harbor patrol cannot find the bag, Eilene recalls hearing a boat whistle and theorizes that Barry may have tossed it onto the passing craft. The port director (Emmett Vogan) denies there was a boat in the area as he is under orders to not to reveal that a secret radio-controlled Navy vessel was there at the time. Having trailed Barry, Hausmer notifies Schiller of the possible whereabouts of the agent list and the enemy spy places a newspaper advertisement saying he has found the packet. Barry is told to go to the Half Moon Bay harbor where the *S.S. Pelican* is anchored. While awaiting his return, Eilene sees the newspaper advertisement and contacts Schiller, who abducts her when she comes to his shop. Finding a torn note in Eilene's possession given to her by Barry revealing the name of the craft he was boarding at Half Moon Bay, Schiller orders Hausmer to pretend to be a port authority chief and he sends out an order for the packet to be sent to San Francisco. When Barry finds out about the agent list going to San Francisco, he has a Port Authority desk sergeant (Eddie Dunn) alert the police. Hausmer is arrested, and they are able to obtain the packet from the officer (Eddie Parker) transporting the package.

Barry goes back to his hotel where he finds a ransom note offering Eilene for the pouch. Barry sets out to rescue Eilene while Devon discovers the recording machine in the back of his clock. Separately both men go to Schiller's shop where Smith gets the drop on Barry. After getting the list, Schiller and Smith plan to kill Barry and Eilene in a gas explosion but the agent manages to write "Hail Japan" on a magnifying glass. When he illuminates it with his cigarette lighter, the sign is seen by passersby who break into the shop just as Devon shows up with the police. The two spies try to escape in the dense fog but after separating they are killed, Smith by the police and Schiller by Barry. Lovers Eilene and Barry go back to the Golden Gate Bridge, the site of her prophetic dream.

Escape in the Fog was one of those mid–1940s *film noir* programmers which used premonitions and dream imagery to beef up an otherwise mundane plotline, in this case spies trying to get hold of a pouch containing the names of double agents operating in Japan. Its use of night sequences, dense fog and the heroine's recurring nightmare added a bit of flavor. Beautiful Nina Foch, replacing Lynn Merrick, handled the leading lady assignment well while Otto Kruger was wasted as the leader of the government undercover agents. William Wright was passable as the lead agent and Konstantin Shayne, Ivan Triesault and Ernie Adams were good as the spies. Don Miller in *B Movies* (1973) noted that the film's heroine was "beset by all manner of nerve-shattering contrivances, not too convincingly."

Eyes of Laura Mars

(1978; 104 minutes; Color) PRODUCER: Jon Peters. EXECUTIVE PRODUCER: Jack H. Harris. ASSOCIATE PRODUCER: Laura Ziskin. DIRECTOR: Irvin Kershner. SCREENPLAY: John Carpenter and David Zelag Goodman. PHOTOGRAPHY: Victor J. Kemper. EDITOR: Michael Kahn. MUSIC: Artie Kane. SONG: John Desautels; sung by Barbra Streisand. ART DIRECTOR: Robert Gunlach. PRODUCTION DESIGN: Gene Callahan. SET DECORATOR: John Godfrey. COSTUME DESIGN: Theoni V. Aldredge. SPECIAL EFFECTS: Edward Drohan. MAKEUP: Vincent Callaghan, Lynn Donahue and Lee Harman. UNIT PRODUCTION MANAGER: Louis A. Stroller. ASSISTANT DIRECTORS: Louis A. Stroller and Mel Howard. CAST: Faye Dunaway (Laura Mars), Tommy Lee Jones (Detective Lieutenant John Neville), Brad Dourif (Tommy Ludlow), Rene Auberjonois (Donald Phelps), Raul Julia (Michael Reisler), Frank Adonis (Detective Sergeant Sal Volpe), Lisa Taylor (Michelle), Darianne Fluegel (Lulu), Rose Gregorio (Elaine Cassell), Bill Boggs (Himself), Steve Marachuk (Robert), Meg Mundy (Doris Spencer), Marilyn Meyers (Sheila Weissman), Gary Bayer, Mitchell Edmonds (Newsmen), Michael Tucker (Bert), Jeff Niki, Toshi Matsuo (Photography Assistants), John E. Allen (Billy T), Anna Anderson, Deborah Beck, Jim Devine, Hanny Friedman, Winnie Hollman, Patty Oja, Donna Palmer, Sterling St. Jacques, Rita Tellone, Kari Page (Models), Dallas Edward Hayes (Douglas), John Randolph Jones, Al Joseph, Gerald Kline, Tom Degidon (Policemen), Sal Richards (Driscoll), Paula Laurence (Aunt Caroline), Joey R. Mills (Makeup Man), John Sahag (Hairdresser), Hector Troy (Cab Driver), Ernie Pysher (Gallery Guest), Linda Kendall (Reporter).

Greatly influenced by the somewhat gory European thrillers being directed by Dario Argento, Mario Bava, Luigi Cozzi, Umberto Lenzi and others, this Jon Peters production was originally intended to star his then-girlfriend Barbra Streisand, who opted to sing the title song instead, leaving the lead role to Faye Dunaway, who had just won an Academy Award for *Network* (1976). It was also one of future director John Carpenter's first filmed scripts although Peters hired David Zelig Goodman to rewrite it and change the identity of the killer. Uncredited Julian Barry, Matt Crowley and Joan Tewkesbury also worked on the screenplay. *Variety* thought it "a very stylish thriller in search of a better ending" while Joe Kane in *The Phantom of the Movies' Videoscope* (2000) found it to be "basically a standard B-movie slasher [given] glitzy mainstream treatment." Janet Maslin in the *New York Times* opined, "It's the cleverness of *Eyes of Laura Mars* that counts, cleverness that manifests itself in superlative casting, drily controlled direction from Irvin Kershner, and spectacular settings that turn New York into the kind of eerie, lavish dreamland that could exist only in the idle noodlings of the very, very hip."

Fashion photographer Laura Mars (Dunaway) has compiled a book of her various layouts but on the eve of its publication she dreams that model Doris Spencer (Meg Mundy) is killed by having her eyes stabbed with an ice pick. Upset, she calls the model but gets no answer. Later she attends a gallery exhibit of her own work where she meets a stranger who turns out to be policeman John Neville (Tommy Lee Jones) although she does not learn his name at the time. When Laura learns that Doris was murdered in the manner she dreamed of, she tells her agent Donald Phelps (Rene Auberjonois). Since Doris was one of her models, the demand for her work escalates. She also gets an order from gallery owner Elaine Cassell (Rose Gregorio) for a photo shoot, unaware that the woman is having an affair with Laura's former husband, Michael Reisler (Raul Julia). The next day at Columbia Circle, while the photography is being supervised by advertising agency liaison Robert (Steve Marachuk), Laura, in her mind, sees Elaine in jeopardy and asks her agent to stop the shoot. She goes to Elaine's apartment and finds she has been murdered in the same manner as Doris. She tells a police sergeant (Frank Adonis) she saw the murder and is taken to headquarters where she and her driver, Tommy Ludlow (Brad Dourif), an ex-convict, are questioned. There Laura again meets Neville, who ridicules her psychic vision. They go back to the dead woman's apartment where Laura recognizes clothes hanging in the closet as belonging to Michael.

Reisler comes to Laura's apartment, claims he is innocent, and asks for money. Laura accompanies Donald and Ludlow to another photo shoot at a Manhattan pier warehouse where Laura comes to feel she is being followed. She becomes hysterical during the session; Neville tries to soothe her nerves by telling her she is overworked. He tells her he believes the stalker may be jealous of her and orders his patrolmen to guard Laura. After models Michelle (Lisa Taylor) and Lulu (Darianne Fluegel) are questioned by the police, Laura has a vision of their murders which comes true. Laura attends the models' funeral with Neville. The two find themselves falling in love and he gives her a gun for protection. At a birthday bash for Donald, Laura gets a call from Michael who claims to be suicidal, so in order for her to get to him, the agents put on her clothes and is tailed by her guards as she goes to help her ex-husband. On his way back to his apartment, Donald is murdered and Laura envisions the killing. Tommy later is shot while trying to escape from the police after they accuse him of being the killer. Laura and Neville decide to go away together but at her apartment, Neville begins to come apart mentally and she realizes he is the culprit. He attacks her with an ice pick, but instead stabs her mirror image and begs her to shoot him. When she fails to do so, Neville forces her to pull the trigger.

Several people involved in the making of *Eyes of Laura Mars* had other genre credits, in addition to scripter John Carpenter who later gained fame as a horror film director. Irvin Kershner went on to direct *The Empire Strikes Back* (1980), while cinematographer Victor J. Kemper also photographed *The Reincarnation of Peter Proud* (1975), *Audrey Rose* (1976) and *Coma* (1977). Executive producer Jack H. Harris financed the sci-fi classic *The Blob* (1958).

The Face Behind the Mask

(1941; 69 minutes) PRODUCER: Wallace MacDonald. EXECUTIVE PRODUCER: Irving Briskin. DIRECTOR: Robert Florey. SCREENPLAY: Paul Jarrico and Allen Vincent. STORY: Arthur Levinson, from the radio play "Interim" by Thomas Edward O'Connell. PHOTOGRAPHY: Franz Planer. EDITOR: Charles Nelson. MUSIC DIRECTOR: M.W. [Morris] Stoloff. ART DIRECTOR: Lionel Banks. SOUND: George Cooper. ASSISTANT DIRECTORS: Milton Carter and William Mull. CAST: Peter Lorre (Janos Szabo), Evelyn Keyes (Helen Williams), Don Beddoe (Lieutenant James O'Hara), George E. Stone (Dinky), John Tyrrell (Watts), Al Seymour [Cy Schindell] (Benson), Stanley Brown (Harry), James Seay (Jeff Jeffries), Warren Ashe (Johnson), Charles Wilson (Chief O'Brien), George McKay (Terry Finnegan), Ben Taggart (Dr. Jones), Mary Currier (Nurse Kritzer), Sarah Edwards (Mrs. Perkins), Frank Reicher (Dr. Ronald Cheever), Ralph Peters (Chef), Al Hill (Horton), Water Soderling (Jonathan Harris), Lee Prather (Immigration Officer), David Oliver (Steward), John Dilson (Anderson), Joel Friedkin (Charlie Perkins), Lee Phelps (Detective Brown), Sam Ash (Pilot Mike Carey), Edwin Stanley (Dr. Alex Beckett), Claire Rochelle (Nurse Bailey), Walter Merrill (Joe), Harry Strang (Stimson), Alan Bridge (Horgan), Lee Shumway (Police Officer), Eddie Foster (Passerby), Chuck Hamilton (Service Station Man), Bill Lally (Wilson), Ernie Adams (Guest), Jack Gardner (Caller).

Janos Szabo (Peter Lorre) arrives in New York from Hungary and meets police Lieutenant O'Hara (Don Beddoe) who gets him a job as a dishwasher at Finnegan's (George McKay) hotel. Janos, who plans to earn enough money to send for his sweetheart, gets his face terribly burned when a fire breaks out in the lodging. While recovering, Janos, with O'Hara's help, is able to get a position with a watchmaker (Walter Soderling). After Janos sees his hideous face, he writes to his girlfriend and breaks off their engagement. When a man drops his wallet after seeing Janos' face, he and crook Dinky (George E. Stone) divide the money found in it and become friends. When Dinky needs medical aid, Janos robs a safe and as a result the two men go into partnership with Benson (Al Seymour) and Watts (John Tyrrell) in pulling off several successful robberies.

Hoping to get plastic surgery for his face, Janos visits Dr. Cheever (Frank Reicher) whose assistant (Edwin Stanley) fashions a face mask for him to wear. After the gang robs an opera house,

Left: Peter Lorre in *The Face Behind the Mask* (1941), and *(right)* the poster that also features Evelyn Keyes.

ex-convict Jeff Jeffries (James Seay) tries to muscle in on their operation but Janos welcomes him into the gang. When Cheever informs Janos he can do nothing for him, Janos hysterically runs into the street, knocking down blind Helen Williams (Evelyn Keyes). Helen and Janos become very close. After she tells him she does not approve of the robbery gang, he decides to give up his criminal activities. Planning to wed Helen and move to a house he has purchased in the country, Janos tells Dinky the location. Jeffries, who thinks Janos is in league with O'Hara, beats the information out of Dinky. The next day Janos and Helen are having breakfast at the country house when Jeffries arrives. While he talks with Janos, gang members place a bomb in his automobile. The injured Dinky tries to call Janos to warn him but before he can get the call through, Helen goes out to unpack the vehicle and the bomb goes off, killing her. Dinky informs Janos that Jeffries and the rest of the gang plan to take a plane to New Mexico. Janos makes Dinky promise to go straight, sends O'Hara a letter informing him of the gang's intent and asks him to give the reward for their capture to Dinky's mother. Janos takes over as pilot of the plane and he flies the gang into the desert where he disables the craft. The gangsters tie Janos to the plane and try to escape on foot but die of thirst. When Lieutenant O'Hara arrives he finds the bodies of Janos and the criminals.

Peter Lorre first worked for Columbia portraying Raskolnikov in *Crime and Punishment* (1935). He also starred for Columbia as the sadistic warden in *Island of Doomed Men* (1940) [q.v.] and in the 1942 horror comedy *The Boogie Man Will Get You* (q.v.). Director Robert Florey had earlier helmed Universal's *Murders in the Rue Morgue* (1932) and would later direct Lorre in Warner Bros'. *The Beast with Five Fingers* (1947). Unfortunately *The Face Behind the Mask* was not one of the better efforts for either the star or director and its main pleasure comes from Evelyn Keyes' work as the blind girl who falls in love with the bitter, disfigured immigrant. Released in Great Britain as *Behind the Mask*, the feature was based on a radio play by Thomas Edward O'Connell.

The *New York Times* opined, "Despite a certain pretentiousness toward things psychological, [the movie] may safely be set down as just another bland melodramatic exercise in which the talents of Peter Lorre again are stymied by hackneyed dialogue and conventional plot manipulations." In *B Movies* (1973), Don Miller called the film "[o]ne of the best Columbia B pictures.... The script was well constructed, Robert Florey's direction rated with his best.... Franz Planer's photography was evocative, and performances were entirely in keeping." *Variety* opined, "Columbia bills this as a 'horror' picture. It's that in spades. It's not so much likely to scare audiences as make them a little sick, between Peter Lorre in a nauseating rubber mask and the femme lead as a blind girl. Production, acting and story, paradoxically, are all of a fairly high order, but it's all too unpleasant."

Fail-Safe

(1964; 112 minutes) PRODUCERS: Max E. Youngstein and Sidney Lumet. ASSOCIATE PRODUCER: Charles H. Maguire. DIRECTOR: Sidney Lumet. SCREENPLAY: Walter Bernstein, from the novel by Eugene Burdick and Harvey Wheeler. PHOTOGRAPHY: Gerald Hirschfeld. EDITOR: Ralph Rosenblum. ART DIRECTOR: Albert Brenner. SETS: J.C. Delaney. COSTUME DESIGN: Anna Hill Jonstone. MAKEUP: Harry Buchman. CONTINUITY: Marguerite James. SPECIAL ANIMATED EFFECTS: Storyboard, Inc. ASSISTANT DIRECTOR: Harry Falk, Jr. CAST: Henry Fonda (U.S. President), Dan O'Herlihy (Brigadier General Warren A. "Blackie" Black), Walter Matthau (Professor Groteschele), Frank Overton (General Bogan), Edward Binns (Colonel Jack Grady), Fritz Weaver (Colonel Cascio), Larry Hagman (Interpreter Buck), William Hansen (Defense Secretary Swenson), Russell Hardy (General Stark), Russell Collins (Gordon Knapp), Sorrell Booke (Representative Raskob), Nancy Berg (Ilsa Wolfe), John Connell (Radio Man Thomas), Frank Simpson (Airman Sullivan), Hildy Parks (Betty Black), Janet Ward (Helen Grady), Dom DeLuise (Technical Sergeant Collins), Dana Elcar (Mr. Foster), Stewart Germain (Lou Cascio), Louise Larabee (Mrs. Cascio), Frieda Altman (Jennie Johnson), Charles Tyner (Voice of Fighter Pilot).

"Covering almost precisely the same territory as *Dr. Strangelove, Or: How I Learned to Stop Worrying and Love The Bomb, Fail Safe* was another anti-nuclear statement — but without the laughs," wrote Clive Hirschhorn in *The Columbia Story* (2000). He added, "[U]nlike the [Stanley] Kubrick film, it was the vulnerability of machines rather than the lunacy of men that set the plot in motion.... Though an element of science fiction was apparent in director Sidney Lumet's suspenseful handling of the material, there was no denying the serious intention behind the enterprise, or the wholehearted dedication to the project by [its] cast ... Lumet's film, despite (or because of?) the earnestness of its approach, failed to find the audience it deserved."

Columbia issued *Dr. Strangelove* to theaters

early in 1964 and ten months later it released *Fail-Safe*. The latter's story begins with a series of events taking place at the same time, 5:30 A.M., at three separate locations. Brigadier General Warren "Blackie" Black (Dan O'Herlihy) awakens from a recurring dream in which a matador kills a bull and he tells his wife (Hildy Parks) that such an event will result in his own death. At a Washington D.C. all-night society gathering, political scientist Professor Groteschele (Walter Matthau) debates with bureaucrat Foster (Dana Elcar) about the outcome of a nuclear conflict and later resists the advances of a society girl (Nancy Berg) who has become aroused over the prospect of a final holocaust. In Omaha, Colonel Cascio (Fritz Weaver) signs out from the Strategic Air Command base and goes to see his alcoholic parents (Stewart Germain, Louise Larabee), where he is found by his commanding officer, General Bogan (Frank Overton). In Alaska, Colonel Jack Grady (Ed Binns) and his men begin another routine day of flying fighters carrying nuclear warheads defending the six points in the sky near the Soviet Union.

That morning Defense Secretary Swenson (William Hansen) meets with Black and other generals in the Pentagon's War Conference Room to listen to a lecture on limited war delivered by Groetschele with Black advocating the end of warfare. At the same time in Omaha, Bogan, Cascio and electronics expert Gordon Knapp (Russell Collins) show Congressman Raskob (Sorrell Booke) how the nation's borders are constantly being protected by the nuclear warhead-carrying planes. A UFO is spotted near Hudson's Bay headed to Detroit and the defense planes are placed on alert for Fail-Safe (orders from the president, done electronically, to launch a nuclear attack). Just before Fail-Safe is set in motion, the UFO is determined to be a low-flying plane and the orders are aborted but a fault indicator in Omaha's master control sets off the Fail-Safe box in Grady's Group Six quintet of bombers. Losing radio contact with Omaha, Grady and his fellow officer, Sullivan (Frank Simpson), open secret orders telling them to head for Moscow with their nuclear cargo. Stationed in a bomb shelter, the president (Henry Fonda) meets with his interpreter, Buck (Larry Hagman), and asks the advice of Swenson and the Pentagon people before ordering the planes shot down. When the Air Force fails to bring down the planes, Black informs the president that two of the bombers will probably make it to Moscow. The president then calls the Soviet premier as the fighters cross over into his country, causing a technical state of war to exist. With two of the planes shot down, the Soviets inform the president that they had jammed U.S. radios with a special device and the premier agrees to lift it so Grady can be contacted. The president tells Grady to return home but the flier, adhering to orders, refuses to accept verbal commands. Meanwhile, another of his squad is knocked out of the sky.

At the Pentagon, Groeteschele urges Swenson to launch a first strike against the Soviets in order to achieve minimal casualties at home but Black opposes the action. The president sends Black to a local airfield and orders the Army to assist the Russians in shooting down the remaining planes. Cascio has a breakdown when Bogan tells him to carry out the president's command and send the Soviets sensitive information about the firing of the nuclear warheads, telling them how to blow up the planes. Cascio claims the Soviets are using the negotiations as a trap and are planning their own strike. When Bogan does not agree to a full nuclear attack, he says his commanding officer is committing treason and tries to knock him out and take over the Omaha command. Cascio is restrained by the other officers and taken away as Technical Sergeant Collins (Dom DeLuise) gives the Russians the information they need to bring down another plane. The president informs the Soviet premier that two 20-megaton bombs will fall on Moscow and he orders the American ambassador to stay there. To avert a world war he also orders the destruction of New York City, and the Russian leader agrees to the terms. When the Soviets shoot down the last protector plane, Grady's craft is able to make it to Moscow as Groeteschele estimates three million people will die immediately in New York and another one to two million will expire within two weeks and that it is urgent to rescue as many corporation records as possible from the city before it is destroyed so the economy will survive. The president tells the Russian leader their countries are both responsible for the situation by letting their machines get out of hand. As the bombs fall on Moscow, he orders Black to drop his nuclear cargo on New York City, where the first lady is visiting. As he does so, Black dies of a heart attack, bringing reality to his dream.

Variety called the picture "a tense and suspenseful piece of filmmaking ... a gripping narrative realistically and almost frighteningly told."

The *New York Times* proclaimed, "If the last few minutes of this doesn't freeze you, nothing will. Covering almost precisely the same ground as *Dr. Strangelove*, it's actually in the science fiction realm, using a classic theme of melodrama — man menaced with destruction by his own machines.... The topical significance of it — with the camera jumping about from the SAC nerve center to the White House, is given crackling urgency by Sidney Lumet's fast-paced, stinging direction." Interestingly, the film carried an epilogue disclaimer assuring viewers that the government felt such a event could not happen.

The similarities between *Fail-Safe* and *Dr. Strangelove* was not without controversy. *Fail-Safe* was based on the 1962 novel by Eugene Burdick and Harvey Wheeler and was originally planned as an independent production by Max E. Youngstein. Columbia Pictures and the producers of *Dr. Strangelove* filed a lawsuit saying that the book *Fail-Safe* plagiarized the novel 1958 novel *Red Alert* by Peter George, the source for their film. The affair was settled when Columbia agreed to finance and distribute *Fail-Safe* with Youngstein as its producer.

With its claustrophobic settings mostly in small, somewhat dark rooms, *Fail-Safe* had the look of a television production. It was remade for the small screen in 2000 from a teleplay by Walter Bernstein, who scripted the 1964 feature. Produced by Warner Bros. Television and Maysville Pictures, this version was broadcast in black-and-white on CBS-TV and done live at the Warner Bros. Studios. The same year, the 1964 film was released on DVD by Columbia TriStar Home Video and an extra on the disc was the short film *Revisiting Fail-Safe* with commentary by the film's star Dan O'Herlihy, director Sidney Lumet, and screenwriter, Walter Bernstein.

The Faker

(1929; 55 minutes) DIRECTOR: Phil Rosen. STORY-SCREENPLAY: Harold J. Green. PHOTOGRAPHY: Teddy [Ted] Tetzlaff. EDITOR: William Hamilton. ART DIRECTOR: Harrison Wiley. TECHNICAL DIRECTOR: Edward Shulter. ASSISTANT DIRECTOR: Tenny Wright. CAST: Jacqueline Logan (Rita Martin), Charles Delaney (Bob Williams), Warner Oland (Hardian), Charles Hill Mailes (John Clayton), Gaston Glass (Frank Clayton), Flora Finch (Emma), David Mir (Believer), Lon Poff (Assistant), Fred Kelsey (Detective).

This silent mystery-comedy dealt with fake spiritualism and today only a few minutes of its footage remain. A contemporary source, the *Mason City (Iowa) Globe-Gazette* called it, "Unique in plot, unusual in treatment, and simple in presentation ... one of the best photodramas to be shown here in many months. Those who are looking for mystery, thrills, chills, suspense and tense drama, interspersed with fitting comedy, will do well to witness a showing.... The séance sequences are exceptionally well handled and no less awe-inspiring, because the spectator is taken behind the scenes and shown just how they are worked." *Photoplay* opined, "Well done expose of spiritualistic charlatans, with Warner Oland fine as the phony spook-chaser."

No-account Frank Clayton (Gaston Glass) hires medium Hardian (Warner Oland) to get his father, wealthy John Clayton (Charles Hill Mailes) to change his will (Frank has been disinherited in favor of his stepbrother Bob Williams [Charles Delaney]). Hardian has his pretty assistant, Rita Martin (Jacqueline Logan), get a job as the elder Clayton's private secretary and then holds a séance in which Rita, pretending to be Clayton's deceased wife, urges him to reinstate Frank in his will. Rita falls in love with Bob and, in order to stop the hoax, she reveals her boss to be a fake and exposes his false tricks. Mr. Clayton refuses to reconcile with Frank. Bob, who has fallen in love with Rita, forgives her past.

In the sound era, prolific director Phil Rosen would helm the genre efforts *The Phantom Broadcast* and *The Sphinx* (both 1933), *Murder by Invitation, Spooks Run Wild* (both 1941), *Mystery of Marie Roget* (1942), *Return of the Ape Man* (1944), *The Strange Mr. Gregory* (1946) and several spooky entries in Monogram's Charlie Chan series, including *The Chinese Cat* and *Black Magic* (both 1944) and *The Scarlet Clue* (1945). Warner Oland, famous for portraying Chan at Fox from 1931 to 1937, also starred as Dr. Fu Manchu in a trio of Paramount features as well as appearing in horror outings like *Drums of Jeopardy* (1931), *Before Dawn* (1933) and *WereWolf of London* (1935).

The Fatal Night

(1948; 50 minutes) PRODUCER-DIRECTOR: Mario Zampi. SCREENPLAY: Gerald Butler and Kathleen Connors, from the story "The Gentleman from America" by Michael Arlen. PHOTOGRAPHY: Cedric Williams. EDITOR: Giulio Zampi. MUSIC: Stanley Black. SOUND: Charles T. Parkhouse. PRODUCTION MANAGER: Donald Wynne. CAST: Lester Ferguson (Puce), Jean Short (Geraldine), Leslie Armstrong (Cyril), Brenda Hogan (Julia), Patrick Macnee (Tony), Aubrey Mallalieu (Yokel).

Made by Mario Zampi Productions in England and released there and in the U.S. by Columbia, this short feature proved to be a very scary affair, with its use of only half-seen horrors via flickering lights and shadows. David Quinlan in *British Sound Films: The Studio Years 1928–1959* (1984) termed it a "[g]enuinely frightening chiller made on record low budget; the best second-feature of its year." The author expounded further on the feature in *Quinlan's Film Directors* (1999) when he called it "one of the most frightening films ever made, full of horror not quite or only half-seen, flickering lights and shadows on walls, a triumph, in fact, of the editor's skill."

Young American Puce (Lester Ferguson) accepts a bet from his British pals Cyril (Leslie Armstrong) and Tony (Patrick Macnee) to spend a night in a reputedly haunted house with only a match, candle and revolver. That evening he reads a book about two girls who were murdered in a remote dwelling. After a draft snuffs out the candle, Puce begins to see ghosts and other supernatural activities and in a panic fires the gun. Cyril and Tony have played a prank on Puce, acting as the ghosts and setting up the fake effects. Months later the two men return from the war and again meet Puce and they admit they were behind the supposed supernatural activities. Puce attacks them, then is led away by two attendants from the asylum from which he recently escaped.

Columbia distributed five films produced by Mario Zampi, including 1950's *Shadow of the Past* (q.v.). *The Fatal Night* was one of Patrick Macnee's first films; he later appeared in *Scrooge* (1951), *Three Cases of Murder* (1955) and *Incense for the Damned (The Bloodsuckers)* (1970). He's best remembered for portraying John Steed in the TV series *The Avengers* and *The New Avengers*. Stanley Black, who composed the music for *The Fatal Night*, had a number of best-selling record albums on the London label in the 1960s.

Faust and the Devil

(1950; 87 minutes) PRODUCER: Gregor Rabinovitch. DIRECTOR: Carmine Gallone. SCREENPLAY: Leopold Marchand, from the poem by Johann Wolfgang Goethe and the opera by Charles Gounod. PHOTOGRAPHY: Arturo Gallea and Vaclav Vinch. MUSIC: Charles Gounod and Arrigo Boito. COSTUME DESIGN: Geoges Annenkov. CAST: Gino Mattera (Faust), Nelly Corradi (Marguerite), Italo Tajo (Mephistopheles), Onelia Fineschi (Singing Voice of Marguerite), Therese Dorny (Martha), Cesare Barbetti Siebel), Gilles Queant (Valentine), Livia Venturini.

Released in Italy in 1948 as *La Leggenda di Faust* (The Legend of Faust), this Cineopera Production was based on Johann Wolfgang Goethe's work "Faust" and the 1859 opera of the same name by Charles Gounod. It was a well-made feature which nicely retold the story of lonely Dr. Faust (Gino Mattera) selling his soul to Mephistopheles (Italo Tajo) in return for being able to live forever and then finding love with the beautiful peasant girl Marguerite (Nelly Corradi), with tragic results.

In the *New York Times*, Bosley Crowther noted, "This solemn Italian-made picture ... is probably as fair and impressive an approximation of the opera as could be got. And yet it is far from a brilliant and dynamic or even dramatic film." He called the production "solid and sumptuous, with gabled houses, pleasure palaces, aerial dreamboats, and the smoking crags of hell all reproduced in a manner that testifies to expended coin. The final episode — the burning of Margaret at the stake — is produced with particular magnificence, full of medieval barbarism and gloom."

Columbia distributed *Faust and the Devil* in the U.S. two years after its original Italian showings and in 1968 issued yet another version, *Doctor Faustus* (q.v.).

Fear Chamber

(1971; 86 minutes; Color) PRODUCER: Luis Enrique Vergara. DIRECTORS: Jack Hill and Juan Ibanez. SCREENPLAY: Jack Hill and Luis Enrique Vergara. PHOTOGRAPHY: Austin McKinney and Raul Dominguez. EDITOR: Felipe Maino. MUSIC: Enrico Cabiati. ART DIRECTORS: Jose Mendez and Octavio Ocamp. SOUND: Heinrich Henkel. SETS: Raul Cardenas. MAKEUP: Tony Ramirez. PRODUCTION MANAGER: Jose Luis Cerrada. Production Coordinator: Guillermo Olivera. DIALOGUE DIRECTOR: Stim Segar. ASSISTANT DIRECTOR: Jose Luis Gonzalez de Leon. CAST: Boris Karloff (Dr. Carl Mandel), Julissa (Corinne Mandel), Carlos East (Mark), Isela Vega (Helga Lund), Yerye Beirute (Roland), Eva Muller (Sally Ransom), Sandra Chavez (Louise Martinez), Santanon [Rafael Munoz] (Dwarf), Pamela Rosas (Dancer), Fuensanta (Said).

In April 1968, Boris Karloff filmed scenes for a quartet of horror features in Los Angeles under the direction of Jack Hill, with photography by Austin McKinney. Producer Luis Enrique Vergara, who had made *La Señora Muerte* (The Death Woman) and *Las Vampiras* (The Vampires) (both 1969) [qq.v.), planned to finish filming the features in Mexico. After completing *The Snake People* (q.v.), Vergara died and the three remaining movies, *Fear Chamber*, *House of Evil* and *The Incredible Invasion* [qq.v.], were not completed for some time. Columbia gave all four outings theatrical release in Spanish-language theaters in the early 1970s. Even then the quartet remained obscure until re-released on video in the 1980s. As with the other three movies, *Fear Chamber* was issued under more than one title with varying running times. Its Spanish-language appellation was *Camara del Terror* (Chamber of Terror), running 87 minutes. The U.S. theatrical release as *Fear Chamber* ran 86 minutes and it was released on video as *The Torture Chamber* and *The Torture Zone*, the latter timed at 71 minutes.

Produced by Azteca Films/Filmica Vergara S.A., *Fear Chamber*'s credits carried the subtitle "With All the Macabre of Edgar Allan Poe." The film opens with scientists Corinne Mandel (Julissa) and Mark (Carlos East) exploring a volcano crevice under the telephone direction of Corinne's father, Dr. Carl Mandel (Karloff). Trying to learn the secrets of the center of the Earth for the good of humanity, they find a pulsating rock that Dr. Mandel believes has crystallized intelligence. It is brought to the Benefical Foundation where six months later a young woman (Sandra Chavez) has been recruited for a job only to be kidnapped from her bed by dim-witted Roland (Yerye Beirute), a dwarf (Santanon) and an Arab (Fuensanta) and taken to a dungeon where she is tortured by the sight of strange people and venomous snakes. After witnessing the supposed murder of another girl, she is tied over a fire pit. After she passes out, Dr. Mandel, who pretends to be performing a black mass, removes body fluids from her which he uses to feed the living rock. Mandel has surmised that the rock needs the fluid to live and develop but only if it can be procured from young women in a state of extreme terror, thus the use of his fear chamber. After a woman (Eva Muller) enlisted for the experiment turns out to be a burglar who is devoured by the rock, Dr. Mandel finds out that the thing is capable of feeding itself via his computer and he decides to abandon the project and destroy the rock. The computer short circuits, causing him to have a seizure. Dr. Mandel recuperates under the care of another assistant, Helga Lund (Isela Vega), unaware that Helga has enlisted the aid of Roland, who thinks the rock is his friend, in reviving the thing. As Dr. Mandel rests in bed, Corinne and Mark go away for a holiday and realize they are in love. Helga has Roland abduct an exotic dancer (Pamela Rosas) and another young woman, both of whom are drained of their body fluids by the rock. When the dwarf and Said try to molest some of the young women, Roland kills them and comes under the delusion the rock will give him diamonds. Corinne and Mark hear a news report about the discovery of Said's body and they drive home. Realizing that the rock is using the computer to learn to adapt to live on the Earth's surface and may be sending messages to others of its kind, Helga decides to destroy it but is stopped by Roland, who feeds her to the creature. Corinne and Mark arrive to find Dr. Mandel using the computer in an attempt to stop the rock but the thing grabs the girl with its tentacle. Telling his daughter to remain calm, Dr. Mandel is joined by Mark and the two of them use the computer's power to reverse the thing's growth process and return it to an inanimate object. Rambling through the volcano crevice in search of diamonds, Roland dies when it erupts.

Although hardly a cinema classic, *Fear Chamber* is not without attributes, including a good performance by Karloff, in a role that extends throughout the feature, and very nice color photography. Thrown into the plot are all kinds of flashing bright lights, the ghastly torture chamber, a lesbian SandM whipping scene, a topless exotic dancer (shown only in the Elite DVD version as a bonus scene) and various kinds of torture. The creature itself looks like some kind of pulsing red orange mass with a tentacle. *Psychotronic Video* #5 (1990) called it "undoubtedly the low point of [Karloff's] career, and is badly put together, but still fascinating."

First Men in the Moon

(1964; 103 minutes; Color) PRODUCER: Charles H. Schneer. ASSOCIATE PRODUCER-SPECIAL EFFECTS: Ray Harryhausen. DIRECTOR: Nathan Juran. SCREENPLAY: Nigel Kneale and Jan Read, from the novel by H.G. Wells. PHOTOGRAPHY: Wilkie Cooper. EDITOR: Maurice Rootes. MUSIC: Laurie Johnson. ART DIRECTOR: John Blezard. SOUND: Buster Ambler and Red Law. PRODUCTION MANAGER: Ted Wallis. CONTINUITY: Eileen Head. ASSISTANT DIRECTOR: George Pollard. CAST: Edward Judd (Arnold Bedford), Martha Hyer (Katherine "Kate" Callender), Lionel Jeffries (Joseph Cavor), Miles Malleson (Registrar), Norman Bird (Astronaut Stuart), Gladys Henson (Matron), Hugh McDermott (Richard Challis), Betty McDowall (Margaret Hoy), Sean Kelly (Colonel Rice), Gordon Robinson (Sergeant Andrew Martin), John Murray Scott (Cosmonaut Nevsky), Marne Millard (Dr. Tok),

Paul Carpenter (Reporter), Erik Chitty (Gibbs), Peter Finch (Bailiff's Man), Laurence Herder (Glushkov), Huw Thomas (Announcer).

Based on H.G. Wells' 1901 novel, *First Men in the Moon* was produced in England by Ameran Films and premiered in London in the summer of 1964 as *H.G. Wells' First Men in the Moon*, receiving stateside shows four months later. Visual effects wizard Ray Harryhausen was the associate producer and his insect-like moon creatures and a giant caterpillar were outstanding. The feature was a visual treat during its Moon sequences, but overall it was too long and plagued by lumbering comedy, especially Lionel Jeffries' performance as the addled inventor. While the feature had its fun moments, *Films in Review* was justified in its comment, "The H.G. Wells yarn now seems old-fashioned."

Astronauts landing on the Moon find a British flag and a letter dated 1899 claiming the orb for Queen Victoria. A United Nations Space Agency team traces the letter to a Dimchurch, England, nursing home where elderly Arnold Bedford (Edward Judd) resides. He tells them that in 1899 he rented a cottage in Dimchurch in order to write a play to free himself of debts. He lies to his fiancée, Kate Callender (Martha Hyer) about his circumstances and they meet an eccentric neighbor, Joseph Cavor (Lionel Jeffries), who tells Arnold he has developed a metallic paste he calls Cavorite that can control gravity. He also shows Arnold a sphere he has built which he plans to use to fly to the Moon. When Arnold learns that the orb may contain a wealth of minerals, he agrees to go along on the trip, much to Kate's chagrin.

When creditors show up with a summons for Arnold, Kate runs to the sphere just as the men are about to take off and she is taken along on the trip to the Moon. After a lunar landing, the two men explore the surface and claim it for England and her queen. They fall through a glass-covered vortex and find ant-like creatures that Cavor calls Selenites; they appear to be hostile. Returning to the surface, the men realize that the sphere, with Kate still inside, has been dragged into a cavern. They manage to get into the area and find the Selenites swarming over the spacecraft. A giant caterpillar attacks the men, with the Moon beings capturing Cavor and killing the beast with a ray. Walking through the underground cavern, Cavor realizes that the Selenites harness power from sunlight to generate oxygen, and an eclipse causes everything to come to a standstill. When the eclipse is over, the Moon men use crystals to translate and Cavor is able to communicate with them. Arnold and Kate do not trust the creatures while Cavor wants to understand and make peace with them. As he tells the Moon's ruler about Earth, Arnold and Kate repair the sphere. After Arnold shoots the ruler, the Selenites go wild and Kate and Arnold blast off back to Earth while Cavor, who has developed a head cold, remains behind. Bedford then watches a television transmission of the United Nations astronauts exploring the Moon's underground, which they

West German poster for *First Men in the Moon* (1964).

find deserted and collapsing. Arnold remembers Cavor's cold and realizes its germs wiped out the Selenites, who had no resistance to the virus.

H.G. Wells also used the theme of germs destroying an alien race in his science fiction classic *The War of the Worlds* (1898). *First Men in the Moon* was initially filmed in Great Britain in 1919 with Bruce Gordon, Heather Thatcher and Hector Abbas.

Ed Naha in *The Science Fictionary* (1980) thought the 1964 feature "[a] visually stunning, adroitly written adaptation of the vintage tale of space..." Phil Hardy wrote in *Science Fiction* (1984) that it was "a jolly version of H.G. Wells' 1901 visionary novel which was the inspiration for George Méliès' *Le Voyage dan la Lune* (1902). A hugely enjoyable piece of fluff, greatly aided by Harryhausen's special effects..." The author also noted the feature was released in Cinerama in West Germany. In his article "H.G. Wells on the Screen" in *Films in Review* (November 1967), Paul Jensen declared, "Once again too much time was spent on Victorian atmosphere before the imaginative action begins. And too little time was spent on Ray Harryhausen's stop-motion photography." Clive Hirschhorn in *The Columbia Story* (2000) called it a "diverting update of H.G. Wells's novel ... clearly aimed at the matinee brigade, though fathers with a touch of the schoolboy in them enjoyed it too." In *The Family Guide to Movies on Video* (1988), Henry Herz and Tony Zaza said it was "an entertaining combination of satirical comedy and fairly serious science fiction."

The film's adaptor, Nigel Kneale, is probably best known for his "Quatermass" series for British television and later films, while director Nathan Juran also helmed such genre features as *The Black Castle* (1952), *The Deadly Mantis* (1957), *20 Million Years to Earth* (1957) [q.v.], *The 7th Voyage of Sinbad* (1958) [q.v.], *Attack of the 50 Foot Woman* and *The Brain from Planet Arous* (both 1958 with Juran billed as Nathan Hertz), *Flight of the Lost Balloon* (1961), *Jack the Giant Killer* (1962), which he co-wrote, and *The Boy Who Cried Werewolf* (1973). He also directed episodes of the sci-fi TV shows *Lost in Space* and *Land of the Giants*.

Five

(1951; 93 minutes) PRODUCER-DIRECTOR-SCREENPLAY-ART DIRECTOR: Arch Oboler. PHOTOGRAPHY: Sidney Lubow and Louis Clyde Stoumen. EDITORS: John Hoffman, Ed Spiegel and Arthur Swerdloff. MUSIC: Henry Russell. SOUND: William Jenkins Locy. CAST: William Phipps (Michael), Susan Douglas (Roseanne Rogers), James Anderson (Eric), Charles Lampkin (Charles), Earl Lee (Oliver Peabody Barnstable).

When an atomic holocaust decimates the planet, one of the few survivors, pregnant Roseanne Rogers (Susan Douglas), goes to a country home belonging to her aunt and meets Michael (William Phipps), an elevator operator who has taken up residence in the house. Both were saved because Michael was inside an elevator and Roseanne was undergoing an x-ray in a hospital. They decide to stay together although the young woman dismisses Michael's romantic advances. Banker Oliver Peabody Barnstable (Earl Lee) and his co-worker, Charles (Charles Lampkin), arrive by automobile and tell how they survived the blast by being in a bank vault. Delusional, Oliver believes they are on a holiday and shows signs of radiation poisoning. After getting electricity by putting in a generator and planting a garden, the group go to the beach at the behest of Oliver and there they rescue a drowning man, explorer Eric (James Anderson). After being on Mt. Everest when the holocaust took place, he had flown across the Pacific Ocean to the United States, but his plane crashed after running out of fuel.

Following Oliver's death, Eric announces that he wants to go to a large city and shows dislike for Charles because he is black. After Roseanne has her baby, Charles says he plans to leave but Michael convinces him to stay. Eric agrees to help with the garden but continues to remain idle. Michael tells Roseanne he loves her. Eric destroys their crops, but Michael tries to protect Roseanne and says a wild animal caused the destruction. Eric convinces Roseanne to go with him to the city. As they sneak away they meet Charles, whom Eric murders. Finding Charles' body and a note left by Roseanne, Michael goes after her. In the city, the young woman finds the skeleton of her husband in the hospital waiting room. When Eric informs Roseanne that he will not go back to the country, she tries to get away from him and he grabs her. Noticing the signs of radiation poisoning on his own arms, he runs away. On her way back to the house, Roseanne's baby dies and Michael finds her. The two return to the country and start a new garden.

This somber, post-atomic war melodrama was made by Arch Oboler Productions and visually is remindful of the neo-realist cinema movement so popular in Europe at the time. Production-wise it was almost a one-man show with

Oboler as producer, director, writer and art director. Even the house used in the film, designed by Frank Lloyd Wright, was Oboler's. A pioneer in radio drama, Oboler was best known for the series "Lights Out," which was broadcast on various networks between 1934 and 1947, and "Arch Oboler's Plays," an anthology series that was on NBC in the 1939–40 season and on Mutual in 1945. He wrote and directed *Strange Holiday* for PRC in 1946 and wrote, directed and produced *Bwana Devil* (1952), the first 3-D theatrical feature, *The Twonky* (1953) and *The Bubble* (1967). In 1952 Oboler sold all rights for *Five* to Columbia Pictures, which had issued the feature theatrically in the spring of 1951.

Bosley Crowther wrote in the *New York Times*, "Obviously, Mr. Oboler, in his manufacture of this film, has some sort of poetic drama or social allegory in mind. For the mood is solemn and ethereal, the pace is portentously slow and the pictorial details, while literal, are blandly illogical. It takes Mr. Oboler a long time to get from here to there, so randomly does he let his camera wander over sea, sky, clouds and hills.... The consequence is that an idea which bears some imaginative thought is reduced to the level of banality and somewhat 'arty' pretense."

The 5000 Fingers of Dr. T

(1953; 89 minutes; Color) DIRECTOR: Roy Rowland. SCREENPLAY: Dr. Seuss [Theodore Geisel] and Allan Scott. STORY: Dr. Seuss. PHOTOGRAPHY: Frank [Franz] Planer. EDITOR: Al Clark. MUSIC: Frederick Hollander. MUSIC DIRECTOR: Morris Stoloff. SONG: Dr. Seuss and Frederick Hollander. ART DIRECTOR: Cary Odell. SOUND: Russell Malmgren. PRODUCTION DESIGN: Rudolph Sternad. SETS: William Kiernan. MAKEUP: Clay Campbell. PRODUCTION MANAGER: Clem Beauchamp. COSTUMES: Jean Louis. Color Consultant: Francis Cugat. CHOREOGRAPHER: Eugene Loring. ASSISTANT DIRECTOR: Frederick Briskin. CAST: Peter Lind Hayes (August Zabladowski), Mary Healy (Heloise Collins), Hans Conreid (Dr. Terwilliker), Tommy Rettig (Bartholomew "Bart" Collins), John Heasley (Uncle Whitney), Robert Heasley (Uncle Judson), Noel Cravat (Sergeant Lunk), Henry Kulky (Stroogo), Diki Lener (Dungeon Ballet Dancer), Tony Butala (Boy Pianist), George [Chakiris] Kerris (Dancer), Kim Charney (Boy), Roy Rowland (Doorman).

Famed children's author Dr. Seuss (Theodore Geisel) conceived the idea for *The 5000 Fingers of Dr. T* and co-wrote the script. He also composed one of the film's songs with Frederick Hollander, whose original music score was nominated for an Academy Award. Apparently an attempt to come up with fantasy-musical in the vein of Victor Herbert's *Babes in Toyland*, the resulting feature was a glitzy but pretentious, boring affair which proved to be a box office bust. Columbia's reissued it as *Crazy Music*. In the 1990s it emerged on video as *Dr. Seuss' 5000 Fingers of Dr. T*.

Youngster Bart Collins (Tommy Rettig) falls asleep and, after a bad dream in which he is pursued by strange creatures in a foreboding land, he is awakened by his assertive piano teacher, Dr. Terwilliker (Hans Conreid), who rebukes him for not practicing his lessons. The boy's young widowed mother, Heloise (Mary Healy), wants her son to play so he continues as she and his instructor leave and plumber August Zabladowski (Peter Lind Hayes) shows up to repair a sink. The bored boy again goes to sleep and dreams he is at a huge keyboard with Terwilliker telling him about the opening the next day of his institute where 500 boys with 5000 fingers will daily play a gigantic piano. Trying to escape, Bart finds August putting in scores of sinks for the opening; the plumber informs the boy that his mother is working with his instructor on the institute. Bart finds his mother with Terwilliker, who tells her she must forget her son because she is going to marry him. When it is learned that Bart is on the loose, Terwilliker commands that he be found and placed in the castle's dungeon. Bart finds August and conveys his wish that he (August) and his mother get married so he can have a happy home. Showing only brief interest, the plumber continues his work until the boy asks him to check on his mother. When he finds her, Terwilliker appears and the two men engage in a magic combat which neither wins. August says he will not install more sinks, but Heloise and Terwilliker flatter the man to the point that he agrees to continue the work. Bart hears the music instructor tell his minions to eliminate August after his work is done and he makes a getaway as Terwilliker puts Heloise in a cell since he feels he can no longer control her thoughts. When the plumber informs Bart he needs the money for the sink jobs, the boy finds the key to Terwilliker's safe, removes $30, leaves an IOU and takes the written order for August's execution. After hearing an announcement for his capture dead or alive, Bart finds August who now believes him and says he will be his stepfather. The two then rescue Heloise. August is forced to kill two skating twins but Terwilliker captures the trio, hypnotizing Heloise and placing

Bart and the plumber in the dungeon. The day of the institute's opening, the piano-playing boys arrive as Bart and August work on a formula for absorbing piano notes. Bart is brought from the dungeon to join the other boys in playing the piano. Just as Terwilliker starts to conduct, Bart opens the formula bottle and all the piano notes vanish. Terwilliker and his minions converge on the boy and he tells them the formula is atomic and they run away. Bart starts to conduct but the bottle explodes and he wakes up to find August and his mother watching. When the two go off together, Bart forgets about music lessons and goes out to play baseball with his dog Sport.

The *New York Times*' Bosley Crowther opined, "Except for one musical number in which a gang of slightly satanic goons, all green and black and chalky, beat out some weird and racy jazz on a variety of grotesque musical instruments in what appears to be a modernistic cave, there is little or no inspiration or real imagination in the thing." According to *The Best, Worst and Most Unusual: Hollywood Musicals* (1983), the feature "may well be the strangest musical fantasy ever made [but it] works well as a children's film."

Co-star Hans Conreid, who played the villainous piano instructor, told Leonard Maltin in *Film Fan Monthly* (May 1970) that the feature "was to be made under the direction and overall oppression of Mr. Harry Cohn. The picture was to be a big one, and Mr. Geisel, or Dr. Seuss, designed it, wrote it, designed the costumes, designed the scenery. A good deal of money was spent; it was a great, beautiful picture.... [It] was badly cut in fear and anguish of the reappraisal after it was made, even if it was evident to those knowledgeable but inartistic heads of [the] studio that it might have been an artistic triumph rather than a financial one. But in an attempt to make it one, they cut out over 11 musical numbers, and re-shot for one whole week. To make this very long and tedious and somewhat tearful story short for me, the picture never made its print money back. It was comparable to *Wilson* [1944] as one of the great money-losers of all time..."

Although *The 5000 Fingers of Dr. T* was a financial bust, it apparently did not hurt the careers of his four lead players. Conreid went on to be one of the most active actors in films and TV, while the husband-and-wife team of Peter Lind Hayes and Mary Healy continued on stage and television. Juvenile lead Tommy Rettig became best known for the role of Jeff Miller in the CBS-TV series *Lassie* from 1954 to 1957.

Flight to Fame

(1938; 67 minutes) DIRECTOR: C.C. [Charles C.] Coleman. SCREENPLAY: Michael L. Simmons. PHOTOGRAPHY: Lucien Ballard. EDITOR: James Sweeney. MUSIC DIRECTOR: Morris Stoloff. ART DIRECTORS: Stephen Goosson and Lionel Banks. SOUND: George Cooper. ASSISTANT DIRECTOR: George Rhein. CAST: Charles Farrell (Captain Robert Lawrence), Jacqueline Wells [Julie Bishop] (Barbara Fiske), Hugh Sothern (Dr. Harlan Fiske), Alexander [Alex] D'Arcy (Perez), Jason Robards [Sr.] (Muller/Drake), Charles D. Brown (Major Loy), Addison Richards (Colonel King), Frederick Burton (General Darrow), Selmer Jackson (Jules Peabody), Reed Howes (Roy Curran), Vernon Steele, Eddie Kane, Lee Prather (Officers), Captain Robby Robinson, James Millican (Pilots), Malcolm [Bud] McTaggart (Page Boy), Oscar G. Hendrian (Sound Sergeant).

Working title: *Wings of Doom*.

"The Weirdest Killer That Ever Stalked the Air Lane Spreads Terror Across the Clouds!" exclaimed the advertising for *Flight to Fame* which Columbia issued in the fall of 1938. Its flying stunts were performed by noted aviator Paul Mantz, who had the same chore in *Air Mail* six years before. *Variety* reported, "Science film which will attract the youngsters with a super-mechanics bug, give the thrill hunters a fair portion, and be generally acceptable, if not hot, in the action spots.... It revives the death ray again, and throws in some test-piloting with more than the usual hazards." Phil Hardy in *Science Fiction* (1984) called it a "routine airplane melodrama which is of interest as one of the earliest films of cinematographer Lucien Ballard."

Although Dr. Harlan Fiske (Hugh Sothern) has perfected a death ray machine with the aid of associates Perez (Alex D'Arcy) and Muller (Jason Robards), the device fails to when it is demonstrated to War Department officials. His former flying squadron commander, General Darrow (Frederick Burton), scoffs at Fiske's claim the death ray will work. At the same time, Captain Robert Lawrence (Charles Farrell), who is in love with Fiske's daughter Barbara (Jacqueline Wells), learns that his new swift pursuit plane has been repudiated by test pilots. General Darrow agrees with Robert that his new plane is safe and to prove it he flies the craft, which is shot down by a device like the one invented by Dr. Fiske. During the investigation, the inventor claims his weapon could not have destroyed the plane because it failed to work during the war department demonstration. Airline pilot Roy Curran (Reed Howes) goes up in Lawrence's new aircraft and he too is brought down by the ray machine. When Robert goes to see Barbara, he learns that her father has received blueprints. Perez sees Robert looking at them and tells the girl. Feeling Robert has been romancing her in order to get to the blueprints, she refuses to see him again. Robert is drummed out of the service and Major Loy (Charles D. Brown) informs him that Fiske had a falling out with Darrow and his "Dirty Dozen" flying squadron after he had defended a flier, Drake (Jason Robards), who was accused of being a coward. In order to trap the killer, Major Loy announces he will fly another of Robert's models. The two men go up in the craft, avoid the ray gun and demolish the weapon. Landing at the site of the attack, the two pilots learn the assassin in Muller, but Loy recognizes him as Drake. The dying killer tells them he made a duplicate of Fiske's model in order to shoot down the men who drummed him out of the "Dirty Dozen" and botched the War Department demonstration. Dr. Fiske is able to prove the worth of his invention and Robert and Barbara are reunited.

Fog

(1933; 70 minutes) DIRECTOR: Albert S. Rogell. SCREENPLAY: Ethel Hill and Dore Schary, from the play by Valentine Williams and Dorothy Rice Sims. PHOTOGRAPHY: Benjamin H. Kline. EDITOR: Richard Cahoon. SOUND: Edward Bernds. COSTUMES: Robert Kalloch. CAST: Donald Cook (Wentworth Brown), Mary Brian (Mary Fulton), Reginald Denny (Dr. Winstay), Robert McWade (Alonzo Holt), Helen Freeman (Madame Alva), Maude Eburne (Mrs. Jackson), G. Pat Collins (Mullaney), Edwin Maxwell (Captain), Samuel S. Hinds (Dickens), Marjorie Gateson (Mrs. Bentley), C. Montague Shaw (Dr. Alloway), Merrill McCormick (Officer), Eddie Fetherston (Passenger).

Alonzo Holt (Robert McWade), an elderly, crotchety rich man, is murdered aboard a fog-enshrouded ocean liner headed for England. His body is found hanging over the side of the ship by Mary Fulton (Mary Brian). The captain (Edwin Maxwell) orders an inquest, making scientific detective Wentworth Brown (Donald Cook) the chief investigator. Wentworth loves Mary who is also being romanced by Dr. Winstay (Reginald Denny), the dead man's personal physician. Among the suspects are medium Madame Alva (Helen Freeman), whom Holt rejected romantically after realizing she was a charlatan. When Dr. Alloway (C. Montague Shaw) prepares to do an autopsy on Holt's body, he is murdered and the corpse vanishes. Wentworth reads Holt's will and finds he is the man's son and sole heir. During a séance in the dining salon, Madame Alva is about to name the killer when she is strangled. Since everyone on board is a suspect, Wentworth calls all the passengers to the captain's cabin and unmasks a stowaway who later helps him reveal the identity of the killer, who confesses and then jumps overboard.

A flavorful murder mystery with horror trappings that included a series of strange murders, a fog-enveloped ship, a medium, a séance and a phantom, *Fog* proved to be quite entertaining. *Harrison's Reports* stated, "This material is just like the material of similar murder-mystery melodramas. There is no appeal to the emotions; success depends on its ability to hold the spectator in suspense.... You may take it for granted that it will turn out to be a good program mystery melodrama." This publication later rated the movie's box office performance as "poor." *Variety* noted, "Commendably directed film, but Reginald Denny makes a poor menace. Thus, because most of the action revolves around Denny's supposed villainy, the dramatic tenor of the story screens unconvincing. Little humor and the picture is also weak on romance. It will need support."

Director Albert S. Rogell also helmed two other Columbia genre releases, *Below the Sea* (1933) and *Air Hawks* (1935) [qq.v.] as well as Universal's 1941 thriller *The Black Cat*. Star Donald Cook was also in *The Mad Genius* (1931), Columbia's *The Circus Queen Murder* (1933) and *The Ninth Guest* (1934) [qq.v.], and *Murder in the Blue Room* (1944). Mary Brian was the leading lady in Columbia's *Killer at Large* (1936) [q.v.]. Co-scripter Dory Schary later became a producer at several major studios, including RKO and MGM.

Footsteps in the Fog

(1955; 90 minutes; Color) PRODUCERS: M.J. Frankovich and Maxwell Setton. DIRECTOR: Arthur Lubin. SCREENPLAY: Dorothy Reid and Lenore Coffee. ADAPTATION: Arthur Pierson, from the story "The Interruption" by W.W. Jacobs. PHOTOGRAPHY: Christopher Challis. EDITOR: Alan Osbiston. MUSIC: Benjamin Frankel. ART DIRECTOR: Wilfred Shingleton. SOUND: A. Ambler and Rex Law. MAKEUP: N. Smallwood. PRODUCTION MANAGER: Fred Gunn. COSTUMES: Beatrice Dawson and Elizabeth Haffenden. CONTINUITY: Betty

Forster. ASSISTANT DIRECTOR: Ronald Spencer. CAST: Stewart Granger (Stephen Lowry), Jean Simmons (Lily Watkins), Bill Travers (David MacDonald), Belinda Lee (Elizabeth "Beth" Travers), Ronald Squire (Alfred Travers), Finlay Currie (Inspector Peters), William Hartnell (Herbert Moresby), Frederick Leister (Dr. Simpson), Percy Marmont (Magistrate), Margery Rhodes (Mrs. Park), Peter Bull (Brasher), Barry Keegan (Constable Burke), Sheila Manahan (Rose Moresby), Norman Macowan (Butler Grimes), Cameron Hall (Corcoran), Victor Maddern (Jones), Peter Williams (Constable Farrow), Arthur Howard (Vicar).

Working titles: *Deadlock*, *Interruption* and *Rebound*.

In 1905 London, Stephen Lowry (Stewart Granger) poisons his wealthy wife. His Cockney maid, Lily Watkins (Jean Simmons), finds out and takes the murdered woman's jewels. When Lowry learns of this, he threatens Lily, who tells him she knows his secret. Keeping the jewels, Lily is promoted to housekeeper much to the chagrin of Lowry's cook, Mrs. Park (Margery Rhodes), who dislikes Lily.

Lowry is asked to become a partner in a business run by his friend Alfred Travers (Ronald Squire). Travers would like Stephen to marry his daughter Elizabeth (Belinda Lee), who is in love with barrister David MacDonald (Bill Travers). While Lowry and Lily become lovers, David finds out Elizabeth is in love with Lowry. When MacDonald broaches the matter of Elizabeth with Lowry, he declares he is still in mourning. Their meeting is interrupted by Mrs. Park and Grimes (Norman Macowan), the butler, who have been dismissed by Lily, who is wearing a broach belonging to Lowry's late wife. When Lily refuses to go abroad, Lowry follows her in a dense fog and beats her to death with his cane. Making a getaway he has a tussle with two men and loses the stick. Back home, Lowry is surprised when Lily returns; noticing blood on his cape, she realizes he planned to kill her. The murder victim was the wife of Constable Burke (Barry Keegan). Lowry is arrested after being identified as the man at the scene of the crime. Elizabeth asks MacDonald to defend Lowry.

At the trial, Lily testifies he was home with her at the time of the murder and he is set free. To protect herself, Lily tells Lowry she has written a letter to be opened by her sister, Rose Moresby (Sheila Manahan), in the event of her death. Lowry decides to join Travers' firm and begins romancing Elizabeth, making Lily jealous. Lowry tells Lily he plans to steal the firm's money so they can run away together to the United States and get married. To placate Lowry, Lily asks Rose to burn the letter but Herbert Moresby (William Hartnell), Rose's husband, gets it out of the fire. In order to frame Lily, Stephen begins giving himself small amounts of poison, calling in a physician (Frederick Leister) as his condition grows worse. MacDonald tells Travers he believes that Lowry murdered his wife. Herbert brings the letter to David who shows it to Elizabeth and her father. Feeling worse, Lowry sends Lily for the doctor and then takes more poison. But she is stopped by the police and taken to Travers' office where she is asked about the letter; she denies writing it. When Lily does not return, Lowry contacts Constable Burke. When she gets home, Burke tells her he believes she poisoned both Lowry and his late wife. Lily then tries to make Lowry confess to the killing but he dies and she is arrested.

Filmed in England, *Footsteps in the Fog* is a disappointing thriller that mutes its horror overtones with a mundane plot. Those involved in its production are much more interesting than the film itself. It was based on a short story by W.W. Jacobs, best known for writing the classic horror tale "The Monkey's Paw." Stars Stewart Granger and Jean Simmons were married at the time the movie was made and it was the fourth and last feature in which they appeared together. Director Arthur Lubin was an old hand at genre efforts, including *The House of a Thousand Candles* (1936), *Black Friday* (1940) *Hold That Ghost* (1941), *Phantom of the Opera* (1943), *Ali Baba and the Forty Thieves* (1944), *The Spider Woman Strikes Back* (1946), six features in Universal's "Francis the Talking Mule" series from 1949 to 1955, *The Thief of Baghdad* (1961) and *The Incredible Mr. Limpet* (1964). He also directed the popular CBS-TV series *Mr. Ed* which ran from 1961 to 1965. Co-scripter Dorothy Reid was a star in the silent days, billed as Dorothy Davenport. The daughter of character actor Harry Davenport, she was married to matinee idol Wallace Reid and later a director of exploitation films like *Human Wreckage* (1923), *The Red Kimono* (1926), *Sucker Money* (1933) and *The Road to Ruin* (1934).

Despite its stars and top-notch production values, *Footsteps in the Fog* ended up at the bottom of dual bills when Columbia issued it in the U.S. in the summer of 1955. In *British Sound Films: The Studio Years 1928–1959* (1984), David Quinlan termed it, "[w]ell-acted but slow." James Robert Parish and Don E. Stanke wrote in *The*

Swashbucklers (1976), "Regardless of its unfavorable reviews, [it] is excellent fodder for devotees of the Victorian Era. The plush settings and costumes make it very easy on the eyes."

Forbidden Island

(1959; 66 minutes; Color) PRODUCER-DIRECTOR-SCREENPLAY: Charles B. Griffith. PHOTOGRAPHY: Gilbert Warrenton. EDITOR: Jerome Thoms. MUSIC: Alexander Laszlo. SONG: Martin Denny and Magoon Eaton, Jr. SOUND: John Livadary and Ben Winkler. PRODUCTION MANAGER: Bart Carre. MAKEUP: Esther Cyr. UNDERWATER PHOTOGRAPHY: Lamar Boren. COLOR CONSULTANT: Henri Jaffa. ASSISTANT DIRECTOR: Lew Borzage. CAST: Jon Hall (Dave Courtney), Nan Adams (Joanne Godfrey), John Farrow (Edward Stuart Godfrey), Jonathan Haze (Jack Maunter), Greigh Phillips (Dean Pike), Dave "Howdy" Peters (Fermin Fry), Tookie Evans (Raoul Estoril), Martin Denny (Marty), Bob LaVarre (Cal Priest), Bill Anderson (Mike), Abraham Kaluna (Abe), Mahi Beamer, Randy Oness (Singers), Arthur Lyman (Marimba Player), Joseja Moe (Dancer).

While drinking in a Manila bar, ex–Navy buddies and divers Dave Courtney (Jon Hall), Jack Maunter (Jonathan Haze) and Dean Pike (Greigh Phillips) are offered a job by Stuart Godfrey (John Farrow), who wants them to retrieve a precious, but unnamed object, from a sunken ship. When he offers a $1,000 bonus to the one who finds the article, the trio agree to go along on the expedition which also includes Joanne (Nan Adams), whom Godfrey is blackmailing because of a gun she stole; he is forcing her to pretend to be his wife in order to fool the local police. When the three men join the expedition they meet several other divers whom Godfrey has also hired. After a few days, Godfrey orders his yacht anchored near a deserted island and he informs the divers they have three weeks to find a huge emerald before Naval Salvage takes over. While diving, Dean locates a sunken wreck with the skeleton of a woman with a belt around its neck in one of the cabins. Not telling what he found, Dean later goes through Godfrey's things. Godfrey catches him and delivers a nasty blow with a whip. Joanne tends to the wound on Dean's neck and when he asks about the state of her marriage she shows him a bracelet her "husband" gave her with the initials E.G., the same as the initials on the belt on the skeleton. Dean then tries to blackmail Godfrey by accusing him of murder. When Joanne walks on the beach with Dean, Godfrey tampers with the man's air tank. When Dean dives again, the tank malfunctions and he is drowned. After another diver brings up the belt and gives it to Godfrey, he tells Joanne she is no longer under obligation to him and encourages her to romance Dave. Godfrey then tries to turn Jack against Dave by telling him he believes Joanne and Dave worked together to get rid of Dean. After both men are told by Godfrey to oversee diving tank valves, Jack attacks Dave with a grappling hook while they are diving and Dave is forced to sever Jack's air hose. When Godfrey suggests Dave may have killed Jack to hide his murder of Dean, Joanne, who is in love with Courtney, reveals the truth about Godfrey and he shoots her. Trying to escape, Godfrey takes a motor launch to his yacht but is pursued by Dave and the other divers. Dave and Godfrey fight it out and Courtney strangles Godfrey with his own whip. Dave and the recovered Joanne return to Manila.

Filmed in Hawaii with underwater sequences lensed at Star Springs in Florida, *Forbidden Island* was the first of five feature films Charles B. Griffith directed between 1959 and 1989. He is, however, best known as a script writer for such Roger Corman outings as *Gunslinger* (1956), *Naked Paradise*, *Not of This Earth*, *The Undead* and *Attack of the Crab Monsters* (all 1957), *A Bucket of Blood* and *Beast from Haunted Cave* (both 1959) and *The Little Shop of Horrors* (1960). Star Jon Hall headlined genre fare like *Invisible Agent* and *Arabian Nights* (both 1942), *Ali Baba and the Forty Thieves*, *Cobra Woman* and *The Invisible Man's Revenge* (all 1944). In 1965 he produced, directed and starred in *Monster from the Surf*, which was also called *Beach Girls and The Monster*. Also in *Forbidden Island* were noted musicians Martin Denny and Arthur Lyman. Denny, who co-wrote the film's title song and played one of the divers, had several best-selling singles and albums on the Liberty label in the late 1950s and early 1960s, including "Quiet Village" in 1959 and "A Taste of Honey" in 1962. Lyman, seen playing the marimba in *Forbidden Island*, recorded for Hi Fi Records and also had popular singles and albums, including the songs "Taboo" (1959), "Yellow Bird" (1961) and "Love for Sale" (1963). Author-director John Farrow played the role of the villain who eschewed his first name Edward, because it was part of the initials E.G. on the belt that proved he was a murderer. Early in his directorial career Farrow helmed Boris Karloff in two Warner Bros. non-horror outings, *West of Shanghai* (1937) and *The Invisible Menace* (1938), and he later did the genre efforts

The Night Has a Thousand Eyes (1948) and *Alias Nick Beal* (1949) for Paramount.

With its subplot of a precious emerald being found on the skeleton of a strangled woman in a sunken wreck, *Forbidden Island* was somewhat of an admixture of Robert Louis Stevenson's *Treasure Island*, Edgar Allan Poe's "The Gold Bug" and Griffith's earlier *Naked Paradise*. Although pleasing to the eye thanks to Gilbert Warrenton's color photography, the overall feature was rather mundane despite its minor horror trappings.

Fury of the Congo

(1951; 69 minutes) PRODUCER: Sam Katzman. DIRECTOR: William Berke. SCREENPLAY: Carroll Young. PHOTOGRAPHY: Ira H. Morgan. EDITOR: Richard Fantl. MUSIC DIRECTOR: Mischa Bakaleinikoff. ART DIRECTOR: Paul Palmentola. SOUND: Josh Westmoreland. SETS: Sidney Clifford. UNIT MANAGER: Herbert Leonard. ASSISTANT DIRECTOR: Wilbur McGaugh. CAST: Johnny Weissmuller (Jungle Jim), Sherry Moreland (Leta), William Henry (Ronald Cameron), Lyle Talbot (Grant), Joel Friedkin (Professor Dunham), George Eldredge (Barnes), Rusty Wescoatt (Magruder), Blanca Vischer (Mahara), Pierce Lyden (Allen), John Hart (Guard), Wally West (Henchman), Tamba (Chimp), James Seay (Narrator).

Working title: *Jungle Menace*.

The sixth entry in producer Sam Katzman's "Jungle Jim" series based on the comic strip by Alex Raymond, *Fury of the Congo* is a mundane African adventure yarn whose only genre ingredients are light-skinned natives worshipping a small horse-like creature called an Okongo and Jungle Jim (Johnny Weissmuller) being attacked by a tatty-looking giant spider during a sandstorm. *Variety* found it to be "mediocre filler fare at best." The *Motion Picture Herald* felt it was "largely juvenile in appeal" and *The Hollywood Reporter* commented, "Though slightly under par for the Jungle Jim series, *Fury of the Congo* packs enough excitement and color to please the juvenile and action fans."

Spotting a small plane about to crash on a lake, Jungle Jim (Weissmuller) swims to the rescue of its pilot, Ronald Cameron (William Henry), who tells him he is a territorial police inspector on the trail of missing Professor Dunham (Joel Friedkin), the dean of biochemistry at Cairo University. Dunham is in the Congo doing a study of the Okongo, a combination of antelope and zebra that is worshipped by a local tribe. Going to a nearby village, the two men find it abandoned. When a woman throws a knife at them, they trail her to a cave where they are captured in a net. Leta (Sherry Moreland), the leader of the tribe's women, sets them free and informs them that white hunters have taken their men and forced them to find the Okongo. She leads Jungle Jim and Cameron in search of the tribesmen while at the hunters' camp Grant (Lyle Talbot) and Barnes (George Eldredge) make Dunham process a narcotic derived from glands of the Okongo after it consumes mandro leaves. When Dunham refuses to continue the operation, he is beaten by henchman Macgruder (Rusty Wescoatt). When one of the natives releases a captured Okongo, it kills henchman Allen (Pierce Lyden).

Jim, Cameron and Leta takes refuge from a sandstorm in a rocky area where Jim is attacked by a giant desert spider. After Dunham sabotages the operation by destroying the bottles containing the narcotic, he tries to escape and is shot at by Macgruder but saved by Jim, who leaves him with Cameron and Leta. The professor recognizes Cameron as the leader of the hunters and Leta goes back to her village where the women have armed themselves in preparation for setting their men free. Jim returns to the camp and attempts to let loose the natives but is captured by Cameron and his men and forced to lead the hunters to the main herd of the Okongo. While scouting for the herd from a tree top, Jim manages to escape as the Okongo herd stampedes, the natives rebel and the women arrive to join the fight. Cameron tries to escape but is pursed through a sandstorm by Jim and falls from a cliff to his death. Leta wants Jim to stay with the tribe for a celebration but he departs to lead Professor Dunham out of the jungle.

Two of the most amusing sequences in *Fury of the Congo* involve Jungle Jim's pesky pet chimp, Tamba. In one scene the simian uses a native hatchet to scare off an attacking lion and in another Jim is trying to cross a quicksand pit when the chimp comes swinging along on a vine and knocks him into the quagmire. It takes the jungle man several attempts before he is able to get hold of the vine and pull himself to freedom only to come face to face with a rhino! Actor Paul Marion received on-screen billing but he does not appear in the feature.

The Gamma People

(1956; 76 minutes) PRODUCER: John Gossage. DIRECTOR: John Gilling. SCREENPLAY: John Gossage and John

Gilling. STORY: Louis Pollock. PHOTOGRAPHY: Ted Moore. EDITOR: Jack Slade. MUSIC: George Melachrino. ART DIRECTOR: John Box. SOUND: Peter Davies. COSTUMES: Olga Lehmann. MAKEUP: George Frost. PRODUCTION SUPERVISOR: John Palmer. CONTINUITY: Pamela Davies. ASSISTANT DIRECTOR: Robert Lynn. CAST: Paul Douglas (Mike Wilson), Eva Bartok (Paula Wendt), Leslie Phillips (Howard Meade), Walter Rilla (Dr. Boronski/Dr. Macklin), Philip Leaver (Commandant Colonel Koerner), Martin Miller (Herr Lochner), Michael Caridia (Hugo Wendt), Pauline Drewett (Hedda Lochner), Jackie [Jocelyn] Lane (Anna), Olaf Pooley (Bikstein), Rosalie Crutchley (Frau Bikstein), Leonard Sachs (Telegrapher), Paul Hardmuth (Hans), St. John Stuart (First Goon), Cyril Chamberlain (Graf).

On their way to Salzburg's annual music festival, newsmen Mike Wilson (Paul Douglas) and Howard Meade (Leslie Phillips) find themselves stranded in the tiny country of Gudavia when their train car becomes uncoupled. Commandant Koerner (Philip Leaver) promptly throws them in jail but they are set free on the orders of Dr. Boronski (Walter Rilla), a scientist who controls the country. The journalists are taken to a hotel run by Lochner (Martin Miller) and there they hear his daughter Hedda (Pauline Drewett) play the piano before being bullied by a boy her own age, Hugo Wendt (Michael Caridia). Bikstein (Olaf Pooley), one of Boronski's assistants, asks hotel maid Anna (Jackie Lane) to give the men a written message asking them to save the country's children from his boss. Bikstein is murdered and that night the two foreigners are harassed by zombie-like goons who are called off by Boronski. The next day Koerner takes Mike and Howard to meet Dr. Boronski, whom Wilson recognizes as Dr. Macklin, who disappeared five years before. The scientist-educator tells him he took a new identity when he gave up research involving the study of aging and instead has concentrated on youth in an attempt to increase intelligence. After the two men witness Bikstein's funeral, his widow (Rosalie Crutchley) gives them a journal her husband took from the doctor's laboratory that details his experiments in using gamma rays. Since the scientist has taken control of Hedda in an attempt to make her the greatest piano player in the world, her father attempts to smuggle her out of the country but the plot is found out by Hugo who informs Boronski. While walking in the coun-

Posters for *The Gamma People* (1956).

tryside, Mike runs into Paula Wendt (Eva Bartok), Hugo's sister and the children's tutor, who tells him she works for Boronski as did her late father. After hearing her brother tell the scientist about Lochner's plan, Paula tries to warn the hotel owner but he refuses to listen and the goons kill him and kidnap Hedda. Paula finds Lochner's body and her screams alert Wilson. When he tries to console her, she flees. Wilson meets Boronski and promises him he will write a story about his activities. The scientists sends the goons after Wilson, who manages to escape back to the village and tell the people about Lochner's murder.

Boronski orders Koerner to cancel an impending carnival but the citizens rebel and celebrate. During the festivities, Frau Bikstein takes Wilson to her house where Paula tells him about Hedda being kidnapped and taken to the scientist's castle, where he conducts his gamma ray experiments. After getting away from the police, Mike and Paula are picked up by Howard in an old auto he obtained from Koerner and they drive to the castle. The trio barely manage to escape when the car explodes. Mike sends Howard back to the village for help as he and Paula proceed to the castle where they set Hedda free. As they try to escape, Hans sets off an alarm and Mike, Paula and Hedda are trapped in a control room where Boronski begins bombarding them with gamma rays. Just as they are about to collapse, Hugo has a change of heart and causes the scientist to fall into his lab equipment, starting a fire. Howard and the villagers arrive and fight it out with the goons as Mike leads Paula and Hedda to safety and then returns for Hans. Boronski tries to stop Wilson, who throws him into the flames and escapes with the boy. The goons are killed and the castle burns. Koerner gives Mike and Howard another auto so they can leave the country with Paula, Hugo and Hedda.

Made by Irving Allen and Albert R. Broccoli's Warwick Film Corporation at MGM's British Studios at Elstree in England, *The Gamma People* was first shown there in 1955. When Columbia issued it in the U.S. at the end of 1956, it was cut by three minutes. Stateside it was double-billed with *1984* (q.v.) which co-starred Jan Sterling who was married to Paul Douglas, the star of *The Gamma People*. The miscasting of Douglas is the feature's main drawback; it would have been much better had Brian Donlevy, who was originally signed, to have played the part. For a film with such an austere theme, the movie contains quite a bit of comedy, mainly involving Leslie Phillips' girl-chasing, stiff-upper-lip Britisher and Philip Leaver's bombastic and bumbling commandant. Eva Bartok's role is hazy and rather hard to believe, especially in Paula's original loyalty to Boronski who she knows killed her father. Performance-wise, the film is best served by Walter Rilla as the mad scientist and Michael Caridia as the brainwashed Hugo. While *The Gamma People* captures the smothering atmosphere of an authoritarian state, its admixture of too many plot themes keeps it from building up any real excitement.

The British *Monthly Film Bulletin* thought it "on a distinctly elementary level" while *The Hollywood Reporter* felt it was a "good suspense yarn." Stephen Jones in *The Essential Monster Movie Guide* (2000) noted, "This is an odd blend of political propaganda, spy thriller, science fiction adventure and comedy..." Joe Kane wrote in *The Phantom of the Movies' Videoscope* (2000), "The offbeat tone and cast manage to transform this Poverty Row polemic about Commie brainwashers and their zombie-making machinery into a fairly engrossing item."

Director and co-writer John Gilling (1912–1984) was an old hand at genre efforts having helmed such outings as *Mother Riley Meets the Vampire* (1952), *The Flesh and the Fiends (Mania)* (1960), *The Shadow of the Cat* (1961), *The Night Caller (Blood Beast from Outer Space)* (1965), *The Plague of the Zombies* and *The Reptile* (both 1966), *The Mummy's Shroud* (1967) and *La Cruz del Diablo (The Devil's Cross)* (1975). Composer George Melachrino had a best-selling record in England in 1956 with his Melachrino Orchestra's disk of "Autumn Concerto" on the HMV label.

The Ghost That Walks Alone

(1944; 63 minutes) PRODUCER: Jack Fier. DIRECTOR: Lew Landers. SCREENPLAY: Richard Shattuck, from his story "The Wedding Guest Sat on a Stone." PHOTOGRAPHY: L.W. O'Connell. EDITOR: Jerome Thoms. MUSIC DIRECTOR: M.W. [Morris] Stoloff. ART DIRECTOR: Lionel Banks and Paul Murphy. SOUND: Phillip Faulkner. SETS: George Montgomery. ASSISTANT DIRECTOR: Louis Germonprez. CAST: Arthur Lake (Eddie Grant), Janis Carter (Enid Turner), Lynne Roberts (Sue McGuire Grant), Frank Sully (Beppo), Warren Ashe (Whitney Burke), Arthur Space (Cedric Jessup), Barbara Brown (Milly Westover), Matt Willis (Tom Walker), Ida Moore (Cornelia Coates), Jack Lee (Macy Turner), Paul Hurst (Sheriff Slim Carson), Robert Williams (Lieutenant Phillips), John Tyrrell (Sergeant Hurd),

Walter Baldwin (Deputy Sheriff), John Dilson (Basbom), Vi Athens (Miss Brady), Eddie Bruce (Announcer), Teddy Mangean (Usher), Earle S. Dewey (Sexton).

The title *The Ghost That Walks Alone* is a cheat in that no specter appears in the feature, which is mainly a comedy murder-mystery set in a spooky old lodge. Star Arthur Lake, as Dagwood Bumstead, headlined a similar outing in *Blondie Has Servant Trouble* (q.v.) in 1940. The year before *The Ghost That Walks Alone* was issued, director Lew Landers helmed Columbia's top-notch horror thriller *The Return of the Vampire* (q.v.) which also featured Matt Willis. In that outing, Willis was the pathetic Andreas, a werewolf victim of the bloodsucker, and here he is cast as a sinister caretaker. Don Miller wrote in *B Movies* (1973), "Lake played the role as if it were Dagwood, which may well have been the sole asset of the film — except for Janis Carter — and the winsome Lynne Roberts as the new bride of Lake."

Radio sound effects man Eddie Grant (Arthur Lake) marries Sue McGuire (Lynne Roberts) over the objections of his producer Macy Turner (Jack Lee), who wants him back in the studio for rehearsals since the sponsor is about to cancel their program, "The Tender Hour." The newlyweds go to a country inn owned by Sue's aunt Milly Westover (Barbara Brown) to spend their honeymoon but as they are about to cut the wedding cake, Macy and the show's cast and crew arrive. When the bride objects, Macy derides her and is hit by Eddie. That night Eddie remembers he left the trunk containing his sound effects downstairs and he goes to get it. Upon returning, he finds his bride gone and Macy's corpse in their bed. Eddie seeks the aid of writer Beppo (Frank Sully) and actor Cedric Jessup (Arthur Space) who figure out that the room numbers have been switched and that the corpse was intended for the one occupied by actor Whitey Burke (Warren Ashe). The trio decide to hide the body in the basement but are interrupted by elderly guest Cornelia Coates (Ida Moore) who is sleepwalking. She insists Eddie go with her for a walk and he does as his pals hide the body. When Sue finds out her husband has been out walking with Cornelia, she locks him out of their room. The next day Enid Turner (Janis Carter), Macy's wife, announces that her husband has disappeared. Beppo says he will look for him while Eddie tries to make amends with Sue. Hearing noises from the basement, Eddie, Beppo and Cedric find handyman Tom Walker (Matt Willis) opening the trunk that is supposed to contain Macy's body but it is empty. Cornelia then asks Eddie to go for a carriage ride with her and along the way she informs him she dreamed of seeing a murder and knows the identity of the killer. When Eddie tries to return to the inn, the horses bolt and run away with Cornelia. Getting back, Eddie finds Los Angeles homicide cops Phillips (Robert Williams) and Hurd (John Tyrrell) there. According to the two investigators, Macy's body was found in Eddie's trunk at the city's train station and Eddie is arrested. Trying to get Eddie out of the clutches of the policemen, Sue and her aunt call in local Sheriff Slim Carson (Paul Hurst) and Sue has her husband arrested for desertion. Put in the town lockup, Eddie spies Cornelia ride by in a wagon. Finding his cell door unlocked, he goes back to the inn where Phillips questions the old lady. When Cornelia denies she saw the crime, Sue asks her about the dream. The killer enters her room and Eddie captures the culprit. Cornelia agrees to sponsor "The Tender Hour" and Eddie is not only reconciled with Sue but is also made the program's producer.

The Giant Claw

(1957; 74 minutes) PRODUCER: Sam Katzman. DIRECTOR: Fred F. Sears. SCREENPLAY: Paul Gangelin and Samuel Newman. PHOTOGRAPHY: Benjamin H. Kline. EDITORS: Saul A. Goodkind and Anthony DiMarco. MUSIC: Mischa Bakaleinikoff. ART DIRECTOR: Paul Palmentola. SOUND: J.S. Westmoreland. SETS: Sidney Clifford. SPECIAL EFFECTS: Ralph Hammeras and George J. Teague. PRODUCTION COORDINATOR: Paul Sterling. ASSISTANT DIRECTOR: Leonard Katzman. CAST: Jeff Morrow (Mitch MacAfee), Mara Corday (Sally Caldwell), Morris Ankrum (General Edward Considine), Louis D. Merrill (Pierre Broussard), Edgar Barrier (Dr. Karol Noymann), Robert Shayne (General Van Buskirk), Ruell Shayne [Frank Griffin] (Pilot Pete), Clark Howat (Major Bergen), Morgan Jones (Radar Officer), Robert Williams (State Trooper), George Cisar (Annoyed Passenger), Dabbs Greer (Fighter Pilot), Dan White (Deputy Joe), Fred F. Sears (Narrator).

Working title: *Mark of the Claw.*

Producer "Jungle" Sam Katzman was known for his budget parsimony and nowhere is this more exemplified than with his Clover Productions' *The Giant Claw.* What could have been an entertaining sci-fi programmer about a giant bird from another dimension attacking the Earth was ruined by Katzman's refusal to shell out enough money for decent special effects. Originally Ray Harryhausen was to have used stop-motion models for the title monster but Katzman instead decided to hire an outfit in Mexico for the technical effects and the result was one of the most ridiculous-looking monsters in movie history. The title creature was nothing more than a tatty giant flying buzzard whose appearance literally caused the film to be laughed out of theaters. This is too bad since the rest of the film as directed by Fred F. Sears, who also served as narrator, was an otherwise well-done, suspenseful thriller that played well until the monster shows up, causing audience derision. Columbia released it in the summer of 1957 on a dual bill with another Katzman-Sears collaboration, *The Night the World Exploded* (q.v.).

While conducting calibration tests on radar at the North Pole for the military, civilian electronics engineer Mitch MacAfee (Jeff Morrow) sees a UFO and reports the incident. After landing he is reprimanded by base commander Major Bergen (Clark Howat) for causing a false alarm that resulted in the loss of a surveillance plane and its crew. Bergen then learns a commercial flight has also been lost after the pilot saw a UFO. Mitch and mathematical systems analyst Sally Caldwell (Mara Corday) are flown to New York City and during the flight the pilot (Ruell Shayne) sees a strange object. The plane is attacked and, with the pilot injured, Mitch brings it down near the U.S.–Canadian border. After crash landing, the pilot dies and Mitch and Sally are taken to the home of farmer Pierre Broussard (Louis D. Merrill). During a storm, Pierre tends to his frightened livestock and sees a giant creature that leaves a huge claw track.

On their return flight, Mitch and Sally playfully argue about the supposed UFO until Mitch sees a pattern in the appearances of the object. When a plane carrying Civil Aeronautics Board members is attacked and destroyed by a giant flying bird, Mitch, Sally and General Van Buskirk (Robert Shayne) are flown to the nation's capitol to consult with General Edward Considine (Morris Ankrum). Considine orders the destruction of the creature but finds out that conventional weapons are useless against it. After studying the wrecked planes and feathers from the bird, the group is told by Dr. Karol Noymann (Edgar Barrier) that the creature has an anti-matter screen which can be opened so it can use its wings, beak and claws. He also says the bird is from an anti-matter star system. As the giant flying monster causes destruction throughout the world, martial law is declared. Sally figures out the bird may have a nest on Pierre's farm and she and Mitch get permission from General Considine to investigate. Along with Pierre, they spot the bird at its nest. Mitch and Sally destroy its huge egg and as Pierre tries to get away the monster kills him and attacks a jalopy carrying four teenagers. Back in

Poster for *The Giant Claw* (1957).

Washington, Mitch, Sally and Dr. Noymann work to develop a weapon that will obliterate the bird's shield. With the creature attacking New York City, Considine and Van Buskirk co-pilot a stripped-down bomber carrying Mitch, Sally, Dr. Noymann and the anti-matter shield destroyer. After the bird demolishes the Empire State Building and attacks the United Nations, the generals are able to get it to chase their plane. Mitch sets off the atom ray that obliterates the bird's shield and it is killed with warheads.

Using footage from the previous Columbia releases *Mission Over Korea* (1953) and *Earth vs. The Flying Saucers* (1956) [q.v.], both directed by Fred F. Sears, *The Giant Claw* also included grainy stock scenes for its military and world-wide crowd scenes. In *The Scarecrow Video Movie Guide* (2004), Spenser Hoyt wrote, "*The Giant Claw* features one of the funniest and stupidest movie monsters ever!...The monster is an obvious papier-mâché marionette and gets lots of screen time as it attacks airplanes and chomps on parachuters ... I'm not sure it's intentional, but at times, *The Giant Claw* comes across as an *Airplane!*-style spoof of the '50s monster movie genre."

The Gladiator

(1938; 72 minutes) PRODUCER: David L. Loew. ASSOCIATE PRODUCER: Edward Gross. DIRECTOR: Edward Sedgwick. SCREENPLAY: Charles Melson and Arthur Sheekman. ADAPTATION: Earle Snell and James Mulhauser, from the play by Philip Wylie. PHOTOGRAPHY: George Schneiderman. EDITOR: Robert Crandall. MUSIC: Victor Young and Arthur Kay. SONG: Walter G. Samuels and Charles Newman. ART DIRECTOR: Albert D'Agostino. SOUND: William R. Fox. COSTUMES: Albert Deanno. CAST: Joe E. Brown (Hugo Kipp), Man Mountain Dean (Himself), June Travis (Iris Bennett), Dickie Moore (Bobby), Lucien Littlefield (Professor Abner Danner), Robert Kent (Tom Dixon), Ethel Wales (Mrs. Danner), Donald Douglas (Coach Robbins), Lee Phelps (Coach Stetson), Eddie Kane (Speed Burns), Wright Kramer (Dr. DeRay), Jack Mulhall (Wrestling Spectator), Richard Alexander (Thug), Marjorie Kane (Miss Taylor), Milton Kibbee (Assistant Coach), William Gould (Professor), Harrison Greene (Trophy Presenter), Edward LeSaint, Lloyd Ingraham (Committee Members), Frank Mills (Movie Patron), Charles Sullivan (Football Fan), Harry Semels (Hamburger Vendor), Charles C. Wilson (Theater Manager), Sam Hayes (Announcer), John Shelton (Student).

Philip Wylie's 1930 play was the basis for *The Gladiator*, the first of Joe E. Brown's two genre spoofs for Columbia; it was followed the next year by *Beware Spooks!* (q.v.), with both features being directed by Edward Sedgwick, who helmed the 1920 Fox serial *Fantomas*. Production on *The Gladiator* had to be halted for two weeks when star Brown injured his leg during a football scene. Second-billed, but not seen until near the end of the movie, was legendary professional wrester Man Mountain Dean, whose real name was Frank S. Leavitt. Regarding the feature, the *New York Times* enthused, "Not since Chaplin have we beheld so unbrokenly successful a pattern of pure cinematic clownery, or one that tickled us so hugely.... People who don't like it may insist that the effect of slapstick is always painful, but the pain *The Gladiator* leaves you with is the kind you get from laughing too much."

Forced to leave Webster College at the end of his freshman year due to monetary problems, Hugo Kipp (Brown) works at a children's hospital where he delights the young boys with his storytelling. After he is replaced by a college graduate, the downhearted Hugo finds a woman's purse. When he attempts to return it to her at a movie theater, he has to buy a ticket and wins $1,500 in a drawing. With the money he goes back to Webster and enrolls as a sophomore, taking rooms at a home with Professor Abner Danner (Lucien Littlefield) and his wife Matilda (Ethel Wales). The addled professor is developing a formula to increase strength by abstracting chemicals from insects. Hugo aids coed Iris Bennett (June Travis) when her car runs out of gasoline. Learning that Hugo's father and grandfather were athletic stars at the school, she vamps him into trying out for the football team. The team captain is Iris' boyfriend Tom Dixon (Robert Kent), who is jealous of Hugo, and he gets his teammates to give the newcomer a humiliating workout. After the professor's formula gives a monkey the strength of a gorilla, he tries it on the exhausted Hugo, who becomes superhuman. His abilities impress the team's coach (Lee Phelps) but Hugo fears his strength will hurt others and he refuses to join the squad. Iris then decides to use Hugo's friendship with hospital patient Bobby (Dickie Moore) as a way to get him on the football team. Hugo wins a major game and becomes a national champion. During the prom, the jealous Dixon tells Hugo how he was conned into joining the squad and the disappointed Hugo goes to his room and finds Bobby there, the boy having run away from the hospital in order to avoid being put in an orphanage. Needing $10,000 to adopt the youngster, Hugo agrees to wrestle Man Mountain Dean (himself) but during the third fall of the match the formula wears off and he returns to his normal strength. By using his wits, Hugo is able to win the match and the money which he uses to adopt Bobby. Since the adoption cannot become legal unless Hugo is married, Iris volunteers to become his wife. Hugo kayoes Dixon.

The Golden Voyage of Sinbad

(1974; 105 minutes; Color) PRODUCERS: Charles H. Schneer and Ray Harryhausen. DIRECTOR: Gordon Hessler. SCREENPLAY: Brian Clemens. STORY: Brian Clemens and Ray Harryhausen. PHOTOGRAPHY: Ted Moore. EDITOR: Roy Watts. MUSIC: Miklos Rozsa. ART DIRECTOR: Fernando Gonzalez. SOUND: Doug Turner. MAKEUP: Jose Antonio Sanchez. PRODUCTION EXECUTIVE: Andrew Donaly. PRODUCTION SUPERVISOR: Roberto Roberts. PRODUCTION DESIGN: John Stoll. SETS: Julian Mateos. COSTUMES: Verena Coleman and Gabriella Falk. SPECIAL VISUAL EFFECTS: Ray Harryhausen. SPECIAL EFFECTS ASSISTANT: Manuel Baquero. CONTINUITY: Eva Del Castillo. ASSISTANT DIRECTOR: Miguel A. Gil, Jr. CAST: John Phillip Law (Sinbad), Caroline Munro (Margiana), Tom Baker (Prince Koura), Douglas Wilmer (Grand Vizier), Martin Shaw (Rachid), Gregoire Aslan (Hakim), Kurt Christian (Haroun), Takis Emmanuel (Achmed), John D. Garfield (Abdul), Ferdinado Poggi (Cassim), Aldo Sombrell (Omar), Porfiria Sanchis (Medium), Mario Debarros (Akbar), Juan Majan (Captain of the Guards), Robert Shaw (Oracle), Robert Rietty (Voices).

The Golden Voyage of Sinbad was the second of a trilogy of Sinbad features producer Charles H. Schneer and special effects expert Ray Harryhausen did for Columbia; it was preceded by *The 7th Voyage of Sinbad* (1958) and followed by *Sinbad and the Eye of the Tiger* (1977) [qq.v]. Filmed for slightly under one million dollars, the production visually looks many times more expensive thanks to location shooting on the island of Majorca and in Spain and the river estuary Torrente de Pareis, along with interiors done at the Verona Studios in Madrid. Equally impressive was the full-scale ship John Stoll designed for Sinbad and his crew. Harryhausen's various creatures (a miniature flying homunculus, a ship's living wooden figurehead, the six-armed goddess Kali, a Cyclops centaur and a winged griffin) were also impressive, although not as foreboding as some of his earlier creations. The best visual effect was stunningly sexy leading lady Caroline Munro, who had little to do, but looked fantastic nonetheless. The feature was in production for almost four years with one year needed to complete the special effects. Allegedly Robert Shaw wanted the role of Sinbad but ended up doing a cameo as the Oracle of All Knowledge.

A strange flying reptile-like creature drops a golden amulet on a ship belonging to Sinbad (John Phillip Law) and he wears it as a good luck charm. That night he dreams of a man calling his name and a dancing girl with an eye in the palm of her right hand. He awakens to a terrible storm. After guiding his ship safely into a harbor he swims ashore where he is assaulted by black arts wizard Prince Koura (Tom Baker), who demands the amulet, and his henchman Achmed (Takis Emmanuel). Sinbad outsmarts the assailants and is able to ride into Marabia where he is welcomed by the Grand Vizier (Douglas Wilmer), whose face is covered by a gold mask. He reveals to Sinbad that his face was badly burned in a fire started by Koura, who wants to rule the empire, and that he owns the second of two more amulets needed to find the Fountain of Destiny on Lemuria. He wants to locate the fountain in order to restore his looks, obtain invisibility and endless wealth. Sinbad agrees to aid the Vizier in finding the fountain but Koura uses a flying homunculus to gain knowledge of their plans.

In town, businessman Hakim (Gregoire Aslan) gives Sinbad beautiful slave girl Margiana (Caroline Munro), the girl he saw in this dream, so he will take his indolent son Haroun (Kurt Christian) on the voyage. Koura also hires a ship and, during the voyage, he casts a spell making the wooden figurehead on Sinbad's ship come to life; it is defeated by being pushed into the sea. Koura then has the figurehead resurface and he takes from it Sinbad's map to Lemuria. Each time Koura calls up the powers of darkness for help, he ages; this happens again when he reanimates the homunculus and tells it to trail Sinbad and his crew. Sinbad and the Vizier locate the Temple of the Oracle of All Knowledge where the Oracle (Robert Shaw) tells them to go north to pagan places to find the gold tablet to complete their plan. Koura and Achmed also arrive on the island and the wizard seals the entrance to the temple, trapping Sinbad and his comrades. Sinbad fashions a rope ladder and tries to climb out of the temple but is attacked by the homunculus, which is killed with an arrow by Haroun. Setting his comrades free, Sinbad leads the party inland where they are captured by savages and taken to the temple of the Goddess Kali. There they find Koura trying to locate the third amulet. He causes the Kali statue to come to life and it fights Sinbad and his men with swords. After a long battle, Haroun gets behind the animated statue and pushes it off a pedestal, causing it to crack into pieces, revealing the third amulet. Koura takes the golden talisman as the savages plan to kill Sinbad and his men and to sacrifice Margiana, who has come on the voyage after being set free by Sinbad, to a Cyclops centaur. The monster carries the girl off into the bowels of the caves below Kali's temple as Sinbad tells the Vizier to reveal his scarred face. The sight frightens the savages, and Sinbad and his men fight their way free and descend into the caves in order to save Margiana. As Koura locates the fountain in the caves, Sinbad finds Margiana and starts to fight the centaur who fights with a winged griffin. During the battle, Koura aids the centaur in killing the griffen but Sinbad and his men fight the centaur which Sinbad manages to stab to death. At the fountain, Koura puts the amulet together and obtains renewed youth and the power of invisibility. He and Sinbad then duel with swords but the invisible Koura steps into the waters of the fountain and is seen by Sinbad who kills him, turning the fountain into a font of blood. The crown containing vast riches is found by Sinbad, who places it on the Vizier's head, returning his face to normal. Going back to Marabia, Sinbad tells Margiana she is the treasure he wants.

Variety reported, "An Arabian Nights saga told with some briskness and opulence for the childish eye, yet ultimately falling short of implied promise as an adventure spree…. Good enough conjuring tricks to impress the kids." *Castle of Frankenstein* #21 (1974) noted, "Harryhausen's animation and special effects *look better* in *Golden Voyage of Sinbad* thanks to the most recent technical advancements…. The new RH process is called Dynarama, successor to Dynamation. Consequently, RH's animation/spcl fx now look so much more natural that it's virtually impossible to see any *traveling matte* work." In *Horrors: From Screen to Scream* (1975), Ed Naha called it "one of [Harryhausen's] most spectacular films ever…. It's all swashbuckling stuff done in the grandest of *Thief of Bagdad* styles." Henry Herz and Tony Zaza in *The Family Guide to Movies on Video* (1988) said, "[This] lighthearted and entertaining adventure movie brings a treat for youngsters and those adults who wish to recapture some of the magic of childhood."

Good Times

(1967; 95 minutes; Color) PRODUCER: Lindsley Parsons. EXECUTIVE PRODUCER: Steve Broidy. DIRECTOR: William Friedkin. SCREENPLAY: Tony Barrett. STORY: Nicholas Hyams. PHOTOGRAPHY: Robert Wychkoff. EDITOR: Melvin Shapiro. MUSIC AND SONGS: Sonny Bono. ART DIRECTORS: Hal Pereira and Arthur Lonergan. SOUND EFFECTS: Delmore Harris and Carlo Lodato. SETS: Arthur Krams. COSTUMES: Leah Rhodes. WARDROBE: Forrest T. Butler. MAKEUP: Edwin Butterworth. PRODUCTION MANAGER: Arthur M. Broidy. CHOREOGRAPHER: Andre Tayir. SCRIPT SUPERVISOR: Marvin Weldon. ASSISTANT DIRECTOR: David Salven. CAST: Sonny [Bono] (Himself), Cher [Bono] (Herself), George Sanders (Mr. Mordicus/Knife McBlade/White Hunter/Zarubian), Norman Alden (Warren), Larry Duran (Smith), Kelly Thordsen (Tough Guy), Lennie Weinrib (Leslie Garth), Peter Robbins (Brandon), Edy Williams, China Lee, Diane Haggerty (Mr. Mordicus' Women), James Flavin (Detective), Phil Arnold (Solly), Hank Worden (Kid), Morris Buchanan (Owner), Charles Smith (Telegrapher), John Cliff (Gangster), Herk Reardon, Bruce Tegner (Wrestlers), Richard Collier (Peddler), Howard Wright (Old Man), Joe Devlin (Bartender), Mike Kopach (Deputy), Guy Wilkerson, Holly Bane (Card Playing Deputies), Micky Dolenz (Jungle Gino), Jess Kirkpatrick (Doorman), Paul Frees (Various Voices).

Singers Sonny and Cher (themselves) are married with a successful career but Sonny longs to be a movie star while Cher wants to continue their current entertainment venues. When Mr. Mordicus (George Sanders), a rich film producer, offers the duo a movie contract, Sonny realizes the script is terrible and he has only ten days to remedy the situation. First he fantasizes about being a lawman in the old west with Cher as a dancehall entertainer and Mordicus as a crooked town boss. Sonny then envisions himself as Tarzan, living in the jungle with Jane (Cher) until their tranquility is disturbed by the arrival of a wicked white hunter (Sanders). Another idea Sonny develops is his being a private eye in a case in which he is involved with a gangster's (Sanders) moll (Cher) and a night club singer (Cher). Not wanting to deal with Mordicus, Sonny and Cher turn down his offer of movie stardom and continue with their singing.

Sonny and Cher, a youthful version of Louis Prima and Keely Smith, had a number of hit singles for Atco Records in the mid–1960s. Thanks to their popularity on stage and television, Columbia headlined them in *Good Times*, which came to theaters in the spring of 1967. It was William Friedkin's directorial debut. The soundtrack, issued on Atco (33-214/SD-33-214), included such songs as "I Got You Babe," a number one hit single for the duo in 1965, "It's the Little Things," "Trust Me," "Don't Talk to Strangers," "I'm Gonna Love You," "Just a Name" and the title tune, all composed by Sonny. In addition to nicely showcasing the married stars, the feature also gave George Sanders four different roles, which he handled with his usual finesse.

Writing in the *New York Times*, Richard F. Shepard called *Good Times* a "colorful, sprightly bit of good-humored silliness.... There are lovely little bits of fun sprinkled throughout the reels ... *Good Times* is part-time tongue-in-cheek, part-time beguiling foot-in-mouth. It's a tasty tidbit of entertainment..." In *The Family Guide to Movies on Video* (1988), Henry Herz and Tony Zaza termed it "a cheerful, unassuming little movie."

Largely overlooked today, *Good Times* was a fantasy feature that served as the springboard for the very popular CBS-TV program *The Sonny and Cher Comedy Hour* (1971–74). From 1976 to 1977 the duo headlined *The Sonny and Cher Show* on the same network; in the interim they divorced and each had unsuccessful tries at solo programs.

Gorath

(1964; 83 minutes; Color) EXECUTIVE PRODUCERS: Edward L. Alperson and Tomoyuki Tanaka. DIRECTOR: Ishiro Honda. SCREENPLAY: Takeshi Kimura. STORY: Jojiro Okamai. PHOTOGRAPHY: Hajime Koizumi. EDITOR: Reiko Kaneko. MUSIC: Kan Ishii. PRODUCTION DESIGN: Teruaki Abe and Takeo Kita. PRODUCTION MANAGER: Yasuaki Sakamoto. SOUND: Toshiya Ban. SOUND EFFECTS: Hisashi Shimoaga. SPECIAL EFFECTS: Sokei Tomioka. ASSISTANT DIRECTORS: Koji Kajita, Shoji Kuroda, Masahi Matsumoto and Katsumune Ishida. CAST: Ryo Ikebe (Dr. Tazawa), Yumi Shirakawa (Kiyo Sonoda), Takashi Shimura (Dr. Kesuke Sonoda), Akira Kubo (Tatsuo Kanai), Kumi Mizuno (Ari), Ken Uehara (Dr. Konno), Fumio Sakamoto (Sumio Sonoda), Ko Nishimura (Space Agency Secretary Murata), Keiko Sata (Murata's Secretary), Akihiko Hirata (Captain Endo), Jun Tazaki (Dr. Sonoda), Nadao Kirino (Dr. Manabe), Patrick Allen, Grant Taylor, Masayoshi Kawabe, Yukihiko Gondo, Kenichiro Maruyama (Officials), Kenji Sahara (First Officer Saiki), Nasanari Nihel (Ito), Hiroshi Tachikawa (Wakabayashi), Takamaru Sasaki (Prime Minister Seki), Eitaro Ozawa (Justice Minister Kinami), Akira Yamada, Rinsaku Ogata (Chief Engineers), Yasuo Araki, Toshihiko Furuta (Navigators), Sachio Sakai (Doctor), Ross Benette (Gibson), George Furness (Hooverman), Kozo Nomura, Tomoo Suzuki (Fuel Checkers), Hiroshi Takagi, Ichior Shioji, Yoshiyuki Uemura, Jiro Kumagai, Junichiro Mukai, Yasushi Matsbara (Astronauts), Seizaburo Kawazu (Minister Tada), Ko Mishima (Sinda), Koichi Sato, Koji Suzuki (Pilots), Tadashi Okabe, Wataru Omae (Mathematicians), Ikio Sawamura (Taxi Driver), Eisei Amamoto (Drunk), Joji Uno (Newsman), Yasuhiko Saijo, Kazuo Imai (Radio Operators), Katsumi Tezuka, Osman Yusuf (Workers), Saburo Iketani (Anchorman).

Columbia released *Gorath* in the United States in the spring of 1964, two years after it appeared in its homeland of Japan as *Yosoi Gorasu*. Produced by the Toho Company, the color production was cut by six minutes when shown stateside; a climactic battle with Magma, a giant walrus, was excised from the feature. Originally the huge walrus, portrayed by Haruo Nakajima in a monster suit, was not included in the film's script but producer Tomoyuki Tanaka demanded the movie contain a prehistoric creature. *Videohound's Sci-Fi Experience: Your Quantum Guide to the Video Universe* (1997) said this is "[o]ne of the few Japanese sci-fi flicks you'll see with a display at the Smithsonian Air and Space Museum.... [R]e-edits and clumsy dubbing (half the actors speak with distinct pipes of voiceover artist Paul Frees) lend a tacky feel to this elaborate space-disaster drama." In *Science Fiction* (1984), Phil Hardy compared sci-fi to reality when he noted that the movie "features a convincingly executed space walk three years before Leonov became the first man to leave his spacecraft in flight..."

In 1979, violent weather patterns and strange cosmic activities in the Earth's solar system results in Japan sending a spacecraft to seek out the cause of the problem, a cosmic force they dub Gorath. While scientists believe Gorath is bigger than Earth with 6,000 times its mass, a spaceship under the command of Dr. Sonada (Jun Tazaki) and his assistant, Dr. Manabe (Nadao Kirino), cannot locate the body. Nearing Saturn, they finally see Gorath as a British craft is drawn into its gravitational pull and crashes. The Japanese spaceship is also caught by Gorath but continues to transmit data until it too is destroyed.

With the information provided by the lost ship, Astrophysical Committeemen Dr. Tazawa (Ryo Ikebe) and Dr. Konno (Ken Uehara) announce that the giant space body will collide with the Earth. Dr. Konno wants to send another ship to track the invader but his request is refused due to budget limitations. He and Dr. Tazawa then ask scientist Kesuke Sonoda (Takashi Shimura) to help them figure out a way to save the Earth. Dr. Tazawa has romantic feelings for Kiyo Sonoda (Yumi Shirakawa), the doctor's grandchild. When Kiyo's brother Sumio (Fumio Sakamoto) makes a humorous comment on the crisis, Dr. Tazawa realizes the only way to keep the planet from being annihilated is to change its orbit so as to avoid contact with Gorath or destroy the mass. Thanks to the work of Dr. Tazawa and Dr. Konno, the nations of the world come together and send out another spacecraft to blow up the invader. When it becomes apparent that Gorath is gaining power and cannot be destroyed, Dr. Tazawa devises a plan to construct a large rocket base in the Antarctic that will be used to alter the planet's orbit when the rocket engines are fired. The first test causes an earthquake and the second melts the continent's ice cap. As Gorath nears the Earth, the Moon's orbit is disturbed, and tidal waves and destruction take place all over the globe. The launching of the rockets results in the Earth changing its orbit and Gorath continuing its journey through space.

The Gorgon

(1964; 83 minutes; Color) PRODUCER: Anthony Nelson Keys. DIRECTOR: Terence Fisher. SCREENPLAY: John Gilling. STORY: J. Llewellyn Devine. PHOTOGRAPHY: Michael Reed. EDITOR: Eric Boyd Perkins. MUSIC: James Bernard. ART DIRECTOR: Don Mingaye. SOUND: Ken Rawkins. PRODUCTION DESIGN: Bernard Robinson. PRODUCTION MANAGER: Don Weeks. SPECIAL EFFECTS: Syd Pearson. MAKEUP: Roy Ashton. CONTINUITY: Pauline Harlow. ASSISTANT DIRECTOR: Bert Batt. CAST: Peter Cushing (Dr. Namaroff), Christopher Lee (Professor Karl Meister), Richard Pasco (Paul Heitz), Barbara Shelley (Carla Hoffman), Michael Goodliffe (Professor Jules Heitz), Patrick Troughton (Inspector Kanof), Jack Watson (Ratoff), Prudence Hyman (Megaera), Joseph O'Connor (Coroner), Redmond Phillips (Hans), Jeremy Longhurst (Bruno Heitz), Toni Gilpin (Sascha Cass), Joyce Hernson (Martha), Alister Williamson (Janus Cass), Michael Peake (Constable), Sally Nesbitt (Nurse).

The Gorgon was the fifth of seven feature films in which Terence Fisher directed the popular horror team of Peter Cushing and Christopher Lee. Unfortunately the two stars shared very little screen time together in this eerie tale with its roots in Greek mythology. Its writer John Gilling directed a number of horror films, including *The Gamma People* (1956) [q.v.]. Columbia released the film in the U.S. early in 1964 on a double-bill with *The Curse of the Mummy's Tomb* (q.v.) but it was not until the fall of the same year that this Hammer Films production, lensed at London's Bray Studios, was seen in its homeland. Director Fisher had a long career in horror with Hammer, including *Four Sided Triangle* (1954), *The Curse of Frankenstein* (1956), *Horror of Dracula* and *The Revenge of Frankenstein* (q.v.) (both 1958), *The Hound of the Baskervilles*, *The Mummy* and *The Man Who Could Cheat Death* (all 1959), *The Brides of Dracula* and *The Two Faces of Dr. Jekyll* (*House of Fright*) (both 1960), *The Curse of the Werewolf* (1961), *The Phantom of the Opera* (1962), *Dracula — Prince of Darkness* (1966), *Frankenstein Created Woman* (1967), *The Devil's Bride* (*The Devil Rides Out*) (1968), *Frankenstein Must Be Destroyed* (1969) and *Frankenstein and the Monster from Hell* (1973).

The movie is set in 1910 in the Eastern European hamlet of Vandorf, where seven murders have occurred in the past five years. Artist Bruno Heitz (Jeremy Longhurst) learns from his model Sascha Cass (Toni Gilpin) that she is pregnant with his child. Against her wishes he goes to see her father, innkeeper Janus Cass (Alister Williamson). When the girl follows him, she meets something that causes her death. Her body, which has turned to stone, is brought to the hospital of Dr. Namaroff (Cushing) and is also seen by his assistant, Carla Hoffman (Barbara Shelley). Inspector Kanof (Patrick Troughton) and his men find Bruno's body hanging from a tree and later, over the objections of the young man's father Professor Jules Heitz (Michael Goodliffe), the constable (Michael Peake) rules the case a murder-suicide.

Vowing to clear his son's name, the professor unsuccessfully tries to enlist the aid of Namaroff and then writes to his other son, Paul Heitz (Richard Pasco), who is at the University of Leipzig, asking him to come to Vandorf. That night the professor hears a siren call and goes to the nearby deserted Castle Borski where he is confronted by the ancient Greek Gorgon Megaera (Prudence Hyman). Running back to the village and slowly turning to stone, the professor writes a letter to Paul and asks his valet (Redmond Phillips) to deliver it to him when he arrives in the village. When Paul shows up, Namaroff informs him that his father died of heart failure but Heitz confronts him with the letter. Paul meets Carla and becomes attracted to her and she tells him the spirit of Megaera roams the area. After Namaroff informs Carla, with whom he is in love, that the Gorgon has taken on human form, Paul sees Megaera's reflection in a pool and ends up in the hospital, where he is cared for by Carla. Upon his release, Paul tells Namaroff he plans to find the Gorgon and destroy it and he digs up his father's corpse, proving the body has turned to stone. That night, when Professor Meister (Lee), Paul's mentor, arrives, Heitz tells him what has happened. The two try to see Namaroff but he refuses to talk with them and confronts Carla about having been with Paul the night before. The next morning Paul and Carla have a rendezvous at the castle where she tells him she wants to go away with him but says it will be too late for them if he stays in the village and tries to kill the Gorgon. Meister sneaks into Namaroff's office and finds Carla's records, proving that five years before she was an amnesiac who was treated by the doctor. Meister then tells Paul he believes Carla houses the Gorgon's spirit and Paul decides to send her to Leipzig. Later the police try to arrest Paul for abducting Carla but he manages to escape and goes to the castle, followed by Meister. At the castle, Paul is confronted by Namaroff and the two fight. The doctor dies when he looks upon the Gorgon. Megaera then tries to get Paul to gaze upon her and just as he does, Meister comes up behind the Gorgon and beheads her. Paul turns to stone as he sees the Gorgon's head become Carla.

James O'Neill wrote in *Terror on Tape* (1994) that *The Gorgon* was a "[h]aunting Hammer movie," adding, "One of Fisher's best, most underrated pictures, this is like a monster movie version of *Vertigo*, with its mood of tragic love and thwarted desire.... The one debit: Roy Ashton's low-budget Gorgon makeup." Alan G. Frank in *Horror Movies* (1974) enthused, "Hammer added another 'classic' monster with Terence Fisher's *The Gorgon* ... Filled with chilling menace ... Roy Ashton's makeup for the Gorgon, haloed with a hissing, striking frieze of serpents, made Megaera a true and unique female monster." Regarding the lead players, Robert W. Pohle, Jr., and Douglas C. Hart stated in *The Films of Christopher Lee* (1983), "Lee had one of his best roles as the Van Helsing–like heroic professor, and Richard Pasco (a notable Hamlet for the Bristol Old Vic) and Cushing also made the most of their opportunities. The truly beautiful Barbara Shelley, as the girl who doesn't know she is the title character, gave one of her own best performances of all..."

Hamlet

(1969; 114 minutes; Color) PRODUCER: Neil Hartley. EXECUTIVE PRODUCERS: Leslie Linder and Martin Ransohoff. DIRECTOR: Tony Richardson. SCREENPLAY: Tony Richardson, from the play by William Shakespeare. PHOTOGRAPHY: Gerry Fisher. EDITOR: Charles Rees. MUSIC: Patrick Gowers. SOUND: Tony Jackson. PRODUCTION DESIGN: Jocelyn Herbert. PRODUCTION MANAGER: Gavrik Losey. ASSISTANT DIRECTOR: Andrew Grieve. CAST: Nicol Williamson (Hamlet), Judy Parfitt (Gertrude), Anthony Hopkins (Claudius), Marianne Faithfull (Ophelia), Mark Dignam (Polonius), Michael Pennington (Laertes), Gordon Jackson (Horatio), Ben Aris (Rosencrantz), Clive Graham (Guildenstern), Peter Gale (Osric), Roger Livesey (Lucianus/Gravedigger), John Carney (Player King), Richard Everett (Player Queen), Robin Chadwick (Francisco), Ian Collier (Priest), Michael Elphick (Captain), Mark Griffith (Messenger), Anjelica Huston, Jennifer Tudor (Court Ladies), Bill Jarvis (Courtier), Roger Lloyd-Pack (Renaldo), John Railton (First Sailor), John Trenaman (Barnardo).

William Shakespeare's 1601 tragedy was made by Filmways and Woodfall Film Productions and filmed on the stage of the Round House in London. When released in the U.S. in the fall of 1969 by Columbia, it was sometimes called *Shakespeare's Hamlet*. The play was shortened for the filming with several roles either made smaller or removed. Its inclusion here is naturally due to the appearance of the king's ghost although the specter was only represented by a bright light. Star Nicol Williamson repeated his stage performance where he got far greater critical acclaim than in this somewhat tattered version where he is forced to talk quickly in order to enact as much of the part as possible in a little under two hours. The British release of the production ran three minutes longer than the U.S. version.

Roger Greenspun wrote in the *New York Times*, "The production is full of ideas. [Director Tony] Richardson has photographed his film against total blackness except for a few dark brick walls and passageways to represent the battlements, with only the most essential properties, often in front of his actors' faces. He thus provides a foreground, but very little background. And, because he is at pains to include among the properties a candle flame of greater or lesser brilliance, we have the notion of 'idea' or, more accurately, an emblem for 'idea' as a metaphor for the play. However, the production only succeeds in making it look as if all of *Hamlet* took place at night." F. Maurice Speed in *Film Review 1970–1971* (1970) called the film a "[s]traightforward transference to celluloid of the Round House theatrical production, considerably photographed in close-up and medium shot." *Castle of Frankenstein* #16 (1971) opined, "Hopelessly stagy, dark, dank and dismal Tony

Richardson version looks like it was shot off a rehearsal stage. Nicol Williamson's performance the sole virtue, but film is worse than TV, with fantasy elements completely glossed over."

This was the fourth and final theatrical version of *Hamlet* to be made in the 1960s. West German television did an adaptation of the theatrical work in 1960, produced by Bavaria Athelier and starring Maximilian Schell in the title role. It did not see U.S. theatrical release until 1968 and was missing ten minutes of its original footage. In 1964 Richard Burton starred in Electronovision Productions' filmed interpretation of the New York City stage play directed by John Gielgud; it was distributed by Warner Bros. Two years later the Soviet company Lenfilm made a version of the play with stateside distribution by Lopert Pictures.

Happy Birthday to Me

(1981; 115 minutes; Color) PRODUCERS: John Dunning and Andre Link. ASSOCIATE PRODUCER: Lawrence Nesis. DIRECTOR: J. Lee Thompson. SCREENPLAY: John Saxton, Peter Jobin and Timothy Bond. PHOTOGRAPHY: Michael A. Jones and Miklos Lente. EDITOR: Debra Karen. MUSIC: Bo Harwood and Lance Rubin. PRODUCTION DESIGN: Earl G. Preston. SOUND: Robert Fernandez. MAKEUP: Jocelyne Bellemare. SPECIAL MAKEUP EFFECTS: Thomas R. Burman. SPECIAL EFFECTS: Gilles Aird and Louis Craig. LINE PRODUCER: Stewart Harding. ASSISTANT DIRECTOR: Charles Braive. CAST: Melissa Sue Anderson (Virginia "Ginny" Wainwright), Glenn Ford (Dr. David Faraday), Lawrence Dane (Hal Wainwright), Sharon Acker (Sharon Wainwright), Frances Hyland (Mrs. Howard), Tracy Bregman (Ann Thomerson), Jack Blum (Alfred Morris), Matt Craven (Steve Maxwell), Lenore Zann (Maggie), David Eisner (Rudi), Lisa Langlois (Amelia), Michel-Rene LaBelle (Ethienne Vercures), Richard Rebiere (Greg Hellman), Lesleh Donaldson (Bernadette O'Hara), Earl Pennington (Lieutenant Tracy), Murray Westgate (Gatekeeper), Jerome Tiberghien (Professor Heregard), Maurice Podbrey (Dr. Feinblum), Vlasta Vrana (Bartender), Walter Massey (Conventioneer Leader), Griffith Brewer (Verger), Allan Katz (Ann's Date), Ron Lea (Amelia's Date), Terry Haig (Dr. Feinblum's Assistant), Karen Stephen (Miss Calhoun), Louis De Grande (Surgeon), Nick Kibertus (Anesthetist), Damir Andrei (Second Surgeon), Gina Dick (Ingrid), Stephanie Miller (Nurse), Stephen Mayoff (Policeman), Nancy Allan, Karen Hynes, Tracy-Marie Langston, Debbie McGellin, Kathy Reid, Lori Timmons, Debbie Tull, Lynn Wilson (Cheerleaders), Mark Zilbert (Student), Aram Barkey, Alan Barnett, Paul Board, Marc DeGagne, Bruce Gooding, Victor Knight, Rollie Nincheri, Keith Sutherland, Herbert Vool, Len Watt, Joe Wertheimer (Conventioneers).

Melissa Sue Anderson starred as Mary Ingalls on the popular NBC-TV series *Little House on the Prairie* from 1974 to 1981. Leaving the program, she headlined *Happy Birthday to Me*, one of the many juvenile-oriented blood-and-gore features popular at the time. Thanks to Anderson's TV exposure, veteran Glenn Ford as the co-star and the directorial skills of J. Lee Thompson, the feature proved to be a well-received outing that was a notch above its ilk in plot, production values and execution. *John Stanley's Creature Features Movie Guide Strikes Again* (1994) termed it an "[a]bove average slasher flick.... While this qualifies as an imitation of *Halloween*, it has ingenious twists and turns of its own.... Pseudopsychiatrist (sic) motivations and mental-breakdown nonsense give the film a compelling perversity and sense of madness." *VideoHound's Complete Guide to Cult Flicks and Trash Pics* (1996) called it "[f]airly tame horror." Henry Herz and Tony Zaza in *The Family Guide to Movies on Video* (1988) found it "[s]impleminded ... senselessly nauseating in its gore and violence." That same year, the film's producers John Dunning and Andre Link made a similar entry, *My Bloody Valentine*, and Melissa Sue Anderson co-starred with *The Waltons'* Mary McDonough in the telefeature *Midnight Offerings*.

"The Top Ten" is a select group of teenage girls who attend the Crawford Academy. One of the members, Bernadette O'Hara (Lesleh Donaldson), is attacked by a strangler on her way to meet the others at a local watering hole, The Silent Woman. She manages to escape her attacker only to have her throat cut by someone she recognizes. Tossed out of the tavern for being too noisy, the other girls decide to try to drive over a raised drawbridge but one of them, Ginny Wainwright (Anderson), refuses and runs away, stopping on the way home to see the grave of her mother. Later her father, Hal Wainwright (Lawrence Dane), tells his daughter not to go to the graveyard again because it upsets her. Before going to bed, Ginny sees a peeping Tom, who turns out to be one of her classmates, Ethienne Vercures (Michel-Rene LaBelle). During the dissection of a frog in biology class the next day, Ginny recalls having surgery following an accident that also involved her mother. She talks to psychiatrist Dr. David Faraday (Glenn Ford) about the flashback and he says it is a step in her regaining her memory. After school she is accosted by Ethienne, who has stolen a pair of panties from Ginny's bedroom. Seeing the underwear, the girl walks away. Ethienne is later strangled when the scarf he is wearing is dropped into the operating motor of his cycle by a mysterious figure. Ginny and her friend Ann Thomerson (Tracy Bregman) break into fellow student Alfred Morris' (Jack Blum) house and find what appears to be Bernadette's head, but it turns out only to be a model made by the weird Morris. Another student, Greg Hellman (Richard Rebiere), is murdered while working with weights, and Ginny is held at knifepoint by Rudi (David Eisner) at the academy's chapel campanile. She gets away and goes to see Dr. Farraday and remembers another episode about her brain surgery. On her way home, Ginny is trailed by Alfred, who is stabbed to death.

After a school dance, Ginny invites date Steve Maxwell (Matt Craven) to her house and she prepares a shish kebob; he is skewered with it, causing him to choke. When Ann comes to Ginny's home the next day to find Steve, Ginny has no recollection of seeing him but does have a flashback about the auto accident that killed her mother. When Ginny finds Ann dead in her bathtub with a slit throat, she calls Dr. Farraday. When he arrives at her home, Ginny tells him she killed Ann but the body cannot be found. The doctor forces the girl to recall the events leading up to the accident and she remembers that a half-dozen of her friends were invited to her birthday party but none came because they went to another party. When her upset mother and Ginny are not allowed to attend the other festivities, her mother got drunk and drove them into a river with Ginny managing to escape while her mother drowned. Dr. Farraday is also murdered. When Ginny's father returns for her birthday party, he finds the psychiatrist's body and goes to the graveyard and sees that his wife's body has been removed. In the house where his dead wife once lived, Hal finds the bodies of all the murdered students placed around a table with Ginny carrying a birthday cake. Hal too is murdered but the killer turns out to be Ann, whose father once had an affair with Ginny's mother. As the two girls fight, Ann reveals they are half-sisters and that she committed the crimes to place the blame on Ginny whose birth caused the breakup of her family. Ginny saves her own life by stabbing Ann to death as a cop (Stephen Mayoff) arrives on the scene.

Harvard, Here I Come

(1941; 64 minutes) PRODUCER: Wallace MacDonald. DIRECTOR: Lew Landers. SCREENPLAY: Albert Duffy. STORY: Karl Brown. PHOTOGRAPHY: Franz Planer. EDITOR: William A. Lyon. MUSIC DIRECTOR: Morris Stoloff. ART DIRECTOR: Lionel Banks. DIALOGUE DIRECTOR: Ted Thomas. CAST: Maxie Rosenbloom ("Slapsie" Maxie Rosenbloom), Arline Judge (Francie Callahan), Stanley Brown (Harrison Carey), Don Beddoe (Hypo McGonigle), Marie Wilson (Zella Phipps), Virginia Sale (Miss Frisbie), Byron Foulger (Professor Nickajack Alvin), Boyd Davis (Professor Hayworth), Julius Tannen (Professor Anthony), Walter Baldwin (Professor MacSquigley), Tom Herbert (Professor Teeter), Larry Parks (Eddie Spellman), George McKay (Blinky), John Tyrrell (Slug), Mary Ainslee (Phyllis), Yvonne De Carlo (Bathing Beauty), Jack Mulhall, Charles Ray (Reporters), Lloyd Bridges (Larry), Al Hill (Doorman), Ed Emerson (Mr. Plunkett), Bobby Watson (Horace), Marion Martin (Oomphie), Dan Tobey (Master of Ceremonies), Tommy Seidel (Boy), Harry Bailey (Guest).

In today's society with its over-saturation of political correctness, *Harvard, Here I Come* seems unlikely for revival seeing that its plot labels star Maxie Rosenbloom as the country's number one moron who later endows a "School for Morons" at Harvard while his business partner forms a corporation called "Twenty Million Jerks, Inc." The film's inclusion here comes from the plot ploy of the pointy-heads at Harvard trying to prove Maxie is a throwback to caveman, thus "the missing link." On the plus side, the feature gives the very funny Rosenbloom the leading role and its cast includes future stars Yvonne De Carlo, Larry Parks and Lloyd Bridges as well as silent screen favorites Jack Mulhall and Charles Ray.

The editor of the *Harvard Lampoon*, Harrison Carey (Stanley Brown), gives club owner Maxie Rosenbloom (himself) the Supreme Pediculousness Award; Maxie does not realize it means he has body lice. When newspapers carry the story, Rosenbloom's cashier-general manager, Francie Callahan (Arline Judge), and sports reporter Hypo McGonigle (Don Beddoe), are upset but Maxie takes the insult in stride and decides to enroll at Harvard to get an education. There Rosenbloom comes under surveillance by Prof. Alvin (Byron Fougler), chairman of Antediluvian studies, who feels he might be the missing link. He offers Maxie a stipend plus room and board so he can test him. After accepting the offer, Rosenbloom learns that Hypo has also enrolled on a newspaper scholarship.

Maxie quickly becomes popular with the students, lives in a dormitory, is initiated into a fraternity and wins the affections of scatterbrained but beautiful Zella Phipps (Marie Wilson). Professor Alvin's tests show Rosenbloom is the country's main moron and he is quickly deluged by offers from various firms seeking his endorsement for their wares. After signing with a slick promotion outfit, Maxie wants to open an inn near the campus and asks Francie to run it for him. She arrives, gets her boss out of the contract and forms their own corporation called Twenty Million Jerks, Inc. Maxie breaks up with Zella when he realizes she only wants a college graduate. Turning down Professor Alvin's offer of a special diploma, he opens the inn and announces he will endow a School for Morons at Harvard as Francie and Hypo decide to get married.

The trade paper *Variety* was enthusiastic about the feature while Don Miller in *B Movies* (1973) was the polar opposite. *Variety* called it "a nicely-gaited, screwball comedy geared for maximum of laughs. Almost the entire hokum is constructed around 'Slapsie' Maxie Rosenbloom's manhandling of the English language.... [T]he glib pace director [Lew] Landers maintains, plus snappy editing by William Lyon, make the most absurd developments shape up for chuckles." Miller, on the other hand, said the film was an "abortion ... so completely devoid of laughs, wit or anything remotely resembling a spark of intelligence that one wonders how it passed the outline stage. What could be done with such an atrocity? Adding to its woes, the film had additional dopey lines written for Marie Wilson, which sounded moronic rather than quaint. If a poll were ever taken attempting to discover the most nauseating comedy of all time, *Harvard, Here I Come* would be high on the list."

Have Rocket, Will Travel

(1959; 76 minutes) PRODUCER: Harry Romm. DIRECTOR: David Lowell Rich. SCREENPLAY: Raphael Hayes. PHOTOGRAPHY: Ray Cory. EDITOR: Danny B. Landres. MUSIC DIRECTOR: Mischa Bakaleinikoff. SONG: George Duning and Stanley Styne. ART DIRECTOR: John T. McCormack. SOUND: Howard Lewis. SETS: Darrell Silvera. RECORDING SUPERVISOR: John Livadary. ASSISTANT DIRECTOR: Floyd Joyer. CAST: The Three Stooges [Moe Howard, Larry Fine, "Curly Joe" De Rita] (Themselves), Jerome Cowan (J.P. Morse), Anna-Lisa (Dr. Ingrid Naarveg), Bob Colbert (Dr. Ted Benson), Marjorie Bennett (Mrs. Huntingford), Don Lamond (Narrator/Reporter's Voice), Nadine Ducas (French Girl), Robert J. Stevenson (Robot's Voice), Dal McKinnon (Unicorn's Voice), Hank Bell (Stagecoach Driver Shot in Movie).

Early in 1958, Columbia's television division, Screen Gems, began releasing the studio's theatrical shorts starring the Three Stooges to TV. The films were so successful that within a year the studio had brought back the comic trio (now made up of originals Moe Howard and Larry Fine plus Joe De Rita) to star in the feature film *Have Rocket, Will Travel*, the title being a take-off on the popular CBS-TV western *Have Gun, Will Travel*. Leonard Maltin in *Movie Comedy Teams* (1985) called the film "an entertaining light-comedy vehicle with a topical outer-space theme. It was vastly superior to the Stooges' last shorts, and proved itself at the box office, leading to a string of low-budget comedy features...." Among these were two 1962 Columbia releases, *The Three Stooges Meet Hercules* and *The Three Stooges in Orbit* (qq.v.).

A $10 million rocket launched at the National Space Foundation crashes near the maintenance men's headquarters, waking its janitors Moe (Howard), Larry (Fine) and Curly Joe (De Rita). They rush out to find the rocket as do J.P. Morse (Jerome Cowan), the president of the foundation, scientist Ingrid Naarveg (Anna-Lisa) and Ted Benson (Bob Colbert), a psychologist. Back at the laboratory, Ted asks Ingrid to marry him but she refuses because of her career. Trying to rescue a monkey trapped in the rocket, the janitors cause the craft to tip as they enter it and are stuck inside. After several bumbling misadventures, the chimp communicates with Curly Joe and shows them the way out of the ship. In the laboratory, Ingrid tells the boys they remind her of her janitor father who worked to put her through school. When Morse informs Ingrid that the board may close the project, she breaks into tears and Moe, Larry and Curly Joe decide they must help find a fuel for the rocket. Larry accidentally drinks their concoction, resulting in his breathing fire. Realizing they have found the right formula, the boys pump the fuel into the rocket but end up flooding the laboratory basement when Curly Joe breaks some water pipes. Morse shows up and all of them nearly drown in the basement before they are washed out into the street through the loading dock doorway. Moe, Larry and Curly Joe run to the rocket with Morse in pursuit. The fuel ignites sending the janitors into space.

During the voyage to Venus, the rocket is bombarded by meteors, the boys are forced to deal with weightlessness and Larry accidentally swallows a tube needed to communicate with Earth. Landing on Venus, the trio set out to explore the planet and are chased by a giant, fire-breathing spider. After escaping from it, they rescue a talking unicorn whose horn has become stuck in a rock. The unicorn leads them to a city where a giant square robot with six tentacles and antenna tells them it is the last of its kind after having destroyed its creators and turned them into electrical energy. The robot reduces the boys in size and uses them as models for their exact doubles. After returning them to their original size, the robot gives Moe, Larry and Curly Joe to his creations as playthings but the boys try to escape. When the replicas try to turn the men into energy, they land near the rocket ship and again meet the unicorn. As they attempt to board the craft, the giant spider returns and its flame causes the ship to take off. The boys return to Earth as heroes and are given a ticker tape parade. Honored at a society ball, Moe, Larry and Curly Joe learn that Ingrid and Ted have married and they promise to name their children after the world's first astronauts. At the affair the boys end up causing a fight between a society woman (Marjorie Bennett) and a statuesque blonde (Nadine Ducas), resulting in a free-for-all. As Moe, Larry and Curly Joe escape to a balcony, their duplicates re-appear and join the fray. The boys go back into the peace of outer space in a flying car with Larry and Curley Joe hitting Moe in the face with pies.

During the course of this very amusing feature, the Three Stooges sing the title song "Have Rocket, Will Travel," composed by George Duning and Stanley Styne. Michael J. Weldon noted in *The Psychotronic Encyclopedia of Film* (1983), "[The movie] made millions. Soon there were Three Stooges comic books, stamps, bubble-gum cards ... They starred in five more films." Phil Hardy stated in *Science Fiction* (1984), "Cheaply made and harshly received by the critics, the film ... was a phenomenal success and revived their careers..."

Her Husband's Affairs

(1947; 85 minutes) ASSOCIATE PRODUCER: Raphael Hakim. DIRECTOR: S. Sylvan Simon. SCREENPLAY: Ben Hecht and Charles Lederer. PHOTOGRAPHY: Charles Lawton, Jr. EDITOR: Al Clark. MUSIC: George Duning. MUSIC DIRECTOR: M.S. [Morris] Stoloff. ART DIRECTORS: Carl Anderson and Stephen Goosson. SOUND: Frank Goodwin. SETS: Louis Diage and Wilbur Menefee. COSTUMES: Jean Louis. ASSISTANT DIRECTOR: Earl McEvoy. CAST: Lucille Ball (Margaret Weldon), Franchot Tone (William "Bill" Weldon), Edward Everett Horton (J.B. Cruikshank), Mikhail Rasumny (Professor Emil Glinka), Gene Lockhart (Peter Winterbottom), Nana Bryant (Mrs. Winterbottom), Jonathan Hale (Governor Fox), Paul Stanton (Dr. Frazee), Mabel Paige (Mrs. Josper), Frank Mayo (Vice President Starrett), Pierre Watkin (Vice President Beitler), Carl Leviness (Vice President Brady), Dick Gordon (Vice President Nicholson), Douglas Wood (Tappel), Jack Rice (Slocum), Clancy Cooper (Window Washer), Charles C. Wilson (Police Captain), Charles Trowbridge (Brewster), Selmer Jackson (Judge), Arthur Space (District Attorney), Cliff Clark (Gus), Douglas D. Coppin (Milkman), Virginia Hunter (Miss Hunter), Doris Houck (Secretary), Stanley Blystone (Ike), Fred Miller (Dan), Larry Parks (Himself), Nancy Saunders, Edythe Elliott, Wanda Cantion (Nurses), Harry Cheshire (Mayor Dandy Jim Harker), Gerald Oliver Smith (Harold), Robert Emmett Keane (Cruise Line Manager), Emmett Vogan (Mr. Miller), Fred F. Sears (Mayor's Party Guest), Philip Morris (Mayor's Bodyguard), John L. "Bob" Cason, Sayre Dearing (Hecklers), Mary Field (Hortense), George Douglas, Stephen Bennett (Vice Presidents), Tommy Lee, James B. Leong, Owen Song, H.W. Gim (Acrobats), Fred Howard (Bailiff), Bill Wallace, Russell Whiteman, Chuck Hamilton (Policemen), Eric Wilton (Governor's Butler), Dan Stowell (Willowcombe), Victor Travers (Jury Foreman), Franklyn Farnum (Juror), Buddy Gorman (Youth), Michael Towne (Photographer), Charles Bates, Buz Buckley, Teddy Infuhr, Darryl Hickman (Boys), Charles Williams (Cruise Line Clerk), William Gould (Jailer), Frank Wilcox (Floorwalker), Susan Simon (Girl), George Magrill (Banquet Policeman), Brooks Benedict (Defense Man).

Cornell Pictures' initial production, *Her Husband's Affairs* was a flimsy flick, with a slight fantasy plotline (an addled scientist concocts an embalming fluid that turns corpses into glass but ends up being promoted as a hair remover). Released in November 1947, the feature met with little enthusiasm as noted by the *New York Times*' Bosley Crowther: "Except for occasional incidents which are good for explosive yaks ... the humor is pretty labored, the going pretty rough." In *TV Movie Almanac and Ratings 1958 and 1959* (1958), Steven H. Scheuer termed it "a meaningless little farce." Lucille Ball ended her Columbia contract headlining producer Sam Katzman's *The Magic Carpet* (1951) [q.v.].

Advertising salesman Bill Weldon (Franchot Tone) and his new bride Margaret (Ball) keep postponing their honeymoon because of his job. Just as they are about to finally depart, hat manufacturer Tappel (Douglas Wood) dismisses Bill's advertising slogan for his product so Weldon tries to get Mayor Dandy Jim Harker (Harry Cheshire) to endorse the product but he refuses. Margaret tricks him into saying her husband's slogan and it is picked up by the news media. J.B. Cruikshank (Edward Everett Horton), Bill's boss, upsets

Here Comes Mr. Jordan

(1941; 94 minutes) PRODUCER: Everett Riskin. DIRECTOR: Alexander Hall. SCREENPLAY: Sidney Buchman and Seton I. Miller, from the play *Heaven Can Wait* by Harry Segall. PHOTOGRAPHY: Joseph Walker. EDITOR: Viola Lawrence. MUSIC: Frederick Hollander. MUSIC DIRECTOR: Morris Stoloff. ART DIRECTOR: Lionel Banks. SOUND: George Cooper. COSTUMES: Edith Head. MAKEUP: Robert J. Shiffer. ASSISTANT DIRECTOR: William Mull. CAST: Robert Montgomery (Joe Pendleton/Bruce Farnsworth/Murdock), Evelyn Keyes (Bette Logan), Claude Rains (Mr. Jordan), Rita Johnson (Julia Farnsworth), Edward Everett Horton (Messenger 7013), James Gleason (Max Corkle), John Emery (Tony Abbott), Donald MacBride (Inspector Williams), Don Costello (Lefty), Halliwell Hobbes (Valet Sisk), Benny Rubin (Bugsy), Ken Christy (Chuck), Lloyd Bridges (Pilot Sloan), Warren Ashe (Charlie), William Newell (Murdock), Billy Dawson (Johnny), Joe Hickey (Lou Gilbert), Maurice Costello (Fight Fan), Heinie Conklin, William Forrest, Eddie Bruce (Newsmen), Joseph Crehan (Doctor), Mary Currier (Secretary), Tom Hanlon (Ring Announcer), Chester Conklin, Joe Conti, Gerald Pierce (News Hawks), Edmund Elton (Old Man), John Ince (Collector), Douglas Wood, Selmer Jackson (Board

him by saying Margaret actually sold the account and Weldon tells his bride to stay out of his work. On their way to a travel agency to get tickets for Jamaica, the newlyweds run into Professor Emil Glinka (Mikhail Rasumny), a muddled inventor who wants to borrow money from them to finance his latest scheme, an embalming compound that will turn a body to glass. He also says the fluid will remove whiskers. Bill gets his boss to let him peddle it to shaving cream magnate Peter Winterbottom (Gene Lockhart). To garner publicity for this new product, Bill invites dignitaries to a banquet but his promotion flops when the fluid results in heavy hair growth, giving Mrs. Winterbottom (Nana Bryant) a mustache and the state's governor (Jonathan Hale) a bushy beard. When the enraged woman wants Bill put in jail, Margaret comes to his defense with the suggestion the fluid be used to restore hair. Although he again becomes upset with what he thinks is his wife's meddling, Bill gets the governor to put the product on his bald head, but it turns it to glass. Bill drives to the professor's tool shed laboratory where Dr. Glinka demonstrates his new invention, an elixir that turns flowers into stone. When the police arrive, the scientist manages to escape but Bill is arrested. When a dead body, which the scientist was using in one of his experiments, is found, Bill is accused of Glinka's murder. After the laboratory explodes, Bill gets the professor to remain in hiding so that his trial can be used to promote the new formula. When Bill makes no attempt to defend himself but instead promotes the fluid, Margaret becomes distraught and testifies that he is out of his mind. As the judge (Selmer Jackson) takes the matter of Bill's sanity under advisement, the newlyweds get into a scrap and Margaret whacks her husband with one of the flowers that has turned to stone. She then rounds up Dr. Glinka and brings him to court, causing the trail to be terminated, and then promises to stay out of Bill's promotions.

Poster for *Here Comes Mr. Jordan* (1941).

Members), John Kerns (Sparring Partner), Bobby Larson (Chip), John Rogers (Escort), Bert Young (Taxi Driver), Abe Roth (Referee).

Working titles: *Heaven Can Wait* and *Mr. Jordan Comes to Town.*

A wonderfully humorous fantasy and one of the most popular films of 1941, *Here Comes Mr. Jordan* earned an Academy Award for Sidney Buchman and Seton I. Miller's screenplay and also garnered five other nominations, including Best Picture. Based on Harry Segall's unproduced play *Heaven Can Wait*, it spawned the Columbia sequel *Down to Earth* (1947) [q.v.], in which Edward Everett Horton and James Gleason repeated their roles and Alexander Hall returned as director; it was remade by Paramount in 1978 as *Heaven Can Wait* and again in 2001 as *Down to Earth*. Robert Montgomery was borrowed from MGM to play the leading role of Joe Pendleton.

Boxer-pilot-musician Joe Pendleton (Montgomery) crashes his plane while flying to a match in New York and Messenger 7013 (Horton) takes him to the Pearly Gates to be registered by Mr. Jordan (Claude Rains), who discovers that Joe's spirit was taken from his body before the crash and that he is not entitled to get into Heaven for another 50 years. Messenger 7013 returns Pendleton to the crash site only to find out that Joe's manager, Max Corkle (Gleason), has already had the body cremated. Jordan orders 7013 to find Joe another body and they end up at the mansion of wealthy Bruce Farnsworth (Montgomery), who is about to be drowned by his wife Julia (Rita Johnson) and her lover, Tony Abbott (John Emery). Joe refuses the offer until he sees beautiful Bette Logan (Evelyn Keyes), who has unwittingly been involved by Farnsworth in a securities fraud scheme. Wanting to help the young woman, Joe agrees to the identity switch and Mr. Jordan informs him that while he will have Bruce's body he will retain his own personality. To the surprise of Julia and Tony, Bruce shows up and gets Bette out of jail and pays off all the bad debts credited to her. When he realizes he will not be able to fight for the world's boxing title, Joe asks to be let out of the bargain but changes his mind when Bette re-appears to thank him. Joe instead decides to train for the fight as Farnsworth and gets Max to help him, convincing him of his real identity by playing his favorite song on the saxophone. As Max tries to set up the title match, Julia and Tony plot to again kill her husband and Pendleton is informed he can no longer stay in the body of Farnsworth. Telling Bette not to forget him, Joe is shot by Tony. Now an invisible spirit, Joe watches as Police Inspector Williams (Donald MacBride) interrogates Max, Bette, Julia and Tony about Farnsworth's disappearance. When Pendleton's opponent, Murdock (Montgomery), is shot at ringside for not throwing the fight, Mr. Jordan lets Joe take over his body. The fight resumes and Pendleton ends up winning the title. When he finds out the new champion is carrying a saxophone, Max suspects it was Joe who won the bout. Now as Murdock, Joe informs Max about Farnsworth's murder and he tells Williams where the body is hidden; Julia and Tony are placed under arrest. Mr. Jordan arrives to let Joe know he will permanently be Murdock and removes all memories of Pendleton from his mind. Murdock then asks Max to be his manager. When he meets Bette, who is immediately attracted to him, he asks her for a date.

The *New York Times* called *Here Comes Mr. Jordan* "rollicking entertainment. ... [The writers and director] have had the rare sense to keep the comedy where it belongs — in the characters and situations rather than in a series of double exposures and process shots of ectoplastic spooks.... The performances, with the exception of the distaff side, are tops. Robert Montgomery's dazed prizefighter keeps his place secure as one of the screen's deftest comedians." *Variety* also liked the acting: "Montgomery's portrayal is a highlight in a group of excellent performances. Keyes displays plenty of charm. James Gleason scores as the fast-gabbing fight manager, who is bewildered by the proceedings. Direction by Alexander Hall sustains a fast pace throughout." In *Ghosts and Angels in Hollywood Films* (1994), James Robert Parish called it "[o]ne of the most delightful feature films of the 1940s.... [It] was largely responsible for the wave of ghost pictures with which Hollywood peppered the Forties.... [A] landmark fantasy comedy."

The H-Man

(1959; 79 minutes; Color) ASSOCIATE PRODUCER: Tomoyuki Tanaka. DIRECTOR: Ishiro [Inoshiro] Honda. SCREENPLAY: Takeshi Kimura. STORY: Hideo Unagami. PHOTOGRAPHY: Hajime Koizumi. EDITOR: Kazuji Taira. MUSIC: Masaru Sato. ART DIRECTOR: Takeo Kita. SOUND: Choshichiro Mikami and Masanobu Miyazaki. SPECIAL EFFECTS: Eiji Tsuburaya. PRODUCTION MANAGER: Teruo Maki. ASSISTANT DIRECTORS: Koji Maurata and Yoshio Nakamura. CAST: Yumi Shirakawa (Chikako Arai), Kenji Sahara (Professor Masada), Akihiko Hirata (Inspector Tominaga), Koreya Senda (Dr. Maki), Makoto Sato (Uchida), Yoshifumi Tajima (Detective Sakata), Eitaro Ozawa (Inspector Miyashita), Yoshio Tsuchiya (Detective Taguchi), Kamayuki Tsubono (Detective Ogawa), Tadao Nakamaru (Detective Seki), Nadao Kirino (Shimazaki), Tetsu Nakamura (Mr. Chin), Naomi Shiraishi (Mineko), Minosuke Yamada (Chief Inspector Kusuda), Katsumi Tezuka (Fishing Boat Captain), Hisaya Ito (Misaki), Jun Fujiro (Nishiyama), Hiroshi Akitsu, Yashuhiro Shigenobu (Fishermen), Nasaki Tachibana (Night Club Manager), Ryutaro Amani, Minoru Ito, Toshio Katsube (Detectives), Ichiro Chiba, Jiro Kumagai, Jiro Mitsuaki, Yutaka Oka (GSDF Officers), Miki Hayashi, Aiko Kusama, Shiro Tsuchiya, Mitzuo Tsuda, Soji Ubutaka (Policemen), Kazuo Higata, Keiichiro Katsumoto, Akira Kichoji, Yasuzo Ogawa (Night Club Patrons), Shoichi Hirose (Fireman), Koji Iwamoto (Waiter), Haruya Kato (Mattchan), Shigeo Kato (Matsu-chan), Machiko Kitagawa (Hanae), Mitsu Matsumoto, Matsue Ono (Apartment Neighbors), Ko Mishima (Kishi), Senkichi Omura, Haruo Nakajima (Dissolved Sailors), Toshkio Nakano (Mrs. Okami), Yutaka Nakayama (An-chan), Yosuke Netsuke (Witness), Shin Otomo (Hamano), Yutaka Sada (Taxi Driver), Akira Sera (Horita), Hideo Shibuya, Rioji Shimizu, Yoshiyuki Uemura (Newsmen), Ren Yamamoto (Saeki), Akira Yamada (Officer Wakasugi), Ayumi Sonoda (Dancer Emi), Yoshiko Ieda (Woman).

Columbia issued Toho's *The H-Man* in the spring of 1959 on a double-bill with the British feature *The Womaneater* (q.v.). It ran 79 minutes in the U.S., eight minutes shorter than its original Japanese release the year before as *Bijo to Ekitainingen* (Beautiful Women and the Hydrogen Man). A combination gangster-horror-science fiction affair, it featured some night club sequences with a chorus line of very scantily attired young women that was rather racy for the time. For the U.S. version, the heroine became the wife instead of the mistress of a gangster and many of the voices were dubbed by Paul Frees. Leading lady Yumi Shirakawa warbled two songs in the feature and was dubbed by Martha Miyake in both the Japanese and stateside versions. The title character, the result of H-Bomb testing, was actually a liquid mass that turned into ghost-like creatures that dissolved humans. Producer Tomoyuki Tanaka and director

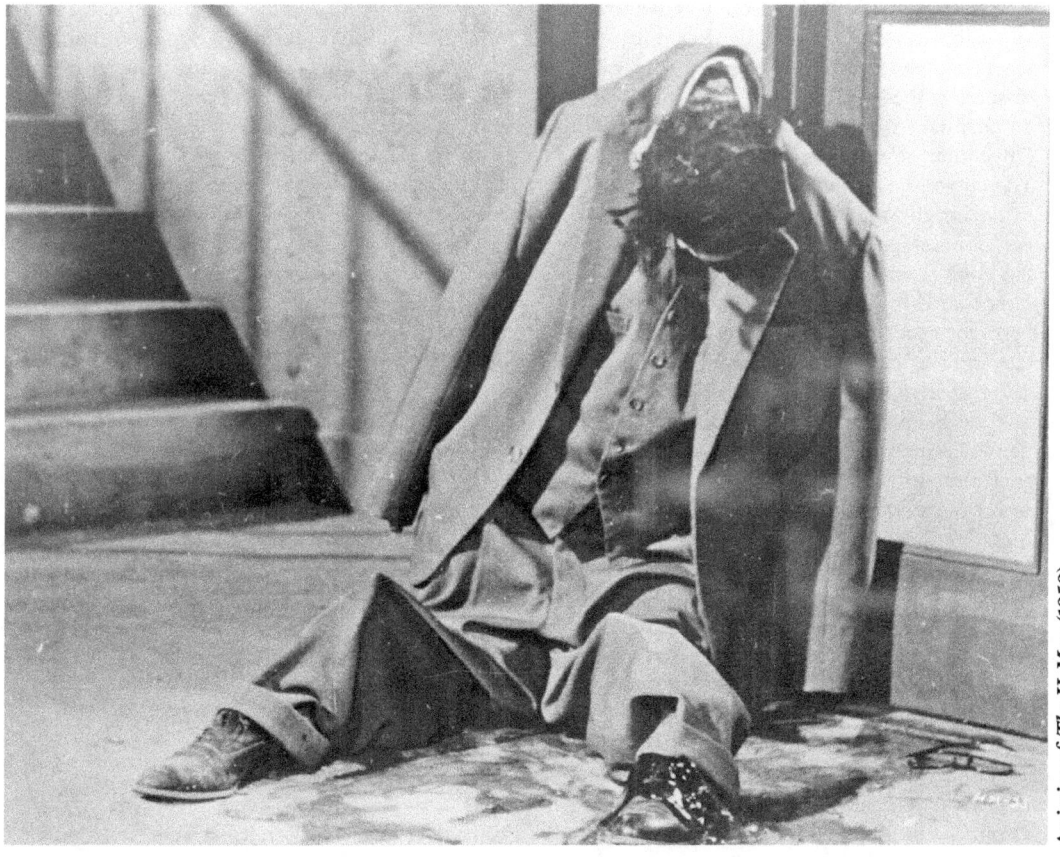

A victim of *The H-Man* (1959).

Ishiro Honda later reworked the plot as *Gas Nigen Daiichigo*, released in the U.S. in 1960 as *The Human Vapor*.

Opening with an atomic blast, *The H-Man* moves to Tokyo where gangster Misaki (Hisaya Ito) attempts to escape with a bag full of heroin only to be hit by a taxi cab and then dissolve, leaving only his clothes and the valise. The police trace the narcotics to gangster Chin (Tetsu Nakamura). The officers find Misaki's wife, night club singer Chikako Arai (Shirakawa) and bring her in for questioning. She claims to know nothing about the heroin and they let her go but plan to use her as bait in capturing her husband. Professor Masada (Kenji Sahara) visits his friend Inspector Tominaga (Akihiko Hirata) and tells him he must find Misaki because he thinks he may have been exposed to a recent H-Bomb test near Christmas Island. The biochemistry professor tells the police he has been studying the effects of nuclear fallout on humans and theorizes a phenomena may have occurred that caused Misaki to dissolve. Although Tominaga is skeptical, he lets the professor question Chikako who is later accosted by another gangster (Jun Fujiro) who also wants to know the whereabouts of her husband. After threatening the singer, the hoodlum leaves and she sees him dissolve in the street. Masada takes Tominaga to a hospital where a fisherman (Yashuhiro Shigenobu) relates how one night his boat found a derelict vessel and boarded it only to be attacked by oozing ghost-like creatures who dissolved several of his shipmates. Masada then produces the log book from the ship showing that six sailors disappeared following the H-Bomb test; he believes their cells were altered, causing them to mutate and become liquid creatures that can reform as transparent figures. Chikako tells Masada she saw the gangster dissolve and asks what is being done to protect the people of Tokyo. He takes her to Tominaga. After Dr. Maki (Koreya Senda), who has conducted experiments on frogs proving Masada's theory, makes his findings public, the young woman agrees to point out the gangsters who frequent the night club where she sings. The police surround the club but a waiter (Koji Iwamoto) alerts hoodlum Uchida (Makoto Sato) and they attempt to escape. The liquid creatures disintegrate the waiter as the gangster leaves behind his own clothes to fool the law. Dr. Maki announces that the two deterrents to the liquid monsters are electricity and fire and he orders gasoline to be poured on the water in the city sewers where the creatures stay. Masada informs Tominaga that Uchida's clothes were not radioactive and that the gangster is still alive. When the professor goes to pick up Chikako, with whom he has fallen in love, he sees her being abducted by Uchida. The gangster forces Chikako to go with him into the sewers to find Misaki's stash of heroin. They locate the narcotics but are hemmed in by soldiers and the crawling slime; he forces the girl to take off her clothes so the police will think she has been dissolved. When the girl's blouse floats out of the sewer, Masada goes underground in search of her just as the military lights the gasoline fires which roars through the sewers. The monsters dissolve Uchida but Masada rescues Chikako and the flames destroy the monsters and part of the city. Dr. Maki warns that if man does not stop nuclear testing, the next rulers of the world may be the H-Men.

Variety said *The H-Man* was "well made" and a "technically excellent production." *Videohound's Sci-Fi Experience: Your Quantum Guide to the Video Universe* (1997) noted, "Genuinely creepy f/x highlight this mixture of two commonly underrated genres of Japanese cinema — science fiction and gangster drama. Though [director] Honda was famous for his giant monster sagas (*Godzilla, War of the Gargantuas,* and many others), he was also adept at these less-epic chillers." Phil Hardy opined in *Science Fiction* (1984), "The plot appears merely as an excuse to string together extraordinary scenes of hallucinatory images as bodies liquefy, enclosed within gelatinous blobs. Such scenes, together with the *film noir* aspects of the gangster plot, make this Honda's most sensual film, a quality not usually associated with his work."

In 1961 the French magazine *Star Cine Cosmos* published a photo novel of *The H-Man* entitled *L'Homme H.*

Homicidal

(1961; 87 minutes) PRODUCER-DIRECTOR: William Castle. ASSOCIATE PRODUCER: Dona Holloway. SCREENPLAY: Robb White. PHOTOGRAPHY: Burnett Guffey. EDITOR: Edwin H. Bryant. MUSIC: Hugo Friedhofer. ART DIRECTOR: Cary Odell. SOUND: Lambert Day. SOUND ENGINEER: Charles G. Rice. SETS: Darrell Silvera. MAKEUP: Ben Lane. ASSISTANT DIRECTOR: Al Shenberg. CAST: Jean Arless [Joan Marshall] (Emily Webster/Warren Webster), Glenn Corbett (Karl Anderson), Patricia Breslin (Miriam Webster), Eugenie Leontovich (Helga Swenson), Alan Bunce (Dr. Jonas), Richard Rust (Jim Nesbitt), James Westerfield (Justice of the Peace Alfred S. Adrims), Gilbert Green (Lieutenant Miller), Wolfe Barzell (Repairman Olie), Hope Summers (Martha Adrims), Teri Brooks (Mrs. Forest), Ralph Moody, Joe Forte (Hotel Clerks), Snub Pollard (Bellhop Eddie), William Castle (Himself/Narrator).

Producer-director William Castle is best remembered for his promotional gimmicks and advertising campaigns for the features he did for Allied Artists, Columbia and Universal in the 1950s and 1960s but in reality he was a very talented craftsman whose association with Columbia Pictures dated back to 1943 when he made his directorial debut with *The Chance of a Lifetime*, a Boston Blackie thriller.

He followed this with a number of solid programmers for the studio, including entries in the Whistler and Crime Doctor series, before going to Universal in 1950 and returning to Columbia in the mid–1950s. With *Macabre* (1958) for Allied Artists, Castle began tying in a gimmick with his films, this one having Lloyds of London insure viewers for $1,000 in case they died of fright from the film. After the hugely successful *House on Haunted Hill* (1959) for Allied Artists, Castle returned to Columbia with *The Tingler* (1959) and *13 Ghosts* (1960) [qq.v], followed by *Homicidal*, a feature often compared to Alfred Hitchcock's *Psycho* (1960).

In a brief epilogue set in Solvang, California, in 1948, two small children have a falling out over a doll. Years later, in Ventura, California, a woman using the name Miriam Webster registers at a hotel where she offers bellhop Jim Nesbitt (Richard Rust) $1,000 to marry her that night with the an immediate annulment. He agrees and at midnight they arrive at the home of justice of the peace Alfred S. Adrims (James Westerfield), who reluctantly carries out the ceremony for a payment of $50. When Antrims attempts to kiss the bride, she stabs him to death and flees in Nesbitt's old car which she soon ditches for another. Later the woman, Emily Webster (Jean Arless), arrives at the home where she lives with her husband Warren, whom she married in Denmark, and his mute, wheelchair-bound ex-nanny Helga Swenson (Eugenie Leontovich). As Emily tells Helga about Adrims' murder, her sister-in-law, the real Miriam Webster (Patricia Breslin), arrives with flowers for Helga from the flower shop her brother purchased for her. Emily asks Miriam to stay with Helga while she goes to Solvang to get

Spanish lobby card for *Homicidal* (1961), Jean Arless and Patricia Breslin in photograph.

a prescription filled at the drugstore owned by Miriam's fiancé Karl Anderson (Glenn Corbett). Emily tries to seduce Karl but is interrupted by the arrival of Dr. Jonas (Alan Bunce). The physician informs them that Helga had once been his nurse and that she delivered Warren and then quit working for him to be the nanny for the infant who she raised in Denmark after his father died.

Going to Miriam's flower shop, Emily destroys several items and a picture of Warren. That evening Karl goes to see Miriam in the shop and, after seeing the destruction, he is clobbered over the head by Emily and is later revived by Warren. Karl asks Warren to keep Miriam at his house that night because of the prowler and after she agrees to stay, they discuss their childhood and their overbearing father who left his $10 million estate to Warren, who will collect it in two days when he becomes 21. That night Miriam wakes up to find Emily in her room. Before leaving, she takes Miriam's doll, the one she and Warren once fought over as children. When Miriam confronts Emily the next morning about the doll, Emily tells her that if she stays in the house any longer, she will kill her. Frightened, Miriam drives back to her shop where he is interrogated by Police Lt. Miller (Gilbert Green). Miller brings along Nesbitt, who fails to identify Miriam as the woman he married. When Karl shows up, Miriam tells him about the policeman and about her name being used by the woman who killed Antrims. Miriam and Karl question Warren about Emily and he admits they are married and he gives Karl a picture of his wife. Karl drives to Ventura with the photo, leaving Miriam at the shop. Emily pays repairman Olie (Wolfe Barzell) two dollars to sharpen her surgical knife but when she appears poised to kill Helga with it, they are interrupted by a visit from Dr. Bunce. Helga tries unsuccessfully to communicate with the physician, and after he leaves Emily murders her. In Ventura, Lieutenant Miller takes Karl to see Nesbitt. Later, Karl calls Miriam, who is with Warren, to tell her that the bellhop identified the photo as that of the woman he married. Warren and Miriam drive to his house but he tells her to remain in the car. Becoming afraid, Miriam goes inside and finds Helga dead, her decapitated head rolling down the stairs. Just then Emily attacks Miriam and she calls for Warren only to have Emily remove her wig, showing that she and Warren are the same person. Saying she will blame Miriam's murder on Emily who will fully become Warren, Emily prepares to stab Miriam but is stopped by the return of Dr. Jonas. As the two struggle, Miriam shoots Emily.

Lieutenant Miller tells Karl, Miriam and Dr. Jonas that Emily was raised as a boy so as not to lose the inheritance, the charade having been carried out by Adrim, who as county clerk signed the birth certificate, and Helga, who raised Emily as Warren. She killed them both to hide the secret and not lose the inheritance, which now belongs to Miriam.

At the film's climax, just as Miriam is about to enter the house, there was a 45-second "Fright Break" enabling patrons to leave the theater if they were too frightened to see the finale. As a further gimmick, Castle offered a full refund to those who left the theatre before the film was over on the condition they walked on a yellow line to the "Coward's Corner" where they had to remain while those who stayed to the finish passed them on the way out. To prevent patrons from staying over and collecting the refund at a second showing, color coded tickets were issued for each performance.

As noted, *Homicidal* was compared to *Psycho*; *Time* magazine proclaimed, "It surpasses *Psycho* in structure, suspense and sheer nervous drive." Certainly the Castle film went a step further than the Hitchcock one in that actress Joan Marshall, billed as Jean Arless, portrayed both Emily and Warren, and the sudden, brutal murder of the justice of the peace was bloodier and more shocking that the shower sequence in *Psycho*. In *The Incredibly Strange Film Book* (1995), Jonathan Ross said, "Bizarre is far too tame a word to describe *Homicidal*. It was insane. Deranged. Fabulous ... [Jean Arless gives] a good, solid and almost convincing dual-performance..."

Arless, under her own name of Joan Marshall, later portrayed Lily Munster in the initial pilot for the CBS-TV series *The Munsters*.

House of Evil

(1978; 89 minutes; Color) PRODUCER: Luis Enrique Vergara [as Henry Berg]. DIRECTORS: Jack Hill and Juan [John] Ibanez. SCREENPLAY: Jack Hill and Luis Enrique Vergara [as Henry Berg]. PHOTOGRAPHY: Raul Dominguez and (uncredited) Austin McKinney. MUSIC: Enrico C. Cabiati and (uncredited) Alice Uretta. ART DIRECTORS: George Mendez and Octavio Ocampo. SOUND: Henrich Henkel, Richard Salder and William Carras. PRODUCTION MANAGER: J.L. Cerrada. PRODUCTION COORDINATOR: William Olivera. SPECIAL EFFECTS: Henry Gordilla. ASSISTANT DIRECTORS: Louis L. Leon and (uncredited) Barry Langley. CAST: Boris

Karloff (Matthias Morteval), Julissa (Lucy Durant), Andres Garcia (Assistant Police Superintendent Charles Beasley), Angel Espinosa (Dr. Emery Horvath), Beatriz Baz (Cordelia Rash), Quintin Buines (Ivar Morteval), Manuel Alvarado (Morgenstern Morteval), Arturo Fernandez (Butler Fodor), Carmen Velez (Girl in Dungeon).

House of Evil was allegedly the last to be completed of a quartet of features Boris Karloff filmed back to back in Hollywood in the spring of 1968 for producer Luis Enrique Vergara. Karloff was paid $100,000 for each film and his scenes were directed by Jack Hill while the films were supposedly finished in Mexico that fall by director Juan Ibanez. Preceded by *The Snake People, Fear Chamber* and *The Incredible Invasion* (qq.vl.), *House of Evil* had brief theatrical showings in U.S. border states in Spanish-language theaters in 1978 as *Serenata Macabre* (Macabre Serenade) but for most viewers it did not surface until the 1980s when Unicorn Video released it under Columbia's U.S. theatrical release title. In 1986 Parasol Video issued a badly cut version of the feature as *Dance of Death*. Like all the Karloff-Vergara collaborations, *House of Evil* had a variety of running times. Its original theatrical release was in Spanish was 93 minutes while the English-language version ran 89 minutes. The Parasol edition has been clocked at both 75 and 82 minutes.

Whatever the running time, *House of Evil* is a sad finale to Karloff's career. It is a monotonous and plodding production with dim photography and bad dubbing. (The star's voice is used in the English-language versions.) The video editions are so badly cut they make little sense. For example, hero Andres Garcia, without explanation, disappears from the side of his fiancée, played by Julissa, ending up in a dungeon with a young woman who appears nowhere else in the film. When the hero manages to escape, he shows up in Julissa's room although in a previous scene she has promised to keep her door bolted. *Psychotronic Video* #5 (1990) called it the worst of the Vergara productions. About the only amusement the film provides is the line, "I'm in perfect health," which Karloff keeps repeating although his character appears to be at death's door.

House of Evil takes place in an unspecified country in 1900 and begins with two men finding the body of a young woman with her eyes plucked out. The action then switches to Morhenge Mansion where Dr. Emery Horvath (Angel Espinosa) informs owner Matthias Morteval (Karloff) that a homicidal maniac is in the area. Matthias has requested that his relatives come to see him and one of them, beautiful Lucy Durant (Julissa), has had her fiancé, policeman Charles Beasley (Andres Garcia), accompany her. Arriving at the mansion, they meet with hostility from the butler, Fodor (Arturo Fernandez), and then join the other relatives, Cordelia Rash (Beatriz Baz), Ivar Morteval (Quintin Bulnes) and Morgenstern Morteval (Manuel Alvarado). All of them are told by Matthias they have inherited the insanity of his late brother Hugo, who became so obsessed with eyes that he plucked out his own. The relatives also learn that Hugo made animated toys for kings and maharajahs that the brothers had the power to make commit murder.

When the villagers bring in Fodor's corpse, Charles is suspected of the crime, and Matthias has a heart attack from the shock and soon dies.

Poster for *House of Evil* (1978).

That night Charles returns to the mansion to check on Lucy but he is captured by the doctor and the servants and placed in a dungeon with a drugged young woman (Carmen Velez). The policeman passes out after drinking from a bottle he finds in his cell. Dr. Horvath informs the relatives that Matthias made a will before his death. After the funeral the next day, Morgenstern goes to his room where he is killed when one of the toy cannons on his dresser fires a bullet into him. Ivar and Cordelia believe the doctor is trying to kill them, but Ivar finds the physician drowned in a well. Cordelia is captured by one of the humanlike dolls and it stabs her to death during a dance. Reviving, Charles is attacked by a group of soldier dolls but escapes and finds that the murdered man is not Horvath. Ivar is murdered by a doll in armor. When it chases Lucy, Charles manages to push it off a balcony. When they investigate, Lucy and Charles find the dying Horvath in the suit of armor. Back in the dungeon, the two see a face mask of Matthias who suddenly reappears and blames Lucy for Fodor's death. Charles tells him that Horvath was the killer since he wanted Matthias' estate. Trapping the young couple in the dungeon with him, the now mad Matthias begins to play the organ, causing flames from wall torches to ignite the place, and all three perish.

The Humanoid

(1979; 100 minutes; Color) PRODUCER: Giorgio Venturini. DIRECTOR: George B. Lewis [Aldo Lado]. SCREENPLAY: Adriano Belzoni and Aldo Lado. STORY: Aldo Lado. PHOTOGRAPHY: Silvano Ippoliti. EDITOR: Mario Morra. MUSIC: Ennio Morricone. ART DIRECTOR: Giacomo Calo Carducci. SOUND: Ugo Celani. SPECIAL EFFECTS: Anthony M. Dawson [Antonio Margheriti]. MAKEUP: Giannetto De Rossi. Production Supervisor: Cecilia Bigazzi. PRODUCTION MANAGER: Viero Spadoni. WARDROBE: Nadia Vitali. COSTUMES: Luca Sabatelli. UNIT MANAGER: Giuliano Principato. CONTINUITY: Flavia Vanin. SECOND UNIT DIRECTOR: Enzo Castellari. CAST: Leonard Mann (Nick), Richard Kiel (Golob), Corinne Clery (Dr. Barbara Gibson), Ivan Rassimov (Lord Graal), Barbara Bach (Lady Agatha), Arthur Kennedy (Dr. Kraspin), Marco Yeh (Tom Tom), Massimo Serato (Great Brother), Kip the Robot (Himself), Steffano Gragnani, Giuseppe Quaglio, Attilio Duse, Vito Fomari, Venantino Venantini.

Filmed in Rome by Maropa Productions and issued as *L'Umanoide* (The Humanoid), this somewhat tongue-in-cheek sci-fi soap opera was released stateside by Columbia Pictures in the summer of 1979 as *The Humanoid*. It was one of many global outings that resulted from the popularity of *Star Wars* (1977). Its theme and international cast was designed to give it worldwide box office potential. For release in the U.S., the distributor emphasized Richard Kiel, the gigantic actor who gained fame in the James Bond adventures *The Spy Who Loved Me* (1977) and *Moonraker* (1979), as well as Corinne Clery, who was also in *Moonraker*, and already established screen favorites Arthur Kennedy and Barbara Bach. Bach, also in *The Spy Who Loved Me*, was very popular in Europe as was top-billed action star Leonard Mann.

In the distant future, the Earth, now called Metropolis, is ruled by the Great Brother (Massimo Serato) but his evil sibling, Mediterranean Lord Graal (Ivan Rassimov), wants to take over. He enlists the aid of mad scientist Dr. Kraspin (Kennedy) who invents a torpedo called the Kappatron that can turn ordinary people into superhuman, killer robots. When space soldier Golob (Kiel) and his pal, a canine robot, attack Kraspin's laboratory, the pilot is subjected to the chemical in the torpedo and changes into a humanoid under the command of Graal. The wicked Kraspin is also engaged in experiments to keep his love Lady Agatha (Bach) eternally youthful by using a device to extract a serum from the bodies of young women. Opposing both tyrants is beautiful scientist Dr. Barbara Gibson (Clarey) and a Tibetan boy mystic, Tom Tom (Marco Yeh), who rallies the citizens of Metropolis as the world is being besieged by the invincible Golob and the superhuman robots. Another space soldier, Nick (Leonard Mann), enters the fray. Eventually the villains are defeated after Golob is again humanized and joins in the fight against them.

Luca M. Palmerini and Gaetano Mistretta's *Spaghetti Nightmares* (1996) featured an interview with veteran director Antonio Margheriti, who did the special effects for *The Humanoid*. He explained, "I tried to get the right effects done properly in five weeks, but the poor characterization of the humanoid represented an insurmountable problem. Also, the film was structured like a poor remake of *Star Wars*, and although [second unit director Enzo] Castellari tried to develop some pretty good duel scenes, the film was basically doomed from the beginning." In *Film Review 1979–1980* (1979), F. Maurice Speed declared it a "science-fiction lark, reminiscent of greater, earlier such spectaculars right down to the comedy robot mascot.... All good, clean, very simple fun!"

Hurricane Island

(1951; 71 minutes; Color) PRODUCER: Sam Katzman. DIRECTOR: Lew Landers. SCREENPLAY: David Mathews. PHOTOGRAPHY: Lester White. EDITOR: Richard Fantl. MUSIC DIRECTOR: Mischa Bakaleinikoff. ART DIRECTOR: Paul Palmentola. SOUND: J.S. Westmoreland. SETS: Sidney Clifford. ASSISTANT DIRECTOR: Paul Donnelly. CAST: Jon Hall (Captain Carlos Montalvo), Marie Windsor (Jan Bolton), Romo Vincent (Jose), Edgar Barrier (Ponce de Leon), Karen Randle (Maria), Jo Gilbert (Okahla), Nelson Leigh (Padre), Marc Lawrence (Angus Macready), Marshall Reed (Rolfe), Don C. Harvey (Valco), Rick Vallin (Coba), Russ Conklin (Owanga), Alex Montoya (Alfredo), Lyle Talbot (Doctor), Rusty Wescoatt (Crandall), Zon Murray (Lynch), Hugh Prosser (Courier), Herman Hack (Sailor), Blackie Whiteford (Helmsman).

In 1513, Spaniard Ponce de Leon (Edgar Barrier) is leading an expedition in the New World when he is shot with a poisoned arrow. Captain Carlos Montalvo (Jon Hall), who is working with de Leon, takes him to a doctor (Lyle Talbot) in Cuba who advises them to seek out the local witch doctor (Rick Vallin) who says the only cure is the golden fountain of youth. Pirate leader Jan Bolton (Marie Windsor) infiltrates the expedition hoping it will lead her to gold. She pretends to be one of several female prisoners sent to help colonize the New World and tries to romance the captain in order to get the map to the fountain. When crew member Jose (Romo Vincent) alerts Montalvo of a nearby pirate ship, the captain sets it on fire as Jane's men, lead by her lover, Angus Macready (Marc Lawrence), escape and then attack the Spaniards. During the battle, Jane gets a gun and tries to make Jose give her the map but she is captured by Montavio and placed in irons. Valco (Don C. Harvey), leader of the local Indians, wants to attack the invaders but he is stopped by Indian princess and high priestess Okahla (Jo Gilbert). The crew members marry the women prisoners and during the celebration the captain brings food to Jane, who had tried to escape. She beings to fall in love with Montalvo who goes into the jungle where he is captured by Valco and his men.

In the Indian village, Valco wants to know the secret of the Spaniards, their guns. Montalvo forms an alliance with Okahla and pretends to shoot her with a firearm; the tribe members then believe their priestess is immortal. In return, Okahla agrees to show Montalvo the fountain of youth as long as he does not try to steal its gold. Valco joins with Macready and the pirates in opposing Okahla and her warriors, the fountain's guardians. Montalvo and Okahla take de Leon to the fountain, whose waters cure him. Valco, Macready and their men attack the fountain and Okahla calls on the god of the winds which causes the Indians to flee. Montalvo and Macready engage in a sword fight with the captain defeating the pirate. As the Spaniards leave the island, Montalvo takes Okahla with them but without the fountain's youth-giving waters she turns into a crone and dies. Ponce de Leon and his expedition leave Hurricane Island, with Montalvo and Jane realizing they are in love.

The *Motion Picture Daily* claimed that *Hurricane Island*'s script "slighted both history and legend." *Variety* said the feature "is a mediocre costume action-drama that drags itself out for 71 minutes. Production values are very light ... Had the script been more adeptly put together and better dialog written for the players it might have had a mild chance for general acceptance in the action-adventure field." In a career article on the film's co-star, Marie Windsor, in *Screen Facts* #16 (1967), Jim Meyer stated, "Aside from much-improved Cinecolor hues, this epic ... had the cast trampling about the Columbia ranch, hopefully got up to resemble the Florida Everglades. The actors toiled hard, as did director Lew Landers, but all were stymied from the start by dizzy dialogue."

I Love a Mystery

(1945; 69 minutes) PRODUCER: Wallace MacDonald. DIRECTOR: Henry Levin. SCREENPLAY: Charles O'Neal. STORY: Carlton E. Morse. PHOTOGRAPHY: Burnett Guffey. EDITOR: Aaron Stell. MUSIC DIRECTOR: Mischa Bakaleinikoff. ART DIRECTOR: George Brooks. SOUND: Edward Bernds. SETS: Joseph Kish. CAST: Jim Bannon (Jack Packard), Nina Foch (Ellen Monk), George Macready (Jefferson Monk), Barton Yarborough (Doc Long), Carole Mathews (Jean Anderson), Lester Matthews (Julian Reeves/Mr. G), Gregory Gaye (Dr. Han), Leo Mostovoy (Vovaritch), Frank O'Connor (Jason Anderson/Peg-leg/The Face), Isabel Withers (Miss Osgood), Joseph Crehan (Captain Quinn), Pietro Sosso (Street Musician/Blind Beggar), Gary Bruce (Intern), Ernie Adams (Morgue Man Gimpy), Carlyle Blackwell, Jr., Kay Dowd (Young Couple), Fred Graff (Reporter Morgan), Cosmo Sardo (Reynolds), Gene Stone (Waiter Sascha), Franklyn Farnum (Reporter), Larry Steers (Diner).

In 1945 Columbia Pictures acquired the rights to the radio show "I Love a Mystery" that was written and directed by Carlton E. Morse. Series stars Jim Bannon and Barton Yarborough were signed to repeat their radio roles in a trio of features, all of which had macabre themes. The initial outing *I Love a Mystery*, released early in 1945, was based on Morse's radio play "The Decapitation of Jefferson Monk." *Variety* called it "a fairly suspenseful low-budget chiller" while Don Miller in *B Movies* (1973) thought it "produced better than average results" and noted "some clever scripting by Charles O'Neal." It was followed by *The Devil's Mask* and *The Unknown* (qq.v.), both 1946 releases.

The decapitated corpse of Jefferson Monk (George Macready), who died in a car wreck, is brought to the San Francisco morgue. Later, at the Silver Samovar night spot, detectives Jack Packard (Bannon) and Doc Long (Yarborough) tell the owner, Vovaritch (Leo Mostovoy), how they became involved in the case. Three nights before at the club, the two sleuths observed a row between Monk and his beautiful companion Jean (Carole Mathews), who he said called him a coward. When a flaming dessert explodes, Monk complains that an unknown person is trying to kill him. After telling Jack and Doc that he will die in three days and that a stranger with a bag big enough to carry his head is after him, Monk convinces the detectives to trail him and Jean when they leave the Silver Samovar. In the fog Jefferson claims he hears footsteps but Jean tells him he is imagining things. A phantom with a hideous face and peg-leg tries to attack Monk but he is frightened away by the arrival of Jack and Doc. Jean disappears.

At Jefferson's home, he tells the detectives he only met the girl that evening and that he lives with his wife Ellen (Nina Foch), who is paralyzed from the waist down. He relates how, a year before, he and Ellen had made a trip to the Orient as a second honeymoon searching for jade and in the mysterious city of Bakaab he heard a strange melody played by a street musician (Pietro Sosso). Upon returning home Monk saw the same man, now a blind beggar, who led him to a hidden monastery where he met Mr. G (Lester Matthews), the high priest of a secret Tibetan society called the Barokan. He was shown the mummified corpse of "The Sacred One," the founder of the cult, dead a thousand years. Since Monk looks

Barton Yarborough, Jim Bannon and George Macready in *I Love a Mystery* (1945).

like the Sacred One, Mr. G offered him $10,000 for his head, which would be used to replace the real one that is decaying. To get away from the place, Monk agreed to the bargain since Mr. G. told him that Ellen was also being held there. Although he was informed by Mr. G that he had only a year to live, Monk disregarded the warning until he started receiving letters counting down to the day of his decapitation. To further add to the prophecy, Ellen lost the use of her legs three days after the receipt of the initial letter.

Monk then introduces Ellen to the detectives; she tells Jack she thinks Jefferson may be contemplating suicide because of remorse over her disability. After the detectives leave Ellen's room, she gets out of her wheelchair and makes a telephone call, and soon her physician, Dr. Han (Gregory Gaye), arrives at the house. He becomes uncomfortable after being interrogated by Han and after he departs, the detective tells Monk he believes the doctor is not Russian as he claims but is Eurasian and may have something to do with Jefferson's troubles. Back at their hotel, Jack informs Doc that he suspects that Ellen may not be a cripple.

The next evening at the Silver Samovar, Doc runs into Jean and is then told by Jack that Monk's father left him two million dollars on the condition he never divorce Ellen. Since he thinks someone is trying to get Jefferson to kill himself in order to get the money, Jack tells Doc they will trail the man that night. Jefferson is followed by the phantom who leaves after a woman screams. The detectives find Jean in a cab and deduce that she did the screaming. After she runs away, the phantom returns to his room where he is murdered. The next day Jack and Doc find Monk in Dr. Han's office undergoing psychotherapy and they inform him of the phantom's death, revealing he was Jean's father. Jack sees antique dealer Justin Reeves (Lester Matthews), whom he believes is not only involved with Ellen, but is also Mr. G. When Jean is found dead, Jack goes to police Captain Quinn (Joseph Crehan) and offers to use himself as bait to trap the killer. After a newspaper story appears saying Jack can identify the murderer, he is allowed to break jail and hides in the Bay Shore Storage Company, owned by Monk. There he tells Doc to send telegrams to Ellen and her nurse, Miss Osgood (Isabel Withers), Dr. Han and Reeves, telling them to meet him at midnight. At the Monk house, the quartet discusses the situation and Ellen exhorts them to carry out their plan so they can collect the inheritance. When Dr. Han and Miss Osgood depart, Justin remains but hides behind a curtain when the suspicious Jefferson visits his wife and accuses her of infidelity. When her husband leaves, Reeves tells Ellen he is getting out of the scheme but as he runs out of the house he is murdered. Jefferson, who finds Ellen standing in her room, tells her he killed her lover and will soon do the same to her and her cohorts. Going to his warehouse, Monk confronts Jack and informs him he found out about the scheme to drive him to suicide by bribing Dr. Han. When he tries to shoot the detective, Jack causes a piano lid to drop on his gun hand and gets away. Doc, who had been knocked out earlier by Jefferson, shows up and Monk gets the drop on him. Jack comes to his rescue and the gunman escapes in a freight elevator and drives away, only to smash into a lamp post. When his body is found, the head is missing. Back at the club, Jack tells Doc and Vovaritch that Ellen, Dr. Han and Miss Osgood will go to jail and ponders what became of Jefferson Monk's head.

El Imperio de Dracula (The Empire of Dracula)

(1967; 85 minutes; Color) PRODUCER: Luis Enrique Vergara. DIRECTOR: Federico Curiel. SCREENPLAY: Ramon Obon, Jr. PHOTOGRAPHY: Alfredo Uribe. EDITOR: Luis Sobreyra. MUSIC: Gustavo Cesar Carreon. ART DIRECTOR: Artis Gener. SOUND: Gonzalo Gavira. PRODUCTION MANAGER: Luis Garcia de Leon. MAKEUP: Armando Islas. ASSISTANT DIRECTOR: Angel Rodriguez. CAST: Lucha Villa (Patricia Brener), Cesar del Campo (Luis Brener), Erick del Castillo (Baron Draculstein), Ethel Carrillo (Diana), Guillermo Zetina (Dr. Wilson), Robin Joyce (Lily), Fernando Oses (Igor), Victor Alcocer (Mr. Brener), Mario Orea (Inspector), Rebecca Ituribbe (Mrs. Brener), Jose Dupeyron (Driver), Atilia Michel, Gigi Monet, Carlos David Ortigoza, Jr., Erick del Castillo, Jr., Judy Ortega.

Another horror film production from Luis Enrique Vergara that Columbia distributed in the U.S. to border state Spanish-language theaters, *El Imperio de Dracula* was allegedly the first Mexican genre outing to be made in color. Its plot was heavily influenced by Hammer Films' *Dracula—Prince of Darkness* (1966) in its story of the vampire (Erick del Castillo), revived by the blood of a woman pouring into his sepulcher, stalking visitors to his remote castle. It was the first of the Vergara-Columbia films helmed by Federico Curiel, who also directed *La Sombra del*

Murciélago (The Shadow of the Bat), *Arañas Infernales* (The Hellish Spiders), both 1968 releases, and *Enigma de Muerte* (Secret of Death) and *Las Vampiras* (The Vampires) [qq.v], both issued in 1969.

Years earlier, Brener (Victor Alcocer) staked vampire Baron Draculstein (del Castillo). On her death bed, his wife (Rebecca Iturbide) begs her now grown son, Luis (Cesar del Campo), to make sure the vampire is not revived. Traveling with his wife Patricia (Lucha Villa) and her sister Lily (Robin Joyce) and friend Diana (Ethel Carrillo), Luis is taken Castle Draculstein by a frightened driver (Jose Dupeyron) and there they meet Igor (Fernando Oses), the caretaker. Igor restores his master, the baron, by killing a young woman whose blood pours into his vault and the vampire begins a reign of terror that includes trying to make the three women his undead brides. When Draculstein attempts to seduce Patricia, Luis saves her by driving the "wooden cross of the Robles" into the bloodsucker, destroying him forever. Luis then hunts down and kills Igor. Using a cross, he also brings about the demise of the lustful Diana, whom Draculstein turned into one of the undead.

In *The Encyclopedia of Horror Movies* (1986), Phil Hardy wrote that *El Imperio de Dracula* "emphasizes eroticism whenever the opportunity arises [The real threat] is most clearly represented, not by the lubricious Count (sic), but by the voracious sexuality of the vampire woman.... [I]t is her sexuality which is presented as the ultimate menace, thus undercutting the implications of the Dracula myth as shaped by Bram Stoker and [Terence] Fisher in Great Britain and substituting a more directly sexual politic relevant to the pathologically macho aspects of Mexican popular culture."

The Incredible Invasion

(1971; 86 minutes; Color) PRODUCER: Luis Enrique Vergara. DIRECTORS: Jack Hill and Juan Ibanez. SCREENPLAY: Karl Schanzer and Luis Enrique Vergara. PHOTOGRAPHY: Raul Dominguez and (uncredited) Austin McKinney. EDITOR: Raul J. Casso. MUSIC: Enrico C. Cabiati. ART DIRECTORS: Jose Mendez and Octavio Ocampo. SOUND: Heinrich Henkel and Victor Rojo. MAKEUP: Tony Ramirez. SPECIAL EFFECTS: Enrique Gordillo. SETS: Raul Cardenas. PRODUCTION MANAGER: Jose Luis Cerrada. DIALOGUE DIRECTOR: Stim Segar. ASSISTANT DIRECTOR: Jose Luis Gonzalez De Leon. CAST: Boris Karloff (Professor John Mayer), Enrique Guzman (Dr. Paul Rosten), Maura Monti (Dr. Isabel Reed), Christa Linder (Laura Mayer), Yerye Beirute (Thomas), Tere Valez (Nancy), Sergio Kleiner (Space Man), Griselda Mejia (Mrs. Anton), Rosangela Balbo (Street Walker), Mariela Flores (Deaf-Mute), Tito Novaro (General Nord), Sergio Virel (Mayor Anton), Victor Jordan, Julian de Meriche (Dignitaries), Jorge Fegan (Officer), Angel D'Estefani (Visitor), Frankestein [Nathanael Leon], Carlos Leon (Villagers), Arturo Fernandez (Peter), Victorio Blanco (Cross Man).

James O'Neill in *Terror on Tape* (1994) called *The Incredible Invasion* "one of the four awful low-budget U.S.-Mexican co-productions the great actor [Boris Karloff] filmed a few months prior to his death in 1969." Regarding Karloff's health status, Michael J. Weldon noted in *The Psychotronic Encyclopedia of Film* (1983), "The ill, 81-year-old horror star is always shown sitting down or leaning against a support of some kind." Columbia Pictures, who co-produced the feature with Azteca Films, distributed it to Spanish-language theaters in the U.S. in 1971; its Mexican title was *Invasion Siniestra* (Sinister Invasion). In 1986, Parasol Video released a truncated version called *Alien Terror*, running 73 minutes. Sinister Cinema issued the film on video as *Sinister Invasion*.

In 1890 in the Central European village of Gutenberg, Professor Mayer (Karloff) works with Dr. Isabel Reed (Maura Monti), whose face has been scarred in a laboratory accident. They are trying to develop a ray gun but the experiment goes awry with a powerful beam shooting through the roof of their lab and into space. A spacecraft from another galaxy intercepts the ray and lands on Earth with an alien (Sergio Kleiner) ordered to destroy the invention before it brings doom to the universe. Sex fiend Thomas (Yerye Beirute) murders a prostitute (Rosangela Balbo) and then confesses the crime to his crippled lover, Nancy (Tere Valez). The alien uses the lovely wife (Griselda Mejia) of the village mayor (Sergio Virel) to aid him in taking over Thomas' mind. Disguised as a gypsy, Thomas goes to Mayer's estate where a group of dignitaries have gathered to watch the scientist demonstrate his new invention. Among those present are government agent Dr. Paul Rosten (Enrique Guzman), the former boyfriend of Laura Mayer (Christa Linder), who lives with her uncle the professor. When Professor Mayer and Dr. Reed show how the ray gun can obliterate a boulder, General Nord (Tito Novaro) wants it for a weapon but Mayer refuses. Laura introduces Paul to her uncle and the scientist invites the young man to stay and work with him and Dr. Reed on the project.

Thomas introduces himself to the professor

and the alien takes over Mayer's mind. Thomas is made the professor's new lab assistant as the aliens make plans to destroy the invention and discredit the scientist. After Paul questions Dr. Reed about Thomas, she goes to the laboratory where she finds a strangely conceived formula. The alien sends Nancy to Thomas and then forces him to kill her. Mayer realizes that both his body and that of Thomas are becoming radioactive and he speeds up plans to destroy the area and its inhabitants. Thomas spies on Laura as she bathes and later comes upon a beautiful blonde deaf-mute (Mariela Flores) whom he strangles. Dr. Reed tries to seduce Paul but he rejects her. When she tries to entice Thomas, he kills her.

Paul confronts Dr. Mayer with the formula that Isabel found but is forced to leave the estate when he learns that the villagers have taken up arms against the scientist. As Mayer tries to regain control of his body, Thomas plans to carry out the destruction of the area but Laura finds Isabel's body. Thomas attacks her but she escapes. Going to her uncle for help, Laura finds out he is in league with Thomas. Paul confronts the villagers, but is forced to flee when they find the body of the murdered mute girl in his wagon. As Thomas tries to strangle Laura, Paul returns to Mayer's house and the two men fight. Mayer regains control of his mind and uses the machine to blind Thomas as the alien takes over Laura's body. The professor tells Paul not to let his niece operate the ray gun. The villagers show up and shoot Thomas. Mayer and Paul strap Laura to a table and the professor uses the ray to burn the alien malignancy out of his niece's brain. The alien leaves Laura's body and Mayer uses his invention to destroy it as well as his home, consuming the ray gun. The space man returns to his craft and goes back into outer space.

The Incredible Invasion was the second of four films Karloff did for Columbia-Azteca to be completed and released theatrically, the first being *The Snake People* (q.v.). Due to the death of producer Luis Enrique Vergara, the other two, *Fear Chamber* and *House of Evil* (qq.v.), were not released until later in the 1970s.

Karloff's scenes for *The Incredible Invasion*

Poster for *Incredible Invasion* (1971).

were filmed at Hollywood's Dored Studios while the rest was shot in Mexico. Some sources claim it is a reworking of the H.P. Lovecraft story "The Whisperers in the Dark." While Karloff is quite good as the scientist and Christa Linder is strikingly beautiful as his niece, the overall production is labored. Far too much time is spent on the activities of the razor-wielding sex fiend portrayed by brutish Yerye Beirute. One of the unintentionally amusing aspects of the plot is having a number of beautiful women lusting for the homely killer. While not as bad as *Fear Chamber* or *House of Evil*, *The Incredible Invasion* must rank as one of Karloff's worst cinema outings.

Invasion U.S.A.

(1952; 73 minutes) PRODUCERS: Albert Zugsmith and Robert Smith. EXECUTIVE PRODUCERS: Joseph Justman and Peter Miller. DIRECTOR: Alfred E. Green. SCREENPLAY: Robert Smith. STORY: Robert Smith and Franz Spencer. PHOTOGRAPHY: John L. Russell. EDITOR: W. Donn Hayes. MUSIC: Albert Glasser. ART DIRECTOR: James Sullivan. SOUND: Frank McWhorter. MAKEUP: Harry Thomas. SPECIAL EFFECTS: Jack Rabin. SETS: John Sturtevant. PRODUCTION MANAGER-ASSISTANT DIRECTOR: Ralph E. Black. CAST: Gerald Mohr (Vince Potter), Peggie Castle (Carla Sanford), Dan O'Herlihy

(Mr. Ohman), Robert Bice (George Sylvester), Tom Kennedy (Bartender Tim), Wade Crosby (Congressman Arthur V. Harroway), Erik Blythe (Ed Mulvry), Phyllis Coates (Mrs. Mulvry), Aram Katcher (Fifth Column Leader), Knox Manning (Himself), Edward G. Robinson, Jr. (Dispatcher), Noel Neill (Ticket Agent), Clarence A. Stoop (Major), William Schallert (Newscaster), Richard Eyer (Boy), Franklyn Farnum (Omaha Man), John Crawford, Jack Lomas (Bar Patrons), Ethan Laidlaw (Russian Sea Captain), Jack Carr, Frank Mills (Plant Workers), Jack Reitzen (Russian), Bert Stevens (Spotter).

Television newsman Vince Potter (Gerald Mohr) interviews a number of people at a New York City bar regarding their opinions on a universal military draft. Cattle rancher Ed Mulvry (Erik Blythe), who is with his wife (Phyllis Coates), dislikes government regulations and exorbitant taxes, while businessman George Sylvester (Robert Bice), who refused to convert his tractor factory to make tanks, feels it is Communistic. A Congressman from Illinois, Arthur V. Harroway (Wade Crosby), announces that the public dislikes Communism but wants to avoid a military conflict with the Soviet Union, while one-time model Carla Sanford (Peggie Castle) complains how factory work during World War II harmed her hands. Another patron, Mr. Ohman (Dan O'Herlihy), states that Americans are blasé and need new leaders. After he leaves, a TV news broadcaster announces that Alaska has been invaded by air and Vince returns to his TV station. It is declared that an atomic bomb has fallen on Alaska and that the government promises to protect and defend its citizens. Vince returns with the news that Washington state has been invaded by a foreign military and that they are moving down the West Coast. Sylvester and Mulvry leave to go home, George to San Francisco and Ed to Arizona. Vince and Carla, who have become romantically involved, remain in the bar as George and Ed take a flight to California. Once there, they find the city under attack by war planes. Sylvester goes to his factory to start making tanks but a fellow traveler (Aram Katcher), working as a window washer, causes trouble among the other workers and blocks his attempt. When the invaders try to make Sylvester help them, he refuses and he is murdered.

Vince decides to join the service and Carla volunteers to become a Red Cross worker. Since more men enlist than there is equipment, Vince is rejected while Ed heads to Arizona by cab, but enemy planes bomb Boulder Dam and he is drowned. Foreign jets attack the Empire State Building and the bartender (Tom Kennedy) is killed while Vince and Carla escape. As Congressman Harroway speaks at the nation's capitol, the invaders arrive and murder the country's elected representatives. Carla listens to a radio broadcast that has been taken over by the Communists who try to force Vince to work for them. When he will not, they shoot him. Carla commits suicide by jumping out of a window to avoid the advances of a lecherous enemy soldier (Jack Reitzen).

Everyone in the bar then comes out of a trance and finds that Ohman, who is really a hypnotist, had put them all under a spell. After buying their drinks, he tells them they have foreseen what will happen if the United States becomes complacent in its fight against Communism. As a result, all the bar patrons agree to work to keep American prepared for a military conflict.

When Columbia issued *Invasion U.S.A.* late in 1952, the Cold War was raging with the United States helping to defend South Korea against North Korean and Red Chinese aggression. On the home front, Joseph McCarthy's Senate committee and the House Committee on Un-American Activities were trying to ferret out Communists stateside. Just as Hollywood produced propaganda films during World War II to fight Fascism, the film capitol was responsible for a number of anti–Communist features like *I Married a Communist* (*The Woman on Pier 13*) (1950) and *I Was a Communist for the F.B.I.* (1951), the latter spawning a same-name radio series starring Dana Andrews and the syndicated TV series *I Led Three Lives* (1953–57), headlining Richard Carlson. The Columbia feature went one step farther and showed what it might be like if the United States was suddenly invaded by a Communist power. The feature neatly interpolated footage supplied by the Atomic Energy Commission and the U.S. military to illustrate the attack on American soil.

As is typical of the *New York Times*, the reviewer complained, "Complacency must be abolished and a warrior's posture assumed. With this premise established, the picture blithely ignores the possibility that peace might be obtained by free strength backing up reason and negotiation, and embarks on a pictorial essay in carnage, devastation, death and spiritual crucifixion ... This frank espousal of raw strength without thought sets it apart from the American heritage of quick thinking and dry powder, in that order."

More in keeping with the feelings of the

time, *Variety* opined, "Columbia has a potent exploitation release.... Idea is spectacularly presented, and Alfred E. Green's direction makes the most of the potential offered in lending credence to the theme.... Startling aspects of the [Robert] Smith screenplay are further parlayed through effective use of war footage.... These scenes, suitably adapted to point up plot motivation, have been subtly edited into the narrative and create a grim realism which should pay off..."

Co-producer Albert Zugsmith had a seesaw career in movies. He produced "A" pictures like *The Tarnished Angels* (1957), *Touch of Evil* (1958) and *Imitation of Life* (1959), as well as the exploitation classic *High School Confidential!* (1958). He produced and directed a number of other features, including *College Confidential* (1960), *Sex Kittens Go to College* and *The Private Lives of Adam and Eve* (both 1960), *Dondi* (1961), *Confessions of an Opium Eater* (1962), and *Dog Eat Dog* (1963), and in the late 1960s and early 1970s he directed a number of sex comedies for Famous Players and other companies.

Island of Doomed Men

(1940; 67 minutes) PRODUCER: Wallace MacDonald. DIRECTOR: Charles Barton. SCREENPLAY: Robert D. [Hardy] Andrews. PHOTOGRAPHY: Benjamin Kline. EDITOR: James Sweeney. MUSIC DIRECTOR: Morris Stoloff. ART DIRECTOR: Lionel Banks. COSTUMES: Kalloch. CAST: Peter Lorre (Stephen Danel), Rochelle Hudson (Lorraine Danel), Robert Wilcox (Mark Sheldon aka No. 64), Don Beddoe (Brand), George E. Stone (Siggy), Kenneth MacDonald (Dr. Rosener), Charles Middleton (Captain Cort), Stanley Brown (Eddie), Earl Gunn (Mitchell), Sam Ash (Ames), Eddie Laughton (Borgo), John Tyrrell (Durkin), Richard Fiske (Hale), Al Hill (Clinton), Bruce Bennett (Guard Hazen), Don Douglas (Justice Department Official), Trevor Bardette (District Attorney), Howard Hickman (Judge), Addison Richards (Jackson/No. 46), Walter Miller (Detective), Raymond Bailey (Killer), Lee Prather (Warden), Forbes Murray (Parole Board Chairman), George McKay (Bookkeeper), Bernie Breakston (Townsend), Harry Strang, Chuck Hamilton (Policemen), Edmund Mortimer (Parole Board Member).

Working title: *Dead Man's Isle*.

Perhaps the most iffy title in this volume is *Island of Doomed Men*, a feature with little horror content. Its main asset is providing Peter Lorre with a sadistic character who beats and works to death parolee slaves, torments his beautiful wife and even shoots and kills his houseboy's pet monkey. To further solidify its horror reputation, the feature was one of 11 Columbia Pictures movies included in Screen Gems' "Son of Shock!" package issued to local television stations in the late 1950s. Co-star Rochelle Hudson finished her 60-plus feature film career in three horror outings, *Strait-Jacket* (1964) [q.v.], *The Night Walker* (1965) and *Dr. Terror's Gallery of Horror* (1967). Columbia reissued *Island of Doomed Men* in 1955, four years before it landed on television.

In Washington D.C., Department of Justice operative Mark Sheldon (Robert Wilcox) meets with an official (Don Douglas) who assigns him the code number 64 and sends him to see another agent at Jackson Securities. There he meets Jackson (Addison Richards), also known as 46, who tells him they are assigned to break up a slave trade operation on a U.S. Pacific island run by Stephen Danel (Lorre), who uses parolees to work his diamond mines. While they are talking, Jack-

Advertisement for *Island of Doomed Men* (1940).

son is shot in the back and Sheldon, mistaken for the murderer, is arrested. Danel, who has an office in the same building, observes the situation. Calling himself John Smith, Sheldon is put on trial, convicted and sent to prison. Believing that Sheldon knows about his operations, Danel gets him released into his custody on Dead Man's Island along with four other prisoners.

Sheldon finds out that Danel lives on the island with his beautiful wife Lorraine (Hudson) and that he is aided by cruel Captain Cort (Charles Middleton), drunken Dr. Rosener (Kenneth MacDonald) and cowardly Brand (Don Beddoe), along with a downtrodden houseboy, Siggy (George E. Stone). The newcomers learn of Danel's brutal ways when Cort kills a fleeing prisoner and they are taken to work on the rock-busting gang and chained in their beds at night. Danel sends for Sheldon and demands to know what Jackson told him. When Mark refuses, Danel tells Cort to torture the information out of the government agent. Lorraine, who hates her husband, tells Siggy to get a message to Sheldon so that she can talk to him. The houseboy delivers the request to the prisoner who is whipped by Cort although he tries to convince the overseer to join him in taking over the island. When Dr. Rosener tends to Sheldon's wounds, the prisoner knocks him out and takes his gun. Danel accuses his wife of falling for the government agent. While Danel, Cort and Brand search for him, Sheldon has Siggy bring Lorraine to him; he tells her to lift her husband's keys so he can get his guns. She begs the prisoner to take her with him when he leaves the island. Smith then lets Cort recapture him and enlists his promise of aid in overthrowing Danel. That night Lorraine takes Danel's keys but he sees her. When she tries to give them to Sheldon, the two are captured by Danel, who sends his wife back to their house; she tells him she will never stop hating him. Danel then turns Sheldon and the traitorous Cort over to Brand. When Brand and a guard (Bruce Bennett) try to lock up the men for the night, the prisoners revolt and Cort takes over, telling Sheldon he will take care of Lorraine. Sheldon manages to crawl through a electrified fence surrounding Danel's house and gets inside where Danel gets the drop on him. Just as Danel is about to shoot Sheldon in front of Lorraine, Cort and the other men show up. Danel shoots Cort but is stabbed in the back by Siggy, who is shot by his boss before he dies. With the parolees set free, Sheldon and Lorraine fly back to the mainland.

The *New York Times* emphasized Lorre's domination of the film: "Always the gentle fiend, Peter Lorre again is offering a study in sadism ... For psychopathic malevolence is his forte and within the routine dimensions of the script Mr. Lorre et al. provide enough vicarious excitement to satisfy the most bloodthirsty of the Globe's patrons." *Variety* noted, "Scare-fodder was the intention of the producers ... but it realizes its purpose only as fare for the extremely young."

It Came from Beneath the Sea

(1955; 79 minutes) PRODUCER: Charles H. Schneer. EXECUTIVE PRODUCER: Sam Katzman. DIRECTOR: Robert Gordon. SCREENPLAY: George Worthington Yates and Hal Smith. STORY: George Worthington Yates. PHOTOGRAPHY: Henry Freulich. EDITOR: Jerome Thoms. ART DIRECTOR: Paul Palmentola. SOUND: J.S. Westmoreland. SETS: Sidney Clifford. SPECIAL EFFECTS: Jack Erickson. SPECIAL TECHNICAL EFFECTS–VISUAL EFFECTS: Ray Harryhausen. UNIT MANAGER: Leon Chooluck. ASSISTANT DIRECTOR: Leonard Katzman. CAST: Kenneth Tobey (Commander Pete Mathews), Faith Domergue (Professor Lesley Joyce), Donald Curtis (Dr. John Carter), Ian Keith (Admiral Burns), Dean Maddox, Jr. (Admiral Norman), Chuck Griffiths (Lieutenant Griff), Harry Lauter (Sheriff Bill Nash), Richard W. Peterson (Captain Stacy), Del Courtney (Assistant Secretary of the Navy Robert David Chase), Tol Avery (Navy Intern), Ray Storey (Newsman), Rudy Puteska (Seaman Hall), Jack Littlefield (Aston), Ed Fisher (McLeod), Jules Irving (King), Sam Hayes (Himself), William Bryant (Helicopter Pilot), Roy Engel (Control Room Officer), William Woodson (Narrator).

Working titles: *The Monster Beneath the Sea* and *Monster of the Deep*.

Double-billed with *Creature with the Atom Brain* (q.v.), *It Came from Beneath the Sea* was issued theatrically by Columbia in the summer of 1955; both features being made by Sam Katzman's Clover Productions. *It* was the initial collaboration between producer Charles H. Schneer and special effects wizard Ray Harryhausen and led to such Columbia releases as *Earth vs. the Flying Saucers* (1956), *20 Million Miles to Earth* (1957), *The 7th Voyage of Sinbad* (1958), *The 3 Worlds of Gulliver* (1960), *Mysterious Island* (1961), *Jason and the Argonauts* (1963), *First Men in the Moon* (1964) and *The Golden Voyage of Sinbad* (1974) [qq.v]. Made on a budget of $150,000, the feature was filmed in a little over a week's time with some on-location work in San Francisco. The highlight of the movie was the giant octopus destroying some of the city,

Unknown, Faith Domergue, Donald Curtis, Kenneth Tobey and unknown in *It Came from Beneath the Sea* (1955).

including a portion of the Golden Gate Bridge. In order to save money, Harryhausen only created a miniature octopus with six arms rather than the normal eight.

The successful testing of an atomic-powered submarine in the Pacific Ocean is interrupted when the vessel comes in contact with a gigantic object that holds it in place.

Commander Pete Mathews (Kenneth Tobey) and Lieutenant Griff (Chuck Griffiths) come to realize that the thing is radioactive and after much maneuvering Mathews is able to get the submarine free. Two divers later find a flesh-like substance attached to the vessel. In Honolulu, Harvard professor Dr. John Carter (Donald Curtis) and Dr. Lesley Joyce (Faith Domergue), an authority on marine biology, examine the substance and after 13 days of testing conclude it was part of a giant octopus. Mathews finds himself attracted to Lesley, who has hidden feelings for Dr. Carter. During a meeting with admirals Burns (Ian Keith) and Norman (Dean Maddox, Jr.) and Assistant Secretary of the Navy Robert David Chase (Del Courtney), the two scientists claim that the Marshall Islands atomic tests caused radioactive fallout in the Mindanao Deep, disturbing the giant creature and causing it to surface in search of prey since its radioactivity causes other sea life to avoid it. The officials scoff at the theory and the two marine biologists are about to leave when word comes that a French ship has been mysteriously destroyed. Some of the survivors are brought to the naval base and questioned but, afraid they'll be called crazy, they refuse to talk. Lesley uses her feminine appeal on one of the men (Rudy Puteska) and records his story of the boat being attacked by the octopus.

The military orders the closing of all Pacific sea traffic. While Carter checks on a lost ship, Mathews and Lesley go to the Oregon coast where fishermen have reported poor catches. After a family and their boat is reported missing near Astoria, the two meet with Sheriff Bill Nash (Harry Lauter) who also scoffs at their tale of a sea monster. After John arrives, the creature rises from the ocean and kills Nash. As a result, the navy mines the coast area. In San Francisco, an electrified net is placed underwater in the bay. The beast, drawn to the city, destroys the net and wraps itself around the Golden Gate Bridge. Panic ensues in the city as the creature's giant arms wreck the area. Mathews and Carter board the submarine, which

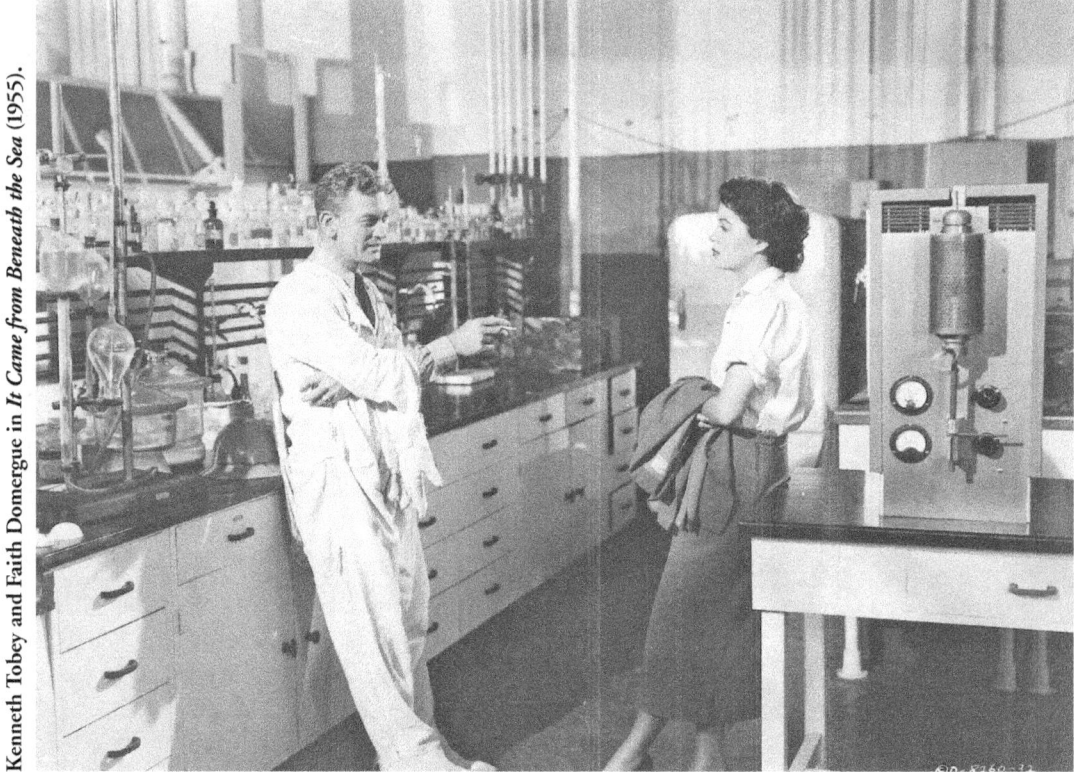

Kenneth Tobey and Faith Domergue in *It Came from Beneath the Sea* (1955).

is armed with a jet-propelled atomic torpedo. The military uses flame throwers to force the creature back into the bay and Mathews hits the beast with the torpedo but it wraps one of his arms around the craft. Donning a diving suit, the commander rams the creature with explosives but is knocked out when they go off. Carter follows him and fires a charge into the octopus' eye, causing it to release the submarine. Once the craft is out of range, Griff follows Mathews' orders and detonates the torpedo which blows the octopus to bits. Mathews and Carter are picked up by the submarine and later, at a night spot, the commander and Lesley cement their romance.

It Came from Beneath the Sea proved to be very popular with sci-fi audiences. The *Motion Picture Herald* opined, "Although not unusually original, it's continuously exciting and the special effects are quite fascinating." Phil Hardy in *Science Fiction* (1984) said that the feature was shot "in the realist manner that dominated American Science Fiction after the success of *Them!* (1954)." James Robert Parish and I noted in *The Great Science Fiction Pictures* (1977), "As in most genre films of the period, there was an implicit message behind the action storyline: a warning against the uncontrolled use of atomic testing." *The Time Out Film Guide* (2001) felt it was a "minor entry in the '50s cycle of radiation-paranoia sci-fi pics" while Spenser Hoyt in *The Scarecrow Video Movie Guide* (2004) claimed it was a "by-the-books giant monster movie ... but it's still memorable for its six-armed octopus.... There's too much stereotypical sci-fi romance (sub captain and hot young scientist) and not nearly enough octopus."

It is interesting that *It*'s finale, with the octopus being speared in order to loosen its hold on the submarine, had been used earlier in *Below the Sea* (1933) [q.v.] when hero Ralph Bellamy carried out a similar action to free a diving bell containing Fay Wray. For its time, the feature also took an fascinating approach to the hinted *menage a trois* relationship between Lesley and the two men in her life.

In 2008, Sony Pictures Home Entertainment released a colorized version of *It Came from Beneath the Sea*.

Jack and the Beanstalk

(1976; 89 minutes; Color) PRODUCER: Katsumi Furukawa and Mikio Nakada. DIRECTOR: Gisaburo Sugli.

ENGLISH-LANGUAGE DIRECTOR-SCREENPLAY: Peter J. Solmo. MUSIC: Takashi Mitsuki, Tadao Inque and Shunichi Tokura. VOICE CAST: Billie Lou Watt (Jack), Jack Grimes (Prince Tulip/Crosby), Corinne Orr (Princess Margaret/Madame Hecuba).

There have been many screen versions of the fairy tale "Jack and the Beanstalk" since Edison first filmed it in 1902, the most noted being the 1952 Bud Abbott–Lou Costello vehicle. Columbia released this animated dubbed version with songs in the U.S. early in 1976 as a kiddie matinee feature; it was produced in Japan by Nippon Herald Films and released there two years earlier as *Jack to mame no ki*. It was subtitled a "Musical Fantasy." Among its forgettable tunes are "Good Old Days Are Here Again," "No One's Luckier Than I," "See the Morning Sunshine" and "Things Are Going to Be All Right."

After being told by his mother to milk the family cow Matilda, young Jack (voice of Billie Lou Watt) finds out that the animal has gone dry and is ordered to sell her to the butcher. Along the way he meets a seller of miracles who trades him a bag of magic beans for the cow. Back home Jack's mother is so angry she whips him with a broom and throws the seeds out of a window. Overnight they grow into a giant beanstalk that reaches beyond the clouds. When he awakes and finds it, Jack is greeted by a mouse who has climbed down the huge vine. He and his dog Crosby follow the mouse up the beanstalk and they go through clouds and find themselves in a castle where they meet the pretty Princess Margaret (voice of Corinne Orr). She tells Jack that her parents were betrayed by a wicked witch and that tomorrow she is to marry the handsome Prince Tulip (voice of Jack Grimes), son of Madame Hecuba (voice of Corinne Orr). When Jack sees a portrait of the ugly prince, he realizes Margaret is under a spell.

The princess takes the boy to meet Madame Hecuba, who gives him a drugged dinner since she plans to eat Jack in order to regain her beauty. When the hulking giant Tulip shows up, he also wants to eat the boy but Jack escapes and finds a room filled with treasure. There a talking harp informs him that the princess' parents were murdered by Madame Hecuba and the girl was put under a spell that has to be renewed daily. The harp also explains that all the people of the kingdom were turned into mice by the witch. The mice want Jack to fight the giant and his mother but he refuses and takes a bag of gold and starts to leave the castle until the sleeping princess calls out his name and asks for help. After being chased by Tulip, the boy climbs back down the beanstalk and returns home with the gold. As he and his mother celebrate their new-found riches, Jack hears Crosby singing and decides to return to the castle and save Margaret. As the wedding ceremony is about to start, the mice mourn but are heartened by the return of Jack and Crosby. The boy forces the harp to reveal that the princess' spell can only be broken when she is kissed by someone who is truly courageous. Jack stops the wedding ceremony and kisses Margaret, bringing her back to reality. When the young girl recognizes Hecuba as the witch who did away with her parents, the evil one orders Tulip to destroy Jack and the princess. They run away and hide in a well. There Jack reveals to Margaret that he took the gold and she tells him it is his reward for saving her. Tulip throws a lance into the well that breaks a rock and causes the water to rise; the two young people are swept back into the castle where they run into Madame Hecuba. The witch orders Tulip to trample them to death but instead he smashes her. The kingdom returns to normal with the mice being transformed back into people. Jack wants Margaret to return with him to his house but she refuses, saying she has obligations to her kingdom and subjects. When Jack and Crosby taunt Tulip, he chases them and they trick the ogre, sending him into the skies. As Jack and Crosby bid farewell to the princess and her subjects, the giant returns and follows them down the vine. When Jack reaches his home, he has his mother bring him an axe and he chops down the beanstalk, hurling Tulip to the ground.

Richard Eder in the *New York Times* complained about the technical aspects of the feature: "The lines are blurry, the colors muddy, and the action is blocklike. When the characters' lips move up and down, the words come out sideways." Somewhat tongue-in-cheek he also noted, "It is the kind of thing grandfathers are sent out to take their grandchildren to. They will sit silently, side by side, and a quiet loathing will spring up between them." Henry Herz and Tony Zaza in *The Family Guide to Movies on Video* (1988) opined, "Its songs are insipid and the animation rather primitive, still it moves along at a lively enough pace and may amuse younger children."

Jason and the Argonauts

(1963; 104 minutes; Color) PRODUCER: Charles H. Schneer. ASSOCIATE PRODUCER-VISUAL EFFECTS CREATOR: Ray Harryhausen. DIRECTOR: Don Chaffey. SCREENPLAY: Jan Reed and Beverley Cross. PHOTOGRAPHY: Wilkie Cooper. EDITOR: Maurice Rootes. MUSIC: Bernard Herrmann. ART DIRECTORS: Jack Maxted, Tony Sarzi Braga and Herbert Smith. SOUND: Cyril Collick and Red Law. PRODUCTION DESIGN: Geoffrey Drake. UNIT MANAGERS: Jimmy Komisarjevsky, Paul Maslansky and Leon Lenoir. CONTINUITY: Phyllis Crocker. TITLE DESIGNER: James Wines. ASSISTANT DIRECTOR: Dennis Bertera. CAST: Todd Armstrong (Jason), Nancy Kovack (Medea), Gary Raymond (Acastus), Laurence Naismith (Argos), Niall MacGinnis (Zeus), Michael Gwynn (Hermes), Douglas Wilmer (Pelias), Honor Blackman (Hera), Jack Gwillim (King Aeetes), John Cairney (Hylas), Patrick Troughton (Phineas), Andrew Faulds (Phalerus), Nigel Green (Hercules), John Crawford (Polydeuces), Davina Taylor (Briseis), Aldo Cristiana (Lynceus), Doug Robinson (Eupaemus), Ennio Antonelli (Ship's Drummer), Tim Turner (Voice of Jason).

Working title: *Jason and the Golden Fleece.*

More than two years in production, *Jason and the Argonauts* was another collaboration between producer Charles H. Schneer and special effects wizard Ray Harryhausen, who claimed the feature was his favorite of more than a dozen such outings for which he created some of the screen's most remembered monsters. For this affair he came up with memorable special effects such as the giant bronze Talos, two pesky and mean-spirited Harpies, the colossal sea god Neptune, a seven-headed Hydra and an army of sword-wielding skeletons. Although somewhat slow in parts, overall the film was colorful and very exciting.

Production began in the fall of 1961 with interior work at the Safa Palatino Studios in Rome. Exteriors were lensed along the sea coast south of Naples in Palinuro. The scenes with the Harpies were done at the site of Paestum's Roman temples. The location filming took around nine weeks and then the filmmakers moved to Shepperton Studios in London where Harryhausen created the movie's visual effects. He spent more than one year working on the production; the scenes with the battling skeletons alone took over four months. Also very complicated was the filming of the fight with the seven-headed Hydra because in every frame each head had to be moved a millimeter and the direction of heads had to be calculated and remembered in conjunction with the movements of the other heads.

Released in the summer of 1963, the feature began with Hermes (Michael Gwynn) predicting that the Greek gods would permit Pelias (Douglas Wilmer) to take over Thessaly by killing his half-brother King Aeson, but that Aeson's children would recover the kingdom from him. Pelias vows to kill all three of Aeson's offspring. After murdering his half-brother, he stabs his niece Briseis (Davina Taylor), who has prayed to Hera (Honor Blackman), the wife of Zeus (Niall MacGinnis). Hera tells Pelias the gods have abandoned him and that in the future Jason will take revenge on him. Zeus then permits Hera to help Jason five times in his attempt to overthrow his uncle.

Twenty years later, Hera causes Pelias' horse to bolt near a river and he nearly drowns before being saved by Jason (Todd Armstrong), who does not know the man is the uncle he vowed to kill. Jason tells Pelias he wants to find the mythical Golden Fleece that has the power to heal, bring peace and end famine. Not revealing himself, Pelias hopes to get Jason out of the way by urging him to follow his dream. Hermes takes the young man to Mount Olympus where Hera tells him he must search in the land of Colchis at the end of the world. Back in Greece, games are arranged and the winners form the crew of the ship that Jason will command. Joining him are Hercules (Nigel Green) and Hylas (John Cairney), who has defeated the strongman in a discus throw. Also among the crew is Acastus (Gary Raymond), Pelias' son, who has been sent by his father to prevent Jason from obtaining the Golden Fleece. Shipbuilder Argos (Laurence Naismith) constructs the craft containing a figurehead of Hera and Jason dubs it the *Argos*. After sailing for some time, the water supply runs low and Jason prays to Hera who tells him to steer north to the Isle of Bronze. There Hercules takes a golden weapon and this awakens a giant Titan named Talos, who tears up the ship. Again turning to Hera, Jason learns that the Titan's weakness is in his ankles and he manages to pry open a portal there, releasing the bronze creature's liquid of life. It cracks and falls apart, killing Hylas as it collapses.

While Hercules stays on the isle trying to find his dead friend, the Argonauts set sail again. Hera gives Jason orders to find the blind prophet Phineas (Patrick Troughton), who is being harassed by two flying Harpies. Before Phineas will give the Argonauts directions to Colchis, he makes them promise to seize the Harpies and they do so by capturing them in a net and putting them in a cage. Phineas informs Jason that the route he must take will go through clashing rocks. During the voyage, an avalanche almost destroys the *Argos* until the giant sea god Neptune arises and holds back the cliffs so the ship can pass safely. Later the men find a wrecked boat and rescue the beautiful Medea (Nancy Kovack). Jason and Acastus fight and the latter jumps overboard followed by Eupaemus (Doug Robinson), whom he kills. On Colchis, Jason meets with King Aeetes (Jack Gwillim), Medea's father, who gives a feast for the Argonauts. During the festivities, the king turns on Jason and announces he will not give up the Golden Fleece. The king has all the Argonauts put in prison, their plan having been revealed to him by Acastus. Medea comes to Jason, whom her father has condemned to death, and frees him and his men and goes with them in search of their quest. When Aeetes realizes either Acastus or Medea betrayed him, he and his soldiers follow the Argonauts as Acastus finds the Golden Fleece. When Jason arrives on the scene he sees that the fleece is defended by a seven-headed Hydra that has captured and killed Acastus. Jason fights and destroys the Hydra. As the Argonauts flee, Medea is struck by a spear. Using the power of the treasure, the young woman is healed and Jason sends her and Argo back to the ship with the Golden Fleece. King Aeetes then uses the teeth of the Hydra to raise seven skeletons to fight Jason and his two comrades. Jason's friends are killed but Jason manages to elude the monsters by jumping into the sea. Zeus tells Hera that Jason will have other adventures as the young man returns to the *Argos* and is reunited with Medea.

Variety declared that *Jason and the Argonauts* contained "spectacular mythological landscape and characters" while Michael J. Weldon in *The Psychotronic Encyclopedia of Film* (1983) called it "[a]nother Ray Harryhausen animated masterpiece ... A classic fantasy.... It was a box-office failure because most people thought it would be another routine muscleman feature." Ed Naha in *Horrors: From Screen to Scream* (1975) termed it "[o]ne of Harryhausen's best ... As is usually the case, the plot is decidedly secondary when compared to Harryhausen's visuals ... A total delight to the senses, *Jason and the Argonauts* blends just the right amount of swashbuckling and distorted mythology." In *Guide for the Film Fanatic* (1986), Danny Peary wrote, "Ray Harryhausen's spectacular special effects highlight this marvelous fantasy-adventure that is even better than his Sinbad movies.... It is directed by Don Chaffey with equal amounts of wit and excitement. It is beautifully filmed by Wilkie Cooper ... Bernard Herrmann's score gives grandeur to the production. Beverley Cross's imaginative, literate script keeps the story on a high intellectual plane so that it will appeal to adults as well as kids ... This film is about the decision by Man, as represented by Jason, to choose his own life's course, to challenge the gods' unfair laws, to no longer be frightened by the gods into blind obedience."

Director Chaffey went on to such genre affairs as *One Million Years B.C.* (1966), containing Harryhausen dinosaurs; *The Viking Queen* (1967), *Creatures the World Forgot* (1971) [q.v.], *Persecution (The Terror of Sheba)* (1974), *Pete's Dragon* (1978) and *C.H.O.M.P.S.* (1979).

Jason and the Argonauts was remade for television in 2000 by Hallmark Entertainment.

Jungle Jim

(1948; 73 minutes) PRODUCER: Sam Katzman. DIRECTOR: William Berke. STORY-SCREENPLAY: Carroll Young. PHOTOGRAPHY: Lester White and Irving Klein. EDITOR: Aaron Stell. MUSIC DIRECTOR: Mischa Bakaleinikoff. ART DIRECTOR: Paul Palmentola. SOUND: George Cooper. SETS: Sidney Clifford. ASSISTANT DIRECTORS: Wilbur McGaugh and Leonard Katzman. CAST: Johnny Weissmuller (Jungle Jim), Virginia Grey (Dr. Hilary Parker), George Reeves (Bruce Edwards), Lita Baron (Zia), Rick Vallin (Kolu), Holmes Herbert (Commissioner Geoffrey Marsden/Narrator), Tex Mooney (Devil Doctor Chief), Neyle Morrow (Fleeing Native), Al Kikume, Max Reid (Bearers).

Alex Raymond's comic strip "Jungle Jim" was distributed by King Features Syndicate from 1934 to 1954. In 1937 Grant Withers headlined Universal's serial *Jungle Jim*; Matt Crowley starred in the radio program "Jungle Jim" that was syndicated from 1935 to 1954 with nearly 1,000 episodes broadcast. In 1948 Columbia obtained the screen rights to the character and producer Sam Katzman signed Johnny Weissmuller to portray the leading role, resulting in 16 features films being released through 1955. (The final trio dropped the Jungle Jim moniker since the studio did not renew its contract with King Features.) The series opener, *Jungle Jim*, was issued late in 1948 and was an inauspicious start with much animal stock footage and seemingly endless jungle trekking to pad its thin storyline.

On the trail of a man-eating leopard, Jungle Jim (Weissmuller) spies a native (Neyle Morrow) fleeing the jungle cat. The fatally mauled man has in his hand a solid gold vial with hieroglyphics on it and containing a dark substance.

Local government commissioner Marsden (Holmes Herbert) meets with cameraman Bruce Edwards (George Reeves), who squandered a fortune left to him. Marsden says that the vial came from the lost temple of Zimbalu and it would be one of the greatest archaeological discoveries of all time along with the possibility of vast treasure. Dr. Hilary Parker (Virginia Grey) arrives to lead the expedition in search of the temple; she is assisted by Jungle Jim and his friend Kolu (Rick Vallin) and his Masai warriors. She informs them that not only will they be seeking treasure but also the substance in the vial, a cure for polio. Jim says the temple may be in the country of a mysterious witch doctor cult that uses the poison to catch victims for human sacrifice. During the safari, the vial is stolen from the archaeologist's tent. It turns out the culprit is Kolu's sister Zia (Lita Baron), who has followed them from Masai country. After an elephant stampede and a falling boulder, Jim sets up a warning device around their camp. That night Bruce shows up and Dr. Parker hires him as the expedition's photographer. The next day as they are walking along a cliff, a supposedly dizzy Edwards pushes Jim over the edge but he is saved by Kolu and the Masai warriors. When Jim and Zia go swimming, Hilary becomes jealous and she joins them only to be menaced by a crocodile which Jim kills.

The expedition finds the temple but Kolu falls into a pit containing a lion. As the devil doctor cult surrounds them, Jim frees Kolu and fights and kills the beast but the rest of the group is captured and taken to the temple. Edwards arrives and tells Hilary, Kolu and Zia that the cult members think he is a god because he can take their pictures. He plans to let them be sacrificed so he can have the treasure for himself. Jim sneaks into the temple as his pet crow Caw-Caw steals the lens from Edwards' camera. When the devil doctor chief (Tex Mooney) demands his picture be taken, Edwards is unable to do so. The natives attack him and he kills the chief. As Edwards flees the cult members, Jim frees Hilary, Kolu, Zia and the Masai warriors, who were left hanging from their ankles. When the devil doctors return, a fight ensues with Edwards falling into a flaming pit. Jim, Kolu and the Masais subdue the cultists. As Hilary plans to take the treasure and the polio cure back to civilization, Jim and Kolu tell her she can join them in future adventures.

Jungle Jim featured Skipper, a white terrier, and the raven Caw-Caw as Jim's pets. The character Kolu was from the comic strip although there he was a Hindu and not a Masai chief. Interestingly the natives in the "Jungle Jim" series appear to be mostly Polynesian, with occasional Orientals or blacks being shown (the series was set in the heart of Africa). Its plot does have the interesting ploy of Jim being pursued by two females with Lita Baron stealing the spotlight as the

Poster for *Jungle Jim* (1948).

seductive Zia, a role originally intended for Acquanetta. *Variety* termed the film "completely juvenile.... [P]roducers might have attracted a broader market had they given it a bit more adult interest." Bosley Crowther in the *New York Times* called star Weissmuller "fat, but physically fearless, and [a] miraculously clever jungle guide.... [I]t's a tired gent that we see in this life-sized comic strip."

Jungle Jim in the Forbidden Land

(1952; 65 minutes) PRODUCER: Sam Katzman. DIRECTOR: Lew Landers. STORY-SCREENPLAY: Samuel Newman. PHOTOGRAPHY: Fayte M. Browne. EDITOR: Henry Batista. MUSIC: Mischa Bakaleinikoff. ART DIRECTOR: Paul Palmentola. SOUND: J.S. Westmoreland. UNIT MANAGER: Herbert Leonard. CAST: Johnny Weissmuller (Jungle Jim), Angela Greene (Dr. Linda Roberts), Jean Willes (Denise), Lester Matthews (Commissioner Kingston), William Tannen (Doc Edwards), George Eldredge (Fred Lewis), Frederic Berest (Zulu), Tex Erickson, Irmard Raschke (Giants), William Fawcett (The Old One), Frank Jaquet (Quigley), Tamba (Chimp).

Wasabi area commissioner Kingston (Lester Matthews) refuses to let Dr. Linda Roberts (Angela Greene) lead an expedition into Central Africa in search of a lost race of giants. Deciding to disobey the commissioner, she is abandoned by her hired men when they are attacked by a hippopotamus at Gamba Lake. Linda swims to shore only to be trailed by a panther. Jungle Jim (Johnny Weissmuller) saves her from the beast and takes her to his camp. There she tells him of her mission.

Jim is called away to speak with a prophet known as The Old One (William Fawcett). At the Old One's camp he finds the commissioner, who brings news of ivory hunters slaughtering an elephant herd surrounded by flood waters. When the commissioner requests that Jim take him to the land of the giants so he can help elephants escape, the jungle man refuses, saying the prehistoric people are very dangerous. Kingston informs him that two of the giants have been captured and Jim tells him not to set them free. Jim then seizes two natives he finds carrying ivory tusks. Quigley (Frank Jaquet), a local merchant, is upset with ivory hunter Fred Lewis (George Eldredge) and his ward Denise (Jean Willes) because they are not supplying him with enough tusks. After Jim informs Quigley of finding the stolen ivory, the trader tells Fred he wants more tusks. Lewis says he is constrained by government regulations. Going back to Wasabi, Fred, Denise and their cohort Doc Edwards (William Tannen) inform the commissioner they will set the giants free, follow them back to their country and aid the elephant herd. In order to control the giants, Denise suggests drugging them but when the giant female

Poster for *Jungle Jim in the Forbidden Land* (1952).

(Irmard Raschke) is given an injection her male mate (Tex Erickson) escapes. Although wounded by a guard, he makes a getaway into the jungle.

As government soldiers search for the giant, he almost attacks Linda but is run off by Jim; the giant later frees his mate. Doc and Denise plan to use the expedition into the land of the giants only to get more ivory. When Fred hears Denise making a deal with tribal chief Zulu (Frederic Berest), he objects and she orders the native to kill him. When Jim returns to camp, he is knocked out by Doc, and he and Denise blame the jungle man for Lewis' murder. When the commissioner shows up, he arrests Jim. Doc, Denise and Zulu then trail the two giants as Jim's pet chimpanzee Tamba and Linda set the jungle man free. They follow the others and come upon the trapped herd of elephants. Jim manages to capture Zulu. When the giants attack Doc and Denise, she kills the female giant, causing her mate to go berserk. The commissioner shows up with his men and tries to take Jim back into custody but Tamba diverts their attention and Jim and Linda get away and trail Zulu. They manage to recapture him and take him to Kingston where he admits killings Fred after being told to do so by Denise. Trying to escape, Zulu is shot by the commissioner but the gunfire causes the elephants to stampede. Jim manages to herd them through a pass as Doc and Denise try to get away. Doc fights with Jim while Denise runs into the clutches of the giant and they fall from a cliff to their deaths. With Edwards in custody, the commissioner tells Jim he is sorry for doubting his word and Linda ends her search for the tribe of giants.

Filmed in sepia, *Jungle Jim in the Forbidden Land* was the eighth entry in Columbia's "Jungle Jim" series. The inclusion of two pre–Cro-Magnon giants in the plot provided the horror element in an otherwise mundane jungle affair about corrupt ivory hunters. Lester Matthews would reprise the role of Commissioner Kingston in the thirteenth series entry *Jungle Man-Eaters* (1954). *Variety* opined, "While a few actionful sequences manage to come across okay, majority of the footage is too implausible to rate interest from any viewer but the sub-teenster." The *Motion Picture Herald* felt "the story is somewhat on the fantastic side."

Jungle Manhunt

(1951; 66 minutes) PRODUCER: Sam Katzman. DIRECTOR: Lew Landers. STORY-SCREENPLAY: Samuel Newman. PHOTOGRAPHY: William Whitley. EDITOR: Henry Batista. MUSIC DIRECTOR: Mischa Bakaleinikoff. ART DIRECTOR: Paul Palmentola. SOUND: J.S. Westmoreland. SETS: Sidney Clifford. CAST: Johnny Weissmuller (Jungle Jim), Bob Waterfield (Bob Miller), Sheila Ryan (Ann Lawrence), Rick Vallin (Chief Bono), Lyle Talbot (Dr. Mitchell Heller), Billy Wilkerson (Maklee Chief), Rusty Wescoatt, Max Reid (Maklee Warriors), Tamba (Chimp).

Producer Sam Katzman got plenty of publicity by co-starring former football hero Bob Waterfield, the husband of Jane Russell, in this "Jungle Jim" episode, the seventh entry in the series, shot at Corriganville. Unfortunately the film is on the bland side with an abundance of poorly matched stock footage of natives and wildlife plus a grainy fight between a shark and an octopus. Also thrown into the mix was a scene from *One Million B.C.* (1940) in which two giant prehistoric lizards battle to the death. *Variety* called it "a routine series entry ... For most adult audiences, *Jungle Manhunt* is implausible and indigestible.... Weissmuller is still the he-man of old and a terrific swimmer as Jungle Jim." The *Motion Picture Herald* was more magnanimous: "[T]he picture stands up to its predecessors and contains a generous amount of action and suspense."

A trio of skeleton men lead a force of Maklee warriors in attacking African villages, killing women and children, carrying off able-bodied men and setting fire to the inhabitants' huts. When they attack the Matusa village, Chief Bono (Rick Vallin) is injured but manages to escape. Newspaper photographer Ann Lawrence (Sheila Ryan) has come to the area in search of one-time football great Bob Miller (Bob Waterfield), whose plane crashed while on a mission nine years before. Her boat capsizes on river rapids and she is saved by Jungle Jim (Weissmuller), whom she hires as a guide. After another village is raided, the local tribal chiefs meet and Bono asks Jim to lead them in finding the leader of the evil spirits, a mysterious white man that Ann speculates might be Miller. At a village in the Sengali area, the natives inform Jim, Ann and Bono that a great white god who throws thunder is nearby. When a strange man shows up in the hut in which the scouting party is sleeping, Jim follows him. The village is soon under attack by the skeleton men and their followers. Jim, Ann and Bono try to get away and are trailed by some of the Maklee warriors, but the stranger leads them to a river and then throws home-made bombs, dispersing the raiders. When their boat comes to some rapids,

Jim orders the party to jump into the water; the stranger saves Ann while Jim helps Bono to shore. Taking them to his village, the stranger identifies himself as Bob Miller; he has improved the lives of the natives with irrigation and a steel forge operated by a seesaw. Later Miller tells Ann that after crashing in the jungle, he stayed to aid the natives who helped him regain his strength.

When news arrives that the skeleton men and their cohorts have raided another village, Bob agrees to join Jim and Bono, with Ann coming along, in battling the marauders. Traveling overland, they reach the mysterious land of the Monagechi and see two giant lizards fight before they are taken prisoner by the skeleton men and the Maklees. Dr. Mitchell Heller (Lyle Talbot) informs them that he is an industrial chemist who has found the secret of making synthetic diamonds and that he needs a constant supply of new workers in his mine since his process involves radiation. He also tells them that the Maklee warriors are his allies in raiding the native villages for more workers. Ann insults Heller, causing a disturbance and Jim escapes. The chemist then tells the young woman she will transport the synthetic diamonds through customs in the cans she uses for film.

Helping Ann to escape, Jim sets up a plan in which she will detonate an explosion, blowing up an inlet and flooding the mine where Miller, Bono and the captured natives are forced to work. Dressing as a native, Jim infiltrates the mine and liberates Bob, who goes for reinforcements. Jim travels to the village where Heller is headquartered and signals with a flaming arrow, causing Ann to detonate the explosion with the flood waters giving Bono the opportunity to lead the prisoners out of the mine as Miller and his tribesmen attack the Maklee natives. Heller grabs a box full of his diamonds and tries to escape but falls from a cliff after being pursued by Jim. The Maklees are turned over to the authorities and Ann throws away her camera, preferring to remain with Bob in the jungle.

In a scene excised from *Jungle Manhunt*, Jungle Jim fights a lizard man (actually a stuntman in a dinosaur suit). Some of the advertising for the film includes a picture of the fight and a snippet of footage from it appeared in the trailer.

Jungle Moon Men

(1955; 70 minutes) PRODUCER: Sam Katzman. DIRECTOR: Charles S. Gould. SCREENPLAY: Dwight V. Babcock and Jo Pagano. STORY: Jo Pagano. PHOTOGRAPHY: Henry Freulich. EDITOR: Henry Batista. MUSIC DIRECTOR: Mischa Bakaleinikoff. ART DIRECTOR: Paul Palmentola. SOUND: J.S. Westmoreland. SETS: Sidney Clifford. UNIT MANAGER: Leon Chooluck. SPECIAL EFFECTS: Jack Erickson. ASSISTANT DIRECTOR: Eddie Saeta. CAST: Johnny Weissmuller (Himself), Jean Byron (Ellen Marston), Helene Stanton (Oma), Bill [William] Henry (Bob Prentice), Myron Healey (Mark Santo), Billy Curtis (Pygmy Chief Damu), Michael Granger (Chief Nolimo), Frank Sully (Max), Benjamin F. Chapman, Jr. [Ben Chapman] (Marro), Kenneth L. Smith (Link), Ed Hinton (Matt Regan), Rory Mallinson (Commissioner Jones), Angelo Rossitto (Pygmy), Kimba (Chimp).

Working title: *Moon Men*.

In the Baku country of Africa, a group of pygmies called Moon Men, led by Damu (Billy Curtis), use drugged darts to capture young Aribis warrior Marro (Ben Chapman), the son of Chief Nolimo (Michael Granger). Also coming to the land of the Aribis is archaeologist Ellen Marston (Jean Byron). She believes that a tribe of whites who lived there in ancient times may have been Egyptian, and that they held the secret of eternal life. She meets jungle man Johnny Weissmuller (himself) and tells him of her theories as Nolimo asks to accompany them in search of his son. Bob Prentice (Bill Henry), Ellen's boyfriend, trails her in the company of trader Mark Santo (Myron Healey). When they meet the expedition, Bob joins up with Jim, Ellen and the Aribis chief. A drugged Marro, who has escaped from his captors, arrives on the scene but the pygmies kill him. Ellen notes that the diamond pendant he is wearing contains hieroglyphics identifying it as belonging to Baku's high priest. The group captures Damu, who tells them that the goddess Oma gave Marro the poison that killed him.

Mark returns to his trading post and informs cohorts Max (Frank Sully), Link (Kenneth L. Smith) and Matt Regan (Ed Hinton) about the pendant and they set out to take it from the expedition. After Nolimo and his tribesmen leave to carry out a ceremonial burial for Marro, the Moon Men free their chief and shoot Johnny with a drugged dart. Ellen revives him and they set out to find Bob, whom the raiders have taken prisoner. They are waylaid by Santo and his pals, who take the pendant from Johnny; they are later shot with drugged darts by the Moon Men, who carry off the necklace as Damu wrecks Santo's Jeep. Coming to, Santo and his cohorts find the pendant gone. When Link and Matt want to go back, Santo shoots them. Johnny and Ellen come

Myron Healey and Frank Sully in *Jungle Moon Men* (1955).

to what looks like the entrance to an ancient Egyptian temple. When Santo and Max show up, the four go into the edifice and are captured by the Moon Men who take them to their ruler, the beautiful blonde Oma (Helene Stanton). She informs them she is a Moon goddess, the high priestess of Baku who has lived for centuries, and that Marro was made a high priest but had to be killed when he tried to escape. She reveals that Bob is her new high priest; when he is brought out by the Moon Men, he is obviously drugged. That night Johnny locates Bob who comes out of his stupor with no memory of being brought to the underground temple. Found by the Moon Men, they are taken to Oma and Johnny agrees to become her new high priest so Bob can be with Ellen. Johnny tells Bob to bring the police after he and Ellen are set free, then catches Santo trying to steal Oma's diamonds. The two fight, and as a result, all of the captives are sent to the death chamber where they will be devoured by lions, the guardians of the temple. Johnny's pet chimpanzee Kimba helps him to escape. The chimp lures the lions through a cavern as Johnny sets the others free. Santo and Max try to steal the diamonds and are killed by the big cats. Oma shows the captives the way out of the temple but says she cannot leave because the sun god Ra will destroy her. Johnny forces her to go with them and when they get outside, the Moon Men are surrounded by Nolimo and his warriors and Oma disintegrates in the sunlight. No longer slaves, the Moon Men now want peace with the Aribis tribe. Kimba wears the pendant that Ellen needs for her book, proving her theories.

After making 13 "Jungle Jim" features, producer Sam Katzman did three more jungle outings with Johnny Weissmuller starting with *Jungle Moon Men* (issued in the spring of 1955) in which the hero used his own moniker. Otherwise the films were a continuation of the Alex Raymond comic strip. This one even used a scene from a previous entry, *Jungle Manhunt*, as well as the usual grainy stock footage scenes of animals and natives. Also padding the proceedings was a lengthy sequence in which the archaeologist and her boyfriend hunt two wild boars and a lion with bow and arrow. *The Hollywood Reporter* noted, "*Jungle Moon Men* will contribute little toward winning back to the theaters a discriminating young audience that can enjoy better stuff free on television." On the other hand, the *Motion Picture*

Herald reported, "[T]here is no reason to suspect that *Jungle Moon Men* will not attract and delight as many youngsters as the previous films."

An interesting aspect of the feature is that it borrowed the themes of eternal life and a beautiful priestess from H. Rider Haggard's 1887 novel *She*.

Just Before Dawn

(1946; 65 minutes) PRODUCER: Rudolph C. Flothow. DIRECTOR: William Castle. SCREENPLAY: Eric Taylor and Aubrey Wisberg. PHOTOGRAPHY: Henry Freulich and Philip Tannura. EDITOR: Dwight Caldwell. MUSIC DIRECTOR: Mischa Bakaleinikoff. ART DIRECTOR: Hans Radon. SOUND: Howard Fogetti. SETS: William Kiernan. ASSISTANT DIRECTOR: Carl Hiecke. CAST: Warner Baxter (Dr. Robert Ordway), Adelle Roberts (Claire Foster), Martin Kosleck (Karl Ganss), Mona Barrie (Harriet Travers), Marvin Miller (Corcello/Casper), Charles D. Brown (Police Inspector Burns), Robert H. Barrat (Clyde Travers), George Meeker (Walter Foster), Wilton Graff (Alec Girard), Peggy Converse (Connie Day), Craig Reynolds (Jack Swayne), Charles Lane (Dr. Steiner), Charles Arnt (Allen S. Tobin), Ted Hecht (Armand Morcel), Irene Tedrow (Florence White), Thomas E. Jackson (Walter Cummings), Byron Foulger (Harris), Egon Brecher (Dr. Evans), Skelton Knaggs (Louie), Walter Soderling (Old Servant), Eric Wilton (Party Guest), Brick Sullivan (Officer Murphy).

Working title: *Exposed by the Crime Doctor*.

The seventh entry in Columbia's long-running "Crime Doctor" series, based on the CBS radio series created by Max Marcin, *Just Before Dawn* did not have the heavy horror overtones of the earlier *Shadows in the Night* (1944) and *The Crime Doctor's Courage* (1946) [qq.v]. Director William Castle, however, imbued the feature with enough eerie details to entertain its intended audience, such as scenes in a spooky funeral home, creepy characters like mortician Karl Ganss (Martin Kosleck) and his bestial henchman Casper (Marvin Miller), and several grisly murders, including that of the leading lady. To further add to the horror element, star Warner Baxter was made up to resemble Boris Karloff when his character impersonated a wanted criminal. (The voice he used sounded more like Marlon Brando in *The Godfather* [1972]). With its horror trappings and a killer hard to identify, *Just Before Dawn* was a sturdy dual bill item from Larry Darmour Productions.

The film opens with repulsive Casper (Miller) going to the Ganss Mortuary where the owner, Karl Ganss (Kosleck), gives him poison disguised as insulin. That evening, famous physician-psychiatrist-criminologist Dr. Robert Ordway (Warner Baxter), aka "The Crime Doctor," is called on by neighbor Harriet Travers (Mona Barrie) who asks him to look at a party guest, Walter Foster (George Meeker), who has passed out. Ordway finds out the man is diabetic and gives him a shot of insulin from the case that Foster carries with him. As the man recovers, Ordway is introduced to Foster's beautiful sister Claire (Adelle Roberts), her boyfriend Jack Swayne (Craig Reynolds), realtor Alec Girard (Wilton Graff) and Harriet's husband, Clyde Travers (Robert H. Barrat). Foster dies within minutes and the next day Police Inspector Burns (Charles D. Brown) asks Ordway to help locate the killer since coroner Dr. Steiner (Charles Lane) diagnosed Foster had been poisoned. Ordway visits Swayne at his health club and learns that the man disliked the victim because he opposed his marrying Claire. He also informs the doctor of his belief that Clyde or Harriet Travers is the culprit because Foster was having an affair with Harriet and also blackmailing her. Foster family attorney Tobin (Charles Arnt) tells Ordway that Walter was dependent on his sister financially since he had squandered the $250,000 left to him by his late father. After Ordway leaves the lawyer's office, Casper goes to see Tobin. Claire telephones the doctor and asks him to come to her home to discuss her brother's last words, which were from *Hamlet*. But Casper shows up first, in a hearse, and abducts the young woman.

Ordway returns to the Travers home which he sees is for sale. Harriet tells him that she and her husband are having marital troubles; Clyde later reveals his wife had sold bonds and given the proceeds to Foster. Mr. Travers also says that Foster was involved with a mortuary worker named Connie Day (Peggy Converse). After several phone calls, Ordway manages to make a date to see the young woman. Her employer, Ganss, overhears the conversation and locks her in a funeral chamber with a corpse and she becomes hysterical. Casper arrives and takes Connie into a room with a masked doctor and she is murdered. The next day Corcello (Miller) and his brother Louie (Skelton Knaggs) consult with Ordway about Louie's mental condition; Corello, who is really Casper, orders Louie to shoot the doctor and he does so but only blinds the physician. Corello then tosses Louie, who is not his sibling but a hired gunman, out of the office window.

Left blind by the murder attempt, Ordway learns from Burns that the appointment card used by the two men bore no fingerprints and he deduces they were removed by plastic surgery. Although his sight returns, Ordway decides to pretend to be blind in order to capture the brains behind the plastic surgery operation. With the help of makeup man Harris (Byron Foulger) he takes on the guise of wanted criminal Pete Hastings. Going to Casper, he makes arrangements to see Ganss in order to get plastic surgery but at the mortuary Karl gets a phone call from Casper who has just heard on the radio that Hastings was gunned down by police in Indianapolis. When Ganss tries to poison Ordway, he knocks out the mortician and calls the police, who arrive and place Karl under arrest. They also apprehend Casper when he arrives at the scene. When Ordway later meets with Burns and Steiner, he learns that the bodies of Claire and Connie were exhumed and both of them had been poisoned. In order to trap the killer, Ordway gives a party at his house and invites everyone involved in the case, telling each person he knows the identity of the murderer. After everyone leaves, Girard returns, gives Ordway a poisoned drink and then confesses to the murders, saying he used to be a plastic surgeon before losing his license, and that he was being blackmailed by Foster. Burns and Steiner are in another room and, after hearing Alec's confession, they arrest the killer. Ordway prepares to have his stomach pumped by Steiner.

Killer Ape

(1953; 68 minutes) PRODUCER: Sam Katzman. DIRECTOR: Spencer Gordon Bennet. SCREENPLAY: Arthur Hoerl and Carroll Young. STORY: Carroll Young. PHOTOGRAPHY: William P. Whitley. EDITOR: Gene Havlick. MUSIC DIRECTOR: Mischa Bakaleinikoff. ART DIRECTOR: Paul Palmentola. SOUND: J.S. Westmoreland. UNIT MANAGER: Herbert B. Leonard. SETS: Sidney Clifford. MAKEUP: Clay Campbell. ASSISTANT DIRECTOR: Carter DeHaven, Jr. CAST: Johnny Weissmuller (Jungle Jim), Carol Thurston (Shari), Max Palmer (Ape Man), Burt Wenland (Ramada), Nestor Paiva (Dr. Andrews), Paul Marion (Mahara), Eddie Foster (Achmed), Rory Mallinson (Perry), Ray Corrigan (Norley), Nick Stuart (Maron), Pedro Regas (Magi), Harry Wilson (Henchman), Michael Fox (Medical Officer), Tamba (Chimp).

The tenth entry in Columbia's "Jungle Jim" series, *Killer Ape* was filmed at Corriganville and its owner, Ray Corrigan, played a supporting role in the feature. Max Palmer, who stood over 7'6", played the title character wearing monster makeup by Clay Campbell. Certainly Palmer's portrayal of the rampaging giant creature was the highlight, and selling point, of the film. *Variety* felt the outing "is no worse, but certainly no better, than predecessors in the series.... The pace is slow, the script obvious and talky, and the direction and playing stereotyped." The *Motion Picture Herald* noted, "The film moves at a fairly brisk pace, climaxed by a surprise finale."

After finding a number of animals acting in a sluggish fashion, Jungle Jim (Weissmuller) consults local authorities who ask him to bring in specimens for testing. Unknown to them, Dr. Andrews (Nestor Paiva), a scientist, has been extracting fluids by using a local ore in trying to develop a serum that will break down resistance on the part of people and animals. Arab trader Ramada (Burt Wenland) and his fiancée Shari (Carol Thurston) are working with her brother, Wasuli chief Mahara (Paul Marion), in capturing wildlife to sell to zoos; Shari nearly takes Jim's pet chimp Tamba before he comes to its rescue. Both the Andrews party and the animal hunters are near a land rumored to be the home of a dangerous giant ape man (Palmer) who tries to kill Tamba. Jim warns both groups about the dangers of the area and becomes suspicious of Andrews after seeing listless animals he has caged. When the antidote Andrews develops to reverse the lethargy fails, he has his men try and purchase the hunters' animals for further experiments. Trailing Andrews, Jim locates his experimental station in a large cave. Later, the ape man finds it and wreaks havoc. Getting away from the giant, Jim tries to halt the sale of the animals as Andrews tells the hunters that Jim's claims about the creature are bogus. Mahara tells Ramada to sell their captured animals to Dr. Andrews as he tries to locate Jim so he can confirm his story. When the ape man attacks Mahara, Jim tries to save him. Mahara is thrown on the jungle man's knife by the creature and dies as the monster escapes back into the jungle. Ramada and Shari accuse Jim of killing Mahara and he is taken to their camp where seer Achmed (Eddie Foster) defends Jim. Tamba opens the animal cages as Jim makes his escape but he is followed by Shari, whom he captures. The ape man raids Jim's camp and he is able to scare him off with fire. Shari, seeing that Jim's story about the giant is true, promises to alert Ramada about the creature. As Jim tries to stop the sale of the animals by Ramada and Achmed to Dr. Andrews, the ape man returns and takes Shari. Ramada and Achmed are not given a reason why Andrews wants the animals and so they refuse to carry out the bargain; the two men and other Wasulis are taken prisoners. Jim manages to set Ramada free but the giant arrives. Shari and Andrews' men overpower the creature and tie him to the ground where they force-feed him the serum. After it fails to work on the ape man, Andrews decides to experiment on Jim, whom he has also captured, and Ramada and Shari. After three days, Tamba shows up with a bevy of jungle simians who raid the camp. In the struggle, Jim and the other captives are set free, as is the ape man. Andrews and his men return to his laboratory where the giant kills them. In a showdown with the ape man, Jim manages to destroy the creature with fire.

Killer at Large

(1936; 58 minutes) ASSOCIATE PRODUCER: Harry L. Decker. DIRECTOR: David Selman. SCREENPLAY: Harold Shumate, from the story "Poker Face" by Carl Clausen. PHOTOGRAPHY: Allen G. Siegler. EDITOR: James Sweeney. SOUND: Lambert Day. ASSISTANT DIRECTOR: Milton Carter. CAST: Mary Brian (Linda Allen), Russell Hardie (Tommy Braddock), George McKay (Sergeant Kelly), Thurston Hall (Inspector O'Hara), Henry Brandon (Mr. Zero), Betty Compson (Kate), Harry Hayden (Bentley), Boyd Irwin (Whitley), Charles R. Moore (High Pockets), Harry Bernard (Sexton), Edward LeSaint (Landlord), Alma Chester (Old Lady), Rolf Ernst (Messenger), Lee Shumway (Police Captain), Billy Arnold (Police Operator), Beatrice Curtis (Shop Girl), Brady Kline (Police Lieutenant), James Millican (Hotel Clerk), Charles Dorety (Driver), Lon Chaney, Jr., Roger Gray (Coffin Men).

Working title: *Poker Face*. Also released as *Killer on the Loose*.

This cheap programmer has several horror elements, mainly a maniac killer and his wax museum. The madman, Mr. Zero (Henry Brandon), is also an illusionist who manages the feat of being able to make himself indistinguishable from the human wax figures he creates. Also of interest to horror film buffs is the casting of future genre star Lon Chaney, Jr., as one of Zero's henchmen. Frank S. Nugent in the *New York Times* called the dual biller "a complete waste of time.... [It] is a literary crime — almost a capital offense."

Lovers Linda Allen (Mary Brian) and Tommy Braddock (Russell Hardie) are employed at Whitley's Department Store, both answering to superintendent William Bentley (Harry Hayden), who has just made Linda chief of security. Tommy, who works in the jewelry area, teases her about the promotion since he wants her to quit so they can get married. After showing customer Kate (Betty Compson) expensive diamond bracelets housed in the store vault, Tommy is scolded by Bentley after the woman is caught trying to shoplift a compact. Kate is not arrested but Tommy is warned by his boss that he will have to make up any losses from future thefts while Linda is praised for capturing the thief. When Linda returns to the store that night to meet her fiancé, who has stayed behind to take inventory, she finds Bentley dead and the vault empty. The police are called and Inspector O'Hara (Thurston Hall) and Sergeant Kelly (George McKay) think Tommy is the culprit; he claims to have been out for a walk when the crimes took place. Placing Tommy in Linda's custody, O'Hara tells Kelly to tail the couple since he suspects they may have been involved. Linda speculates that the crimes were perpetrated by a mystery man called Mr. Zero (Brandon), the operator of a wax museum who has set up a store window display where has installed his wax figures and then tries to get passersby to guess which ones are real and which one is him. Realizing that Mr. Zero could have seen Tommy showing Kate the bracelets in the vault, Linda convinces Tommy to go with her to the eerie museum where Mr. Zero is berating his accomplice Kate for nearly ruining his plans by shoplifting. When the woman asks for more money, he kills her and hides her body along with the stolen bracelets. Linda and Tommy enter the museum through a window but they are overheard by Mr. Zero who pretends to be a wax figure. When the police locate Kate's body and the bracelets, O'Hara is convinced that Mr. Zero is the killer and he sets a trap to capture him. The police chief tells Linda and Tommy to go to their usual Sunday dinner site, a rural hotel; during the trip, Mr. Zero tries to shoot them. Kelly is hiding in the backseat of their auto and he uses a machine gun to end Mr. Zero's reign of terror. With the case solved, Tommy informs Linda that she will now have to quit her job and be his wife.

Kiss the Girls and Make Them Die

(1966; 106 minutes; Color) PRODUCERS: Salvatore Argento and Arduino Maiuri. EXECUTIVE PRODUCER: Dino De Laurentiis. DIRECTORS: Henry Levin and Arduino Maiuri. SCREENPLAY: Dino [Arduino] Maiuri and Jack Putnam. PHOTOGRAPHY: Aldo Tonti. EDITORS: Alberto Ballitti and Ralph Kempton. MUSIC: Mario

Nascimbene. SONG: Mario Nascimbene and Howard Greenfield. ART DIRECTOR: Mario Garbuglia. SETS: Emilio D'Andria. COSTUME DESIGN: Maria De Matteis and Piero Gherardi. SPECIAL EFFECTS: Augie Lohman. SECOND UNIT DIRECTORS: Alberto Pieralisi and Leopoldo Savona. ASSISTANT DIRECTOR: Sanin Cherques. CAST: Michael Connors (CIA Agent 409 Kelly), Dorothy Provine (Susan Fleming), Raf Vallone (Mr. Ardonian), Terry-Thomas (Lord Aldric/James), Margaret Lee (Grace), Nicoletta Machiavelli (Sylvia), Beverly Adams (Karin), Marilu Tolo (Gioia), Seyna Seyn (Wilma Soong), Oliver MacGreevy (Ringo), Sandro Dori (Omar), Jack Gwillim (British Ambassador), Andy Ho (Ling), K. Wang (Kasai), Hans Thorner (Kruger), Nerio Bernardi (Papal Envoy), Michael Audley (Major Davis), Edith Peters (Maria).

In Brazil, CIA agent Kelly (Michael Connors) learns that several beautiful young women have disappeared after coming into contact with Omar (Sandro Dori) and Ringo (Oliver MacGreevy), thugs who work for Ardonian (Raf Vallone), an industrial scientist whose business in located in Rio de Janeiro. Kelly meets vacationing Britisher Susan Fleming (Dorothy Provine) and begins to fear for her safety. Checking into Ardonian's activities, Kelly is captured by his men but manages to free himself, letting the scientist and Susan think he has been killed. At a party for the British ambassador (Jack Gwillim) given by Ardonian, Kelly shows up and steals a notebook left behind by noted archaeologist Lord Aldric (Terry-Thomas), who was murdered in a remote village. The scientist, who was responsible for the homicide, does not want the notebook made public but Susan manages to get it away from Kelly. That night the CIA man breaks into her house and learns she is a British agent working with her chauffeur James (Terry-Thomas) in trying to expose Ardonian. Teaming up, they head into the interior to locate the village where Aldric was killed, find that the natives, due to Ardonian's experiments, are sexually quelled. Men working for the scientist kidnap Susan and fly her via helicopter to his ocean laboratory where she learns that Ardonian has constructed a satellite that, when placed in orbit, will give off a cobalt ray that will sterilize the world's population. To preserve the human race he has kidnapped beautiful young women and placed them in a state of hibernation until they will be needed to repopulate the planet. The madman agrees to sell the Red Chinese the satellite for $500 million but once he gets the money he uses the ray to destroy that country's populace. Ardonian plans to rule the world and add Susan to his collection of hibernating women. Kelly locates his lair and, sending James to get the country's army, he infiltrates it and saves her. During a fight with Ardonian, Kelly pushes the scientist into his own hibernation vault. The army arrives and takes over the complex.

Filmed in Brazil by Dino De Laurentiis Cinematografica as *Se Tutte le Donne del Mondo* (If All the Women in the World...), this production was also called *Operazione Paradiso* (Operation Paradise) before its release in the U.S. by Columbia late in 1966 as *Kiss the Girls and Make Them Die*. A tongue-in-cheek "James Bond" spoof, it not only sported a stalwart, banana-eating CIA hero and a suave, murderous villain, it contained the usual modicum of beautiful women, exotic gadgets and weapons, a state-of-the-art Rolls-Royce, various ingenious methods of murder and Rio carnival scenes. Howard Thompson (*The New York Times*) failed to see the fun in the proceedings when he called the film "a strictly one-horse James Bonded adventure... A meandering, coy script simply slides most of the incidents around some nice Brazilian

Dorothy Provine, Oliver MacGreevy in *Kiss the Girls ...* (1966).

scenery in color, wasting both." More on the mark was David Deal in *The Eurospy Guide* (2004) when he wrote that the feature "is a tongue-in-cheek Bondian adventure that rivals the official product in all departments...All the pleasing nonsense is presented in a matter-of-fact way without the grandiose posturing of Bond or the mugging comedy of other spoofs." In *The Family Guide to Movies on Video* (1988), Henry Herz and Tony Zaza called it a "[f]ailed Italian spy spoof.... [T]he result is largely unamusing and mildly sexually suggestive."

Co-director Henry Levin went on to direct Dean Martin in two tongue-in-cheek Matt Helm spy features for Columbia, *Murderer's Row* (1966) and *The Ambushers* (1967) [qq.v.].

Ladies in Retirement

(1941; 91 minutes) PRODUCER: Lester Cowan. ASSOCIATE PRODUCER: Gilbert Miller. DIRECTOR: Charles Vidor. SCREENPLAY: Reginald Denham, Edward Percy and Garrett Fort, from the play by Reginald Denham and Edward Percy. PHOTOGRAPHY: George Barnes. EDITOR: Al Clark. MUSIC: Ernst Toch. SONG: Morris Stoloff and Ernst Toch. ART DIRECTORS: Lionel Banks and George Montgomery. PRODUCTION DESIGN: David S. Hall. COSTUME DESIGN: Walter Plunkett. ASSISTANT DIRECTOR: George Rhein. CAST: Ida Lupino (Ellen Creed), Louis Hayward (Albert Feather), Evelyn Keyes (Lucy Gilham), Elsa Lanchester (Emily Creed), Edith Barrett (Louisa Creed), Isobel Elsom (Leonora Fiske), Emma Dunn (Sister Theresa), Queenie Leonard (Sister Agatha), Clyde Cook (Bates).

Reginald Denham and Edward Percy's play *Ladies in Retirement* debuted on the London stage late in 1939 starring Mary Clare, who repeated the role of Ellen Creed in a second production in the late summer of 1941. In the interim it opened on Broadway in the spring of 1940 starring Flora Robson, Estelle Winwood, Evelyn Ankers and Isobel Elsom, who would repeat the role of retired actress Leonora Fiske when the property was filmed by Columbia in 1941. The feature's top-billed stars, Ida Lupino (who replaced Rosalind Russell) and Louis Hayward, were married during its filming. The movie garnered two Academy Award nominations for Morris Stoloff and Ernst Toch's song and Lionel Banks and George Montgomery's dark, foreboding art direction. Theodore Strauss in the *New York Times* said the film was "an exercise in slowing accumulating terror with all the psychological trappings of a Victorian thriller. It has been painstakingly done, beautifully photographed and thoughtfully played ... and for the most part, it catches all the script's nuances of horror quite as effectively as did the original play version." *Photoplay* said, "In a subdued and quiet vein [the play is] translated to the screen in a superb manner, creeps up on its audience slowly, eerily, stealthily." *Variety* complained that the film's "sordid combination of a murderess and two mentally deranged sisters is too strong to catch general audience reaction on a favorable plane," but added, "Production itself is a fine example of the best in motion picture technique. Script is compactly written; Charles Vidor's direction is of outstanding excellence; the small cast carefully etches each particular characterization; and every technical advantage has been provided for an artistic presentation."

At a remote farmhouse near the marshes of a Thames River estuary, Ellen Creed (Ida Lupino) is the housekeeper for onetime stage star Leonora Fiske (Isobel Elsom). Ellen receives a letter informing her that she must take immediate custody of her mentally ill sisters Emily (Elsa Lanchester) and Louisa (Edith Barrett) and she asks her employer's permission for them to visit her. Ellen's nephew Albert Feather (Louis Hayward) shows up and convinces Leonora to loan him money he needs to cover what he stole from his bank employer. After he departs, Ellen returns with her sisters who upset Leonora to the point that she orders her housekeeper to send them away. Ellen refuses, the two argue and she is dismissed. When Leonora refuses to change her mind, Ellen strangles her and walls her body in an old oven the woman used as a safe. Two nuns (Emma Dunn, Queenie Leonard) request some oil; Ellen tells them Leonora has gone on a sea voyage and sends maid Lucy Gilham (Evelyn Keyes) to a shed for it. There she finds the hiding Albert. When Lucy informs him his aunt is not aware of his previous visit, he goes to the front door and introduces himself. He tells Ellen the police are after him, so she permits him to remain until she can get him safely out of England.

Albert becomes suspicious when he learns that the oven has been bricked up and that Emily and Louisa believe Leonora sold Ellen the house. Later he finds out that Ellen has forged Leonora's name on a check and he gets Lucy, who has fallen in love with him, to help him blackmail his aunt. After Albert takes apart the oven, Ellen is badly frightened when she thinks she sees Leonora playing the piano, although it turns out to be Lucy wearing the woman's favorite wig. Albert then gets the slowly unraveling Ellen to admit that she murdered Leonora. He runs away when the nuns show up saying that the police are on his trail. Lucy also escapes from the house as Emily and Louisa inform Ellen that Albert has been captured. Ellen bids her sisters farewell and leaves to surrender to the law.

Ladies in Retirement was done three times in the early days of television, the first being a presentation in 1948 on WBKB-TV's *Chicago Playhouse* starring Catherine Payne. Lillian Gish portrayed Ellen Creed in a 1951 NBC-TV production telecast on *Lucky Strike Theatre*. Una O'Connor and Betty Sinclair played the deranged sisters and Robert Montgomery served as producer. In December 1954, Claire Trevor starred in another NBC-TV presentation of the work on *Lux Video Theatre* with Elsa Lanchester and Edith Barrett repeating their film roles. In 1969, Columbia remade the feature as *The Mad Room* (q.v.).

Ladrón de Cadaveres (Body Snatcher)

(1957; 80 minutes) DIRECTOR: Fernando Mendez. SCREENPLAY: Fernando Mendez and Alejandro Verbitzky. PHOTOGRAPHY: Victor Herrera. EDITOR: Jorge Butos. MUSIC: Federico Ruiz. SOUND: James L. Fields. SPECIAL EFFECTS: Juan Munoz. PRODUCTION DESIGN: Gunther Gerzso. MAKEUP: Margarita Ortega. PRODUCTION CHIEF: Armando Espinosa. ASSISTANT DIRECTOR: Americo Fernandez. CAST: Columba Dominguez (Lucia), Crox Alvarado (Captain Carlos Robles), Wolf Rubinski [Ruvinskis] (Guillermo Santana/El Vampiro), Carlos Riquelme (Don Panchito/Mad Scientist), Arturo Martinez (Felipe Dorantes), Eduardo Alcaraz (Chief of Police), Guillermo Hernandez ["Lobo Negro"] (El Lobo), Yerye Beirute (Cosme Ramirez), Alberto Catala (Rubio), Lee Morgan (City Official), Ignacio Navarro (Henchman), Alejandro Cruz ["Black Shadow"] (El Tigre), Jose Pardave (Waiter), Roberto Meyer (Forensic Doctor), Hector Mateos (Ring Doctor), Antonio Padilla "Picoro" (Ring Announcer), Jesus Murcielago Velazquez (Wrestler), Salvador Lozano (Minister), Armando Acosta, Pepe Nave, Oscar Ortiz de Pinedo (Spectators).

Ladrón de Cadaveres, an admixture of professional wrestling, the Frankenstein theme, telepathy and romance, was one of several Mexican horror thrillers Columbia distributed in the United States to Spanish-language theaters. Released stateside in the fall of 1957, it was made by Internacional Cinematográfica at the Churubusco Azteca studios and issued in its homeland in 1956. Like most Mexican horror films of the 1950s and 1960, it was quite atmospheric, especially in the initial graveyard scene and the sequences in the mad scientist's laboratory. Unfortunately these were few in comparison to the wrestling footage and the romantic interludes. In *The Encyclopedia of Fantastic Film* (2000), R.M. Young called it a "[g]risly horror-thriller ... [Mexico's] answer to *Invasion of the Body Snatchers*."

At night in a graveyard, a mad scientist (Carlos Riquelme) and his assistant Cosme (Yerye Beirute) dig up and steal a recently buried corpse. The scene switches to Mexico City where country boy Guillermo Santana (Wolf Rubinski) looks up his old pal Carlos Robles (Crox Alvarado), now a captain on the police force. Santana tells Robles he wants to be a cowboy but the cop instead introduces him to wrestling promoter Felipe Dorantes (Arturo Martinez), in the hopes that Santana will be hired as a grappler. While at Dorantes' gym, Santana meets secretary Lucia (Columba Dominguez), who he finds very attractive. He also witnesses a ring fight between El Lobo (Guillermo Hernandez) and El Tigre (Alejandro Cruz), after which El Lobo shoves an old man, Don Panchito (Carlos Riquelme), who is selling lottery tickets. After the two are separated, El Lobo goes to the showers where he is stabbed by Don Panchito, who is really the mad scientist in disguise. Cosme removes the wrestler's body to the doctor's laboratory where the medico attempts to make him a superman by putting a monkey's brain in his head. Although the experiment fails, the scientist vows to continue his work.

Robles suggests that Santana bill himself in the ring as El Vampiro. El Vampiro wins his first match and soon becomes a popular wrestling sensation. At his master's behest, Cosme attacks El Vampiro before a match and cuts his arm but as he runs away he is shot and killed by Robles. Don Panchito switches antiseptic with poison in the ring doctor's (Hector Mateos) bag. After being treated with the supposed medication, El Vampiro collapses during a match and is declared dead. The scientist's other henchman (Ignacio Navarro) takes Santana's body from the morgue and transfers it to the lab and this time a brain transplant using a gorilla is a success, but Santana is turned into a superhuman fiend. To prove the success of his work, the scientist has Santana kill a masked wrestler and take his place, but the creature goes berserk, throws his opponent (Jesus Murcielago Velazquez) out of the ring and tears off his mask, revealing a hideous countenance. The crowd stampedes from the arena, trampling the henchman to death. When the doctor tries to control his creation with fire, he is impaled by the beast, who begins to take on simian facial features. The creature escapes and seeks out Lucia, abducting her from her apartment and taking her to the roof. There he is confronted by Robles. When Santana tries to kill his friend, the chief of police (Eduardo Alcaraz) shoots him and he falls to his death. Later Lucia is given a commendation by a city official (Lee Morgan) honoring Santana and his sacrifice.

The film's hero-monster was played by professional wrestler Wolf Ruvinskis, billed here as Wolf Rubinski. Not only was Ruvinskis (1925–99) a popular grappler of the 1940s and 1950s, he also appeared in over 120 films between 1944 and 1996. He was best known for his portrayal of the superhero wrestler Neutron in a series of movies from 1960 to 1965. The film featured two other ring warriors who worked in Mexican movies, Guillermo Hernandez, "Lobo Negro" and Alejandro Cruz, "Black Shadow." Also in the movie was Yerye Beirute, who was known as the Mexican Boris Karloff due to his gaunt build and sinister looks. In addition to this outing, he was in *El Ataud del Vampiro* (The Vampire's Coffin) (1958), *La Casa del Terror* (The House of Terror) (1959) with Lon Chaney, Jr., and two of Karloff's final films, *Fear Chamber* and *The Incredible Invasion* [qq.v.]) which Columbia co-produced and distributed in the U.S. in the 1970s.

The League of Frightened Men

(1937; 71 minutes) ASSOCIATE PRODUCER: Edward Chodorov. DIRECTOR: Alfred E. Green. SCREENPLAY: Eugene Solow and Guy Endore, from the novel by Rex Stout. PHOTOGRAPHY: Henry Freulich. EDITOR: Gene Milford. ART DIRECTOR: Stephen Gooson. COSTUMES: Robert Kalloch. CAST: Walter Connolly (Nero Wolfe), Lionel Stander (Archie Goodwin), Eduardo Ciannelli (Paul Chapin), Irene Hervey (Evelyn Hibbard), Victor Kilian (Pitney Scott), Nana Bryant (Agnes Burton), Allen Brook (Mark Chapin), Walter Kingsford (Ferdinand Bowen), Leonard Mudie (Professor Hibbard), Kenneth Hunter (Dr. Burton), Charles Irwin (Augustus Farrell), Rafaela Ottiano (Dora Chapin), Edward McNamara (Inspector Cramer), Jameson Thomas (Michael Ayres), Ian Wolfe (Nicholas Cabot), Jonathan Hale (Alexander Drummond), Herbert Ashley (Fritz Brenner), James Flavin (Joe).

Columbia obtained the screen rights to Rex Stout's brainy, lazy, self-indulgent, portly and surly private detective Nero Wolfe with plans to do a series of features based on the character. *Meet Nero Wolfe* (1936) starred Edward Arnold in the title role with Lionel Stander as his associate, Archie Goodwin. It was a fairly interesting murder mystery except Arnold was too jovial to capture the character properly and Stander did not fit the Goodwin role either mentally or physically (although he repeated it in *The League of Frightened Men*). The second outing, based on Stout's 1935 novel, completely miscast Walter Connolly as a chocolate-loving (rather than a beer drinker as in the novels and the first film), mild-mannered Wolfe. By the time it was released, Stout refused to let Columbia tamper further with his works. The film's plot, however, was interesting and the *New York Times* termed it "a well-knit mystery, and well played out." Its chief horror element was having a mysterious fiend doing away with aging members of a college club whose long-ago prank left another associate a mangled cripple.

Professor Hibbard (Leonard Mudie) receives a menacing missive and, since two of his friends died after receiving similar notes, he calls on reclusive private detective Nero Wolfe (Connolly) for help. Wolfe learns that more than two decades before, Hibbard and nine other wealthy Harvard University club members pulled a hazing prank on Paul Chapin (Eduardo Ciannelli), a scholarship freshman whose family was not rich; as a result, the young man was permanently crippled. Chapin, now a noted writer, hates the former club members for what they did to him and Hibbard thinks he is responsible for the killings. The professor's daughter Evelyn (Irene Hervey) loves Chapin's brother Mark (Allen Brook).

When Hibbard disappears, Wolfe asks all the remaining members of the club to meet with him at his Gotham brownstone and all agree except cabbie Pitney Scott (Victor Kilian). One of the men, banker Ferdinand Bowen (Walter Kingsford), informs Wolfe that the two murdered men were broke. Since Wolfe rarely moves from his home, he orders his associate, Archie Goodwin (Stander), to watch Chapin's abode. Another party is doing the same thing. After club member Dr. Burton (Kenneth Hunter) is shot when Chapin is in his house, Wolfe comes to find out that the victim's wife Dora (Rafaela Ottiano) once had an affair with Chapin. Wolfe is able to clear Chapin by proving the shot that killed the doctor was fired from a closet in his home just as Chapin arrived on the scene. Upset about his brother being a suspect, Mark drugs Archie and kidnaps Wolfe but the detective manages to settle him down before the arrival of police Inspector Cramer (Edward McNamara). Back at the brownstone, Wolfe has another meeting with the survivors and reveals that the phantom trailing Paul was Professor Hibbard, who disappeared in order to save his own life. The detective also proves that Chapin sent the missives to frighten his former tormenters but the murders were actually committed by Bowen to cover up his embezzlement of the murdered men's money.

The plot involving murder for the revenge of a college hazing was also used in Paramount's *College Scandal*, released the previous year.

Little Prince and the Eight Headed Dragon

(1964; 86 minutes; Color) EXECUTIVE PRODUCER: Hiroshi Okawa. ASSOCIATE PRODUCERS: Shin Yoshida, Isanu Takahashi and Takashi Ijima. DIRECTOR: Yugo Serikawa. SCREENPLAY: Takashi Iijima and Ichiro Ikeda. PHOTOGRAPHY: Mitsuaki Ishikawa and Hideaki Sugawara. EDITOR: Ikuzo Inaba. MUSIC: Akira Ifukube. ART DIRECTOR: Reiji Koyama. SOUND: Sachio Ishii and Takeshi Mori. VISUAL EFFECTS: Ryuzo Iwato. ANIMATORS: Yasuo Otsuka and Sadao Tsukioka. ANIMATION DIRECTOR: Yasuhi Mori. SUPERVISORS: Sanae Yamamoto and Koji Fukiya. ASSISTANT DIRECTORS: Isao Takeaway and Kimio Yabuki. ENGLISH-LANGUAGE VERSION: DIRECTOR-SCREENPLAY: William Ross. VOICE CAST: Tomohito Sumida (Susanoo), Yukiko Okada (Princess Kushinada), Chiharu Kuri (Akahana), Kiyoshi Kawakubo, Masato Yamanouchi.

One of the earliest Japanese *anime* features produced by Tokyo's Toei Animation Studios, this production was released in Japan in 1963 as *Wanpaku Oji No Orochi Taiji* with Columbia issuing it in the U.S. early in 1964 as *Little Prince and the Eight Headed Dragon*. It was also known as *Prince in Wonderland* and *Rainbow Bridge*. Billed as "An Ancient Japanese Fairy Tale," the widescreen feature proved to be very satisfying with kiddie matinee audiences because of its interesting story, lovely Magnacolor, well-done animation and the highly entertaining finale with the little prince in a fight to the death with the eight-headed monster. Akira Ifukube's score reused battle music from *The Mysterians* (1959) and some of it was also in a couple of episodes of the *anime* TV series *Mazinger Z*. The English-language version of the film, written and directed by William Ross, was done by United Services in Tokyo.

The Lord of the Universe tells god Izanagi and his wife Izanami to create a land where people can live and be happy. With their three children, the Crystal Prince, the Sun Goddess and Prince Susanoo (voice of Tomoshito Sumida), they use a magic spear to form the islands of the world. When the tiger Taro harasses his talking rabbit Akahana (voice of Chiharu Kuri), Susanoo beats the big cat but his mother advises him to show mercy. His father informs the boy that his mother has been called to a place called Heaven; Susanoo throws a temper tantrum after being told he cannot follow her. Finally falling asleep, the boy dreams that his mother gives him an amulet that will protect him from danger but that he cannot locate the place where she has gone. Determined to find her, the little prince builds a boat but all his animal friends except Akahana desert him. The two set sail but are soon attacked by a giant fish that Susanoo kills. The King of the Sea guides them to the Land of Night at the lowest depths of the ocean. There they enter the Crystal Cave and find the boy's older brother, the Crystal Prince, whose war chief thinks Susanoo has come to do battle and encases him in ice. When he is thawed, the boy fights with the crystal soldiers until his brother tells him that he does not know how to find their mother. As the angry Susanoo leaves, the Crystal Prince gives Akahana a crystal ball that will thwart danger. A wind tunnel tosses the little prince and his dog into the desolate Land of Fire where they meet a kindly giant, Big Taitanbo, who tells them a Fire God has decimated the area. When Susanoo confronts the Fire God, a fight ensues. Each time the boy attacks the deity, it multiplies. Finally the boy uses the crystal ball to disperse the flames. Taking Big Taitanbo with them, Susanoo and Akahana leave for the Land of Light; the repentant Fire God gives them a magic bird to fly them there. The boy's sister, the Sun Goddess, rules the Land of Light and she asks him to stay and make a place there for the people of the fire country. The boy, his dog and the giant cause so many unintended problems that the Sun Goddess' subjects become agitated and she leaves, causing their land to become dark. In order to get her to return, they have a celebration and pretend to replace her. After the Sun Goddess retakes her throne, she tells her brother and his friends to leave her kingdom but for him to be brave, fight evil and protect those who suffer.

The trio travels to the Land of Morning Sun where the boy saves a small mouse from drowning and meets pretty Kushinada (voice of Yukiko Okada), a little princess who resembles his mother. She takes him to her father who warns that an eight-headed dragon, the Yamata no Orochi, is about to arrive. Since it has carried off seven maidens in as many years, it is now coming for the princess. Susanoo vows to destroy the monster. The mouse's father advises him to fly high and attack the dragon; to do so, he must capture a magic flying horse. That night when the animal comes to drink, he jumps on its back and asks for its help in defeating the monster. The fire-breathing dragon arrives and drinks the wine the prince and his friends have left for it, hoping to get the creature drunk. Riding the magic horse, the little prince attacks the hydra and after a grueling battle kills the monster. Exhausted by the battle, Susanoo is awakened by Kushinada as the magic horse flies back to the Land of Light where it came from at the behest of the Sun Goddess. Susanoo's mother appears and tells him she has always been in his heart as the little prince and his friends decide to remain in the Land of the Morning Sun which is engulfed by a rainbow.

Lost Horizon

(1937; 132 minutes) PRODUCER-DIRECTOR: Frank Capra. SCREENPLAY: Robert Riskin and Sidney Buchman, from the novel by James Hilton. PHOTOGRAPHY: Joseph Walker. EDITORS: Gene Havlick and Gene Milford. MUSIC: Dimitri Tiomkin. MUSIC DIRECTOR: Max Steiner. ART DIRECTOR: Stephen Goosson. SOUND: John Livadary. COSTUME DESIGN: Ernest Dryden. SPECIAL EFFECTS: Harry Redmond, Jr., E. Roy Davidson and Ganahl Carson. TECHNICAL ADVISOR: Harrison Forman. CAST: Ronald Colman (Robert Conway), Jane Wyatt (Sondra Bizet), John Howard (George Conway), Thomas Mitchell (Henry "Barney" Barnard), Edward Everett Horton (Alexander P. Lovett), H.B. Warner (Chang), Margo (Maria), Isabel Jewell (Gloria Stone), Sam Jaffe (High Lama/Father Parrault), Hall Johnson Choir (Voices), David Torrence (British Prime Minister), Hugh Buckler (Lord Gainsford), Val Durand (Hijacker Talu), Milton Owen (Hijacked Pilot Fenner), Richard Loo (Shanghai Airport Officer), Willie Fung (Fuel-Stop Bandit Leader), Victor Wong (Bandit Leader), John Burton (Wynant), John Miltern (Carstairs), John T. Murray (Meeker), Dennis D'Auburn (Aviator), Noble Johnson (Return Journey Porter Leader), John Tetterner (Montaigne), Matthew Carlton (Pottery Maker), Joe Herrera (Candle Maker), Carl Stockdale, Margaret McWade, Ruth Robinson, Wyrley Birch (Missionaries), Richard Masters, Alex Shoulder, Ernesto Zambrano, Manual Kalilli (Servants), Max Rabinowitz (Pianist Selveking), Boyd Irwin (Assistant Foreign Secretary), Leonard Mudie (Security Secretary), Neil Fitzgerald, Darby Clark (Radio Operators), Patricia Curtis, Mary Lou Dix, Beatrice Blinn, Arthur Rankin (Passengers), Norman Ainsley, David Clyde (Club Stewards), George Chan (Chinese Priest), Robert Cory, Barry Winton, Eric Wilton, Henry Mowbray, Wedgwood Nowell (Britishers), Lawrence Grant (First Man), Sonny Bupp (Carried Boy), David Cavendish (First Aviator), Chief Big Tree, Richard Robles, James P. Smith, Eli Casey, Charles Dempsey, Robert Lugo, Moning Gonzales, George Kaluma, Delmar Ingraham, Ira Walker, Tom Campbell, Glenn Howard, Antonio Herrara, Pat Tapia, Joe Shoulder, Ed Thorpe, Joe Molina, Harry Lishman (Porters).

While *It Happened One Night* (1934) is credited with giving Columbia Pictures its first major production, lifting the studio from the ranks of Poverty Row, it was *Lost Horizon* that gave it the prestige it needed to compete with the majors in feature filmmaking. Budgeted at $2.5 million, nearly half the expenditure for all of Columbia's 1937–38 releases, the film was nearly a disaster since its opening scenes drew derision at an early preview. Studio boss Harry Cohn and producer-director Frank Capra then removed the first reel of the production, resulting in a much better received version. When the feature was issued theatrically late in the summer of 1937 it ran 118 minutes although its road show prints, released earlier (in March), ran 132 minutes; reissued in the early 1940s as *Lost Horizon of Shangri-La*, it was cut further to 107 minutes in an effort to minimize its pacifistic leanings. It was nominated for seven Academy Awards, including Best Picture, Best Supporting Actor (H.B. Warner) and Sound (John Livadary) and it won Oscars for Gene Havlick and Gene Milford's editing and art direction by Stephen Goosson. Despite raising Columbia to the position of being a major studio, *Lost Horizon* failed to initially recoup its costs and caused the company to fail to turn a profit the year of its release.

A revolution takes place in the Chinese city of Baskul on March 10, 1935, and British diplomat Robert Conway (Ronald Colman) assists in helping 90 British subjects get out of the city by airplane. He takes the last flight out of the city accompanied by his brother George (John Howard), expatriate businessman Henry "Barney" Barnard (Thomas Mitchell), paleontologist Alexander P. Lovett (Edward Everett Horton) and American Gloria Stone (Isabel Jewell), who is suffering from tuberculosis. On the flight to Shanghai, Robert discusses the possibility he may be Britain's next foreign secretary with George, not knowing the plane has been hijacked. The next morning the passengers realize the plane is heading west and after a stopover for fuel at a remote village, it heads for Tibet where it crash lands, killing the pilot (Val Durand). As Robert is about to go for help, a group of porters led by the English-speaking Chang (H.B. Warner) arrives and prepares them for the difficult journey to his monastery, Shangri-La.

After climbing for miles along treacherous mountain ledges, the group arrives at their destination, an earthly paradise protected on all sides by high mountains. While the others are not comfortable in their new surroundings, Robert finds contentment. During dinner, Chang gives them the history of Shangri-La, which was started more than 200 years before by a Belgian priest, Father Perrault; the community has little outside contact with the rest of the world. George tells the group he thinks they were kidnapped and tries to find Chang while brandishing a gun. Robert is forced to slug him. When Chang comes to their rooms, they inform him that they will hold him hostage unless he tells them the truth. Chang then takes Robert to the High Lama (Sam Jaffe), who turns out to be the still living Perrault. He tells Robert he has read his books and feels they contain the same ideals as his community and that he hopes they will eventually be spread throughout the world. The next day, Robert meets Sondra Bizet (Jane Wyatt), who was brought up in Shangri-La after the deaths of her missionary parents. She informs him it was her idea for him to be brought to the monastery. As time passes the two fall in love.

Barnard finds gold and makes plans to steal it while Gloria begins to regain her health and George becomes attracted to beautiful Maria (Margo) although Chang informs Robert she is over 60 years old and is kept youthful by living in Shangri-La. Barnard and Lovett soon come under the spell of the community; forgetting about the gold, Barnard draws up plans to bring modern plumbing to the village while Lovett gets Chang's permission to teach geology classes. During Robert's second visit with the High Lama, the old man asks him to be his replacement, and then peacefully dies. When George learns that porters are at the border of the community and will take the party back home, he tries to get the others to go with him but fails. Finally he has Maria tell Robert how she was kidnapped by Chang and is being forced to live in Shangri-La against her will. Robert agrees to go with George and Maria and he reluctantly leaves the community but on the trip back they are shot at by the porters who are buried when their gunshots sets off an avalanche. As the trio struggles on, Maria begins to age and when George sees she has physically withered he goes mad and falls off a cliff. After many torturous days, Robert winds up in a Tibetan village with amnesia. Lord Gainsford (Hugh Buckler) is

Ronald Colman, Sam Jaffe and director Frank Capra on the set of *Lost Horizon* (1937).

sent to bring him home but, regaining his memory, he escapes. Gainsford chases him for ten months before giving up the quest. Returning to England he tells the story to members of his club. After a long struggle, Robert finds his way back to Shangri-La and Sondra.

Variety reported, "So canny are the ingredients that where credulity perhaps rears its practical head, audiences will be carried away by the histrionic illusion, skill and general Hollywood legerdemain which so effectively capture the best elements in this $2.5 million saga of Shangri-La ... Whether it's James Hilton's original novel or Robert Riskin's celluloid transmutation, the scripting contribution is one of the picture's strongest assets." In *Guide for the Film Fanatic* (1986), Danny Peary wrote, "Frank Capra's classic has dated badly ... Don't miss the film's subtle anti-communist propaganda: the only person dissatisfied with this true utopia is Margo, who is a Russian." Joe Kane in *The Phantom of the Movies' Videoscope* (2000) states, "While not quite the flawless masterpiece many have proclaimed it, *Lost Horizon* certainly ranks as quality offbeat entertainment..." and *Time Out Film Guide* (2001) opined, "Classic fantasy epic ... Not at all the sort of film one could make in these considerably more jaundiced times, as was evident with the appearance of the atrocious remake in 1973."

The fantasy elements of *Lost Horizon* deal mainly with longevity, the High Lama (played by Sam Jaffe) having lived for over 200 years before passing on the mantle of Shangri-La's leadership to Bob Conway. More horrific is Maria's transformation scenes as the beauty becomes a hag when she leaves the youth-protective confines of the Valley of the Blue Moon.

Lost Horizon

(1973; 150 minutes; Color) PRODUCER: Ross Hunter. ASSOCIATE PRODUCER: Jacques Mapes. DIRECTOR: Charles Jarrott. SCREENPLAY: Larry Kramer, from the novel by James Hilton. PHOTOGRAPHY: Robert Surtees. EDITOR: Maury Winetrobe. MUSIC: Burt Bacharach. SONG: Burt Bacharach and Hal David. Title Song Sung by Shawn Phillips. ART DIRECTOR: E. Preston Ames. SOUND: Dan Wallin, Richard Tyler, Jack Solomon and Arthur Piantadosi. SETS: Jerry Wunderlich. COSTUME

Peter Finch and Liv Ullmann in *Lost Horizon* (1973).

DESIGN: Jean Louis. CHOREOGRAPHER: Hermes Pan. ASSISTANT DIRECTORS: Jerry Ziesmer, Russ Saunders and Malcolm R. Harding. CAST: Peter Finch (Richard Conway), Liv Ullmann (Catherine), Sally Kellerman (Sally Hughes), George Kennedy (Sam Cornelius), Michael York (George Conway), Olivia Hussey (Maria), Bobby Van (Harry Lovett), James Shigeta (To Len), Charles Boyer (High Lama), John Gielgud (Chang), Kent Smith (Bill Ferguson), John Van Dreelen (Dr. Verden), Hedley Mattingly (Colonel Rawley), Miiko Taka (Nurse), Bruce Davis Bayne (Airplane Passenger), Larry Duran (Asian Pilot), Jessie Salve (Bridegroom), Michael Bernal, Sharann Hisamoto, Jackie Torn (Student Dancers).

In 1973 Columbia released its disastrous $6 million remake of *Lost Horizon* to almost unanimous critical contempt and audience apathy. While the storyline remained virtually the same, music was added: Peter Finch's singing voice was provided by Jerry Hutman, Diana Lee sang for Liv Ullmann and Andrea Willis for Olivia Hussey. There was also some character name changes: Robert Conway in the original became Richard Conway in the remake; crooked industrialist Barnard became engineer-businessman Sam Cornelius; tubercular Gloria Stone was turned into magazine photojournalist Sally Hughes; paleontologist Alexander P. Lovett was now USO entertainer Harry Lovett; and Conway's brother George became a pushy newspaper reporter. To explain Chang's perfect English, the script had him educated at Oxford. Ullmann's character remained a schoolteacher but her name was changed from Sondra Bizet to Catherine. The remake used sets from the 1967 feature *Camelot* since this was Columbia's first film after moving to the Warner Bros. lot.

As noted, the critics were harsh. Charles Champlin in the *Los Angeles Times* called the remake "[c]umbersome, unlyrical and tedious." *Esquire* was more blunt, dubbing it the "Worst Movie of the Year." Rex Reed in the *New York Daily News* said it was "[t]rash" and "an empty, wooded-headed musical.... The dance numbers are like half-time at the Super Bowl. The songs are dreadful.... The dialogue is dumbfoundedly simple-minded." In *The Family Guide to Movies on Video* (1988), Henry Herz and Tony Zaza noted it "wastes a fine cast and good story in a welter of forgettable Burt Bacharach-Hal David tunes." James Robert Parish and I reported in *The Great Hollywood Musical Pictures* (1992), "It recouped less than half [the $6 million budget] when shown in theaters. Not only had the plot of the Hilton fantasy dated badly, but the music score contributed by Burt Bacharach and Hal David was one of their worst and Hermes Pan's choreography (which included a dancing bear!) is almost unbearable, including the steps given to wisecracking hoofer Bobby Van ... The acting, script and sets were sub-par."

The Lost Tribe

(1949; 72 minutes) PRODUCER: Sam Katzman. DIRECTOR: William Berke. SCREENPLAY: Arthur Hoerl and Don Martin. STORY: Arthur Hoerl. PHOTOGRAPHY: Ira H. Morgan. EDITOR: Aaron Stell. MUSIC: Mischa Bakaleinikoff. ART DIRECTOR: Paul Palmentola. SOUND: Russell Malgren. SETS: Sidney Clifford. ASSISTANT DIRECTOR: Wilbur McGaugh. CAST: Johnny Weissmuller (Jungle Jim), Elena Verdugo (Li Wanna), Myrna Dell (Norina), Joseph Vitale (Calhoun), Ralph Dunn (Captain Rawlings), Paul Marion (Chot), Nelson Leigh (Zoron), George J. Lewis (Wilson), Gil Perkins (Dojek), Rube Schaeffer (Lerch), George DeNormand (Avery), Wally West (Sam Welker), John Merton (Kessler), Jody Gilbert (Barmaid Zulta), Blackie Whiteford (Rifleman), Ray Corrigan (Zimba), Holmes Herbert (Narrator).

Working title: *Jungle Jim's Adventure*.

The Lost Tribe, the second "Jungle Jim" feature, arrived in theaters in the spring of 1949. Basically a reworking of the initial film in the series, *Jungle Jim* (q.v.), its opening narration was by Holmes Herbert, who had the same job in the first film as well as playing the area commissioner. Mike Mazurki and Jack Ingram were originally intended for two of the villain roles but were replaced by Joseph Vitale and George J. Lewis. Like many of the features in the series, *The Lost Tribe* was filmed in part at Corriganville and its owner, Ray Corrigan, played the role of Zimba the gorilla. Photographically, the film was a ragtag affair with scenes ranging from very clear to grainy wild animal footage. In addition to the antics of Jim's pets Skipper the dog and Caw Caw the crow, the production had star Johnny Weissmuller in the expected swimming sequences plus doing battle with a crocodile, a lion and two sharks. *Variety* called the film "an action-packed entry that will prove surefire entertainment for youthful filmgoers" while *The Motion Picture Herald* said it was a "film providing a generous measure of the expected excitement.... [The] story is routine."

Two men (Wally West, George DeNormand) working for Captain Rawlings (Eddie Dunn) shoot and kill natives they are trailing in an effort to find the lost city of Dzamm. The natives were escorting Li Wanna (Elena Verdugo) who has come in search of Jungle Jim (Weissmuller). Caw Caw leads the jungle man to the scene of the crime only to find the murderers have been mauled to death by a lion. Jim manages to get Li Wanna into a tree before a group of lions attack them but the beasts are scared away by an elephant. Jim then goes with Li Wanna to Dzamm and meets with her father, high priest Zoron (Nelson Leigh), who believes that white men are after diamonds and other treasures in the city's temple. Since his people oppose combat, Zoron asks Jim to give some of the diamonds to the white men if they will promise to leave the city and its inhabitants alone. Jim agrees, not knowing that Zoron's son Chot (Paul Marion) has come under the spell of Norina (Myrna Dell), the niece of trading post owner Calhoun (Joseph Vitale), who is in cahoots with Rawlings and his associate Wilson (George J. Lewis).

On the way back to the sea coast town where Calhoun has his establishment, Jim saves gorilla Zimba (Corrigan) and its baby from a lion. Chot informs Calhoun that Jim is bringing a peace offering from his people and that he cannot see Norina again, although he soon learns she has betrayed him to her uncle. When Calhoun tries to follow Chot into the jungle, Jim stops him with a rigged rope. Jim then meets Norina who introduces him to her uncle and he gives the trader half the diamonds and takes the rest to Rawlings, who is aboard his ship. That night Norina tries to convince Jim to take her away from the jungle but he thinks she only wants to find the way to Dzamm. Rawlings, Wilson and their men capture Jim and beat him in order to try and learn the route to the lost city. As Li Wanna leaves Dzamm in search of Jim, Norina tries to set him free and is stabbed to death by her uncle. Caw Caw pecks at its master's rope bonds and frees him. Jim beats up both Wilson and Calhoun and escapes but Calhoun and Rawlings capture Li Wanna when she arrives in the village. Jim swims to Rawlings' ship and rescues the girl but as they attempt to get to shore they are captured. When Calhoun threatens Li Wanna, Jim agrees to lead them to the lost city, but along the way they run into Zimba and a gorilla band who follow them to Dzamm. Once in the city, the marauders and the natives raid the temple, stealing its treasures. Chot attacks the men guarding the jungle man and Li Wanna and sets the two free before being shot. The gorillas attack the invaders and kill most of them but Rawlings and Wilson take Jim and Li Wanna captive. When the two crooks try to escape, they are killed by Zimba. Chot asks Jim and Li Wanna for forgiveness before dying as the natives restore the treasure to the temple.

Macbeth

(1971; 141 minutes; Color) PRODUCER: Andrew Braunsberg. EXECUTIVE PRODUCER: Hugh M. Hefner. ASSOCIATE PRODUCER: Timothy Burrill. DIRECTOR: Roman Polanski. SCREENPLAY: Roman Polanski and Kenneth Tynan, from the play by William Shakespeare. PHOTOGRAPHY: Gil Taylor. EDITOR: Alastair McIntyre. MUSIC: The Third Ear Band. ART DIRECTOR: Fred Carter. PRODUCTION DESIGN: Wilfred Shingleton. SETS: Bryan Graves. COSTUMES: Anthony Mendleson. WARDROBE: Jackie Breed and Phil Pickford. MAKEUP: Tom Smith. SPECIAL EFFECTS: Ted Samuels. CONTINUITY: Angela Allen. ARTISTIC ADVISOR: Kenneth Tynan. ASSISTANT DIRECTOR: Hercules Bellville. CAST: Jon Finch (Macbeth), Francesca Annis (Lady Macbeth), Nicholas Selby (King Duncan), Martin Shaw (Banquo), Terence Baylor (Macduff), John Stride (Ross), Stephan Chase (Malcolm), Paul Shelley (Donalbain), Maisie MacFarquhar, Elsie Taylor, Noelle Rimmington (Witches), Noel Davis (Seyton), Sydney Bromley (Porter), Richard Pearson (Doctor), Patricia Mason (Gentlewoman), Michael Balfour, Andrew McCullough (Murderers), Keith Chegwin (Fleance), Andrew Laurence (Lennox), Bernard Archard (Angus), Bruce Purchase (Caithness), Frank Wylie (Menteith), Diane Fletcher (Lady Macduff), Mark Dightam (Macduff's Son), Bill Drysdale, Roy Jones (King's Grooms), Vic Abbott (Thane of Caudor), Iag Hogg, Geoffrey Reed, Nigel Ashton (Thanes), William Hobbs (Young Seyward), Alf Joint (Old Seyward), Paul Hennen (Doctor's Apprentice), Ronald Lacey (Banquo's Killer), Howard Lang, David Ellison (Old Soldiers), Terence Mountain (Soldier), Lynette Reade (Witch), Anna Willoughby, Olga Anthony, Don Vernon, Maxine Skelton, Roy Desmond, Pamela Foster, Christina Paul, Dickie Martyn, John Gordon, Janie Kells, Beth Owen (Dancers), Clement Freud (Hanged Man).

Upon its U.S. release late in 1971, Columbia's *Macbeth* was considered quite a controversial adaptation of William Shakespeare's 1605–06 play due to its nudity and violence. (By today's standards it seems rather tame.) Filmed in North Wales and at Shepperton Studios in London by Playboy Productions for Caliban Films, it was also issued as *The Tragedy of Macbeth*. A good deal of the play's text was removed from the shooting script and some of the dialogue was done as voiceover rather than being spoken directly by the characters on-screen. In addition, the finale of Donalbain seeking out the witches was tacked onto the production, whose highlight was a colorful reproduction of 13th century Scotland and its violent times. Jon Finch and Francesca Annis portrayed the youthful Macbeths; Finch's performance lacked the ferocity the character needed and the strikingly beautiful Annis was more neurotic than grasping as Lady Macbeth. Nonetheless, *Macbeth* was declared the best English-language film of 1971 by National Board of Review of Motion Pictures.

Three witches (Maisie MacFarquhar, Elsie Taylor, Noelle Rimmington) bury a hand holding a dagger in the sand. Later, the Scots route Norwegian invaders and triumphant King Duncan (Nicholas Selby) is told of the heroism of one of his thanes, Macbeth (Finch). Riding home to his castle at Dunsinane with his comrade Banquo (Martin Shaw), Macbeth meets the three witches who tell him he will be Thane of Cawdor and a king, while Banquo will never rule but will father kings. That night a messenger informs Macbeth that the Thane of Cawdor (Vic Abbott) is a traitor and that Duncan has bestowed upon him the thane's title. Stopping at Duncan's court, Macbeth is received as a hero but is soon disappointed when he learns the king plans to be succeeded by his son Malcolm (Stephan Chase). Lady Macbeth (Annis) has received a letter from her husband detailing the prophecies of the witches and she realizes she may soon become queen of Scotland but doubts her husband's ability to take the title by murder. When Macbeth returns home and she finds out that Duncan and his entourage will be their guests that night, she urges her husband to look like an innocent flower but be the serpent under it. As a storm brews, the king arrives and is feasted. Macbeth has doubts about killing him and wants to give up the quest for the throne but his wife calls him a coward and tells him to carry out the deed. Lady Macbeth drugs the drinks of Duncan's grooms (Bill Drysdale, Roy Jones) and her husband sneaks into the king's bedroom and stabs him to death. When he returns to his bedchamber with blood on his hands and carrying the murder daggers, Lady Macbeth takes the weapons and leaves them with the grooms and smears Duncan's blood on their bodies. They both wash the blood off their hands with Lady Macbeth telling her husband that a little water has cleansed them of their deeds.

Yugoslav poster for *Macbeth* (1971).

The next morning Macduff (Terence Bayler), another thane, arrives to see the king. When he goes with Macbeth to his bedchamber, he finds Duncan murdered. Macduff alerts the castle to the crime as Macbeth slays the awakening grooms. After Malcolm and his lame younger brother Donalbain (Paul Shelley) see their father's bloody corpse, they decide to split up and flee the country. As Duncan's funeral procession leaves Dunsinane, Macbeth is crowned Scotland's new king. He remembers the witches' prophecy about Banquo siring kings and dreams that his friend and small son Fleance (Keith Chegwin) try to kill him. After the new king bids farewell to Banquo and Fleance as they leave for a hunting trip, Macbeth convinces two assassins (Michael Balfour, Andrew McCulloch) to murder them. Banquo is killed but Fleance manages to escape. Macbeth gets rid of the killers by luring them into a dungeon. That night he and Lady Macbeth host a feast but the king sees the bloody ghost of Banquo. After his behavior upsets the court, his wife orders everyone to leave. Macbeth rides to the witches' cave where the naked coven gives him a potion and he is told that no man born of woman can harm him and that he will reign until Burnham Wood comes to Dunsinane. Confidently returning home, Macbeth finds out that Macduff has gone to join Malcolm in England and the king orders the murders of Lady Macduff (Diane Fletcher) and her children. Seeing blood on her hands, a naked Lady Macbeth wanders the castle pining over the murder of Duncan and trying to wash away his blood. Her servant (Patricia Mason) calls in a doctor (Richard Pearson) who tells the king of his wife's condition and is commanded to cure her. When Ross (John Stride), who aided Macbeth in the killings of Banquo and Lady Macduff, his sister-in-law, is denied the Thane of Caudor, he rides to join Malcolm and Macduff. He tells his brother-in-law of how Macbeth ordered the massacre of his family and Macduff vows revenge as he and Malcolm put together a large army to take the Scottish throne. After couriers bring news of the uprising, Macbeth orders his castle prepared for battle, the doctor departs and Lady Macbeth jumps off a wall to her death. As the invaders carry trees from Brunham Wood in front of them, the inhabitants of Dunsinane loot and desert the castle, leaving Macbeth alone on his throne. He fights off several of Malcolm's men and then does battle with Macduff who tells him he was not born of woman since he was torn from his mother's womb. After a lengthy fight, Macduff pierces Macbeth with his sword and then decapitates him. Ross removes the crown from Macbeth's head and places it on Malcolm as the invaders rejoice in their victory. Donalbain then rides to confer with the witches.

Roger Greenspun in the *New York Times* noted,

> *Macbeth* is a drama of unusual dark disruption, and in [Roman] Polanski's version the countervailing sense of order is either ironically undercut (as in the speeches of the smugly callous Duncan) or cut out entirely. I can imagine a much better *Macbeth*, but in point of fact all the other productions I've seen have been much worse ... I think that there is a principle of subordination at work here, and that Polanski means to develop a world in which no individual matters too much or, indeed, differs too greatly from his fellows....
> [I]t represents excellent Shakespearean moviemaking, a real interpretation of the text on the part of Polanski and his co-scenarist Kenneth Tynan.

In *Film Review 1972–1973* (1972), F. Maurice Speed said the feature "turned out to be a far more successful and impressive Shakespearean exercise than might have been thought likely, relating in visual terms of the cinema the horrors of this rough episode of Scots history." *Films in Review* (February, 1972) stated, "[T]he screenplay ... *expands* some of the scenes, and Polanski's direction protracts them further. Result: a bloody play has been made bloodier, and the essence of it has been lost."

The Mad Magician

(1954; 72 minutes) PRODUCER: Bryan Foy. DIRECTOR: John Brahm. STORY-SCREENPLAY: Crane Wilbur. PHOTOGRAPHY: Bert Glennon. EDITOR: Grant Whytock. MUSIC: Arthur Lange and Emil Newman. ART DIRECTOR: Frank Sylos. SOUND: John K. Kean. MAKEUP: George Bau and Gustaf Norin. SPECIAL EFFECTS: Dave Koehler. MAGIC EFFECTS: Bob Haskell. SETS: Howard Bristol. WARDROBE: Robert Martien. ASSISTANT DIRECTOR: Hal Herman. CAST: Vincent Price (Don Gallico), Mary Murphy (Karen Lee), Eva Gabor (Claire Gallico Ormond), John Emery (The Great Rinaldi), Donald Randolph (Ross Ormond), Lenita Lane (Alice Prentiss), Patrick O'Neal (Lieutenant Alan Bunce), Jay Novello (Frank Prentiss), Tom Powers (Police Chief), Lyle Talbot (Program Seller), Roland Varno (Master of Ceremonies), George Eldredge (Theater Manager), Robert B. Williams, Roy Engel (Carriage Drivers), Corey Allen (Stagehand Gus), Jack Kenny (Stagehand), Fred Keating (Theater Doorman), Keith Richards (Telephone User).

Columbia's final 3-D effort, *The Mad Magician* was their answer to *House of Wax*, released the previous year by Warner Bros. In fact the films had the same producer (Byron Foy), script writer (Crane Wilbur), cinematographer (Bert Glennon), makeup man (George Bau) and star (Vincent Price), and each took place in the Gaslight era with the protagonist being a basically honest artist whose work, hopes and dreams are confiscated by evil men with horrific results. Both features were lensed in 3-D although a regular version of *The Mad Magician* was also available to theaters. While *Variety* declared that Price "gives a realist interpretation," the film was a pale reminder of the much more entertaining and scary *House of Wax*. The *Los Angeles Daily News* felt *The Mad Magician* was a "grim little film of murder by hacksaw and crematory furnaces." Filmed on the Samuel Goldwyn lot, the feature was made in conjunction with Edward Small Productions.

Around the turn of the 20th century in New

York City, illusion inventor Don Gallico (Price), billed as "Gallico the Great," is preparing to open his new stage act called the Lady Buzz Saw. During the final rehearsal, his beautiful assistant Karen Lee (Mary Murphy) introduces Gallico to her boyfriend, police lieutenant Alan Bunce (Patrick O'Neal). On opening night, Gallico first performs in disguise as another trickster, the Great Rinaldi, but when his main act is about to begin the curtain drops and the theater manager (George Eldredge) tells the audience the performance cannot continue. Gallico's employer, Ross Ormond (Donald Randolph), the owner of Illusions, Inc., produces an injunction saying that everything Gallico invents belongs to him.

The next day Gallico shows Bunce his contract with Ormond and the policeman declares it valid. Ormond then appears with Rinaldi (John Emery) to whom he has promised the buzz saw illusion. When Rinaldi leaves, Gallico and Ormond argue over their agreement and the fact that Ross stole Gallico's wife Claire (Eva Gabor) and has abandoned her. When Ormond makes castigating remarks about Claire, the two men fight and Gallico ends up killing his boss with the buzz saw and hiding his decapitated head in a satchel. Karen briefly visits Gallico and mistakenly takes the valise, later leaving it in a cab before he regains possession of the bag. Finding out from Karen that a local campus is having a bonfire, Gallico puts on a face mask of Ormond he has developed, takes the dead man's body to the event and places it on the pile of items to be burned.

Wearing the Ormond mask, Gallico rents rooms under the name Ward Jameson with Frank Prentiss (Jay Novello) and his mystery novelist wife Alice (Lenita Lane). Returning from Europe, Claire comes to Illusions, Inc., to find her estranged husband. When Gallico refuses to help her, she goes to the police. When Ormond's picture is published in the newspaper, Alice sees the article and invites Claire to her home, telling her that Ormond is staying there under an assumed name. That night Gallico, disguised as Ormond, returns to the Prentiss home and is surprised by Claire, who can tell that the man is not her husband. Removing the mask, she realizes Gallico has killed Ormond. When she tries to seduce him, he murders her. The woman's screams alert the Prentisses but by the time they get to Ormond's room he has departed. The next day, the police chief (Tom Powers) declares that Ormond is the killer. After Alice shows interest in his work, Gallico invites her and Frank to see his latest illusion, a crematorium. Following the demonstration, Rinaldi appears, accuses Gallico of murdering Ormond and demands the new magic trick for himself. Gallico then murders his rival and takes on his guise while Bunce tries to solve the murders with a new method using fingerprints. Suspicious because Rinaldi will not submit his prints, Bunce tells the police chief who is leery of such evidence but assigns two men to trail the magician. Alice comes to the conclusion that Gallico, Ormond and Jameson are all the same person and she confides in Bunce and Karen. The policeman thinking that Gallico might also be impersonating Rinaldi. After seeing the magician's show, Bunce and Alice go to Illusions, Inc., to get a set of Gallico's fingerprints, leaving Karen to stall Rinaldi. Instead Gallico, who claims he also came to see the magician, comes out of the theater and offers to take Karen home. Once he has gone, she tries to telephone Bunce to warn him that Gallico is on his way to the workshop and when she finally gets through it is Gallico who answers the call. Pretending to submit to having his prints taken, Gallico knocks out the policeman and fires up the crematorium, planning to roast the lawman alive. Alice, who is hiding on a ledge outside the workshop, sees Karen and tells her to divert Gallico's attention. When Karen demands entrance into the workshop, Alice is able to set Alan free. The two men fight with Gallico being knocked onto the crematorium's conveyor belt and killed by his own invention.

The Mad Magician later became the first 3-D movie to be shown on television. Andre DeToth, who directed *House of Wax*, was originally signed to repeat on *The Mad Magician* but he had trouble working with the 3-D effects and was replaced by John Brahm, who incorporated story ideas from a couple of earlier Gaslight era thrillers he did for 20th Century–Fox. The subplot of the use of fingerprints came from *The Lodger* (1944) and a bonfire to dispose of a corpse was used in *Hangover Square* (1945). Both starred Laird Cregar.

The Mad Room

(1969; 93 minutes; Color) PRODUCER: Norman Maurer. DIRECTOR: Bernard Girard. SCREENPLAY: Bernard Girard and A.Z. Martin, from the play by Reginald Denham and Edward Percy and the 1941 screenplay by Reginald Denham and Garrett Fort. PHOTOGRAPHY: Harry Stradling, Jr. EDITOR: Pat Somerset. MUSIC: Dave

Grusin. ART DIRECTOR: Sydney Z. Litwack. SOUND: James Z. Flaster and Arthur Piantadosi. SETS: Sidney Clifford. COSTUMES: Moss Mabry. MAKEUP: Ben Lane. ASSISTANT DIRECTOR: Rusty Meek. CAST: Stella Stevens (Ellen Hardy), Shelley Winters (Mrs. Armstrong), Skip Ward (Sam Aller), Carol Cole (Chris), Severn Darden (Nate), Beverly Garland (Mrs. Racine), Michael Burns (George Hardy), Barbara Sammeth (Mandy Hardy), Lloyd Haynes (Dr. Marion Kincaid), Jenifer Bishop (Mrs. Ericson), Gloria Manon (Edna), Lou Kane (Armand Racine), Allen Pinson (Security Guard), Emil Sitka (Old Man).

Filmed in Vancouver, British Columbia, *The Mad Room* was a remake of Columbia's 1941 *Ladies in Retirement* (q.v.) with a somewhat altered plot. Instead of the two loony sisters from the original, this outing replaced them with teenage siblings who may have committed murder. Norman Maurer, the son-in-law of Moe Howard of the Three Stooges, produced the remake. Actress Carol Cole was the daughter of singer Nat (King) Cole.

At a remote island mansion, Mrs. Armstrong (Shelley Winters), a rich widow, resides with her stepson Sam Aller (Skip Ward), his fiancée Ellen Hardy (Stella Stevens), who is also the woman's paid companion, and Chris (Cole), who works as both secretary and maid. Just as Ellen and Sam are about to wed, she finds out that her teenage siblings, George (Michael Burns) and Mandy (Barbara Sammeth), are being let out of an insane asylum where they have been confined since childhood. Years before their parents were savagely stabbed to death in their beds and the two youngsters were suspected of the slayings but it was never proved which one of them was guilty. Afraid that Mrs. Armstrong will find out about the teenagers' pasts, Ellen lies that they have been residing with an uncle and convinces her employer to let them come and live in the mansion.

Upon their arrival, George and Mandy demand a private place they can call their own. Without informing Mrs. Armstrong, Ellen lets them use the attic, where they can vent their emotional bitterness. Eventually Mrs. Armstrong learns about their using the attic, which she has kept locked since her husband died because he used it as a study. Finding out about George and Mandy's supposed involvement in their parents' deaths, Mrs. Armstrong tells Ellen to get them out of the house. Ellen murders her employer with one of the woman's husband's sabers. When George and Mandy learn of the killing, they at first suspect the other but come to realize it was Ellen who not only murdered Mrs. Armstrong but also their parents. Ellen throws the corpse in a nearby river and tries to make the death appear accidental but the woman's dog finds one of Mrs. Armstrong's severed hands. When Ellen sees it she goes berserk and attempts to slaughter the animal, but is caught by her fiancé.

Howard Thompson in the *New York Times* called the feature "a fine suspense-shocker ... a dandy chiller that is original, civilized, well played, exquisitely directed and scenic. Threading it all is a current of electric tension that triggers a jolting surprise and a hair-raising postscript." *Variety* said *The Mad Room* was a "[w]eak story which pretends to be a psycho-suspense yarn ... Script has a patent mystery plot in which the real murderer isn't exposed until the film's end but any astute filmgoer will perceive the twist long before it comes on the screen." *Time Out Film Guide* (2001) thought the film's plot was "rather disastrously renovated for contemporary consumption.... Skeletons in the cupboard, hacked-up bodies, and severed hands still can't make it anything more than routine." *Castle of Frankenstein* #19 (1972) felt it was "[s]uspenseful, at times slow shocker.... A few tingling moods amid ample sickish moments, adequately directed by Bernard Girard."

The Magic Carpet

(1951; 84 minutes; Color) PRODUCER: Sam Katzman. DIRECTOR: Lew Landers. SCREENPLAY: David Mathews. PHOTOGRAPHY: Ellis W. Carter. EDITOR: Edwin Bryant. MUSIC DIRECTOR: Mischa Bakaleinikoff. ART DIRECTOR: Paul Palmentola. SOUND: J.S. Westmoreland. SETS: Sidney Clifford. UNIT MANAGER: Herbert B. Leonard. SPECIAL EFFECTS: Jack Erickson. COSTUMES: Jean Louis. ASSISTANT DIRECTOR: Wilbur McGaugh. CAST: Lucille Ball (Princess Narah), John Agar (Ramoth aka The Scarlet Falcon), Patricia Medina (Lida), George Tobias (Razi), Raymond Burr (Grand Vizier Boreg), Gregory Gaye (Caliph Ali), Rick Vallin (Abdul), Jo Gilbert (Maras), William Fawcett (Ahkmid), Doretta Johnson (Queen Yasmina), Linda Williams (Estar), Perry Sheehan (Copah), Eileen Howe (Vernah), Winona Smith (Ziela), Minka Zorka (Nedda), Leonard Penn (Caliph Omar), Aram Katcher (Mecca Governor), Rodolfo Hoyos, Jr. (Sergeant), Terry Frost (Beggar), Edward Colmans (Wine Steward), John George (Seller), Suzanne Ridgeway (Harem Girl), James Dime (Palace Guard).

The story behind the production of *The Magic Carpet* is far more interesting than the resulting fantasy programmer that Columbia issued theatrically in the fall of 1951. Lucille Ball had been lured to Columbia with a contract calling for her to star in a trio of features with a salary of

$85,000 per film, all to be produced by S. Sylvan Simon. After starring in *Miss Grant Takes Richmond* (1949) and *The Fuller Brush Girl* (1950), both directed by Lloyd Bacon, Ball was set to do a third feature but Simon died in 1951 and she agreed to appear in Cecil B. DeMille's *The Greatest Show on Earth* (1952) for Paramount. Columbia chief Harry Cohn wanted to get out of paying Ball for the contracted third film so he offered her the low-budget *The Magic Carpet* thinking she would decline it and thus nullify their agreement. Upon the advice of her friend, director Edward Sedgwick, she accepted the assignment for this ten-day Sam Katzman quickie with her salary making up almost half the budget. During production at the Iverson Ranch in Chatsworth, Ball found she was pregnant and had to drop out of the DeMille film. But this led to her and husband Desi Arnaz starring in television's *I Love Lucy* (CBS-TV, 1951–57).

In ancient Arabia, Caliph Omar (Leonard Penn) plans to declare his infant son his successor but he is murdered by rival Ali (Gregory Gaye). Ali's ally, grand vizier Boreg (Raymond Burr), attempts to slay Omar's wife, Queen Yasmina (Doretta Johnson), and her baby but she puts the baby on a magic carpet with a locket emblazoned with Omar's royal seal. As Boreg murders Yasmina, the carpet carries the baby to her uncle, Ahkmid (William Fawcett), who names him Ramoth and raises him as his own son. Ali becomes the new caliph and rules with his sister Princess Narah (Lucille Ball) and Boreg, tyrannically robbing the populace of their possessions. When be becomes a man, Ramoth (John Agar) is a doctor like his uncle but he is also the Scarlet Falcon, who with his friend Razi (George Tobias) fights Ali's oppressive rule. When Razi's sister Lida (Patricia Medina) demands to go with Ramoth and his men on a mission to capture weapons, she is nearly killed in an ambush but the Scarlet Falcon saves her life.

Wanting to infiltrate Ali's court, Ramoth contaminates his wine shipment with an herb; after curing the caliph, he becomes his doctor. Princess Narah becomes infatuated with Ramoth and when he rejects her she tears off his locket. It is found by Boreg, who stabs Ahkmid when he learns about Ramoth's family origins. Before dying, Ahkmid informs Ramoth of his history and tells him where he can find the carpet. Vowing revenge, Ramoth tells Razi and Lida he will use the carpet to bring down Ali and his regime. After he gets word of another weapons shipment, Ramoth informs Razi and Lida. Boreg tries unsuccessfully to have the physician assassinated; the princess' attendant Maras (Jo Gilbert) sees the attempt and informs her mistress. When the princess tells Boreg to stay away from Ramoth, he informs her of his royal past. Most of the Scarlet Falcon's men are arrested. Lida takes on the guise of a dancer in order to warn Ramoth but he does not recognize her until she insults the princess and is arrested. Although Lida is able to tell Ramoth of the arrests, the princess finds his Scarlet Falcon red robe. She confronts him, and he accuses her of killing his uncle. Narah informs him it was Boreg who killed Ahkmid and then has the physician arrested by her guards. The princess gives Ramoth to her brother, telling the caliph that he is the Scarlet Falcon. Orders are given for his execution.

Lida escapes from her dungeon cell, goes to Ramoth's room, finds the magic carpet and sends it to rescue him. He flies to Razi and his band who are planning to rob the caravan carrying the weapons shipment. As the caliph's soldiers try to stop the robbery, Ramoth uses the magic carpet to douse them with pepper. After the Falcon's men get the weapons, they attack Ali's stronghold. During the fight, Ramoth kills Boreg and sets Lida free. Ali is also eliminated. Once he is installed as the new caliph, Ramoth puts Princess Narah in a dungeon and he asks Lida to marry him. The two then use the magic carpet to inspect their new kingdom.

Variety called the feature a "fair escapist picture ... Lucille Ball is wasted in her role of a princess but does supply a fair amount of marquee value." *Showmen's Trade Review* stated, "Exceptionally well-made for a program offering, it carries an abundance of action, has top-budget production values and is a treat to the eye because of its beautiful Supercinecolor photography." In *Lucy at the Movies* (2007), Cindy De La Hoy called it a "routine adventure film."

The Magic World of Topo Gigio

(1965; 75 minutes; Color) DIRECTOR: Luca De Rico and (uncredited) Federico Caldura. SCREENPLAY: Federico Caldura, Mario Faustinelli, Maria Perego and Guido Stagnaro. PHOTOGRAPHY: Giorgio Battilana. EDITOR: Franco Alessandri. SONGS: Aldo Rossi. ANIMATORS: Maria Perego, Grazia Curti, Annabella Spadon,

Emanuele Pagani and Emy Ricciotti. PRODUCTION DESIGN: Franco Serino. SETS: Mario Milani. COSTUMES: Sandro Negri. SPECIAL EFFECTS: Ettore Catallucci. VOICE CAST: Giuseppe "Peppino" Mazzulo (Topo Gigio), Federica Milani (Rosy), Armando Benetti (Giovannino), Ignazio Colnaghi, Carlo Delfini, Ignazio Dolce, Ermanno Roveri, Milena Zini.

Topo Gigio, the ten-inch-high foam rubber mouse puppet, was very popular in the United States in the 1960s due to its 91 appearances on CBS-TV's *The Ed Sullivan Show* between 1963 and 1971. Maria Perego created Topo Gigio (translated as Louie Mouse in English) in 1958 for an Italian television puppet show with Giuseppe "Peppino" Mazzulo supplying the voice. The character became so popular in Italy that it also appeared in children's magazines, cartoons, records and various merchandising. In 1961 Cinecidi/Jolly Film produced the animated feature *Le Avventure di Topo Gigio* (The Adventure of Topo Gigio). Four years later, Sullivan Enterprises acquired the film for U.S. release by Columbia. Luca De Rico directed a new ending and ten minutes were lopped off its original running time; it was retitled *The Magic World of Topo Gigio*. *Castle of Frankenstein* #17 (1971) called it a "[c]utesy-poo Italian children's film. Mickey [Mouse] need not fear the competition." Reviewing it under the title *Topo Gigio*, Henry Herz and Tony Zaza in *The Family Guide to Movies on Video* (1988) felt it was a "[d]elightful little movie ... Young children will love it and the puppet characterization is droll enough to please their parents."

Italian mouse Topo Gigio (voice of Mazzulo) constructs a rocket ship so he can go to the Moon with his girlfriend Rosy (voice of Federica Milani) and cowardly worm Giovannino (voice of Armando Benetti), but after takeoff it plunges into an amusement park. There the three meet a puppeteer and join his act, much to the delight of his audience. This causes problems with a magician whose fans leave him in order to see Topo Gigio. The magician puts Rosy under his spell and abducts her. Topo Gigio and the worm discover how the illusionist does his trickery and ruin his act, making him a laughingstock. The two are then able to set Rosy free and get away from the magician.

The Italian version of the feature ended differently with Topo Gigio ingratiating himself with the magician, who teams up with the puppeteer. Although Topo Gigio's popularity in the U.S. declined after leaving Ed Sullivan's program, the character remains a favorite in Italy, Spain, Japan and Central and South American to this day. Topo Gigio returned to Italian television and in the 1980s headlined the Japanese animated program *Topo Gigio* as a time-traveling astronaut. In 2004 the character starred in the Spanish video movie *El Show del Topo Gigio: Especial de Navidad* (The Topo Gigio Show: Christmas Special).

The Man Called Flintstone

(1966; 89 minutes; Color) PRODUCERS-DIRECTORS: William Hanna and Joseph Barbera. SCREENPLAY: Ray Allen and Harvey Bullock. ADDITIONAL STORY MATERIAL: Alex Lovy, Warren Foster, William Hanna and Joseph Barbera. ANIMATION DIRECTOR: Charles A. Nichols. EDITORS: Milton Krear, Dave Horton, Larry Cowan and Pat Foley. MUSIC: Marty Paich and Ted Nichols. SONGS: John McCarthy and Doug Goodwin. ART DIRECTOR: Bill Perez. SOUND: Bill Getty and Richard Olson. PRODUCTION SUPERVISOR: Howard Hanson. SPECIAL EFFECTS: Brooke Lindon. VOICE CAST: Alan Reed (Fred Flintstone), Mel Blanc (Barney Rubble), Jean Vander Pyl (Wilma Flintstone/Pebbles Flintstone), Gerry Johnson (Betty Rubble), Don Messick (Bamm Bamm Rubble), Paul Frees (Rock Slag), Harvey Korman (Green Goose/Triple X), John Stephenson (Chief Boulder), June Foray (Tanya Malichite), Henry Corden (Singing Voice of Fred Flintstone), Janet Waldo.

Set in the Stone Age, ABC-TV's animated series *The Flintstones* (a takeoff on Jackie Gleason's *The Honeymooners*) was telecast from 1960 to 1966. The series then ran on Saturday mornings on NBC from 1967 to 1970 and on CBS from 1972 to 1974 before returning to NBC from 1979 to 1984. Following the series' initial small-screen run, Columbia released the spy comedy *The Man Called Flintstone*, produced and directed by William Hanna and Joseph Barbera for their Hanna-Barbera Productions, the makers of the TV program. The big-screen production, which was aimed at the Saturday kiddie matinee crowd, featured the voices of the television cast and contained seven songs, the best being Louis Prima singing "Pensate Amore."

In the Stone Age town of Bedrock, Fred Flintstone (voice of Alan Reed), his wife Wilma and daughter Pebbles (voice of Jean Vander Pyl) are planning to start a camping trip with their best friends and neighbors Barney (voice of Mel Blanc) and Betty Rubble (voice of Gerry Johnson) and little boy Bamm Bamm (voice of Don Messick). After taking their pets Dino the dinosaur and Hoppy the kangaroo to stay at the animal hospital, Fred and Barney are involved in an accident. At the hospital, Fred is mistaken for super agent Rock Slag (voice of Paul Frees) who is recovering from injuries sustained while trying to get away from the Goon Twins, Bobo and Ollie, who work for the madman Green Goose (voice of Harvey Korman), the chief of SMIRK, who wants to control the world. Chief Boulder (voice of John Stephenson) of the Stone Age Secret Service realizes that Fred is a double for Slag and convinces him to go to Paris and capture Green Goose, although he does not tell Fred that the master villain is not a bird.

The Flintstone and the Rubbles fly to Paris and once they are there Boulder informs Fred he must go to Rome where he will be aided by Agent Triple X (voice of Harvey Korman). There Fred meets exotic Tanya (voice of June Foray) who is to take him to Green Goose. After escaping from several amorous women who think he is Slag, Fred tells Boulder he wants to quit being a spy. The chief informs him that Green Goose is really a master criminal out to take over the planet. Fred insists on giving up the search but, after realizing Pebbles and Bamm Bamm's futures rest with him, he changes his mind and goes to the Papa Piccola Pizza Palace to meet Tanya. Boulder tells him to keep her there until the recovered Slag arrives to take over for him. Fred sees Wilma, Barney and Betty at the pizza place and when he dances with Tanya, Wilma gets jealous; she, Betty and Barney attack and incapacitate the recently arrived Slag, thinking he is Fred.

Tanya takes Fred to Green Goose's hideout, an unused amusement park. When Barney follows them, he is tortured on a rack by Tanya since Green Goose believes Fred is really Slag and has information on the country's new missile. Bobo and Ollie tell their boss they have stolen a report from Boulder saying the missile is not ready and Green Goose makes plans to launch his own rocket. Fred and Barney manage to escape but Fred runs into Triple X and realizes he is really Green Goose. After Barney falls into a pit, Fred rescues him and the two take refuge in the rocket which they program to blast into space. Green Goose then offers Fred a million dollars for a cheap imitation diamond necklace he bought to appease Wilma and the boys manage to trap the villain and his cohorts in the rocket just before it is launched. Fred is then feted as a hero before he, Wilma and Pebbles go fishing with Barney, Wilma and Bamm Bamm. The vacation does not last because one of Slag's admirers arrives with her brother, demanding marriage. Fred flees.

The *New York Times* said, "Unfortunately the fun gets much too frantic and cluttered with James Bond riggings, which don't enhance such unsophistication." (The feature was made at the height of the Bond and cinema spying craze of the mid–1960s). James Robert Parish and I noted in *The Great Spy Pictures* (1974), "The attention catcher of this comic strip entry was always its presentation of prehistoric life in contemporary terms, but here the premise wore very thin..." In *The Espionage Filmography* (2001), Paul Mavis wrote, "This feature-length animated spy spoof doesn't succeed very well as spy film or spoof, but it's pretty to look at, with rich, saturated colors and interesting backgrounds. The original songs are cute, too, but the pace drags badly and the timing is way off— cartoons should *move*."

Man in the Dark

(1953; 70 minutes) PRODUCER: Wallace MacDonald. DIRECTOR: Lew Landers. SCREENPLAY: George Bricker and Jack Leonard. ADAPTATION: William Sackheim. STORY: Henry Altimus and Tom Van Dycke. PHOTOGRAPHY: Floyd Crosby. EDITOR: Viola Lawrence. MUSIC DIRECTOR: Ross DiMaggio. ART DIRECTOR: John Meehan. SOUND: Lodge Cunningham. SETS: Robert Priestly. ASSISTANT DIRECTOR: Irving Moore. CAST: Edmond O'Brien (Steve Rawley aka James Brooks), Audrey Totter (Peg Benedict), Ted de Corsia (Lefty), Horace McMahon (Arnie), Nick Dennis (Cookie), Dayton Lummis (Dr. Marston), Dan Riss (Jawald), John Harmon (Herman), Shepard Menken (Interne), Ruth Warren (Mayme), Mickey Simpson (Flanagan), Carleton Young (Second Surgeon), Paul Bryar (Bartender Freddie), William Tannen (Slaven), Chris Alcaide, Frank Fenton, Howard Negley (Detectives), Leonard Bremen (Clinic Guard), Frank Sully (Cab Driver), Frank O'Connor (Gate Guard), Guy Way (Armored Car Guard), Ted Stanhope (Post Office Clerk), Sayre Dearing (Wheelchair Patient), Mary Alan Hokanson (Nurse), Maudie Prickett (Receptionist Nurse), Robert Williams, Fred Aldrich (Policemen).

Working title: *The Man Who Lived Twice*.

Columbia's first foray into the realm of 3-D came with *Man in the Dark*, a programmer produced by Wallace MacDonald's "B" picture unit and released in the spring of 1953. It was a remake of the 1936 feature *The Man Who Lived Twice* (q.v.) and like that outing it had tinges of horror in the story of a man who is given a new personality through experimental brain surgery. Despite the stereoscopic effects, Bosley Crowther in the *New York Times* dubbed the feature "a thoroughly unspectacular affair ... Withal, it is not exciting. The story is a drably written thing, unimaginative, unintelligent and undistinguished by visual stunts. And the direction is wholly pedestrian." *Variety* noted that 3-D was played "to the hilt and [uses] the added dimension for some first-rate shock effects that should thrill customers." The trade paper added, however, "Preoccupation with spotlighting what 3-D can do detracts some from the picture's entertainment value. Story, scripting and performances all are mediocre..."

After serving one year of a ten-year stretch for a payroll robbery, convict Steve Rawley (Edmond O'Brien) agrees to undergo experimental brain surgery performed by Dr. Marston (Dayton Lummis). Steve is given a new personality, with no memory of his past: He becomes James Brooks, and he is told he was in an automobile accident that caused amnesia. Insurance investigator Jawald (Dan Riss), who is trying to find the $130,000 Rawley stole, is informed by Dr. Marston that the ex-con will now lead a normal life.

Just as Rawley is about to be released from the hospital, his former cohorts Lefty (Ted de Corsia), Arnie (Horace McMahon) and Cookie (Nick Dennis) abduct him and take him to their hideout next to an amusement park. They try to get him to tell them where he hid the money but he has no memory of what happened and he fails to recognize Peg Benedict (Audrey Totter), his girlfriend. The gang members tell Steve how he planned the robbery and carried it out with his hiding the money and refusing to divulge its location. Arnie thinks Rawley hid the loot in his house and he goes there with Steve, Lefty and Cookie. They find only a piece of paper containing numbers. Back at the hideout, Arnie and Cook beat Rawley when he continues to deny any recollection of the holdup. As Rawley recovers from the beating he dreams of the amusement park and a box of candy. By now Peg believes that Rawley is telling the truth. When he refuses Lefty's offer of half the take from the robbery, he reverts to his former angry self and Peg begs him to remain the new man he has become. Managing to escape, Rawley takes Peg to the amusement park but they are followed by Lefty, Arnie, Cook and, separately, by Jawald. Rawley comes to realize the numbers he found at his former home are to a claim check and eventually locates the money in a box of chocolates. Peg informs Rawley that she will leave him if he keeps the money. When the gang appears, he dashes onto a roller coaster, getting off at the top. He and Lefty fight but the latter is knocked in front of a car and dies. The police, called by Jawald, shoot Arnie. Reunited with Peg, Steve gives the money to the insurance man and decides to start over again.

The Man They Could Not Hang

(1939; 72 minutes) PRODUCER: Wallace MacDonald. DIRECTOR: Nick Grinde. SCREENPLAY: Karl Brown. STORY: Leslie T. White and George W. Sayre. PHOTOGRAPHY: Benjamin H. Kline. EDITOR: William A. Lyon. MUSIC DIRECTOR: M.W. [Morris] Stoloff. ART DIRECTOR: Lionel Banks. SOUND: George Cooper. ASSISTANT DIRECTOR: Thomas Flood. CAST: Boris Karloff (Dr. Henryk Savaard), Lorna Gray [Adrian Booth] (Janet Savaard), Robert Wilcox (Scoop Foley), Roger Pryor (District Attorney Drake), Don Beddoe (Lieutenant Shane), Ann Doran (Betty Crawford), Joe De Stefani (Dr. Stoddard), Charles Trowbridge (Judge Bowman), Byron Foulger (Lang), Dick Curtis (Clifford Kearney), James Craig (Watkins), John Tyrrell (Sutton), Ian MacLaren (Priest), Harlan Briggs (Defense Attorney Parker), George Anderson (Warden), Stanley Brown (Bob Roberts), John Dilson (Mr. King), Robert Sterling, Franklin Parker (Reporters), Frank Jaquet, Chuck Hamilton, Flo Campbell (Jurors), Charles F. Miller (Dr. Avery), Cyril Thornton (Butler), Sam Ash (Druggist), Larry Lund (Court Clerk), Bill Lally, Perc Launders (Bailiffs), Stanley Blystone (Guard), Walter Sande (Newsroom Typist), Charles McAvoy (Prison Official).

In 1939 Boris Karloff signed a five-film contract with Columbia to star, *sans* monster makeup, in a series of movies in which he portrayed mad scientists, beginning with *The Man The Could Not Hang*, which the studio issued in the summer of the same year. The second half of the film was an uncredited remake of *The Ninth Guest* (1934) [q.v.]. When the feature was issued in Great Britain it was shorn of four of its original 72 minutes. It was cut even more when Favorite Films reissued it in the late 1940s, this time running 64 minutes. Like most of the features Karloff made under the Columbia pact, it was produced by Wallace MacDonald and directed by Nick Grinde.

Dr. Henryk Savaard (Karloff), working with his assistant Lang (Byron Foulger), has developed a mechanical heart which he believes will revive the dead. To prove his theory, medical student Bob Roberts (Stanley Brown), the fiancé of Savaard's nurse Betty (Ann Doran), agrees to let himself be scientifically put to death and then re-

Don Beddoe, Robert Wilcox, Boris Karloff and Lorna Gray in *The Man They Could Not Hang* (1939).

vived by the doctor's device. As the three men conduct the experiment, Betty panics and goes to Police Lt. Shane (Don Beddoe) for help. Overhearing the nurse's story, newspaperman Scoop Foley (Robert Wilcox) drives to the Savaard home where he meets the doctor's daughter Janet (Lorna Gray). Shane and his men arrive with Betty and upset the experiment as medical examiner Dr. Stoddard (Joe De Stefani) declares Roberts dead. Shane refuses Savaard's pleas for one hour to revive the young man and the doctor is arrested. Lang goes into hiding with the mechanical heart.

Savaard is put on trial for murder and is defended by lawyer Parker (Harlan Briggs) as District Attorney Drake (Roger Pryor) demands the death penalty. Jury foreman Clifford Kearney (Dick Curtis) leads his colleagues in convicting the doctor, and Judge Bowman (Charles Trowbridge) sentences him to be hanged. Savaard addresses the court and declares that those who condemned him will face a terrible judgment. Just before he is hung, Savaard signs over his body to "Dr. Bruckner," who is really Lang in disguise. Lang takes the body back to the clinic where he uses the mechanical heart to revive Savaard. Three months later, Scoop, who has fallen in love with Janet, realizes that six of the jurors who convicted Savaard have died by hanging. His editor (John Dilson) orders Scoop to investigate "the Savaard Curse." When the reporter learns that Judge Bowman has been called to the Savaard home, he informs Shane. Driving to Savaard's, Scoop finds the judge, Drake, Shane, Dr. Stoddard, Betty Crawford and the remaining jurors are also there.

When the servants leave, Savaard appears and invites those present to join him for dinner, telling them that Lang used the mechanical heart to bring him back to life. Saying his death is a perfect alibi, the scientist informs his guests they will all die. Judge Bowman is electrocuted as he tries to leave. Scoop realizes they are trapped in the house (all the doors and windows are sealed). Juror Kearney is killed when a poison needle is shot through his brain. As Savaard prepares to kill the others, Janet lets herself into the house. When the survivors tells her that her father is alive, she locates him and he informs her of his retribution and that he also murdered Lang who threatened to expose his plans. After Savaard fails in an attempt to shoot Betty, he tells his daughter to leave the house but instead she touches an electrified grill and is killed. When he runs to Janet, Savaard is shot by Shane. Savaard tells Stoddard to get the girl to his laboratory where the mechanical heart is used to save her. After Janet is revived, the scientist destroys his life-saving device and dies with its secret.

Tongue-in-cheek, the *New York Times* said that star Karloff "does another amusing encore to life" in the film, adding, "He fails, of course, but the failures of Mr. Karloff are more interesting than the successes of ordinary homicides." *Variety* complained, "Plot is inconsistent with the deep interest of Karloff in promoting life by his discovery to deliberately turn murderer in the end. The unexpected and implausible revenge doesn't jell, but Karloff turns in his usual good performance." The British *Kinematograph Weekly* opined, "The initial experiment and the trial scene are impressive, it is during the second half that the picture falls foul of conviction.... However, Karloff is the key to the film's macabre appeal, and his presence, augmented by ambitious technical presentation, enables the thriller to be given the benefit of the doubt for industrial circles."

In *The Films of Boris Karloff* (1974), Richard Bojarksi and Kenneth Beale noted that the storyline "was inspired by actual experiments conducted by Dr. Robert E. Cornish. The biochemist attracted publicity during the thirties by restoring dead dogs back to life after gassing them with nitrogen gas. Cornish also tried to obtain permission to restore life to executed convicts in order to further test his theories. But he did not obtain the opportunity to do so." Universal made a feature film about Cornish's experiments, *Life Returns* (1935), which Scientart Pictures reissued three years later.

It is interesting to note that what was science fiction in 1939 had become science fact by the end of the 20th century with the use of heart transplants and mechanical hearts.

The Man Who Lived Twice

(1936; 73 minutes) EXECUTIVE PRODUCER: Irving Briskin. ASSOCIATE PRODUCER: Ben Pivar. DIRECTOR: Harry Lachman. SCREENPLAY: Tom Van Dycke, Fred Niblo, Jr., Arthur Strawn. STORY: Tom Van Dycke and Henry Altimus. PHOTOGRAPHY: James Van Trees. EDITOR: Byron Robinson. SPECIAL EFFECTS: Kenneth Wheeler. CAST: Ralph Bellamy (Johnny "Slick" Rawley/Dr. James Blake), Marian Marsh (Janet Haydon), Thurston Hall (Dr. Clifford L. Schuyler), Isabel Jewell (Peggy Russell), Ward Bond (John "Gloves" Baker), Henry Kolker (Judge Henry Treacher), Willard Robertson (Inspector Logan), Ann Doran (Miss Cameron), Kathryn Clare Ward (Aggie), Mary Lou Dix, Beatrice Curtis, Nell Roy (Prisoners), Edward Keane (Police Commissioner), Edward Le Saint (Judge), Betty Farrington (Matron), G. Raymond Nye (Fingerprint Man), Bruce Mitchell (Cleary), Bert Moorhouse (Carney), Eric Mayne (Montage).

The Man Who Lived Twice most likely would have been a forgotten Columbia programmer had it not been included in Screen Gems' "Son of Shock!" syndicated TV package of horror films released in the late 1950s. It was one of 11 Columbias included in the collection of 20 horror films and no doubt caused much disappointment for young viewers used to seeing Dracula, the Frankenstein Monster, the Mummy and their ilk, since it was basically a crime melodrama with only borderline sci-fi elements. In fact, the only other Columbia feature in the package that was less of a chiller was *Island of Doomed Men* (1940) [q.v.], that offered Peter Lorre as a sadistic island prison commandant. Despite its lack of fright, *The Man Who Lived Twice* was a well-made and entertaining dual bill item. *Castle of Frankenstein* #17 (1971) called it a "[f]ascinating marginal melodrama.... Would have been more effective if ending came about two minutes earlier."

Running from the law, as well as his girlfriend Peggy Russell (Isabel Jewell) and henchman "Gloves" Baker (Ward Bond), scar-faced hoodlum Johnny "Slick" Rawley (Ralph Bellamy) seeks asylum at the Baldwin Medical College. Dr. Clifford L. Schuyler (Thurston Hall) is delivering a lecture on his brain surgery experiments that have transformed wild animals into peaceful ones. Rawley approaches Schuyler about giving him a new face but during the operation the doctor also removes tumors from Rawley's brain, turning him into a docile man without memories of his past. The doctor tells the recovering gangster that his name is James Blake and that he has amnesia from a car wreck. As he grows stronger, Blake comes to respect Dr. Schuyler and wants to become a doctor, eventually graduating from medical school. After several years Blake goes to work at Belmore Island Prison where he hopes to use inmates to further Dr. Schuyler's study of the criminal mind. Homeless Janet Haydon (Marian Marsh), who was sent to the facility for stealing food, becomes the doctor's secretary and the two eventually fall in love. One day Blake gives Peggy a vaccination and she suspects he may be Rawley since he has the same habit as her ex-boyfriend of twirling a key chain. Peggy informs "Gloves" about her theory, and the thug tries to rob Blake who ends up hiring him as his driver. Dr. Schuyler confides in "Gloves" about Blake's past, which he agrees to keep secret. Peggy hopes to collect the reward money for Rawley by going to police Inspector Logan (Willard Robertson), whose partner was murdered by the gangster. Using fingerprints, Logan learns that Rawley and Blake are the same person; he confronts Schuyler, who tells Blake about his past. When Gloves learns that his mother has died, he takes Peggy, who plans to testify against Blake, for a drive and intentionally causes a wreck that takes both their lives. When James comes to trial, Judge Treacher (Henry Kolker), who appointed him prison doctor, works as his defense attorney. He admits that Rawley and Blake are the same person but tells the jury that the gangster ceased to exist after Schuyler performed brain surgery on him. Although he is found guilty, Blake gets a pardon through the efforts of his fellow doctors and he resumes practice and asks Janet to marry him.

The movie's associate producer, Ben Pivar, later worked at Universal where he produced a number of their horror films. Columbia reworked the plot of *The Man Who Lived Twice* as *Man in the Dark* (1953) [q.v.], the studio's first 3-D feature production.

The Man Who Turned to Stone

(1957; 71 minutes) PRODUCER: Sam Katzman. DIRECTOR: Leslie Kardos. SCREENPLAY: Raymond T. Marcus [Bernard Gordon]. PHOTOGRAPHY: Benjamin H. Kline. EDITOR: Charles Nelson. MUSIC: Ross DiMaggio and George Duning. ART DIRECTOR: Paul Palmentola. SOUND: J.S. Westmoreland. SETS: Sidney Clifford. ASSISTANT DIRECTOR: Sam Nelson. CAST: Victor Jory (Dr. Murdock), Charlotte Austin (Carol Adams), Ann Doran (Mrs. Ford), William Hudson (Dr. Jess Rogers), Jean Willes (Tracy), Paul Cavanagh (Dr. Cooper), George Lynn (Dr. Freneau), Victor Varconi (Dr. Myer), Frederick Ledebur (Eric), Tina Carver (Marge), Barbara Wilson (Anna Sherman), Don C. Harvey (Coroner Griffin), Jean Harvey (Head Matron).

Working title: *The Petrified Man*.

Several inmates at the LaSalle Detention Home, a facility for incorrigible young women, have died. After newcomer Anna Sherman (Barbara Wilson) is diagnosed with a heart murmur by administrator Mrs. Ford (Ann Doran), inmate Marge (Tina Carver) is put in isolation for questioning her decision. Following the death of inmate Angie Collins, another prisoner, Tracy (Jean Willes), asks social worker Carol Adams (Charlotte Austin) to look into the matter. Mrs. Ford finds Carol reading the home's records and informs the house doctor, Murdock (Victor Jory), who orders his brain-damaged assistant Eric (Frederick Ledebur) to bring Anna to his laboratory which is concealed in the building's attic. She is placed in a tub of water and Dr. Murdock drains the girl's life force out of her body to rejuvenate Eric over the objections of colleague Dr. Cooper (Paul Cavanagh). Later Anna is found hanging from a rafter in the prison dormitory and the inquest coroner (Don C. Harvey) declares her death a suicide. During the hearing, Carol questions the assumption that the girl killed herself. Murdock intimates that her lack of job experience may have led to Anna's suicide. Dr. Jess Rogers (William Hudson), a psychiatrist, agrees to investigate the charge but when Carol informs him about the rash of deaths at LaSalle he asks her to help him find the truth.

Rogers learns that 11 inmates have died in the past two years after Murdock and his associates, Mrs. Ford, Eric, Dr. Cooper, Dr. Freneau (George Lynn) and Dr. Myer (Victor Varconi), began to run the institution. All of the doctors dress in 19th century clothing. Mrs. Ford informs Rogers that the girls' death records have been destroyed. He and Carol talk to Marge who tells them that she heard Anna screaming before her alleged suicide. Murdock refuses to perform an autopsy on Anna, so Rogers performs one himself but later deceives the doctor and his cohorts by telling them he agrees with the suicide verdict although he determined that the young woman was dead before she was hanged. When Rogers talks to Dr. Cooper, whose heartbeat is loud enough to be heard, the older man tells him he expects to die soon and that Rogers will then be mailed instructions. Murdock meets with his colleagues and tells them that Dr. Cooper has become a danger to their work and that he will have to die. As he begins to turn to stone, Dr. Cooper informs them he has written out his history and mailed it to an unnamed person. After receiving the dead man's letter, Rogers finds Cooper's diary hidden in a cliff and it relates how, 170 years earlier, the doctors had learned how to harness bioelectric energy to indefinitely extend life. The process involves transferring the life force of young women into their own bodies to keep them alive forever, although the females die as a result of the procedure. The document also details the mismanagement of Eric's operation, causing him to use up the energy faster and needing more transfers despite the fact he is slowly turning to stone. Eric has followed Rogers and tries to take the diary but falls over a cliff as the psychiatrist escapes.

The crazed Eric goes back to LaSalle, abducts Marge and forces Dr. Murdock to use her for an energy transfer. Rogers tells Carol about the diary, then tries to call the police but finds that Murdock has shut down the switchboard. Since Tracy can operate the switchboard, Rogers tells her to make the call. Dr. Myer shoots at the switchboard and destroys it. Rogers manages to get the gun from him and goes to the basement, shutting off the water supply and disconnecting the electricity. There he finds the petrified body of Dr. Cooper and Marge's corpse. Eric abducts Carol to be his next donor, knocks out Rogers and drags them both to the laboratory. As Murdock, Mrs. Ford and Dr. Frenau plan to delay the transfer so Eric will turn to stone, Rogers awakens and puts a saline neutralizer in the tub, saving Carol's life and making Eric even more desperate. When he attacks Dr. Freneau, the physician shoots at Eric who dies of a heart attack. Murdock straps Rogers in the transfer chair and tries to get him to reveal the location of Dr. Cooper's diary. Rogers refuses to help him until the doctor threatens to shoot Carol; he turns over the fuses and Murdock tells Freneau to restore the power. When the lights return, Tracy and the other inmates escape while a fire in the cellar, started by Dr. Frenau when he dropped a candle searching for the fuse box, engulfs the institution. Rogers manages to overpower Murdock and rescue Carol and they get away before an explosion kills Murdock and Mrs. Ford, who remained behind to complete their experiment notes.

The Man Who Turned to Stone was released in March, 1957 on a double bill with *Zombies of Mora Tau* (q.v.), both features being made by Sam Katzman's Clover Productions. The *Monthly Film Bulletin* termed it "a grim and grisly little piece" but *Castle of Frankenstein* #17 (1971) thought it an "illiterate horror of retard level." Stephen Jones in *The Essential Monster Movie Guide* (2000) called it a "typically silly low-budget premise from producer Sam Katzman, but the scenes where the scientist's flesh turns to stone when their energy dissipates are quite effective." Phil Hardy in *Science Fiction* (1984) felt it was a "silly, charmless film," while Welch Everman summed up his essay on the feature in *Cult Science Fiction Films* (1995) by stating: "Well, this one won't spark your intellect, but you might want to include it, along with *Cat-Women of the Moon*, in your next Victor Jory Film Festival."

Leading lady Charlotte Austin, who appeared in other genre efforts like *Gorilla at Large* (1954), *The Bride and the Beast* (1958) and *Frankenstein 1970* (1958), was the daughter of crooner Gene

Austin. Top-billed Victor Jory, who gave a surprisingly low-key performance as the mad scientist, headlined Columbia's 1940 cliffhanger *The Green Archer* (q.v.). Hero William Hudson appeared in several horror efforts but is best remembered as the two-timing husband who met a bad end in *Attack of the 50 Foot Woman* (1958). Paul Cavanagh had supporting roles in a whole string of horror and science fiction features as did Ann Doran. Beautiful Barbara Wilson went from playing the victim Anna in the film to starring in the 1958 U.S.-Swedish production *Rymdinvasion i Lapland* (Space Invasion of Lapland), which was announced for release in the United States in 1960 as *Terror in the Midnight Sun*. The feature did not reach American screens until 1962 when producer Jerry Warren issued a hacked-up version called *Invasion of the Animal People* through his ADP Productions.

The Man with Nine Lives

(1940; 74 minutes) PRODUCER: Wallace MacDonald. DIRECTOR: Nick Grinde. SCREENPLAY: Karl Brown. STORY: Harold Shumate. PHOTOGRAPHY: Benjamin H. Kline. EDITOR: Al Clark. MUSIC DIRECTOR: Morris Stoloff. ART DIRECTOR: Lionel Banks. SOUND: Edward Bernds. TECHNICAL ADVISOR: Dr. Ralph S. Willard. CAST: Boris Karloff (Dr. Leon Kravall), Roger Pryor (Dr. Tim Mason), Jo Ann Sayers (Judith Blair), Stanley Brown (Bob Adams), John Dilson (District Attorney John Hawthorne), Hal Taliaferro [Wally Wales] (Sheriff Ed Stanton), Byron Foulger (Dr. Henry Bassett), Charles Trowbridge (Dr. Harvey), Ernie Adams (Pete Daggett), Lee Willard (Jasper Adams), Ivan Miller (Sheriff Hadley), Bruce Bennett (State Trooper), Minta Durfee (Patient), Charles F. Miller, Eddie Dew, Landers Stevens, Cyril Ring, Wedgwood Nowell, William Marion, James Conaty (Medical Observers).

A patient (Minta Durfee) suffering from cancer is subjected to frozen therapy by Dr. Tim Mason (Roger Pryor), who demonstrates the technique before a panel of doctors: He places the woman in suspended animation by freezing her in order to arrest the disease and prolong her life. When news of the experiment's success reaches the public, hundreds of requests come in for the procedure and the hospital's chief, Dr. Harvey (Charles Trowbridge), tells Mason to take a leave of absence while his work is double-checked by experts. With his nurse and fiancée Judith Blair (Jo Ann Sayers), Dr. Mason travels to Silver Lake, near the Canadian border, to try and find records belonging to Dr. Leon Kravall (Boris Karloff), who disappeared ten years before after writing a book on his own experiments with frozen therapy. Kravall's deserted home is on Crater Island; local boat owner Pete Daggett (Ernie Adams) warns the young couple not to go there, explaining that it has been deserted ever since the doctor and four other men disappeared a decade before. Disregarding the warning, Tim and Judith row to the island. While exploring the Kravall home, the nurse falls through the floor into a basement laboratory, and behind an iron door they find the missing doctor's body encased in ice. Tim digs out Kravall and uses his experimental techniques to bring the doctor back to life. Kravall relates that in 1930 he was using frozen therapy to aid cancer patient Jasper Adams (Lee Willard) but the man's nephew Bob Adams (Stanley Brown) accused him of murdering his uncle. To prove him wrong, Kravall took Bob, Sheriff Stanton (Hal Taliaferro), District Attorney Hawthorne (John Dilson) and Dr. Bassett (Byron Foulger), the coroner, to his underground laboratory to show them the process. When Bassett declared the patient dead, Stanton arrested Kravall, who claimed that the man was alive but frozen. He concocted a formula with which to bring the man back to life but instead released poisonous vapors and the five men took haven in an ice-filled room, part of a glacier. Realizing that inhaling the vapors caused him and the other men to survive in a state of suspended animation after being frozen, Kravall enlists the aid of Mason and Judith in reviving the others. Once they are brought back to life, Bob is told by Hawthorne that he has been legally dead for longer than the law allows for him to inherit his late uncle's one million dollar estate. Angered, Adams burns Kravall's formula and the doctor shoots him. Determined to reconstruct the formula by using the men as guinea pigs, Kravall takes Mason and Judith prisoner and ends up killing Stanton, Hawthorne and Bassett when he experiments on them. Now mad, Kravall decides to run tests on Judith after knocking out Mason. Daggett arrives with the local lawman (Ivan Miller) and a state trooper (Bruce Bennett), who shoots Kravall as Tim saves his fiancée. At the hospital, Dr. Harvey informs Mason that he has his colleagues' support in completing Dr. Kravall's work.

The Man with Nine Lives was the second of five features Karloff did for Columbia from 1939 to 1942 and like the initial outing, *The Man They Could Not Hang* (q.v.), it was produced by Wallace MacDonald and directed by Nick Grinde. The feature, which was reissued later in the decade by Favorite Films, was shown in Great Britain as *Behind the Door*, running seven minutes less than when released in the U.S. Like its predecessor, it proved to be medically prophetic in its plot involving the use of freezing to prolong life.

The *New York Daily News* thought the feature was "not as horrendous as some have been, but it is unusual and interesting to a certain degree." The *New York Times* warned, "[F]or casual and literal-mined moviegoers *The Man with Nine Lives* may seem hard to take." *Variety* was far more enthusiastic, saying it "carries plenty of sock as a horror thriller.... Film stacks up with the best screen chillers and one that will appease the most choosey patrons of this sort of entertainment." The British *Kinematograph Weekly* reported, "Now and again the film runs past itself and is in danger of inviting laughter in the wrong places, but, in the main, showmanship and a keen imagination back its versatile and colorful collation of macabre thrills."

Maniac

(1963; 86 minutes) PRODUCER-SCREENPLAY: Jimmy Sangster. DIRECTOR: Michael Carreras. PHOTOGRAPHY: Wilkie Cooper. EDITOR: Tom Simpson. MUSIC: Stanley Black. ART DIRECTOR: Edward Carrick. SOUND: Cyril Swern. PRODUCTION DESIGN: Bernard Robinson. PRODUCTION MANAGER: Bill Hill. MAKEUP: Basil Newall. CONTINUITY: Kay Rawlings. ASSISTANT DIRECTOR: Ross MacKenzie. CAST: Kerwin Mathews (Geoff Farrell), Nadia Gray (Eve Beynat), Donald Houston (Georges Beynat/Andre), Liliane Brousse (Annette Beynat), George Pastell (Inspector Etienne), Arnold Diamond (Janiello), Norman Bird (Salon), Justine Lord (Grace), Jerold Wells (Giles), Leon Peers (Blanchard), Andre Maranne (Voice of Salon).

Filmed on location in England and France, *Maniac* was produced by Hammer Films in 1961 and released in the United States two years later by Columbia. It was one of Hammer's weaker productions, coming at a time when the company was making psychological horror thrillers like *Scream of Fear* (1961) [q.v.], *Paranoiac* (1963) and *Nightmare* (1964). Phil Hardy reported in *The Encyclopedia of Horror Movies* (1986), "The typical [Jimmy] Sangster script, a mechanical structure with the traditional surprise ending as just one more arbitrary device to close the narrative when a respectable running time has been reached.... The French Camargue setting is virtually wasted, and suspense is reduced to a few sensationalist images of a blowtorch approaching the hero's face." In *Little Shoppe of Horrors* #4 (1978), Richard E. Klemensen called it a "boring 'thriller'": "Don't watch this at night because you'll never be able to stay awake." The main asset of the feature was lovely Liliane Brousse as Annette, the young girl who is raped, and four years later falls in love with a man only to have him seduced by her stepmother.

On her way home from school, teenager Annette Beynat (Brousse) is given a ride by neighbor Janiello (Arnold Diamond), who brutally rapes her. When her father, Georges Beynat (Donald Houston), finds out, he exacts a terrible revenge by torturing the rapist to death with a blowtorch. He is placed in an insane asylum for life. Beynat owns a rural inn in Southern France and his wife Eve (Nadia Gray) continues to run it with the help of her stepdaughter Annette. Four years after Georges is committed, Geoff Farrell (Kerwin Mathews), an artist from the United States, comes to stay at the inn after deserting his rich lover Grace (Justine Lord), and is attracted to Annette. Geoff goes on a picnic with Eve and she tells him about her husband whom she believes is sane. The next day Geoff and Eve go horseback riding and they make love on the beach. The stepmother enlists Geoff's help in getting her husband out of the asylum, telling him that a male nurse, Andre (Donald Houston), will arrange for Georges' escape; she says that her husband plans to disappear and let them get married. Geoff and Eve go to the asylum to await Georges. When he does not come over the wall they return to their auto, find him already there and drive him to Marseille, letting him off at a dock. While shopping the next day with Eve, Geoff finds a dead body in the car's trunk and assumes that Georges murdered the nurse. That night they dispose of the body by dropping it off a bridge. Annette sees a light in the garage where her attacker was tortured and discovers that someone has lit a blowtorch. The next day Inspector Etienne (George Pastell) questions Eve about why her husband should suddenly escape from the asylum after being a model prisoner. Annette receives a telegram from her father asking her to meet him in an amphitheater. Eve drives her there only to find it deserted. Geoff sees the body he got rid of in the garage and he ends up being captured by Georges. Georges sets explosives, planning to blow up the place, thus burning Geoff and the corpse beyond recognition and making the police think Georges died and not the artist. When the women return home they find the police there and are told about the explosion and that one of the men survived and is in the hospital. Eve slips into his room and disconnects the life support system. Back at the inn, Annette begs her stepmother to tell the law about her father dying in the explosion and she agrees but drives the girl to an abandoned building where Andre is waiting to kill her. Geoff, who managed to escape before the explosion with the help of a handyman (Jerold Wells), goes to Inspector Etienne and the two set out to trick Eve, who planned the whole affair by having her lover, the male nurse, kill Georges and then pretend to be him. When Andre corners Annette on a ledge, she pushes him off just as Geoff arrives with the police. He rescues the girl as Eve is taken into police custody.

Mark of the Gorilla

(1950; 68 minutes) PRODUCER: Sam Katzman. DIRECTOR: William Berke. SCREENPLAY: Carroll Young. PHOTOGRAPHY: Ira H. Morgan. EDITOR: Henry Batista. MUSIC: Mischa Bakaleinikoff. ART DIRECTOR: Paul Palmentola. SOUND: J.S. Westmoreland. SETS: George Montgomery. UNIT MANAGER: Herbert Leonard. ASSISTANT DIRECTOR: Paul Donnelly. CAST: Johnny Weissmuller (Jungle Jim), Trudy Marshall (Barbara Bentley), Suzanne Dalbert (Princess Nyobi), Onslow Stevens (Dr. Brandt), Robert Purcell (Kramer), Pierce Lyden (Gibbs), Neyle Morrow (Chief Ranger), Selmer Jackson (Warden Frank R. Bentley), Holmes Herbert (Narrator), Steve Calvert (Gorilla Man).

On the Nairobi Game Preserve in the Nagudi District, a messenger is murdered by a giant gorilla. The event is witnessed by Caw Caw, a crow, who flies to Jungle Jim (Johnny Weissmuller), who is fishing with two other pets, his dog Skipper and a chimpanzee. Jim follows the bird to the dead man and reads the letter he was carrying, which was addressed to the jungle man, asking him to meet with the preserve's warden, Frank Bentley (Selmer Jackson). On the way to see Bentley, Jim stops the gorilla from ambushing beautiful Nyobi (Suzanne Dalbert) and throws his knife into the beast. The young woman accompanies Jim to the preserve's headquarters where they meet Bentley's niece Barbara (Trudy Marshall), who is in charge since her uncle is ill and being cared for by Dr. Brandt (Onslow Stevens), a professor of zoology. Jim uses a native fever remedy to help Bentley, who tells him that treasure hunters are on the preserve searching for over a million dollars in gold bullion buried there by the Nazis after they took it from the Shalikari nation. When Brandt finds out about Jim treating Bentley, he orders Kramer to kill the warden and then frees a leopard which attacks Jim. Another attempt is made on Jim's life with his own knife. Tracking the attacker, he finds gorilla footprints and blood. Kramer (Robert Purcell), who was wearing the gorilla suit, goes to his boss, Brandt, for medical aid.

The next day, local rangers are frightened by the sight of two gorillas (also men in suits working for Brandt). The doctor is the leader of a group digging in a hidden cave in search of the buried gold. The rangers seek out Jim who unmasks one of the men, Gibbs (Pierce Lyden). The man is taken back to headquarters where Nyobi tries to get him to tell her the location of the treasure. Jim intercedes and she informs him she is the princess of Shalikari. When Brandt finds out that Jim and the two women are suspicious of him, he frees Gibbs and then shoots him, claiming that he did it to avenge Bentley's murder. Searching for the other gorilla, Jim and Barbara climb a dangerous cliff

Advertisement for Mark of the Gorilla *(1950).*

while Brandt stays behind with Nyobi, who is kidnapped by his men. Brandt then joins Jim and Barbara, who have an encounter with an eagle that causes them to fall into a lake. Jim saves Barbara from a huge water snake and Brand tries to shoot them. Thanks to Caw Caw, Jim and Barbara find the camouflaged entrance to the cave. He sends her for the rangers and then puts on one of the gorilla suits but is soon captured by Brandt's men. After shooting at a small group of rangers, Brandt's cohorts bring Barbara to the cave but the head ranger (Neyle Morrow) goes for reinforcements. Finding the treasure, whose location was told to Brandt by a war criminal, the crooks prepare to leave. One of them throws down a lit cigar; Caw Caw brings it to Jim, who uses it to burn off his bonds. When Kramer tries to shoot him, Jim knocks him out and frees Barbara and Nyobi. More rangers arrive and shoot it out with the treasure seekers. When most of the invaders are killed, Brandt takes some of the gold and tries to escape but is followed by Jim. Brandt falls to his death from a cliff. Later, Nyobi prepares to take the treasure back to her country.

Mark of the Gorilla was the fifth Jungle Jim feature made by producer Sam Katzman, based on the *Comic Weekly* cartoon character created by Alex Raymond. The feature opens with a lengthy narration by Holmes Herbert about African wildlife and the necessity for game preserves. Like the others in the series, the feature is stuffed with animal stock footage and the comedy antics of Jungle Jim's animal pals. Although this outing gave the aquatic star little time in the water, he did have the opportunity to do battle with a leopard, lion, eagle and a large water snake. *Variety* stated, "Followers of the cartoon series from which it is fashioned will find it exciting," while the *New York Times* felt, "[T]he only ones who really earn their salaries are the chimp and Caw Caw, who nimbly unearth clues the others stumble over, keep a sharp watch for skullduggery and actually keep the plot going."

In 1963 a photo story magazine of *Mark of the Gorilla* was published in France as *L'Empreinte Due Gorille*.

Marooned

(1969; 129 minutes; Color) PRODUCER: M.J. Frankovich. ASSOCIATE PRODUCER: Frank Capra, Jr. DIRECTOR: John Sturges. SCREENPLAY: Mayo Simon, from the novel by Martin Caidin. PHOTOGRAPHY: Daniel Fapp. EDITOR: Walter Thompson. SOUND: Les Fresholtz and Arthur Piantadosi. PRODUCTION DESIGN: Lyle Wheeler. SETS: Frank Tuttle. PRODUCTION MANAGER: William O'Sullivan. SPECIAL VISUAL EFFECTS: Robie Robinson, Lawrence W. Butler and Donald C. Glouner. TECHNICAL ADVISORS: George Smith and Martin Caidin. SECOND UNIT DIRECTOR: Ralph Black. ASSISTANT DIRECTOR: Daniel J. McCauley. CAST: Gregory Peck (Charles Keith), Richard Crenna (Jim Pruett), David Janssen (Ted Dougherty), James Franciscus (Dr. Clayton "Stoney" Stone), Gene Hackman (Buzz Lloyd), Lee Grant (Celia Pruett), Nancy Kovack (Teresa Stone), Mariette Hartley (Betty Lloyd), Scott Brady (Public Affairs Officer), John Carter (Flight Surgeon), Craig Huebing (Flight Director Wheeler), Vincent Van Lynn (Cannon), George Gaynes (Mission Director), Tom Stewart (Houston Cap Com Frank), Dube Hibbie (Air Force Titan Specialist), Walter Brooke (Newsman), Dennis Robertson (Launch Director), George Smith (Weather Officer), Mauritz Hugo (Hardy), Bill Couch (Cosmonaut), Mary Linda Rapelye (Priscilla Keith), Bruce Rhodewalt (Computer Technician), George R. Robertson (Dignitary).

Famed director Frank Capra began work on *Marooned*, based on the 1964 novel by Martin Caidin, and stayed with it for two years before abandoning the project as being too costly. His son, Frank Capra, Jr., eventually became the associate producer on the feature which Columbia made on an $8 million budget, releasing it at the end of 1969. Filmed in Panavision, the feature had no music score and was filmed at Cape Kennedy in Florida and at the Mission Space Center in Houston, Texas. It was nominated for three Academy Awards and won for Robie Robinson's special visual effects. A picturesque movie, it was low-key, slow-paced and methodical in telling its science fiction tale of a disabled space probe, something that too soon became fact just four months after its release when NASA aborted the Apollo-Saturn 13 Moon mission when a service module oxygen tank ruptured.

Astronauts Jim Pruett (Richard Crenna), Dr. Clayton "Stoney" Stone (James Franciscus) and Buzz Lloyd (Gene Hackman) blast off in a space probe that docks with the Saturn Orbital Laboratory. The mission is to test their endurance in space, in preparation for interplanetary deep space missions, over a seven-month period in a station 285 miles above the Earth and orbiting the globe every 94 minutes. After five months the Houston team notices a dramatic decline in the astronauts' abilities. Mission supervisor Charles Keith (Gregory Peck) orders them home with the public affairs officer (Scott Brady) announcing the closing of the laboratory and their imminent return to

Earth. After Houston's senior astronaut Ted Dougherty (David Janssen) has a hard time contacting the crew, Pruett informs him of negative retrofire and Dougherty suggests he try manual re-entry. With no backup thrusters, the craft cannot move out of its orbit. The astronauts' wives Celia Pruett (Lee Grant), Teresa Stone (Nancy Kovack) and Betty Lloyd (Mariette Hartley) are told that their husbands are stranded in space. Keith informs the press that NASA is trying to correct the situation but at a meeting with his staff he discusses contingency plans, including the loss of the astronauts since they have only 42 hours of oxygen left. Dougherty offers to lead a rescue mission but Keith rejects the proposal until overridden by orders from the president. Tired of waiting, the three astronauts want to try and repair the engines themselves but Keith tells them they do not have the oxygen to spare and they agree to a power down. The astronauts' wives are brought in to talk with them but Lloyd loses his composure and has to be sedated. Just as Dougherty is about to lift off in the one-man XRV Rescue Craft, a hurricane hits and Keith orders the mission scrubbed. When he gets word that the eye of the storm will pass over the base, giving them 14 minutes to launch, he re-instates the effort but by now the men in space will not have enough oxygen to survive until Dougherty reaches them. When Keith suggests to the astronauts that one of them sacrifice himself, they talk it over but reject the idea. Pruett leaves the craft in an attempt to repair the engines and his suit is torn on a propeller blade and he drifts into space. Keith informs Celia of her husband's death while Stone gives Lloyd his oxygen supply and tries to breathe the air in the capsule. As Dougherty approaches the probe, a Russian vessel also arrives on the scene and since it is closer to the astronauts, Dougherty tells Stone and Lloyd to try and reach the cosmonaut (Bill Couch) who has left his ship. The Russian's life line is not long enough and Lloyd floats by him but Dougherty is able to reach Lloyd and give him oxygen. Stone goes back into the probe. When Dougherty arrives, he finds the cosmonaut giving him the oxygen he needs to survive. Jubilation breaks out at the space headquarters when Dougherty informs Keith that the men have been saved and they are returning to Earth.

Howard Thompson wrote in the *New York Times*, "This ambitious, conscientious Columbia movie is admirably intelligent all the way, with a good cast ... It is simply not the thriller it was intended to be.... Even with a story surprise, the stratospheric climax seems curiously antiseptic, after a long, claustrophobic wait inside the space ship, with the desperate men — and the picture — running low on oxygen. Minus a vital, culminate wallop, the film remains workmanlike. Leanly structured, crisply performed and beautifully directed by John Sturges, it neatly interweaves human behavior and scientific savvy." In *Castle of Frankenstein* #15 (1970), Calvin T. Beck said, "*Marooned* is so disjointed and uneven in quality that it would be easy to believe more than one or two directors had their hands in the stew. As is and on superficial examination, *Marooned* is erratic on a wholesale basis; when it is good, though, it's very, very good, but when it's bad ... well, you know the rest.... Not a classic by any means, it's still well made and entertaining ... and recommended." Philip Strick in *Science Fiction Movies* (1976) called it "a big, glossy and absorbing production directed with neutral efficiency by John Sturges ... There are some oddities in the special effects — the Russian arrives in what looks like a hand grenade — but the film has a pleasingly ironic edge." *Variety* opined, "The film is superbly crafted, taut and an technological cliff-hanger. The production's major flaw is a hokey old-fashioned Hollywood Renfrew-to-the-rescue climax that is dramatically, logically and technologically unconvincing."

The Menace

(1932; 64 minutes) PRODUCER: Sam Nelson. DIRECTOR: Roy William Neill. SCREENPLAY: Dorothy Howell and Charles Logue, from the novel *The Feathered Serpent* by Edgar Wallace. DIALOGUE: Roy Chanslor. PHOTOGRAPHY: L. William O'Connell. EDITOR: Gene Havlick. SOUND: George Cooper. ASSISTANT DIRECTOR: Gene Anderson. CAST: H.B. Warner (Inspector Tracy), Walter Byron (Ronald Quayle), Bette Davis (Peggy Lowell), Natalie Moorhead (Caroline Quayle), William B. Davidson (John "Jack" Utterson), Crauford Kent (Sam Lewis), Halliwell Hobbes (Phillips), Charles Gerrard (Bailiff), Murray Kinnell (Carr), Frank Rice (Jim Anderson), Oscar Apfel (Dr. Jorgenson), Frank Atkinson (Cartier Man).

Working title: *The Feathered Serpent*.

The Menace was Bette Davis' fifth feature film. It was based on Edgar Wallace's 1927 novel *The Feathered Serpent* and marketed as a Wallace movie in 1932, when anything with the author's name on it was box office. With its murder mystery plot set in creepy Quayle Manor, which had a room featuring esoteric items like the statue of a large feathered serpent and a mummy case, the film took on the trappings of a horror effort. It even included a Halloween party with a costumed band. The *New York Times* said, "[I]t toys with a routine assortment of shadows and murderous symbol [but] is hardly adult entertainment." For Davis, who had the romantic lead, the film was an important one because through fellow cast member Murray Kinnell she was introduced to George Arliss who put her in his Warner Bros. feature *The Man Who Played God* (1932), thus sending her on the path to movie stardom.

Falsely accused of murdering his father by his stepmother Caroline Quayle (Natalie Moorhead), Ronald Quayle (Walter Byron) breaks out of an English prison with his pal Jim Anderson (Frank Rice) and goes to the United States. While working at an oil field, Ronald's face is badly scarred by an explosion. A plastic surgeon (Oscar Apfel) restores his looks by giving him a different face. Determined to clear himself and find the real killer, Ronald returns to England using the name Robert Crockett. Suspecting that the guilty parties are Caroline and her lover Jack Utterson (William B. Davidson), who masquerades as her brother, he learns that his stepmother has run through his father's money and is selling Quayle Manor. Posing as a buyer for the property, Ronald is able to fool both his stepmother, who flirts with him, and his former sweetheart Peggy Lowell (Davis). As Crockett, the young man begins a romance with Caroline while Peggy goes to work for Inspector Tracy (H.B. Warner) of Scotland Yard, who has her help inventory the mansion looking for clues that might exonerate Ronald. Quayle tells Caroline's pal Sam Lewis (Crauford Kent) that he plans to elope with her to New York City and when Lewis tells Utterson, both men fear that Caroline will deceive them. During a Halloween party at the manor, Crockett places an expensive necklace he boasted about giving Caroline on Sam and when Utterson finds out he murders Lewis, thinking he stole the gems. Peggy discovers Lewis' body in the mummy case and faints as Ronald calls Inspector Tracy, who arrives to investigate. Ronald and Utterson have a falling-out over Caroline and engage in a fistfight with the huge statue of a feathered serpent crushing Utterson. Dying, he confesses to killing the senior Quayle on Caroline's behalf. With his stepmother taken into police custody, Ronald reveals his identity to Peggy and they resume their romance.

Two years after the release of *The Menace*, the property was remade by Columbia at its British studios under the work's original title, *The Feathered Serpent*. Outside of a subplot about a secret society, the story had none of the mystery-horror elements of the U.S. version in its tale of a newsman (Tom Helmore) proving that an actress (Enid Stamp-Taylor) was not involved in robbery or murder. "Confused thriller" is how David Quinlan described the quota programmer in *British Sound Films: The Studio Years 1928–1959* (1984).

A Midsummer Night's Dream

(1967; 93 minutes; Color) PRODUCER: Dick Davis. SUPERVISOR-CHOREOGRAPHER: George Balanchine. DIRECTOR: Dan Eriksen. From the play by William Shakespeare. EDITOR: Armond Lebowitz. MUSIC: Felix Mendelssohn. ART MUSIC CONDUCTOR: Robert Irving. DIRECTOR: Albert Brenner. COSTUMES: Barbara Karinska. CAST: Suzanne Farrell (Queen Titania), Edward Villella (King Oberon), Arthur Mitchell (Puck), Mimi Paul (Helena), Nicholas Magallanes (Lysander), Patricia McBride (Hermia), Roland Vazquez (Demetrius), Francisco Moncion (Theseus), Gloria Gorvin (Hippolyta), Richard Rapp (Bottom), Jacques d'Amboise, Allegra Kent (Court Dancers), The New York City Ballet and Children of the School of American Ballet (Dancers).

Since Vitagraph headlined Maurice Costello in a 1,000-foot version of William Shakespeare's *A Midsummer Night's Dream* in 1909, there have been more than a dozen screen versions of the 1495 comedy-fantasy, the best known being Warners' 1935 all-star production. Early in 1967, Columbia released this Films Oberon version of the play, a ballet based on Shakespeare's work told by performance *sans* dialogue and using the 1827 music composed by Felix Mendelssohn. A filmed version of George Balanchine's New York City Ballet production, it was photographed in a studio with the stage setting redesigned; the choreography closely followed Balanchine's original ballet. Columbia's distribution was a brief one for the film had its "world premiere" in August 1967 at the New York State Theatre, a solo benefit showing for the city's Ballet Fund. A month later *McCall's* magazine announced it would underwrite showings of the feature in 28 cities with funds raised going to those community's symphony orchestras, with an option for 42 more screenings in other venues. Showcorporation handled the release for these benefit outings.

The ballet tells the basic story of the Shakespeare work about beautiful Hermia (Patricia McBride) being forced to marry Demetrius (Roland Vazquez), who loves her, although she wants Lysander (Nicholas Magallanes). Under threat of exile or execution, Hermia and Lysander head for Athens to be married at his aunt's home. Her best friend Helena (Mimi Paul), who loves Demetrius even though he left her for Hermia, tells her ex-lover about the elopement. Demetrius heads into the forest determined to bring back Hermia and he is followed by Helena. The woods also houses a group of Athenian craftsmen who want to perform a play at the wedding of Theseus (Francisco Moncion), the duke of Athens, and Hippolyta (Gloria Gorvin), the queen of the Amazons. A group of fairies led by King Oberon (Edward Villella) and Queen Titania (Suzanne Farrell) have come to bless the nuptials.

Unhappy about a young man given to his wife, Oberon sends his servant Puck (Arthur Mitchell) to find a magical flower whose juices, when spread over a sleeper's eyes, will cause that person to love the first thing they see upon waking. When he sees Demetrius being cruel to Helena, he spreads the juice over his eyes and the two young men both end up loving Helena while the jealous Hermia wants to fight her best friend. After having the juice spread over her eyes, Titania awakes to see one of the craftsmen, weaver Bottom (Richard Rapp), whose head Puck has made into that of a jackass. Titania immediately falls in love with him while Puck puts the potion on Lysander's eyes and he awakes to fall in love with Hermia. When Theseus and Hippolyta find the four lovers asleep in the woods, they take them back to Athens where they are married in a dual ceremony. The court then watches the amateurish play by the craftsmen. Later the fairies bless the sleeping newlyweds with a charm and vanish. Puck stays to tell the audience the play was only a dream.

The *New York Times*' Clive Barnes felt those behind the production "had more ambitious plans than that of simple record. It appears that recreation was their aim, the synthesis of a genuine ballet film able to hold its own with the original ballet on its own terms. In this they have failed. The attempt has been a brave one ... Both the dance and the dancers produce nothing that really approximates to the effect they create on stage, and the choreography in particular seems to undervalue itself, so that even passages that look magical on stage here occasionally look trite." In *The Family Guide to Movies on Video* (1988), Henry Herz and Tony Zaza noted, "A treat for those who could not otherwise see this lavish, seldom-performed ballet with the music of Felix Mendelssohn."

After the ballet version of Shakespeare's play was released theatrically, a Czech puppet feature of *A Midsummer Night's Dream* was showcased in theaters. This outing had been made in 1959 but its English-language version did not come out until 1971 with Richard Burton narrating and the Royal Shakespeare company providing the speaking voices. Although a dozen years old and aimed at kiddie audiences, this version got more attention than its ballet counterpart.

The Missing Juror

(1944; 66 minutes) PRODUCER: Wallace MacDonald. DIRECTOR: Oscar Boetticher, Jr. [Budd Boetticher] SCREENPLAY: Charles O'Neal. STORY: Leon Abrams and Robert Hill Wilkinson. PHOTOGRAPHY: L.W. O'Connell. EDITOR: Paul Borofsky. MUSIC DIRECTOR: Mischa Bakaleinikoff. ART DIRECTOR: George Brooks. SOUND: John Goodrich. SETS: George Montgomery. ASSISTANT DIRECTOR: Ivan Volkman. CAST: Jim Bannon (Joe Keats), Janis Carter (Alice Hill), George Macready (Harry Wharton/Jerome K. Bentley), Jean Stevens (Tex Tuttle), Joseph Crehan (Willard Apple), Carole Mathews (Marcy), Cliff Clark (Inspector Davis), Mike Mazurki (Cullie), Edmund Cobb (Detective Cahan), George Lloyd (George Szabo), Alan Bridge (Deputy Sheriff), William Newell (Wally), Victor Travers (Clem Poskins), John Tyrrell (Sergeant Regan), Walter Baldwin (Sheriff), William Hall (Officer Gannett), Danny Desmond (Newsboy), Harry Strang (Sergeant Lewton), Charles C. Wilson (Mac Ellis), Cecil Weston (Mrs. Jackson), Nancy Brinckman (Nurse), Shelby Payne (Marie Chappel), Pat O'Malley (Priest), Sam Flint (Judge), Del Henderson, Frank O'Connor (Train Conductors), Trevor Bardette (Pierson), Ernest Hilliard (Doctor), Ray Teal (Line-Up Detective), Forbes Murray (District Attorney), Edwin Stanley (Warden), Jesse Graves (Porter), Milton Kibbee (Train Engineer Joe), George Anderson (Defense Attorney), Chuck Hamilton (Bailiff), Jack Gardner (Reporter), Stuart Holmes (Juror), Bud Fine (Waiter), Pat Lane (Court Clerk).

Working title: *Tomorrow We Die*.

The Missing Juror is best known as the directorial debut of Budd Boetticher, then billed under his given name Oscar. The next year he would helm *Escape in the Fog* (q.v.) at Columbia and in 1948 he directed the horror favorite *Behind Closed Doors* for Eagle Lion. Changing his name to Budd Boetticher, the former bullfighter co-wrote and directed his favorite feature, *The Bullfighter and the Lady* for Republic in 1951. Later in the decade he directed Randolph Scott in a series of Columbia westerns that have developed cult status. Charles O'Neal's script for *The Missing Juror* borrows its main theme from two previous Columbia features, *The Ninth Guest* (1934) and *The Man They Could Not Hang* (1939) [qq.v.], in its tale of a falsely convicted man taking revenge "from beyond the grave." It was filmed on a two-week schedule. Don Miller in *B Movies* (1973) said the feature was a "suspense thriller [with] a fairly exciting script and a good cast ... but it was Boetticher's strong handling that gave the minor item its value."

Former crime reporter and now feature editor Joe Keats (Jim Bannon) becomes interested in the murder of leather manufacturer Jason Sloan, whose corpse was put in a car run over by a train. Sloan was the fourth juror in the Wharton murder case to die recently; Keats had covered the trial in which Harry J. Wharton (George Macready) was sentenced to be hanged for the murder of his girlfriend Marie Chappel (Shelby Payne). The main witness, private eye George Szabo (George Lloyd), testified that he was outside Marie's apartment when she was killed and he saw Harry at the scene. After his appeal is denied, Wharton lapses into madness as he awaits execution. When Keats tries to interview Szabo he refuses to talk. While walking home, Szabo is gunned down; before dying he tells Keats that Wharton was framed. A pardon is given to Wharton but when he is told by the warden (Edwin Stanley) that he is a free man, Wharton says he is one of the living dead and is sent to a private hospital for treatment. There he receives visitors, including some of the jurors who convicted him, such as foreman Jerome K. Bentley. A fire breaks out in Wharton's room; after it is put out, his body is found hanging from the ceiling, so badly burned it cannot be identified.

Keats then suggests to his editor, Willard Apple (Joseph Crehan), that he interview the surviving jurors and he starts with beautiful antique store owner Alice Hill (Janis Carter), who refuses to cooperate. Her assistant-roommate, Tex Tuttle (Jean Stevens), gives Keats a picture of Alice to use in his story. Alice is visited by Bentley (George Macready) who tells her he has purchased a new home and that he wants to buy its furnishings from her. When another juror, housewife Mrs. Stagler, is murdered, Police Lt. Davis (Cliff Clark) accuses Keats of starting a crime wave because of his stories reviving the Wharton case. Keats finds himself attracted to Alice. When he goes to meet her and Tex at their apartment, Bentley shows up saving he picked up the women's key by mistake when he ordered a shipment of antiques from them. On his way home, Keats is met by Bentley who tells him he thinks he knows the killer's identity and takes him to a police line-up before promising to reveal the culprit's identity at dawn. Bentley then insists that Keats accompany him to Cullie's Steam Bath where Bentley gets a neck massage from the owner, Cullie (Mike Mazurki), before the two men take a steam bath. Bentley locks Keats in the steam room and tries to kill him by turning up the temperature, but Cullie manages to rescue the newsman and call a doctor. Keats is taken to a hospital where he tells Willard he thinks Bentley tried to murder him. His editor refutes the statement by saying that the police are questioning a man named Pierson (Trevor Bardette) who has confessed to the homicides. The two men go to the police station where the suspect is being interrogated by Davis and Detective Cahan (Edmund Cobb). Keats become leery when Pierson cannot name the still extant jurors. Although Keats asks Davis not to release a new story on Pierson, it becomes headline news.

Keats tries to contact one of the remaining jurors, Peter Jackson, but is only able to talk with his wife (Cecil Weston) who informs him that her husband was called to Buckminster to meet someone. Keats goes to the address, Bentley's new home, finds Jackson's corpse and goes to inform the sheriff (Walter Baldwin). When a deputy (Alan Bridge) and his pal (Victor Travers) tell the lawman there is no body, Joe is put in a jail cell. Alice gets a message to meet Keats at Glen Lock. After she leaves, Willard calls her and talks to Tex, who becomes fearful when she finds out Keats is really in jail. Willard picks up Tex and the two drive to Glen Lock. Keats is set free when Jackson's body is located in a nearby river. Calling Willard, Keats finds out from his secretary Marcy (Carole Mathews) that her boss and Tex have gone to Glen Lock where Alice arrives to find Bentley, who has gotten rid of his disguise and she recognizes him as Harry Wharton. He makes her go with him to his house where he plans to hang the young woman. Just as he starts to put a noose around her neck, Keats fires at him through a window, killing the madman. Keats finishes his series by saying that Wharton murdered Bentley and took his identity, planning to kill all the remaining jurors who convicted him of a crime he did not commit.

Mr. Sardonicus

(1961; 89 minutes) PRODUCER-DIRECTOR: William Castle. ASSOCIATE PRODUCER: Dona Holloway. STORY-SCREENPLAY: Ray Russell. PHOTOGRAPHY: Burnett Guffey. EDITOR: Edwin Bryant. MUSIC: Von Dexter. ART DIRECTOR: Cary Odell. SOUND: James Z. Flaster. SETS: James M. Crowe. MAKEUP: Ben Lane. WARDROBE: Jack Angel and Paul Barto. ASSISTANT DIRECTOR: R. Robert Rosenbaum. CAST: Oscar Homolka (Krull), Ronald Lewis (Sir Robert Cargrave), Audrey Dalton (Baroness Maude Randall Sardonicus), Guy Rolfe (Baron Sardonicus aka Marek Toleslawski), Vladimir Sokoloff (Henryk Toleslawski), Erika Peters (Elenka Toleslawski), Lorna Hanson (Anna), Edith Atwater (Hospital Sister), James Forrest (Wainwright), Tina Woodward, Annalena Lund, Ilse Burkert (Girls), Constance Cavendish (Mrs. Higgins), Mavis Neal (Head Nurse), Charles H. Radilac (Stationmaster), David Janti (Janku), Franz Roehn (Gravedigger), Albert D'Arno (Gatekeeper), William Castle (Himself/Narrator).

Mr. Sardonicus was the fourth "gimmick" horror feature that producer-director William Castle made for Columbia. For this one he used the "Punishment Call ballot" that allegedly allowed the film's audience to decide the fate of the title character. (Most sources claim that only one ending was actually made.) Released in Great Britain as *Sardonicus*, the film was very atmospheric with its fog-enshrouded and barren countryside, spooky graveyard and medieval castle replete with a torture chamber. The title character looked like Conrad Veidt in *The Man Who Laughs* (1928). Oscar Homolka added to the horrific proceedings as Sardonicus' sadist valet who gleefully places leeches on the face and feet of a blonde maid. Guy Rolfe's makeup for the part of Sardonicus involved five facial appliance fittings that could only be worn for about one hour.

The feature opens in whirling London fog with a delightful prologue in which Castle, calling the audience his "homicidal friends" (a reference to his shocker *Homicidal* [q.v.], issued the same year), says this new film was about "gallantry, graciousness and ghouls." Set in the Victorian Era, the plot had facially scarred Krull (Homolka) arriving at Queens College Hospital with a missive for eminent surgeon Sir Robert Cargrave (Ronald Lewis). The doctor, who has been experimenting with poisons in an effort to cure certain types of paralysis, reads the letter and finds out his ex-fiancée Maude Randall (Audrey Dalton), now Baroness Sardonicus, needs his help. Canceling all his work, Cargrave travels by ship and train to the Central European locale of Gorslava where the stationmaster (Charles H. Radilac) shows fright when he hears the name Sardonicus. Krull calls for Cargrave and takes him to the castle where the doctor finds Anna (Lorna Hanson), a maid, screaming from pain due to leeches placed on her face. As the doctor removes the leeches, Krull tells him he put them on the girl on the orders of his master, Baron Sardonicus (Rolfe).

After being reunited with Maude in the castle's salon, Cargrave notices that all the picture frames in the castle are empty. He also sees a padlocked door and Krull jokingly refers to the room as the "chamber of horrors." At dinner, Maude introduces Cargrave to her husband, Baron Sardonicus, who wears a face mask. That night Krull brings five young girls to the castle's dungeon and Sardonicus picks one of them to stay. The girl (Tina Woodward)

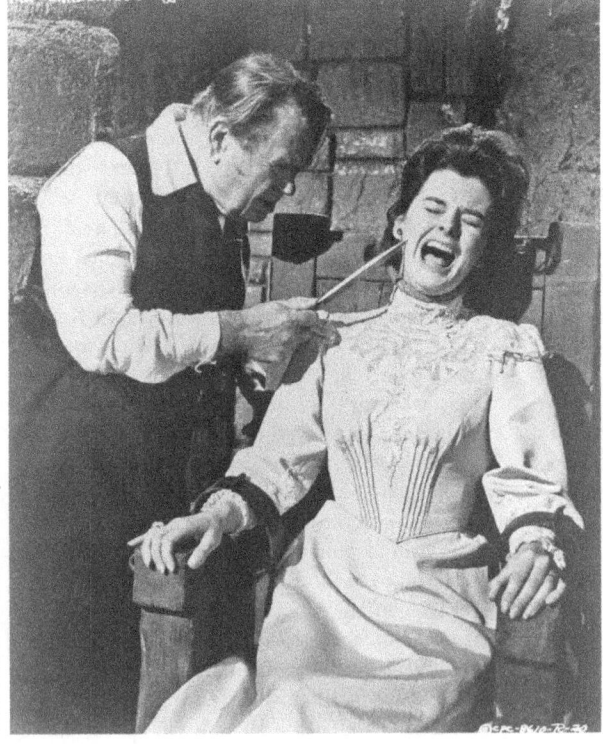

Oscar Homolka and Audrey Dalton in *Mr. Sardonicus* (1961).

pulls off his mask and screams. Cargrave spends a restless night in the castle and the next day finds out that Sardonicus forbids mirrors in his home. When Sardonicus informs Maude that he plans to tell the doctor the truth about himself, he warns her she had better use her feminine charms to convince her ex-lover to carry out his wishes or she will have to face the consequences. In the castle's overgrown garden, Sardonicus tells Cargrave he was once a peasant named Marek Toleslawski and that his father (Vladimir Sokoloff) had purchased a lottery ticket that was inadvertently buried with him. Months later, after the ticket is announced as the winner of a huge amount of money, Marek's wife Elenka (Erika Peters) forces him to agree to dig up his father's grave to retrieve it. That night Marek carries out her wishes but the sight of his father's corpse causes his mouth to freeze in a perpetual grin. Seeing her husband's face, Elenka becomes insane and commits suicide.

With the fortune he received from the lottery, Marek buys his title and a barony and takes the name Sardonicus. After unsuccessfully trying to get treatment from several renowned doctors, Sardonicus let Krull use an ancient folk remedy in which leeches were used to draw blood from young girls, but this too was not a success. When Cargrave informs Sardonicus he will not help him, he is taken to the castle's torture chamber where he finds Maude chained to a chair. Sardonicus orders Krull to cut her face so she too will have a perpetual grim. When Krull resists, Sardonicus reminds him that he (Krull) once had two eyes before his previous art of disobedience. Cargrave agrees to help Sardonicus and he sends to London for equipment and drugs for the serum he hopes to perfect. When Cargrave asks Maude why she married Sardonicus, she tells him her father got into financial troubles and that Sardonicus paid off the debts and threatened to expose him as an embezzler, thus forcing her into the marriage. When Cargrave says that his new treatment is not ready, Sardonicus takes Maude to the padlocked room and forces her to stay there with his father's corpse. To free the woman he loves, Cargrave agrees to try the serum, ties Sardonicus to a chair in the padlocked room and gives him a shot that results in his face returning to normal. Told not to talk for a time, Sardonicus writes out an annulment decree and Robert, Maude and Anna leave the castle. While they are waiting at the train station, Krull shows up and tells the doctor that his master cannot open his mouth. Cargrave says that Sardonicus' cure must come from within himself since the serum used was only distilled water. Returning to the castle, Krull remembers his lost eye, lies that he missed Cargrave at the station and begins gorging himself, leaving Sardonicus to starve.

Phil Hardy in *The Encyclopedia of Horror Movies* (1986) noted, "This is one of Castle's brighter films, though it borrows shamelessly from *The Man Who Laughs* (1928), probably because it's far better scripted than his usual efforts." *Castle of Frankenstein* #19 (1972) called it a "[l]urid but compelling horror tale." "Enjoyable gimmick film" was the verdict in *John Stanley's Creature Feature Movie Guide Strikes Again* (1994).

Misterios de la Magia Negra (Mysteries of Black Magic)

(1958; 86 minutes) PRODUCER: Sergio Kogan. DIRECTOR: Miguel M. Delgado. SCREENPLAY: Ulises Petit de Murat. PHOTOGRAPHY: Victor Herrera. EDITOR: Jorge Bustos. MUSIC: Gustavo Cesar Carreon. ART DIRECTOR: G. Gunther Gerzso. SOUND: James L. Fields and Javier Mateos. SPECIAL EFFECTS: Juan Munoz and Antonio Neira. PRODUCTION MANAGER: Fidel Pizarro. MAKEUP: Ana Guerrero. ASSISTANT DIRECTOR: Jaime Contreras. CAST: Nadia Haro Oliva (Egle Elohim), Carlos Riquelme (Professor Elodio Tejeda), Aldo Monti (Raul/Galli), Lourdes Parga (Maria Tejeda), Angelines Fernandez (Laura), Carlos Ancira (Kerobal), Diana Ochoa, Elvira Lody, Reynaldo Rivera, Gerardo del Castillo, Ada Carrasco, Eloida Hernandez.

Conductor of a stage magic act, Elge Elohim (Nadia Haro Oliva) is really a 400-year-old witch who practices black magic with her deformed assistant Kerobal (Carlos Ancira). She also keeps the mummy of her ancient lover Galli (Aldo Monti) in a hidden crypt. When Elodio Tejeda (Carlos Riquelme), a professor of black magic, challenges Elge's powers, she is determined to destroy him and his family but ends up falling in love with Raul (Aldo Monti), the boyfriend of the professor's daughter Maria (Lourdes Parga) and the reincarnation of Galli. She puts Raul under a spell and tells him to murder Maria. The jealous Galli arises from his tomb and kills the witch, thus releasing the young man from her spell. Raul and Maria make their escape.

In *The Encyclopedia of Horror Movies* (1986), Phil Hardy called the feature "ludicrous.... The effects are rudimentary and the script's possibilities (a witch performing her tricks on stage as a spectacle could have yielded some nice cinematic paralells) wasted as [director Miguel M.] Delgado opts for a crude melodramatic approach devoid of humor and beset with decidedly anti-semitic overtones."

Filmed at Estudios Churubusco Azteca in Mexico City and produced by Alfa Films S.A., *Misterios de la Magia Negra* was one of several Mexican horror film acquired by Columbia in the 1950s and 1960s and issued theatrically in border states in their original Spanish-language versions. Like some south-of-the-border terror outings, it was very atmospheric but suffered from a weak plot. Among its highlights were the not quite human assistant Kerobal, the revived mummy Galli, various stage illusions and some voodoo rituals.

El Monstruo Resucitado (The Resuscitated Monster)

(1953; 85 minutes) PRODUCER: Sergio Kogan. DIRECTOR-SCREENPLAY: Chano Urueta. STORY: Dino Maiuri. PHOTOGRAPHY: Victor Herrera. EDITOR: Jorge Bustos. MUSIC: Federico Ruiz. PRODUCTION DESIGN: Gunther Genszo and Mario Padilla. SOUND: Jose de Perez. MAKEUP: Armando Meyer. SPECIAL EFFECTS: Jorge Benavides. CAST: Miroslava (Nora), Carlos Navarro (Ariel/Serguei Rostov), Jose Maria Linares Rivas (Dr. Hermann Ling), Fernando Wagner (Gherasimos), Alberto Mariscal (Mischa), Estefan Berne (Crommer).

Subtitled "Dr. Crimen," *El Monstruo Resucitado* popularized horror films in Mexico (the genre in that country dates back to the early 1930s). Along with its follow-up *La Bruja* (The Witch), released the next year, director-writer Chano Urueta created the atmospheric background that would dominate Mexican horror movies for the next two decades. Especially impressive were the cemetery and old house sets, both beautifully photographed by Victor Herrera. The story was a mixture of Frankenstein and Phantom of the Opera themes but its main plot twist came in having the mad scientist as a repulsive monster while his revived creature was an Adonis. Top-billed Miroslava committed suicide at age 30 in 1955, the year the movie was officially released in the U.S. as *The Revived Monster*. Its other stateside titles include *The Monster Lives* and *The Monster Who Lived Again*; it was issued in Italy as *Dr. Crimen*. The feature was produced by Internacional Cinematografica and was distributed by Columbia in Mexico and in border states' Spanish-language theaters. Its 1955 stateside issuance was by the Mexican company Azteca Films. The Czech-born Miroslava (Sternova) had starred in Columbia's *The Brave Bulls* (1951).

Balkan news reporter Nora (Miroslava) is bored with her job and her editor, Gherasimos (Fernando Wagner), suggests she glean the newspaper's personal columns for a story. She is intrigued by one submitted by Dr. Hermann Ling (Jose Maria Linares Rivas) and she makes an appointment with the man only to find he wears a black mask and dark glasses. Although uneasy, Nora accepts his invitation to go to his house which is reached through an eerie graveyard. The house contains statues of morose women, mirrors covered in black and a dim-witted, simian-like servant, Crommer (Estefan Berne). Nora continues to question Ling, who tells her he is a plastic surgeon, an outcast from his profession and the world because he was born deformed. Showing sympathy for the man, Nora convinces him to remove his mask, revealing his hideous face. She faints but after recovering she apolo-

Poster for *El Monstruo Resucitado* (The Resuscitated Monster) (1953).

gizes and kisses his forehead. Ling, who has fallen in love with Nora, vows to become a better man and follows her back to the city where she meets with Gherasimos in a restaurant and relates her adventures. Unknown to the young woman, Dr. Ling is behind a partition and hears her conversation and realizes she was only using him to get a news story. He vows revenge and steals the corpse of a handsome young man, Rostov (Carlos Novarro), who has committed suicide. Ling gives him a new brain and Crommer's life force, renaming him Ariel. He orders his creation to kill a woman and then romance Nora. Nora and Ariel meet in the restaurant and are immediately attracted to each other and soon fall in love. When Ling attempts to harm the young woman, Ariel turns on him and kills his creator but goes mad as Gherasimos arrives and shoots him. Nora holds the resurrected man as he dies.

This proved to be the first of a slew of Mexican horror films distributed by Columbia.

Most Dangerous Man Alive

(1961; 82 minutes) PRODUCER: Benedict Bogeaus. DIRECTOR: Allan Dwan. SCREENPLAY: James Leicester and Phillip Rock. STORY: Phillip Rock and Michael Pate. PHOTOGRAPHY: Carl Carvahal. EDITOR: Carlo Lodato. MUSIC: Louis Forbes. SOUND: Joe Kavigan. PRODUCTION SUPERVISOR: Clarence Eurist. COSTUMES: Gwen Wakeling. CAST: Ron Randell (Eddie Candell), Debra Paget (Linda Marlow), Elaine Stewart (Carla Angelo), Anthony Caruso (Andy Damon), Gregg Palmer (Lieutenant Fisher), Morris Ankrum (Captain Davis), Tudor Owen (Dr. Meeker), Steve Mitchell (Devols), Joel Donte (Franscotti), Jay Novello (Policeman).

Gangster Eddie Candell (Ron Randell) is framed for murder by rival Andy Damon (Anthony Caruso), who also steals Candell's girlfriend, Linda Marlow (Debra Paget). Escaping from the law, Candell goes into a desert area about to become the site of atomic testing. He is caught in a low-level blast and absorbs a great deal of radiation before seeking refuge in a shack. The supervisor of the test, Dr. Meeker (Tudor Owen), viewed the hoodlum on a monitor but was unable to halt the experiment. He informs policemen Captain Davis (Morris Ankrum) and Lieutenant Fisher (Gregg Palmer) that Candell may mutate as a result of the explosion.

When Eddie awakes he sees that the steel handcuffs he was wearing are being absorbed by his body. He steals a truck loaded with dynamite and plans to take revenge on Damon. When a trap he sets for Candell fails, Damon realizes that Candell's body can withstand bullets. Linda is forced to go with her ex-lover. The two drive to the home of Carla Angelo (Elaine Stewart), a friend of Candell's who thinks he is being hounded by the police; he tells her about the changes in his body from the radiation. When the police show up, Candell and Linda go to Damon's headquarters where Candell kills two gang members. Dr. Meeker informs Carla that Candell will slowly turn to steel and at the same time begin giving off atomic radiation, but she does not believe him. When the gangsters fail in an attempt to kidnap Carla, the young woman goes to Dr. Meeker for help and the two visit Candell, who is becoming mentally deranged as his body solidifies. Damon and his men abduct Dr. Meeker and force him to set up a meeting with Candell at a brewery. Planning to electrocute Candell, Damon sees his plan foiled by the now invincible man, who kills more of the gang and takes Damon, Linda and Carla by car into hilly terrain. The police detectives and the National Guard trail the quartet. When Damon murders Linda, Candell throws him over a cliff. Just as they are about to use a flamethrower on Candell, Carla steps next to him. He pushes her aside and is reduced to dust by the flames.

This low-budget excursion into the effects of radiation on humans, combining the sci-fi and gangster genres, was a minor effort made by producer Benedict Bogeaus' Trans-Global Films in Mexico, on a one-week schedule, as a two-part pilot for a television series. When the series failed to materialize, Bogeaus sold the production as a feature to Columbia, which released it theatrically in the summer of 1961. It was the last of over 250 films directed by Allan Dwan, who began his career in 1911, becoming one of the cinema's most celebrated helmsmen. It was also the last of 11 features Dwan directed for Bogeaus; they included *Passion* (1954) and *The River's Edge* (1957). In an interview for the book *Allan Dwan: The Last Pioneer* (1971), the director told Peter Bogdanovich that *Most Dangerous Man Alive* was a "misfit from start to end." *Variety* called the feature "shopworn, absurd and tasteless."

Mothra

(1962; 91 minutes; Color) PRODUCER: Tomoyuki Tanaka. DIRECTOR: Inoshiro Honda. SCREENPLAY: Shinichi Sekizawa. STORY: Shinichiro Nakamura, Takehijo Fukunaga and Yoshie Hotta. PHOTOGRAPHY: Hajime Koizumi. EDITOR: Kazuji Taira. MUSIC: Yuji Koseki. ART DIRECTORS: Takeo Kita and Teruaki Abe. SOUND: Shoichi Fijinawa and Masanobu Miyazaki. PRODUCTION MANAGER: Shin Morita. SPECIAL EFFECTS DIRECTOR: Eiji Tsuburaya. SPECIAL EFFECTS PHOTOGRAPHER: Sadamasa Arikawa. ASSISTANT DIRECTOR: Masaji Nonagase. ENGLISH-LANGUAGE VERSION: PRODUCER: David D. Horn. DIRECTOR: Lee Kresel. SCREENPLAY: Robert Myerson. CAST: Emi Ito, Yumi Ito (The Peanuts), Hiroshi Koizumi (Dr. Shinichi Chujo), Jelly [Jerry] Ito (Clark Nelson), Franky Sakai (Senichiro "Bulldog" Fukuda), Kyoko Kagawa (Michi Hanamura), Ken Uehara (Dr. Harada), Takashi Shimura (Newspaper Editor), Tetsu Nakamura (Yakamura), Akihiro Tayama (Shinji Chujo), Akihiko Hirata (Doctor), Seizaburo Kawazu (General), Yoshifumi Tajima (Military Advisor), Obel Wyatt (Dr. Roff), Harold Conway (Rolisican Ambassador), Robert Dunham (Rolisican Policeman), Johnny Yuseph, Akira Wakamatsu, Hiroshi Akitsu, Hiroshi Iwamoto, Toshio Miura (Henchmen), Yoshio Kosugi (Ship Captain), Ren Yamaoto, Haruya Kato, Ko Mishima, Rinsaku Ogata (Surviving Sailors), Kenji Sahara (Helicopter Pilot), Akira Yamada (Native Worshipper), Takeo Nagashima, Aral Hayamizu (Native Dancers), Kazuo Imai (Announcer), Wataru Omae, Kazuo Higata (Officials), Toshihiko Furuta, Shoichi Hirose (Dam Workers), Koji Uno (Reporter), Tadashi Okabe, Akio Kusama (Surveyors), Mitsuo Matsumoto, Hiroyuki Satake (Policemen), Haru Nakajima, Katsumi Tezuka (Larva Mothra).

Mothra is a polarizing film; either loved or hated. James O'Neill in *Terror on Tape* (1994) said it was "[a] colorful and enjoyable Japanese monster film with elaborate but unconvincing effects." *Videohound's Sci-Fi Experience* (1997) raved about it being a "[c]lassic Japanese monster shenanigans ... one of the best of the '60s Japanese giant monster epics, a colorful, fast-moving fantasy with an unforgettable monster." *Castle of Frankenstein* #19 (1972) dubbed it an "[i]diotically childish Japanese fantasy-horror actioner ... Between poor dubbing, papier-mâché Tokyo and set are leveled again." Produced by the Toho Company and filmed in TohoScope, the feature was first issued in Japan in 1961 as *Mosura* running 101 minutes. When Columbia released it in the U.S. in the spring of 1962 as *Mothra*, the feature was cut by ten minutes. The tiny women who control Mothra are often dubbed the Twin Fairies but the film's title card bills them as The Peanuts.

During a typhoon, a ship runs into a reef and the crew is forced to abandon the craft. Later a helicopter spots four survivors on a remote island. Following their rescue, they are questioned by several doctors as well as ace reporter "Bulldog" Fukuda (Franky Sakai) and his lovely photographer, Michi Hanamura (Kyoko Kagawa). When the sailors tell of being given juice by natives on the island, Dr. Chujo (Hiroshi Koizumi) suggests leading an expedition to the island. It includes Dr. Harada (Ken Uehara) and Clark Nelson (Jelly Ito), a representative of the nation of Rosilica which has been using the area for an atomic testing ground. The medical men do not like Nelson since he declares all information must go through him and he also does not permit news reporters on the expedition. Nelson becomes upset when he finds "Bulldog" aboard their ship disguised as a cabin boy. Harada appoints him one of the expedition's guards.

On the island they find a jungle with strange, mutated flora. Chujo is caught by a giant vampire plant but is saved by the appearance of two tiny women (Emi Ito, Yumi Ito). Nelson captures the girls but the explorers are surrounded by natives and he is forced to free them. After the expedition returns home, Dr. Chujo shows "Bulldog" a scroll he found on the island which refers to Mothra. Nelson and his men go back to the isle and find the two girls, recapture them and then shoot their way out as a giant egg appears. Nelson plans to exhibit the tiny women on stage in Tokyo. As the girls sing a siren song on stage, the natives of the island also sing and dance to the same refrain. Nelson permits Dr. Chujo, "Bulldog" and Michi to converse with the tiny maidens who communicate through telepathy. The girls warn them that Mothra will come to their rescue. On the island, the egg cracks open and a giant larva emerges and begins swimming toward Tokyo, destroying a ship. When Nelson refuses to release the girls, Dr. Chujo asks them to stop Mothra but they tell him nothing can halt the creature. He decides to use telepathy to block their communication with the creature. Rosilican bombers attack the larva and Nelson thinks it has been killed but the creature re-emerges at the city docks and breaks through a dam. Dr. Chujo's little brother Shinji (Akihiro Tayama) attempts to rescue the girls but he is stopped by Nelson and his henchmen. The Rosilican embassy orders Nelson to release the tiny women but when Dr. Chujo and "Bulldog" find Shinji, he tells them that Nelson and his men took them away. Michi arrives to say that Mothra is crawling through the city causing mass destruction. After knocking down Tokyo Towers, the larva begins spinning a cocoon. Nelson and his henchmen fly to Rosilica with the girls as the country sends atomic heat guns to Tokyo to set fire to the cocoon. The heat causes the emergence of a giant flying moth which heads for Rosilica, its massive wings causing violent wind storms along its path of destruction. Dr. Chujo, "Bulldog" and Michi fly to Rosilica's Newkirk City where the police shoot Nelson when he tries to escape with the tiny women. Upon their arrival, Dr. Chujo, "Bulldog" and Michi take the girls to the city's airport where a huge symbol, like the one on the island scroll, is painted on the runway. As church bells ring, Mothra lands, the girls are set free and the giant moth flies them back to their island home.

While a nicely paced and entertaining monster-fantasy, *Mothra* is basically a mediocre outing with a rather benign title creature, one that only causes havoc when fighting human greed and saving the island girls. The special effects are satisfactory but Mothra, both as a larva and a giant flying moth, is a rather hokey-looking creature. The film appears to have a political slant in that the villain Nelson is non–Japanese; he was probably an American in the original Japanese version but in the dubbed U.S. prints he seems to be Russian.

Mothra would reappear in such Japanese monster rallies as *Gojira Tai Mosura* (Godzilla vs. Mothra) (1964), which was shown in the U.S. as *Godzilla vs. the Thing*; *Monster Zero* (1967), which had alternate titles like *Battle of the Astros, Godzilla vs. Monster Zero, Invasion of Astro-Monster* and *Invasion of Planet X*; *Destroy All Monsters* (1968), and *Godzilla and Mothra: The Battle for Earth* (1998).

Murderers' Row

(1966; 105 minutes; Color) PRODUCER: Irving Allen. ASSOCIATE PRODUCER: Euan Lloyd. DIRECTOR: Henry Levin. SCREENPLAY: Herbert Baker, from the novel by Donald Hamilton. PHOTOGRAPHY: Sam Leavitt. EDITOR: Walter Thompson. MUSIC: Lalo Schifrin. SONGS: Tommy Boyce, Bobby Hart, Howard Greenfield and Lalo Schifrin. ART DIRECTOR: Joe Wright. SOUND: Lambert Day and Jack Haynes. SETS: George R. Nelson. COSTUMES: Moss Mabry. MAKEUP: Ben Lane. PRODUCTION SUPERVISOR: Ivan Volkman. SPECIAL EFFECTS: Danny Lee. CHOREOGRAPHY: Miriam Nelson. ASSISTANT DIRECTOR: Ray Gosnell. CAST: Dean Martin (Matt Helm), Ann-Margret (Suzie Solaris), Karl Malden (Julian Wall), Camilla Sparv (Coco Duquette), James Gregory (MacDonald), Beverly Adams (Lovey Kravezit), Richard Eastham (Dr. Norman Solaris), Tom Reese (Ironhead), Duke Howard (Billy Orcutt), Ted Hartley, Nick Dimitri, Dirk Evans, Richard Gardner, Morry Ogden, Bob Peoples, Alex Rodine (Guards), Marcel Hillaire (Captain Deveraux), Corinne Cole (Miss January), Robert Terry (Dr. Rogas), Mary Jane Mangler, Amadee Chabot, Lynn Hartoch, Rena Horten, Mary Hughes, Marilyn Tindall, Jan Watson, Dale Brown, Luci Ann Cook, Dee Duffy, Barbara Burgess, Karen Lee (Slaygirls), Jacqueline Fontaine (Wake Singer), Frank Gerstle (Agent Furnace), Robert Glenn (FBI Agent), Dale Van Sickel (Fortress Guard), Lou Robb (International Agent), Soon-Tek Oh (Japanese Agent), George Takei (Agent Tempura), Joe Gray (Agent Ames), Vincent Barbi (Agent Philippe), Dino, Desi and Billy [Dean Paul Martin, Desi Arnaz, Jr. and Billy Hinsche] (Themselves).

After demonstrating how a newly developed heat ray destroys a model of Washington, D.C., Julian Wall (Karl Malden) claims he will actually demolish the city in ten days after the powerful weapon has been fully developed. In order to accomplish his mission, he kidnaps the playboy inventor of the helio-beam, Dr. Norman Solaris (Richard Eastham), and gives orders for Dr. Rogas (Robert Terry), to torture information out of the scientist. He also orders the elimination of four interventional secret agents, including Matt Helm (Martin), by his assistant Ironhead (Tom Reese), who has an iron plate on the top of his skull. While photographing Miss January (Corinne Cole) for a calendar layout, Helm is allegedly electrocuted along with his model, one of Julian's agents. Matt's boss at Intelligence and Counter-Espionage (ICE), MacDonald (James Gregory), attends his wake. Later MacDonald meets with Matt and shows him films of Solaris, who he says has constructed a weapon that utilizes the rays of the sun. He orders Matt to find the missing scientist, warning him that time is of the essence since the ore needed to perfect the weapon is missing. MacDonald also informs the secret agent that there is a security breach in their organization and that he will be working alone. Matt flies to the Riviera to meet his contact, singer Dominique, but he finds she has been murdered. Going to the disco where the singer worked, Matt meets swinger Suzie (Ann-Margret), the dead entertainer's roommate. As Ironhead is about to shoot Matt, the police arrive at the disco and inform Suzie that her friend has been killed. She blames Matt and slaps him, causing a riot. The secret agent is arrested and taken to police headquarters where Wall identifies him as the man he saw leaving Dominique's room. Wall is thwarted by his mistress Coco Duquette (Camilla Sparv) and Suzie, who claim not to recognize Helm. Suzie informs Matt that she believes Coco hired him to kill Dominique since Solaris, who is her father, was involved with Coco, but he denies the charge. The agent then travels to Wall's wharf where he is captured and put on a hover craft where he is drugged by Coco. Wall gets word from his ICE informant that his prisoner (Matt) is a Chicago hit man and he hires him to rub out MacDonald. When Matt finds out Wall has sent Suzie a gift that will kill her, he goes back to the disco and rescues the girl just before a pin bomb she is wearing explodes. They are pursued by Ironhead but manage to elude him. That night Matt and Suzie take a speedboat to Wall's island fortress where the needed ore is being processed in order to perfect the helio-beam. Matt and Suzie separately search for Solaris but both are captured and taken to Wall who decides to torture the young woman so her father will provide the information needed to complete the beam. After Wall gets a call informing him that MacDonald is in Monte Carlo, Matt offers to kill him but Ironhead realizes the agent's true identity. Matt agrees to talk to MacDonald and claim his mission has been successful. During the call, Matt drops several clues that make MacDonald order the evacuation of the nation's capitol as well as realize the identity of the ICE traitor, agent Furnace (Frank Gerstle). The latter commits suicide by jumping out of a window but before dying he transmits to Wall the information that he has been double-crossed by Matt. Ironhead seals Matt in a tube as Solaris agrees to give Wall the information he needs. Using a hairpin, Suzie causes the controls on the island to malfunction and Matt escapes from the tube and fights Ironhead, who is killed when his skull plate fastens onto a steel pillar on which Helm has attached a bomb. When Coco tries to stop Wall from killing Solaris, who she still loves, Julian instead shoots her and heads to the hover craft, where he controls the beam. Matt, Suzie and her father follow in a boat. As Matt fights with Wall, Suzie disables the boat's pilot. Wall attempts to murder Matt with his own gun, but it's a trick gun that kills him. Planting a bomb on the hover craft, Helm and Suzie escape and are picked up by MacDonald in a helicopter. The boat is destroyed, ending Wall's plans to demolish Washington, D.C.

Filmed in the U.S., on the French Riviera and the Isle of Wight, *Murderer's Row* was the second Matt Helm screen outing starring Dean Martin. It was based on Donald Hamilton's 1962 novel but followed the example of the initial entry *The Silencers* (q.v.), issued the same year, in that Helm was no longer the taciturn hero of literature but instead exemplified star Martin's hard-drinking, girl-chasing and laid-back stage persona. The film even gave the star an opportunity to croon "I'm Not the Marrying Kind" (which he recorded for Reprise Records), along with a snippet of "An Old Spinning Wheel." His son Dean Paul Martin appeared with Desi Arnaz, Jr., and Billy Hinsche as Dino, Desi and Billy in a disco sequence performing "If You're Thinking What I'm Thinking." Like most take-offs of its ilk, the film featured an array of spy contrivances like a delayed firing gun that shoots in reverse, a freeze pistol, a cigarette shooting a poison dart, a futuristic car, and a harmonica that can be used to eavesdrop. It was also a step down in entertainment from the initial outing and the series would continue its slide when producer Irving Allen and director Henry Levin teamed for the third Helm entry, *The Ambushers* (q.v.), the next year.

Regarding *Murderer's Row*, Paul Mavis wrote in *The Espionage Flimography* (2001), "If you saw the first one, you got the joke, and the next three sequels just hit you over the head with it, again and again. Martin is not so funny this time; the bored act doesn't look like an act.... This is a weak film from a series that should have stopped after the first film." Phil Hardy complained in *Science Fiction* (1984) that it was "decidedly inferior" to *The Silencers*, adding, "Not only is the film dull and, like those that were to follow, wholly derivative of the Bond films, but unlike its similarly derivative Italian counterparts, it lacks and sense of style." In *The Family Guide to Movies on Video* (1988), Henry Herz and Tony Zaza noted, "[It] is meant to be a spoof of spy-spoof movies but offers little more than a leer-filled bag of crude sexual innuendo and puerile naughtiness with Martin's lumbering characterization providing a paltry few unintentional guffaws."

The Mutations

(1974; 92 minutes; Color) PRODUCER: Robert D. Weinbach. EXECUTIVE PRODUCER: J. Ronald Getty. ASSOCIATE PRODUCERS: Brad Harris and Herbert G. Luft. SCREENPLAY: Robert D. Weinbach and Edward Mann. PHOTOGRAPHY: Paul Beeson. EDITOR: John Trumper. MUSIC: Basil Kirchin and Jack Nathan. ART DIRECTOR: Herbert Smith. SOUND: Danny Daniel. SETS: Josie MacAvin. PRODUCTION SUPERVISOR: Jack Smith. PRODUCTION MANAGER: Al Marcus. MAKEUP: Charles E. Parker. CONTINUITY: Doreen Soan. ASSISTANT DIRECTOR: Brian Dunbar. CAST: Donald Pleasence (Dr. Nolter), Tom Baker (Lynch), Brad Harris (Dr. Brian Redford), Julie Ege (Hedi), Michael Dunn (Burns), Scott Anthony (Tony Croydon), Jill Haworth (Lauren

Bates), Olga Anthony (Bridget), Lisa Collings (Suzanne), Joan Scott (Landlady), Toby Lennon (Tramp), John Wineford (Policeman), Richard Davies (Doctor), Eithne Dunne (Nurse), Tony Mayne (Tony), Molly Tweedlie (Molly), Kathy Kitchen (Kathy), Fran Fullenwider (Fat Woman), Lesley Roose (Skinny Lady Lesley), Fay Bura (Bearded Lady Diane), Bob Bura (Fire Eater), O.T. (Human Pincushion George), Madge Garnett (Monkey Woman Mary Louise), Willie Ingram (Popeye), Hugh Bailey (Pretzel Boy), Felix Duarte (Frog Boy Mardico), Esther Blackmon (Alligator Woman).

Filmed at London's Pinewood Studios by Getty Pictures Corporation, and released in that country in 1973, *The Mutations* was shown theatrically in the U.S. in the fall of 1974 by Columbia. This R-rated production, on which co-star Brad Harris served as associate producer, was basically a combination of director Tod Browning's *Freaks* (1932) and the Japanese-made *The Double Garden* (1970), also known as *Revenge of Dr. X*, scripted by Edward D. Wood, Jr. The former film dealt with circus freaks and the latter had a mad scientist trying to create an intelligent, man-like plant which turned out to be a blood seeking monster. *The Mutations* starred Donald Pleasence as yet another off-track scientist, here more addled than mad, who tries to design a "super race" by combining humans and plants into one being. The film's stunt work was performed by Eddie Powell, who played the mummy in *The Mummy's Shroud* (1967). In addition to the true live grotesqueries of the freak show subplot, the movie's monsters varied in quality. The briefly seen lizard woman was truly horrific while the human Venus fly trap looked more like a walking pile of lettuce.

At a London university, Dr. Nolter (Pleasence) lectures about inducing mutations to improve various species and is scoffed at by one of his students, Tony Croydon (Scott Anthony). When class lets out, student Bridget (Olga Anthony) goes for a walk in a deserted park and is stalked by two dwarfs, Burns (Michael Dunn) and Tony (Tony Mayne), before being abducted by Lynch (Tom Baker), a tall man whose face is deformed by a glandular disease. He takes her to Nolter who experiments on the girl in an attempt to create a new being that is both plant and human. The resulting lizard woman is then showcased in the oddities show Lynch and Burns own.

Tony, his girlfriend Lauren Bates (Jill Haworth) and another student, Hedi (Julie Ege), go to the airport to meet visiting scientist Dr. Brian Redford (Harris). The next day they hear Nolter discuss his theories on combining plants and animals. Nolter takes Redford to his home and shows him the results of his decade of work in the field as he attempts to create a new race of humans with the properties of plants. A few days later, Redford and Hedi, who have become lovers, go with Tony and Lauren to a carnival and they attend a freak show hosted by Burns. They are denied admission to see the lizard woman upon orders from Lynch. After dropping off Lauren at the apartment, Tony returns to the show and sneaks into the lizard woman display. Lynch chases him through the show's haunted gold mine, knocks him out and takes him to Nolter to be his next guinea pig. The freaks have a birthday party for Kathy (Kathy Kitchen), a midget; when Lynch refuses to join them, they taunt him and he goes berserk, disrupting the festivities. He then drives into the city and seeks out Suzanne (Lisa Collings), a prostitute, and pays her three pounds for her services. Lauren informs Redford and Hedi that Tony is missing. Now a mutation, Tony escapes from Nolter's laboratory and calls Lauren but when she sees him, he has become such a monstrosity she goes into a catatonic state. That night Burns informs Lynch that he and his co-workers want nothing more to do with him. Tony murders an alcoholic tramp (Toby Lennon).

Feeling uneasy, Hedi calls Brian to come stay with her. While taking a bath, she is visited by Tony who keeps himself covered while relating to her what Nolter did to him. As Redford arrives, Lynch abducts Hedi, and Tony runs away. Bradford drives to Nolter's estate where he fights with Lynch, who knocks him out. Lynch is cornered and repeatedly stabbed by the freaks and then devoured by a pack of watchdogs. As Nolter experiments on Hedi, Tony arrives and sucks the life out of the scientist and sets fire to his laboratory. Coming to, Redford saves Hedi and gets her out of the house. But as they embrace she begins to mutate.

Despite its cockeyed plot and sleazy presentation, *The Mutations* is a surprisingly fast paced and entertaining sci-fi effort.

My Name Is Julia Ross

(1945; 65 minutes) PRODUCER: Wallace MacDonald. DIRECTOR: Joseph H. Lewis. SCREENPLAY: Muriel Roy Bolton, from the novel *The Woman in Red* by Anthony Gilbert. PHOTOGRAPHY: Burnett Guffey. EDITOR: James Sweeney. MUSIC DIRECTOR: Mischa Bakaleinikoff. ART DIRECTOR: Jerome Pycha, Jr. SOUND: Lambert Day. SETS: Milton Stumph. ASSISTANT DIRECTOR: Milton

Lobby card for *My Name Is Julia Ross* (1945), picturing Dame May Whitty, George Macready and Nina Foch.

Feldman. CAST: Nina Foch (Julia Ross), Dame May Whitty (Mrs. Williamson Hughes), George Macready (Ralph Hughes), Roland Varno (Dennis Bruce), Anita Bolster (Mrs. Sparkes), Doris Lloyd (Mrs. Mackie), Leonard Mudie (Peters), Joy Harington (Bertha), Queenie Leonard (Nurse Alice), Harry Hays Morgan (Mr. Robinson), Ottola Nesmith (Mrs. Susan Robinson), Olaf Hytten (the Rev. Jonathan Lewis), Evan Thomas (Dr. Keller), Marilyn Johnson (Nurse), Milton Owen, Leyland Hodgson (Policemen), Reginald Sheffield (James B. McQuarrie), Charles McNaughton (Gatekeeper).

Working title: *The Woman in Red*.

Following surgery, Julia Ross (Nina Foch) obtains an interview with employment agency owner Mrs. Sparkes (Anita Bolster) who gets her a job as private secretary to Mrs. Hughes (Dame May Whitty). Going to her London flat to pack, Julia sees Dennis Bruce (Roland Varno), her ex-boyfriend, and they agree to have dinner the next night. Before leaving for Mrs. Hughes' home on Hendrique Square, Julia gives maid Bertha (Joy Harington) the rent money she owes her landlady, Mrs. Mackie (Doris Lloyd), as well as her forwarding address. Disliking the young woman, Bertha destroys the address and keeps the money for herself. When Julia does not show up for their date, Dennis goes to the Hughes home only to be told that the owners have moved. In talking with Mrs. Mackie and Bertha, he learns from the maid about Julia getting the job through the employment agency but he when he goes there the landlord (Reginald Sheffield) tells him it has closed. At the Hughes estate, Sea House in Beverton, Cornwall, Julia discovers that her clothes and purse are missing and she is referred to as Mrs. Hughes by Alice (Queenie Leonard), a nurse. When Julia becomes upset, Alice calls for her employer. Mrs. Hughes and her son Ralph (George Macready) inform Julia that she is Ralph's wife Marian and that she is mentally ill and under the delusion she is Julia Ross. Going for a walk with Ralph to tour the estate, Julia comes to realize that the man who claims to be her husband is mad. When Reverend Lewis (Olaf Hytten), his sister (Ottola Nesmith) and her husband (Harry Hays Morgan) call on Mrs. Hughes, Julia tells them she is being held prisoner but they are informed she is having a nervous breakdown. The young woman manages to hide in the back seat of their car but when she is found, the trio return her to Ralph. Back in her room, Ralph tries to kiss Julia who slaps him. He becomes angry and attempts to push her out of a window. When Alice arrives, he makes it look like he tried to save Julia from committing suicide. Mrs. Hughes and her son find a missive penned by Julia to Dennis and replace it with blank paper. Ralph later takes her and Alice to town so she can mail it, not knowing

Julia has written another plea for help to Bruce. That night Julia discovers a secret passage and she hears her keepers planning her murder by throwing her off a cliff. She learns that Ralph killed his wife Marian and, in order for them to collect her insurance, he and his mother plan to do away with Julia and make her death appear to be the wife's suicide. Making it look like she took poison, Julia feigns illness; when a doctor (Leonard Mudie) arrives, she tells him about the murder and her letter to Bruce. The "doctor," a fake, reports to Mrs. Hughes who sends him to London to obtain the letter before it gets to Bruce. A real doctor (Evan Thomas) says Julia should be placed in a hospital for her own good.

In London, Peters finds the letter but Mrs. Mackie becomes suspicious of him and goes for the police. That night Ralph and his mother try to lure the girl to her death by dislodging a panel from the staircase but she realizes what is happening, locks herself in her room and pretends to kill herself by jumping from a window. Seeing what they think is her body, Mrs. Hughes and her son tell the doctor that Ralph's wife committed suicide. To make sure Julia is dead, Ralph plans to drop a huge rock on her. Dennis and a policeman (Leyland Hodgson) show up and when he tries to run away Ralph is shot and killed by the officer. Mrs. Hughes is arrested and Dennis takes Julia back to London. On the way he asks her to marry him.

Over the years *My Name is Julia Ross* has taken on somewhat of a cult status, mainly as a forerunner of the type of psychological horror film that would become so popular in the 1960s. When it was initially released late in 1945, the *New York Times* noted that director Joseph H. Lewis and writer Muriel Roy Bolton "strived earnestly to whip up excitement and suspense, but somehow that electrifying quality which distinguishes good melodrama is lacking ... The elements of a mystifying entertainment with psychological overtones are present in this story ... [Lewis] succeeds in creating an effectively ominous atmosphere [but] he has not been as adept in handling the players." In *Focus on Film* #5 (November–December 1970), Don Miller stated, "It would be easy to overrate *My Name is Julia Ross* due to its reputation through the years, which would be unfair to the film. By any standards it's a superior, well-knit thriller, proceeding at a pace that makes the brief running time seem even briefer. However, the glowing accolades attributed to it since its initial release would lead the unwary to expect something of a masterpiece, which it most definitely is not.... The script proceeds without frills or fancies in a manner calculated to maintain maximum interest, and the leading roles are in more than capable hands..." *Castle of Frankenstein* #19 (1972) thought it a "[n]early obscure, but suspenseful and exciting grade-B mystery." Geoff Andrew wrote in *Time Out Film Guide, 9th Ed.* (2000), "Handling the various plot twists with ease and eliciting superior performances from his three leads, Lewis repeatedly displays his ability to convey mood and meaning through visuals: Burnett Guffey's camera prowls nervously through shadowy interiors, [George] Macready's madness is vividly evoked by his endless knife-playing. A small, dark gem in the *Rebecca* tradition..."

The film was released in Argentina as *Prisionera del Destino* (Prisoner of Destiny) and in Mexico as *Noche Tragica* (Tragic Night).

"My Name is Julia Ross" was done as an episode of NBC-TV's *Lux Video Theatre* on March 31, 1955, starring Fay Bainter and Beverly Garland. The film's plot was reworked for *Dead of Winter*, a 1987 MGM release.

Mysterious Island

(1961; 101 minutes; Color) PRODUCER: Charles H. Schneer. DIRECTOR: Cy Enfield. SCREENPLAY: John Prebble, Daniel Ullman and Crane Wilbur. PHOTOGRAPHY: Wilkie Cooper. EDITOR: Frederick Wilson. MUSIC: Bernard Herrmann. ART DIRECTOR: Bill Andrews. SOUND: Peter Handford and Bob Jones. SPECIAL VISUAL EFFECTS: Ray Harryhausen. Production Supervisor: Raymond Anzarut. PRODUCTION MANAGER: Bob Sterne. CONTINUITY: Marjorie Lavelly. ASSISTANT DIRECTOR: Rene Dupont. CAST: Michael Craig (Captain Cyrus Harding), Joan Greenwood (Lady Mary Fairchild), Michael Callan (Herbert Brown), Gary Merrill (Gideon Spillit/Narrator), Herbert Lom (Captain Nemo), Beth Rogan (Elena Fairchild), Percy Herbert (Sergeant Pencroft), Dan Jackson (Corporal Neb Nugent).

Also called *Jules Verne's Mysterious Island*, this colorful adventure outing, lensed in Superdynamation, was a U.S.–British co-production made by Ameran Films and released in the U.S late in 1961 by Columbia with showings in England six months later. Filmed in Britain and Spain, it was based on Verne's 1874 novel which was filmed on several occasions (the best-known being MGM's *The Mysterious Island* [1929] featuring undersea humanoids). Another teaming of producer Charles H. Schneer and visual effects artist Ray

Harryhausen, was one of their least satisfying efforts from a monster standpoint. The film offered giant versions of a crab, wingless bird (a Phorohacos), honey bees and a giant coiled cephalopod. None of the creatures were particularly interesting, let alone frightening. While the island scenery was nice and the production well-made, the highlight, at least for male viewers, was lovely Beth Rogan in a brief animal skin outfit.

As the Civil War is ending, three Union prisoners, Captain Cyrus Harding (Michael Craig), Herbert Brown (Michael Callan) and Corporal Neb Nugent (Dan Jackson), plot to escape from a Confederate prison and use an observation balloon to take back to their regiment. Making their getaway, the three are pursued by Southern Sergeant Pencroft (Percy Herbert) and New York *Herald* correspondent Gideon Spillit (Gary Merrill). Taking off in the craft, the Yankees realize they need Pencroft to steer the vessel and he agrees after they promise to set him free once they land. The worst storm in the nation's history grips the craft and carries it for days in a westward pattern and eventually they spot an island. Cutting loose the balloon's basket, the men are carried to the atoll by a strong wind. Brown, Pencroft and Nugent are separated from Harding and fear he has been killed. While exploring the island they find Harding, who has no recollection of reaching shore. Going through a valley filled with huge plants, they are attacked by a giant crab. The men manage to turn it over on its back and push it into a boiling pit of water, and then eat it.

After finding a herd of mountain goats, the men see a small boat floating to shore. Aboard are a dead sailor and two women, Lady Mary Fairchild (Joan Greenwood) and her niece Elena (Rogan), whose ship was wrecked while sailing from Chile. Planning to find timber to build a boat, the men come across a cave where they see a skeleton and the diary of Tom Ayerton, who hanged himself after being left on the island by pirates in 1862. After moving their headquarters into the cave and reaching it by a rope elevator, Herbert finds a chest that has washed ashore. It contains weapons and tools they will need to built an escape craft. They realize these things came from the *Nautilus*, a submarine the supposedly dead Captain Nemo (Herbert Lom) used to destroy war ships. The craft was reportedly lost off the coast of Mexico eight years before.

While fishing, Spillit is attacked by a giant wingless bird which follows him and captures Elena. Herbert stabs the creature, and after they cook and eat it they find a bullet in its flesh. Elena and Herbert fall in love and, while exploring the island, they find a cave with a giant honeycomb. Attacked by huge bees, they take refuge in one of the chambers only to be sealed inside it by the insects. Using fire, Herbert burns the back off the chamber and they escape into a grotto where they come across the *Nautilus*. A pirate ship arrives in the lagoon and three men row ashore looking for water; they find the islanders' camouflaged craft. A battle between the pirates and the islanders ensues, and suddenly the pirate ship sinks. A man in a diving suit emerges from the water; he turns out to be Nemo, who invites the castaways aboard his submarine.

Nemo tells them he has been experimenting with horticulture on the island for eight years in an effort to fight famine and economic competition. He says his craft can no longer function underwater and that he wants to join them in leaving the island, which is about to be destroyed by the vol-

West German poster for Mysterious Island *(1961).*

cano, and take the results of his work back to civilization. He also tells them of his plans to bring up the Spanish craft, repair it and sail away from the island. Their efforts appear doomed when the volcano begins to erupt before they can raise the ship. Harding comes up with the idea of using the *Nautilus'* air compressors to raise the vessel but as they are trying to repair the hole in the craft the men are attacked by a giant snail-like Phorohacos which they kill with Nemo's underwater electric gun. The ship is brought up by pumping air into the observation balloon and the group gets aboard but Nemo, who has stayed on his craft to operate the air compressors, is killed when the *Nautilus* is crushed by falling debris.

Eugene Archer noted in the *New York Times*, "Under Cy Enfield's spirited direction, events glide swiftly past a colorful variety of cardboard backdrops." In *Film Review 1963/1964* (1963), F. Maurice Speed called *Mysterious Island* a "[r]ip-roaring adaptation" and Ed Naha in *The Science Fictionary* (1980) stated, "Special effects galore and fine acting makes this Jules Verne adaptation a winner."

Nigel Green was filmed in scenes as Tom Ayerton but the footage was deleted before the film's theatrical debut. In 1962 the French publication Star Cine Cosmos issued a photo novel of the film in magazine format called *Ile Mysterreruse*.

The Charles H. Schneer production of *Mysterious Island* was Columbia's second association with the Jules Verne novel since the studio made a serial based on the work in 1951 with Leonard Penn as Nemo; that script was embellished to include a beautiful alien invader (Karen Randle) and her minions. This 15-chapter version of *Mysterious Island* (q.v.) top-billed Richard Crane as Captain Harding.

The Mystery of Thug Island

(1966; 88 minutes; Color) EXECUTIVE PRODUCER: Nino Battiferri. DIRECTOR: Luigi Capuano. SCREENPLAY: Arpad DeRiso and Ottavio Poggi, from the novel *I Misteri della Giungla Nera* (The Mystery of the Black Jungle) by Emilio Salgari. PHOTOGRAPHY: Guglielmo Mancori. EDITOR: Antonietta Zitta. MUSIC: Carlo Rustichelli. ART DIRECTOR: Ernest Kromberg. SOUND: Victor Massi. SETS: Camilio Del Signore. PRODUCTION MANAGER: Gino Fanano. MAKEUP: Anacieto Giustini. ASSISTANT DIRECTOR: Francesco Massaro. CAST: Guy Madison (Souyadhana), Inga Schoner (Ada MacPherson), Giacomo Rossi-Stuart (Tremal Naik), Peter Van Eyck (Captain MacPherson), Ivan Desny (Machadi), Giulia Rubini (Gundali), Nando Poggi (Kammamuri), Aldo Bufi Landi (Sergeant Barata), Aldo Cristiani (Windy), Romano Giomini (General).

The 1895 novel *I Misteri della Giungla Nera* by Emilio Salgari (1862–1911) was filmed under that title in Italy in 1954 by Venturini Films starring Lex Barker as tiger hunter Tremal Naik. The feature was released in the U.S. in two parts with Republic distributing its first half as *Mystery of the Black Jungle* in 1955 and Medallion Pictures issuing the second part as *Killers of the East* in 1958. Filmed at Fert Studios in Turin, Italy, the original features' history got more complicated when *Mystery of the Black Jungle* was shown in Great Britain as *Black Devils of Kali* and *Killers of the East* was sold to U.S. TV as *Mystery of the Jungle*. To further complicate matters, *Killers of the East* was also issued to television in the 1980s by Stacofilms as *Dawn of the Pirates* although there were no pirates in the production.

In 1964 Eichberg-Film of West Germany and Italy's Liber Film co-produced a remake of the 1954 production called *I Misteri della Giungla Nera* (Mystery of the Black Jungle) in Italy and *Das Geheimnis der Lederschling* (The Secret of the Leather Noose) in West Germany. Columbia issued a dubbed version of the film in the United States in May 1966 as *The Mystery of Thug Island*. Filmed in Rome, the production was also called *Kidnapped to Mystery Island*. In 1986 Wizard Video released it on tape as *The Snake Hunter Strangler*. In *The Family Guide to Movies on Video* (1988), Henry Herz and Tony Zaza wrote: "Failed European adventure story ineptly directed.... Stylized Violence."

In Colonial India, the three-year-old daughter of Captain MacPherson (Peter Van Eyck) is kidnapped by Machadi (Ivan Desny) and his band of Tugs, a secret sect that worships the goddess Kali. Sergeant Barata (Aldo Bufi Landi) tries to save the child but is left with a facial scar after losing a knife fight with Machadi, who takes the little girl to the Black Jungle where the Tugs and their high priest, Souyadhana (Guy Madison), live in underground caverns accessed through a hidden door in a giant banyon tree. MacPherson leaves the British army and exhausts his fortunes and energy in a 15-year quest to find his child. The area's commanding general (Romano Giomini) has him reinstated and gives him soldiers and he heads to the Snake Islands to find the Tugs and retrieve his daughter Ada (Inga Schoner), who is now 18 and the sacred virgin incarnation of Kali.

Snake hunters Tremal Naik (Giacomo Rossi-Stuart) and Kammamuri (Nando Poggi) and their men come to the Black Jungle in search of giant reptiles. Tremal Naik sees Ada walking alone and saves her from a poisonous serpent. The two young people are attracted to each other but Ada returns to the cavern where Souyadhana tells her that all India awaits a sign from her for the Tugs to drive out the British. Sick of the human sacrifices the Tugs make to Kali, Ada again meets Tremal Naik and he promises to fight for her. He and Kammamuri find the entrance to the caverns and after a battle with the Tugs they are hidden by Ada in her chambers. When Tremal Naik asks her to marry him, Ada agrees to help the two men escape and promises to go with them. Souyadhana sends his pet tiger, Kali-Bag, to kill the intruders, but Tremal Naik stabs the tiger to death. He and his friend are captured by the Tugs, and Souyadhana tells him that Ada will be burned alive unless he kills the Tugs' moral enemy, Captain MacPherson. Agreeing to the high priest's demands, Tremal Naik goes with Machadi to the soldiers' camp but finds out that MacPherson is Ada's father. Sergeant Barata spies Machadi and the two men fight. Barata takes revenge on the Tug for scarring his face by strangling him.

Tremal Naik returns to the caverns with a wrapped body as MacPherson and Barata prepare their men to attack the Tugs' stronghold. When Souyadhana sees the body, he tells Ada that her lover has murdered her father but the corpse is revealed to be that of Machadi. As Tremal Naik and Kammamuri fight the Tugs, Ada's beautiful lady in waiting, Gundali (Giulia Rubini), is mortally wounded as MacPherson arrives with the soldiers and invades the caverns. Souyadhana plans to flood the grotto and kill both his own men and the soldiers, but he is stopped by Tremal Naik, who drowns him. Ada is reunited with her father who stays in the Black Jungle since she plans to marry Tremal Naik.

Eichberg-Film and Liber Film had previously teamed to make two other features based on the works of Emilio Salgari, *Sandokan Alla Riscossa* (Sandokan to the Rescue), released in the U.S. as *Sandokan Fights Back* and *Throne of Vengeance*, and *Sandokan Contro il Leopardo di Sarawak* (Sandokan Against the Leopard of Sarawak), both 1964 releases directed by Luigi Capuano, who also did *The Mystery of Thug Island*. Ray Danton had the title role in the Sandokan features. Co-starring was one-time film idol and TV star Guy Madison whose voice was dubbed as the lead villain in *The Mystery of Thug Island*. The latter feature used stock footage of a water buffalo stampede from the Sandokan films but this matched far better than a grainy scene in which a mongoose kills a cobra. The fight between Tremel Naik and the tiger is also poorly staged. Overall, the feature is nicely photographed with scenic locales but the plot is mundane and it is disconcerting to hear another actor dubbing for Madison.

In the 1990s, Salgari's novel was filmed again, this time as the Italian TV miniseries "I Misteri della Giungla Nera" (The Mystery of the Black Jungle).

The Night Club Lady

(1932; 66 minutes) DIRECTOR: Irving Cummings. SCREENPLAY: Robert Riskin, from the novel *About the Murder of the Night Club Queen* by Anthony Abbot (Fulton Oursler). PHOTOGRAPHY: Teddy [Ted] Tetzlaff. EDITOR: Maurice Wright. CAST: Adolphe Menjou (Thatcher Colt), Mayo Methot (Lois Carewe), Skeets Gallagher (Tony), Ruthelma Stevens (Miss Kelly), Blanche Friderici (Mrs. Carewe aka Mrs. Bouchet), Nat Pendleton (Detective Mike MacDougal), Albert Conti (Vincent Rowland), Greta Granstedt (Eunice), Gerald Fielding (Guy Everett), Ed Brady (Detective Bill), Lee Phelps (Detective Joe), George Humbert (Andre), Niles Welch (Dr. Baldwin), William von Brincken (Dr. Lengle), Teru Shimada (Mura), Frank Darien (Dr. Mangus), Olaf Hytten (Butler).

Working title: *About the Murder of the Night Club Lady*.

In 1932 Columbia optioned three murder mysteries about New York City Police Commissioner Thatcher Colt by "Anthony Abbot," a pen name for Fulton Oursler. The first outing for the series was *The Night Club Lady*, released in the summer of 1932 and based on his book *About the Murder of the Night Club Lady*, published a year earlier. As portrayed by Adolphe Menjou, Thatcher Colt was a lip-reading, multi-lingual chain smoker with a penchant for thinking up wrestling holds. He was aided in his sleuthing efforts by tipsy pal Tony (Skeets Gallagher) and sexy secretary Miss Kelly (Ruthelma Stevens), who had a definite affinity for her boss. Nat Pendleton added comedy relief as a bumbling member of the police force but overall the film was on the horrific side with the killer using scorpions to dispatch three victims, the initial murder taking place on a windy New Year's at exactly midnight. Further adding to the spooky feel of the proceedings was Ted Tetzlaff's excellent camerawork that included a variety of angles and dolly shots. *Harrison's Reports* noted, "The material is gruesome and unpleasant to sensitive natures, but very good for a horror murder mystery melodrama."

As the wind howls on New Year's Eve, speakeasy owner Lola Carewe (Mayo Methot) is visited by Vincent Rowland (Albert Conti). He takes her to her club despite the objects of her mother, Mrs. Carewe (Blanche Friderici), who is concerned because Lola has received several death threats. At the club are Police Commissioner Thatcher Colt (Menjou) and his girl-chasing, heavy-drinking friend Tony (Gallagher). When Lola gets another missive saying she will die at midnight, Colt uses his lip-reading powers to find out the source of her anxiety. Just as Colt offers to take Lola home, a shot is fired at her. Back at her penthouse apartment the two are joined by Tony and Thatcher's secretary Miss Kelly (Stevens), plus several detectives, including bumbling Mike (Nat Pendleton). Colt, Tony, Miss Kelly and the policemen form a ring around Lola as midnight approaches but when the clock strikes the woman jumps up, screams and drops dead. Mrs. Carewe calls in Lola's physician Dr. Lengle (William von Brincken), who says the woman died of a heart attack as she was subject to such seizures. Colt is suspicious and brings in Dr. Baldwin (Niles Welch) who agrees to perform an autopsy.

While searching Lola's apartment and questioning her mother, maid Eunice (Greta Granstedt) and houseboy Mura (Teru Shimada), Colt finds a picture of Basil Bouchet, whom Mrs. Carewe says was one of her daughter's admirers; he has been dead for six years. The commissioner finds it interesting that the man's picture is covered with lipstick kisses. One of the detectives, Joe (Lee Phelps), finds an empty bamboo box on the terrace. Colt is told by Mura that actor Guy Everett (Gerald Fielding), who has been dating Lola's roommate Christine Quires, Mrs. Carewe and Dr. Lengle all had motives for killing Lola. Everett is brought in and Thatcher tells him about the murder; he says Christine came back to the apartment at 11 o'clock. Eunice faints after seeing a face at the window of Lola's bedroom. After finding Christine's body hanging outside the window, Colt sends photographs of all of Lola's close associates to police departments around the world. Thatcher then brings in all the suspects and informs them that he knows they were being blackmailed by Lola because of their pasts. After they leave, Colt notices the bamboo box is missing. Miss Kelly informs him that Dr. Lengle took it.

At the morgue, Colt examines Lola's arm and has Dr. Baldwin give him an injection like the one Dr. Lengle gave the victim when he tried to revive her with adrenalin. Comparing the two puncture marks, Thatcher deduces that Lengle's shot was used to cover up the bite of a scorpion on the woman's arm. Figuring out that Christine was murdered because she came home too early and caught the killer making plans to slay Lola, Colt, Tony and Miss Kelly go to see Dr. Lengle but find him dead from the bite of a scorpion which had been housed in the bamboo box. Colt visits Dr. Mangus (Frank Darien) who informs him that Dr. Lengle brought back two scorpions from Mexico, allegedly for medical research. Learning from the French police that Basil Bouchet killed himself six years earlier because he was being blackmailed by Lola, Colt accuses Everett of the two murders. The actor denies the charge and says that he and Christine were in love and planned to be married; Christine wanted to kill Lola because her roommate was blackmailing him since he was an ex-convict. That evening, Colt assembles all the suspects in Lola's apartment and re-enacts the murder, even putting on the dead woman's dressing gown. Exactly at midnight, Thatcher collapses and Mrs. Carewe begs him not to die so that he can bring in her daughter's killer. As the old lady goes to her room, Colt gets up and finds a scorpion concealed in her glove. She admits to killing Lola, saying she was only hired to play the woman's mother and that her motive was revenge for the death of her son, Basil Bouchet. She also says she did not want to kill Christine and that she killed her accomplice Dr. Lengle because he was about to confess. Admitting that she kissed the picture of her son when Lola died, Mrs. Carewe jumps out of the apartment window, falling 14 floors to her death. Later, while wrestling with Tony at the athletic club, Colt reveals that he was wearing a rubber shirt which prevented his being stung by the scorpion.

The Night Club Lady was an eerie and slightly horrific murder mystery. Adolphe Menjou and Ruthelma Stevens returned as Thatcher Colt and Miss Kelly in the second and last series entry, *The Circus Queen Murder* (q.v.), the next year.

Night of Terror

(1933, 65 minutes) PRODUCER: Bryan Foy. DIRECTOR: Benjamin Stoloff. SCREENPLAY: Beatrice Van and William Jacobs. STORY: Willard Mack. PHOTOGRAPHY:

174 *Night of Terror*   FEATURE FILMS

Joseph A. Valentine. EDITOR: Walter Hilton. SOUND: Lambert Day. TECHNICAL DIRECTOR: W.L. Vogue. ASSISTANT DIRECTOR: Lester Neilson. CAST: Bela Lugosi (Degar), Sally Blane (Mary Rinehart), Wallace Ford (Tom Hartley), Tully Marshall (Prof. Richard Rinehart), Bryant Washburn (John Rinehart), Gertrude Michael (Sarah Rinehart), George Meeker (Arthur Hornsby), Mary Frey (Sika), Matt McHugh (Detective Bailey), Edwin Maxwell (Maniac), Oscar Shaw (Chauffeur Martin), Eric Mayne (Professor John Andre), Frank Austin (Short Professor), Dave O'Brien (First Murder Victim), Pat Harmon (Double for the Maniac).

Two years after ushering in the first sound horror film cycle with *Dracula* (1931), Bela Lugosi headlined this Columbia programmer, one of the studio's few excursions into the genre in the early years of talking pictures. Nicely photographed by Joseph A. Valentine and kept moving by director Benjamin Stoloff, the feature was a flavorful outing enhanced by its shadowy old mansion setting and the histrionics of top-billed Lugosi as the mysterious servant Degar, a red herring who solves a series of baffling murders at Rinehart Manor.

The feature opens with the cast and credits emerging via a crystal ball. Nearly all its action takes place on the grounds of the Rinehart estate, where a mad killer called the Maniac (Edwin Maxwell), who leaves newspaper clippings on his victims' bodies, is lurking. Having already murdered a dozen people, the madman attempts to knife scientist Arthur Hornsby (George Meeker) but is frightened away by the arrival of Hornsby's uncle, Professor Richard Rinehart (Tully Marshall). Hornsby has developed a formula which suspends animation and respiration and he plans to demonstrate it by being buried alive for eight hours. When Hindu servant Degar (Lugosi) brings word that the Maniac is in the area, both Rinehart and Hornsby worry about the professor's niece Mary (Sally Blane), who is returning home from the theater with newspaperman Tom Hartley (Wallace Ford). Tom is trying to romance Mary although she is engaged to Hornsby. After Degar's wife Sika (Mary Frey) warns that death hovers over the mansion, Professor Rinehart is murdered in his laboratory. When Hartley and bumbling police detective Bailey (Matt McHugh) arrive on the scene, they discover that the man hired to dig the grave for Hornsby's experiment has also been killed.

A week later, the professor's will is read and his estate is divided between his relatives, which also include his brother John Rinehart (Bryant Washburn) and wife Sarah (Gertrude Michael), with Degar and Sika each getting equal portions. Hornsby makes final preparations for his experiment with the aid of several visiting professors and Degar, who is entrusted with the key to the cabinet containing the restorative which will revive him. Mary sees the Maniac outside her bedroom window and calls for Sika, who remains with

Poster for *Night of Terror* (1933).

Tully Marshall and Bela Lugosi in *Night of Terror* (1933).

her. After the burial, the Maniac murders a cab driver who has brought Hartley to view the interment. John is killed when he tries to steal the restorative. Bailey returns with his men to investigate the homicides as the household members hold a séance conducted by Sika. As she is about to reveal the killer's identity, she too is murdered. Sarah accuses Degar of the killings and Bailey arrests him but he manages to outwit them. A hooded figure abducts Mary and takes her to the cellar. Mary screams for help as Degar and Hartley come to her rescue, with the newsman shooting the Maniac. The police dig up Hornsby's coffin but find it empty. Degar and the Rinehart's killer emerge from the grave with the servant detailing how the murders were carried out. Tom and Mary embrace as the Maniac rises from the cellar floor and warns the audience not to reveal the ending of the film.

Perhaps the weakest part of *Night of Terror* is its finale, with the grotesque Maniac's reappearance taking the edge off an otherwise entertaining thriller. *Variety* was not overly impressed with the proceedings: "Follows the usual lines of the direct-suspicion type of plot.... Entire cast works hard." Jefferson, Missouri's, *Daily Capitol News and Post Tribune* called it a "sensational mystery" and the *Lincoln* (Nebraska) *Sunday Journal and Star* enthused, "It's the terror picture of the season and a better mystery than any since 1933 was officially ushered in." New Mexico's *The Deming Headlight* thought Lugosi was "even better in *Night of Terror* than he was in *Dracula*.... [Y]ou'll sit on the edge of your seat and forget that it's only a movie after all, as this weird story unfolds on the screen."

Two years after making *Night of Terror*, Lugosi returned to Columbia to co-star with Edmund Lowe and Jack Holt in the thriller *Best Man Wins* and in 1944 he headlined one of Columbia's best genre efforts, *The Return of the Vampire* (q.v.). Wallace Ford played a smart-aleck, fast-taking reporter in two other Lugosi vehicles, *Mysterious Mr. Wong* (1935) and *The Ape Man* (1943), both made by Monogram. Lugosi and George Meeker re-teamed for the 1935 Imperial-Cameo release *Murder by Television*. The pre-release titles for *Night of Terror* were *He Lived to Kill* and *Terror in the Night*.

The Night the World Exploded

(1957; 64 minutes) PRODUCER: Sam Katzman. DIRECTOR: Fred F. Sears. SCREENPLAY: Jack Natteford and Luci Ward. PHOTOGRAPHY: Benjamin H. Kline. EDITOR: Paul Borofsky. MUSIC DIRECTOR: Ross DiMaggio. ART DIRECTOR: Paul Palmentola. SOUND: J.S. Westmoreland. SETS: Sidney Clifford. ASSISTANT DIRECTOR: Willard Sheldon. CAST: Kathryn Grant (Laura "Hutch" Hutchinson), William Leslie (Dr. David Conway), Tris [Tristram] Coffin (Dr. Ellis Morton), Raymond Greenleaf (Governor Chaney), Charles Evans (General Bortes), Frank Scannell (Sheriff Quinn), Marshall Reed (General's Aide), Fred Coby (Ranger Brown), Paul Savage (Ranger Kirk), Terry Frost (Rescue Foreman), Otto Waldis (Professor Hagstrom), John Zaremba (Assistant Secretary of Defense Daniel J. Winters), Dennis Moore (Radio Operator), Natividad Vacio (Doctor), Robert King (Scientist), Sam Harris (Board Member), John Close (Soldier), Fred F. Sears (Narrator).

Dr. David Conway (William Leslie) has invented a mechanism that can predict earthquakes and he shows it to his boss at the University Seismology Laboratory, Dr. Ellis Morton (Tristram Coffin). The invention alerts them to the possibility of an imminent quake 50 miles north of the area, in Southern California. They go to see Governor Chaney (Raymond Greenleaf) in hopes that he will evacuate the locale. Although sympathetic, Chaney rejects their notion of an impending disaster. Back at the laboratory, Laura "Hutch" Hutchinson (Kathryn Grant), Conway's assistant, tells Morton that she plans to quit her job and marry her boyfriend. Morton realizes that Hutch really loves David and tries to talk her out of it. Following a huge quake that shifts the Earth's axis three degrees, Morton flies to Washington and meets with General Bortes (Charles Evans), who gives him carte blanche to carry out whatever experiments are necessary to save the planet. David, Morton and Hutch go to New Mexico's Carlsbad Caverns in an effort to find the origin of the pressure causing the tremors. David descends into the deepest part of the cavern followed by Hutch who freezes on their rope ladder but is finally talked down by David. Park Service Ranger Kirk (Paul Savage) finds a strange rock which he adds to his collection. Later, as he is examining it in his cabin, it grows, ignites and explodes, resulting in Kirk's death. Another rock does the same thing in the cavern but falls into a pool before it can explode.

Spanish lobby card for *The Night the World Exploded* (1957), Kathryn Grant pictured.

Dubbing the rock Element 112, David theorizes that it is what is causing the Earth to expand, creating the quakes. David then flies to the nation's capitol and meets with an official (John Zaremba) who sets up a conclave of world scientists at the Smoky Ridge Proving Ground. At the session, David informs the scientists about Element 112 and the need for them to return to their countries and initiate plans to use water to stop the planet's imminent destruction.

After being informed that Hutch has been trapped in the cavern during a tremor, David returns to the site and supervises her rescue. Later, at the local hospital, he gives her perfume, realizing how much she means to him. Using the information he has fed into a computer, he learns that the Earth has 28 days before it will be destroyed by Element 112. As panic and destruction grips the populace, Morton and David mobilize a worldwide effort to seed clouds to produce enough rain to halt the upward movement of the element. When a newly formed volcano in Nevada threatens the Earth, David and Hutch go to Horseshoe Dam so it can be opened for its waters to flood the volcano. The two are nearly trapped as they set the fuses to blow up the dam, but they manage to escape by helicopter as it explodes, saving the world. David and Hutch then look forward to being together.

This Clover Production from Sam Katzman was issued in the summer of 1957 on a double-bill with *The Giant Claw* (q.v.), both films being directed and narrated by Fred F. Sears. Although running only slightly over one hour, *The Night the World Exploded* was a drab affair punctuated by loads of grainy stock footage of floods and buildings collapsing. Its only exciting sequence was the rescue of Hutch from the cavern as a quake destroys the locale. Kathryn Grant was a fetching leading lady and it was good to see usual villain Tristram Coffin in a starring role. The feature was hampered by the leaden performance of hero William Leslie. The feature was scripted by Jack Natteford and Luci Ward, who were associated with "B" westerns. Even next to *The Giant Claw*, *The Night the World Exploded* was lacking. Phil Hardy in *Science Fiction* (1984), like a number of other critics, noted its plot similarity to Universal's far better *The Monolith Monsters*, issued the same year. In *Keep Watching the Skies!* (1982), Bill Warren said, "This has a more intelligent idea than most of the Sam Katzman–produced science fiction films of this period, but the idea is too ambitious for the budget, and pedestrian direction and an undeveloped plot sink the promise of the premise rather rapidly.... There's very little suspense at any point. Needless to say, the sensational promise of the title is never delivered."

Nightwing

(1979; 105 minutes; Color) PRODUCER: Martin Ransohoff. EXECUTIVE PRODUCER: Richard R. St. Johns. ASSOCIATE PRODUCER-UNIT PRODUCTION MANAGER: Peter V. Herald. DIRECTOR: Arthur Hiller. SCREENPLAY: Steve Shagan, Bud Shrake and Martin Cruz Smith, from the novel by Martin Cruz Smith. PHOTOGRAPHY: Charles Rosher. EDITOR: John C. Howard. MUSIC: Henry Mancini. PRODUCTION DESIGN: James Vance. SETS: Richard Kent. MAKEUP: Del Armstrong. SPECIAL EFFECTS: Milt Rice. ASSISTANT DIRECTOR: Gary Daigler. CAST: Nick Mancuso (Deputy Sheriff Youngman Duran), David Warner (Phillip Payne), Kathryn Harrold (Dr. Anne Dillon), Stephen Macht (Walker Chee), Strother Martin (Selwyn), George Clutesi (Abner Tasupi), Ben Piazza (Roger Piggott), Donald Hotton (John Franklin), Charles Hallahan (Henry), Judith Novgrod (Judy), Alice Hirson (Claire Franklin), Pat Corley (Vet), Charles L. Bird (Beejay), Danny Zapien (Joe Marnoa), Peter Prouse (Doctor), Jose Toledo (Harold Masito), Richard Romancito (Ben Mamoa), Flavio Martinez (Isla Laloma), Lena Carr (Pregnant Woman), Virginia P. Maney (Squaw), Wade Stevens (Ambulance Man), Robert Dunbar, John R. Leonard (Helicopter Pilots).

Released to theaters in the summer of 1979, this Polyc International production was a politically correct sci-fi effort. Its retread plot about vampire bats attacking humans had been used in an earlier studio offering, *Chosen Survivors* (1974) [q.v.]. Despite the bloodsuckers, the real villains were the big business bosses of a mining company attempting to desecrate tribal burial grounds found to contain large deposits of shale. Since the tribal medicine man called out the bats to destroy the world and save his people from such capitalist intrusions, the flying creatures became a symbol of nature's revenge for mankind's greed. Despite the political philosophy, *Nightwing* turned out to be as arid as the Southwest landscape in which it took place.

In New Mexico's Maskai Indian territory, lawman Youngman Duran (Nick Mancuso) and fellow tribesman Walker Chee (Stephen Macht) look out for the welfare of their people with the help of Duran's girlfriend, Dr. Anne Dillon (Kathryn Harrold), despite the area's difficult living conditions and poverty. When representatives of the Peabody Mining Company discover

Spanish lobby card for *Nightwing* (1979), Kathryn Harrold and David Warner inset.

shale deposits in the tribe's sacred burial grounds and want to mine it, medicine man Abner Tasupi (George Clutesi) calls for evil spirits to destroy their enemies and save his people. A horse is found dead from multiple bites and smelling of ammonia. Duran and Chee are at odds as how to handle the case. Duran wants to keep the investigation within the confines of the tribe while Chee insists on calling in federal authorities and notifying the mining company officials. Anne and some tourists are attacked by a pack of vampire bats. The lawman is joined by British biologist and bat hunter Phillip Payne (David Warner) in trying to find the bloodsuckers. Payne hates bats because the creatures murdered his father and he vows to wipe out the vermin. Using an electrified cage to protect themselves, Duran, Anne and Payne track the killers to a cave, trap them there and set it on fire, thus ending the mining company's plans and fulfilling the medicine man's prediction of saving the tribe.

Despite the fact *Nightwing* had some prestigious credits like director Arthur Hiller and producer Martin Ransohoff, plus a music score by Henry Mancini, it was not well received. Vincent Canby complained in the *New York Times*, "Mr. Hiller is credited as the director of the film but it looks as if it had been put together from a child's instruction book. The screenplay ... is terrible and the special effects third-rate." Phil Hardy in *The Encyclopedia of Horror Movies* (1986) said, "[T]he film has little atmosphere or momentum.... [T]he bat attacks themselves are repetitious in the extreme." In *Videohound's Horror Show* (1998), Mike Mayo contended, "The main problem is the bats — they're never remotely believable or frightening. The script isn't much better. The flaky characters from Smith's novel have been replaced by a series of clichés." James O'Neill reported in *Terror on Tape* (1994), "Absurd adaptation of the Martin Cruz Smith novel ... Even worse than *The Swarm*, this has ludicrous scenes of silly-looking actors running from Carlo Rambaldi's bat puppets (which are so dumb-looking they hardly appear) augmented by lots of dull 'romantic' scenes involving Mancuso and Harrold. Beautiful photography and one of Warner's great ranting performance are the only reasons to endure this guano." The feature found a booster in Stephen Jones when he wrote in *The Essential Monster Movie*

Guide (2000), "This interesting blend of Red Indian mysticism and modern science is stylishly directed and beautifully photographed. Henry Mancini supplies an evocative score, and Carlo Rambaldi's mechanical bats look better than the dodgy optical work."

The year of its release, the film was the subject of a picture book, *Nightwing: A Fotonovel* by Fotonovel Publications.

1984

(1955; 90 minutes) PRODUCER: N. Peter Rathvon. ASSOCIATE PRODUCER: Ralph Gilbert Bettinson. DIRECTOR: Michael Anderson. SCREENPLAY: William R. Templeton and Ralph Gilbert Bettinson, from the novel by George Orwell. PHOTOGRAPHY: C.M. Pennington-Richards. EDITOR: Bill Lewthwaite. MUSIC: Malcolm Arnold. MUSIC CONDUCTOR: Louis Levy. ART DIRECTOR: Len Townsend. SOUND: Arthur Bradbum and Harold King. MAKEUP: L.V. Clark. COSTUMES: Barbara Gray. PRODUCTION DESIGN: Terence Verity. PRODUCTION SUPERVISOR: John Croydon. PRODUCTION MANAGERS: Gerry Mitchell and G.R. Mitchell. SPECIAL EFFECTS: George Blackwell, Bryan Langley and Norman Warwick. CONTINUITY: Gladys Goldsmith. Assistant Director: Fred Stark. CAST: Edmond O'Brien (Winston Smith), Jan Sterling (Julia), Michael Redgrave (O'Connor), David Kossoff (Charrington), Mervyn Johns (Jones), Donald Pleasence (Parsons), Carol Wolveridge (Selina Parsons), Ernest Clark (Outer Party Announcer), Patrick Allen (Inner Party Officer), Ronan O'Casey (Rutherford), Michael Ripper, Ewen Solon (Outer Party Orators), Kenneth Griffith (Prisoner), Bernard Rebel (Calidor), Barbara Cavan, Anthony Jacobs (Telescreen Voices), Barbara Keogh (Woman), John Vernon (Voice of Big Brother).

By the time *1984* came to television in the late 1950s, some younger fans of horror and science fiction films were taken aback by the movie's dour plot premise and lack of thrills, despite being set in the future. The film's message was simply too powerful to be fully absorbed, even at a time when the western world was at the height of the Cold War with the Soviet Union and Red China. Based on George Orwell's 1949 novel, the production stayed as close to the novel as the censorship of the time allowed in its depiction of a nation under the rule of a totalitarian government. Most readers took Orwell to mean that the government was Communistic and its leader, Big Brother, represented Josef Stalin. The bleak, depressing world of such a society was exemplified in the person of Winston Smith, who was beautifully translated to the big screen by Edmond O'Brien. While perhaps a bit beefy for the part, O'Brien brought out the desperation of a man caught in the vise of a political system that demanded total subservience to the state, even to the point of mind control. *1984* brilliantly told what could happen to a nation whose citizens, through complacency and other factors, let government become supreme.

Following a nuclear strike on London in 1966, atomic weapons are abolished but wars continued as the absolute rulers of the world's three nations fight endless conflicts with each other to keep themselves in power. In the spring of 1984, Oceania, with its capitol in London, is battling Eurasia after declaring peace with East Asia. During an air raid, Winston Smith (O'Brien), a Outer Party member who does historical rewrites for the Records Department, meets Julia (Jan Sterling), and fears that she is a member of the Thought Police spying on him. At his shabby one-room flat, Smith has his briefcase examined by a telescreen as he slyly hides an old 1960 diary he bought at a junk shop. In defiance of the state and in an act that can cost him his life if caught, Smith plans to write his secret thoughts, including "Down with Big Brother." As he begins, Selina Parsons (Carol Wolveridge), a young neighbor, vaults into his apartment and accuses him of being a thought criminal. Her father, Parsons (Donald Pleasence), arrives and tells Smith the child is practicing to be a spy for the party and asks Smith to have a drink with him at a local canteen. Going to the Chestnut Tree, the two men see Jones (Mervyn Johns) and Rutherford (Ronan O'Casey), one-time Inner Party members who have been rehabilitated by the Ministry of Love after being exposed as traitors. Smith and Parsons are uneasy at the presence of the two, who are arrested not longer after Julia arrives.

Skipping his night at the community center, Smith walks among the common people, something that is frowned upon for Outer Party members, and is followed by the young woman as he enters the shop where he bought the diary. The owner, Charrington (David Kossoff), is an old man and Smith questions him about life before the revolution. The proprietor shows Smith a furnished room above the shop. When Julia arrives, Smith leaves quickly, is stopped by the police and ordered to attend an interrogation session the next day. There an officer (Patrick Allen) is not pleased with his replies to questions but Inner Party Minister O'Connor (Michael Redgrave) ends the matter by telling Smith to pay attention to regulations in the future.

Back at his desk at the Records Department, Smith finds a photograph of Jones and Rutherford that proves they were with Big Brother at the time they were later accused of being traitors. When he attempts to show the picture to O'Connor, the minister says it does not exist and Smith vaporizes it. During a Two Minute Hate Rally, Julia gives Smith a note saying "I Love You" and, later while eating at a canteen, they make a date to meet in Victory Square. There they agree to see each other the next Sunday in a rural area where they make love in defiance of the party's Anti-Sex League. After another rendezvous at a bell tower, Smith rents the furnished apartment from Charrington and they begin meeting on a regular basis, although they both feel that eventually they will be caught. One day Smith sees a rat in the flat and becomes almost hysterical, telling Julia the rodents are the things he fears most. After finding a note saying "Down with Big Brother" in his diary, Smith believes it was written by O'Connor. He and Julia accept the minister's invitation to meet him at his home. There O'Connor talks of the underground resistance to Big Brother and they both ask to join him. He tells them they will have to fight in the dark and will get no help. The only thing they ask of him is that they not be separated. At a Hate Week rally, Smith exchanges briefcases with a man and gets a copy of a book by Underground leader Calidor (Bernard Rebel). At the flat, he and Julia discuss the volume and she informs him she wants to have a child. As Julia tells Smith that only love can bring down the party, they hear a voice saying, "You are the Dead" coming from a telescreen behind a mirror in the room. Immediately the Thought Police arrive and place them under arrest; Charrington orders them to be taken to the Ministry of Love. There Smith is joined by Parsons who has been accused of being a thought criminal by his daughter. O'Connor arrives and informs Smith that he (Smith) is there to be cured. He is given shock treatments in an effort to numb his mind and bend his will to the authority of the party. Despite the degradation and pain, Smith refuses to betray Julia until O'Connor takes him to Room 101 where he is confronted by hundreds of rats. As a result, Smith collapses mentally and begs O'Connor to let the rats devour Julia and not himself. The minister then pronounces him cured and Smith is allowed to go back into the city. During a Hate Rally he spies Julia in a park area. They sit together and both admit having betrayed the other. As Big Brother announces the defeat of the Eurasian forces, Julia wanders away and Smith shouts that he loves Big Brother.

Holiday Film Productions made this prophetic feature in England, shooting two different endings. The one in the version released by Columbia in the fall of 1956 in the U.S. shows Smith and Julia totally subjugated by Big Brother while the one screened in Great Britain has the two killed, with Smith being shot after his torture and Julia meeting the same fate when she tries to go to him.

George Orwell's novel was first dramatized on television on September 21, 1953, as a segment of *Studio One* on CBS-TV with Eddie Albert, Norma Crane and Lorne Greene. The BBC telecast *1984* on November 12, 1954, starring Peter Cushing as Winston Smith.

In 1984 the novel was remade theatrically and issued by Atlantic Releasing Corporation, starring John Hurt as Winston Smith, Suzanna Hamilton as Julia and Richard Burton as O'Connor. Burton's final movie, it was dedicated to his memory.

The Ninth Guest

(1934; 67 minutes) DIRECTOR: Roy William Neill. SCREENPLAY: Garnett Weston, from the play by Owen Davis and the novel *The Invisible Host* by Bruce Manning and Gwen Bristow. PHOTOGRAPHY: Benjamin H. Kline. EDITOR: Gene Milford. MUSIC: Louis Silvers. CAST: Donald Cook (James "Jim" Daley), Genevieve Tobin (Jean Trent), Hardie Albright (Henry Abbott), Edward Ellis (Timothy "Tim" Cronin), Edwin Maxwell (Jason Osgood), Vince Barnett (William Jones), Helen Flint (Sylvia Inglesby), Samuel S. Hinds (Dr. Murray Reid), Nella Walker (Margaret Chisholm), Sidney Bracey (Butler Hawkins), Arthur Hoyt (Osgood's Secretary), Mary MacLaren (Guest), Charles C. Wilson (Burke), Mildred Gover (Maid).

Telegrams sent by "Your Host" are received by eight people who are invited to a party in their honor at a swank art-deco penthouse apartment. When they arrive at the appointed time, each of the guests finds they have an enemy among the assembled. Attending the outing are writer James "Jim" Daley (Donald Cook); Jean Trent (Genevieve Tobin), Jim's former girlfriend who is now involved with another guest, academic extremist Henry Abbott (Hardie Albright); Dr. Murray Reid (Samuel S. Hinds), Abbott's rival; mobster Jason Osgood (Edwin Maxwell); lawyer Sylvia Inglesby (Helen Flint), district attorney

Timothy "Tim" Cronin (Edward Ellis); and society lady Margaret Chisholm (Nella Walker). The guests are made welcome by the butler (Sidney Bracey) and his bumbling assistant (Vince Barnett) who depart after turning on a radio. A voice from the radio announces that a ninth guest, death, will make an appearance and that each will die. The group finds out they are prisoners in the apartment which has barred windows and an electrified gate. After a corpse is discovered in a closet, Jason accidentally takes poison he planned to use on the other guests. Jean then informs the group that Mrs. Chisholm committed bigamy and had her husband placed in an asylum to cover up her crime. After the society matron commits suicide, the others start to quarrel. When Cronin is found to have a gun, they try to take it. Sylvia, Cronin's lover, accidentally shoots the district attorney. Running into the electrified gate, Sylvia also kills herself. Later, while the lights are extinguished, Reid is murdered and Abbott survives a gun shot. Daley then binds Henry's hands and declares that he is the murderer. He informs Jean that Abbott killed the electrician who wired the penthouse for him and then left his body in the closet. He also tells her it was Abbott who used a remote control device to play the radio recording of the host. Abbott confesses to the killings, saying that Mrs. Chisholm had put his brother in the asylum and had been abetted in the crime by Sylvia, who was her lawyer, and the district attorney. Asking to be set free of his bonds, Abbott tells Jean to go with Jim. After they leave, he dies by electrocution.

The Ninth Guest was a flavorful, spooky murder mystery based on the 1930 Owen Davis play which was novelized that year by Bruce Manning and Gwen Bristow as *The Invisible Host*. Without credit, part of the plot was reworked in Columbia's 1939 Boris Karloff vehicle *The Man They Could Not Hang* (q.v.) and the 1944 release *The Missing Juror* (q.v.). Some sources have also claimed it was the inspiration for Agatha Christie's 1939 novel *And Then There Were None* which was staged in 1945 as *Ten Little Indians*. The Christie work was filmed in 1945 as *And Then There Were None* and in 1965, 1976 and 1989 as *Ten Little Indians*.

In the *New York Times*, Mordaunt Hall thought *The Ninth Guest* "is neatly staged, well photographed and contains an adequate amount of slaughter, [but] it is all far too unconvincing to be even mildly spine-chilling ... As comedy relief there is the conduct of Vincent [sic] Barnett, the assistant butler, who during one episode tackles a large piece of ice, which he finally gets rid of by putting it in the oven." *Harrison's Reports* stated, "None one can have any doubt that this material will hold the spectator interested and in tense suspense. But the material in the second half, where the murders occur, may prove too strong for sensitive natures, and too demoralizing for weak natures. The sight of people dropping dead one after another certainly is not a very pleasant sight. Perhaps Columbia intended to make it a horror melodrama, with the horror served by the bushel..." The same trade paper later reported that the film's box office performance was "fair."

The Old Dark House

(1963; 86 minutes; Color) PRODUCER-DIRECTOR: William Castle. ASSOCIATE PRODUCER: Dona Holloway. SCREENPLAY: Robert Dillon, from the novel *Benighted* by J.B. Priestley. PHOTOGRAPHY: Arthur Grant. EDITOR: James Needs. MUSIC: Benjamin Frankel. SOUND: Jock May. SPECIAL EFFECTS: Les Bowie. PRODUCTION DESIGN: Bernard Robinson. PRODUCTION MANAGER: John Draper. COSTUMES: Molly Arbuthnot. MAKEUP: Roy Ashton. CONTINUITY: Pauline Wise. DRAWINGS: Charles Addams. ASSISTANT DIRECTOR: Douglas Hermes. CAST: Tom Poston (Tom Penderel), Robert Morley (Roderick Femm), Janette Scott (Cecily Femm), Joyce Grenfell (Agatha Femm), Mervyn Johns (Petiphar Femm), Fenella Fielding (Morgana Femm), Peter Bull (Caspar Femm/Jasper Femm), Danny Green (Morgan Femm), John Harvey (Club Host), Amy Dalby (Gambler).

Universal's 1932 thriller *The Old Dark House* was so good, it spawned a subgenre of mystery-horror films. Expertly directed by James Whale and containing a wonderful cast (Boris Karloff, Gloria Stuart, Charles Laughton, Melvyn Douglas, Raymond Massey, Lillian Bond, Ernest Thesiger, Eva Moore), it told the tale of several people stranded on a stormy night in a spooky Welsh home inhabited by a group of eccentrics, two of them capable of murder. In 1963, producer-director William Castle joined forces with England's Hammer Films for a comedy remake, which itself had been co-adapted by J.B. Priestley from his 1928 novel *Benighted*. Filmed at Bray Studios, it was released in the U.S. by Columbia in 1963; it was not shown in its homeland until three years later and with nine minutes shorn from the original running time. While the remake got top play dates stateside, it was used as the lower half of double bills in England when Columbia issued it there.

Although the 1932 version had not been shown for years, thus leaving audiences nothing

Spanish lobby card for *The Old Dark House* (1963), picturing Robert Morley, Mervyn Johns, Janette Scott, Tom Poston, Joyce Grenfell (Poston and Johns inset).

to compare the remake with, the Castle version is still a disappointment. While the gimmick king excelled at comedy in promoting his straight horror product, he was not at his best in directing lighter material, instead being more at home with the *film noir* and fright features. Although Castle's film had a superb cast of great British actors (Robert Morley, Joyce Grenfell, Mervyn Johns, Peter Bull) and two sexy leading ladies (Janette Scott, Fenella Fielding), its main drawback seems to be Tom Poston as the American protagonist caught up in the homicidal antics of the Femm family. Like many comedians of the time whose popularity came from television, Poston excelled in cameo work but his screen persona was not enough to carry the load of a feature film. As a result, this *Old Dark House*, while nicely photographed by Arthur Grant and containing Bernard Robinson's colorful production design, was not very funny and not at all scary.

At London's Mayfair Casino, American car salesman Tom Penderel (Poston) visits Casper Femm (Bull), bringing him the new auto he sold the man, with whom he shares a London flat. The two rarely see each other as Femm occupies the apartment by day and Penderel stays there at night. After losing a large amount of money gambling, Casper asks Tom to drive the car to Femm Hall, his ancestral home near Dartmoor. He also tells Tom he wants him to meet his pretty cousin and that he must return home immediately so he has hired an airplane. During a terrible storm, Tom drives to the Femm home. While trying to open the gates, a huge statue of a lion falls on the car's hood, wrecking the vehicle. Attempting to gain entrance to the hall, Tom pulls a lever and falls through a trap door into a cellar where he is met by gun-toting Petiphar Femm (Johns), Casper's uncle. Accompanying Petiphar upstairs, Tom finds his client has died and is lying in state. The female cousin, beautiful Cecily (Scott), tells Tom that Casper was murdered and that he must not stay at Femm Hall, a dilapidated edifice with a leaking roof. As she takes him to the door, they are met by the head of the household, Roderick Femm (Morley), who is obsessed with guns. He soon meets other house members: Casper's twin Jasper (Bull), who has a phobia about dying; their father Morgan (Danny Green). a prude with homicidal tendencies; and their mother Agatha (Grenfell), a knitting addict. Morgan's brother Petiphar believes the world is coming to an end and has built a replica of Noah's Ark. Also in the house is nymphomaniac daughter Morgana (Fenella Fielding), who takes a shine to Tom, much to Cecily's chagrin. After dinner, Roderick informs Tom that the Femms are descended from Morgan the Pirate, who built their home, and that each of them must always be at the mansion by midnight or they will lose their portion of the family estate. Roderick also hints that the American might be a descendant of Morgan's daughter and is there to try and collect the family fortune, which Tom denies. Events occur that cause Tom to feel Caspar may not be dead. Mrs. Femm is murdered with a knitting needle driven through her throat. An hour later, Jasper is done in; then Roderick is found dead from a gunshot wound. Wanting to get Cecily out of the house before she becomes the next victim, Tom tries to stop the killer but he has to fend off the seductive advances of Morgana, who is encouraged to pursue Tom by her addled father. Realizing the murderer is a woman, Tom tries to trap Morgana but then deduces that Cecily is the culprit. Near hysteria, the pretty cousin tells him she plans to murder all her relatives in order to get the family's fortune and that she has placed bombs in the hall's clocks that are set to explode when they strike in unison. Tom hastens through the mansion trying to defuse all the clocks. When he throws the last one out of a window it lands near Cecily, killing her. With the killer out of the way, Tom now finds himself with the gloomy prospect of being forced to marry Morgana by her threatening father.

A "somewhat less than successful [remake]" is how Ed Naha referred to the 1963 *Old Dark House* in *Horrors: From Screen to Scream* (1975). *Castle of Frankenstein* #21 (1974) said the feature was an "unrecognizable remake.... Slim plot, hardly a patch on quality gothic, but fun because of great cast and William Castle's slick, likeable pro' touches." Richard Klemensen wrote in *Little Shoppe of Horrors* #4 (April 1978) that it was "an enjoyable little film." Regarding the making of the feature, Allen Eyles, Robert Adkinson and Nicholas Fry said in *The House of Horror: The Story of Hammer Films* (1973), "*The Old Dark House* was a rare instance of Hammer ceding creative authority to another filmmaker — William Castle, then a skillful practitioner in exploitation 'quickies.' However, despite the presence of entertaining artists ... this remake of James Whale's classic of 1932 was such a misfire blend of comedy and shock that it only escaped into a quiet second-feature niche in Britain four [sic] years after it was made." Phil Hardy in *The Encyclopedia of Horror Movies* (1984) thought the remake was "[s]o outrageously bad that it becomes enjoyable." *Films in Review* (December 1963) termed it a "[f]air spoof of the horror genre."

Uncredited, Anthony Hinds was one of the feature's producers. The macabre drawings used during the credits were done by Charles Addams, the cartoon great who created "The Addams Family."

1001 Arabian Nights

(1959; 75 minutes; Color) PRODUCER: Stephen Bosustow. DIRECTOR: Jack Kinney. SCREENPLAY: Czenzi Ormonde. STORY: Ted Allen, Pete Burness, Lew Keller, Dick Kinney, Ed Notziger, Leo Salkin, Margaret Schneider, Paul Schneider and Dick Shaw. EDITORS: Carl Bennett and Skip Craig. MUSIC: George Duning. MUSIC CONDUCTOR: Morris Stoloff. SONGS: Ned Washington and George Duning. SOUND: Marne Ellis and John P. Livadary. PRODUCTION DESIGN: Robert Dranko. EXECUTIVE PRODUCTION MANAGER: Bud Getzler. UNIT MANAGERS: Robert C. Brown and Paul Marron. VOICE CAST: Jim Backus (Uncle Abdul Azziz Magoo), Kathryn Grant (Princess Yasminda), Dwayne Hickman (Aladdin), Hans Conreid (The Wicked Wazir), Herschel Bernardi (The Jinni of the Lamp), Alan Reed (The Sultan), Daws Butler (Omar the Rug Maker), The Clark Sisters (The Three Little Maids from Damascus).

Working title: *Magoo's Arabian Nights*.

During the 1950s, Columbia released scores of popular "Mr. Magoo" seven-minute cartoons to theaters with Jim Backus providing the voice of the myopic, bumbling and lovable character. Stephen Bosustow produced the cartoons for United Productions of America (UPA) and in 1959 they did the first "Mr. Magoo" movie, *1001 Arabian Nights*, the studio's first feature-length color cartoon. Issued at Christmas in 1959, it again employed Backus as the voice of Magoo. Howard Thompson in the *New York Times* noted "the perennial Magoo joke — his nearsightedness — simply isn't enough to galvanize an oft-told tale.... All told, Mister Magoo's package is a satisfactory one — if you don't confuse the old boy with Santa Claus."

In ancient Arabia, lamp seller Abdul Azziz Magoo (voice of Jim Backus) urges his nephew Aladdin (voice of Dwayne Hickman) to marry. Aladdin runs away when his uncle shows him three eligible girls. Magoo, who is very nearsighted, is continuously followed by the yarn that

Omar the Rugmaker (voice of Daws Butler) is using to make a magic carpet for the Wicked Wazir (voice of Hans Conreid), who wants to get control of the country by marrying the beautiful Princess Yasminda (voice of Kathryn Grant), daughter of the sultan (voice of Alan Reed). Since the Wazir has been stealing from the country's treasury and her father is in jeopardy because of this, Yasminda says she will marry the evil one. But as she travels through the town, Aladdin sees her and is smitten. Needing a magic lamp hidden in a secret cave, Wazir finds out from his oracle, the evil flame, that only Aladdin has the power to unlock the door to the cavern. Finding out that the young man loves Yasminda, the Wazir poses as Magoo's brother Ben and says that he will help him get riches so he can win the heart of the princess. The day of the wedding, the Wazir takes Aladdin to the cave and steals the lamp but Magoo arrives and causes the wicked one to drop it. Aladdin finds the lamp and releases the Jinni (voice of Herschel Bernardi), who grants him the wish of going back to Magoo's shop with a treasure trove of jewels for the princess. The young man has his uncle go to the palace with the gems and ask the sultan to let Yasminda marry him. The myopic Magoo mistakes the Wazir, who is standing behind a picture of the ruler, for the sultan and agrees to his demand that Aladdin bring the magic lamp to him. After the Wazir's men fail to steal the lamp, Aladdin asks the Jinni to stop the wedding. When the command is carried out, the sultan and his daughter see the young man's wealth, and the potentate agrees to let him marry Yasminda. The Wazir manages to cheat Magoo out of the lamp and once it is in his possession, the wicked one orders the Jinni to make Aladdin's riches vanish, which he does, causing the sultan to cancel the marriage plans and have the young man jailed. The Wazir takes Yasminda to his seaside palace. Magoo, using the magic carpet, finds her but is driven into the sea by a storm brought on by the Jinni at the behest of the Wazir. Magoo and the carpet outride the storm and return to the palace where he finds the magic lamp. When the Wazir tries to murder Magoo, the Jinni throws him into the ocean where he is eaten by sharks. Magoo then wishes for Aladdin and Yasminda to be together. After the sultan marries the young couple, they ride away on the magic carpet along with Magoo.

The year of the film's release, Columbia's record division, Colpix, issued the soundtrack (CP/SCP-410) with cast members Backus and the Clark Sisters along with the Jud Conlon Singers. It was reissued in 1981 on the Varese Sarabande (STV-81138) label.

In 1962, NBC-TV telecast the TV movie *Mr. Magoo's Christmas Carol* with Backus as Magoo portraying Ebeneezer Scrooge. Following a successful 1963 re-broadcast, the network presented the half-hour cartoon series *The Famous Adventures of Mr. Magoo* with Backus providing the voice of Magoo as famous fictional characters. The program was shown on Saturday nights during the 1964–65 season.

Pacto Diabólico (Diabolical Pact)

(1969; 87 minutes; Color) PRODUCER: Luis Enrique Vergara. EXECUTIVE PRODUCER: Jorge Garcia Besne. DIRECTOR: Jaime Salvador. SCREENPLAY: Ramon Obon. STORY: Adolfo Torres Portillo, from the novel *Dr. Jekyll and Mr. Hyde* by Robert Louis Stevenson. PHOTOGRAPHY: Alfredo Uribe. EDITOR: Juan Jose Mungula. MUSIC: Gustavo Cesar Carrion. ART DIRECTORS: Jose Mendez and Octavio Ocampo. SOUND: Guillermo Carrasco. ASSISTANT DIRECTOR: Tito Novaro. CAST: John Carradine (Dr. Halbeck), Regina Torne (Di Nora Jekyll), Miguel Angel Alvarez (Frederick Halbeck), Guillermo Zetina (Doyle), Andres Garcia (Dr. Alphonse Bennett), Isela Vega (Melessa Jackson), Laura Ferlo (Melessa's Sister), Gloria Mungula (Singer), Silvia Villalobos (Guillotine Victim), Angel De Stefani (Policeman), Enriqueta Carrasco (Victim), Carlos Suarez (Waiter).

Pacto Diabólico was the second film in the quartet that John Carradine did for producer Luis Enrique Vergara in which he received top screen billing (he appeared after co-stars Regina Torne and Miguel Angel Alvarez in the feature's advertising). He has less screen here than in the others, *Enigma de Muerte* (Secret of Death), in which he was also first-billed on screen but not in the advertising, *La Señora Muerte* (The Death Woman) and *Las Vampiras* (The Vampires) [qq.v.], all of which were released theatrically in 1969; in all of them, Carradine's voice is dubbed. He is in *Pacto Diabólico* for the first 22 minutes, makes a brief appearance at about the midway point and then returns at the finale. Carradine opens the film, as he did in *Enigma de Muerte*, explaining to the audience the feature's plot. He is seated at a desk with a skull he calls his "companion angelic." Mr. Hyde, shown in the film with hairy hands and a dark facial countenance, otherwise is hardly hor-

Lobby card for *Pacto Diabólico* (1969), picturing John Carradine and Andres Garcia; note Fredric March visage as Hyde from the 1932 *Dr. Jekyll and Mr. Hyde*.

rific although throughout the proceedings he is referred to as "el monstruo."

Columbia issued the feature in the U.S. to Spanish-language theaters only. It was the fourth Columbia release based on Robert Louis Stevenson's 1886 novel *Dr. Jekyll and Mr. Hyde*, the first being *The Son of Dr. Jekyll* (q.v.) (1951) followed by the Hammer Films–produced comedy *The Ugly Duckling* (q.v.) (1959). In 1961 the studio again collaborated with Hammer on *The Two Faces of Dr. Jekyll* but when it was shown in the U.S. it was distributed by American International Pictures as *House of Fright*. *Pacto Diabólico* has also been issued on DVD as *Jekyll and Hyde—Satanic Pact* and *Pact with the Devil*.

Aged Dr. Halbeck (Carradine), a disciple of his old friend Dr. Edward Jekyll, works with his associate, Dr. Alphonse Bennett (Andres Garcia), in trying to develop a formula that will restore youth. Jekyll's beautiful daughter, Di Nora (Regina Torne), comes to visit Halbeck and that night he drinks an elixir that causes him to have a seizure and become the evil Edward Hyde. Di Nora hears his cries but after investigating the doctor's laboratory she finds no one. The next day she meets his nephew, Frederick Halbeck (Miguel Angel Alvarez), who tells her the scientist is away working on an experiment. Alphonse arrives with Melessa Jackson (Isela Vega), an old friend of Di Nora's, and Frederick finds he is attracted to both women.

Frederick goes to a cabaret where he meets a singer (Gloria Mungula). They go back to her apartment where they make love but he turns into Hyde and strangles her. Back in the laboratory, Frederick drinks a formula that returns him to normal but he becomes jealous when he spies on Di Nora and Alphonse, who have fallen in love. Frederick concocts another potion and after drinking it he becomes Dr. Halbeck, who goes mad when he sees his hairy hands. Reverting again to Frederick, the doctor abducts Melessa and removes her eyes and, after throwing her body in a furnace, he uses them in a formula that restores him to physical normality. Di Nora thwarts Frederick's advances and he again turns into a fiend and frightens the young woman. As Hyde he later sneaks into Di Nora's room and tries to kill her but her screams cause him to panic and run away. She tells Alphonse and Halbeck's butler Doyle

(Guillermo Zetina) about seeing a monster. When Alphonse goes to the laboratory he is attacked by Hyde, who is scared away by Doyle. The next day Melessa's sister (Laura Ferlo) comes looking for her. Frederick pretends to take her to her sibling but in a remote woods he tries to kill her but is run off by a policeman (Angel De Stefani). Going back to the laboratory, Frederick drinks the elixir and returns to normal and then informs Di Nora he will take her to Dr. Halbeck. Back in the laboratory he tries to attack her but Doyle hears her cries and goes for Alphonse. As the two try to break into the lab, Frederick downs another concoction and reverts back to Dr. Halbeck, who attempts to strangle Di Nora but comes to his senses when he hears a refrain from a music box she has given him. Appalled by his actions and hairy hands, Dr. Halbeck throws himself into the fiery furnace.

A drawing of Fredric March as Edward Hyde, from the 1932 Paramount release *Dr. Jekyll and Mr. Hyde*, was used on the advertising material for *Pacto Diabólico*. The feature was given an R-rating for drugs, sex (there is a very brief nude scene) and violence.

The Phantom Thief

(1946; 65 minutes) PRODUCER: John Stone. DIRECTOR: D. Ross Lederman. SCREENPLAY: Richard Wormser and Richard Weil. STORY: G.A. Snow. PHOTOGRAPHY: George B. Meehan, Jr. EDITOR: Al Clark. MUSIC DIRECTOR: Mischa Bakaleinikoff. ART DIRECTOR: Robert Peterson. SOUND: George Cooper. SETS: George Montgomery. ASSISTANT DIRECTOR: Milton Feldman. CAST: Chester Morris (Boston Blackie), Jeff Donnell (Anne Duncan), Richard Lane (Inspector Farraday), Dusty Anderson (Sandra), George E. Stone (The Runt), Frank Sully (Sergeant Matthews), Marvin Miller (Dr. Nejino), Wilton Graff (Rex Duncan), Murray Alper (Eddie Alexander), Forbes Murray (Dr. Purcell Nash), Joseph Crehan (Jumbo Madigan), Eddie Dunn, Eddie Featherston (Police Sergeants), George Magrill (Officer Kowalski), Pat O'Malley (Older Policeman), Charles C. Wilson (Police Lieutenant), Tom Dillon (Officer Denny McGonagle), Doris Houck (Waitress), Adele Roberts (Nurse), George Eldredge, Charles Jordan (Hospital Policemen), John Tyrrell (Patrolman), Brick Sullivan (Police Escort).

Working title: *Boston Blackie's Private Ghost*.

Between 1941 and 1949 Columbia Pictures released 14 feature films based on Jack Boyle's fictional reformed safecracker, Boston Blackie. *The Phantom Thief* was the eleventh adventure involving Blackie (Chester Morris) and his pal Runt (George E. Stone) and, like *Boston Blackie's Rendezvous* (1945) [q.v.], it had horror elements. The earlier entry dealt with a maniac; this outing centered on spiritualism with hefty doses of comedy from the Runt and dim-witted policeman Sergeant Matthews (Frank Sully). The feature also included the continuing rivalry between Blackie and his nemesis, Inspector Farraday (Richard Lane), although in this one they became allies in trapping a would-be killer and a murderer. With two séances involving spirits, a skeleton, spectral voices, floating hands and a ghostly trumpet, the production had more than enough genre trappings to satisfy horror film fans. Jim Bannon, who appeared in several other studio chillers, was originally cast in the role eventually played by Wilton Graff.

Paroled ex-convict Eddie Alexander (Murray Alper) seeks the aid of his pal Runt (Stone) when he is hunted by the police for stealing a leather case from a swami, Dr. Nejino (Marvin Miller). When Eddie finds a diamond necklace in the case he worries about being sent back to prison. Runt asks his roommate, Boston Blackie (Morris), to aid Alexander, who works as a chauffeur for Anne Duncan (Jeff Donnell) and her blueblood husband, Rex (Graff). Since Eddie was getting the case for Anne, who said it contained letters, the three men take it back to Dr. Nejino who informs them he does not believe in spirits but conducts séances as therapy treatments for his clients. Telling them Mrs. Duncan is mentally unbalanced, the swami has Blackie, Runt and Eddie attend a séance with her and Rex, and then tells his secretary Sandra (Dusty Anderson) to call in Inspector Farraday (Lane). During the séance, Nejino conjures up the voice of Anne's father who says he cannot remove a barrier between them since there is something evil in the room. When Anne screams, the lights are turned on and Eddie is found stabbed in the back. Farraday and his associate, Sergeant Matthews (Sully), show up and Dr. Nash (Forbes Murray), who has an office next door, is brought in since Nejino is in a state of shock. Knowing Farraday is going to try and pin the killing on them, Black and Runt make a getaway through a trap door. They hide in Anne's car and she helps them escape and then asks Blackie's aid since Nejino, her ex-husband, has been blackmailing her. She tells Blackie and Runt that the swami was her dramatic coach in college but that her father had their marriage annulled. After she married Rex, a member of a prominent Southern family, Nejino informed her that he was still married to her, and she agreed to give him the necklace to keep quiet. Blackie tells Anne he will help her and he and Runt return to Nejino's home but he gets the drop on them. Nejino orders Sandra to call the police but she aids the two men in escaping. Later they meet her at a restaurant and she tells them she has lost faith in Nejino who is involved in mysterious business. When Blackie learns from her that Nejino has a file in Dr. Nash's office, they go there but find the physician, who has lost his license to practice medicine, murdered with Sandra using a secret signal which tells her boss to call the law. Just as the boys start to leave, Farraday and Matthews arrive and try to arrest them but they escape after an explosion caused by a formula Blackie concocted to open the doctor's safe. Blackie tells Runt to hide while he pretends to be drunk and gets put in the slammer overnight. When Matthews brings in Runt, Blackie is told to leave and he uses the station's public phone to get his pal set free by calling Farraday. When the inspector and Matthews finally trace the call, Blackie and Runt have escaped and gone to the pawnshop of their friend Jumbo Madigan (Joseph Crehan), who looks over the necklace and informs them that Rex Duncan was broke before marrying Anne. Blackie then calls the young woman and when she arrives at the pawnshop he tells her that Rex is working with Nejino to get her money. While they are talking, someone shoots her through a window. After calling a doctor for Anne, Blackie tells Runt to give himself up to the police and then leaves while the girl is taken to the hospital where Rex is told his wife has died. Blackie trails Duncan to Nejino's home where Farraday orders the swami to hold a séance in an attempt to get Anne's spirit to reveal her murderer. Blackie confronts Nejino and the two men have a fistfight. Nejino enters the room where the séance is to be held and is strapped to a table and goes into a trance, with Anne's specter appearing and accusing her husband of killing her. Rex pulls a revolver and fires at the ghost, breaking a mirror. As the police grab Duncan, Blackie appears and shows how Nejino used a dummy as a substitute while he murdered Eddie and that he also killed his former ally, Dr. Nash. Blackie and Farraday confirm they worked together to solve the case as Nejino and Duncan are arrested.

The Phantom Thief was one of over 50 feature films that D. Ross Lederman directed for Columbia between 1931 and 1950. In a 1978 interview with me, actor Benny Baker talked about working with Lederman on *Panic on the Air* (1936): "D. Ross Lederman directed *Panic on the Air* and he was a perfect director for Harry Cohn because at that time Columbia had to make pictures in six days. There was no convenience of rehearsing, you just went in and shot it. I had a scene with Lew Ayres and an actor playing a Chinese houseboy. What Lederman would do was set up a scene and then yell 'roll it' and then go away to set up another scene and the assistant would holler 'cut' and Lederman would ask him how it was. If there was a mistake he would say 'closeup' and you would do the line and then go on to the next setup. In the scene the Chinaman blew the line and Lederman kept making setups and after three takes we all left the set and went and did other setups. After that we went back to the original setup and there was a new Chinaman. Lederman wasted no time. That's why Harry Cohn liked him. He didn't waste time."

The Phantom Wagon

(1940; 93 minutes) DIRECTOR: Julien Duvivier. SCREENPLAY: Julien Duvivier and Alexandre Arnoux, from the novel *Korkarlen* by Selma Lagerlof. PHOTOGRAPHY: J. Kruger. EDITORS: L. Bognar and Jean Feyte. MUSIC: Jacques Ibert. ART DIRECTORS: Jacques Krauss and [Andre] Trebuchet. SOUND: Marcel Courmes. MAKEUP: Tourjansky. PRODUCTION MANAGER: Jean Levy-Strauss. UNIT MANAGERS: De Masure and Klein. ASSISTANT DIRECTOR: Pierre Duvivier. CAST: Pierre Fresnay (David Holm), Marie Bell (Sister Maria), Micheline Francey (Sister Edith), Louis Jouvet (Georges), Jean Mercanton (Pierre Holm), Ariane Borg (Suzanne), Alexandre Rignault (The Giant), Le Vegan (Father Martin), Palau (Mr. Benoit), Genin (The Eternal Father), Marie-Helene Daste (Prostitute), Philippe Richard (Cabaret Patron), Georges Mauloy (Pastor), Jottre (Prison Guard), [Marcel] Peres (Customer), Claudio, Jean Buquet (Children), Andree Mery (Old Repentant), Mila Parely (Anna), Henri Nassiet (Gustave), Marguerite de Morlaye (Rich Woman), George Douking (Drunkard), Michel Francois (David Holm's Son), Edouard Francomme (Cabaret Man), Mme. Lherbay (Murdered Old Lady), Suzanne Morlot, Eugene Evernes, Sylvain, Jean Paredes, Genia Vaury (Greeters).

In May 1940, Columbia Pictures released *The Phantom Wagon* in the United States. Made in France by Transcontinental Film Productions as *La Charrette Fantome* (The Phantom Wagon), it was in French with English subtitles. It was directed and co-written by Julien Duvivier who had earlier helmed *Le Golem* (The Golem) in 1936 and who, during a World War II sojourn in Hollywood, co-produced and directed *Flesh and Fantasy*

(1943) for Universal. Based on the novel *Korkarlen* by Selma Lagerlof, it was first filmed under that title in Sweden in 1921 by director Victor Sjostrom and was remade in that country in 1958 under its original title by Norsk Tonefilm with direction by Arne Mattsson.

In a small French village the poor are given a free meal and then told that thanks to Edith (Micheline Francey) they can live at a new homeless shelter. Student Georges (Louis Jouvet) tells his fellow drinkers the story of the Phantom Wagon, a ghostly hearse that takes the deceased to the afterworld and how its creaky wheels can be heard just as the dead depart. He also relates that anyone who dies at midnight is doomed to drive the wagon for a year. After getting into a fight at the cabaret, Georges is taken to a hospital where he wants to die before the New Year; running away, he perishes just at midnight. Drunken glass blower David Holm (Pierre Fresnay) shows up at the shelter and wakes up the next day to find Edith has sewn his clothes. She tells him to go back to work and return a year later to inform her how his life has improved. Several months later the young woman tries to find David but his wife Anna (Mila Parely) says he has returned to drinking and has vanished. When Edith, who loves David, finds him, she convinces the wayward man to go with her to the Salvation Army's church service but when one of his cohorts repents he becomes angry and goes home to beat his wife and ends up behind bars. David is released and Edith, who has developed tuberculosis from contact with him, says his wife and children are being taken care of by the Salvation Army. When she tries to take him to them, he leaves her after hearing what he thinks are the creaking wheels of the Phantom Wagon. Going to a camp for vagabonds, David is beaten by a man (Andree Mery) because of his treatment of Edith. Since it is New Year's Eve, Georges, the Phantom Wagon driver, tells him it will be his turn to take over the position. Going to see his family, David stops his wife from killing their children and then visits Edith, who dies peacefully. Since he has repented, David is allowed by Georges' ghost to go back to his family as Edith's specter gives thanks.

Like most dubbed foreign films of the time, *The Phantom Wagon* got little distribution outside cosmopolitan areas. It was further hampered by its downbeat plot and locales with its main protagonist a drunken tubercular who abandons his wife and children and fatally infects a saintly Salvation Army Sister who tries to reform him. For horror followers there was the Phantom Wagon and its ghost passengers and driver but they were little compensation for an otherwise depressing melodrama mired among the lower depths of humanity.

The Power of the Whistler

(1945; 66 minutes) PRODUCER: Leonard S. Picker. DIRECTOR: Lew Landers. SCREENPLAY: Aubrey Wisberg. PHOTOGRAPHY: L.W. O'Connell. EDITOR: Reg Browne. SOUND: Hugh McDowell, Jr. ART DIRECTORS: John Datu. SETS: Sidney Clifford. ASSISTANT DIRECTOR: Leonard J. Shapiro. CAST: Richard Dix (William Everest), Janis Carter (Jean Lang), Jeff Donnell (Francie Lang), Loren Tindall (Charlie Kent), Tala Birell (Constantina Ivaneska), John Abbott (Kaspar Andropolous), Cy Kendall (Druggist), Kenneth MacDonald (Dr. John Crawford), Walter Baldwin (Station Master), Murray Alper (Joe Blainey), Margia Dean (Mary), Nina Mae McKinney (Flotilda), Forrest Taylor (Stage Doorman), Crane Whitley (Police Captain), I. Stanford Jolley (Car Owner), Stanley Price (Printer), John Tyrrell (Clerk), Eddie Parker (Motorcycle Cop), Robert Williams, Frank J. Scannell (Patrolmen), Frank Hagney (Cake Delivery Man), Jack George (Locksmith), Otto Forrest (Voice of the Whistler).

In 1944 Columbia acquired the screen rights to the popular radio program "The Whistler" (CBS, 1942–55) and in the next five years turned out eight programmers, all but the last starring Richard Dix. William Castle directed the first two series entries, *The Whistler* and *The Mark of the Whistler* (both 1944) [qq.v.], but with the third outing, *The Power of the Whistler*, Lew Landers took over as helmsman, resulting in a basically lackluster effort highlighted by beautiful Janis Carter who had the same amount of screen time as top-billed Dix. In each of the series' features, Dix portrayed someone caught in destiny's web, with some of the outings, like this tale of a psychotic killer, bordering on the horrific. Another such effort was the follow-up to this release, *The Voice of the Whistler* (q.v.), issued the same year.

Walking in Greenwich Village on his way to carry out a ghastly mission, William Everest (Dix) is hit by a car and knocked out. Coming to, he cannot remember his identity and goes into The Salt Shaker café for a drink in an attempt to clear his head. Also there are beautiful department store buyer Jean Lang (Carter), her sister Francie (Jeff Donnell) and Charlie Kent (Loren Tindall), Francie's boyfriend. Jean is using a deck of cards to predict the future and, spotting Everest, she jokingly predicts his fortune but finds that on both tries she comes up with cards saying he will die within 24 hours. When Everest leaves the café, Jean follows to tell him about the prediction but learns he cannot recall his name, only remembering he has someone to see and something important to accomplish. While resting in a vacant car, Everest and Jean go through his belongings. When the driver (I. Stanford Jolley) returns, he offers to take them to the Civic Theatre since Everett has a voucher for flowers sent to dancer Constantina Ivaneska (Tala Birell), the headliner. The woman, who is about to be married, claims she does not know Everest so next Jean and Everest go to see a doctor who wrote a prescription found on the amnesiac. The address turns out to be a bookstore in a shabby part of town. Everest waits outside talking to a small girl who has a kitten. He gives her money for ice cream and agrees to tend to the pet while Jean talks with the store owner, Kaspar Andropolous (John Abbott), who knows nothing about the doctor although he recognizes the name as that of the author of *The Art of Poison*, published 50 years before. He tells her that Everett was in the shop the week before looking for the book. As Jean and Everest leave in a taxi, the little girl cries after finding her kitten has been killed. Everest agrees to stay with Jean and Francie at their apartment. That night, Francie tells her sister that Charlie has asked her to marry him. She also confronts Jean about her romantic feelings for Everest. Francie finds her pet canary dead in its cage and to ease her suffering over its loss, Jean asks her to trace some of the contents found in Everest's pockets. While checking on a license number on a Canadian dollar in his possession, Everest finds out it belongs to Judge Edward Nesbitt and this causes him to regain his memory. From a printer (Stanley Price) who made up the prescription, Francie goes to the druggist (Cy Kendall) who filled it and learns it was for a poison. She also traces a cake order form found on Everest and locates the Elite Bakery truck driver (Murray Alper) who sold the cake; he informs her that the buyer returned with it and had it mailed to Dr. John Crawford (Kenneth MacDonald). Meeting Jean in a park, Everest tells her he has fallen in love with her and that he remembers the name Edward Nesbitt and asks her to accompany him to the man's home in Woodville. As they leave, Jean is upset to see a dead squirrel who had playfully jumped on Everest's lap before her arrival. When Jean does not return to their apartment, Francie tells Charlie she is afraid for her sister since she no longer trusts Everest. As Francie goes to the police captain (Crane Whitley) with her concerns, Charlie brings the dancer, druggist and bakery driver to the policeman. Constantina admits that Everest was a former suitor. Francie tells the police that she suspects that Everest has mailed a poisoned cake to Dr. Crawford, the head of the Hudson Mental Institution. A bulletin is put out on Everest as the local police arrive in time to stop Crawford and his son from eating the cake. Crawford informs them that Everest is an escaped mental patient who wants to kill Judge Nesbitt for having him committed. Arriving by train in Woodville, Everest and Jean borrow the station master's (Walter Baldwin) car to go to Nesbitt's house. Everest overhears a radio broadcast announcing that he is wanted by the police. Stopped by highway patrolmen (Robert Williams, Frank J. Scannell), Bill tells them he is Dr. Crawford and that Jean is his nurse, Miss Carroll, and they are looking for the escaped Everest. When Jean tries to get the truth out of Everest, he takes out a knife and tells her he plans to kill her. She runs from the car and Everest pursues her through a wooded area. The police see the abandoned car and follow the two as Everest traps Jean in a barn and climbs a ladder to the haymow to murder her. Jean stabs him with a pitchfork and he dies, just as the cards had predicted. Later, back at the café with Francie and Charlie, Jean agrees to abandon fortunetelling.

In *B Movies* (1973), Don Miller noted, "Aside from an excellent bit of photography (L.W. O'Connell) introducing the Dix character in full closeup, *The Power of the Whistler* failed to approach the story and entertainment values set by the first two. Significantly or not, [William] Castle did not direct..."

Profanadores de Tumbas (Profaners of Tombs)

(1966; 89 minutes) PRODUCER: Luis Enrique Vergara. DIRECTOR: Jose Diaz Morales. SCREENPLAY: Rafael Garcia Travesi. PHOTOGRAPHY: Eduardo Valez Correa. EDITOR: Jose Juan Mungula. PRODUCTION MANAGER: Raul Manjarrez. COSTUMES: Bertha Mendoza Lopez. MAKEUP: Armando Islas. ASSISTANT DIRECTOR: Angel Rodriguez. CAST: Santo (Himself), Gina Romand (Marta), Mario Orea (Dr. Toicher), Jorge Peral (Carlos Resendiz), Jesus Camacho (Quasimodo), Jessica [Mungula] (Abduction Witness), Fernando Oses

(Henchman), Bigoton Castro (Inspector Mendoza), Lobo Negro [Guillermo Hernandez] (Gorilla), Estela Peral (Estela), Jorge Fegan (Violinist), Martha Lasso Renteria (Dancer), Fernando Saucedo (Artist), Nathanael Frankenstein [Nathanel Leon] (Gallery Owner), Julio Ahuet (Spying Henchman), Leonor Gomez, Juan Garza (Spectators).

One of four features in which masked professional wrestler Santo starred for producer Luis Enrique Vergara, *Profanadores de Tumbas*, also called *Grave Robbers*, is one of the Enmascarado de Plata's more obscure movies. It was the first of several Vergara productions distributed in the United States for Spanish-language theaters by Columbia. A relatively tacky affair, it contains the usual modicum of wresting sequences with Santo always besting his opponent. It also includes several songs by leading lady Gina Romand in addition to a singing trio. Santo drives a nifty white convertible sports car and has a futuristic communications center in which he keeps in contact with his Interpol employers. The most interesting characters are the villains. Mario Orea portrays the sadistic and thoroughly evil Dr. Toicher. The madman has a laboratory in an abandoned factory and with two thuggish henchmen (Fernando Oses, Lobo Negro) and a deformed hunchback (Jesus Camacho) he carries out a number of loony experiments that require fresh corpses. When riled, the scar-faced Toicher is apt to use a whip on his cohorts, especially the hunchback. The actor playing that role, Jesus Camacho, is billed twice, first under his own name and then as his character, Quasimodo.

Two graves are robbed by Dr. Toicher (Orea), his thugs (Oses, Lobo Negro) and Quasimodo (Camacho), a hunchback. Back in his laboratory, the scientist nearly revives one of the corpses but a machine explodes. Toicher thinks he needs a superior body to complete his work and he sends a messenger to the home of wrestler Santo (Himself) with a lamp that will send out vibrations to incapacitate the grappler. Although nearly disabled by the apparatus, Santo is able to unplug the lamp. When Quasimodo returns without the wrestler, he is beaten by his enraged master.

Having read about the grave robbers, Santo calls his friend Carlos (Jorge Peral) who is in love with singer Marta (Romand). After another experiment goes awry, Toicher and his men attempt to rob a grave but are caught by Santo; they knock him out and bury him alive. Managing to claw his way out of the grave, Santo finds a hat with the doctor's name on it and calls his bosses at Interpol who later inform him the scientist is a wanted criminal. When a henchman (Julio Ahuet) phones Toicher and tells him that Santo is still alive, the angry scientist beats his associates. Santo and Carlos inform Inspector Mendoza (Bigoton Castro) that Toicher is behind the grave desecrations. During a wrestling match, Santo's opponent is punctured in the leg with a needle by Quasimodo and the grappler goes haywire, runs out of the arena and dies. That night while Marta is singing at a club, she is nearly killed when her wig starts vibrating thanks to a device placed in it by the madman. Santo arrives and fights the doctor and his henchmen but they manage to escape. Later the two thugs try to kidnap Marta and again they are stopped by Santo. When the hunchback again places the lamp in Santo's home, the singer and her boyfriend are called to the house by Toicher, pretending to be Santo, and are abducted. Santo returns home to find the lamp and unplugs it as Toicher forces Marta

Poster for *Profanadores de Tumbas* (1966), released by Columbia.

to phone Santo and beg him to rescue her. The wrestler drives to the abandoned factory where the scientist is headquartered but he is knocked out by an electric charge and tied up in a store room. Santo manages to escape and he fights and kills both the thugs as Toicher prepares to give Marta a heart transplant. Wanting the heart for himself, Quasimodo turns on Toicher and the scientist kills him. The madman then fights with Santo as Carlos manages to free Marta and call Mendoza. As the crazed doctor lunges at Santo with an iron rod, the wrestler moves to the side and Toicher falls head first into a fire pit and is consumed as the police arrive on the scene.

Santo (Rudolfo Guzman Herta) (1917–84) was Mexico's most popular professional wrestler and a pop culture hero. He was the hero of a comic book series, and from 1958 to 1982 he appeared in over 50 feature films, fighting various monsters, sometimes in tandem with mat rivals like Blue Demon and Mil Mascaras. In addition to *Profanadores de Tumbas*, he also starred in *El Podor Satánico* (The Satanic Power), *Atacan las Brujas* (The Witches Attack) and *El Hacha Diabólica* (The Diabolical Hatchet), all 1964 releases, for Filmica Vergara.

Pygmy Island

(1950; 69 minutes) PRODUCER: Sam Katzman. DIRECTOR: William Berke. SCREENPLAY: Carroll Young. PHOTOGRAPHY: Ira H. Morgan. EDITOR: Jerome Thoms. MUSIC DIRECTOR: Mischa Bakaleinikoff. ART DIRECTOR: Paul Palmentola. SOUND: J.S. Westmoreland. SETS: Sidney Clifford. PRODUCTION MANAGER: Herbert B. Leonard. ASSISTANT DIRECTOR: R.M. Andrews. CAST: Johnny Weissmuller (Jungle Jim), Ann Savage (Captain A.R. Kingsley), David Bruce (Major Bolton), Steven Geray (Leon Marko), William Tannen (Kruger), Tris [Tristram] Coffin (Novak), Billy Curtis (Makuba), Tommy Farrell (Captain), Pierce Lyden (Lucas), Rusty Wescoatt (Anders), Billy Barty (Kimba), Selmer Jackson (Pentagon Officer), Larry Steers (General), Harry Wilson (Machine Gun Henchman), Angelo Rossitto, John George (Pygmies), Steve Calvert (Gorilla), Tamba (Chimp).

Following news reports that Captain A.R. Kingsley (Ann Savage) is missing in the African jungle while on special assignment, a Pentagon officer (Selmer Jackson) reports to his superior (Larry Steers) that Kingsley was trying to locate the source of the N'goma plant in Bugandi country. He informs the general that Jungle Jim (Johnny Weissmuller) found a dead pygmy with Kingsley's dogtags and a rope that was fireproof. He further stated that the rope was made from N'goma fibers that had the strength needed for military use. The Pentagon decides to send a caravan lead by Major Bolton in search of Kingsley. At the Bugandi Trading Company, Bolton meets the proprietor, Leon Marko (Steven Geray), and Jim, who learns from the major that Kingsley is the army's expert in tropical plants and a woman. As Jim goes with Bolton and his men, foreign spy Marko and his henchman Kruger (William Tannen) try to kill the jungle man but are frightened away by a gorilla (Steve Calvert) who attacks Jim. When Jim tries to get away from the creature, the beast dislodges a suspension bridge but Jim manages to make it to safety. When an arrow belonging to a mysterious cult called the Bush Devils is fired into the army camp, Jim finds a boot print that proves the shooter was not a native. Marko, who is trying to find the source of the N'goma plant for his country, and Kruger cause an elephant stampede that nearly kills the soldiers. Jim's pet chimp Tamba finds a spent rifle shell and gives it to its master, who tells Bolton the stampede was not an accident. At a remote cave, a tribe of pygmies lead by Makuba (Billy Curtis) manufactures rope from the N'goma plant which grows nearby and they shelter Kingsley, who wants to get to Bugandi in order to inform the army of the location of the plant. Since Marko's men, masquerading as members of the Bush Devil cult, have been harassing the pygmies, Makuba constructs a driftwood island and he and the captain float down the river but are nearly seen by gang members Novak (Tristram Coffin) and Lucas (Pierce Lyden). Spotting Marko's boat, the captain and Makuba board the craft but find a Bush Devil mask. When they try to escape, Marko and Kruger stop them. Jim shows up and saves the woman and the pygmy and gets them to shore where Kingsley tells Bolton that Marko appears to be a foreign agent. With Makuba leading them back to the cave, Bolton and his men are joined by the captain as Jim scouts ahead and gets rid of two of Marko's men, Lucas and Anders (Rusty Wescoatt). Novak is killed when he falls from a cliff while being pursued by the jungle man. After fighting in quicksand with Kruger, Jim is captured by Marko and his men as Makuba sends his friend Kimba (Billy Barty) for the rest of the pygmy tribe. Marko sets a trap for the soldiers. When Bolton arrives with his men, they are attacked with hand grenades but the pygmies ambush the crooks and they are captured. Makuba and his tribe then agree to cultivate more N'goma plants since they are now "good neighbors" with America.

Also called *Jungle Jim in Pygmy Island*, this was the third Sam Katzman production based on the comic strip created by Alex Raymond. The series was already beginning to show signs of wear. A somewhat tepid affair, its main action consisted of Jim fighting a crocodile and a gorilla, an elephant stampede and the finale battle between the army and the foreign agents. Its marginal horror elements consisted of the supposed supernatural masked Bush Devils. *Variety* complained that the film was "overlong for release intentions" and that it had a "[r]outine plot." The *Hollywood Reporter* felt it was "an over-plotted and confusing adventure film with little chance of being popular with anyone but juveniles." *Film Daily* opined, "Here is another number for the youngsters. It is quite harmless and provides simple adventure and excitement to provoke imaginative response on their part."

Ransom

(1928; 58 minutes) PRODUCER: Harry Cohn. DIRECTOR-STORY: George B. Seitz. SCREENPLAY: Dorothy Howell. ADAPTATION: Elmer Harris. TITLES: Mort Blumenstock. PHOTOGRAPHY: Joseph Walker. ART DIRECTOR: Joseph C. Wright. ASSISTANT DIRECTOR: Joe Nadel. CAST: Lois Wilson (Lois Brewster), Edmund Burns (Burton Meredith), William V. Mong (Wu Fang), [Edgar] Blue Washington (Oliver), James B. Leong (Scarface), Jackie Combs (Bobby Brewster).

Columbia's first foray into the horror genre came in 1928 with the silent entry *Ransom*, based on a story by its director, George B. Seitz. A melodrama in the then popular Yellow Peril vein, the feature was fashioned around a newly developed gas weapon that is coveted by a Chinese gangster. Still considered a part of Poverty Row in the closing days of the silent era, Columbia hired Lois Wilson to headline the effort, which *Photoplay* called "[t]hird rate." Wilson was best known for headlining releases *The Covered Wagon* (1923), *Ruggles of Red Gap* (1923) and *Monsieur Beaucaire* (1924) and for playing Daisy Buchanan in *The Great Gatsby* (1926). She easily made the transition to sound and continued to make films until 1949.

Wu Fang (William V. Mong), a leader in San Francisco's Chinese gangland, learns that government chemist Burton Meredith (Edmund Burns) has developed a poisonous gas formula and he sets out to obtain it. He blackmails Burton's fiancée, Lois Brewster (Wilson), by abducting her little boy Bobby (Jackie Combs) and holding him hostage until she obtains the formula and hands it over to him. With no other recourse, Lois meets Meredith at this laboratory and pleads with him to give her the formula so she can save her son. When Meredith denies her request, Lois takes a vial she thinks contains the gas and gives it to Wu Fang. Finding out he has been duped, the hoodlum threatens to torture Lois. Meredith, who has trailed her to the gangster's den, arrives and stops him, saving the woman he loves and her son. Wu Fang and his gang are arrested and Lois agrees to marry Meredith.

Ravagers

(1979; 90 minutes; Color) PRODUCER: John W. Hyde. ASSOCIATE PRODUCER: Saul David. DIRECTOR: Richard Compton. SCREENPLAY: Donald S. Sanford, from the novel *Path to Savagery* by Robert Edmond Alter. PHOTOGRAPHY: Vincent Saizis. EDITOR: Maury Winetrobe. MUSIC: Fred Karlin. PRODUCTION DESIGN: Ron Hobbs. COSTUMES: Ronald Talsky. MAKEUP: Bob Westmoreland and Dorothy J. Pearl. ASSISTANT DIRECTORS: Pat Kehoe and Ed Milkovich. CAST: Richard Harris (Falk), Art Carney (Sergeant), Anthony James (Gang Leader), Ann Turkel (Faina), Alana Stewart (Miriam), Woody Strode (Brown), Ernest Borgnine (Rann), Seymour Cassel (Blind Lawyer), Bob Westmoreland (Hank), Brian Carney (Foy), Kurt Grayson (Coop), Cecily Hovanes (Grace), Gordon Hyde (Bert), George Stokes (Bant), Oliva Barton (Mushroom Woman), Kim Crow (Flocker Woman), Steve Lashley, Arch Archambault (Gang Members), Billy Carmack (Sickle Thug), Harvey Evans (Guard), Andre Tayir (Prisoner).

Produced by Cinecorp Productions and filmed at the Alabama Space and Rocket Center Museum and Rocket Park, *Ravagers* was one of a series of 1970s–80s features dealing with a post-apocalyptic world in which a group of people try to build new lives out of anarchy and chaos. Unfortunately it was not one of the better examples of this genre, as noted by Phil Hardy in *Science Fiction* (1984) who called it, "[a] commercial disaster ... a vapid blending of *Death Wish* (1974) and *Mad Max* (1979) ... limply scripted by [Donald S.] Sanford, the film updates the vigilante theme to no purpose and wastes its strong cast." Michael J. Weldon concurred in *The Psychotronic Encyclopedia of Film* (1983): "Nothing good has been said about this end-of-the-world movie..."

In 1991 the planet has been desolated by a nuclear war that has left the oceans poisoned and the land barren and depopulated. Those who have survived are menaced by the Ravagers, gangs who pillage and murder. Falk (Richard Harris) and his girlfriend Miriam (Alana Stewart) reside in the ruins of a factory in New York City. When she is raped and murdered by a Ravager leader (Anthony James) and his gang, Falk tries to take revenge by killing several of the rapists. Forced to leave the city by the Ravagers, he meets Sergeant (Art Carney), an addled career officer looking for a commander, and Faina (Ann Turkel), a young girl who is seeking a safe haven called Genesis. The leader and his men trail the trio as they eventually come upon Rann (Ernest Borgnine), who has set up a community in two abandoned freighters with the purpose of rebuilding civilization. The Ravagers show up and Falk, Sergeant, Rann and the others are forced into a final showdown to save the world from evil.

Ravagers was based on the 1969 novel *Path to Savagery* by Robert Edmond Alter (1925–66), the author of the crime paperback favorites *Carny Kill* and *Swamp Sister*. Alter, who had many works published posthumously, wrote in various genres, including children's and historical novels, and for magazines like *Argosy, Bizarre! Mystery Magazine, Ellery Queen's Mystery Magazine, Intrigue, The Man from U.N.C.L.E., Mike Shayne Mystery Magazine, Suspense* and *Trapped Detective Star Magazine*.

A Reflection of Fear

(1973; 89 minutes; Color) PRODUCER: Howard B. Jaffe. DIRECTOR: William A. Fraker. SCREENPLAY: Lewis John Carlino and Edward Hume, from the novel *Go to Thy Deathbed* by Stanton Forbes. PHOTOGRAPHY: Laszlo Kovacs. EDITOR: Richard Brockway. MUSIC: Fred Myrow. ART DIRECTOR: Joe Schiller. SOUND: Whitey Ford and Arthur Piantadosi. SETS: Phil Abramson. COSTUMES: Patti Norris. MAKEUP: Emile LaVigne. SPECIAL EFFECTS: Milton Burrow. ASSISTANT DIRECTOR: John Chulay. CAST: Robert Shaw (Michael Heffernan), Sally Kellerman (Anne Haverd), Mary Ure (Katherine Heffernan), Sondra Locke (Marguerite Heffernan), Signe Hasso (Julia Sterling), Mitch Ryan (Inspector McKenna), Gordon Devol (Hector), Gordon Anderson (Voice of Aaron), Victoria Risk (Peggy), Leonard John Crofoot (Aaron), Michael St. Clair (Kevin), Liam Dunn (Coroner), Michelle Marvin (Nurse), Michele Montau (Mme. Caraquet).

Working titles: *Autumn Child* and *Labyrinth*.

Teenager Marguerite Heffernan (Sondra Locke) lives a secluded life in a New England coastal town with her mother Katherine (Mary Ure) and wealthy grandmother Julia (Signe Hasso). She keeps busy with at-home schooling, science hobbies and an enormous collection of dolls; she calls one of her dolls Aaron and carries on secret conversations with it. When she finds out that her father, Michael Heffernan (Robert Shaw), whom she has not seen in over a decade, plans to visit her, she gets into an argument with Aaron, who is jealous of her father. Michael comes to town with his girlfriend Anne Haverd (Sally Kellerman) and they stay at the local inn where they meet the owner's son, vacationing medical student Hector (Gordon Devol). Michael informs Katherine that he wants a divorce in order to marry Anne but is unhappy to find his daughter so isolated and without companions her own age. Marguerite goes into hysterics when she finds her garden has been destroyed, claiming it was done by Aaron; her grandmother is forced to take her to her room. Katherine slaps Michael when he accuses her of giving their daughter a bad upbringing but he later informs Anne that his wife will divorce him if he promises never again to see his daughter.

Michael and Anne come to have dinner with Marguerite, who secretly requests that her father meet her in the garden. He returns Anne to the inn and tells her he plans to get Marguerite away from her mother and grandmother. Marguerite has another argument with the jealous Aaron and while Michael waits for his daughter, Julia and Katherine are murdered. When the maid (Victoria Risk) finds the corpses, she calls the police and Inspector McKenna (Mitch Ryan) finds out from the gardener (Michael St. Clair) that he saw a young person climbing over a wall surrounding the house. McKenna questions Michael and Anne and tells them not to leave town while Marguerite again argues with Aaron. The next day the policeman informs Michael that Marguerite has inherited her grandmother's vast estate and that he is her legal guardian. When Michael and Anne take Marguerite to the beach, Anne becomes wary of the young girl but later tries to make friends with her and shows interest in her hobbies. Anne begins to wonder if Aaron is real as Marguerite tells her father that she wants to live with him and his girlfriend. Hector starts coming to see Marguerite and she becomes upset with him when he forces her to listen to her father and Anne having sex. When Anne and Michael have a falling out over his failure to control Marguerite's outbursts, she drives away in the rain and stops to pick up someone she thinks is Hector. The person attacks her but is scared away by an oncoming vehicle.

She goes back to the house and calls the police and the next day Hector takes Marguerite for a boat ride and tries to kiss her. When the boat is found wrecked, McKenna attempts to talk to the hysterical Marguerite before finding Hector's dead body. Michael feels that his daughter needs psychiatric care and makes plans to put her in a Boston sanitarium. When Marguerite finds out, she throws a fit and destroys her science projects. Although Anne tries to stop him, Michael goes to face Marguerite who comes at him with a club. After he subdues her, he realizes that the person he thought was his daughter is actually a teenage boy.

Based on Stanton Forbes' 1968 novel *Go to Thy Deathbed*, *A Refection of Fear* used the plot premise of William Castle's *Homicidal* (1961)(q.v.) but was not nearly as entertaining. The feature was filmed in 1970 but underwent several editing changes before being distributed by Columbia in the spring of 1973. Its strongest aspect was the cast: Robert Shaw and Mary Ure, who were married at the time, gave excellent performances as did Sally Kellerman as the girlfriend, Signe Hasso as the stern mother-in-law and Mitch Ryan as the police inspector. The film was dominated by Sondra Locke as the mentally fragile Marguerite; Locke is best known as the one-time co-star and girlfriend of Clint Eastwood before their acrimonious breakup. The *New York Times* complained, "[T]here is such density of atmospheric haze that half the film looks as if it had been photographed through a jellyfish." John Stanley in *John Stanley's Creature Features Movie Guide Strikes Again* (1994) called it a "[w]eak imitation of *Psycho*, with surprise twists more baffling than enthralling.... The cast is good but the ending muddled."

Repulsion

(1965; 105 minutes) PRODUCER: Gene Gutowski. EXECUTIVE PRODUCERS: Tony Tenser and Michael Klinger. ASSOCIATE PRODUCERS: Robert Sterne and Sam Waynberg. DIRECTOR: Roman Polanski. SCREENPLAY: Roman Polanski and Gerard Brach. PHOTOGRAPHY: Gilbert Taylor. EDITOR: Alastair McIntyre. MUSIC: Chico Hamilton. ART DIRECTOR: Seamus Flannery. SOUND: Stephen Dalby. MAKEUP: Tom Smith. ASSISTANT DIRECTOR: Ted Sturgis. CAST: Catherine Deneuve (Carol Ledoux), Ian Hendry (Michael), John Fraser (Colin), Yvonne Furneaux (Helene Ledoux), Patrick Wymark (Landlord), Renee Houston (Miss Balch), Valerie Taylor (Madame Denise), James Villiers (John), Helen Fraser (Bridget), Hugh Futcher (Reggie), Monica Merlin (Mrs. Rendlesham), Imogen Graham (Manicurist), Mike Pratt (Workman), Roman Polanski (Spoon Player).

Director Roman Polanski received international recognition in 1962 with his Polish film *Knife in Water* but it was his first English-language film three years later, *Repulsion*, that cemented his reputation. He followed it with other genre efforts, *The Fearless Vampire Killers, or Pardon Me, But Your Teeth Are in My Neck* (1967), the box office blockbuster *Rosemary's Baby* (1968), produced by William Castle, and *Macbeth* (1971) [q.v.]. More popular in its time than today, *Repulsion* is a dark, slow-moving, low-key and terrifying film that intricately explores the facets of the mind leading to a mental collapse and murder, along with sexual guilt and repression. While Polanski's direction is fine, the film could not have worked without the meticulous performance of Catherine Deneuve as a young woman who spirals into insanity and homicide. Despite its flaws, *Repulsion* remains a milestone in mid–1960s horror films. Filmed on a $300,000 budget and released in the U.S. by Columbia in the fall of 1965, the film was made by Compton Film/Tekli-British Productions and was named one of the top ten films of the year by the *New York Times* film critics.

During a London heat wave, beautiful blonde French manicurist Carol Ledoux (Deneuve) becomes withdrawn, especially with her roommate-sister Helene (Yvonne Furneaux), who is having an affair with Michael (Ian Hendry), an older man. Lethargic, uptight and nail-biting, Carol refuses to see her boyfriend Colin (John Fraser) that night, saying she is having dinner with her sister. Their landlord (Patrick Wymark) calls and demands his back rent and Helene promises that Carol will give it to him the next day. Carol does not like Michael and does not want her sister going away with him to Italy. At work the next day, Carol finds out that her co-worker Bridget (Helen Fraser) is having boyfriend problems. That night she forgets about a dinner date with Colin, who finds her staring at a crack in the sidewalk. He takes Carol home but when he kisses her he jumps out of his car and runs to her apartment. After listening to the sounds of Helene and Michael making love during the night, Carol is so despondent when her sister leaves the next morning that her boss, Madame Denise (Valerie Taylor), sends her home. That night she dreams of being raped. When Colin calls, she hangs up.

After three days, Carol goes back to work but is so depressed that she cuts a customer's (Renee Houston) finger and is again sent home. Colin comes to see Carol but she will not let him in so he breaks open the door. When he tries to talk to her, she uses a candle holder to kill him. She drags his body into the bathroom, dumps it in a water-filled tub and barricades the apartment door. The landlord shows up wanting the rent money, finds the door unlocked and breaks through the barricade. He sees Carol in a passive state and she gives him the rent money. When she sits nonchalantly in front of him in a flimsy nightgown and baring most of her legs, the man mistakes her pose as an invitation for sex but when he tries to kiss her she kills him with Michael's razor. As Carol's mind completely snaps she sees the walls crack with hands emerging to grope her and the ceiling close in on her bed. Helene and Michael return from their trip and Helene discovers the apartment is a mess. She nearly goes into shock when she finds Colin's body. Michael goes to telephone for the police. Helene sees Carol in a catatonic state under her bed; when Michael returns he picks up the young woman and carries her out of the apartment.

Variety reported, "*Repulsion* is a classy, truly horrific psychological drama in which Polish director Roman Polanski draws out a remarkable performance from young French thesp, Catherine Deneuve. Polanski ... uses his technical resources and the abilities of his thesps to build up a tense atmosphere of evil ... Deneuve, without much dialog, handles a very difficult chore with insight and tact." Phil Hardy wrote in *The Encyclopedia of Horror Movies* (1986), "Although flawed ... *Repulsion* sets up the major lines of force that structure the whole of his [Polanski] work: a cinema that relentlessly questions the relation of fascination between the viewer and an audiovisual spectacle. He plays a complex game with audience expectations, identification, perceptions and generic conventions, simultaneously fascinating and unsettling the viewer, exploring the fundamental fantasies, desires and anxieties at stake in our relationship with cinema as spectacle." Ed Naha in *Horrors: From Screen to Scream* (1975) stated, "Critically acclaimed but average melodrama benefits from the directorial skills of Roman Polanski."

In *Horror in the Cinema* (1971), Ivan Butler devoted a chapter to the production in which he said, "On the bare framework of this horror story Polanski has constructed a film of such complexity and subtlety that an entire book could be written about it.... [L]ike any noteworthy film, *Repulsion* demands more than a single viewing. There is not hardly a frame which has not a dual purpose — simultaneously developing and commenting on the story."

The Return of October

(1948; 98 minutes; Color) PRODUCER: Rudolph Mate. DIRECTOR: Joseph H. Lewis. SCREENPLAY: Melvin Frank and Norman Panama. STORY: Karen DeWolf and Connie Lee. PHOTOGRAPHY: William Snyder. EDITOR: Gene Havlick. MUSIC: George Duning. MUSIC DIRECTOR: M.W. [Morris] Stoloff. ART DIRECTORS: Stephen Goosson and Rudolph Sternad. SOUND: George Cooper. SETS: William Kiernan and Wilbur Menefee. MAKEUP: Clay Campbell. COSTUMES: Jean Louis. COLOR CONSULTANT: Francis Cugat. ASSISTANT DIRECTOR: Sam Nelson. CAST: Glenn Ford (Professor Bentley "Bass" Bassett, Jr.), Terry Moore (Terry Ramsey), Albert Sharpe (Vince the Tout), James Gleason ("Uncle Willie" Ramsey), Dame May Whitty (Martha Grant), Henry O'Neill (President Hotchkiss), Frederic Tozere (Mitchell), Samuel S. Hinds (Judge Northridge), Nana Bryant (Therese), Lloyd Corrigan (Dutton), Roland Winters (Colonel Wood), Stephen Dunne (Professor Stewart), Gus Schilling (Benny), Murray Alper (Little Max), Horace McMahon (Big Louie), Victoria Horne (Margaret Grant), Byron Foulger (Jonathan Grant), Bill Pearson (Tommy), Russell Hicks (Taylor), Robert Malcolm (Detective), Ray Walker (Joe), Sam Finn, Fred F. Sears (Newsmen), Myron Healey, Paul Campbell, George Carleton (Assistant Lawyers), Charles Marsh (Court Clerk), Eddie Parker (Motorcycle Policeman), Symona Boniface (Hedwig), Arthur Space (Radio Salesman), Boyd Irwin (Jennings), Edith Arnold (Louise), Harry Tyler (Mac), Mary Newton (Posture Instructor), Eric Wilton (Butler), Matt McHugh (Ticket Seller), Garry Owen (Stable Hand Charlie), Eddie Acuff (Stable Hand), Harry Harvey (Auction Cashier), Charles Edward Adams (Auctioneer), Ralph Volkie (Court Policeman), Polly Bailey (Pekinese), Cy Schindell (Court Bailiff), Frank Wilcox (Mr. Rawlins), Esther Zeitlin (Mrs. Northridge), Emmett Vogan (Veterinarian), Virginia Wave (Stenographer), James Flavin (Detention Guard), Hazel Dohlman (Wife), Teddy Infuhr (Racetrack Imp), Jimmy Lloyd (Racetrack Man), Freeman F. Gosden, Charles J. Correll (Voices of Amos 'n' Andy), Eddie Dunn (Racetrack Cop), Hal J. Moore (Radio Announcer), Hal Mohr (Voice of Radio Announcer), Highland Dale (October the Horse).

Director Joseph H. Lewis is highly regarded in some circles for his dark, moody, horror-tinged melodramas like Columbia's *My Name is Julia Ross* (1945) and *So Dark the Night* (1946) [qq.v.], as well as his penchant for interesting camera angles and setups. In that respect his best work may be in the gangster genre with *Deadly Is the Female (Gun Crazy)* (1949) and *The Big Combo* (1955). Here Lewis helms a comedy-fantasy horse racing story that "while not calculated to change things at tracks, is an affable, whimsical comedy in which the cast, horses and backgrounds are panoplied in the pleasant hues of Technicolor and the comedy is chucklesome, if not downright abdominal ... It gives you a nice run for your money" (*New York Times*). Released in Great Britain as *A Date with Destiny*, the feature was partly shot at the University of Southern California at Los Angeles and the Del Mar Race Track and it employed Technicolor race horse footage from the 1938 20th Century–Fox feature *Kentucky*.

A sanity trial takes place to decide the competence of Terry Ramsey (Terry Moore), an eighteen-year-old who is about to inherit a fortune after the death of her aunt, Martha Grant (Dame May Whitty), and who believes her late Uncle Willie Ramsey (James Gleason) has been reincarnated as a racehorse, October (Highland Dale). Racetrack denizen Vince the Tout (Albert Sharpe), a pal of Willie's, tells how Ramsey raised his niece and bet all he had on his horse Sunset to win a big race. After the horse loses, Willie, who always claimed he would come back to life as a thoroughbred, dies, causing his niece to live with her rich Aunt Martha who is being secretly swindled by three greedy cousins (Nana Bryant, Victoria Horne, Byron Foulger). When Terry sees October at a horse auction she buys him because she believes he is her reincarnated uncle since both of them suffered from a goldenrod allergy. She outbids college psychology professor Bass Bassett (Glenn Ford). Bassett wants the horse for experimentation and agrees to pay for the animal when Terry cannot come up with the money. In return he houses the animal at the university until the teenager can repay the loan, although the president (Henry O'Neill) of the academic establishment becomes upset when he find out Bass has used school funds to buy the horse. In order to justify his actions, Bassett tells his boss he plans on writing a book on Terry's mental fixation on October since she believes it is her late uncle. As Martha is dying, the greedy relatives have their lawyer (Frederic Tozere) begin a court case to prove Terry is mentally unbalanced and not fit to inherit her aunt's estate. After writing the book, Bass begins to feel that her notion about the horse is not irrational and he tries to stop his book's publication but fails to do so just as Martha passes away. Thinking that Bass has betrayed her, Terry does not want him to testify in her defense but he is finally called and announces that his work is incorrect and that the teenager is sane. Upon his suggestion, the judge and jury go to the track with Terry to watch October race. When she starts cheering for Uncle Willie she is joined by the crowd as the horse wins. October drops dead at the finish line, but Terry knows that is the way Uncle Willie would have wanted it, and she and Bass realize they are in love.

The Return of the Vampire

(1944; 69 minutes) PRODUCER: Sam White. DIRECTOR: Lew Landers. SCREENPLAY: Griffin Jay. STORY: Kurt Neumann. ADDITIONAL DIALOGUE: Randall Faye. PHOTOGRAPHY: L.W. O'Connell and John Stumar. EDITOR: Paul Borofsky. MUSIC: Mario C. Tedesco. MUSIC DIRECTOR: M.W. [Morris] Stoloff. ART DIRECTORS: Lionel Banks and Victor Greene. SETS: Louis Diage. SPECIAL EFFECTS: Aaron Nibley. MAKEUP: Clay Campbell. CAST: Bela Lugosi (Dr. Armand Tesla), Nina Foch (Nicki Saunders), Frieda Inescort (Lady Jane Ainsley), Miles Mander (Sir Frederick Fleet), Roland Varno (John Ainsley), Matt Willis (Andreas Obry), Gilbert Emery (Dr. Walter Saunders), Leslie Denison (Detective Lynch), Ottola Nesmith (Elsa), William Austin (Detective Gannett), Jeanne Bates (Miss Norcutt), Billy Bevan (Civil Defense Worker Horace), Harold De Becker (Civil Defense Worker), Donald Dewar (John Ainsley as a Child), Sherlee Collier (Nicki Saunders as a Child), Marianne Mosner, Audrey Manners (Nurses), George McKay (Caretaker), Frank Dawson, Clara Reid (Old Couple), Jean Fenwick (Street Girl), Syd Chatton (Desk Clerk), Olaf Hytten (Butler), Stanley Logan (Colonel Mosley), Nelson Leigh (Scotland Yard Assistant).

When *The Return of the Vampire* was released early in 1944, the *Brooklyn Citizen* enthused that it "is a horror film of the first order. It is certain to send thrills and chills up and down one's spine." Seeing the financial success of Universal's return to the horror genre in the World War II years, studio chief Harry Cohn commissioned Griffin Jay to write a Dracula script for the studio, one that would star Bela Lugosi. Unfortunately for Columbia, Universal owned the rights to the Bram Stoker character and thus the title creature was dubbed Dr. Armand Tesla, but Dracula in any other guise is still the King of the Vampires, especially when enacted by Lugosi. The film's visuals were obviously influenced by the Universal horror efforts; *Return* boasts spooky, foggy graveyard and forest sets that in some ways topped the rival studio in horrific atmosphere, thanks to decorator Louis Diage and art directors Lionel Banks and Victor Greene. The feature was shot over a four-week period in the fall of 1943 with a budget slightly under $140,000; its initial box office gross was nearly four times that amount and the film remained in continual theatrical release well into the 1950s. Roland Varno replaced Michael Duane in the role of music conductor John Ainsley. The film marked Lugosi's first legitimate vampire part since *Dracula* in 1931 and it was definitely his finest horror starring role of the 1940s.

On October 15, 1918, a young woman (Jeanne Bates) is attacked by a vampire. The next night in Priory Cemetery near London, the bloodsucker, Dr. Armand Tesla (Lugosi), is called from his coffin by his servant, werewolf Andreas Obry (Matt Willis). Supposedly dead for 200 years, the Rumanian Tesla sets out to find new victims as sanitarium owner Lady Jane Ainsley (Frieda Inescort) aids Walter Saunders (Gilbert Emery), an Oxford University professor who is trying to save the life of the young girl attacked by Tesla. When she dies after an hysterical fit, Saunders tells Lady Jane that the problem is deeper than science or medicine. That night he reads an essay written by Tesla on vampirism as the bloodsucker attacks his small daughter Nicki (Sherlee Collier). When she is found near death the next morning, her father realizes she has been the victim of a vampire. Following a blood transfusion that saves the little girl's life, Saunders and Lady Jane seek out the vampire's lair and find his coffin. As Saunders drives a stake through Tesla's heart, Andreas shows up; freed from the evil curse of the vampire, he reverts to human form.

Poster for *The Return of the Vampire* (1944).

For the next two decades, Andreas works with Lady Jane as her laboratory assistant while her son John (Varno), who has returned to his work as a music conductor after being injured fighting the Germans, has become engaged to Nicki (Nina Foch), whose father was recently killed in a plane crash. Saunders' notes on the Tesla case fall into the hands of Scotland Yard chief commissioner Sir Frederick Fleet (Miles Mander), who interviews Lady Jane and tells her he plans to dig up Tesla's grave; if Tesla has a spike through his heart she may be prosecuted for murder. Before the exhumation can take place, the Germans bomb the area, destroying Priory Cemetery. Two Civil Defense workers (Billy Bevan, Harold De Becker) find Tesla's corpse and remove the stake before reburying him. That night the vampire rises from the grave, finds Andreas, turns him back into a werewolf and orders him to do his bidding. Andreas takes the vampire's coffin to the bombed ruins of a church and then follows his master's wishes in killing Dr. Hugo Bruckner, a concentration camp victim brought to England to aid the war effort. Andreas gives Tesla the murdered man's identification papers and the vampire pretends to be Bruckner and attends the engagement party Lady Jane gives for her son and Nicki. There Tesla charms Nicki and meets Sir Frederick. During the night the vampire attacks Nicki; when she is found near death the next morning, Lady Jane gives her a blood transfusion. Lady Jane meets with Sir Frederick who is skeptical of her tales of a vampire but orders two of his detectives (Leslie Denison, William Austin) to follow Andreas. The two policemen spot Andreas outside the hotel where Tesla has taken rooms, and when they try to restrain him he turns into a werewolf and flees. That night Tesla tells Nicki to kill John, whom he wants out of the way so he can have the young woman for himself. When John fails to show up to conduct a concert, his mother is alerted and she finds him with the same throat bites as Nicki. When she is sure that John will not die, Lady Jane calls in Sir Frederick and the two talk to Andreas, who runs away after they see his furry hands. The two then search Tesla's hotel room where they find Tesla's ring, convincing both of them that Bruckner is being impersonated by Tesla and that he is the vampire who attacked Nicki. Lady Jane plays the organ in her home when Tesla materializes and informs her he plans to make Nicki his own but she frightens him away with the image of a cross. When Nicki leaves the house under Tesla's command, she is followed by Sir Frederick and Lady Jane; she leads them to the cemetery where the vampire and his servant await her. The young woman faints when Sir Frederick shoots Andreas but the werewolf manages to carry her to the vampire's lair where Tesla prepares to make her his own. When Andreas implores his master to help him, Tesla orders him aside. Andreas locates a crucifix in the dust and uses it to hold off the vampire, whom he vows to destroy forever. German planes bomb the area and Tesla and Andreas, who has returned to human form, are buried in the rubble. Reviving, the dying Andreas drags the vampire into the sunlight and drives a stake through his heart. Lady Jane and Sir Frederick arrive to find Nicki free of the vampire's spell and she tells them it was Andreas who destroyed the vampire.

Regarding *The Return of the Vampire*, Arthur Lennig wrote in *The Count: The Life and Films of Bela "Dracula" Lugosi* (1974), "The film was not as good as the original *Dracula* but far better than many of Lugosi's other films. It contained some excellent atmospheric effects, especially in the graveyard, but unfortunately it had more incident than mood and more adventure than fright. Although the wolf-man creature was not very believable, Lugosi was quite impressive as the vampire." In truth, Matt Willis as the lycanthrope was no Lon Chaney when it came to pathos or being fearsome, and a talking werewolf was certainly the feature's weakest element. Clay Campbell's makeup for the wolfman, however, was very realistic and it would be used in several other studio releases, most notably the 1956 Sam Katzman production *The Werewolf* (q.v.). The film's other main weakness is having the Scotland Yard man look directly at the audience at the end and inquire if they believe in vampires.

While *The Return of the Vampire* is probably the highlight of Columbia's 1940s horror output, and one of the studio's finest genre efforts, it is not without controversy. When the vampire perishes as the finale, the special effects of melting hot wax leaving exposed facial bones showing was indeed horrific, so much so the scene was excised from British prints. The plot ploy of having the vampire attack a small girl strongly hints of pedophilia, although it should be noted that in various versions of *Dracula*, the Lucy Weston character victimized children. In one scene, Frieda Inescort, as the girl's future mother-in-law, gets a bit too touchy with Nina Foch, in a sequence that surprisingly survived the censors. Finally, even for a vampire, the Armand Tesla character was particularly evil, especially when he tells the always faithful Andreas to "crawl into the corner and die" as he plans to put the bite on Nicki.

The Revenge of Frankenstein

(1958; 90 minutes; Color) PRODUCER: Anthony Hinds. EXECUTIVE PRODUCER: Michael Carreras. ASSOCIATE PRODUCER: Anthony Nelson-Keys. DIRECTOR: Terence Fisher. SCREENPLAY: Jimmy Sangster. ADDITIONAL DIALOGUE: Hurford Janes. PHOTOGRAPHY: Jack Asher. EDITOR: Alfred Cox. MUSIC: Leonard Salzedo. PRODUCTION DESIGN: Bernard Robinson. SOUND: Jock May. MAKEUP: Philip Leakey. PRODUCTION MANAGER: Don Weeks. WARDROBE: Rosemary Burrows. CONTINUITY: Doreen Dearnaley. ASSISTANT DIRECTOR: Robert Lynn. CAST: Peter Cushing (Baron Victor Frankenstein), Francis Matthews (Dr. Hans Kleve), Eunice Gayson (Margaret Conrad), Michael Gwynn (The Monster), John Welsh (Bergman), Lionel Jeffries (Fritz), Oscar Quitak (Karl), Richard Wordsworth (Sweeper), Charles Lloyd Pack (Medical Council Head), John Stuart (Police Inspector), Michael Ripper (Kurt), Arnold Diamond (Dr. Molke), Marjorie Cresley (Countess Barscynska), Anna Walmsley (Vera Barscynska), George Woodbridge (Janitor), Ian Whittaker (Young Man), Avril Leslie (Gerda), Julia Nelson (Inga), Robert Brooks Turner (Joseph), Alex Gallier (Priest), Raymond Hodge (Exhumation Official), Eugene Leahy (Kleiner), Gordon Needham (Male Nurse), John Gayford (Footman), Middleton Woods, Freddie Watts, George Hirste, Michael Mulcaster (Patients).

Between 1958 and 1971 Columbia released 29 features in the United States made by England's Hammer Films. The fourth release was *The Revenge of Frankenstein*, issued stateside in the summer of 1958; it was a sequel to *The Curse of Frankenstein* (1957) and its plot began where the first film ended, with the execution of Baron Frankenstein (Peter Cushing). While Columbia would distribute eleven more Hammer horror films in the U.S., this was its only "Frankenstein" release.

In 1860 in the village of Ingstad, Baron Victor Frankenstein (Cushing) is led to the guillotine for the brutal murders committed by the monster he created from dead bodies. Following the execution, two grave robbers, Fritz (Lionel Jeffries) and Kurt (Michael Ripper), dig up his body for the ten marks buried with it, but when they open the grave the find the beheaded corpse of the priest (Alex Gallier) who presided over Frankenstein's execution. The baron and his crippled helper Karl (Oscar Quitak) appear, causing Fritz to die of fright as Kurt runs away. Frankenstein was not executed because Karl bribed the local officials. Three years later, the scientist and his assistant are in the village of Carlsbruck where Frankenstein is known as Dr. Victor Stein. Not only does he have a successful medical practice but he also ministers to indigents at the Poor Hospital. After refusing an offer to join the local Medical Council, Frankenstein is visited by one of its members, Dr. Hans Kleve (Francis Matthews), who tells him that he knows his true identity and that he wants to work with him in his experiments. Frankenstein agrees to Kleve's request in return for his silence and shows him the laboratory where he has continued his experiments in creating life. He exhibits a human body awaiting only a brain which he tells Hans will be given by Karl, who wants to be normal. Margaret Conrad (Eunice Gayson), the niece of a countess (Margery Cresley), volunteers to work at the hospital and Karl becomes infatuated with her. Frankenstein and Kleve successfully place Karl's brain in his new body but they are forced to keep him strapped in bed in an attic room until his wounds heal. They are spied upon by the hospital's sweeper (Richard Wordsworth). When Kleve informs Karl that Frankenstein plans to show him off to other scientists along with his now embalmed former body, the newly created man becomes upset. The sweeper brings Margaret to see Karl and she feels pity for him, loosens his bonds and tells him to come see her at the countess' estate. While talking with the sweeper, Kleve realizes that Frankenstein's pet chimp, also a brain transplant experiment, is a meat eater while chimpanzees only consume plants. He confronts Frankenstein about his but the scientist tells him there was an accident with the chimp and that Karl will not become a cannibal. Karl escapes from the attic and goes to Frankenstein's laboratory and burns his old body. But he is seen by the sadist janitor (George Woodbridge) and during a fight he kills the man. Frankenstein and Kleve find Karl has gone and at the laboratory they come across the murdered janitor.

Karl hides in the barn at the countess' estate. Margaret finds him there and goes for Kleve when Karl begs her not to tell Frankenstein of his whereabouts. Karl begins to lose feeling in his right side and when Kleve and Margaret go to find him, they realize the creation has escaped. Developing a lust for human flesh, Karl attacks and murders a young woman (Avril Leslie). That night Frankenstein and Kleve question Margaret about Karl. During a musical recital the creation shows up in a deformed physical state and calls out the name Frankenstein before dying. Later Dr. Molke (Arnold Diamond) urges the Medical Council to declare that Dr. Stein is really Baron Frankenstein but the scientist denies the charge. The council orders Frankenstein's body exhumed and finds the decapitated priest. Frankenstein is attacked and brutally beaten by the Poor Hospital's inhabitants; Kleve takes the dying scientist back to the laboratory where he removes his brain. When the police inspector (John Stuart) arrives with the Medical Council members, Kleve declares Baron Frankenstein is dead. After they leave, Kleve transplants the baron's brain into a new body that the scientist had earlier created. Several months later, the two men are set up in medical practice in London's Harley Street West with Frankenstein now using the name Dr. Franck.

Although tame by today's standards, *The Revenge of Frankenstein* offered its audiences such then-stomach turners as floating eyeballs, dismembered body parts and bloody brain removals. Richard Klemensen in *Little Shoppe of Horrors* #4 (1978) felt the feature was "much superior to its predecessor.... [A] very, very well done film, that benefits from the ingenious characters like the 'monster' played by Michael Gwynn. By now, Hammer had realized it was the Baron as personified by Peter Cushing that interested the movie goers — not any lumbering monster." In *The Encyclopedia of Horror Movies* (1986), Phil Hardy noted, "[Jack] Asher's gloriously saturated Technicolor photography helps to make this one of the most complex and intelligent treatments of the story to date." David Quinlan in *British Sound*

Riders in the Sky

(1949; 69 minutes) PRODUCER: Armand Schaefer. DIRECTOR: John English. SCREENPLAY: Gerald Geraghty, from the story "A Fool and His Gold" by Herbert A. Woodbury. PHOTOGRAPHY: William Bradford. EDITOR: Henry Batista. MUSIC DIRECTOR: Mischa Bakaleinikoff. MUSIC SUPERVISOR: Paul Mertz. SONGS: Jimmie Davis, Stan Jones and Floyd Tillman. ART DIRECTOR: Harold MacArthur. SOUND: George Cooper. SETS: Frank Kramer. ASSISTANT DIRECTOR: Paul Donnelly. CAST: Gene Autry (Himself), Champion (World's Wonder Horse), Pat Buttram (Chuckwalla Jones), Gloria Henry (Anne Lawson), Mary Beth Hughes (Julie Stewart), Robert Livingston (Rock McCleary), Steve Darrell (Ralph Lawson), Alan Hale, Jr. (Marshal Riggs), Tom London (Pop Roberts), Hank Patterson (Stagecoach Driver Luke), Ben Welden (Bartender Dave), Dennis Moore (Bud Dwyer), Joe Forte (Willard Agnew), Kenne Duncan (Travis), Frank Jaquet (Coroner), Roy Gordon (District Attorney J.B. Galloway), Loie Bridge (Widow Cathart), Vernon Johns (Blaisdale), Pat O'Malley (Lowry), John Parrish (Sam Devlin), Bud Osborne (Parkhurst), Lynton Brent (Croupier), Isabel Withers (Secretary Companion), Stan Jones (Singing Cowboy), Boyd Stockman, Kermit Maynard (Henchmen), Sandy Sanders (Sandy), Tom Smith, Cactus Mack (Bar Customers), Herman Hack, Lee Phelps (Jurors), Robert Walker, Denver Dixon, Jack Evans (Citizens).

Working title: *Beyond the Purple Hills.*

While working in Death Valley, Ranger Stan Jones composed the song "Ghost Riders in the Sky," which he later sold to Gene Autry, who was making the feature *Beyond the Purple Hills* for Columbia with filming at the Iverson Ranch and Pioneertown. Columbia executives were so impressed with the song that they incorporated it into the movie, changing the film title to *Riders in the Sky*. Based on a *Ranch Romances* magazine story by Herbert A. Woodbury, it was a typical sagebrush yarn that was greatly highlighted by Autry singing Jones' song with phantom horsemen on 20 white steeds riding through the skies. Don Miller in *Hollywood Corral* (1976) termed the feature "superior," adding, "It had a clever screenplay ... and particularly noteworthy directorial touches by John English, including an atmospheric depiction of the title tune enacted by Tom London as the old cowpoke who went ridin' out one dark and windy day, etc. English and [cinematographer William Bradford] teamed for some brooding photographic effects combined with apt use of close-ups of London's seamed and weather-beaten face, to produce one of the more haunting vignettes in Westerns." *Variety* called it "a fairly entertaining range fable that adds up into strong b.o. [box office] entry for the action situations."

Gene Autry (playing himself) tells friends of the events behind the song "Ghost Riders in the Sky": Gambler Sam Devlin (John Parrish) is murdered and Pop (London), an old cowboy, witnesses the crime. At a coroner's jury, rancher Ralph Lawson (Steve Darrell) testifies that he shot the gambler in self-defense after finding out he was cheating in a card game they were playing. Gambler Rock McCleary (Robert Livingston) dominates the town and keeps other witnesses from speaking out; Lawson is convicted and sent to jail. Real estate broker Anne Lawson (Gloria Henry), Ralph's daughter, blames state investigator Autry for her father's conviction. Autry, who has inherited a great deal of money from his late uncle, rides to Desert Wells with his pal Chuckwalla Jones (Pat Buttram) and enlists Anne's help in looking for a ranch to buy, although the area is plagued with alkaline water. McCleary has purchased Lawson's ranch and sells the water rights to mining engineer Willard Agnew (Joe Forte), who plans to mine beneath the property. The gambler has some of his henchmen ambush Pop, causing his water wagon to crash and fatally injuring the old man. Found by Autry just before dying, Pop confirms Lawson's testimony about shooting Devlin in self-defense. Autry gets into a card came with McCleary and reveals he is cheating. A brawl ensues but is halted when the sheriff (Alan Hale, Jr.) arrives, saying Lawson broke jail. Locating the escapee at his daughter's real estate office, Autry learns the truth about Devlin's killing and turns Lawson over to a posse for safekeeping. Julie Stewart (Mary Beth Hughes), who entertains in McCleary's saloon, confirms Lawson's side of the story and agrees to testify for him if Gene will purchase the Lawson ranch from McCleary without water rights. Gene checks the well on the ranch and learns that its water comes from an irrigation ditch; Anne informs him that state law does not permit land and water rights be divided. In a confrontation with McCleary, Gene forces him to own up to the Devlin and Pop Roberts killings. Lawson is freed from jail, becoming Autry's associate.

Made by Gene Autry Productions, *Riders in the Sky* not only highlighted the Jones song but also had the star singing the traditional western ballad "Streets of Laredo," along with Governor

Jimmie Davis and Floyd Tillman's country classic "It Makes No Difference Now." "Ghost Riders in the Sky" was one of the most popular songs in 1949–50: It was a million-selling record for Vaughn Monroe on Victor Records plus charted platters for Burl Ives and Bing Crosby on Decca and Peggy Lee on Capitol.

The ballad has been revived successfully several times, including recordings by the Ramrods on the Amy label and Lawrence Welk on Dot Records in 1961, the Baja Marimba Band on A&M in 1966, Roy Clark on Dot in 1973, Johnny Cash on Columbia in 1979 and the Outlaws on the Ari label in 1981. The Shadows charted with the song in England in 1980 on the EMI label.

A Safe Place

(1971; 94 minutes; Color) PRODUCER: Bert Schneider. DIRECTOR-SCREENPLAY: Henry Jaglom. PHOTOGRAPHY: Richard C. Kratins. EDITOR: Pieter Bergems. PRODUCTION DESIGN: Harold Schneider. SOUND: Fred Bosch. PRODUCTION MANAGER: Robert Barron. COSTUMES: Barbara Flood. CAST: Tuesday Weld (Susan/Noah), Orson Welles (Magician), Phil Proctor (Fred), Jack Nicholson (Mitch), Dov Lawrence (Dov), Gwen Welles (Bari), Sylvia Zapp (Young Susan), Fanny Birkenmier (Maid), Rhonda Alfaro (Little Girl), Francesca Hilton, Barbara Flood, Jennifer Walker, Julie Robinson, Richard Finnochio, Roger Garrett, Jordan Hohn (Friends).

British actor Henry Jaglom made his film directorial debut with *A Safe Place*, which he originally wrote as a play. Upon the recommendation of Dennis Hopper, with whom Jaglom had appeared in *Easy Rider* (1969), Columbia agreed to finance the project, which debuted at the New York Film Festival in the fall of 1971, causing a near riot due to heated audience division over its artistic merits. *The Free Press* called it "an important milestone in the art of the motion picture" while *Leonard Maltin's 2004 Movie and Video Guide* (2003) felt it was a "[s]paced-out, waterlogged fantasy..." *Time Out Film Guide, 9th Edition 2001* (2000) noted, "Jaglom's composition is sufficiently coherent, and Tuesday Weld's performance adds a real focus point. The result is sometimes indulgent, often fragile, and occasionally enchanting." Henry Herz and Tony Zaza in *The Family Guide to Movies on Video* (1988) opined, "[T]he movie has no substance beyond its self-conscious attempt to reflect the way a disoriented mind copes with the passage of time." The feature got virtually no release in the United States and only minor showings in Great Britain and Europe before Columbia pulled it from circulation, taking a financial loss on the production.

The muddled plot concerns a strange young woman (Tuesday Weld), who calls herself Noah, a name she has taken from a toy Noah's Ark given to her by a magician (Orson Welles) in New York's Central Park when she was a little girl (Sylvia Zapp). He also gave her a levitating silver ball and a star ring and now that she is grown up and living alone he often reappears in her life, much of which is a fantasy as she yearns for her past. Noah has a level-headed but vapid boyfriend, Fred (Phil Proctor), and a lusty lover, Mitch (Jack Nicholson), but neither of them can make her happy or bring fulfillment to her life. While she desires to be a productive, independent woman, Noah also longs for the security of her childhood. The combination and the pressures of the various forces in her life result in Noah's literally disappearing.

Jaglom called the feature "an essay on time and memory." Its soundtrack included vintage vocals by Fred Astaire, Buddy Clark, Helen Forrest, Vera Lynn, Dinah Shore, Charles Trenet and Edith Piaf. Footage of Welles as the magician also appeared as a TV movie in Jaglom's 1983 feature *Can She Bake a Cherry Pie?* The play *A Safe Place* was staged in Los Angeles in 2003 starring Tanna Frederick.

Savage Mutiny

(1953; 73 minutes) PRODUCER: Sam Katzman. DIRECTOR: Spencer G. Bennet. SCREENPLAY: Sol Shor. PHOTOGRAPHY: William Whitley. EDITOR: Henry Batista. MUSIC DIRECTOR: Mischa Bakaleinikoff. ART DIRECTOR: Paul Palmentola. SETS: Sidney Clifford. UNIT MANAGER: Herbert Leonard. ASSISTANT DIRECTOR: Carter DeHaven, Jr. CAST: Johnny Weissmuller (Jungle Jim), Angela Greene (Joan Harris), Lester Matthews (Major Walsh), Nelson Leigh (Dr. Parker), Charles Stevens (Chief Wamai), Paul Marion (Lutembi), Gregory Gaye (Carl Kroman), Leonard Penn (Emil Bruno), Ted Thorpe (Paul Benek), George Robotham (Johnson), Tamba (Chimp).

Savage Mutiny, the eleventh film in Columbia's "Jungle Jim" adventure series, was one of its weaker outings, stuffed with stock footage and putting too much emphasis on the comic antics of Jim's (Johnny Weissmuller) pet chimp Tamba. The most exciting scene was a battle between the jungle man and a panther; much of the footage was lifted from *Jungle Jim in the Forbidden Land* (q.v.), issued the previous year. Only borderline horror elements like superstitious natives, devil masks and evil omens were part of Sol Shor's script although the introduction of a near-futuristic radioactive uranium sprayer was somewhat novel, especially since the U.S. government was considering such a weapon at the time of the feature's release early in 1953. *Variety* opined, "Latest 'Jungle Jim' entry lacks the straightforward approach of former entries in series, which will cause it to be sloughed even in the program market ... Spencer G. Bennet generally is unable to rise above the unconvincing elements of script in his direction ... and Sam Katzman apparently gave the film the once-over-lightly treatment..."

After rounding up foreign spies near Mogamba, Jungle Jim (Weissmuller) reports to Major Walsh (Lester Matthews) in Dangor and is introduced to Dr. Parker (Nelson Leigh), an atomic weapons expert, who informs him that, with the enemy agents out of the way, the path is clear for Jungle Project X, the first atom bomb test in Africa. Parker asks Jim to help evacuate the natives from the island of Tulongan, where the bomb will be dropped. Traders Carl Kroman (Gregory Gaye) and Emil Bruno (Leonard Penn) are unhappy when they can no longer barter with the Tulongans although in reality they are spies blackmailing Paul Benek (Ted Thorpe), Parker's associate, for information about the atomic test. World Health Organization worker Joan Harris (Angela Greene) goes with Jim to the island to inoculate the natives and help him get them to the mainland. When they arrive on Tulongan, Jim and Joan find Kroman and Bruno there, not realizing they are provoking tribe member Lutembi (Paul Marion) in trying to keep the natives in their villages. After Jim beats Lutembi in a fight, Chief Wamai (Charles Stevens) agrees to the evacuation. The spies set up several evil omens along the trail, causing the tribe to halt their journey to the coast. As Jim looks into the matter, Kroman sets loose a panther that attacks the chief. Jim kills the beast, but the chief is badly injured. By the next day, Wamai is able to go to the mainland with his tribe and settle near Dangor. When Kroman learns from Benek that the test is all set, he uses a machine to spray radioactive dust on the tribe which results in the natives becoming ill and planning to return to their island. The spies want to use photographs of the destroyed island, with the Tulongans on it, to get worldwide support for the stoppage of U.S. and British atomic testing. As Joan and Dr. Parker try to find the source of the radioactive contamination, Jim trails Benek to Kroman's camp and overhears him objecting to the plans to kill off the tribe. When Jim confronts the men, Kroman stabs Benek. Carl and Bruno head to the Tulongan camp to convince the chief to return to his island. There the spies tie up Joan and Dr. Parker while the wounded Benek tells Major Walsh of his traitorous activities. The major wants to halt the test but finds Kroman has sabotaged his only radio. Jim heads down river in a canoe in a desperate attempt to stop the tribes' return home. He is forced to kill both the spies when they try to stop him. After he unties the natives' canoes, he is captured by the tribesmen. He tells the chief and Lutembi that they can kill him if the great fire god does not destroy their island. Just after sunrise, the atomic bomb is dropped on Tulonga. Chief Wamai, witnessing its destructive power, frees Jim, Joan and Dr. Parker.

Scream of Fear

(1961; 81 minutes) PRODUCER-SCREENPLAY: Jimmy Sangster. EXECUTIVE PRODUCER: Michael Carreras. DIRECTOR: Seth Holt. PHOTOGRAPHY: Douglas Slocombe. EDITOR: Eric Boyd-Perkins. MUSIC: Clifton Parker. MUSIC SUPERVISOR: John Hollingsworth. PRODUCTION DESIGN: Bernard Robinson. SOUND: E. Mason and Len Shilton. SPECIAL EFFECTS: Les Bowie. PRODUCTION MANAGER: Bill Hill. MAKEUP: Basil Newall. CONTINUITY: Pamela Mann. ASSISTANT DIRECTOR: David Tomblin. CAST: Susan Strasberg (Penelope "Penny" Appleby/Maggie Fencheau), Ronald Lewis (Robert), Ann Todd (Jane Appleby), Christopher Lee (Dr. Pierre Gerrard), John Serret (Inspector Legrand), Leonard Sachs (Mr. Spratt), Anne Blake (Marie), Fred Johnson (Mr. Appleby), Bernard Browne (Gendarme), Richard Klee, Frederick Rawlings (Detective Sergeants), Frederick Schrecker, Heinz Bernard, Brian Jackson (Police Officers), Rodney Burke (Policeman), Madame Lobegue (Airline Hostess).

In the early 1960s, Hammer Films made a series of psychological horror thrillers commencing with *Taste of Fear*, which Columbia distributed in the United States in the late summer of 1961 as *Scream of Fear*.* Contemporary

---

*Columbia also issued stateside two other titles in this series, Maniac *(1963)* and Die! Die! My Darling! *(1965) [qq.v.].*

reviewers took a shine to the feature as *Time* dubbed it "[c]hiller con carne.... A couple of nasty surprises have been stirred into the routine ingredients of this unsavory little chiller..." Brendan Gill in *The New Yorker* thought it "one of the most complicated thrillers on record." Allen Eyles, Robert Adkinson and Nicholas Fry in *The House of Horror: The Story of Hammer Films* (1973) felt it was "a splendid exercise in squeezing thrills out of a clichéd story ... well scripted by Jimmy Sangster, superbly photographed by Douglas Slocombe, and directed with dazzling skill for precisely right effect by Seth Holt." In *The Encyclopedia of Horror Movies* (1986), Phil Hardy called the feature a "a contrived but excellently directed [Seth] Holt movie, which also marks [Jimmy] Sangster's production debut. The script, as usual with Sangster, is a mechanical piece of suspense-mongering, which sacrifices logic and verisimilitude to achieve the mandatory number of shocks and 'twists' at the end.... [T]he picture's main asset is Holt's canny direction which, skillfully assisted by Slocombe's photography, expertly builds up the mood of incipient insanity."

Three weeks after the police bring up the body of a young woman from a lake in Switzerland, the wheelchair-bound Penelope "Penny" Appleby (Susan Strasberg) arrives in the French Riviera to stay with her father (Fred Johnson) and stepmother, Jane Appleby (Ann Todd), at their villa near Nice. Penny is picked up at the airport by the handsome family chauffeur, Robert (Ronald Lewis), and taken to the villa where she meets Jane for the first time. Robert tells Penny that her father had gone away on business four days before and that he has been ill for some time. At dinner, Penny informs her stepmother that she and her mother lived in Italy after her parents divorced and three weeks ago her best friend Maggie drowned. That night Penny is awakened by a slamming door and goes in her wheelchair to the villa's summer house where she finds her father's dead body in a chair. Hysterically she rolls away and falls into a swimming pool but is saved by Robert. He later takes her back to the building where there is no corpse. She is treated by Pierre Gerrard (Christopher Lee), her father's physician, who tells her it is her imagination and that she is suffering from the strain of travel. The next day Penny tells Robert that she was a neurotic child who was afraid of everything. The two go to the shore where Penny informs the chauffeur that she lost the use of her legs nine years before when a horse fell on her. Later she gets a telephone call from a man claiming to be her father, saying he will be home in two days. At dinner Gerrard warns the girl to be careful of her mental state. That night Penny goes into the garage and sees the small car her father was supposed to have driven when he went away. Hearing someone playing the piano in the music room, she goes there only to find it empty. Later in her room she again sees her father propped up in a chair but by the time she gets Robert they find the chair empty although he feels its fabric and finds it to be soaking wet. Robert then surmises to Penny that if she was declared incompetent and her father was dead, her stepmother would inherit the estate. She begins to feel that Jane and Dr. Gerrard, whom she believes are lovers, are trying to drive her mad. At dinner Gerrard tells Penny she may not be able to walk because of hysterical paralysis and she informs him that the horse fall broke her back in two places. The next day she tells Robert that she wants to go to the police but he says they have no proof against Jane and Gerrard. Later, when Robert kisses Penny, they are observed by her stepmother. The next night, Robert dives into the pool and finds Penny's father's body. They set out for the police station at Cannes but on the road they are flagged down by Jane. As Robert gets out of the car to go to Jane, the vehicle begins to roll backward and just before it plunges into the sea Penny sees her father's corpse in the front seat. Back at the villa, Robert informs Jane that he killed her husband and she expresses regret at having to murder Penny in order for them to get the estate. In an interview with Inspector Legrand (John Serret), Jane says her husband and Penny had gone for a drive when the accident occurred. Her solicitor, Mr. Spratt (Leonard Sachs), informs her that she cannot inherit until after the coroner's verdict is rendered. As the police raise the vehicle from the sea and only find the corpse of a man in it, Spratt informs Jane that her stepdaughter committed suicide three weeks before in Switzerland. Jane then sees Penny sitting in her wheelchair on a bluff over the ocean and goes to talk with her. The woman she thought was Penny is really her best friend Maggie, who reveals that she became suspicious because Penny's father knew about her suicide. She then contacted Dr. Gerrard for help and when Jane and Bob tried to kill her, she jumped out of the car before it crashed. The solicitor meets Robert, who is returning to the villa after seeing the car raised, and tells him to go to Jane. Maggie leaves and

Jane absent-mindedly sits in the wheelchair. Seeing Jane from the back, Robert thinks it is Penny and pushes her over the bluff onto the rocks below. Inspector Legrand then arrests the chauffeur as Maggie and Dr. Gerrard leave the villa.

Scream of Fear ran 81 minutes although some United Kingdom prints clocked in at 78 minutes. When the feature was issued to British television in 1972, its running time was 90 minutes.

See No Evil

(1971; 89 minutes; Color) PRODUCERS: Martin Ransohoff and Leslie Linder. ASSOCIATE PRODUCER: Basil Appleby. DIRECTOR: Richard Fleischer. SCREENPLAY: Brian Clemens. PHOTOGRAPHY: Gerry Fisher. EDITOR: Thelma Connell. MUSIC: Elmer Bernstein. ART DIRECTOR: John Hoesli. SETS: Hugh Scaife. COSTUMES: Evelyn Gibbs. MAKEUP: Stuart Freeborn. PRODUCTION MANAGER: Jilda Smith. CONTINUITY: Pamela Carlson. ASSISTANT DIRECTOR: Terry Marcel. CAST: Mia Farrow (Sarah), Dorothy Alison (Betty Rexton), Robin Bailey (George Rexton), Diane Grayson (Sandy Rexton), Brian Rawlinson (Barker), Norman Eshley (Steve Reding), Paul Nicholas (Jacko), Max Faulkner (Frost), Scott Fredericks, Reg Harding (Stablemen), Lila Kaye (Gypsy Mother), Barrie Houghton (Jack), Michael Elphick (Tom), Donald Bisset (Doctor).

Near an English town, Sarah (Mia Farrow) is driven by her uncle George Rexton (Robin Bailey) and his wife Betty (Dorothy Alison) to their country place, Manor Farm. The young woman, who recently lost her sight due to falling from a horse, has come to live with her relatives, including George and Betty's daughter, Sandy (Diane Grayson). After a few days, Sarah's former boyfriend, Steve Reding (Norman Eshley), invites her to go horseback riding at his farm and there she meets Reding's horse groom, Jacko (Paul Nicholas). While she is riding with Steve, a maniac kills her relatives. After she gets home, Sarah is unaware they are dead. The next morning Steve comes back with a chestnut horse for Sarah, who had planned to go to London to study physiotherapy. She tells him she will stay at Manor Farm and they go for a ride and resume their romance. Back home she starts to take a bath, stumbles over the corpses of her relatives and runs through the house, falling into the cellar. Getting back upstairs, she finds the family gardener, Barker (Brian Rawlinson), who tells her he was shot by a man who killed her aunt, uncle and cousin. Before dying, he informs her that the murderer left a bracelet behind. As the man returns, Sarah attempts to phone the police but finds the lines cut. She runs to the stable, cutting her foot on a piece of glass. Sarah manages to ride away on her horse but is knocked off by a tree branch in the forest.

Finding her way to a gypsy camp, she is helped by a woman (Lila Kaye) whose son Tom (Michael Elphick) agrees to drive her to the police. After finding out about the bracelet, Tom thinks it belongs to his brother Jack (Barrie Houghton) and drives Sarah to a deserted building near a clay pit and locks her inside. The horse goes back to Reding, who enlists the aid of Jacko and another worker (Max Faulkner) in trying to locate the girl; they go to Manor Farm where they find the four dead bodies. Breaking out of the shack, Sarah tries to draw attention by pounding scrap metal. The men hear her and Steve takes her home where a doctor (Donald Bisset) bandages her cut foot. Thinking the gypsies are the culprits, Reding leaves Sarah with Jacko and goes to find them while Tom locates his brother and confronts him with the bracelet. Jack denies owning it and claims to have gone to Manor Farm to see Sandy but found no one there. When Steve finds the two men, they show him the bracelet which has the killer's name inscribed on it. They all head back to Reding's place where Jacko is trying to drown Sarah in a bathtub. Reding saves her from the maniac.

Filmed in Great Britain by Filmways Pictures and Genesis Productions, *See No Evil* was distributed in the U.S. by Columbia in the fall of 1971 with the studio also releasing it in its homeland as *Blind Terror*. Costing over $1 million, the production failed to recoup that amount in stateside showings. This is somewhat surprising since star Mia Farrow had a popular following at the time due to her appearing for two seasons (1964–66) on the ABC-TV series *Peyton Place* and starring in the feature films *Rosemary's Baby* (1968) and *John and Mary* (1969). It was not until she did *The Great Gatsby* (1974) that her box-office pull revived from the downturn it took with *See No Evil*.

Video Hound's Golden Movie Retriever 1991 (1991) thought the film was "[c]hilling and well crafted." James O'Neill in *Terror on Tape* (1994) wrote, "Farrow is great in this tense mix of *Psycho* and *Wait Until Dark*.... Edge-of-your-seat thrills until a somewhat slack final third; nice autumnal photography and a pretty Elmer Bernstein score." The author also noted that the film was the final first-run movie screened at Radio City Music Hall in New York City. In *The Family Guide to Movies on Video* (1988), Henry Herz and Tony Zaza called it an "[e]ffective British thriller," adding, "Though director Richard Fleischer doesn't play quite fair in his emotional manipulations, he achieves some high-intensity terror found in the best of Hitchcock. The violence is more implicit than explicit but its aura of psychological horror is not meant for youngsters to handle."

One interesting aspect of this taut horror thriller was the juxtaposition of the peaceful family and riding scenes with those of the crazed killer who is shown leaving a porno movie house, vandalizing the Rextons' auto, watching female dancers in a bar and discovering his missing bracelet while washing the blood of his hands following the murders. The killer's face is not revealed until the finale when he tries to drown Sarah while she bathes.

La Señora Muerte (The Death Woman)

(1969; 85 minutes; Color) PRODUCER: Luis Enrique Vergara. EXECUTIVE PRODUCER: Jorge Garcia Besne. DIRECTOR: Jaime Salvador. SCREENPLAY: Ramon Obon, Jr. PHOTOGRAPHY: Alfred Uribe. EDITOR: J. Juan Munguia. MUSIC: Gustavo Cesar Carreon. SOUND: Ing. Heinrich and Guillermo Carrasco. SETS: Raul Cardenas. PRODUCTION DESIGN: Jose Mendez and Octavio Ocampo. ASSISTANT DIRECTOR: Tito Novaro. CAST: John Carradine (Dr. Fadel), Regina Torne (Marlen), Elsa Cardenas (July), Miguel Angel Alvarez (Tony Winter), Isela Vega (Lisa), Victor Junco (Andres), Fernando Oses (Lieutenant Henry), Alicia Ravel (Patricia), Patricia Ferrer (Sara), Carlos Ortigoza (Luis), Carlos Ancira (Laor), Mario Orea (Doctor), Nathanael Leon (Coroner), Cristine Rubisles, Lucrecia Munoz (Models), Tito Novaro (Pianist), Marcelo Villami (Spectator).

In the late 1960s, John Carradine starred in four Mexican horror films for producer Luis Enrique Vergara filmed at Estudios America in Mexico City. In both *La Señora Muerte* and *Las Vampiras* (q.v.), the actor found himself to be the only English-speaking performer in the casts and his voice was dubbed in the Spanish-language versions that were released in the United States by Columbia. Both features were lensed in 1967 but it took two years before they got stateside showings. Carradine did two other horror features for Vergara, *Enigma de Muerte* (Enigma of Death) and *Pacto Diabólico* (Diabolical Pact)

Regina Torne in *La Señora Muerte* (1969).

Advertisement for *La Señora Muerte* (1969).

(both 1969), which Columbia released. There was also a fifth Mexican horror film done by Carradine during the same period, *Autopsia de un Fantasma* (Autopsy of a Ghost) (1967), for Películas Nacionales.

La Señora Muerte opens with Carradine introducing what he calls a "story of love and death." The film begins with middle-aged Andres (Victor Junco) making love to his beautiful young wife Marlen (Regina Torne). Andres has cancer and when he suffers from terrible pain he begs Marlen to call Dr. Fadel (Carradine), much against her wishes. Fadel's experiments have caused him to be expelled from the medical profession and he operates in his own laboratory assisted by the deformed Laor (Carlos Ancira). Fadel uses his new inventions on Andres but without success and when he mixes the blood of the married couple it causes Marlen to suffer from premature aging. The doctor offers them a cure if they will provide him with fresh blood for needed transfusions. For the love of her husband and fear of the aging process and Fadel, Marlen begins a series of murders to get the necessary blood. The first victim is Patricia (Alicia Ravel), a designer at the House of Models, who works with Marlen. Tony Winter (Miguel Angel Alvarez), Patricia's boyfriend, is suspected of the killing since he has been having an affair with another model, Lisa (Isela Vega). Marlen murders Lisa for her blood, leaving the body in the basement of the modeling business. When questioned about the killings by Lieutenant Henry (Fernando Oses), Marlen hints at the coincidence of the two murdered women both being involved with Tony. Marlen goes to her friends Sara (Patricia Ferrer) and Luis (Carlos Ortigoza) who have opened a wax museum which includes a chamber of horrors with figures of Dracula, Frankenstein's monster and the wolf man. When the two find out about Marlen's murders, she is forced to kill them. She then calls July (Elsa Cardenas) to the House of Models on the pretext of giving her a job but the hysterical model manages to escape and go to the police. The dying Marlen returns to Fadel so he can save her with the blood she has taken from her victims. Laor is attracted to her; when she rejects him, he connects high voltage cables to the equipment being used by his master, electrocuting Dr. Fadel and destroying the laboratory. Marlen dies trying to escape. As Lieutenant Henry explains the case to the coroner (Nathanael Leon), Laor watches as Marlen's face returns to normal.

The 7th Voyage of Sinbad

(1958; 88 minutes; Color) PRODUCER: Charles H. Schneer. ASSOCIATE PRODUCER–SPECIAL VISUAL EFFECTS: Ray Harryhausen. DIRECTOR: Nathan Juran. SCREENPLAY: Kenneth Kolb. PHOTOGRAPHY: Wilkie Cooper. EDITORS: Edwin Bryant and Jerome Thoms. MUSIC: Bernard Herrmann. ART DIRECTOR: Gil Parrendo. SOUND: John Livadary. SETS: Jose Alguero. PRODUCTION SUPERVISOR: Luis Roberts. SPECIAL EFFECTS ASSISTANT: George Lofgren. COLOR CONSULTANT: Henri Jaffa. STUNT SUPERVISOR: Enzo Musumeci-Greco. TITLE DESIGN: Bob Gill. ASSISTANT DIRECTORS: Eugenio Martin and Pedro de Juan. CAST: Kerwin Mathews (Captain Sinbad), Kathryn Grant (Princess Parisa), Richard Eyer (Barani the Genie), Torin Thatcher (Sokurah), Alec Mango (Caliph of Bagdad), Danny Green (Karim), Harold Kasket (Sultan of Chandra), Alfred Brown (Harufa), Nana de Herrera (Handmaiden Sari), Nino Falanga, Luis Guedee (Sailors), Virgilio Telxeira (Ali).

One of the all-time great adventure film classics, *The 7th Voyage of Sinbad* was released late in 1958 by Columbia, having been filmed earlier in the year in Spain using Dynamation, "The New Miracle of the Screen." The special visual effects by Ray Harryhausen were then done in London over a six-month period. This was the first complete color film to use stop motion animation. A Morningside Production, it was filmed at a cost of $650,000 but has a much more expensive look. The giant creatures created by Harryhausen include a Cyclops, a four-armed dancing part-human, part-serpent woman, a two-headed Roc bird and its hatchling, a sword-wielding skeleton and a fire-breathing serpent. Kerwin Mathews was acceptable as Sinbad although Kathryn Grant was too cutesy as the princess. Torin Thatcher was excellent as the evil magician, a part that would have been perfect for Bela Lugosi. The same year *The 7th Voyage of Sinbad* was released, director Nathan Juran, billed as Nathan Hertz, also did *Attack of the 50 Foot Woman* and *The Brain from Planet Arous*.

On the way back to Bagdad with a peace promise from the sultan of Chandra (Harold Kasket) and with the ruler's daughter, Princess Parisa (Grant), as his fiancée, Captain Sinbad (Mathews) anchors his ship off the coast of the island of

Kerwin Mathews battles a skeleton in *The 7th Voyage of Sinbad* (1958).

Colossa in order to get food and water for his crew. On the isle they find huge cloven hoof prints in the sand as they search for fresh water; they spy a cave whose opening is the mouth of a stone mask. Magician Sokurah (Thatcher) comes running out of the cave, pursed by a giant Cyclops. As the monster attacks the intruders, the magician calls up a genie (Richard Eyer) from the magic lamp he possesses and orders him to put up an invisible barrier between them and the creature. The men make it to their boats but the magician drops the lamp, which is retrieved by the monster. Back aboard Sinbad's ship, Sokurah wants to return to the island for the lamp, saying that 100 years of treasure gathered by the Cyclops from sunken ships awaits them. Sinbad refuses his request because he must be back in Bagdad to preserve the peace between it and Chandra.

In Bagdad, the caliph (Alec Mango) is pleased with Sinbad's peace mission as well as his beautiful betrothed. Parisa's father soon joins them for a wedding feast at which Sokurah displays his magic that includes turning the princess' shrewish handmaiden (Nana de Herrera) into a dancing, four-armed snake woman and then returning her to normal. Both the caliph and the sultan ask Sokurah to foretell the future and he announces there will be war between Bagdad and Chandra and again asks for support in returning to Colossa. This angers the caliph, who warns the seer to be out of the city by the next day or his eyes will be plucked out. Sokurah goes to the princess' bedchamber that night and produces a mist which causes her to become tiny. When she is discovered the next day, the caliph informs the sultan that his city will be turned to rubble as Sinbad finds Sokurah and asks him to help return his fiancée to normal. The magician agrees but says he will need to return to Colossa for various charms that he needs to brew a potion to restore Parisa to her right size. Unable to get a crew, Sinbad and his loyal friend Harufa (Alfred Brown) go to the city's prison yard where he enlists criminals who are about to be hung, promising them the riches gathered on Colossa by the Cyclops. Placing Parisa in a small decorated container, Sinbad and Harufa set sail with the new crew whose leader Karim (Danny Green) plans to mutiny. On board is a giant crossbow and arrow which Sinbad plans to use to kill the Cyclops.

After a week, the crew mutinies and the captured Sinbad, Harufa and Sokurah are locked in the hold. The magician predicts destruction for the mutineers and a strong wind blows the ship southward to an island where wailing demons drive the crew to madness; the captured men shut out the sounds by putting waxed rags in their ears. Set free, Sinbad takes control of the vessel and they land near Colossa with the surviving men bringing the crossbow and arrow on shore. Sinbad leads one group of men into the valley of the Cyclops while Sokurah and another group try to find the magic lamp. When Sinbad's men locate the treasure in the Cyclops' cave, the giant beast appears and places them in a cage. Hearing the commotion, the magician goes to see what has happened while his men get drunk from a pool of wine. The intoxicated sailors then try to attack the Cyclops, who crushes them with a tree trunk. The princess manages to push the lock off the top of the cage and set the men free. The magician finds the lamp as the Cyclops puts Harufa over a spit, planning to roast him for dinner. The giant chases the seer into some rocks where he and Sinbad fight the giant with Sinbad using a torch to put out the creature's eye. He then leads him to the edge of a gorge where the Cyclops falls to his death. Refusing to give Sokurah the lamp, Sinbad and his crew climb treacherous cliffs in order to find the egg of the giant two-headed Roc bird. A piece of the egg is needed for the potion to return Parisa to normal. Two starving sailors break open the first egg they find; a two-headed hatchling attacks them and they kill and eat it. With the egg shell, Sokurah tells Sinbad he must return to his underground castle to get the other elements needed for the potion but since Sinbad does not trust the magician he has Parisa enter the magic lamp to ask the genie the secret of how to call him out. She finds the genie is a young boy named Barani who tells her he is lonely but cannot return to the real world until his name is called. She promises to help him get free and returns to Sinbad with the phrase he needs to call the genie. A huge Roc bird attacks Sinbad, causing him to drop the lamp. Harufa throws it to Sinbad; Sokurah kills Harufa. The bird carries Sinbad to its nest and then flies away.

Reviving, Sinbad climbs out of the nest and calls up the genie who tells him Sokurah has taken Parisa to his castle where the entrance is protected by a chained, fire-breathing dragon. Getting past the giant reptile, Sinbad confronts the magician and forces him to mix the potion that restores his fiancée to normal. As the two try to leave the grotto, Sokurah calls up a skeleton that engages in a sword fight with Sinbad, who lures it to a rock bluff and knocks it over, causing the skeleton to shatter. Sokurah then destroy a bridge over a river of lava that Sinbad and Parisa need to cross in order to get out the cave. They beckon the genie who gives them a rope so they can get free. Once they are safe, Sinbad and the princess throw the lamp into the lava, so the genie can be released from his captivity. As they leave the cave, another Cyclops arrives; Sinbad frees the dragon which kills the beast. As they run to the ship, Sokurah orders the dragon to follow and destroy the lovers but they get back to the ship's crew on the beach and Sinbad uses the giant crossbow and arrow to slay the dragon, who falls on the magician and crushes him. Back on the ship, Sinbad and Parisa are pleased to find Barani is their cabin boy. He tells them he has prepared a feast for them, which turns out to be the treasure of the Cyclops.

Variety called *The 7th Voyage of Sinbad* "a bright, noisy package.... [T]his isn't the sort of film in which performers matter very much. It's primarily entertainment for the eye, and the action moves swiftly and almost without interruption. Ray Harryhausen, who was responsible for the visual effects, emerges as the hero of this piece." "A spectacle to end all spectacles brought to life by the expert hand of Ray Harryhausen ... A superb screen fantasy for both old and young," is how Ed Naha referred to the feature in *Horrors from Screen to Scream* (1975). *The Phantom's Ultimate Video Guide* (1989) termed it "[o]ne of the most popular fantasy films ever made" while Danny Peary in *Guide for the Film Fanatic* (1986) raved, "Wondrous adventure is a major source of inspiration for most of today's fantasy-film directors, who were kids when it came out and had never seen anything like it." Dennis Fischer in *Science Fiction Film Directors, 1895–1998* (2000) called it "one of the most rousing adventure movies ever made."

One of the highlights of the feature is the music score by Bernard Herrmann. The soundtrack was issued by Colpix Records (CP-504) in 1959, but only on monaural; the first stereo recording was released on LP in 1983 by Varese Saraland (STV-81135). In 1998 the same label released the complete score on compact disc (5961), with the soundtrack performed by the Royal Scottish National Orchestra conducted by John Debney.

There was also a tie-in comic book of *The 7th Voyage of Sinbad*, published by Dell Comics in 1958. The feature was reissued theatrically in 1975.

The Shadow

(1937; 58 minutes) ASSOCIATE PRODUCER: Wallace MacDonald. DIRECTOR: C.C. Coleman, Jr. SCREENPLAY: Arthur T. Horman. STORY: Milton Raison. PHOTOGRAPHY: Lucien Ballard. EDITOR: Byron Robinson. MUSIC DIRECTOR: Morris Stoloff. ART DIRECTORS: Stephen Goosson and Lionel Banks. SOUND: John Livadary. COSTUMES: Kalloch. ASSISTANT DIRECTOR: Bob Farfan. CAST: Rita Hayworth (Mary Gillespie), Charles Quigley (Jim Quinn), Marc Lawrence (Kid Crow), Arthur Loft (Sheriff Jackson), Dick Curtis (Carlos), Vernon Dent (Dutch Schultz), Marjorie Main (Hannah Gillespie), Donald Kirke (Senor Peter Martinet), Dwight Frye (Vindecco), Bess Flowers (Marianne), William Irving (Deputy Sheriff Mac), Eddie Featherston (Deputy Sheriff Woody), Sally St. Clair (Dolores), Sue St. Clair (Rosa), John Tyrrell (Mr. Moreno), Beatrice Curtis (Mrs. Moreno), Ann Doran, Beatrice Blinn (Shaw Sisters), Bud Jamison, Harry Strang (Ticket Takers), Francis Sayles (Mr. Shaw), Edward Hearn (Doctor), Edward LeSaint (Coroner Bascomb), Harry Bernard (Night Watchman Jerry), Ernie Adams (Dan), Ted Mangean (Masked Figure), George Hickman (Messenger).

Working title: *Carnival Lady*.

Between 1937 and 1939 Columbia teamed Rita Hayworth and Charles Quigley in six feature films, four of them for producer Irving Briskin's unit. *The Shadow*, issued late in 1937, was the third release. Called *The Circus Shadow* in England, it marked the first movie in which Hayworth got top billing, thus starting her on the path to becoming "The Love Goddess" of the next decade. The highlight of *The Shadow*, which has no relationship with the long-running radio show of the same title, is Lucien Ballard's low-key photography, with most of the action taking place at night in shadowy circus backgrounds. Besides the plot of a black-cloaked phantom killer using poisoned darts, the production also offers genre favorite Dwight Frye as yet another physically deformed character, this time a groom who hates his sadistic master. Overall, the film is a compact murder mystery with horror overtones augmented by good production values and a superb cast.

Following the sudden death of her father, Mary Gillespie (Hayworth) has to manage a circus, Col. Gillespie's Big Show. She does so with the help of publicist Jim Quinn (Quigley), her boyfriend. Members of the carnival troupe include Mary's aunt, Hannah Gillespie (Marjorie Main), who acts as ringmaster Mademoiselle Laverne; ex-boxer and roustabout Kid Crow (Marc Lawrence); famed bareback rider Senor Martinet (Donald Kirke), who is physically abusive to his deformed groom Vindecco (Frye); knife thrower Carlos

(Dick Curtis), clown Dutch Schultz (Vernon Dent), palm reader Marianne (Bess Flowers) and Siamese twins Dolores (Sally St. Clair) and Rosa (Sue St. Clair).

When the show opens at a new locale, Sheriff Jackson (Arthur Loft) pays a courtesy call. Mary shows him a Jivaro blow gun and darts that her father had acquired for his trophy board. That night Mary informs the troupe that the circus is now solvent and she will be able to pay their salaries but Martinet produces notes signed by her father for $60,000 and says that unless they are settled he will take possession of the show the next day. Jim tells Mary he will try to help her save the outfit and he asks the other employees to loan her money but Marianne predicts there will be a trio of murders. Later, Jim stops Martinet from beating Vindecco. A cloaked figure steals the blow gun and darts but is spied by Crow who gives chase but is knocked out by the phantom. When someone throws a knife at Jim, they suspect Carlos but he claims one of his knives is missing. Just before a performance, Martinet informs the Siamese twins that show freaks will not be allowed in the main tent when he takes over the circus. During the show, the bareback rider falls from his horse and is pronounced dead and the sheriff takes over the investigation as the performance continues. The lawman later questions all the circus folk and Hannah tells him that everyone hated Martinet. Vindecco finds a poisoned dart in an ornament on the horse his master was riding and hides it. Jim and the sheriff go through the dead man's possessions and learn that he was once married. Vindecco goes to see Mary and they discover that the blow gun and darts are missing. The groom tells her that the murdered man was his brother and they had once rode together in an act with yet another Martinet, whom Vindecco suspects is the killer. Mary confides to Jim about Vindecco being Martinet's brother as Jim finds the dart. He places it in Mary's safe, where he also finds the missing promissory notes, just as they are informed by Crow that Vindecco has been murdered by another poisoned missile. As Jim goes to investigate, Mary is attacked in her quarters by the cloaked phantom but manages to fight off the killer. When Sheriff Jackson questions the performers, Jim informs him that Mary had the motive, darts and notes and that she should be arrested for the murders. As the lawman takes Mary to jail, Kid Crow slugs Jim who then tells everyone that their boss' life is in danger and that he framed her so that she would be put behind bars where she will be safe. When Jim promises to catch the murderer, Crow tells him and Hannah that he was the one who put the notes in the safe (the colonel had given him the combination). While searching the circus grounds, Jim is attacked by the phantom and left for dead after he has bitten the killer's wrist. The publicist then calls the sheriff who brings Mary back to the circus where Jim eliminates each of the performers by calling up their alibis, saying the killer is a woman, Martinet's wife. Marianne then confesses to the crimes but Jim uses a saber to cut the strap binding Dolores to Rosa and accuses Dolores of killing her husband and brother-in-law by revealing the bite mark on her wrist. The young woman confesses to the murders and is taken away by the sheriff as Mary promises to let Jim be her man.

In *The Films of Rita Hayworth* (1974), Gene Ringgold wrote that the feature must "have impressed screenwriters Aben Kandel and Herman Cohen because, some thirty years later, they devised an almost identical 'original' story, *Berserk* (q.v.), which, filmed in England by Columbia Pictures, starred a ludicrously miscast Joan Crawford. Granted they expanded the plot and changed the killer's identity but other similarities between the films are too numerous to have been totally coincidental."

Shadow of the Hawk

(1976; 92 minutes; Color) PRODUCERS: John Kemeny and Herbert Wright. DIRECTOR: George McGowan. SCREENPLAY: Norman T. Vane. STORY: Norman T. Vane, Lynette Cahill, Peter C. Jensen and Herbert Wright. PHOTOGRAPHY: John Holbrook and Reginald H. Morris. EDITOR: O. Nicholas Brown. MUSIC: Robert McMullin. ART DIRECTOR: Keith Pepper. SETS: Peter Young. SOUND: George Mulholland. COSTUMES: Bob Watts and Ilse Richter. MAKEUP: Phyllis Newman. PRODUCTION MANAGER: Bob Gray. SPECIAL EFFECTS: Richard Albain and John Thomas. ASSISTANT DIRECTORS: Ronald L. Schwarz and Jim Scott. CAST: Jan-Michael Vincent (Mike aka Young Hawk), Marilyn Hassett (Maureen), Chief Dan George (Old Hawk), Pia Shandel (Faye), Marianne Jones (Dsonqua), Jacques Hubert (Andak), Cindi Griffith (Secretary), Anna Hagan (Desk Nurse), Murray Lowry (Intern), Terry York (Monster).

Filmed near Vancouver, British Columbia, during the spring of 1976 on a $1.8 million budget, *Shadow of the Hawk* was released theatrically by Columbia in the summer of that year to tepid box office returns. Highlighted by beautiful Canadian forest scenery, the feature top-billed then-popular Jan-Michael Vincent and Marilyn Hassett but it did nothing to enhance their careers. Vincent later headlined the TV series *Airwolf* in which he played a pilot called Hawke, the same character name as in this outing. For horror fans the feature offered a 200-year-old witch and her evil curse, wildlife (bear, snake) gone awry, a rope bridge that self-destructs, a bewitched automobile, Indian spirits, devil dolls, a water monster and an invisible wall. Despite all of these genre ingredients, the feature was no more than a "tired, TV-style chase movie" according to *Time Out Film Guide, 9th Ed. 2001* (2000). Donald C. Willis in *Horror and Science Fiction Films II* (1982) thought it was "[t]he poor-man's *Manitou*.... The dialogue is equally pathetic." *Shadow of the Hawk* did predate *The Manitou* by two years as a Native American supernatural thriller but overall it was mostly a combination of *The Devil Rides Out* (1968) and *The Exorcist* (1973). In *The Family Guide to Movies on Video* (1988), Henry Herz and Tony Zaza called it a "[t]erribly amateurish movie.... [T]he story is awfully far-fetched and not particularly scary."

Canadian businessman Mike (Vincent) is visited in his Vancouver home by his dying grandfather, Old Man Hawk (Chief Dan George), who wants the young man to take him on a 200-mile journey to his native village. Mike, who has long forsaken the ways of his Indian people, has been having visions of a white-faced mystical mask that disturbs his sleep and even torments him while swimming with Faye (Pia Shandel), his girlfriend. The old man tells Mike that a 200-year-old tribal feud has erupted between himself and Dsonqua (Marianne Jones), a witch who was executed two centuries before but who has returned and is trying to kill him. Since Mike is his grandson, thus Young Hawk, the sorceress is also out to eliminate him. The elder Hawk needs to return to his people in order to be able to destroy the enchantress for good.

Journalist Maureen (Hassett) becomes interested in the old man's story and asks to accompany them to the Indian village. Driving through the dense, misty Canadian forests, they are harassed by white-painted faced tribesmen who appear and vanish, a bear and a snake, a strange car with black windows and several mechanical failures of Mike's vehicle. Despite the witch's attempts to kill them, the trio reaches the village where Mike confronts Dsonqua in a mystic ritual in which the demon takes on other forms.

Shadow of the Past

(1950; 83 minutes) PRODUCERS: Mario Zampi and Mae Murray (not the popular Hollywood star of the silent era). DIRECTOR: Mario Zampi. SCREENPLAY: Ian Stuart Black and Aldo De Benedetti. STORY: Aldo De Beneditti. PHOTOGRAPHY: Hone Glendinning. EDITOR: Guilio Zampi. MUSIC: Stanley Black. ART DIRECTOR: Ivan King. SOUND: Tommy Meyers. PRODUCTION MANAGER: Victor Peck. CAST: Joyce Howard (The Lady in Black), Terence Morgan (John Harding), Michael Medwin (Dick Stevens), Andrew Osborn (George Bentley), Wylie Watson (Caretaker), Marie Ney (Mrs. Bentley), Ella Redford (Daily Help), Ronald Adam (Solicitor), Louise Gainsborough (Susie).

Mario Zampi (1903–63), a native of Italy, worked in British cinema for more than three decades and from 1938 to 1961 he directed a number of features including 1948's *The Fatal Night* (q.v.). His *Shadow of the Past* was a co-production of Anglofilm and Mario Zampi Productions, with distribution in Great Britain and the U.S. by Columbia Pictures. David Quinlan in *British Sound Films: The Studio Years 1928–1959* (1984) called it "[m]odest but quite tense; twists in the plot are well concealed."

John Harding (Terence Morgan) is staying with friends (Andrew Osborn, Marie Ney) when he spies a deserted house across the street and sees the ghostly Woman in Black (Joyce Howard) prowling around the place. He learns the house is owned by Dick Stevens (Michael Medwin), whose wife was killed two years before in an automobile wreck; since that time the house has been vacant except for a caretaker (Wylie Watson). John investigates and discovers the specter is really the twin sister of the dead woman; she suspects that her brother-in-law killed his wife and made it look like an accident. Harding agrees to aid her in exposing the killer.

Shadows in the Night

(1944; 67 minutes) PRODUCER: Rudolph C. Flothow. DIRECTOR: Eugene J. Forde. SCREENPLAY-STORY: Eric Taylor, from the radio series by Max Marcin. PHOTOGRAPHY: James S. Brown, Jr. EDITOR: Dwight Caldwell. ART DIRECTOR: John Dafu. SETS: Sidney Clifford. CAST: Warner Baxter (Dr. Robert Ordway), Nina Foch (Lois Garland), George Zucco (Frank Swift), Edward Norris (Jess Hilton), Lester Matthews (Stanley Carter), Ben Welden (Nick Kallus), Jeanne Bates (Adele Carter), Minor Watson (Frederick Gordon), Charles C. Wilson (Sheriff), Charles Halton (Dr. Stacey), Arthur Hohl (Riggs), Isabel Withers (Mrs. Riggs).

Working title: *Crime Doctor's Rendezvous*.

At 3 A.M. during a violent thunderstorm, Dr.

Robert Ordway (Warner Baxter), a psychiatrist, is visited by commercial artist Lois Garland (Nina Foch), a beautiful young woman who asks for his help. She tells him that she has been having terrible nightmares about the specter of a woman who comes into her bedroom out of the fog, dripping wet. The figure motions for Lois to follow her to the sea near her coastal home at Rocky Point. Afraid she will not live until morning, the young woman says she fears she may be going insane; Ordway questions her about suicidal tendencies, which she denies. When he declines her invitation to come to her home and recommends she check into a hotel for the night, Lois angrily leaves, unaware that she is being followed by Nick Kallus (Ben Welden), her cook. Ordway realizes they had been spied upon when he finds wet footprints on the hall carpet and an open window with its lock broken. The next night the psychiatrist drives to Ravencliff, the woman's home, where he is met at the gate by Kallus and welcomed by Lois who introduces him to her sister Adele Carter (Jeanne Bates) and Adele's out-of-work actor husband Stanley (Lester Matthews). Lois suggests to Ordway that they exchange bedrooms for the night. While he is sleeping, a vapor engulfs the psychiatrist's room and he falls into a trance as the apparition of a woman beckons him to follow her to the sea. He falls over some rocks and is awakened by Frank Swift (George Zucco), Lois' uncle.

Going back to the house, Ordway sees a dead body at the top of the stairs and awakens Lois, but now the corpse is missing. When he tells her he too saw the specter, the woman realizes she is not going mad. The next morning the doctor finds the corpse on the beach and Lois identifies him as her employer, textile manufacturer Raymond Shields. Ordway tells Lois to call the police. Back at the house, her lawyer Frederick Gordon (Minor Watson) says Shields died accidentally while Nick implies it was murder. The local sheriff (Charles C. Wilson) and coroner (Charles Halton) are both skeptical when Ordway tells them about the disappearing body. At breakfast the doctor meets another houseguest, Jess Hilton (Edward Norris), who was Shields' partner. Ordway stumbles onto Swift's laboratory in a shack on the beach and learns from the industrial chemist that he is developing a new fabric that can be made cheaply and that all the proceeds will go to his niece. The doctor intentionally drops a vial containing a substance he has mixed, causing a gaseous vapor, and

Warner Baxter, Ben Welden, Nina Foch, Edward Norris in *Shadows in the Night* (1944).

Swift orders him back to the house. Lois and Jess discuss the fact that Shields' death has removed an impediment to their being wed since the deceased had also asked to marry the girl. Wanting to talk to Gordon, Ordway goes to the wrong room and finds a picture of a young boy; Adele says he is her stepson. The lawyer informs Ordway that Carter's first wife was from a wealthy steel manufacturing family and that he has been trying to convince Lois to stop opening her home to practically all comers, since it is keeping her broke. Exploring the house, the doctor goes into the cellar where he finds a laundry chute and stairs going to a cave that leads to the sea. Near the mouth of the cave he finds a broken candlestick. Nick follows him and uses a gun to force Ordway to go back upstairs. The psychiatrist manages to get the weapon, and the cook admits following his boss to Ordway's house on the night of the storm, fearing she was being blackmailed. He asks the doctor to testify at the inquest that Shields' death was accidental so that Lois will not be accused of the crime.

Ordway goes to Lois' room and shows her the candlestick, which he says was the weapon used to kill Shields. She informs him that Nick once served time for accidental homicide. She begs the doctor not to tell the sheriff about the candlestick, fearing that Jess will be blamed for the murder since he will inherit the textile business (being Shields' partner). While Ordway is asleep that night, he is again put in a stupor by the vapor and a figure wearing a gas mask comes into the room and finds the candlestick. Riggs (Arthur Hohl), the caretaker, is killed by the intruder. When the doctor awakens and finds Riggs, he calls the sheriff and alerts the household. Carter says that his wife is unconscious. Ordway finds out she has been drugged and when the sheriff and coroner return he tells them the two killings took place because the victims knew the identity of the person using the hypnotic vapor. He also says that Shields' body was moved by pushing it down the laundry chute. When the coroner slides down the same route to the basement, Ordway goes to Lois' room and then climbs into the attic where he finds out that an air conditioning duct could have been used by someone to overhear their conversation about his finding the candlestick. In the attic he also sees an envelope addressed to Gordon containing a white powder and a bottle of acid; when he pours it on the powder, the vapor materializes. Gordon tells him he threw away the envelope which contained legal papers regarding his representing Carter in a custody case over his son. Lois accuses the lawyer and her brother-in-law of trying to use the boy to extort money out his rich former in-laws; she had promised to testify against Carter since he has stolen $4,000 from a charity. When the candlestick along with a rubber mask and wig are tossed down the laundry chute, they are found by the sheriff and the coroner who take them to Ordway. The trio find Carter bound hand and foot in the locked clothes closet, saying he had been accosted. When all of the members of the household are together, Ordway and the sheriff have the coroner pretend to be the apparition and the doctor uses the vapor to turn the coroner into a sleepwalker. He has Nick demonstrate how a person can tie themselves hand and foot and announces that the key to the locked closet was found hidden inside that small room. Ordway says that Carter was trying to drive Lois insane so she could not testify against him in the custody battle. When Carter tries to escape, he is shot and wounded by the sheriff.

Shadows in the Night was the third entry in Columbia's "The Crime Doctor" series, based on the popular CBS radio program of the same title that was broadcast from 1940 to 1947. This polished murder mystery, with a superb cast, veered into the realm of the horror film with its creepy underground passage, fog-like vapor and the appearance of a ghostly figure that was used to drive the heroine insane. To further solidify its genre status, horror favorite George Zucco was cast as a red herring, the heroine's uncle and an industrial chemist who suffered a nervous breakdown after fifteen people died as a result of one of his formulas gone awry.

Critics liked *Shadows in the Night*. *Variety* called it "better than average" and the *New York Daily News* said it was "satisfactorily suspenseful." Jon Tuska in *The Detective in Hollywood* (1978) thought it "was by far the best entry in the Crime Doctor series." Director Eugene J. Forde was an old hand at borderline horror in mysteries like *Charlie Chan in London* (1934), *The Great Hotel Murder* (1935), *Charlie Chan's Murder Cruise* (1940), *Sleepers West* (1941) and *The Crimson Key* (1947).

The series would also touch on the supernatural in its next outing, *Crime Doctor's Courage* (q.v.), issued the following year.

The Silencers

(1966; 102 minutes; Color) PRODUCER: Irving Allen. ASSOCIATE PRODUCER: Jim Schmerer. DIRECTOR: Phil Karlson. SCREENPLAY: Oscar Saul, from the novels *The Silencers* and *Death of a Citizen* by Donald Hamilton. PHOTOGRAPHY: Burnett Guffey. EDITOR: Charles Nelson. MUSIC: Elmer Bernstein. SONGS: Elmer Bernstein and David Mack. ART DIRECTOR: Joe Wright. SOUND: Lambert Day. SETS: George R. Nelson. UNIT MANAGERS: Ralph Black and Sergei Petschnikoff. COSTUMES: Moss Mabry. MAKEUP: Ben Lane. CHOREOGRAPHY: Robert Sidney. ASSISTANT DIRECTOR: Clark Paylow. CAST: Dean Martin (Matt Helm), Stella Stevens (Gail Hendricks), Daliah Lavi (Tina), Cyd Charisse (Sarita), Victor Buono (Tung-Tze), Arthur O'Connell (Wigman), Robert Webber (Sam Gunther), James Gregory (MacDonald), Nancy Kovack (Barbara), Roger C. Carmel (Andreyev), Beverly Adams (Lovey Kravezit), Richard Devon (Domino), David Bond (Dr. Naldi), John Reach (Traynor), John Willie (Master of Ceremonies), Frank Gerstle (Frazer), Grant Woods (Radio Operator), Robert Phillips, Bill Couch, Dirk Evans, Chuck Hicks, Gary Lasdun (Armed Men), Todd Armstrong, Myron Cook, Scotty Perry, Tom Steele, Thomas A. Sweet, Richard Treeter (Guards), Barbara Burgess, Susan Holloway, Karen Lee, Victoria Lockwood, Gay MacGill, Gigi Michel, Pamela Rodgers, Margaret Teele, Rita Thiel, Marilyn Tindell, Jan Watson (Slaymates), Guy Wilkerson (Farmer), John Daheim (Student Guard), Pat Hawley (Bartender Eddie), Harry Holcombe (Agent X), Robert Glenn (FBI Agent), Ray Montgomery (Agent C), Leoda Richards, Jeffrey Sayre (Club Patrons), Larri Thomas, Anna Lavele (Specialty Dancer), Inga Nielsen (Statue), Vincent Van Lynn (Agent Z), Amadee Chabot (Blonde), Carol Cole (Waitress), Sol Gorss (Pilot), Frank Hagney (Drunk), Thomas Horton, Bruce Ritchey (Hunters), Art Koulias (Engineer), Grace Lee (Oriental), Nelson Leigh, Ted Jordan, Pat Renella, Robert Ward, Cosmo Sardo, Joe Gray (Men), Vicki Carr (Singing Voice of Sarita).

The Silencers was originally intended as a spy thriller in the same vein as the popular James Bond series starring Sean Connery. But with the signing of crooner Dean Martin to play Matt Helm, the script was turned into a tongue-in-cheek spoof whose outlandish plot involved world domination by a secret organization, gadgets (a pistol that shoots backwards, exploding buttons, a station wagon with a folding bed and bar), plenty of scantily clad young women and music. The admixture resulted in an empty-headed, silly, colorful, fast-moving and fairly entertaining affair that spawned three follow-ups (*Murderers' Row* [1966], *The Ambushers* [1967] and *The Wrecking Crew* [1969] (qq.v.)), each descending after the other in quality. In *The Great Spy Pictures* (1974), James Robert Parish and I noted, "Martin's portrayal lies in his tried and true public assets: a sleepy-eyed delivery put across in the casualest of manner, with heavy (pseudo) emphasis on booze, broads and boorishness. As an added attraction, Martin's Matt Helm occupies an idealized bachelor pad, complete with a motorized round bed, swimming pool, and a bevy of 'Slaygirls.'" The film proved to be a big success with a domestic gross of over $7 million.

The Brotherhood for International Government and Order (Big O) orders a hit on retired ICE (Intelligence and Counter Espionage) agent Matt Helm (Martin), who now works as a photographer. MacDonald (James Gregory), the head of ICE, recommends Helm for a new assignment but Helm prefers his companion, Lovey Kravezit (Beverly Adams). Big O agents Andreyev (Roger C. Carmel) and Domino (Richard Devon) are summoned to a secret subterranean bunker by Tung-Tze (Victor Buono) who announces that American scientist Dr. Naldi (David Bond) is going to provide them with the plans for an underground atomic test. Sent by Big O, beautiful Barbara (Nancy Kovack) shows up at Helm's house and tells him she has been sent by MacDonald but when she tries to stab him she is shot by Tina (Daliah Lavi), Helm's former partner at ICE. She announces the young woman was a Big O agent and when the two are attacked by more of the organization's minions they make a successful escape and head to Phoenix where Naldi is to deliver the plans. At the hotel, Helm has a run-in with clumsy Gail Hendricks (Stella Stevens), who is there with her boyfriend, Sam Gunther (Robert Webber). That night Helm and Tina attend a show starring singer-dancer Sarita (Cyd Charisse), who is shot while performing. Before dying, she gives Gail the tape from Naldi. The two ICE agents abduct the young woman and take her to Helm's room where he strips her and gets the tape. When Gail tries to make a telephone call, a deadly gas is released from the phone and they barely survive. MacDonald arrives and tells Helm about Operation Fallout, a nuclear conspiracy hatched by Big O; the tape contains the timetable for a planned U.S. underground atomic test. He also says that the person behind the plot is known as Cowboy. When Gail admits Sarita gave her the tape, MacDonald arrests her. In order to keep out of prison, Gale agrees to accompany Matt to the small town of San Juan where Big O agents are supposed to get the tape. MacDonald and Helm secretly agree to use the young woman to catch the conspirators and Matt is provided with two secret weapons, a gun that shoots in reverse and exploding buttons. On their way to San Juan, Helm and Gail are attacked by Andreyev and Domino who try to crush them in separate cars but the ICE agent manages to elude them and the two Big O operators end up crashing into each other. After spending the night together in Helm's station wagon in the desert, he and Gail reach San Juan and stop at a service station run by Wigman (Arthur O'Connell). MacDonald informs Helm that he has only five hours to stop Big O from firing a rocket that will crash into the area of the underground test and cause radiation fallout over the entire Southwest. He also tells him that Tina has been abducted by the conspirators. Wigman, a Big O operative, overhears the conversation and with Gunther captures Helm and Gail, who are taken to the underground bunker. There Tung-Tze says the U.S. will blame the Russians for the atomic fallout, thus leading to a nuclear conflict with his organization taking over the world. Cowboy turns out to be Tina, who tells Helm that she wants to keep him alive but he refuses her advances. Tina is killed by one of Helm's button bombs; he also blows up an underground control room. When Gunther tries to shoot Gail, he kills himself with the reverse firing gun. Tung-Tze asks Helm to join his organization and he promises to save Gail but when Helm refuses, the madman turns a laser weapon on him. After Helm blows up more of the complex, killing Wigman, Tung-Tze gets the drop on him but Helm shoots the Oriental with the gun and then causes the Big O rocket to crash. After returning home, Helm refuses MacDonald's phone calls in favor of being with Gail.

Reviews for *The Silencers* were mixed. *Newsweek* said, "It's no story at all, but rather a succession of diffuse, adolescent references to eccentric events." The *New York Times* opined, "Another parody of James Bond, spies and sex, this one is loud, fast, obvious and occasionally funny, with Martin behaving exactly as you'd expect, with a continual wink and ready fists.... Phil Karlson's direction is speedy and most of the girls are knockouts." In *The Espionage Flexography* (2001), Paul Mavis wrote, "[I]t's funny for what it is—a cheap Bond imitation—but nothing more. It should never have been a series, but this one cleaned up at the box office and spawned three more sequels.... Funny as camp—once."

Vicki Carr dubbed Cyd Charisse singing the title song in *The Silencers* and she also did the same for the dancer's tune "Santiago" in the film's big production number. These vocals, along with the film's other music (conducted by composer Elmer Bernstein), were issued on the movie's soundtrack album in 1966 by Victor Records (LOC/LSO-1120). The same year Reprise Records released "Dean Martin as Matt Helm Sings Songs from *The Silencers*" (R/RS-6211). Besides crooning part of his theme song, "Everybody Loves Somebody Sometime," Martin did snippets of a number of popular tunes in the movie although the lyrics were changed to fit the film's plotline. These included "Anniversary Song," "Empty Saddles," "The Glory of Love," "If You Knew Susie," "The Last Roundup," "On the Sunny Side of the Street," "Red Sails in the Sunset," "Side By Side" and "South of the Border." Joi Lansing also sang the movie's title theme on a Scopitone short and Vicki Carr's rendition was later on the soundtrack of *Confessions of a Dangerous Mind* (2002).

Silent Rage

(1982; 103 minutes; Color) PRODUCERS: Anthony B. Unger and Andy Howard. ASSOCIATE PRODUCER: Aaron Norris. DIRECTOR: Michael Miller. SCREENPLAY: Joseph Fraley. PHOTOGRAPHY: Robert C. Jessup and Neil Roach. EDITOR: Richard C. Meyer. MUSIC: Peter Bernstein and Mark Goldenberg. ART DIRECTOR: Jack Marty. MAKEUP: Del Armstrong. SETS: Derek R. Hill. COSTUMES: Christy Haines. EXECUTIVE IN CHARGE OF PRODUCTION: Paul Lewis. ASSISTANT DIRECTORS: Robert P. Cohen and Alice West. CAST: Chuck Norris (Sheriff Dan Stevens), Ron Silver (Dr. Tom Halman), Steven Keats (Dr. Phillip "Phil" Spires), Toni Kalem (Alison Halman), William Finley (Dr. Paul Vaughn), Brian Libby (John Kirby), Stephen Furst (Deputy Charlie), Stephanie Dunnam (Nancy Halman), Joyce Ingle (Mrs. Sims), Jay De Plano (Biker Leader), Lillette Zoe Raley (Tattooed Biker Woman), Mike Johnson (Café Biker), Linda Tatum, Kathleen Lee (Biker Women), James Bodeen (Bar Biker), John Barrett (Institute Doctor), Desmond Dhooge (Guard Jimmy), Joe Farago (Emergency Room Doctor), Russel Higginbotham, Eddie Galt, David Unger (Boys), Sonny Jones, Sandy Lang (Deputies), Paul Selzer (Waitress).

Martial arts expert and karate champion Chuck Norris headlined a number of popular violent action films in the late 1970s and 1980s, including *Good Guys Wear Black* (1979), *The Octagon* (1980), *Eye for an Eye* (1981), *Forced Vengeance* (1982), *Lone Wolf McQuade* (1983), *Missing in Action* (1984), *Missing in Action 2: The Beginning* (1985), *Code of Silence* and *The Delta Force* (both 1986). Sandwiched among these combat outings was the sci-fi affair *Silent Rage*, filmed in Texas by Topkick Productions and distributed by Columbia, which had a domestic gross of $10.5 million. Way too long at 103 minutes, it was padded with slow-paced drug and suspense sequences that tried to augment a slim plot. The only real excitement came in an out-of-context sequence in which Norris wipes up a gang of bikers in a sleazy roadside bar. While the feature tended to borrow plot themes from *Carrie* (1976), *Halloween* (1978) and *The Shining* (1980), it mainly appears to be a reworking of *Indestructible Man* (1956), without the positive presence of Lon Chaney.

In a small Texas town, mentally unstable John Kirby (Brian Libby) calls his physician, Dr. Tom Halman (Ron Silver), and warns him he can no longer cope. Unable to bear the strain of living at his boarding house, Kirby takes an axe and murders his landlady (Joyce Ingle) and another boarder before being taken into custody by Sheriff Dan Stevens (Norris). The madman breaks his handcuffs and tries to escape before being shot by the police; near death, he is taken to a nearby by institute dealing in genetic research. There he is operated on by Halman, Dr. Spires (Steven Keats) and Dr. Vaughn (William Finley); in trying to save Kirby's life, Spires uses an untested drug, Monogen 35, on him.

At the institute, Stevens sees Alison Halman (Toni Kalem), Tom's sister and the sheriff's former lover, who is now the office manager. She and the lawman have not seen each other for six years. The three doctors agree to let Kirby die, but after Halman leaves, Spires and Vaughn bring the killer back to life although he remains unconscious. Stevens and Alison resume their sexual relationship. Later, the sheriff has a run-in with a biker (Jay De Plano) and his gang, ordering them out of town. At the institute, Spires and Vaughn show Dr. Halman the accelerated healing process on Kirby but Halman still wants to terminate the psychopath's life. Unbeknownst to the doctors, he has regained consciousness. Stevens and his deputy Charlie (Stephen Furst) have a showdown with the bikers at a bar and the lawman uses his martial arts abilities to defeat the gang. Unsure about getting back together with Stevens, Alison tells him she wants a relationship and the two plan a trip to the country. Kirby escapes from the institute and goes to Dr. Holman's house and tries to kill him. The doctor shoots him but his wounds quickly heal. Holman's artist wife Nancy (Stephanie Dunnam) returns home to find her husband murdered. Trying to elude the madman, she too is killed. Alison, who lives with her brother and his wife, gets ready to go off with Stevens but sees the dead bodies and becomes hysterical. Stevens arrives at the house as Kirby escapes. Going back to the institute, Kirby is met by Spires and Vaughn. Spires tells the sheriff he will give him Halman's files as the lawman is seeking clues to who killed the doctor and his wife. Realizing that Kirby killed their colleague, Spires and Vaughn agree to terminate the now superhuman fiend but after Vaughn gives him a shot of sulfuric acid, Kirby revives and plunges a syringe through his neck. Spires finds Vaughn's body and is then murdered by Kirby, who also attempts to kill Alison, who has come to the clinic accompanied by Deputy Charlie. When Charlie tries to defend her, Kirby crushes his spine. Kirby is pushed out of a high window by Stevens as the two fight. As Stevens and Alison leave the institute, Kirby revives. Alison hits him with a van she is driving but he clings to the vehicle. Stevens and Alison jump out of the van as it bursts into flames and crashes. Kirby, who is on fire, jumps into a river and emerges. He chases the lawman and the young woman to a deserted cabin where the two men fight. Stevens eventually knocks out Kirby and drops him down a deep well. As Stevens and Alison leave, Kirby rises from the well's depths.

The editors of *Consumer Guide* and Jay A. Brown in *Rating the Movies: From Home Video, TV, and Cable* (1985) stated, "There's an interesting sci-fi angle here, but it's handled awkwardly.... This could be stuff of which sequels are made." Stephen Jones in *The Essential Monster Movie Guide* (2000) thought it was an "[e]ntertaining action thriller," while the *Time Out Film Guide, 9th Edition* (2001) called the film "disappointingly incompetent." In *The Family Guide to Movies on Video* (1988), Henry Herz and Tony Zaza said, "[I]t is an utterly inconsequential effort of deadening predictability. Considerable violence, though stylized, and some fleeting nudity."

Sinbad and the Eye of the Tiger

(1977; 113 minutes; Color) PRODUCERS: Charles H. Schneer and Ray Harryhausen. DIRECTOR: Sam Wanamaker. SCREENPLAY: Beverly Cross. STORY–SPECIAL VISUAL EFFECTS: Ray Harryhausen. PHOTOGRAPHY: Ted Moore. EDITOR: Roy Watts. MUSIC: Roy Budd. ART DIRECTORS: Fred Carter and Fernando Gonzalez. PROduction Design: Goeffrey Drake. Costumes: Cynthia Tingey. Makeup: Colin Arthur. Assistant Director: Miguel Gil, Jr. Cast: Patrick Wayne (Captain Sinbad), Taryn Power (Dionae), Margaret Whiting (Queen Zenobia), Jane Seymour (Princess Farah), Patrick Troughton (Melanthius), Kurt Christian (Rafi), Nadim Sawalha (Hassan), Damien Thomas (Prince Kassim), Bruno Barnabe (Grand Vizier Balsora), Bernard Kay (Zabid), Salami Coker (Maroof), David Sterne (Aboo-Seer), Peter Mayhew (Minoton).

While overlong, *Sinbad and the Eye of the Tiger* is a more than passable adventure-fantasy film, but compared to the other collaborations of producer Charles H. Schneer and special effects wizard Ray Harryhausen, it is tepid, both plotwise and in its monsters. Costing over $7 million, it was the most expensive of their screen ventures and after principal filming in places like the rock tombs of Petra, Picor de Europa and the glaciers of the Spanish Pyrenees, it took Harryhausen eighteen months (October 1975 to March 1977) to complete the animation (in Dynamation) at his home studio. His most impressive creation was a giant prehistoric man, the Troglodyte, followed by a massive walrus. A hulking bronze minotaur was not particularly momentous nor were a trio of skeleton demons, a baboon or an oversized fly, but the worst of the lot was a tatty-looking sabertoothed tiger. Patrick Wayne (John Wayne's son) looked the part of Sinbad, replacing John Phillip Law who had done the role in *The Golden Voyage of Sinbad* (1974) [q.v.], but he was not good with dialogue. Taryn Power (daughter of Tyrone Power) and Jane Seymour served as eye candy; the film's strongest performance came from Patrick Troughton as the wise man Melanthius. The evil Queen Zenobia was adequately played by British actress Margaret Whiting (not to be confused with the popular American singer with the same name).

As Prince Kassim (Damien Thomas) is about to be crowned caliph, a tremendous explosion takes place. When his friend Captain Sinbad (Wayne) and his men arrive in Bagdad, they find the city silent. Merchant Rafi (Kurt Christian) informs them the place has been quarantined by plague and he offers the men the hospitality of his tent. When one of his men dies from drinking poisoned wine, Sinbad and the others fight Rafi and his minions but are soon at odds with a trio of demons raised from hell by Queen Zenobia (Whiting), Rafi's mother. Sinbad manages to destroy the creatures by causing them to be crushed under falling logs and he finds out from his fiancée, Kassim's sister Princess Farah (Seymour), that her brother has been put under an evil spell by their stepmother Zenobia, a witch whose son will become caliph unless her brother is crowned in seven months. She also says she will marry Sinbad when her brother is again himself.

The next day Farah's uncle, the Grand Vizier Balsora (Bruno Barnabe), comes aboard Sinbad's ship and tells him that all the skilled doctors and wise men in the Middle East have been consulted but no one can help Kassim. Zenobia shows up and taunts Balsora and the princess by saying that nothing can help Kassim and that her son will become the caliph. Sinbad agrees to aid his friend by voyaging to a mythical island that is supposedly the home of a black arts alchemist called Melanthius (Troughton). To combat this effort, Zenobia creates a colossus of bronze called Minoton (Peter Mayhew) that will row the boat she and Rafi will use to follow Sinbad. On board Sinbad's vessel, his friend Hassan (Nadim Sawalha) sees Farah playing chess with a baboon and he soon finds out the animal is really her brother who has become a simian because of his stepmother's spell. Upon reaching the island, Sinbad and his crew and the princess are met by rock-throwing natives but are saved by a young girl, Dionae (Power), who has an immediate rapport with Kassim. She takes them to her father, Melanthius, who cannot help the prince but he tells them of an ancient civilization, located at the top of the world in the temperate valley of Hyperborea, who can transform matter. He says a shrine there contains extraordinary powers and agrees to accompany them on the voyage. During the trip, Zenobia uses a potion to turn herself into a bird and board Sinbad's craft and finds out their location by becoming a miniature being. When she is captured, the witch creates a giant bee that attacks Melanthius but Sinbad kills it. Zenobia then uses the last of the potion to become a gull again; back on her own vessel she resumes human form but finds out she has the right leg of a bird. When they reach the land of ice mountains, Sinbad realizes that his ship is too big to go through a tunnel that will take them to Hyperborea and they are forced to sail a longer route and end up marooned on an ice cap. As they move forward through a blinding snowstorm they are attacked by a monstrous walrus that kills one of the sailors. Find the temperate valley, Sinbad and the group meet up with a horned ancestor of man called Troglodyte who they tame after he is attracted to Dionae. The giant leads them to the Shrine of the Four Elements and uses his power to open the huge doors, revealing a pyramid. Zenobia and Rafi sail their boat manned by the Minoton through the ice tunnel filled with frozen corpses and end up near the pyramid. As Sinbad and his men try to find an opening in the structure, Zenobia orders the Minoton to push back a giant boulder that reveals an entrance into the pyramid. The bronze colossus is crushed when the block falls on it. As Zenobia and Rafi reach the shrine just before Sinbad and his party, they find it guarded by a giant saber-tooth tiger encased in ice. Rafi tries to kill Kassim but instead is mauled to death by the baboon. Melanthius puts the prince in a cage and passes him through the rays of the shrine, restoring him to his normal state. In revenge, Zenobia thaws out the saber-tooth tiger which fights and kills the Trogloyte. The witch vanishes and Sinbad orders the others to leave. The pyramid beings to disintegrate while he kills the beast by impaling it on the Minoton's golden lance. Later in Bagdad, Kassim is crowned caliph and looks forward to marrying Dionae. Sinbad and the princess also plan to wed.

In *The Family Guide to Movies on Video* (1988), Henry Herz and Tony Zaza called it a "[s]low-paced bit of leaden whimsy ... The acting is undistinguished, Sam Wanamaker's direction is haphazard and only a few special effects merit anything more than passing interest."

The book *Sinbad and the Eye of the Tiger*, a novelized version of the movie's script by John Ryder Hall, was published in 1977 as a Pocket Fiction paperback movie tie-in.

Siren of Bagdad

(1953; 73 minutes; Color) PRODUCER: Sam Katzman. DIRECTOR: Richard Quine. SCREENPLAY: Robert E. Kent. PHOTOGRAPHY: Henry Freulich. EDITOR: Jerome Thoms. MUSIC: Mischa Bakaleinikoff. ART DIRECTOR: Paul Palmentola. MAGIC EFFECTS: Bob Haskell. CAST: Paul Henreid (Kazah the Great/Grand Vizier Hazak), Patricia Medina (Princess Zendi), Hans Conreid (Ben Ali), Charlie Lung (Sultan El Malid), Laurette Luez (Orena), Anne Dore (Leda), George Keymas (Grand Vizier Soradin), Michael Fox (Telar/Sultan Ahmand the Just), Karl Davis (Morab), Carl Milletaire (Hamid), Eddie Foster (Turan), Vivian Mason (Harem Girl), Suzanne Ridgeway (Palace Show Girl), Steven Ritch (Soldier), Ethan Laidlaw, Jack Chefe (Magic Show Watchers), Frankie Darro (Raid Survivor), Tommy Farrell (Palace Guard), Eugene Borden (Man who Faints), Terry Frost (Hamid's Henchman), Jack Ingram (Kazah's Henchman), Joseph Mell (Auctioneer), Sol Gorss (Human Catapult), Henry Rowland (Raider), Blackie Whiteford (Telar's Henchman), Richard Reeves (Soradin's Guard), Blue Washington (Palace Servant), Sylvia Lewis (Dancer).

After providing entertainment for a desert caravan, Kazah the Great (Paul Henreid), a magician, and his cowardly assistant Ben Ali (Hans Conreid) follow the bandit leader Hamid (Carl Milletaire) and his men to Bagdad since they have abducted Kazah's two favorite dancing girls, Orena (Laurette Luez) and Leda (Anne Dore); he sends the rest of his troupe, including acrobats, to Besserah. Finding the two young women about to be sold as slaves in Bagdad, Kazah and Ben Ali attempt to free them only to be set upon by soldiers. They are saved by the giant Morab (Karl Davis) and a grimy gypsy maiden, Zendi (Patricia Medina). At the camp of Zendi's father, Telar (Michael Fox), the two men are told that the women were stolen by Hamid who works for Grand Vizier Soradin (George Keymas), the brains behind Sultan El Malid (Charlie Lung). Refusing Telar's offer to join him in taking over the kingdom, Kazah returns to Bagdad hoping to perform his magic tricks for the sultan. There the sultan gives the dancing girls to the grand vizier in return for approving his marriage to the unseen Princess Alexia. Kazah dresses Ben Ali as a dancing girl and has him infiltrate the palace where he learns of the marriage plans. Soradin is attracted to the new blonde dancer.

Showing off his magic, Kazah makes Ben Ali, Orena and Leda disappear in his magic trunk. When the sultan demands their return, Kazah is forced to escape from the palace. Returning to Telar's camp, the magician tells him of the marriage proposal and the now bathed and beautiful Zendi agrees to masquerade as Alexia. Telar informs him that he is really Sultan Ahmand the Just; he was overthrown by the grand vizier, who thinks he is dead. Kazah tries to talk Zendi out of marrying the sultan but she insists on helping her father so he decides to go along with her wishes. He and Morab obtain the marriage proposal being carried to the real Alexia and the magician then enlists his troupe of acrobats as the princess' royal court. Two weeks later under the guise of Grand Vizier Hazak, Kazah arrives in Bagdad with Zendi and her court. The sultan falls in love with the girl but Soradin is reluctant because of her demand of ten thousand pieces of gold for agreeing to the nuptials. Ben Ali finds out that the sultan and Soradin plan to force Zendi into the marriage as the two leaders learn their old enemy Ahmand is still alive. Soradin enlists the help of Hamid and his men in saving the kingdom and Kazah tries to help Zendi escape from the palace but she refuses to go. Joining Telar and his army, Kazah helps them construct a barricade around the palace to hold off Hamid's forces and the magician and Ben Ali try to rescue Zendi. When the sultan and Soradin find the two men with Zendi, they engage them in a swordfight with the grand vizier being captured and the Sultan fainting. Hamid and his men flee when Kazah shows them he can make the sultan and Soradin vanish in his magic trunk. With Telar back in power, Kazah and Zendi plan to marry and Ben Ali dreams of having his own show.

Eschewing the usual Arabian Nights fantasy elements such as flying carpets, magic lamps and genies, this color Sam Katzman production was pretty much a comedy actioner with the exception of the magician's bag of tricks and a trunk that could make people vanish. Probably the highlight was the scene in which Paul Henreid's Kazah lights two hookahs (water pipes), one for himself and another for his lady fair, a takeoff of his famous scene with Bette Davis in *Now, Voyager* (1942). It was a rather anemic affair; *Variety* noted, "Fans who like this type of romantic action played straight aren't likely to go for the heavy-handed comedy introduced as farce to derrin'-do fiction. Such escapism has enough chuckles for the more sophisticated viewer when offered unadulterated, so there was no need to hoke it up further."

The Sleeping Beauty

(1966; 90 minutes; Color) DIRECTORS: Apollinari Dudko and Konstantin Sergeyev. SCREENPLAY: Konstantin Sergeyev and Iosif Shapiro, from the fairy tale by Charles Perrault and the ballet by Peter Ilyitch Tchaikovsky. PHOTOGRAPHY: Anatoli Nazarov. MUSIC DIRECTORS: V. Gamaliya and B. Khajkin. ART DIRECTORS: Ysevolod Ultimo and T. Vasilkovskaya. SETS: Ye. Yakuba. SPECIAL EFFECTS: Mikhail Krotkin and Nikolai Pokoptsev. CHOREOGRAPHY: Konstantin Sergeyev. CAST: Alla Sizova (Princess Aurora), Yuri Solovyov (Prince Desire), Natalya Dudinskaya (Carabosse, the Wicked Fairy), Irina Bazhenova (Lilac Fairy), Vsevolod Ukhov (King), Olga Zabotkina (Queen), Natalya Makarova (Princess Florina), Valeri Panov (Blue Bird), V. Ryazanov (Master of Ceremonies), E. Minchenok (Tenderness), I. Komeyeva (Playfulness), L. Kovalyova

Spanish lobby card for *The Sleeping Beauty* (1966), with Alla Sizova and Yuri Solovyou.

(Generosity), K. Fedicheva (Courage), N. Sakhnovskaya (Lightheartedness), G. Kekisheva (White Pussy), Shura Kuznetsov (Puss 'n Boots), Sergei Vykulov (Dancer).

When the baby Princess Aurora is about to be christened, the Wicked Fairy Carabosse (Natalya Dudinskaya) places a curse on the infant and predicts she will die when her finger is pricked. The Lilac Fairy (Irina Bazhenova), who has come to the palace to give the child a gift, counteracts the Wicked Fairy's curse by altering it to where Aurora will not die but will descend into a deep sleep. When Princess Aurora (Alla Sizova) turns 16, Carabosse returns in the guise of a kindhearted old peasant and gives her some beautiful flowers in which a knitting needle is hidden. The princess' finger is pricked and she goes to sleep. The Lilac Fairy then causes the entire realm to slumber. A century passes and the domain is covered by an impenetrable forest where the Lilac Fairy meets a handsome prince, Desire (Yuri Solovyov), and she causes him to see the image of the sleeping princess in her castle. Using a magic boat called up by the Lilac Fairy, Prince Desire arrives at the palace, finds Aurora and brings her back to reality with a kiss. Everyone in the realm then wakes up and Princess Aurora and Prince Desire plan to wed.

Produced in the Soviet Union by Lenfilm Studio and released there in 1964 as *Spyaschchaya Krasavitsa*, *The Sleeping Beauty* got limited theatrical release in the United States via Columbia in the spring of 1966. Based on the 1696 fairy tale by Charles Perrault and the Tchaikovsky ballet, the film featured the Kirov State Academic Corps De Ballet and Students of Vaganova Dancing School. *John Stanley's Creature Feature Movie Guide Strikes Again* (1994) called it "[p]ure form and beauty in a rewarding series of dances."

Snake People

(1971; 90 minutes; Color) PRODUCER: Henry Verg [Luis Enrique Vergara] and (uncredited) Juan Ilbanez. DIRECTORS: Jhon [Juan] Ibanez and (uncredited) Jack Hill. SCREENPLAY: Jack Hill. PHOTOGRAPHY: Austin McKinney and (uncredited) Raul Dominquez. EDITOR: John Munyea. MUSIC: Alice Uretta. ART DIRECTOR: Ray Markham. SOUND: Heinrich Henkel. PRODUCTION MANAGER: J.L. Cerad. PRODUCTION SUPERVISOR: Dick Compton. MAKEUP: Louis Lane. SPECIAL EFFECTS: Ross Hahn. DIALOGUE DIRECTOR: Stim Segar. ASSISTANT DIRECTORS: Louis G. Leon and Henry von Seyfried. CAST: Boris Karloff (Carl Van Molder/Damballah), Julissa (Annabella Vanderberg), Charles [Carlos] East (Lieutenant Andrew Wilhelm), Ralph [Rafael] Bertrand (Captain Pierre Labesch), Tongolele [Yolanda Montes] (Kalea), Quintin Bulnes (Klinsor), Santanon [Rafael Munoz] (Dwarf), Martinique (Maria), Julie Marichal (Mary Ann Vandenberg), Yol Duhalt (Captain Tony), Quentin Miller (Gomez).

Snake People was the first of a quartet of films Boris Karloff did for Columbia in 1968 to be released theatrically, albeit not until 1971. While some sources claim it is the best of the four features, in some respects it is the most incoherent. The plotline about voodoo is hard to follow and the feature balloons to 90 minutes with filler scenes like a resurrection, a snake dance, a man dancing with a zombie and seemingly endless voodoo ceremonies. There are also obviously edited sequences with Karloff glued onto scenes filmed in Mexico, and continuity gaffes, such as the scene where the voodoo priestess enters the heroine's bedroom: The doorknob is glass, but when she leaves it is metal and a little later it is glass again. A map at the beginning of the film shows the island where the action takes place being in the Pacific Ocean, halfway around the world from where voodoo is practiced. There is also the repugnant scene of a dwarf cutting off a chicken's head. Karloff only shows up in about three scenes, leaving audiences to endure an otherwise poorly dubbed and watery-colored farrago. Karloff's scenes were filmed on a small soundstage in Los Angeles by director Jack Hill, who also wrote the script, in the spring of 1968 with the rest of the feature being finished in Mexico that fall.

On the island of Coaibai, a French possession, a demented dwarf (Santanon) uses voodoo rites to resurrect a native girl (Martinique) for her lover, plantation overseer Klinsor (Quintin Bulnes). The island is visited by Annabella Vandenberg (Julissa), who has come to stay with her uncle, plantation owner Carl Van Molder (Karloff), and Captain Pierre Labesch (Rafael Bertrand), who has been assigned to re-establish law and order. Locating lazy Lieutenant Andrew Wilhelm (Carlos East) and introducing him to Annabella, the captain and his subordinate take the young woman into the interior to her uncle's plantation. Along the way they witness a voodoo funeral where a corpse is buried and guarded so it will not be turned into a zombie that works in the fields. Von Molder welcomes his niece and she asks his aid in helping her with the temperance movement on the island. Labesch informs Von Molder that he plans to put and end to the natives' voodoo practices. The plantation owner shows his guests his laboratory where he studies the local culture in hopes of unlocking the power of the human mind. When Labesch scoffs at the old man's demonstration of moving an object, housekeeper Kalea (Tongolele) uses her mind to set fire to twigs and Von Molder warns the police officer it would be dangerous for him to involve himself in the island's affairs. That night Labesch and Wilhelm break up a voodoo ceremony and leave behind three guards who are killed while a young girl is beaten to death and cannibalized. As a result, the captain orders a curfew. Wilhelm tells Von Molder and his niece that the natives are not afraid of the police but they do fear zombies. The plantation owner informs Annabella and Wilhelm that the natives believe Damballah, the servant of Baron Zombie, will conduct a voodoo ceremony that will raise the evil one. Klinsor, who works for Von Molder, tells his boss there is danger in the air and later he has the natives kill a policeman (Yol Duhalt). Kalea and the dwarf enter Annabella's room and use magic to make her dream that she is in a coffin; after arising from it in a cave she sees her lookalike (Julie Marichal) who chases her with a snake and passionately kisses her. Labesch is also taunted by visions of snakes. A zombie girl entices a policeman and she and four others devour him while a spy is caught in the voodoo cave and cannibalized. When Klinsor tries to have sex with his zombie girlfriend Maria, Von Molder beats him and then has Kalea set fire to the dead girl. Seeking revenge, Klinsor goes to Labesch and informs him there will an invocation of Baron Zombie that night with a human sacrifice. Wilhelm tells Annabella he loves her but they have to part so he can help Labesch. The young woman is kidnapped by two zombies. Arming themselves with high explosives, the officers go to the voodoo cave incognito while Klinsor is killed by Kalea and several zombie girls. The masked Damballah murders the dwarf. At the voodoo ceremony, Kalea invokes Damballah as Annabella is brought for sacrifice. Labesch then shows himself and unmasks Damballah as Von Molder, who calls for Baron Zombie. Kalea uses a snake to bite Labesch but he shoots Von Molder as Wilhelm rescues Annabella. The dying Labesch jumps into a fire pit and sets off an explosion that blows up the voodoo cave.

Columbia co-financed the four Karloff features with Mexico's Azteca Films but when producer Luis Enrique Vergara died not long after their completion, *Snake People* and *The Incredible Invasion* (q.v.) remained unreleased and *The Fear Chamber* and *House of Evils* (qq.v.) were unfinished. The first two features did get some theatrical release in Spanish-language theaters in the U.S. in 1971 with *Snake People* being called *La Muerte Viviente* (The Living Dead) and *Isla de los Muertos* (Island of the Dead). The film was issued to American television by Horror International Pictures as *Isle of the Snake People* and a truncated version was released on video in 1987 by MPI as *Cult of the Dead*, 15 minutes shy of its original running time.

So Dark the Night

(1946; 67 minutes) PRODUCER: Ted Richmond. DIRECTOR: Joseph H. Lewis. SCREENPLAY: Dwight Babcock and Martin Berkeley. STORY: Aubrey Wisberg. PHOTOGRAPHY: Burnett Guffey. EDITOR: Jerome Thoms. MUSIC: Hugo Friedhofer. MUSIC DIRECTOR: M.W. [Morris] Stoloff. ART DIRECTOR: Carl Anderson. SOUND: Frank Goodwin. SETS: William Kiernan. CAST: Steven Geray (Henri Cassin), Micheline Cheirel (Nanette Michaud), Eugene Borden (Pierre Michaud), Ann Codee (Madame "Mama" Michaud), Egon Brecher (Dr. Boncourt), Helen Freeman (Madame Bridelle), Theodore Gottlieb (Georges the Hunchback), Gregory Gay (Commissaire Grande), Jean Del Val (Dr. Manet), Paul Marion (Leon Archard), Emil Rameau (Father Cortot), Louis Mercier (Jean Duval), Billy Snyder (Chauffeur Billy), Frank Arnold (Antoine), Adrienne D'Ambricourt (Newspaper Woman), Marcelle Corday (Proprietor), Alphonse Martell (Bank President), Andre Marsaudon (Postmaster), Francine Bordeaux (Flower Girl), Esther Zeitlin (Peasant), Cynthia Gayford (Little Shoeshine Girl).

Following their initial foray into *film noir* with *My Name Is Julia Ross* (1945) [q.v.], director Joseph H. Lewis and cinematographer Burnett Guffey collaborated on *So Dark the Night*, a similar but less frenzied psychological horror melodrama that was filmed at the Rowland V. Lee Ranch in Canoga Park, California. This taut featured top-billed middle-aged character actor Steven Geray, who even shared a love scene with much younger co-star Micheline Cheirel. While the *New York Times* called it "a pretentious and drab little film," Don Miller in *Focus on Film* #5 (1970) was more on the mark when he noted, "The script spins the tale methodically, garnished by Geray's meticulous portrayal of the detective and the tense direction of Lewis, whose work here proved that *Julia Ross* was no fluke ... [Lewis'] penchant for shots above and below eye-level add greatly to the atmospherics, while the prevailing

Steven Geray, Micheline Cheirel, Emil Rameau, Ann Codee and Eugene Borden in *So Dark the Night* (1946).

aura, as in all his most successful melodramas, is one of melancholia."

Paris Police Commissaire Grande (Gregory Gay) tells Dr. Manet (Jean Del Val) that he is worried that his most valuable detective, Henri Cassin (Geray), has not gone on holiday, his first in eleven years. After saying farewell to Grande and Manet, Cassin is driven to the rural village of St. Margot where he has a room reserved at Le Chavel Noir tavern owned by Pierre Michaud (Eugene Borden) and his wife Mama (Ann Codee). Upon arrival the detective spies the owners' daughter, pretty Nanette (Cheirel), and she is attracted to his obvious affluence. At the inn he is greeted by the local physician, Dr. Boncourt (Egon Brecher), who tells him that Nanette is an admirer of his work. Widowed housekeeper Madame Bridelle (Helen Freeman) is also attracted to the policeman.

While Henri is getting settled at the inn, Mama urges her daughter to ingratiate herself with the policeman although her upcoming marriage to farmer Leon Archard (Paul Marion) has been approved by her father. Seeing that Nanette is attracted to Cassin, Leon tells her he would kill her rather than lose her to someone else. The next day Madame Bridelle informs Leon that Nanette has gone off with Cassin. When he finds her kissing the detective on a river bank, he threatens the policeman and Nanette rebuffs him. After the local priest (Emil Rameau) tells him he appears to be in good health, Cassin proposes to Nanette and she accepts, much to the chagrin of the jealous Madame Bridelle. At a betrothal party, Dr. Manet informs Cassin he is too old to marry Nanette. Leon breaks up the festivities by telling the engaged couple that he will win the girl back. As he leaves, Nanette follows Leon and she does not return. Cassin spends time brooding while Henri tells him he thinks his daughter and Leon have eloped. After several days, local policeman Jean Duval (Louis Mercier) asks Cassin's help in finding the missing girl and Georges (Theodore Gottlieb), a hunchback, brings word that her body has been found. Henri investigates and says Nanette was strangled. He and a search party go to Leon's farm where the hunchback finds the young farmer dead in the barn. Cassin finds a footprint under the body and makes a plaster cast of it. Madame Bridelle brings him a note saying another person will die.

When Pierre gets an identical note he goes

to Cassin for help and they find the body of Mama, who has been murdered in the inn's kitchen. After finding Madame Bridelle snooping in his room, Cassin begins to suspect the housekeeper of the murders. She begs him to take her with him when he leaves the village. Returning to Paris alone by train, Cassin goes to police headquarters where he meets with Grande and admits he has failed to find the killer. Grande calls in sketch artist Antoine (Frank Arnold) who draws a composite picture of the murderer from the clues gathered by Cassin. After seeing the sketch, Henri realizes that he is the murderer. Grande tells him he has been under an emotional strain and that he will be guarded while an investigation is made. Grande then consults Dr. Manet who tells him that Cassin may have a split personality due to being schizophrenic and that he may have had amnesia and not remembered committing the crimes. While writing out a detailed report of his activities in St. Margot, Cassin is overcome by a dark vision. When Grande and Dr. Manet come to see him, they find his guard has been murdered. Returning to the inn by train, Cassin tells Madame Bridelle not to interfere and he goes in search of Pierre, who he blames for having lost Nanette. The two fight and as Cassin starts to bludgeon Pierre with a poker, he is shot by Grande, who has followed him to St. Margot along with Dr. Manet. Dying, Cassin sees himself and Nanette as he was when he first came to the village. Breaking a huge glass window with the poker, he dies telling Grande that he has killed the murderer.

Another horrific aspect of *So Dark the Night* was the inclusion of the grotesque hunchback Georges, who was instrumental in finding the bodies of both the murdered lovers. The role was played by Theodore Gottlieb (1908–2001), who was better known as Brother Theodore, a monologue comedian. In addition to numerous television appearances from the 1960s into the 1990s, he also appeared in (or narrated) a number of films, including such genre efforts as *Horror of the Blood Monsters* (1970), and the telefilms *The Hobbit* (1977) and *The Return of the King* (1980).

The script of *So Dark the Night* seems to have been influenced by Clifford Orr's 1932 novel *The Wailing Rock Murders* in which aged hunchbacked detective Spider Meech tries to solve several homicides only to discover he is the killer.

La Sombra del Murciélago (The Shadow of the Bat)

(1968; 87 minutes) PRODUCER: Luis Enrique Vergara. DIRECTOR: Federico Curiel. SCREENPLAY: Jesus "Murcielago" Velazquez. PHOTOGRAPHY: Eduardo Valdes. EDITOR: Raul Caso. MUSIC: Jorge Perez Herrera. SONGS: Alvaro Carrillo, Federico Curiel and Amando Manzanero. PRODUCTION DESIGN: Artis Gener. PRODUCTION MANAGER: Raul Manjarrez. WARDROBE: Bertha Mendoza Lopez. SPECIAL EFFECTS: Ricardo Sainz. ASSISTANT DIRECTOR: Angel Rodriguez. CAST: Blue Demon (Himself), Jaime Fernandez (Daniel), Marta Romero (Marta), Fernando Oses (Ring Opponent), Mario Orea (Comandante), Gerardo Cepeda (Corrado), Murcielago Velazquez (The Bat), Rene Barrera (Lieutenant), Maria Antonieta Olivera (Crone), Marco Antonio Arzate, Enriqueta Reza, Eduardo Bonada, Jose Loza, Juan Garza, Vicente Lara "Cacama," Victor Jordan.

While producer Luis Enrique Veraga is credited with the idea for this Mexican horror outing, professional wrestler Jesus Velazquez wrote the script and played the part of the villain. Velazquez was known in the ring as El Murcielago, which translates as The Bat. The character he played was much like that of Erik in *The Phantom of the Opera*, an organ-playing madman with a hideously disfigured face. The hero was another professional heavyweight wrestler, Blue Demon, who earlier in the year had the lead in Vergara's *Arañas Infernales* (q.v.). Like most such outings, the film was padded with wrestling footage and songs; co-star Marta Romero sang three tunes while a vocal trio did a number, and there was even an instrumental of "Wooly Bully" complete with disco girls. Apparently all of Romero's vocals were filmed simultaneously because the same audience members are seen in each of them although they are spread throughout the feature. The Bat wore a mask topped by animal hair and large ears but when he reveals his countenance to Romero the left side of his face is badly scarred and he sports a bulging eye.

The Bat (Velazquez) yearns for his glory days in the wrestling ring and lusts for vocalist Marta (Romero), whom he watches as she sings on television. In his underground grotto, the Bat instructs his moronic giant henchman Corrado (Gerardo Cepeda) and his deformed helpers to kidnap women and imprison them in an underground cell. The Bat orders his men to abduct Marta but she is saved by her boyfriend Daniel (Jaime Fernandez). Corrado knocks out Daniel and begins to carry off Marta when Blue Demon (himself) arrives and, after a tussle, runs off the kidnapper. Corrado reports back to his master and the Bat vows vengeance on Blue Demon. When he finds a strange leaf outside his dressing room, the masked wrestler goes to an old crone (Maria Antonieta Olivera), a herbalist who identifies it as being from a charm. After finishing her work at a club and meeting with Daniel, Marta goes home and is kidnapped by Corrado. The Bat puts Marta in a cell and offers her his kingdom but she calls him crazy. The Bat shows off for her by defeating a wrestler he has abducted; afterward, Corrado strangles the loser.

Blue Demon and Daniel trace the leaf to a remote area where the Bat is headquartered, as the madman reveals his hideous face to Marta. Finding his way into the grotto, Blue Demon is captured and taken to the Bat and the two wrestle. Blue Demon defeats the Bat as Daniel locates Marta and the other women but he is attacked by Corrado. Blue Demon comes to Daniel's rescue as the Bat shoots Corrado and then falls to his death in a pit filled with rats. Blue Demon and Daniel set Marta and the other women free and flee from the building as it is destroyed by fire.

The songs sung by Marta Romero in *La Sombra del Murciélago* are "¡Aye! Que Cruz," composed by the film's director, Federico Curiel, "Con un Poquito Este Noche" and "La Mentira."

The Son of Dr. Jekyll

(1951; 77 minutes) DIRECTOR: Seymour Friedman. SCREENPLAY: Edward Huebsch. STORY: Mortimer Braus and Jack Pollexfen. PHOTOGRAPHY: Henry Freulich. EDITOR: Gene Havlick. MUSIC: Paul Sawtell. MUSIC DIRECTOR: Morris Stoloff. ART DIRECTOR: Walter Holscher. SOUND: Jack A. Goodrich. SETS: William Kiernan. MAKEUP: Clay Campbell. GOWNS: Jean Louis. ASSISTANT DIRECTOR: James Nicholson. CAST: Louis Hayward (Edward Jekyll), Jody Lawrance (Lynn), Alexander Knox (Sir Curtis Lanyon), Lester Matthews (John Utterson), Gavin Muir (Richard Daniels), Paul Cavanagh (Inspector Stoddard), Rhys Williams (Michaels), Doris Lloyd (Lottie Sarelle), Claire Carleton (Hazel Sarelle), Patrick O'Moore (Joe Sarelle), Leslie Denison, James Logan (Constables), Hamilton Camp (Willie Bennett), Bruce Lester (Newsman), Holmes Herbert (Local Constable), Matthew Boulton (Inspector Grey), Patrick Aherne (Landlord), Wheaton Chambers (Magistrate), Vesey O'Davoren (Butler), Harry Martin (Detective), Olaf Hytten (Prosecutor), Stapleton Kent (Mr. Arnim), Betty Fairfax (Woman in Window), Keith Hitchcock (Bobby), Ottola Nesmith (Nurse), Carol Savage (Young Woman), David Dunbar, Frank Hagney (Pub Patrons), Guy Kingsford (Male Nurse), Leonard Mudie (Druggist), Phyllis Morris (Tea Shop Owner), Robin Hughes (Alec), Alex Harford (Clerk), David Cole (Copy Boy), Joyce Jameson (Barmaid), Denver Dixon (Lanyon's Coachman), Benita Booth (Woman), Bob Reeves, Jimmie Long (Men), Ida MacGill, Ola Lorraine (Women).

"He would better have remained childless" is how Ivan Butler described *The Son of Dr. Jekyll* in *Horror in the Cinema* (1970) and his point is well taken in that except for a couple of brief shots of star Louis Hayward in monster makeup, the feature is basically a complicated, but not overly interesting, melodrama. The star looks at least a decade too old to be playing the part of a thirty-year-old medical student although he handles the role well, as does the rest of the cast. The film's production values are polished and it moves along at a fairly good clip but the story itself is rather turgid and does not contain the monster effects needed for its intended audience.

In 1860 a mob chases the terror of London, Mr. Hyde (Hayward), to his Mayfair home, which is set on fire. The evil Hyde reverts to his normal self, Dr. Henry Jekyll, after falling to his death from a rooftop. Curtis Lanyon (Alexander Knox), Jekyll's student, and John Utterson (Lester Matthews), the doctor's lawyer, are summoned to Soho by police Inspector Grey (Matthew Boulton) who shows them Jekyll's small son, whom Utterson agrees to raise as his own, keeping his identity a secret, while Lanyon will be the child's guardian. Three decades later, newspaper editor Daniels (Gavin Muir) receives word that Edward (Hayward), the lawyer's adopted son, has been dismissed from the Royal Academy of Sciences for conducting experiments edging on witchcraft. Elated about his expulsion, Edward asks Lynn Utterson (Jody Lawrance), with whom he was raised, to marry him and she accepts and they plan to move abroad so he can continue his studies. When he finds out about his daughter's engagement to Edward, Utterson tells Lanyon, who runs a sanatorium, that the young man must be told of his true heritage. Lanyon informs Edward that he is the son of the infamous Dr. Jekyll and an actress, Jane Bellman, who was murdered by his father when he was in the guise of Mr. Hyde, the evil alter ego he created. Going to Lynn, Edward asks her to delay the marriage until he can find out the truth about his father and she agrees.

At his father's abandoned house, Edward finds his dad's book *Studies in Abnormalities* and begins to read it. The next day Daniels' newspaper reports his presence in the abode and hints that it is haunted. Using money from his father's estate, Edward fixes up the house and moves in, revitalizing the laboratory with Lanyon giving him Jekyll's notes on his experiments. After getting a letter from Lottie Sarelle (Doris Lloyd), who says she knew his mother, Edward goes to visit the woman in the hovel where she lives with her son Joe (Patrick O'Moore) and his wife Hazel (Claire Carleton). The drunken Lottie tells Edwards she saw his father murder his mother but he refuses to believe her and vows to carry out the necessary experiments to prove Dr. Jekyll was not a fiend. His father's assistant Michaels (Rhys Williams) learns of Edward's work and volunteers to assist him, much to Lynn's relief since she has begun to worry about the strain the bad press and the experiments are having on her fiancé. One night Lanyon secretly visits the laboratory and tampers with Jekyll's unfinished experiment. The next day Edward completes the experiment and drinks the formula that causes him to pass out and turn into a hideous creature. Considering the experiment a success, the back-to-normal Edward demonstrates it for Lynn, Lanyon and Daniels; without the drug Anacracon that Lanyon added to the formula, it fails. Running into Joe, Edward returns to the Sarelle flat to see an old scrapbook that belonged to his mother. After leaving he is arrested on suspicion of attacking a young boy (Hamilton Camp) who had earlier hurled a rock through his laboratory window. Arrested by Inspector Stoddard (Paul Cavanagh), Edward goes before a magistrate (Wheaton Chambers) and is turned over to Lanyon, who takes him to his sanatorium after the Sarelles fail to provide him with an alibi.

Escaping his confinement, Edward returns to see the Sarelles but the landlord (Patrick Aherne) informs him they have skipped, leaving only an empty trunk and a music box. Taking the music box, he goes to its place of purchase, Arnim's Music Shop, and learns from the owner (Stapleton Kent) where he can find the Sarelles. Hazel appears ready to help Edward but her husband provokes him into a fight and he is again arrested with Lanyon getting him released. Finding a message from Hazel to meet her at her former home, Edward goes there only to find her dead. At Utterson's home, Edward is told that he may be suffering from hallucinations and that he should plead temporary insanity. Edward tells Lynn and Michaels he suspects Lanyon of being behind his troubles. When Michaels mentions the drug Anacracon used by his father, Edward realizes it was not included in the notes given him by Lanyon. Lynn gets the notes from Lanyon; Edward believes they are not his father's and returns to his laboratory for the originals and is followed by an angry mob. Lanyon gets to the lab before Edward and tries to burn Dr. Jekyll's notes and the two confront each other with Lanyon telling the young man he needed the Jekyll estate since his association with his mentor had nearly cost him his fortunes. The two fight and a fire is started in the lab with Lanyon knocking out Edward and leaving him to die. As Lanyon tries to get out of the house, the mob thinks he is Jekyll and forces him back into the burning building. Michaels braves the inferno and drags Edward to safety, bringing along the original notes proving that Lanyon had forged an altered copy. As the fire mounts, Lanyon runs to the roof where falls to his death, meeting the same fate as Mr. Hyde.

In the film, Louis Hayward used the sword cane that John Barrymore carried in the 1920 feature *Dr. Jekyll and Mr. Hyde*, in which he played the title roles. Jack Pollexfen, who co-wrote the story for *The Son of Dr. Jekyll*, was involved with another of the infamous scientist's offspring six years later when he wrote and produced the Allied Artists release *Daughter of Dr. Jekyll*, starring Gloria Talbott in the title role. The story had a similar theme to the Columbia film in that Jekyll's daughter is being driven to madness by a doctor (Arthur Shields) she thinks is her friend.

The Soul of a Monster

(1944; 61 minutes) PRODUCER: Ted Richmond. DIRECTOR: Will Jason. SCREENPLAY: Edward Dein. PHOTOGRAPHY: Burnett Guffey. EDITOR: Paul Borofsky. MUSIC DIRECTOR: Mischa Bakaleinikoff. ART DIRECTORS: Lionel Banks and George Brooks. SETS: Faye Holbrook. CAST: Rose Hobart (Lilyan Gregg), George Macready (Dr. George Winson), Jim Bannon (Dr. Roger Vance), Jeanne Bates (Ann Winson), Erik Rolf (Fred Stevens), Ernest Hilliard (Wayne), Harry Strang (Frightened Policeman), Ray Teal (Truck Driver), Milton Kibbee, Ruth Lee (Couple in Car), Brian O'Hara (Police Driver), Ida Moore (Mrs. Kirby), Grace Lenard (Woman in Bar), Edith Evanson (Housekeeper), Ann Loos (Mrs. Jameson), Clarence Muse (Entertainer), John Tyrrell (Police Lieutenant), Charles Perry, Cy Malin (Street Workmen), Norman Salling, Buddy Swan (Newsboys), Al Hill (Waiter), Charles Sullivan (Bar Patron), Al Thompson (Disabled Worker), Ervin Nyiregyhazi (Pianist Ervin).

Working titles: *They Walked by Night* and *Death Walks Alone*.

Double-billed with *Cry of the Werewolf*

(q.v.), *The Soul of a Monster* gave the promise of being a scary horror thriller, especially with its poster featuring two shots of a corpse-like ghoul. Instead, this late 1944 summer release was probably the studio's worst genre effort. Although done in a *Film noir* style, it was basically a talky, pointless and vapid affair punctuated by long, drawn-out sequences, such as "The Mephisto Waltz" being played during a thunderstorm and an almost endless stalking sequence; there was even a scene with five young tenors singing "Ave Maria." The *New York Times* felt it was a "cheap way to go nuts…. Brother, this one's an entry for the all-time looney prize!" Don Miller in *B Movies* (1973) was charitable when he wrote, "This balderdash was patterned after the successful Val Lewton–produced horror thrillers at RKO, and while not a patch on them was passably managed by director Will Jason and photographer Burnett Guffey."

Noted surgeon Dr. George Winson (George Macready) is on his death bed after contracting an infection when a rubber glove split during a surgery. When his partner, Dr. Roger Vance (Jim Bannon), and pastor Fred Stevens (Erik Rolf) fail to help him, Winson's wife Ann (Jeanne Bates) calls to the powers of both good and evil to save her husband. A couple (Milton Kibbee, Ruth Lee) driving near the Winson house hit a woman who disappears and then turns up at the doctor's residence. Upon admission to the home the woman, Lilyan Gregg (Rose Hobart), tells Ann she has answered her summons and demands to be left alone with George. Eight hours later the doctor is better and despite the protests of Vance and Stevens she insists on staying and nursing the doctor back to health. George makes a complete recovery but his personality has changed from that of a kind man into a cruel, suspicious person. After Ann tells Stevens she thinks Lilyan has poisoned her husband's mind, Lilyan leaves and Stevens finds the Winsons' dog dead. On the way to a party at the home of a friend (Ernest Hilliard), Stevens buys flowers for Ann and when the jealous George pins them on her they wilt. As they listen to a pianist (Ervin Nyiregyhazi) at the party, a thunderstorm arises, frightening Ann. George hears Lilyan's voice beckoning and he joins her at a café where she tells him those she has helped now resent her. George informs her he will kill the ones who would hurt her. Later, Ann confronts the woman and says she wants both her and her husband dead. Ann then meets Stevens, who sends her home. After confronting Lilyan he leaves and she tells George to stab him with an ice pick. George follows Stevens who picks up a holy cross and as the doctor is about to kill him he sees the crucifix and runs away. Later the two meet at a café and the pastor tells his friend a story about a man who let evil take over his soul. Upset, George goes back to Lilyan who urges him to kill anyone who gets in his way. George decides to work with Vance again but after treating a young boy, the two have an argument. When Vance grasps Winson's wrist, he notices he has no pulse. He then accidentally stabs George with a pair of scissors and George does not bleed and feels no pain. Vance informs Stevens of what happened and the pastor advises him to stay away from George but instead he confronts George. They are interrupted by Lilyan who says Vance wants all the

Poster for *The Soul of a Monster* (1944).

glory for their medical work. At his home, Vance gets an emergency call and when he steps out into the street he is run down by Lilyan's car. Unable to get Vance to a hospital, George decides to perform an operation but upon Lilyan's urging he lets his friend die. As a result he is forced to face a grand jury indictment for murder. Out on bail, he asks Ann and Stevens for their help. Stevens tells Ann to pray for her husband. George accuses Lilyan of trying to take over his life. She shoots him and he pushes her out of a window. The driver and wife, along with Stevens, find Lilyan lying dead in the street. Ann and Vance are relieved when George begins to recover although he does not know if what happened to him was a dream.

Will Jason made his directorial debut with *The Soul of a Monster*. During the next nine years he would helm 17 more features, mostly for Columbia; he would end his career at the studio with the fantasy *Thief of Damascus* (q.v.) in 1952. *Soul* was so bad that its co-star, Jim Bannon, had no kind words for it in his mid–1970s self-published autobiography *The Son That Rose in the West*: "It's classed as a 'low-budget B picture' but I've an idea the critics may treat it like a 'no-budget Z picture.' This is one of those forgettable productions that they don't release — it has to escape."

The Stepford Wives

(1975; 115 minutes; Color) PRODUCER: Edgar J. Scherick. EXECUTIVE PRODUCER: Gustave M. Berne. ASSOCIATE PRODUCER: Roger M. Rothstein. DIRECTOR: Bryan Forbes. SCREENPLAY: William Goldman, from the novel by Ira Levin. PHOTOGRAPHY: Enrique Bravo and Owen Roizman. EDITOR: Timothy Gee. MUSIC: Michael Small. PRODUCTION DESIGN: Gene Callahan. SETS: Robert Drumheller. UNIT MANAGER: Neil Machlis. COSTUMES: Anna Hill Johnstone. MAKEUP: Andy Ciannella. ASSISTANT DIRECTOR: Mike Haley and Peter Scoppa. CAST: Katharine Ross (Joanna Ingalls Eberhart), Paula Prentiss (Bobbie Markowe), Peter Masterson (Walter Eberhart), Nanette Newman (Carol Van Sant), Tina Louise (Charmaine Wimpiris), Carol Rossen (Dr. Fancher), Patrick O'Neal (Dale "Diz" Coba), William Prince (Ike Mazzard), Carole Mallory (Kit Sunderson), Toni Reid (Marie Axhelm), Judith Baldwin (Patricia Cornell), Barbara Rucker (Mary Ann Stavros), George Coe (Claude Axhelm), Franklin Cover (Ed Wimpiris), Robert Fields (Raymond Chandler), Michael Higgins (Mr. Cornell), Josef Somer (Ted Van Sant), Paula Trueman (Column Writer), Martha Greenhouse (Mrs. Kirgassa), Simon Deckard (Dave Markowe), Remak Ramsey (Mr. Atkinson), Mary Stuart Masterson (Kim Eberhart), Ronny Sullivan (Amy Eberhart), John Aprea (Policeman), Matt Russo, Anthony Crupi (Movers), Kenneth McMillan (Store Manager), Dee Wallace (Maid Nettie), Tom Spratley (Doorman Charlie), Dennis Kear (Grocery Boy), Emma Forbes (Alison Van Sant).

Lawyer Walter Eberhart (Peter Masterson), his photographer wife Joanna (Katharine Ross) and their two daughters (Mary Stuart Masterson, Ronny Sullivan) move from New York City to Stepford Village in rural Connecticut. Both Walter and Joanna find the townspeople a bit different. Joanna is unhappy with the change and she tells a local gossip columnist (Paula Trueman) she misses the city's noise. Joanna realizes that Walter has become upset over an offer to join the town's Men's Association but he agrees to do so in order to ingratiate himself with his peers. Joanna sees her neighbor, scientific researcher Ted Van Sant (Josef Somer), fondle his wife Carol (Nanette Newman) in their yard. Later she and Walter see the woman become disoriented after being involved in a minor traffic accident. Free-spirited Bobbie Markowe (Paula Prentiss), the wife of realtor Dave Markowe (Simon Deckard), reads the newspaper article about Joanna and the two quickly become good friends. That night Walter brings some of the club's members, including founder Dale "Diz" Coba (Patrick O'Neal), to their house to discuss a local fundraiser; one of the men, famous artist Ike Mazzard (William Prince), makes sketches of Joanna. At the fundraiser, Carol drinks too much and begins repeating the same phrase until Ted takes her home. Later she apologizes to Joanna and Bobbie for her behavior, saying she is a recovered alcoholic.

Joanna and Bobbie decide to form a local Women's Lib organization but no housewife shows interest other than tennis player Charmaine Wimpiris (Tina Louise), the wife of television executive Ed Wimpiris (Franklin Cover). The group's only meeting fizzles when most of the women discuss housework. Later Joanna and Bobbie are dismayed to find Charmaine has become a passive wife and has joyfully permitted Ed to tear up her tennis court to make room for a swimming pool. Bobbie comes up with the theory that the water in the area is making the women passive and Joanna thinks the culprit might be Coba Biochemical Associates, which is owned by Diz. Since Joanna's first lover was a chemist, Raymond Chandler (Robert Fields), they take a water sample to him to be analyzed and the results are negative. Joanna finds out that Raymond, who is married, is still interested in her.

When Joanna tells Walter she is unhappy in Stepford, he agrees to let her look for a new place to live. She and Bobbie go house hunting, aided by realtor Mrs. Kirgasa (Martha Greenhouse). Joanna submits some of her photographs to a gallery and is elated to have them accepted but when she tries to share the good news with Bobbie she finds her once sloppy, outgoing friend is now meticulous and reserved. Afraid she will be the next woman to be changed, Joanna meets with Dr. Francher (Carol Rossen), a psychiatrist, who advises her to take the children and get out of Stepford. Returning home during a thunderstorm, Joanna learns from Walter that their girls are staying elsewhere; she goes to Bobbie's house thinking they might be there. When she confronts her friend, Joanna thinks Bobbie is lying and ends up stabbing her. There is no blood and Bobbie suddenly becomes a human robot, continually repeating the same phrase. Walter alerts the police, a roadblock is placed around the town and a dragnet is issued for Joanna, who returns home. When Walter again refuses to reveal the whereabouts of their children, Joanna hits him in the head with a stove poker and he tells her they are at the Men's Association mansion. Joanna goes to the estate, where Coba informs her that he is the mastermind behind the procedure that replaces local wives with their obedient robot doubles. When Joanna tries to get away from him and find her children, she ends up in a room with her lookalike, an automaton with black eyes. Later the now passive Joanna shops at the local market with the other Stepford wives.

Filmed in Connecticut by Fadsin Cinema Associates/Palomar Pictures International and based on Ira Levin's 1972 novel, *The Stepford Wives* had a domestic gross of $4 million. Coming out near the height of frenzy over the Congressional adoption of the Equal Rights Amendment, the film satirized both the women's movement and the horror and sci-fi genres in its plot of authoritarian men using skewed science to program beautiful, subservient and sexually charged "perfect" wives. While a fairly low-budget effort, the feature contained outstanding performances, especially by Katharine Ross as a strong-willed young woman who begins to fear for her very existence after her husband comes under the influence of the men of Stepford. *Variety* called the film "a quietly freaky suspense-horror story ... The black humor and sophistication of the plot is handled extremely well." Phil Hardy in *Science Fiction* (1982) noted, "Despite the slow pace [it] remains an intriguing film.... The chilling climax ... is overlong in coming and the film's satirical intentions too deeply buried in the melodramatic execution of the plot. In short, a film, which was mistakenly attacked as anti-feminist, that lacks the bite of Ira Levin's original novel." Perhaps *Video Hound's Golden Movie Retriever 1991* (1991) best summed it up by calling the feature "creepy."

The Stepford Wives was produced by Edgar J. Scherick and in 1980 his company, Edward J. Scherick Associates, made a sequel, *Revenge of the Stepford Wives*, for NBC-TV. It starred Sharon Gless, Julie Kavner, Audra Lindley, Don Johnson, Mason Adams and Arthur Hill, who played the character of Diz from the original feature. Scherick did two more *Stepford* telefilms, *The Stepford Children* (NBC, 1987) and *The Stepford Husbands* (CBS, 1996). The former headlined Barbara Eden and Don Murray; Donald Mills, Michael Ontkean and Cindy Williams starred in the latter production. In 2004 *The Stepford Wives* was remade theatrically by Paramount, starring Nicole Kidman and Matthew Broderick.

Storm Over Tibet

(1952; 87 minutes) PRODUCERS: Ivan Tors and Laslo Benedek. DIRECTOR: Andrew Marton. SCREENPLAY: Ivan Tors and Sam Meyer. PHOTOGRAPHY: Richard Angst and George E. Diskant. EDITOR: John Hoffman. MUSIC: Leith Stevens and Arthur Honegger. SOUND: Richard Van Hessen. PRODUCTION DESIGN: George Van Marter. SETS: Al Orenbach. PRODUCTION SUPERVISOR: Herman E. Webber. MAKEUP: Ernest Young. SPECIAL EFFECTS: Harry Redmond, Jr. WARDROBE: Jack Miller. ASSISTANT DIRECTOR: Marty Moss. CAST: Rex Reason (David Simms), Diana Douglas (Elaine March Simms), Myron Healey (Bill March), Robert Karnes (Radio Operator), Strother Martin (Co-Pilot), Harold Fong (Sergeant Lee), Harald Dyrenforth (Professor Faber), Jarmila Marton (Jarmila Faber), William Schallert (Aylen), John Dodsworth (Philip Malloy), M. Concepcion (High Lama), R. Lal Singh (Priest), John Dako (Native).

Working title: *The Mask of the Himalayas*.

After collapsing upon his arrival in a remote Tibetan village, David Simms (Rex Reason) is taken to a temple where relates the story of how he arrived in the area. He tells of being an Army captain during World War II, flying airlift cargo from China to India, and after 75 missions plans to return home to the United States. He learns that his roommate, pilot Bill March (Myron Healey), has stolen a sacred Tibetan mask from a temple and plans to take it home as a present for his wife Elaine (Diana Douglas). The two men fight over the cursed object, which Simms wants to return. Simms accidentally cuts his hand and is replaced by March on the homebound flight. March's plane crashes over Tibet. Simms goes to the temple and tries to pay for the stolen mask but the priest (R. Lal Singh) informs him that the debt has been fulfilled. Back home the troubled Simms goes to visit Elaine and the two soon fall in love and marry. When a package containing the Buddhist mask arrives one day, both Simms and Elaine feel it must have been sent to them by March and they vow to return the sacred object to its home. After much red tape they get permission from UNESCO to join an Himalayan expedition led by Professor Faber (Harald Dyrenforth) and his wife Jarmila (Jarmila Marton). Fighting the brutal elements, the group reaches a Tibetan monastery where they see a ritual dance. Simms has visions of an avalanche that kills a number of people.

While Elaine wants her husband to abandon the quest and remain at the monastery with Jarmila, Simms meets with the High Lama (M. Concepcion) who warns him that the god Sindja is angry because of the expedition. Despite his warnings and Elaine's pleas, Simms and Faber continue on. After a rockslide, the porters quit, fearing the wrath of Sindja. A native (John Dako) replaces the group's kerosene supply with water but they do not find out until they reach the top of a high precipice. One of the natives returns to tell Jarmila about the kerosene and she sets out with several natives to rescue her husband and Simms. She reaches the expedition, and eventually Simms and two others arrive at a summit where they suspect March's plane crashed. Two of the men are blown off the precipice and die when their rope breaks. Simms then prays to Sindja and the whole mountain is inundated by snow. Back at the temple, Simms is reunited with his wife. The High Lama tells them he was the one who sent the mask in order to bring the pilot closure over the death of his friend.

Storm Over Tibet, issued in the summer of 1952, was a patchwork effort made up of new footage filmed by director Andrew Marton at Hollywood's General Service Studios to accompany scenes he did for the 1936 Swiss feature *Demon of the Himalayas*. The new movie also interpolated about 20 minutes of footage he shot in 1936 that did not appear in the Swiss production.

Marton's wife Jarmila is in both movies in the role of the wife of the expedition leader. Norman Dyrenforth was the head of the 1936 expedition to the Karakoram region of the Himalayas and for the 1952 movie his son Harald played the part. *Variety* said, "Exhibitors' best sales approach on this entry probably lies in emphasizing the picture's pictorial values.... From a scenic standpoint there are some fine clips of the rugged Himalayan mountain peaks along with snow avalanches and sudden storms amid the lofty crags." The trade paper, however, noted, "Even though something allegedly supernatural is involved, the plots gets a little incredulous when flier No. 1 returns to the U.S. and weds the widow of flier No. 2, apparently on the spur of the moment."

Although *Demon of the Himalayas* never saw U.S. release, some of the on-location footage in *Storm Over Tibet* had been used previously in Columbia's *Lost Horizon* (q.v.) in 1937.

Strait-Jacket

(1964; 93 minutes) PRODUCER-DIRECTOR: William Castle. ASSOCIATE PRODUCER: Dona Holloway. SCREENPLAY: Robert Bloch. PHOTOGRAPHY: Arthur Arling. EDITOR: Edwin Bryant. MUSIC: Van Alexander. PRODUCTION DESIGN: Boris Leven. SOUND: Lambert Day. SETS: Frank Tuttle. MAKEUP: Ben Lane and Monty Westmore. SPECIAL EFFECTS: Richard Albain. ASSISTANT DIRECTOR: Herbert Greene. CAST: Joan Crawford (Lucy Harbin), Diane Baker (Carol Harbin), Leif Erickson (Bill Cutler), Howard St. John (Raymond Fields), John Anthony Hayes (Michael Fields), Rochelle Hudson (Emily Cutler), George Kennedy (Leo Krause), Edith Atwater (Mrs. Fields), Mitchell Cox (Dr. Anderson), Lee Yeary [Lee Majors] (Frank Harbin), Patricia Crest (Stella Fulton), Vicki Cos (Carol Harbin as a Child), Patty Lee, Laura Hess (Little Girls), Robert Ward (Shoe Clerk), Lyn Lundgren (Beautician), Howard Hoffman (Man).

When producer-director William Castle first submitted the script of *Strait-Jacket* to Columbia for filming, the project was to have starred Joan Blondell and Anne Helm. The studio was unhappy that Castle had not planned it as another of his "gimmick" pictures but when Blondell dropped out and Joan Crawford was signed to star, Columbia executives realized that her box office draw was better than any stratagem that could be devised to promote the production. Helm started rehearsals for the film but Crawford insisted she be replaced by Diane Baker with whom she had earlier worked in *The Best of Everything* (1959). Coming off the success of *What Ever*

Happened to Baby Jane? (1962), in which Crawford co-starred with Bette Davis, *Strait-Jacket* proved to be another box office winner for the perpetual star with a domestic gross of $3.2 million. The feature was rather gory for its time with the depictions of several decapitations and severed heads. To demonstrate the plot's two-decade time span, the popular 1940s tune "There Goes That Song Again" was used throughout the proceedings and at the end Castle added a bit of macabre humor to an otherwise highly entertaining horror film by showing the famous Columbia Pictures torch-carrying female statue without her head. Also of interest was the casting of Pepsi Corporation executive Mitchell Cox in the pivotal role of a psychiatrist and the placement of a Pepsi advertisement in one of the scenes. (At the time Crawford was on the board of directors of the Pepsi Corporation.)

In the early 1940s, farmer Frank Harbin (Lee Majors) meets pretty Stella Fulton (Patricia Crest) at a roadhouse while his wife Lucy (Crawford), who is seven years his senior, is out of town. He takes the girl back to his farm and goes to bed with her, not realizing they are seen by his and Lucy's three-year-old daughter Carol (Vicki Cos). That night Lucy arrives home on a train a day early and walks to the farm where she sees her husband and Stella asleep in bed. Going berserk, she decapitates Frank and Stella with an axe as Carol watches in horror. Lucy is sent to an Ohio asylum and Carol is adopted by Lucy's brother Bill Cutler (Leif Erickson) and his wife Emily (Rochelle Hudson).

Two decades pass and Carol (Baker), now an accomplished sculptress, lives on the Cutler Ranch with her aunt and uncle and dates Michael Fields (John Anthony Hayes), the scion of wealthy dairy cattle raisers. Lucy is released from the asylum and comes to live at the ranch but appears nervous and looks haggard. Carol shows her mother around the place and also unveils a sculpture she did of Lucy. Carol and Michael find an old family album in which Frank's head has been cut out of various photographs. Carol treats her mother to new clothes, jewelry and a wig, making her appear as she did when she (Carol) was a child. That night Lucy awakens to find two severed heads and an axe in her bed and becomes hysterical. When the other family members investigate, the bedroom appears normal and Lucy thinks she had a nightmare. Later she becomes upset when she sees farmhand Krause (George Kennedy) cut off a chicken's head with an axe. When Michael comes a second time to meet Lucy, she is very seductive toward him and becomes upset when she gets a telephone call from Dr. Anderson (Cox), the psychiatrist who treated her at the asylum. His arrival at the ranch disturbs Lucy; the doctor informs Carol that her mother is only on probation and that he plans to take her back to the asylum. As he searches for Lucy, Anderson enters an outbuilding and is murdered with an axe. When Carol finds Anderson's car, she hides it in a barn but is observed by Krause. Carol questions her mother about Anderson, and Lucy claims he left hours earlier. When Carol sees Krause painting Anderson's car she tells him to get off the ranch and he defies her. Krause finds the doctor's body in a refrigerator in the ice house and he too is beheaded.

Lucy goes with Carol, Bill and Emily to Michael's home to meet his parents, Raymond Fields (Howard St. John) and his

West German poster for Strait-Jacket *(1964).*

wife (Edith Atwater). When Carol goes with Michael, Bill and Emily to look over a new dairy barn, Lucy chats with the Fieldses and mentions her daughter's upcoming marriage to their son. The snobbish Mrs. Fields denounces the idea, causing Lucy to become upset, talk about her incarceration and run out of the house. Michael and Bill search for her as Carol and Emily return home. Raymond prepares to go to bed but is attacked and murdered. When his wife investigates, she too is assaulted by an axe-wielding woman. Lucy bursts into the bedroom and stops the killer, pulling off a wig and face mask, revealing Carol. As Lucy runs down the stairs she meets Michael. Carol calls from the landing, telling him her mother murdered his parents. When Lucy shows Michael the mask with a face made to look like her, he realizes the murderer is Carol, who tells him she had planned to kill his parents (because they objected to their marriage) and pin the rap on her mother. Later Lucy packs Carol's possessions and informs her brother that she plans to go back to the asylum and take care of her daughter.

Elaine Rothschild in *Films in Review* (February 1964) stated, "I must say I am full of admiration for Joan Crawford, for even in drek like this she gives a performance ... Robert Bloch, who wrote *Psycho*, also wrote *Strait-Jacket*. At least five heads are chopped off in this one, and there are other scares for the booboisie. There is also a lot of good acting ... Considering the low-budget production values, Arthur Arling's black-and-white photography is unusually good." Tongue in cheek, *Time* said that Joan Crawford "plainly plays her mad scenes For Those Who Think Jung," a word twist of a popular Pepsi jingle of the time. Judith Crist in the *New York Herald Tribune* was unhappy with the script, acting and direction: "These make a disappointing, low-level melodrama of this madness-and-murder tale that might have been a thriller, given Class A treatment."

Variety cutely termed it "a chip off the old Bloch," adding, "Crawford does well by her role, delivering an animated performance. Baker is pretty and histrionically satisfactory as her daughter. Some of Castle's direction is stiff and mechanical, but most of the murders are suspensefully and chillingly constructed." The *New York Times* described the feature as "disgusting claptrap." Mike Mayo in *Videohound's Horror Show* (1998) opined, "[T]he work is still an effective period piece that's not without its moments."

While *Strait-Jacket* was not a gimmick picture, some theaters did hand out tiny, artificially blood-stained axes to customers. Crawford reteamed with Castle in 1965 for *I Saw What You Did* which was released by Universal. Leif Erickson was in the cast.

The Stranglers of Bombay

(1960; 80 minutes) PRODUCER: Anthony Hinds. EXECUTIVE PRODUCER: Michael Carreras. ASSOCIATE PRODUCER: Anthony Nelson Keys. DIRECTOR: Terence Fisher. SCREENPLAY: David Z. Goodman. PHOTOGRAPHY: Arthur Grant. EDITORS: Alfred Cox and James Needs. MUSIC: James Bernard. PRODUCTION DESIGN: Bernard Robinson. SOUND: Jock May. PRODUCTION MANAGER: Don Weeks. MAKEUP: Roy Ashton. ASSISTANT DIRECTOR: John Peverall. CAST: Guy Rolfe (Captain Harry Lewis), Jan Holden (Mary Lewis), Andrew Cruickshank (Colonel Henderson), George Pastell (High Priest), Marne Maitland (Patel Shari), Paul Stassino (Lieutenant Silver), Allan Cuthbertson (Captain Christopher Connaught-Smith), Michael Nightingale (Sidney Flood), John Harvey (Burns), David Spenser (Gopali Das), Tutte Lemkow (Ram Das), Margaret Gordon (Dorothy Flood), Ewen Solon (Camel Vendor), Marie Devereux (Karim), Jack McNaughton (Captain Roberts), Steven Scott (Walters), Roger Delgado (Bundar), Warren Mitchell (Merchant).

Working title: *The Stranglers of Bengal*.

Following its success with straight horror films in the late 1950s, Hammer Films launched a series of genre offshoots into the action field, starting with *The Stranglers of Bombay*, which Columbia distributed in the U.S. in the spring of 1960. It was directed by Terence Fisher who had previously directed the Hammer flicks *Four-Sided Triangle*, *Spaceways* (both 1953), *The Curse of Frankenstein* (1957), *Dracula* (*Horror of Dracula*), *The Revenge of Frankenstein* [q.v.] (both 1958), *The Hound of the Baskervilles*, *The Man Who Could Cheat Death* and *The Mummy* (all 1959). In the same action-horror vein, Hammer followed *The Stranglers of Bombay* with *Terror of the Tongs* (q.v.) the next year and *Captain Clegg* (*Night Creatures*) in 1962. The feature was originally intended to star Peter Cushing in the role of Captain Harry Lewis, who was based on the real-life Major General William Sleeman, and Christopher Lee as the high priest of the Goddess Kali.

In 1826 India, a cult group of stranglers, the Thuggees, worship the Hindu Goddess Kali whose high priest (George Pastell) tells of its beginnings and the use of a sacred silk cloth to strangle their enemies. In Bengal, members of the British East Indian Company demand that Colonel Henderson (Andrew Cruickshank), the chief of the British military there, do something to stop the robberies of their caravans and the abduction of workers. Arriving late for the meeting is Captain Harry Lewis (Guy Rolfe), who has been investigating the disappearance of over 1,000 people each year. After company executive Burns (John Harvey) threatens to file a complaint with the captain's superiors in Bombay, Lewis suggests the appointment of an envoy to solely handle the problem. Going home to discuss the matter with his wife Mary (Jan Holden), Lewis tells her he thinks he will get the nod but is disappointed when a message comes from Henderson announcing the appointment of Captain Christopher Connaught-Smith (Allan Cuthbertson). Riding to meet Connaught-Smith, Lewis and his men spy a merchant's wagon being attacked. They apprehend the two thieves and confiscate their silk scarves; the attackers manage to escape. Lewis informs Henderson of the details but the colonel tells him to submit a report to Connaught-Smith, the polo-playing son of Henderson's former schoolmate, who discounts the matter.

At the shrine of Kali, the high priest orders the two thieves punished by having their eyes and tongues removed. When Lewis' manservant Ram Das (Tutte Lemkow) thinks he sees his long-lost brother Gopali Das (David Spenser) in a caravan passing through the city, the captain gives him permission to find his sibling. Ram Das leaves behind his beloved pet, a mongoose. During his instructions to initiates, the high priest is told of the capture of Ram Das and at the same time he teaches Gopali Das how to ingratiate himself with caravans in order to rob them. After Connaught-Smith refuses to accept Lewis' aid in stopping the abductions, Lewis is attacked by two Thuggees who take the silk scarves he obtained from the bandits. Again the investigator refuses to heed Lewis' warnings about the abductions. When Lewis and his wife play cards with their neighbors, company executive Sidney Flood (Michael Nightingale) and his wife Dorothy (Margaret Gordon), a wrapped object is thrown through their window and it turns out to be Ram Das' severed hand. When the colonel and Connaught-Smith again refuse to listen to him, Lewis resigns his post and begins a search for his servant but finds the locals unwilling to cooperate. When he and Sidney go on a tiger hunt, the mongoose uncovers a shallow mass grave but neither Henderson or former area ruler Patel Shari (Marne Maitland) exhibit any interest in the matter. Following the execution of a thief who broke into Burns' home, Lewis follows the burial party out of the city and finds the Kali shrine but is captured. When the high priest lets lose a cobra to kill him, the mongoose stops it. The death of the snake appears to be a evil omen to the priest who orders the captain set free. Back in Bengal, Lewis tells Henderson and Connaught-Smith that a vast religious organization worshipping the goddess Kali is behind the killings but when he fails to get corroboration from the locals, the matter is dropped. The high priest orders the murders of the two thieves and Ram Das and he forces Gopali Das to strangle his own brother. Patel and Henderson's half–Hindu associate Lieutenant Silver (Paul Stassino) tells the merchants to combine their caravans into one and they agree, not knowing the two men are also members of the Kali cult. The high priest orders his men to kill Lewis but make it look like a robbery by ransacking his home and also murdering Sidney. Following Sidney's death, Lewis and Silver set out to find the caravan which has been infiltrated by Gopali Das and other cult members. During the night the caravan members are strangled. When Connaught-Smith and his men try to fight them, they too are killed, and all the victims are buried in a mass grave. The next day Lewis and Silver locate the vacant caravan camp but the lieutenant accidentally reveals the cult's brand on his right arm and Lewis is forced to kill him. After finding the mass grave, Lewis goes back to the Kali shrine where he is again captured and ordered to be sacrificed by the high priest. Gopali Das turns on the cult and helps free Lewis, who throws the high priest onto the sacrificial pyre. The two men escape back to Bengal where Gopali Das exposes Patel Shari as a cult member. Henderson now believes Lewis and promises to send a full report to Bombay along with recommending Lewis to lead the opposition to the Thuggees. At home, Lewis tells his wife the struggle against the cult of Kali is only beginning.

In reality over 100,000 people died in India in the 19th century before the Thuggee cult was finally eradicated. Other films dealing with the Thuggees and/or the cult of Kali include *Gunga Din* (1939), *Mystery of the Black Jungle* (1954), *Killers of the East* (1958), *The Mystery of Thug Island* (1966) [q.v.] and *Indiana Jones and the Temple of Doom* (1984).

The Stranglers of Bombay was filmed at the Bray Studios in Berkshire, England, in Mega-

Scope. Its most exciting sequence was an actual battle between a cobra and a mongoose. In *The House of Horror: The Story of Hammer Films* (1973), Allen Eyles, Robert Adkinson and Nicholas Fry noted, "Mercifully, and perhaps respecting the more realistic basis of the film, Hammer shot in monochrome, dispensing with the opportunity to sensationalize in colour." Donald C. Willis in *Horror and Science Fiction Films: A Checklist* (1972) called the film "[b]rutal, with the most evil, bloodthirsty cult on film. [James] Bernard's score almost as exciting as his score for *Horror of Dracula*. Better-than-average Hammer." In *Little Shoppe of Horrors* #4 (1978), Richard Klemensen rated it as "a very good actioner with lots of thrills and suspense ... This film is little noted today, but was a step in another direction for Hammer that proved that they could make good films even when not making older horror-types."

The film's graphic violence was illustrated by Paul M. Jensen in *The Men Who Made the Monsters* (1996): "*The Stranglers of Bombay* is a catalogue of physical atrocities performed by this corrupt and inhuman cult: The arms of initiates are slit and the wound seared with a heated iron; men are blinded, their tongues cut out, and they are kept in a cage until they act like ravenous animals; Lewis is staked out on the ground, his arm slit, and a cobra let loose; many strangulations occur, and the corpses' stomachs are slit so they will not swell and disclose their shallow graves; other corpses are placed on a funeral pyre to provide Kali with 'the greatest gift of all — human flesh.' Few of these horrors are shown in detail, but they are presented with [director Terence] Fisher's usual directness."

Guy Rolfe, who starred as Captain Lewis, headlined William Castle's *Mr. Sardonicus* (q.v.) the next year for Columbia.

Streets of Ghost Town

(1950; 54 minutes) PRODUCER: Colbert Clark. DIRECTOR: Ray Nazarro. SCREENPLAY: Barry Shipman. PHOTOGRAPHY: Fayte Browne. EDITOR: Paul Borofsky. MUSIC: Stephen Foster. ART DIRECTOR: Charles Clague. SETS: George Montgomery. ASSISTANT DIRECTOR: R.M. Andrews. CAST: Charles Starrett (Steve Woods aka The Durango Kid), Smiley Burnette (Smiley), George Chesebro (Bill Donner), Mary Ellen Kay (Doris Donner), Stanley Andrews (Sheriff Dodge), Frank Fenton (Bart Selby), Don Reynolds "Brown Jug" (Tommy Donner), Ozie Waters and His Colorado Rangers (Musicians), John L. Cason (John Wicks), Jack Ingram (Deputy Sheriff Kirby), Robert Kortman (Sackett), Emmett Lynn, Doris Houck (Homesteaders), Dick Rush (Banker), John Tyrrell (Deputy Sheriff), Ted

Stanley Andrews, Smiley Burnette and Charles Starrett in *Streets of Ghost Town* (1950) (courtesy of Wayne Lackey).

French, George Russell (Gang Members), Raider, Ring Eye (Horses).

In *Western Film Series of the Sound Era* (2009), I noted that *Streets of Ghost Town* "was akin to a picture puzzle in that it was made up of whole parts and bits and pieces of previous Durango [Kid] films strung together with new footage to create a surprisingly entertaining programmer." At the time of its release, in the summer of 1950, *Variety* thought it "a mighty confusing sagebrusher," adding, "Stock footage from past oaters comes back to haunt this one, storyline featuring constant switches back and forth between old and new scenes. This frequent flashback manner of staging doesn't help clarity or interest." While most of the older footage came from the Durango Kid entries *Gunning for Vengeance* and *Landrush* (both 1946), it also had snippets from other movies in the series along with the new storyline scenes featuring a spooky ghost town, a haunted mine with a locked vault where two outlaws were left to die, a blind madman and a sadistic gang leader. Most of the macabre activities take place at the beginning and end with its middle mainly made up of the older footage.

Lawman Steve Woods (Charles Starrett), his sidekick Smiley (Smiley Burnette) and Dusty Creek Sheriff Dodge (Stanley Andrews) ride into the allegedly haunted ghost town of Shadeville where over one million dollars in stolen funds is supposed to be hidden. Skittish Smiley is unhappy about the decision to spend the night there and becomes even more distraught after finding a human skull outside the Shadeville Hotel. Dodge spies a man running away from the area; Smiley claims it is a ghost that protects the treasure while Steve believes it may be a member of Bart Selby's (Frank Fenton) gang. That night Steve relates to Dodge how the area was opened to settlement and that Selby and gang member Bill Donner (George Chesebro) tried to dissuade newcomers so they could keep the area as their headquarters. After a land rush led by the masked crusader known as the Durango Kid (Starrett), the gang decides to take their loot and find a new locale but Donner and another gang member, John Wicks (John L. Cason), double-cross Selby by stealing the money and hiding it in Devil's Cave, an old Spanish mine. After they put the loot in the mine's vault, Donner locks Wicks and another outlaw in the

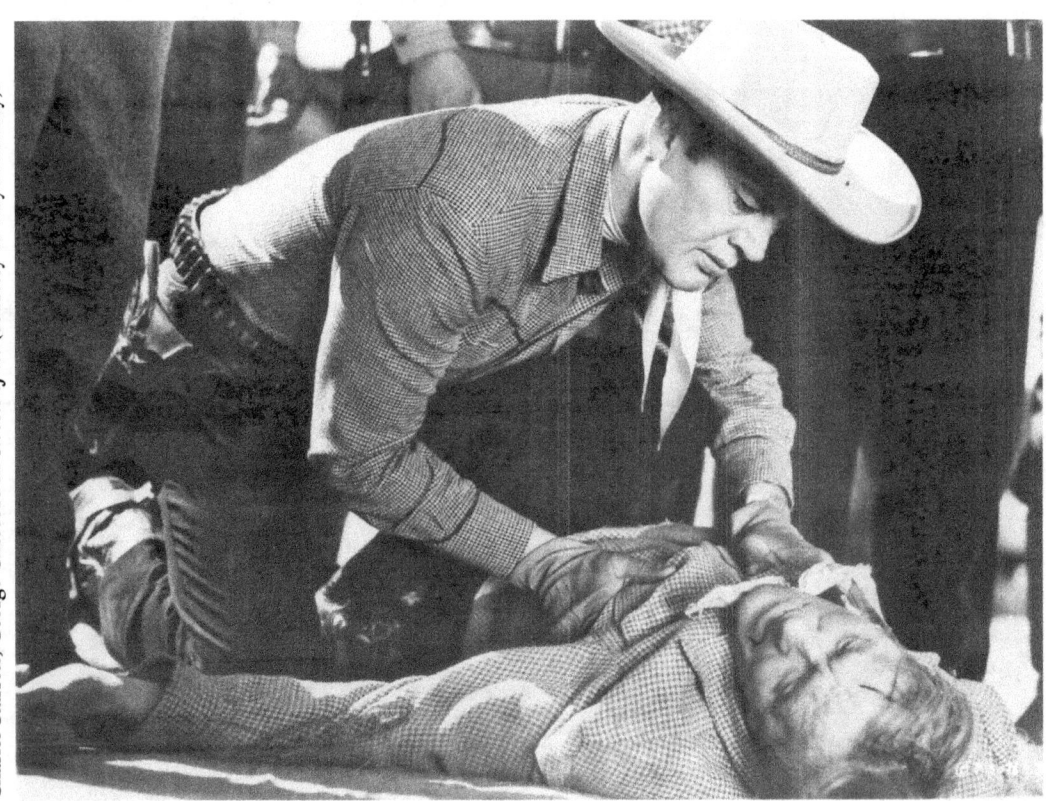

Charles Starrett, George Chesebro in *Streets of...* (courtesy of Wayne Lackey).

crypt, leaving them to die. Later Steve and Smiley hear a tapping noise and see a man they believe to be Donner, who is supposed to be dead, and Smiley thinks it is the outlaw's ghost. Returning to the hotel, the three men find their grub has been stolen and see a youngster's handprints in the dust on a window ledge. The next day they return to Dusty Creek for more supplies and meet Donner's niece Doris (Mary Ellen Kay) who is looking for her younger brother Tommy (Don Reynolds "Brown Jug'), who has run away from boarding school. She thinks he may be looking for the treasure and she asks the three men to take her with them when they return to the ghost town. Before leaving, Steve tells her and Dodge how Selby put together a new gang and raided Shadeville so often that all the citizens left and the outlaws were then free to try and find the hidden gold, but without success. When Donner tries to rob a stagecoach he is captured by Steve but busted out of jail by the Durango Kid. Selby's men get the drop on them and Donner is taken to Selby. Weeks later he rides into Split Rock, now blind after having his eyes put out by Selby for refusing to reveal the treasure's location. Donner is sent to prison but keeps his secret and is supposedly killed in a fire. Steve, Smiley, Doris, the sheriff and Deputy Kirby (Jack Ingram) ride to Shadeville as Tommy tells his Uncle Bill, who survived the prison fire, he has found the location to the mine under the Mansion House hotel. Selby has been informed by Kirby, who is actually a gang member, about the hunt for the treasure and he overhears Tommy and shoots Donner. As Tommy is being forced to take the gang to the Mansion House, the Durango Kid saves him. Kirby takes Doris and Tommy to Selby who forces them to go with him to the mine. As he opens the vault door, Selby finds the now deranged Donner, who was only winged, holding a gun on him and counting the money. Selby kills the old man as Doris and Tommy run away. As Selby grabs them, the gang leader is shot and killed by the Durango Kid. Durango then informs the siblings the money must be returned but Tommy will get a reward.

Like most "Durango Kid" features, *Streets of Ghost Town* contained music. Ozie Waters and His Colorado Rangers sang "Oh, Susanna" in footage from *Landrush* while Smiley Burnette performed "Streets of Laredo," including new lyrics about ghosts. In the new footage, Jock Mahoney can be seen doubling for Starrett.

A Study in Terror

(1966; 95 minutes; Color) PRODUCER: Henry E. Lester. EXECUTIVE PRODUCER: Herman Cohen. ASSOCIATE PRODUCER: Sam Waynberg. DIRECTOR: James Hill. PHOTOGRAPHY: Desmond Dickinson. EDITOR: Henry Richardson. MUSIC: John Scott. PRODUCTION DESIGN: Vetchinsky. SOUND: John Cox. PRODUCTION SUPERVISOR: Robert Sterne. SPECIAL EFFECTS: Wally Veevers. MAKEUP: Tom Smith. COSTUMES: Motley [Sophie Devine]. ASSISTANT DIRECTOR: Barry Langley. CAST: John Neville (Sherlock Holmes), Donald Houston (Dr. John H. Watson), John Fraser (Edward Osborne, Lord Carfax), Anthony Quayle (Dr. Murray), Robert Morley (Mycroft Holmes), Barbara Windsor (Annie Chapman), Adrienne Corri (Angela Osborne), Frank Finlay (Inspector Lestrade), Judi Dench (Sally Young), Cecil Parker (Prime Minister), Georgia Brown (Entertainer), Barry Jones (Osborne, Duke of Shires), Kay Walsh (Cathy Eddowes), Edna Ronay (Mary Kelly), Terry Downes (Chunky), Peter Carsten [O.W. Fischer] (Max Steiner), Charles Regnier (Joseph Beck), Dudley Foster (Home Secretary), John Cairney (Michael Osborne), Christiane Maybach (Polly Nichols), Avis Bunnage (Landlady), Barbara Leake (Mrs. Hudson), Patrick Newell (Benson), Jeremy Lloyd (Rupert), Corin Redgrave (Rupert's Pal), Harriet Devine, Sally Douglas (Pub Girls), Donna White (First Victim), Norma Foster (Elizabeth Stride) Michael Ripper (Man in Crowd).

Considered in some circles to be one of the finest screen Sherlock Holmes movies, *A Study in Terror* was released in the U.S. late in 1966 by Columbia Pictures after having had its debut in England the previous year; it was also called *Fog*. Produced there by Compton Film/Sir Nigel Film, the feature for the first time had the famous sleuth at odds with Jack the Ripper. It received an "X" certificate in its homeland for sexual overtones. Although not a big-budget item, the production was a posh one with a particularly fine reproduction of the Victorian Era, seedy Whitechapel locales and a solid cast. John Neville was exceedingly good as Holmes, with his physical appearance very close to the character as created by Sir Arthur Conan Doyle. While Donald Houston's Watson was only a younger version of Nigel Bruce's interpretation of the part, the rest of the cast was superb, including Anthony Quayle as a crusading doctor, Judi Dench as his niece, John Fraser as a philanthropist, Frank Finlay as Inspector Lestrade, Charles Regnier (a regular in the West German Edgar Wallace *Krimis*) as a pawnbroker, and Robert Morley humorously portraying Sherlock's older, portly brother Mycroft. Even small roles were nicely cast as in the case of slaughterhouse worker Chunky who was portrayed by Terry Downes, former World's Middleweight boxing champion and British Empire Middleweight title holder. He later appeared in Roman Polanski's *The Fearless Vampire Killers* (1967). Nicely incorporated into the proceedings was singer Georgia Brown as a pub entertainer performing "Ta Ra Ra Boom De Eh" and "In These Hard Times."

In 1888 in London's Whitechapel, a poverty-ridden area, a streetwalker (Donna White) is brutally murdered. Three nights later Angel and Crown pub owner Max Steiner (Peter Carsten) throws out hooker Polly Nichols (Christiane Maybach) after she tries to fleece a customer (Jeremy Lloyd). She is also killed. At 221B Baker Street, Dr. John H. Watson (Houston) is upset by the newspaper accounts of the murder because the killer appears to have medical training. His roommate, Sherlock Holmes (Neville), surmises that the victim was a prostitute and decides to investigate. That night Annie Chapman (Barbara Windsor) tries to get into her room but her landlady (Avis Bunnage) evicts her for non-payment of rent. The feather-headed girl tries unsuccessfully to get funds from butcher Chunky (Downes) and later ends up being killed and disemboweled by a man carrying a medical case. By now the newspapers are referring to the murderer as Jack the Ripper.

Holmes receives a parcel containing a surgical instrument case missing a large scalpel, the post mortem knife. After finding out that the case bears the family crest of the Duke of Shires (Peter Jones), Holmes and Watson go to the Duke's country estate where they are informed that the case belonged to his oldest son, Michael (John Cairney), whom he disinherited. As they are leaving, the two meet Lord Carfax (Fraser), the duke's other son, who says Michael left medical school in France and returned to England but has not been heard from in two years. Going to Whitechapel, Holmes and Watson learn from a pawnshop owner (Regnier) that the medical case was brought to him two years before by Angela Osborne (Adrienne Corri) and he sold it just a few days earlier. Holmes views the body of Annie Chapman and questions the examining physician, Dr. Murray (Quayle), who also operates a soup kitchen for the poor. While there he meets with Scotland Yard Inspector Lestrade (Finlay) and warns him there will be more murders. The next day Holmes sends Watson to the soup kitchen with a demand to see Angela, and Sally Young (Dench), Murray's niece and a volunteer, takes him to her uncle who refuses his request. Pretending to be angry, Watson leaves as Holmes, disguised as a beggar, follows Sally to a nearby house where he finds Lord Carfax, who informs him that his brother married Angela, a prostitute, and that his family has been blackmailed by Steiner. Sally also tells the detective that Carfax secretly financed her uncle's efforts to help the people of Whitechapel.

That night Holmes and Watson go to the Angel and Crown pub to dine and meet with Steiner who says Angela as disappeared. Walking home, they are accosted by three thugs sent by the pub owner but they defeat them. After Elizabeth Stride (Norma Foster), another prostitute, is murdered, Murray speaks to a crowd in Whitechapel calling for the closing of places like the Angel and Crown. He nearly causes a riot, forcing Lestrade to use his police force to disperse the gathering. At Downing Street, the prime minister (Cecil Parker) informs the home secretary (Dudley Foster) that he will lose his post if the Ripper murders are not solved and he calls in Mycroft Holmes (Morley), hoping he can persuade his brother Sherlock to catch the fiend. When Mycroft goes to Baker Street to enlist his sibling's help, Lestrade shows up with a letter

Advertisement for *A Study in Terror* (1966).

from the Ripper promising more murders. After Lestrade says the government will not publish the missive, Holmes warns him that the Ripper will strike again. When Dr. Murray admits to Holmes that a medical man may be the killer, Holmes suggests to him that Michael Osborne is a prime suspect. The next night Holmes and Watson return to Whitechapel in a heavy fog searching for the Ripper. Hearing a woman's scream, the detective chases a man into Murray's mortuary but loses him. At the soup kitchen, Holmes sees Lord Carfax and Sally and he also finds a scalpel and again questions Dr. Murray about Michael. The doctor informs him that the younger Osborne had once been his assistant but had found out that his wife Angela and her lover, Steiner, were blackmailing his father. During a fight with Steiner, Michael accidentally threw acid in Angela's face, the experience causing him to have a mental breakdown. Murray then takes him to the sleeping Michael, now a pathetic simpleton. As Murray examines the body of the latest mutilated hooker, Holmes and Watson return to the pub and demand that Steiner take them to Angela. In her upstairs bedroom, the woman tells them it was she who sent Holmes the medical case, hoping he would investigate the murders. The badly scarred Angela says Michael came up with the blackmail scheme and that he deliberately threw acid at her. After Holmes and Watson return Michael to his father, the detective informs his associate that he knows the identity of the madman but needs proof. That night Holmes hides in Angela's bedroom and when the Ripper appears to kill her, he turns out to be Carfax. As Holmes fights with the Ripper, the latter throws a lamp, setting the room on fire. The flames quickly spread, killing Angela and Steiner as they try to escape, and ending the life of the Ripper when the ceiling falls on him. Back at Baker Street, Holmes tells Watson he had found a history of insanity in the Osbornes and that he would not disclose the identity of Jack the Ripper to protect the family.

In *Film Review 1966–1968* (1967), F. Maurice Speed called *A Study in Terror* a "neat idea of script writers Donald and Derek Ford ... Better in conception than execution but amusing enough and with some exciting moments and nice reconstruction of the gaslight London of the late 1880s." The *Motion Picture Herald* opined, "A fine production.... John Neville is superb as Sherlock Holmes; he may very well be the best interpreter of the detective.... [The movie is] an intelligent and exciting vehicle for the return of Sherlock Holmes." *Time* thought it "[s]ly and stylish." *Films in Review* (August-September 1966) stated, "John Neville is a credible Holmes, and the direction of James Hill, the production design of Vetchinsky, and the costumes of Motley, lift this inexpensive [film] above the level of routine entertainment." Ron Haydock in *Deerstalker! Holmes and Watson on Screen* (1978) called it an "entertaining, well-produced Victorian adventure"; in *The Films of Sherlock Holmes* (1978), Chris Steinbrunner and Norman Michaels termed the feature "an excellent contribution to the genre ... realistically recreating the sordid East End, setting of the Ripper murders, in detail, sparing neither the depravity of the period nor the sadistic horror of the times." Alan Barnes in *Sherlock Holmes on Screen* (2002) noted, "Famously, *A Study in Terror* was luridly promoted in the States by reference to the then-hot pop cultural phenomena of James Bond and, especially, Batman." In *Holmes at the Movies* (1968), David Stuart Davies said, "[T]he film failed to impress at the box office, and it did in fact sound the death knell of Compton Films. As well as spending an above average amount on the production, they went all-out in their promotional campaign, producing giant-sized press books and folders. It was to be the first in a series of new Holmes adventures authorized by the Conan Doyle estate, but its failure at the box office put an end to these exciting and ambitious plans."

The feature did result in an interesting novel by Ellery Queen (Frederic Dannay and Manfred B. Lee) in which the Fords' script was reworked to show both Holmes and Queen, in their own times, trying to solve the Ripper case. A paperback original, it was published in the U.S. by Lancer Books in 1966 and later reprinted by Lodestone Books. It was published in England in 1967 as *Sherlock Holmes vs. Jack the Ripper* by Victor Gollancz.

The *Study in Terror* soundtrack was issued by Roulette Records (OS/OSS-801) in 1966. It was recorded in England by the film's composer, John Scott, and his orchestra. The album cover contained the subtitle "Sherlock Holmes vs. Jack the Ripper."

John Neville had been the choice of the film's producer, Henry E. Lester, to appear as Sherlock Holmes in the 1964 Broadway musical *Baker Street* and a decade later the actor did the part on the Great White Way in an adaptation of the 1899 William Gillette play "Sherlock Holmes." Executive producer Herman Cohen had a long genre career on the production end of such features as *Bride of the Gorilla* (1951), *Bela Lugosi Meets a Brooklyn Gorilla* (1952), *Target Earth* (1954), *Blood of Dracula*, *I Was a Teenage Werewolf* and *I Was a Teenage Frankenstein* (all 1957), *How to Make a Monster* (1958), *Horrors of the Black Museum* and *The Headless Ghost* (both 1959), *Circus of Horrors* (1960), *Konga* (1961), *Black Zoo* (1963), *Berserk* (1967) [q.v.], *Trog* (1970) and *Craze* (1974).

In 1979, another cinematic version of an encounter between the famous Baker Street sleuth and Saucy Jack was issued: The U.S.-Canadian co-production *Murder by Decree*, released stateside by Avco–Embassy, headlined Christopher Plummer as Holmes with James Mason underplaying Watson. Frank Finlay returned (as Lestrade) as did Anthony Quayle, this time as the commissioner of the Metropolitan Police. Although nicely made and entertaining, it did not compare well with the Columbia release.

Superargo vs. Diabolicus

(1968; 88 minutes; Color) PRODUCER: Ottavio Poggi. EXECUTIVE PRODUCER: Nino Battiferri. DIRECTOR: Nick Nostro. SCREENPLAY: Jesus Balcazar and Mino Giarda. PHOTOGRAPHY: Francisco Marin. EDITOR: Teresa Alcocer. MUSIC: Franco Pisano. ART DIRECTOR: Juan Alberto Soler. PRODUCTION SUPERVISOR: Gino Fanano. PRODUCTION MANAGER: Valentin Sallent. MAKEUP: Anacieto Giustini. ASSISTANT DIRECTOR: Ferruccio Castronuovo.

CAST: Ken Wood [Giovanni Cianfrigilia] (Superargo), Gerhard [Gerard] Tichy (Diabolicus), Loredana Nusciak (Mistress), Monica Randall (Lidia), Francisco Castillo Escalona (Colonel Alex Kinski), Emilio Messina, Geoffrey Copleston, Valentino Macchi, Guilio Battiferri, Bruno Arie, Fortunato Arena, Sergio Testori.

A Spanish-Italian co-production filmed in Spain, *Superargo contro Diabolicus* (Superargo Against Diabolicus) was made by Liber Film, S.E.C. Film and Producciones Cinematográficas Balcazar in Eastmancolor-Cromoscope. It was released in Italy late in 1966 and in Spain early the next year. Columbia acquired the feature and showed it in the U.S. in 1968 as *Superargo vs. Diabolicus*. The spy sci-fi offering was so successful in Europe that it resulted in a 1967 sequel, *Superargo el Gigante* (Superargo the Giant), with Ken Wood repeating the title role.

Famed wrestler Superargo (Wood) gives up his ring career when one of his opponents dies following a match. An international organization fighting corruption hires him because of his great physical strength and ability to absorb pain. He is assigned to investigate the thefts of cargos of uranium and mercury and traces this activity to a small island where he discovers underground tunnels leading to a subterranean lake. He has been under the surveillance of Diabolicus (Gerard Tichy), who uses involved electronic devices to capture the wrestler. Diabolicus, who lives on the island with his mistress (Loredana Nusciak), informs Superargo he has invented a gold isotope that he plans to use to take over the planet and that he is behind the thefts in order to get the materials he needs to carry out his mission. Superargo refuses to reveal to Diabolicus why he has come to the island and after lengthy interrogations he manages to escape. Diabolicus has his men abduct the wrestler's fiancée Lidia (Monica Randall), and bring her to the island. Superargo goes back to the isle to save Lidia as well as rid the world of Diabolicus, who realizes he is in danger and decides to escape aboard a missile he has built. Superargo turns the tables on Diabolicus, who is blown to bits when the missile explodes.

Super-Speed

(1935; 53 minutes) ASSOCIATE PRODUCER: Irving Briskin. DIRECTOR: Lambert Hillyer. STORY-SCREENPLAY: Harold Shumate. PHOTOGRAPHY: Benjamin H. Kline. EDITOR: Otto

Meyer. SOUND: George Cooper. ASSISTANT DIRECTOR: Cliff Broughton. CAST: Norman Foster (Randy Rogers), Florence Rice (Billie Devlin), Mary Carlisle (Nan Gale), Charley Grapewin (Terry Devlin), Arthur Hohl (Philip Morton), Robert Middlemass (Wilson Gale), George McKay (George Stone), Thurston Hall (Investor), Gene Morgan (Master of Ceremonies), Edward Earle (Holmes), Emmett Vogan (Ward), Edward LeSaint (Coach), Stanley Blystone (Policeman), Nick Copeland (Assistant Coach), Eddy Chandler (Joe), Russ Clark (Charles Smith), Franklyn Farnum (Ralph Grey), Hal Price (Mac), Bob Furher (Burton), Billy Atkins (Head Waiter), Hal Cole (Driver), Steve Clark (Superintendent), Lynton Brent, Roger Kane (Newsmen), Jerome Storm, Christian Frank (Garage Men).

In 1925 Rayart Pictures starred Reed Howes in the programmer *Super Speed*, dealing with a newly developed race car supercharger and the machinations of crooks to steal the invention. A decade later Columbia used the title and basic story line for its dual biller *Super-Speed* that came to theaters late in 1935. The futuristic aspect of the feature involved the invention of a supercharged engine that could attain the speed of 150 miles per hour, something unheard of at the time.* *Super-Speed* is a pleasant, compact and (pardon the joke) fast-moving low-budget affair, ably directed by the always reliable Lambert Hillyer and highlighted by Norman Foster as the hero and two lovely leading ladies, Florence Rice and Mary Carlisle.

Football hero Randy Rogers (Foster) has invented a high-speed engine, and his girlfriend, Nan Gale (Carlisle) gets her father, Golden Arrow Automobile Company president Wilson Gale (Robert Middlemass), to give him a job. Finding out that Gale only wants him as a salesman, Randy mentions his invention to Golden Arrow general manager Philip Morton (Arthur Hohl), who is secretly working with rival United Motors in taking over Gale's business. Realizing that the new engine could be Gale's salvation, Morton has Randy work clandestinely at George Stone's (George McKay) machine shop. Although the completed engine is put in an old car, it registers 150 miles per hour and Nan sets up a demonstration for her father. In order to sabotage the test, Morton and Stone dilute the engine's oil, causing it to overheat and burn. As a result, Gale has to sell his business to United Motors. Morton becomes chief of Golden Arrow and offers to hire Randy.

Realizing the double cross, Randy refuses Morton's proposal and finds himself blacklisted. While looking for work, Randy meets a former acquaintance, Billie Devlin (Rice), and her speedboat-maker father, Terry (Charley Grapewin). Billie suggests that Randy place his new engine in one of their speedboats and try it out in an upcoming race. When Nan finds out about Randy meeting with Billie she becomes jealous and takes his engine out of her own boat which is later sabotaged by Morton and Stone, who do not realize they have not harmed Randy's invention. Billie's father gets Randy another boat which he pilots in the race. When Billie's boat catches fire, Randy, who is in the lead, turns around, rescues his lady love and finally wins the contest.

Swan Lake

(1960; 81 minutes; Color) DIRECTOR: Z. Tulubyeva. SCREENPLAY: A. Messerer and Z. Tulubyeva. PHOTOGRAPHY: A. Khavchin, M. Silyenko, O. D. Rimarev, O. Sugint, V. Khodyokov and V. Tsistron. MUSIC: Peter Ilyitch Tchaikovsky. MUSIC DIRECTOR: Yuri Faier. CAST: Maya Plisetskaya (Odette/Odile), Nicolai Fadeyechev (Prince Siegfried), Vladimir Levashev (Rothbart), V. Khomyakov.

Produced in the Soviet Union by Central Documentary Film Studio and released there in 1957 as *Lebedinoe Ozero*, *Swan Lake* saw stateside showings in 1960 when it was released by Columbia. Like most other screen versions of the classic 1877 ballet with music by Tchaikovsky, this production was a cinematic reproduction of the 1895 version of the work choreographed by Lev Ivanov and Marius Petipa. In 1967 Russian ballet star Rudolph Nureyev choreographed and starred with Margo Fonteyn and the Vienna State Opera Ballet in a version of *Swan Lake* filmed in Munich and released in the U.S. by UPA–7 Arts. The next year the Soviets did a 70mm production of the work produced by Lenfilm.

In medieval Germany, Prince Siegfried (Nicolai Fadeyechev) celebrates his coming of age at a ball and later he and his friends set out to hunt a flock of swans. When they locate them on a lake, one of the birds is wearing a crown. Later the beautiful Odette (Maya Plisetskaya) implores the prince to stop the hunt, saying she and her companions are only human between midnight

---

*When Kelly Petrillo won the Indianapolis 500 Mile Race in 1935, it was with a speed of a little over 106 mph. It would not be until 1965 that 150 mph would be attained, when Jim Clark won the 500 Mile Race with a little over that speed.

and dawn thanks to having been placed under a spell by Rothbart (Vladimir Lavashev), an evil sorcerer. The rest of the time they are swans. She also tells him that only when someone promises her eternal love and will die for her can the spell be broken. The prince invites Odette to another ball but she declares she can attend only after midnight. By morning she and her companions are again swans. Rothbart, disguised as an owl, has overheard the conversation. During the ball, the sorcerer shows up with his daughter Odile (also Plisetskaya), Odette's doppelganger, and Siegfried is deceived into believing she is the princess with whom he has fallen in love. When the prince chooses Odile for his bride, her father makes him swear eternal fealty to her. After Siegfried agrees, Odette as a swan flies at a palace window. After it breaks, Rothbart declares his daughter's real identity and the two disappear as the prince tries to find his true love. Odette joins her companions at a lake, followed by Siegfried. Rothbart causes a terrible storm as Siegfried asks the princess to forgive him for making a pledge of loyalty to Odile. When Odette tells him they must part forever, he grabs her crown and tosses it into the boiling lake and they are swallowed by its waters. When the sun comes out, all is calm and swans swim across the water.

The Terror of the Tongs

(1961; 76 minutes) PRODUCER: Kenneth Hyman. EXECUTIVE PRODUCER: Michael Carreras. ASSOCIATE PRODUCER: Anthony Nelson Keys. DIRECTOR: Anthony Bushell. STORY-SCREENPLAY: Jimmy Sangster. PHOTOGRAPHY: Arthur Grant. EDITOR: Eric Boyd-Perkins. MUSIC: James Bernard. ART DIRECTOR: Thomas Goswell. SOUND: Jock May. PRODUCTION DESIGN: Bernard Robinson. PRODUCTION MANAGER: Clifford Parkes. MAKEUP: Roy Ashton. COSTUMES: Molly Arbuthnot. CONTINUITY: Tilly Daly. ASSISTANT DIRECTOR: John Peverall. CAST: Christopher Lee (Chung King), Yvonne Monlaur (Lee), Geoffrey Toone (Captain Jackson Sale), Marne Maitland (The Beggar), Brian Worth (District Commissioner Harcourt), Ewen Solon (Tang How), Roger Delgado (Tang Hao), Richard Leech (Inspector Bob Dean), Marie Burke (Maya), Charles Lloyd Pack (Dr. Fu Chao), Barbara Brown (Helena Sale), Burt Kwouk (Mr. Ming), Bandana Das Gupta (Anna Chang), Andy Ho (Lee Chung), Milton Reid (The Guardian), Michael Hawkins (Priest), Tom Gill (Beamish), Eric Young (Confucius), Johnny Arlen (Executioner), June Barry, Mary Rose Barry, Audrey Burton, Ruth Calvert, Marialla Capes, Katy Cashfield, Patty Dalton, Louise Dickson, Pauline Dukes, Hazel Gardner, Valerie Holman, Julie Shearing, Valerie Shevaloff, Barbara Smith (Tong Girls), Barbara Brown (Helena Sale).

Hong Kong in 1910 is under the control of the British but a corrupt terrorist group, the Red Dragon Tong, keeps the city in its grasp of vice and corruption, including the opium and slave trades in addition to murdering its opponents and demanding protection money from the people, thus keeping them in a state of poverty. Returning to the city with his cargo ship, Captain Jackson Sale (Geoffrey Toone), who has lived there for 15 years, doubts the stories about the Tong told to him by businessman Mr. Ming (Burt Kwouk), who gives him a book of Chinese verse for his teenage daughter Helena (Barbara Brown). Unknown to the captain, Ming has concealed a list of Tong leaders in the volume's back sleeve. As Ming leaves the ship he is murdered.

At his home, Sale gives Helena the book along with a ring he bought for her on his voyage. At his café, Tong leader Chung King (Christopher Lee) learns that the list has not been found and tells his minions to locate it. The first officer of Sale's ship is found dead on the vessel, which has been ransacked. Returning home, the captain finds his house in disarray and his daughter murdered. Police Inspector Dean (Richard Leech) investigates and East India Company District Commissioner Harcourt (Brian Worth) tells Sale to help him. After they leave, the captain finds the book with the back panel torn out and he goes to question his housekeeper, Anna Chang (Bandana Das Gupta), and finds she has also been murdered. Long-time friend and shopkeeper, Maya (Marie Burke), refuses to help Jackson, as do several of the locals. Sale does not know that the woman and a man called the Beggar (Marne Maitland) are behind a movement to bring down the Tong. Hoping to get Sale to aid them, the Beggar has Maya invite him to tea the next day when Tang Hao (Roger Delgado), a pier supervisor and Tong collector, arrives to get protection money. With him is his beautiful young half-caste concubine Lee (Yvonne Monlaur). When Tang Hao gets rough with Maya, the captain tries to stop him but he is held at bay by the Tong man with a pistol. Feeling confident, Tang Hao tells Jackson about the Tong's involvement in vice but before he can shoot, Lee knocks him over the head. Telling Maya to get rid of Tang Hao, Jackson takes Lee to his house where she will be safe and then goes to an opium den where he tries to get information on the secret society. The next day the captain informs Harcourt of the Tong's activities; he scoffs at the accusations but he does say that Tang Hao has been found murdered. When Sale informs Lee of Tang Hao's death, she tells him it was a Tong killing and that the man had bought her when she was 15. After accidentally mentioning Chung King's establishment, she begs the captain not to go but he does not listen and while there his drink is drugged. Chung King has him tortured by the Guardian (Milton Reid) using the method of bone-scraping and Sale faints from the pain. The Beggar shows up and rescues him. As they escape, the Guardian tries to stop them and Jackson kills him with a sacred Tong hatchet. Back at his house, Lee takes care of Jackson, with whom she has fallen in love, but she becomes suspicious when Dr. Fu Chao (Charles Lloyd Pack), who is really a Tong operative, arrives to check on him instead of his regular physician. While Lee is out of the room, the doctor tries to stab the captain with a drug-filled syringe but the girl stops him and uses the poison to kill the Tong man. After being questioned by Dean, Jackson goes back to the café where he sees the ring he gave Helena on a Chinese who attacks him. He chases the man who is cornered and beaten to death by the Beggar and his followers. Chung King orders Sale eliminated in a ceremonial killing but his associate Tang How (Ewen Solon) objects, saying such an action will bring too much attention to the Tong. Chung King disagrees and orders Harcourt, who is in the pay of the society, to have Jackson at the pier the next night. At Maya's shop, the Beggar tells the captain he will be the target of the Tong and Sale agrees to join him and his men in destroying the organization. After he leaves, Harcourt forces Lee to reveal where Jackson has gone. When she goes to warn the captain, she is killed by the assassin (Johnny Arlen) sent to carry out Chung King's orders. Before dying, the girl informs Sale that Harcourt is a Tong man. The Beggar and his men defeat the Tongs in a fight on the wharf and Sale goes to the café where he sees Harcourt killed on the owner's orders. When Chung King finds himself surrounded by the Beggar and his minions, he plans to commit suicide but Tang How kills him.

Made by Hammer Films and Merlin Film Productions at the Bray Studios in England, *The Terror of the Tongs* was filmed in color and released in Great Britain in 1960. When Columbia issued it in the U.S. in the summer of 1961 it was shown in black and white and sometimes called *Terror of the Hatchet Men*. Basically the feature was a reworking of Hammer's *The Stranglers of Bombay* (q.v.), issued earlier in 1960, with the locale changed from India to Hong Kong and the villainous Thuggees of the first film becoming the Red Dragon Tong. Although Christopher Lee had been a staple in the genre since 1956, this feature marked the first time he got top billing in either a horror or Hammer film. Lee's sinister and well modulated performance in *The Terror of the Tongs* led to his playing the role of Dr. Fu Manchu in five features between 1965 and 1970. "Quite nicely done Oriental thriller.... Rather gruesome in parts but holds your attention throughout," wrote Richard Klemensen in *Little Shoppe of Horrors* #4 (1978). Michael J. Weldon in *The Psychotronic Encyclopedia of Film* (1983) called it a "good violent adventure."

Lee and beautiful Yvonne Monlaur were the highlights of the film. The interesting supporting cast included Burt Kwouk, who gained prominence in the *Pink Panther* movies with Peter Sellers, and Milton Reid, a wrestler who was Hammer's answer to Tor Johnson. The feature marked the debut of producer Kenneth Hyman, who later became the head of Warner Bros. Although an austere movie, *The Terror of the Tongs* did elicit some mirth when shown in the United States because of Lee's character name Chung King, since that was also the name of a company that sold food products and advertised heavily in the American media.

These Are the Damned

(1965; 77 minutes) PRODUCER: Anthony Hinds. EXECUTIVE PRODUCER: Michael Carreras. ASSOCIATE PRODUCER: Anthony Nelson Keys. DIRECTOR: Joseph Losey. SCREENPLAY: Evan Jones, from the novel *The Children of Light* by H.L. Lawrence. PHOTOGRAPHY: Arthur Grant. EDITOR: James Needs. MUSIC: James Bernard. SONG: James Bernard and Evan Jones. ART DIRECTORS: Bernard Robinson and Don Mingaye. SOUND: Jock May. PRODUCTION MANAGER: Don Weeks. MAKEUP: Roy Ashton. CONTINUITY: Pamela Davies. SCULPTURES: Elizabeth Frink. ASSISTANT DIRECTOR: John Peverall. CAST: Macdonald Carey (Simon Wells), Shirley Anne Field (Joan), Viveca Lindfors (Freya Neilson), Alexander Knox (Bernard), Oliver Reed (King), Walter Gotell (Major Holland), James Villiers (Captain Gregory), Thomas Kempinski (Ted), Kenneth Cope (Sid), Brian Oulton (Mr. Dingle), Barbara Everest (Miss Lamont), Alan McClelland (Mr. Stuart), James Maxwell (Mr. Talbot), Rachel Clay (Victoria), Caroline Sheldon (Elizabeth), Rebecca Dignam (Anne), Siobhan Taylor (Mary), Nicolas Clay (Richard), Kit Williams (Henry), Christopher Witty (William), David Palmer

(George), John Thompson (Charles), Edward Harvey (Doctor), Fiona Duncan (Control Room Guard), Neil Wilson (Guard), Larry Martyn, Anthony Valentine, Geremy Phillips, Lon Garcia, David Gregory (Gang Members).

Working title: *On the Brink.*

Hammer Films made this sci-fi thriller based on H.L. Lawrence's 1960 novel *The Children of Light* at Bray Studios in HammerScope in 1961. It was issued in its homeland of England in 1963 as *The Damned* and ran 87 minutes; it did not see stateside issuance by Columbia until the summer of 1965 when it was showcased with *The Old Dark House* (q.v.) as *These Are The Damned* and running 77 minutes. A 91-minute version of the feature was released in a dubbed version in France. It 1964 it won the Trieste Science Fiction Film Festival's Golden Asteroid award. Despite its title, the feature was not a sequel to MGM's *Village of the Damned* (1960).

Poster for *These Are the Damned* (1965), the U.S. release of *The Damned* (1963).

At the English seaside town of Weymouth, middle-aged American Simon Wells (Macdonald Carey), while on holiday, attempts to entice a beautiful young woman named Joan (Shirley Anne Field) and ends up being beaten and robbed by a gang of Teddy-Boys led by her brother King (Oliver Reed). Wells is found by Major Holland (Walter Gotell) and Captain Gregory (James Villiers), military men under the command of Scotland scientist Bernard (Alexander Knox). They take him to a café where their boss is with his ex-lover, sculptor Freya Neilson (Viveca Lindfors), who offers him aid. Later, while aboard his boat, Wells again meets Joan who leaves with him when her brother and his gang show up. King vows to kill Wells. On board the boat, the American kisses Joan who asks to be put ashore.

At his laboratory, a secret government project sealed off by electric fence, Bernard talks to nine children via television. Wells and Joan come ashore at a cliffside home owned by Freya, next to the military compound. That night Wells asks Joan to marry him but they are forced to leave when Freya arrives, followed by King, who is looking for his sister and Wells. He and the gang follow the duo who manage to get over the compound's fence but Joan slips down a cliff wall and Wells follows her. The children, who they discover are cold to the touch, find them and take Wells and Joan into a cave they call their hideout. The youngsters, who are all 11 years old, ask the adults if they are there to rescue them. When King falls from a cliff into the water, he is rescued by one of the children, Henry (Kit Williams), as another child, Victoria (Rachel Clay), tells Wells and Joan that the youngsters have always been at the facility. When Henry brings King into the cave, Joan asks her brother to touch the boy's face and King exclaims the child is dead. Wells and Joan inform Victoria they will stay and help the youngsters and the next day Bernard comes to Freya's house and she tells him about the break-in there. Bernard and his associates learn that Wells, Joan and King are with the children and all three adults begin to feel ill. After a visit from Gregory, Freya meets gang member Sid (Kenneth Cope) who is trying to find King. Via the TV receiver, Bernard tells the children he knows about the "big people" being with them and asks they turn them over to him but the group rebels. Henry leads Wells, Joan and King through the cave tunnels into the complex. Wells and King overcome Major Holland and his men but Wells finds out the place is radioactive as are the children. The adults take the youngsters into the outside world but the military recaptures most of them. King and Henry manage to escape in a car. Freya and Sid witness the children's capture as Wells confronts Bernard. The scientist permits Wells and Joan to leave in their boat and he tells Freya the pair will soon die of radiation poisoning. He also informs her that the children all came from mothers who were accidentally exposed to radiation and they are being conditioned to live in a post-nuclear world. Two helicopters chase King and Henry and military men recapture the boy. King speeds away in his car only to careen off a bridge and drown. As Wells and Joan drift at sea in their boat, Bernard shoots Freya. The children can be heard calling for help from within the military compound.

In *The House of Horror: The Story of Hammer Films* (1973), Allen Eyles *et al.* noted, "Hammer had a problem film that took some time to come down off the shelf ... Cut even before its British release, then sheared more drastically for its eventual American appearance *The Damned* was paired off [in England] with Hammer's equally unsuccessful adult thriller *Maniac* [q.v.]." The feature contained the song "Black Leather Rock," written by scripter Evan Jones and music composer James Bernard.

In *Science Fiction in the Cinema* (1970), John Baxter stated, "Butchered by the producers when they saw whatever commercial appeal the story had removed by [director Joseph] Losey's adroit symbolism, *The Damned* remains alarmingly prophetic sf.... [T]here are still some fine moments, and a sense of social relevance which only Losey can attain." *Castle of Frankenstein* #8 (1965) noted the cut American version of the feature "still has disturbing fascination" while *Time Out Film Guide* (2001) wrote, "Certainly the strangest Hammer film ever made, this combines apocalyptic sci-fi, teen rebellion, and portentous philosophizing to awkward but riveting effect.... [A]s an ambitious oddity, it exerts not a little fascination." Philip Strick opined in *Science Fiction Movies* (1976), "Losey made a stylish and grimly ironic study of manipulation ... He points out, as science fiction seldom bothers to do, that the right to pass on knowledge does not include the right to dictate how it will be used — or even the right to expect that it will be absorbed. It's important to be able to concede that the truths of one generation may be the lies of the next." In *Films of Science Fiction and Fantasy* (1988), Baird Searles claimed that the film has "achieved a certain reputation because of its early warnings about the dangers of government-run scientific experimentation on human beings."

Thief of Damascus

(1952; 78 minutes; Color) PRODUCER: Sam Katzman. DIRECTOR: Will Jason. STORY-SCREENPLAY: Robert E. Kent. PHOTOGRAPHY: Ellis W. Carter. EDITOR: William Lyon. MUSIC DIRECTOR: Mischa Bakaleinikoff. ART DIRECTOR: Paul Palmentola. SOUND: J.S. Westmoreland. SETS: Sidney Clifford. UNIT MANAGER: Herbert Leonard. SPECIAL EFFECTS: Jack Erickson. ASSISTANT DIRECTOR: Carl Hiecke. CAST: Paul Henreid (Abu Amdar), John Sutton (Khalid), Jeff Donnell (Sheherazade), Lon Chaney, Jr. (Sinbad), Elena Verdugo (Neela), Helen Gilbert (Princess Zafir), Robert Clary (Aladdin), Edward Colmans (Sultan Raudah), Nelson Leigh (Ben Jammal), Philip Van Zandt (Ali Baba), Leonard Penn (Habayah), Larry Stewart (Hassan), Robert Conte (Horse Trader), Rick Vallin, Jack Ingram (Gate Guards), Terry Frost, John Hart, Rusty Wescoatt (Soldiers), Suzanne Ridgeway (Handmaiden), Belle Mitchell (Old Woman).

In seventh century Damascus, invaders lead by Khalid (John Sutton) and his general, Abu Amdar (Paul Henreid), take the city after a two-month siege as Sultan Raudah (Edward Colmans) tells his daughter Princess Zafir (Helen Gilbert) and her companion Sheherazade (Jeff Donnell) of the defeat. Ali Baba (Philip Van Zandt), the sultan's main counsel, flees but the two women decide to stay. The princess and Sheherazade go to see the general under a flag of truce and he tells them he will not destroy the city as long as Khalid gets all the area's wealth and is accepted as its new sovereign. Once Khalid takes control of the city, he orders Amdar arrested. The general escapes using a sword he takes from Ben Jammal (Nelson Leigh), a weapons maker. Putting the sultan in prison, the new ruler claims the princess for his bride. When Amdar goes to see her, the young woman tries to kill him but he informs her he plans to free the sultan. Leaving the city, he meets Sinbad (Lon Chaney, Jr.) and Aladdin (Robert Clary) who take him to their mountain cave whose door opens to the phrase "Open sesame."

There Amdar sees his friend Neela (Elena Verdugo), who his new allies think is a spy. He has her freed. He also finds Ali Baba and agrees to help him reclaim the city.

Needing weapons, the general goes back to Damascus with Sinbad, Aladdin and Neela to enlist the aid of Ben Jammal. Disguised as merchants, they meet with Jammal who informs them of the upcoming wedding. In the guise of a half-blind waiter, Amdar crashes the wedding feast and, enlisting the help of Sheherazade, he drugs Khalid. Rescuing the princess, the general finds out where the city's gold is hidden, and she gives him her jewels to pay Jammal for the new swords. While the princess remains in Damascus to be with her father, Amdar and his friends return to the cave realizing they are being followed by two of Khalid's men. The spies report back to their ruler but when his regiment of men surrounds the cave the next day they find it deserted. Ali Baba, who is nearby, calls out an incantation that closes the cave door, locking the regiment inside. When Khalid learns that the princess and Sheherazade have aided Amdar, he puts them in the dungeon with the sultan and orders all three beheaded. Finding out about the ruler's plans, Amdar and his friends return to Damascus with their weapons concealed in large barrels. As the executions are about to take place, Sinbad rallies the citizens to rise up against Khalid. Amdar and his followers overcome the invader's soldiers although Neela dies. Amdar engages Khalid in a sword fight with the general killing the tyrant, freeing Damascus and its sultan and winning the hand of Princess Zafir.

Thief of Damascus was one of three Arabian Nights fantasy adventures that producer Sam Katzman made for Columbia; it was preceded by *The Magic Carpet* (q.v.) in 1951 and followed in 1953 by *Siren of Bagdad* (q.v.). Filmed in Technicolor and released in the spring of 1952, the film was mainly a costume adventure drama that featured the fantasy elements of a magic incantation that opens a cave fortress door and super-powerful swords forged from an arcane formula. Also of interest for genre fans is the casting of Lon Chaney, Jr., in the role of the hero's ally, Sinbad. Jeff Donnell plays the part of Sheherazade with both allure and comedic overtones.

Variety noted, "Cast does a good job under Will Jason's breezy direction. None takes his role seriously, and the film comes off more as a satire on an Arabian Nights tale than as pure adventure ... Ellis W. Carter's Technicolor camerawork framed the physical values excellently." The *New York Times* called it a "harmless but preposterous entertainment package with an Arabian Nights background.... The battle sequences contain plenty of slam-bang gymnastics and one or two shots are surprisingly spectacular ... Typical of the tired jauntiness of the whole affair is the labored wisecracking of Jeff Donnell as the snappiest Sheherazade in screen history."

13 Ghosts

(1960; 84 minutes) PRODUCER-DIRECTOR: William Castle. ASSOCIATE PRODUCER: Dona Holloway. SCREENPLAY: Robb White. PHOTOGRAPHY: Joseph Biroc. EDITOR: Edwin Bryant. MUSIC: Von Dexter. ART DIRECTOR: Cary Odell. SOUND: Harry Mills. MAKEUP: Ben Lane. SETS: Louis Diage. ASSISTANT DIRECTOR: Max Stein. CAST: Charles Herbert (Buck Zorba), Jo Morrow (Medea Zorba), Martin Milner (Benjamin Rush), Rosemary De Camp (Hilda Zorba), Donald Woods (Cyrus Zorba), Margaret Hamilton (Elaine Zacharides), John Van Dreelen (Mr. Van Allen), David Hoffman (Delivery Man), John Burnside, Roy Jenson, Jeanne Baker (Ghosts), William Castle (Himself).

Producer-director William Castle followed *The Tingler* (1959) [q.v.] with *13 Ghosts*, which the studio issued in the summer of 1960. Filmed in "Illusion-O" with special glasses needed by the audience to see ghosts, the movie was done in black and white except when color was used for the rather blurred spook sequences. Regarding Castle's showmanship in promoting the picture, Jonathan Ross wrote in *The Incredibly Strange Film Book* (1995), "For *13 Ghosts* Castle performed his most generous stunt. He purchased a haunted house in France and had 20 million keys made up. Only one matched the house, and the lucky cinema-goer who received that key would also get the house." As to the "ghost viewer" given the film's watchers, he said, "Castle claims that it was a trip to the opticians that stumbled on the idea behind Illusion-O. Audiences would be given cardboard glasses, rather like those used to watch 3-D movies. These glasses would reveal the 13 ghosts of the title. Without the glasses, you would see nothing."

While lecturing on the La Brea Tar Pits at the Los Angeles County Museum, Cyrus Zorba (Donald Woods), a poorly paid paleontologist, gets a phone call from his wife Hilda (Rosemary De Camp) saying their furniture is being repos-

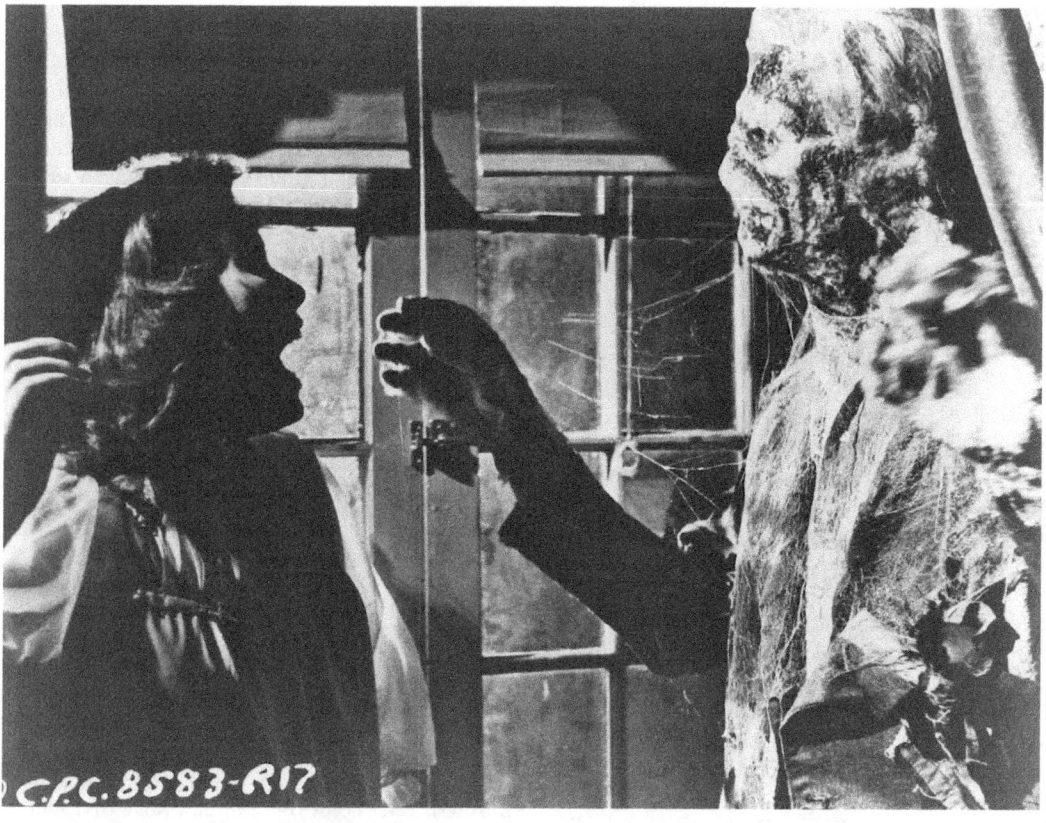

Jo Morrow being menaced in *13 Ghosts* (1960).

sessed. That night the two celebrate the birthday of their young son Buck (Charles Herbert), who receives a book on ghosts. Also present is their grown daughter Medea (Jo Morrow). A gnome-like man (David Hoffman) brings Cyrus a telegram asking him to meet the next day with attorney Benjamin Rush (Martin Milner), who informs them they have inherited a house that belonged to Cyrus's eccentric uncle, Dr. Plato Zorba. The place is allegedly haunted because Plato had been conducting experiments on contacting the dead. With the property comes a box containing special glasses invented by Plato which he believed could be used to see specters.

The next day the family moves into the dilapidated house which is also occupied by housekeeper Elaine Zacharides (Margaret Hamilton), who Buck thinks is a witch. That night Ben checks on the Zorbas, and Buck finds a Ouija board and a book written in Latin in a panel behind a book shelf. Using a planchette, they ask the board how many ghosts are in the house and get the answer 12. When the board is asked who will be the next one, the planchette jumps into the air and drops on Medea. Since the terms of Plato's will state that the family must remain in the house or it will become part of the state's park system, they try to ignore the warning. That night Cyrus uncovers a sliding panel and when he goes into a concealed room he puts on the glasses and sees a skeleton surrounded by flames. When the vision vanishes he sees a book; when he touches it the number 13 is burned on his hand. Taking the Latin book to his boss Van Allen (John Van Dreelen), Cyrus finds out it details Plato's experiments, saying he harnessed 11 ghosts from around the world and that he became the twelfth specter with plans to take revenge on his killer. Hilda then calls Cyrus and asks him to come home. There he finds the kitchen in a mess with objects floating around the room. Buck tells them that Elaine says the ghost of Emilio, a butcher who murdered his unfaithful wife and her relatives, is the cause of the disorder. Talking to the housekeeper, Cyrus finds out that she had often helped Plato with his work but he had come to distrust her and that he had taken all his money out of the bank and hidden it; and that while his death was ruled suffocation, he was murdered. She urges the family to leave the house that night.

While examining his uncle's bedroom, Cyrus finds a knob which causes the top of the canopy bed to raise and lower. After returning home from being with Rush, Medea awakens to the sound of a slamming window and is accosted by a hideous rotting corpse. The next morning Buck slides down the banister, causing two century notes to fall from the staircase. He takes the now recovered Medea her breakfast and goes to the cellar where he finds an old trunk belonging to lion tamer Shadrack the Great. Putting on the glasses, the boy sees the headless ghost of Shadrack working with a lion. Going upstairs, Buck finds the money and shows it to Rush when he arrives to see his father, who is at the museum. Rush has Buck promise not to tell his parents about the money until after he returns that night so they can find the rest of the loot. Rush goes to the museum to tell Cyrus that the state may buy the Zorba house. While Cyrus and Rush are talking, Van Allen shows up and says that Plato's writing indicates his money is concealed in the house and that Elaine is a medium.

That night Cyrus, Hilda, Medea and Elaine conduct a séance in order to contact Plato regarding the money's whereabouts but they will not let Buck attend. As Buck again slides down the banister, more money appears. Rush arrives and tells Buck to get a good night's sleep so they can have an early start on finding the rest of the money. During the séance, the specter of Plato comes out of his portrait, takes over Cyrus's body and promises death to one of them before returning to the picture. Elaine declares the spirits in the house are restless and angry. Later that night the moldering corpse carries Buck to Plato's bed and sets the canopy lever to smash the boy. The specter of Plato materializes and attacks the cadaver, who turns out to be Rush in makeup. Buck awakens and escapes from the room as the spirit drives Rush onto the bed where he is crushed to death. The next day the family counts the money as Cyrus reveals it was Rush who tried to scare them away so he could find the inheritance since he was Plato's killer. Although the Zorbas decide to stay, Elaine tells them the ghosts will be back.

13 Ghosts was hardly Castle's finest schlock hour although it did greatly benefit from the casting of Margaret Hamilton, famous as the Wicked Witch of the West in *The Wizard of Oz* (1939), as the eerie housekeeper. Howard Thompson in the *New York Times* referred to the production as a "mild little spook melodrama" and "a simple, old-fashioned haunted house yarn." Ed Naha in *Horrors: From Screen to Scream* (1975) called it a "[j]uvenile, gimmicky, and pretty entertaining William Castle film which parodies the 3D thrillers of old..." In *Terror on Tape* (1994), James O'Neill thought it a "[f]un Castle thriller.... Vastly entertaining, if a bit silly..."

In 2001 Warner Bros. reworked the plot for its release *Thir13en Ghosts*.

The 30 Foot Bride of Candy Rock

(1959; 75 minutes) PRODUCER: Lewis J. Rachmil. EXECUTIVE PRODUCER: Edward Sherman. DIRECTOR: Sidney Miller. SCREENPLAY: Rowland Barber and Arthur A. Ross. STORY: Lawrence L. Goldman. PHOTOGRAPHY: Frank G. Carson. EDITOR: Al Clark. MUSIC: Raoul Kraushaar and Rudy Schrager. ART DIRECTOR: William Flannery. SOUND: George Cooper. SPECIAL EFFECTS: Jack Rabin, Louis De Witt and Irving Block. SETS: James Crowe. MAKEUP: Clay Campbell. ASSISTANT DIRECTOR: William Dorfman. CAST: Lou Costello (Artie Pinsetter), Dorothy Provine (Emmy Lou Rossiter), Gale Gordon (Raven Rossiter), Jimmy Conlin (Justice of the Peace Magruder), Charles Lane (Standard Bates), Robert Burton (General), Will Wright (Pentagon General), Lenny Kent (Sergeant), Ruth Perrott (Aunt May Rossiter), Peter Leeds (Bill Burton), Robert Nichols (Bank Manager), Veola Vonn (Jackie Delaney), Jack Straw (Pilot), Russell Trent, Bobby Barber, Joe Greene, Doodles Weaver, Joey Faye, Jack Rice (Booster Club Members), Arthur Walsh (Lieutenant), Michael Hagen (Military Policeman), Mark Scott (Announcer), James Bryce (Soldier).

Working titles: *Lou Costello and His 30 Foot Bride* and *The Secret Bride of Candy Rock*.

Three years after his final film with Bud Abbott, Lou Costello returned to the screen to star in *The 30 Foot Bride of Candy Rock*, made by D.R.B. Productions and filmed at the Iverson Ranch in Chatsworth, California. Columbia released the feature in August 1959, five months after Costello's death. *Variety* found it "mildly amusing" and Jim Mulholland in *The Abbott and Costello Book* (1975) stated, "It was an innocuous little film similar to the Disney comedies." Leonard Maltin noted in *Movie Comedy Teams* (1985), "The humor in the film was aimed at younger viewers, who responded appropriately when the film was released." Unfortunately Costello was over 50 when he made the feature and looked it in deference to his young lady love, played by pretty Dorothy Provine. Columbia released the Three Stooges comeback feature *Have Rocket, Will Travel* (q.v.) just a few weeks before the Costello film and its huge success greatly overshadowed this pedestrian effort, which almost seemed to be a comedy takeoff of *Attack of the 50 Foot Woman* (1958).

Refuge collector Artie Pinsetter (Costello) has the only business in Candy Rock not owned by Raven Rossiter (Gale Gordon), who is planning to run for governor of the state. Artie is also an inventor and he has built a thinking machine he calls Max; he goes to Rossiter's radio station to get parts for his creation. Since Rossiter does not approve of Artie dating his pretty niece Emmy Lou (Provine), he gives the broke inventor credit for the parts in return for agreeing to not see the girl. Emmy Lou tells Aunt Mary (Ruth Perrott), Rossiter's wife, how much she cares for Artie. She proposes to him and when he refuses her upon the recommendation of Max, the girl hides in a cave. There she comes in contact with mystic dinosaur springs and grows into a 30-foot giant. The frightened Artie tells Rossiter his niece has gotten big; Rossiter thinks he means she is pregnant and he quickly arranges for Justice of the Peace Macgruder (Jimmy Conlin) to tie the knot between the garbage man and Emmy Lou. Artie gets a parachute for Emmy Lou to use as a wedding gown and the blind justice of the peace marries them only to discover the bride's size when he kisses her. The next day Artie collects a huge amount of food to satisfy Emmy Lou's appetite. To keep her out of sight, Rossiter has her relocated to a remote barn. When Emmy Lou is given a shower with a water hose by Artie she is seen by a military helicopter pilot participating in war games. The general (Robert Burton) in charge of the games gets the report about Emmy Lou and cancels the maneuvers; his Pentagon superior (Will Wright) sends out a warning of a possible space invasion. While campaigning at the Booster's Club, Rossiter is informed by Artie that Emmy Lou continues to grow and to get the garbage man out of the way he makes him a club member and gives him a new car. As he leaves, the new vehicle draws the attention of flirt Jackie Delaney (Veola Vonn) and she rides with him to the barn where the jealous Emmy Lou runs her off and accuses Artie of being unfaithful. Also angry with her uncle, the giantess heads to town where she climbs on top of a building and heckles the people. Artie goes to Max for help as the military fires missiles at Emmy Lou. When Max uses his powers to cause the missiles to crash into each other, the army sends in foot soldiers with bazookas. Artie has Max take the three of them back to the Civil War era and prehistoric times. Artie tells his invention to return Emmy Lou to her normal size but it turns her into a tiny being just as the military men arrive wanting to find the outer space giant. Rossiter and TV show host Bill Burton (Peter Leeds) show up and Artie tells them about Max's achievements. Burton snubs Raven and asks Pinsetter to be a guest on his program. Emmy Lou becomes normal again although Artie's dog Corporal has become a giant.

The story idea for *The 30 Foot Bride of Candy Rock* was conceived by Jack Rabin and Irving Block, who along with Louis De Witt did the film's special effects.

The star's stunt work in the production was performed by his brother, Pat Costello.

A Thousand and One Nights

(1945; 94 minutes; Color) PRODUCER: Sam Bischoff. DIRECTOR: Alfred E. Green. SCREENPLAY: Wilfred H. Pettitt, Richard English and Jack Henley. STORY: Wilfred H. Pettitt. PHOTOGRAPHY: Ray Rennahan. EDITOR: Gene Havlick. MUSIC: Marlin Skiles. MUSIC DIRECTOR: Morris Stoloff. SONGS: Saul Chapin and Eddie De Lange. ART DIRECTORS: Stephen Goosson and Rudolph Sternad. SOUND: Lambert Day. SETS: Frank Tuttle. COSTUMES: Jean Louis. SPECIAL EFFECTS: L.W. Butler and Ray Bomba. PROCESS PHOTOGRAPHY: Ray Cory. DIALOGUE COACH: Mel Ferrer. TECHNICOLOR CONSULTANT: Natalie Kalmus. ASSISTANT TO PRODUCER: Norman Deming. ASSISTANT DIRECTOR: Rex Bailey. CAST: Cornel Wilde (Aladdin of Cathay), Evelyn Keyes (Babs the Genie), Phil Silvers (Abdullah), Adele Jergens (Princes Armina), Dusty Anderson (Novira), Dennis Hoey (Sultan Kamar Al-Kir/Prince Hadji), Philip Van Zandt (Grand Wazir Abu-Hassan), Gus Schilling (Jafar), Nestor Paiva (Captain Kahim), Rex Ingram (Giant), Richard Hale (Sorcerer Kofir), John Abbott (Ali the Tailor), Murray Leonard (Camel Driver), Cy Kendall (Auctioneer), Trevor Bardette (Hasson), Dick Botiller (Ramud), Harold De Becker (Physician), Patrick Desmond, Frank Scannell (Retainers), Nina Foch, Jeff Donnell, Janis Carter, Diana Murphy, Dorothy Bailer, Virginia Cruzon, Carol Rush (Harem Girls), Shelley Winters, Carole Mathews, Adele Roberts, Francine Ames, Pat Parrish (Handmaidens), Tommy Cook (Salim), Frank Lackteen (Man with Camel), Lester Sharpe, Ethan Laidlaw, Pietro Sosso (Merchants), Napoleon Simpson, Noble Blake (Blackamoors), Eddie Abdo (Muezzin), Alfred Allegro, David Bond (Heralds), Rebel Randall, Claire James, Pauline Derby, Georgia Lange, Barbara Slater (Seamstresses), Vivian Mason (Exotic Girl), Janet Warren, Nancy Brinckman (Girls), Mari Jenishian (Dancer), Charles La Torre (Innkeeper), Harry Semels (Caravan Leader), Bud Wolfe (Messenger), John George (Dwarf), Dorothy Koster, Lois James

(Slave Girls), Tom Clark (Aladdin's Singing Voice), Frank Sinatra (Abdullah's Singing Voice).

This sumptuous production, filmed in gorgeous Technicolor, with location shooting at the Iverson Ranch in Chatsworth and Vasquez Rocks Natural Area Park, was a delightful mixture of the Arabian Nights and modern lingo combined into an entertaining comedy-fantasy. Sporting a bevy of beautiful women, a fast-moving and "actionful" plot, a singing hero and his wisecracking sidekick, this escapist entertainment also had star Cornel Wilde (dubbed by Tom Clark) singing the Saul Chapin–Eddie De Lange tunes "Beauty for Sale," "I Can't Believe My Eyes" and "Nor More Women," while at the finale Phil Silvers croons "All or Nothing at All," dubbed by Frank Sinatra, to a flock of bobby-sox–wearing harem girls. Bosley Crowther commented in the *New York Times*, "There are no magic carpets in this one, no horses with sky-beating wings; there are just a lot of elegant females and a couple of gents who make colloquial gags. In other words, it's a typical Hollywood harem-scare 'em film, with the comedy cut to the fashion of the modern swoon-spooning school." The feature cast a number of future female stars (Nina Foch, Jeff Donnell, Shelley Winters, Carole Mathews, Janis Carter, Adele Roberts, Rebel Randall) as eye candy while Mel Ferrer functioned as its dialogue coach. Rex Ingram as the giant had a similar role in *The Thief of Bagdad* (1940).

In ancient Arabia the daredevil Aladdin of Cathay (Wilde) sings songs in the town's bazaar as his jive-talking, glasses-wearing pal Abdullah (Silvers), who claims to have been born 1200 years too soon, uses sleight of hand to steal valuables from bystanders. When Abdullah is caught in the act, he and Aladdin escape with the crooner taking refuge in the covered litter of the veiled Princess Armina (Adele Jergens), whom no man may gaze upon and live. The romantic vagabond not only persuades the princess to drop her veil, he also kisses her and she falls in love with him. Armina returns to the palace where he father, Sultan Kamar Al-Kir (Dennis Hoey), is recovering from an assassination attempt by his twin brother, Prince Hadji (Hoey), which has left a scar on his arm. Hadji is in the palace incognito and he conspires with Abu-Hassan (Philip Van Zandt), the grand wazir, in a plot to kidnap the sultan and take his place with Abu-Hassan getting to marry the princess. The two carry out the coup as Aladdin sings to Armina and is captured by Captain Kahim (Nestor Paiva) and his men and taken to the grand wazir who orders that he be hanged the next day.

Aladdin is put in the same cell with Abdullah, who has been arrested for stealing, but they are able to escape when Armina orders her lady-in-waiting Novira (Dusty Anderson) to pass them the key to their cell while she sweet-talks Kahim, who is in love with her. Having been provided with horses by Novira, Aladdin and Abdullah ride away from the palace and take refuge in a cave. There they meet Kofir (Richard Hale), a sorcerer who uses a magic crystal to see present events and he tells Aladdin that deceit surrounds the palace and that if he will follows his orders, the singer will marry Armina. Kofir has Aladdin and Abdullah enter a mountain tunnel and search for a magic golden lamp that has more power than all the forces of nature. Inside the tunnel the two men are stalked by a giant (Ingram) but find the lamp and elude the ogre. When they return to the entrance they find it blocked. Kofir tells them to give him the lamp in return for their freedom but Aladdin doubts his sincerity. When he accidentally rubs the lamp, a beautiful genie named Babs (Evelyn Keyes) appears. She sets the two men free but since only Aladdin can see her the Genie convinces Abdullah of her existence by providing him with a banquet. When she finds out Aladdin loves the princess, the Genie becomes jealous but bows to his command to return to the palace, turning him into Prince Alushan of Hindustan and providing him with an entourage. When Alushan shows interest in the princess, the fake sultan agrees to their marriage but the girl rejects her new suitor, not recognizing him as Aladdin. Upon his request, Babs turns Aladdin into a small dog who sneaks into Armina's bedchamber where he hears her say her heart belongs to him. The Genie then returns Aladdin to his former self and he shows his true identity to the princess who agrees to marry him. The jealous Babs vows to stop the nuptials and she is able to get Novira to give the lamp to an old peddler, who turns out to be Kofir. During the wedding ceremony, Kofir uses the lamp to reveal Aladdin's true identity and he is arrested and condemned to death by the fake sultan. Abu-Hassan then blackmails the princess in agreeing to marry him in exchange for Aladdin's freedom once she denounces him. With this done, Aladdin and Abdullah are set free but the singer is deeply hurt until Novira tells him the truth and he learns about Kofir getting possession of the lamp. The two men return to the cave where the crystal shows them the sorcerer is at a tavern but when they go there they find Kofir has died and the owner (Charles La Torre) has given the lamp to his young son (Tommy Cook) who traded it to a camel driver (Murray Leonard) for sugar. When they find out that the camel driver bartered the lamp to Ali (John Abbott), a tailor, they go to his shop where he has learned the secret of the lamp and has been given the sultan's robe and a bevy of beautiful seamstresses. Babs causes the fake Sultan to lose the robe while he performs the marriage ceremony between Abu-Hassan and Armina. The princess sees that the man she thought was her father had no scar on his arm, realizing he is her uncle Hadji. As Aladdin and Abdullah swipe the lamp from Ali, causing him to lose the robe and the girls, Abu-Hassan learns from the princess that she knows the sultan is a fake and she plans to denounce him. When the grand wazir informs Hadji, the prince decides to kill his niece. Abu-Hassan tries to stop him and is murdered. As Hadji attempts to carry out his plan, he finds Aladdin and Abdullah in Armina's bedchamber, and he and Aladdin fight with swords. Aladdin forces Hadji to reveal the whereabouts of the sultan and the prince dies in a fall. With Sultan Kamar Al-Kir returned to power, Aladdin is made grand wazir and he and Armina plan to marry. The disappointed Babs is given the lamp by Aladdin and she wishes for his doppelganger who does not know Abdullah. The Genie then makes Abdullah a Frank Sinatra sound-alike who croons "All or Nothing at All" to swooning harem girls.

A Thousand and One Nights received Academy Awards nominations for Art Direction-Set Direction (Stephen Goosson, Rudolph Sternad, Frank Tuttle) and for L.W. Butler and Ray Bomba's special effects.

The Three Stooges in Orbit

(1962; 87 minutes) PRODUCER-STORY: Norman Maurer. DIRECTOR: Edward Bernds. SCREENPLAY: Elwood Ullman. PHOTOGRAPHY: William P. Whitley. EDITOR: Edwin H. Bryant. MUSIC: Paul Dunlap. ART DIRECTOR: Don Ament. SOUND: William Bernds. SETS: Richard Mansfield. ASSISTANT DIRECTOR: Eddie Saeta. CAST: The Three Stooges [Moe Howard, Larry Fine, "Curly Joe" De Rita] (Themselves), Carol Christensen (Carol Danforth), Edson Stroll (Captain Tom Andrews), Emil Sitka (Professor Danforth), George N. Neise (Ogg/Pilot), Rayford Barnes (Zogg/Co-Pilot), Norman Leavitt (Williams the Butler), Nestor Paiva (Martian Chairman), Don Lamond (Colonel Smithers), Peter Brocco (Dr. Appleby), Thomas Glynn (George Galveston), Jean Charney (WAF Sergeant), Peter Dawson (General Bixby), Maurice Manson (Lansing), Duane Ament (Personnel Clerk), Bill Dyer (Colonel Lane), Roy Engel (Detective Welby), Jane Wald (Woman in Bathtub), Cheerio Meredith (Woman in TV Commercial), Marjorie Eaton (Mrs. McGinnis), Rusty Wescoatt (Cook).

Released six months after *The Three Stooges Meet Hercules* (q.v.), *The Three Stooges in Orbit*, like its predecessor, was produced by Moe Howard's son-in-law, Norman Maurer, and directed by Edward Bernds and scripted by Elwood Ullman, both of whom had worked with the Stooges on their earlier Columbia short comedies. Some of the footage in this sci-fi comedy came from a Maurer-produced 1960 TV pilot called *The Three Stooges Scrapbook*; that title was used as the trio's TV show in the film's plot. Brief scenes from *Earth vs. the Flying Saucers* (1956) [q.v.] also appeared in the production, which might have been tedious for some viewers but was a delight to Stooges fans and children of all ages. Some nice underplayed political satire in the proceedings included having the Martian language sound Russian and in one scene the chairman (Nestor Paiva) of Mars rants, raves and slams a book on the table parodying Soviet leader Nikita Khrushchev's outburst at the United Nations. George N. Neise and Rayford Barnes plays the Martian invaders but they are not recognizable in alien makeup so they also have brief bits as airplane pilots.

After their landlady (Marjorie Eaton) throws them out of their room for cooking, television stars the Three Stooges (Moe Howard, Larry Fine, "Curly Joe" De Rita) take residence at a remote, spooky house owned by addled Professor Danforth (Emil Sitka), who tells them that spies from outer space are trying to steal his invention. The professor's butler, Williams (Norman Leavitt), is a Martian agent transmitting information on Danforth's activities to the Chairman (Paiva) of the Red Planet by telescreen. That night Curly Joe sees a clawed hand and runs for Moe as a phantom carries off Larry. When the menace again tries to scare Curly Joe, he and Moe capture Williams, who is trying to run the Stooges away. The boys inform the professor but the butler uses a ray gun to escape and calls Mars, being informed that Ogg (George N. Neise) and Zogg (Rayford Barnes) will be sent as the vanguard of an invasion. When police detective Welby (Roy Engel) refuses to listen to Danforth's story of Mar-

Larry Fine, Joe De Rita and Moe Howard in *The Three Stooges in Orbit* (1962).

tians, the professor follows the Stooges to the TV studio where they are doing their program. There the show's sponsor (George Galveston) and his hateful assistant (Maurice Manson) inform the boys that if they do not come up with a new cartoon format they will be cancelled. Danforth says he has invented a revolutionary process, electronic cartoons, and that he will give it to the Stooges if they will help him thwart a Martian invasion.

Back at the professor's Lompoc home, the boys meet his pretty visiting daughter Carol (Carol Christensen). Ogg and Zogg arrive and forcefully send the incompetent Williams back to Mars. The professor shows the Stooges his new invention, a military weapon that combines the features of a helicopter, submarine and tank, as well as his electronic cartoon machine. When the Air Force expresses an interest in the weapon, Colonel Tom Andrews (Edson Stroll) arrives to see it and promptly falls for Carol. The Chairman orders Ogg and Zogg to spare the humans until the weapon is finished so they can take it to Mars. Although a miniature of the weapon goes awry and scares a woman (Jane Wald) taking a bath, Tom is so infatuated with Carol that he agrees to set up a demonstration of the actual device for his superiors. The Stooges help Danforth put the finishing touches on the invention but louse up the Martian's telescreen, causing the Chairman to order the Earth destroyed. As Danforth and his daughter head to the demonstration site, the Stooges drive the weapon to the Air Force base where it is to be viewed by area commander General Bixby (Peter Dawson). During the demonstration, Moe, Larry and Curly Joe mess up the controls, making the weapon to go haywire and eventually causing all the military brass to be hit with pies from the base's cook house. As Andrews apologizes to the general, he calls Danforth an old crackpot and this causes Carol to become angry and return home with her father. The Stooges end up driving the weapon to an atomic testing site where Curly Joe accidentally installs a bomb, thinking it is a carburetor. They take off again in the invention and orbit the planet before going back to the laboratory. Tom returns to apologize to Carol and the professor films the boys doing the twist with the electronic cartoon device. Ogg and Zogg mount a death ray on the professor's invention and after a confrontation with the Stooges leave in the vehicle. Moe, Larry and Curly Joe get aboard just before takeoff. The military attacks the weapon with missiles as the Martians use the ray gun on various buildings and the general orders a red alert. Eventually Moe uses the Martians' ray gun to cut off the bottom of the craft, sending it into the sea where it explodes, killing the invaders. The boys fly the top part of the invention to their TV studio where they arrive in time to get their contract renewed thanks to Danforth's electronic cartoons.

While *Videohound's Sci-Fi Experience* (1997) termed the feature "For die-hard fans and kids only," one of the best summations of *The Three Stooges in Orbit* was written by Bill Warren in *Keep Watching the Skies! Volume II* (1986) when he said it "is undemanding, trivial fun for kids and the childlike; it's not badly made, it delivers the goods and for its intended audience, and even provides some laughs for adults." Before ending their screen careers, the Three Stooges would headline more Columbia features, *The Three Stooges Go Around the World in a Daze* (1963) and *The Outlaws Is Coming* (1965), two of their best-received films. They also provided nicely etched cameos in a duo of 1963 releases, *It's a Mad Mad Mad Mad World* and *4 for Texas*. Emil Sitka, who was practically a fourth Stooge in *The Three Stooges in Orbit*, was to have become a part of the comedy trio in 1975: Following Larry Fine's death, he was supposed to join Moe Howard and Joe De Rita as the Stooges in *Blazing Stewardesses* (1975). Moe's death, however, caused them to be replaced by the Ritz Brothers.

The Three Stooges Meet Hercules

(1962; 89 minutes) PRODUCER-STORY: Norman Maurer. DIRECTOR: Edward Bernds. SCREENPLAY: Elwood Ullman. PHOTOGRAPHY: Charles S. Welbourne. EDITOR: Edwin H. Bryant. MUSIC: Paul Dunlap. ART DIRECTOR: Don Ament. SOUND: James Z. Flaster. SETS: William F. Calvert. ASSISTANT DIRECTOR: Herb Wallerstein. CAST: The Three Stooges [Moe Howard, Larry Fine, "Curly Joe" De Rita] (Themselves), Vicki Trickett (Diane Quigley), Quinn Redeker (Schuyler Davis), George N. Neise (Ralph Dimsal/King Odius), Samson [Sammy] Burke (Hercules), The McKeever Twins [Martin McKeever and Mike McKeever] (Two-Headed Cyclops), Emil Sitka (Sheep Herder), Hal Smith (King Theseus), John Cliff (Ulysses), Lewis Charles (Achilles the Heel), Barbara Hines (Anita), Terry Huntingdon (Hecuba), Diana Piper (Helen), Gregg Martell (Simon), Gene Roth (Ship Captain), Eddie Foster (Freddie the Fence), Cecil Elliott (Matron), Rusty Wescoatt (Philo the Drummer), Don Lamond (Narrator).

The Three Stooges (Moe Howard, Larry Fine, "Curly Joe" De Rita) work for nasty Ralph Dimsal (George N. Neise) at his Ithaca Pharmacy and they are friendly with inventor Schuyler Davis (Quinn Redeker), who is trying to perfect a time machine. Dimsal and Davis are rivals for the affections of pretty Diane Quigley (Vicki Trickett), who is employed by Ralph but loves Schuyler. One of the inventor's experiments goes awry, causing havoc in the drug store by setting off a lather-making machine. Diane gives Schuyler two days to perfect his contrivance or get a job and if he does not she will leave him. When Dimsal finds the plans for Schuyler's time travel apparatus he makes changes. The Stooges decide to help their friend by trying to fix the contraption. Curly Joe feeds it his recently develops tranquilizers and the machine goes haywire. As the Stooges, Schuyler and Diane board the craft it lifts off and hurls them through time back to Greece in 900 B.C. There they witness a battle between the forces of King Odius (Neise) of Ithaca and Ulysses (John Cliff), who is defeated. Odius believes the visitors and their flying chariot were sent by the gods to give him victory. The king's strong man, Hercules (Samson Burke), secures the machine with boulders and the time travelers are taken to the king's palace where they are honored. Odius has designs on Diane.

When Ulysses is brought in as a prisoner and ordered executed, the Stooges help him get free and incur the wrath of Hercules. Trying to escape the strongman, the three zanies masquerade as female slaves and end up in a girls' bath before being exposed and carried by Hercules to Odius who condemns them to be galley slaves along with the cowardly Schuyler. After three months in the galley, Curly Joe uses his tranquilizers to incapacitate the ship's drummer (Rusty Wescoatt) and they get free. A storm wrecks the vessel and they end up on the island of Rhodes. There they meet a shepherd (Emil Sitka) who takes them to the island's harbor where a ship's captain (Gene Roth) drafts them as rowers on a ship belonging to King Theseus (Hal Smith). After months of rowing, Schuyler is turned into a muscleman. The king mistakes him for Hercules and offers him and the Stooges their freedom if they can kill a two-headed Cyclops (The McKeever Twins). The Stooges manage to subdue the behemoth by shooting the tranquilizers into its mouths and they then convince Schuyler he was responsible for bringing down the giant. The king next pays the strongman to defeat a Cretan bull; he later brings down a nine-headed Hydra. After all the money they saved to buy a boat is taken by crooks Achilles the Heel (Lewis Charles) and Freddie the Fence (Eddie Foster), the Stooges take Schuyler on a tour where he defeats an array of wild beasts, thus replenishing their fortunes. When the crooks try to get their money a second time, Schuyler knocks them out. He and the boys buy a boat and return to Ithaca where Hercules has become infuriated that Schuyler has been using his name. Odius has placed Diane under a spell with a potion and he warns Hercules that Ulysses is trying to overthrow him. When the Stooges and Schuyler arrive at Odius' palace, Odius tricks them into falling into a dungeon and then decides to pit Schuyler against Hercules in the local arena. The next day the two strongmen do battle with Schuyler defeating Hercules and making him promise to help Ulysses. Hercules frees the Stooges as Schuyler saves Diane and they all rush to the time machine in a chariot followed by Odius. They get it started and take off with Odius hanging on; after traveling through the centuries and witnessing the Crusades and Lord Nelson's victory at Trafalgar, they push him off in the Old West where the king is chased by Indians. Returning to the present, the group is confronted by Dimsal who is sent into Puritan times and comes back in a pillory. As the Stooges saw him free, Schuyler and Diane kiss.

Following their successful return to films in *Have Rocket, Will Travel* (q.v.) in 1959, The Three Stooges teamed with Moe Howard's son-in-law, Norman Maurer, to form Normandy Productions. Previously Maurer had worked as a writer and artist on Three Stooges comic books. *The Three Stooges Meet Hercules*, which Columbia issued early in 1962, was the first in a series of new Stooges movies that was followed six months later by *The Three Stooges in Orbit* (q.v.). Filmed in "Glorious Black and White," the feature was a mildly entertaining affair that had great appeal to moppet audiences. The Stooges are in good form and work well with director Edward Bernds, who had helmed many of their Columbia short subjects. Ed Naha in *Horrors: From Screen to Scream* (1975) noted that the film contained "[s]ome genuinely funny scenes and nice spoofing of the Italian grunt parades." When the feature came out on video (in 1988 from Goodtimes), *The Phantom's Ultimate Video Guide* (1989) opined, "The Stooges' determinedly violent take on the human condition is more popular today than it's ever been." With the film's release in Great Britain in the summer of 1963, *The Monthly Film Bulletin* termed it "[l]amentable slapstick rubbish.... [T]he production is tawdry, the comedy very tired indeed."

Hercules was portrayed by Samson Burke, a Canadian body builder, swimmer and professional wrestler who billed himself in the ring as Sammy Berg. He appeared in over a dozen films, and played other mythological characters like Ursus in *La Vendetta di Ursus* (The Revenge of Ursus, 1961), Maciste in *Toto Contra Maciste* (Toto vs. Maciste, 1961) and the Cyclops Polyphemus in the TV miniseries *L'Oddesea* (1976), which was released theatrically as *The Adventures of Ulysses*.

The 3 Worlds of Gulliver

(1960; 98 minutes; Color) PRODUCER: Charles H. Schneer. DIRECTOR: Jack Sher. SCREENPLAY: Arthur Ross and Jack Sher, from the novel by Jonathan Swift. PHOTOGRAPHY: Wilkie Cooper. EDITOR: Raymond Poulton. MUSIC: Bernard Herrmann. SONG: George Duning and Ned Washington. ART DIRECTORS: Gil Parrondo and Derek Barrington. SOUND: Gordon K. McCallum. SPECIAL VISUAL EFFECTS: Ray Harryhausen. PRODUCTION SUPERVISOR: Luis Roberts. COSTUMES: Eleanor Abbey. ASSISTANT DIRECTORS: Eugenio Martin and Paul Ganspoler. CAST: Kerwin Mathews (Dr. Lemuel Gulliver), Jo Morrow (Gwendolyn Bermogg), June Thorburn (Elizabeth Whitley), Lee Patterson (Reldresal), Gregoire Aslan (King Brob of Brobdingnag), Basil Sydney (Emperor of Lilliput), Charles Lloyd Pack (Makovan), Martin Benson (Flimnap), Mary Ellis (Queen of Brobdingnag), Marion Spencer (Queen of Lilliput), Peter Bull (Lord Bermogg), Alec Mango (Minister of Lilliput), Sherri Alberoni (Glumdalclitch), Noel Purcell (Captain Pritchard), Doris Lloyd (Mrs. Dewsbury), Joan Hickson (Patient), Waveney Lee (Shrike), John Breslin (Guard).

Working title: *Gulliver's Travels*.

The fifth screen collaboration between producer Charles H. Schneer and special effects animator Ray Harryhausen, *The 3 Worlds of Gulliver*, Columbia's Christmas release for 1960, lacked the excitement and entertainment value of its predecessors. Filmed in Spain and London's Pinewood Studios in Super Dynamation by Morningside Productions, the feature failed to properly evoke the satire and social commentary of Jonathan Swift's 1726 novel, and its visual effects were mediocre compared to the previous Harryhausen efforts. Outside of brief appearances by a couple of giant rodents, the film's only excitement was a fight between the diminutive Gulliver and an oversized crocodile. To add to its obvious appeal to youngsters, the feature include two songs by George Duning and Ned Washington, "Gentle Love," crooned by star Kerwin Mathews, and "What a Wonderful, Wonderful World."

In the rural English village of Wapping in 1699, Lemuel Gulliver (Mathews) is fed up with being a poor country physician and financially unable to marry his fiancée Elizabeth Whitley (June Thorburn). He decides to join Captain Pritchard (Noel Purcell) as a ship's doctor but Elizabeth objects. After they quarrel over a tumbledown cottage she wants to buy for their home, Gulliver sets sail with Pritchard not realizing that Elizabeth is a stowaway on the ship. When she is discovered the captain vows to put the young woman off at their first stop but a storm erupts and Gulliver is thrown overboard. He is washed ashore on the island of Lilliput where handsome Reldresal (Lee Patterson) is in love with beautiful Gwendolyn (Jo Morrow), who is about to be exiled with her belligerent father Lord Bermogg (Peter Bull), who had a falling-out with the island's emperor (Basil Sydney) on how to crack an egg. When Gulliver awakens he finds himself staked to the shore since he is a giant among the tiny Lilliputians. Minister of Defense Flimnap (Martin Benson) urges the emperor to have his army kill the giant with poisoned arrows but Gulliver proves his kindness by using his breath to blow away a sudden storm. The emperor orders him freed and the physician begins to build a boat to take him home. When Flimnap complains about how much the newcomer eats and drinks, Gulliver removes trees to make way for farm land and brings in tons of fish in his hat. Claiming he can make Lilliput an island without greed or envy, Gulliver becomes a citizen but the emperor will not permit him to continue building his boat until he aids in the fight with the people of the island of Blefscu. A contest involving tightrope walking is set up between Flimnap and Reldresal to see who will lead the island's army against Blefscu. When the defense minister's men use dirty tricks to defeat his opponent, Gulliver sneezes, causing them to fall down, with Reldresal winning the contest. The vengeful Flimnap informs the emperor about Reldresal's love for Gwendolyn; when the young warrior refuses to renounce her, he is placed in prison.

Gulliver breaks Reldresal out of jail and then swims to Blefscu whereby bringing back that island's naval armada, he ends any chance of war. On Lilliput, Gulliver is praised by the populace and the emperor gives him a medal and then orders to him wipe out the people of Blefscu but he refuses.

When Reldresal tells him the emperor plans to have him killed, Gulliver boards his finished boat and sets sail, eventually landing on another island, Brobdingnag, where he is captured by Glumdalclitch (Sherri Alberoni), who is 40 feet tall. In this land of giants, he is taken to the king's (Gregoire Aslan) castle, where he finds Elizabeth, who wound up there after a shipwreck. While the king makes the young girl the guardians of the little people, sorcerer Makovan (Charles Lloyd Pack) warns him they are evil. Given their own small castle, Gulliver and Elizabeth are so happy that they wake up Glumdalclitch in the middle of the night and ask to be married. She rouses the king and the rest of the court and a marriage ceremony is performed. After everyone goes back to bed, the newlyweds sneak out of the castle for their honeymoon. The next morning the girl goes searching for them. In a wooded area, a chipmunk grabs Gulliver and drags him into its lair. Glumdalclitch finds Elizabeth, rescues Gulliver and takes them back to the castle where Makovan declares the physician is a witch after he formulates a remedy for the queen's (Mary Ellis) upset stomach from chemicals in the sorcerer's laboratory. In order to save Elizabeth and himself, Gulliver denounces science but Makovan tricks him into revealing his true beliefs and the king condemns him to death by having him fight his pet crocodile. After a lengthy battle, the physician kills the reptile and he and Elizabeth are carried away by Glumdalclitch in a covered basket. As the king, his sorcerer and the court follow her, the girl takes the little people to a forest but the ruler orders a brush fire set to trap them. Before they can stop her, Glumdalclitch throws the basket into a stream which goes into the sea. When they come to on a beach, Gulliver and Elizabeth realize their love is the only important thing in life, happily finding out they are near Wapping.

Eugene Archer in *The New York Times* opined, "While the adults will find it all too mechanical to really capture the imagination, and may resent the unclear ending that seems certain to provoke some youthful queries, they should be grateful for a children's film that treats a classic without condescension or burlesque." *Variety* proclaimed,

"Jonathan Swift's 18th-century stinging satire has been considerably softened and drastically romanticized, but enough of its telling caustic comment remains ... The picture is notable for its visuo-cinematic achievements and its bold, bright and sweeping score by Bernard Herrmann. Special visual effects expert Ray Harryhausen, whose Superdynamation process makes the motion-pictured Gulliver plausible and workable, rates a low bow for his painstaking, productive efforts."

The *3 Worlds of Gulliver* soundtrack was issued on Colpix Records (CP-414) in 1961; it included not only music but also dialogue and sound effects. Citadel Records reissued the soundtrack in stereo in 1981 (CT-7018). More of the movie's score was included in the 1976 London Records album "Mysterious Film World of Bernard Herrmann" (SPC-21137).

Although a sequel to *The 3 Worlds of Gulliver* (to be called *The New Travels of Master Gulliver*) was planned by Schneer and Harryhausen, with Mathews again in the title role, it was never made. The two collaborators did make an NBC-TV series pilot in 1963 called *Gulliver*, produced by Screen Gems. Again filmed in Dynamation, it starred John Cairney as Gulliver and Christina Gregg as his lady love. The project failed to sell as a series.

The Tingler

(1959; 82 minutes) PRODUCER-DIRECTOR: William Castle. PRODUCER'S ASSOCIATE: Dona Holloway. SCREENPLAY: Robb White. PHOTOGRAPHY: Wilfrid M. Cline. EDITOR: Chester W. Schaeffer. MUSIC: Von Dexter. ART DIRECTOR: Phil Bennett. SOUND: Harry Mills. SETS: Milton Stumph. ASSISTANT DIRECTOR: Herb Wallerstein. CAST: Vincent Price (Dr. Warren Chapin), Judith Evelyn (Martha Higgins), Darryl Hickman (David Morris), Patricia Cutts (Isabel Chapin), Pamela Lincoln (Lucy Stevens), Philip Coolidge (Oliver "Ollie" Higgins), Dal McKinnon (Projectionist), Bob Gunderson (Ryerson), Clarence Straight, Gail Bonney, Amy Fields, Pat Colby (Audience Members), William Castle (Host).

Working title: *The Chiller*.

A good, old-fashioned horror film that boasted a genre star (Vincent Price), a deadly monster and a variety of shock effects, *The Tingler* was the first of eight such features producer-director William Castle made for Columbia from 1959 to 1964. It was due to these films that Castle got the reputation of being a "gimmick" filmmaker, one who used various methods to promote his features, resulting in big box office returns. In this case the trick was "Percepto," a hidden seat buzzer used in selected theatres to cause audience members to allegedly feel the effect of the title monster. In reality the buzzers were war surplus vibrating motors. In some audiences, "plants" would scream and "faint" at the proper time.

Filmed at the Columbia Ranch in Burbank, California, *The Tingler* cost $400,000 to make but its final budget ended up at nearly one million dollars thanks to the added ballyhoo bills. The production made a bundle for Columbia and Castle followed it with *13 Ghosts* (q.v.) the next year.

Following the execution of the killer (Bob Gunderson) of two women, pathologist Dr. Warren Chapin (Price) performs an autopsy on the electrocuted man in front of the deceased's brother-in-law Ollie Higgins (Philip Coolidge). Chapin finds the dead man's spinal column has splintered and he speculates it was due to fear, a phenomenon he has been researching for many years. Ollie suggests that the doctor refer to this force of fear as "the Tingler." Once the autopsy is finished, Ollie hitches a ride into town with Chapin who takes him to the silent film theatre Ollie runs with his deaf-mute wife Martha (Judith Evelyn). While having a cup of coffee with Ollie, the doctor accidentally cuts his finger and the sight of blood causes Martha to become terrified and faint. When she recovers, Chapin theorizes that her fainting was a psychosomatic escape since she could not scream to relieve her fright. When he goes home, Chapin is met by his beautiful sister-in-law, Lucy Stevens (Pamela Lincoln), who tells him his wife Isabel (Patricia Cutts) has gone out. She also complains that her sister will not share their family inheritance with her so she can marry her fiancé, Chapin's assistant David Morris (Darryl Hickman). When David arrives to take Lucy to dinner, the doctor tells him about Martha's reaction and speculates that something solid in the spinal cord causes a reaction in people at the instant of complete terror. At one o'clock in the morning, Chapin sees Isabel kissing a man outside their home; when she comes inside they argue over her infidelities and her treatment of Lucy. Isabel warns her husband she controls the family's money and that she could put an end to his work. Chapin forces his wife at gunpoint into his laboratory where he fires the weapon and she collapses. He places her on an examining table and takes x-rays of her spine and when she comes to he informs her that the gun contained blanks and that she fainted due to terror.

The next day Chapin shows the x-rays to David and they reveal a hardened substance along the contour of the spine which the doctor thinks is caused by terror and can only be dispelled by screaming. Attempting to create a Tingler in himself, the doctor injects LSD into his arm and this causes him to have uncontrolled fears of being crushed by the laboratory walls moving in on him. Screaming, the doctor collapses. He later realizes that people who cannot scream can produce the Tingler. Returning to the theater with the excuse he is worried about Martha, Chapin examines the woman and gives her an injection. The woman goes to sleep only to wake up and see a chair rocking in her bedroom as the lights go out and doors open and close. When she tries to get out of the bedroom, a deformed hand with an axe appears, followed by a walking, putrid corpse. In the kitchen a cabinet door opens and on it is her death certificate stating that she died of fright. Martha runs into the bathroom where she sees a blood-filled bathtub with a hand emerging from it. Unable to scream, she dies of fright.

Well after midnight, Ollie arrives at Chapin's home telling him that his wife is dead and that he brought her body for an autopsy. During the procedure the corpse rises up due to a muscular reaction. The doctor removes a black crustacean-like creature from Martha's spine. The thing tries to wrap itself around Chapin's arm before he manages to lock it in a medical case. Isabel witnesses the event, congratulates her husband on proving his theory and suggests they reconcile. She then gives him a doped drink and releases the Tingler which tries to strangle him; it is immobilized when Lucy arrives and screams. Ollie returns home with the corpse of his wife and then cleans up the place, removing items like a fright mask and hand that he used to scare Martha to death. The next day Chapin tries to destroy the creature but fails and speculates that the only way to end its existence is to return it to Martha's body. Finding out that the dead woman's corpse is not at the local funeral home, Chapin goes back to the theater and confronts Ollie, who was about to leave with the money his wife had hoarded in their home safe. Ollie admits killing Martha, saying she had threatened to do the same to him on several occasions. The Tingler, which Chapin has brought with him in a case, breaks loose and escapes through a loose floor board and enters the movie theatre showing the 1921 feature *Tol'able David*. When a woman (Gail Bonney) screams after the Tingler attacks her leg, Chapin turns out the theater lights and tells the audience members to scream in order to save their lives. The doctor and Ollie see the creature's shadow on the movie screen and go to the projection room where it is trying to strangle the projectionist (Dal McKennon). Chapin puts the monster in a film case, hurries to the Higgins home and put it back onto Martha's spine. When Chapin informs Ollie he plans to call the police, the man pulls a gun on him and the doctor leaves. The bedroom door and window slam shut and Ollie sees Martha sit up in bed, staring with dead eyes. Ollie tries to scream but cannot and dies of fright.

While audiences flocked to *The Tingler*, the critics were less than enthusiastic. Some looked at it in with a tongue-in-cheek reaction like *Variety*: "The film abounds in hokum, camouflaged in science ... Overall, it's a highly entertaining property." *The Hollywood Reporter* felt it was "a lot of fun." Douglas Brode in *Lost Films of the Fifties* (1991) called it "a dull, dumb, dreary item which nonetheless caught on big owing to a brilliant gimmick"; Phil Hardy said it was "Castle's best film" in *The Encyclopedia of Horror Movies* (1986). Mike Mayo took a sociological approach to the film in *Videohound's Horror Show* (1998) when he observed, "Beyond the loopy horror aspects, which are a ton of fun, the film's subtext of male-female sexual and economic competition in the 1950s is fascinating." Perhaps Lucy Chase Williams summed up *The Tingler* best in *The Complete Films of Vincent Price* (1995) when he dubbed it "one of Vincent Price's most ridiculous, most enjoyable, and most popular films."

While *The Tingler* has some genuine fright moments and a lovingly absurd plot, the title monster is anything but ferocious; this black, rubber giant centipede is tugged around by strings. The invitation to the audience to scream when the creature makes its rounds is one of the most endearing aspects of the production. Also fun is the prologue in which Castle hawks the shenanigans, warning that certain audience members may experience mysterious electronic impulses along with strange, tingling sensations. He claims the only relief to these is screaming.

For silent film buffs, the showing of portions of the 1921 feature *Tol'able David* featuring scenes with star Richard Barthelmess and villain Ernest Torrence is of interest. Filmed in black and white, *The Tingler* has a color sequence in which the blood in Martha's bathroom is bright red.

The feature was later the subject of a 1994 video documentary, *Scream for Your Lives! William Castle and the Tingler*.

Torture Garden

(1967; 100 minutes; Color) PRODUCERS: Max J. Rosenberg and Milton Subotsky. DIRECTOR: Freddie Francis. SCREENPLAY: Robert Bloch. PHOTOGRAPHY: Norman Warwick. EDITOR: Peter Elliott. MUSIC: Don Banks and James Bernard. ART DIRECTORS: Don Mingaye and Scott Slimon. SOUND: Ken Rawkins. Production Supervisor: Ted Wallis. PRODUCTION MANAGER: Tony Wallis. PRODUCTION DESIGN: Bill Constable. MAKEUP: Jill Carpenter. CONTINUITY: Barbara Rowland. ASSISTANT DIRECTOR: Derek Parr. CAST: Jack Palance (Ronald Wyatt), Burgess Meredith (Dr. Diabolo), Beverly Adams (Carla Hayes), Peter Cushing (Lancelot Canning), Michael Bryant (Colin Williams), John Standing (Leo Winston), Robert Hutton (Bruce Benton), John Phillips (Eddie Storm), Michael Ripper (Gordon Roberts), Bernard Kay (Dr. Otto Heim), Catherine Finn (Nurse Parker), Maurice Denham (Uncle Roger), Ursula Howells (Maxine Chambers), David Bauer (Mike Charles), Niall MacGinnis (Doctor), Nicole Shelby (Millie), Barbara Ewing (Dorothy Endicott), Clytie Jessop (Atropos), Hedger Wallace (Edgar Allan Poe), Michael Hawkins (Constable), Timothy Bateson (Barker).

Max J. Rosenberg and Milton Subotsky formed Amicus Productions in the mid–1960s and the company quickly became a rival to Hammer Films in making horror movies. Since the late 1950s, Columbia had been releasing some of the Hammer product in the U.S. and in 1967 the studio picked up Amicus' second outing, *Torture Garden*, and in some venues double-billed it with *Berserk* (q.v.). As a promotional gimmick, packets of garden seeds were given to theatrical patrons who viewed the movie, which was shown stateside early in 1967 and not until the end of the year in its homeland of Great Britain, where it was made at the Shepperton Studios in Middlesex. Amicus majored in anthology productions and *Torture Garden* was no exception, being based on stories by Robert Bloch who also wrote the screenplay. Bloch had scripted *The Skull* and *The Psychopath* (both 1965) and *The Deadly Bees* (1966) for Amicus. Following the financial success of *Torture Garden* he penned *The House That Dripped Blood* (1971) and *Asylum* (1972) for the company.

At his "Torture Garden," a fair sideshow exhibit, Dr. Diabolo (Burgess Meredith) presents an electrocution before his audience and for extra money offers to let them experience real horrors in his inner sanctum. Accepting his proposal are playboy Colin Williams (Michael Bryant), Hollywood actress Carla Hayes (Beverly Adams) and her cousin Dorothy Endicott (Barbara Ewing), Edgar Allan Poe collector Ronald Wyatt (Jack Palance) and businessman Gordon Roberts (Michael Ripper). For five pounds they each are placed before a statue of Atropos (Clytie Jessop), goddess of destiny who holds the shears of fate, and Diabolo promises to reveal to them the horror hidden within themselves.

Williams, the first to look at the shears, has a vision where he goes to visit his elderly Uncle Roger (Maurice Denham), whom he has not seen in three years. When the old man refuses to tell his nephew the source of his apparent wealth, Williams keeps his heart medicine from him and Roger dies. Ransacking his uncle's cottage looking for the miser's gold he goes into the cellar where he digs up a coffin. When he opens it, a cat springs out. That night the feline puts Williams under its power and demands he kill an old beggar. The next day Williams digs up a chest of gold in the cellar but later is forced by the cat to kill his uncle's nurse (Catherine Finn). That night Williams is about to leave the area when a constable (Michael Hawkins) notices blood on his clothes trunk and he is arrested for decapitating the nurse and the vagrant. In his cell, Williams tells the local doctor (Niall MacGinnis) about being under the spell of the cat and that it feeds on the heads of his vic-

Jack Palance in *Torture Garden* (1967).

tims. That night the cat returns for Williams' head and then places the constable under its spell. Back in the Torture Garden, the playboy admits he was planning a trip to see his uncle.

Next starlet Carla Hayes faces the shears: In the apartment she shares with another actress, Millie (Nicole Shelby), she deliberately ruins the girl's dress in order to go out with the young woman's date, middle-aged film producer Mike Charles (David Bauer). At a restaurant they meet film star veteran Bruce Benton (Robert Hutton) and the producer of his current film, Eddie Storm (John Phillips). Mike soon has a falling-out with Storm and leaves. Millie becomes friendly with Benton, who suggests to Storm that she should test for a part in their production. When she gets the role, Carla buys Benton an expensive watch. Storm advises her to leave him alone. Later the star drives off with two hoodlums and is trailed by Storm and Carla. They find him shot in the forehead in a secluded area. He is rushed to Dr. Heim's (Bernard Kay) sanatorium; Storm later tells Carla that Benton has had a complete recovery. When she expresses doubt, Storm admits that it was Benton's double who was murdered because he owned gambling debts. Carla questions Storm about his past and he becomes very upset. When she embraces Benton, she accidentally scratches his face with her fingernails and finds he is made of metal. He confesses to her that both he and Storm are automatons whose brains were transplanted into robots so they could live forever. Storm arrives with Dr. Heim, and Benton suggests to them that Carla also become a robot.

The next patron to look at the shears is Dorothy, a writer who gets an interview with renowned pianist Leo Winston (John Standing), who shows her his grand piano, a present from his late mother. Winston and Dorothy fall in love. He has a row with his manager (Ursula Howells) over the girl and agrees to postpone a concert tour in order to be with her. Winston has told Dorothy that the piano resents her and it smashes a photo of her that she gave Winston. When Winston goes to pack to go away with Dorothy, she hears the piano playing and investigates. It pursues her around the room and pushes her out of a window to her death.

Wyatt faces the shears and ends up at a party given in honor of fellow Poe fancier Lancelot Channing (Peter Cushing), who invites him to his home to see his complete collection. There Channing informs Ronald that both his father and grandfather were Poe collectors and he takes him to the basement where Wyatt sees a previously unpublished Poe work, "The House of the Worm," and other unknown works by the famed writer. Channing informs Wyatt that his grandfather not only collected the ashes of the author but used the occult to resurrect him. Channing is killed by Wyatt when he tries to stop him from entering a locked room adjacent to the cellar. There Wyatt finds Poe, who demands that Wyatt let him finally die by fire. He carries out the author's wishes only to become a disciple of the Devil.

Finally, when it is Roberts' turn to face the shears he goes berserk and stabs Diablo to death as Williams and the two women quickly depart. Diabolo then pays off Gordon, who is really his shill in the act — but they are seen by Wyatt, who remained behind to make a deal with the showman.

An interesting aspect of the plot had the character of Atropos not only as a lifelike statue but also being seen in the various vignettes, such as a nurse during Benton's operation, the portrait of the mother of pianist Winston and a patron at the display of Channing's Poe memorabilia. Many critics were taken with Jack Palance's overwrought performance as a Poe collector in deference to the more underplayed work of Peter Cushing, in a surprisingly small role, as his rival. As to be expected, Burgess Meredith chewed up the scenery as the Mephistopheles-like Dr. Diabolo.

Ed Naha in *Horrors: From Screen to Scream* (1975) thought it was "above average." In *The Encyclopedia of Horror Movies* (1986), Phil Hardy opined, "[Director Freddie] Francis's workmanlike professionalism is here enhanced by [Robert] Bloch's adaptations of his own stories. The result is an omnibus movie far better than Francis's *Dr. Terror's House of Horrors* (1964) and an improvement on previous Francis-Bloch collaborations such as *The Skull* and *Psychopath* ... or the execrable *The Deadly Bees*." James O'Neill in *Terror on Tape* (1994) said it was an "[e]ntertaining anthology.... Solid Robert Bloch script derived from some of his *Weird Tales* stories and slick direction from Francis make this a fun omnibus."

Trapped by Television

(1936; 63 minutes) ASSOCIATE PRODUCER: Ben Pivar. DIRECTOR: Del Lord. SCREENPLAY: Harold Buchman and Lee Loeb. STORY: Sherman Lowe and Al Martin. PHOTOGRAPHY: Allen G. Siegler. EDITOR: James Sweeney. SPECIAL CAMERA EFFECTS: E. Roy Davidson.

Advertisement for *Trapped by Television* (1936).

CAST: Mary Astor (Barbara "Bobby" Blake), Lyle Talbot (Fred Dennis), Nat Pendleton (Rocky O'Neil), Joyce Compton (Mae Collins), Thurston Hall (John Curtis), Henry Mollison (Thornton), Wyrley Birch (Paul Turner), Robert Strange (Mr. Standish), Marc Lawrence (Frank "Griff" Griffin), Wade Boteler (J.W. Greggs), Lillian Leighton (Mrs. Leary), Russell Hicks, Lloyd Whitlock, William Gould, Howard C. Hickman, Boyd Irwin, George Webb, Bruce Sidney, Harry Stafford (Board Members), Max Wagner (Al), Mary Blake (Miss Walsh), Eddie Featherston (Radio Broadcaster), Robert Gordon (Delivery Man), Neil Moore (Mason), Lillian Stuart (Boarder), Harry Tenbrook, Chuck Hamilton (Policemen), Ralph McCullough (Salesman), Caroline Houseman (Secretary).

Working title: *Caught by Television.*

Trapped by Television is a good example of a film whose science fiction plot has long since become science fact: The story involves the invention of a perfect TV and the machinations of rivals to destroy the device. While television had been in the experimental stage since the 1920s, it was still considered futuristic in the summer of 1936, when Columbia issued this programmer; it had already been the plot ploy of other features like *International House* (1933) and *Murder By Television* (1935). The film marked the re-teaming of stars Mary Astor and Lyle Talbot, who had been in Warner Bros'. 1934 horror-mystery *The Return of the Terror*, and it was the second feature film to be directed by Del Lord, best known for the three dozen–plus two-reelers he did with the Three Stooges at Columbia from 1935 to 1945. The film's associate producer, Ben Pivar, made a number of horror films at Universal in the 1940s. The feature was released in Great Britain as *Caught By Television*, its working title. The *New York Times* dubbed it "a breezy, illogical concoction of comedy and melodrama."

Acme Collection Agency manager Greggs (Wade Boteler) threatens to fire collector Rocky O'Neil (Nat Pendleton), a science addict, unless he brings in business. Rocky tries to get money owed by electrical engineer Fred Dennis (Talbot) who needs two more months to complete his invention, a television that sends out pictures and sound over the air. Fascinated by the concept, Rocky agrees to give Fred more time and he also attempts to pacify the inventor's landlady (Lillian Leighton), who is owed back rent. In order for Fred to earn money, Rocky takes him to Greggs who hires him to collect an account owned by Blake Enterprises, a business promotion outfit run by Barbara "Bobby" Blake (Mary Astor) and her best friend Mae Collins (Joyce Compton). Fred goes to see Bobby and falls for her; after seeing his invention she becomes his manager. When Rocky meets Mae, he is immediately attracted to the pert blonde.

Engineer Paul Turner (Wyrley Birch) and his assistant Griffin (Marc Lawrence) have disappeared and John Curtis (Thurston Hall), the head of Paragon Broadcasting Company, is in a quandary since Turner is developing a television device for his company. He does not know that his assistant Standish (Robert Strange) is in league with Griffin in kidnapping Turner, since they plan to re-sell Curtis his own invention. Standish urges

Curtis to get bids on the TV project, planning to have Thornton (Henry Mollison), another crook, present Turner's plan as his own. When Turner threatens to go to the law, Griffin shoots him. Bobby meets with Curtis and asks for $2,000 to finish work on Fred's invention but ends up only with $200, which she gives to Fred, with whom she has fallen in love. With Rocky's help, Fred finishes the TV and tells Bobby it is ready for a demonstration. Bobby gets Curtis to call a meeting of his company's board of directors in order to show off the new invention as Standish makes plans with Griffin to sabotage the TV. Rocky and Mae set up the television camera at a football game as Fred and Bobby take the receiver to the Paragon company where Griffin has one of his stooges break a tube. When the machine blows up, Curtis throws the inventor and Bobby out of his office. The next day Fred tells Bobby that someone crossed the wires on his machine and the expensive broken tube must be replaced for the TV to work again. After the two have a tiff, Fred gets a package in the mail with the tube and he thinks Rocky paid for it. Mae learns that Bobby pawned her fur coat to buy the tube; when Fred finds out, he and Bobby make up. The two go to see Curtis again but he refuses to give them an audience although they tell Standish the invention is fixed and ready for operation. Getting a list of the board members, Bobby and Mae send out false invitations from Curtis inviting them to another demonstration at the Paragon building. Standish, Griffin and gang member Al (Max Wagner) go to Fred's apartment to destroy the television. Rocky and Mae arrive at the board room and set up the TV receiver. When the gangsters fight with Fred over the invention, the pictures are broadcast to the board members. In a cab followed by the police, Rocky goes to Fred's place and waylays the crooks. The hoodlums are arrested, Paragon buys Fred's TV and the two sets of lovers look forward to the future.

Trapped in the Sky

(1939; 61 minutes) PRODUCER: Larry Darmour. ASSOCIATE PRODUCER: Rudolph Flothow. DIRECTOR: Lewis D. Collins. STORY-SCREENPLAY: Eric Taylor. PHOTOGRAPHY: James S. Brown, Jr. EDITOR: Dwight Caldwell. SOUND: Tom Lambert. ASSISTANT DIRECTOR: Carl Hiecke. CAST: Jack Holt (Major Roston), Ralph Morgan (Colonel Whalen), C. Henry Gordon (William Fornay), Katherine DeMille (Carol Rayder), Paul Everton (General Moody), Sidney Blackmer (Jules Mann), Ivan Lebedeff (Joseph Dure), Regis Toomey (Lieutenant Gray), Holmes Herbert (Walter Fielding), Guy D'Ennery (Henry the Butler).

Working titles: *Army Spy* and *Sabotage*.

Like *Trapped by Television* (q.v.), *Trapped in the Sky*'s sci-fi plot (involving an electronically driven, high speed, noiseless airplane) has since become passé, but in the summer of 1939, when the feature was released, it was still a futuristic weapon. The film was one of over 50 Jack Holt–Columbia vehicles made between 1927 to 1941; among these were blockbusters like *Submarine* (1928) and *Dirigible* (1931), along with the genre efforts *Behind the Mask* (1932) and *Black Moon* (1934) [qq.v.]. *Variety* said of the feature, "Aviation mystery actioner produced with skillful economy and making the most of an unpretentious script and Jack Holt's talents.... [T]he picture ambles along at a leisurely pace.... Director hasn't provided enough suspense to create more than mild interest in the proceedings." In *The Fabulous Holts* (1976), Buck Rainey noted, "It was typical Holt all the way as our hero fought for justice and country."

Aviation inventor Walter Fielding (Holmes Herbert) designs a new high-speed aircraft which he offers to sell to the government until William Fornay (C. Henry Gordon), an agent for a foreign power, offers him a much bigger amount of money for the airplane. In order to get rich, the inventor decides to sabotage the tests on the aircraft which are to be conducted under the auspices of Major Roston (Holt). The army flyer commander chooses his good friend Lieutenant Gray (Regis Toomey) to run the test flight, since he feels there is little danger due to Fornay's reputation. The plane crashes and Gray is killed, with Roston doubting the plane's failure was an accident. Suspecting spies, the major sets up a court martial for himself and blames the army for the crash that killed his friend. Drummed out of the service, Roston comes in contact with pretty Carol Rayder (Katherine DeMille), who turns out to be a foreign operative. When the major attempts to connect the plane crash to her organization, the young woman and her immediate superior Joseph Dure (Ivan Lebedeff) are eliminated. Looking into the murders, Roston finds a connection to Fornay that convinces him the inventor was responsible for his plane's sabotage. He manages to get Fielding to go with him on another test flight and sets up an explosion that causes the terrified inventor to admit his guilt. Roston, who never left the army, then arrests the foreign spies.

12 to the Moon

(1960; 74 minutes) PRODUCER-STORY: Fred Gebhardt. ASSOCIATE PRODUCER: Thom E. Fox. DIRECTOR: David Bradley. SCREENPLAY: DeWitt Bodeen. PHOTOGRAPHY: John Alton. EDITOR: Edward Mann. MUSIC: Michael Anderson. ART DIRECTOR: Rudi Feld. SOUND: Herman Lewis. SETS: John Burton. PRODUCTION SUPERVISOR: Joel Freeman. ASSISTANT TO PRODUCER: Ned Roberts. SPECIAL PHOTOGRAPHIC EFFECTS: Howard A. Anderson Co. ADDITIONAL SPECIAL EFFECTS: E. Nicholson. ASSISTANT DIRECTOR: Gilbert Mandelik. CAST: Ken Clark (Captain John Anderson), Michi Kobi (Dr. Hideko Murata), Tom Conway (Dr. Feodor Orloff), Anthony Dexter (Dr. Luis Vargas), Francis X. Bushman (Secretary General of the International Space Order/Narrator), John Wengraf (Dr. Erich Heinrich), Anna-Lisa (Dr. Sigrid Bomark), Tema Bey (Dr. Selim Hamid), Philip Baird (Dr. William Rochester), Richard Weber (Dr. David Ruskin), Roger Til (Dr. Ethienne Martel), Cory Devlin (Dr. Asmara Makonen), Bob Montgomery, Jr. (Roddy Murdock).

A dozen people with scientific backgrounds, from various parts of the world, are assigned to make the first voyage to the Moon in a rocket dubbed "Lunar Eagle." Named by the Secretary General of the International Space Order (Francis X. Bushman) to go on the expedition are its leader, Captain John Anderson (Ken Clark), an American; Japanese pharmacist Dr. Hideko Murata (Michi Kobi); Soviet Dr. Feodor Orloff (Tom Conway); Brazilian pilot Dr. Luis Vargas (Anthony Dexter); German scientist Dr. Erich Heinrich (John Wengraf); Swedish physician Dr. Sigrid Bomark (Anna-Lisa); Turkish doctor Selim Hamid (Tema Bey); British geophysicist Dr. William Rochester (Philip Baird); Dr. David Ruskin (Richard Weber), an Israeli; Dr. Ethienne Martel (Roger Til), a French engineer; African astronomer Dr. Asmara Makonen (Cory Devlin); and 19-year-old mathematics genius Roddy Murdock (Bob Montgomery, Jr.). Also along on the voyage are various animals, including a dog, cats and monkeys, to be used in a breeding experiment on the lunar satellite. During the voyage the international crew bickers, with the pompous Orloff bragging about his country's space feats. The Israeli and the German become good friends while the Frenchman takes a dislike to young Roddy.

After surviving a meteor shower, the rocket lands on the lunar surface and 11 of the astronauts go out to explore while Martel remains to oversee communications. Proclaiming the Moon interna-

Anthony Dexter, Michi Kobi, Bob Montgomery, Jr., Ken Clark, Cory Devlin and Tom Conway in *12 to the Moon* (1960).

tional territory by planting a flag, the eleven engage magnets to dodge meteors. Orloff finds a fiery rock he dubs the Medea Stone as Hamid and Ingrid enter a cave with air and water, locate a mushroom-like substance that explodes, and disappear into a strange mist. When Orloff touches flowing ore, his space gloves are damaged, forcing him to return to the ship with Dr. Murata. Hamid and Ingrid do not appear and the other nine astronauts follow their trail into the cave but only find a wall of ice. Dr. Rochester dies when he falls into a pumice pit and Captain Anderson nearly meets the same fate until Roddy saves him with one of the magnets. With dwindling air supplies, the astronauts return to the rocket only to find communication with Earth has stopped. The ship's magnetic tape recorder begins sending printed characters that Dr. Murata translates as being from a civilization that lives deep inside the Moon. They are told to leave the orb although Hamid and Sigrid have agreed to stay to help them to understand love. They also ask that the cats be left behind so they too can be studied. Dr. Ruskin believes the communication to be faked. Erich suffers a heart attack and reveals that his father was the Nazi responsible for the murders of the Israeli's family and later asks for David's friendship. The rocket blasts off but when it approaches Earth the crew finds that North America has been frozen. The Moon people inform them that they have done this as a warning and the scientists decide to unthaw the area by dropping an atomic bomb on Popocatepetl, a Mexican volcano. David and Eric draw the lots to pilot the space shuttle that will unleash the bomb. Orloff and Martel are assigned to prepare the explosive but Martel tries to destroy it so the continent will stay frozen. Although both men are Communists, Orloff fights to stop his colleague and is aided by Anderson. The two shuttle pilots drop the bomb but are unable to land on Earth due to gravity changes and die after completing their mission. While the continent thaws, the rocket becomes frozen by the Moon people. But after they witness the heroics of David and Erich they reverse the procedure and issue an invitation to again visit the Moon. With communications reestablished with Earth, the surviving crew members prepare to return home.

12 to the Moon was made by Luna Productions in eight days at a cost of $150,000 and sold to Columbia Pictures, who issued it on double bills with *Battle in Outer Space* and *13 Ghosts* [qq.v.]. A rather bland, darkly photographed production with acceptable special effects, the feature is more interesting for its participants than its plot. Produced by Fred Gebhardt, from his original story, the feature was scripted by DeWitt Bodeen, who wrote the Val Lewton horror thrillers *Cat People* (1942) and *The Seventh Victim* (1943), both starring Tom Conway, who played the Russian scientist. Ironically, the actor was born in Russia of British parents. Gebhardt went on to produce and write *The Phantom Planet* (1961) that also starred Anthony Dexter and Francis X. Bushman, who appeared in *12 to the Moon*. Top-billed Ken Clark had earlier headlined *Attack of the Giant Leeches* (1959) and would star in a number of European genre spy efforts. Cinematographer John Alton had filmed *The Lady and the Monster* (1944) and *The Ghost Goes Wild* (1947). The director, David Bradley, was a film historian and teacher who gained early recognition for semi-professional features like *Peer Gynt* (1941) and *Julius Caesar* (1949) but afterward helmed the tacky *The Madmen of Mandoras* (1964), which had a later reincarnation as *They Saved Hitler's Brain*.

Critics were not kind to *12 to the Moon*. *Variety* thought it "crude and cliché-ridden," while the *Monthly Film Bulletin* said it was a "juvenile piece of hokum." In *Science Fiction* (1984), Phil Hardy found it to be a "decidedly minor offering." Steven H. Scheuer's *Movies on TV 1975–76* (1974) proclaimed, "Spaceship takes off for lunar territory and boredom."

One ironic aspect of the film's plot had the Russian astronaut, while self-important and overbearing, fighting to save the United States in opposition to his fellow Communist who wants North America to remain frozen. Such a plot wrinkle is quite surprising, coming near the apex of the Cold War. A prophetic aspect of the script included the discovery of ice on the Moon, something not confirmed until a half century later by lunar probes. Probably the film's most (unintentional) humorous scene was the one in which looker Anna-Lisa take a waterless shower by means of ultrasound! The Moon beings are shown only briefly as giant shadows.

20 Million Miles to Earth

(1957; 82 minutes) PRODUCER: Charles H. Schneer. DIRECTOR: Nathan Juran. SCREENPLAY: Bob Williams and Christopher Knopf. STORY: Charlotte Knight and (uncredited) Ray Harryhausen. PHOTOGRAPHY: Irving Lippman and Carlo Ventimiglia. EDITOR: Edwin

Bryant. MUSIC DIRECTOR: Mischa Bakaleinikoff. ART DIRECTOR: Cary Odell. SOUND: Lambert Day. SETS: Robert Priestley. TECHNICAL VISUAL EFFECTS: Ray Harryhausen. ASSISTANT DIRECTORS: Eddie Saeta and Ottavio Oppo. CAST: William Hopper (Colonel Robert Calder), Joan Taylor (Marisa Leonardo), Frank Puglia (Dr. Leonardo), John Zaremba (Dr. Judson Uhl), Thomas Browne Henry (Major General McIntosh), Tito Vuolo (Police Commissioner Charra), Jan Arvan (Signore Contino), Arthur Space (Dr. Sharman), Bart Bradley (Pepe), George Pelling (Maples), George Khoury (Verrico), Don Orlando (Mondello), Rollin Moriyama (Dr. Koroku), Sid Cassel (Farmer), Barry Russo (Pentagon Staff Officer), Ray Harryhausen.

Working title: *The Giant Ymir*.

20 Million Miles to Earth was the third Columbia Pictures collaboration between producer Charles H. Schneer and stop motion animator Ray Harryhausen, following the successful *It Came from Beneath the Sea* (1955) and *Earth vs. the Flying Saucers* (1956) [qq.v.]. Although he got no writing credit, the film was based on a story idea by Harryhausen, one he first conceived in 1954; it went through several plot changes before emerging in its released form. For this outing, Schneer formed Morningstar Productions, an independent entity that kept his association with Columbia but gave him and Harryhausen more artistic freedom and less studio meddling. There was considerable on-location filming in Italy, including such Rome sites as the Coliseum, Forum, Palace of Justice and the Temple of Saturn. The remainder of the production was lensed at Columbia and at Corriganville. The highlight of the feature was its monster, the Ymir, a dinosaur-like creature from Venus who was somewhat akin to King Kong in that it was removed from its natural habitat and forced to defend itself in a hostile new world. Like Kong, the Ymir aroused some pathos except for the scene when it killed an elephant. The Ymir is one of Harryhausen's best stop motion–animated creations. For the scenes with the elephant, both a model and a live animal were used and it is almost impossible to tell the difference between the two on screen. It was a good thing the monster was so realistic because the Ymir has to carry the film: The plot is mundane and

The Ymir attacks Rome in *20 Million Miles to Earth* (1957).

top-billed William Hopper is one of the blandest heroes in 1950s sci-fi cinema. Leading lady Joan Taylor has little to do and is harshly photographed in several scenes.

Thanks to the monster and good production values, *20 Million Miles to Earth* proved to be a box office success. *Variety* called it "[a]nother 'monster' film to scare the kids the way they like to be scared. Good bet for the fantasy addicts." Phil Hardy in *Science Fiction* (1984) opined, "Special-effects master Harryhausen's first attempts at monster-making are only partially successful in this low-budget, poorly scripted would-be epic.... Director [Nathan] Juran ... builds flatly around the effects of Harryhausen..." In *Science Fiction Film Directors, 1895–1998* (2000), Dennis Fischer noted, "[T]he Ymir is one of Harryhausen's most expressive creations ... Juran's direction is also an improvement over that in previous Harryhausen films, involving a livelier sense of pacing and editing..."

While fishing near their Sicilian village, Verrico (George Khoury), Mondello (Don Orlando) and young Pepe (Bart Bradley) spot a flying craft fall into the sea. The three take their boat to the site and find that part of the ship's hull has been torn away. The two men enter and rescue Colonel Robert Calder (Hopper) and Dr. Sharman (Arthur Space) before the craft submerges. At the Pentagon, Major General McIntosh (Thomas Browne Henry) is informed that a returning spacecraft from Venus has sunk off the coast of Sicily and he and Dr. Judson Uhl (John Zaremba) make plans to go to Sicily.

As the rescued men are taken to a nearby hospital, Pepe finds a metal capsule on the beach; inside is a rubbery substance that he sells to zoologist Dr. Leonardo (Frank Puglia) for 200 lire. At the hospital the zoologist's niece, Marisa Leonardo (Taylor), a medical student, looks after the two men. When Calder regains consciousness he tries to communicate with the badly burned Sharman, who gives the colonel his notes before dying. As Marisa returns to her uncle's trailer she finds a small lizard-like being has come out of the substance Pepe sold her uncle. Dr. Leonardo puts the unknown specimen in a locked trailer. The next morning the creature is three times bigger and the zoologist decides to drive to Rome with it for further study. General McIntosh and Dr. Uhl arrive in Gerra, the small village near the crash site, and meet with Calder and a representative of the Italian government, Signore Contino (Jan Arvan).

They inform Contino about the Venus space flight: Thirteen months earlier, the U.S. launched a secret, manned probe of the second planet from the Sun with 17 crew members. Only Calder had survived. On board the spaceship was an Ymir, a small animal that lives in Venus' low density. McIntosh offers to pay a half-million lire for the return of the container with the specimen. Pepe tells him about finding it and selling it to Dr. Leonardo. Calder and Uhl go after the trailer.

When the zoologist and his niece stop to rest that night, they check on the Ymir and find it is now bigger than a man. It twists the bars of its cage and escapes as Calder and Uhl arrive. They track it to a nearby farm where the creature excites the horses and sheep and becomes trapped in a barn. When Calder tries to get the alien into a cage, it breaks through a wall and runs away. The local police commissioner, Charra (Tito Vuolo), announces it must be killed. Calder and McIntosh get Contino's permission to try and capture the beast and they track it to an area with sulfur pits. After the Italian military chases it with flame throwers, Calder leaves several bags with sulfur in an open area; when the Ymir finds them and begins eating, he and the soldiers surround the spot as Uhl pilots a helicopter that drops an net over the creature. Calder uses electric shock to subdue the alien and it is taken to the zoo in Rome for further examination.

McIntosh invites the press to a briefing on the creature. When asked about its size, Calder says he believes the Earth's atmosphere has upset the Ymir's metabolic rate; the more air it breathes, the more tissue it builds. Now 30 feet tall, the alien is strapped to a table at the zoo where Dr. Uhl and Dr. Koroku (Rollin Moriyama) conduct tests on it. The power in the room goes off after a large piece of equipment smashes into another machine. The creature begins to revive and Calder orders everyone out of the area. The alien attempts to leave the zoo area but is forced into combat with an elephant that it eventually kills. Calder trails the Ymir to the Tiber River where it submerges. The army shoots bombs into the water, causing the alien to rise up and go to the Roman Coliseum where it becomes lost in the labyrinth. When the creature is spotted, the soldiers use bazookas to make it climb to the top of the structure where Calder is able to knock it off with a mortar round. The Ymir plunges to its death on the pavement below and is immediately surrounded by gawkers as Calder and Joan embrace.

Six years after *20 Million Miles to Earth* was released, the French publication Star Cine Cosmos published a magazine photo novel of the film.

The 27th Day

(1957; 75 minutes) PRODUCER: Helen Ainsworth. EXECUTIVE PRODUCER: Lewis J. Rachmil. DIRECTOR: William Asher. SCREENPLAY: John Mantley, from his novel. PHOTOGRAPHY: Henry Freulich. EDITOR: Jerome Thoms. MUSIC DIRECTOR: Mischa Bakaleinikoff. ART DIRECTOR: Ross Bellah. SOUND: Ferrol Redd. SETS: Frank A. Tuttle. ASSISTANT DIRECTOR: Willard Sheldon. CAST: Gene Barry (Jonathan Clark), Valerie French (Eve Wingate), George Voskovec (Professor Klaus Bechner), Arnold Moss (The Alien), Stefan Schnabel (Soviet General), Ralph Clanton (Mr. Ingram), Friedrich Ledebur (Dr. Karl Neuhaus), Paul Birch (Admiral), Azemat Janti (Private Ivan Godofsky), Marie Tsien (Su Tan), Ed Hinton (Commander), Grandon Rhodes (United Nations Secretary General), Jerry Janger (Officer), Don Spark (Harry Bellows), David Bond (Dr. Schmidt), Eric Feldary (Soviet Sergeant), Weaver Levy (Chinese Sergeant), Monty Ash (Soviet Prison Doctor), Hank Clemin (Hans), Theodore Marcuse (Colonel Gregor), Peter Norman (Interrogator), John Bleifer (Spokesman), Mel Welles (Soviet Marshal), Sigrid Thor (General Zamke), John Dodsworth (BBC Announcer), Jacques Gallo (French Announcer), Charles Evans, Thomas Browne Henry (Army Generals), Robert Forrest (Air Force General), Mark Bennett (Gorky), Arthur Lovejoy (Brakovich), John Bryant (Agent Kelly), John Mooney (Military Police Captain), Paul Power (Army Doctor), Michael Harris (FBI Agent), Walda Winchell (Nurse), Tom Daly (Joe), Don Rhodes (Television Technician), Emil Sitka (Newspaper Seller), Philip Van Zandt (Cab Driver), Paul Frees (Newscaster Ward Mason), Ralph Brooks, Harold Miller (Pentagon Officers), Ralph Montgomery (Bar Patron).

While swimming off the coast of Cornwall in England on an outing with her painter boyfriend (Don Spark), Eve Wingate (Valerie French) is summoned by a mysterious figure to accompany him. Jonathan Clark (Gene Barry), a writer for the Los Angeles *Record Telegram*, gets the same summons, as does Su Tan (Marie Tsien), whose Chinese village is under siege by government troops. On his way to the United States to watch a satellite launch, Professor Klaus Bechner (George Voskovec), a West German scientist, gets the call and so does a Soviet prison guard, Private Ivan Godofsky (Azemat Janti). All five people next find themselves aboard a spaceship heading away from the Earth and they are greeted by a being called

Spanish-language lobby card for *The 27th Day* (1957).

the Alien (Arnold Moss). He tells them his planet, located in a nearby universe, is dying and its sun will explode in 35 days. His people want to take over the Earth but are non-violent and he has called the five of them together as representatives of the human race. He gives them each three capsules that are capable of wiping out humanity but if they are not used in 27 days the Earth will survive and his people will perish.

Back on Earth, Eve tosses her capsules into the ocean and Su Tan, after seeing the body of her dead mother and her village destroyed, kills herself, thus making her capsules useless. Clark receives a telephone call from Eve telling him she is flying to Los Angeles as the professor goes to the same city for his scientific meeting. The Alien interrupts all broadcasts around the world to state the names of the people who have been given the deadly capsules, global causing alarm. While walking across a street, Bechner is struck by an automobile and taken to Hudson Hospital where noted atomic scientist Dr. Karl Neuhaus (Friedrich Ledebur) tries to uncover the secrets of the professor's capsules. In the Soviet Union, Private Godofsky is seized by the government and the top Soviet General (Stefan Schnabel) tells his associate, Colonel Gregor (Theodore Marcuse), to make him talk. Jonathan meets Valerie at the airport and, after getting supplies, the two take refuge in an off-season race track in order to wait out the remaining 25 days. Gregor tries to torture the information he needs from Godofsky but the pain sends the young man into shock. As the professor recovers in the hospital, Dr. Neuhaus and government officials try to get him to reveal how to open the box containing the capsules but he claims he does not know the answer. Two foreign agents attempt to get the box from Bechner but they are shot and killed by federal agents. When Jonathan hears over the radio that a man looking like him was murdered by a mob, he decides to turn himself over to the authorities. Truth serum is administered to Godofsky, causing him to reveal how the capsules can be activated. The Soviets announce to the world they know the secret of the weapon and Pentagon officials attempt to get the professor, Jonathan and Eve to divulge the same information to them. When Bechner finally opens the box, Dr. Neuhaus expresses doubt as to the alien claims about the weapon and offers to serve as a guinea pig to see if it works. The Soviet general releases a letter telling the West to withdraw from all other countries or the people of North America will be obliterated. Dr. Neuhaus disintegrates when the weapon is tested and the United States removes all its troops in nations outside its borders. Realizing that the Soviets are probably still planning to use the weapon on North America, Bechner asks Jonathan to give him his capsules so he can try and mathematically decipher a code written on them. As the Soviet general begins to unleash the power of the alien weapon, Godofsky tries to stop him, causing the capsules to fall from a balcony to the street below. At the same time Bechner, who has broken the code, locks himself in a ship's cabin and sets off the power of his altered capsules, killing only the enemies of freedom. On the 27th day, Bechner contacts the aliens from the United Nations and offers them refuge in the uninhabited parts of the planet and they accept the invitation to live in peace and harmony on Earth.

Made by Romson Productions, *The 27th Day* was released by Columbia in the summer of 1957, often on a double-bill with *20 Million Miles to Earth* (q.v.). The pictures were almost direct opposites plot-wise, with the former being a slow-paced, cerebral exercise in Cold War dramatics in a sci-fi setting, while the latter was an action production focusing on a well-conceived monster. That creature, a Ymir, was created by Ray Harryhausen; some sources claim that he also did the briefly seen UFO in *The 27th Day*. *Videohound's Sci-Fi Experience* (1997) observed, "Despite some outdated philosophy and all-too-obvious preaching about the good and bad guys of the Cold War, this extremely literate film should have most viewers thinking along with the onscreen characters ... Despite flaws, an intelligent film adaptation of the John Mantley novel, still to be published when Columbia Pictures purchased the rights." The author also wrote the feature's script.

In an interesting bit of propaganda, the Soviet general (portrayed by Stefan Schnabel, in a strong performance) bore a resemblance to Josef Stalin. Top-billed Gene Barry previously headlined *The War of the Worlds* (1953) and co-star Valerie French would go on to appear in *The Four Skulls of Jonathan Drake* (1959). Director William Asher is best remembered as the producer-director of the popular ABC-TV series *Bewitched* (1964–72) that starred his wife, Elizabeth Montgomery. In 1961, *The 27th Day* was the subject of a French photo novel entitled *Les 27 Jours de Sigma*, published by Star Cine Cosmos.

The Ugly Duckling

(1959; 84 minutes) EXECUTIVE PRODUCER: Michael Carreras. ASSOCIATE PRODUCER: Tommy Lyndon-Haynes. DIRECTOR: Lance Comfort. SCREENPLAY: Sid Collin and Jack Davies. STORY: Sid Collin. PHOTOGRAPHY: Michael Reed. EDITORS: James Needs and John Dunsford. MUSIC: Douglas Gamley. ART DIRECTOR: Bernard Robinson. CAST: Bernard Breslaw (Henry Jekyll/Teddy Hyde), Jon Pertwee (Victor Jekyll), Reginald Beckwith (Reginald), Maudie Edwards (Henrietta Jekyll), Jean Muir (Snout), Richard Wattis (Barclay), Elwyn Brook-Jones (Dandy Kingsley), Michael Ripper (Benny), David Lodge (Pee Wee), Keith Smith (Figures), Michael Ward (Pasco), Mary Wilson (Lizzie), Geremy Phillips (Tiger), Ian Ainsley (Fraser), Heather Downham (Margo), Helen Pohlman (Amanda), Vicky Marshall (Kitten), Ann Mayhew (Lucienne), Jacqueline Perrin (Ursula), Helga Wahlrow (Rosemary), Jill Carson (Yum Yum), Reginald Marsh, Roger Avon, Robert Statman (Newsmen), Nicholas Tanner (Commissionaire), Cyril Chamberlain (Police Sergeant), Alan Coleshill (Willie), Robert Desmond (Dizzy), Shelagh Dey (Miss Angers), Jean Driant (M. Blum), Sheila Hammond (Receptionist), Ian Wilson (Little Man), Malika Alamont (Fifi), Lucy Griffiths (Cellist), Akline Harvey (Jane), Alexander Dore (Customer), Joe Loss (Himself), Verne Morgan (Barman), Jack Armstrong, Jamie Barnes, Richard Dake, Stella Kernball, Aileen Lewis, Peter Mander, Lola Morice, Alecia St. Leger (Old Time Dancers).

Having no relationship to Hans Christian Andersen's famous children's story of the same title, *The Ugly Duckling* was Hammer's first attempt to film the 1886 novel *Dr. Jekyll and Mr. Hyde* by Robert Louis Stevenson, albeit tongue-in-cheek. Apparently it was never released in the U.S.; Columbia distributed it in the United Kingdom in the summer of 1959 and today it is one of Hammer's most obscure titles. Perhaps the reason it got no stateside showings is that it had a British cast headed by ungainly TV comedian Bernard Bresslaw, an unknown in America. Another reason may be that U.S. audiences simply would not have understood the film's humor. Hammer filmed a more literate version of the Stevenson novel a year later as *The Two Faces of Dr. Jekyll*, which Columbia released in England (its stateside showings came by way of American International Pictures).

Gawky Henry Jekyll (Bresslaw) is the nephew of Victor Jekyll (Jon Pertwee), a bandleader who operates a dance team with his sister Henrietta (Maudie Edwards). Although they get plenty of bookings, the clumsy Henry always manages to mess things up with his dim-witted doings. Henry's greatest desire is to be a member of a gang called The Rockets and he is befriended by one of their minions, tomboy Snout (Jean Muir), although the rest of the teenagers reject him. Unhappy with his life, Henry begins tampering in the family's chemist shop where he finds his great-great grandfather Dr. Henry Jekyll's notes and concocts a formula that causes an explosion. When he recovers, Henry is changed into worldly Teddy Hyde, a master criminal and ladies man who becomes a dance hall favorite. Corrupt Dandy Kingsley (Elwyn Brook-Jones), a theater proprietor, hires Teddy to join his gang in carrying out a daring jewel robbery. When Henry returns to his old self and finds the proceeds of the robbery in his pockets, he sets out to capture the gang and ends up a hero.

In *British Sound Films: The Studio Years 1928–1959* (1984), David Quinlan wrote, "Comedy fails to build on its original good idea." The film's plot premise was used far more successfully in the 1963 and 1996 film versions of *The Nutty Professor*.

The Underwater City

(1962; 78 minutes) PRODUCER: Alex Gordon. DIRECTOR: Frank McDonald. SCREENPLAY: Owen Harris [Orville H. Hampton]. STORY: Alex Gordon and Ruth [Gordon] Alexander. PHOTOGRAPHY: Gordon Avil. EDITORS: Al Clark and Donald W. Starling. MUSIC: Ronald Stein. ART DIRECTOR: Don Ament. SOUND: George Cooper. MAKEUP: Ben Lane. PRODUCTION ASSISTANT: Jack Cash. SPECIAL EFFECTS: Howard A. Anderson Company. SPECIAL EFFECTS SUPERVISOR: Howard Lydecker. ASSISTANT DIRECTOR: Robert Agnew. CAST: William Lundigan (Bob Gage), Julie Adams (Dr. Monica Powers), Roy Roberts (Tim Graham), Carl Benton Reid (Dr. Junius Halstead), Chet Douglas (Chuck Marlow), Paul Dubov (George Burnett), Karen Norris (Phyllis Gatewood), Kathie Browne (Dotty Steele), Edward Mallory (Lieutenant Wally Steele), George DeNormand (Dr. Carl Wendt), Edmund Cobb (Meade), Roy Damron (Winchell), Paul Power (Author), Vince Williams (Narrator).

The Underwater City is one of the sorrier examples of poor theatrical distribution on the part of Columbia, which promised a major release for the production in the summer of 1962 but instead shipped it to theaters earlier in the year on the bottom half of dual bills. To add insult to injury, the movie was made in Eastman Color but ended up in theaters in black and white. Shot in a week on a $350,000 budget by Neptune Productions, the feature had several weeks of post-production work, including the destruction of the title city. Ed Naha elaborated on the film's troubles in *The Science Fictionary* (1980): "The production was plagued by front-office warfare throughout, and it shows. Per the instructions of the studio, all the 'underwater' shots were filmed 'dry' on a sound stage, through a fish tank. Making matters worse, the film was initially released in black and white (much to the surprise of the producer), which turned most of the underwater scenes a murky gray." Naha described the film as a "fairly excruciating excursion into soggy space."

Although he would prefer working with NASA on its space project, marine engineer Bob Gage (William Lundigan) agrees to oversee the building of a city beneath the ocean where people will live and harvest food for the planet (and can take refuge in the event of a nuclear war). One of the reasons Gage is won over to the project is his attraction to Dr. Monica Powers (Julie Adams), the niece of the designer of the futuristic city, Dr. Junius Halstead (Carl Benton Reid) of the Institute of Oceanography. A huge eel kills a geologist (George DeNormand) making a survey of the ocean floor; completing the survey, Halstead unknowingly situates the underwater city on the rim of a large ravine. The city is built on land in sections that are taken to the site and submerged with frogmen assembling them and they are then united and made habitable. Called Amphibia City, the project is about to be inspected by government executives when Gage finds out the site is sinking due to its placement and calls for an evacuation. Halstead and some of his associates die when several of the sections collapse, falling into the gorge. When Gage and Monica realize that one of the sections has survived, they are determined to see Halstead's dream of a productive underwater city fulfilled.

Basil Rathbone and Raymond Massey were considered for the part of Dr. Halstead but both had to turn it down due to prior commitments. Producer Alex Gordon was an old hand at genre productions, among them an earlier underwater sci-fi adventure, *The Atomic Submarine* (1959). William Lundigan had starred in *Riders to the Stars* (1954) as well as the TV series *Men Into Space* (CBS-TV, 1959–60), while Julie Adams had adorned *Creature from the Black Lagoon* (1954).

Gordon and Orville H. Hampton, the film's writer, sued Columbia for breach of contract because the studio released *The Underwater City* in black and white instead of color as originally projected. The suit was eventually dropped. The film was issued to television in its original color version.

The Unknown

(1946; 70 minutes) PRODUCER: Wallace MacDonald. DIRECTOR: Henry Levin. SCREENPLAY: Charles O'Neal and Dwight V. Babcock, from the radio play by Malcolm Stuart Boylan and Julian Harmon. PHOTOGRAPHY: Henry Freulich. EDITOR: Arthur Seid. MUSIC DIRECTOR: Mischa Bakaleinikoff. ART DIRECTOR: George Brooks. SOUND: George Cooper. SETS: George Montgomery. ASSISTANT DIRECTOR: Carl Hiecke. CAST: Karen Morley (Rachel Martin Arnold), Jim Bannon (Jack Packard), Jeff Donnell (Nina Arnold), Robert Scott [Mark Roberts] (Reed Cawthorne), Robert Wilcox (Richard Arnold), Barton Yarborough (Doc Long), James Bell (Edward Martin), Wilton Graff (Ralph Martin), Helen Freeman (Phoebe Martin/Narrator), J. Louis Johnson (Joshua), Boyd Davis (Captain Selby Martin), Robert [Kellard] Stevens (James Wetherford), Russell Hicks (Colonel Wetherford).

Working title: *The Coffin.*

At their Bluegrass State plantation, Captain Selby Martin (Boyd Davis) and his wife Phoebe (Helen Freeman) host a party to announce the engagement of their daughter Rachel (Karen Morley) to her childhood sweetheart, James Wetherford (Robert Stevens), the son of wealthy Colonel Wetherford (Russell Hicks). The captain finds his daughter in the mansion's study with Richard Arnold (Robert Wilcox) who she says is her husband. Martin orders Arnold out of the house at gunpoint, and the two struggle over the weapon. Helen comes into the room and orders Rachel to go to her room as her husband collapses and dies. The distraught matron accuses Richard of killing the captain and then has her children, deaf Edward (James Bell) and Ralph (Wilton Graff), along with Rachel, help her inter his remains in the study's fireplace which they brick up.

Phoebe cuts the family off from the rest of the world. Twenty years pass with the property falling into ruin as Rachel becomes deranged, Edward a sculptor and Ralph an alcoholic. When Phoebe dies, her granddaughter, Nina Arnold (Jeff Donnell), the offspring of Rachel and Richard, arrives for the reading of her grandmother's will, accompanied by private detectives Jack Packard (Jim Bannon) and Doc Long (Barton Yarborough). They are met by the Martin's butler, Joshua (J. Louis Johnson), who has been with the family for many years, and lawyer Reed Cawthorne (Robert Scott), who questions Nina about her past as she reveals she was supported by a mysterious benefactor, Adam Franklin. Since the will cannot be read until the next day, Nina and her hirelings stay the night and she is awakened by the sound of a baby's cry. She finds her mother tending to a nonexistent infant and tries to calm her fears as Ralph demands the will be read since it is after midnight. Cawthorne cannot find the document and Ralph tells Nina she will receive nothing since without a legal instrument everything will go to him and his siblings. When Nina again hears the cries of an infant she investigates. Packard and Long also hear it and see a mysterious figure running across the lawn to the family mausoleum. There Jack discovers one of the coffins is empty and that it leads to a tunnel where they find a room while Nina is lured by the calls of a cloaked figure who shoves her down a staircase. The tunnel leads the detectives to the locked study. After Jack bangs on the door, they are let out by the revived Nina, Cawthorne and the Martin brothers. Packard inspects the fireplace in the study and thinks it is hollow behind its brick covering. Nina finds a note telling Rachel to meet her husband in the crypt; there they see Edward, who has been stabbed. Jack and Doc join them and see Ralph hiding in the hollow coffin (he reveals he has hidden a case of liquor there). A seaman shows up at the mansion, having been summoned by Adam Franklin, and the detectives learn he is Richard Arnold. At first Arnold tells Nina he does not care about her but after seeing Rachel he realizes he still loves his wife and tells his daughter he will try and help her. Jack announces to Joshua that he plans to tear open the fireplace front in the study and when he attempts to do so he is confronted by Phoebe who tells him she faked her death in order to try and atone for her past crimes against her family. She informs him that she is Adam Franklin and that she sent for Arnold hoping to make amends with Rachel. While they are talking, a mysterious figure knocks out Jack and carries off Phoebe. Jack and Doc go to the crypt where they find the old woman in her coffin. Jack deduces she died of shock and in the tunnel they find the mechanism that caused the baby's cries. The detectives are locked in the tunnel's room as Nina and Rachel come to the crypt after hearing the infant. There they are confronted by Ralph who tells them he hates his family and he plans to eliminate the two so he can have the estate for himself. Joshua gets Jack and Doc out of the locked room, and Jack gets the drop on Ralph who tries to escape but is stopped by Joshua. Phoebe's will is found on Ralph. Nina is happy to see her parents reunited.

Released in the summer of 1946, *The Unknown* was the last of three Columbia features based on Carlton E. Morse's popular radio series *I Love a Mystery*, which ran from 1939 to 1952 on NBC, CBS and Mutual. Preceded by *I Love a Mystery* (1945) and *The Devil's Mask* (1946) [qq.v], the feature continued the first outing's casting of Jim Bannon and Barton Yarborough in their radio roles of Jack Packard and Doc Long. The feature opens with a lengthy narration by the Phoebe Martin character, detailing how she brought misery to her home and broke her daughter's heart. Top-billed Karen Morley nicely portrayed the mentally unbalanced Rachel (in early scenes she looks much too old to be playing an 18-year-old). Definitely the weakest of the "I Love a Mystery" trio (it was based on the radio play "Faith, Hope and Charity Sisters" by Malcolm Stuart Boylan and Julian Harmon), it still managed some modicum of entertainment in its dreary old mansion setting with its spooky crypt, cloaked killer and a woman who literally returns to the grave. Writing flippantly in the *New York Times*, Bosley Crowther opined, "It is something about a bunch of loonies inhabiting an old Southern house which has underground rooms, sliding panels, a mausoleum and no electric lights. It also has some sort of killer lurking menacingly in the gloom and a very dead Southern colonel [*sic*] walled up in a brick fireplace."

The reason for the series' sudden halt was noted by the film's star, Jim Bannon, in his self-published mid–1970s autobiography *The Son That Rose in the West*: "The writing is so bad that it almost seems as though they're content to let it die. It's very sad because it had excellent potential if it had been done right. Instead of continuing with the Carlton Morse stories they have just turned the studio's staff writers loose on the scripts and what they've turned out couldn't even earn them a passing grade in a high school play-writing class."

Valley of the Dragons

(1961; 79 minutes) PRODUCER: Byron Roberts. EXECUTIVE PRODUCER: Alfred Zimbalist. DIRECTOR-SCREENPLAY: Edward Bernds, from the novel *Hector Servadac* by Jules Verne. STORY: Donald Zimbalist. PHOTOGRAPHY: Brydon Baker. EDITOR: Edwin H. Bryant. MUSIC: Ruby Raksin. ART DIRECTOR: Don Ament. SOUND: Lambert Day. MAKEUP: Ben Lane. SPECIAL EFFECTS: Richard Albain. ASSISTANT DIRECTOR: George Rhein. CAST: Cesare Danova (Captain Hector Servadac), Sean McClory (Michael Denning), Joan Staley (Deena), Danielle De Metz (Nateeta), Gregg Martell (Od-Loo), Gil Perkins (Tarn/Doctor), I.

Stanford Jolley (Patoo), Mike Lane (Anoka), Roger Til (Vidal), Mark Dempsey (Andrews), Jerry Sunshine (LeClerc), Dolly Grey (Mara).

While preparing to fight a duel in Algeria in 1881, Captain Hector Servadac (Cesare Danova) and adventurer Michael Denning (Sean McClory) are swept away by a comet and find themselves on a landscape filled with prehistoric creatures. They run into a cave in order to escape a huge lizard that has a fight to the death with one of its own kind. In the cave they are confronted with a giant spider; after killing it, the two men decide to unite in order to survive. When they spot the Earth in the heavens, Hector and Michael realize they are on another planet. In the cave they see members of a tribe who run from them. The two men dress in the animal skins they find there but when they go outside Hector is pursued by a mammoth and falls over a precipice with Michael believing he has been killed. Deena (Joan Staley), part of a tribe called the River People, comes upon Hector and takes him to her home where he is welcomed. When a giant ox gores Patoo (I. Stanford Jolley), a member of the Cave People, Michael saves him and is taken to meet the man's daughter, Nateeta (Danielle de Metz), but in order to have her he is forced to fight and defeat the giant Anoka (Mike Lane). While at the encampment of the River People, Hector saves a small child when she is attacked by a dinosaur and he also finds the components necessary to make gunpowder. He and Deena explore a cave where they are attacked by sub-humans. The girl escapes, only to be taken prisoner by the Cave People, the enemies of her tribe. When the young woman speaks English, Michael realizes Hector is still alive. The River People come for Deena and the two tribes begin fighting but are stopped when a volcano erupts. In trying to escape, Michael and Deena run into Hector who uses his explosives to kill a pack of giant lizards attacking the Cave People. The tribes unite in friendship and the two men decide to enjoy the company of their pretty companions while they await the time, in seven years, when the comet will bring them back to Earth.

Allegedly based on Jules Verne's 1877 novel *Hector Servadac* (aka *The Career of a Comet* and *Off on a Comet*), *Valley of the Dragons* was produced by Z.R.B. Productions and released by Columbia late in 1961 on a dual bill with William

Spanish lobby card for *Valley of the Dragons* (1961).

Castle's *Mr. Sardonicus* (q.v.). In the United Kingdom it was called *Prehistoric Valley*. Outside of using Verne's premise of having someone lifted off the Earth by a comet, the film mainly fashioned its story around footage from *One Million B.C.* (1940), where most of its monster scenes originated. A mountain set was utilized from the studio's *The Devil at 4 O'Clock* (1961) while its giant spider footage was lifted from Allied Artists' *World Without End* (1956), which Edward Bernds also helmed. *Variety* called this tepid, tedious production a "corny caveman spectacle that is shopworn even by 20-year-old cinema standards." Dennis Fischer wrote in *Science Fiction Film Directors, 1895–1998* (2000), "The film's pace and story are lethargic and dull, its science fictional believability tenuous at best ... and the Verne association is cynically exploited. It is not so much a movie as a bad business deal involving how to throw together some product with exploitable associations and minimal expense."

The Verne work was far better served by Czech director-scripter Karel Zeman's 1970 production *Na Komete* (Off on a Comet).

Las Vampiras (The Vampires)

(1969; 91 minutes; Color) PRODUCERS: Luis Enrique Vergara and Jesus Fragoso Montoya. DIRECTOR: Federico Curiel. SCREENPLAY: Adolfo Torres Portillo and Federico Curiel. PHOTOGRAPHY: Alfred Uribe. EDITOR: Juan Jose Mungula. MUSIC: Gustavo Cesar Carrion. PRODUCTION DESIGN: Jose Mendez and Octavia Ocampo. CAST: Mil Mascaras (Himself), John Carradine (Branus/Count Dracula), Maria Duval (Veria), Martha Romero (Aura), Maura Monti (Marian), Pedro Armendariz, Jr. (Carlos Mayer), Dagoberto Rodriguez (Police Inspector), Elsa Maria, Jessica Mungula, Sara Benitez, Rossy Cabellos (Vampire Women), Joe Carson (Himself), Nathanael Leon, Manuel Garay, Sergio Beauregard, Juan Ortiz Hernandez, Felipe del Castillo.

Released by Columbia in the United States to Spanish-language theaters, *Las Vampiras* was the second of two Mexican horror features (the other being *La Señora Muerte* (The Death Woman) (q.v.) produced by Filmica Vergara, S.A., starring John Carradine, who voice was dubbed in both movies. Carradine has previously portrayed Count Dracula in Universal's *House of Frankenstein* (1944) and *House of Dracula* (1945) and *Billy the Kid Versus Dracula* (1966) as well as a 1956 episode of TV's *Matinee Theatre*. In *Las Vampiras*, as Dracula, he was surrounded by a

Poster for *Las Vampiras* (The Vampires) (1969).

bevy of beautiful vampire brides wearing tights. Not only did he battle rebellious wives but also the masked wrestling hero Mil Mascaras (playing himself) and his reporter friend (Pedro Armendariz Jr.). The wrestler, known as "The Thousand Masks," wears various colored head gear throughout, a carryover from his ring wars, some of which are shown early in the film. Mil Mascaras was an internationally known grappler who held the world's heavyweight title.

When his girlfriend is murdered by the undead, Mascaras teams with newsman pal Carlos Mayer (Armendariz) to document the existence of vampires. At a remote castle, Branus, better known as Count Dracula (Carradine), sends his brides to get victims for his bloodlust. The count, however, is being kept in a dungeon cell by his wives Aura (Martha Romero) and Veria (Maria Duval).

The wrestler and the reporter go to the castle but fall into a pit and are almost killed by a huge swinging ball with spikes. Escaping, they next witness a dance by the vampire women. When Dracula promises to make Veria his queen, she sets him free. Seeing Mascaras and Carlos, the vampires chase them through the castle but with the arrival of dawn the undead are forced to return to their coffins. After reporting to the police, the two men head back to the castle but are nearly waylaid by the specters of two vampire women along the road. In the castle, the men are brought before Dracula. After they defeat his undead gladiators, Mil Mascaras is named King of the Vampires. Aura puts both men under a spell. When the count realizes he is losing his powers, Veria willingly lets him drink her blood. Dracula attacks Mayer's girlfriend Marian (Maura Monti) and brings her to the castle as Aura tries to get Carlos to kill his friend. Mascaras uses fire to make Aura break her spell on Carlos. When Aura sees her husband with Marian, she turns into a bat and tries to stop him from biting the young woman. Mascaras and Carlos set fire to the castle, trapping the vampires, and escape with Marian.

The feature was released in Great Britain as *The Vampires* and was later issued on video in the U.S. as *The Vampire Girls*. While it was nicely photographed and fairly entertaining, with lots of fights and some wrestling sequences, the feature suffered from poor special effects, and its music score was reworked from the Japanese sci-fi feature *Atragon* (1964).

Voice of the Whistler

(1945; 60 minutes) PRODUCER: Rudolph C. Flothow. DIRECTOR: William Castle. SCREENPLAY: Wilfred H. Pettitt and William Castle. STORY: Alan Radar. PHOTOGRAPHY: George Meehan. EDITOR: Dwight Caldwell. MUSIC DIRECTOR: Mischa Bakaleinikoff. SOUND: Jack Goodrich. ASSISTANT DIRECTOR: Chris Beute. CAST: Richard Dix (John Sinclair aka John Carter), Lynn Merrick (Joan Martin Sinclair), Rhys Williams (Ernie Sparrow), James Cardwell (Dr. Fred Graham), Tom Kennedy (Ferdinand), Douglas Wood (Paul Kitridge), Frank Reicher (Dr. Rose), Gigi Perreau (Bobbie), Byron Foulger (Georgie), Minerva Urecal (Georgie's Wife), John Hamilton (Doctor), Martin Garralaga (Tony), Charles Coleman (Butler), Frank J. Scannell, Robert Williams (Druggists), Clinton Rosemont (Porter), Stuart Holmes, Sam Ash, Forbes Murray, Wilbur Mack, Harold Miller, Charles Marsh (Company Executives), Otto Forrest (Voice of the Whistler), Ken Carpenter (Newsreel Narrator).

Working title: *Checkmate for Murder.*

William Castle returned to Columbia's "The Whistler" series for its fourth entry, *Voice of the Whistler*, released in the fall of 1945. Previously Castle had helmed *The Whistler* (q.v.) and *Mark of the Whistler* (both 1944) and he would also do a fourth outing, *Mysterious Intruder* (1946). The feature was made by Larry Darmour Productions and was based on the popular CBS radio series *The Whistler* which was broadcast from 1942 to 1955. This entry was a brooding psychological horror drama with its beginning and finale in a lonely old New England lighthouse. *Variety* opined, "Despite its eerie buildup, *Voice of the Whistler* isn't as haunting as ballyhooed. A minor item." Jon Tuska in *The Detective in Hollywood* (1978) declared, "Lynn Merrick, perhaps the best *femme fatale* working in the Columbia 'B' unit, renders a performance which nearly qualifies the picture to be considered a *film noir*."

The voice (Otto Forrest) of the Whistler tells the story of a recluse living at a remote Maine lighthouse and the circumstances that brought her there. At the office of industrial giant John Sinclair (Richard Dix), a newsreel detailing the man's life is screened. Afterward he tells his executives he wants his privacy separated from his public presence. Going home, he collapses; his doctor (John Hamilton) urges him to take a vacation. He travels to Chicago by train but at Union Station he collapses and is cared for by taxi driver Ernie Sparrow (Rhys Williams) who gets him a room at the place he lives. Using the name John Carter, Sinclair and Sparrow become friends. The cabbie tells him he once was the British lightweight boxing champion but he only found mental peace as an obscure taxi driver with lots of friends.

Sparrow takes Sinclair to a free medical clinic where he meets nurse Joan Martin (Lynn Merrick), the fiancée of Dr. Fred Graham (James Cardwell), who has six months before he can go into private practice. After tests are run, the head of the clinic, Dr. Rose (Frank Reicher), informs Sinclair that he has only a few months to live and suggests he take a trip to the coast of Maine for a rest. When Sinclair tells Sparrow of the doctor's suggestion, the cabbie offers him his savings to make the trip and instead Sinclair invites Sparrow to be his guest. After the cabbie jokingly suggests that Joan join them, Sinclair tells her his real name and asks her to marry him. He explains that in return for her being with him in his last days, she will inherit his entire fortune. That night in the park, Joan tells Graham she plans to marry Sinclair, and he calls her selfish and leaves. The newlyweds, along with Sparrow, move to a renovated lighthouse in Gull Point, Maine, and after six months Sinclair regains his health while Joan becomes cold and unresponsive. By now Sinclair loves Joan but she tells him she misses the outside world and that she plans to leave him. He asks her to reconsider and promises to take her anywhere she wishes to travel. Joan agrees to stay. Graham comes to see her and asks that she leave Sinclair and return with him. Sinclair overhears their conversation but asks Graham to stay for awhile and later, over a chess board, suggests to him the perfect murder. Graham goes to a local drug store and gets sleeping powder for Sinclair and then tells Sparrow to get locks for the lighthouse windows since he saw Sinclair sleepwalking. The night before the Sinclairs plan to close the beach home and return to New York City, Graham enters Sinclair's room intending to kill him but only bludgeons pillows that Sinclair has covered on his bed. Sinclair then kills the doctor and tries to throw his body out of a window into the ocean but he finds it will not open. He carries the corpse to the shore but he is seen by Sparrow. Sinclair tells Sparrow that Graham fell out of a window to his death but the cabbie informs him he had nailed all the lighthouse windows shut the day before. Sinclair then claims he killed Graham in self-defense and they return to the lighthouse so Sparrow can see the smashed pillows. As they enter, Sinclair tells Joan about Graham's death but she accuses him of murdering her ex-fiancée and calls the police. A jury convicts Sinclair of murder and he is executed. The now-wealthy Joan goes on a world tour but eventually ends up at the lighthouse, a lonely and bitter recluse.

Poster for *Voice of the Whistler* (1945).

Voodoo Tiger

(1952; 67 minutes) PRODUCER: Sam Katzman. DIRECTOR: Spencer Gordon Bennet. STORY-SCREENPLAY: Samuel Newman. PHOTOGRAPHY: William P. Whitley. EDITOR: Gene Havlick. MUSIC DIRECTOR: Mischa Bakaleinikoff. ART DIRECTOR: Paul Palmentola. SETS: Sidney Clifford. UNIT MANAGER: Herbert Leonard. ASSISTANT DIRECTOR: Charles Gould. CAST: Johnny Weissmuller (Jungle Jim), Jean Byron (Phyllis Bruce), James Seay (Abel Peterson), Jean Dean (Shalimar), Charles Horvath (Wombulu), Robert Bray (Major Bill Green), Michael Fox (Karl Werner aka Heinrich Schultz), Rick Vallin (Sergeant Bono), John L. Cason (Jerry Masters), Paul Hoffman (Michael Kovacs), Richard Kipling (Commissioner Kingston), William Bryant (Co-Pilot), Frederic Berest (Headhunter Chief), Billy Wilkerson (Voodoo Cultist), Alex Montoya (Native Leader), Joanne Dean, Diane Garrett, Josephine Parra (Show Girls), Tamba (Chimp).

Voodoo Tiger was the ninth entry in Columbia's Jungle Jim series based on the cartoon character created by Alex Raymond. Its genre connections were minor and mainly dealt with natives worshipping a voodoo tiger god, Tambura, that called for ritual human sacrifice. Since the tiger is not indigenous to Africa, the plot had the beast brought to the jungle via a crashed plane with another subplot having a British Museum representative looking into the cult and trying to find out how it could exist if tigers never populated the continent. Most of the tiger footage came from the 1932 RKO Radio feature *Bring 'Em Back Alive* starring Frank Buck, which included battles with a small crocodile, water buffalo and a leopard. Unlike some of the stock stuff used in other series entries, these scenes fit quite well with the rest of the picture. *Variety* thought the film "stacks up as okay program filler. The jungle adventure yarn abounds with blood-and-thunder, and moppets will go for this aspect of it." *The Hollywood Reporter* said the feature "has movement and suspense in spades."

A native is about to be sacrificed in voodoo ritual to the tiger god Tambura by witch doctor Wombulu (Charles Horvath), a high priest of the cult, when Jungle Jim (Johnny Weissmuller) stops the proceedings, beats up the witch doctor and sets fire to the tiger idol worshipped by the bloodthirsty natives. As Wombulu attempts to stab Jim, he is shot and grazed by big game hunter Abel Peterson (James Seay), who is accompanied by his associates, Jerry Masters (John L. Cason) and Michael Kovacs (Paul Hoffman). Jim is serving as guide for British Museum researcher Phyllis Bruce (Jean Byron), who is researching the tiger cult legend, and they are accompanied by a local lawman, Sergeant Bono (Rick Vallin). Peterson invites Jim, Phyllis and Bono to his camp where he tells them he is hunting an animal of the two-legged variety. Before he can say more, Jim gets a missive ordering him to see Commissioner Kingston (Richard Kipling) at the airfield in Watusi. There Jim meets U.S. Army Major Bill Green (Robert Bray) who works for military archives. Kingston asks the jungle man to take them inland to the Werner Trading Post to see its proprietor, Karl Werner (Michael Fox). The two men are seeking knowledge of the whereabouts of the $2 million Schulman art collection that was stolen in Southern France during World War II and taken to Germany and is now missing. Werner is asked if he knows how to find Heinrich Schultz, a Nazi who aided in the heist. When Werner says he knows nothing of Schultz, Green accusing him of being the thief. Peterson and his cohorts show up at the trading post and Green says they are international art thieves. A fight ensues with Peterson getting the drop on Jim and his friends and traps them in a supply closet. Werner escapes during the fracas, drives Jim's Jeep to a nearby airfield and hijacks a plane, forcing the co-pilot (William Bryant) to fly inland. Also on board are night club dancer Shalimar (Jean Dean), her showgirls and pet tiger Baby, which she uses in her act. Peterson and his men just miss the takeoff. Jim and Green break through the barricade and also head to the airstrip. The plane's left engine catches on fire and it is forced down in a swamp in Crescent Valley, a hotbed of voodoo in the Valley of the Headhunters. The local natives surround the crash victims but when Baby appears the voodoo cultists think the tiger is Tambura and worship the beast. When the commissioner gets word of the plane crash, he asks Jim to guide Green to the site, and Phyllis goes along to investigate the rumored appearance of Tambura. Peterson enlists the aid of Wombulu in leading him to the plane crash site. In the narrow Dundee Pass, Peterson sets up explosives to get rid of anyone who follows them. The headhunter chief (Frederic Berest), an ally of Wombulu, takes Peterson and his party to his village where Werner is held captive. At Dundee Pass, Tamba, Jim's pet chimp, uncovers the explosive wires and its master cuts them. When the jungle man goes on ahead to scout the area, the headhunters capture Phyllis, Green and Kingston and murder Bono. Following Baby, Jim finds Shalimar and the others in the crash but she tells him to go back since they are safe because the natives think she has magical powers over the tiger. Back at Dundee Pass, Jim finds the murdered sergeant and then goes to the headhunters' village where Peterson and his men have been ordered to leave by the chief who says Werner will be sacrificed to Tambura. Jim is taken prisoner and witnesses a voodoo ceremony in which Green is almost killed. The chief orders Jim to endure a voodoo trial by fighting a lion. Tamba procures a knife for its master and while Jim fights and kills the giant cat, Shalimar frees Green and the co-pilot as Peterson and his cohorts abduct Werner. Jim gets the drop on the chief and Baby comes back, scaring off the natives as the jungle man takes the former captives back into the jungle. The tiger fights off a leopard as Jim pursues Peterson and his men and takes Werner away from them. The headhunters murder Peterson, Masters and Kovacs and pursue Jim and company to Dundee Pass where the jungle man resets the explosives. When the voodoo cultists trip the wire, an explosion causes them to be buried in a rock slide. At Watusi, Kingston orders a platoon to destroy the voodoo cults and their idols. He gives Jim his appreciation in helping capture Werner, who has confessed to being Schultz and revealed the hiding place of the art collection. The two men are then amused when they see Green and Phyllis kiss.

One of the locales in the film, the Valley of the Headhunters, was used as the title of the twelfth "Jungle Jim" feature *Valley of Head Hunters*, a 1953 release that had no genre overtones in its tale of the jungle man trying to stop a local tyrant.

Warlords of Atlantis

(1978; 96 minutes; Color) PRODUCER: John Dark. DIRECTOR: Kevin Connor. SCREENPLAY: Brian Hayles. PHOTOGRAPHY: Alan Hume. EDITOR: Bill Blunden. MUSIC: Mike Vickers. ART DIRECTOR: Jack Maxsted. SOUND: Ken Barker and George Stephenson. PRODUCTION DESIGN: Elliot Scott. PRODUCTION SUPERVISOR: Graham Easton. MAKEUP: Robin Grantham. VISUAL EFFECTS: John Richardson, Roger Dicken and George Gibbs. ASSISTANT DIRECTOR: Ray Frift. CAST: Doug McClure (Greg Collinson), Peter Gilmore (Charles Aitken), Shane Rimmer (Captain Daniels), Lea Brodie (Delphine), Cyd Charisse (Atsil), Daniel Massey (Atraxon), Michael Gothard (Atmir), Hal Galili (Grogan), John Ratzenberger (Fenn), Derry Power (Jacko), Donald Bissett (Professor Aitken), Ashley Knight (Sandy), Robert Brown (Briggs).

Working title: *Seven Cities of Atlantis*.

In 1892, British archaeologist Professor Aitken (Donald Bissett) heads a scientific expedition in Bermuda. Also on board the ship *Texas Rose* is his son Charles (Peter Gilmore), another archaeologist; American engineer Greg Collinson (Doug McClure), boatswain Grogan (Hal Galili), crewmen Fenn (John Ratzenberger) and Jacko (Derry Power), cabin boy Sandy (Ashley Knight) and Captain Daniels (Shane Rimmer). The professor is supposedly after a rare fish; Charles and Collinson go down in a diving bell looking for it and they are attacked by a sea monster which Collinson electrocutes. The two divers see a gold statue and have it taken aboard the ship where it is examined by the professor. While the crew plots to steal the object, the captain insists that the professor terminate the expedition but he refuses. Grogan cuts off communication with the diving bell and when a huge octopus approaches the ship, Collinson and Charles are unable to warn the men aboard. When Grogan cuts the line to the diving bell, Sandy tells the professor who is then shot. Just as Grogan is about to bludgeon the captain, the octopus attacks the ship, carries off the crew and then attaches itself to the diving bell, carrying it into a cavern.

Collinson and Charles end up in a brightly lit cave in a lagoon. They leave the diving bell and find the captain, who has survived the octopus attack. The three men swim to shore where they see Grogan, Fenn and Jacko. The six survivors are confronted by a man in a white robe, Atmir (Michael Gothard), and a group of armored soldiers, the Guardians. On board the ship, Sandy ministers to the professor who deliriously calls the gold statue cursed. As the ship's survivors travel with the soldiers, Atmir tells them they are in the realm of Atlantis which consists of seven cities. Collinson accuses Charles of knowing about Atlantis all along. Charles admits that he and his father were really in search of the fabled kingdom and not hunting for rare sea life. As the group crosses a wood bridge they are confronted by the Mogdaan, a huge black fish, but it submerges and they proceed to Troi, a city in ruins. In the city of Vaar the newcomers see Briggs (Robert Brown), a big man with a beard, ordering cannons set on the town walls. Collinson is attracted to Delphine (Lea Brodie) and tries to help her carry pails of water but she refuses his aid. Collinson has a confrontation with one of the soldiers, and the rest of the men join in. After a fracas, Atmir orders the newcomers taken to a dungeon. All of the men except Charles are incarcerated; he is brought by Atmir to the nearby city of Cinqua, where he meets Atsil (Cyd Charisse), who leads him to the Hall of Contemplation to see the ruler of Atlantis, Atraxon (Daniel Massey). Along the way she explains to him that Atlanteans came to Earth from Mars in a meteor that crashed into the ocean and they are still living inside it. In the seventh city of Zefft, Atsil takes Charles to Atraxon's throne room while Delphine and Briggs, who is her father, tries to help the prisoners. Briggs tells Captain Daniels he was once a sailor who two decades before was captured by the Atlanteans and that he must help them defend their cities against attack. He also says the men will be enlisted to aid their captors and then shows them he has gills.

Two giant spiked creatures with huge tusks

and tails called Zaargs attack the city and Briggs goes to help with the defenses and is killed. When one of the monsters breaks the wall outside their cell, the sailors manage to escape. Delphine agrees to help the men get away from Atlantis and shows them a tunnel that leads to Zefft where Atraxon and Atsil place a crystal helmet on Charles' head, permitting him to see the future that will allow the Atlanteans to leave the Earth. The survivors and Delphine arrive in the palace and Daniels sees Charles as Collinson tears the helmet from his head. When Charles berates him, Collinson kayoes the archaeologist and carries him away. As they head back through the tunnel, the group is pursed by the Atlantean soldiers on the orders of Atsil. Returning to Vaar, Delphine offers to help them get back to the diving bell. The men manage to obtain rifles which Collinson and Charles use to shoot the Mogdaan when it tries to block their path to the lagoon. Everyone gets over the bridge except Jacko, who is devoured by the monster. Atmir calls to Charles to give himself up in return for his friends' safe departure. Saying goodbye to Delphine, Collinson gets control of the diving bell as Charles joins the other men and they successfully return to the *Texas Rose*. Once on board, Collinson and Charles are told by Sandy that someone tried to shoot the professor. The captain takes the gun away and puts them in the brig. The giant octopus returns, attacks the ship and carries off the gold statue with Daniels being killed. Collinson, Charles, Sandy and the professor get aboard a lifeboat and are followed by Grogan and Fenn.

Two Amicus Films alumni, producer John Dark and director Kevin Connor, reunited to make *Warlords of Atlantis*, sometimes called *Warlords of the Deep*, for EMI Films with financial backing and distribution by Columbia. Doug McClure, who had previously starred for the duo in Amicus' Edgar Rice Burroughs trilogy *The Land That Time Forgot* (1975), *At the Earth's Core* (1976) and *The People That Time Forgot* (1977), returned to headline this effort. Perhaps the feature's most interesting casting is that of 57-year-old Cyd Charisse as the beautiful and sexy Atsil, the ageless associate of the ruler of Atlantis. For monster fans there are also a trio of giants: an octopus called the Sentinel, two armored lizards, the Zaargs, and the Mogdaan, a black fish. Unfortunately, *Warlords of Atlantis* came along too late in the monster-fantasy cycle of the 1970s and failed to gain the audience attention of the earlier Burroughs-based productions.

F. Maurice Speed in *Film Review 1979–1980* (1979) called the feature a "well-made portion of good old Hollywood hokum ... Lots of clever model work, highly incredible escapes and, in spite of all the travail that besets them, a sense of enjoyment as the heroes and villains battle their way in and out of the Lost Continent." In *The Family Guide to Movies on Video* (1988), Henry Herx and Tony Zaza noted "there's plenty of papier-mâché monsters, wooden dialogue and leaden comic relief." *Time Out Film Guide, 9th Edition 2001* (2000) found it to be "a rehash of exactly the same old fantasy formula used by Connor and producer John Dark.... As always, Connor's approach is commendably stolid, but this production lacks almost all the more pleasing elements of the earlier movies."

The year the film was released, Futura Publications published a novel based on *Warlords of Atlantis*, written by Paul Victor.

Watermelon Man

(1970; 97 minutes; Color) PRODUCER: John B. Bennett. EXECUTIVE PRODUCER: Leon Mirrell. DIRECTOR-MUSIC: Melvin Van Peebles. SCREENPLAY: Herman Raucher. PHOTOGRAPHY: W. Wallace Kelley. EDITOR: Carl Kress. ART DIRECTORS: Malcolm C. Bert and Sydney Z. Litwack. SETS: John Burton. MAKEUP: Ben Lane. COSTUMES: Gene Ashman and Edna Taylor. CAST: Godfrey Cambridge (Jeff Gerber), Estelle Parsons (Althea Gerber), Howard Caine (Mr. Townsend), D'Urville Martin (Bus Driver), Mantan Moreland (Counterman), Kay Kimberley (Erica), Kay E. Kuter (Dr. Wainwright), Scott Garrett (Burton Gerber), Erin Moran (Janice Gerber), Irving Selbat (Mr. Johnson), Emil Sitka (Delivery Man), Lawrence Parke, Robert Dagny, Ray Ballard (Passengers), Karl Lukas (Second Policeman), Paul H. Williams (Employment Office Clerk), Ralph Montgomery (Drugstore Proprietor), Charles Lampkin (Dr. Catlin), Vivian Rhodes (Gladys), Erik Nelson (Doorman), Matthias Uitz (Cab Driver), Rhodie Cogan (Mrs. Johnson), Donna Dubrow (Receptionist), Frank Farmer (Andy Brandon), Hazel Medina (Widow), Mae Clarke (Woman), Almira Sessions (Woman on Bus), Melvin Van Peebles (Sign Painter).

Working title: *The Night the Sun Came Out*.

Bombastic and bigoted white life insurance salesman Jeff Gerber (Godfrey Cambridge) wakes up and finds he has turned black due to a biological accident. After trying to rid himself of his new skin color via water, bleach and milk, he decides to blame his condition on over-exposure to the sun and soy products. His feather-headed wife Althea (Estelle Parsons) is at first horrified and then sympathetic while their children Burton

(Scott Garrett) and Janice (Erin Moran), who do not like their father to begin with, are complacent. After being told by his doctor to consult a black physician, Jeff's employer (Howard Caine) has his contacts checked before formulating the idea that Jeff could now exploit his new color by selling insurance to the black market. To complicate his life further, Jeff finds that the office secretary, Erica (Kay Kimberley), a blonde from Norway, has fallen for him. Finally becoming alienated from her husband, Althea takes their children and goes home to her mother in Indianapolis. This causes Jeff to reject his boss' business proposition and Erica's romantic advances and take up residence in the black community, start his own insurance business and join a self-defense class.

The sci-fi aspect of *Watermelon Man* is the unspecified biological accident that changes the skin color of the title character. Other than that the film is an R-rated comedy vehicle for Godfrey Cambridge that is an attempt at social satire. In both respects, it got mixed reviews. *Variety* noted, "A few chuckles are evident, but as entertainment, *Watermelon Man* is a trifle; as an interracial social document, it's nothing." F. Maurice Speed in *Film Review 1971–1972* (1971) opined, "Thoroughly amusing one-off comedy which by its humour and general good nature illuminates with impact the harsh facts of being an American Negro...." Henry Herx and Tony Zaza in *The Family Guide to Movies on Video* (1988) stated, "[S]atire is crude, embarrassing, and at times consciously offensive. Though terribly uneven, it at least attempts to deal with the festering ulcer of everyday racial prejudice." *Time Out Film Guide, 9th Edition 2001* (2000) said, "Often very funny in its topsy-turvy comments on racism, the script unfortunately has to battle against a director determined to use every gaudy trick in the book." The *TLA Video and DVD Guide 2004* (2003) termed it a "[s]ocial comedy with bite ... Cambridge's broad playing helps greatly in the enjoyment of this racial parable." Marc Sigoloff wrote in *The Films of the Seventies* (1984) that the film was an "[u]nusual fantasy comedy.... The premise is clever, a bizarre variation of *Gentleman's Agreement*, but the storyline runs out of steam. Unfortunately Cambridge's makeup is imperfect and he is unconvincing as a white man."

The Werewolf

(1956; 79 minutes) PRODUCER: Sam Katzman. DIRECTOR: Fred F. Sears. SCREENPLAY: Robert Kent and James B. Gordon. PHOTOGRAPHY: Edward Linden. EDITOR: Harold White. MUSIC CONDUCTOR: Mischa Bakaleinikoff. ART DIRECTOR: Paul Palmentola. SOUND: Ferrol Redd. SETS: Dave Montrose. ASSISTANT DIRECTOR: Willard Sheldon. CAST: Don Megowan (Sheriff Jack Haines), Joyce Holden (Amy Standish), Steven Ritch (Duncan Marsh), Eleanore Tanin (Helen Marsh), Kim Charney (Chris Marsh), Harry Lauter (Deputy Sheriff Ben Clovy), Larry J. Blake (Hank Durgis), Ken Christy (Dr. Jonas Gilchrist), James Gavin (Mark Fanning), S. John Launer (Dr. Emery Forrest), George M. Lynn (Dr. Morgan Chambers), George Cisar (Hoxie), Marjorie Stapp (Min), Jean Charney (Cora), Jean Harvey (Ma Everett), Don C. Harvey (Deputy Sheriff), Charles Horvath (Joe Mitchell), Ford Stevens (Newsman), Fred F. Sears (Narrator).

When Columbia issued the double-bill of *Earth vs. the Flying Saucers* (q.v.) and *The Werewolf* in July 1956, the studio put out one of its most entertaining theatrical combos. Both features were made by Sam Katzman's Clover Productions and directed by Fred F. Sears. While the sci-fi item was highlighted by Ray Harryhausen's special effects, *The Werewolf* was a combination science fiction–horror affair that benefited from filming in rural Northern California locales, a literate script, a fine cast (particularly Steven Ritch as the haunted title character) and uncredited Clay Campbell's monster makeup, which he had developed 12 years earlier for *The Return of the Vampire* (q.v.). While *The Werewolf* remains in the shadow of its more showy co-feature, the movie is a solid tale of science gone awry with an innocent man victimized by two crazed scientists out to prove their theories at all cost. (The theme was also utilized the same year *Indestructible Man* starring Lon Chaney, Jr.) *Variety* had little faith in *The Werewolf*, however: "Once its premise of a man changing back and forth into a wolf is posed, the Sam Katzman production seldom rises above a plodding monotone and won't create much reaction in the minor program market for which it is headed."

Duncan Marsh (Ritch) shows up in Mountaincrest, a small town, and buys a drink at Chad's Café. As he leaves he is followed by burly Joe Mitchell (Charles Horvath) who tries to mug him. A fight ensues, the brawl witnessed by an old lady (Jean Harvey). Her screams bring the patrons of the bar, including Deputy Sheriff Ben Clovy (Harry Lauter), who finds Joe's throat has been torn out. Clovy, along with bartender Hoxie (George Cisar) and fellow drinker Mack Fanning (James Gavin), follow Marsh's footprints in the snow and see them change from human to wolf tracks. The deputy sends the two men back to town for the sheriff, Jack Haines (Don Megowan). Hours later the lawman arrives, with Clovy suffering from a severe arm wound. Warning the locals to remain quiet about the matter, the sheriff takes his deputy to the home of "Doc" Jonas Gilchrist (Ken Christy) where he is treated by Doc's niece, nurse Amy Standish (Joyce Holden), Jack's fiancée. When Clovy tells the trio about the attack on him and how the predator had hairy hands, the sheriff theorizes they may be dealing with a werewolf.

The barefoot Marsh wakes up in a culvert in a wooded area and thinks he has had a bad dream and goes back to the place where Clovy was attacked and finds his shoes and socks. The sheriff sends for deputies from a nearby community and sets up roadblocks while refusing to let hunters into the nearby woods. Newspapermen from out of town arrive after having received a tip from an undertaker about Mitchell's murder and the sheriff permits them to stay. After seeing one of the roadblocks, Marsh comes down from the hills and goes to the doctor's house where he is admitted by Amy. Marsh tells them he has lost his memory and the last thing he remembers is seeing two doctors following an automobile accident. When Amy tries to give the man a sedative he becomes agitated and runs away. Amy calls Haines and both she and her uncle ask him to go easy on the obviously troubled stranger.

Forty miles away, doctors Morgan Chambers (George M. Lynn) and Emery Forrest (S. John Launer) read a newspaper story about Mitchell's killing and surmise the culprit must be Marsh, who they treated following a car wreck. The two men have been experimenting with a serum that will keep people alive following a nuclear war, one that Chambers thinks may be imminent. Fearing that Marsh may expose their work, Chambers vows to kill him and the two physicians make plans to go to Mountaincrest. Before they can leave, Marsh's wife Helen (Eleanore Tanin) shows up looking for him; Chambers tells her he left without being treated. Although worried about her missing husband, Helen goes back home with their young son Chris (Kim Charney).

Hunted by a posse led by Haines and Clovy, Marsh takes sanctuary near a mine tunnel where he is discovered by Chambers and Forrest. Chambers orders Forrest to go into the tunnel to find Marsh; when the doctor tries to kill him, Marsh transforms into a werewolf and attacks him but

Steven Ritch as *The Werewolf* (1956).

is scared away by Chambers' gunfire. The sheriff and his men arrive and deride the doctors for scaring off the wolfman. After the beast kills and devours two sheep, Haines orders the evacuation of nearby ranches. When Helen finds out that her husband's abandoned auto has been found near Mountaincrest, she drives there with Chris. The sheriff and several locals set a series of baited bear traps in hopes of capturing Marsh. Coming upon one of the traps, the werewolf gets caught in it but manages to break it open and get away before transforming back to human. Doc and Amy extend the hospitality of their home to Helen and Chris. Helen overhears the sheriff tell his fiancée that Marsh broke one of the bear traps; she asks why Marsh is being hunted. After being told by Haines what he suspects has happened to Marsh, he lets her and Chris join him, Amy and Clovy in the search. Using a loudspeaker, Haines calls out to Marsh as the party looks for him in the wooded hills. Helen urges him to give himself up while Chris sees his father and runs to him. Marsh is taken back to town and put in a jail cell. There he tells his family to leave before he transforms into a werewolf. After they do so, Doc takes a blood sample in hopes of developing a serum to cure Marsh. That night a deputy (Don C. Harvey) takes first watch over the prisoner as Clovy gets some needed rest. Chambers and Emery knock out Durgis (Larry J. Blake), a braggart who claimed he nearly caught the wolfman, and place him in front of the jail. When Clovy comes out to investigate, they drug him and go into Marsh's cell to kill him. Transforming into a werewolf, Marsh slaughters both doctors and escapes, causing Haines to order a torch-carrying posse to track the beast. After scaring him into the hills with the torches, the sheriff decides to wait until the next day to try and capture the werewolf. The following morning, Marsh is spotted and gunned down by his pursuers. Dying, he transforms back into human form.

The Werewolf is a nice integration of the horror and science fiction genres; the scene where the two doctors get their comeuppance by being murdered by the werewolf in his jail cell is one of the scariest in 1950s horror. The film was also unique in another respect as reported by Denis Gifford in *Movie Monsters* (1969): "*The Werewolf* was the first horror film to break away from the tradition of studio sets and take its monster into the streets among real people. A technique developed by low-budget science-fiction film makers, it worked well for this werewolf..."

In 1963 a French company, Star Cine Cosmos, published a photo novel magazine of *The Werewolf* entitled *L'Empreinte du Loup-Garou*.

When a Stranger Calls

(1979; 97 minutes; Color) PRODUCERS: Doug Chapin and Steve Feke. EXECUTIVE PRODUCERS: Barry Krost and Melvin Simon. ASSOCIATE PRODUCER: Larry Kostroff. DIRECTOR: Fred Walton. SCREENPLAY: Steve Feke and Fred Walton. PHOTOGRAPHY: Don Peterman. EDITOR: Sam Vitale. MUSIC: Dana Kaproff. PRODUCTION DESIGN: Elayne Barbara Ceder. SETS: Lee Poll. MAKEUP: Bob Mills. STUNT COORDINATOR: Stan Bennett. ASSISTANT DIRECTORS: Ed Ledding and Lynn Morgan. CAST: Charles Durning (John "Cliff" Clifford), Carol Kane (Jill Johnson, later Jill Lockhart), Colleen Dewhurst (Tracy Pollard), Tony Beckley (Curt Duncan), Rachel Roberts (Dr. Monk), Ron O'Neal (Lieutenant Charlie Garber), Steven Anderson (Stephen Lockhart), Carmen Argenziano (Dr. Alexander Mandrakis), Rutanya Alda (Mrs. Mandrakis), Sara Damman (Bianca Lockhart), Richard Ball (Stevie Lockhart), William Boyett (Sergeant Sacker), Kirsten Larkin (Nancy), Carol O'Neal (Mrs. Garber), Ed Wright, Louise Wright (Elderly Couple), Joseph Reale (Bartender), Heetu (Servant), Michael Champion (Bill), Dennis McMullen (Janitor), Wally Taylor (Cheater), John Tobyansen (Bar Customer), Lenora May (Sharon), Randy Holland (Maitre D'), Trent Dolan, Frank DiElsi, Arell Blanton (Policemen), DeForrest Covan, Charles Boswell (Officers), Cheryl Wilson (Mrs. Shifrin).

Teenager Jill Johnson (Carol Kane) arrives at the home of Dr. Mandrakis (Carmen Argenziano) and his wife (Rutanya Alda) to babysit for their two children while they go out to dinner. During the evening she begins getting telephone calls from a man asking her if she has checked on the children. Becoming distraught, Jill tries to contact the Mandrakises and, failing to get them, she contacts the police and a dispatcher tries to calm her fears. After more calls the police promise to trace them and find out they are coming from within the house. As Jill tries to escape, she sees the figure of a man at the top of the stairs and runs into police officer John Clifford (Charles Durning) who has come to investigate with his partner Charlie Garber (Ron O'Neal). They arrest British seaman Curt Duncan (Tony Beckley), who has been in the country less than six months. A jury finds Duncan guilty of killing the Mandrakis children, declare him insane and order him institutionalized. Seven years later Dr. Mandrakis hires now private detective Clifford to find Duncan, who has escaped from the asylum. Going to the institution, Clifford talks to its director, Dr. Monk (Rachel Roberts), who doubts Duncan is dangerous although she says he may revert to violence since he is off medication.

The killer walks into Torchy's Bar where he sees Tracy (Colleen Dewhurst) and tries to become friendly with her. When she resists his advances, a bar patron (Michael Champion) beats him. When Tracy gets home she finds Duncan waiting for her. To get him out of her apartment she makes a tentative date to meet him the next evening for coffee. Clifford goes to a party at Garber's house and informs him that he plans on not bringing in Duncan alive. After questioning a number of indigents, the detective finds out about Duncan meeting Tracy and he goes to see the woman who reluctantly agrees to help him capture the psychopath. That night Duncan does not keep his date with Tracy. Clifford, who has been following her, tells the woman to lock her door, not knowing Duncan is hiding in her closet. When he emerges, Tracy's screams alert Clifford but the madman manages to get away. He takes refuge in a flophouse where he has flashbacks of killing the two children. Clifford traces Duncan to the flophouse and then chases him through a warehouse and an apartment building before the escapee manages to elude him. Back on the street, Duncan finds a newspaper with a picture of Jill, who is now married to salesman Stephen Lockhart (Steven Anderson) and the mother of two children (Sara Damman, Richard Ball). That night the Lockharts plan to go to dinner to celebrate

Stephen's recent promotion and teenager Sharon (Lenora May) comes to sit with the kids. While they are dining, Jill gets a phone call from a man asking if she has checked on the children and she becomes hysterical, knowing the caller is Duncan. Stephen checks with Sharon and finds out the little ones are peacefully sleeping. Garber learns of the call and informs Clifford who tries unsuccessfully to talk with Jill but learns her phone is out of order. During the night, a distraught Jill checks on her children and then returns to bed only to hear Duncan's voice. As she tries to wake her husband she finds the psychopath in bed with her. When she tries to escape he attempts to rip off her gown and strangle her. Jill hears gunfire and sees Clifford kill Duncan. He finds Stephen is alive and comforts Jill.

Made on a modest budget of $740,000, this 1979 Halloween release from Columbia grossed $21 million at the domestic box office and has since gained a reputation as a top-notch horror thriller. Leisurely paced and surprisingly lacking in blood and gore, it is well-acted and well-produced, with very interesting color effects. Many of the scenes with Charles Durning are filmed in various brown hues while the night sequences often have green tones. Also very effective is the presentation of the character change in the babysitter played by Carol Kane. As a teenager she is presented as rather passive, dull and not very attractive but the passing of seven years finds her outgoing, bright, quite feminine and sexy. Also interesting is how the film duplicates the beginning and ending sequences with the babysitter, now a mother, faced with the same horrific circumstances — a brutal psychopath planning to murder two small children — only this time they are her own.

Variety opined, "Thanks to a fine cast, a rich and atmospheric score by Dana Kaproff, and astute direction by co-writer Fred Walton, *Stranger* is unquestionably a scary film.... [S]cript has chills a-plenty.... [It] resembles a good, old-fashioned grade B thriller." James O'Neill in *Terror on Tape* (1994) wrote, "A stunning first 15 minutes and a suspenseful wrap-up are the best things about this *Halloween* imitation ... Strikingly photographed and very well acted, but a dull midsection ... and a foredoomed attempt to make the maniac into a sympathetic character mar an otherwise taut tale." In *The Phantom of the Movies' Videoscope* (2000), Joe Kane noted, "While the pic gets pretty predictable ... it does offer a great hook, and Kane convincingly conveys high anxiety of the hysterical kind." Writing in *The Encyclopedia of Horror Movies* (1986), Phil Hardy said, "Part woman-in-peril film, part desperate manhunt, *When a Stranger Calls* is equally successful on both and manages to avoid the worst gory excesses of the former ... As a tight, economical thriller the film works very well and it would be a pity if its apparent proximity to the stalk-'n'-slash subgenre were to consign it to comparative oblivion." Hardy need not have worried since the feature went on to influence numerous genre efforts in the next two decades. The sequel *When a Stranger Calls Back*, a 1993 television movie made by Producers Entertainment Group, reunited director Walton with stars Kane and Durning, who repeated their roles. *When a Stranger Calls* was remade in 2006 by Screen Gems, starring Camilla Belle and Katie Cassidy.

The Whistler

(1944; 61 minutes) PRODUCER: Rudolph C. Flothow. DIRECTOR: William Castle. SCREENPLAY: Eric Taylor. STORY: J. Donald Wilson. PHOTOGRAPHY: James S. Brown. EDITOR: Jerome Thoms. MUSIC: Wilbur Hatch. ART DIRECTOR: George Van Marter. SETS: Sidney Clifford. SOUND: Hugh McDowell. ASSISTANT DIRECTOR: Richard Monroe. CAST: Richard Dix (Earl C. Conrad), Gloria Stuart (Alice Walker), J. Carrol Naish (The Killer/Mr. Smith), Don Costello (Lefty Vigran aka Gorss), Joan Woodbury (Antoinette "Toni" Vigran), Cy Kendall (Bartender Gus), Trevor Bardette (Flophouse Thief), Robert Emmett Keane (Charles McNear), Clancy Cooper (Repairman), Byron Foulger (Flophouse Clerk), Charles Coleman (Jennings), Robert Homans (Dock Watchman), Otto Forrest (Voice of the Whistler), Kenneth MacDonald, Jack Ingram, Pat O'Malley (Detectives), Billy Benedict (Deaf Mute), George Lloyd (Bill Tomley), Kermit Maynard (Dock Sergeant), Ralph Dunn (Patrolman), Dick Gordon (Tomley's Clerk), Walter Soderling, Charles Wagenheim (Flophouse Bums).

Several of the series produced by Columbia's "B" unit, such as "Boston Blackie" and "The Crime Doctor," made entries with genre trappings. Larry Darmour Productions began making films based on the popular radio series *The Whistler* in 1944 and several of these fit into that category, beginning with the first outing, *The Whistler*, released in the spring of 1944. Richard Dix headlined the first seven series films, playing a different character in each, and William Castle directed the debut entry which had elements of *film noir* as well as psychological horror, in this case a man being hounded by the assassin he hired to kill him. The killer, who also keeps pet mice and reads about necrophobia, considers his mission a psychological experiment in which he tries to frighten his employer to death by "rough shadowing."

Bosley Crowther in the *New York Times* felt it was a "weary, illogical imitation of an Alfred Hitchcock (plus an early Fritz Lang) film.... [A]ll very serious and phony — and, consequently, very dull." Don Miller in *B Movies* (1973) noted, "[Eric] Taylor's script was suspenseful and without wasted motion, and Castle heightened the tenseness with excellent economy of means while eliciting exemplary performances from Dix and J. Carrol Naish as the killer ... *The Whistler* attracted more than the normal amount of attention from trade-press reviewers and commanded several glowing critiques from various newspaper critics."

At the Crow's Nest, a waterfront bar, businessman Earl C. Conrad (Dix) meets Lefty Vigran (Don Costello) and hires him to set up his, Conrad's, murder. Instructions for the hit are passed on by a deaf mute (Billy Benedict) to the killer (J. Carrol Naish). As Lefty leaves the bar he is cornered by three detectives (Kenneth MacDonald, Jack Ingram, Pat O'Malley) who accuse him of being cop killer Gorss and in a shootout Lefty is shot. Going home, Conrad gives his butler (Charles Coleman) $5,000 and terminates his employment, saying he plans to sell the house.

At his business, Phoenix Ceramics, which he co-owns with Charles McNear (Robert Emmett Keane), Conrad tells his loyal secretary, Alice Walker (Gloria Stuart), that he blames himself for his wife's death two years before and that he feels his friends think he murdered her (he was unable to save her when their cruise boat sank). Insurance salesman Smith (Naish) tries to sell Conrad a life insurance policy but the businessman throws him out of his office. That night Conrad finds a window broken at his home. When a repairman (Clancy Cooper) arrives to fix his telephone, Conrad thinks he is the hired killer, who is hiding in the house. Alice arrives to check on Conrad. When the killer starts to fire through a window, he is caught off guard by a tune from the Whistler (Otto Forrest). Returning to his rooming house, the killer finds Gorman (Alan Dinehart) waiting for him with a job offer. The killer turns him down, saying he has to complete his present contract, and decides to get rid of Conrad by causing him to die of fright. When Conrad finds out from the Red Cross that his wife is still alive in a Japanese interment camp and is about to be released, he realizes he wants to live and tries to find Lefty in order to stop his killing. After he departs, McNear tells Alice he knows that she is in love with Conrad.

Conrad goes to see Bill Tomley (George Lloyd), the man who introduced him to Lefty, but he refuses to help. He next revisits the saloon where the bargain was made but the bartender (Cy Kendall) is of no assistance. A young woman (Joan Woodbury) shows up and, overhearing their conversation, tells Conrad she used to sing at the High Hat Roadhouse on Mountain View Drive, a place where Vigran spent a lot of time. She agrees to drive Conrad there but along the way she tells him that she is Lefty's widow and that she blames him for her husband's shooting. As the woman drives at a terrific speed, Conrad tries to get control of the wheel and causes the car to veer off the road and into a ravine. The woman is killed and the badly beat-up businessman walks home and finds Alice waiting there for him. When two cops show up, Conrad escapes through the back entrance and buys a bed in a flophouse with the killer sleeping there. When the flophouse clerk (Byron Foulger) phones the police, one of the bums (Trevor Bardette) helps Conrad escape and takes him to a basement where he plans to rob him. As the bum starts to bludgeon Conrad, he is shot by the killer. Everywhere he goes, Conrad sees the killer on his trail and in desperation he runs to a pier where he falls down and is helped by the dock watchman (Robert Homans), who recognizes him from a newspaper story about Conrad being an amnesia victim. The watchman telephones Phoenix Ceramics and talks to Alice who arranges to come to the dock. By the time she arrives, Earl has vanished. Conrad attempts to go aboard a Red Cross Swedish exchange ship as a cargo carrier but he stopped by a dock detective (Kermit Maynard) and taken in for questioning. Alice shows up while her boss is being interrogated. The killer attempts to shoot Conrad but misses. As he runs away, the killer is fatally shot by the dock detective, giving Conrad a new chance at life.

Two other series entries, *The Power of the Whistler* and *The Voice of the Whistler* (both 1945) [qq.v.] also had genre overtones. The radio series *The Whistler*, an anthology presenting psychological mysteries, was broadcast from 1942 to 1955 on CBS. Among those portraying the title character were Joseph Kearns, Bill Forman, Everett

Clarke and Bill Johnstone. Marvin Miller served as the announcer for the bulk of the programs.

Womaneater

(1959; 71 minutes) PRODUCER: Guido Coen. DIRECTOR: Charles Saunders. STORY-SCREENPLAY: Brandon Fleming. PHOTOGRAPHY: Ernest Palmer. EDITOR: Seymour Logie. MUSIC: Edwin Astley. ART DIRECTOR: Herbert Smith. SOUND: Mickey Jay. PRODUCTION MANAGER: Frank Bevis. MAKEUP: Terry Terrington. CONTINUITY: Vera Pavey. ASSISTANT DIRECTOR: Douglas Hermes. CAST: George Coulouris (Dr. James Moran), Vera Day (Sally Norton), Peter Wayn (Jack Venner), Joyce Gregg (Margaret Santor), Joy Webster (Judy), Jimmy Vaughn (Tanga), Edward Higgins (Sergeant Bolton), Maxwell Foster (Inspector Brownlow), Peter Lewiston (Detective Sergeant Freeman), Robert MacKenzie (Lewis Carling), Norman Claridge (Dr. Patterson), Marpessa Dawn (Native Girl), Sara Leighton (Susan Curtis), Harry Ross (Barker), Alexander Field (Gun Booth Man), David Lawton (Judy's Date), John A. Tinn (Explorer's Club Waiter), Roger Avon (Constable), John Grant (Rescuer), Susan Neil (Fair Counter Girl), Stanley Platts (Explorer's Club Steward), Shief Ashanti (Cult Leader), Marie Devereux (Girl).

Joy Webster is devoured in *Womaneater* (1959).

Produced in England by Fortress Films and released there in 1957 by Eros Films with an X certificate, this horror thriller was picked up by Columbia for U.S. issuance as the bottom half of a double with *The H-Man* (q.v.) and was shown stateside in the summer of 1959. Its title *Womaneater* was retained on release prints but on all advertising material the feature was called *The Woman Eater*. Under either title it took a critical lambasting. The British *Monthly Film Bulletin* declared, "[T]he production is poor and the acting, if anything, worse." David Quinlan in *British Sound Films: The Studio Years 1928–1959* (1984) called it "[d]aft without being horrific." Bill Warren in *Keep Watching the Skies!, Volume II* (1986) dismissed it as "an old-fashioned, uninteresting disaster, barely even a footnote in film history." In *Terror on Tape* (1994), James O'Neill felt the feature was a "tacky, Monogram-like mad doctor flick ... with plenty of [George] Coulouris hamming and a monster tree about as scary as your average weeping willow." For all its faults, and there are many, *Womaneater* is an unpretentious, low-grade and likable monster flick. It has ingredients dear to the hearts of fans of cheap horror movies: a screwy scientist, out to perfect a formula for eternal life, who falls in love with a lovely, but empty-headed blonde; her stalwart boyfriend, a jealous housekeeper, a crazed voodoo drum-beating native, police on the prowl, sacrificed comely maidens and a tentacled, carnivorous tree. In addition, the feature includes a classic line from the mad scientist, "What are a few lives compared to what I am giving the world — turning death into life."

At a meeting of the Explorer's Club in London, Dr. James Moran (Coulouris) asks Lewis Carling (Robert MacKenzie) to accompany him on an expedition into the Amazon jungle in search of a juju, a tree that can bring the dead back to life. After trekking through the jungle, with Moran coming down with fever, the two men witness the sacrifice of a native girl (Marpessa Dawn) to a flesh-eating tree. When Carling tries to stop the ceremony, he is killed. Days later Moran is found unconscious by a rescue party. Five years pass and at his English estate, Moran works in his laboratory basement with native Tanga (Jimmy Vaughn) in developing a serum from the tree, which the scientist has brought back from South America, that will revive the dead. The two men sacrifice a young woman (Sara Leighton) to the tree. Sergeant Bolton (Edward Higgins) shows up looking for the girl and talks to the doctor and his housekeeper, Margaret Santor (Joyce Gregg). Later, at a local fun fair, garage mechanic Jack Venner (Peter Wayn) meets dancer Sally Norton (Vera Day); when he asks her for a date, it upsets her employer, the carnival barker (Harry Ross); the two men fight. The next day Sally shows up at Jack's garage and tells him she was fired. He suggests she see Moran for a servant position. He drives her to the doctor's house and over the objections of Margaret, who is the scientist's ex-lover, she is given the job of assistant housekeeper.

Bolton returns to the estate with his superior, Inspector Brownlow (Maxwell Foster), and they ask permission to go over the grounds because they think the missing girl may have been abducted in the area. That night Moran goes to London where he follows a young woman, Judy (Joy Webster), to a cheap club. After she has an argument with her date (David Lawton), Moran asks her to accompany him for a night on the town. Instead he drives her back to his laboratory where he and Tanga feed her to the tree. When Margaret accuses Moran of doing evil things, he warns her he will send her away and she begs to stay with him. The next day Sally goes to see Jack and he proposes to her but they soon have a row and she returns to the estate where Moran informs her he plans to send Margaret away and offers her the full-time job of housekeeper. She hesitates to accept and returns to Jack, telling him she can no longer stand to remain with Moran. Margaret accuses Moran of being in love with Sally. They argue, she tries to stab him with an Amazon knife and he strangles her. When Sally returns she informs Moran of her plans to leave but he tells her he loves her and that he wants her to share in his success. He takes Sally to his laboratory.

Brownlow gets confirmation that Moran had a tree sent to his estate from Rio and he and Bolton return to inspect the doctor's property. When Sally does not show up at his service station as promised, Jack goes to the police station. In the laboratory, Moran uses his new serum to revive Margaret but he realizes she has no mind. Tanga mocks him for wanting the secrets of his people. Margaret attempts to strangle Sally but collapses as Jack arrives at the doctor's house with the police. Tanga attempts to feed Sally to the tree and Moran tries to stop him. As the two men fight, Jack locates the laboratory and rescues Sally. Moran knocks out Tanga and sets fire to the juju tree. Moran runs away and Tanga hurls a knife into his back. The native is consumed in the fire that incinerates his idol.

The Wrecking Crew

(1969; 105 minutes; Color) PRODUCER: Irving Allen. ASSOCIATE PRODUCER: Harold F. Kress. DIRECTOR: Phil Karlson. SCREENPLAY: William McGivern, from the novel by Donald Hamilton. PHOTOGRAPHY: Sam Leavitt. EDITOR: Maury Winetrobe. MUSIC: Hugo Montenegro. SONG: Mack David and Frank De Vol. ART DIRECTOR: Joe Wright. SOUND: James Flaster and Arthur Piantadosi. SETS: Frank Tuttle. MAKEUP: Ben Lane. COSTUMES: Moss Mabry. UNIT PRODUCTION MANAGER: Ralph Black. KARATE ADVISOR: Bruce Lee. ASSISTANT DIRECTOR: Jerome Siegel. CAST: Dean Martin (Matt Helm), Elke Sommer (Linka Karensky), Sharon Tate (Freya Carlson), Nancy Kwan (Yu-Rang), Nigel Green (Count Massimo Contini), Tina Louise (Lola Medina), John Larch (MacDonald), John Brascia (Karl), Weaver Levy (Kim), Wilhelm von Homburg (Gregor), Bill Saito (Ching), Fuji (Toki), Ted Jordan (Guard), Pepper Martin (Frankie), Whitney Chase (Miss Natural Gas), Bill M. Ryusaki (Henri), Chuck Norris (House of 7 Joys Guest), David Chow (Bartender), John Kowai (Kelly), Allen Pinson (Page), Tony Giorgio (ICE Gadget Man), Noel Drayton (British Bureaucrat), Josephine James (Girl), Byron Morrow, Kenner G. Kemp (Hospital Room Officers), James Lloyd (Desk Clerk), Bartlett Robinson (President's Spokesman).

Working title: *The House of 7 Joys*.

After three descending box offices successes (*The Silencers, Murderer's Row, The Ambushers* [q.v.]) with its Matt Helm films, Columbia tried to breathe new life into the declining series by bringing back director Phil Karlson, who helmed the initial outing, in addition to surrounding star Dean Martin with a quartet of sexy leading ladies (Elke Sommer, Sharon Tate, Nancy Kwan, Tina Louise) and an improved, if not more realistic, screenplay. Although mostly set in Denmark, the feature was made in California and its link to sci-fi and fantasy was its use of futuristic weaponry, in this case a camera that emits blinding smoke, a collapsing helicopter and puppet bombs. Based on Donald Hamilton's 1963 novel, the feature also included two future martial arts film stars: Chuck Norris had a bit as a man in the House of 7 Joys and Bruce Lee served as the production's karate advisor. During the course of the feature, Martin crooned various popular tunes with new lyrics to suit the script including "Anniversary Song," "Cry," "Exactly Like You," "The Glory of Love," "Let Me Call You Sweetheart," "My Melancholy Baby," "On the Sunny Side of the Street" and "Red Sails in the Sunset."

Multimillionaire crook Count Massimo Contini (Nigel Green) is the mastermind behind the theft of a billion dollars worth of gold. He directs the hijacking in Denmark while ordering his agents to stop ICE director MacDonald (John Larch) from contacting top agent Matt Helm (Martin). After the effort fails, MacDonald finds Matt with a bevy of scantily clad beauties and assigns him to retrieve the gold before its loss causes an international financial panic. Contini is the only link they have to the theft and Matt has 48 hours to recover the stolen shipment. MacDonald also informs the agent that Contini dropped his former lover, stripper Lola Medina (Louise), in favor of Linka Karensky (Sommer).

Dean Martin in *The Wrecking Crew* (1969).

Arriving at his Copenhagen hotel, Matt is spotted by both Lola and Linka and has a run-in with clumsy Danish tourist bureau representative Freya Carlson (Tate). That night he goes to meet Lola at her apartment and she tells him she knows the location of the stolen gold but in return for the information she wants Contini destroyed and one million dollars. As the two are about to go to bed to consummate their deal, Lola is killed by an exploding Scotch bottle. The police nearly arrest Matt but Contini shows up and vouches for him and gives Matt, who is masquerading as a photographer, and Freya permission to take pictures of his chateau the next morning. After Linka informs Contini that she set up Lola's killing, Matt and Freya arrive at the chateau where the count introduces Matt to his fiancée and then tells him he knows his true identity and assignment. After Matt refuses Contini's offer of two million dollars to give up his work for ICE and go to South America, the count tries to kill the agent but Matt uses his camera, which gives off a blinding fog, to escape with Freya. They are chased by Yu-Rang (Kwan), one of Contini's agents, and her men but manage to elude them. Contini tells Linka to eliminate Helm.

Back at his hotel room, Matt finds Yu-Rang who offers him half the stolen gold but before she can stab him Freya shows up and announces that MacDonald is on his way. Yu-Rang makes a hasty retreat. Ignoring Freya's pleas, Matt goes to meet Linka, who plans to shoot him, and she too offers him a partnership but Freya intrudes, breaking up their dalliance. When he returns to his hotel, Matt is greeted by a very sexy Freya. MacDonald shows up and informs him that the young woman is with British Intelligence. The agent goes to the House of 7 Joys to meet Yu-Rang but ends up being captured in a revolving booth. He is soon joined by MacDonald, who has been lured there by Linka. After Contini orders Yu-Rang to kill the two ICE agents, Freya grabs a gun and sets the men free. In a shootout, MacDonald is wounded by Linka. As he and Freya make a getaway, Matt throws Linka and her cohort Karl (John Brascia) into the revolving booth and when Yu-Rang gives the order to kill the ICE agents she ends up causing the deaths of Linka and Karl. With Contini planning to go to Luxembourg with the gold, Matt and Freya follow in his car which Yu-Rang and her men try to intercept. When Freya accidentally dismantles their auto with a puppet bomb, Matt assembles a helicopter and the two fly to the count's chateau. There Matt is trapped in a room as Contini has a truck containing the gold placed on a car attached to a locomotive which he engineers. Matt manages to escape as Freya has a showdown with Yu-Rang. As Matt and Freya leave, Contini uses a remote device to try and blow them up but instead kills Yu-Rang. Back in the helicopter, the two agents follow the locomotive and land on top of the truck. As Matt fights the count's guards, Freya enters the locomotive compartment and nearly falls through a trap door. Matt saves Freya and throws Contini to his death through the trap door. He then gets orders from MacDonald to take the gold to Copenhagen. Putting the locomotive on automatic pilot, Matt and the sexy Freya decide to have "a little talk."

Variety said *The Wrecking Crew* "emerges as a very entertaining, relaxed spy comedy ... Film rolls pleasantly through its 105 minutes, featuring the recurring music of Hugo Montenegro and a song by Mack David and Frank De Vol." James Robert Parish and I wrote in *The Great Spy Pictures* (1974), "Production-wise, this is the most pleasing of the four Matt Helm films ... Director Phil Karlson, who also did the first in this series, boosted the sagging property with visual techniques (split screen effects) and gadgetry (excessive variations of electronically devised booby traps)..." Still star Dean Martin appeared even more lackadaisical than ever, as Paul Mavis noted in *The Espionage Filmography* (2001): "The look of contempt and boredom on Dino's ravaged, overtanned face couldn't be recreated by Laurence Olivier."

At the finale of *The Wrecking Crew*, a fifth Matt Helm film was announced: *The Ravagers*. Because of *The Wrecking Crew*'s disappointing box office showing, this feature was never made. Columbia did use the title *The Ravagers* for its 1979 post-nuclear holocaust sci-fi release (q.v.).

Anthony Franciosa had the title role in ABC-TV's *Matt Helm*, a one-hour series that ran from September 1975 to January 1976 on Saturday nights. The show bore a stronger resemblance to the Columbia films with Dean Martin than the more straightforward spy novels of Donald Hamilton.

Zombies of Mora Tau

(1957; 69 minutes) PRODUCER: Sam Katzman. DIRECTOR: Edward L. Cahn. SCREENPLAY: Raymond T. Marcus [Bernard Gordon]. PHOTOGRAPHY: Benjamin Kline. EDITOR: Jack Ogilvie. MUSIC: Mischa Bakaleinikoff. ART DIRECTOR: Paul Palmentola. SOUND: J.S. Westmoreland. SETS: Sidney Clifford. ASSISTANT DIRECTOR: Jerrold Bernstein. CAST: Gregg Palmer (Jeff Clark), Allison Hayes (Mona Harrison), Autumn Russell (Jan Peters), Joel Ashley (George Harrison), Morris Ankrum (Dr. Jonathan Eggert), Marjorie Eaton (Mrs. Peters), Gene Roth (Sam), Leonard Geer (Johnny), Ray Corrigan (First Mate), Karl "Killer" Davis, William Baskin, Rube Schaffer (Zombies), Mel Curtis (Johnson), Frank Hagney (Captain Jeremy Peters), Lewis Webb (Art).

Director Edward L. Cahn (1907–63) is not highly regarded by film critics but he was prolific and made an impressive number of genre outings. (His finest effort was probably the 1932 Universal western *Law and Order*.) Beginning in 1955 with Columbia's *Creature with the Atom Brain* (q.v.), Cahn turned out ten horror, sci-fi and fantasy features, with some like *The She-Creature* (1956), *It! The Terror from Beyond Space* (1958) and *Beauty and the Beast* (1963) being above average. He also contributed what might be called "guilty pleasure" horror items like *Curse of the Faceless Man* (1958) and *Invisible Invaders* (1959), along with *Zombies of Mora Tau*. Released in England as *The Dead That Walk*, *Zombies of Mora Tau* was doublebilled in the U.S. with *The Man Who Turned to Stone* (q.v.) when Columbia issued it in March 1957.

Despite being a fun, briskly paced affair with enough horrific touches to satisfy most terror film fans, the feature is not given much respect. Rose London in *Zombie: The Living Dead* (1976) did say it "was pretty faithful to old legend" while Ed Naha in *Horrors: From Screen to Scream* (1975) declared it a "[n]ice try." In *The Phantom of the Movies' Videoscope* (2000), Joe Kane called it "a tame, cheap, but occasionally atmospheric '50s fright flick." James O'Neill in *Terror on Tape* (1994) noted, "Although marred by phony underwater FX and sound effects that sound like Three Stooges leftovers (they probably were), this is worth watching for some creepy graveyard scenes and the always welcome presence of [Allison] Hayes as the expedition leader's slutty wife." Stephen Jones in *The Essential Monster Movie Guide* (2000) felt it was "[m]ore low-budget nonsense produced by 'Jungle' Sam Katzman" but he did commend Cahn who "creates a few creepy moments with the zombies emerging from their coffins..." In the context that the feature was made by quickie, fast-buck producer Katzman, Welch Everman's comments in *Cult Horror Films* (1993) are of interest. While he calls *Zombies of Mora Tau* "a more or less forgettable film with mediocre acting and abysmal special effects," he goes on to claim the feature exposes "white North American entrepreneurs do what white North American entrepreneurs do — invade and plunder a third-world country." Having discovered this alleged political subtext in the script (written by blacklisted Bernard Gordon under the name Raymond T. Marcus), he adds, "This is a pretty strong message addressed to 1950s America that had business

Joel Ashley, Allison Hayes, Gregg Palmer, Lewis Webb and Marjorie Eaton in *Zombies of Mora Tau* (1957).

interests all over the world and that faced anti–American sentiments and revolutions in many third-world nations. For this reason alone, *Zombies of Mora Tau* is probably worth another look." One has to wonder how much this supposedly subliminal anti-capitalist message soaked into the minds of the popcorn munchers at 1957 kiddie matinees.

After being away from her family for more than a decade, Jan Peters (Autumn Russell) arrives at her great-grandmother's (Marjorie Eaton) African estate near the bay of Mora Tau. While being driven to the house, Jan sees Sam (Gene Roth), a servant, run over a man (Karl "Killer" Davis) and then refuse to help him. When she is reunited with Mrs. Peters, Jan tells her what happened but the old lady dismisses the event.

On a salvage ship owned by George Harrison (Joel Ashley), anchored in the bay near the Peters home, Harrison, his sexy wife Mona (Hayes), researcher Jonathan Eggert (Morris Ankrum) and diver Jeff Clark (Gregg Palmer) go over plans to bring up a treasure in diamonds from a ship called *The Susan B* that sunk there in 1894. From her window, Jan sees a man submerge into the lagoon and a few minutes later he climbs aboard the sloop and murders a crew member (Mel Curtis). The victim is carried to shore and Mrs. Peters declares he must be buried at once and takes the visitors to the graveyard where Mona becomes hysterical after falling into an open grave. The old lady then relates how five other expeditions came to the area in search of the diamonds and shows them their graves. After inviting the expedition members to stay with her, Mrs. Peters tells Dr. Eggert how her husband, Captain Jeremy Peters (Frank Hagney), commanded a ship whose crew stole a cache of diamonds from a local temple and that he was one of ten men killed over them. Later he and the others rose from their graves, murdered the survivors and sunk the ship. Fifty years ago she got word her husband's corpse was seen walking in the vicinity and she moved there and built her home, hoping someday to help him find eternal rest.

She and the scientist hear Jan and Mona screaming and find them being attacked by a zombie. The old lady scares it off with fire. After her great-grandmother tells Jan she hopes the newcomers will destroy the treasure and free the zombies, the young woman asks Jeff to help her find the man Sam hit on the road. They go to the spot and the zombie abducts Jan, taking her to a jungle graveyard where his shipmates await in their coffins in a mausoleum. Using flares, Jeff holds off the undead, rescues Jan and returns her to her home where the next day he tells Harrison he is leaving the expedition. Desperate to get the diamonds, Harrison finally offers him half of the treasure and Jeff agrees. That day Jeff dives into the bay and finds the ship but is attacked by a zombie who tears off his air hose; he is brought up unconscious. Taken back to the house, Jeff is nursed by Jan as her great-grandmother gives him a medication that helps him breathe. When Jeff regains consciousness, he and Jan are confronted by Mona, who wants to seduce the diver; she accuses Jan of trying to take him away from her. When her husband finds out he slaps Mona and she runs away. When she does not show up by nightfall, Mrs. Peters says the zombies have her. Harrison, Jeff and Eggert drive to the graveyard in search of Mona and find her in the mausoleum surrounded by the undead. Again using flares, Jeff and Harrison manage to spirit her away as Eggert spreads gasoline around the building and Jeff sets it on fire, holding back the zombies as the four escape back to the house. Mrs. Peters informs Harrison that his wife is dead but he refuses to believe her. That night Mona gets up and stabs one of the ship's crew (Lewis Webb) and threatens another (Leonard Geer). To keep Mona in her room she is placed in bed and surrounded by candles as Harrison and Jeff return to the bay to retrieve the treasure. Jeff dives to the ship and locates a box containing the diamonds but is jumped by zombies and barely makes it back aboard Harrison's ship. The crew is attacked by the walking dead and to get them away from the sloop, Jeff takes the treasure chest and goes back to the house by boat. There, with Mrs. Peters' help, the box is opened and the diamonds are revealed. Harrison shows up and holds Jeff and the women at bay with a gun, takes the box and Mona and returns to the vessel. There his wife kills Harrison, retrieves the box and returns to the jungle with the other zombies. Jeff has placed the diamonds in a sack and asks Jan to leave with him but she does not want to desert her great-grandmother. He then orders both women to accompany him to the boat. As they are about to leave, Mona arrives with the undead to take the diamonds. When Mrs. Peters sees her husband she begs Jeff to let her throw away the treasure. Because he has fallen in love with Jan, he agrees. Mrs. Peters tosses the diamonds into the bay and sees her husband evaporate.

Zotz!

(1962; 87 minutes) PRODUCER-DIRECTOR: William Castle. ASSOCIATE PRODUCER: Dona Holloway. SCREENPLAY: Walter Karig, from the novel by Ray Russell. PHOTOGRAPHY: Gordon Avil. EDITOR: Edwin Bryant. MUSIC: Bernard Green. ART DIRECTOR: Robert Peterson. SOUND: J.S. Westmoreland. SETS: James M. Crowe. MAKEUP: Ben Lane. ASSISTANT DIRECTOR: Carter De Haven, Jr. CAST: Tom Poston (Professor John Jones), Julia Meade (Professor Virginia Fenster), Jim Backus (Professor Horatio Kellgore), Fred Clark (General Bullivar), Cecil Kellaway (Dean Joshua Updike), Margaret Dumont (Persephone Updike), James Millhollin (Dr. R.A. Kroner), Carl Don (Josh Bates), Mike Mazurki (Igor), Jimmy Hawkins (Jimmy Kilgore), Bart Patton (Mr. Crane), Judee Morton (Miss Blakiston), Michael Westfield (Captain Nestor Byron), Russ Whiteman (Major Percy Foulger), George Moorman (First Lieutenant John G. Stefanski), Elaine Martone (Secretary), Susan Dorn (Nurse), Albert Glasser (Nikita Khrushchev), Louis Nye (Hugh Fundy), Frank J. Scannell (Pentagon Newsman), Fred Aldrich (Policeman), Bess Flowers, Phil Arnold (Party Guests), William Castle (Himself), Zeme North (Cynthia Jones).

For his fifth "gimmick" feature for Columbia, producer-director William Castle did *Zotz!*, based on the 1947 novel by Ray Russell; it was released in July 1962. Unlike his previous efforts for the studio (*The Tingler, 13 Ghosts, Homicidal* and *Mr. Sardonicus* [qq.v.]), this outing was not a horror film but a comedy thriller about an ancient artifact with magical powers. For publicity purposes, thousands of plastic Zotz coins were distributed to theater patrons. The film also utilized stock footage of Patricia Breslin from 1961's *Homicidal*. While a fairly entertaining production, *Zotz!* suffered from a rather lethargic script compounded by the star casting of laconic comedian Tom Poston, a part better suited for a Cary Grant or a Robert Montgomery. Poston, like many comedians whose origins are in television, was fine handling cameo roles but he did not have the screen persona to carry an entire feature, as witnessed by his next outing for Castle, 1963's *The Old Dark House* (q.v.). Louis Nye, who like Poston was an alumnus of Steve Allen's TV programs, was excellent in *Zotz!* in a small role as the addled inventor of a death ray.

Cynthia Jones (Zeme North), who lives with her uncle, health food nut Professor John Jones (Poston), is sent an old coin from a friend involved in an archaeological expedition. Prof. Jones, who is a teacher of Ancient Eastern Languages at Saracen Valley College, comes to realize that the artifact has magical properties: It can give its bearer the power to cause pain and when the word

"Zotz" is spoken it slows motion. When both methods are used in tandem, the result can be fatal. Jones is attracted to another member of the faculty, Professor Virginia Fenster (Julia Meade), and through his use of the coin, he meets and falls in love with her. Thanks to his activities with the coin, the dean of the college, Joshua Updike (Cecil Kellaway), thinks Jones should see psychiatrist Dr. Kroner (James Millhollin), while Professor Horatio Kellgore (Jim Backus) tries to convince Updike that Jones, his rival for the position of dean of the Languages Department, is unfit for the job. Dr. Kroner diagnoses Jones as being not sane, prompting Jones to plead his case with the Pentagon and meets with General Bullivar (Fred Clark). While the military sees no advantage in the artifact and thinks it is a joke, Soviet spies report to Nikita Khrushchev (Albert Glasser) about the object and he orders it stolen. Russian agents kidnap Cynthia and Virginia and will hold them hostage until Jones turns over the coin. He decides to play along with the kidnappers and finds out where the two women are being held prisoners. He then uses the power of the coin to set them free and stop the Soviets from obtaining the artifact. During a fight with the agents, Jones drops the object and it falls into the street and down a sewer manhole. The spies are apprehended and Jones returns to Saracen Valley College, happy he no longer has to deal with the coin and grateful that he and Virginia got promotions.

One of Castle's lesser efforts, *Zotz!* got mixed reviews. The *New York Times* found it to be "[g]rade Z, or perhaps Y. A flaccid little farce." Ed Naha in *Horrors: From Screen to Scream* (1975) thought it was "[c]ute but lightweight." Paul Mavis in *The Espionage Filmography* (2001) wrote, "[T]he funny cast goes along with the silly premise, and the movie doesn't ask the audience to do anything but laugh along with it. *Zotz!* is an amusing mixture of comedy, fantasy and the spy genre.

Julia Meade, Tom Poston, Mike Mazurki and Zeme North in *Zotz!* (1962).

SERIALS

Adventures of Captain Africa

(1955; 15 chapters) PRODUCER: Sam Katzman. DIRECTOR: Spencer Gordon Bennet. STORY-SCREENPLAY: George H. Plympton. PHOTOGRAPHY: Ira H. Morgan. EDITOR: Earl Turner. MUSIC DIRECTOR: Mischa Bakaleinikoff. ART DIRECTOR: Paul Palmentola. SOUND: J.S. Westmoreland. SETS: Sidney Clifford. PRODUCTION MANAGER: Herbert Leonard. UNIT MANAGER: Jack Erickson. ASSISTANT DIRECTOR: Horace Hough. CAST: John Hart (Captain Africa), Rick Vallin (Ted Arnold), Ben Welden (Omar), June Howard (Princess Rhoda), Bud Osborne (Nat Coleman), Paul Marion (Abdul el Hamid), Lee Roberts (Boris), Terry Frost (Greg), Ed Coch (Balu), Michael Fox (Prime Minister), Kermit Maynard (Gang Member).

CHAPTER TITLES: (1) Mystery Man of the Jungle; (2) Captain Africa to the Rescue; (3) Midnight Attack; (4) Into the Crocodile Pit; (5) Jungle War Drums; (6) Slave Traders; (7) Saved By Captain Africa; (8) The Bridge in the Sky; (9) Blasted by Captain Africa; (10) The Vanishing Princess; (11) The Tunnel of Terror; (12) Fangs of the Beast; (13) Renegades at Bay; (14) Captain Africa and the Wolf Dog; (15) Captain Africa's Final Move.

Columbia's fifty-fifth serial, and its last non-western cliffhanger, *Adventures of Captain Africa* was subtitled "Mighty Jungle Avenger." Filmed at the Iverson Ranch, it was basically a remake of *The Phantom* (1943) [q.v.], allowing star John Hart to wear the same costume Tom Tyler donned as the Phantom. Co-star Rick Vallin wore the same attire as Gilbert Roland in *The Desert Hawk* (1944) so that action footage from that chapterplay could also be incorporated into the cheapie production. This 15-chapter outing was not the first time star Hart played a masked hero: He portrayed the title role in the ABC-TV series *The Lone Ranger* from 1952 to 1954.

Captain Africa (Hart) joins forces with daring Ted Arnold (Vallin), wild animal trainer Nat Coleman (Bud Osborne) and Coleman's assistant Omar (Ben Welden). The three follow Omar to a jungle hideaway where he meets with Princess Rhoda (June Howard) and his former caliph, Abdul el Hamid (Paul Marion), who is trying to regain his title. Boris (Lee Roberts) and Greg (Terry Frost) are out to get rid of Hamid and his disciples, including Omar. When Arnold and Coleman convince Omar of their good intentions, he takes Captain Africa and Arnold to meet with Hamid and they find out that the former caliph's prime minister (Michael Fox) is held captive in a castle. Captain Africa attempts to rescue him and is nearly killed by the castle gate spikes. He and Ted learn the location of the prime minister and Arnold rescues him. With Arnold, Omar and Hamid leading their men in an attack on the castle, Captain Africa prevents Boris' henchmen from blowing up the citadel. During the melee, the usurper caliph (Ed Coch) is killed by Hamid, who regains his throne. As Arnold and Rhoda plan to marry, Captain Africa goes in search of more adventures.

Adventures of Sir Galahad

(1949; 15 chapters) PRODUCER: Sam Katzman. DIRECTOR: Spencer Gordon Bennet. SCREENPLAY: George H. Plympton, Lewis Clay and David Mathews. PHOTOGRAPHY: Ira H. Morgan. EDITORS: Dwight Caldwell and Earl Turner. MUSIC DIRECTOR: Mischa Bakaleinikoff. ART DIRECTOR: Paul Palmentola. SETS: Sidney Clifford. PRODUCTION MANAGER: Herbert B. Leonard. CAST: George Reeves (Sir Galahad), Nelson Leigh (King Arthur), William Fawcett (Merlin), Hugh Prosser (Sir Lancelot), Lois Hall (Lady of the Lake), Charles King (Sir Bors), Pat Barton (Morgan le Fay), Don C. Harvey (Bartog), Jim Diehl (Sir Kay), Marjorie Stapp (Queen Guinevere), John Merton (Saxon King Ulric), Pierce Lyden (Cawker), Rick Vallin (Sir Gawain), Leonard Penn (Modred aka The Black Knight), Ray Corrigan (Innkeeper One-Eye), Al Ferguson (Captain of the Guards), Rusty Wescoatt

(Bartog's Thug), Frank Ellis (Outlaw), Paul Frees (Voice of the Black Knight).

CHAPTER TITLES: (1) Stolen Sword; (2) Galahad's Daring; (3) Prisoners of Ulric; (4) Attack on Camelot; (5) Galahad to the Rescue; (6) Passage of Peril; (7) Unknown Betrayer; (8) Perilous Adventure; (9) Treacherous Magic; (10) The Sorcerer's Spell; (11) Valley of No Return; (12) Castle Perilous; (13) The Wizard's Vengeance; (14) Quest for the Queen; (15) Galahad's Triumph.

There have been scores of films dealing with the legend of King Arthur but the only Hollywood serial to cover the subject is Sam Katzman's *Adventures of Sir Galahad*. George Reeves had the title role in the chapterplay, several years before gaining fame in the syndicated television series *Adventures of Superman* (1951–57). Discussing Reeves in *Superman: Serial to Cereal* (1976), Gary Crossman noted, "The serial served up a potpourri of traditional Mack Sennett chase/Doug Fairbanks fight formula. Reeves squared off against the magic of Merlin, clinging vines, fire monsters, catapults, arrows and a nasty encounter or two with the Black Knight. Except for the uniform, it all sounds like an audition for Superman. But Reeves was actually put through paces in *Galahad* that were in many ways more difficult than any he faced as the Man of Steel." Alan G. Barbour wrote in *Cliffhanger: A Pictorial History of the Motion Picture Serial* (1977), "One of [Columbia's] better efforts was put forward in *Adventures of Sir Galahad* with George Reeves ... Part of the fun of watching this serial was in seeing veteran Western heavy Charles King play a comic foil — a type of role he began his career with in silent films. King engaged in various slapstick sequences, even donning a dress when the situation called for such an extreme." Filmed at Corriganville, the serial cast a bevy of "B" western players as characters from the Dark Ages, making for somewhat amazing viewing.

Denied admission to King Arthur's (Nelson Leigh) famed Round Table, Sir Galahad (Reeves), along with his bumbling pal Sir Bors (King), sets out to find the magic sword Excalibur that can make its owner unconquerable. Saxon King Ulric (John Merton) leads an invasion force into Arthur's kingdom and Galahad attempts to get the weapon from the invader's henchman Bartog (Don C. Harvey), who obtained it from the Black Knight (Leonard Penn), a traitor who wants Arthur's throne. Each time Galahad tries to get the sword he is vexed by the aged magician Merlin (William Fawcett) but he is aided by Morgan le Fay (Pat Barton), Arthur's sister. The Black Knight and his cohorts kidnap Arthur's queen, Guinevere (Marjorie Stapp), causing Merlin to help Galahad by telling him to see the Lady of the Lake (Lois Hall), who presents him with the sword which he takes to the king. One of the Round Table, Modred (Penn), is unmasked as the Black Knight and Galahad is made a member of Arthur's circle.

Atom Man vs. Superman

(1950; 15 chapters) PRODUCER: Sam Katzman. DIRECTOR: Spencer Gordon Bennet. SCREENPLAY: David Mathews, George H. Plympton and Joseph F. Poland. PHOTOGRAPHY: Ira H. Morgan. EDITOR: Earl Turner. MUSIC: Mischa Bakaleinikoff. ART DIRECTOR: Paul Palmentola. SETS: Sidney Clifford. PRODUCTION MANAGER: Herbert B. Leonard. SPECIAL EFFECTS: Howard Swift. CONTINUITY: Violet Newfield. SECOND UNIT DIRECTOR: Derwin Abrahams. ASSISTANT DIRECTOR: R.M. Andrews. CAST: Kirk Alyn (Clark Kent/Superman), Noel Neill (Lois Lane), Lyle Talbot (Luthor), Tommy Bond (Jimmy Olsen), Pierre Watkin (Perry White), Jack Ingram (Foster), Don C. Harvey (Albor), Rusty Wescoatt (Carl), Terry Frost (Baer), Wally West (Dorr), Paul Stader (Killer Lawson), George Robotham (Earl), Pierce Lyden (Garland), Fred Kelsey (Chief Forman), Edward Hearn (Professor Stone), Stanley Blystone (Joe Evans), Marshall Bradford (Mr. Taylor), Jack Chefe (Eddie), Charles King (Robber), Rick Vallin (Power Company Trucker), William Fawcett (Metropolis Mayor), Creighton Hale (Observer), Tommy Farrell (Briggs), Frank Ellis (Police Escort/Bogus Cameraman), Guy Teague (Bridge Policeman), Chuck Roberson (Road Policeman), George Morrell (Bank Guard), Eddie Parker (Power Company Driver), Eddie Foster, Eddie Featherston (Truck Loaders), Frank O'Connor (Train Passenger), John Hart, Hugh Prosser (Gang Members), Kit Guard (Cave Guard), Frank Hagney (Bridge Man), John Elliott, Michael Vallon (Councilmen), Knox Manning (Narrator).

CHAPTER TITLES: (1) Superman Flies Again; (2) Atom Man Appears; (3) Ablaze in the Sky; (4) Superman Meets Atom Man; (5) Atom Man Tricks Superman; (6) Atom Man's Challenge; (7) At the Mercy of Atom Man; (8) In the Empty Room; (9) Superman Crashes Through; (10) Atom Man's Heat Ray; (11) Luthor's Strategy; (12) Atom Man Strikes; (13) Atom Man's Flying Saucer; (14) Rocket of Vengeance; (15) Superman Save the Universe.

Following the success of the 1948 serial *Superman* (q.v.), based on the comic book characters created by Joe Shuster and Jerry Siegel, producer Sam Katzman did a sequel, *Atom Man vs. Superman*, again starring Kirk Alyn as the Man of Steel with Lyle Talbot as his arch-enemy, Luthor. Filmed at the Iverson Ranch and Bronson

Poster for *Atom Man vs. Superman* (1950).

Canyon, this action-filled chapterplay paved the way for the syndicated television series *Adventures of Superman* (1951–57), starring George Reeves. Jim Harmon and Donald F. Glut in *The Great Movie Serials: Their Sound and Fury* (1972) reported that the second Superman serial was "far more gimmicky and gadget-prone than the first ... but was flawed by the same Katzman cheapness in production values..." In *Those Fabulous Serial Heroines: Their Lives and Films* (1990), Buck Rainey noted, "The serial proved profitable and highly popular with juvenile audiences..."

Mild-mannered reporter Clark Kent (Alyn), Lois Lane (Noel Neill) and Jimmy Olsen (Tommy Bond) are assigned by *Daily Planet* newspaper editor Perry White (Pierre Watkin) to cover the story of evil Luthor's (Talbot) promise to destroy the city of Metropolis. The madman uses a number of his inventions, including one that can break up and reassemble people, to cause havoc but each time he is thwarted by Superman (Alyn). Luthor then invents synthetic Kryptonite; Superman loses his powers when near the substance. As the steel mask-wearing Atom Man, Luthor and his henchmen take the weakened Superman to his hideout and launch him into space. The master criminal and his gang ransack the city; when Superman returns he is unable to stop the crime wave. Luthor becomes fearful when a *Daily Planet* news story announces that the Man of Steel will reappear and he decides to destroy Metropolis with a sonic vibrator, abduct Lois and escape from the Earth in a flying saucer. A rejuvenated Superman saves the city and then flies after the spaceship, rescuing Lois and putting Luthor in jail.

In 1978 Alyn and Neill had cameo roles as Lois Lane's parents in *Superman*, the first of three theatrical films to star Christopher Reeve as the Man of Steel.

Batman

(1943; 15 chapters) PRODUCER: Rudolph C. Flothow. DIRECTOR: Lambert Hillyer. SCREENPLAY: Victor McLeod, Leslie J. Swabacker and Harry Fraser. PHOTOGRAPHY: James S. Brown, Jr. EDITORS: Dwight Caldwell and Earl Turner. MUSIC: Lee Zahler. ASSISTANT DIRECTOR: Gene Anderson. CAST: Lewis Wilson (Bruce Wayne/Batman), Douglas Croft (Dick Grayson/Robin), J. Carrol Naish (Dr. Tito Daka/Prince Daka), Shirley Patterson (Linda Page), William Austin (Alfred), Charles C. Wilson (Captain Arnold), Charles Middleton (Ken Colton), George Chesebro (Brennan), Robert Fiske (Foster), Michael Vallon (Preston), Gus Glassmire (Martin Warren), Frank Shannon (Dr. Hayden), George J. Lewis (Burke), Dick Curtis (Agent Croft), Earle Hodgins (Joe), Tom London (Andrews), John Maxwell (Sam Fletcher), Kenne Duncan (Fred), Sam Flint (Dr. G.H. Borden), Terry Frost (Male Nurse), Robert Fiske (Foster), Karl Hackett (Wallace), Jack Ingram (Klein), I. Stanford Jolley (Brett), Michael Vallon (Preston), Anthony Warde (Stone), Billy Wilkerson (Steve), Ted Oliver (Marshall), Bud Osborne (Brown), Lester Dorr (Lawson), Jack Gardner (Jim Bramwell), Al Hill (Detective), Eddie Kane (Bondsman Hanson), Mauritz Hugo (Doctor), Warren Jackson (Club Owner Bernie), Pat O'Malley, Sam Lufkin (Policemen), George Magrill (Club Henchman), Harry Tenbrook (Bartender), Lynton Brent (Replaced Pilot), Frank Austin (Desk Clerk), Jerry Frank (Thug), Stanley Price (Driver), George Robotham, Harry Wilson (Gang Members), Blackie Whiteford, Roy Bucko (Bar Customers), Cyril Ring, Harold Miller (Restaurant Patrons), Knox Manning (Narrator).

CHAPTER TITLES: (1) The Electrical Brain; (2) The Bat's Cave; (3) The Mark of the Zombies; (4) Slaves of the Rising Sun; (5) The Living Corpse; (6) Poison Peril; (7) The Phony Doctor; (8) Lured by Radium; (9) The Sign of the Sphinx; (10) Flying Spies; (11) A Nipponese Trap; (12) Embers of Evil; (13) Eight Steps Down; (14) The Executioner Strikes; (15) The Doom of the Rising Sun.

Gotham City is the target of Japanese spy Dr. Daka (J. Carrol Naish) who is after radium that he needs to manufacture an atom-smashing ray gun. He plans to use this weapon to help the New Order of the Axis defeat the Allies and take over the United States. He is opposed by two masked crusaders, Batman (Lewis Wilson) and Robin (Douglas Croft), who are really millionaire Bruce Wayne and his ward Dick Grayson, both secret government agents. Daka has also invented a device that will transform people into zombies. His cohorts abduct Martin Warren (Gus Glassmire), the uncle of Wayne's girlfriend Linda Page (Shirley Patterson). In his secret laboratory behind a Chamber of Horrors exhibit, Daka turns the old man into a zombie and later tries to do the same to Robin but is foiled by Batman. To stop the masked duo, Daka abducts Linda and makes her a zombie, but Batman manages to rescue the young woman and her uncle. The evil Daka then sets several traps to destroy Batman and Robin but his entire spy ring is captured and the Axis agent meets death in his own alligator pit.

Batman was the first DC Comics character to star in a serial; he was created for comic books in 1939 by Bob Kane. Filmed at the Iverson Ranch in Chatsworth, *Batman* was a cheap affair, laughable even in its time. The two heroes were bland and J. Carrol Naish almost chewed up the sets in his outlandish portrayal of the Axis agent. Due to the shoddiness of the production, Batman no longer had his super Batmobile but instead drove a luxury car. The Bat Cave and Utility Belt from the comics were retained for the serial. Alan G. Barbour commented in *Days of Thrills and Adventure* (1970) that Batman was "portrayed by Lewis Wilson in the most ill-fitting costume one could imagine. Douglas Croft as Robin was equally unappealing."

Because of the continued popularity of the DC Comics character, a serial sequel, *Batman and Robin* (q.v.), came out in 1949. In the mid–1960s the property obtained its greatest success with ABC-TV's *Batman* series starring Adam West and Burt Ward as the caped crusaders; it ran from 1965 to 1967 and also resulted in a 1966 feature film, *Batman*, starring West and Ward. This breathed new life into the old serial and it was reissued by Columbia in 1965 (with new narration by Garry Owens) as *An Evening with Batman and Robin*.

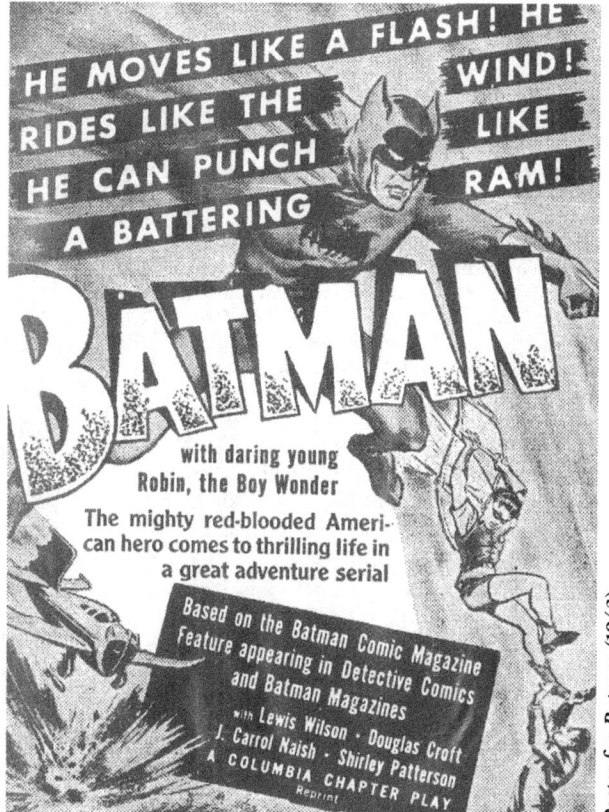

Poster for *Batman* (1943).

In the summer of 1974 the initial chapter of the 1943 serial was included in the Columbia compilation feature release *The Three Stooges Follies*.

Batman and Robin

(1949; 15 chapters) PRODUCER: Sam Katzman. DIRECTOR: Spencer Gordon Bennet. SCREENPLAY: George H. Plympton, Joseph F. Poland and Royal K. Cole. PHOTOGRAPHY: Ira H. Morgan. EDITORS: Dwight Caldwell and Earl Turner. MUSIC DIRECTOR: Mischa Bakaleinikoff. ART DIRECTOR: Paul Palmentola. SETS: Sidney Clifford. PRODUCTION MANAGER: Herbert Leonard. ASSISTANT DIRECTOR: R.M. Andrews. CAST: Robert Lowery (Bruce Wayne/Batman), John Duncan (Dick Grayson/Robin), Jane Adams (Vicki Vale), Lyle Talbot (Commissioner Gordon), Ralph Graves (Winslow Harrison), Don C. Harvey (Nolan), William Fawcett (Professor Hammil/The Wizard), Leonard Penn (Carter), Rick Vallin (Barry Brown), Michael Whalen (Dunne), Greg McClure (Evans), House Peters, Jr. (Earl), Jim Diehl (Jason), Rusty Wescoatt (Ives), Eric Wilton (Alfred Pennyworth), Marshall Bradford (Wesley Morton), Emmett Vogan (Mr. Williams), James Craven (Norwood), Myron Healey (Officer Walker), Lee Roberts (Neal), Harold Landon (Jimmy Vale), Allan Ray (Mac Lacey), Eddie Parker (Holt), Phil Arnold

(Doctor), John Hart (John Hench), Frank O'Connor (Gate Guard), Wally West (Patrol Policeman), Guy Teague (Guard/Aircraft Janitor), Frank Hagney, Jack Chefe (Plant Guards), John Doucette (Gang Member), Frank Ellis (Policeman), Richard Cramer (Newspaper Office Worker), George Cisar (Alley Policeman), George Robotham (Gang Member Driver), Knox Manning (Narrator).

CHAPTER TITLES: (1) Batman Takes Over; (2) Tunnel of Terror; (3) Robin's Wild Ride; (4) Batman Trapped; (5) Robin Rescues Batman; (6) Target — Robin; (7) The Fatal Blast; (8) Robin Meets the Wizard; (9) The Wizard Strikes Back; (10) Batman's Last Chance; (11) Robin's Ruse; (12) Robin Rides the Wind; (13) The Wizard's Challenge; (14) Batman vs. Wizard; (15) Batman Victorious.

When the mysterious, cloaked Wizard steals a remote control device invented for the government by wheelchair-bound Professor Hammil (William Fawcett) and his associate Carter (Leonard Penn), Gotham City Police Commissioner Gordon (Lyle Talbot) calls in Batman (Robert Lowery) and Robin (John Duncan). Eventually Batman unmasks the Wizard as the eccentric Hammil, who wanted the invention for himself.

In regards to this second Batman serial (Columbia's fortieth cliffhanger), Jim Harmon and Donald F. Glut wrote in *The Great Movie Serials: Their Sound and Fury* (1972), "As usual on a [Sam] Katzman production, the low budget showed everywhere in money-saving shortcuts and inadequacies. Even Batman's costume was so cheap it looked as if it might have been made by his grandmother for a Halloween party. The cowl or hood fitted so poorly, it was obvious that the actor beneath it could neither see nor breathe very well ... The fabled Batmobile was in for the lowest casting of all. No longer even impersonated by a limousine, it was replaced by a 1949 Mercury."

The year after the serial was shown in theaters, an attempt was made to bring the caped duo to radio with an audition show for a proposed series called *Batman and Robin* (broadcast on September 5, 1950), starring John Emery and Ronald Liss. Apparently the effort never made it to a full-blown series.

Blackhawk

(1952; 15 chapters) PRODUCER: Sam Katzman. DIRECTORS: Spencer Gordon Bennet and Fred F. Sears. SCREENPLAY: George H. Plympton, Sherman L. Lowe and Royal K. Cole. PHOTOGRAPHY: William Whitley. EDITOR: Earl Turner. MUSIC DIRECTOR: Mischa Bakaleinikoff. ART DIRECTOR: Paul Palmentola. SETS: Sidney Clifford. PRODUCTION MANAGER: Herbert Leonard. SPECIAL EFFECTS: Jack Erickson. CONTINUITY: Moree Herring. ASSISTANT DIRECTOR: Charles S. Gould. CAST: Kirk Alyn (Blackhawk), Carol Forman (Laska), John Crawford (Chuck), Michael Fox (Mr. Case/The Leader), Don C. Harvey (Olaf), Rick Vallin (Stanislaus/Boris), Larry Stewart (Andre), Weaver Levy (Chop Chop), Zon Murray (Bork), Nick Stuart (Cress), Marshall Reed (Aller), Pierce Lyden (Dyke), William Fawcett (Dr. Rolph), Rory Mallinson (Hodge), Frank Ellis (Hendrickson), Marshall Bradford (Malcolm Smith), Charles Horvath (Otto Helger), Jack Mulhall, Frank O'Connor (Defense Councilmen), Terry Frost (The Leader's Secretary), Eddie Foster (Jose), Frank Gerstle (Dawson), Wally West, David Sharpe (Gang Members), Jack Chefe (Guard), Knox Manning (Narrator).

CHAPTER TITLES: (1) Distress Call from Space; (2) Blackhawk Traps a Traitor; (3) In the Enemy's Hideout; (4) The Iron Monster; (5) Human Targets; (6) Blackhawk's Leap for Life; (7) Mystery Fuel; (8) Blasted from the Sky; (9) Blackhawk Tempts Fate; (10) Chase for Element X; (11) Forced Down; (12) Drums of Doom; (13)

Poster for *Blackhawk* (1952).

Blackhawk's Daring Plan; (14) Blackhawk's Wild Ride; (15) The Leader Unmasked.

Blackhawk was Kirk Alyn's final Columbia serial after having headlined *Superman* (1948) and *Atom Man vs. Superman* (1950) [qq.v.], plus Republic's *Daughter of Don Q* (1948), *Federal Agents vs. Underworld, Inc.* (1949) and *Radar Patrol vs. Spy King* (1950). It was based on characters created by Will Eisner and drawn by Reed Crandall that made their debut in 1941 in *Military Comics*. Also called *Blackhawk: Fearless Champion of Freedom*, the serial had been preceded by the Wednesday night ABC radio series *Blackhawk* that ran from September 1950 to January 1951.

Blackhawk (Alyn), the leader of the International Brotherhood, an organization dedicated to fighting crime, finds out one of his men, Stanislaus (Rick Vallin), has been drafted by enemy agent Laska (Carol Forman) in a scheme to steal Dr. Rolph's (William Fawcett) electronic death ray machine. When he refuses, Stanislaus is captured by the spies and replaced by a lookalike, Boris (Vallin), who is revealed by another organization member, Hendrickson (Frank Ellis). Boris manages to defeat Henrickson and his pal Chop Chop (Weaver Levy) and almost kills Blackhawk. After demonstrating his death ray to Blackhawk, Dr. Rolph is abducted by the foreign agents along with his invention. Eventually Blackhawk and fellow crime fighter Chuck (John Crawford) locate and rescue the scientist but not before Blackhawk is nearly killed by the death ray. Laska, who works for a mystery man called the Leader, flies to the Mexican town of Valdez but is followed by Blackhawk who enlists the help of the local police in tracking the spies. A tribe of Yaqui Indians attack Blackhawk and his men but he is aided by local rancher Bork (Zon Murray), and the assailants are thwarted. After one of Laska's operatives, Case (Michael Fox), is caught by the Blackhawks, they try to trap the female spy but she makes a getaway, not knowing that the Leader plans to eliminate her. When Laska arrives at the Leader's headquarters she confronts the master spy and kills him but is then arrested by the Blackhawks as the gang is rounded up.

Brick Bradford

(1947; 15 chapters) PRODUCER: Sam Katzman. DIRECTOR: Spencer Gordon Bennet. SCREENPLAY: George H. Plympton, Arthur Hoerl and Lewis Clay. PHOTOGRAPHY: Ira H. Morgan. EDITOR: Earl Turner. MUSIC DIRECTOR: Mischa Bakaleinikoff. ART DIRECTOR: Paul Palmentola. SETS: Sidney Moore. PRODUCTION MANAGER: David Katzman. SECOND UNIT DIRECTOR: Thomas Carr. ASSISTANT DIRECTOR: R.M. Andrews. CAST: Kane Richmond (Brick Bradford), Rick Vallin (Sandy Sanderson), Linda [Leighton] Johnson (June Salisbury), Pierre Watkin (Professor Salisbury), Charles Quigley (Laydron), Jack Ingram (Albers), Fred Graham (Black), John Merton (Dr. Gregor Tymak), Leonard Penn (Eric Byrus), Wheeler Oakman (Louis Walthar), Carol Forman (Queen Khana), Charles King (Creed), John Hart (Dent), Helene Stanley (Carol Preston), Nelson Leigh (Edward Preston), Robert Barron (Zuntar),

Poster for *Brick Bradford* (1948).

George DeNormand (Meaker), Noel Neill (Lulah), Stanley Blystone (Stevens), Frank Ellis (Rork), Al Ferguson (Bucaneer), Gene Roth (Akbar), Marshall Reed (Moon Soldier), Stanley Price (Chief).

CHAPTER TITLES: (1) Atomic Defense; (2) Flight to the Moon; (3) Prisoners of the Moon; (4) Into the Volcano; (5) Bradford at Bay; (6) Back to Earth; (7) Into Another Century; (8) Buried Treasure; (9) Trapped in the Time Top; (10) The Unseen Hand; (11) Poison Gas; (12) Door of Disaster; (13) Sinister Rendezvous; (14) River of Revenge; (15) For the Peace of the World.

Columbia's thirty-fifth serial and its initial sci-fi cliffhanger, *Brick Bradford* was based on the King Features Syndicate comic strip by Clarence Gray and William Ritt. Not only did the script have the title hero going to the Moon and then back in time, it also included an anti-guided missile interceptor ray, a transporter and an invisibility mechanism. Unfortunately the chapterplay was hampered by producer Sam Katzman's usual cost-cutting along with a choppy scenario concocted by three writers (George H. Plympton, Arthur Hoerl, Lewis Clay) that ran the gamut from exciting science fiction to tongue-in-cheek comedy and mediocre plotting. *Brick Bradford* proved to be star Kane Richmond final serial. His other cliffhangers included Mascot's *The Adventures of Rex and Rinty* (1935); *The Lost City* (1935), an independent release by Sherman Krellberg; Republic's *Spy Smasher* (1942) and *Haunted Harbor* (1944); and two 1945 Columbia releases, *Brenda Starr, Reporter* and *Jungle Raiders* (q.v.).

Working for the United Nations, Brick Bradford (Richmond) is assigned to keep crooks from stealing Dr. Tymak's (John Merton) anti-guided missile interceptor ray. He is aided by the inventor's daughter, June (Linda Johnson), and his pal Sandy Sanderson (Rick Vallin). Gangster Laydron (Charles Quigley) wants the weapon but is thwarted for a time when Dr. Tymak uses his Crystal Door to travel to the Moon where he hopes to find Lunarium, a mineral he needs to perfect the weapon. He is soon captured by the Moon rulers; he is followed by Brick and Professor Salisbury (Pierre Watkin) and they too are taken prisoners. When the two men learn that a group of rebels want to overthrow the dictators ruling the Moon, they help them in their quest and then return home with Dr. Tymak. After the inventor is kidnapped by Laydron and his gang, he is rescued by Brick who then travels with Sandy in a Time Top to Central America in the 1700s in order to obtain a formula Dr. Tymak needs. The two men are captured by natives and nearly burned alive and also have to do battle with pirates before finding the formula and getting back to their own time. Back home, Brick and Sandy continue to combat Laydron and his men until they trap them in their hideout as the inventor finishes the ray weapon.

Bruce Gentry

(1949; 15 chapters) PRODUCER: Sam Katzman. DIRECTORS: Spencer Gordon Bennet and Thomas Carr. SCREENPLAY: George H. Plympton, Joseph F. Poland and Lewis Clay. PHOTOGRAPHY: Ira H. Morgan. EDITORS: Dwight Caldwell and Earl Turner. MUSIC DIRECTOR: Mischa Bakaleinikoff. ART DIRECTOR: Paul Palmentola. SETS: Sidney Clifford. PRODUCTION MANAGER: Herbert Leonard. ASSISTANT DIRECTOR: R.M. Andrews. CAST: Tom Neal (Bruce Gentry), Judy Clark (Juanita Farrell), Ralph Hodges (Frank Farrell), Forrest Taylor (Dr. Alexander Benson), Hugh Prosser (Paul Radcliffe), Tristram Coffin (Krendon), Jack Ingram (Allen), Terry Frost (Chandler), Eddie Parker (Gregg), Charles King (Ivor), Stephen Carr (Adrian Hill), Dale Van Sickel (Gregory), Rusty Wescoatt, George DeNormand, Al Wyatt (Gang Members), Knox Manning (Narrator).

CHAPTER TITLES: (1) The Mystery Disk; (2) Fiery Furnace; (3) The Man of Menace; (4) Grade Crossing; (5) Danger Trail; (6) A Fight for Life; (7) The Flying Disk; (8) Fate Takes the Wheel; (9) Hazardous Heights; (10) Over the Falls; (11) Gentry at Bay; (12) Parachute of Peril; (13) Menace of the Mesa; (14) Bruce's Strategy; (15) The Final Disk.

After flier Bruce Gentry (Tom Neal) is attacked by a flying saucer on his way to Los Angeles, he meets with scientist Dr. Alexander Benson (Forrest Taylor) regarding the incident. The Recorder, an enemy agent who speaks only through recordings, has his henchmen Krendon (Tristram Coffin), Allen (Jack Ingram) and Chandler (Terry Frost) abduct the scientist and bring him to his headquarters where he is interrogated. Businessman Paul Radcliffe (Hugh Prosser) hires Gentry to locate the disks, which are electronically controlled and can be directed at any target, to see if they can be used for commercial purposes. Gentry is aided in his quest by rancher Frank Farrell (Ralph Hodges) and his sister Juanita (Judy Clark). After many near-fatal encounters, Gentry traces the Recorder and his gang to their remote hideout and unmasks the enemy agent as Benson. Krendon electronically guides one of the disks to destroy the Panama Canal but Gentry follows it in his plane and knocks it out of the air. As Gentry parachutes to safety, the control panel at the Recorder's headquarters explodes, killing the gang.

Based on the newspaper comic strip by Ray Bailey, *Bruce Gentry* was fairly entertaining but was hampered by shoddy special effects that presented the flying saucers as animated cartoons. In *Days of Thrills and Adventure* (1970), Alan G. Barbour said it "did have a little action, thanks to Tom Steele and Dale Van Sickel, who did the action work, but the serial provided more laughs than excitement."

Captain Midnight

(1942; 15 chapters) PRODUCER: Larry Darmour. DIRECTOR: James W. Horne. SCREENPLAY: Basil Dickey, George H. Plympton, Jack Stanley and Wyndham Gittens. PHOTOGRAPHY: James S. Brown, Jr. EDITORS: Dwight Caldwell and Earl Turner. MUSIC: Lee Zahler. ASSISTANT DIRECTOR: Carl Hiecke. CAST: Dave O'Brien (Captain Albright/Captain Midnight), Dorothy Short (Joyce Edwards), James Craven (Ivan Shark), Sam Edwards (Chuck Ramsey), Guy Wilkerson (Ichabod "Iggy" Mudd), Bryant Washburn (John Edwards), Luana Walters (Fury Shark), Joe Girard (Major Steele), Ray Teal (Borgman), George Pembroke (Dr. James Jordan), Chuck Hamilton (Martel), Al Ferguson (Gardo), Jack Perrin (Policeman), Franklyn Farnum (Federal Agent Allen), George Magrill (Red), Ted Mapes (Slim), Ed Peil, Sr. (Fang), Lee Shumway (Federal Agent Burns), Slim Whitaker (Police Car Patrolman), Dick Botiller (Kraus), John Elliott (Police Chief), Charles Sherlock (Spotter), Bert Young (Taxi Cab Driver), Charles McMurphy (Air Dispatcher/Guard).

CHAPTER TITLES: (1) Mysterious Pilot; (2) Stolen Range Finder; (3) The Captured Plane; (4) Mistaken Identity; (5) Ambushed Ambulance; (6) Weird Waters; (7) Menacing Fates; (8) Shells of Evil; (9) The Drop of Doom; (10) The Hidden Bomb; (11) Sky Terror; (12) Burning Bomber; (13) Death in the Cockpit; (14) Scourge of Revenge; (15) The Fatal Hour.

Captain Midnight was based on the popular radio series of the same title that was first heard only in the Midwest from 1938 to 1940. In 1940 Mutual broadcast the series nationwide and continued to do so for two seasons until the NBC Blue network ran it from 1942 to 1945. Thereafter it was back on Mutual until the conclusion of its run in 1949. Over the years the title character was portrayed by Ed Prentiss, Bill Bouchey and Paul Barnes. Dell Comics put out a *Captain Midnight* comic book in 1941; Fawcett took over the property and issued the comics from 1942 to 1948. Dave O'Brien played Captain Midnight in the serial which was an action-packed and nicely made affair that had the hero facing any number of death-defying situations including being bombed, avoiding death traps and being shot out of the air. The serial villain, Ivan Shark (James Craven), was carried over from the radio serial although transformed from just a general bad guy into the evil head of an enemy sabotage ring out to destroy the United States in keeping with the war fervor of the time.

Famed World War I aerial fighter Captain Albright (O'Brien), aka Captain Midnight, is asked to stop criminal Ivan Shark (Craven), now working for an enemy power, from stealing a futuristic range finder that will help his forces invade the country. The new weapon, invented by John Edwards (Bryant Washburn), is sought by Shark's agent Martel (Chuck Hamilton). The scientist gives the mechanism to his daughter Joyce (Dorothy Short), who he tells to pass it on to Captain Midnight. Shark's men kidnap Edwards but Captain Midnight finds the remote cabin where he is held prisoner; Shark bombs the place hoping to kill the crime fighter. Captain Midnight manages to escape and continues his pursuit of Shark and his minions. After several more adventures he traces Shark and his gang to their underground lair where they are holding Edwards and his daughter, along with Major Steele (Joe Girard). Now possessing the range finder, Shark plans to eliminate his prisoners by electrocution. Captain Midnight and his followers break into the hideout and during the ensuing fight Shark is killed when he accidentally touches electrical wires.

In 1954 the character came to television: CBS's *Captain Midnight* was a 30-minute series starring Richard Webb in the title role with Sid Melton as Iggy, Renee Beard as Chuck Ramsey, Jan Shepard as Marcia Stanhope, another Secret Squadron agent, and Olan Soule as scientist Tut. Like its radio counterpart, the TV program was sponsored by Ovaltine, which owned the property. The series ran until 1958 when it went into syndication as *Jet Jackson, Flying Commando*. Due to Ovaltine's ownership of *Captain Midnight*, all references to the title character had to be redubbed.

Captain Video, Master of the Stratosphere

(1951; 15 chapters) PRODUCER: Sam Katzman. DIRECTORS: Spencer Gordon Bennet and Wallace A. Grissell. SCREENPLAY: Royal K. Cole, Sherman L. Lowe and Joseph F. Poland. STORY: George H. Plympton. PHOTOGRAPHY: Fayte Browne. EDITOR: Earl Turner. MUSIC DIRECTOR: Mischa Bakaleinikoff. ART DIRECTOR: Paul Palmentola. SETS: Sidney Clifford. PRODUCTION MANAGER: Herbert Leonard. SPECIAL EFFECTS: Jack

Erickson. CONTINUITY: Moree Herring. ASSISTANT DIRECTOR: Charles S. Gould. CAST: Judd Holdren (Captain Video), Larry Stewart (Ranger), George Eldredge (Dr. Tobor), Gene Roth (Vultura), Don C. Harvey (Gallagher), William Fawcett (Alpha), Jack Ingram (Aker), I. Stanford Jolley (Zarol), Skelton Knaggs (Retner), Jimmy Stark (Ranger Rogers), Rusty Wescoatt (Beal), Zon Murray (Elko), George Robotham (Drock), Rick Vallin (Ranger Brown), Tristram Coffin (Professor Anton Dean), Oliver Cross (Professor Markham), Terry Frost (Agent 29/Agent 172), Selmer Jackson (Deputy Commissioner Wade), Bruce Edwards (Agent 34), Eddie Foster (Charlie), Tommy Farrell (Atoma Captain), Lee Roberts, Frank Hagney, Frank Marlowe, Wally West (Gang Members), Fred Kelsey (Laboratory Guard), Herman Hack, Jack Tornek (Theros Citizens), Roy Butler (Vault Guard), Frank Ellis (Hijacker), Pierce Lyden (Space Platform Operator), Frank O'Connor (Vultura's Soldier), Knox Manning (Narrator).

CHAPTER TITLES: (1) Journey into Space; (2) Menace to Atoma; (3) Captain Video's Peril; (4) Entombed in Ice; (5) Flames of Atoma; (6) Astray in the Atmosphere; (7) Blasted by the Atomic Eye; (8) Invisible Menace; (9) Video Springs a Trap; (10) Menace of the Mystery Metal; (11) Weapon of Destruction; (12) Robot Rocket; (13) Mystery of Station X; (14) Vengeance of Vultura; (15) Video vs. Vultura.

The first motion picture serial to be based on a television program was *Captain Video, Master of the Stratosphere* (more commonly known as *Captain Video*), released theatrically late in 1951. Although filmed in black and white, for most of its running time it did employ watery Cinecolor for scenes on the planets Atoma (red) and Theros (green). No women appeared in the 15 chapters. The robots used by the evil Vultura were first seen in Mascot's chapterplay *The Phantom Empire* (1935), starring Gene Autry. Filmed at the Iverson Ranch in Chatsworth, California, the serial was reissued as *Captain Video, Hero of Outer Space!* Under any title it was a tatty affair as noted by Jim Harmon and Donald F. Glut in *The Great Movie Serials: Their Sound and Fury* (1972): "[W]ith its shoddy sets, unbelievable costumes, phony special effects, unconvincing action, and laughable plotting and dialogue [*Captain Video*] showed that the serial had but a few remaining years before extinction."

At his mountain retreat, Captain Video (Judd Holdren) is informed by fellow crime fighter Gallagher (Don C. Harvey) that a signal has been received by Ranger (Larry Stewart), a young recruit who has compiled a secret report about an invention perfected by Dr. Tobor (George Eldredge). Ranger gives his report on Tobor's magnetic impulse invention that affects the world's weather. Captain Video and Ranger to go the scientist's laboratory where he works with Retner (Skelton Knaggs), his strange assistant. Many adventures on Earth and on the planet Atoma, ruled by dictator Vultura (Gene Roth), ensue. Vultura attacks the Earth with strange mechanical monsters but Captain Video and Ranger save their planet and also the planet Theros from the madman. Finally, Captain Video takes on the guise of one of Vultura's men and uses a ray cannon to eliminate the dictator.

Among the tacky futuristic devices utilized by Captain Video in the serial were an electronic wave detector scan scope, a scanning device (aka television), an astro-viewer, a psychomatic weapon, a cosmic vibrator, the jet mobile, a paralysis ray gun, the detograph and a radionic guide.

Poster for *Captain Video* (1951).

Captain Video and His Video Rangers debuted on television in 1949 on the DuMont network with the plots set in the twenty-third century. For the first season Richard Coogan played the title role and Don Hastings was the Video Ranger, his teenage assistant. In 1950 Al Hodge took over the role of Captain Video and remained with it until the series left the air in 1956. Until 1953 the program was shown as a continuing serial but that year it had a different plot each week and was shown as *The Files of Captain Video*. In 1956 the program became *Captain Video's Cartoons* with Hodge hosting Betty Boop cartoons and episodes of the 1951 Columbia serial. Fawcett Comics published six issues of the *Captain Video* comic book in 1951.

Congo Bill

(1948; 15 chapters) PRODUCER: Sam Katzman. DIRECTORS: Spencer Gordon Bennet and Thomas Carr. SCREENPLAY: George H. Plympton, Arthur Hoerl and Lewis Clay. PHOTOGRAPHY: Ira H. Morgan. EDITORS: Dwight Caldwell and Earl Turner. MUSIC DIRECTOR: Mischa Bakaleinikoff. ART DIRECTOR: Paul Palmentola. SETS: Sidney Clifford. PRODUCTION MANAGER: Herbert Leonard. ASSISTANT DIRECTOR: R.M. Andrews. CAST: Don McGuire (Congo Bill), Cleo Moore (Lureen aka Ruth Culver), Jack Ingram (Cameron), I. Stanford Jolley (Bernie MacGraw), Leonard Penn (Andre Bocar), Nelson Leigh (Dr. Greenway), Charles King (Kleeg), Armida (Zalea), Hugh Prosser (Morelli), Neyle Morrow (Kahla), Fred Graham (Villabo), Rusty Wescoatt (Ivan), Anthony Warde (Rogan), Stephen Carr (Tom MacGraw), William Fawcett (Blinky), Frank Lackteen (Witch Doctor Nagu), Stanley Price (Nagu's Ally), Frank O'Connor (Frank), Eddie Parker (Torturer), Wally West (Circus Worker), Knox Manning (Narrator). CHAPTER TITLES: (1) The Untamed Beast; (2) Jungle Gold; (3) A Hot Reception; (4) Congo Bill Springs a Trap; (5) White Shadows in the Jungle; (6) The White Queen; (7) The Black Panther; (8) Sinister Schemes; (9) The Witch Doctor Strikes; (10) Trail of Treachery; (11) A Desperate Chance; (12) The Lair of the Beast; (13) Menace of the Jungle; (14) Treasure Trap; (15) The Missing Letter.

Congo Bill, also called *Congo Bill, King of the Jungle*, was another serial based on a comic book hero, in this case an African adventurer created by *Action Comic*'s executive editor Whitney Ellsworth. The chapterplay was mainly an average jungle outing but its plot did include the legend of a white goddess along with a killer ape. Leading lady Cleo Moore later starred in Columbia's 1954 melodrama *Bait* (q.v.), produced and directed by Hugo Haas, who headlined Moore in several of his features. Jim Harmon and Donald F. Glut wrote in *The Great Movie Serials: Their Sound and Fury* (1972), "The cliffhangers in *Congo Bill* were mild compared to some of those faced by Tarzan, Kioga, and even Jungle Jim. A boulder was rolled down on him, he was shot, and stabbed. Some imagination went into the climax of Chapter Eight, 'Sinister Schemes.' wherein a device with revolving blades was lowered toward his reclining frame."

Brothers Bernie (I. Stanford Jolley) and Tom (Stephen Carr) MacGraw will inherit $500,000 and a circus if the long-lost daughter of its late owner is not found within one year. Hearing rumors of a white goddess in the wilds of Africa, Tom thinks she might be Ruth Culver (Moore), the heiress. Wanting his brother out of the way so he can have the money and the circus for himself, Bernie knocks out Tom and leaves him at the mercy of a killer ape but animal trainer Congo Bill (Don McGuire) comes to his rescue. Before dying, Tom asks Bill to find Ruth Culver. Bill is put in charge of a safari in search of the goddess, unaware that Bernie is in cahoots with trader Andre Bocar (Leonard Penn), who smuggles gold supplied to him by the white queen's witch doctor Nagu (Frank Lackteen). Several attempts are made to get rid of Bill but he is aided by Cameron (Jack Ingram), a Colonial Intelligence agent investigating the smugglers. Bill eventually locates Lureen (Moore), the white goddess, and finds out she is really Ruth Culver. Bill and Cameron expose the machinations of Bernie and Bocar and bring them to justice, while the gold is handed over to the colonial government. Bill and Ruth plan to return to the United States and with her inheritance enhance the circus.

Deadwood Dick

(1940; 15 chapters) PRODUCER: Larry Darmour. DIRECTOR: James W. Horne. SCREENPLAY: Wyndham Gittens, Morgan B. Cox, George Morgan and John Cutting. PHOTOGRAPHY: James S. Brown, Jr. EDITORS: Dwight Caldwell and Earl Turner. MUSIC DIRECTOR: Lee Zahler. SOUND: Tom Lambert. ASSISTANT DIRECTOR: Carl Hiecke. CAST: Don Douglas (Dick Stanley/Deadwood Dick), Lorna Gray [Adrian Booth] (Anne Butler), Lane Chandler (Wild Bill Hickok), Marin Sais (Calamity Jane), Harry Harvey (Dave Miller), Jack Ingram (Buzz Rickert), Charles King (Tex), Edward Cassidy (Tennison Drew/The Skull), Robert Fiske (Ashton), Lee Shumway (Bentley), Edmund Cobb (Steele), Edward Hearn (Tom Sharp), Karl Hackett (Jack McCall), Roy Barcroft (Jim Bridges), Bud Osborne (Stagecoach

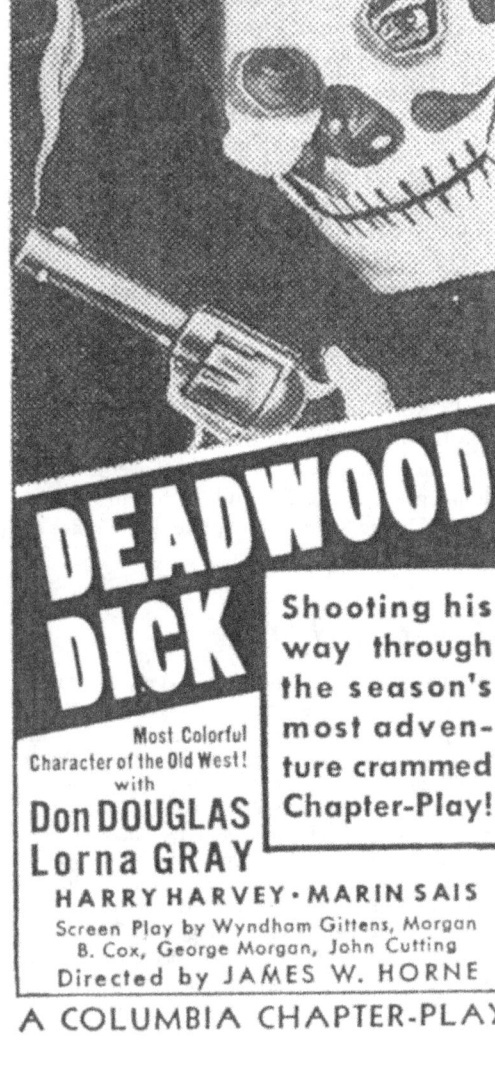

Poster for *Deadwood Dick* (1940).

Driver Strong), Fred Kelsey (Bartender Bottles), Edward Cecil (Attorney), Joe Girard, Arthur Millett (Judges), Tom London (Jake), Kit Guard (Buck), Al Ferguson (Mike), Constantine Romanoff (Butch), Franklyn Farnum (Clayton), Kenne Duncan (Two-Gun), Chuck Hamilton (Chuck), Eddie Featherston (Land Registrar), Jim Corey (Steve), Yakima Canutt, Eddie Laughton, Tex Palmer, Dick Botiller, Blackie Whiteford, Blackjack Ward, Bob Woodward (Gang Members), Fern Emmett (Miranda), Forrest Taylor (The Masked Skull), Murdock MacQuarrie (Kenyon), Herman Hack (Juror), Edward Peil, Sr. (Sears), Dick Rush (Deputy Sheriff), George Morrell (Station Agent), Horace B. Carpenter (Old Man), Jack C. Smith (Luke), Jack Ingram, Denver Dixon, Helen Gibson, Bob Burns (Citizens), Art Dillard, Bert Dillard (Laborers).

CHAPTER TITLES: (1) A Wild West Enterprise; (2) Who Is the Skull?; (3) Pirates of the Plains; (4) The Skull Baits a Trap; (5) Win, Lose or Draw; (6) Buried Alive; (7) The Chariot of Doom; (8) The Secret of Number Ten; (9) The Fatal Warning; (10) Framed for Murder; (11) The Bucket of Death; (12) A Race Against Time; (13) The Arsenal of Revolt; (14) Holding the Fort; (15) The Deadwood Express.

While most Columbia serials were taken from comics, magazine stories or radio programs, *Deadwood Dick* was based on the dime novels written by Edward Lytton Wheeler between 1877 and 1897. Although Deadwood Dick was a fictional character, several men took the nickname and claimed Wheeler's works were based on their exploits. *Deadwood Dick* was a traditional western cliffhanger but its hero and villain both wore masks, the latter's a terrifying skull, combined with a black hat, cloak and gloves. To add to the mystery of The Skull, as the bad man was known, the character was played by two actors: Edward Cassidy, who also played supposedly honest committee man–banker Tennison Drew, and Forrest Taylor, when the villain was masked. Set in Deadwood, South Dakota, the cliffhanger included a trio of historical characters: Wild Bill Hickok (Lane Chandler), Calamity Jane (Marin Sais) and Jack McCall (Karl Hackett).

With Dakota Territory about to vote for statehood, an outlaw band led by The Skull, who is determined to keep out the railroad and have his own empire, terrorizes the area. In Deadwood, newspaper editor Dick Stanley (Don Douglas) leads the Statehood for Dakota Committee, whose members include banker Tennison Drew (Cassidy). Also fighting the Skull is masked man Deadwood Dick, who is really Stanley in disguise. Aiding the masked avenger are Anne Butler (Lorna Gray) and Calamity Jane (Sais), plus Jane's lover Wild Bill Hickok (Lane Chandler) until he is shot in the back by cowardly Jack McCall (Karl Hackett). Deadwood Dick captures McCall and brings him in for trial. The Skull's gang intimidates the jury and McCall is sent free and ordered to Cheyenne by the gang leader. Deadwood Dick, Anne Butler and Jack are nearly killed when their stagecoach plunges into a canyon after The Skull orders his henchman Buzz Rickert (Jack Ingram) to eliminate McCall. McCall attempts to make a getaway but is shot and killed by The Skull. With the aid of Anne and Calamity Jane, Deadwood Dick unmasks The Skull as Drew and puts and end to his crime wave. Deadwood Dick then removes his own mask as he and Anne plan to get married.

The Green Archer

(1940; 15 chapters) PRODUCER: Larry Darmour. DIRECTOR: James W. Horne. SCREENPLAY: Morgan B. Cox, John Cutting, Jesse A. Duffy and James W. Horne, from the novel by Edgar Wallace. PHOTOGRAPHY: James S. Brown, Jr. EDITORS: Dwight Caldwell and Earl Turner. MUSIC: Lee Zahler. SOUND: Tom Lambert. ASSISTANT DIRECTOR: Carl Hiecke. CAST: Victor Jory (Spike Holland), Iris Meredith (Valerie Howett), James Craven (Abel Bellamy), Robert Fiske (Savini), Dorothy Fay (Elaine Bellamy), Forrest Taylor (Parker Howett), Jack Ingram (Brad), Joe Girard (Inspector Ross), Fred Kelsey (Captain Thompson), Kit Guard (Dinky Stone), Kenne Duncan (Michael Bellamy), Charles King (Tardoni), Franklyn Farnum (Pete), Edmund Cobb (Stevens), Harry Harvey (Martin), Lloyd Ingraham (Worthington), Anthony Warde (Lefty Brent), Mary MacLaren (Mrs. Patton), Kernan Cripps (Frank), Eddie Feather-

Advertisements for *The Green Archer* (1940).

ston (Turk Martin), Warren Jackson (Charlie), Jack Cheatham (Detective Charlie), Bert Young (Biff), Johnny Kascier (Jake), Duke York (Martel/Harry Madison), Bud Osborne (Lanton), Harry Tenbrook (Vrooner), Constantine Romanoff (West), Cy Schindell (Darcy), Chuck Hamilton (Kardak), Edward Hearn, Bruce Mitchell, Dick Rush (Policemen), Herbert Evans (Butler Henderson), Sam Lufkin, Charles Dorety (Thugs), Knox Manning (Narrator).

CHAPTER TITLES: (1) Prison Bars Beckon; (2) The Face at the Window; (3) The Devil's Dictograph; (4) Vanishing Jewels; (5) The Fatal Spark; (6) The Necklace of Treachery; (7) The Secret Passage; (8) Garr Castle is Robbed; (9) The Mirror of Treachery; (10) The Dagger That Failed; (11) The Flaming Arrow; (12) The Devil Dogs; (13) The Deceiving Microphone; (14) End of Hope; (15) The Green Archer Exposed.

The Green Archer, released in the fall of 1940, was the second of three screen adaptations of the same-name 1923 Edgar Wallace novel, one of his most popular and enduring thrillers. The first version was also done as a serial in 1925 by Pathe in ten chapters under the direction of Spencer Gordon Bennet and starring Allene Ray, Walter Miller, Burr McIntosh and Frank Lackteen. The third outing, *Der Grüne Bogenschutze* (The Green Archer), was produced in West Germany in 1961 by Horst Wendlandt and directed by Jurgen Roland. The feature starred Gert Frobe, Karin Dor and Eddi Arent and was shown on U.S. television as *The Green Archer*. A nicely conceived chapterplay, Columbia's *The Green Archer* did not always take itself too seriously and its main horror aspect was the supposedly ghostly archer. Alan G. Barbour commented in *Cliffhanger: A Pictorial History of the Motion Picture Serial* (1977) that the serial "had a colorful character who came to the frequent aid of star Victor Jory, even though a bogus Green Archer would pop up from time to time to confuse viewers."

When his brother Michael Bellamy (Kenne Duncan) inherits Garr Castle, Abel Bellamy (James Craven) has him put in prison on a false charge and takes possession of the place. Michael's wife Elaine (Dorothy Fay) shows up to confront her brother-in-law, who has her put in a dungeon. Suspecting something is amiss, Elaine's father, Parker Howett (Forrest Taylor), and sister, Valerie Howett (Iris Meredith), hire detective Spike Holland (Victor Jory) to help them find Elaine and the trio rent an estate next to Bellamy's. Abel has his henchman Brad (Jack Ingram) dress as the ghostly Green Archer; when Valerie follows the specter to Garr Castle, Spike trails them and is thrown into a pit where he is set upon by savage hounds. The real Green Archer saves Spike. Spike and Valerie are captured and imprisoned in a burning warehouse but manage to escape. After the Green Archer steals Abel's jewels, Spike returns to the castle where he nearly meets death by sharp, descending knives but again is saved by the Archer. When Abel tries to frame Spike on a jewel theft charge, the detectives goes back to the castle and is nearly drowned in a pit before the Green Archer shuts off the water. Spike's real identity as an insurance investigator is revealed as he goes to a dock warehouse where the jewels are hidden and is captured by Abel's gang and thrown into a river with an anchor wired to him. Again the Green Archer comes to his rescue. Abel orders his treasure returned to Garr Castle. Spike and Valerie retrieve it and are taken prisoners at a roadhouse but manage to escape. Abel goes after them in an airplane and drops bombs on the shack where they take refuge but they get to safety. Spike goes back to the castle and is nearly killed by a shotgun device when he tries to open Abel's safe but its door stops the force of the blast. When a fight ensues between the detective and Abel's henchmen, the police show up. Abel tries to get them to arrest Spike on several trumped-up charges but again he manages to escape with a radium formula kept in the safe. Although he is nearly killed in a car crash when pursued by the gangsters, Spike manages to give the formula to Valerie but she is later kidnapped and taken to the castle. Abel's henchmen try to get the formula from Spike but it is destroyed in a fight. Savini (Robert Fiske), one of Abel's minions, betrays him to Elaine and tells her he can prove Michael's innocence. Wanting Spike out of the way for good, Abel has his gang place bombs in the detective's furnace; when they explode, he is knocked unconscious but is pulled from the burning house by the Green Archer. After the Archer informs Spike that Valerie and her father have been abducted by Abel, Spike rushes to the castle and tries to save them but is again captured. As Abel prepares to murder the trio, the Green Archer appears, stops him and reveals himself to be Michael Bellamy. Abel and his gang are arrested by the police as Michael and Elaine are reunited and Spike proposes to Valerie.

Hop Harrigan

(1946; 15 chapters) PRODUCER: Sam Katzman. DIRECTOR: Derwin Abrahams. SCREENPLAY: George H. Plympton and Ande Lamb. PHOTOGRAPHY: Ira H. Morgan. EDITOR: Earl Turner. MUSIC: Lee Zahler. ASSISTANT DIRECTOR: Mike Eason. CAST: William Bakewell (Hop Harrigan), Jennifer Holt (Gail Nolan), Robert "Buzz" Henry (Jackie Nolan), Sumner Getchell (Tank Tinker), Emmett Vogan (J. Westley Arnold), Claire James (Gwen Arnold), John Merton (Dr. Tobor), Wheeler Oakman (Alex Ballard), Ernie Adams (Retner), Peter Michael (Mark Craven), Terry Frost (Barry), Anthony Warde (Edwards), Jackie Moran (Fraser), Bobby Stone (Gray), Jack Buchanon (Deputy Sheriff), Jim Diehl (Carter), Jack Ingram (Lieutenant Riley), Charles King (Thief), Jack Rockwell (Sheriff), Tiny Brauer (Hunter).

CHAPTER TITLES: (1) A Mad Mission; (2) The Secret Ray; (3) The Mystery Plane; (4) Plunging Peril; (5) Betrayed by a Madman; (6) A Flaming Trap; (7) One Chance for Life; (8) White Fumes of Fate; (9) Dr. Tobor's Revenge; (10) Juggernaut of Fate; (11) Flying to Oblivion; (12) Lost in the Skies; (13) No Escape; (14) The Chute That Failed; (15) The Fate of the World.

Filmed in Arizona, *Hop Harrigan* was based on the character created by John Blummer for *All American Comics* in 1941 and the radio program *Hop Harrigan* that starred Chester [Chet] Stratton in the title role and Ken Lynch as his pal Tank Tinker. The series was broadcast on the ABC Blue network from 1942 to 1946 and on Mutual from 1946 to 1948. In *The Fabulous Holts* (1976), Buck Rainey noted of the cliffhanger, "As true of many Columbia serials, *Hop Harrigan* was, overall, a shoddy production. [Jennifer] Holt was perhaps its one redeeming feature." Noting the title character's appeal, Jim Harmon and Donald F. Glut opined in *The Great Movie Serials: Their Sound and Fury* (1972), "Hop Harrigan was not a super crusader such as Captain Midnight. He wore no distinctive uniform and was satisfied with his flying jacket. He was only an ex-serviceman, like the brothers and fathers of his young audience. He was a celebration of the 'average man' as hero, but he and his kind would lose their popularity to the 'superhero' like the mysterious leader of the Secret Squadron."

Pilot Hop Harrigan (William Bakewell) and his pal Tank Tinker (Sumner Getchell) operate an airfield they lease from Gail Nolan (Jennifer Holt) and her brother Jackie (Robert "Buzz" Henry). After saving the life of businessman Arnold (Emmett Vogan), Hop agrees to fly the man's friend, scientist Dr. Tobor (John Merton), to his secret laboratory. The eccentric scientist has invented a super motor he claims can out-power atomic energy. A mystery man called the Chief Pilot and his gang are after the invention and they follow Hop and Tank as they fly Tobor to his destination. Although they are attacked by the rival plane, Hop manages to get away only to have the scientist make him and Tank put on blindfolds as they follow his directions to the hidden laboratory. The plane nearly crashes into a mountain but Hop saves the day. The ungrateful Tobor ignites a gas bomb in the craft and bails out. Hop and Tinker continue to battle the Chief Pilot, escaping death from a ray machine, until the mystery man is done in by one of his own agents. By now Dr. Tabor is completely mad and plans to demolish the Earth with his invention but Hop finds his hiding place and fights the scientist and his associate Retner (Ernie Adams). During the melee, the madman is killed when one of his inventions explodes.

The Iron Claw

(1941; 15 chapters) PRODUCER: Larry Darmour. DIRECTOR: James W. Horne. SCREENPLAY: Basil Dickey, George H. Plympton, Jesse A. Duffy, Charles R. Condon and Jack Stanley. STORY: Arthur Stringer. PHOTOGRAPHY: James S. Brown, Jr. EDITORS: Dwight Caldwell and Earl Turner. MUSIC DIRECTOR: Lee Zahler. ASSISTANT DIRECTOR: Carl Hiecke. CAST: Charles Quigley (Bob Lane), Joyce Bryant (Patricia Benson), Forrest Taylor (Anton Benson), Walter Sande (Jack "Flash" Strong), Norman Willis (Roy Benson), Alex Callam (James Benson), James Metcalfe (Culver Benson), Allen Doone (Simon Leach), Edythe Elliott (Milly Leach), John Beck (Gyves), Charles King (Silk Langdon), James C. Morton (Casey), Hal Price (O'Malley), Frank LaRue (Inspector Cramer), Marin Sais (Housekeeper Hannah), Jack Perrin (Mine Guard), Cy Schindell (Red), Eddie Hart (Jake), Lloyd Ingraham (Managing Editor), Ted Mapes (Slim), Richard Alexander (Henchman), Knox Manning (Narrator).

CHAPTER TITLES: (1) The Shaft of Doom; (2) The Murderous Mirror; (3) The Drop to Destiny; (4) The Fatal Fuse; (5) The Fiery Fall; (6) The Ship Log Talks; (7) The Mystic Map; (8) The Perilous Pit; (9) The Cul-de-Sac; (10) The Curse of the Cave; (11) The Doctor's Bargain; (12) Vapors of Evil; (13) The Secret Door; (14) The Evil Eye; (15) The Claw's Collapse.

Miser Benson hoarded a fortune in gold he took from a sunken Spanish galleon and murdered all who tried to get it away from him. After his death, various relatives arrive at his remote country house, Bensonhurst, hoping to find the hidden treasure. A mysterious masked figure called the Iron Claw, sporting a talon-like weapon on his left hand, murders Culver Benson (James Metcalfe), who has argued with his brothers Anton (Forrest Taylor) and Roy (Norman Willis), over the proceeds from the treasure. Newspaperman Bob Lane (Charles Quigley), who is in love with Anton's daughter Patricia (Joyce Bryant), and his photographer pal Jack "Flash" Strong (Walter Sande) arrive at the estate and investigate the Claw's threat to eliminate other family members. Gangsters are also after the gold. The Iron Claw tries to kill Patricia, who turns out to be the sole heir to the treasure.

Although it used the same title as a 1916 Pathe serial starring Pearl White, Creighton Hale and Sheldon Lewis, *The Iron Claw* was from an original story by Arthur Stringer. It took five screenwriters to complete the 15-chapter outing, proving again that too many cooks can spoil the brew. A slow-moving affair, it was Columbia's seventh serial from the team of producer Larry Darmour and director James W. Horne. In *Cliffhanger: A Pictorial History of the Motion Picture Serial* (1977), Alan G. Barbour found little to commend Horne's work in the field: "[Horne's] serials like *The Iron Claw*, *Deadwood Dick*, *The Green Archer* and *The Spider Returns* set serial fans' funny bones in motion with their ludicrous sight gags and ridiculous situations (i.e., gangsters playing jacks, hanging out their laundry, wearing silly party hats, etc.). Columbia certainly seemed to be slipping..." Regarding the appearance of the Iron Claw, Jim Harmon and Donald F. Glut commented in *The Great Movie Serials: Their Sound and Fury* (1972) that the villain "not only wore the glove-like device which gave him his name, but also facial bandages, dark glasses, and a pulled-down hat that made him look more like the Invisible Man of Universal features." In 1945 Columbia reworked *The Iron Claw* as *Who's Guilty?* (q.v.).

Jack Armstrong

(1947; 15 chapters) PRODUCER: Sam Katzman. ASSOCIATE PRODUCER: Melville De Lay. DIRECTOR: Wallace Fox. SCREENPLAY: Arthur Hoerl, Lewis Clay, Royal K. Cole and Leslie Swabacker. STORY: George H. Plympton. PHOTOGRAPHY: Ira H. Morgan. EDITOR: Earl Turner. MUSIC: Lee Zahler. ART DIRECTOR: Paul Palmentola. SPECIAL EFFECTS: Ray Mercer. ASSISTANT DIRECTORS: Mike Eason and Leonard Shapiro. CAST: John Hart (Jack Armstrong), Rosemary La Planche (Betty Fairfield), Claire James (Princess Alura), Joe Brown (Billy Fairfield), Pierre Watkin (Uncle Jim Fairfield), Wheeler Oakman (Professor Hobart Zorn), Jack Ingram (Blair), Eddie Parker (Slade), Hugh Prosser (Vic Hardy), John Merton (Gregory Pierce), Frank Merlo (Naga), Charles Middleton (Jason Grood/The Ruler), Russ Vincent (Umala), Gene Roth (Dr. Albour), Terry Frost (Jackman), Frank Ellis (Lobard), Lane Bradford (Lesseps), Stanley Blystone (Marlin), Zon Murray (Wechsler), George DeNormand (Traffic Officer), Augie Gomez (Selford), Kenneth Terrell (Tabori), Joe Palma (Blake), Rito Punay (Songuri), Tiny Brauer (Burr), Jack Kenny (Pop), Jack Buchanan (Pilot Blackburn), Gary Garrett (Haines), Carmen D'Antonio (Panther Woman), Knox Manning (Narrator).

CHAPTER TITLES: (1) Mystery of the Cosmic Ray; (2) The Far World; (3) Island of Deception; (4) Into the Chasm; (5) The Space Ship; (6) Tunnels of Treachery; (7) Cavern of Chance; (8) The Secret Room; (9) Human Targets; (10) Battle of the Warriors; (11) Cosmic Annihilator; (12) The Grotto of Greed; (13) Wheels of Fate; (14) Journey into Space; (15) Retribution.

Jack Armstrong was another example of the studio bringing a radio hero to the big screen. In this case it was *Jack Armstrong, All American Boy*, which was broadcast from 1933 to 1951, first on Chicago's WBBM and later on the ABC, NBC and CBS networks. The program was created by Robert Hardy Andrews. Jim Ameche played the title role from 1936 to 1938; Armstrong was also done by St. John Terrell, Stanley Harris, Charles Flynn and Michael Rye. In the waning days of the series, Dick York portrayed the hero's pal Billy Fairfield. Over 3,000 episodes aired in a 15-minute time slot over its many years on the air.

Scientist Vic Hardy (Hugh Prosser), an employee of aviation company owner Uncle Jim Fairfield (Pierre Watkin), is kidnapped by Gregory Pierce (John Merton) and his men, who want to find out about cosmic radiation experiments he has been investigating. Searching for the scientist are Jim's niece Betty (Rosemary La Planche) and nephew Billy (Joe Brown), along with their college friend Jack Armstrong (John Hart). As Uncle Jim, Jack, Betty and Bill hunt for Hardy in Jim's new jet-propelled aircraft, the scientist is taken to see Professor Zorn (Wheeler Oakman), who works for a mystery man called The Ruler. Vic finds out they are working on a cosmic ray that will control the Earth from outer space and his help is enlisted in perfecting the weapon. When Jack's plane gets too near his laboratory, Zorn causes the controls to freeze and the aircraft is forced to land on a remote island where they meet trading post operator Jason Grood (Charles Middleton), who is really The Ruler. To get the intruders out of the way, Grood has his henchman Blair (Jack Ingram) murder a native and orders his ally, Princess Alura (Claire James), to condemn them to die in the Pit of Ever Lasting Fire at the Temple of Xalta. While Uncle Jim and Billy make a getaway, Jack and Betty are thrown into the pit. Umala (Russ Vincent), a native opposed to Grood, saves them. Taking Jack and Betty to Uncle Jim and Billy, Umala leads the quartet to his village. Grood demonstrates his aeroglobe, the satellite he plans to use to house the cosmic ray, and returns it to its hiding place inside the pit of fire. Jack and his friends are nearly killed while investigating the pit but continue their struggle against Grood and Zorn. Grood gets the cosmic ray weapon installed on the aeroglobe and decides to destroy a city to show the world its power. As Hardy prepares to accompany Grood on the flight, Jack knocks him out and dresses in his spacesuit. As the satellite lifts off, he is found by Zorn and the two fight. During the melee, the aeroglobe malfunctions and hurtles back to Earth. Zorn and Grood's gang are killed but Jack parachutes unharmed to the ground. Hardy gets the drop on Jason and demands he sign a confession but the madman knocks him out as Jack arrives. When Grood tries to do him in with a hand grenade, the weapon misfires and kills the maniac.

The serial's plot harkened back to the earlier days of the radio show since by 1947 Jack Armstrong was an operative of the Scientific Bureau of Investigation. The cliffhanger brought back the character of Uncle Jim Fairfield although it also retained his radio replacement, Vic Hardy. Regarding the casting in the chapterplay, Alan G. Barbour noted in *Days of Thrills and Adventure* (1970), "John Hart appeared too old to play the 'hero of Hudson High' in 1947's *Jack Armstrong*, although Pierre Watkin was ideal as Uncle Jim Fairfield." Hart would later have the title role in another Columbia serial, *Adventures of Captain Africa* (1955) [q.v.]. Leading lady Rosemary La Planche, a former Miss America, was here re-teamed with villain Charles Middleton after the two had appeared the eerie PRC horror thriller *Strangler of the Swamp* (1946).

During its final season on the air, *Jack Armstrong, All American Boy* was re-titled *Armstrong of the SBI* and was broadcast three times a week in a 30-minute timeslot on ABC. In 1997 Timothy Bottoms portrayed Jack Armstrong in the Inter-Active Production *American Hero*.

Jungle Raiders

(1945; 15 chapters) PRODUCER: Sam Katzman. DIRECTOR: Lesley Selander. SCREENPLAY: Ande Lamb and George H. Plympton. PHOTOGRAPHY: Ira H. Morgan. EDITOR: Earl Turner. MUSIC: Lee Zahler. ART DIRECTOR: Paul Palmentola. PRODUCTION MANAGER: Melville De Lay. CAST: Kane Richmond (Bob Moore), Eddie Quillan (Joe Riley), Veda Ann Borg (Cora Bell), Carol Hughes (High Priestess Zara), Janet Shaw (Ann Reed), John Elliott (Dr. Horace Moore), Jack Ingram (Tom Hammil), Charles King (Jake Raynes), Ernie Adams (Charlie), I. Stanford Jolley (Brent), Kermit Maynard (Cragg), Budd Buster (Dr. Murray Reed), Nick Thompson (Aztec Chief), Alfredo de Sa (Matu), Ted Adams, Jack Gordon, P.J. Kelly (Witch Doctors), George Turner (Carter), Jimmie Aubrey (Mark).

CHAPTER TITLES: (1) Mystery of the Lost Tribe; (2) Primitive Sacrifice; (3) Prisoners of Fate; (4) Valley of Destruction; (5) Perilous Mission; (6) Into the Valley of Fire; (7) Devil's Brew; (8) The Dagger Pit; (9) Jungle Jeopardy; (10) Prisoners of Peril; (11) Vengeance of Zara; (12) The Key to Arzac; (13) Witch Doctor's Treachery; (14) The Judgment of Rama; (15) The Jewels of Arzac.

Beginning with *Brenda Starr, Reporter* (1945), Sam Katzman took over production of Columbia's serials and he would remain in that position until cliffhangers ran their course in 1956. While Katzman's regime returned a more serious note to the plotting of the chapterplays that has been absent in those directed by James S. Horne, the producer's penchant for cheapness often gave the outings a tacky look that compromised their entertainment value. A good example of this is the first genre serial Katzman handled for Columbia, *Jungle Raiders*, which was released theatrically beginning in the fall of 1945. Despite its title it had no jungle, only a rocky terrain background, and a mythical lost city in the plot was hardly more than a skip and a jump from the villain's trading post. One of the enticements for young viewers to watch all the serial's episodes was membership in the Jungle Raiders Club; they received a card that could be punched each week and provided free admission to the theater in the playdate of the final chapter if all the previous 14 weeks outings were verified. This come-on was often used by theaters to keep up cliffhanger attendance.

Dr. Horace Moore (John Elliott) leads a jungle expedition in search of missing colleague Dr. Murray Reed (Budd Buster), who has discovered a powder that will cure diseases. Accompanying Dr. Moore is his guide Tom Hammil (Jack Ingram). The two stop for supplies at Jake Raynes' (Charles King) trading post before seeking out the hidden village of the Arzecs tribe. Going with them on the journey are Raynes' employees, Brent (I. Stanford Jolley), Charlie (Ernie Adams) and Cragg (Kermit Maynard). When Dr. Reed's daughter Ann (Janet Shaw) arrives she is met by Cora Bell (Veda Ann Borg), a cohort of Raynes, who locks her up. Moore and his group are taken prisoners by the Arzecs for sacrifice to their god Rana.

Ann escapes into the jungle where she is found by Bob Moore (Kane Richmond), Dr. Moore's son, and his pal Joe Riley (Eddie Quillan). The two men take her back to the trading post and then go to the village where Dr. Moore has cured the tribe's dying chief (Nick Thompson). A jealous witch doctor (Ted Adams) sentences him to be sacrificed in a ceremony presided over by the high priestess of Rana, Zara (Carol Hughes). Matu (Alfredo de Sa), the chief's son, saves Dr. Moore as the witch doctor flees into the jungle. When Bob and Joe hear Ann calling for help over their Jeep's radio, they return to the trading post and stop Rayne from molesting her and return to the Arzec village only to be followed by Raynes and his men. Natives abduct Ann and take her back to their village where the witch doctor tampers with Dr. Moore's medication. When he fails to heal some of the wounded villagers, he and the young woman are sentenced to be sacrificed to Rana. Bob and Joe, joined by Hammil, trek through the Valley of Sounds. When the witch doctor begins the sacrifice by beating a huge gong, it causes a landslide nearly trapping the trio. Just as the scientist and Ann are about to be sacrificed, the doctor requests that Ann be allowed to go to the trading post for special medicine. Matu agrees to take her place if she does not return. She treks to the post and, during a fight between Joe and Bob and Raynes' men, a sacred necklace given to her by Matu is taken by Brent. Cora makes Brent give her the necklace as she heads for the village where Dr. Moore and Matu are about to be sacrificed (more of the villagers have become ill). Taken prisoners by Raynes' men, Joe and Tom are in the village when Bob and Ann are brought back. Joe manages to get a gun and free them, taking Raynes' henchmen prisoners. Matu's friends lead Bob through the Valley of the Fire God; he reaches the top of the volcano as Dr. Moore and Matu are pushed into the crater. He rescues them after they land on a ledge. Fearing that his father will be the next victim of the witch doctor, who is responsible for all the sickness, Matu leads the expedition back to the village while Raynes, who has been keeping Dr. Reed a prisoner, tries to force the scientist to reveal the location of the Arzecs' hidden treasure. When Charlie observes Ann and Joe approaching the trading post, he tells his boss who rigs up explosives that will kill them; they are saved by Hammil. At the behest of Zara, Cora drugs coffee given to Dr. Moore and Bob and they pretend to be asleep. The witch doctor has them taken to the Dagger Pit where they are to be executed but Bob escapes with his father. Disliking Zara, Cora decides to help Dr. Moore while Raynes enlists the help of a tribe of pygmies in retaking his trading post and capturing Joe, Ann and Tom. When Bob, his father and Cora arrive at the post, they too are taken prisoners. The father and son escape and Charlie tells them he will lead them to the pygmy village to aid Joe, Ann and Tom. Instead he takes them to a crocodile-infested swamp. Escaping from the reptiles, the Moores go to the pygmy village where Joe, Tom and Raynes are being tortured (the tribe wants to find the Arzec treasure). Bob informs the pygmies that his father will take them to the Arzec village if the others are set free. Matu gets the chief to banish Zara. When Cora and her men fire on Bob, Joe and Tom, the trio pretend to be hit. Cora promises Zara she will again rule her tribe if she helps her find the treasure. When the pygmies imprison Dr. Moore, his son and Joe get gun powder from the post and return to rescue him. After an explosion caused by the powder, Zara and the pygmies run away and the expedition returns to the trading post where Rayne locks Bob in a cellar that also houses Dr. Reed. Joe and Tom fight with the trader as Bob and Reed escape. Dr. Reed leads Bob, Joe and Tom to the hidden Arzec village where the witch doctor has imprisoned Cora, Zara, Matu and Raynes and his men. He then captures Bob and his father along with Reed, his daughter and Hammil. Joe manages to stay outside the village and frees Ann and her father, Tom and Dr. Moore. As the witch doctor plans to sacrifice Cora, Brent and Cragg, Dr. Reed leads Bob to the scene and gets him to fight the native in a fire test in which both go into the volcanic crater to retrieve the bracelet of Rana, thrown there by Zara. The witch doctor arranges for Raynes to shoot Bob but he misses and the trader is killed by Matu. Taking Cora, Brent and Cragg to the Dagger Pit in hopes of getting both the treasure and the medical powder, the witch doctor murders the two men. Zara arrives and fights with Cora, with both women falling into the pit of daggers and dying. As the witch doctor tries to escape with a box containing the healing powder, Bob arrives and grabs the box as the native plunges to his death into the volcano's crater. Bob gives the medicine to Dr. Moore as he, Joe, Ann and Dr. Reed leave to return home.

King of the Congo

(1952; 15 chapters) PRODUCER: Sam Katzman. DIRECTORS: Spencer Gordon Bennett and Wallace A. Grissell. SCREENPLAY: George H. Plympton, Arthur Hoerl and Royal K. Cole. PHOTOGRAPHY: William Whitley. EDITOR: Earl Turner. MUSIC DIRECTOR: Mischa Bakaleinikoff. PRODUCTION MANAGER: Herbert Leonard. ASSISTANT DIRECTOR: Charles S. Gould. CAST: Buster Crabbe (Thunda/Captain Roger Drum), Gloria Dee (Princess Pha), Leonard Penn (Boris), Jack Ingram (Clark), Rick Vallin (Andreov), Nick Stuart (Degar), William Fawcett (High Priest), Neyle Morrow (Nahee), Bart Davidson (Alexis), Rusty Westcoatt (Kor), Bernie Gozier (Zahlia), Lee Roberts (Lieutenant Blake), Alex Montoya (Lipah), Frank Ellis (Ivan).

CHAPTER TITLES: (1) Mission of Menace; (2) Red Shadows in the Jungle; (3) Into the Valley of Mist; (4) Thunda Meets His Match; (5) Thunda Turns the Tables; (6) Thunda's Desperate Chance; (7) Thunda Trapped; (8) Mission of Evil; (9) Menace of the Magnetic Rocks; (10) Lair of the Leopard; (11) An Ally from the Sky; (12) Riding Wild; (13) Red Raiders; (14) Savage Vengeance; (15) Judgment of the Jungle.

On a secret mission to Africa to investigate foreign agents, Air Force Captain Roger Drum (Buster Crabbe) crash-lands in the jungle and is saved by Princess Pha (Gloria Dee), ruler of the Rock People. She takes him to an ancient temple. When a group of strangers led by Boris (Leonard Penn) shows up, a gong is sounded and this causes the structure to collapse, burying Drum. The captain emerges from the debris unscathed, so impressing the primitive people that they dub him Thunda. He aids them in their struggle with a prehistoric tribe of Cave Men. Boris thinks Drum is actually working on his side and this alienates Thunda from Pha and her people but eventually his allegiance to the Rock People is re-established as he fights the cave dwellers and the spies, who are after a mineral more powerful than uranium. Thunda faces many dangers, including a gorilla. After being captured by the Cave Men and nearly killed by a descending hatchet, Thunda blows up the spies while the fleeing Boris is killed by jungle animals. Thunda brings peace to the land by joining together the two warring tribes.

King of the Congo was Columbia's final jungle cliffhanger. It was star Buster Crabbe's seventh and last chapterplay; his first cliffhanger was two decades before when he had the title role in Principal's 12-episode *Tarzan the Fearless* (1933). Filmed at the Iverson Ranch in Chatsworth, California, and also called *The Mighty Thunda*, *King of the Congo* was a typically cheap Sam Katzman outing. Jim Harmon and Donald F. Glut in *The Great Movie Serials: Their Sound and Fury* (1972) said it had "barely more extravagancies than a studio jungle set, prefabricated ancient temple, and a number of 'wild' animals." *King of the Congo* was based on the *Thunda* comic strip created by Frank Frazetta. In 1989 AC Comics published *The Mighty Thunda—King of the Congo*. The same company also featured Thunda stories in its compilations *AC Comics Annual #1* (1990), *Bill Black's Comic Book Jungle* (1999) and *Men of Mystery #80* (2009).

The Lost Planet

(1953; 15 chapters) PRODUCER: Sam Katzman. DIRECTOR: Spencer Gordon Bennet. SCREENPLAY: George H. Plympton and Arthur Hoerl. PHOTOGRAPHY: William Whitley. EDITOR: Earl Turner. MUSIC DIRECTOR: Ross Di Maggio. ART DIRECTOR: Paul Palmentola. SOUND: J.S. Westmoreland. SETS: Sidney Clifford. SPECIAL EFFECTS: Jack Erickson. CONTINUITY: Moree Herring. ASSISTANT DIRECTOR: Charles S. Gould. CAST: Judd Holdren (Rex Barrow), Vivian Mason (Ella Dorn), Michael Fox (Dr. Ernst Grood), Forrest Taylor (Professor Edmund Dorn), Gene Roth (Reckov), Ted Thorpe (Tim Johnson), Karl "Killer" Davis (Karlo/Robot R-4), Jack George (Jarva), Frederic Berest (Alden), John L. [Bob] Cason (Hopper), Lee Roberts (Wesley Brenn/Robot R-9), Nick Stuart (Dari), Leonard Penn (Ken Wopler), I. Stanford Jolley (Robot Number 9), Joseph Mell (Lah), Pierre Watkin (Ned Hilton).

CHAPTER TITLES: (1) The Mystery of the Guided Missile; (2) Trapped by the Axial Propeller; (3) Blasted by the Thermic Disintegrator; (4) The Mind Control Machine; (5) The Atomic Plane; (6) Disaster in the Stratosphere; (7) Snared by the Prysamic Catapult; (8) Astray in Space; (9) The Hypnotic Ray Machine; (10) To Free the Planet People; (11) Dr. Grood Defies Gravity; (12) Trapped in the Cosmic Jet; (13) The Invisible Enemy; (14) In the Grip of the De-Thermo Ray; (15) Sentenced to Space.

Following the success of 1951's *Captain Video* (q.v.), producer Sam Katzman reunited director Spencer Gordon Bennet, screenwriter George H. Plympton and star Judd Holdren for another outer space adventure, *The Lost Planet*, which also brought back Gene Roth as a villain. Like its predecessor, this cliffhanger was loaded with all kinds of futuristic gadgets, some of which were named in the titles of its various episodes, but overall it was just as cheap and proved to be the studio's final sci-fi chapterplay. Holdren also headlined the Republic serial *Zombies of the Stratosphere* (1952) as well as being the *Sky Marshal of the Universe*, the title hero in the 1955 NBC-TV series *Commando Cody*.

Judd Holdren and Vivian Mason in *The Lost Planet* (1953).

Professor Edmund Dorn (Forrest Taylor) is kidnapped by Dr. Ernst Grood (Michael Fox) and taken to his planet, Ergro, where he is forced to work on electronic devices Grood wants to use to conquer the universe. On a second trip to Earth, Grood's cosmojet crashes into Mount Vulcan and Dorn's daughter Ella (Vivian Mason) and fellow reporter Rex Barrow (Judd Holdren) are sent to cover the event along with Tim Johnson (Ted Thorpe), a photographer. They are abducted by the aliens and taken to Ergro where they are made to hunt for a metal called cosmonium. Dorn helps them to escape to a cave which Grood blasts with a death ray. The professor manages to destroy the weapon. Grood's human robots capture Johnson and later Ella. Rex and Dorn then work together to combine cosmonium with another alloy called dornite to make a ray which turns the reporter invisible. When Grood orders Rex's cosmojet destroyed, Rex becomes invisible and makes a getaway only to be captured again when he becomes visible. Grood orders Rex to help Dorn, who tells him of a spacecraft that can return him to Earth. When Rex prepares to take off, Grood shoots at the craft with nuclear rays, but space junk obstructs them and Rex is able to return home. After the professor informs him by radio that Grood is back on Earth at his hidden laboratory, Rex tries to find the alien but learns he has returned to his planet and the newsman follows and is again captured by the robots. As he is about to be killed by a hypnotic ray weapon, Rex is made invisible by Dorn and he manages to free Ella and Tim from their prison inside a defunct volcano. As they escape, Grood uses his solar-thermo furnace to try and kill them but Dorn blocks him by reversing the heat generated by the weapon. The Earthlings return to their spaceship, go back home and destroy Grood's laboratory. Returning to Ergro, they are nearly killed when Grood fires a missile at their ship. Trapped, Grood gets into his cosmojet and sets off into space but one of his robots mistakenly sets the wrong controls, heading the ship into deep space with no hope of return.

Mandrake the Magician

(1939; 12 chapters) PRODUCER: Jack Fier. DIRECTORS: Sam Nelson and Norman Deming. SCREENPLAY: Joseph F. Poland, Basil Dickey and Ned Dandy. PHOTO-

GRAPHY: Benjamin H. Kline. EDITORS: Richard Fantl and Jerome Thoms. MUSIC: Lee Zahler. CAST: Warren Hull (Mandrake the Magician), Doris Weston (Betty Houston), Al Kikume (Lothar), Rex Downing (Tommy Houston), Edward Earle (Dr. Andre Bennett), Forbes Murray (Professor Houston), Kenneth MacDonald (James Webster), Don Beddoe (Frank Raymond), Dick Curtis (Dorgan), John Tyrrell (Dirk), Stanley Brown (Green), Beatrice Curtis (Nurse), Sam Ash (George Regan), Lester Dorr (Gray), Ernie Adams (Brown), Eddie Featherston, Buel Bryant, Bert Young (Rest Home Thugs), Eddie Foster (Ed), Russell Simpson (Parsons), George Chesebro (Baker), Art Mix (Iron Works Thug), Harry Tenbrook (Streeter), Frank Hagney (Harris), Ernie Alexander (Taxi Cab Driver), Eddie Hart (Williams), Jerry Jerome (Ward), Eddie Laughton (Kidnapper), Harry Bernard (Watchman), Stanley Blystone (CX-12), Ralph Peters (Ship Steward), Budd Buster, Blackie Whiteford (Construction Camp Thugs), Tom London, Charles Dorety (Inn Thugs), Jerry Frank (Harper Drive Thug), Tom Steele, Kit Guard, Oscar "Dutch" Hendrian (Power House Thugs), Chuck Hamilton, Cy Schindell (Bank Robbers), Pat McKee (Dam Henchman), Frank Mills (Gas Station Shooter), Cyril Ring (Magic Mart Henchman), Charles Sullivan (Driver), George Turner (Hall), Bud Wolfe (Tower Henchman), Steve Clark, Eddie Parker, Frank Wayne (Gang Members), Rose Plummer (Ship Passenger), Charles Sherlock (Ship Henchman), Knox Manning (Narrator).
CHAPTER TITLES: (1) Shadow on the Wall; (2) Trap of the Wasp; (3) City of Terror; (4) The Secret Passage; (5) The Devil's Playmate; (6) The Fatal Crash; (7) Gamble for Life; (8) Across the Deadline; (9) Terror Rides the Rails; (10) The Unseen Monster; (11) At the Stroke of Eight; (12) Reward of Treachery.

Columbia's first serial to be based on a comic strip character, *Mandrake the Magician* was released starting in the spring of 1939 with Warren Hull playing the title role. Hull previously headlined the studio's cliffhanger *The Spider's Web* (q.v.) in 1938 and did the same for its sequel *The Spider Returns* (q.v.) in 1941. At Universal he had the title role in another chapterplay, *The Green Hornet Strikes Again* (1940). The Mandrake serial was based on the popular King Features newspaper comic strip by Lee Falk and Phil Davis; Falk also created "The Phantom" for King Features, which Columbia filmed as a serial (q.v.) in 1943. The Columbia Mandrake cliffhanger was one of its best with 12 chapters of exciting action surrounding the title magician's constant attempts to stop a masked gang leader, The Wasp, from acquiring a futuristic weapon. Both the hero and the villain were nattily attired. Mandrake wore a tuxedo-like outfit replete with a cape, top hat and cane, while The Wasp dressed in light colors, contrary to most masked serial villains. Emblazoned on his silk outfit was an embroidered wasp; he also a wore silver mask and hat.

Returning from Tibet with the formula needed by Professor Houston (Forbes Murray) to perfect his radium energy machine, Mandrake the Magician (Hull) and his assistant Lothar (Al Kikume) meet the scientist and his daughter Betty (Doris Weston) on a cruise ship. Not only is Mandrake bringing the professor the platonite steel alloy formula but he also wants to resume his romance with Betty. While the professor plans to use his invention for medical purposes, the mysterious gang leader The Wasp wants it as a weapon. The Wasp has his minions kidnap Professor Houston and steal a working model of the machine. To further his attempts to get the perfected weapon, The Wasp orders the destruction of a radio station, powerhouse and a dam as Mandrake battles his minions at various locales including a rest home, a construction camp, an inn, a power plant and on board the cruise liner. Eventually the magician is able to round up The Wasp and his henchmen and unmasks him as a scientist who pretended to be Houston's ally. Mandrake is then able to resume his romance with Betty and see her father receive scientific acclaim for a powerful new medical treatment.

By the time the serial was ending its initial theatrical run, *Mandrake the Magician* was being broadcast on the Mutual Radio Network five times a week in a 15-minute time slot. Raymond Edward Johnson played the title character during the series run (November 1940 to February 1942). A dozen years later, 1954, Mandrake the Magician came to television with the half-hour syndicated series starring Coe Norton, a real-life magician, as Mandrake and Woody Strode as Lothar. On January 24, 1979, NBC-TV showed the two-hour telefeature *Mandrake* starring Anthony Herrera in the title role and Ji-Tu Cumbuka as Lothar. It was the pilot for a series that did not sell.

The Monster and the Ape

(1945; 15 chapters) PRODUCER: Rudolph C. Flothow. DIRECTOR: Howard Bretherton. SCREENPLAY: Royal K. Cole and Sherman L. Lowe. PHOTOGRAPHY: L.W. O'Connell. EDITORS: Dwight Caldwell and Earl Turner. MUSIC: Lee Zahler. SOUND: Hugh McDowell. ASSISTANT DIRECTOR: Leonard J. Shapiro. CAST: Robert Lowery (Ken Morgan), George Macready (Professor Ernst), Ralph Morgan (Professor Franklin Arnold), Carole Mathews (Babs Arnold), Willie Best (Flash), Jack Ingram (Dick Nordik), Anthony Warde (Joe Flint), Ted

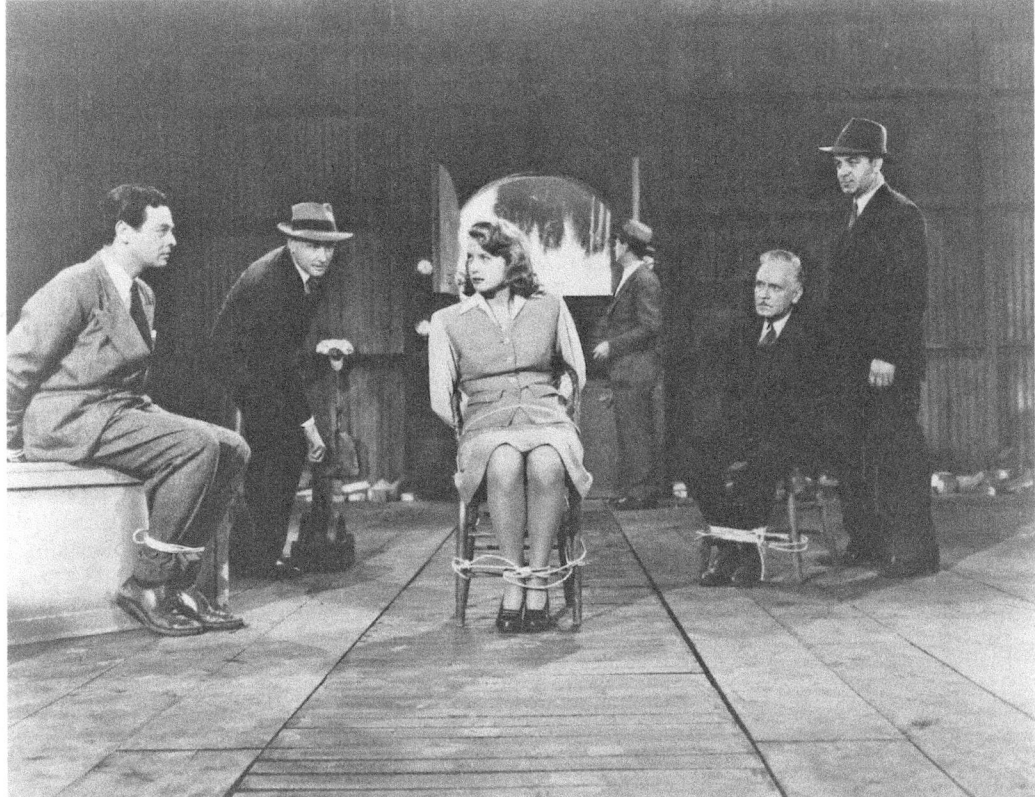

Robert Lowery, George Macready, Carole Mathews, Ted Mapes, Ralph Morgan and Anthony Warde in *The Monster and the Ape* (1945).

Mapes (Joe Butler), Eddie Parker (Blake), Stanley Price (Mead), Bud Osborne, Kit Guard (Zoo Guards), Kenneth MacDonald (Inspector Hamilton), Charles King (Policeman), Lee Shumway (Hardy), Ray Corrigan (Thor the Gorilla).

CHAPTER TITLES: (1) The Mechanical Terror; (2) The Edge of Doom; (3) Flames of Fate; (4) The Fatal Search; (5) Rocks of Doom; (6) A Friend in Disguise; (7) A Scream in the Night; (8) Death in the Dark; (9) The Secret Tunnel; (10) Forty Thousand Volts; (11) The Mad Professor; (12) Shadows of Destiny; (13) The Gorilla at Large; (14) His Last Flight; (15) Justice Triumphs.

The Metalogen is a robot invented by Professor Franklin Arnold (Ralph Morgan) at the Bainbridge Research Foundation. He shows his invention to a fellow scientist, Professor Ernst (George Macready), not knowing he is the head of a spy ring that wants the robot and its metal for his country's war effort. The company who wants to buy the invention sends Ken Morgan (Robert Lowery) to protect its investment; Morgan is attracted to Arnold's beautiful daughter and assistant Babs (Carole Mathews). Using his trained gorilla Thor (Ray Corrigan), Ernst and his gang try to obtain the robot, kidnapping Babs and holding her prisoner. When the gorilla tries to kill Morgan, Arnold destroys the creature. When Ernst tries to escape from Morgan and Arnold he falls off a cliff.

The Monster and the Ape is one of Columbia's most entertaining and visually satisfying serials. It was the last of five cliffhangers Rudolph C. Flothow produced for the company and it was enhanced by Howard Bretherton's direction; Bretherton is mainly remembered as a western director who helmed some top-notch Hopalong Cassidy features, including the initial *Hop-Along Cassidy* (1935), along with *The Eagle's Brood* (1935), *Heart of the West* (1936), *Hopalong Cassidy Enters* (1938) and *In Old Colorado* (1941). Bretherton also co-directed the Columbia serial *Who's Guilty?* (1945) [q.v.] with Wallace Grissell for producer Sam Katzman. Unlike Katzman's cheap chapterplays, this Flothow production had some impressive sets, including the villain's mansion, that sported secret passages, a cave, a hidden laboratory and a zoo. The exteriors were shot at Bronson Canyon. Some screen time was given over to Ray Corrigan's antics as the killer gorilla. The two titles monsters actually have little to do in the proceedings where hero Morgan is mainly at odds with Ernst and his foreign agent henchmen. Robert Lowery played the lead in the studio's *Batman and Robin* (q.v.) in 1949.

Mysterious Island

(1951; 15 chapters) PRODUCER: Sam Katzman. DIRECTOR: Spencer Gordon Bennet. SCREENPLAY: George H. Plympton, Royal K. Cole and Lewis Clay, from the novel by Jules Verne. PHOTOGRAPHY: Fayte Browne. EDITOR: Earl Turner. MUSIC DIRECTOR: Mischa Bakaleinikoff. ART DIRECTOR: Paul Palmentola. SOUND: J.S. Westmoreland. SETS: Sidney Clifford. PRODUCTION MANAGER: Herbert Leonard. ASSISTANT DIRECTOR: R.M. Andrews. CAST: Richard Crane (Captain Cyrus Harding), Marshall Reed (Jack Pencroft), Karen Randle (Rulu), Ralph Hodges (Herbert "Bert" Brown), Gene Roth (Captain Shard), Hugh Prosser (Gideon Spillett), Leonard Penn (Captain Nemo), Terry Frost (Ayrton), Rusty Wescoatt (Moley), Bernie Hamilton (Neb), William Fawcett (Mr. Jackson), George Robotham (Mercury Man), Tom Tyler (Union Dispatch Rider), Stanley Blystone, Frank O'Connor (Rebel Soldiers), Zon Murray, Roy Butler (Park Thugs), Frank Ellis (Pirate), Top (Dog).

CHAPTER TITLES: (1) Lost in Space; (2) Sinister Savages; (3) Savage Justice; (4) Wild Man at Large; (5) Trail of the Mystery Man; (6) The Pirates Attack; (7) Menace of the Mercurians; (8) Between Two Fires; (9) Shrine of the Silver Bird; (10) Fighting Fury; (11) Desperate Chance; (12) Mystery of the Mine; (13) Jungle Downfall; (14) Men from Tomorrow; (15) The Last of Mysterious Island.

Columbia made two versions of Jules Verne's 1874 novel *Mysterious Island*, first as a serial in 1951 and a decade later as a feature (q.v.) that sported animated creatures by Ray Harryhausen. While the second is the better known of the two, the cliffhanger, despite producer Sam Katzman's usual penchant for cheapness, is a fairly faithful adaptation of the book except for the addition of outer space aliens. Filmed at Corriganville, the chapterplay headlined Richard Crane, who later gained fame in the title role of the syndicated TV series *Rocky Jones, Space Ranger* (1954–55). In *The Great Movie Serials: Their Sound and Fury* (1972), Jim Harmon and Donald F. Glut dubbed the production "[p]erhaps the strangest, and outright boldest, alternation of a classic novel for a cliffhanger," adding, "Although fantastic beyond credibility, *Mysterious Island* actually contained more elements from the original source than most such adaptations of the sound era."

Toward the end of the Civil War, Confederate prisoners Captain Cyrus Harding (Crane), sailor Jack Pencroft (Marshall Reed) and his adopted son Bert Brown (Ralph Hodges), war correspondent Gideon Spillet (Hugh Prosser), and Harding's servant Neb (Bernie Hamilton) escape in a hot air balloon and drift for five days before crashing on an island where Harding vanishes after being attacked by a sea monster. Also landing on the island are Rulu (Karen Randle) and two other aliens from Mercury. The Union castaways are buried when a cave roof collapses but Pencroft digs them out. Harding, who was actually rescued

Poster for *Mysterious Island* (1951).

from the sea by Captain Nemo (Leonard Penn) in his submarine *Nautilus*, is taken to a secret grotto while wild man Ayrton (Terry Frost), an outcast who has gone mad, attacks Bert, who is rescued by his comrades. The castaways are chased by hostile natives but escape. Next they are nearly burned alive while Rulu and her aides search for a mysterious metal. The natives find Harding and take him to their village. Jack and Spillett follow them while Bert and Neb return to the balloon for weapons. After driving off the natives, the castaways find Ayrton's hut and he tells them he escaped from pirates who use the island to hide their stolen loot. When he promises them food, Pencroft and Spillett go with Ayrton but he betrays them and the two men are nearly killed when he causes an avalanche. Surviving the trap, they are joined by Harding and Bert and after capturing two natives they go to see the witch doctor, who says they must die because the gods are angry they have come to the island. The trio make a getaway and are taken to a cave by Ayrton where they are knocked out by an electrical blast. Ayrton is taken prisoner by pirates led by Captain Shard (Gene Roth), and the castaways are forced to fight them as Bert is placed in a trance by Rulu. When the pirates set off an explosion, Harding and Neb run into a cave where they find a secret tunnel that leads them to Nemo, who later helps the captured Pencroft and Spillett escape. When the pirates fire on them with their cannons, the castaways run away and are joined by the natives who fear the buccaneers. Shard has one of the natives killed and the tribe blames the castaways. When Harding and his men fight off pirates, the natives again become friendly and take them to the Shrine of the Silver Bird where they find a plastic box. Bert, who has been under the power of Rulu, escapes with some of her ray guns but is captured by Ayrton. The Mercurians surround the castaways and the natives. Rulu destroys the box with a ray gun and flees, followed by Harding and Pencroft. Harding is taken by her aides but Rulu then agrees to help the castaways get off the island. When Harding finds out that Shard plans to attack Rulu, he realizes this gives the castaways a chance to take over the pirate ship. While the castaways escape, Ayrton is killed by the blast. Bert is captured by Shard and his men but freed by Rulu, who again places him in a trance. Harding and Pencroft follow their friend as the aliens enter a mine where the Mercurians are seeking a radioactive metal. Shard asks the castaways to join the pirates in getting off the island. When they try to get the natives to help them, they are thwarted by Rulu who puts the locals under a spell. Harding and Shard follow Rulu to the mine where she finds the metal. The aliens take the men prisoners but they are rescued by Nemo who tells Harding and Shard that the explosive Rulu has found could destroy the planet. When another spacecraft arrives from Mercury, Harding and Shard are attacked by the invaders, and the pirate captain is killed. Bert trails Rulu who nearly captures him. Cyrus intervenes and the two men overpower the aliens. Rulu gets away and uses her discovery to create an explosion that destroys the island. Before it sinks into the sea, the castaways are rescued by a passing ship.

The Phantom

(1943; 15 chapters) PRODUCER: Rudolph C. Flothow. DIRECTOR: B. Reeves Eason. SCREENPLAY: Morgan B. Cox, Victor McLeod, Sherman L. Lowe and Leslie J. Swabacker. PHOTOGRAPHY: James S. Brown, Jr. EDITORS: Dwight Caldwell and J. Henry Adams. MUSIC: Lee Zahler. ART DIRECTOR: George Van Marter. ASSISTANT DIRECTOR: Richard Monroe. CAST: Tom Tyler (Geoffrey Prescott/The Phantom), Jeanne Bates (Diana Palmer), Kenneth MacDonald (Dr. Max Bremmer), Frank Shannon (Professor Davidson), Ace the Wonder Dog (Devil), Guy Kingsford (Guy Anderson), Joe Devlin (Singapore Smith), Ernie Adams (Rusty Fenton), John S. Bagni (Moku), Edmund Cobb (Grogan), George Chesebro (Marsden), Pat O'Malley (Joe Miller), Sol Gorss (Andy Kriss), I. Stanford Jolley (Watson), Anthony Caruso (Count Silento), Paul Marion (Rocco), Kermit Maynard (Drake), Eddie Parker (Scott), Wade Crosby (Long), Pierce Lyden (Paul), Dick Curtis (Tartar Chief), Reed Howes (Tartar Guard), Robert Barron (King), John Maxwell (Larkin), Dan White (Braddock), Lal Chand Mehra (Suba), Anthony Warde (Karak), Stanley Price (Chief Chota), Early Cantrell (Ruby Dawn/Fire Princess), Angel Cruz (Chief Zarka), Al Hill (Collins), John Indrisano (Perry), Al Ferguson (Henchman), Ernesto Morelli (Desk Clerk), Jay Silverheels (Astari Warrior), Iron Eyes Cody (Native), Alex Havier (Houseboy), Knox Manning (Narrator).

Lee Falk and Ray Moore created the comic character The Phantom for King Features, and Columbia brought the masked hero to the screen in a serial produced by Rudolph C. Flothow, who earlier did another of Falk's creations, *Mandrake the Magician* (1939) [q.v.], for the studio. Filmed in Newhall, California, and initially released to theaters in the 1943 Christmas season, *The Phantom* was directed by veteran serial helmsman B. Reeves "Breezy" Eason and starred cowboy hero Tom Tyler in the title role. Two years before, Tyler had starred as another masked avenger in Republic's *Adventure of Captain Marvel*, a comic book hero. In *The Great Movie Serials: Their Sound and Fury* (1972), Jim Harmon and Donald F. Glut called *The Phantom* "one of Columbia's better serials." Alan G. Barbour opined in *Cliffhanger: A Pictorial History of the Motion Picture Serial* (1977), "Tom Tyler cut a striking figure in the title role of *The Phantom*, but the serial itself was a meaningless fiasco."

In the 1500s, a seaman was left on an African shore by buccaneers. Using his skills with gunpowder he became The Phantom, the masked king of a pygmy jungle tribe. He vowed to end piracy and all injustice. The mantel of The Phantom, the Ghost Who Walks, passed from father to son. As the latest Phantom dies from a gunshot wound, his son, Geoffrey Prescott (Tom Tyler), takes on the guise and vows to avenge his father's murder. The Phantom comes to the aid of Professor Davidson (Frank Shannon) and his daughter Diana (Jeanne Bates), Geoffrey's fiancée. They possess three of the seven ivory pieces needed to locate Zoloz, a lost city of historical importance and great wealth. Crook Singapore Smith (Joe Devlin) has three other parts and the seventh is missing. Getting financial backing from Byron Andrews (Guy Kingsford), Davidson is about to set forth on an expedition to find the lost city when Smith steals his three puzzle sections. The Phantom retrieves all six pieces and returns them to the professor, not knowing that Dr. Max Bremmer (Kenneth MacDonald), a foreign spy, wants Zoloz for a clandestine enemy airport. (It was Bremmer who murdered The Phantom's father when he learned of the foreign agent's nefarious plans.) While Bremmer and his gang try to causes disharmony among the native tribes, The Phantom uses his influence and mystic powers in thwarting the crook, although at times it nearly costs him his life as well as those of the professor and his daughter. The Phantom and the other members of the expedition are taken prisoner by the Tartar tribe chief (Dick Curtis), who claims to possess the needed ivory puzzle piece. He informs The Phantom he can have it if he takes it from a chain around the neck of a huge gorilla. After a fierce battle with the beast, The Phantom obtains the puzzle part and leads his friends to Zoloz where he finds Bremmer has set up a bogus Phantom to fool the natives into helping him build an air strip. When The Phantom shows the natives he is their true protector and that Bremmer has deceived them, they turn on the spy and murder him and his henchmen.

In 1961 the King Features Syndicate partnered with Tele Screen Productions to make a pilot for a TV series of *The Phantom*, starring Roger Creed in the title role, with guest stars Paulette Goddard, Lon Chaney, Jr., and Reginald Denny. It failed to sell. Five years later a Philippine feature version of the Lee Falk character was filmed as *Alyas Phantom*, starring Bob Soler as The Phantom.

Pirates of the High Seas

(1950; 15 chapters) PRODUCER: Sam Katzman. DIRECTORS: Spencer Gordon Bennet and Thomas Carr. SCREENPLAY: Joseph F. Poland, David Mathews, George H. Plympton and Charles R. Condon. PHOTOGRAPHY: Ira H. Morgan. EDITOR: Earl Turner. MUSIC DIRECTOR: Mischa Bakaleinikoff. ART DIRECTOR: Paul Palmentola. SETS: Sidney Clifford. PRODUCTION MANAGER: Herbert B. Leonard. CAST: Buster Crabbe (Jeff Drake), Lois Hall (Carol Walsh), Tommy Farrell (Kelly Walsh), Gene Roth (Governor Frederick Whitlock), Tristram Coffin (Walter Castell), Stanley Price (Lamar), Marshall Reed (Shark Wilson), Rusty Wescoatt (Adams), Terry Frost (Carter), Pierce Lyden (Durk), Neyle Morrow (Kalana), Symona Boniface (Lotus Lady), Hugh Prosser (Roper), Lee Roberts (Barker), William Fawcett (Ben Wharton), John Hart (Jenkins/Earl Turner), Charles Quigley (Merkel), I. Stanford Jolley (Turner), John Zaremba (Dr. Schmidt), Charles Horvath (Temple Native), Knox Manning (Narrator).

CHAPTER TITLES: (1) Mystery Mission; (2) Attacked by Pirates; (3) Dangerous Depths; (4) Blasted to Atoms; (5) The Missing Mate; (6) Secret of the Ivory Case; (7) Captured by Savages; (8) The Vanishing Music Box; (9) Booby Trap; (10) Savage Snare; (11) Sinister Cavern; (12) Blast from the Depths; (13) Cave In; (14) Secret of the Music Box; (15) Diamonds from the Sea.

Buster Crabbe made a trio of serials for producer Sam Katzman, beginning with *The Sea Hound* (1947) and ending with *King of the Congo* (1952) [qq.v.]. Sandwiched between them was *Pirates of the High Seas*, a modern-day story of piracy that revolved around the search for five million dollars worth of diamonds and a ghostly phantom ship. Mostly filmed at the Iverson Ranch in Chatsworth, it was basically a reworking of *The Sea Hound*.

In the South Pacific, Kelly Walsh (Tommy Farrell) operates a freighter that is being assaulted by a phantom pirate ship. He requests help from his friend Jeff Drake (Crabbe) who sails his vessel, the *Viking*, to the island of Taluha. On board are Kelly's sister Carol (Lois Hall), war criminal hunter Walter Castell (Tristram Coffin), and the island's governor, Frederick Whitlock (Gene Roth). As Jeff investigates the raids on Kelly's cargo ship he encounters many dangers but eventually comes to realize that Whitlock is behind the ghost ship and in cahoots with Walter, who is really a wanted war criminal after five million dollars worth of diamonds he hid at the end of the last conflict. With the help of the siblings, Drake is able to bring both Whitlock and Castell to justice and find the diamonds.

Roar of the Iron Horse

(1951; 15 chapters) PRODUCER: Sam Katzman. DIRECTORS: Spencer Gordon Bennet and Thomas Carr. SCREENPLAY: George H. Plympton, Sherman L. Lowe and Royal K. Cole. PHOTOGRAPHY: Fayte Browne. EDITOR: Earl Turner. MUSIC DIRECTOR: Mischa Bakaleinikoff. ART DIRECTOR: Paul Palmentola. SETS: Sidney Clifford. PRODUCTION MANAGER: Herbert Leonard. SCRIPT SUPERVISOR: Violet Newfield. ASSISTANT DIRECTOR: R.M. Andrews. CAST: Jock O'Mahoney [Jock Mahoney] (Jim Grant), Virginia Herrick (Carol Lane), William Fawcett (Rocky), Hal Landon (Tom Lane), Jack Ingram (Homer Lathrop), Mickey Simpson (Cal), George Eldredge (Karl Ulrich/The Baron), Myron Healey (Ace), Rusty Wescoatt (Scully), Frank Ellis (Outlaw), Pierce Lyden (Erv Hopkins), Dick Curtis (Campo), Hugh Prosser (Lefty), Tommy Farrell (Del), Milton Kibbee (Telegrapher Ezra), Rick Vallin (White Eagle), Charles Horvath (Bodyguard), Wally West (Henchman), Bud Osborne (Camp Outlaw), Knox Manning (Narrator).

CHAPTER TITLES: (1) Indian Attack; (2) Captured by Redskins; (3) Trapped by Outlaws; (4) In the Baron's Stronghold; (5) A Ride for Life; (6) White Indians; (7) Fumes of Fate; (8) Midnight Marauders; (9) Raid on the Pay Train; (10) Trapped on a Trestle; (11) Redskin's Revenge; (12) Plunge of Peril; (13) The Law Takes Over; (14) When Killer Meet; (15) The End of the Trail.

Released in the spring of 1951, *Roar of the Iron Horse* was a retread of the studio's 1947 modern western cliffhanger *The Vigilante* (q.v.). Outside of the heroics of athletic star-stuntman Jock Mahoney, here billed as Jock O'Mahoney, the serial had little to offer. What places it in the realm of this volume is that its plot crux was the search for a diamond-stuffed meteor. Thus a small sci-fi element crept into what was otherwise a routine entry in a dying genre.

When a government-built railroad appears to be the target of sabotage, its chief engineer, Tom Lane (Hal Landon), makes a request to superintendent Homer Lathrop (Jack Ingram) for a special investigator to look into the matter. Over the objections of railroad foreman Scully (Rusty Wescoatt), Lathrop wires Washington D.C. and asks for help. Jim Grant (Mahoney), sent to look into the trouble, meets prospector Rocky (William Fawcett). The two men are attacked by marauders but are aided by White Eagle (Rick Vallin), an Indian chief who is fighting crooked Karl Ulrich (George Eldredge), also known as The Baron. Ulrich is enslaving White Eagle's tribesmen and making them dig for a meteor that legend says contains diamonds. Working with Lane and his sister Carol (Virginia Herrick), Jim eventually finds out that Ulrich is the mastermind behind the sabotage that is being carried out by his henchmen, Lathrop and Scully. In a showdown, the superintendent and foreman are killed and Ulrich and his gang are captured. After Rocky announces he has uncovered the meteor, Jim and Carol decide to get married.

The Sea Hound

(1947; 15 chapters) PRODUCER: Sam Katzman. DIRECTORS: Walter B. Eason and Mack V. Wright. SCREENPLAY: George H. Plympton, Arthur Hoerl and Lewis Clay. PHOTOGRAPHY: Ira H. Morgan. EDITOR: Earl Turner. MUSIC DIRECTOR: Mischa Bakaleinikoff. ART DIRECTOR: Paul Palmentola. SOUND: J.S. Westmoreland. SETS: Sidney Moore. PRODUCTION MANAGER: David Katzman. CAST: Buster Crabbe (Captain Silver), Jimmy Lloyd (Tex), Pamela Blake (Ann Whitney), Ralph Hodges (Jerry), Spencer Chan (Cookie Kukai), Robert Barron (The Admiral), Hugh Prosser (Stanley Rand), Rick Vallin (Manila Pete), Jack Ingram (Murdock), Milton Kibbee (John Whitney), Al Baffert (Lon), Stanley Blystone (Black Mike), Robert [Bob] Duncan (Sloan), Pierce Lyden (Vardman), Rusty Wescoatt (Singapore Manson), Carl LeViness (John Lawson), Dolores Castle (Ilani), Gene Roth (Store Owner), Britt Wood (Van Wart), William Fawcett (Andre), Terry Frost, Wally West (Henchmen), Harry Vejar (Chief Kalahama), Tom Balbuena (Naylah), Knox Manning (Narrator).

CHAPTER TITLES: (1) Captain Silver Sails Again; (2) Spanish Gold; (3) The Mystery of the Map; (4) Menaced by Ryaka; (5) Captain Silver's Strategy; (6) The Sea Hound at Bay; (7) In the Admiral's Lair; (8) Rand's Treachery; (9) On the Water Front; (10) On the Treasure Trail; (11) Sea Hound Attacked; (12) Dangerous Waters; (13) The Panther's Prey; (14) The Fatal Doublecross; (15) Captain Silver's Last Stand.

While sailing his schooner *The Sea Hound* in the South Seas, Captain Silver (Buster Crabbe) gets a distress call saying a yacht is being attacked by pirates at Typhoon Cove. Going there with his crew, cowboy Tex (Jimmy Lloyd), teenager Jerry (Ralph Hodges), Chinese scientist-inventor Kukai (Spencer Chan), and Flecha, a dog, they find the yacht's owner, Stanley Rand (Hugh Prosser) and his guests, Ann Whitney (Pamela Blake) and Vardman (Pierce Lyden), besieged by the henchmen of a hijacker, The Admiral (Robert Barron), who pretends to be a rubber planter-trader. Silver and his crew rescue the trio and find out they have come their to meet Ann's father, John Whitney (Milton Kibbee), who has found a long-lost Spanish treasure. The group sets out to find a sunken Spanish galleon; Silver dives down and locates the wreck but its treasure chest is empty. After nearly being killed by a native diver, Silver learns that the natives have secreted the treasure. The Admiral pretends to be friendly with the newcomers and helps save them when they are attacked by a gang of thugs. He then invites the party to be his guests at his plantation. After hearing that Rand and Vardman had robbed John Whitney, whom the natives took into the island's interior, he locks the group in his house and sets it on fire. Silver manages to help his friends escape but they are later followed by the island's Ryak warriors. Ann disappears. Jerry and Vardman save Silver and Rand from the warriors but in the jungle Rand and Vardman fall into a pit filled with pointed stakes while Ann is captured by a huge carnivorous plant. After all are rescued, they head back to the schooner not knowing The Admiral's henchman have taken control of the vessel. Using The Admiral's boat, the group attacks *The Sea Hound* and retake it.

That night, the crooks steal one of the treasure maps. When Silver pursues them, he is caught in a tidal wave in a cave but is saved by Tex. Rand and Vardman ally themselves with The Admiral, who needs them to decipher the treasure map. The Admiral later turns on Rand and Vardman and orders them to be tortured. The natives capture the pair; Silver and Jerry are seized by The Admiral and his men. When Silver refuses to help read the treasure map, The Admiral tries to drown him but Tex comes to his and Jerry's rescue. The three men return to camp to find that Ann has been kidnapped by Rand and Vardman. They free her but are attacked by the Ryak warriors. Escaping, the group sets out to find John Whitney. When Silver locates him, he is taken prisoner by the warriors who try to kill him but Tex and Jerry come to the rescue. The three men learn that Whitney is on The Admiral's boat and Silver goes to set him free but they are pursed by the crooks. Silver and Whitney fall off a cliff but are saved by a log that cushions their fall into the ocean. They return to the jungle where they join Tex and Jerry.

Poster for *The Sea Hound* (1947).

Ann is reunited with her father. Rand and Vardman abduct Whitney and his daughter and take them to The Admiral in return for a cut of the treasure. Ann is nearly killed when a jealous native girl (Dolores Castle) turns a black panther loose on her but Silver comes to the rescue. As Silver and Ann retreat into the jungle, The Admiral promises to torture John Whitney unless he reveals the location of the treasure. When Rand tries to double-cross him, The Admiral orders his execution; Rand is shot despite Silver's attempt to save him. During the melee, Whitney escapes as the warriors capture Tex and Jerry. When The Admiral and his men tries to pursue the old man, they too are captured. The Admiral bargains for his life with the Ryaks but one of his men kills him and then tries to abduct the chief but is thwarted by Silver and falls from a cliff. The warriors set Silver and his party free and give him the Spanish treasure.

The cliffhanger was based on a mid–1940s comic book character as well as a children's radio adventure series, *The Sea Hound*, which was also called *Captain Silver's Log of the Sea Hound* and *Captain Silver and the Sea*. The 15-minute series starred Ken Daigneau as Captain Silver and was broadcast first on ABC from 1942 to 1944, then on Mutual until 1947 and then back on ABC until the end of its run in August 1951.

Filmed on and near Catalina Island, *The Sea Hound* was the first of a trio of Buster Crabbe serials for Columbia producer Sam Katzman. It was followed by *Pirates of the Highs Seas* (1950) and *King of the Congo* (1952) [qq.v.]. Outside of Crabbe's athletic heroics at age 40 and its scenic locales, the serial had little to recommend it.

The Secret Code

(1942; 15 chapters) PRODUCER: Larry Darmour. DIRECTOR: Spencer Gordon Bennet. SCREENPLAY: Basil Dickey, Robert Beche and Leighton Brill. PHOTOGRAPHY: James S. Brown, Jr. EDITOR: Earl Turner. MUSIC: Lee Zahler. ASSISTANT DIRECTOR: Carl Hiecke. CAST: Paul Kelly (Lieutenant Dan Barton/The Black Commando), Anne Nagel (Jean Ashley), Trevor Bardette (Jensen), Robert O. Davis [Rudolph Anders] (Rudi Thysson), Clancy Cooper (Sergeant Pat Flanagan), Gregory Gay (Feldon), Louis [Ludwig] Donath (Professor Metzger), Beal Wong (Quito), Eddie Parker (Beck), Wade Boteler (Police Chief Burns), Charles C. Wilson (Sergeant Cullen), Alex Callam (Investigator Hogan), Robert Fiske (Inspector Ryan), Selmer Jackson (Major Henry Barton), Jacqueline Dalya (Linda), Jack Gardner (Wolper), Kenne Duncan (Marvin), George Lynn (Chief Stover), Frank Shannon (Police Commissioner), Gus Glassmire (Mr. Stevens), John Elliott (Professor Clyde), Jack Rice (Clerk Fred), Sigund Tor (Lieutenant Kurtz), Joe Girard (Colonel Drake), Dick Botiller (Hans Steufel), Lucien Prival (U-499 Commander), Rose Plummer (Flower Lady), Lester Dorr (Otto Stahl), Peter Leeds (Carl Hiecke), Kit Guard (Corrick), Warren Jackson (Ralph), Lee Shumway (Police Dispatcher), Eddie Woods (Kurt), Joseph Crehan (Chief Henry Burns), James Millican (Bill), Franklyn Farnum, Tom Steele (Federal Agents), Harry Gribbon (First Mate), Zon Murray, Roy Brent, Frank McCarroll (Military Policemen), Tom London (Weather Bureau Guard), Frank LaRue, Eddie Dunn (Weather Bureau Workers), Eddie Polo (Special Delivery Messenger), Steve Clark, Ted Mapes (Nazi Agents), Stanley Brown (Police Laboratory Technician), Eddie Kane (Counterman), Wally West, Dick Rush, Ed Peil, Sr. (Policemen), Charles Sullivan (Truck Driver), Lee Phelps (Jailer), Harry Strang, Chuck Hamilton, Bert Young, Ray Henderson (Gang Members), Bobby Stone (Newsboy), Joe Caits (Messenger), Ken Carpenter (Newscaster), Knox Manning (Narrator).

CHAPTER TITLES: (1) Enemy Passport; (2) The Shadows of the Swastika; (3) Nerve Gas; (4) The Sea Spy

Advertisement for *The Secret Code* (1942).

Strikes; (5) Wireless Warning; (6) Flaming Oil; (7) Submarine Signal; (8) The Missing Key; (9) The Radio Bomb; (10) Blind Bombardment; (11) Ears of the Enemy; (12) Scourge of the Orient; (13) Pawn of the Spy Ring; (14) Dead Men of the Deep; (15) The Secret Code Smashed.

The chief protagonist of *The Secret Code* was a superhero dubbed The Black Commando because he wore black clothes, including a hood and gloves. In reality he was a supposedly disgraced police lieutenant on the trail of a gang of foreign agents out to steal a new synthetic rubber formula. Paul Kelly, who once served time for killing his future wife's ex-husband, played the hero. An interesting aspect of the plot was that each chapter had a different kind of code and one of the characters, Major Barton (Selmer Jackson), demonstrated how to unravel the ciphers. The code lessons were written by Henry Lysing. Jim Harmon and Donald F. Glut in *The Great Serial Heroes: Their Sound and Fury* (1972) called the serial "above average" but noted its resemblance to an earlier Republic chapterplay, *Spy Smasher*, issued earlier the same year. An inside joke in *The Secret Code* had Peter Leeds playing spy Carl Hiecke, the name of the film's assistant director.

Expelled from the police force for dereliction of duty, Dan Barton (Kelly) gets on the trail of spy ring leader Rudi Thyssen (Robert O. Davis) who has learned from agent Feldon (Gregory Gay) that the government has a new formula for making synthetic rubber. Feldon has come from Berlin with a secret spy code. He and Thyssen capture Barton after he pretends to try and steal the formula. Finding out the Nazis' plans, Barton meets with his girlfriend, newspaper reporter Jean Ashley (Anne Nagel), and gives her the story, and then takes on the guise of the masked Black Commando in an attempt to thwart the spies. Barton pretends to be a prisoner of the spies while respected businessman Jensen (Trevor Bardette), the real leader of the enemy agents, orders the finding of the formula and the killing of the Black Commando. Barton manages to turn over the secret document to his friend, Detective Sergeant Pat Flanagan (Clancy Cooper). Jenson has his men rob the Sub-Treasury for funds but the Black Commando thwarts him only to become hunted by the police. When Barton is accepted into the spy ring after becoming a fugitive, he finds out that the agents plan to bomb a troop ship. As the Black Commando he stops the mission. When the spies find out that the Japanese need a weather report in order to plan a bombing of the West Coast, Barton goes with Thyssen and Feldon to the Mount Wilson Observatory to steal the forecast bulletin; The Black Commando gets away with it.

The Black Commando learns of the spies' plan to hijack gasoline and oil from a warehouse. When the saboteurs set off an explosion in an attempt to rid themselves of the Black Commando, the avenger's fireproof suit saves his life and he gets away. Supposed insurance broker Stahl (Lester Dorr) gives Jensen film that later is shown to picture a coded message. The Black Commando saves Hogan (Alex Callam), a federal agent on Stahl's trail, when the insurance man tries to destroy a navy ship. Stahl is arrested by Flanagan and handed over to Hogan for questioning but the spies plan to rescue him. As he is being taken from city prison to a federal facility, Jean is kidnapped by the spies while the enemy agents free Stahl. The Black Commando pursues the saboteurs and saves Jean when their car crashes. The spies then kidnap the reporter and try to make her tell them the identify of the Black Commando but he raids their headquarters and frees her. After escaping from the bombing of a cargo ship, the Black Commando finds out that the saboteurs plan to destroy war production sites and tries to find a list of the locations. Thyssen and the masked man fight over the list but Barton manages to escape and hands the site locations to Flanagan and tells him that Jensen is the spy ring chief. Jean is given the list to give to Hogan who finds Barton's fingerprints on it and pursues the ex-cop with his men. Escaping the police, Barton learns that Jensen is bringing in an enemy pilot from Canada. Flanagan helps him capture the flier. Barton puts on the spy's uniform and is found out by the agents but he escapes on Flanagan's motorcycle. Barton goes back to the landing site and pretends to have been attacked by the Black Commando. Jensen orders the kidnapping of Flanagan and shoots at him but Barton knocks away his gun just as Hogan and his men, along with Jean, arrive. Barton, Pat and Jean make a getaway. After he recaptures Flanagan, Jensen fears being apprehended and uses a secret code to send for a submarine on which to leave the country. The Black Commando finds Jensen in his secret headquarters but the spy manages to escape, leaving Dan and Flanagan to die by poison gas. The two men get free by breaking a glass panel. Barton locates the key to the enemy's secret code and, along with Jean, travels to Point Grayson. There Barton sees laundry on a line at a ranch house and it forms Roman numerals giving the time and locale of the enemy submarine's arrival. Barton contacts the police and Jensen and his gang are arrested and a destroyer sinks the sub. The Black Commando retires for good to marry Jean, who cannot reveal his identity to her readers.

The Secret of Treasure Island

(1938; 15 chapters) PRODUCER: Jack Fier. ASSOCIATE PRODUCER: Louis Weiss. SUPERVISING PRODUCER: George M. Merrick. DIRECTOR: Elmer Clifton. SCREENPLAY: George Rosener, Elmer Clifton and George M. Merrick. STORY: L. Ron Hubbard. PHOTOGRAPHY: Edward Linden and Edward Schopp. EDITOR: Earl Turner. MUSIC DIRECTOR: Abe Meyer. ART DIRECTOR: James Altwies. SOUND: Corson Jowett. SETS: Paul Palmentola. PRODUCTION MANAGER: Clarence Bricker. SPECIAL EFFECTS: Ken Pach and Earl Bunn. ASSISTANT DIRECTOR: Adrian Weiss. CAST: Don Terry (Larry Kent), Gwen Gaze (Toni Morrell), Grant Withers (Roderick Gridley), Hobart Bosworth (Dr. X), William Farnum (George Brennan Westmore), Walter Miller (Carter Collins/The Shark), George Rosener (Captain Samuel Cuttle), Dave O'Brien (Detective Jameson), Yakima Canutt (Dreer), Warner Richmond (Captain Tom Stanton/Captain Tom Faxton), William Royle (Paul Thorndyke), Sandra Karina (Zanya), Joe Caits (Saltwater Jerry), Colin Campbell (Butler Hawkins), Patrick J. Kelly (Professor Gault), Ted Adams (Moore), Frank Lackteen (Pedro), Clara Kimball Young (Hotel Maid), Josef Swickard (Ship Doctor), Blackie Whiteford (Andy), Robert Frazer, Edward Cassidy (Passenger Ship Captains), Reed Howes (Thug), Jack Perrin, Lane Chandler, Wally West, Milburn Morante, Louis Caits (Gang Members), Joe Girard (Newspaper Executive), Harry Harvey (Kidnapper), Carl Mathews (Fishing Boat Captain), Robert Walker, Jerry Frank (Mole Men), Eddie Foster (Guard), Willy Castello, Harry Burns (Pirates).

CHAPTER TITLES: (1) The Isle of Fear; (2) The Ghost Talks; (3) The Phantom Duel; (4) Buried Alive; (5) The Girl Who Vanished; (6) Trapped by the Flood; (7) The Cannon Roars; (8) The Circle of Death; (9) The Pirate's Revenge; (10) The Crash; (11) Dynamite; (12) The Bridge of Doom; (13) The Mad Flight; (14) The Jaws of Destruction; (15) Justice.

L. Ron Hubbard (1911–86), a science fiction writer and founder of the Church of Scientology, contributed the original story for this 15-chapter serial that Columbia released in March 1938. The

Grant Withers, Patrick J. Kelly and Gwen Gaze in *The Secret of Treasure Island* (1938).

studio advertised it as being based on Robert Louis Stevenson's 1883 novel *Treasure Island* but outside of the fact it dealt with the search for hidden wealth on a remote island it had little to do with the literary classic. Columbia's third cliffhanger was solid entertainment from genre veterans: producer Jack Fier (who told his production units there was nothing to fear but Fier himself), associates Louis Weiss and George M. Merrick, and director Elmer Clifton, who had been helming films for two decades. Fier produced the studio's first eight chapterplays before Larry Darmour took over that chore in 1940.

In the 1700s, buccaneers buried their treasure on an island near the Coast of Mexico but they were killed when a volcano erupted. For years there were attempts to find the hidden wealth but without success. Carter Collins (Walter Miller), known as The Shark, takes over the island after obtaining part of a map leading to the treasure. He has hidden bombs buried around the place to keep out other searchers and moves into the island's huge old mansion with the nearly mad Dr. X (Hobart Bosworth), nurse Zanya (Sandra Karina), butler Hawkins (Colin Campbell) and associate Roderick Gridley (Grant Withers), who also has part of the map and wants the treasure for himself. When reporter Paul Thorndyke (William Royle) disappears while investigating the mystery of the island, his editor, Westmore (William Farnum), assigns news hawk Larry Kent (Don Terry) the task of finding him. Larry's girlfriend Toni Morrell (Gwen Gaze) learns from a dying sea captain that she may be the heir to the treasure since her father supposedly found it. She joins Larry on his investigation and the two come up against not only The Shark, who is using slaves called Mole Men to dig for the gold, but also a mysterious skull-masked buccaneer called the Ghost of the Black Pirate. After nearly meeting death in a variety of ways, such as nearly being buried alive, killed by bombs and fighting a sword duel with the pirate ghost, Larry manages to solve the case by unmasking the culprit, reuniting Toni with her father and locating the treasure.

The Shadow

(1940; 15 chapters) PRODUCER: Larry Darmour. DIRECTOR: James W. Horne. SCREENPLAY: Joseph Poland, Ned Dandy and Joseph O'Donnell. PHOTOGRAPHY: James S. Brown, Jr. EDITOR: Dwight Caldwell. MUSIC: Lee Zahler. SOUND: Tom Lambert. ELECTRICAL EFFECTS: Kenneth Strickfaden. ASSISTANT DIRECTOR: Carl Hiecke. CAST: Victor Jory (Lamont Cranston/The Shadow/Lin Chang), Veda Ann Borg (Margo Lane), Roger Moore (Harry Vincent), Robert Fiske (Stanford Marshall), J. Paul Jones (Mr. Turner), Jack Ingram (Flint), Chuck Hamilton (Roberts), Ed Peil, Sr. (Inspector Joe Cardona), Frank LaRue (Commissioner Ralph Weston), George Turner (Jimmy), Philip Ahn (Wu Yung), Griff Barnett (Stephen Prescott), Hal Cooke (Mr. Kent), Franklyn Farnum (Sparks), Charles King (Russell), Rex Lease (Garage Thug), Henry Tenbrook (Adams), Lee Shumway (Frank Milford), Eddie Featherston (Williams), Cy Schindell (Streeter), Charles K. French (Joseph Rand), Constantine Romanoff (Harvey), Kit Guard (Clark), Jack Rice (Taylor), Gordon Hart (Albert Hill), Murdock MacQuarrie (Butler Richards), Lloyd Ingraham (Judge), Sam Lufkin (Kirk), Edward LeSaint (Dr. Grant), Jack Perrin (Mechanic), Frank Hagney (Kidnapper), Tom London (Truck Driver), Jack Low (Mallory), Horace B. Carpenter (Auto Driver), Joe Caits (Radio Shop Thug), Kernan Cripps (Shipyard Guard), Dick Botiller (Green), Bert Young, Lewis Sargent, Duke York, Joe Devlin, Frank Mills, Lester Dorr, Charles Dorety, Johnny Kascier (Gang Members), Jack Kennedy (Oriental Bazaar Policeman), Charles Sullivan (Café Counterman), Mary MacLaren, Marin Sais (Nurses), Lew Meehan (Dispatcher), Budd Buster (Beggar), Dick Rush, William Lally (Policemen), George Morrell (Newspaper Seller), Charles McAvoy (Police Guard), Richard Cramer (Voice of The Black Tiger).

CHAPTER TITLES: (1) Doomed City; (2) The Shadow Attacks; (3) The Shadow's Peril; (4) In the Tiger's Lair; (5) Danger Above; (6) The Shadow's Trap; (7) Where Horror Waits; (8) The Shadow Rides the Rails; (9) The Devil in White; (10) The Underground Trap; (11) Chinatown at Dark; (12) Murder by Remote Control; (13) Wheels of Death; (14) The Sealed Room; (15) The Shadow's Net Closes.

Using the name Maxwell Grant, Walter B. Gibson created the character of Lamont Cranston, The Shadow, for *Shadow Magazine* novels around 1930, the same year the character came to radio as part of CBS's *Detective Story Hour* with James La Curto as the first Cranston. Frank Readick, Jr., took over the part; the next season the show was called *Blue Coal Radio Revue* until it ended in June 1932. From October 1931 to September 1932, Readick played the role on the same network's *Love Story Drama*, also called *Love Story Hour*. Early in 1932, while still appearing on *Love Story Drama/Hour*, Readick starred in *The Shadow*. (From October 1932 to April 1933 the show was called *Blue Coal Mystery Revue*.) The program permanently became *The Shadow* in the fall of 1934 and Readick continued in the part until March 1935. From 1937 to 1938 Orson Welles starred as Cranston on the Mutual network; its sponsor continued to be Blue Coal, which had backed the program since 1931 and would continue to do so until 1949. In 1938 Welles also recorded 26 syndicated broadcasts of *The Shadow*, sponsored by Goodrich. In 1938 Bill Johnstone took over the starring role on Mutual's *The Shadow* and continued in the part until March 1943. In the fall of that year, Bret Morrison became the longest running radio Lamont Cranston, playing the part on the Mutual network until the series ended its radio run in 1954. There were also separate *The Shadow* radio shows broadcast in Australia, Brazil, Great Britain, Mexico and South Africa.

Rod La Rocque portrayed Lamont Cranston in two Grand National programmers, *The Shadow Strikes* (1937) and *International Crime* (1938), before Columbia acquired the rights to the character in 1940 and made *The Shadow*, a 15-chapter serial starring Victor Jory, who would also headline the cliffhanger *The Green Archer* (q.v.) for the company the same year. Both chapterplays were produced by Larry Darmour and directed by James W. Horne. Alan G. Barbour complained in *Days of Thrills and Adventure* (1970), "[T]he film was mediocre. The writers took too many liberties with the character, including having Lamont Cranston frequently pose as a ridiculous-looking Oriental called Lin Chang. Audiences looked forward to seeing a man with the incredible ability to 'cloud men's mind so they could not see him.' Instead there was only a typical masked hero behaving rather like an imbecile." In *The Great Movie Serials: Their Sound and Fury* (1972), Jim Harmon and Donald F. Glut concurred: "All the mystery and menace of the Shadow was lost by having him often appear in broad daylight and brightly lit rooms. The weapons and schemes of the Black Tiger were far from fantastic. All in all, the serial was simply a detective story in which the hero chose to wear a black cloak and slouch hat for no justifiable motive." Buck Rainey in *Those Fabulous Serial Heroines: Their Lives and Films* (1990) called it "a thrilling chapterplay."

A mysterious madman, The Black Tiger, is terrorizing and destroying parts of a city for no known reason. He sends his henchmen to steal the formula for a super-explosive invented by Stanford Marshall (Robert Fiske), who works for rich society man Lamont Cranston (Jory). They take the formula from Cranston's laboratory after overwhelming his secretary-companion Margot Lane (Veda Ann Borg). Cranston is really The Shadow, a mystery man in a black cloak who fights for law and justice. To catch The Black Tiger, Cranston asks Police Commissioner Ralph Weston (Frank LaRue) to let one of the maniac's henchmen go so he can be trailed to his boss. Disguising himself as Lin Chang, Lamont ingratiates himself into the gang and tells them of an approaching police raid and then manages to make a getaway with the aid of Harry Vincent (Roger Moore), Cranston's chauffeur and assistant. When The Black Tiger tries to sabotage a television demonstration, The Shadow tells those in attendance to leave. He is attacked by Flint (Jack Ingram), the Tiger's chief henchman, and his men, and during the melee the device is destroyed. In order to perfect a death ray, the madman has his men steal chemicals and electronic equipment. Cranston and Weston work with a citizen's committee that includes Marshall and businessmen Stephen Prescott (Griff Barnett), Joseph Rand (Charles K. French), Albert Hill (Gordon Hart), Frank Milford (Lee Shumway) and Kent (Hal Cooke). During his various confrontations with The Black Tiger and his men, The Shadow saves Margot from being crushed by a falling elevator and eventually, as Lin Chang, he has Cranston accused of a murder. Finally The Shadow and Marshall locate The Black Tiger's secret headquarters and rescue the businessmen he had kidnapped and imprisoned there so they would sign their fortunes over to him. In a fight with The Black Tiger, The Shadow reveals him to be Marshall, who is killed when one of his inventions electrocutes him.

The Shadow returned to the screen in 1946 when Monogram starred Kane Richmond as Lamont Cranston in three well-done "B" productions, *The Shadow Returns*, *Behind the Mask* and *The Missing Lady*. In the mid–1950s Republic Pictures made two pilot episodes for a proposed *The Shadow* TV series that never sold; 1958 they were pasted together into a feature film, *Invisible Avenger*. Richard Derr starred as Lamont Cranston. In 1962 new footage was added to the movie and it was reissued as *Bourbon Street Shadows*. With the success of *Batman* (1989) and its sequels, Universal starred Alec Baldwin as Lamont Cranston in a big-budget 1994 feature called *The Shadow* but it failed to recoup its production costs.

The Spider Returns

(1941; 15 chapters) PRODUCER: Larry Darmour. DIRECTOR: James W. Horne. SCREENPLAY: Jesse A. Duffy and George H. Plympton. STORY: Morgan B. Cox,

Lawrence E. Taylor, John Cutting and Harry Fraser. PHOTOGRAPHY: James S. Brown, Jr. EDITORS: Dwight Caldwell and Earl Turner. MUSIC DIRECTOR: Lee Zahler. SOUND: Tom Lambert. ASSISTANT DIRECTOR: Carl Hiecke. CAST: Warren Hull (Richard Wentworth/Blinky McQuade/The Spider), Mary Ainslee (Nita Van Sloan), Dave O'Brien (Jackson), Joseph W. Girard (Police Commissioner Kirk), Kenne Duncan (Ram Singh), Corbet Harris (McLeod/The Gargoyle), Bryant Washburn (Steve Westfall), Charles F. Miller (Mr. Van Sloan), Anthony Warde (Trigger), Harry Harvey (Stephen), Alden [Stephen] Chase (Jenkins), Dale Van Sickel (Taylor), Jack Mulhall, Tom London (Detectives), Lane Chandler (Fingerprint Expert), Jack Perrin (Armored Car Guard), Ruth Findlay (Secretary), Irving Mitchell (Holden), Lee Phelps (Mulligan), Stanley Blystone (Policeman), Kenneth Terrell (Cahill), George Chesebro, Steve Clark, George Larkin, Michael Vallon, Chuck Hamilton, Joe McGuinn, George Magrill (Gang Members), Arthur Belasco (Butler), Forrest Taylor (Voice of the Gargoyle).

CHAPTER TITLES: (1) The Stolen Plans; (2) The Fatal Time-Bomb; (3) The Secret Meeting; (4) The Smoke Dream; (5) The Gargoyle's Trail; (6) The X-Ray Eye; (7) The Radio Boomerang; (8) The Mysterious Message; (9) The Cup of Doom; (10) The X-Ray Belt; (11) Lips Sealed by Murder; (12) A Money Bomb; (13) Almost a Confession; (14) Suspicious Telegrams; (15) The Payoff.

Poster for *The Spider Returns* (1941).

Following the success of 1938's *The Spider's Web* (q.v.), Columbia made a sequel, *The Spider Returns*, issued in the spring of 1941. James W. Horne, who had co-directed the first outing with Ray Taylor, returned to helm this one solo. George H. Plympton was also back as one of the script writers. Warren Hull again starred in the title role and Kenne Duncan repeated his earlier character of Ram Singh, the hero's Hindu chauffeur. Like most of the cliffhangers that Larry Darmour produced for Columbia, and Horne directed, the chapterplay did not take itself very seriously, which upset some serial fans and amused others. At the time the production was released, the *Motion Picture Exhibitor* commented, "Columbia's latest serial has timeliness as its asset ... This should satisfy all the kids and action fans. It has plenty of chase episodes, gun-play, and occultism."

National defenses are being sabotaged by a gang of foreign agents led by the masked and cloaked fiend The Gargoyle. Socialite Richard Wentworth (Hull), alias The Spider, renews his battle with lawlessness. In his second guise as one-eyed hoodlum Blinky McQuade he learns of the fifth columnists' activities. He calls a meeting of the nation's most important industrialists but The Gargoyle's men use tear gas to break it up and kidnap Wentworth. At an airport he is knocked unconscious and placed aboard a plane which goes into the air with the pilot ejecting. Richard manages to get into a parachute and jump to safety before the plane crashes. At the airport he learns the locale of the madman's headquarters. Disguised as The Spider, he goes there but after a fight the saboteurs get away. Wentworth finds out that The Gargoyle plans to blow up a gas plant. At the plant The Spider is knocked out by the spies but escapes from an explosion they set only to be blamed for it by the police. Calling a meeting with defense work executives, including Holden (Irving Mitchell) and McLeod (Corbet Haris), Wentworth suggests they place their secret plans in a safe. He later follows the armored car taking the documents. The Gargoyle's henchmen try to hijack the car but Wentworth drives away in it only to be forced off the road and over a cliff by a heavy truck. After surviving the crash, he again becomes Blinky and, at the spies' headquarters, he learns of their plans to destroy Van Sloan's (Charles F. Miller) new airplane motor. The Spider tries to stop the sabotage at the motor's demonstration but is trapped inside the plant when the agents set off gas bombs. Unhurt, The Spider finds out that Van Sloan has been kidnapped. He goes to The Gargoyle's headquarters and sends in his aide Jackson (Dave O'Brien), who is apprehended. The Spider frees Jackson and has him take Van Sloan to a hospital. As he investigates the place he is trapped as the floor collapses and he slides into a bed of hot coals but uses his cape to stop the fall and then escapes. Blinky goes with the spies as they sabotage a defense plant and as The Spider he escapes in a truck but is nearly killed when he speeds toward a washed-out bridge.

Wentworth finds out that Police Commissioner Kirk (Joe Girard) plans to arrest members of the spy gang and as Blinky he warns The Gargoyle's men of the impending raid. When The Gargoyle refuses to meet with Blinky, who takes a radio from the hideout but as Wentworth he tries unsuccessfully to communicate with the madman. The Gargoyle sends his men to raid Wentworth's home and they kidnap his fiancée Nita Van Sloan (Mary Ainslee). When Wentworth tries to rescue her, he is knocked unconscious and tied to railroad tracks. Wentworth breaks his bonds in time to escape. Next he learns that The Gargoyle has demanded the plans to Van Sloan's new invention and threatens to torture Nita, the inventor's niece. When Van Sloan shows up with the documents, Blinky takes them. The Gargoyle imprisons the inventor and captures Wentworth. The trio are taken to a boat and nearly killed by a heavy crane but The Spider rescues Van Sloan and his niece. Wentworth concludes that The Gargoyle is really one of the defense plant executives. To trap the enemy agent he announces that Van Sloan's motor is being shipped by train for flying tests; The Spider stops the spies from stealing the invention. At an airport, The Spider takes the controls of the plane after recognizing the pilot as one of the enemy agents. The craft explodes in midair but the crime fighter survives. The Gargoyle becomes suspicious of Blinky and orders his man Trigger (Anthony Warde) to kill him. When Blinky tries to hide from the gang in a car trunk, the spies run the vehicle over a cliff but he manages to jump clear. The Gargoyle kidnaps Commissioner Kirk and demands a ransom from Wentworth, who takes bogus money to a waterfront dive. As The Spider he tries to rescue the police chief. Following the agents as they flee, The Spider escapes death when his motorboat explodes. The Gargoyle again kidnaps Nita and wants to exchange her for his henchman Trigger who has been arrested. Blinky serves as the go-between and takes Trigger to The Gargoyle's lair. As he starts to leave with Nita, three walls of knives and one of flames encroach on them but they are saved by the police. The Gargoyle abducts Nita, her uncle and three of the businessmen. As he attempts to kill them with poison gas, The Spider stops him and after a terrific fight rounds up the gang. He then unmasks The Gargoyle as McLeod.

The Spider's Web

(1938; 15 chapters) PRODUCER: Jack Fier. EXECUTIVE PRODUCER: Irving Briskin. DIRECTORS: Ray Taylor and James W. Horne. SCREENPLAY: Robert E. Kent, George H. Plympton, Basil Dickey and Martie Ransom. PHOTOGRAPHY: Allen G. Siegler. EDITOR: Richard Fantl. MUSIC DIRECTOR: Morris Stoloff. CAST: Warren Hull (Richard Wentworth/Blinky McQuade/The Spider), Iris Meredith (Nita Van Sloan), Richard Fiske (Jackson), Kenne Duncan (Ram Singh), Forbes Murray (Police Commissioner Kirk), Donald Douglas (Butler Jenkins), Charles C. Wilson (Chase), Marc Lawrence (Steve Harmon), John Tyrrell (Crafton), Beatrice Curtis (Kate Sands), Paul Whitney (Gray), Gene Anderson, Jr. (Johnnie Sands), Gordon Hart (J. Mason), Byron Foulger (Allen Roberts), Lane Chandler (Trigger), Nestor Paiva (Red), Al Ferguson, Robert Kortman (Mechanics),

Tom London (Bank Guard), Edmund Cobb (Police Dispatcher), Ann Doran (Secretary), Frank Bruno (Monk), Eddie Foster (Lefty), Lee Prather (Editor Morris), Eddie Featherstone (Tom), Gloria Blondell (Chase's Secretary), Beatrice Blinn (Adams' Stenographer), Bentley Hewlett (Joseph Crane), Stanley Mack (Nick), Chet Lynn (Florist Jim), Dick Curtis (Malloy), Lester Dorr (Frank Martin), Bob Perry (Tim Spencer), Dick Stanley (Steve), Ernie Adams (Beggar/Merkel), Roger Williams, Curley Dresden, Brooks Benedict (Drivers), Sam Ash (Ticket Clerk Dover), King Mojave (Mike), Edward LeSaint (Doctor), Harry Depp (Oswald), Ed Peil, Sr. (Officer Jones), Al Herman (Spike Malean), Johnny Sinclair (Writer), Rose Plummer, Anne Schaefer, Jessie Perry (Women at Bus Station), Richard Terry [Jack Perrin] (Intern), Al Klein (Saber), Edward Earle (J.R. Adams), Steve Clark (Masked Gang Member), Edward Hearn (Desk Sergeant), Harry Myers, Charles Sherlock (Detectives), John Roy (Chemist), Lee Shumway (Police Sergeant), Gene Stone (Cashman), Harry Tenbrook, Jimmie Baker, Ed Randolph (Powerhouse Employees), Francis Walker, Cap Severn (Farm Couple), Bruce Mitchell, William Witney, Frank O'Connor, Carl Faulkner, Jack Richardson, Charles McMurphy (Policemen), James Carlisle (Fire Department Captain), Sidney D'Albrook (Spike), Kernan Cripps (Officer Mullvaney), Lew Meehan (Burke), Dick Dickinson (Bus Customer), Tony Merlo, Jack Hennessy (Chauffeurs), William Worthington (Canton), Harry A. Bailey (Dr. Gaylord), Harry Bernard (Watchman), Harry Hollingsworth (Police Inspector), Roy Brent (Ted), Ralph Brooks (Chambers), Russell Heustis (James), Buel Bryant (Airport Policeman), Jack Harvey (Marvin), Lew Caits (Blade), Chuck Hamilton (Gorman), Harry Cornell (Brownie), Bill Gavier (Louis), Lew Davis (Harry Stone), Art Dupuis (Radio Operator), Dick Durrell (Charlie Dennis), Jerry Jerome (Sparks), Cy Schindell (Cadman), Bud Marshall (Police Dispatcher), Cyril Ring (Henry Blake), Ralph McCullough (Motorist), Gus Reed (Frank), Wedgwood Newell (Allen), Claude Peyton (Radarez), Dick Scott (Joe), Reginald Simpson (Gordon), Tom Steele (Bank Robber), Larry Wheat (Carter), Henry Taylor (Wilson), Victor Travers (Benefit Director), Jack Gardner (Reporter), Malcolm "Bud" McTaggart (Elevator Boy), Harry Cornell (Brownie), Reed Howes, Dirk Thane, Frank Hagney, Bud Geary, Kit Guard, Earle Bunn, Bing Connolly, Roger Gray, Charles Haefeli, George De Normand, George Hoey, Dick Jensen, Al Rhein, Ray Johnson, Charles Phillips, Sam Lufkin, Frank Mills, Jack Lowe, Ed McCabe, Bill Patton, Joe Palma, Walter Stiritz, George Turner, Joe Sully (Gang Members), Bess Flowers (Carlotta Cobb).

CHAPTER TITLES: (1) Night of Terror; (2) Death Below; (3) High Voltage; (4) Surrender or Die; (5) Shoot to Kill; (6) Sealed Lips; (7) Shadows of the Night; (8) While the City Sleeps; (9) Doomed; (10) Flaming Danger; (11) The Road to Peril; (12) The Spider Falls; (13) The Man Hunt; (14) The Double Cross; (15) The Octopus Unmasked.

The crime fighter The Spider first appeared in *The Spider*, a pulp magazine, in 1933 in popular monthly novelettes written by Grant Stockbridge (Norvell Page). Columbia acquired the rights to the character and filmed *The Spider's Web*, a serial issued in the fall of 1938. It contained one of the largest casts of character actors ever assembled for a cliffhanger and also some interesting casting twists in that usual villains Kenne Duncan and Richard Fiske played the hero's aides rather than his nemeses. At the time of its release, the *Motion Picture Exhibitor* wrote, "The first two episodes reveal a smashing action serial, with more thugs being killed in five reels than most in most other complete serials. In addition to the blood, action, it has good production, fast pace, with Warren Hull a very convincing hero." The chapterplay's success resulted in the sequel *The Spider Returns* (q.v.) three years later.

When a crime wave grips his city, Police Commissioner Kirk (Forbes Murray) asks for help from noted criminologist Richard Wentworth (Warren Hull), who refuses because he plans to marry Nita Van Sloan (Iris Meredith). The Octopus, a masked and robed madman who plans to control the country's transportation system, tries to get Wentworth out of the way by causing his plane to crash. After fighting with some of the evildoer's henchmen, Richard has Nita leave town with his trusted servant Ram Singh (Duncan). Taking on the guise of underworld denizen Blinky McQuade, Wentworth visits a number of dives and learns that The Octopus plans to blow up a passenger bus. Wentworth then becomes The Spider, who fights the saboteurs and drives off in the bus which explodes. The Spider is blamed by the police for the attack. Trying to avoid capture by both the madman and the law, The Spider continues his fight against the master criminal, who has kidnapped Nita and his aide Jackson (Fiske). As Blinky, he learns that a secret radio tube in the possession of a person he suspects is The Octopus. He traces the tube manufacturer to a building where messages from the outlaw gang have emanated. Wentworth sets off smoke bombs that bring the fire department as The Spider uses one of their ladders to get into the building. Locating the gang's headquarters, the spider and the evil one have a shootout with The Octopus being killed. The Spider removes the mask from the dead man, revealing banker Chase (Charles C. Wilson). Wentworth sets Nita and Jackson free as he and his fiancée plan to carry on with their wedding plans.

Superman

(1948; 15 chapters) PRODUCER: Sam Katzman. DIRECTORS: Spencer Gordon Bennet and Thomas Carr. SCREENPLAY: Arthur Hoerl, Lewis Clay and Royal K. Cole. ADAPTATION: George H. Plympton and Joseph F. Poland. PHOTOGRAPHY: Ira H. Morgan. EDITOR: Earl Turner. MUSIC DIRECTOR: Mischa Bakaleinikoff. ART DIRECTOR: Paul Palmentola. SOUND: Josh Westmoreland and Phillip Faulkner. SETS: Sidney Clifford. ASSISTANT DIRECTOR: R.M. Andrews. CAST: Kirk Alyn (Clark Kent/Superman), Noel Neill (Lois Lane), Tommy Bond (Jimmy Olsen), Carol Forman (The Spider Lady), George Meeker (Driller), Jack Ingram (Anton), Pierre Watkin (Perry White), Terry Frost (Brock), Charles Quigley (Dr. Hackett), Herbert Rawlinson (Dr. Arnold Graham), Forrest Taylor (Professor Arnold Leeds), Stephen Carr (Morgan), Charles King (Conrad), Rusty Wescoatt (Elton), Nelson Leigh (Jor-El), Luana Walters (Lara), Robert Barron (Ro-Zon), Ed Cassidy (Eben Kent), Virginia Carroll (Martha Kent), Alan Dinehart III (Clark Kent as a Boy), Ralph Hodges (Clark Kent as a Teenager), Jack George (Railroad Man), Gene Roth (Train Conductor Carson), Peggy Wynne (Switchboard Operator Gloria), Frank Ellis (Mine Security Guard), Rube Schaefer (Grady), Stanley Price (Crandall), Paul Stader (Irwin), Reed Howes (Jackson), Leonard Penn (Ward), Wheeler Oakman (Dr. Frederick Larkin), Edmund Cobb (Mechanic), Emmett Vogan (National Security Secretary), I. Stanford Jolley (Sheriff), Frank Lackteen (Hawkins), Frank O'Connor (Fire Chief Forman), Wally West (State Trooper), Jimmie Aubrey (Wave Tracer), George DeNormand (Crandall's Agent), William Fawcett (Fake News Hawk), Eddie Parker (Truck Driver), Tom London (Pop Andrews), Phil Arnold (Taxi Cab Driver), Jack Chefe (Dupe), Fred Aldrich (Museum Policeman), Eddie Foster (Fred Collier), Al Wyatt, Frank Hagney (Gang Members), Bert Stevens (Station Helper), Chuck Hamilton (Prison Guard), Charles Sherlock (Newspaper Employee), George Magrill (Bank Robber), Knox Manning (Narrator).

CHAPTER TITLES: (1) Superman Comes to Earth; (2) Depths of the Earth; (3) The Reducer Ray; (4) Man of Steel; (5) A Job for Superman; (6) Superman in Danger; (7) Into the Electrical Furnace; (8) Superman to the Rescue; (9) Irresistible Force; (10) Between Two Fires; (11) Superman's Dilemma; (12) Blast in the Depths; (13) Hurled to Destruction; (14) Superman at Bay; (15) The Payoff.

Written by Jerry Seigel and drawn by Joe Shuster, the character of Superman was first seen in *Action Comics* in 1938 (and later in *Superman* comics) and for the next two years it was broadcast on a trial basis in different parts of the country before debuting on the Mutual network in February 1942. The radio series *The Adventures of Su-*

Emmett Vogan (seated left), Herbert Rawlinson (seated center with white hair) and Kirk Alyn as Superman (1948) (others unknown).

perman starred Bud Collyer in the title role, a part he would play until 1950 when Michael Fitzgerald took over when the series switched to ABC, where it concluded its run in March 1951. From 1949 to 1954 there was also an Australian version of *The Adventures of Superman* starring Leonard Teale. Collyer also provided the voice of Superman in 19 cartoons made by Fleischer Studios and released by Paramount between 1941 and 1943. After several years of haggling among various studios, the character came to the big screen in 1948 with Sam Kazman's production of *Superman* starring Kirk Alyn as the Man of Steel and his alter ego, newspaperman Clark Kent. Alyn, leading lady Noel Neill and Pierre Watkin, who played editor Perry White, all had journalism backgrounds. The cliffhanger was a good one and very popular with audiences. Its main weakness was that when Superman was called on to fly, he became a cartoon character, a cost-cutting device that cheapened the look of the production.

Following the storyline set forth in the *Superman* comics, the serial begins on the doomed planet Krypton where scientist Jor-El (Nelson Leigh) and his wife Lara (Luana Walters) fear for their infant as their world is being drawn into its sun. To save the boy, the scientist places him in a rocket and sends it to Earth where the infant is found by farmer Eben Kent (Ed Cassidy) and his wife Martha (Virginia Carroll) who adopt him and name him Clark. As he grows up, the boy (Alan Dinehart III) realizes he has powers that others his age do not have and as a teenager (Ralph Hodges) he attains great strength, speed, x-ray vision and feels no pain. Having grown into manhood, Clark Kent (Alyn) goes to Metropolis where as Superman he saves reporter Lois Lane (Neill) and cameraman Jimmy Olsen (Tommy Bond) when their train is nearly derailed by twisted tracks. Going to the *Daily Planet* newspaper, Kent is given a writing job by editor Perry White (Watkin) and learns that the city is being besieged by the evil Spider Lady (Carol Forman) and her henchmen Driller (George Meeker), Anton (Jack Ingram), Brock (Terry Frost), Conrad (Charles King), Elton (Rusty Wescoatt) and the corrupt Dr. Hackett (Charles Quigley). Kent and Lois are nearly trapped in a mine cave-in but Superman comes to their rescue. As Kent interviews scientist Professor Leeds (Forrest Taylor), he collapses after being exposed to a meteor that contains Kryptonite, the one element that can disable the Man of Steel. The Spider Lady finds out about the radioactive material and sets out to obtain it in order to get rid of her nemesis. She also wants to get a revolutionary disintegrating gun called the Reducer Ray which she forces Dr. Graham (Herbert Rawlinson) to perfect. Lois and Jimmy are nearly killed in a number of additional ways, including electrocution, being burned alive and in a runaway car, but are always saved by Superman. The Spider Lady bombards Superman with the ray gun and Kryptonite but he deflects the Reducer Ray and, thanks to a lead lining in his costume, he is now immune to the alien element. The ray machine explodes, killing The Spider Lady and her gang.

Location filming for this chapterplay took place at Bronson Canyon in Griffith Park, Lone Pine and the Iverson Ranch in Chatsworth. Jim Harmon and Donald F. Glut wrote in *The Great Movie Serials: Their Sound and Fury* (1972), "Despite the flaws in special effects, the cast and director managed to make the whole thing come off. The serial became a tremendous financial success, playing first-run theatres that had never before booked a serial." Some sources claim that *Superman* was the top-grossing cliffhanger of all time. Its success led to Columbia filming a sequel, *Atom Man vs. Superman* (q.v.), in 1950.

Terry and the Pirates

(1940; 15 chapters) PRODUCER: Larry Darmour. DIRECTOR: James W. Horne. SCREENPLAY: Mark Layton, George Morgan and Joseph Levering. PHOTOGRAPHY: James S. Brown, Jr. EDITORS: Dwight Caldwell and Earl Turner. MUSIC: Lee Zahler. CAST: William Tracy (Terry Lee), Granville Owen [Jeff York] (Pat Ryan), Joyce Bryant (Normandie Drake), Allen Jung (Connie), Victor De Camp (Big Stoop), Sheila Darcy (The Dragon Lady), Dick Curtis (Master Fang), J. Paul Jones (Dr. Herbert Lee), Forrest Taylor (Mr. Drake), Jack Ingram (Stanton), Kit Guard (Borden), Charles King (Blackie), Eddie Featherston (Thompson), Constantine Romanoff (Krench), Jack Perrin (Mr. Harris), Louis Vincenot (Gori), Harry Harvey (Talman), John Ince (High Priest), Cy Schindell (Morgan), Jack O'Shea (Guard/Gang Member), Chuck Hamilton (Hayes).

CHAPTER TITLES: (1) Into the Great Unknown; (2) The Fang Strikes; (3) The Mountain of Death; (4) The Dragon Queen Threatens; (5) At the Mercy of the Mob; (6) The Scroll of Wealth; (7) Angry Waters; (8) The Tomb of Peril; (9) Jungle Hurricane; (10) Too Many Enemies; (11) Walls of Doom; (12) No Escape; (13) The Fatal Mistake; (14) Pyre of Death; (15) The Secret of the Temple.

After making *The Shadow* (1940) [q.v.], Columbia again turned to a radio series for cliff-

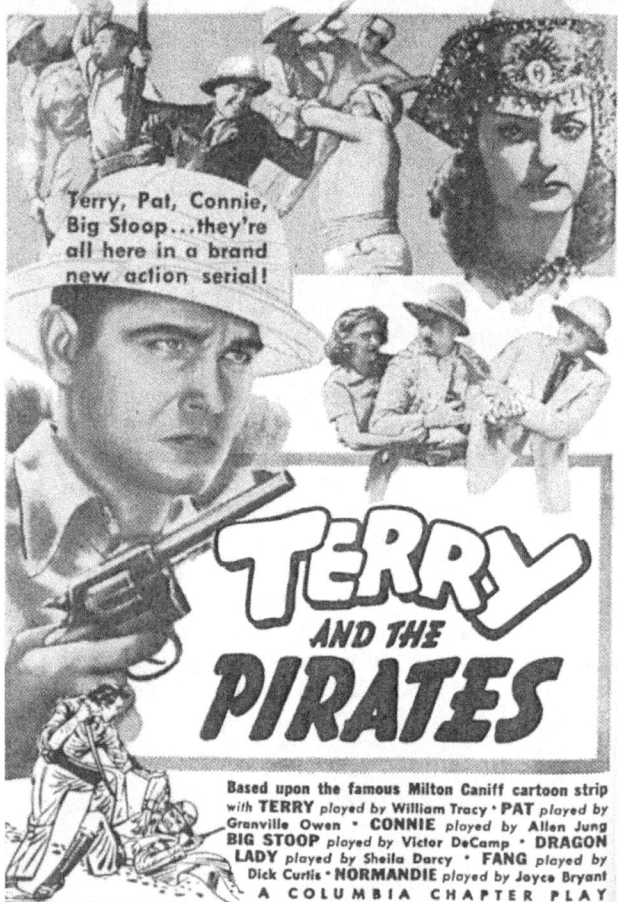

Poster for *Terry and the Pirates* (1940).

hanger material and issued *Terry and the Pirates* in the spring of 1940. Originally a newspaper comic first written by Milton Caniff in 1934, "Terry and the Pirates" came to radio in 1937 on NBC's Red network before being broadcast on the NBC Blue network during the 1938–39 season. After a two-year hiatus, the program resumed out of WGN in Chicago as a weekday show from 1941 to 1943; it continued in that format when broadcast on ABC from 1943 to 1948. Among the actors to portray leading character Terry Lee were Jackie Kelk, Cliff Carpenter, Owen Jordan and Bill Fein. Regarding the chapterplay, Alan G. Barbour in *Cliffhanger: A Pictorial History of the Motion Picture Serial* (1977) called it an "exciting and humorous film" but complained that director James W. Horne "found it impossible to do a straight serial without having his actors 'ham' up their dialogue and overreact (as though they were in a silent movie) with exaggerated gestures."

Arriving in the Asiatic outpost of Wingpoo, teenager Terry Lee (William Tracy) and Pat Ryan (Granville Owen), Terry's father's assistant, are bringing important documents needed by the young man's father, archaeologist Dr. Herbert Lee (J. Paul Jones). Dr. Lee is leading an expedition investigating a lost civilization and is being opposed by Fang (Dick Curtis), a half-caste warlord who rules the area and wants a treasure hidden underneath a remote jungle temple of the god Mara. Opposing Fang is the Dragon Lady (Sheila Darcy) and her followers, worshippers of Mara. At the trading post in Wingpoo, Terry and Pat meet with hostility and only find friendship with trader Allen Drake (Forrest Taylor) and his daughter Normandie (Joyce Bryant). When Terry is attacked by a gorilla, Pat drives off the creature but the documents are stolen. Fang's henchmen ambush Dr. Lee's expedition. Terry and Pat, along with Connie (Allen Jung), a Chinese servant, and Big Stoop (Victor De Camp), a tall street magician, trek into the jungle in search of the explorers. That night the safari is attacked by Fang's Tiger Men but Terry and Pat manage to escape. Fang asks Dr. Lee to translate a native inscription and he reveals that it predicts an era of happiness when Mara speaks. When Fang informs Dr. Lee he will never see his son again unless he helps him find the treasure, the archaeologist runs away.

Terry and Pat return to Wingpoo where a huge gorilla carries off Normandie. When Tiger Men attack Terry, Pat and Drake, Connie and Big Stoop frighten them away with firecrackers and the five men set out to rescue the young woman. Led by its keeper Gori (Louis Vincenot), the gorilla carries Normandie to the slope of a volcano but it erupts and they are trapped in the debris. Dr. Lee arrives to see his daughter taken behind a stone door and is then recaptured by Stanton (Jack Ingram), one of Fang's henchmen. Terry and Pat rescue the girl, and the three trek to the Temple of the Dawn to enlist the aid of the

Dragon Lady. When they stop a human sacrifice, they are sentenced to death. Connie and Big Stoop save them but the Dragon Lady nearly has the party executed. They are saved when Stanton and the Tiger Men arrive to steal the statue of Mara. Terry and Pat escape but are later apprehended by the locals and charged with taking the statue. When Normandie goes to help them, she falls into a tiger trap and is again attacked by the gorilla. Gori saves the girl. When Terry and Pat arrive, Gori uses the gorilla to capture them and they are taken to Fang. As the despot attempts to torture Terry, Big Stoop comes to his rescue and aids Terry, Pat and Dr. Lee in making a getaway. When they offer to help the Dragon Lady recover the statue, she sends Dr. Lee with some followers to do this but holds Terry, Pat and Normandie as hostages. Renegades ambush the expedition. The Dragon Lady orders Normandie killed by a descending sword but Pat saves her with a hand grenade. They escape through a wall opening but the girl is recaptured. The high priest of Mara (John Ince) proclaims that Normandie must be sacrificed to appease his god but Terry and Pat disguise themselves as guards and free the young woman.

Fang finds a scroll inside the idol. Fang places a phonograph inside the head of the idol to make it talk. Terry and Pat discover this but the warlord's henchmen force them into an underground passage that fills with water. Pat manages to release a lever controlling the water and he and Terry escape and find Dr. Lee, who refuses to leave before again getting the scroll. Fang and his henchmen go to return to the idol to its temple and Terry and Pat, disguised as Tiger Men, join them. When Fang makes the idol talk, the natives bow to his supremacy and the Tiger Lady is forced to flee with Terry and Pat through a secret exit. Lee falls into a deep pit and is attacked by an alligator. Pat kills the giant reptile with his knife and the Dragon Lady helps them out of the pit. She then goes to Fang and agrees to reveal the treasure's location if he and his henchmen leave the temple. As the gorilla guards the Dragon Lady, the high priest takes Fang and Stanton into the catacombs beneath the temple. Terry and Pat rescue the priestess.

Normandie, Connie and Big Stoop are captured by Fang's henchmen. A hurricane blows up as Lee and the girl manage to cling to a cliff. The henchmen capture Drake and try to drown him in a vat of molten rubber; he recognizes one of them as a business rival, Thompson (Eddie Fetherston). Terry and Pat save Drake but natives set fire to the trader's home. Lee, Pat and Normandie go to the authorities for help but their speedboat is blown up by their enemies. Terry, Pat and Normandie attempt to contact the authorities by breaking into a radio station in Thompson's store. They are overpowered by Stanton and his men but manage to escape and set out to find Dr. Lee at the ancient temple, not knowing he has gone with the key to the scroll. Using radio parts he finds in the temple, Terry plans to make the statue of Mara speak in favor of the Dragon Lady but he and Pat are thrown into a torture room by the Tiger Men. Using a pipe to prevent the closing walls from crushing them, Terry and Pat escape and imprison their enemies. Terry and Pat disguise themselves as Tiger Men and join an expedition to the Temple of the Dawn. Fang picks them to guard the statue of Mara. When the disguises are removed, the two fight back but are caught in a barrage of hand grenades. They escape and head to Fang's headquarters where Pat is knocked unconscious but is saved by Terry. The duo trek to the ancient temple and are met by Dr. Lee, Connie and Big Stoop. The two women are captured by the Tiger Men. After escaping from an explosion set by the renegades, Terry and Pat go to the Dragon Lady's villa. Dr. Lee, Connie and Big Stoop are captured by the Tiger Men and taken to Fang, who also holds Normandie and the Dragon Lady. When Fang orders the women searched, Dr. Lee shoves him into the grasp of the gorilla. As Gori struggles to control the beast, the Dragon Lady disappears through a secret passage. She goes back to her villa and meets with Terry and Pat. The Tiger Men attack them and carry off the scroll. The Dragon Lady, Terry and Pat rescue Dr. Lee and Normandie and the five go to a hidden room where the Golden Hand of Mara points the way to the treasure. The Tiger Men attack them but Terry escapes as the others are bound to a lighted funeral pyre. Using a powderkeg to scare off the renegades, Terry saves the others as Pat, pretending to be the voice of Mara, informs the high priest and his people of Fang's treachery. As the natives go after Stanton, Fang learns some of his henchmen have found the treasure of Mara, a huge diamond, and he kills them in order to get possession of the gem. When Fang murders Gori, the gorilla breaks free from its chains and crushes the warlord. Pat gives the diamond to the Dragon Lady who again becomes the high priestess of Mara. She then passes the gem to Dr. Lee and also gives him access to the history of her people.

Terry and the Pirates came to television on the DuMont network in 1952. William Tracy, who played Terry Lee in the Columbia serial, co-starred as the hero's pal, Hotshot Charlie, while John Baer portrayed Terry Lee and Gloria Saunders was the Dragon Lady.

The Vigilante

(1947; 15 chapters) PRODUCER: Sam Katzman. DIRECTOR: Wallace Fox. SCREENPLAY: George H. Plympton, Lewis Clay and Arthur Hoerl. PHOTOGRAPHY: Ira H. Morgan. EDITOR: Earl Turner. MUSIC DIRECTOR: Mischa Bakaleinikoff. ART DIRECTOR: Paul Palmentola. SETS: George Montgomery. PRODUCTION MANAGER: Herbert Leonard. SPECIAL EFFECTS: Ray Mercer. ASSISTANT DIRECTOR: Mike Eason. CAST: Ralph Byrd (Greg Sanders/The Vigilante), Ramsay Ames (Betty Winslow), Lyle Talbot (George Pierce/X-1), George Offerman, Jr. (Stuff), Robert Barron (Prince Amil), Hugh Prosser (Captain Riley), Jack Ingram (Silver/X-2), Eddie Parker (Doc/X-3), Bill Brauer (Thorne/X-9), George Chesebro (Walt), Edmund Cobb (Miller/X-7), Frank Merlo (Rabin), John Fostine (Azar), Frank Ellis (Sadlow/X-8), Terry Frost (Lefty/X-4), Ted Mapes (Tex Collier), Wally West (Stagecoach Driver Scar), Ted Adams (Hamid), Al Ferguson (Stolen Car Ring Boss), Bud Osborne (Waldron), Wallace Fox (Movie Director Sid), Lane Bradford (Andy), Emmett Lynn (Pop), Rusty Wescoatt (Blacksmith Garrity), Pierre Lyden (Merk), Jack Chefe (Headwaiter Andre), Bob Duncan, Baynes Barron (Policemen), Al Wyatt, Tex Palmer (Movie Henchmen), George DeNormand (Rocky/Barker Jackson/Driver), Knox Manning (Narrator).
CHAPTER TITLES: (1) The Vigilante Rides Again; (2) Mystery of the White Horses; (3) Double Peril; (4) Desperate Flight; (5) In the Gorilla's Cage; (6) Battling the Unknown; (7) Midnight Rendezvous; (8) Blasted to Eternity; (9) The Fatal Flood; (10) Danger Ahead; (11) X-1 Closes In; (12) Death Rides the Rail; (13) The Trap That Failed; (14) Closing In; (15) The Secret of the Skyroom.

Based on the *Action Comics* character, the serial *The Vigilante* had as its title character a motorcycle-riding government undercover agent who masquerades as a western film star. Ralph Byrd, a veteran cliffhanger and action star best known for playing Dick Tracy in serials, features and on television, played the role. The part afforded him a chance to sing "Saturday Night in San Antone" in the initial episode. An inside joke had the chapterplay's director, Wallace Fox, cast as a movie director during the filming of a western starring the Vigilante's alter-ego, Greg Sanders. While *The Vigilante* was a modern-day western, the film's plot was reworked as an all-out oater in the studio's 1951 cliffhanger *Roar of the Iron Horse* (q.v.). *The Vigilante*'s genre connection is the search for the "100 tears of blood," a cursed string of pearls whose origins are shrouded in the mists of time.

Although he is known to the world as a cowboy film star, Greg Sanders (Byrd) works as an government undercover agent called The Vigilante. He and his assistant Stuff (George Offerman, Jr.) are assigned to masquerade as guests of rich rancher George Pierce (Lyle Talbot) while locating a set of red pearls called the "100 tears of blood." Also at the ranch are beautiful rodeo rider Betty Winslow (Ramsay Ames), Arabian potentate Prince Amil (Robert Barron) and his assistant Hamid (Ted Adams), sheriff's squad member Captain Reilly (Hugh Prosser), and rancher Tex Collier (Ted Mapes). Pierce is really X-1, the leader of a gang out to steal the pearls. As the government agent investigates the case, several attempts are made to eliminate the ranch guests (Pierce suspects that one or more of them may possess the valuables). Sanders learns from Prince Amil that Hamid took the pearls and has come under their curse. The tears of blood are hidden in the hooves of five stallions that belong to the ranch visitors. Working with Hamid, The Vigilante comes to suspect that Pierce and his men are behind a series of crimes related to the pearls. When the ranch owner tries to make a getaway with the tears of blood, he is killed. To rid the world of the pearls' curse, Prince Amil and Hamid destroy them with acid.

Who's Guilty?

(1945; 15 chapters) PRODUCER: Sam Katzman. DIRECTORS: Howard Bretherton and Wallace Grissell. SCREENPLAY: Ande Lamb and George H. Plympton. PHOTOGRAPHY: Ira H. Morgan. EDITOR: Earl Turner. MUSIC: Lee Zahler. ART DIRECTOR: Paul Palmentola. PRODUCTION MANAGER: Melville De Lay. CAST: Robert Kent (Bob Stewart), Amelita Ward (Ruth Allen), Tim Ryan (Duke Ellis), Jayne Hazard (Rita Royle), Minerva Urecal (Mrs. Dill), Charles Middleton (Patton/Walter Calvert), Davison Clark (Henry Calvert), Sam Flint (Horace Black), Bruce Donovan (Curt Bennett), Jack Ingram (Sergeant Smith), Milton Kibbee (Morgan Calvert), Nacho Galindo (Pancho), Roberto Tafur (Jose), Wheeler Oakman (Smiley), Charles King (Burke), Anthony Warde (Edwards), Belle Mitchell (Sara Caldwell).
CHAPTER TITLES: (1) Avenging Visitor; (2) The Unknown Strikes; (3) Held for Murder; (4) A Killer at Bay; (5) Human Bait; (6) The Plunge of Doom; (7) A Date with Fate; (8) Invisible Hands; (9) Fate's Vengeance;

(10) The Unknown Killer; (11) Riding to Oblivion; (12) The Tank of Terror; (13) White Terror; (14) A Cry in the Night; (15) The Guilty One.

Detective Bob Stewart (Robert Kent) is hired to investigate the mysterious death of Henry Calvert (Davison Clark), who was killed in an automobile wreck. Hiding at a remote and spooky mansion, Henry is visited by his brother Walter (Charles Middleton), who wants his share of the family's wealth. When Henry refuses his request, Walter warns that he will get rid of his brother and get all the fortune for himself. Accompanied by newspaper reporter Duke Ellis (Tim Ryan), Bob goes to the old house where he meets Ruth Allen (Amelita Ward), whose father was a business partner of Henry Calvert. Also there are the dead man's sister Mrs. Dill (Minerva Urecal), his half-brother Morgan Calvert (Milton Kibbee), his nephew Curt Bennett (Bruce Donovan) and his fiancée Rita Royle (Jayne Hazard), and the butler, Patton (who is actually Walter, pretending to be the butler). A mysterious figure called The Voice attempts to kill off the various relatives. Bob, who is attracted to Ruth, teams with her in trying to unmask the phantom killer. When Bob proves that Henry is still alive and in league with Walter to murder all the other relatives and divide the estate among themselves, Henry, who is really The Voice, tries to murder Bob. He is accidentally shot by Patton, who is revealed to be Walter Calvert. With the two homicidal siblings out of the way, the rest of the family members divide the estate.

Filmed at Corriganville, *Who's Guilty?*, a reworking of Columbia's earlier cliffhanger *The Iron Claw* (1941) [q.v.], was released late in 1945. It was one of the few Columbia serials to be shown in Great Britain as a feature film.

Short Subjects

All Gummed Up

(1947; 18 minutes) Producer-Director: Jules White. Story-Screenplay: Felix Adler. Photography: Allen Siegler. Editor: Edwin Bryant. Art Director: Charles Clague. Cast: The Three Stooges [Moe Howard, Larry Fine, Shemp Howard] (Themselves), Christine McIntyre (Serena Flint), Emil Sitka (Amos Flint), Cy Schindell (Prescription Customer), Florence Lake (Light Bulb Customer), Victor Travers (Bubble Gum Customer), Al Thompson (Fountain Pen Customer), Symona Boniface (Mother-in-Law).

The Three Stooges (themselves) operate the Cut Throat Drug Store but their miser landlord, Amos Flint (Emil Sitka), plans to evict them. He also deserts his wife Serena (Christine McIntyre) because she has become old. The Stooges let her live in their spare room. The trio concoct a vitamin formula that restores Cerina's youth. When Amos sees her, he signs the store over to the Stooges on the condition they give him the potion. They overestimate the formula and cause Flint to revert to childhood. To celebrate her recovered youth, Cerina bakes a cake but instead of decorating it with marshmallows, Shemp accidentally uses bubble gum. The Stooges remade the short in 1953 as *Bubble Trouble* (q.v.).

In 1934 the trio, then consisting of brothers Moe and Jerry "Curly" Howard and Larry Fine, joined the Columbia short subjects department; they became the company's most popular and long-lasting stars of two-reel comedies. The Stooges made 190 Columbia shorts between 1934 and 1959 with a third Howard brother, Samuel "Shemp," taking over when Curly suffered a stroke in 1946. Shemp died in 1955 and was replaced by Joe Besser.

All Work and No Pay

(1942; 16 minutes) Producers: Del Lord and Hugh McCollum. Director: Del Lord. Screenplay: Monte Collins and Elwood Ullman. Photography: George Meehan. Editor: Burton Kramer. Cast: Andy Clyde (Himself), Frank Lackteen, Duke York (Jewel Thieves), Eddie Laughton (Billings), Vernon Dent (A.B. Glass), John Tyrrell (Captain), Bud Jamison (Jackson), Blanche Payson (Newsstand Woman), Johnny Kascier (Gorilla).

A native of Scotland, Andy Clyde starred in over 50 comedy short subjects for Mack Sennett between 1929 and 1932 before making 14 more comedies for Education between 1932 and 1934. In 1935 he joined the Columbia short subject roster and for the next 21 years he headlined more than 70 two-reelers for the studio.

Released in the summer of 1942, *All Work and No Pay* had Andy as a security guard who finds out that thieves (Frank Lackteen, Duke York) have lifted a valuable gem from a vault. When they head for a ship he follows, not realizing the vessel houses a wild gorilla (Johnny Kascier).

Bedlam in Paradise

(1955; 16 minutes) Producer-Director: Jules White. Screenplay: Felix Adler and Zion Myers. Photography: Paul Cory. Editor: Paul Borofsky. Art Director: Carl Anderson. Assistant Director: Jerrold Bernstein. Cast: The Three Stooges [Moe Howard, Larry Fine, Shemp Howard] (Themselves), Philip Van Zandt (The Devil/Mr. Heller), Vernon Dent (I. Fleecem), Victor Travers (Mr. De Puyster), Symona Boniface (Mrs. De Puyster), Marti Shelton (Miss Jones), Sylvia Lewis (Helen Blazes), Judy Malcolm (Celestial Switchboard Girl).

A remake of 1949's *Heavenly Daze* (q.v.), and made up mostly of footage from that two-reeler, *Bedlam in Paradise* had Shemp (Shemp Howard) on his deathbed with hoof and heart disease. At the Pearly Gates he meets his Uncle Mortimer (Moe Howard), who informs him that he will not be admitted until he reforms his pals Moe (also Moe Howard) and Larry (Larry Fine). Crooked lawyer Fleecem (Vernon Dent) reads Shemp's will to Moe and Larry and it leaves them $140 which he takes for his fee. Disguised as Mr. Heller (Philip Van Zandt), the Devil entices the boys to swindle a couple (Victor Travers, Symona Boniface) out of $50,000 by selling them a bogus fountain pen that will write under whipped cream. Shemp throws a monkey wrench into the pen's demonstration and then wakes up with his bed on fire from smoking (it was all a dream).

A Bird in the Head

(1946; 16 minutes) PRODUCER: Hugh McCollum. DIRECTOR-SCREENPLAY: Edward Bernds. PHOTOGRAPHY: Burnett Guffey. EDITOR: Henry Batista. ART DIRECTOR: Charles Clague. CAST: The Three Stooges [Moe Howard, Larry Fine, Curly Howard] (Themselves), Vernon Dent (Professor Panzer), Robert Williams (Mr. Beedle), Frank Lackteen (Nikko), Art Miles (Igor the Ape).

Wallpaper hangers Moe (Moe Howard), Larry (Larry Fine) and Curly (Curly Howard) are hired by Mr. Beedle (Robert Williams) to redecorate a room in the home of Professor Panzer (Vernon Dent), who with his assistant Nikko (Frank Lackteen) wants to put a human brain in the head of an ape (Art Miles). When the boys louse up the job, Beedle fires them. Panzer hires them to work for him since he wants to place Curly's brain into the ape's head. The ape befriends Curly and shoots up the professor's laboratory with a machine gun.

A Bird in the Head was the first of 33 Three Stooges shorts Edward Bernds directed for Columbia, although it was the second to be filmed, following *Microphonies* (1945), which was issued ahead of it.

Boobs in the Night

(1943; 16 minutes) PRODUCER: Jules White. DIRECTOR: Del Lord. SCREENPLAY: Elwood Ullman. CAST: El Brendel (Himself), Monte Collins (Monty), Charles Middleton (Mad Scientist), Frank Lackteen (Assistant).

Home Defense workers El Brendel (himself) and Monty (Monte Collins) investigate a spooky old house and find a mad scientist (Charles Middleton) and his assistant (Frank Lackteen) needing a human head to perfect a mechanical man they have constructed. This was remade as The Three Stooges' 1950 comedy *Dopey Dicks* (q.v.).

Bubble Trouble

(1953; 17 minutes) PRODUCER-DIRECTOR: Jules White. SCREENPLAY: Felix Adler and Jack White. PHOTOGRAPHY: Ray Cory. EDITOR: Edwin Bryant. ART DIRECTOR: Cary Odell. ASSISTANT DIRECTOR: James Nicholson. CAST: The Three Stooges [Moe Howard, Larry Fine, Shemp Howard] (Themselves), Emil Sitka (Amos Flint), Christine McIntyre (Serena Flint), Victor Travers (Bubble Gum Customer).

Moe (Moe Howard), Larry (Larry Fine) and Curly (Curly Howard) operate the Cut Throat Drug Store but their mean landlord, Amos Flint (Emil Sitka), plans to evict them so he can sell out to the Pinch Penny Market. He also rejects his wife Serena (Christine McIntyre) because she has grown old. After the boys develop a youth formula, Serena becomes young again and celebrates by making a cake which Shemp accidentally decorates with bubble gum instead of marshmallows. When Amos sees Serena he offers to deed the store to the Stooges if they give him their formula. The elixir turns the old man into a rampaging gorilla. After he is subdued, Moe accidentally swallows the stuff and reverts to a simian.

The short gets most of its footage from the 1947 release *All Gummed Up* (q.v.) with new scenes making up only the last few minutes of the production.

Creeps

(1956; 16 minutes) PRODUCER-DIRECTOR: Jules White. SCREENPLAY: Felix Adler and Jules White. PHOTOGRAPHY: Henry Freulich. EDITOR: Harold White. ART DIRECTOR: Ross Bellah. ASSISTANT DIRECTOR: Eddie Saeta. CAST: The Three Stooges [Moe Howard, Larry Fine, Shemp Howard] (Themselves), Phil Arnold (Voice of Sir Tom the Knight).

A remake of *The Ghost Talks* (1949) [q.v.], this short opens with Moe (Moe Howard), Larry (Larry Fine) and Shemp (Shemp Howard) telling their infant sons a bedtime story. In it the trio are express movers who are hired to empty out an old castle where they find a suit of armor that houses the invisible ghost of a knight, Sir Tom (voice of Phil Arnold). The spirit tells the boys he does not want to be moved because unscrupulous antique dealers plan to sell his armor and that bad luck will pursue them if they carry out their job. As the Stooges try to escape from the castle, a skeleton named Red emerges from a chest and Shemp is nearly done in by a guillotine.

Crime on Their Hands

(1948; 17 minutes) PRODUCER: Hugh McCollum. DIRECTOR: Edward Bernds. STORY-SCREENPLAY: Elwood Ullman. PHOTOGRAPHY: Henry Freulich. EDITOR: Henry DeMond. ART DIRECTOR: Charles Clague. CAST: The Three Stooges [Moe Howard, Larry Fine, Shemp Howard] (Themselves), Kenneth MacDonald (Dapper Malone), Christine McIntyre (Bea), Charles C. Wilson (J.L. Cameron), Lester Allen (Runty), Cy Schindell (Muscles), Frank O'Connor (Policeman), George Lloyd (Squid McGuffey), Jimmy Aubrey (Hawkins), Heinie Conklin (Bartender), Blackie Whiteford (Sailor), Ray Corrigan (Gorilla).

A remake of the 1942 Andy Clyde two-reeler *All Work and No Pay* (q.v.), *Crime on Their Hands* finds Moe (Moe Howard), Larry (Larry Fine) and Shemp (Shemp Howard) working as janitors at a newspaper office. When the editor (Charles C. Wilson) goes to lunch, the boys get a tip on the location of the recently stolen Punjab Diamond. Wanting to be reporters, the Stooges go to Squid's Café where sailor Hawkins (Jimmy Aubrey) keeps a gorilla (Ray Corrigan) he brought back from Africa. Dapper Malone (Kenneth MacDonald), his moll Bea (Christine McIntyre) and henchman Muscles (Cy Schindell) have the gem hidden in a bowl of candy. As the Stooges question the crooks, Shemp swallows the diamond and Dapper and Muscles plan to cut it out of him. Moe and Larry accidentally let the gorilla loose and when the beast hits Shemp, it causes him to cough up the gem.

Cuckoo on a Choo-Choo

(1952; 15 minutes) PRODUCER-DIRECTOR: Jules White. SCREENPLAY: Felix Adler. PHOTOGRAPHY: Henry Freulich. EDITOR: Edwin Bryant. ART DIRECTOR: Charles Clague. CAST: The Three Stooges [Moe Howard, Larry Fine, Shemp Howard] (Themselves), Patricia Wright (Nora), Victoria Horne (Roberta), Reggie Dvorak (Carrie).

Working title: *A Train Called Schmow*.

Meant to poke fun at *A Streetcar Named Desire* (1951), this is one of the oddest of the Three Stooges shorts in that the boys have separate characters and do not work as a team. All of the action takes place on a train car that Larry (Larry Fine) has stolen. He wants to marry his girlfriend Nora (Patricia Wright) but she will not consent unless her homely older sister Roberta (Victoria Horne) weds rummy Shemp (Shemp Howard), who is in love with a giant white canary named Carrie (Reggie Dvorak). Moe (Moe Howard), who works for the Penciltucky Railroad, locates the missing car and recognizes Roberta as his long-lost love. After several adventures like eating limburger cheese and being interrupted by a skunk, Moe and Larry learn that the sisters both want Shemp but he still prefers the canary.

Dizzy Detectives

(1943; 18 minutes) PRODUCER-DIRECTOR: Jules White. SCREENPLAY: Felix Adler. PHOTOGRAPHY: Benjamin Kline. EDITOR: Jerome Thoms. ART DIRECTOR: Carl Anderson. CAST: The Three Stooges [Moe Howard, Larry Fine, Curly Howard] (Themselves), Bud Jamison (Police Commissioner Doolittle), John Tyrrell (Mr. Dill), Lynton Brent, Dick Jenson (Henchmen), Ray Corrigan (Bonzo the Gorilla).

Carpenters Moe (Moe Howard), Larry (Larry Fine) and Curly (Curly Howard) become policemen and are assigned to solve a series of robberies thought to be carried out by a man disguised as a gorilla. Dill (John Tyrrell), the head of the Citizens League, tells the police commissioner (Bud Jamison) the crimes must be solved. When they get a tip that a robbery is taking place at the Gysum Good Antiques store, the boys go to investigate and run into a real gorilla (Ray Corrigan) who is being used by Dill, who wants the commissioner's job, and his henchmen (Lynton Brent, Dick Jenson), to carry out the thefts. During a fight with the hoodlums, Curly goes wild and subdues them. The gorilla drinks a bottle full of nitroglycerin and when Curly charges into the beast, it explodes.

Dizzy Detectives was remade twice by Columbia, as *Fraidy Cat* (q.v.) in 1951 and as *Hook a Crook* (q.v.) in 1955. Both two-reelers headlined a future Stooge, Joe Besser.

Dopey Dicks

(1950; 15 minutes) PRODUCER: Hugh McCollum. DIRECTOR: Edward Bernds. SCREENPLAY: Elwood Ullman. PHOTOGRAPHY: Vincent Farrar. EDITOR: Henry DeMond. ART DIRECTOR: Charles Clague. CAST: The Three Stooges [Moe Howard, Larry Fine, Shemp Howard] (Themselves), Christine McIntyre (Louise), Philip Van Zandt (Professor), Stanley Price (Ralph).

After moving detective Sam Shovel into his new office, Stooges Moe (Moe Howard), Larry (Larry Fine) and Shemp (Shemp Howard) are visited by beautiful Louise (Christine McIntyre) who tells them she is being followed by a strange man and that her life is in danger. She is abducted but leaves a note asking the boys to go to Mortuary Road. During a thunderstorm they arrive at a remote house where the Professor (Philip Van Zandt) and his assistant Ralph (Stanley Price), escapees from a mental institution, are trying to make an army of mechanical men. Seeking a human head, the Professor decides to use Moe's. Eventually the Stooges are able to rescue Louise and subdue the madmen. This short was a remake of the 1943 El Brendel vehicle *Boobs in the Night* (q.v.).

Fiddlers Three

(1948; 17 minutes) PRODUCER-DIRECTOR: Jules White. SCREENPLAY: Felix Adler. PHOTOGRAPHY: Allen G. Siegler. EDITOR: Edwin Bryant. ART DIRECTOR: Charles Clague. CAST: The Three Stooges [Moe Howard, Larry Fine, Shemp Howard] (Themselves), Vernon Dent (King Cole), Virginia Hunter (Princess Alisha), Philip Van Zandt (Murgittroyd the Magician), Frank Sully (Court Courier), Cy Schindell, Joe Palma (Guards), Al Thompson (Attendant).

In the mythical kingdom of Coleslaw-vania, court jester–musicians Moe (Moe Howard), Larry (Larry Fine) and Shemp (Shemp Howard) entertain King Cole (Vernon Dent). They ask the king's permission to marry their girlfriends and he tells them they may do so when his daughter, Princess Alisha (Virginia Hunter), weds Prince Valiant. Evil magician Murgittroyd (Philip Van Zandt) has his men abduct the princess since he wants to marry her himself. The Stooges decide to find the girl and, after having trouble shoeing their mule Sue, they locate her tied up in a chamber in the palace. The magician gets the king's permission to wed Alisha if his magic will conjure her up but it is the Stooges who come out of his magic box. When the princess shows up, Murgittroyd is arrested.

This two-reeler was remade by the Stooges in 1954 as *Musty Musketeers* (q.v.).

Flagpole Jitters

(1956; 16 minutes) PRODUCER-DIRECTOR: Jules White. SCREENPLAY: Felix Adler and Jules White. PHOTOGRAPHY: Irving Lippman. EDITOR: Harold White. ART DIRECTOR: Cary Odell. ASSISTANT DIRECTOR: Will Sheldon. CAST: The Three Stooges [Moe Howard, Larry Fine, Shemp Howard] (Themselves), David Bond (Svengarlic), Mary Ainslee (Mary), Vernon Dent (Insurance Adjuster), Don C. Harvey, Frank Sully (Henchmen), Richard Alexander (Policeman), Beverly Thomas, Barbara Bartay (Show Girls), Ned Glass (Manager), Johnny Kascier (Bicycle Rider).

This Stooges outing was a remake of their 1949 *Hokus Pokus* (q.v.), made up mostly of footage from that production with a few additional scenes tacked on to make it seem like a new product.

Moe (Moe Howard), Larry (Larry Fine) and Shemp (Shemp Howard) have befriended handicapped Mary (Mary Ainslee) and are trying to earn money so she can have an operation by working at the Garden Theatre where they put up advertising posters. The theater's headliner, hypnotist Svengarlic (David Bond), is the head of a robbery gang; he puts the boys under his spell and has them walk on a flagpole as a diversion while his henchmen (Don C. Harvey, Frank Sully) rob the Gottrox Jewelry Company. When the hypnotist is knocked out by a man (Johnny Kascier) riding by on a bicycle, the spell is broken and the Stooges fall into the store and thwart the heist.

While *Flagpole Jitters* was a remake of *Hokus Pokus* it completely changed two major characters. In the 1949 short the character of Mary was actually a crook out to fleece an insurance company by pretending to be handicapped while in the remake this plot ploy is eliminated. The 1956 film has the hypnotist Svengarlic as the leader of a hold-up gang while in the original he is simply trying to pull off a publicity stunt.

Flying Saucer Daffy

(1958; 17 minutes) PRODUCER-DIRECTOR: Jules White. SCREENPLAY: Jack White and Warren Wilson. PHOTOGRAPHY: Fred Jackman, Jr. EDITOR: Saul A. Goodkind. ART DIRECTOR: Cary Odell. SETS: Milton Stumph. ASSISTANT DIRECTOR: Jerrold Bernstein. CAST: The Three Stooges [Moe Howard, Larry Fine, Joe Besser] (Themselves), Gail Bonney (Mother), Emil Sitka (Magazine President), Bek Nelson (Tyrin), Diana Darrin (Elektra), Joe Palma (Government Man), Harriette Taylor (Party Girl).

Joe (Joe Besser) plans to go on a two-week camping vacation but he lives with his slovenly aunt (Gail Bonney) and her two sons, Moe (Moe Howard) and Larry (Larry Fine), and she insists he take them along. Moe and Larry read about a $10,000 prize for getting a picture of a flying saucer. When Joe accidentally takes a photo of a flying paper plate, they think it is a UFO and enter the contest. The president (Emil Sitka) of Facts and Figures Magazine awards Moe and Larry the prize and they go on a wild spending spree with their mother, pushing Joe into the background as their servant. When the picture is proved to be a hoax, Joe is thrown out of the house but meets two beautiful aliens (Bek Nelson, Diana Darrin) who let him take a picture of their spacecraft. The photo makes Joe a hero. Moe and Larry end up in straitjackets.

Flying Saucer Daffy was the 189th Three Stooges short for Columbia and the last one of the series, although it was released after *Sappy Bullfighters* (1959). While the 16 Joe Besser-Stooges shorts are considered the worst of the series, this entry is pretty entertaining and moves at a good clip.

For Crimin' Out Loud

(1956; 16 minutes) PRODUCER-DIRECTOR: Jules White. SCREENPLAY: Felix Adler. STORY: Edward Bernds. PHOTOGRAPHY: Irving Lippman. EDITOR: Harold White. ART DIRECTOR: Cary Odell. ASSISTANT DIRECTOR: Will Sheldon. CAST: The Three Stooges [Moe Howard, Larry Fine, Shemp Howard] (Themselves), Christine McIntyre (Dolores Goodrich), Ralph Dunn (Gang Leader), Emil Sitka (John Goodrich), Charles Knight (Crandall), Barbara Bartay (News Girl), Duke York (Nikko the Goon).

For Crimin' Out Loud was Shemp's final Three Stooges short; several others followed in which he was billed as one of the Stooges but in each of them he was doubled in new scenes by Joe Palma. It was a remake of the team's 1949 *Who Done It?* (q.v.) with brief new footage at the beginning. The storyline was first used in the 1940 Walter Catlett short *You're Next* (q.v.) and then refashioned for the Gus Schilling-Richard Lane two-reeler *Pardon My Terror* (1947) [q.v.] which, ironically, was intended as a Stooges short until to Curly Howard left the team due to a stroke.

Miracle Detective Agency operators Moe (Moe Howard), Larry (Larry Fine) and Shemp (Shemp Howard) get a frantic call from councilman John Goodrich (Emil Sitka) who claims his life is in danger. As the boys go to protect him, he is abducted by a goon (Duke York) working for a gangster (Ralph Dunn) who is in cahoots with Goodrich's niece Dolores (Christine McIntyre) and his butler (Charles Knight) in stealing Goodrich's fortune. When the Stooges arrive, Dolores suggests they separate. Shemp goes with her and she drugs his drink. Too scared to stay in the house, the detectives try to get away but are stalked by the goon until he is knocked out by Shemp. The trio find Goodrich who says the crooks tried to torture him. In a fight with gang members, Shemp manages to knock them out as well as his partners and, finally, himself.

Fraidy Cat

(1951; 16 minutes) PRODUCER-DIRECTOR-SCREENPLAY: Jules White. STORY: Felix Adler. CAST: Joe Besser (Joe), Jim Hawthorne (Jim), Tom Kennedy (Detective Agency Chief), Eddie Baker (Nick), Joe Palma (Henchman), Steve Calvert (Gorilla).

Working title: *Silly Sleuths*.

A remake of The Three Stooges' 1943 short *Dizzy Detectives* (q.v.), this two-reeler teamed future Stooge Joe Besser and Los Angeles radio and television personality Jim Hawthorne. Most of its footage remained when it was remade in 1955 as *Hook a Crook* (q.v.). The head (Tom Kennedy) of the Wide Awake Detective Agency assigns Joe (Besser) and Jim (Hawthorne) to investigate a series of robberies committed by a gorilla (Steve Calvert). This leads them to the Jeweler Antique Building where they are frightened by devil masks, dummies and a guillotine before running into the beast, who is controlled by two crooks (Eddie Baker, Joe Palma).

Fuelin' Around

(1949; 16 minutes) PRODUCER: Hugh McCollum. DIRECTOR-SCREENPLAY-STORY: Edward Bernds. PHOTOGRAPHY: Vincent Farrar. EDITOR: Henry Batista. ART DIRECTOR: Robert Peterson. CAST: The Three Stooges [Moe Howard, Larry Fine, Shemp Howard] (Themselves), Christine McIntyre (Vera Sneed), Emil Sitka (Professor Sneed), Vernon Dent (General), Philip Van Zandt (Captain Rork), Jacques O'Mahoney [Jock Mahoney] (Guard), Tiny Brauer (Leon), Andrea Pola [Hans Schumm] (Cluttz).

Professor Sneed (Emil Sitka) has invented a rocket fuel that is wanted by the country of Anemia. Carpet layers Moe (Moe Howard), Larry (Larry Fine) and Shemp (Shemp Howard) are working at the Sneed home when Captain Rork (Philip Van Zandt) and two other spies (Andre Pola, Tiny Brauer) mistake Larry for the inventor. They kidnap him, along with Moe and Shemp, and take them to Anemia where the boys pretend to work on the formula so the professor and his daughter Vera (Christine McIntyre) will be safe. They concoct a phony recipe that burns through wood. An Anemian general (Vernon Dent) shows up with the professor and Vera and they are all placed under arrest. Rork is demoted while a lovesick guard (Jock Mahoney) falls for

Vera. Sneed obtains the keys to their jail cell. Using the fake formula, Moe and Larry burn a hole in the laboratory floor and fall into the Sneeds' jail cell. Shemp also drops into the cell and they all escape in a Jeep using the phony formula for fuel.

Most of the footage in *Fuelin' Around* was reused when it was remade in 1956 as *Hot Stuff* (q.v.).

A Gem of a Jam

(1943; 17 minutes) PRODUCER: Hugh McCollum. DIRECTOR-SCREENPLAY: Del Lord. PHOTOGRAPHY: John Stumar. EDITOR: Paul Borofsky. ART DIRECTOR: Victor Greene. CAST: The Three Stooges [Moe Howard, Larry Fine, Curly Howard] (Themselves), Fred Kelsey (Police Chief), Dudley Dickerson (Watchman), John Tyrrell (Joe), Al Hill (Hoodlum), Frank O'Connor, Al Thompson (Policemen).

In one of the more memorable Three Stooges ventures, cleaning men Moe (Moe Howard), Larry (Larry Fine) and Curly (Curly Howard) are working in the office of doctors Hart, Burns and Belcher when crooks bring in their boss (John Tyrrell) who has been shot. Ordered to operate on the robber, the boys accidentally cause him to slide off a table and through an open window, landing in the car of the police chief (Fred Kelsey). Moe and Larry replace him with Curly and then with a skeleton to fool the crooks. Believing the law is after them, the boys hide in the basement where Curly falls into a vat of plaster and comes out resembling a dummy. The crooks try to hide their stolen loot inside him, but they are frightened away when he talks and are captured by the police. Moe, Larry and the building's watchman (Dudley Dickerson) then run from Curly, who they think is a monster.

Get Along Little Zombie

(1946; 17 minutes) PRODUCER: Jules White. DIRECTOR-SCREENPLAY: Edward Bernds. CAST: Hugh Herbert (Himself), Christine McIntyre (Millie Mulligan), Dick Curtis (Moe Mulligan), Dudley Dickerson (Fauntleroy Jones), Jack Roper (Frankie), Symona Boniface (Mrs. Herbert), Jessie Arnold.

One of 23 two-reel shorts Hugh Herbert headlined for Columbia between 1943 and 1952, *Get Along Little Zombie* had him as an bungling realtor who shows a house to a married couple (Christine McIntyre, Dick Curtis), not realizing it is the domicile of an ape man. Herbert also starred in the studio's scare comedies *Tall, Dark and Gruesome* (1948) and *One Shivery Night* (1950) [qq.v.].

The Ghost Talks

(1949; 16 minutes) PRODUCER-DIRECTOR: Jules White. SCREENPLAY: Felix Adler. PHOTOGRAPHY: M.A. Anderson. EDITOR: Edwin Bryant. ART DIRECTOR: Charles Clague. CAST: The Three Stooges [Moe Howard, Larry Fine, Shemp Howard] (Themselves), Nancy Saunders (Lady Godiva), Phil Arnold (Voice of Peeping Tom).

Working title: *That's the Spirit*.

A to Z Express Company movers Moe (Moe Howard), Larry (Larry Fine) and Shemp (Shemp Howard) go to a remote castle on a stormy night to take away the furnishings, including a suit of armor. They soon learn that the armor contains the spirit of Peeping Tom (voice of Phil Arnold) who has spent the last thousand years encased in it after being beheaded for watching his lover, Lady Godiva (Nancy Saunders), take her famous ride. He tells them if they take the armor away, bad luck will follow them.

When they do not listen, a talking skeleton named Red comes out of a chest, an owl flies around inside a skull and two skeletons play chess. Lady Godiva shows up riding a horse and takes the armor away with her. Watching them leave, the boys are hit with pies.

A fairly amusing two-reeler, this was remade in 1956 as *Creeps* (q.v.); most of *Creeps*' footage comes from *The Ghost Talks*.

Gum Shoes

(1935; 21 minutes) ASSOCIATE PRODUCER: Jules White. DIRECTOR: Del Lord. CAST: Tom Kennedy (Tom), Monte Collins (Monty), Wilfred Lucas (Mr. Aldrich), James C. Morton (Hotel Clerk), Lynton Brent, William Irving (Crooks), Leo Willis, Al Thompson (Hotel Guests), Charles Gemora (Gorilla).

In 1935 Columbia teamed Monte Collins and Tom Kennedy in a series of two-reelers, beginning with the March release *Gum Shoes*. In *The Columbia Comedy Shorts: Two-Reel Hollywood Film Comedies, 1933–1958* (1986), Ted Okuda and Edward Watz noted, "Director Del Lord keeps things moving at a breezy clip; a sizable laugh content compensates for the film's lack of subtlety." The team headlined a dozen shorts for the studio until 1938, including another horrific outing, *Midnight Blunders* (q.v.) in 1936.

Working as house detectives at the Marberry Hotel, Monty (Monte Collins) and Tom (Tom Kennedy) are awakened from their nap by the clerk (James C. Morton) who informs them that several guests have reported items beings stolen from their rooms. A radio drama makes them think the culprit is someone clad in a fur coat and they harass several guests (Wilfred Lucas, Leo Willis, Al Thompson) before finding out the thief is a gorilla (Charles Gemora). The beast takes Tom's gun and fires it. When Monty locks himself in a closet, the gorilla chases his partner; trying to elude the simian, Monty ends up in the closet with the animal who is controlled by two crooks (Lynton Brent, William Irving) after a bag of jewels. Monty and Tom eventually run onto the hotel roof and climb a flag pole that is pulled up by the gorilla and the two detectives are left hanging over a street. The gorilla jiggles the pole and Monty shoots the beast. The two gumshoes fall onto a car.

Heavenly Daze

(1948; 17 minutes) PRODUCER-DIRECTOR: Jules White. SCREENPLAY: Zion Meyers. PHOTOGRAPHY: Allen G. Siegler. EDITOR: Edwin Bryant. ART DIRECTOR: Charles Clague. CAST: The Three Stooges [Moe Howard, Larry Fine, Shemp Howard] (Themselves), Vernon Dent (I. Fleecem), Sam McDaniel (Butler Spiffingham), Victor Travers (Mr. De Puyster), Symona Boniface (Mrs. De Puyster), Marti Shelton (Miss Jones), Judy Malcolm (Celestial Switchboard Girl).

At the Pearly Gates, Shemp (Shemp Howard) is informed by his Uncle Mortimer (Moe Howard) that he will not be eligible for admittance unless he can reform his pals Moe (Moe Howard) and Larry (Larry Fine). Back on Earth, Moe and Larry hear lawyer I. Fleecem (Vernon Dent) read Shemp's will that leaves them $140 but he takes the money as his fee. Although Moe and Larry realize Shemp has come back to haunt them, they go ahead with their plan to sell a fountain pen that writes under whipped cream for $50,000 to a gullible couple (Victor Travers, Symona Boniface). After scaring off a hired butler (Sam McDaniel), Shemp keeps the couple from being gypped by messing up the pen's demonstration. Everyone gets hit with whipped cream. Shemp then wakes up to find it was all a dream and that his bed is on fire.

Columbia remade *Heavenly Daze* in 1955 as *Bedlam in Paradise* (q.v.). Like most of the studio's short subject retreads, it was made up mostly of footage from the original.

Hokus Pokus

(1949; 16 minutes) PRODUCER-DIRECTOR: Jules White. SCREENPLAY: Felix Adler. PHOTOGRAPHY: Vincent Farrar. EDITOR: Edwin Bryant. ART DIRECTOR: Robert Peterson. CAST: The Three Stooges [Moe Howard, Larry Fine, Shemp Howard] (Themselves), Mary Ainslee (Mary), Vernon Dent (Insurance Adjustor), Jimmy Lloyd (Cliff), David Bond (Svengarlic), Ned Glass (Manager), Johnny Kascier (Bicycle Rider).

Mary (Mary Ainslee) and her boyfriend Cliff (Jimmy Lloyd) have cooked up a scheme in which she pretends to be unable to walk so she can collect $25,000 from the Calamity Insurance Company. The woman uses Moe (Moe Howard), Larry (Larry Fine) and Shemp (Shemp Howard) as witnesses since they believe she is crippled and are caring for her. At the theater where they work as advertisement hangers, the boys hope to convince hypnotist Svengarlic (David Bond) to help Mary. When Svengarlic's manager (Ned Glass) tells him he needs to do a big publicity stunt to improve business, he hypnotizes the boys and has them walk on a flagpole high above the street before a huge crowd. When a bicyclist (Johnny Kascier) runs into Svengarlic the spell is broken and the pole snaps, dropping the Stooges into the office where Mary is about to collect from an insurance adjustor (Vernon Dent). Their sudden arrivals causes her to jump to her feet, proving she is a crook.

Most of this short's footage was used in its 1956 remake *Flagpole Jitters* (q.v.), but the plot was somewhat changed.

Hold That Monkey

(1950; 16 minutes) PRODUCER-DIRECTOR: Jules White. CAST: Gus Schilling (Gus), Richard Lane (Dick), Jean Willes, Margie Liszt, Joe Palma.

The last of 11 two-reelers Gus Schilling and Richard Lane headlined for Columbia between 1945 and 1950, *Hold That Monkey* was a remake of the Monte Collins-Tom Kennedy 1935 short *Gum Shoes* (q.v.) and it utilized footage from that production. Schilling had worked in burlesque and also played supporting roles in many Columbia features and shorts while Lane was a busy character actor who gained his greatest fame as the announcer for the TV wrestling and roller derby from the late 1940s well into the 1970s.

Following the plotline of *Gum Shoes* fairly closely, the production had two hotel detectives (Schilling, Lane) on the trail of a burglar who turns out to be a gorilla trained by crooks to steal valuables.

Hoofs and Goofs

(1957; 16 minutes) PRODUCER-DIRECTOR: Jules White. SCREENPLAY: Jack White. PHOTOGRAPHY: Gert Andersen. EDITOR: Harold White. ART DIRECTOR: Paul Palmentola. ASSISTANT DIRECTOR: Willard Shelton. CAST: The Three Stooges [Moe Howard, Larry Fine, Joe Besser] (Themselves), Benny Rubin (Mr. Dinklespiel), Harriette Tarler (Miss Dinklespiel/Voice of Birdie), Tony the Wonder Horse (Birdie), Joe Palma (Drunk).

Working title: *Galloping Bride.*

Hoofs and Goofs was the first of 16 shorts Joe Besser made as one of The Three Stooges, replacing Shemp Howard, who died in 1955. Released in January 1957, it was practically a family affair production-wise with Jules White producing and directing, his brother Jack writing the script, and his son Harold the editor. One of the weakest of the Stooges shorts, it was followed by an even worse sequel, *Horsing Around*, (q.v.), the same year.

Joe (Joe Besser) reads a book about reincarnation and thinks that his and Moe (Moe Howard) and Larry's (Larry Fine) late sister Birdie has returned in another form. When the three run into a talking horse (voice of Harriette Tarler) it tells them it is Birdie and they take her home even though she says she is in love with another horse. They sneak the animal into their hotel but it kicks the floor, causing plaster to fall onto the landlord (Benny Rubin) and his daughter (Harriette Tarler). The landlord comes to the Stooges' apartment looking for the horse but they hide her in a closet. After he leaves, they give Birdie a bath and she tells them she is going to have a baby. Joe tries to use ether on the horse but ends up knocking himself out. After the colt is born, Joe wakes up to find it was all a dream. When he tells Birdie (Moe Howard) about the dream, she dumps a bowl of salad on his head.

Hoofs and Goofs was one of six Besser-Stooges shorts that was included in Columbia's compilation feature *Three Stooges Fun-O-Rama* (1959).

Hook a Crook

(1955; 16 minutes) PRODUCER-DIRECTOR: Jules White. SCREENPLAY: Jack White. STORY: Felix Adler. EDITOR: Harold White. CAST: Joe Besser (Joe), Jim Hawthorne (Jim), Tom Kennedy (Agency Chief), Steve Calvert (Gorilla), Lela Bliss, Barbara Bartay, Joe Palma.

Working title: *Daffy Detectives.*

The penultimate comedy short co-starring Joe Besser and Jim Hawthorne, *Hook a Crook* was a remake of their earlier *Fraidy Cait* (q.v.), and most of its footage came from that 1951 release. (It had been done eight years before as the Three Stooges vehicle *Dizzy Detectives* [q.v.].) The now very tired plot had bumbling private detectives Joe (Besser) and Jim (Hawthorne) assigned by their boss (Tom Kennedy) to find jewels stolen by a gorilla (Steve Calvert) trained by crooks.

Horsing Around

(1957; 16 minutes) PRODUCER-DIRECTOR: Jules White. SCREENPLAY: Felix Adler. PHOTOGRAPHY: Ray Cory. EDITOR: William Lyon. ART DIRECTOR: Cary Odell. SETS: Fay Babcock. ASSISTANT DIRECTOR: Herb Wallerstein. CAST: The Three Stooges [Moe Howard, Larry Fine, Joe Besser] (Themselves), Emil Sitka (Horse Trainer), Tony the Wonder Horse (Birdie), Harriette Tarler (Voice of Birdie).

Working titles: *Just Fooling Around* and *Just Horsing Around.*

One of the worst of Stooges' two-reelers, *Horsing Around* was a sequel to the only slightly better *Hoofs and Goofs* (q.v.), issued nine months before this sorry affair. In the first outing, the plot of the Stooges' sister Birdie being reincarnated as a horse proved to be a dream but in this sequel it is a fact. The story has Moe (Moe Howard), Larry (Larry Fine) and Joe (Joe Besser) reading that famous circus horse Schnapps is about to be destroyed. This makes their sister Birdie, who has been reborn as a mare, unhappy since Schnapps is the father of her colt. Promising to save the animal, the boys and Birdie travel by wagon to the Brooks Circus; the Stooges end up pulling the tram because their sister's feet hurt. While having lunch in a deserted shack, they hear a radio report that Schnapps is about to be shot and they rush to the fairgrounds where Joe locates the horse. The trainer (Emil Sitka), who is about to shoot Schnapps, thinks Moe and Larry have stolen him. To elude their nearly blind pursuer they dress up in a horse costume. When the trainer mistakes Moe and Larry for Schnapps and tries to give them a tranquilizer, they run away as Birdie and Schnapps are reunited.

Host to a Ghost

(1941; 17 minutes) PRODUCERS: Del Lord and Hugh McCollum. DIRECTOR: Del Lord. STORY-SCREENPLAY: Elwood Ullman and Harry Edwards. PHOTOGRAPHY: L.W. O'Connell. EDITOR: Burton Kramer. CAST: Andy Clyde (Andy), Dudley Dickerson (Henry), Frank Mills (Frank), Lew Kelly (Ghoul), Monte Collins (Policeman), Vernon Dent (Client), Bud Jamison (Detective/Southern General's Voice), Johnny Kaiser (Man).

Andy (Andy Clyde), owner of the Clyde Wrecking Company, is hired by a client (Vernon Dent) to demolish an old mansion. With his helpers Henry (Dudley Dickerson) and Frank (Frank Mills), he begins work only to become involved with ghosts still battling the Civil War. Clyde remade the short in 1955 as *One Spooky Night* (q.v.).

Hot Ice

(1955; 16 minutes) PRODUCER-DIRECTOR: Jules White. SCREENPLAY: Elwood Ullman and Jack White. PHOTOGRAPHY: Fred Jackman, Jr. EDITOR: Tony DiMarco. ART DIRECTOR: Cary Odell. ASSISTANT DIRECTOR: Willard Sheldon. CAST: The Three Stooges [Moe Howard, Larry Fine, Shemp Howard] (Themselves), Kenneth MacDonald (Dapper Malone), Christine McIntyre (Bea), Barbara Bartay (Woman in Café), Cy Schindell (Muscles), Budd Fine (Runty), Charles Knight (Inspector McCormick), James Logan (Scotland Yard Assistant), Blackie Whiteford (Sailor), George Lloyd (Bartender), Jimmy Aubrey (Gorilla Owner), Ray Corrigan (Gorilla).

This remake of 1948's *Crime on Their Hands* (q.v.) got most of its footage from that short. *Hot Ice* borrowed its opening sequence from another Three Stooges vehicle, *The Hot Scots* (1948) [q.v.].

Moe (Moe Howard), Larry (Larry Fine) and Shemp (Shemp Howard) have just graduated from a mail order detective school and apply for work at Scotland Yard. Needing some men for yard work, Inspector McCormick (Charles Knight) assigns them to clean up trash. In doing so, they find a missive about the recently stolen Punjab Diamond. Deciding to retrieve the gem and prove their worth as detectives, the boys head to the café where the diamond can supposedly be located. There they meet a young Englishwoman (Barbara Bartay) who they suspect is involved in the theft but they end up being slapped by her. Searching the premises they find beautiful Bea (Christine McIntyre), the moll of Dapper (Kenneth MacDonald), who with henchmen Muscles (Gus Schilling) and Runty (Budd Fine) stole the gem. Bea has it hidden in a candy dish. Shemp is infatuated with Bea and while eating candy swallows the diamond. When Dapper finds out, he and Muscles decide to operate to recover the jewel. Moe and Larry try to help Shemp, but are locked in a closet by Muscles. While sawing through a wall they let loose a gorilla (Ray Corrigan) that has been housed there by its owner (Jimmy Aubrey). As Dapper is about to cut Shemp open, the gorilla attacks him and Muscles. Shemp makes a getaway.

The Hot Scots

(1948; 17 minutes) PRODUCER: Hugh McCollum. DIRECTOR: Edward Bernds. SCREENPLAY: Elwood Ullman. PHOTOGRAPHY: Allen Siegler. EDITOR: Henry DeMond. ART DIRECTOR: Harold MacArthur. CAST: The Three Stooges [Moe Howard, Larry Fine, Shemp Howard] (Themselves), Herbert Evans (The Earl), Christine McIntyre (Lorna Doone), Charles Knight (Inspector McCormick), Theodore Lorch (MacPherson), George Pembroke (Angus), James Logan (Scotland Yard Assistant).

When Moe (Moe Howard), Larry (Larry Fine) and Shemp (Shemp Howard) show up at Scotland Yard looking for jobs as detectives, Inspector McCormick (Charles Knight) gives them the task of cleaning up the grounds. His assistant (James Logan) leaves a message on McCormick's desk saying that three men are needed to guard Glenheather Castle. When the paper blows out a window, Moe finds it and the boys decide to take the case in order to get promotions. Arriving at the remote, spooky citadel they are greeted by the earl (Herbert Evans) and his beautiful secretary Lorna Doone (Christine McIntyre). The earl wants the boys to guard his valuables while he is away at a meeting of the Clans. Moe and Shemp keep guard as a masked figure begins stealing items. The phantom wakes Larry and locks him in a closet; escaping, Larry manages to get the bag containing the valuables. Lorna, who is in cahoots with the thieves, dances with Shemp and Moe. When two masked figures try to retrieve the bag, the Stooges subdue them and unmask the thieves as the earl's servants MacPherson (Theodore Lorch) and Angus (George Pembroke). The earl arrives with the police, and the servants and Lorna are arrested. To show his appreciation, the earl goes to the liquor cabinet to get the Stooges a drink and they see a bagpipe-playing skeleton.

The Hot Scots was remade in 1954 as *Scotched in Scotland* (q.v.). Its opening scenes were also incorporated into 1955's *Hot Ice* (q.v.).

Hot Stuff

(1956; 16 minutes) PRODUCER-DIRECTOR: Jules White. SCREENPLAY: Felix Adler. STORY: Elwood Ullman. PHOTOGRAPHY: Irving Lippman. EDITOR: Harold White. ART DIRECTOR: Ross Bellah. ASSISTANT DIRECTOR: Willard Sheldon. CAST: The Three Stooges [Moe Howard, Larry Fine, Shemp Howard] (Themselves), Christine McIntyre (Vera Sneed), Emil Sitka (Professor Sneed), Philip Van Zandt (Captain), Gene Roth (Ambassador), Vernon Dent (General), Tiny Brauer (Chauffeur Leo), Jock Mahoney (Guard), Andre Pola [Hans Schumm] (Colonel Klotz), Barbara Bartay (Trailed Woman), Evelyn Lovequist, Connie Cezan (Uranian Officers), Joe Palma (Shemp Howard's Double).

Shemp Howard died during the production of *Hot Stuff* and his scenes were completed by double Joe Palma. The two-reeler was a remake of the Stooges' *Fuelin' Around* (q.v.) and got most of its footage from that 1949 production.

While Shemp (Joe Palma) trails a pretty girl (Barbara Bartay), his fellow Uranian agents Moe (Moe Howard) and Larry (Larry Fine) are told that the trio is to guard a rocket fuel invented by Professor Sneed (Emil Sitka). The ambassador (Gene Roth) of the rival country of Anemia orders his captain (Philip Van Zandt) to get the formula. With two other agents, the captain goes to the professor's home and mistakes Larry for the scientist. He and his men kidnap Larry, Moe and Shemp (Shemp Howard) and take them to Anemia. There the Stooges decide to pretend to work to perfect the formula in order to protect the professor and his daughter Vera (Christine McIntyre). The boys come up with a recipe that eats through wood and are about to pass it off as the rocket fuel when an Anemian general (Vernon Dent) shows up with the professor and Vera, who are put in a jail cell when Sneed refuses to reveal his formula. The Stooges use their invention to burn a hole in the floor and eventually all five Uranians escape using the fake fuel to power a Jeep.

Hula-La-La

(1951; 16 minutes) PRODUCER-DIRECTOR: Hugh McCollum. SCREENPLAY: Edward Bernds. PHOTOGRAPHY: Henry Freulich. EDITOR: Edwin Bryant. ART DIRECTOR: Charles Clague. CAST: The Three Stooges [Moe Howard, Larry Fine, Shemp Howard] (Themselves), Jean Willes (Luana), Kenneth MacDonald (Verulu), Emil Sitka (Mr. Baines), Joy Windsor (Native Girl), Heinie Conklin (King), Maxine Doviat (Kawana), Lei Aloha (Idol).

The president of B.O. Pictures, Mr. Baines (Emil Sitka), is in a dither because he has purchased a South Seas island in order to film a musical there and has found out the natives cannot dance. He sends three musicians, choreographer Moe (Moe Howard), pianist Larry (Larry Fine) and dancer Shemp (Shemp Howard), to the headhunter-infested isle to teach the inhabitants a few steps. Upon their arrival they are taken to the Witch Doctor, Verulu (Kenneth MacDonald), who tells them he plans to add their heads to his collection. The king's (Heinie Conklin) daughter Luana (Jean Willes) promises to help the boys because she does not want to marry Verulu. The Stooges escape into the jungle. The witch doctor recaptures Shemp as Moe and Larry do battle with a four-armed idol (Lei Aloha) who guards a box of hand grenades which Moe finally steals. As Verulu is about to behead Shemp, Moe and Larry trick him into proving his skill with an axe by chopping into the box. It explodes, eliminating the witch doctor. The natives then accept the Stooges as their new rulers and the boys teach them to dance.

This is the only Stooges short directed by producer Hugh McCollum. It features a very amusing sequence where Shemp hides under a bed only to have baby and adult alligators crawl up his leg.

Idle Roomers

(1944; 17 minutes) PRODUCER: Hugh McCollum. DIRECTOR: Del Lord. STORY-SCREENPLAY: Del Lord and Elwood Ullman. PHOTOGRAPHY: Glen Gano. EDITOR: Henry Batista. ART DIRECTOR: Charles Clague. CAST: The Three Stooges [Moe Howard, Larry Fine, Curly Howard] (Themselves), Christine McIntyre (Mrs. Leander), Vernon Dent (Mr. Leander), Duke York (Lupe the Wolf Man), Esther Howard (Frightened Woman in Bed), Eddie Laughton (Desk Clerk), Joanne Frank (Hazel).

The Leanders (Christine McIntyre, Vernon Dent), carnival performers, check into Hotel Snazzy Plaza with a trunk that houses their new attraction, Lupe the Wolf Man (Duke York), who goes insane when he hears music. Bellhops Moe (Moe Howard), Larry (Larry Fine) and Curly (Curly Howard) take the trunk to the couple's room where all three flirt with the beautiful Mrs. Leander. When the couple leaves, the boys are told to clean the room. As Curly sweeps the floor he turns on a radio whose music causes the wolf man to go wild and break out of his cage. After terrorizing two sleeping women (Esther Howard, Joanne Frank), Lupe stalks the Stooges and goes berserk when Curly plays a trombone. The boys try to escape by getting into an elevator but he ends up inside with them. They push the up-down buttons so often the contrivance goes haywire and catapults them and Lupe into the skies.

The most interesting aspect of this amusing Three Stooges opus is the makeup worn by Duke York as the wolf man. It was created by the uncredited Clay Campbell, whose earlier design for the lycanthrope played by Matt Willis in *The Return of the Vampire* (1944) [q.v.] was far superior to the poor facsimile in *Idle Roomers*. When Campbell again did the makeup (for Steven Ritch to wear in the title role of *The Werewolf* [1956] [q.v.]), it reverted to the much better 1944 model.

If a Body Meets a Body

(1945; 18 minutes) PRODUCER-DIRECTOR: Jules White. SCREENPLAY: Jack White. STORY: Gil Pratt. PHOTOGRAPHY: Benjamin Kline. EDITOR: Charles Hochberg. ART DIRECTOR: Charles Clague. CAST: The Three Stooges [Moe Howard, Larry Fine, Curly Howard] (Themselves), Theodore Lorch (Jerkington), Fred Kelsey (Detective), Victor Travers, Dorothy Vernon (Relatives), Joe Palma (Housekeeper), John Tyrrell (Deceased Lawyer), Al Thompson (Deceased Professor Robert O. "Bob" Link).

One of the best of the Stooges' 1940s comedies, *If a Body Meets a Body* is a loose remake of *The Laurel and Hardy Murder Case* (1930) with Fred Kelsey repeating his part of the harried detective he first played in the original Hal Roach production.

Hobos Moe (Moe Howard) and Larry (Larry Fine) throw out their fellow bum Curly (Curly Howard) after he makes them soup flavored with a horseshoe. When they read that Curly is the heir to the estate of the late millionaire Professor Robert O. Link, they claim they were only kidding and go with their pal, whose real name is Curly Q. (Q for Cuff) Link to a remote mansion on a stormy night for the reading of the will. They are admitted by butler Jerkington (Theodore Lorch) and join other relatives who are told by a police detective (Kelsey) that their benefactor was murdered. When a lawyer (John Tyrrell) is also killed and Link's body (Al Thompson) disappears along with the will, the policeman orders everyone to stay the night. The butler takes the Stooges to the bedroom where Curly's uncle was murdered. During the night the lights go out and a parrot escapes from its cage and gets into a human skull and flies around their room. The Stooges escape into the professor's laboratory where they find his body. When they come back to the room with the detective, the corpse is gone. Running into another bedroom, the boys see the corpses of both the professor and his lawyer. As they try to escape, they run over the housekeeper (Joe Palma), who turns out to be a man and the killer with the will. When the document is read, Curly is bequeathed 67 cents.

I'm a Monkey's Uncle

(1948; 16 minutes) PRODUCER-DIRECTOR: Jules White. SCREENPLAY: Zion Myers. PHOTOGRAPHY: George F. Kelly. EDITOR: Edwin Bryant. ART DIRECTOR: Charles Clague. CAST: The Three Stooges [Moe Howard, Larry Fine, Shemp Howard] (Themselves), Dee Green (Baggie), Virginia Hunter (Aggie), Nancy Saunders (Maggie), Cy Schindell, Joe Palma, Bill Wallace (Rivals), Heinie Conklin (Milkman).

Moe (Moe Howard), Larry (Larry Fine) and Shemp (Shemp Howard) are cavemen who have problems trying to obtain something to eat for lunch and dinner. Moe introduces Larry and Shemp to his girlfriend Aggie (Virginia Hunter) and her friends Maggie (Nancy Saunders) and Baggie (Dee Green). The beautiful Maggie goes for Larry while homely Baggie takes a shine to the reluctant Shemp. Three other cavemen (Cy Schindell, Joe Palma, Bill Wallace) show up wanting the women. The Stooges use a tree limb to catapult rocks and other debris at them and finally scare away their rivals with a skunk.

With its threadbare plot, *I'm a Monkey's Uncle* is one of the lesser Stooges offerings. It was even duller when remade in 1955 as *Stone Age Romeos* (q.v.), comprised mostly of stock footage from the original.

Merry Mavericks

(1951; 16 minutes) PRODUCER: Hugh McCollum. DIRECTOR-SCREENPLAY: Edward Bernds. PHOTOGRAPHY: Allen Siegler. EDITOR: Edwin Bryant. ART DIRECTOR: Charles Clague. CAST: The Three Stooges [Moe Howard, Larry Fine, Shemp Howard] (Themselves), Don C. Harvey (Red Morgan), Marion Martin (Gladys), Paul Campbell (Clarence Cassidy), John Merton (Shotgun), George Chesebro (Pete), Victor Travers (Editor Higgins), Ernie Adams (Banker), Emil Sitka (Jailer Mort), Blackie Whiteford (Al), Al Thompson (Bartender).

Wanted for vagrancy, Moe (Moe Howard), Larry (Larry Fine) and Shemp (Shemp Howard) decide to go to Peaceful Gulch, unaware that it is plagued by Red Morgan (Don C. Harvey) and his gang. The town's newspaper editor (Victor Travers) and banker (Ernie Adams) decide to fool the outlaws by claiming the Stooges are really tough lawmen who will clean up the town. When the trio arrive they meet big-talking, but cowardly, Clarence Cassidy (Paul Campbell) and then ask Morgan for jobs. When Red learns the truth about the Stooges he and his gang start a fight with them.

The boys manage to subdue the outlaws and Cassidy puts them in jail but they are sprung by another gang member (Blackie Whiteford) and a crooked jailer (Emil Sitka). The Stooges go to a house, reputed to be haunted by the spirit of an Indian chief looking for its head, to guard the town's money that has been hidden there from the outlaws. The headless chief shows up as the gang members dress as phantoms to scare off the lawmen. Red captures Moe and Larry and demands to know the whereabouts of the money. The headless ghost knocks out Red and henchman Pete (George Chesebro) with the specter turning out to be Shemp. Cassidy goes to arrest the crooks but faints at the sight of blood.

Fast-paced and quite entertaining, *Merry Mavericks* was a remake of an earlier Stooges short, 1943's *Phony Express*, which did not have "supernatural" plot elements. *Merry Mavericks* kidded the then-popular Hopalong Cassidy craze by having a stalwart hero named Cassidy being a weakling and a coward.

Microspook

(1949; 16 minutes) PRODUCER: Hugh McCollum. DIRECTOR-SCREENPLAY: Edward Bernds. CAST: Harry Von Zell (Himself), Christine McIntyre, Emil Sitka, Dudley Dickerson, Jimmy Aubrey, Harry Tyler.

Harry Von Zell was a popular radio actor and announcer whose greatest fame was as a foil to Gracie Allen on television. Between 1946 and 1950 he headlined eight two-reel comedies for Columbia, the next to last being *Microspook*. It had Von Zell broadcasting from a supposedly haunted house, a scheme set up by his co-workers who are fed up with his practical jokes. They decide to scare him with one of the troupe dressed in a gorilla outfit. Unbeknownst to them and Harry, the abode is the hiding place of a real gorilla and its keeper.

Midnight Blunders

(1936; 17 minutes) ASSOCIATE PRODUCER: Jules White. DIRECTOR: Del Lord. SCREENPLAY: Preston Black [Jack White] and Harry McCoy. STORY: Jack Leonard and Monte Collins. PHOTOGRAPHY: Benjamin Kline. EDITOR: Charles Hochberg. CAST: Tom Kennedy (Tom), Monte Collins (Monte), Wilfred Lucas (Professor Oscar Millstone), Phyllis Crane (Miss Millstone), Val Durand (Dr. Wong), Sam Lufkin (Policeman), Harry Semels (Professor), Eddie Lee, Beal Wong (Henchmen), Eddie Lee (Chinese), Jack "Tiny" Lipson (Monster).

After appearing in the scare comedy *Gum Shoes* (q.v.), Tom Kennedy and Monte Collins headlined *Midnight Blunders*, released in the spring of 1939. It cast them as bumbling beat cops who run into two villains, a Fu Manchu–like Oriental madman and a huge human monster. Obviously an attempt to imitate the Stan Laurel-Oliver Hardy comedies produced by Hal Roach, the two-reeler moves at a good clip and is somewhat amusing although its wrap-up comes so fast it stretches viewer credulity.

Thick-headed policemen Tom (Kennedy) and Monte (Collins) fail to see all the crimes being committed on their Chinatown beat. Dr. Wong (Val Durand), who has a wooden leg, has financed an experiment by Professor Millstone (Wilfred Lucas) that has resulted in the creation of a superhuman creature (Jack "Tiny" Lipson). When the professor refuses to give Wong the secret of how to make such a being, the Oriental has his henchmen kidnap Millstone and tie up his daughter (Phyllis Crane). Miss Millstone tells Tom and Monte her father was abducted by a Chinese with a wooden leg and the two check all the men they see on their beat for such a false limb until they have a run-in with a fellow officer (Sam Lufkin). They eventually locate Dr. Wong and follow him to his home where he plans to torture the secret out of the professor. In attempting to turn on the lights in Wong's laboratory, Tom starts a vitalizer that revives the monster. The creature drinks a can of liquid explosives and blows up when some of Wong's men shoot him. Tom and Monte round up the baddies and free the professor.

Mummy's Dummies

(1948; 16 minutes) PRODUCER: Hugh McCollum. DIRECTOR: Edward Bernds. SCREENPLAY: Elwood Ullman. PHOTOGRAPHY: Allen G. Siegler. EDITOR: Henry DeMond. ART DIRECTOR: Charles Clague. CAST: The Three Stooges [Moe Howard, Larry Fine, Shemp Howard] (Themselves), Vernon Dent (King Rootentootin), Philip Van Zandt (Futamon), Ralph Dunn (Rhadames), Dee Green (Princess Fatima), Suzanne Ridgeway, Wanda Perry, Virginia Ellsworth (Court Girls).

In Ancient Egypt, Moe (Moe Howard), Larry (Larry Fine) and Shemp (Shemp Howard) peddle used chariots and try to swindle Rhadames (Ralph Dunn), chief of the palace guard. He takes them before King Rootentootin (Vernon Dent) who orders them tossed to the crocodiles. When the boys find out the king has a bad tooth, they tell him Shemp is a dentist known as the "Painless Papyrus." After accidentally pulling Moe's molar, Shemp manages to remove Rootentootin's bad tooth and he makes them royal chamberlains. Rhadames is in cahoots with tax collector Futamon (Philip Van Zandt), who has been hoarding the kingdom's assessments. When the Stooges overhear the two men dividing up the tax collections Futamon and Rhadames order their execution. Moe and Larry hide in an oracle while Shemp pretends to be a mummy in order to elude the palace guards. The boys eventually expose the two crooks and return the tax money. As a reward the king gives Shemp his ugly daughter (Dee Green) in wedlock.

Musty Musketeers

(1954; 16 minutes) PRODUCER-DIRECTOR: Jules White. SCREENPLAY: Felix Adler and Jack White. PHOTOGRAPHY: Gert Andersen. EDITOR: Edwin Bryant. ASSISTANT DIRECTOR: Irving Moore. CAST: The Three Stooges [Moe Howard, Larry Fine, Shemp Howard] (Themselves), Vernon Dent (King Cole), Philip Van Zandt (Mergatroid), Virginia Hunter (Princess Alisha), Frank Sully (Court Courier), Heinie Conklin, Joe Palma (Guards), Sherry O'Neil (Girl in Box), Ruth White (Tillieth), Diana Darrin (Millieth), Norma Randall (Lillieth), Wanda Perry (Court Girl).

Musty Musketeers was a remake of 1948's *Fiddlers Three* (q.v.) and, like most of the Stooges shorts of the period, it was made up mostly of footage from the original. The two-reeler opens with new shots of the Stooges, Moeth (Moe Howard), Larryeth (Larry Fine) and Shempeth (Shemp Howard), as swains who propose marriage to their sweethearts Tillieth (Ruth White), Millieth (Diana Darrin) and Lillieth (Norma Randall). The rest of the short is *Fiddlers Three* footage with the boys going to King Cole (Vernon Dent) and getting permission to marry their lady loves; he says they may not wed until after his daughter, Princess Alisha (Virginia Hunter) weds Prince Valiant. The wicked court magician, Mergatroid (Philip Van Zandt), wants the princess for himself and orders her kidnapped by his guards. The Stooges find the princess bound and gagged; as Moeth and Larryeth get her guards to follow them, Shempeth sets her free. Mergatroid makes the king promise to let him marry Alisha if his magic returns her; he plans to have the guards place her in his magic box. But the Stooges climb in and then break it open. The princess tells her father that Mergatroid kidnapped her and, after a battle with the magician and the guards, the Stooges subdue them.

Nervous Shakedown

(1947; 16 minutes) PRODUCER: Hugh McCollum. DIRECTOR: Del Lord. CAST: Hugh Herbert (Mr. Penn), Kenneth MacDonald, Dick Wessel (Crooks), Vernon Dent (Prison Guard), Dudley Dickerson (Baldwin), Frank Lackteen (Dr. Flint).

Working title: *A-Haunting We Will Go*.

Due to a bad case of nerves, millionaire Mr. Penn (Hugh Herbert) goes to Dr. Flint's (Frank Lackteen) Sanitarium, a rest home that houses two fugitives (Kenneth MacDonald, Dick Wessel) pretending to be doctors. The escaped convicts plan to get the two men out of the way.

Of Cash and Hash

(1955; 15 minutes) PRODUCER-DIRECTOR: Jules White. SCREENPLAY: Del Lord and Jack White. PHOTOGRAPHY: Ray Cory. EDITOR: Robert B. Hoover. ART DIRECTOR: Edward L. Ilou. ASSISTANT DIRECTOR: Eddie Saeta. CAST: The Three Stooges [Moe Howard, Larry Fine, Shemp Howard] (Themselves), Christine McIntyre (Gladys Harmon), Kenneth MacDonald (Lefty Loomis), Frank Lackteen (Red Watkins), Vernon Dent (Captain Mullins), Duke York (Angel), Stanley Blystone (Café Customer), Cy Schindell (Officer Jackson), Joe Palma (Lie Detector Policeman).

The Three Stooges, Moe (Moe Howard), Larry (Larry Fine) and Shemp (Shemp Howard), get caught in the crossfire between robbers Lefty Loomis (Kenneth MacDonald) and Red Watkins (Frank Lackteen) and the police. After they are caught hiding in a barrel, the Stooges are taken to police headquarters where they are given lie detector tests by Captain Mullins (Vernon Dent), who suspects them of being the thieves. Back at their jobs at the Elite Café, the boys decide they need to find the real hoodlums in order to clear themselves. Mullins shows them a picture of Lefty and they identify him as one of the robbers. Red enters at the café and they recognize him. The trio, along with their friend Gladys (Christine McIntyre), follow Red to a remote house where he is hiding with Lefty and a sub-human goon, Angel (Duke York). As the Stooges try to get into the house, Gladys is abducted and Loomis orders Angel to bump off the boys. The goon stalks the Stooges with a machete but Shemp drops a large barrel over him and also captures Lefty and Red in the same manner. Moe, Larry and Shemp tie up the hoodlums, Gladys frees herself and the money is recovered.

Largely made up of footage from *Shivering Sherlocks* (1948) [q.v.], *Of Cash and Hash* was a fair Stooges outing. It is best remembered as being the final screen appearance of Christine McIntyre, who had been a major asset to the Columbia comedy shorts department since the mid-1940s.

One Shivery Night

(1950; 16 minutes) PRODUCER: Hugh McCollum. DIRECTOR: Del Lord. SCREENPLAY: Elwood Ullman. PHOTOGRAPHY: Henry Freulich. EDITOR: Henry DeMond. ART DIRECTOR: Charles Clague. CAST: Hugh Herbert (Mr. Herbert), Vernon Dent (Mr. Fordice), Dudley Dickerson (Julius), Philip Van Zandt, Robert Williams (Crooks).

Mr. Herbert (Hugh Herbert) runs the Herbert Construction Company and he and his employee Julius (Dudley Dickerson) are broke. Mr. Fordice (Vernon Dent) hires them to remodel an old mansion that belonged to his late uncle, a hermit who supposedly hid a fortune in the abode. Going there at night, Herbert and Julius find two men (Philip Van Zandt, Robert Williams) tearing up the place and claiming to be electricians. During a storm the two crooks dress like ghosts and try to scare away the construction company men.

One Shivery Night was one of several Columbia shorts that teamed Hugh Herbert with black comedian Dudley Dickerson; the others include the genre efforts *Get Along Little Zombie* (1946), *Nervous Shakedown* (1947) and *Tall, Dark and Gruesome* (1948) [qq.v.].

One Spooky Night

(1955; 16 minutes) PRODUCER-DIRECTOR: Jules White. SCREENPLAY: Harry Edwards and Elwood Ullman. EDITOR: Harold White. CAST: Andy Clyde (Andy), Barbara Bartay (Girlfriend), Dudley Dickerson (Henry), Frank Mills (Frank), Lew Kelly (Ghoul), Monte Collins (Policeman), Norman Ollestad, Carol Coombs, Dorothy Granger, Joe Palma.

A remake of 1941's *Host to a Ghost* (q.v.), *One Spooky Night* had construction company owner Andy (Andy Clyde) telling his girlfriend (Barbara Bartay) that he is not afraid to work in a supposedly haunted house. He goes there with his co-workers (Dudley Dickerson, Frank Mills) to demolish the place but the trio are harassed by ghosts who turn out to be a counterfeiting gang.

Operation Universe

(1959; 28 minutes; Color) Producer-Director-SCREENPLAY: Peter Bryan. PHOTOGRAPHY: Len Harris. EDITOR: Bill Lenny. CAST: Robert Beatty (Narrator).

Columbia co-financed, with Hammer Films, and released this docudrama in Great Britain; it got little or no issuance in the United States. Filmed in Technicolor and HammerScope, the short detailed the work of British scientists in the field of atomic power and space travel. It showed the experiments being done at research stations and also depicted the efforts of an RAF officer involved in rocket research.

Outer Space Jitters

(1957; 17 minutes) PRODUCER-DIRECTOR: Jules White. SCREENPLAY: Jack White. PHOTOGRAPHY: William Bradford. EDITOR: Harold White. ART DIRECTOR: Walter Holscher. SETS: Sidney Clifford. ASSISTANT DIRECTOR: Max Stein. CAST: The Three Stooges [Moe Howard, Larry Fine, Joe Besser] (Themselves), Emil Sitka (Professor Jones), Gene Roth (Grand Slitz), Philip Van Zandt (High Mucky Muck), Diana Darrin, Arline Hunter, Harriette Tarler (Sunev Girls), Don [Dan] Blocker (Giant Goon), Joe Palma (Soldier).

Joe Besser made 16 shorts as part of the Three Stooges between 1957 and 1959; the trio of sci-fi comedies they did were more entertaining than most of the others. Sandwiched between *Space Ship Sappy* (1957) and *Flying Saucer Daffy* (1958) [qq.v.] was the amusing and fast-paced *Outer Space Jitters*.

On the planet Sunev, the Grand Slitz (Gene Roth) is told by his general, the High Mucky Muck (Philip Van Zandt), that a rocket ship from Earth has landed. Professor Jones (Emil Sitka) and his aides Moe (Moe Howard), Larry (Larry Fine) and Joe (Joe Besser), are brought before the ruler. After the general takes the Stooges to see the local females, the Grand Slitz informs the professor that everything on Sunev is made up of atomic electricity. He demonstrates his ability to bring back to life a prehistoric goon (Dan Blocker) and then announces he has an army of such zombies to destroy the Earth. Moe, Larry and Joe kiss the Sunev girls but find they are charged with energy. The ruler plans to turn the professor and his men into zombies. Trying to find Jones, the boys accidentally revive the giant goon but manage to elude him and untie the professor, who uses a machine to stop the giant. The four Earthlings set about destroying the ruler's machinery and then return to Earth in their rocket. The whole thing is just a story told by the Stooges to their young sons but when the babysitter shows up she looks like the goon and the boys jump out of their apartment window.

Pardon My Terror

(1946; 17 minutes) PRODUCER: Hugh McCollum. DIRECTOR-SCREENPLAY: Edward Bernds. PHOTOGRAPHY: Glen Gano. EDITOR: Paul Borofksy. ART DIRECTOR: Charles Clague. CAST: Gus Schilling (Gus), Richard Lane (Dick), Christine McIntyre (Alice Morton), Lynne Lyons (Mrs. Bruce), Kenneth MacDonald (Mr. Bruce), Emil Sitka (Mr. Dugan), Philip Van Zandt (Butler Jarvis), Vernon Dent (Jonas Morton), Dick Wessel (Duke), Dudley Dickerson (Janitor).

Wide Awake Detective Agency private eyes Gus (Gus Schilling) and Dick (Richard Lane) are so broke they give their landlord (Emil Sitka) their only gun when he demands the rent. Beautiful Alice Morton (Christine McIntrye) hires the bumbling duo to find her wealthy grandfather, Jonas Morton (Vernon Dent), who has disappeared and may have been murdered. They accompany her to his remote, spooky mansion where they meet a married couple, the Bruces (Kenneth MacDonald, Lynne Lyons), and their henchman Duke (Dick Wessel), along with a creepy butler, Jarvis (Philip Van Zandt). They see a ghostly white figure, find sliding panels, etc. Mrs. Bruce tries to poison Gus, and her husband attempts to electrocute both detectives. Morton shows up alive. Gus and Dick capture the crooks and are paid $10,000 for their services.

Pardon My Terror is a fast-paced and fairly entertaining scare comedy that was originally scheduled for The Three Stooges but Curly Howard suffered a stroke while making *Half Wits Holiday* (1946) and the script was re-tooled for the comedy team of Gus Schilling and Richard Lane. The plotline had its origins in the 1940 Walter Catlett vehicle *You're Next* (q.v.); it was remade by The Three Stooges as *Who Done It?* (1949) and *For Crimin' Out Loud* (1956) [qq.v.].

Phoney Cronies

(1942; 18 minutes) PRODUCERS: Del Lord and Hugh McCollum. DIRECTOR-SCREENPLAY: Harry Edwards. CAST: El Brendel (Oley), Tom Kennedy (Tom), Monte Collins (Homeowner), Dudley Dickerson (Petty Larsen), Stanley Blystone (Crook).

Swedish dialect comedian El Brendel was very popular in the early sound era in films like *The Big Trail* and *Just Imagine* (1930) but his brand of comedy soon wore thin and by 1936 he was working in Columbia's comedy short subject unit. Between 1936 and 1945 he headlined 18 shorts. *Phoney Cronies*, released in the summer of 1942, was one of a trio of scare comedies Brendel did for the studio; it was preceded by *Sweet Spirits of Nighter* (1941) [q.v.] and followed by *Boobs in the Night* (1943) [q.v.]. Tom Kennedy co-starred with Brendel in *Sweet Spirits of Nighter* and *Phoney Cronies*.

Transfer company operatives Oley (Brendel) and Tom (Kennedy) get a job delivering a large crate to a spooky museum in the middle of the night, not knowing it houses a hoodlum on the lam. Once there they find themselves at odds with the hoodlum's gang, who are after a priceless Buddha statue.

The short was originally conceived as a vehicle for The Three Stooges.

Scotched in Scotland

(1954; 15 minutes) PRODUCER-DIRECTOR: Jules White. SCREENPLAY: Elwood Ullman and Jack White. PHOTOGRAPHY: Ray Cory. EDITOR: Robert B. Hoover. ART DIRECTOR: Carl Anderson. ASSISTANT DIRECTOR: Irving J. Moore. CAST: The Three Stooges [Moe Howard, Larry Fine, Shemp Howard] (Themselves), Philip Van Zandt (Dean O.U. Gonza), Christine McIntyre (Lorna Doone), Herbert Evans (Earl), Theodore Lorch (McPherson), George Pembroke (Angus).

Working title: *Hassle in the Castle*.

O.U. Gonza (Philip Van Zandt), the head of the Wide Awake Detective School, gives McMoe (Moe Howard), McLarry (Larry Fine) and McShemp (Shemp Howard) their diplomas after they graduate with the lowest honors in the institution's history. He sends them on their first case to Scotland's Glenheather Castle, which is allegedly haunted, where they meet the earl (Herbert Evans) and his beautiful secretary Lorna Doone (Christine McIntyre). The earl wants the boys to guard his valuables that night when he goes to a meeting of the Clans. Lorna is in cahoots with servants McPherson (Theodore Lorch) and Angus (George Pembroke) in robbing the castle; the two men dress up in costumes to scare the detectives, McPherson as a sheik and Angus as a masked phantom. A parrot gets inside a skull and flies around the castle frightening the sleuths. When McMoe catches Lorna and McPherson stealing heirlooms, he calls the police. McMoe, McLarry and McShemp succeed in subduing the two men while Lorna is arrested when the earl arrives with the law. As a reward the earl takes the boys to his liquor cabinet for a snifter and there they see a bagpipe-playing skeleton.

Released in November 1954, *Scotched in Scotland* was a remake of *The Hot Scots* (q.v.) and most of it was made up of footage from that 1948 release; only the opening detective school sequence was newly made for this production. Charles Knight is given on-screen credit but he does not appear in the film.

Scrambled Brains

(1951; 16 minutes) PRODUCER-DIRECTOR: Jules White. STORY-SCREENPLAY: Felix Adler. PHOTOGRAPHY: Henry Freulich. EDITOR: Edwin Bryant. ART DIRECTOR: Charles Clague. CAST: The Three Stooges [Moe Howard, Larry Fine, Shemp Howard] (Themselves), Babe London (Nora), Emil Sitka (Dr. Gazuntite), Vernon Dent (Nora's Father), Royce Milne (Mary Belle).

Moe (Moe Howard) and Larry (Larry Fine) have placed Shemp (Shemp Howard) in a sanitarium for his nerves but since they cannot afford to keep him there they decide to take him home and try to cure his problems. Shemp has fallen madly in love with nurse Nora (Babe London) who he thinks is very beautiful although she is just the opposite. He proposes marriage to her and she accepts. When he cannot relax at home, Moe and Larry tell him to practice the piano to calm his nerves. When he does so, he sees two other hands playing jazz and gets violent. Deciding to take him to another doctor, Moe and Larry lead Shemp to their hotel lobby where they plan to call ahead to see if the physician is in his office. They have a confrontation with an angry man (Vernon Dent) and all four end up in a telephone booth which they demolish. Later at Shemp's marriage to Nora, her father shows up and he turns out to be the man in the phone booth. As he goes to beat up the Stooges, Nora carries off Shemp.

Somewhat of an oddity in the Three Stooges canon, *Scrambled Brains* actually pokes fun at mental illness and has no sensitivity to Shemp's nervous condition. The confrontation scene in the telephone booth, however, is quite hilarious. The film's genre content is Shemp's hallucinations, especially the appearance of his extra pair of hands. Babe London, who plays the homely romantic foil, had a similar role in the Stan Laurel-Oliver Hardy classic short *Our Wife* (1931); she was much thinner in the Stooges vehicle.

Shivering Sherlocks

(1948; 17 minutes) PRODUCER: Hugh McCollum. DIRECTOR: Del Lord. SCREENPLAY: Del Lord and Elwood Ullman. PHOTOGRAPHY: Allen Siegler. EDITOR: Henry DeMond. ART DIRECTOR: Charles Clague. CAST: The Three Stooges [Moe Howard, Larry Fine, Shemp Howard] (Themselves), Christine McIntyre (Gladys Harmon), Vernon Dent (Captain Mullins), Kenneth MacDonald (Lefty Loomis), Frank Lackteen (Red Watkins), Duke York (Angel), Cy Schindell (Officer Jackson), Stanley Blystone (Café Customer), Joe Palma (Lie Detector Policeman).

While searching for robbers, the police find Moe (Moe Howard), Larry (Larry Fine) and Shemp (Shemp Howard) hiding in a trash can and take them to Captain Mullins (Vernon Dent) who gives them lie detector tests. Mullins shows the Stooges a picture of Lefty Loomis (Kenneth MacDonald) and they identify him as one of the robbers. Elite Café owner Gladys (Christine McIntyre) informs the boys that someone wants to buy her late father's country homestead and they go to look at the place. The house is being used as a hideout by Lefty, his partner Red Watkins (Frank Lackteen) and their subhuman goon, Angel (Duke York). When the four show up, Gladys is abducted. Lefty tells the goon to get rid of the Stooges. Angel stalks the boys but Shemp drops a huge barrel over him; he also subdues Lefty and Red in the same fashion. The police show up and arrest the crooks as Shemp drops a flour barrel on Moe and Larry.

One of the highlights of *Shivering Sherlocks* was the use of a routine involving a live clam eating crackers. Curly Howard had been the protagonist when the bit was done earlier but this time his brother Moe took over as the harried diner. *Shivering Sherlocks* was remade as *Of Cash and Hash* (q.v.) in 1955 by the Stooges with most of the original footage retained.

Shivers

(1934; 20 minutes) PRODUCER: Jules White. DIRECTOR: Arthur Ripley. SCREENPLAY: Arthur Ripley and John Grey. EDITOR: Edgar A. Lyon. CAST: Harry Langdon (Ichabod Somerset Crop), Florence Lake, Dick Elliott, Chester Gan, Louis Vincenot.

During the 1920s Harry Langdon had rivaled Charles Chaplin, Buster Keaton and Harold Lloyd as a comedy film giant but by the time the sound era came along those palmy days were long gone and he was reduced to starring in two-reel comedies for Hal Roach–MGM, Educational and Paramount before joining Columbia in 1934. Langdon made 20 short comedies for the studio until his death in 1944 and *Shivers* was the second to be released. In it he played a mystery writer who moves into a supposedly haunted house for inspiration and finds plenty of it.

Near the end of his Columbia tenure, Langdon co-starred with Una Merkel in another scare comedy, *To Heir Is Human* (1944) [q.v.].

Space Ship Sappy

(1957; 16 minutes) PRODUCER-DIRECTOR: Jules White. SCREENPLAY: Jack White. PHOTOGRAPHY: Henry Freulich. EDITOR: Saul A. Goodkind. ART DIRECTOR: Walter Flannery. SETS: Frank Tuttle. ASSISTANT DIRECTOR: Donald Gold. CAST: The Three Stooges [Moe Howard, Larry Fine, Joe Besser] (Themselves), Doreen Woodbury (Lisa Rimple), Benny Rubin (Professor A.K. Rimple), Lorraine Crawford (Flora), Harriette Tarler (Fauna), Marilyn Hanold (Venusian), Emil Sitka (Master of Ceremonies).

Of the 16 comedies Moe Howard, Larry Fine and Joe Bessser did as The Three Stooges between 1957 and 1959, *Space Ship Sappy* is probably the pick of the litter. While it retains the Poverty Row look of these last Stooges two-reelers, it is a genuinely funny film and the boys are in good form with the production moving at a good pace. The giant lizard footage used in the short came from *One Million B.C.* (1940).

Hobos Moe (Howard), Larry (Fine) and Joe (Besser) read an advertisement wanting three sailors. They go to the address given and board a rocket ship where they meet scientist Professor Rimple (Benny Rubin) and his daughter Lisa (Doreen Woodbury). They are hired on the spot and are soon on their way to Venus. The professor sends the boys out to explore the planet and they meet three beautiful maidens (Lorraine Crawford, Harriette Tarler, Marilyn Hanold) who turn out to be vampires. The women tie up Moe, Larry and Joe and tickle their feet but are scared off by the arrival of a huge prehistoric lizard. The Stooges race back to the rocket and accidentally knock out Rimple and his daughter. They take control of the vessel and launch it into space but Joe breaks off the control lever and the craft falls downward. The Stooges are then given an award for being the world's biggest liars.

Spook Louder

(1943; 16 minutes) PRODUCERS: Del Lord and Hugh McCollum. DIRECTOR: Del Lord. SCREENPLAY: Clyde Bruckman. PHOTOGRAPHY: Jack Stumar. EDITOR: Paul Borofsky. ART DIRECTOR: Carl Anderson. CAST: The Three Stooges [Moe Howard, Larry Fine, Curly Howard] (Themselves), Stanley Blystone (Chief Spy), Lew Kelly (Professor J. Ogden Dunkfeather), Theodore [Ted] Lorch (Mr. Graves), Charles Middleton (Butler), Stanley Brown (Mr. Wells), Shirley Patterson (Miss Perkins), William Kelly (Devil), Symona Boniface (Drenched Customer).

Special Investigator Professor J. Ogden Dunkfeather (Lew Kelly) is interviewed by a newspaper reporter (Stanley Brown) about the breakup of a spy ring. He tells him a story about master salesmen Moe (Moe Howard), Larry (Larry Fine) and Curly (Curly Howard) going to a creepy mansion. There they are met by a gun-toting butler (Charles Middleton) who takes them to the owner, Graves (Theodore Lorch), who mistakes them for the new caretakers. He tells them to be on the lookout for spies since he has been called to Washington D.C. on a secret mission to demonstrate his new death ray machine. Graves gives them a bomb to use in case of an emergency. The spy chief (Stanley Blystone), along with two cohorts dressed in Halloween costumes, plan to scare off the Stooges. The leader is hit in the face with a pie. As the boys search the house, a clawed hand reaches for Moe and he runs away and also gets hit with a pie. As the phantoms stalk the Stooges they hear maniacal laughter. When they are cornered by the spies, Curly hurls the bomb at them, ending their espionage activities. The Stooges then are all hit with pies. When the reporter asks Dunkfeather who threw the pies, he says *he* did and then gets one in the face.

Spook Louder is a very funny Stooges vehicle that nicely balances the trio's zany comedy with the spy and haunted house themes. It was a remake of the 1931 Educational two-reeler *The Great Pie Mystery*, produced by Mack Sennett and starring Harry Gribbon.

The Spook Speaks

(1940; 18 minutes) PRODUCER-DIRECTOR: Jules White. SCREENPLAY: Clyde Bruckman, Elwood Ullman and Ewart Adamson. PHOTOGRAPHY: Henry Freulich. EDITOR: Mel Thorsen. CAST: Buster Keaton (Buster), Elsie Ames (Elsie), Don Beddoe, Dorothy Appleby (Newlyweds), Lynton Brent (Mordini), John Tyrrell (Mordini's Assistant), Bruce Bennett (Mordini's Ex-Assistant).

Buster Keaton's career as a top comedy star of the silent and early sound era had faded when he came to work at Columbia in 1939. He did ten shorts for the Columbia unit between 1939 and 1941. In *The Great Movie Shorts* (1972), Leonard Maltin called *The Spook Speaks* "one of the worst.... [I]ts gags are stale and the haunted-house gimmicks are predicable." Ted Okuda and Edward Watz concurred in *The Columbia Comedy Shorts: Two-Reel Hollywood Film Comedies, 1933–1958* (1986): "Scared reaction comedy wasn't Buster's forte, and *The Spook Speaks* falls flat because of it." The same volume, however, reprinted exhibitor comments from the *Motion Picture Herald* where a Massachusetts theater owner wrote, "Buster Keaton in all his glory. Went over big with our audiences..."

A magician (Lynton Brent) believes someone is trying to steal his magic tricks and he hires Buster (Keaton) and Elsie (Elsie Ames) to guard his home. When the two come across what they think is a homicide, they decide to solve the crime and become entangled in all kinds of problems with the gadget-filled abode. Eventually they come to find out what they thought was murder was really a part of the owner's magic act.

Spook to Me

(1945; 18 minutes) PRODUCER: Jules White. DIRECTOR-SCREENPLAY: Harry Edwards. STORY: Edward Bernds. CAST: Andy Clyde (Andy), Violet Barlowe, Dudley Dickerson, Frank Hagney, Wally Rose, Dick Botiller, Lulu Mae Bohrman.

Working title: *Be Prepared*.

Andy (Andy Clyde) is the scoutmaster of the Bloodhound Boys Patrol. When he and his handyman (Dudley Dickerson) take the youngsters on a camping trip, they find an old house that is supposed to be haunted and decide to investigate.

Spooks!

(1953; 16 minutes) PRODUCER-DIRECTOR: Jules White. SCREENPLAY: Felix Adler. PHOTOGRAPHY: Lester White. EDITOR: Edwin Bryant. MUSIC: Mischa Bakaleinikoff. ART DIRECTOR: Carl Anderson. ASSISTANT DIRECTOR: Eddie Saeta. CAST: The Three Stooges [Moe Howard, Larry Fine, Shemp Howard] (Themselves), Philip Van Zandt (Dr. Jekyll), Tom Kennedy (Mr. Hyde), Norma Randall (Mary Bopper), Frank Mitchell (George B. Bopper), Steve Calvert (Congo the Gorilla).

Originally released in 3-D and filmed in Sepiatone, *Spooks!* was somewhat of a special short subject for Columbia in that it was the first film comedy to be released in the three-dimensional format. It was followed by *Pardon My Backfire* (1953). Leonard Maltin noted in *Movie Comedy Teams* (1985), "The comic value of these two-reelers is strictly second-rate, but the actual 3-D effects are quite good ... *Spooks!* has one of the most effective 3-D gimmicks ever filmed — a lingering shot of a mad doctor coming toward the camera, with a long, long hypodermic needle! The idea of throwing pies at the camera didn't work quite as well." With or without 3-D, *Spooks!* is one of the better Stooges offerings of the Shemp period and overall one of the team's best horror spoofs, especially in atmosphere and sets. A 3-D home video version of the production was called *Tails of Horror*.

Super Sleuth Detective Agency owners Moe (Moe Howard), Larry (Larry Fine) and Shemp (Shemp Howard) are hired by a man (Frank Mitchell) to find his missing daughter Mary (Norma Randall). Disguised as chefs, the trio trail her to an old house where she is being held hostage by mad scientist Dr. Jekyll (Philip Van Zandt) and his associate Mr. Hyde (Tom Kennedy). The two plan to put the young woman's brain in the head of Congo (Steve Calvert), a gorilla. The detectives hear the girl scream and break in, and are promptly harassed by a bat that looks like Shemp. The madmen chase the Stooges with a meat cleaver, a blowtorch and a pitchfork. Shemp interrupts Jekyll as he prepares to operate on Mary and unties the girl but accidentally frees Congo. The Stooges are cornered by Jekyll and Hyde but defend themselves by throwing pies. Congo turns on his masters and locks them in his cage, then tosses pies at Mary and the boys.

Stone Age Romeos

(1955; 15 minutes) PRODUCER-DIRECTOR: Jules White. SCREENPLAY: Felix Adler and Zion Myers. PHOTOGRAPHY: Ira H. Morgan. EDITOR: Paul Borofsky. ART DIRECTOR: Carl Anderson. ASSISTANT DIRECTOR: Jerrold Bernstein. CAST: The Three Stooges [Moe Howard, Larry Fine, Shemp Howard] (Themselves), Emil Sitka (B. Bopper), Virginia Hunter (Aggie), Nancy Saunders (Maggie), Dee Green (Baggie), Cy Schindell, Joe Palma, Bill Wallace (Rivals), Barbara Bartay (Secretary).

A remake of 1948's *I'm a Monkey's Uncle* (q.v.), *Stone Age Romeos* used scenes from that short to make up most of its content with newly filmed wraparound footage at the beginning and end. Like most such efforts by the Columbia short subject department, the transition is a smooth one and the short stands on its own as a respectable comedy filler.

Museum of Natural History curator B. Bopper (Emil Sitka) hires explorers Moe (Moe Howard), Larry (Larry Fine) and Shemp (Shemp Howard) to find living cavemen and bring back the evidence on film. On the expedition the trio see footprints of Stone Age beings and follow them. Three cavemen, Moe, Larry and Shemp, awake and as Shemp prepares breakfast, Moe and Larry go for a dip. Moe tries to capture a duck but it outsmarts him. Moe introduces his pals to his girlfriend Aggie (Virginia Hunter) and her friends Maggie (Nancy Saunders) and Baggie (Dee Green). Maggie falls for Larry and the ugly Baggie wants Shemp. Three cavemen rivals (Cy Schindell, Joe Palma, Bill Wallace) show up and try to take the women. The boys fight them off with a catapult, launching rocks, mud and eggs, before finally running them off with a skunk. The explorers finish showing this footage to Bopper, who leaves to get their money. Bopper then overhears the trio bragging how they made the film in Hollywood. He returns with a gun and chases them away.

Sweet Spirits of Nighter

(1941; 18 minutes) PRODUCERS: Del Lord and Hugh McCollum. DIRECTOR: Del Lord. STORY-SCREENPLAY: Harry Edwards and Al Giebler. PHOTOGRAPHY: Benjamin Kline. EDITOR: Burton Kramer. CAST: El Brendel (Brendel), Tom Kennedy (Tom), Lew Kelly (Mad Scientist), Frank Lackteen (Assistant), Duke York (Monster), Vernon Dent (Mr. Watkins), Bud Jamison (Purdy), Hank Mann (Policeman), John Tyrrell (Crook), Marjorie Deanne (Receptionist).

El Brendel's fifth Columbia short, *Sweet Spirits of Nighter* is a remake of the studio's 1936 frightfest, *Midnight Blunders* (q.v.), with co-star Tom Kennedy repeating his role from the first outing. Incompetent cops Brendel (Brendel) and Tom (Kennedy) look for a missing person and stumble upon a mad scientist (Lew Kelly) and his assistant (Frank Lackteen), who are experimenting with bringing the dead back to life and end up creating a monster (Duke York).

Ted Okuda and Edward Watz in *The Columbia Comedy Shorts: Two-Reel Hollywood Film Comedies, 1933–1958* (1986) felt the short was "laden with tasteless gags" and noted that when it was released in England it was with "an adults-only 'H' certificate, a rating usually reserved for genuine horror pictures." In *The Great Movie Shorts* (1972), Leonard Maltin complained that Brendel's Columbia shorts "are only sporadically funny, laden as they are with predicable and overly mechanical gags. Brendel's portrayal of a simpleton had lost all its charm, and instead he emerges as an idiot."

Tales of Frankenstein

(1958; 28 minutes) PRODUCER: Michael Carreras. ASSOCIATE PRODUCER-DIRECTOR-STORY: Curt Siodmak. TELEPLAY: Catherine and Henry Kuttner. PHOTOGRAPHY: Gert Andersen. EDITOR: Tony DiMarco. ART DIRECTOR: Carl Anderson. SETS: James M. Crowe. MAKEUP: Clay Campbell. PRODUCTION ASSISTANT: Seymour Friedman. ASSISTANT DIRECTOR: Floyd Joyer. CAST: Anton Diffring (Baron Frankenstein), Helen Westcott (Christina Halpert), Don Megowan (Monster), Ludwig Stossel (Wilhelm), Richard Bull (Paul Halpert), Raymond Greenleaf (Doctor), Peter Brocco (Caretaker Gottfried), Sydney Mason (Police Chief).

Tales of Frankenstein was intended as a weekly television series and was a joint collaboration of Columbia and Hammer Films. Only the pilot "Face in the Tombstone Mirror" was filmed; after the series failed to sell, it showed up in the late 1950s as an episode of TV's *The Award Theatre* and then disappeared until the early 1990s when it reappeared on home video. In recent years it has been made available on DVD by companies like Alpha Video and Mill Creek Entertainment. Some sources claim Columbia and Hammer disagreed on the future course of the series with the former desiring an anthology horror–sci-fi format while Hammer wanted to remain with stories centered on Dr. Frankenstein. The monster resembles the Universal version of the creature with makeup by Clay Campbell, who created the lycanthrope for Columbia's *The Return of the Vampire* (1944) and *The Werewolf* (1956) [qq.v.]. James M. Crowe's graveyard and laboratory sets are impressive and the pilot retains the atmospheric flavor of the Universal horrors. In fact, the brief opening sequences include the three vampire women from Universal's *Dracula* (1931) and the talking head that introduced most of its "Inner Sanctum" films from the mid-1940s.

Baron Frankenstein (Anton Diffring), experimenting with bringing life to the dead, creates a monster (Don Megowan) who tries to kill him because it has a criminal brain. An electrical malfunction disables the thing and Frankenstein vows to find a normal brain for his creation. On the same stormy night, Christina Halpert (Helen Westcott) arrives in a nearby village with her critically ill husband Paul (Richard Bull). When they inquire about Frankenstein at the inn, its owner (Ludwig Stossel) and the villagers show fear. The two go to the scientist's castle and ask for his help in keeping Paul alive but the baron tells them he can do nothing. Paul dies and Christina places a locket around his neck. After he is buried, Frankenstein pays the cemetery caretaker (Peter Brocco) to keep the grave open; he later removes the dead man's brain and places it in the head of his creation. When Helen comes to place flowers on her husband's grave she finds the locket. She goes back to the inn and confronts the drunken caretaker who admits what he did. Christina goes to see Frankenstein and sees the creature trying to break free of its chains. She realizes it has Paul's brain. When it spies her the creature breaks the chains and tries to murder the baron. Knocking down its creator, the monster pursues Christina but goes berserk when seeing its reflection in a mirror. Frankenstein shoots the monster but fails to stop the creature who follows him through the forest to the graveyard. There Christina begs the monster not to commit murder and it falls into an open grave as the police come to arrest the baron.

Tall, Dark and Gruesome

(1948; 16 minutes) PRODUCER: Jules White. DIRECTOR: Del Lord. SCREENPLAY: Clyde Bruckman. EDITOR: Henry DeMond. CAST: Hugh Herbert (Hugh Sherlock), Dudley Dickerson (Dudley), Charles C. Wilson (Charlie Hunter), Christine McIntyre (Costumed Party Guest), Myron Healey (Devil-Costumed Party Guest), Heinie Conklin (Delivery Man).

Playwright Hugh Sherlock (Hugh Herbert), along with his valet Dudley (Dudley Dickerson), rents a remote cabin in order to have solitude in order to work. Mayhem ensues when a crate containing a live gorilla is brought to the cabin and gets loose. In *The Columbia Comedy Shorts: Two-Reel Hollywood Film Comedies, 1933–1958* (1986), Ted Okuda and Edward Watz called it "one of the best-received Columbia shorts of that year."

Three Arabian Nuts

(1951; 16 minutes) PRODUCER: Hugh McCollum. DIRECTOR: Edward Bernds. SCREENPLAY: Elwood Ullman. EDITOR: Henry DeMond. ART DIRECTOR: Charles Clague. CAST: The Three Stooges [Moe Howard, Larry Fine, Shemp Howard] (Themselves), Philip Van Zandt (Ahmed), Vernon Dent (John Bradley), Dick Curtis (Hassan), Wesley Bly (Amos the Genii).

In this spritely Three Stooges adventure, wealthy John Bradley (Vernon Dent) hires Moe (Moe Howard), Larry (Larry Fine) and Shemp (Shemp Howard) to move a shipment of valuables he has purchased to his home. When Shemp rubs an old lamp, a genie (Wesley Bly) appears and grants him his wish for a spiffy new suit. Two Arabs, Ahmed (Philip Van Zandt) and Hassan (Dick Curtis), are after the lamp but Moe gets it from Shemp and packs it in a storage box. They unknowingly nail Ahmed in another box and take the collection to Bradley's home where Shemp digs out the lamp and Bradley gives it to him. Just as Shemp is about to ask for a million dollars, he drops the lamp into a fireplace and the genii disappears. Hassan sets Ahmed free and then pretends to be the genii and tries to do in Moe. The two Arabs chases the Stooges through the house and Larry ends up knocking out Bradley. Shemp locates the lamp in the fireplace and calls up the genii who traps the Arabs and then gives the boys a harem and a treasure in jewels.

Three Little Sew and Sews

(1939; 16 minutes) ASSOCIATE PRODUCER: Jules White. DIRECTOR: Del Lord. STORY-SCREENPLAY: Ewart Adamson. PHOTOGRAPHY: Lucien Ballard. EDITOR: Charles Nelson. CAST: The Three Stooges [Moe Howard, Larry Fine, Curly Howard] (Themselves), Phyllis Barry (Miss Arnold), Harry Semels (Count Alfred Gehrol), James C. Morton (Admiral H.S. Taylor), John Ince (Butler), John Tyrrell (Lieutenant), Bud Jamison (Policeman), Cy Schindell (Brig Guard), Ned Glass (Telegram Deliverer), Vernon Dent, Al Thompson, Lew Davis (Party Guests).

A boisterous, fast-moving Stooges entry, this outing has a fantasy sequence at its finale when the boys are shown as angels with wings.

At a naval base in the Republic of Televania, Moe (Moe Howard), Larry (Larry Fine) and Curly (Curly Howard) are navy tailors aboard Admiral Taylor's (James C. Morton) ship. He has been invited to a party given by Count Gehrol (Harry Semels), who is suspected of being a spy. Told to press the admiral's uniform, Curly instead puts it on and is mistaken for the head man. When Moe and Larry hit him, they are put in the brig. They pay Curly five dollars each to get them out and then attend the swank party posing as Taylor and his aides. Gehrol tells beautiful spy Miss Arnold (Phyllis Barry) to pump the navy men for information and she sets her sights on Curly and tries to get secrets about submarines out of him. Taylor shows up in civilian clothes and the Stooges refuse to identify him; he is taken away by a policeman (Bud Jamison). With the boys as hostages, the two spies steal a submarine and leave port. As Miss Arnold holds a gun on the Stooges she sees a mouse and faints. Curly knocks out the count but the sub sinks to the ocean floor where they hear a radio message that the vessel is to be destroyed. The Stooges try to get the submarine to the surface as the admiral orders his batteries to open fire. After a ceasefire, Taylor and his men board the ship and the boys display the captured spies. When Taylor asks how they were caught, Curly shows him a bomb that landed in the ship, when he hits it, it explodes. The Stooges, with wings, fly toward Heaven trying to keep ahead of the admiral and his aides.

Three Missing Links

(1938; 18 minutes) ASSOCIATE PRODUCER-DIRECTOR: Jules White. STORY-SCREENPLAY: Searle Kramer. PHOTOGRAPHY: Henry Freulich. EDITOR: Charles Nelson. CAST: The Three Stooges [Moe Howard, Larry Fine, Curly Howard] (Themselves), Monte Collins (Mr. Herbert), Jane Hamilton (Mirabel), James C. Morton (B.O. Botswaddle), John Lester Johnson (Ba Loni Somi), Naba [Ray Corrigan] (Gorilla).

Super Terrific Productions star Mirabel (Jane Hamilton) has been assigned to make a film in Africa called *Jilted in the Jungle*. During a story conference with director Herbert (Monte Collins) and company president B.O. Botswaddle (James C. Morton), cleaning men Moe (Moe Howard), Larry (Larry Fine) and Curly (Curly Howard) cause such a disturbance that B.O. fires them. Convincing the studio chief and director they are actors, the Stooges are hired for the production with Curly to play the missing link and Moe and Larry as Neanderthal men. After reaching the jungle, Moe, Larry and Curly are captured by a cannibal witch doctor (John Lester Johnson) who sells Curly love candy which he hopes to use to attract Mirabel. They escape from the witch doctor but that night while sleeping in their tent, they are awakened by a lion. The next day Mirabel dresses as a jungle girl and Herbert begins filming with Curly as a gorilla and Moe and Larry playing cave men. A real gorilla (Ray Corrigan) shows up and they mistake him for Curly. When Curly arrives on the scene, Moe and Larry realize they are fighting an actual beast and run away, as does Herbert. Curly manages to knock out the gorilla but now the boys mistake him for the ape. When the beast revives, he chases them into the witch doctor's hut. The gorilla manages to get inside as Moe and Larry escape and Curly nails the door shut. Eating some of the witch doctor's love candy, Curly falls in love with the gorilla, who runs away.

Three Missing Links is a typically funny Three Stooges production of the late 1930s and does a nice job of satirizing Hollywood and jungle movies. The gorilla, Naba, is given on screen billing although it was really actor Ray Corrigan in his ape suit. The next year Corrigan appeared as Naba the Gorilla in Republic's "Three Mesquiteers" western *Three Texas Steers* in which he also starred as one of the title characters.

Three Pests in a Mess

(1945; 15 minutes) PRODUCER: Hugh McCollum. DIRECTOR-SCREENPLAY: Del Lord. PHOTOGRAPHY: Benjamin Kline. EDITOR: Henry Batista. ART DIRECTOR: Charles Clague. CAST: The Three Stooges [Moe Howard, Larry Fine, Curly Howard] (Themselves), Christine McIntyre (Secretary), Brian O'Hara (I. Cheatham), Vernon Dent (Philip Black), Snub Pollard (Cemetery Watchman), Heinie Conklin (Devil), Victor Travers (Patent Office Official), Robert Williams (Skeleton).

I. Cheatham (Brian O'Hara), owner of the Cheatham Investment Company, is out to fleece three men who won a sweepstakes ticket worth $100,000. His pretty blonde secretary (Christine McIntyre) mistakes the Three Stooges, Moe (Moe Howard), Larry (Larry Fine) and Curly (Curly Howard), for the suckers after they show up at the same office building trying to get a patent on a fly catcher. When she finds out they do not have the money, Cheatham and his associates chase them and Curly accidentally shoots a dummy. The boys think they have killed one of their pursuers and take the body to the Everett Pet Cemetery to bury it. The night watchman (Snub Pollard) calls Black (Vernon Dent), the owner of the property. As the boys try to bury the dummy, Black and two friends (Heinie Conklin, Robert Williams) show up in Halloween costumes and scare them. The trio of costumed men fall into a hole; when the Stooges try to throw the dummy in it, the men keep tossing it back at them. When the costumed men rise up out of the grave the Stooges run in fright.

Three Sappy People

(1939; 18 minutes) ASSOCIATE PRODUCER–DIRECTOR: Jules White. SCREENPLAY: Clyde Bruckman. PHOTOGRAPHY: George Meehan. EDITOR: Charles Nelson. CAST: The Three Stooges [Moe Howard, Larry Fine, Curly Howard] (Themselves), Lorna Gray [Adrian Booth] (Sherry Rumsford), Don Beddoe (Mr. Rumsford), Bud Jamison (Butler Williams), Ann Doran (Countess), Forbes Murray (Dr. York), Victor Travers (Uncle John), Beatrice Blinn (Switchboard Operator), Richard Fiske, Eddie Laughton (Partygoers).

One of the best-loved of the Three Stooges comedies, the daffy *Three Sappy People* veers into the realm of fantasy in one very brief sequence where a statue comes to life and kicks Curly. Moe (Moe Howard), Larry (Larry Fine) and Curly (Curly Howard) are telephone repairmen who intercept a call for psychiatrists Ziller, Zeller and Zoller, to come to the home of wealthy Mr. Rumsford (Don Beddoe) to consult with him about his much younger, and scatterbrained wife, Sherry (Lorna Gray). Needing money, the boys disguise themselves as the medical men and arrive at the Rumsford mansion on a bicycle. Sherry invites them inside to her swank birthday party where they spike the punch and turn the dinner into a food fight. Rumsford pays them $1,500 for helping his wife enjoy herself.

To Heir Is Human

(1944; 20 minutes) PRODUCER: Hugh McCollum. DIRECTOR: Harold Godsoe. SCREENPLAY: Monte Collins and Elwood Ullman. PHOTOGRAPHY: George Meehan. EDITOR: Paul Borofsky. ART DIRECTOR: Charles Clague. CAST: Una Merkel (Una), Harry Langdon (Harry Fenner), Christine McIntyre (Velma), Eddie Gribbon (Bobo), Lew Kelly (A. Raven Sparrow), Vernon Dent (Board Chairman), Heinie Conklin (Dentist), John Tyrrell (Dr. I.M. Calm), Eddie Laughton (Exit Man), Al Thompson (Dental Patient).

The teaming of Una Merkel and Harry Langdon in *To Heir Is Human* resulted in a bigger budget, more production care and a slightly longer running time for this two-reeler that includes a very amusing sequence involving an electric bed. Otherwise, it was not very special; Ted Okuda and Edward Watz pinpointed the reason in *The Columbia Comedy Shorts: Two-Reel Hollywood Film Comedies, 1933–1958* (1986): "Harold Godsoe was a curious choice to direct the picture; he had no previous credits with the department and never worked for the unit after that. Godsoe's leaden direction dulls the impact of several potentially funny scenes."

Una (Merkel) wants to be a private eye but ends up delivering telephone books out of an office given to her by a harried dentist (John Tyrrell). The mysterious A. Raven Sparrow (Lew Kelly) mistakes Una for an agent of the Missing Persons bureau and agrees to pay her a thousand dollars to find heir Harry Fenner (Langdon). She locates Harry, a window washer, and the two go to the eerie estate of his late uncle where they encounter his beautiful kissing cousin Velma (Christine McIntyre), Sparrow, who claims to be his uncle, and an oafish handyman, Bobo (Eddie Gribbon). Una and Harry learn that the trio plan to do away with Fenner in order to divide his inheritance.

The Tooth Will Out

(1951; 16 minutes) PRODUCER: Hugh McCollum. DIRECTOR-SCREENPLAY: Edward Bernds. PHOTOGRAPHY: Fayte Browne. EDITOR: Edwin Bryant. ART DIRECTOR: Charles Clague. CAST: The Three Stooges [Moe Howard, Larry Fine, Shemp Howard] (Themselves), Margie Liszt (Miss Beebe), Vernon Dent (Dr. Keefer), Dick Curtis (Mean Patient), Emil Sitka (Italian Chef), Slim Gaut (First Patient).

Trying to get away from an angry chef (Emil Sitka), Moe (Moe Howard), Larry (Larry Fine) and Shemp (Shemp Howard) take refuge in a dentist's office and end up paying four dollars to take a course in dentistry offered by Dr. Keefer (Vernon Dent) and his nurse, Miss Beebe (Margie Liszt). After a week they get their diplomas and take Keefer's advice and go West, ending up in Coyote Pass where they start to work on a patient (Slim Gaut) before being forced to pull a tough guy's (Dick Curtis) tooth. Shemp mistakenly gets instructions from a carpentry book and yanks the wrong tooth.

Footage of the Stooges as dentists in the Old West was shot for *Merry Mavericks* (1951) but not used; director Edward Bernds convinced the hierarchy at Columbia to let him expand the story into a separate short. Its only horrific moments come when the boys fashion a set of living vampire dentures as their final school assignment.

We Want Our Mummy

(1939; 16 minutes) ASSOCIATE PRODUCER: Jules White. DIRECTOR: Del Lord. SCREENPLAY: Elwood Ullman and Searle Kramer. PHOTOGRAPHY: Allen G. Siegler. EDITOR: Charles Nelson. CAST: The Three Stooges [Moe Howard, Larry Fine, Curly Howard] (Themselves), James C. Morton (Curator), Dick Curtis, Theodore [Ted] Lorch (Crooks), Bud Jamison (Dr. Cromwell), Robert Williams (Professor Tuttle), Eddie Laughton (Cab Driver).

When Professor Tuttle (Robert Williams) of the Museum of Ancient History disappears while looking for the tomb of King Rootintootin III, the curator (James C. Morton) of the Egyptian Room hires the three "best" investigators in the city, Moe (Moe Howard), Larry (Larry Fine) and Curly (Curly Howard), to find him. Unknowingly, the boys help carry out a crate in which Tuttle has been hidden by kidnappers (Dick Curtis, Theodore Lorch) who want to find the tomb and its treasure. The curator and Dr. Cromwell (Bud Jamison) send the sleuths on an expedition to Egypt to bring back Rootintootin's mummy; they are driven there in a taxi cab. The trio fall into the king's tomb where they hear a mysterious voice and see a skeleton. Moe and Larry are abducted by the baddies and put in a cell but escape. Curly locates a room that houses a living mummy (Lorch). The boys end up in a secret chamber with Rootintootin's mummy. Curly accidentally topples onto the mummy, crushing it. When they hear the kidnappers hounding Tuttle, Curly wraps up like a mummy. The crooks decide to cut him open to obtain jewels hidden inside the mummy; when he objects they chase him and fall into a well. Tuttle informs the boys that the king was actually a midget. Alligator scares them out of the catacomb.

We Want Our Mummy had few chills but lots of laughs with the Three Stooges engaging in their usual brand of comic mayhem inside an ancient tomb. The one genuinely scary scene comes when Theodore Lorch, wrapped as a mummy, comes to life. Curly Howard in the same costume was benign indeed.

Who Done It?

(1949; 16 minutes) PRODUCER: Hugh McCollum. DIRECTOR-SCREENPLAY: Edward Bernds. PHOTOGRAPHY: Ira H. Morgan. EDITOR: Henry DeMond. ART DIRECTOR: Charles Clague. CAST: The Three Stooges [Moe Howard, Larry Fine, Shemp Howard] (Themselves), Christine McIntyre (Dolores Goodrich), Ralph Dunn (Gang Leader), Charles Knight (Crandall), Emil Sitka (Mr. Goodrich), Duke York (Nikko), Dudley Dickerson (Janitor).

The Three Stooges vehicle *Who Done It?* had plot similarities to the 1940 Walter Catlett two-reeler *You're Next* (q.v.) and was a remake of *Pardon My Terror* (1947) [q.v.], which was itself redone by the Stooges as *For Crimin' Out Loud* (q.v.) in 1956. *Pardon My Terror* was intended as a Stooges comedy but when Curly Howard suffered a stroke and had to leave the team, it was instead done as part of the short subject series starring Gus Schilling and Richard Lane.

Fearing for his life, wealthy Mr. Goodrich (Emil Sitka) calls the Alert Detective Agency for help. Owners Moe (Moe Howard), Larry (Larry Fine) and Shemp (Shemp Howard) accept Goodrich's offer. Goodrich is kidnapped by Nikko (Duke York), a goon who works with the Phantom Gang, whose leader (Ralph Dunn) is in cahoots with Dolores Goodrich (Christine McIntyre) in getting her uncle out of the way so they can have his fortune. The boys show up at the ghostly Goodrich mansion and meet Dolores, who tries to drug Shemp's drink. The boys are chased by the Phantom Gang but Shemp manages to knock out the goon. The sleuths locate Goodrich who says he was tortured by the crooks, who want to find the location of his money. Shemp manages to waylay the entire gang.

The Yoke's On Me

(1944; 16 minutes) PRODUCER-DIRECTOR: Jules White. STORY-SCREENPLAY: Clyde Bruckman. PHOTOGRAPHY: Glen Gano. EDITOR: Charles Hochberg. ART DIRECTOR: Charles Clague. CAST: The Three Stooges [Moe Howard, Larry Fine, Curly Howard] (Themselves), Emmett Lynn (Mr. Smithers), Bob McKenzie (Pa), Eva McKenzie (Ma), Al Thompson (Sheriff), Victor Travers (Deputy Sheriff).

A married couple (Bob McKenzie, Eva McKenzie) brag about their soldier sons Moe

(Moe Howard), Larry (Larry Fine) and Curly (Curly Howard), until they find out they have failed the draft. When the old man orders them to work on a farm as their part in the war effort, they buy a rundown place from Mr. Smithers (Emmett Lynn) for a thousand dollars and their flivver. A group of Japanese, escaping from a nearby relocation center, go to the farm. After stopping an ostrich from eating blasting powder, the boys decide to carve pumpkins into jack-o-lanterns in order to make money. When the escapees surround the farm, the Stooges use the ostrich's eggs as bombs to subdue them. The sheriff (Al Thompson) and his deputy (Victor Travers) round up the fugitives.

The fantasy element in *The Yoke's on Me* comes when the Stooges use the ostrich eggs as explosives. This is the only Three Stooges short to be removed from television showings. In the 1970s it was an early victim of the politically correct crowd since World War II relocation centers became controversial at that time.

You're Next

(1940; 18 minutes) PRODUCERS: Del Lord and Hugh McCollum. DIRECTOR: Del Lord. SCREENPLAY: Elwood Ullman and Harry Edwards. PHOTOGRAPHY: George Meehan. EDITOR: Arthur Seid. CAST: Walter Catlett (Slocum), Monte Collins (Pruitt), Dudley Dickerson (Sam), Roscoe Ates (Mr. Tillson), John T. Murray (Baby Face Wessel), Chester Conklin (Janitor).

Eagle Eye Detective Agency operatives Slocum (Walter Catlett) and Pruitt (Monte Collins) try to find a wealthy man (Roscoe Ates) who has been kidnapped by a mad scientist (John T. Murray). The trail leads them to a weird old house with secret panels and passages, along with a marauding ape.

Character actor Walter Catlett appeared in scores of films, mainly as a cad or slick crook, and between 1934 and 1940 he headlined a handful of shorts for Columbia. *You're Next* had all the elements needed for a fast-moving comedy-horror entry and it proved to be durable plot-wise since it was reworked for the team of Gus Schilling and Richard Lane as *Pardon My Terror* (q.v.) in 1947 and for the Three Stooges' *Who Done It?* (1949) and *For Crimin' Out Loud* (1956) [qq.v.].

TELEFEATURES

Black Noon

(1971; 74 minutes; Color) PRODUCER-TELEPLAY: Andrew J. Fenady. DIRECTOR: Bernard L. Kowalski. PHOTOGRAPHY: Keith Smith. EDITOR: Dann Cahn. MUSIC: George Duning. ART DIRECTORS: John Beckman and Ross Bellah. MAKEUP: Ben Lane. SETS: William Stevens. SPECIAL EFFECTS: Chuck Gaspar. ASSISTANT DIRECTOR: Floyd Joyer. CAST: Roy Thinnes (the Rev. John Keyes), Yvette Mimieux (Deliverance), Ray Milland (Caleb Hobbs), Gloria Grahame (Bethia), Lyn Loring (Lorna Keyes), Henry Silva (Moon), Hank Worden (Joseph), William Bryant (Jacob), Stan Barrett (Man in Mirror), Joshua Bryant, Jennifer Bryant, Charles McCready, Leif Garrett (Towheads), Dave Cass, Suzan Sheppard (Settlers), Bobby Bellyacher (Boy), Buddy Foster (Ethan).

Produced by Screen Gems Television and Fenady Associates, *Black Noon* was first telecast on CBS-TV on November 5, 1971. Set in the Old West, it had circuit-riding preacher John Keyes (Roy Thinnes) and his wife Lorna (Lyn Loring) stranded in a small town where they are welcomed by leader Caleb Hobbs (Ray Milland) but soon find themselves involved with a mute young woman (Yvette Mimieux) and a gunman (Henry Silva). They eventually discover the locale is populated by witches who wear cat masks and white sheets. "Only die-hard occult nuts will want to be beset by the mechanics of this 1971 made-for-television quickie-flick," wrote Judith Crist in *Judith Crist's TV Guide to the Movies* (1974).

The Curse of King Tut's Tomb

(1980; 98 minutes; Color) PRODUCER: Peter Graham Scott. EXECUTIVE PRODUCERS: Hunt Stromberg Jr. and Stoddard W. Kerby. SUPERVISING PRODUCER: Patrick Dromgoole. DIRECTOR: Philip Leacock. TELEPLAY: Herb Meadow, from the book *Behind the Mask of Tutankhamen* by Barry Wynne. PHOTOGRAPHY: Bob Edwards. EDITOR: Adrian Brenard. MUSIC: Gil Melle. ART DIRECTOR: John Biggs. SOUND EDITOR: Geoff Shepherd. SETS: Heather Armitage. COSTUMES: Joan Bridge. MAKEUP: Christine Penwarden. UNIT PRODUCTION MANAGER: Keith Webber. SPECIAL EFFECTS SUPERVISOR: Ted Grumbt. CONTINUITY: Elaine Matthews. ASSISTANT DIRECTORS: Stuart Freeman and Douglas Thorpe. CAST: Eva Marie Saint (Sarah Morrissey), Robin Ellis (Howard Carter), Raymond Burr (Jonash Sabastian), Harry Andrews (Lord George Carnarvon), Wendy Hiller (Princess Vilma), Angharad Rees (Lady Evelyn Herbert), Tom Baker (Hasan), Barbara Murray (Giovanna Antoniella), Faith Brook (Lady Almina Carnarvon), Patricia Routledge (Posh Lady), John Palmer (Fishbait), Darien Angadi (Ahmed Nahas), Rupert Frazer (Collins), Rex Holdsworth (Physician), Stefan Kalipha (Daoud), Andy Pantelidou (Lieutenant), Alfred Hoffman (Stallholder), Paul Scofield (Narrator).

Partially filmed in the Valley of the Kings in Egypt and possessing a fine cast, including Academy Award winners Wendy Hiller and Paul Scofield (the latter as narrator), *The Curse of King Tut's Tomb* was originally telecast in two parts on May 8 and 9, 1980, on NBC-TV. Produced by Columbia Pictures Television in conjunction with Stromberg-Kerby Productions, part one placed thirteenth in its weekly ratings and the two episodes were later telecast as a single film. It was issued theatrically in West Germany at 90 minutes, eight minutes shy of its original running time. Steven H. Scheuer in *Movies on TV 1982–83* (1981) opined, "Hard to take seriously. Chuckles and terror, as cobras strike and scorpions attack."

In the early 1920s, archaeologist Howard Carter (Robin Ellis) and Lord Carnarvon (Harry Andrews) are joined by journalist Sarah Morrissey (Eva Marie Saint) in searching for the tomb of Egyptian Pharaoh Tutankhamen. They locate the burial site and its precious artifacts but find themselves opposed by local crook Jonash Sabastian (Raymond Burr) who wants the treasures to remain in his homeland so he can profit from them.

Desire, the Vampire

(1982; 95 minutes; Color) PRODUCER: Audrey A. Blasdel. EXECUTIVE PRODUCERS: Jim Green and Allen S. Epstein. ASSOCIATE PRODUCER: Pat Butler. DIRECTOR: John Llewellyn Moxey. TELEPLAY: Robert Foster. PHOTOGRAPHY: Robert L. Morrison. EDITOR: Donald R. Rode. MUSIC: Don Peake. ART DIRECTORS: Ross Bellah and Frederick P. Hope. COSTUMES: Grady Hurst. CAST: David Naughton (David Balsiger), Dorian Harewood (Detective Jerry Van Ness), Marilyn Jones (Cheryl Gillen), Barbara Stock (Mona), Arthur Rosenberg (Milton King), James Victor (Dr. Herrera), Brad Dourif (Paul), Anne Bloom (Marge Bookman), Linda Lawrence (Undercover Policeman), Adele Rosse (Head Nurse), Marc Silver (Larry), James Oliver (Restaurant Manager), Ann Blessing (Pat), John Bennick, Nigel Bullard, Cathy Green (Broadcasters), Timothy Stack (Daryl), Stacy MacGregor (Detective), Gary A. McMillan (Plainclothes Policeman), Holly McCarver (Ward Secretary), Liis Kailey (Nurse's Aide), Laurel Rosenberg (Nurse), Jim Veres (Vice Policeman), Herb Mitchell (Bernard McDougal), Bruce Wright (Preacher).

Los Angeles law student David Balsiger (David Naughton), who works part-time at a mortuary, comes to believe that a series of murders that leave men drained of their blood are being committed by a vampire. Both his girlfriend Cheryl Gillen (Marilyn Jones) and police Detective Jerry Van Ness (Dorian Harewood) find his theory unthinkable but ex-priest Paul (Brad Dourif), a long-time vampire hunter, agrees with him. After several false leads, Balsiger is about to give up when he meets enticing prostitute Mona (Barbara Stock) and learns the shocking truth behind the killings.

Also called *I, Desire*, the ABC-TV telefeature was initially shown on November 15, 1982. *John Stanley's Creature Feature Movie Guide Strikes Again* (1994) said it contained a "fascinating man vs. supernatural premise." The telefilm's director, John Llewellyn Moxey, was an old hand at atmospheric horror thrillers, including *City of the Dead* (*Horror Hotel*) (1960), *Circus of Fear* (*Psycho-Circus*) (1966) and the telefilms *The House That Would Not Die* (1970), *The Last Child* (1971), *The Night Stalker* (1972), *Ghost Story* (1972), *Genesis II* (1973), *The Strange and Deadly Occurrence* (1974), *Where Have All the People Gone?* (1974) and *The Power Within* (1979).

Fantasy Island

(1977; 100 minutes; Color) PRODUCERS: Aaron Spelling and Leonard Goldberg. DIRECTOR: Richard Lang. TELEPLAY: Gene Levitt. PHOTOGRAPHY: Archie R. Dalzell and Sherman Kunkel. EDITORS: John Farrell and John M. Woodstock. MUSIC: Laurence Rosenthal. ART DIRECTOR: Paul Sylos. ASSISTANT DIRECTORS: Candace Suerstedt and Kalai Strode. CAST: Ricardo Montalban (Mr. Roarke), Bill Bixby (Arnold Greenwood), Sandra Dee (Francesca Hamilton), Peter Lawford (Grant Baines), Carol Lynley (Elizabeth "Liz" Hollander), Hugh O'Brian (Paul Henley), Eleanor Parker (Eunice Hollander Baines), Victoria Principal (Michelle), Dick Sargent (Charles Hollander), Christina [Tina] Sinatra (Connie Raymond), Herve Villechaize (Tattoo), Peter MacLean (Alex Davidson), Nancy Cameron (World's Most Beautiful Girl), Cedric Scott (Second Hunter), John McKinney (Hugh Addams), Elizabeth Dartmoor (Barmaid), Ian Abercrombie (Bartender), Patrick O'Hara (Air Raid Warden), Richard Ryal (Dart Player), Freddy Weller (Himself), Herb Mendelssohn (Hollandar Ghoast), Joan Roberts (Linda Larson), Toby Holguin (Child).

Mr. Roarke (Ricardo Montalban) and his associate Tattoo (Herve Villechaize) are the hosts of Fantasy Island, a tropical paradise where a number of tourists pay $50,000 to have their deepest desires fulfilled. The telefilm was broadcast by ABC on January 14, 1977, and was produced by Columbia Pictures Television along with Spelling Productions and Goldberg Productions. Its ratings success led to a 1978 sequel, *Return to Fantasy Is-*

Ricardo Montalban, *Fantasy Island* (1977) and *Return ...* (1978).

land (q.v.) followed by the weekly series *Fantasy Island* that ran on ABC-TV from 1978 to 1984 with Montalban and Villechaize repeating their roles.

A Fire in the Sky

(1978; 150 minutes; Color) PRODUCER: Hugh Benson. EXECUTIVE PRODUCER: Bill Driskill. DIRECTOR: Jerry Jameson. TELEPLAY: Michael Bankfort and Dennis Nemec. STORY: Paul Gallico. PHOTOGRAPHY: Matthew F. Leonetti. EDITOR: J. Terry Williams. MUSIC: Paul Chihara. ART DIRECTORS: Ross Bellah and Dale Hennesy. UNIT PRODUCTION MANAGER: Larry Kostroff. SPECIAL EFFECTS: Lee Redmond and Joseph Unsinn. STUNT COORDINATOR: Stan Barrett. CAST: Richard Crenna (Jason Voight), Elizabeth Ashley (Sharon Allan), David Dukes (David Allan), Joanna Miles (Jennifer Dreiser), Lloyd Bochner (Paul Gilliam), Merlin Olsen (Stan Webster), Andrew Duggan (President), Maggie Wellman (Carol), Marj Dusay (Ellen Gilliam), John Larch (Johnson), Kip Niven (Mac), William Bogert (Lustus), Jenny O'Hara (Ann Webster), Michael Biehn (Tom Rearden), Diana Douglas (Mrs. Rearden), Cindy Eilbacher (Paula Gilliam), Bill Williams (Dale Turner), Al White (Sergeant Lockett), George Petrie (Hank), Elta Blake (Co-ed), Roy Gainter (Dr. Jesse), Pat McMahon (News Director), Cecelia Allen (Elizabeth Richie), Dino Bachelor (Danny), Hank Kendrick (Launch Director), Bill Heywood (TV Announcer), David Burke Rhind (Chief Controller), Brad Zinn (Hutton), Bud Conlan (General Kloman), John Ross (Soldier), David Lee Rawlings (Air Guardsman), Dean Ricca (Laboratory Technician), Tom Noga (Airport National Guardsman), M.C. Brennan (Scared Child), Dewey Webb (Newsman).

Special effects and miniatures were the highlights of this lengthy telefilm that NBC-TV initially showed on November 26, 1978. Made by Columbia Pictures Television and Paul Driskill Productions, it told of an astronomer (Richard Crenna) predicting that a large comet is about to hit Phoenix, Arizona; his warnings fall on deaf ears. Filmed on location in Phoenix and Tucson, Arizona, the telefeature used nearly 6,000 extras for its evacuation sequences.

Goliath Awaits

(1981; 200 minutes; Color) PRODUCERS: Hugh Benson and Richard Bluel. EXECUTIVE PRODUCER: Larry White. ASSOCIATE PRODUCER: Pat Fielder. DIRECTOR: Kevin Connor. TELEPLAY: Richard Bluel and Pat Fielder. STORY: Hugh Benson, Richard Bluel and Pat Fielder. PHOTOGRAPHY: Al Francis. EDITORS: Donald Douglas and J. Terry Williams. MUSIC: George Duning. SOUND EDITOR: John Bushelman. PRODUCTION DESIGN: Ross Bellah. SETS: Audrey A. Blasdel and David Horowitz. UNIT PRODUCTION MANAGER: Robert J. Anderson. COSTUMES: Grady Hunt. MAKEUP: Carl Silvera. SPECIAL EFFECTS: Joe Unsinn. SCRIPT SUPERVISOR: Lee Walkling. ASSISTANT DIRECTORS: Mark R. Schilz and Jonathan Giles Zimmerman. CAST: Mark Harmon (Peter Cabot), Christopher Lee (John McKenzie), Eddie Albert (Admiral Wiley Sloan), John Carradine (Ronald Bentley), Alex Cord (Dr. Sam Marlowe), Robert Forster (Commander Jeff Selkirk), Frank Gorshin (Dan Wesker), Jean Marsh (Dr. Goldman), John McIntire (Senator Oliver Bartholomew), Jeanette Nolan (Mrs. Bartholomew), Duncan Regehr (Paul Ryker), Emma Samms (Lea McKenzie), Alan Fudge (Lew Bascomb), Kirk Cameron (Liam), Kip Niven (Gantman), Hedley Mattingly (Bailey), George Innes (Dave Miller), Alan Caillou (*Goliath* Captain), Warwick Sims (Luke Crane), Belinda Mayne (Sally Crane), Christina Nigra (Beth Crane), Michael Evans (Eric Whittaker), Peter von Zemeck (Hoffman), Laurence Haddon (Selma Captain Volero), Lori Lethin (Maria), Julie Bennett (Sylvia King), Clete Roberts (Anchorman), Irene Harvey (Carrie), Sandy Simpson (Moore), Peter Stader (Ed Linder), John Brandon (Chief Engineer), Lawrence Benedict (Young Bailey), Bruce Heighley (Technician), John Berwick (Crewman), Michael Vendress (Robby Cole), Larry Westman (Bowman), Peter Ashton (Enterprise Four Commander), Karen Lustgarten (Nurse), Larry Levine (Enterprise Four Officer), Tony Ballem (Edward R. Murrow), Michael White (PC18 Officer), Laird Stuart (Paul), John Ratzenberger (Bill Sweeney), Colin Drake (Old Man), Tom Dunstan (Agra Worker).

While searching for salvage, oceanographer Peter Cabot (Mark Harmon) comes upon the wreck of the British luxury liner *Goliath* that sunk in the Atlantic in 1939 after being hit by a U-boat torpedo. Over 1,800 passengers were thought to be lost in the tragedy but Cabot and his crew find the vessel is inhabited: Over 300 people, some descendents of the original passengers and crew, live in the wreckage in a Utopian society under the rulership of the ship's engineer, John McKenzie (Christopher Lee). McKenzie and most of the ship's inhabitants do not want to leave their world. The scientists are unaware that the vessel houses sensitive wartime documents that Admiral Wiley Sloan (Eddie Albert) has ordered destroyed.

Hugh Benson produced this posh, lengthy TV movie. It was telecast November 16 and 17, 1981, on Operation Prime Time in two parts and was also shown the same way in West Germany minus 14 minutes of its original 200-minute running time. Benson had previously done *A Fire in the Sky* (q.v.) in 1978 for Columbia and both telefilms had production design by Ross Bellah and special effects by Joseph A. (Joe) Unsinn. Filmed on location about the RMS *Queen Mary*, the telefilm was issued on laserdisc in a truncated

110-minute format. It marked the first time horror film greats John Carradine and Christopher Lee appeared together in the same film.

The Hunchback of Notre Dame

(1982; 102 minutes; Color) PRODUCER: Norman Rosemont. ASSOCIATE PRODUCER: Malcolm Christopher. DIRECTOR: Michael Tuchner. TELEPLAY: John Gay, from the novel by Victor Hugo. PHOTOGRAPHY: Alan Hume. EDITOR: Keith Palmer. ART DIRECTOR: Bill Bennison. PRODUCTION DESIGN: John Stoll. SETS: Harry Cordwell. COSTUMES: Phyllis Dalton. MAKEUP: Beryl Leman and Michael Morris. PRODUCTION MANAGER: Donald Toms. SPECIAL EFFECTS: John Morris. CONTINUITY: June Randall. ASSISTANT DIRECTOR: Ken Baker. CAST: Anthony Hopkins (Quasimodo), Lesley-Anne Down (Esmeralda), Derek Jacobi (Dom Claude Frollo), David Suchet (Clopin Troulliefou), Gerry Sundquist (Pierre Gringoire), Tim Piggot-Smith (Philippe), John Gielgud (Charmolue), Robert Powell (Phoebus), Nigel Hawthorne (Trial Magistrate), Roland Culver (Bishop of Paris), Rosalie Crutchley (Simons), Alan Webb (Trial Judge), David Kelly (Tavern Owner), Joseph Blatchley (Albert), Dave Hill (Coppenhole), Donald Eccles (Judge), Timothy Bateson (Commerce), Jack Klaff (Officer), Timothy Morand (Maurice), Martin Carroll (Herald), Hugo De Vernier (Nobility), Eunice Black (Clergy), Kenny Baker (Pickpocket), Michael Burrell (Clerical Aide), Anthony Carrick (Auditor), John Kidd (Doctor), Stanley Lebor (Torturer), Norman Lumsden (King's Advocate), Wally Thomas, John Rutland (Old Men), June Brown, Pam St. Clement (Cathedral Women).

CBS-TV's *The Hunchback of Notre Dame* was the eighth filming of the 1831 Victor Hugo novel; it was done by Columbia Pictures Television and Rosemont Productions and made at England's Pinewood Studios. Anthony Hopkins as Quasimodo was nominated for an Emmy Award. The novel first came to the screen in 1905 as *Esmeralda* and there were subsequent filmings under the novel's title in 1922 (a British production starring Sybil Thorndike and Booth Conway, also called *Esmeralda*), 1923 (the Universal classic starring Lon Chaney and Patsy Ruth Miller), 1939 (the well-done RKO production with Charles Laughton and Maureen O'Hara), 1956 (a French version co-starring Anthony Quinn and Gina Lollobrigida), 1965 (a BBC-TV production with Peter Woodthorpe and Gay Hamilton), and 1977 (an NBC-TV movie with Warren Clarke and Michelle Newell). Subsequent versions were made in 1996 by Disney as an animated feature and in 1997 with Mandy Patinkin as Quasimodo in TNT-TV's *The Hunchback*, shown in England the next year as *The Hunchback of Notre Dame*.

In medieval Paris, the hideous hunchback Quasimodo (Hopkins) is made "King of Fools" by the peasants. He later saves the beautiful Esmeralda (Lesley-Anne Down) from the courts and gives her refuge in the Notre Dame Cathedral where he is the bell ringer. Power-hungry Archdeacon Dom Claude Frollo (Derek Jacobi), who adopted the hunchback when he was an outcast infant, lusts for the peasant girl and tries to sacrifice Quasimodo to the masses so he can have the young woman, with tragic results.

Tony Schwartz wrote in the *New York Times*, "[Director Michael Tuchner] moves it along with a brisk economy, eschewing tangents and soliloquies in favor of telling the compelling tale in a lean, unfettered style.... [It] contains more than its share of gory scenes. But unlike so many television dramas, this one suggests the violence without dwelling exploitively on it. Nor is any of the drama's considerable power — including the stark final scene — diminished as a result."

Institute for Revenge

(1979; 74 minutes; Color) PRODUCERS: Bill Driskill and Bert Gold. EXECUTIVE PRODUCER: Otto Salamon. DIRECTOR: Ken Annakin. TELEPLAY: Bill Driskill. STORY: Bill Driskill and Otto Salamon. PHOTOGRAPHY: Roland "Ozzie" Smith. EDITOR: J. Terry Williams. MUSIC: Lalo Schifrin. ART DIRECTORS: Ross Bellah and Richard Lawrence. SETS: James Duffy and Audrey A. Blasdel. COSTUMES: Grady Hunt. UNIT PRODUCTION MANAGER: Berg Gold. MAKEUP: Ben Lane and Joe Hailey. ASSISTANT DIRECTORS: Nick Smirnoff and George Wagner. CAST: Sam Groom (John Schroeder), Lauren Hutton (Lilla Simms), Lane Binkley (Joanne Newcomb), T.J. McCavitt (T.J. Bradley), Robert Coote (Wellington), Murray Salem (Sam), Leslie Nielsen (Counselor Hollis Barnes), Ray Walston (Frank Anders), George Hamilton (Alan Roberto), Dennis O'Flaherty (Pilot Arthur), Robert Emhardt (Senator), James Karen (Power Broker), Harlee McBride, John Davey, Rawn Hutchinson (IFR Crew Members), Ron Roy, Anne Bellamy (IFR Clerks), Lisle Wilson (Graphologist), Ernie Fuentes (Mexican Police Officer), John Yates (Airport Guard), Paul Laurence (Designer), Jim Hess (Geologist), Patience Cleveland (Woman), Natalie Core (Woman in Bar), Gavin Mooney (Police Officer), Mo Lauren (Telephone Girl), John Hillerman (IFR Computer Voice).

A computer group plans to stop a corrupt Palm Springs realtor (George Hamilton) by putting together a bogus land deal to swindle him out of his money and put him behind bars. The whole thing is orchestrated by a computer dubbed IFR (Institute for Revenge) that supervises its agents in bringing wrongdoers to justice.

Columbia Pictures Television made this telefilm that was co-produced and written by Bill Driskill, who had earlier done *A Fire in the Sky* (1978) [q.v.] for the company. It was the pilot for a series that did not sell. Leonard Maltin in *TV Movies 1983–84* (1982) dubbed it "[t]ongue-in-cheek sci-fi ... Average."

The Magnificent Magical Magnet of Santa Mesa

(1977; 73 minutes; Color) PRODUCERS: Hy Averback and Jim Brown. EXECUTIVE PRODUCER: David Gerber. DIRECTOR: Hy Averback. TELEPLAY: Dee Caruso and Gerald Gardner. PHOTOGRAPHY: William K. Jurgensen. EDITOR: Asa Boyd. MUSIC: Jack Elliott and Allyn Ferguson. ART DIRECTORS: Ross Bellah and James Hulsey. COSTUMES: Grady Hunt. CAST: Michael Burns (Freddie Griffin), Dick Blasucci (Cal Bixby), Jane Connell (Ida Griffith), Keene Curtis (Mrs. Undershaft), Susan Blanchard (Marcie Hamilton), Conrad Janis (Mr. Kreel), Tom Poston (William Bensinger), Susan Sullivan (C.B. Macauley), Harry Morgan (J.J. Strange), Loni Anderson (Mrs. Daroon), Alex Sharp (Alex), Zachary Charles, Linda McClure (Van Riders), Jack Frey (Photographer), Martin Azarow (Lombardi), Hal Floyd (Hessler), Gary Glenn (Executive), William Hubbard Knight (Security Guard), Lindy Davis (Western Union Delivery Boy).

Another failed small-screen series pilot, this sci-fi comedy was originally scheduled to be shown by NBC in March 1977 as *The Adventures of Freddie*. Telecast on June 19, 1977, it was made by Columbia Pictures Television and David Gerber Productions. Steven H. Scheuer in *Movies on TV 1978–79* (1977) called it "a throwback to the situation comedies of the early sixties, with an updated energy crisis plot thrown in," and declared it had a "thin premise."

Good-natured mental wiz Freddie Griffith (Michael Burns) accidentally invents a disk whose force field can solve the planet's energy problems. His employers decide to take the invention for themselves in order to make a fortune.

Return to Fantasy Island

(1978; 100 minutes; Color) PRODUCER: Michael Fisher. EXECUTIVE PRODUCERS: Aaron Spelling, Leonard Goldberg and Shelley Hull. DIRECTOR: George McGowan. TELEPLAY: Marc Brandell. PHOTOGRAPHY: Archie R. Dalzell. EDITOR: John Woodcock. MUSIC: Laurence Rosenthal. ART DIRECTOR: Alfeo Bocchicchio. CAST: Ricardo Montalban (Mr. Roarke), Adrienne Barbeau (Margo Dean), Horst Buchholz (Charles Fleming), Joseph Campanella (Brian Faber), George Chakiris (Pierre), Joseph Cotten (Simon Grant), Pat Crowley (Lucy Faber), Laraine Day (Mrs. Grant), George Maharis (Lowell Benson), Cameron Mitchell (Raoul), France Nuyen (Kito), Karen Valentine (Janet Fleming), Herve Villechaize (Tattoo), John Zaremba (Dr. Croyden), Kevi Kendall (Pat), Kristine Ritzke (Carol), Nancy McKeon (Ann), Larry Moran (Second Runner).

Working title: *Fantasy Island II*.

Made by Columbia Pictures Television and Spelling-Goldberg Productions, *Return to Fantasy Island* was a follow-up to the previous year's *Fantasy Island* (q.v.). It was telecast January 20, 1978, eight days before the *Fantasy Island* series (ABC-TV, 1978–84) debuted.

Mr. Roarke (Ricardo Montalban) and his minuscule assistant Tattoo (Herve Villechaize) host a trio of couples on the remote tropical island they rent out at a hefty price to people who want to fulfill their dreams. Years before, Brian Faber (Joseph Campanella) and his wife Lucy (Pat Crowley) gave up the child they now want back; Charles Fleming (Horst Buchholz) hopes his wife Janet (Karen Valentine) will regain her memory; and businessman Benson (George Maharis) is out to win the love of his bad-tempered employer Margo Dean (Adrienne Barbeau).

Salvage

(1979; 100 minutes; Color) PRODUCERS: Norman S. Powell and Mike Lloyd Ross. EXECUTIVE PRODUCERS: Harve Bennett and Harris Katleman. DIRECTOR: Lee Phillips. TELEPLAY: Mike Lloyd Ross. PHOTOGRAPHY: Fred J. Koenekamp. EDITOR: Ronald LaVine. MUSIC: Walter Scharf. ART DIRECTORS: John Beckman and Ross Bellah. SOUND: Lee Strosnider. SPECIAL EFFECTS: Kevin Pike. ASSISTANT DIRECTOR: Bruce Hanson. CAST: Andy Griffith (Harry Broderick), Joel Higgins (Addison "Skip" Carmichael), Trish Stewart (Melanie "Mel" Slozar), Richard Jaeckel (Jack Klinger), J. Jay Saunders (Mack), Raleigh Bond (Fred), Jacqueline Scott (Lorene), Peter Brown (Bill Kelly), Lee DeBroux (Hank Beddoes), Richard Eastham (Commentator).

California scrap and salvage company owner Harry Broderick (Andy Griffith) enlists the aid of ex-astronaut "Skip" Carmichael (Joel Higgins) and NASA fuel expert Melanie Slozar (Trish Stewart) in constructing a spaceship that will take them to the Moon in order to bring back the machinery left there by the Apollo missions. They build a rocket ship, the *Vulture*, from a semi-trailer with a cement mixer and fueled by a concoction they dub mono-hydrazine. They successfully make the trip to the lunar surface and return with their cargo.

Telecast January 20, 1979, this ABC telefilm served as the pilot for the series *Salvage 1* that the network began showing nine days later (a dozen one-hour episodes ran through May of that year). In November 1979, two more episodes were shown while another quartet were not aired. These last four shows finally made it to the small screen in the early 1990s via The Nostalgia Channel.

Shadow on the Land

(1968; 100 minutes; Color) PRODUCER: Matthew Rapf. DIRECTOR: Richard C. Sarafian. TELEPLAY: Nedrick Young, from the novel *It Can't Happen Here* by Sinclair Lewis. PHOTOGRAPHY: Fred J. Koenekamp. EDITOR: Henry Batista. MUSIC: Sol Kaplan. ART DIRECTORS: John Beckman and Ross Bellah. CAST: Jackie Cooper (Lieutenant Colonel Andy Davis), John Forsythe (General Wendell Bruce), Gene Hackman (the Rev. Thomas Davis), Carol Lynley (Abigail "Abby" Tyler), Marc Strange (Major Shepherd McCloud), Janice Rule (Captain Everett), Michael Margotta (Timothy Willing), Bill Walker (Arnold), Scott Thomas (Felting), Myron Healey (General Hempstead), Frederic Downs (Drucker), Jonathan Lippe (Lieutenant Allen), Mickey Sholdar (Paul), Ronnie Eckstine (David), Sandy Kevin (Ben), Peter Jason (Man at Airport), Paulene Myers, Ken Swofford, Kay Stewart, Paul Sorensen.

Working title: *United States: It Can't Happen Here*.

Columbia Pictures-Screen Gems' first foray into the then new field of feature films made for television was *Shadow on the Land*, telecast by ABC-TV on December 4, 1968. An adaptation of the 1945 Sinclair Lewis novel *It Can't Happen Here*, the telefeature was called "one of the most peculiar things in movie history" by Jack Edmund Nolan in *Films in Review* (February 1969). He added, "I defy anyone, no matter how sophisticated politically, to explain who was shooting at whom during this film's last half-hour. The script of this by no means a political mess marks the return of Nedrick Young to American films." Steven H. Scheuer in *Movies on TV 1978–79* (1977) called it "[u]ninspiring ... Sloppy, energyless production." In *Judith Crist's TV Guide to the Movies* (1974) the reviewer termed it "sententiously grim and dreary."

In an effort to take over the government, Army General Wendell Bruce (John Forsythe) plans a raid on several California electric power depots, planning to make the attacks appear to be the work of left-wing extremists. He then wants to use the public momentum from the raids to start a national revolution which he would stop and then declare himself the country's ruler. Following the success of his plans, an underground group is started to restore the nation's freedom.

CHRONOLOGY

Feature Films

In order of release:

1928
Ransom (June)

1929
The Faker (January)

1930
Africa Speaks (August)

1932
The Menace (January)
Behind the Mask (February)
By Whose Hand? (July)
The Night Club Lady (August)

1933
Below the Sea (March)
The Circus Queen Murder (April)
Night of Terror (June)

1934
The Ninth Guest (January)
Black Moon (June)
Before Midnight (November)
Fog (November)

1935
Air Hawks (May)
The Black Room (July)
Super-Speed (December)

1936
Trapped by Television (June)
The Man Who Lived Twice (August)
Killer at Large (October)

1937
Lost Horizon (September)
The Shadow (December)

1938
Chinatown Nights (March)
League of Frightened Men (May)
The Gladiator (August)
Flight to Fame (October)

1939
Clouds Over Europe (June)
The Man They Could Not Hang (August)
Beware Spooks! (October)

1940
The Man with Nine Lives (April)
Island of Doomed Men (May)
The Phantom Wagon (May)
Blondie Has Servant Trouble (July)
Before I Hang (September)

1941
The Face Behind the Mask (January)
The Devil Commands (February)
Here Comes Mr. Jordan (August)
Ladies in Retirement (September)
Harvard, Here I Come (December)

1942
The Boogie Man Will Get You (October)

1944
The Return of the Vampire (January)
The Ghost That Walked Alone (February)
The Whistler (March)
Shadows in the Night (July)
Cry of the Werewolf (August)
The Soul of a Monster (August)
The Missing Juror (November)

1945
I Love a Mystery (January)
Crime Doctor's Courage (February)
Escape in the Fog (April)
Power of the Whistler (April)
Boston Blackie's Rendezvous (May)
A Thousand and One Nights (July)
Voice of the Whistler (October)
My Name Is Julia Ross (November)

1946
Just Before Dawn (March)
The Devil's Mask (May)
The Phantom Thief (May)
The Unknown (July)
Crime Doctor's Man Hunt (October)
So Dark the Night (October)

1947
Down to Earth (August)
Her Husband's Affairs (November)

1948
The Fatal Night (April)

The Return of October (October)
Jungle Jim (December)

1949
The Lost Tribe (May)
Riders in the Sky (December)

1950
Faust and the Devil (April)
Mark of the Gorilla (May)
Shadow of the Past (May)
Captive Girl (July)
Streets of Ghost Town (August)
Counterspy Meets Scotland Yard (November)
Pygmy Island (November)

1951
Fury of the Congo (February)
Five (April)
Hurricane Island (July)
Jungle Manhunt (October)
The Magic Carpet (October)
The Son of Dr. Jekyll (October)

1952
Jungle Jim in the Forbidden Land (February)
Thief of Damascus (April)
Storm Over Tibet (July)
Voodoo Tiger (November)
Invasion U.S.A. (December)

1953
Man in the Dark (May)
Siren of Bagdad (May)
The 5000 Fingers of Dr. T (July)
Savage Mutiny (September)
Killer Ape (December)
El Monstruo Resucitado

1954
Bait (February)
The Mad Magician (May)
Cannibal Attack (November)

1955
Jungle Moon Men (April)
Footsteps in the Fog (June)
Creature with the Atom Brain (July)
It Came from Beneath the Sea (July)
Devil Goddess (October)

1956
Earth vs. the Flying Saucers (July)
The Werewolf (July)
1984 (September)
The Gamma People (December)

1957
The Man Who Turned to Stone (March)
Zombies of Mora Tau (April)
The Giant Claw (June)
The Night the World Exploded (June)
20 Million Miles to Earth (June)
The 27th Day (July)
Ladrón de Cadaveres (September)

1958
Bell Book and Candle (January)
The Revenge of Frankenstein (June)
Curse of the Demon (July)
El Castillo de los Monstrous (October)
Misterio de la Magia Negra (November)
The 7th Voyage of Sinbad (December)

1959
Forbidden Island (March)
City of Fear (April)
The H-Man (May)
The Tingler (July)
Womaneater (July)
Have Rocket, Will Travel (August)
The 30 Foot Bride of Candy Rock (August)
The Ugly Duckling (August)
1001 Arabian Nights (December)

1960
Swan Lake (January)
The Electronic Monster (May)
Stranglers of Bombay (May)
12 to the Moon (June)
Battle in Outer Space (July)
13 Ghosts (July)
The 3 Worlds of Gulliver (December)

1961
Homicidal (June)
Most Dangerous Man Alive (June)
Terror of the Tongs (July)
Scream of Fear (August)
Mr. Sardonicus (October)
Valley of the Dragons (November)
Mysterious Island (December)

1962
The Three Stooges Meet Hercules (February)
Mothra (February)
The Underwater City
The Three Stooges in Orbit (July)
Zotz! (July)

1963
Jason and the Argonauts (June)
Maniac (October)
The Old Dark House (October)

1964
Little Prince and the Eight-Headed Dragon (January)
Dr. Strangelove or: How I Learned to Stop Worrying and Love the Bomb (January)
Strait-Jacket (January)
Gorath (May)
Fail-Safe (October)
First Men in the Moon (November)
The Curse of the Mummy's Tomb (December)

1965
Die! Die! My Darling (March)
These Are the Damned (July)
Repulsion (October)

1966
The Magic World of Topo Gigio (January)
The Silencers (February)
Profanadores de Tumbas (April)
The Sleeping Beauty (April)
A Study in Terror (April)
Mystery of Thug Island (May)
Superargo vs. Diabolicus (June)
Birds Do It (August)

The Man Called Flintstone (August)
Kiss the Girls and Make Them Die (November)
Murderer's Row (December)

1967
A Midsummer Night's Dream (January)
Casino Royale (April)
Good Times (May)
Torture Garden (December)
El Imperio de Dracula

1968
Berserk (January)
Corruption (February)
Doctor Faustus (February)
The Ambushers (March)
Arañas Infernales (May)
La Sombra del Murciélago (July)

1969
The Wrecking Crew (January)
Pacto Diabólico (February)
Las Vampiras (June)
Hamlet (September)
Enigma de Muerte (November)
The Mad Room (December)
Marooned (December)
La Señora Muerte (December)

1970
Watermelon Man (May)

1971
The Brotherhood of Satan (August)
Creatures the World Forgot (September)
See No Evil (September)
Macbeth (October)
A Safe Place (October)
Fear Chamber
The Incredible Invasion
Snake People

1973
The Creeping Flesh (February)
Reflections of Fear (May)
Lost Horizon (September)

1974
The Golden Voyage of Sinbad (April)

The Mutations (September)
Chosen Survivors (December)

1975
The Stepford Wives (December)

1976
Jack and the Beanstalk (February)
Shadow of the Hawk (July)

1977
Sinbad and the Eye of the Tiger (June)
Close Encounters of the Third Kind (November)

1978
Warlords of Atlantis (May)
The Eyes of Laura Mars (August)
House of Evil

1979
The Ravagers (May)
The Humanoid (June)
Nightwing (June)
When a Stranger Calls (October)

1981
Happy Birthday to Me (May)

1982
Silent Rage (April)

Serials

1938
The Secret of Treasure Island (March)
The Spider's Web (October)

1939
Mandrake the Magician (May)

1940
The Shadow (January)
Terry and the Pirates (May)
Deadwood Dick (July)
The Green Archer (October)

1941
The Spider Returns (May)
The Iron Claw (August)

1942
Captain Midnight (February)
The Secret Code (September)

1943
Batman (April)
The Phantom (December)

1945
The Monster and the Ape (April)
Jungle Raiders (September)
Who's Guilty? (December)

1946
Hop Harrigan (March)

1947
Jack Armstrong (February)
The Vigilante (May)
The Sea Hound (September)

1948
Superman (July)
Congo Bill (October)
Brick Bradford (December)

1949
Bruce Gentry (February)
Batman and Robin (May)
Adventures of Sir Galahad (December)

1950
Atom Man vs. Superman (July)

1951
Roar of the Iron Horse (May)
Mysterious Island (August)
Captain Video (December)

1952
King of the Congo (May)
Blackhawk (July)

1953
The Lost Planet (June)

1955
Adventures of Captain Africa (June)

Short Subjects

1934
Shivers (December)

1935
Gum Shoes (March)

1936
Midnight Blunders (April)

1938
Three Missing Links (July)

1939
Three Little Sew and Sews (January)
We Want Our Mummy (February)
Three Sappy People (December)

1940
You're Next (May)
The Spook Speaks (September)

1941
Host to a Ghost (August)
Sweet Spirits of Nighter (December)

1942
All Work and No Pay (July)
Phony Cronies (August)

1943
Dizzy Detectives (February)
Spook Louder (April)
Boobs in the Night (June)
A Gem of a Jam (December)

1944
To Heir Is Human (January)
The Yoke's On Me (May)
Idle Roomers (July)

1945
Three Pests in a Mess (January)
If a Body Meets a Body (August)
Spook to Me (December)

1946
A Bird in the Head (February)
Get Along Little Zombie (April)
Pardon My Terror (September)

1947
Nervous Shakedown (March)
All Gummed Up (December)

1948
Shivering Sherlocks (January)
Tall, Dark and Gruesome (April)
Fiddlers Three (May)
The Hot Scots (July)
Heavenly Daze (September)
I'm a Monkey's Uncle (October)
Mummy's Dummies (November)
Crime on Their Hands (December)

1949
The Ghost Talks (February)
Who Done It? (March)
Microspook (June)
Fuelin' Around (July)
Hokus Pokus (August)

1950
Hold That Monkey (February)
Dopey Dicks (March)
One Shivery Night (July)

1951
Three Arabian Nuts (January)
Scrambled Brains (June)
Merry Mavericks (September)
The Tooth Will Out (October)
Hula-La-La (November)
Fraidy Cat (December)

1952
Cuckoo on a Choo-Choo (December)

1953
Bubble Trouble (January)
Spooks (June)

1954
Musty Musketeers (May)
Scotched in Scotland (November)

1955
Of Cash and Hash (February)
Bedlam in Paradise (April)
Stone Age Romeos (June)
One Spooky Night (September)
Hot Ice (October)
Hook a Crook (November)

1956
Creeps (February)
Flagpole Jitters (April)
For Crimin' Out Loud (May)
Hot Stuff (September)

1957
Hoofs and Goofs (January)
Space Ship Sappy (April)
Horsing Around (September)
Outer Space Jitters (December)

1958
Flying Saucer Daffy (October)

1959
Operation Universe
Tales of Frankenstein

Telefeatures

1968
Shadow on the Land (December)

1971
Black Noon (November)

1977
Fantasy Island (January)
The Magnificent Magnet of Santa Mesa (June)

1978
Return to Fantasy Island (January)
A Fire in the Sky (November)

1979
Institute for Revenge (January)
Salvage (January)

1980
The Curse of King Tut's Tomb (May)

1981
Goliath Awaits (November)

1982
The Hunchback of Notre Dame (April)
Desire the Vampire (November)

BIBLIOGRAPHY

Books

Alvarez, Max Joseph. *Index to Motion Pictures Reviewed by* Variety, *1907–1980*. Metuchen, NJ: Scarecrow, 1982.

Alyn, Kirk. *A Job for Superman!* Hollywood, CA: Kirk Alyn, 1971.

Bannon, Jim. *The Son That Rose in the West*. Plano, TX: Devil's Hole, c. 1974.

Barbour, Alan G. *Cliffhanger: A Pictorial History of the Motion Picture Serial*. New York: A&W, 1977.

_____. *Days of Thrills of Adventure*. New York: Collier, 1970.

_____. *The Serials of Columbia*. Kew Gardens, NY: Screen Facts, 1967.

Barnes, David. *Sherlock Holmes on the Screen: The Complete Film and TV History*. London: Reynolds and Hearn, 2002.

Blake, David, and David Deal. *The Eurospy Guide*. Baltimore, MD: Luminary, 2004.

Bleiler, David, ed. *TLA Video & DVD Guide 2004*. New York: St. Martin's Griffin, 2003.

Bojarski, Richard. *The Films of Bela Lugosi*. Secaucus, NJ: Citadel, 1980.

_____, and Kenneth Beale. *The Films of Boris Karloff*. Secaucus, NJ: Citadel, 1974.

Brode, Douglas. *Lost Films of the Fifties*. New York: Citadel/Carol, 1991.

Brooks, Tim, and Earle Marsh. *The Complete Directory to Prime Time Network TV Shows, 1946-Present*. New York: Ballantine, 1988.

Bruskin, David N. *The White Brothers: Jack, Jules, & Sam White*. Metuchen, NJ: Scarecrow, 1990.

Butler, Ivan. *The Horror Film*. South Brunswick, NJ: A.S. Barnes, 1969. (Revised as *Horror in the Cinema*. New York: New Paperback Library, 1971.)

Cocchi, John. *Second Feature: The Best of the "B" Films*. New York: Citadel/Carol, 1991.

Crist, Judith. *Judith Crist's TV Guide to the Movies*. New York: Popular, 1974.

Davies, David Stuart. *Holmes at the Movies: The Screen Career of Sherlock Holmes*. New York: Bramhall House, 1976.

Everman, Wade. *Cult Horror Films*. New York: Citadel/Carol, 1995.

_____. *Cult Science Fiction Films*. New York: Citadel/Carol, 1995.

Eyles, Allen, Robert Adkinson and Nicholas Fry, eds. *The House of Horror: The Story of Hammer Films*. London: Lorrimer, 1973.

Fischer, Dennis. *Science Fiction Film Directors, 1895–1998*. Jefferson, NC: McFarland, 2000.

Frank, Alan. *Horror Films*. London: Spring, 1977.

Gifford, Denis. *The British Film Catalogue 1895–1985*. New York: Facts on Film, 1986.

_____. *Karloff: The Man, the Monster, the Movies*. New York: Curtis, 1973.

_____. *Movie Monsters*. New York: Studio Vista/E.P. Dutton, 1969.

_____. *A Pictorial History of Horror Movies*. London: Hamblyn, 1973.

_____. *Science Fiction Films*. New York: Studio Vista/E.P. Dutton, 1971.

Glut, Donald F. *Classic Movie Monsters*. Metuchen, NJ: Scarecrow, 1978.

Grossman, Gary. *Superman: Serial to Cereal*. New York: Popular Library, 1976.

Hardy, Phil, ed. *The Encyclopedia of Horror Movies*. New York: Harper and Row, 1986.

_____. *Science Fiction*. New York: William Morrow, 1984.

Herx, Henry, and Tony Zaza. *The Family Guide to Movies on Video*. New York: Crossroad, 1988.

Hickerson, Jay. *The New, Revised Ultimate History of Network Radio Programming and Guide to All Circulating Shows*. Hamden, CT: Jay Hickerson, 1996.

Hirschhorn, Clive. *The Columbia Story*. London: Hamblyn, 1999.

Hunter, Allan. *Chambers Film Facts*. Edinburgh: Chambers, 1993.

_____. *The Wordsworth Book of Movie Classics*. Hertfordshire: Cumberland House, 1996.

Jenson, Paul M. *The Men Who Made the Monsters*. London: Twayne, 1996.

Jones, Stephen. *The Essential Monster Movie Guide*. New York: Billboard, 2000.

_____. *The Frankenstein Scrapbook.* New York: Citadel/Carol, 1995.
_____. *The Illustrated Werewolf Movie Guide.* London: Titan, 1996.
Kane, Joe. *The Phantom of the Movies' Videoscope.* New York: Three Rivers, 2000.
Kaplan, Phillip J. *The Best, Worst & Most Unusual: Hollywood Musicals.* New York: Beekman, 1983.
Katz, Ephraim. *The Film Encyclopedia.* New York: Harper Perennial, 1994.
Lee, Walt. *Reference Guide to Fantastic Films* (3 vols.). Los Angeles: Chelsea-Lee, 1972–74.
Lentz, Harris M., III. *Science Fiction, Horror & Fantasy Film and Television Credits* (2 vols.). Jefferson, NC: McFarland, 1983.
London, Rose. *Zombie: The Living Dead.* New York: Bounty, 1976.
Lucas, Tim. *The Video Watchdog Book.* Cincinnati: Video Watchdog, 1972.
Maltin, Leonard. *The Great Movie Shorts.* New York: Crown, 1972.
_____, ed. *Leonard Maltin's 2004 Movie & Video Guide.* New York: Signet, 2003.
_____. *Movie Comedy Teams.* New York: New American Library, 1985.
Mank, Gregory William, James T. Coughlin and Dwight D. Frye. *Dwight Frye's Last Laugh.* Baltimore, MD: Luminary, 1997.
Marill, Alvin H. *Movies Made for Television: The Telefeature and the Mini-Series, 1964–1984.* New York: New York Zoetrope, 1984.
Martin, Len D. *The Columbia Checklist: The Feature Films, Serials, Cartoons and Short Subjects of Columbia Pictures Corporation, 1922–1988.* Jefferson, NC: McFarland, 1990.
Mavis, Paul. *The Espionage Filmography.* Jefferson, NC: McFarland, 2001.
Mayo, Mike. *Videohound's Horror Show.* Detroit: Invisible Ink, 1998.
Miller, Don. *B Movies.* New York: Curtis, 1973.
_____. *Hollywood Corral.* New York: Popular Library, 1976.
Mulholland, Jim. *The Abbott and Costello Book.* New York: Popular Library, 1975.
Naha, Ed. *From Screen to Scream.* New York: Avon, 1975.
_____. *The Science Fictionary.* Wideview, 1989.
Okuda, Ted, with Edward Watz. *The Columbia Comedy Shorts: Two-Reel Hollywood Film Comedies, 1933–1958.* Jefferson, NC: McFarland, 1986.
O'Neill, James. *Terror on Tape.* New York: Billboard, 1994.
Ottoson, Robert. *A Reference Guide to American Film Noir: 1940–1958.* Metuchen, NJ: Scarecrow, 1981.
Parish, James Robert. *Ghosts and Angels in Hollywood Films.* Jefferson, NC: McFarland, 1994.
_____. *The Hollywood Celebrity Death Book.* Las Vegas NV: Pioneer, 1993.
_____, and Michael R. Pitts. *The Great Detective Pictures.* Metuchen, NJ: Scarecrow, 1990.
_____, and _____. *The Great Science Fiction Pictures.* Metuchen, NJ: Scarecrow, 1977.
_____, and _____. *The Great Science Fiction Pictures II.* Metuchen, NJ: Scarecrow, 1990.
_____, and _____. *The Great Spy Pictures.* Metuchen, NJ: Scarecrow, 1974.
Parish, James Robert, and Stephen Whitney. *Vincent Price Unmasked: A Biography.* New York: Drake, 1974.
Perry, Danny. *Guide for the Film Fanatic.* New York: Fireside/Simon & Schuster, 1986.
Pitts, Michael R. *Famous Movie Detectives.* Metuchen, NJ: Scarecrow, 1979.
_____. *Famous Movie Detectives II.* Metuchen, NJ: Scarecrow, 1991.
_____. *Horror Film Stars,* 3rd ed. Jefferson, NC: McFarland, 2002.
_____. *Radio Soundtracks: A Reference Guide,* 2d ed. Metuchen, NJ: Scarecrow, 1986.
_____. *Western Film Series of the Sound Era.* Jefferson, NC: McFarland, 2009.
Pohle, Robert, Jr., and Douglas C. Hart. *The Films of Christopher Lee.* Metuchen, NJ: Scarecrow, 1983.
Price, Michael H., and George E. Turner. *Human Monsters: The Definitive Edition.* Baltimore, MD: Luminary, 2004.
Pym, John, ed. *Time Out Film Guide, 9th Edition, 2001.* London: Penguin, 2000.
Quinlan, David. *British Sound Films: The Studio Years, 1928–1959.* Towowa, NJ: Barnes and Noble, 1985.
_____. *Quinlan's Film Directors: The Ultimate Guide to the Directors of the Big Screen.* London: B.T. Batsford, 1999.
_____. *Quinlan's Film Stars: The Ultimate Guide to the Stars of the Big Screen,* 5th ed. Washington, DC: Brassey's, 2000.
Rainey, Buck. *The Fabulous Holts.* Nashville, TN: Western Film Collector, 1976.
_____. *Serials and Series: A World Filmography, 1912–1956.* Jefferson, NC: McFarland, 1999.
_____. *Those Fabulous Serial Heroines: Their Lives and Films.* Metuchen, NJ: Scarecrow, 1990.
Ross, Jonathan. *The Incredibly Strange Film Book.* London: Simon & Schuster, 1993.
Scaramazza, Paul A. *Ten Years in Paradise.* Arlington, VA: Pleasant, 1974.
The Scarecrow Video Movie Guide. Seattle, WA: Sasquatch, 2004.
Scheuer, Steven H. *Movies on TV and Videocassette, 1991–1992.* New York: Bantam, 1990.
_____, ed. *TV Movie Almanac & Ratings, 1958 and 1959.* New York: Bantam, 1958.
Searles, Baird. *Films of Science Fiction & Fantasy.* New York: AFI/Harry N. Abrams, 1988.
Senn, Bryan. *Drums of Terror: Voodoo in the Cinema.* Baltimore, MD: Luminary, 1998.

_____. *Golden Horrors: An Illustrated Critical Filmography, 1931–1939*. Jefferson, NC: McFarland, 1996.
Sigoloff, Marc. *The Films of the Seventies*. Jefferson, NC: McFarland, 1984.
Soister, John T. *Up from the Vault: Rare Thrillers of the 1920s and 1930s*. Jefferson, NC: McFarland, 2004.
Speed, F. Maurice. *Film Review, 1962–1963*. London: MacDonald, 1962.
_____. *Film Review, 1963–1964*. London: MacDonald, 1963.
_____. *Film Review, 1964–1965*. London: MacDonald, 1964.
_____. *Film Review, 1966–1968*. South Brunswick, NJ: A.S. Barnes, 1967.
_____. *Film Review, 1968–1969*. South Brunswick, NJ: A.S. Barnes, 1968.
_____. *Film Review, 1969–1970*. South Brunswick, NJ: A.S. Barnes, 1969.
_____. *Film Review, 1970–1971*. South Brunswick, NJ: A.S. Barnes, 1970.
_____. *Film Review, 1972–1973*. South Brunswick, NJ: A.S. Barnes, 1972.
_____. *Film Review, 1979–1980*. New York: Hawthorn, 1979.
Stanley, John. *John Stanley's Creature Feature Movie Guide Strikes Again*. Pacifica, CA: Creatures at Large, 1994.
Steinbrunner, Chris, and Norman Michaels. *The Films of Sherlock Holmes*. Secaucus, NJ: Citadel, 1978.
Strick, Philip. *Science Fiction Movies*. London: Octopus, 1976.
Terrace, Vincent. *The Complete Encyclopedia of Television Programs, 1947–1976* (2 vols.). Cranbury, NJ: A.S. Barnes, 1976.
Thomas, Bob. *King Cohn: The Life and Times of Hollywood Mogul Harry Cohn*. Beverly Hills, CA: New Millennium, 2000.
Thomson, David. *The New Biographical Dictionary of Film*. New York: Alfred A. Knopf, 2002.
Truitt, Evelyn Mack. *Who Was Who on Screen*. New York: R.R. Bowker, 1974.
Turner, George E., and Michael H. Price. *Forgotten Horrors: The Definitive Edition*. Baltimore, MD: Midnight Marquee, 1999.
Tuska, Jon. *The Detective in Hollywood*. Garden City, NY: Doubleday, 1978.
TV Feature Film Sourcebook (two volumes). New York: Broadcast Information Bureau, 1978.
Vale, V., and Andrea Juno. *Incredibly Strange Films*. San Francisco, CA: Re/Search, 1986.
Van Hise, James. *Hot Blooded Dinosaur Movies*. Las Vegas, NV: Pioneer, 1993.
Video Hound's Complete Guide to Cult Flicks and Trash Pics. Detroit: Visible Ink, 1996.
Video Hound's Golden Movie Retriever 1991. Detroit: Visible Ink, 1991.
Video Hound's Sci-Fi Experience: Your Quantum Guide to the Video Universe. Detroit: Visible Ink, 1997.
Warren, Bill. *Keep Watching the Skies! Vol. 1: 1950–1957*. Jefferson, NC: McFarland, 1982
_____. *Keep Watching the Skies! Vol. 2: 1958–1962*. Jefferson, NC: McFarland, 1986.
Weiss, Ken, and Ed Goodgold. *To Be Continued...* New York: Crown, 1972.
Weldon, Michael J., with Charles Beesley, Bob Martin and Akira Fitton. *The Psychotronic Encyclopedia of Film*. New York: Ballantine, 1983.
_____. *The Psychotronic Film Guide*. New York: St. Martin's Griffin, 1996.
Williams, Lucy Chase. *The Complete Films of Vincent Price*. New York: Citadel/Carol, 1995.
Willis, Donald C. *Horror and Science Fiction Films: A Checklist*. Metuchen, NJ: Scarecrow, 1972.
_____. *Horror and Science Fiction Films II*. Metuchen, NJ: Scarecrow, 1982.
Young, R.G. *The Encyclopedia of Fantastic Films: Ali Baba to Zombies*. New York: Applause, 2000.

Periodicals

Castle of Frankenstein (North Bergen, NJ)
Cinefantastique (Oak Park, IL)
Cliffhanger (Waynesville, NC)
Famous Monsters of Filmland (New York)
Fangoria (New York)
Film Fan Monthly (Teaneck, NJ)
Filmfax (Evanston, IL)
Filmograph (Alexandria, VA)
Films in Review (New York)
The Films of Yesteryear (Waynesville, NC)
Focus on Film (London, England)
Harrison's Reports (New York)
Horror Monsters (Derby, CT)
Little Shoppe of Horrors (Waterloo, IA)
Mad Monsters (Derby, CT)
Monster World (New York)
Monsters of the Movies (New York)
Photon (Brooklyn, NY)
Psychotronic Video (Chincoteague, VA)
Screen Facts (Kew Gardens, NY)
Screen Thrills Illustrated (Philadelphia, PA)
Serial Quarterly (Kew Gardens, NY)
Spacemen (Philadelphia, PA)
Variety (New York)
Video Watchdog (Cincinnati, OH)
Views & Reviews (Milwaukee, WI)

Websites

American Film Institute (www.afi.com)
Creepy Classics (www.creepyclassics.com)
Internet Movie Database (www.imdb.com)
Newspaper Archive (www.newspaperarchive.com)

Index

Abbas, Hector 80
Abbot, Anthony *see* Oursler, Fulton
Abbott, Bud 119
Abbott, John 50, 189, 249
Abbott, Vic 141
Adams, Beverly 5, 18, 214, 256
Adams, Dorothy 55
Adams, Ernie 70, 71, 152, 301, 303, 339
Adams, Julie 267
Adams, Mason 228
Adams, Nan 85
Adams, Ted 326
Adkinson, Robert 183, 203, 233
Adonis, Frank 72
Adrian, Iris 26
The Adventures of Captain Africa 288, 361
The Adventures of Freddie see *The Magnificent Magnet of Santa Mesa*
The Adventures of Sir Galahad 288–89, 361
The Adventures of Superman 322–23
Africa Speaks 3, 22, 359
Agar, John 7, 144
Aherne, Patrick 225
Ahuet, Julio 190
Ainslee, Mary 320, 331, 334
Air Hawks 3–4, 21, 83, 359
Alberoni, Sherri 253
Albert, Eddie 180, 354
Albright, Hardie 180
Alcazar, Eduardo 133
Alcocer, Victor 112
Alda, Rutanya 278
Alien Terror see *The Incredible Invasion*
Alison, Dorothy 204
All Gummed Up 328, 329, 362
All Work and No Pay 328, 330, 362
Allen, Gracie 339
Allen, Irving 88, 166
Allen, Joseph A., Jr. 30
Allen, Patrick 179
Allen, Robert 21

Allen, Steve 286
Allen, Woody 32
Aloha, Lei 337
Alper, Murray 186, 189
Alpert, Herb 32
Alter, Robert Edmond 193
Alton, John 261
Alvarado, Crox 132
Alvarado, Manuel 107
Alvarez, Miguel Angel 184, 185, 206
Alyas Phantom 311
Alyn, Kirk 289, 290, 293, 322, 323
The Ambushers 4–6, 131, 214, 282, 361
Ameche, Jim 302
American Hero 303
Ames, Ramsay 326
Amicus Productions 256, 275
Andersen, Hans Christian 266
Anderson, Dusty 186
Anderson, James 80
Anderson, Melissa Sue 97, 98
Anderson, Steven 278
Andress, Ursula 32
Andrews, Dana 52, 114
Andrews, Harry 352
Andrews, Robert Hardy 302
Andrews, Stanley 233, 234
Anirca, Carlos 161, 206
Ankers, Evelyn 131
Ankrum, Morris 65, 90, 163, 285
Ann-Margret 165
Anna-Lisa 99, 260, 261
Annis, Francesca 140
Anthony, Olga 167
Anthony, Scott 167
Apfel, Oscar 157
Arañas Infernales (Hellish Spiders) 6–7, 112, 223, 361
Arch Oboler Productions 80
Archer, Eugene 253
Archer, John 37
Arent, Eddi 300
Argenziano, Carmen 278

Arlen, Johnny 241
Arless, Jean 105, 106
Arling, Arthur 231
Arliss, George 20, 157
Armendariz, Pedro, Jr. 34, 271
Armstrong, Leslie 77
Armstrong, Todd 120
Arnaz, Desi 144
Arnold, Edward 133
Arnold, Phil 329, 333
Arsenic and Old Lace 24
Arvan, Jan 263
Ash, Arty 34
Ashe, Warren 89
Asher, William 265
Ashley, Joel 285
Ashton, Roy 96
Aslan, Gregoire 92, 253
Associated British Pictures 51, 53, 59
Astaire, Fred 201
Astor, Mary 258
Ates, Roscoe 351
Atom Man vs. Superman 289–90, 293, 323, 361
Attack of the 50 Foot Woman (1958) 207, 247
Atwater, Edith 231
Atwill, Lionel 14
Auberjonois, Rene 72
Aubrey, Jimmy 330, 336
Austin, Charlotte 150, 151
Austin, Gene 50–51
Austin, Harold 3
Austin, William 197
Autry, Gene 200, 297
Averback, Hy 14
Le Avventure di Topo Gigio see *The Magic World of Topo Gigio*
Axmaker, Sean 60
Ayres, Lew 187

Babcock, Barbara 34
Bach, Barbara 108
Bacharach, Burt 138
Backus, Jim 183, 184
Bacon, Lloyd 140
Baer, John 326
Bagni, John 5
Bailey, Ray 295
Bailey, Robin 205

Bainter, Fay 169
Baird, Phillip 260
Bait 7, 297, 360
Baja Marimba Band 200
Baker, Benny 187
Baker, Diane 229, 230
Baker, Eddie 332
Baker, Tom 92, 167
Bakewell, William 301
Balachine, George 157
Balboa, Rosangela 112
Baldwin, Alec 318
Baldwin, Walter 55, 159, 189
Balfour, Michael 140
Ball, Lucille 100, 143, 144
Ball, Richard 278
Ballard, Lucien 82, 209
Bankhead, Tallulah 58, 59
Banks, Lionel 131, 196
Bannon, Jim 58, 109, 110, 159, 186, 226, 227, 267, 268
Barbeau, Adrienne 356
Barbera, Joseph 145
Barbour, Alan G. 289, 291, 295, 302, 303, 311, 324
Barcroft, Roy 66
Bardette, Trevor 159, 280
Barker, Lex 171
Barnabe, Bruno 217
Barnes, Alan 237
Barnes, Clive 158
Barnes, Paul 295
Barnes, Rayford 249
Barnett, Grif 318
Barnett, Vince 181
Baron, Lita 122
Barrat, Robert H. 127
Barrett, Edith 131, 132
Barrie, Mona 58, 127
Barrier, Edgar 90, 109
Barron, Robert 313, 326
Barrow, Janet 52
Barry, Gene 264, 265
Barry, Julian 72
Barry, Phyllis 348
Barrymore, John 21, 58, 225
Bartay, Barbara 336, 341
Barthelmess, Richard 255
Bartok, Eva 88
Barton, Pat 289

367

Barty, Billy 191
Barwise, Richard 161
Barzell, Wolfe 106
Bateman, Charles 27
Bates, Jeanne 212, 226, 311
Batman (1943) 290–91, 361
Batman (1966) 291
Batman and Robin 291–92, 309, 361
Battle in Outer Space 7–9, 66, 360
Battle in Outer Space 2 9
Bau, George 141
Bauer, David 257
Bava, Mario 71
Baxter, John 243
Baxter, Warner 46, 47, 48, 127, 212
Bayler, Terence 140
Baz, Beatriz 107
Bazhenova, Irina 220
Beale, Kenneth 149
Beard, Renee 295
The Beast with Five Fingers 74
Beck, Calvin T. 156
Beck, Michael 63
Beckley, Tony 278
Beckwith, Reginald 52
Beddoe, Don 9, 18, 24, 73, 98, 116, 148, 349
Bedlam in Paradise 328–29, 334, 362
Before I Hang 9–10, 55, 359
Before Midnight 4, 10–11, 359
Behind the Door see *The Man with Nine Lives*
Behind the Mask (1932) 9, 11–12, 21, 55, 259, 359
Beirute, Yerye 78, 112, 113, 133
Bell, James 267
Bell Book and Candle 12–14, 360
Bellamy, Ralph 4, 10, 15, 118, 149
Belle, Camilla 279
Below the Sea 4, 14–16, 20, 83, 118, 359
Benedict, Billy 280
Benjamin, Adrian 61
Bennet, Spencer Gordon 202, 300, 305
Bennett, Bruce 9, 116, 152
Bennett, Charles 51
Bennett, Joan 13
Bennett, Linda 42
Bennett, Marjorie 100
Benson, Hugh 354
Benson, Martin 253
Berest, Frederic 124, 273
Berg, Nancy 75
Berger, Santa 5
Bernard, James 243
Bernardi, Herschel 184
Bernds, Edward 249, 252, 270, 329, 350
Berne, Estafon 162
Bernstein, Elmer 204, 215
Bernstein, Walter 76
Berserk 16–17, 67, 210, 238, 256, 361
Bertrand, Rafael 220

Besser, Joe 330, 331–32, 335, 342, 344
Bevan, Billy 197
Beware Spooks! 17–18, 91, 359
Bey, Tema 260
Bice, Robert 114
Bijo to Ekitainingen see *The H-Man*
Billy Smart Circus 17
Binns, Edward (Ed) 75
Birch, Wyrley 258
A Bird in the Hand 329, 362
Birds Do It 18–19, 360
Birell, Tala 4, 189
Bisset, Donald 204, 274
Black, Stanley 77
Black Angel 20
Black Moon 14, 19–20, 21, 259, 359
Black Noon 352, 362
The Black Room 9, 20–22, 55, 359
Black Shadow see Cruz, Alejandro
Blackhawk 292–93, 361
Blackman, Honor 120
Blackmer, Sidney 36
Blair, Patricia 37
Blake, Amanda 41
Blake, Larry J. 65, 277
Blake, Pamela 313
Blanc, Mel 145
Bland, Trevor 15
Blane, Sally 174
Blind Terror see *See No Evil*
Bloch, Robert 231, 256, 257
Block, Irving 247
Blocker, Dan 342
The Blonde Captive 22–23
Blondell, Joan 229
Blondie Has Servant Troubles 23, 89, 359
Blood from the Mummy's Tomb 53
Blue Demon 6, 68, 69, 191, 223, 224
Blum, Jack 98
Blummer, John 301
Bly, Wesley 347
Blystone, Stanley 344
Blythe, Betty 10
Blythe, Erik 114
Bodeen, De Witt 262
Body Snatchers see *Ladrón de Cadaveres*
Boetticher, Budd (Oscar, Jr.) 158, 159
Bogdanovich, Peter 163
Bogeaus, Benedict 163
Bojarski, Richard 149
Bolster, Anita 168
Bolton, Muriel Roy 169
Bomba, Ray 249
Bond, David 214, 331, 334
Bond, Lillian 181
Bond, Tommy 290, 323
Bond, Ward 149
Boniface, Symona 334
Bonner, Tony 44
Bonney, Gail 255
Bono, Sonny 93, 94

Boobs in the Night 329, 331, 342, 362
The Boogie Man Will Get You 23–25, 55, 74, 359
Booke, Sorrell 75
Booth, Anthony 39
Borden, Eugene 222
Borelli, Carlo 67
Borg, Veda Ann 303, 318
Borgnine, Ernest 193
Boston Blackie's Private Ghost see *The Phantom Thief*
Boston Blackie's Rendezvous 25–27, 186, 359
Bosworth, Hobart 317
Boteler, Wade 258
Bottoms, Timothy 303
Bouchey, Bill 295
Boulton, Matthew 224
Boyer, Charles 138
Boylan, Malcolm Stuart 268
Boyle, Jack 186
Bracey, Sidney 181
Bracia, John 283
Brackett, Leigh 47
Bradford, William 200
Bradley, Bart 263
Bradley, David 261
Brady, Scott 155
Brahm, John 142
Brando, Marlon 127
Brandon, Henry 129
Brandt, Joe 1
Brauer, Tiny 332
Bray, Robert 273
Brecher, Egon 21, 222
Bregman, Tracy 98
Brent, Lynton 330, 334
Breslin, Patricia 105, 286
Bresslaw, Bernard 266
Bretherton, Howard 309
Brian, Mary 83, 129
Brick Bradford 293–94, 361
Bridge, Alan (Al) 159
Bridges, Lloyd 98
Briggs, Harlan 148
Briskin, Irving 209
Bristow, Gwen 181
Britton, Barbara 23
Brocco, Peter 347
Broccoli, Albert R. 88
Brode, Douglas 255
Broderick, Matthew 228
Brodie, Don 42
Brodie, Lea 274
Brook, Alan 133
Brook-Jones, Elwyn 266
Brooke, Hillary 46
Brother Theodore 222, 223
The Brotherhood of Satan 27–28, 361
Brousse, Liliane 153
Brown, Alfred 208
Brown, Barbara 89, 240
Brown, Charles D. 83, 127
Brown, Georgia 238
Brown, Jay A. 216
Brown, Joe 302
Brown, Joe E. 17, 18, 91
Brown, Robert 274
Brown, Stanley 98, 147, 152, 344

Brown Jug see Reynolds, Don Kay
Browning, Tod 167
Bruce, David 30
Bruce Gentry 294–95, 361
Bryant, Joyce 302, 324
Bryant, Michael 256
Bryant, Nana 101, 196
Bryant, William 273
Bubble Trouble 329, 362
Buchholz, Horst 356
Buchman, Sidney 102
Buck, Frank 273
Buckler, Hugh 136
Buckler, John 22
Bugarini, Ramon 6
Bull, Peter 62, 182, 253
Bull, Richard 347
Bulnes, Quintin 107, 220
Bunce, Alan 106
Bunnage, Avis 236
Buono, Victor 214
Burdick, Eugene 76
Burgess, Dorothy 19
Burke, Marie 240
Burke, Samson "Sammy" 251, 252
Burnette, Smiley 233, 234
Burns, Edmund 191
Burns, Michael 143, 356
Burns, Paul E. 49
Burr, Raymond 144, 353
Burroughs, Edgar Rice 275
Burton, Frederick 82
Burton, Peter 17
Burton, Richard 60, 61, 97, 158, 180
Burton, Robert 247
Bushman, Francis X. 260, 261
Buster, Budd 303
Butler, Daws 184
Butler, Ivan 195, 224
Butler, L.W. 249
Buttram, Pat 200
By Whose Hand? 29, 359
Byrd, Ralph 326
Byron, Jean 125, 273
Byron, Walter 157

Cahn, Edward L. 42, 284
Caine, Howard 276
Cairney, John 120, 236, 254
Callam, Alex 315
Callan, Michael 170
Callard, Kay 67
Calvert, Steve 191, 332, 335, 345
Camacho, Jesus 190
Camacho, Jose Moreno 33
Camara del Terror (Chamber of Terror) see *Fear Chamber*
Cambridge, Godfrey 275, 276
Cameron, Kate 24
Cameron, Rod 66, 67
Camp, Hamilton 225
Campanella, Joseph 356
Campbell, Clay 128, 198, 276, 338, 346
Campbell, Colin 317

Campbell, Paul 339
Canby, Vincent 178
Candoli, Conte 14
Candoli, Pete 14
Caniff, Milton 324
Cannibal Attack 29–30, 360
Capra, Frank 135, 136, 137, 155
Capra, Frank, Jr. 155
Capri, Ahne 27
Captain Midnight 295, 361
Captain Silver and the Sea 314
Captain Silver's Log of the Sea Hound 314
Captain Video, Hero of Outer Space! see *Captain Video, Master of the Stratosphere*
Captain Video, Master of the Stratosphere 295–97, 361
Captive Girl 30–31, 360
Captive Wild Woman 54
Capuano, Luigi 172
Cardenas, Elsa 206
Cardwell, James 271
Carey, Macdonald 242
Caridia, Michael 87, 88
Carleton, Claire 47, 225
Carlisle, Mary 17, 239
Carlson, Richard 114
Carmel, Roger C. 214
Carnage see *Corruption*
Carney, Art 193
Carpenter, Cliff 324
Carpenter, John 71, 72
Carpenter, Ken 46
Carr, Stephen 297
Carr, Vicki 215
Carradine, John 68, 69, 184, 185, 205, 206, 270, 271, 355
Carreras, Michael 44, 53
Carrillo, Ethel 112
Carroll, Virginia 323
Carsten, Peter 236
Carter, Ellis W. 244
Carter, Janis 89, 159, 188, 248
Caruso, Anthony 46
Carver, Tina 150
Carwardine, Richard 61
Cash, Johnny 201
Casino Royale (1967) 31–32, 361
Casino Royale (2006) 32
Cason, John L. 234, 273
Cassidy, Edward (Ed) 298, 323
Cassidy, Katie 279
Casting the Runes 151
Castle, Dolores 314
Castle, Peggy 114
Castle, William 47, 105, 106, 127, 160, 161, 181, 182, 183, 188, 189, 194, 229, 230, 231, 233, 244, 246, 254, 255, 256, 269–70, 271, 279, 286, 287
El Castillo de los Monstruos (The Castle of the Monsters) 32–34, 360
Castro, Bigoton 90
Castro, Fidel 62

The Cat Creeps (1930) 51
Caught by Television see *Trapped by Television*
Cavanagh, Paul 150, 152, 225
Cepada, Gerardo 223
Cervantes, Martha Elena 6
Cey, Jacques 67
Chaffey, Don 44, 121
Chambers, Wheaton 55, 225
Champion, Michael 278
Champlin, Charles 138
Chan, Spencer 312
Chandler, Lane 42, 298, 299
Chaney, Lon, Jr. 129, 133, 198, 216, 243, 244, 276, 311
Chaney, Lon, Sr. 117, 355
Chapin, Saul 248
Chaplin, Charles 344
Chapman, Ben 125
Charisse, Cyd 214, 215, 274, 275
Charles, Lewis 252
Charney, Kim 277
La Charrette Fantome see *The Phantom Wagon*
Chase, Stephan 140
Chavez, Sandra 78
Chegwin, Kevin 140
Cheirel, Micheline 24, 222
Cher (Bono) 93, 94
Chesebro, George 234, 339
Cheshire, Harry 100
Chester, Hal E. 51
Chinatown Nights 34, 359
Chopra, Ram 61
Chosen Survivors 34–35, 177, 361
Christensen, Carol 250
Christian, Kurt 92, 217
Christie, Agatha 181
Christy, Ken 277
Cianfriglia, Giovanni see Wood, Ken
Ciannelli, Eduardo 133
Cimarro, Thomas 16
Cinecorp Productions 192
Circus of Blood see *Berserk*
Circus of Terror see *Berserk*
The Circus Queen Murder 35–36, 83, 359
The Circus Shadow see *The Shadow* (1937)
Cisar, George 276
City of Fear 36–37, 360
Clare, Mary 131
Clark, Buddy 201
Clark, Cliff 159
Clark, Colbert 24
Clark, Davison 327
Clark, Fred 54, 287
Clark, Jim 239
Clark, Judy 294
Clark, Ken 260, 261
Clark, Roy 200
Clark, Tom 248
The Clark Sisters 184
Clarke, Everett 280–81
Clarke, Warren 355
Clary, Robert 243
Clavillazo (Antonio Espino) 33, 34

Clay, Lewis 294
Clay, Rachel 242
Claydon, George 17
Clery, Corinne 108
Cliff, John 251
Clifton, Elmer 317
Close Encounters of the Third Kind 37–38, 361
Clouds Over Europe 38–39, 359
Clover Productions 42, 89, 116, 151, 177, 276
Clutesi, George 178
Clyde, Andy 328, 330 336, 341
Coates, Phyllis 114
Cobb, Edmund 159
Coch, Edward (Ed) 42, 288
Cochran, Steve 26
Codee, Ann 222
Coffin, Tristram 42, 176, 177, 191, 294, 312
Cohen, Herman 16, 17, 210, 238
Cohn, Harry 2, 19, 135, 144, 187, 196
Cohn, Jack 1
Colbert, Robert 99
Cole, Carol 143
Cole, Corinne 165
Cole, Nat (King) 143
Coleman, Charles 280
College Scandal 134
Collings, Lisa 167
Collins, Cora Sue 19
Collins, Monty (Monte) 329, 333, 334, 339, 351
Collins, Ray 47
Collins, Russell 75
Collyer, Bud 323
Collyer, June 10
Colman, Ronald 135, 136
Colmans, Edward 243
Colpix Records 184, 209
Combs, Jackie 191
Compson, Betty 129
Compton, Joyce 258
Conan Doyle, Arthur 235
Congo Bill 297, 361
Conklin, Heinie 337, 349
Connery, Sean 31, 214
Connolly, Walter 133
Connor, Kevin 275
Connors, Michael 130
Conreid, Hans 81, 82, 218
Conti, Albert 173
Converse, Peggy 127
Conway, Booth 355
Conway, Tom 260, 261
Coogan, Richard 297
Cook, Donald 35, 83, 180
Cook, Tommy 248
Cooke, Hal 318
Coolidge, Philip 254
Cooper, Clancy 280, 315
Cooper, George 10
Cooper, Jackie 34
Cooper, Terence 32
Cooper, Wilkie 121
Cope, Kenneth 242
Corbett, Glenn 106
Cord, Alex 34

Corday, Mara 90
Corman, Roger 85
Cornell Pictures 100
Cornish, Dr. Robert 149
Corradi, Neely 77
Corri, Adrienne 236
Corrigan, Lloyd 46
Corrigan, Ray 128, 138, 139, 308, 330, 336
Corruption 39–40, 361
Cos, Vicki 230
Costello, Don 280
Costello, Lou 119, 246, 247
Costello, Maurice 157
Costello, Pat 247
Couch, Bill 156
Coulouris, George 281
Counterspy 40
Counterspy Meets Scotland Yard 40–42, 360
Courtney, Del 117
Cover, Franklin 227
Cowan, Jerome 46, 99
Cowling, Bruce 30
Cox, Mitchell 230
Cozzi, Luigi 71
Crabbe, Buster 30, 31, 305, 311, 314
Craig, Daniel 32
Craig, Michael 170
Crandall, Reed 293
Crane, Norma 180
Crane, Phyllis 339
Crane, Richard 171, 309
Crane, Stephen 46, 50
Cravat, Noel 70
Craven, James 295, 300
Craven, Matt 98
Crawford, Joan 16, 17, 59, 67, 210, 229, 230, 231
Crawford, John 293
Crawford, Lorraine 344
Crazy Music see *The 5,000 Fingers of Dr. T*
Creature with the Atom Brain 42–43, 116, 284, 360
Creatures the World Forgot 43–44, 121, 361
Creed, Roger 311
The Creeping Flesh 44–46, 361
Creeps 329, 333, 362
Cregar, Laird 142
Crehan, Joseph 11, 111, 159, 187
Crenna, Richard 155, 354
Cresley, Margery 199
Crest, Patricia 230
Crime Doctor's Courage 46–47, 127, 213, 359
The Crime Doctor's Man Hunt 47–49, 359
Crime Doctor's Rendezvous see *Shadows in the Night*
The Crime of Helen Stanley 11
Crime on Their Hands 330, 336, 362
Criner, Lawrence 19
Crist, Judith 231, 352, 357
Croft, Douglas 291
Crosby, Bing 201
Crosby, Wade 114

Cross, Beverley 121
Cross, Larry 67
Crowe, James M. 347
Crowley, Matt 72, 121
Crowley, Pat 356
Crowther, Bosley 7, 63, 77, 81, 82, 100, 123, 146, 267, 280
Cruickshank, Andrew 232
Crutchey, Rosalie 44, 87
Cruz, Alejandro 132, 133
Cry of the Werewolf 49–51, 225, 359
Cuckoo on a Choo-Choo 330, 362
Cult of the Dead see *Snake People*
Culver, Roland 63
Cumbuka, Ji-Tu 307
Cummings, Constance 11
Cummins, Peggy 52
Curiel, Federico 68, 111, 224
The Curse of Frankenstein 198, 199, 231
The Curse of King Tut's Tomb 352–53, 362
Curse of the Demon 51–53, 360
Curse of the Mummy's Tomb 53–54, 95, 360
Curtis, Billy 125, 191
Curtis, Dick 148, 209, 311, 324, 333, 347, 349, 350
Curtis, Donald 65, 117
Curtis, Mel 285
Curzon, George 38
Cushing, Peter 39, 40, 44, 46, 95, 96, 180, 199, 231, 257
Cuthbertson, Allan 232
Cutting, Dick 42
Cutts, Patricia 254

Daigneau, Ken 314
Dalbert, Suzanne 154
Dale, Esther 23
Dalton, Aubrey 160
Damman, Sara 278
The Damned see *These Are the Damned*
Dance of Death see *House of Evil*
Dane, Alexandra 39
Dane, Lawrence 97
Danforth, Jim 44
Dannay, Frederic 237
Danova, Cesare 269
Danton, Ray 172
D'Arcy, Alexander (Alex) 82
Darcy, Sheila 324
Darien, Frank 173
Dark, John 275
Darmour, Larry 127, 271, 279, 302, 317, 319
Darrell, Steve (Steven) 130, 200
Darrin, Diana 332, 340
Das Gupta, Bandana 240
A Date with Destiny see *The Return of October*
Daughter of Dr. Jekyll 225
Davenport, Harry 84

David, Hal 138
David, Mack 284
Davidson, William B. 157
David Harding, Counterspy 41
Davies, David Stuart 237
Davis, Bette 59, 156, 157, 219, 230
Davis, Boyd 267
Davis, Jimmie 201
Davis, Karl (Killer) 42, 218, 285
Davis, Owen 181
Davis, Phil 307
Davis, Robert O. 315
Dawn, Marpessa 281
Dawson, Peter 250
Day, Vera 282
Dea, Gloria 305
Dead of Winter 169
The Dead That Walk see *Zombies of Mora Tau*
Deadwood Dick 297–99, 302, 361
Deal, David 131
Dean, Jean 273
De Camp, Rosemary 244
De Camp, Victor 324
De Carlo, Yvonne 98
de Cordoba, Pedro 9
de Corsia, Ted 147
Dee, Sandra 354
De Havilland, Olivia 59
de Herrera, Nana 208
Dehner, John 31, 41
De La Hoy, Cindy 144
Delaney, Charles 76
De Lange, Eddie 248
De Laurentiis, Dino 130
del Campo, Cesar 112
del Castillo, Erick 69, 111, 112
Delgado, Miguel M. 162
Delgado, Roger 240
Dell, Myrna 138
De Luise, Dom 75
De Metz, Danielle 269
De Mille, Cecil B. 144
De Mille, Katherine 21, 259
Demon of the Himalayas 229
Dench, Judi 235, 236
Deneuve, Catherine 194, 195
Denham, Maurice 52, 256
Denham, Reginald 131
Denison, Leslie 70, 197
Denning, Richard 42
Dennis, Nick 147
Denny, Martin 85
Denny, Reginald 83, 311
De Normand, George 138, 267
Dent, Vernon 210, 329, 331, 332, 334, 336, 337, 340, 341, 342, 343, 347, 349
De Plano, Jay 216
De Rita, Joe 99, 249–52
Derr, Richard 318
de Sa, Alfredo 304
Desire, the Vampire 353, 362
Desny, Ivan 171
De Stefani, Angel 186
De Stefani, Joseph 148

De Toth, Andre 142
De Val, Jean 222
The Devil Commands 54–55, 359
Devil Goddess 55–57, 360
The Devil's Mask 57–58, 110, 268, 359
Devlin, Cory 260
Devlin, Joe 26, 311
De Vol, Frank 284
De Vol, Gordon 193
Devon, Richard 214
Dewhurst, colleen 278
De Witt, Louis 247
Dexter, Anthony (Tony) 260, 261
Diabolical Pact see *Pacto Diabólico* (Diabolical Pact)
Diage, Louis 196
Diamond, Arnold 153, 199
Dickerson, Dudley 333, 336, 341, 347
Die! Die! My Darling! 58–60, 202, 360
Diffring, Anton 347
Dillman, Bradford 34
Dillon, Melinda 37
Dilson, John 148, 152
Dinehart, Alan 280
Dinehart, Alan, III 323
Dino, Desi and Billy 166
Dix, Richard 188, 271, 279, 280
Dizzy Detectives 300, 332, 335, 362
Dmytryk, Edward 54
Dr. Crimen see *El Monstruo Resucitado*
Doctor Faustus 60–61, 77, 361
Dr. Jekyll and Mr. Hyde (1932) 185, 186
Dr. Seuss (Theodore Geisel) 81, 182
Dr. Seuss' 5,000 Fingers of Dr. T see *The 5,000 Fingers of Dr. T*
Dr. Strangelove or: How I Learned to Stop Worrying and Love the Bomb 61–62, 74, 76, 360
Dr. Syn 20
Doctor X 14
Domergue, Faith 117, 118
Dominguez, Columba 132
Donaldson, Leslie 97
Donath, Ludwig 58
Donlevy, Brian 88
Donnell, Jeff 24, 25, 186, 188, 243, 244, 248, 267
Donovan, Bruce 327
Dopey Dicks 329, 330–31, 362
Dor, Karin 300
Doran, Ann 147, 150, 152
Dore, Anne 218
Dori, Sandro 130
Dorr, Lester 315
Dors, Diana 16, 17
Doucette, John 42
Douglas, Diana 229

Douglas, Donald (Don) 115, 298
Douglas, Melvyn 181
Douglas, Paul 87, 88
Douglas, Susan 80
Dourif, Brad 72, 353
Down, Lesley-Anne 355
Down to Earth 62–64, 102, 359
Downes, Terry 235–36
Dracula (1931) 12, 47, 174, 347
Dracula A.D. 1972 1
Dracula — Prince of Darkness 111
D.R.B. Productions 246
Drew, Ellen 48
Drewett, Pauline 87
Dreyfuss, Richard 37
Driskill, Bill 354, 356
Drysdale, Bill 140
Duane, Michael 58, 197
Ducas, Nadine 100
Dudinskaya, Natalya 220
Duering, Carl 67
Duff, Amanda 55
Dugan, Tom 29
Dumbrille, Douglass 4
Dunaway, Faye 71
Duncan, John 292
Duncan, Kenne 300, 319, 321
Dunham, Stephanie 216
Duning, George 130, 253
Duning, John 97
Dunn, Eddie 71, 138
Dunn, Emma 131
Dunn, Michael 167
Dunn, Ralph 332, 340, 350
Dupeyrou, Jose 112
Durden-Smith, Richard 61
Durfee, Minta 152
Durning, Charles 278, 279
Duval, Maria 68, 69, 271
Duvivier, Julien 187
Dvorak, Reggie 330
Dwan, Allan 163
Dyrenforth, Harold 229
Dyrenforth, Norman 229

Earle, Edward 58
Earth vs. the Flying Saucers 2, 41, 64–66, 116, 249, 262, 276, 360
Eason, B. Reeves 310
East, Carlos (Charles) 78, 220
Eastham, Richard 165
Eastwood, Clint 194
Eaton, Marjorie 249, 284
Eburne, Maude 24
Eden, Barbara 228
Eder, Richard 119
Edwards, Frank 65
Edwards, Maudie 266
Edwards, Meredith 67
Edwards, Vince 36
Ege, Julie 44, 167
Eisner, David 98
Eisner, Will 293
El Brendel 329, 331, 342, 346

Elcar, Dana 75
Eldredge, George 50, 86, 123, 142, 296, 312
The Electronic Monster 9, 66–68, 360
Elizondo, Evangelina 33
Elliott, John 58, 70, 303
Elliott, Peter 52
Ellis, Anita 63
Ellis, Edward 181
Ellis, Frank 293
Ellis, Mary 253
Ellis, Robin 352
Ellsworth, Whitney 297
Elphick, Michael 204
Elsom, Isobel 131
Emery, Gilbert 197
Emery, John 102, 142
Emmanuel, Takis 92
The Empire of Dracula see *Il Imperio de Dracula*
Enfield, Cy 171
Engel, Roy 249
English, John 200
Enigma de Muerte 68–69, 112, 184, 205, 361
Erickson, Leif 230, 231
Erickson, Tex 124
Escape in the Fog 69–71, 158, 359
Escapement see *The Electronic Monster*
Eshley, Norman 204
Espino, Antonio see Clavillazo
Espinosa, Angel 107
Evans, Charles 30, 42, 176, 336
Evans, Douglas 41
Evans, Herbert 342–43
Evelyn, Judith 254
Everman, Welch 151, 284
Ewing, Barbara 256
Eyer, Richard 208
The Eyes of Laura Mars 71–72, 361
Eyles, Allen 183, 203, 233, 243

The Face Behind the Mask 72–74, 359
The Face in the Tombstone Mirror 346
Fadeyecheu, Nicolai 239
Fail-Safe (1964) 74–76, 360
Fail-Safe (2000) 76
The Faker 76, 359
Falk, Lee 307, 310, 311
Famous Artists Productions 32
Fanatic see *Die! Die! My Darling!*
Fantasy Island 353–54, 356, 362
Farnum, William 317
Farrell, Charles 82
Farrell, Suzanne 158
Farrell, Tommy 311
Farrow, John 85–86
Farrow, Mia 204
The Fatal Night 76–77, 211, 359

Faulkner, Max 264
Faust and the Devil 77, 360
Fawcett, William 123, 144, 289, 292, 293, 312
Fay, Dorothy 300
Fear Chamber 68, 77–78, 107, 113, 133, 221, 361
Fearmaker see *The Mutations*
The Feathered Serpent 1, 157
Fein, Bill 324
Fenton, Frank 234
Ferguson, Lester 77
Ferlo, Laura 186
Fernandez, Abel M. 57
Fernandez, Arturo 107
Fernandez, Jaime 223
Ferrer, Mel 27
Ferrer, Patricia 206
Fiddlers Three 331, 340, 362
Field, Shirley Anne 242
Fielding, Fenella 182, 183
Fielding, Gerald 173
Fields, Robert 227
Fier, Jack 2, 24, 317
Films Oberon 157
Finch, Jon 140
Finch, Peter 138
Fine, Budd 336
Fine, Larry 99, 249–52, 328–51
Finlay, Frank 235, 236, 237
Finley, William 216
Finn, Catherine 256
A Fire in the Sky 354, 356, 362
First Men in the Moon 78–80, 116, 360
Fischer, Dennis 209, 263
Fisher, Terence 95, 112, 231, 233, 270
Fiske, Richard 55, 321
Fiske, Robert 300, 318
Fitzgerald, Michael 323
Five 80–81, 360
The 5,000 Fingers of Dr. T 81–82, 360
Flagpole Jitters 331, 362
Fleischer, Richard 205
Fleming, Ian 32
Fletcher, Diane 141
Flight to Fame 82–83, 359
Flint, Helen 180
Flores, Mariela 113
Florey, Robert 74
Flothow, Rudolph C. 2, 308, 310
Flowers, Bess 210
Fluegel, Darianne 72
Flying Saucer Daffy 331–32, 341, 362
Flying Saucers from Outer Space 64
Flying Saucers—Here and Now 65
Flying Saucers—Serious Business 65
Flynn, Charles 302
Foch, Nina 26, 50, 51, 70, 71, 110, 168, 197, 198, 212, 248
Fog 83, 359

Fonda, Henry 75
Fonteyn, Margot 239
Foo, Wong 70
Footsteps in the Fog 83–85, 360
For Crimin' Out Loud 332, 342, 350, 351, 362
Foray, June 146
Forbes, Stanton 194
Forbidden Island 85–86, 360
Ford, Derek 237
Ford, Donald 237
Ford, Glenn 97, 196
Ford, Wallace 174, 175
Forde, Eugene J. 213
Forman, Bill 280
Forman, Carol 323
Forrest, Helen 201
Forrest, Otto 271, 280
Forsythe, John 357
Forte, Joe 200
Foster, Dudley 236
Foster, Eddie 128, 252
Foster, Maxwell 282
Foster, Norma 236
Foster, Norman 239
Foulger, Byron 98, 127, 147, 152, 196, 280
Fowler, Karin J. 32
Fox, Michael 218, 273, 288, 293, 306
Fox, Wallace 326
Foy, Bryan 141
Fraidy Cat 330, 332, 335, 362
Francey, Micheline 188
Franciosa, Anthony 284
Francis, Freddie 45, 46, 257
Francis, Vera M. 57
Franciscus, James 155
Franco, Jess 40
Frank, Allen G. 40, 96
Frankenstein (1931) 9, 11, 12
Frankestein (Nathanael Leon) 68, 69
Frankenstein Meets the Wolfman 20
Fraser, Helen 194
Fraser, John 194, 235, 236
Frawley, William 48, 63
Frazetta, Frank 305
Frederick, Tanna 201
Freeman, Helen 83, 222, 267
Frees, Paul 65, 103, 146
French, Charles K. 318
French, Valerie 264, 265
Fresnay, Pierre 188
Frey, Mary 174
Friderici, Blanche 173
Friedkin, Joel 86
Friedkin, Willilam 93
Friedlander, Louis see Landers, Lew
Frobe, Gert 300
Frost, Terry 288, 294, 310, 323
Fry, Nicholas 183, 203, 233
Frye, Dwight 29, 35, 36, 209
Fuelin' Around 332, 337, 362

Fujiro, Jun 104
Furneaux, Yvonne 194
Furst, Stephen 216
Fury of the Congo 83, 360
Futter, Walter 3

Gabor, Eva 142
Galili, Hal 274
Gallagher, Skeets 172
Gallier, Alex 199
Galveston, George 250
The Gamma People 86–88, 95, 360
Garcia, Andreas 107, 185
Garland, Beverly 169
Garr, Teri 37
Garrett, Scott 276
Gaut, Slim 349
Gavin, James 276
Gay (Gaye), Gregory 42, 111, 144, 202, 221, 315
Gayson, Eunice 199
Gaze, Gwen 316, 317
Gebhart, Fred 261
Geer, Leonard 286
Geeson, Judy 17
A Gem of a Jam 333, 362
Gemora, Charles 334
Gene Autry Productions 200
George, Chief Dan 211
George, Peter 62, 76
Geray, Steven 191, 221, 222
Germain, Stewart 75
Gerstle, Frank 166
Get Along Little Zombie 333, 341, 362
Getchell, Sumner 301
Getty Pictures Corporation 167
Ghost Crazy 25
Ghost Riders in the Sky 200, 201
The Ghost Talks 329, 333, 362
The Ghost That Walked Alone 88–89, 359
The Ghost Walks 23
The Giant Claw 41, 66, 89–91, 177, 360
Gielgud, John 97
Gifford, Alan 67
Gifford, Denis 278
Gilbert, Helen 243
Gilbert, Jo 109, 144
Gill, Brendan 203
Gillette, William 237
Gilling, John 88, 95
Gillingwater, Claude 10
Gilmore, Peter 274
Gilpin, Toni 95
Gingold, Hermione 14
Giomini, Romano 171
Girard, Bernard 143
Girard, Joseph W. (Joe) 295, 320
Girl in Danger 11
Gish, Lillian 132
The Gladiator 17, 91–92, 359
Glass, Everett 41
Glass, Gaston 76
Glass, Ned 334

Glasser, Albert 287
Glasmire, Gus 391
Gleason, Jackie 145
Gleason, James 63, 102, 196
Glennon, Bert 141
Gless, Sharon 228
Glut, Donald F. 33, 290, 292, 296, 297, 301, 302, 305, 309, 311, 315, 318, 323
Goddard, Paulette 311
Godsoe, Harold 349
Goethe, Johann Wolfgang 77
Gold Key Entertainment 9
The Golden Voyage of Sinbad 92–93, 116, 217, 361
Goliath Awaits 354–55, 362
Good Times 93–94, 361
Goodliffe, Michael 95
Goodman, David Zelig 72
Goosson, Stephen 135, 249
Gorath 94–95, 360
Gordon, Alex 267
Gordon, Bernard 284
Gordon, Bruce 80
Gordon, C. Henry 259
Gordon, Gale 247
Gordon, Margaret 232
Gordon, Richard 36
The Gorgon 53, 95–96, 361
Gorvin, Gloria 158
Gotell, Walter 242
Gothard, Michael 274
Gottlieb, Theodore *see* Brother Theodore
Gough, Michael 16, 17
Gounod, Charles 17
Graff, Wilton 127, 186, 267
Granger, Michael 42
Granger, Stewart 84
Granstedt, Greta 173
Grant, Arthur 182
Grant, Cary 286
Grant, Kathryn 176, 177, 184, 207
Grant, Lee 156
Grapewin, Charley 239
Grave Robbers see *Profanadores de Tumbas* (Profaners of Tombs)
Gray, Clarence 294
Gray, Lorna 148, 349
Gray, Nadia 153
Grayson, Diane 204
Green, Alfred E. 115
Green, Danny 182, 208
Green, Dee 338, 340, 346
Green, Gilbert 106
Green, Nigel 120, 283
The Green Archer (1925) 300
The Green Archer (1940) 152, 299–300, 302, 318, 361
The Green Archer (1961) 300
Greene, Angela 123, 202
Greene, Harrison 70
Greene, Lorne 180
Greene, Victor 196
Greenhouse, Martha 228
Greenleaf, Raymond 176
Greenspun, Roger 96, 141
Greenwood, Joan 13, 170

Greenwood, Rosamund 52
Gregg, Christopher 254
Gregg, Joyce 282
Gregorio, Rose 72
Gregory, James 5, 165, 214
Grenfell, Joyce 182
Grey, Anne 34
Grey, Shirley 11
Grey, Virginia 122
Gribbon, Harry 345, 349
Griffith, Andy 356
Griffith, Charles B. 85
Griffith, William M. 56
Griffiths, Chuck 117
Grimes, Jack 119
Grinde, Nick 9, 147, 152
Grissell, Wallace 308
Grossman, Gary 289
Guffey, Burnett 169, 221, 226
Guffey, Cary 37
Gulliver 254
Gum Shoes 333, 334, 362
Gunderson, Bob 254
Guzman, Enrique 112

The H-Man 102–4, 281, 360
Haas, Hugo 7, 297
Hackett, Karl 298, 299
Hackman, Gene 155
Haggard, H. Rider 127
Hagman, Larry 75
Hagney, Frank 285
Hale, Alan, Jr. 200
Hale, Creighton 302
Hale, Jonathan 23, 101
Hale, Richard 58
Hall, Alexander 63, 102
Hall, John Ryder 218
Hall, Jon 85, 109
Hall, Lois 289, 311
Hall, Mordaunt 3, 10, 181
Hall, Thurston 21, 129, 149, 258
Halton, Charles 212
Hamilton, Bernie 309
Hamilton, Chuck 295
Hamilton, Donald 4, 166, 282, 284
Hamilton, Gay 355
Hamilton, George 355
Hamilton, John 271
Hamilton, Margaret 245, 246
Hamilton, Suzanne 180
Hamlet 96–97, 361
Hammer Films 1, 44, 53, 59, 95, 96, 153, 181, 183, 198, 199, 202, 231, 233, 241, 243, 256, 341, 346
Hampton, Orville H. 267
Hangover Square 142
Hanna, William 145
Hanna-Barbera Productions 145
Hanold, Marilyn 344
Hansen, William 75
Hanson, Lorna 160
Happy Birthday to Me 97–98, 361
Hardie, Russell 129
Hardin, Ty 16, 17
Hardwicke, Sir Cedric 7

Hardy, Phil 39, 40, 45, 53, 66, 80, 82, 94, 100, 104, 112, 118, 151, 153, 161, 166, 177, 178, 183, 192, 195, 199, 203, 227, 255, 261, 263, 279
Hare, Ken 44
Hare, Lumsden 19
Harewood, Dorian 353
Harington, Joy 168
Harmon, Jim 290, 292, 296, 297, 301, 302, 305, 309, 311, 315, 318, 323
Harmon, Julian 267
Harmon, Mark 354
Harris, Brad 167
Harris, Corbett 320
Harris, Jack H. 72
Harris, Richard 193
Harris, Stanley 320
Harris, Theresa 19
Harrison, Rex 13
Harrold, Kathryn 177, 178
Harryhausen, Ray 44, 64, 66, 79, 80, 89, 92, 93, 116, 117, 120, 121, 169–70, 207, 209, 217, 252, 254, 262, 263, 265, 276, 310
Hart, Bobby 5
Hart, Dorothy 63
Hart, Douglas C. 96
Hart, Gordon 318
Hart, Henry 62
Hart, John 288, 302, 303
Hartley, Mariette 156
Hartnell, William 84
Harty, Patricia 23
Harvard, Here I Come! 25, 98–99, 359
Harvey, Don C. 42, 43, 109, 150, 277, 289, 296, 331, 339
Harvey, Jean 276
Harvey, John 232
Hassett, Marilyn 211
Hasso, Signe 193, 194
Hastings, Don 297
Have Rocket, Will Travel 99–100, 246, 252, 360
Havlick, Gene 135
Hawkins, Michael 256
Haworth, Jill 167
Hawthorne, Jim 332, 335
Hawthorne, Nathaniel 45
Hayden, Frank 44
Hayden, Harry 26, 129
Hayden, Sterling 62
Haydock, Ron 237
Hayes, Allison 284, 285
Hayes, John Anthony 230
Hayes, Peter Lind 81, 82
Hayward, Louis 131, 224, 225
Hayworth, Rita 63, 209, 210
Hazard, Jayne 327
Haze, Jonathan 85
Healey, Myron 47, 125, 126, 228
Healy, Mary 81, 82
Heavenly Daze 328, 334, 362
Hecht, Ben 32
Hector Servadac 269

Heffer, Richard 61
Heilborn, Lorna 45
Heller, Joseph 32
Hellish Spiders see *Arañas Infernales* (Hellish Spiders)
Hell's Cargo see *Below the Sea*
Helm, Anne 229
Helmore, Tom 157
Hendry, Ian 194
Henreid, Paul 218, 219, 243
Henry, Gloria 200
Henry, Robert "Buzz" 301
Henry, Thomas Browne 65, 263
Henry, William (Bill) 86, 125
Her Husband's Affairs 100–1, 359
Herbert, Charles 245
Herbert, Holmes 122, 138, 154, 259
Herbert, Hugh 333, 340, 341, 347
Here Comes Mr. Jordan 63, 101–102
Hernandez, Guillermo 132, 133
Herrara, Anthony 307
Herrera, Victor 162
Herrick, Virginia 312
Herrmann, Bernard 209, 254
Hertz, Nathan *see* Juran, Nathan
Hervey, Irene 133
Herx, Henry 18, 28, 38, 45, 80, 93, 94, 97, 119, 131, 138, 145, 158, 166, 171, 201, 205, 211, 216, 218, 275, 276
Hickman, Darryl 254
Hickman, Dwayne 183
Hicks, Russell 267
Hiecke, Carl 315
Higgins, Edward 282
Higgins, Joel 356
Highland Dale (horse) 196
Hill, Arthur 228
Hill, Jack 77, 107, 220
Hill, James 237
Hiller, Arthur 178, 179
Hiller, Wendy 352
Hilliard, Ernest 226
Hillyer, Lambert 11, 239
Hilton, James 137, 138
Hinds, Samuel S. 5, 180
Hinton, Ed 56, 125
Hirata, Akihiko 104
Hirschhorn, Clive 18, 74, 80
Hitchcock, Alfred 51, 59, 105, 280
Hobart, Rose 226
Hobbs, Robeert 34
Hobson, Valerie 38
Hodge, Al 297
Hodges, Ralph 294, 309, 312, 323
Hodgson, Leyland 169
Hoefler, Paul L. 3
Hoerl, Arthur 294
Hoey, Dennis 248
Hoffman, David 245

Hoffman, Paul 42, 273
Hohl, Arthur 23, 213, 239
Hokus Pokus 331, 334, 362
Hold That Monkey 334–35, 362
Holden, Jan 232
Holden, Joyce 277
Holdren, Judd 296, 305, 306
Holiday Film Productions 180
Hollander, Frederick 81
Holman, Harry 35
Holt, Jack 11, 19, 175, 259
Holt, Jennifer 301
Holt, Seth 53, 203
Homans, Robert 280
Homicidal 2, 104–6, 194, 286, 360
Homolka, Oscar 160
Hondo, Ishiro 8, 9, 104
Hoofs and Goofs 335, 362
Hook a Crook 330, 335, 362
Hop Harrigan 300–1, 361
Hopkins, Anthony 355
Hopper, Dennis 201
Hopper, William 263
Horne, James W. 302, 303, 319
Horne, Victoria 196, 330
Horsing Around 335, 362
Horton, Edward Everett 63, 100, 102, 135
Horvath, Charles 273, 276
Host to a Ghost 336, 341, 362
Hot Ice 336, 362
The Hot Scots 336, 343, 362
Hot Stuff 333, 337, 362
Houghton, Barrie 204
House Committee on Un-American Activities 114
House of Evil 68, 78, 106–8, 113, 361
House of Wax 141, 142
House on Haunted Hill (1959) 105
Houston, Donald 153, 235, 236
Houston, Renee 194
Howard, Curly 328–30, 333, 337–38, 342, 343, 344, 348–51
Howard, Esther 15
Howard, John 135
Howard, Joyce 211
Howard, June 288
Howard, Moe 99, 143, 249–52, 328–51
Howard, Ronald 54
Howard, Shemp 328–34, 336–38, 340, 342–43, 345–47, 349, 350
Howat, Clark 90
Howe, James Wong 14
Howells, Ursula 257
Howes, Reed 83, 239
Howland, Olin 48
Hoyt, Spencer 91, 118
Hubbard, L. Ron 316
Huby, Roberta 67
Hudson, Rochelle 115, 116, 230

Hudson, William 150, 152
Huerta, Rudolfo Guzman see Santo
Hughes, Carol 304
Hughes, Mary Beth 200
Hugo, Victor 355
Hula-La-La 307, 319, 362
Hull, Warren 307, 319, 321
The Human Vapor 104
The Humanoid 108, 361
Humphreys, Justin 28
The Hunchback of Notre Dame (1982) 355, 362
Hunter, Allan 38
Hunter, Kenneth 133
Hunter, Tab 18
Hunter, Virginia 331, 338, 340, 346
Hurricane Island 109, 360
Hurst, Paul 89
Hurt, John 180
Hussey, Olivia 138
Huston, John 32
Hutchins, Will 23
Hutman, Jerry 138
Hutton, Robert 257
Hyer, Martha 79
Hyman, Kenneth 241
Hyman, Prudence 95
Hytten, Olaf 168

I Love a Mystery 57, 109–11, 268, 359
I Saw What You Did (1965) 231
I Walked with a Zombie 51
Ibanez, Juan 107
Idle Roomers 337–38, 362
If a Body Meets a Body 338, 362
Ifukube, Akira 8, 9, 134
Ikele, Ryo 94
Illing, Peter 67
I'm a Monkey's Uncle 338, 346, 362
Imperial Pictures 22
El Imperio de Dracula (The Empire of Dracula) 111–12, 361
The Incredible Invasion 68, 78, 107, 112–13, 133, 221, 361
Inescort, Frieda 197, 198
Ingle, Joyce 216
Ingram, Jack 138, 235, 280, 294, 297, 299, 300, 302, 303, 312, 318, 323, 324
Ingram, Rex 248
Institute for Revenge 355–56, 362
Invasion Siniestra (Sinister Invasion) see *The Incredible Invasion*
Invasion U.S.A. 113–15, 360
The Iron Claw 301–2, 327, 361
Irving, William 334
Irwin, Coulter 58
Island of Doomed Men 74, 115–16, 149, 359
Isle of the Snake People see *Snake People*

It Came from Beneath the Sea 16, 42, 116–18, 262, 260
It Came from Hollywood 6
Ito, Emi 164
Ito, Hisaya 104
Ito, Jelly 164
Ito, Yumi 164
Ituribe, Rebecca 112
Ivan Tors Productions 19
Ivanov, Lev 239
Ives, Burl 201
Iwamoto, Koji 104

Jack and the Beanstalk 118–19, 361
Jack Armstrong 302–3, 361
Jack to mame no ki see *Jack and the Beanstalk*
Jackson, Dan 170
Jackson, Selmer 56, 101, 154, 191, 315
Jackson, Thomas E. 11, 58
Jacobi, Derek 355
Jacobs, W.W. 84
Jaeckel, Richard 34
Jaffe, Carl 67
Jaffe, Sam 136, 137
Jaglom, Henry 201
James, Anthony 193
James, Claire 302
James, Montague R. 51, 53
Jamison, Bud 348, 350
Janssen, David 156
Janti, Azemat 264
Jaquet, Frank 123
Jason, Will 226, 227, 244
Jason and the Argonauts 116, 120–21, 360
Jay, Griffin 196
Jeffrey, William 10
Jeffries, Lionel 79, 199
Jekyll and Hyde—A Satanic Pact see *Pacto Diabólico* (Diabolical Pact)
Jensen, Paul M. 45, 80, 233
Jenson, Dick 330
Jergens, Adele 63, 248
Jessop, Clytie 256
Jewell, Isabel 135, 149
John, Robert 44
Johns, Mervyn 179, 182
Johnson, Don 228
Johnson, Doretta 144
Johnson, Fred 203
Johnson, Gerry 145
Johnson, J. Louis 267
Johnson, Linda 294
Johnson, Marilyn 26
Johnson, Raymond Edward 307
Johnson, Rita 102
Johnson, Tor 241
Johnstone, Bill 280, 318
Jolley, I. Stanford 189, 269, 297, 303
Jolson, Al 63
Jones, Evan 243
Jones, J. Paul 324
Jones, L.Q. 27, 28
Jones, Marianne 211
Jones, Marilyn 353
Jones, Peter 236

Jones, Roy 140
Jones, Stan 200
Jones, Stephen 151, 178, 216, 284
Jones, Tommy Lee 72
Jordan, Owen 324
Jory, Victor 150, 151, 300, 318
Jouvet, Louis 188
Joyce, Robin 112
Joyce, Yootha 59, 60
Judd, Edward 79
Judge, Arline 98
Judi the Chimp 19
Julia, Raul 72
Julissa 78, 109, 220
Junco, Victor 68, 69, 206
Jung, Allen 324
Jungle Jim 29, 121–23, 360
Jungle Jim in Pygmy Island see *Pygmy Island*
Jungle Jim in the Forbidden Land 123–24, 201, 360
Jungle Man-Eaters 124
Jungle Manhunt 124–25, 126, 360
Jungle Moon Men 125–26, 360
Jungle Raiders 294, 303–4, 361
Juran, Nathan 80, 207, 263
Just Before Dawn 47, 127–28, 359

Kagawa, Kyoko 164
Kaiser, Erwin 55
Kalem, Toni 216
Kandel, Aben 210
Kane, Bob 291
Kane, Carol 278, 279
Kane, Eddie 55
Kane, Joe 22, 88, 137, 279, 284
Kaproff, Dana 279
Karina, Sandra 317
Karloff, Boris 9, 10, 11, 20, 21, 24, 25, 54, 55, 68, 77, 78, 85, 107, 112, 113, 127, 133, 152, 181, 220, 221
Karlson, Phil 215, 282, 284
Kascier, Johnny 328, 331, 334
Kashey, Abe "King Kong" 47
Kasket, Harold 207
Kasznar, Kurt 5
Katcher, Aram 114
Katzman, Sam 2, 29, 31, 42, 56, 57, 86, 89–90, 100, 116, 121, 124, 126, 144, 151, 177, 191, 198, 202, 219, 244, 276, 284, 289, 290, 294, 303, 305, 308, 309, 311, 314, 323
Kaufman, Maurice 59
Kavner, Julie 228
Kay, Bernard 257
Kay, Mary Ellen 235
Kaye, Lila 204
Keane, Robert Emmett 280
Kearns, Joseph 280
Keaton, Buster 344
Keats, Stephen 216

Keegan, Barry 84
Keen, Geoffrey 17
Keith, Ian 117
Kelk, Jackie 324
Kellard, Robert *see* Stevens, Robert
Kellaway, Cecil 287
Kellerman, Sally 193, 194
Kelly, Gene 63
Kelly, Lew 344, 346, 349
Kelly, Patrick J. 316
Kelly, Paul 315
Kelly, William J. 15
Kelsey, Fred 333, 338
Kemper, Victor J. 72
Kendall, Cy 189, 280
Kendall, Kay 13
Kennedy, Arthur 108
Kennedy, George 230
Kennedy, Tom 26, 114, 332, 333, 334, 335, 339, 342, 345, 346
Kent, Crauford 157
Kent, Robert 91, 327
Kent, Stapleton 225
Kenyon, Ethel 29
Kerr, Deborah 32
Kershner, Irv 72
Keyes, Evelyn 9, 73, 102, 131, 248
Keyhoe, Maj. Donald E. 64–65
Keymas, George 218
Khoury, George 263
Khrushchev, Nikita 62, 249
Kibbee, Milton 313, 327
Kidman, Nicole 228
Kiel, Richard 108
Kikume, Al 307
Kilian, Victor 4, 133
Killer Ape 128–29, 360
Killer at Large 83, 129, 359
Kilpatrick, Lincoln 34
Kimba the Chimp 29, 30
Kimberley, Kim 276
King, Charles 289, 303, 323
King, Claude 11
King Kong (1933) 14, 19
King Kong *see* Kashey, Abe "King Kong"
King of the Congo 305, 311, 314, 361
Kingsford, Guy 311
Kinnell, Murray 157
Kipling, Richard 273
Kirino, Nadao 94
Kirke, Donald 209
Kiss Me Deadly 37
Kiss the Girls and Make Them Die 129–31, 361
Kitchen, Kathy 167
Kleiner, Sergio 112
Klemensen, Richard 44, 153, 183, 199, 233, 241
Knaggs, Skelton 127
Kneale, Nigel 80
Knight, Ashley 274
Knight, Charles 332, 336, 343
Knox, Alexander 224, 242
Kobi, Michi 260
Koizumi, Hiroshi 164

Kolb, Clarence 18
Kolker, Henry 19, 21, 150
Korda, Alexander 39
Korff, Arnold 19
Korman, Harvey 146
Kortman, Robert 10
Kosleck, Martin 127
Kossoff, David 179
Kovack, Nancy 121, 156, 214
Kovacs, Ernie 14
Kramer, Wright 9
Kruger, Otto 70, 71
Kubrick, Stanley 74
Kuri, Chiharu 134
Kwan, Nancy 282, 283
Kwouk, Burt 240, 241

LaBelle, Michel-Rene 97
Lackteen, Frank 56, 297, 300, 328, 340, 343, 346
La Curto, James 317
Ladies in Retirement 131–32, 143, 359
Ladrón de Cadaveres (Body Snatcher) 132–33, 360
Lagerlof, Selma 188
Lake, Arthur 23, 89
Lamble, Lloyd 53
Lampkin, Charles 80
Lanchester, Elsa 13, 14, 131, 132
Landers, Lew 24, 89, 99, 109, 188
Landi, Aldo Bufi 171
Landon, Hal 312
Lane, Charles 127
Lane, Jackie 87
Lane, Richard 26, 186, 332, 334, 335, 342, 350, 351
Lang, Fritz 280
Langdon, Harry 344, 349
Lange, Kelly 34
Lansing, Joi 225
La Planche, Rosemary 302, 303
Larabee, Louise 75
Larch, John 283
La Rocque, Rod 318
LaRue, Frank 318
Laser Killer see Corruption
La Torre, Charles 249
Laughton, Charles 181, 355
Laughton, Eddie 24
Launer, S. John 42, 43, 277
The Laurel and Hardy Murder Case 338
Lauter, Harry 41, 66, 117, 276
Lavashev, Vladimir 240
Lavi, Dahlia 32, 214
Law, John Philip 92, 217
Lawrence, H.L. 242
Lawrence, Jody 224
Lawrence, Marc 18, 109, 209
Lawton, David 282
The League of Frightened Men 133–34, 359
Leaver, Philip 87, 88
Lebedeff, Ivan 259
Lebedinoe Ozero see Swan Lake
Lebedur, Frederick 150, 265

Lederman, D. Ross 11, 187
Lee, Belinda 84
Lee, Bruce 282
Lee, Christopher 45, 46, 95, 96, 203, 231, 240, 241, 354, 355
Lee, Diana 138
Lee, Earl 80
Lee, Jack 48, 89
Lee, Manfred B. 237
Lee, Peggy 201
Leech, Richard 53, 240
Leeds, Peter 247, 315
La Leggenda di Faust (The Legend of Faust) *see Faust and the Devil*
Leiber, Fritz 50
Leigh, Nelson 31, 138, 202, 243, 289, 323
Leighton, Lillian 258
Leighton, Sara 282
Leister, Frederick 84
Lemkow, Tutte 232
Lemmon, Jack 13
Lennig, Arthur 198
Lennon, Toby 167
Lenoir, Leon 49
Lenzi, Umberto 71
Leon, Nathanael (Frankestein) 206
Leonard, Don 44
Leonard, Murray 248
Leonard, Queenie 131, 168
Leontovich, Eugenie 105
Le Saint, Edward 10
Leslie, Avril 199
Leslie, William 176, 177
Lester, Henry E. 237
Levin, Henry 131, 166
Levin, Ira 228
Levy, Weaver 293
Lewis, George J. 17, 138, 139
Lewis, Joseph H. 169, 195, 221
Lewis, Ronald 160, 203
Lewis, Sheldon 302
Lewis, Sinclair 357
Lewton, Val 51, 225, 261
Lhoest, Anita 31
Libby, Brian 216
Life Returns 149
Lights Out 81
Lincoln, Pamela 254
Linder, Christa 112, 113
Lindfors, Viveca 242
Lindley, Audra 228
Link, Andre 97
Lipson, Tiny 339
Liszt, Margie 349
Little Prince and the Eight-Headed Dragon 134–35, 360
Littlefield, Lucien 91
Livardy, John 135
Livingston, Robert 200
Lloyd, Doris 168, 225
Lloyd, George 159, 280
Lloyd, Jeremy 236
Lloyd, Jimmy 41, 312, 334
Lloyd, Sue 39
Lobo Negro (Guillermo Hernandez) 190

Locke, Sondra 193, 194
Lockhart, Gene 101
Lodge, David 39, 40
The Lodger (1944) 142
Loft, Arthur 210
Logan, Jacqueline 76
Logan, James 336
Lollobrigida, Gina 355
Lom, Herbert 170
London, Babe 343
London, Rose 284
London, Tom 200
London Films 39
Longhurst, Jeremy 95
Lorch, Theodore 336, 338, 343, 344, 350
Lord, Del 258, 333
Lord, Justine 153
Lord, Phillips H. 40
Loring, Lyn 352
Lorre, Peter 23, 24, 73, 74, 115, 116, 149
Losey, Joseph 243
Lost Horizon (1937) 2, 135–37, 138, 229, 359
Lost Horizon (1973) 137–38, 361
The Lost Planet 305–6, 361
The Lost Tribe 29, 138–39, 360
Louise, Anita 58
Louise, Tina 227, 282, 283
Loukens, Nicholas 61
Lovecraft, H.P. 113
Lowe, Edmund 175
Lowery, Robert 292, 308, 309
Lubin, Arthur 84
Lucas, Wilfred 334, 339
Luez, Laurette 218
Lufkin, Sam 339
Lugosi, Bela 29, 174, 175, 196, 197, 198, 207
Lumet, Sidney 74, 76
Lummis, Dayton 147
Luna Productions 261
Lundigan, William 267
Lung, Charlie 218
Lupino, Ida 131
Lyden, Pierce 86, 154, 191, 313
Lyman, Arthur 85
Lynch, Ken 301
Lynn, Emmett 7, 351
Lynn, George 150, 277
Lynn, Vera 201
Lyon, Ben 29
Lyon, William 99
Lyons, H. Agar 34
Lyons, Lynne 342

Macabre 105
Macabre Serenade (Macabre Serenade) *see House of Evil*
Macbeth (1971) 139–41, 194, 361
MacBride, Donald 102
MacDonald, Kenneth 116, 189, 280, 311, 330, 336, 337, 340, 342, 343
MacDonald, Wallace 9, 146, 147, 152

MacFarquhar, Maisie 140
MacGinnis, Niall 52, 120, 256
MacGreevy, Oliver 130
MacGregor, Scott 28
Macht, Stephen 177
MacKenzie, Robert 281
MacLane, Barton 50, 51
MacLaughlin, Don 40
Macnee, Patrick 77
Macowan, Norman 84
Macready, George 63, 110, 159, 168, 169, 226, 308
The Mad Magician 141–42, 360
The Mad Room 132, 142–43, 361
Maddox, Dean, Jr. 117
Madison, Guy 171, 172
Madoc, Philip 16
Magallanes, Nicholas 158
The Magic Carpet 100, 143–44, 244, 360
The Magic World of Topo Gigio 144–45, 360
The Magnificent Magical Magnet of Santa Mesa 356, 362
Maharis, George 356
Mahoney, Jock 235, 312, 332
Mailes, George Hill 76
Main, Marjorie 209
Maine, Charles Eric 66
Maitland, Marne 232, 240
Majors, Lee (Lee Yeary) 230
The Making of Close Encounters of the Third Kind 38
Malden, Karl 165
Maltin, Leonard 82, 99, 201, 246, 345, 346, 356
The Man Called Flintstone 145–46, 361
Man in the Dark 146–47, 150, 360
Man Mountain Dean 91
The Man They Could Not Hang 9, 55, 147–49, 152, 159, 181, 359
The Man Who Laughs 160, 161
The Man Who Lived Twice 4, 146, 149–50, 359
The Man Who Turned to Stone 150–52, 284, 360
The Man with Nine Lives 9, 55, 152–53, 359
Manahan, Sheila 84
Mancini, Henry 178, 179
Mancuso, Nick 177, 178
Mander, Miles 197
Mandrake the Magician 306–7, 310, 361
Mango, Alec 208
Maniac (1963) 153–54, 202, 243, 360
Manikum, Philip 39
Mann, Bertha 11
Manning, Bruce 181
Manson, Maurice 250
Mantley, John 265
Mantz, Paul 82
Mapes, Ted 308, 326

Marachuk, Steve 72
Marburgh, Betram 9
March, Fredric 185, 186
Marcin, Max 46, 47, 127
Marcus, Raymond T. *see* Gordon, Bernard
Marcuse, Theodore 265
Margheriti, Antonio 108
Margo 136
Marichal, Julie 221
Marion, Paul 42, 128, 138, 202, 222, 288
Mark of the Gorilla 29, 154–55, 360
The Mark of the Whistler 188, 271
Marlowe, Christopher 60, 61
Marlowe, Hugh 65
Marooned 155–56, 361
Marsh, Marian 21, 150
Marshall, Joan *see* Arless, Jean
Marshall, Trudy 154
Marshall, Tully 174, 175
Martin, Dean 4, 5, 131, 165, 166, 214, 215, 282, 283, 284
Martin, Lewis 41
Martin, Strother 27
Martinez, Arturo 132
Martinique 220
Marton, Andrew 229
Marton, Jarmila 229
Mask of the Himalayas see *Storm Over Tibet*
Maslin, Janet 72
Mason, Patricia 141
Mason, Vivian 306
Massen, Osa 50
Massey, Daniel 274
Massey, Raymond 181, 267
Masterson, Peter 327
Mateos, Hector 132
Matheson, Richard 60
Mathews, Carole 110, 159, 248, 308
Mathews, Kerwin 153, 207, 253, 254
Matt Helm 284
Mattera, Gino 77
Matthau, Walter 75
Matthews, Francis 199
Matthews, Lester 110, 111, 123, 124, 202, 212, 224
Mattson, Arne 188
Maurer, Norman 143, 249, 252
Mauro, David 5
Mavis, Paul 5, 146, 166, 215, 284, 287
Maxwell, Edwin 83, 174, 180
May, Lenora 279
Mayhew, Peter 217
Maynard, Kermit 280, 303
Mayne, Tony 167
Mayo, Frank 58
Mayo, Mike 28, 138, 231, 255
Mazurki, Mike 138, 159, 287
Mazzulo, Peppino 145
McBride, Patricia 158

McCarthy, John 67
McCarthy, Joseph 114
McClory, Sean 269
McClure, Doug 274, 275
McCollum, Hugh 2, 337
McCulloch, Andrew 140
McDaniel, Sam 334
McEveety, Bernard 28
McGuire, Don 297
McHugh, Matt 174
McIntosh, Burr 300
McIntosh, David 61
McIntyre, Christine 328, 329, 330, 332, 333, 336, 337, 341, 342, 343, 348, 349, 350
McKay, George 24, 73, 129, 239
McKeever, Martin 251
McKeever, Mike 251
McKennon, Dal 255
McKenzie, Bob 350
McKenzie, Eva 350
McKinney, Austin 77
McLeod, Gordon 38
McMahon, Horace 147
McNamara, Edward 134
McQuade, Robert 83
McStay, Michael 54
McVey, Patrick 24
Meade, Julia 287
Medina, Patricia 144, 218
Medwin, Michael 211
Meeker, George 127, 174, 175, 323
Meet Nero Wolfe 133
Megowan, Don 277, 347
Meija, Griselda 112
Melachrino, George 88
Méliès, Georges 80
Mell, Joseph 37
Melton, Sid 295
The Menace 20, 156–57, 359
Mendelssohn, Felix 157
Menjou, Adolphe 35, 172, 173
Mercier, Louis 222
Meredith, Burgess 256, 257
Meredith, Charles 42
Meredith, Iris 300, 321
Merkel, Una 344
Merrick, Lynn 71, 271, 272
Merrill, Gary 170
Merrill, Louis D. 90
Merritt, George M. 38, 317
Merry Mavericks 338–39, 350
Merton, John 289, 294, 301
Mery, Andree 188
Messick, Don 145
Methot, Mayo 173
Meyer, Jim 109
Meyer, Torben 21
Michael, Gertrude 174
Michaels, Norman 237
Microspook 339, 362
Middlemass, Robert 4, 239
Middleton, Charles 116, 302, 303, 327, 329, 344
Midnight Blunders 333, 339, 346, 362

A Midsummer Night's Dream (1967) 157–58, 361
The Mighty Thunda see *King of the Congo*
Mil Mascaras 68, 69, 191, 271
Milani, Frederica 145
Milar, Adolph 36
Miles, Art 329
Milford, Gene 135
Milhollin, James 287
Milland, Ray 352
Millard, Helene 29
Miller, Charles F. 320
Miller, Don 71, 74, 89, 99, 110, 159, 169, 189, 200, 221, 226, 280
Miller, Ivan 152
Miller, Martin 87
Miller, Marvin 127, 186, 281
Miller, Patsy Ruth 355
Miller, Seton I. 102
Miller, Walter 300, 317
Milletaire, Carl 218
Mills, Donald 228
Mills, Frank 336, 341
Milner, Martin 245
Mimieux, Yvette 14, 352
Miroslava 152
The Missing Juror 158–60, 181, 359
Mr. Magoo 183, 184
Mr. Sardonicus 160–61, 233, 270, 286, 360
I Misteri della Giungla Nera (The Mystery of the Black Jungle) see *The Mystery of Thug Island*
Misterios de la Magia Negra (Mysteries of the Black Magic) 161–62, 360
Mistretta, Gaetano 108
Mitchell, Arthur 158
Mitchell, Frank 24, 345
Mitchell, Irving 320
Mitchell, Thomas 135
Miyake, Martha 103
Mohr, Gerald 114
Mollison, Henry 259
Moncion, Francisco 158
Mong, William V. 29, 191
Monlaur, Yvonne 240, 241
The Monolith Monsters 177
Monroe, Vaughn 201
The Monster and the Ape 307–9, 361
El Monstruo Resucitado (The Resuscitated Monster) 162–63, 360
Montalban, Ricardo 353, 358
Montenegro, Hugo 284
Montgomery, Bob, Jr. 260
Montgomery, Elizabeth 265
Montgomery, George 131
Montgomery, Robert 102, 132, 286
Monti, Aldo 161
Monti, Maura 112, 271
Mooney, Tex 122
Moore, Alvy 27, 28
Moore, Cleo 7, 297

Moore, Dennis 46
Moore, Dickie 91
Moore, Eva 181
Moore, Ida 89
Moore, Ray 310
Moore, Roger 318
Moore, Terry 196
Moorhead, Natalie 157
Moran, Erin 276
Moreland, Sherry 86
Moreno, Alejandro Munoz *see* Blue Demon
Morgan, Harry Hays 168
Morgan, Lee 133
Morgan, Ralph 308
Morgan, Terence 54, 211
Moriyama, Rollin 263
Morley, Karen 267, 268
Morley, Robert 182, 235, 236
Morningside Productions 207, 252, 262
Morris, Chester 26, 186
Morrison, Bret 318
Morrow, Jeff 90
Morrow, Jo 245, 253
Morrow, Neyle 121, 154
Morse, Carlton E. 109, 268
Morton, James C. 24, 334, 348, 350
Moss, Arnold 265
The Most Dangerous Game 14
Most Dangerous Man Alive 163, 360
Mostovoy, Leo 110
Mosura see Mothra
Mothra 163–65, 360
Moxey, John Llewellyn 353
Mudie, Leonard 133, 169
La Muerte Viviente (The Living Dead) *see Snake People*
Muir, Gavin 224
Muir, Jean 266
Muldaur, Diana 34
Mulhall, Jack 98
Mulholland, Jim 246
Muller, Cora 78
The Mummy (1959) 53
Mummy's Dummies 339–40, 362
Mundy, Meg 72
Mungula, Jessica 6
Munro, Caroline 92
The Munsters 35, 106
Murderers' Row 6, 131, 165–66, 214, 282, 361
Murphy, Mary 67, 142
Murphy, Michael 14
Murray, Billy 39, 40
Murray, Don 228
Murray, Forbes 186, 307, 321
Murray, John T. 351
Murray, Zon 293
Muse, Clarence 19
Musty Musketeers 331, 340, 362
The Mutations 166–67, 361
My Name Is Julia Ross 167–69, 195, 221, 359
The Mysterians 8, 134

Mysterious Island (1951) 171, 309–10, 361
Mysterious Island (1961) 116, 169–71, 310, 360
Mystery of the Black Jungle 171
The Mystery of Thug Island 171–72, 232, 360

Na Komete 270
Naha, Ed 66, 80, 93, 121, 171, 183, 195, 209, 246, 252, 257, 266, 284, 287
Naish, J. Carrol 280, 290, 291
Naismith, Laurence 120
Nakajima, Haruo 94
Nakamura, Tetsu 104
National Investigating Committee on Aerial Phenomena (NICAP) 65
Natteford, Jack 177
Naughton, David 353
Neal, Tom 294
Nedell, Bernard 48
Neill, Noel 290, 323
Neill, Roy William 20, 21
Neise, George N. 249, 251
Nelson, Barry 32
Nelson, Bek 332
Nervous Shakedown 340, 341, 362
Nesmith, Ottola 168
Neville, John 235, 236, 237
Newell, Michelle 355
Newman, Nanette 227
Newton, Mary 48, 70
Newton-John, Olivia 63
Ney, Marie 211
Nicholas, Paul 204
Nicholson, Jack 231
The Night Club Lady 36, 172–73, 359
Night of Terror 29, 173–75, 359
Night of the Demon see Curse of the Demon
The Night the World Exploded 66, 176–77, 360
Nightingale, Michael 232
Nightwing 177–79, 361
1984 (1956) 88, 179–80, 360
The Ninth Guest 20, 83, 147, 159, 180–81, 359
Nippon Herald Films 119
Nissen, Greta 35
Niven, David 32
Nolan, Jack Edmund 357
Normandy Productions 252
Norris, Chuck 215, 216, 282
Norris, Edward 212
North, Zeme 286, 287
Norton, Coe 307
Novak, Kim 13, 14
Novaro, Tito 112
Novarro, Carlos 163
Novarro, Ignacio 132
Novello, Jay 142
Nugent, Frank S. 129
Nureyev, Rudolph 239
Nusciak, Loredana 238

Nye, Louis 286
Nyiregyhazi, Ervin 226

Oakman, Wheeler 302
Obler, Arch 80–81
O'Brien, Dave 295, 320
O'Brien, Edmund 147, 179
O'Casey, Ronan 179
O'Connell, Arthur 18, 215
O'Connell, L.W. 189
O'Connell, Thomas Edward 79
O'Connolly, Jim 67
O'Connor, Una 132
O'Donovan, Elizabeth 61
Of Cash and Hash 340–41, 343–44, 362
Offerman, George, Jr. 326
O'Hara, Brian 348
O'Hara, Maureen 355
O'Herlihy, Dan 75, 76, 114
Okada, Yukiko 135
Okuda, Ted 333, 346, 347, 349
Oland, Warner 76
The Old Dark House (1932) 181
The Old Dark House (1963) 181–83, 242, 286, 360
Oliva, Nadia Haro 161
Olivera, Maria Antonieta 224
Olivier, Laurence 38
O'Mahoney, Jock *see* Mahoney, Jock
O'Malley, Pat 280
O'Mara, Kate 39
O'Moore, Patrick 225
One Is Guilty 11
One Million B.C. 124, 270, 344
One Million Years B.C. 44, 121
One Shivery Night 333, 341, 362
One Spooky Night 336, 341, 362
1001 Arabian Nights 183–84, 360
O'Neal, Charles 110, 159
O'Neal, Patrick 142, 227
O'Neal, Ron 278
O'Neill, Henry 196
O'Neill, James 28, 44, 96, 112, 164, 178, 204, 246, 252, 279, 281, 284
Operation Universe 1, 341, 362
Orea, Guillermo 33
Orea, Mario 190
Orlando, Don 263
Orr, Clifford 223
Orr, Corinne 119
Ortelana, Carlos 33
Ortigoza, Carlos 206
Orwell, George 179, 180
Osborn, Andrew 211
Osborne, Bud 288
Oses, Fernando 6, 112, 190, 206
O'Shaughnessy, Brian 44
Ottiano, Rafaela 133

Oursler, Fulton 172
Ouspenskaya, Maria 50
Outer Space Jitters 341–42, 362
Outkean, Michael 228
The Outlaws 201
Overton, Frank 75
Owen, Dickie 54
Owen, Granville *see* York, Duke
Owen, Tudor 163
The Oxford University Dramatic Society 60, 61

Pack, Charles Lloyd 240, 253
Pact with the Devil see Pacto Diabólico (Diabolical Pact)
Pacto Diabólico (Diabolical Pact) 68, 184–86, 205, 361
Page, Bradley 10
Page, Norvell 321
Page, Paul 15
Paget, Debra 163
Paiva, Nestor 128, 248, 249
Palance, Jack 256, 257
Palma, Joe 332, 337, 338, 346
Palmer, Gregg 163, 285
Palmer, Lilli 13
Palmer, Max 128
Palmerini, Luca M. 108
The Panther's Claw 36
Pardon My Terror 332, 342, 350, 351, 362
Parely, Mila 188
Parga, Lourdes 161
Parish, James Robert 32, 38, 84, 102, 118, 138, 146, 214, 284
Parker, Cecil 236
Parker, Eddie 71
Parks, Hildy 75
Parks, Larry 24, 63, 98
Parnell, Emory 46
Parrish, John 200
Parsons, Estelle 275
Parsons, Milton 50
Penney, Ralph 55
Peral, Jorge 190
Percy, Edward 131
Perego, Mario 145
Perrault, Charles 220
Perrott, Ruth 247
Perry, Jack 30
Pertwee, Jon 266
Peters, Erika 161
Peters, Jon 71
Petipa, Marius 239
Petrillo, Kelly 239
Pettet, Joanna 32
The Phantom (1943) 288, 310–11, 361
The Phantom Empire 276
The Phantom Thief 27, 186–87, 359
The Phantom Wagon 187–88, 359
Phelps, Lee 91, 173
Phillips, Greigh 85

INDEX

Phillips, John 257
Phillips, Leslie 87, 88
Phillips, Redmond 95
Phipps, William 80
Phony Cronies 342, 362
Piaf, Edith 201
Pickens, Slim 62
Pierlot, Francis 48
Pierson, Arthur 10
Pirates of the High Seas 311–12, 314
Pivar, Ben 4, 258
Pizor, William M. 22
Plan 9 from Outer Space 6
Planer, Franz 74
Pleasence, Donald 167, 179
Pleshette, John 14
Plisetskaya, Maya 239
Plympton, George H. 294, 305, 319
Poe, Edgar Allan 86
Poggi, Nando 172
Pohle, Robert W., Jr. 96
Pola, Andre 332
Polanski, Roman 141, 194, 195, 236
Pollard, Snub 349
Pollexfen, Jack 225
Pooley, Olaf 87
Post, Wiley 4
Poston, Tom 182, 286, 287
Powell, Eddie 167
Power, Derry 274
Power, Taryn 217
Power, Tyrone 217
The Power of the Whistler 188–89, 280, 359
Powers, Stephanie 59
Powers, Tom 142
Prehistoric Valley see *Valley of the Dragons*
Prentiss, Ed 295
Prentiss, Paula 227
Price, Dennis 13
Price, Sherwood 37
Price, Stanley 189, 331
Price, Vincent 141, 142, 254, 255
Priestley, J.B. 181
Prima, Louis 93, 145
Prince, William 227
Proctor, Phil 201
Profanadores de Tumbas (Profaners of Tombs) 189–91, 360
Prosser, Hugh 294, 302, 309, 312, 326
Provine, Dorothy 130, 246, 247
Prowse, Dave 32
Pryor, Roger 152
Psycho (1960) 105
Puglia, Frank 24, 263
Purcell, Noel 253
Purcell, Robert 154
Pygmy Island 191–92, 360
Pyl, Jean Vander 145

Q Planes see *Clouds Over Europe*
Quayle, Anthony 235, 236, 237
Queen, Ellery 237
Quigley, Charles 209, 294, 301, 323
Quillan, Eddie 304
Quinlan, David 34, 39, 53, 67, 77, 84, 157, 199, 211, 266, 281
Quinn, Anthony 355
Quirk, Lawrence J. 17
Quitak, Oscar 199

Rabin, Jack 247
Radilac, Charles H. 160
Rain or Shine 36
Rainey, Buck 259, 290, 301, 318
Rains, Claude 63, 192
Raker, Lorin 29
Rambaldi, Carlo 178, 179
Rameau, Emil 222
Randall, Monica 238
Randall, Norma 340, 345
Randall, Rebel 248
Randall, Ron 41, 163
Randle, Karen 309
Randolph, Donald 142
Ransohoff, Martin 178
Ransom 1, 192, 359
Rapp, Richard 158
Rasckle, Irmard 124
Rassimov, Ivan 108
Rasumny, Mikhail 101
Rathbone, Basil 267
Ratzenberger, John 274
The Ravagers 192–93, 284, 361
Ravel, Alicia 206
The Raven (1935) 24
Rawlinson, Brian 204
Rawlinson, Herbert 322, 323
Ray, Allene 300
Ray, Charles 98
Raymond, Alex 57, 86, 121, 126, 154, 191, 273
Raymond, Gary 120
Readick, Frank, Jr. 317
Reason, Rex 228
Rebel, Bernard 54, 180
Rebiere, Richard 98
Red Alert 62, 76
Redeker, Quinn 251
Redgrave, Michael 179
Redmond, Liam 52
Reed, Alan 145, 184
Reed, Marshall 309
Reed, Oliver 242
Reed, Rex 138
Reese, Tom 175
Reeve, Christopher 290
Reeves, George 122, 289, 290
A Reflection of Fear 193–94, 361
Regnier, Charles 235, 236
Reicher, Frank 73, 271
Reid, Carl Benton 256
Reid, Dorothy (Davenport) 84
Reid, Milton 17, 241
Reischl, Geri 27
Reitzen, Jack 114
Repulsion 194–95, 360
Rettig, Tommy 81, 82
Return from the Beyond see *Misterios de la Magia Negra* (Mysteries of the Black Magic)
The Return of October 195–96, 360
The Return of the Vampire 2, 50, 89, 175, 196–98, 338, 347, 359
Return to Fantasy Island 353–54, 356, 362
The Revenge of Frankenstein 95, 198–200, 231, 360
Revenge of the Stepford Wives 228
Revere, Anne 55
Revisiting Fail Safe 76
The Revived Monster see *El Monstruo Resucitado* (The Resuscitated Monster)
Rey, Dolores 29
Reynolds, Craig 127
Reynolds, Don Kay 235
Rhodes, Grandon 65
Rhodes, Margery 84
Rice, Florence 239
Rice, Frank 157
Richards, Addison 115
Richards, Frank 9
Richardson, Ralph 38, 39
Richardson, Tony 96–97
Richmond, Kane 294, 304, 318
Riders in the Sky 200–1, 360
Rilla, Walter 87, 88
Rimmer, Shane 274
Rimmington, Noelle 140
Ringgold, Gene 210
Ripper, Michael 54, 199, 256
Riquelme, Carlos 132, 161
Risk, Victoria 193
Riskin, Robert 137
Riss, Dan 147
Ritch, Steven 37, 276, 277, 338
Ritt, William 294
Rivas, Jose Maria Linares 162
Roar of the Iron Horse 312, 326, 361
Robards, Jason (Sr.) 82
Roberts, Adelle (Adele) 26, 127, 248
Roberts, Doris 14
Roberts, Ewan 52
Roberts, Lee 288
Roberts, Lynne 89
Roberts, Mark see Scott, Robert
Robertson, Willard 11, 150
Robinson, Bernard 182
Robinson, Charles 27
Robinson, Robie 155
Robles, German 33
Robson, Flora 131
Rodriguez, Dagoberto 68, 69
Rogan, Beth 170
Rogell, Albert S. 83
Rohmer, Sax 34
Roland, Gilbert 200
Roland, Jeanne 54
Roland, Jurgen 300
Roley, Sutton 35
Rolfe, Guy 160, 232, 233
Romand, Gina 190
Romero, Martha 223, 224, 271
Romson Productions 265
Rosas, Pamela 70
Rosen, Phil 76
Rosenberg, Max 256
Rosenbloom, Maxie 24, 25, 98, 99
Rosener, George 35
Ross, Harry 282
Ross, Jonathan 106, 246
Ross, Katharine 227, 228
Ross, Michael 42
Ross, William 134
Rossen, Carol 228
Rossi-Stuart, Giacomo 172
Roth, Gene 251, 285, 296, 305, 306, 312, 337, 341
Rothschild, Elaine 231
Royle, William 317
Rubin, Benny 335, 344
Rubin, Giulia 172
Rubinski, Wolf 132, 133
Rule, Janice 5, 13
Russell, Autumn 284
Russell, Jane 124
Russell, Ray 286
Russell, Rosalind 13, 131
Rust, Richard 105
Rutherford, Ann 23
Ruvinski, Wolf see Rubinski, Wolf
Ryan, Mitch 193, 194
Ryan, Sheila 124
Ryan, Tim 327
Rye, Michael 302

Sabre Film Productions 51
Sachs, Leonard 203
A Safe Place 201, 361
Sahara, Kenji 104
Saint, Eva Marie 352
St. Clair, Michael 193
St. Clair, Sally 210
St. Clair, Sue 210
St. John, Howard 41, 230
Sais, Marin 298
Sakai, Franky 164
Sakamoto, Fumio 94
Sales, Soupy 18
Salgari, Emilio 171, 172
Salmi, Albert 5
Salvage 356–57, 362
Sammeth, Barbara 143
Sanchez, Blanca 6
Sande, Walter 302
Sanders, George 94, 94
Sands, Dorothy 13
Sanford, Donald S. 192
Sangster, Jimmy 153, 203
Santanon 78, 220
Santo 6, 9, 68, 69, 190, 191
Sardonicus see *Mr. Sardonicus*
Sato, Makoto 104
Saunders, Gloria 326
Saunders, Nancy 338, 346

Savage, Ann 191
Savage, Paul 176
Savage Mutiny 56, 201–2, 360
Sawalha, Nadim 217
Sayers, Jo Ann 152
Scannell, Frank J. 189
Schary, Dore 83
Schell, Maximilian 97
Scherick, Edgar J. 228
Scheuer, Stephen H. 100, 261, 352, 356, 357
Schilling, Gus 332, 336, 342, 350, 351
Schindell, Cy 330, 334, 335, 338, 346
Schnabel, Stefan 265
Schneer, Charles H. 92, 116, 120, 169, 171, 217, 252, 254, 262
Schoner, Inga 171
Schwartz, Tony 355
Scofield, Paul 352
Scotched in Scotland 336, 342–43, 362
Scott, George C. 62
Scott, Janette 182
Scott, John 237
Scott, Randolph 159
Scott, Robert 46, 267
Scott, Zachary 13
Scrambled Brains 343, 362
Scream for Your Lives! William Castle and The Tingler 256
Scream of Fear 153, 202–4, 360
Se Tutte le Donne del Mondo see *Kiss the Girls and Make Them Die*
The Sea Hound 311, 312–14, 361
Searles, Baird 243
Sears, Fred F. 41, 66, 90, 91, 177, 276
Seay, James 74, 273
The Secret Code 314–16, 361
The Secret of Treasure Island 316–17, 361
Sedgwick, Edward 18, 91, 144
See No Evil 204–5, 361
Segall, Harry 102
Seitz, George B. 192
Sellers, Peter 32, 62
Semels, Harry 348
Senda, Koreya 8, 104
La Señora Muerte (The Death Woman) 68, 77, 205–6, 270, 361
Senwalt, Andre 4
Serato, Massimo 108
Serenata Macabre (Macabre Serenade) see *House of Evil*
Serret, John 203
Sertoroclos, Dr. Fraime 50
The 7th Voyage of Sinbad 2, 80, 92, 116, 207–9, 360
Seyler, Athene 52
Seymour, Al 73
Seymour, Jane 217

The Shadow (1937) 63, 209–10, 359
The Shadow (1940) 317–18, 323, 361
The Shadow of the Bat see *La Sombra del Murciélago* (The Shadow of the Bat)
Shadow of the Hawk 210–11, 316
Shadow of the Past 211, 360
Shadow on the Land 2, 357, 362
The Shadows 201
Shadows in the Night 46, 47, 127, 211–13
Shakespeare, William 96, 139
Shandel, Pia 211
Sharp, Don 46
Sharpe, Albert 196
Shaw, C. Montague 83
Shaw, Janet 303
Shaw, Martin 140
Shaw, Robert 92, 193–94
Shayne, Konstantin 70, 71
Shayne, Robert 90, 193, 194
Shayne, Ruel 90
Sheffield, Reginald 168
Shelby, Nicole 257
Shelley, Barbara 95, 96
Shelley, Paul 140
Shepard, Jan 295
Shepard, Richard F. 94
Shields, Arthur 225
Shigenobu, Yashuhiro 104
Shimada, Teru 173
Shimura, Takashi 94
Shirakawa, Yumi 94, 103, 104
Shivering Sherlocks 341, 343–44, 362
Shivers 344, 362
Shore, Dinah 201
Short, Dorothy 295
Shumway, Lee 318
Shuster, Joe 289, 322
Siegel, Jerry 289, 322
Siegler, Allen G. 21
Sigoloff, Marc 276
The Silencers 6, 166, 213–14, 282, 360
Silent Rage 215–16, 361
Silva, Henry 352
Silver, Ron 216
Silvers, Phil 248
Simmons, Jean 84
Simms, Larry 23
Simon, S. Sylvan 144
Simpson, Frank 75
Sinatra, Frank 248, 249
Sinbad and the Eye of the Tiger 92, 216–18, 361
Sinclair, Betty 132
Singh, R. Lal 229
Singleton, Penny 23
Sinister Invasion see *The Incredible Invasion*
Siodmak, Curt 42, 64
Siren of Bagdad 218–19, 244, 360
Sitka, Emil 249, 251, 328, 329, 331, 332, 335, 337, 339, 341, 342, 346, 350

Sizova, Alla 219, 220
Sjstrom, Victor 188
Sleeman, William 221
The Sleeping Beauty 219–20, 360
Slocomb, Douglas 203
Smith, Hal 251
Smith, Keely 93
Smith, Kenneth L. 125
Smith, Robert 115
Snake Hunter Strangler see *The Mystery of Thug Island*
Snake People 68, 77, 107, 113, 220–21, 361
So Dark the Night 195, 221–23, 359
Soderling, Walter 73
Soiter, John T. 20
Sokoloff, Vladimir 161
Soler, Bob 311
Solon, Ewan 240
Solovyov, Yuri 219, 220
La Sombra del Murciélago (The Shadow of the Bat) 6, 111–12, 223–24, 361
Somer, Josef 227
Sommer, Elke 282, 283
The Son of Dr. Jekyll 185, 224–25, 360
Sosso, Pietro 110
Sothern, Hugh 82
The Soul of a Monster 50, 225–27, 359
Southern, Terry 32
Space, Arthur 89, 263
Space Ship Sappy 341, 344, 362
Space Travelers see *Marooned*
Spark, Don 264
Sparv, Camilla 165
Speed, F. Maurice 61, 96, 108, 141, 171, 237, 275, 276
Spenser, David 232
The Spider Returns 302, 307, 318–20, 321, 361
The Spider's Web 307, 319, 320–21, 361
Spielberg, Steven 38
Spillane, Mickey 37
Spook Louder 344–45, 362
The Spook Speaks 345, 362
Spook to Me 345, 362
Spooks! 345, 362
Spyaschchaya Krasavitsa see *The Sleeping Beauty*
Squire, Ronald 84
Stafford, Hanley 13, 36
Staley, Joan 269
Stalin, Josef 179, 265
Stamp-Taylor, Enid 157
Stander, Lionel 133
Standing, John 257
Stanford, Leonard 9
Stanke, Don E. 84
Stanley, Edwin 73, 159
Stanley, John 28, 40, 97, 161, 194, 220, 353
Stanton, Helene 126
Stapp, Marjorie 289
Starr, Kay 63

Starrett, Charles 233, 234
Stassino, Paul 232
Steele, Tom 295
Steers, Larry 191
Steinbrunner, Chris 237
The Stepford Children 228
The Stepford Husbands 228
The Stepford Wives (1975) 227–28, 361
Stephenson, John 146
Sterling, Jan 88, 179
Sternad, Rudolph 249
Stevens, Angela 42, 56
Stevens, Charles 202
Stevens, Jean 159
Stevens, Onslow 154
Stevens, Robert 267
Stevens, Ruthelma 35, 36, 172, 173
Stevens, Stella 143, 214
Stevenson, Robert Louis 86, 185, 266, 317
Stewart, Alana 193
Stewart, Elaine 163
Stewart, James 13
Stewart, Larry 296
Stewart, Trish 356
Stock, Barbara 353
Stockbridge, Grant 321
Stoker, Bram 53, 112, 196
Stoloff, Benjamin 29, 174
Stoloff, Morris 131
Stone, George E. 26, 73, 116, 186
Stone Age Romeos 338, 346, 362
Storm Over Tibet 228–29, 360
Stossel, Ludwig 347
Stout, Rex 133
Stowell, Dan 27
Strait-Jacket 115, 229–31, 360
Strang, Harry 58
Strange, Robert 258
Stranglers of Bengal see *Stranglers of Bombay*
Stranglers of Bombay 231–33, 241, 360
Strasberg, Susan 203
Stratton, Chester (Chet) 301
Strauss, Theodore 131
Strayer, Frank L. 23
Streets of Ghost Town 233–35, 360
Streisand, Barbra 71
Strick, Philip 156, 243
Stride, John 141
Stringer, Arthur 302
Stroll, Edson 250
Stuart, Gloria 181, 280
Stuart, John 199
A Study in Terror 235–38, 360
Sturges, John 156
Styne, Stanley 100
Subotsky, Milton 256
Sul-Te-Wan, Madame 19
Sullivan, Ed 145
Sully, Frank 24, 26, 48, 89, 125, 126, 186, 331
Sumida, Tomohito 134

Super Speed 238–39, 359
Superargo vs. Diabolicus 238, 360
Superman (1948) 2, 289, 293, 332–23, 361
Sutherland, Donald 60
Sutton, John 243
Swan Lake (1960) 239–40, 360
Swart, Fred 44
Sweet Spirits of Nighter 342, 346, 362
Swift, Jonathan 252, 254
Sydney, Basil 253

Taggart, Ben 9
Tails of Horror see *Spooks!*
Talbot, Lyle 37, 86, 125, 258, 289, 290, 292, 326
Talbott, Gloria 225
Tales of Frankenstein 346–47, 362
Taliaferro, Hal (Wally Wales) 152
Tall, Dark and Gruesome 333, 341, 347, 362
Talmadge, Richard 32
Tanaka, Tomoyuki 8, 94, 103
Tanin, Eleanor 277
Tannen, William 56, 123, 191
Tapley, Colin 21
Tarler, Harriette 335, 344
Taste of Fear see *Scream of Fear*
Tate, Sharon 282, 283
Tayama, Akihiro 164
Taylor, Davina 120
Taylor, Elizabeth 60, 61
Taylor, Elsie 140
Taylor, Forrest 294, 300, 301, 306, 323, 324
Taylor, Joan 65, 263
Taylor, Lisa 72
Taylor, Ray 321
Taylor, Valerie 194
Tazaki, Jun 94
Tchaikovsky, Peter Ilyitch 220, 239
Teale, Leonard 323
Tenbrook, Harry 11
Terrell, St. John 302
Terror of the Hatchet see *The Terror of the Tongs*
The Terror of the Tongs 231, 240–41, 360
Terry, Don 317
Terry, Robert 165
Terry and the Pirates 323–26, 361
Terry-Thomas 130
Teuber, Andress 61
Tewkesbury, Joan 72
Thatcher, Heather 80
Thatcher, Torin 207
These Are the Damned 241–43, 360
Thesiger, Ernest 181
Thief of Damascus 227, 243–44, 360
Thinnes, Roy 352

13 Ghosts 66, 105, 244–46, 254, 286, 360
The 30 Foot Bride of Candy Rock 246–47, 360
Thomas, Damien 217
Thomas, Evan 169
Thomas, Gwydion *61*
Thomas, Lowell 22
Thompson, Al 304, 334, 351
Thompson, Howard 5, 17, 44, 130, 156, 183, 246
Thompson, J. Lee 97
Thomson, David 59
Thomson, Kenneth 29
Thornburn, June 253
Thorndike, Sybil 355
Thorpe, Ted 202, 306
A Thousand and One Nights 2, 247–49, 359
Three Arabian Nuts 347, 362
Three Little Sews and Sews 347–48, 362
Three Missing Links 348, 362
Three Pests in a Mess 348–49, 362
Three Sappy People 349, 362
The Three Stooges 2, 99, 100, 143, 246, 249–52, 258, 328–51
The Three Stooges Follies 291
The Three Stooges Fun-O-Rama 335
The Three Stooges in Orbit 99, 249–51, 252, 360
The Three Stooges Meet Hercules 99, 249, 251–52, 360
The Three Stooges Scrapbook 249
The 3 Worlds of Gulliver 116, 252–54, 360
Thurston, Carol 128
Tichy, Gerhard (Gerard) 238
Tigon Pictures 46
Til, Roger 260
Tillman, Floyd 201
Tindall, Loren 188
The Tingler 105, 244, 254–56, 286, 360
To Heir Is Human 344, 349, 362
Tobey, Kenneth 117, 118
Tobias, George 144
Tobin, Genevieve 180
Toch, Ernst 131
Todd, Ann 203
Toei Animation Studios 134
Toho Company 8, 94, 103, 164
Tol'able David (1921) 255
Tone, Franchot 100
Tongolele 221
Toomey, Regis 259
Toone, Geoffrey 260
The Tooth Will Out 349–50, 362
Topkick Productions 216
Torne, Regina 184, 185, 206
Torrence, Ernest 255
Tors, Ivan 19

The Torture Chamber see *Fear Chamber*
Torture Garden 46, 256–57, 361
The Torture Zone see *Fear Chamber*
Totter, Audrey 147
Tourneur, Jacques 51, 53
Tovar, Lupita 46
Tozere, Frederic 196
Tracy, William 324, 326
The Tragedy of Macbeth see *Macbeth* (1971)
The Tragical History of Doctor Faustus 160, 161
Trans-Global Films 163
Trapped by Television 257–59, 359
Trapped in the Sky 259, 359
Travers, Bill 84
Travers, Victor 159, 334, 339, 351
Travis, June 91
Trenet, Charles 201
Trevarthen, Noel 39
Trevor, Claire 132
Trickett, Vicki 251
Triesault, Ivan 48, 50, 70, 71
Troughton, Patrick 95, 120, 217
Trowbridge, Charles 148, 152
Trueman, Paula 227
Truffaut, François 37
Trumbell, Douglas 38
Tsuburaya, Eiji 8, 9
Tsuchiya, Yoshio 8
Tuchner, Michael 355
Turkel, Ann 193
Turner, Ray 23
Turner, Roscoe 4
Tuska, Jon 213, 271
Tuttle, Frank 249
12 to the Moon 9, 260–61, 360
20 Million Miles to Earth 80, 116, 261–64, 265
The 27th Day 264–65, 360
The Two Faces of Dr. Jekyll 1, 185, 266
Tyler, Tom 288, 310, 311
Tyrrell, John 73, 89, 330, 338, 349

Uch Daiseno see *Battle in Outer Space*
Uehara, Ken 94, 164
The Ugly Duckling 1, 185, 266, 360
Ullman, Elwood 249
Ullman, Liv 138
L'Umanoide see *The Humanoid*
The Underwater City 266–67, 360
United Productions of America (UPA) 183
United States: It Can't Happen Here see *Shadow on the Land*
The Unknown (1946) 57, 110, 267–68, 359
Unsinn, Joseph A. (Joe) 354

Ure, Mary 193, 194
Urecal, Minerva 48, 327
Urueta, Chano 162

Valentine, Joseph A. 174
Valentine, Karen 356
Valez, Tere 112
Valley of the Dragons 268–70, 360
Valley of the Headhunters 274
Vallin, Rick 31, 41, 109, 122, 124, 273, 288, 293, 294, 312
Vallone, Raf 130
Las Vampiras (The Vampires) 68, 77, 112, 184, 205, 270–71, 361
The Vampire Bat 14, 23
The Vampire Girls see *Las Vampiras* (The Vampires)
The Vampires see *Las Vampiras* (The Vampires)
Van Cleve, Patricia 23
Van Dreelen, John 245
Van Druten, John 13, 14
Van Eyck, Peter 171
Van Ost, Valerie 39
Van Sickel, Dale 295
Van Sloan, Edward 4, 9, 11, 12, 21
Van Zandt, Philip 26, 243, 248, 331, 332, 337, 340, 341, 342, 345, 347
Vanaire, Jacques 55
Varconi, Victor 150
Varnals, Wendy 39
Varno, Roland 168, 197
Vasquez, Roland 158
Vaughan, Peter 60
Vaughn, Jimmy 281
Vega, Isela 68, 69, 78, 185, 206
Veidt, Conrad 160
Velasquez, Jesus "Murcielago" 132, 223
Verdugo, Elena 138, 244
Vergara, Luis Enrique 6, 68, 77, 107, 111, 113, 184, 190, 205, 221, 223
Verne, Jules 171, 269, 270, 309
Vetchinsky 237
Victor, Paul 275
Vidor, Charles 131
The Vigilante 312, 326, 361
Vilely, Edward 158
Villa, Lucha 112
Villechaize, Herve 353, 356
Villiers, James 242
Vincenot, Louis 324
Vincent, Jan-Michael 211
Vincent, June 41
Vincent, Romo 109
Vincent, Russ 302
Virell, Sergio 6, 112
Vitale, Joseph 138, 139
Vogan, Emmett 71, 301, 322
Vogeding, Frederick 14
Voice of the Whistler 188, 271–72, 280, 359
Volkman, Ivan 37
von Brincken, William 173

Von Zell, Harry 339
Vonn, Veola 247
Voodoo Tiger 273–74, 360
Voskovec, George 264
Vuolo, Tito 263

Wagner, Fernando 162
Wagner, Max 259
The Wailing Rock Murders 223
Wald, Jane 250
Wales, Ethel 91
Walker, Nella 181
Wallace, Bill 338, 346
Wallace, Edgar 156, 236, 300
Walsh, Judy 30
Walter Futter Productions 3
Walters, Luana 323
Walton, Fred 279
Wanamaker, Sam 218
Wanpaku Oji No Orochi Taiji see *Little Prince and the Eight Headed Dragon*
War of the Worlds (1953) 66
Ward, Amelita 327
Ward, Burt 291
Ward, Luci 177
Ward, Robert 28
Ward, Skip 143
Warde, Anthony 308, 320
Warde, Shirley 55
Warlords of Atlantis 274–75, 361
Warlords of the Deep see *Warlords of Atlantis*
Warner, David 178
Warner, Frank 38
Warner, H.B. 135, 136, 157
Warren, Bill 177, 251, 281
Warren, Jerry 152
Warren, Kenneth J. 45
Warrenton, Gilbert 86
Warwick Film Corporation 88
Washburn, Bryant 174, 295
Washington, Ned 252
Waterfield, Bob 124
Watermelon Man 275–76, 361
Waters, Jan 39
Waters, Ozie 235
Watkin, Pierre 42, 290, 294, 302, 303, 323
Watson, Minor 212
Watson, Wylie 211
Watt, Billie Lou 119
Watts, Gwendolyn 60
Watz, Edward 333, 346, 347, 349
Wayn, Peter 282
Wayne, John 12, 217

Wayne, Patrick 217
We Want Our Mummy 350, 362
Weaver, Fritz 75
Webb, Lewis 285, 286
Webb, Richard 295
Webber, Richard 260, 295
Webber, Robert 214
Webster, Joy 281, 282
Weeks, Barbara 29
Weiler, A.H. 35
Weiss, Louis 317
Weissmuller, Johnny 29, 30, 56, 57, 86, 121, 123, 138, 139, 154, 191, 201, 273
Welch, Raquel 44
Welch, William 28
Weld, Tuesday 201
Welden, Ben 212, 288
Weldon, Michael J. 100, 112, 121, 192, 241
Welk, Lawrence 201
Welles, Orson 32, 201, 317, 318
Wells, H.G. 78, 79
Wells, Jacqueline (Julie Bishop) 82
Wells, Jerold 154
Wendlandt, Horst 300
Wengraf, John 260
Wenland, Burt 138
The Werewolf 2, 37, 41, 66, 198, 276–78, 338, 347, 360
Wescoatt, Rusty 86, 191, 251, 312, 323
Wessel, Dick 340, 342
Wesselhoeft, Eleanor 19
West, Adam 291
West, Wally 138
Westcott, Helen 347
Westerfield, James 105
Weston, Cecil 159
Weston, Doris 307
Whale, James 181, 183
Wheeler, Edward Lytton 298
Wheeler, Harvey 76
When a Stranger Calls (1979) 278–79, 361
When a Stranger Calls (2006) 279
When a Stranger Calls Back 279
When Dinosaurs Ruled the Earth 44
The Whistler 188, 271, 279–81, 359
White, Alice 23
White, Donna 236
White, Harold 335

White, Jack 335
White, Jules 2, 335
White, Pearl 302
White, Ruth 340
Whiteford, Blackie 339
Whiting, Margaret 217
Whitley, Crane 189
Whitty, Dame May 168, 196
Who Done It? 332, 342, 350, 351, 362
Who's Guilty? 302, 308, 326–27, 361
Wilbur, Crane 141
Wilcox, Frank 58
Wilcox, Robert 115, 148, 267
Wilde, Brian 52
Wilde, Cornel 248
Wilder, Billy 32
Wilhelmy, Jose Munoz 33
Willard, Lee 152
Willes, Jean 123, 150, 337
Williams, Cindy 228
Williams, Hugh 61
Williams, Kit 242
Williams, Lucy Chase 255
Williams, Rhys 225, 271
Williams, Robert 71, 89, 189, 329, 341, 349, 350
Williamson, Alister 95
Williamson, Nicol 96, 97
Willis, Andrea 138
Willis, Donald C. 211, 233
Willis, Matt 89, 197, 198, 338
Willis, Norman 301
Wilmer, Douglas 92, 120
Wilson, Barbara 150, 152, 236
Wilson, Charles C. 212, 321, 330
Wilson, Lewis 291
Wilson, Lois 191
Wilson, Marie 98, 99, 109
Wilson, Sue 44
Windom, William 13
Winston, Helene 27
Winters, Shelley 143, 248
Winwood, Estelle 131
Withers, Grant 121, 316, 317
Withers, Isabel 111
Withington, Dr. Paul 22
The Wolfman (1941) 50, 64
Wolveridge, Carol 179
The Woman Eater see *Womaneater*
Womaneater 103, 280–81, 360
Wood, Douglas 100
Wood, Edward D., Jr. 167
Wood, Ken 238
Woodbridge, George 199

Woodbury, Doreen 394
Woodbury, Herbert A. 200
Woodbury, Joan 280
Woods, Donald 244
Woodthrope, Peter 355
Woodward, Tina 160
World Film Services 46
World Without End 270
Worth, Brian 240
Wray, Fay 14, 15, 19, 118
The Wrecking Crew 6, 214, 282–84, 361
Wright, Frank Lloyd 81
Wright, Patricia 330
Wright, Will 247
Wright, William 70, 71
Wyatt, Jane 136
Wylie, Philip 91
Wyman, George 8
Wymark, Patrick 194
Wynn, Keenan 62

Xanadu 63

Yamaoka, Otto 10
Yarborough, Barton 58, 109, 110, 267, 268
Yeary, Lee see Majors, Lee
The Yoke's on Me 350–51, 362
York, Dick 302
York, Duke 328, 332, 337, 338, 341, 343, 346, 350
Yosei Gorsau see *Gorath*
Young, Chic 23
Young, Nedrik 357
Young, R.M. 132
Youngstein, Max E. 76
You're Next 332, 342, 350, 351, 362
Yurka, Blanche 50

Zampi, Mario 77, 211
Zapp, Sylvia 201
Zaremba, John 66, 177, 263
Zaza, Tony 18, 28, 38, 45, 80, 93, 94, 97, 119, 131, 138, 145, 158, 166, 171, 201, 205, 211, 216, 218, 275, 276
Zeman, Karel 270
Zetina, Guillermo 186
Zex, the Electronic Monster see *The Electronic Monster*
Zombies of Mora Tau 151, 284–86, 360
Zotz! 286–87, 360
Z.R.B. Productions 269
Zsigmond, Vilmos 38
Zucco, George 212, 213
Zugsmith, Albert 115

www.ingramcontent.com/pod-product-compliance
Lightning Source LLC
Chambersburg PA
CBHW081534300426
44116CB00015B/2627